NOUS·SOMMES·PRETS

SIMON FRASER UNIVERSITY
W.A.C. BENNETT LIBRARY

SOURCEBOOK OF PARALLEL COMPUTING

SOURCEBOOK OF PARALLEL COMPUTING

JACK DONGARRA

University of Tennessee

IAN FOSTER

Argonne National Laboratory

GEOFFREY FOX

Indiana University

WILLIAM GROPP

Argonne National Laboratory

KEN KENNEDY

Rice University

LINDA TORCZON

Rice University

ANDY WHITE

Los Alamos National Laboratory

MORGAN KAUFMANN PUBLISHERS

AN IMPRINT OF ELSEVIER SCIENCE

AMSTERDAM BOSTON LONDON NEW YORK
OXFORD PARIS SAN DIEGO SAN FRANCISCO
SINGAPORE SYDNEY TOKYO

Senior Editor   Denise Penrose
Publishing Services Manager   Edward Wade
Production Editor   Howard Severson
Editorial Coordinator   Emilia Thiuri
Cover Design   Frances Baca
Text Design   Detta Penna
Illustration   Dartmouth Publishing, Inc.
Composition   Windfall Software, using ZzTEX
Copyeditor   Barbara Kohl
Proofreader   Carol Leyba
Indexer   Steve Rath
Printer   The Maple-Vail Book Manufacturing Group

Cover credit: Paul Klee, Green church steeple at center, 1917. © Nimatallah/Art Resource, NY.

Designations used by companies to distinguish their products are often claimed as trademarks or registered trademarks. In all instances in which Morgan Kaufmann Publishers is aware of a claim, the product names appear in initial capital or all capital letters. Readers, however, should contact the appropriate companies for more complete information regarding trademarks and registration.

Morgan Kaufmann Publishers
An imprint of Elsevier Science
340 Pine Street, Sixth Floor
San Francisco, CA 94104-3205
www.mkp.com

Library of Congress Control Number: 2002107244
ISBN: 1-55860-871-0

This book is printed on acid-free paper.

CONTENTS

              20.1   Dense Linear Algebra Algorithms   576
              20.2   The Influence of Computer Architecture
                     on Performance   580
              20.3   Dense Linear Algebra Libraries   583
              20.4   Sparse Linear Algebra Methods   590
              20.5   Direct Solution Methods   591
              20.6   Iterative Solution Methods   596
              20.7   Sparse Eigenvalue Problems   603
              20.8   Conclusion   619

CHAPTER 21   SOFTWARE FOR THE SCALABLE SOLUTION OF
              PARTIAL DIFFERENTIAL EQUATIONS   621

              21.1   PDE Background   622
              21.2   Challenges in Parallel PDE Computations   623
              21.3   Parallel Solution Strategies   627
              21.4   PETSc Approach to Parallel Software for PDEs   628
              21.5   Software for PDEs   645
              21.6   Conclusion   647

CHAPTER 22   PARALLEL CONTINUOUS OPTIMIZATION   649

              22.1   Local Optimization   651
              22.2   Global Optimization   653
              22.3   Direct Search Methods   659
              22.4   Optimization of Linked Subsystems   663
              22.5   Variable and Constraint Distribution   666
              22.6   Conclusion   669

CHAPTER 23   PATH FOLLOWING IN SCIENTIFIC COMPUTING AND
              ITS IMPLEMENTATION IN AUTO   671

              23.1   Local Continuation   673
              23.2   Global Continuation and Degree Theory   675
              23.3   Folds and Bifurcations   677

PREFACE

During its 11-year lifetime, the Center for Research on Parallel Computation (CRPC), a National Science Foundation (NSF) Science and Technology Center, was focused on research and technology development that would be needed to make parallel computing "truly usable." Over that period, a remarkable number of applications were converted to work on scalable parallel computers, and an equally remarkable number of software tools were developed to assist in that process. These developments emerged both from within CRPC and from the community at large. Although the tools and strategies developed and refined during this period are widely known in the community of professional parallel application developers, to our knowledge there exists no compendium of material describing these advances in a form suitable for use by a newcomer to the field. This volume attempts to fill that gap by bringing together a collection of works covering both applications and the technologies used to convert them to run on scalable parallel systems.

The principal goal of this book is to make it easy for newcomers to the field of parallel computing to understand the technologies available and how to apply them. The book is intended for students and practitioners of technical computing who need to understand both the promise and practice of high-performance parallel computation. It assumes that the reader has a good background in either applications or computational science, but not in parallel computation. Thus, the book includes a significant amount of tutorial material.

We also intend that the book serve as a useful reference for the practicing parallel application developer. Thus, it contains in-depth treatments of specific technologies and methods that are useful in parallel computing. These methods are easily accessible by starting from the application overview sections or by reading the technology overview chapters provided at the beginning of each major part.

We hope that you find this book useful and that it helps you exploit the knowledge gained over the past fifteen years, while avoiding some of the pitfalls that we ourselves encountered in gaining that knowledge.

Overview of Content

The book is organized into five major parts. Part I, entitled *Parallelism*, is a tutorial introduction to the field of parallel computers and computing, with separate chapters providing a broad overview of the field, an in-depth treatment of the architecture of modern parallel computer systems, and a survey of the issues that should be taken into consideration when programming them.

Part II, *Applications*, is designed to help new developers understand how high-performance computation can be applied in a variety of specific application areas. It consists of an overview of the process by which one identifies appropriate software and algorithms and the issues involved in implementation. This treatment is complemented by chapters containing in-depth studies in the areas of computational fluid dynamics, environmental engineering and energy, and computational chemistry, and by a separate chapter with 11 vignettes that briefly describe successful uses of parallel systems in other areas. These have been chosen to cover a broad range of both scientific areas and numerical approaches. The applications are cross-referenced to the material in later chapters that cover the needed software technologies and algorithms in depth.

Part III, *Software Technologies*, discusses the progress made on a variety of technological strategies for application development, including message-passing libraries; run-time libraries for parallel computing, such as class libraries for HPC++, languages like HPF, Co-Array Fortran, and HPC++; performance analysis and tuning tools such as Pablo; and high-level programming systems. The goal of this part is to provide a survey of progress with hints to the user that will help in selecting the right technology for use in a given application.

Part IV, *Enabling Technologies and Algorithms*, treats numerical algorithms and covers parallel numerical algorithms for a variety of problems in science and engineering, including linear algebra, continuous and discrete optimization, and simulation. Each chapter covers a different algorithmic area. The goal here is to serve as a resource for the application developer seeking good algorithms for difficult problems.

The final part of the book is devoted to a summary of the issues and a discussion of important future problems for the high-performance science and engineering community, including distributed computing in a grid environment.

Using This Book

This book can be used in several different ways. The newcomer to parallel computation seeking a tutorial introduction should read all of Part I, along with Chapters 4, 9, 16, 17, and 25. Chapters 4, 9, and 17 provide overviews of Parts II, III, and IV, respectively, so these may provide hints on other chapters that may be of interest to the reader.

On the other hand, the developer wishing to understand technologies that can help with a specific application area should start with Part II, which covers a number of applications along with the strategies used to parallelize them. Once the developer has identified a similar application, he or she can follow the cross-references to find in-depth treatments of the useful technologies in Parts III and IV.

Finally, the parallel computing professional can use the book as a reference. The introductory chapters at the beginning of each major part provide excellent guides to the material in the rest of the part.

The book should serve as a resource for users of systems that span the range from small desktop SMPs and PC clusters to high-end supercomputers costing $100 million or more. It focuses on software technologies, along with the large-scale applications enabled by them. In each area, the text contains a general discussion of the state of the field followed by detailed descriptions of key technologies or methods. In some cases, such as MPI for message passing, this is the dominant approach. In others, such as the discussion of problem-solving environments, the authors choose systems representing key concepts in an emerging area.

Supplementary Online Material

Look for links to the *Sourcebook of Parallel Computing* website at *www.mkp.com*, where you can find numerous supplementary materials. In addition to updates and corrections discovered after publication, the reader will find links to servers (such as Netlib) from which software tools and libraries can be downloaded.

Acknowledgments

This book was inspired by the research carried out in the high-performance parallel computing commmunity during the lifetime of the CRPC, an NSF Science and Technology Center that included Rice University, California Institute of Technology, Argonne National Laboratory, Los Alamos National Laboratory, Syracuse University, the University of Tennessee–Knoxville, and the University of Texas–Austin. Without the original grant from the NSF that established CRPC, the book would not have been possible. In addition, the support for research provided through other grants and contracts from NSF, the Department of Energy, the Department of Defense (especially the Defense Advanced Research Projects Agency), and the National Aeronautics and Space Administration has been critical to the advances described in this volume. Substantive additional support for research and technology development was provided by the CRPC home institutions, and the home institutions of many of the chapter authors. In particular, matching funds for CRPC from Rice University were used to provide technical support for the completion of this volume after the NSF funding for CRPC ended.

The editors would also like to thank the people who helped us finish this volume. Teresa Parks improved the entire manuscript with her editorial and technical writing skills. Sarah Gonzales provided technical support and prepared the graphics for publication. Gail Pieper carefully and knowledgeably edited some of the chapters. Keith Cooper consulted with us on the deeper mysteries of LaTeX. Ellen Butler and Shiliang Chang collected, collated, merged, and corrected the bibliographic entries for this volume. Penny Anderson managed a number of production tasks on the Rice side, including assembling author biographies and collecting copyright transfer forms and permissions for use of copyrighted materials. Ellen Butler, Kathryn O'Brien, Penny Anderson, and Theresa Chatman arranged the meetings and teleconferences, handled the correspondence, managed the many contact lists, and lent hands wherever they were needed. All these people deserve our thanks; without their efforts, this volume would not have been finished.

Denise Penrose, our editor at Morgan Kaufmann, provided valuable advice on the preparation of the manuscript and arranged for independent reviews of the manuscript that were very helpful. Emilia Thiuri provided editorial support and extensive guidance as the final manuscript neared completion. Howard Severson, the production editor, did a superb job of bringing the book to completion on a tight schedule and managed to keep his sense of humor throughout the process. The production staff, including the copyeditor Barbara Kohl, the proofreader Carol Leyba, and the indexer Steve Rath, were tireless in their efforts to bring out a high-quality book on time. We are also grateful to those who contributed to the overall appearance of the book: Detta Penna for text design, Frances Baca for cover design, Dartmouth Publishing for illustration, and Windfall Software for composition. We especially appreciate the compositor's efforts to incorporate the substantive number of changes we made late in the production cycle. Finally, the reviewers provided many intelligent and helpful comments on the book that significantly affected its structure, content, and quality.

To all of these people, and to the authors of individual chapters in this text, we extend our heartfelt thanks.

I Parallelism

1

Introduction

Jack Dongarra • Ken Kennedy • Andy White

"Nothing you can't spell will ever work."
—Will Rogers

Parallel computing is more than just a strategy for achieving high performance—it is a compelling vision for how computation can seamlessly scale from a single processor to virtually limitless computing power. This vision is decades old, but it was not until the late 1980s that it seemed within our grasp. However, the road to scalable parallelism has been a rocky one and, as of the writing of this book, parallel computing cannot be viewed as an unqualified success.

True, parallel computing has made it possible for the peak speeds of high-end supercomputers to grow at a rate that exceeded Moore's Law, which says that processor performance doubles roughly every 18 months. Unfortunately, the scaling of application performance has not matched the scaling of peak speed, and the programming burden for these machines continues to be heavy. This is particularly problematic because the vision of seamless scalability cannot be achieved without having the applications scale automatically as the number of processors increases. However, for this to happen, the applications have to be programmed to be able to exploit parallelism in the most efficient possible way. Thus, the responsibility for achieving the vision of scalable parallelism falls on the application developer.

The Center for Research on Parallel Computation (CRPC) was founded in 1989 with the goal of making parallel programming easy enough so that it would be accessible to ordinary scientists. To do this, the Center conducted research on software and algorithms that could form the underpinnings of an infrastructure for parallel programming. The result of much of this research was captured in software systems and published algorithms, so that it could be widely used in the scientific community. However, the published work has never been collected into a single resource and, even if it had been, it would not incorporate the broader work of the parallel-computing research community.

This book is an attempt to fill that gap. It represents the collected knowledge of and experience with parallel computing from a broad collection of leading parallel computing researchers, both within and outside of the CRPC. It attempts to provide both tutorial material and more detailed documentation of advanced strategies produced by research over the last 2 decades.

In the remainder of this chapter we delve more deeply into three key aspects of parallel computation—hardware, applications, and software—to provide a foundation and motivation for the material that will be elaborated later in the book. We begin with a discussion of the progress in parallel computing hardware. This is followed by a discussion of what we have learned from the many application efforts that were focused on exploitation of parallelism. Finally, we briefly discuss the state of parallel computing software and the prospects for such software in the future. We conclude with some thoughts about how close we are to a true science of parallel computation.

1.1   Parallel Computing Hardware

In the last 50 years, the field of scientific computing has undergone rapid change—we have experienced a remarkable turnover of vendors, architectures, technologies, and systems usage. Despite all these changes, the long-term evolution of performance seems to be steady and continuous, following the famous Moore's Law rather closely. In Figure 1.1, we plot the peak performance over the last 5 decades of computers that could have been called "supercomputers." This chart shows clearly how well Moore's Law has held over almost the complete life span of modern computing—we see an increase in performance averaging two orders of magnitude every decade.

In the second half of the 1970s, the introduction of vector computer systems marked the beginning of modern supercomputing. These systems offered a performance advantage of at least one order of magnitude over conventional systems of that time. Raw performance was the main, if not the only, selling point for supercomputers of this variety. However, in the first half of the 1980s the integration of vector systems into conventional computing environments became more important. Only those manufacturers who provided standard programming environments, operating systems, and key applications were successful in getting the industrial customers who became essential for survival in the marketplace. Performance was increased primarily by improved chip technologies and by producing shared-memory multiprocessor systems.

Fostered by several government programs, scalable parallel computing using distributed memory became the focus of interest in the late 1980s. Overcoming the hardware scalability limitations of shared memory was the main goal of these new systems. The increase of performance of standard microprocessors after the RISC revolution, together with the cost advantage of large-scale parallelism, formed the basis for the "attack of the killer micros" [143]. The transition from ECL to CMOS chip technology and the usage of "off-the-shelf" microprocessors instead of custom processors for massively parallel systems was the consequence.

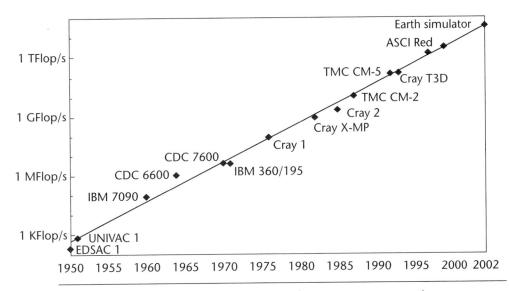

Figure 1.1 Moore's Law and peak performance of various computers over time.

In the early 1990s, while the multiprocessor vector systems reached their widest distribution, a new generation of massively parallel processor (MPP) systems came on the market, claiming to equal or even surpass the performance of vector multiprocessors. To provide a more reliable basis for statistics on high-performance computers, the Top500 [287] list was begun. This report lists the sites that have the 500 most powerful installed computer systems. The best LINPACK benchmark performance [282] achieved is used as a performance measure to rank the computers. The Top500 list has been updated twice a year since June 1993. In the first Top500 list in June 1993, there were already 156 MPP and single-instruction multiple-data (SIMD) systems present (31% of the total 500 systems).

The year 1995 saw remarkable changes in the distribution of the systems in the Top500 according to customer type (academic sites, research labs, industrial/commercial users, vendor installations, and confidential sites). Until June 1995, the trend in the Top500 data was a steady decrease of industrial customers, matched by an increase in the number of government-funded research sites. This trend reflects the influence of governmental high-performance computing (HPC) programs that made it possible for research sites to buy parallel systems, especially systems with distributed memory. Industry was understandably reluctant to follow this path, since systems with distributed memory have often been far from mature or stable. Hence, industrial customers stayed with their older vector systems, which gradually dropped off the Top500 list because of low performance.

Beginning in 1994, however, companies such as SGI, Digital, and Sun began selling symmetric multiprocessor (SMP) models in their workstation families. From

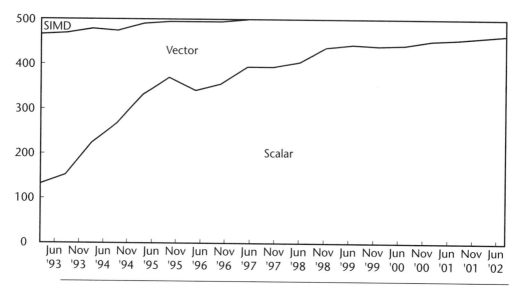

Figure 1.2   Processor design used as seen in the Top500.

the very beginning, these systems were popular with industrial customers because of their architectural maturity and superior price–performance ratio. At the same time, IBM SP2 systems began to appear at a reasonable number of industrial sites. While the SP was initially intended for numerically intensive applications, in the last half of 1995 the system began selling successfully to a larger commercial market, with dedicated database systems representing a particularly important component of sales.

It is instructive to compare the performance growth rates of machines at fixed positions in the Top500 list with those predicted by Moore's Law. To make this comparison, we separate the influence of increasing processor performance and the increasing number of processors per system on the total accumulated performance. (To get meaningful numbers, we exclude the SIMD systems for this analysis, as they tend to have extremely high processor numbers and extremely low processor performance.) In Figure 1.3, we plot the relative growth of the total number of processors and of the average processor performance, defined as the ratio of total accumulated performance to the number of processors. We find that these two factors contribute almost equally to the annual total performance growth—a factor of 1.82. On average, the number of processors grows by a factor of 1.3 each year and the processor performance by a factor 1.4 per year, compared to the factor of 1.58 predicted by Moore's Law.

Based on the current Top500 data (which cover the last 9 years) and the assumption that the current rate of performance improvement will continue for some time to come, we can extrapolate the observed performance and compare these values

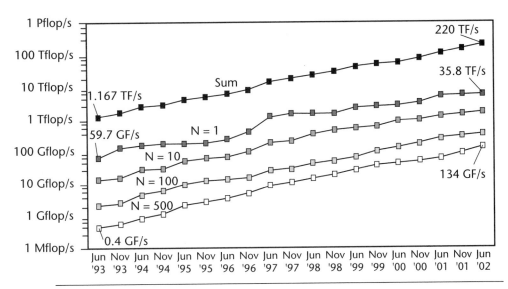

Figure 1.3 Performance growth at fixed Top500 rankings.

with the goals of government programs such as the High Performance Computing and Communications initiative. In Figure 1.4, we extrapolate observed performance using linear regression on a logarithmic scale. This means that we fit exponential growth to all levels of performance in the Top500. This simple curve fit of the data shows surprisingly consistent results. Based on the extrapolation from these fits, we can expect to see the first 100 teraflop/s system by 2005, which is about 1 to 2 years later than the original ASCI projections. By 2005, no system smaller than 1 teraflop/s should be able to make the Top500.

Looking even further in the future, we speculate that based on the current doubling of performance every year, the first petaflop/s system should be available around 2009. Due to the rapid changes in the technologies used in HPC systems, there is currently no reasonable projection possible for the architecture of the petaflop/s systems at the end of the decade. Even as the HPC market has changed substantially since the introduction 3 decades ago of the Cray 1, there is no end in sight for these rapid cycles of architectural redefinition.

There are two general conclusions we can draw from these figures. First, parallel computing is here to stay. It is the primary mechanism by which computer performance can keep up with the predictions of Moore's Law in the face of the increasing influence of performance bottlenecks in conventional processors. Second, the architecture of high-performance computers will continue to evolve at a rapid rate. Thus, it will be increasingly important to find ways to support scalable parallel programming without sacrificing portability. This challenge must be met by the development

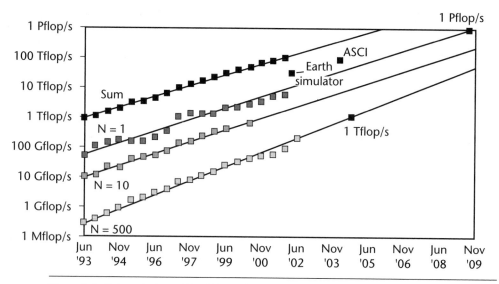

Figure 1.4   Extrapolation of Top500 results.

of software systems and algorithms that promote portability while easing the burden of program design and implementation.

1.2   What Have We Learned from Applications?

Remarkable strides have been taken over the last decade in utilization of high-end, that is, parallel, computers. Federal agencies, most notably the National Science Foundation, Department of Energy, National Aeronautics and Space Administration, and Department of Defense, have provided increasingly powerful, scalable resources to scientists and engineers across the country. We discuss a handful of lessons learned that punctuate the lifetime of the CRPC and provide important context for the next millennium.

Parallel computing can transform science and engineering.   Scalable, parallel computing has transformed a number of science and engineering disciplines, including cosmology, environmental modeling, condensed matter physics, protein folding, quantum chromodynamics, device and semiconductor simulation, seismology, and turbulence [447]. As an example, consider cosmology [729]—the study of the universe, its evolution and structure—where one of the most striking paradigm shifts has occurred. A number of new, tremendously detailed observations deep into the universe are available from such instruments as the Hubble Space Telescope and the Digital Sky Survey. However, until recently, it has been difficult, except in relatively simple circumstances, to tease from mathematical theories of the early universe enough information to allow comparison with observations.

However, scalable parallel computers with large memories have changed all of that. Now, cosmologists can simulate the principal physical processes at work in the early universe over space–time volumes sufficiently large to determine the large-scale structures predicted by the models. With such tools, some theories can be discarded as being incompatible with the observations. High-performance computing has allowed comparison of theory with observation and thus has transformed the practice of cosmology.

To port or not to port. That is not the question.   "Porting" a code to parallel architectures is more than simply bringing up an existing code on a new machine. Because parallel machines are fundamentally different from their vector predecessors, porting presents an opportunity to reformulate the basic code and data structures and, more importantly, to reassess the basic representation of the processes or dynamics involved. As an example, consider ocean modeling, where the standard Bryan–Cox–Semtner (BCS) code was retargeted from Cray vector architecture to the CM-2 and CM-5 [874]. The BCS model was inefficient in parallel for two reasons: the primary loop structure needed to be reorganized, and global communications were required by the stream-function formulation of the BCS representation. The latter feature of the BCS model required that independent line integrals be performed around each island in the calculation. The model was reformulated in surface-pressure form, where the solution of the resulting equations does not require line integrals around islands and is better conditioned than the mathematically equivalent stream-function representation. An additional change to the original model relaxed the "rigid-lid" approximation that suppressed surface-gravity waves (and allowed longer time steps) in the BCS model.

In addition to a more efficient code on either a vector or parallel architecture, this reformulation brought several remarkable benefits:

1. Islands were treated with simple, pointwise boundary conditions, thereby allowing all island features to be included at a particular resolution.

2. Unsmoothed bottom topography could be used without adverse effects on convergence.

3. A free-surface boundary at the ocean–air interface made the sea-surface height a prognostic variable and allowed direct comparison with Topex–Poseidon satellite altimeter data.

Satellite data have become a key feature in the verification and validation of global ocean models [104].

Parallel supercomputing can answer challenges to society.   Computational science has just begun to make an impact on problems with direct human interest and on systems whose principal actors are not particles and aggregations of particles, but rather are humans and collections of humans.

Perhaps the most oft-asked and rarely answered question about scientific computing concerns predicting the weather. However, there are some things that can be said. Hurricane tracks are being more accurately predicted [561], which directly reduces the cost of evacuations and indirectly reduces loss of life. This increased fidelity is equal parts computation and observation—more accurate and detailed data on hurricane wind-fields is available using dropwindsondes that report not only the meteorological variables of interest, but also an accurate position by using the Global Positioning System. Another significant development over the last decade has been the Advanced Regional Prediction System [826] developed by the NSF Science and Technology Center for the Analysis and Prediction of Storms *(www.caps.ou.edu)*.

However, basically this work still concerns modeling of physical systems, in this case severe weather, which have significant impacts on society. A more difficult job is effectively modeling society itself, or a piece thereof. For example, detailed environmental impact statements are required prior to any significant change in metropolitan transportation systems. In order to meet this regulatory requirement, the Department of Transportation commissioned development of a transportation model. The result, TRANSIMS [940], models traffic flow by representing all of the traffic infrastructure (e.g., streets, freeways, lights, and stop signs), developing a statistically consistent route plan for the area's population, and then simulating the movement of each car, second by second. The principal distinction here is that we believe that precise mathematical laws exist that accurately characterize the dynamics and interplay of physical systems. No such systems of laws, with the possible exception of Murphy's, is contemplated for human-dominated systems.

It's not the hardware, stupid.   The focus has often been on computing hardware. The reasons are straightforward: Big systems cost a lot of money and take a lot of time to acquire; they have measurable, often mysterious except to the fully initiated, properties; and we wonder how close they are getting to the most famous computer of all, HAL. However, if we contrast the decade of the Crays to the tumultuous days of the MPPs, we realize that it was the consistency of the programming model, not the intricacies of the hardware, that made the former "good old" and the latter "interesting."

A case in point is seismic processing [247]. Schlumberger acquired two, 128-node CM-5s to provide seismic processing services to their customers. They were successful simply because it was possible, in this instance, to write an efficient post-stack migration code for the CM-5 and provide commercial-quality services to their customers, all within the 2 to 4 year operational window of any given high-end hardware platform. Those programs or businesses that could not profitably, or possibly, write new applications for each new hardware system were forced to continue in the old ways. However, the Schlumberger experience teaches us an important lesson: a successful high-end computing technology must have a stable, effective programming model that persists over the lifetime of the application. In the case of the Stockpile Stewardship Program, this is on the order of a decade.

In conclusion, applications have taught us much over the last 10 years.

1. Entire disciplines can move to a firm scientific foundation by using scalable, parallel computing to expand and elucidate mathematical theories, thus allowing comparison with observation and experiment.

2. High-end computing is beginning to make an impact on everyday life by providing more accurate, detailed, and trusted forecasts and predictions, even on human-dominated systems.

3. New approaches to familiar problems, taken in order to access high capacity, large memory parallel computers, can have tremendous ancillary benefits beyond mere restructuring of the computations.

4. A persistent programming model for scalable, parallel computers is absolutely essential if computational science and engineering is to realize even a fraction of its remarkable promise.

5. The increase in the accuracy, detail, and volume of observational data goes hand in hand with these same improvements in the computational arena.

1.3   Software and Algorithms

As we indicated at the beginning of this chapter, the widespread acceptance of parallel computation has been impeded by the difficulty of the parallel programming task. First, the expression of an explicitly parallel program is difficult—in addition to specifying the computation and how it is to be partitioned among processors, the developer must specify the synchronization and data movement needed to ensure that the program computes the correct answers and achieves high performance.

Second, because the nature of high-end computing systems changes rapidly, it must be possible to express programs in a reasonably machine-independent way, so that moving to new platforms from old ones is possible with a relatively small amount of effort. In other words, parallel programs should be portable between different architectures. However, this is a difficult ideal to achieve because the price of portability is often performance.

The goal of parallel computing software systems should be to make parallel programming easier and the resulting applications more portable while achieving the highest possible performance. This is clearly a tall order.

A final complicating factor for parallel computing is the complexity of the problems being attacked. This complexity requires extraordinary skill on the part of the application developer along with extraordinary flexibility in the developed applications. Often this means that parallel programs will be developed using multiple programming paradigms and often multiple languages. Interoperability is thus an important consideration in choosing the development language for a particular application component.

The principal goal of the CRPC has been the development of software and algorithms that address programmability, portability, and flexibility of parallel applications. Much of the material in this book is devoted to the explication of technologies developed in the CRPC and the broader community to ameliorate these problems. These technologies include new language standards and language processors, libraries that encapsulate major algorithmic advances, and tools to assist in the formulation and debugging of parallel applications.

In the process of carrying out this research we have learned a number of hard but valuable lessons. These lessons are detailed in the next few paragraphs.

Portability is elusive.   When the CRPC began, every vendor of parallel systems offered a different application programming interface. This made it extremely difficult for developers of parallel applications because the work of converting an application to a parallel computer would need to be repeated for each new parallel architecture. One of the most important contributions of the CRPC was an effort to establish cross-platform standards for parallel programming. The Message Passing Interface (MPI) and High Performance Fortran (HPF) standards are just two results of this effort.

However, portability is not just a matter of implementing a standard interface. In scientific computing, most users are interested in *portable performance*, which means the ability to achieve a high fraction of the performance possible on each machine from the same program image. Because the implementations of standard interfaces are not the same on each platform, portability, even for programs written in MPI or HPF, has not been automatically achieved. Typically, the implementor must spend significant amounts of time tuning an application for each new platform.

This tuning burden even extends to programming via portable libraries, such as ScaLAPACK. Here the CRPC approach has been to isolate the key performance issues in a few kernels that could be rewritten by hand for each new platform. Still the process remains tedious.

Algorithms are not always portable.   An issue impacting portability is that an algorithm does not always work well on every machine architecture. The differences arise because of the number and granularity of processors, connectivity and bandwidth, and the performance of the memory hierarchy on each individual processor. In many cases, portable algorithm libraries must be parameterized to do algorithm selection based on the architecture on which the individual routines are to run. This makes portable programming even more difficult.

Parallelism isn't everything.   One of the big surprises on parallel computers was the extent to which poor performance arises because of factors other than insufficient parallelism. The principal problem on scalable machines, other than parallelism, is data movement. Thus, the optimization of data movement between processors is a critical factor in performance of these machines. If this is not done well, a parallel application is likely to run poorly no matter how powerful the individual processors are. A second and increasingly important issue affecting performance is the bandwidth from main memory on a single processor. Many parallel machines use processors that have so little bandwidth relative to the processor power that the processor cycle time could be dialed down by a factor of two without affecting the running time of most applications. Thus, as parallelism levels have increased, algorithms and software have had to increasingly deal with memory hierarchy issues, which are now fundamental to parallel programming.

Community acceptance is essential to the success of software.   Technical excellence alone cannot guarantee that a new software approach will be successful. The scientific community is generally conservative, in the sense that they will not risk their effort on software strategies that are likely to fail. To achieve widespread use, there has to be the expectation that a software system will survive the test of time. Standards are an important part of this, but cannot alone guarantee success. A case in point is HPF. In spite of the generally acknowledged value of the idea of distribution-based languages and a CRPC-led standardization effort, HPF failed to achieve the level of acceptance of MPI because the commercial compilers did not mature in time to gain the confidence of the community.

Good commercial software is rare at the high end.   Because of the small size of the high-end supercomputing market, commercial software production is difficult to sustain unless it also supports a much broader market for medium-level systems, such as symmetric (shared-memory) multiprocessors. OpenMP has succeeded because it targets that market, while HPF was focused on the high end. The most obvious victim of market pressures at the high end are tools—tuners and debuggers—that are usually left until last by the vendors and often abandoned. This has seriously impeded the widespread acceptance of scalable parallelism and has led to a number of community-based efforts to fill the gap based on open software. Some of these efforts are described in later chapters.

1.4   Toward a Science of Parallel Computation

When the CRPC began activities in 1989, parallel computing was still in its infancy. Most commercial offerings consisted of a few processors that shared a single memory. Scalable parallel systems, although long a subject of research, had just graduated from laboratories to become prototype commercial products. Almost every parallel computer had a different proprietary programming interface. Since that time, many machines (and companies) have come and gone.

To deal with the rapid pace of change in parallel systems, application developers needed principles and tools that would survive in the long term and isolate them from the changing nature of the underlying hardware. On the other hand, they also needed new parallel algorithms and an understanding of how to match them to different architectures with differing numbers of processors. In short, they needed a science of parallel computation.

Fostering such a science was a major goal of the High-Performance Computing and Communications (HPCC) initiative, launched by the federal government in 1991. With the help of this initiative, the CRPC and the entire parallel-computing research community have made major strides toward the desired goal. Message-passing interfaces have been standardized; a variety of higher-level programming interfaces have been developed and incorporated into commercial products; debugging systems and I/O interfaces have matured into useful standards; and many new parallel algorithms have been developed and incorporated into widely distributed libraries and templates.

Why, in the face of these advances, is the science of parallel computation still interesting to study? In 1989, many of us felt that we could develop a higher-level parallel programming interface that would supplant the message-passing paradigms then being used. However, our expectation that explicit message passing would routinely be hidden from the developer has not been realized. Today, most developers must use explicit message passing, albeit via a more sophisticated portable interface, to generate efficient scalable parallel programs. This is but one example demonstrating that the science of parallel computation is incomplete.

It is possible that our original goal was unrealistic and that the desired science cannot be achieved. We doubt this, as we now understand much better the demands of applications and the intricacies of high-performance architectures. We understand better where parallel performance is essential and where the developer needs programming paradigms optimized more for functionality than performance; this corresponds to the emerging picture of hybrid systems as a Grid of loosely coupled high performance parallel "kernels." Furthermore, we now have better technologies than those available a decade ago. These technologies come not only from deeper understanding of the problem of parallel computing, but also from new ideas. These include the broader acceptance of object-based languages, powerful scripting environments, and the growing understanding of the role of meta-data in defining how computation should be applied dynamically. Java, Python, and the Semantic Web are illustrative of technologies reflecting these new ideas.

Our intent is that this book document the current science of parallel computation, including the best methods, algorithms, and tools that were developed during the 11 years of CRPC activities, and thus serve as a useful resource for practicing application developers. In addition, we hope it will motivate new approaches to the support of parallel programming that could lead finally to the realization of our original dream.

2

Parallel Computer Architectures

William Gropp • **Rick Stevens** •
Charlie Catlett

Parallel computers provide great amounts of computing power, but they do so at the cost of increased difficulty in programming and using them. Certainly, a uniprocessor that was fast enough would be simpler to use. To explain why parallel computers are inevitable and to identify the challenges facing developers of parallel algorithms, programming models, and systems, in this chapter we provide an overview of the architecture of both uniprocessor and parallel computers. We show that while computing power can be increased by adding processing units, memory latency (the irreducible time to access data) is the source of many challenges in both uniprocessor and parallel processor design. In Chapter 3, some of these issues are revisited from the perspective of the programming challenges they present.

Parallel architectures and programming models are not independent. While most architectures can support all major programming models, they may not be able to do so with enough efficiency to be effective. An important part of any parallel architecture is any feature that simplifies the process of building (including compiling), testing, and tuning an application. Some parallel architectures put a great deal of effort into supporting a parallel programming model; others provide little or no extra support. All architectures represent a compromise among cost, complexity, timeliness, and performance. Chapter 12 discusses some of the issues of parallel languages and compilers; for parallel computers that directly support parallel languages, the ability to compile efficient code is just as important as it is for the single-processor case.

In Section 2.1, we briefly describe the important features of single-processor (or uniprocessor) architecture. From this background, the basics of parallel architecture are presented in Section 2.2; in particular, we describe the opportunities for performance improvement through parallelism at each level in a parallel computer, with references to machines of each type. In Section 2.3, we examine potential future parallel computer architectures. We conclude the chapter with a brief summary of the key issues motivating the development of parallel algorithms and programming models.

This chapter discusses only parallel architectures used in high-performance computing. Parallelism is widely used in commercial computing for applications such as databases and Web servers. Special architectures and hardware have been developed to support these applications, including special hardware support for synchronization and fault tolerance.

2.1   Uniprocessor Architecture

In this section we briefly describe the major components of a conventional, single-processor computer, emphasizing the design tradeoffs faced by the hardware architect. This description lays the groundwork for a discussion of parallel architectures, since parallelism is entirely a response to the difficulty of obtaining ever greater performance (or reliability) in a system that inherently performs only one task at a time. Readers familiar with uniprocessor architecture may skip to the next section. Those interested in a more detailed discussion of these issues should consult Patterson and Hennessy [759].

The major components of a computer are the central processing unit (CPU) that executes programs, the memory system that stores executing programs and the data that the programs are operating on, and input/output systems that allow the computer to communicate with the outside world (e.g., through keyboards, networks, and displays) and with permanent storage devices such as disks. The design of a computer reflects the available technology; constraints such as power consumption, physical size, cost, and maintainability; the imagination of the architect; and the software (programs) that will run on the computer (including compatibility issues). All of these have changed tremendously over the past 50 years.

Perhaps the best-known change is captured by Moore's Law [679], which says that microprocessor CPU performance doubles roughly every 18 months. This is equivalent to a thousandfold increase in performance over 15 years. Moore's Law has been remarkably accurate over the past 36 years (see Figure 2.1), even though it represents an observation about (and a driver of) the rate of engineering progress and is not a law of nature (such as the speed of light). In fact, it is interesting to look at the clock speed of the *fastest* machines in addition to (and compared with) that of microprocessors. In 1981, the Cray 1 was one of the fastest computers, with a 12.5 ns clock. In 2001, microprocessors with 0.8 ns clocks are becoming available. This is a factor of 16 in 20 years, or equivalently a doubling every 5 years.

Remarkable advances have occurred in other areas of computer technology as well. The cost per byte of storage, both in computer memory and in disk storage, has fallen along a similar exponential curve, as has the physical size per byte of storage (in fact, cost and size are closely related). Dramatic advancements in algorithms have reduced the amount of work needed to solve many classes of important problems; for example, the work needed to solve n simultaneous linear equations has fallen,

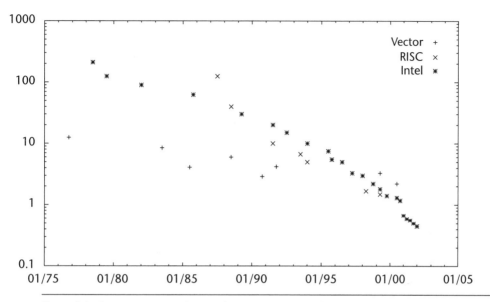

Figure 2.1 Improvement in CPU performance measured by clock rate in nanoseconds.

in many cases, from n^3 to n. For 1 million equations, this is an improvement of 12 orders of magnitude!

Unfortunately, these changes have not been uniform. For example, while the density of storage (memory and disk) and the bandwidths have increased dramatically, the decrease in the time to access storage (latency) has not kept up. As a result, over the years, the balance in performance between the different parts of a computer has changed. In the case of storage, increases in clock rates relative to storage latency have translated Moore's Law into a description of *inflation* in terms of the relative cost of memory access from the point of view of potentially wasted CPU cycles. This has forced computer architectures to evolve over the years, for example, moving to deeper and more complex memory hierarchies.

2.1.1 The CPU

The CPU is the heart of the computer; it is responsible for all calculations and for controlling or supervising the other parts of the computer. A typical CPU contains the following (see Figure 2.2):

- *Arithmetic logic unit (ALU)*. Performs computations such as addition and comparison.
- *Floating-point unit (FPU)*. Performs operations on floating-point numbers.
- *Load/store unit*. Performs loads and stores for data.

- *Registers*. Fast memory locations used to store intermediate results. These are often subdivided into floating-point registers (FPRs) and general purpose registers (GPRs).

- *Program counter (PC)*. Contains the address of the instruction that is executing.

- *Memory interface*. Provides access to the memory system. In addition, the CPU chip often contains the fastest part of the memory hierarchy (the top-level cache); this part is described in Section 2.1.2.

Other components of a CPU are needed for a complete system, but the ones listed are the most important for our purpose.

The CPU operates in steps controlled by a clock: In each step, or *clock cycle*, the CPU performs an operation.[1] The speed of the CPU clock has increased dramatically; desktop computers now come with clocks that run at over 2 GHz (2×10^9 Hz).

One of the first decisions that a computer architect must make is what basic operations can be performed by the CPU. There are two major camps: the complex instruction set computer (CISC) and the reduced instruction set computer (RISC). A RISC CPU can do just as much as a CISC CPU; however, it may require more instructions to perform the same operation. The tradeoff is that a RISC CPU, because the instructions are fewer and simpler, may be able to execute each instruction faster (i.e., the CPU can have a higher clock speed), allowing it to complete the operation more quickly.

The specific set of instructions that a CPU can perform is called the instruction set. The design of that instruction set relative to the CPU represents the instruction set architecture (ISA). The instructions are usually produced by compilers from programs written in higher-level languages such as Fortran or C. The success of the personal computer has made the Intel x86 ISA the most common ISA, but many others exist, particularly for enterprise and technical computing. Because most programs are compiled, ISA features that either aid or impede compilation can have a major impact on the effectiveness of a processor. In fact, the ability of compilers to exploit the relative simplicity of RISC systems was a major reason for their development.

We note that while the ISA may be directly executed by the CPU, another possibility is to design the CPU to convert each instruction into a sequence of one or more "micro" instructions. This allows a computer architect to take advantage of simple operations to raise the "core" speed of a CPU, even for an ISA with complex instructions (i.e., a CISC architecture). Thus, even though a CPU may have a clock speed of over 1 GHz, it may need multiple clock cycles to execute a single instruction in the ISA. Hence, simple clock speed comparisons among different architectures are deceptive. Even though one CPU may have a higher clock speed than another, it may

---

[1] Note that we did not say an instruction or a statement. As we will see, modern CPUs may perform both less than an instruction and more than one instruction in a clock cycle.

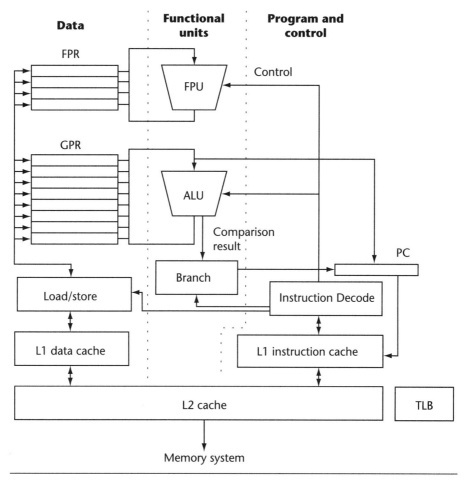

Figure 2.2   Generic CPU diagram. This example has a separate L1 cache for data and for program instructions and a unified (both data and instructions) L2 cache. Not all data paths are shown.

also require more clock cycles than the "slower" CPU in order to execute a single instruction.

Programs executed by the CPU are stored in memory. The *program counter* specifies the address in memory of the executing instruction. This instruction is fetched from memory and decoded in the CPU. As each instruction is executed, the PC changes to the address of the next instruction. Control flow in a program (e.g., if, while, or function call) is implemented by setting the PC to a new address.

One important part of the ISA concerns how memory is accessed. When memory speeds were relatively fast compared with CPU speeds (particularly for complex operations such as floating-point division), the ISA might have included instructions that read several items from memory, performed the operation, and stored the result into memory. These were called memory-to-memory operations. However, as CPU speeds increased dramatically relative to memory access speeds, ISAs changed to emphasize a "load-store" architecture. In this approach, all operations are performed by using data in special, very fast locations called *registers* that are part of the CPU. Before a value from memory can be used, it must first be loaded into a register, using an address that has been computed and placed into another register. Operations take operands from registers and put the result back into a register; these are sometimes called register-to-register operations. A separate store operation puts a value back into the memory (generally indirectly by way of a cache hierarchy analogous to the register scheme just described). Load operations and store operations are often handled by a load/store functional unit, much as floating-point arithmetic is handled by a floating-point unit (FPU).

Over the years, CPUs have provided special features to support various programming models. For example, CISC-style ISAs often include string search instructions and even polynomial evaluation. Some current ISAs support instructions that make it easy to access consecutive elements in memory by updating the register holding the load address; this corresponds closely to the a=*x++; statement in the C programming language and to typical Fortran coding practice for loops.

One source of complexity in a CPU is the difference in the complexity of the instructions. Some instructions, such as bitwise logical or, are easy to implement in hardware. Others, such as floating-point division, are extremely complicated. Memory references provide a different kind of complexity; as we will see, the CPU often cannot predict when a memory reference will complete. Many different approaches have been taken to address these issues. For example, in the case of floating-point operations, *pipelining* has been used. Like the RISC approach, pipelining breaks a complex operation into separate parts. Unlike the RISC approach, however, each stage in the pipeline can be executed at the same time by the CPU, but on different data. In other words, once a floating-point operation has been started in a clock cycle, even though that operation has not completed, a new floating-point operation can be started in the next clock cycle. It is not unusual for operations to take 2 to 20 cycles to complete. Figure 2.3 illustrates a pipeline for floating-point addition. Pipelines have been getting deeper (i.e., have more stages) as clock speeds increase. Note also that this hardware approach is very similar to the use of pipelining in algorithms described in Section 3.3.2. As CPUs have become faster, pipelining has been used more extensively. In modern CPUs, many other instructions (not just floating-point operations) may be pipelined.

From this discussion, we can already see some of the barriers to achieving higher performance. A clock rate of 1 GHz corresponds to a period of only 1 ns. In 1 ns, light travels only about 1 foot in a vacuum, and less in an electrical circuit. Even in the best case, a single processor running at 10 GHz (three more doublings in CPU performance or, if Moore's Law continues to hold, appearing in less than 5 years) and its memory could be only about 1 inch across; any larger and a signal could not cross the chip during a single clock cycle. At that size, heat dissipation, already a concern

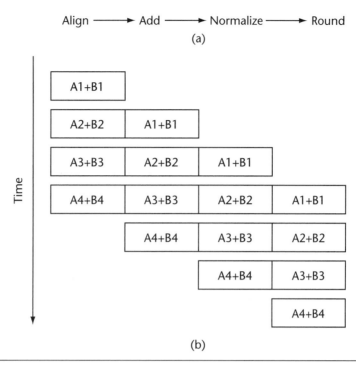

Align ⟶ Add ⟶ Normalize ⟶ Round

(a)

(b)

Figure 2.3 Example of a floating-point pipeline. (a) The separate stages in the pipeline. (b) Four pairs of numbers are added in 7 clock cycles. Note that after a 3-cycle delay, one result is returned every cycle. Without pipelining, 16 clock cycles would be required to add four pairs of numbers.

for many CPUs, becomes a major problem. Approaches such as pipelining (already a kind of parallelism) require that enough operations and operands be available to keep the pipeline full. Other approaches begin to introduce a very fine scale of parallelism. For example, multiple *functional units* such as multiple floating-point adders and multipliers may be provided. In such cases, however, the program must be rewritten and/or recompiled to make use of the additional resources. (These enhancements are discussed in Section 2.2.3.)

Once on-chip clock latency is addressed, the designer must face an even more challenging problem: latency to storage, beginning with memory.

2.1.2 Memory

While a computer is running, active data and programs are stored in memory. Memory systems are quite complex, introducing a number of design issues. Among these are the following:

- *Memory size*. Users never have enough computer memory, so the concept of *virtual memory* was introduced to fool programs into thinking that they have large amounts of memory just for their own use.

- *Memory latency and hierarchy.* The time to access memory has not kept pace with CPU clock speeds. Levels or *hierarchies* of memory try to achieve a compromise between performance and cost.

- *Memory bandwidth*. The rate at which memory can be transferred to and from the CPU (or other devices, such as disks) also has not kept up with CPU speeds.

- *Memory protection*. Many architectures include hardware support for memory protection, aimed primarily at preventing application software from modifying (intentionally or inadvertently) either system memory or memory in use by other programs.

Of these, memory latency is the most difficult problem. Memory size, in many ways, is simply a matter of money. Bandwidth can be increased by increasing the number of paths to memory (another use of parallelism) and using techniques such as interleaving. Latencies are related to physical constraints and are harder to reduce. Further, high latencies reduce the effective bandwidth of a given load or store. To see this, consider a memory interconnect that transfers blocks of 32 bytes with a bandwidth of 1 GB/s. In other words, the time to transfer 32 bytes is 32 ns. If the latency of the memory system is also 32 ns (an optimistic figure), the total time to transfer the data is 64 ns, reducing the effective bandwidth from 1 GB/s to 500 MB/s. The most common approach to improving bandwidth in the presence of high latency is to increase the amount of data moved each time, thus amortizing the latency over more data. However, this helps only when all data moved are needed by the running program. Chapter 3 discusses this issue in detail from the viewpoint of software.

An executing program, or *process*, involves an address space and one or more program counters. Operating systems manage the time sharing of a CPU to allow many processes to appear to be running at the same time (for parallel computers, the processes may in fact be running simultaneously). The operating system, working with the memory system hardware, provides each process with the appearance of a private address space. Most systems further allow the private memory space to appear larger than the available amount of physical memory. This is called a *virtual address space*. Of course, the actual physical memory hardware defines an address space, or *physical address space*. Any memory reference made by a process, for example, with a load or store instruction, must first be translated from the virtual address (the address known to the process) to the physical address. This step is performed by the *translation lookaside buffer* (TLB), which is part of the memory system hardware. In most systems, the TLB can map only a subset of the virtual addresses (it is a kind of address cache); if a virtual address can't be handled by the TLB, the operating system is asked to help out, and in such case, the cost of accessing memory greatly increases.

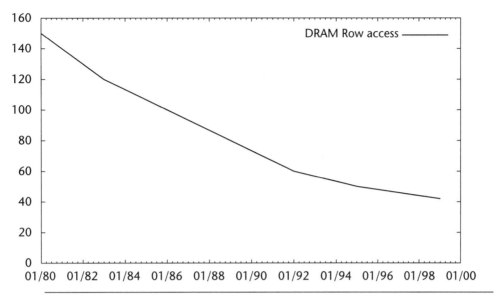

Figure 2.4 DRAM latency in nanoseconds versus time. Note that, unlike the CPU times in Figure 2.1, the vertical axis is linear, and the improvement in performance is little more than a factor of two in 10 years.

For this reason, some high-performance systems have chosen not to provide virtual addressing.

Finding ways to decrease memory latency is a difficult problem. To understand why, we must first look at how computer memory works. Semiconductor memory comes in two main types: static random access memory (SRAM), in which each bit of memory is stored in a latch made up of transistors, and dynamic random access memory (DRAM), in which each bit of memory is stored as a charge on a capacitor. SRAM is faster than DRAM but is much less dense (has fewer bits per chip) and requires much greater power (resulting in heat). The difference is so great that virtually all computers use DRAM for the majority of their memory. However, as Figure 2.4 shows, the performance of DRAM memory has not followed the Moore's Law curve that CPU clock speeds have. Instead, the density and price/performance of DRAMs have risen exponentially. The scale of this problem can be seen by comparing the speeds of DRAMs and CPUs. For example, a 1-GHz CPU will execute 60 instructions before a typical (60 ns) DRAM can return a single byte. Hence, in a program that issues a load for a data item that must come from DRAM, at least 60 cycles will pass before the data will be available. In practice, the delay can be longer because there is more involved in providing the data item than just accessing the DRAM.

To work around this performance gap, computer architects have introduced a hierarchy of smaller but faster memories. These are called *cache memories* because they work by caching copies of data from the DRAM memory in faster SRAM memory, closer to the CPU. Because SRAM memory is more expensive and less dense and consumes much more power than does DRAM memory, cache memory sizes are small relative to *main memory*. In fact, there is usually a hierarchy of cache memory, starting from level 1 (L1), which is the smallest (and fastest) and is on-chip on all modern CPUs. Many systems have two or three levels of cache. A typical size is 16 KB to 128 KB for L1 cache memory to as much as 4 MB to 8 MB for L2 or L3 cache memory. Typical DRAM memory sizes, on the other hand, are 256 MB to 4 GB—a factor of about a thousand larger.

Memory hierarchy brings up another problem. Because the cache memory is so much smaller than the main memory, it often isn't possible for all of the memory used by a process to reside in the L1 or even L2 cache memory. Thus, as a process runs, the memory system hardware must decide which memory locations to copy into cache. If the cache is full and a new memory location is needed, some other item must be removed from the cache (and written back[2] to the main memory if necessary). If the CPU makes a request for data, and the requested data are not in cache, a *cache miss* occurs. The rate at which this happens is called the *cache miss rate*, and one of the primary goals of a memory system architect is to make the miss rate as small as possible. Of course, the rate depends on the behavior of the program, and this in turn depends on the algorithms used by the program. Many different strategies are used to try to achieve low miss rates in a cache while keeping the cache fast and relatively inexpensive. To reduce the miss rate, programs exploit *temporal locality*: reusing the same data within a short span of time, that is, reusing the data before they are removed from the cache to make room for some other data. This process, in turn, requires the algorithm developer and programmer to pay close attention to how data are used in a program.

As just one example, consider the choice of the *cache-line size*. Data between cache and main memory usually are transferred in groups of 64, 128, or 256 bytes. This group is called a *cache line*. Moving an entire cache line at one time allows the main memory to provide relatively efficient bursts of data (it will be at least 60 ns before we can get the first byte; subsequent consecutive bytes can be delivered without much delay). Thus, programs that access "nearby" memory after the first access will find that the data they need are already in cache. For these programs, a larger line size will improve performance. However, programs that access memory in a less structured way may find that they spend most of their time reading data into cache that are never used. For these programs, a large line size reduces performance compared with

---

[2] Write-back caches wait until an item is displaced from the cache before writing the data back into memory. Write-through caches store data to memory and into the cache at the same time. Other approaches can be used as well.

a system that uses a shorter cache line. Chapter 3 discusses these issues in more detail, along with strategies for reducing the impact of memory hierarchies on performance.

Many other issues also remain, with similarly difficult tradeoffs, such as associativity (how main memory addresses are mapped into the cache), replacement policy (what data are ejected to make room for new data), and cache size. Exploiting the fact that memory is loaded in larger units than the natural scalar objects (such as integers, characters, or floating-point numbers) is called *exploiting spatial locality*. Spatial locality also requires temporal locality.

The effective use of cache memory is so important for high-performance applications that algorithms have been developed that are tailored to the requirements of these memory hierarchies. On the other hand, the most widely used programming models ignore cache memory requirements. Hence, problems remain with the practical programming of these systems for high performance. We also see in Section 2.2.1 that the use of copies of data in a cache causes problems for parallel systems.

In recent years, there has been rapid progress in memory system design, particularly for personal computers and workstations. Many of these designs have focused on delivering greater bandwidth and have names like RAMBUS, DDR (for double data rate), and EDO. See Cuppu et al. [240] and other articles in the same issue for a discussion of high-performance DRAM technologies.

2.1.3 I/O and Networking

Discussions of computers often slight the issues of I/O and networking. I/O, particularly to the disks that store files and swap space for supporting virtual memory, has followed a path similar to that of main memory. That is, densities and sizes have increased enormously (25 years ago, a 40-MB disk was large and expensive; today, a 40-GB disk is a commodity consumer item), but latencies have remained relatively unchanged. Because disks are electromechanical devices, latencies are in the range of milliseconds or a million times greater than CPU speeds. To address this issue, some of the same techniques used for memory have been adopted, particularly the use of caches (typically using DRAM memory) to improve performance.

Networking has changed less. Although Ethernet was introduced 22 years ago, only relatively modest improvements in performance were seen for many years, and most of the improvement has been in reduced monetary cost. Fortunately, in the past few years, this situation has started to change. In particular, the 100-MB Ethernet has nearly displaced the original 10-MB Ethernet, and several gigabit networking technologies are gaining ground, as are industry efforts, such as Infiniband [503], to accelerate the rate of improvement in network bandwidth. Optical technologies have been in use for some time but are now poised to significantly increase the available bandwidths. Networks, are, however, fundamentally constrained by the speed of light. Latencies can never be less than 3 ns per meter. Another constraint is the way in which the network is used by the software. The approaches that are currently used by most software involve the operating system (OS) in most networking operations, including most data transfers between the main memory and the network. Involving the OS significantly impacts performance; in many cases, data must be moved several times. Recent developments in networking [962, 964] have emphasized transfers that are executed without the involvement of the operating system, variously called *user-mode, OS bypass,* or *scheduled transfer.* These combine hardware support with a programming model that allows higher network performance.

2.1.4   Design Tradeoffs

The design of a single-processor computer is a constant struggle against competing constraints. How should resources be allocated? Is it better to use transistors on a CPU chip to provide a larger fast L1 cache, or should they be used to improve the performance of some of the floating-point instructions? Should transistors be used to add more functional units? Should there be more registers, even if the ISA then has to change? Should the L1 cache be made larger at the expense of the L2 cache? Should the memory system be optimized for applications that make regular or irregular memory accesses? There are no easy answers here. The complexity has in fact led to increasingly complex CPU designs that use tens or even hundreds of millions of transistors and that are enormously costly to design and manufacture. Particularly difficult is the mismatch in performance between memory and CPU. This mismatch also causes problems for programmers; see, for example, Karp [534] for a discussion of what should be a simple operation (bit reversal) but whose performance varies widely as a result of the use of caches and TLBs. These difficulties have encouraged computer architects to consider a wide variety of alternative approaches for improving computer system performance. Parallelism is one of the most powerful and most widely used.

2.2   Parallel Architectures

This section presents an overview of parallel architectures, considered as responses to limitations and problems in uniprocessor architectures and to technology opportunities. We start by considering parallelism in the memory systems, since the choices here have the most effect on programming models and algorithms. Parallelism in the CPU is discussed next; after increases in clock rates, this is a source of much of the improvement in sustained performance in microprocessors. For a much more detailed discussion of parallel computer architectures, see Culler et al. [236].

2.2.1   Memory Parallelism

One of the easiest ways to improve performance of a computer system is simply to replicate entire computers and add a way for the separate computers to communicate data. This approach, shown schematically in Figure 2.5, provides an easy way to increase memory bandwidth and aggregate processing power without changing the CPU, allowing parallel computers to take advantage of the huge investment in commodity microprocessor CPUs. The cost is in increased complexity of the software

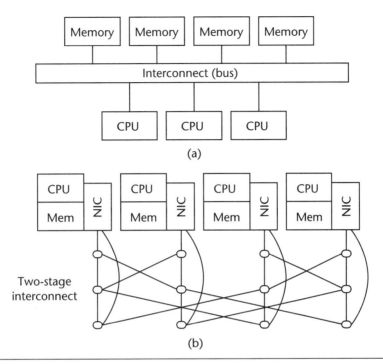

Figure 2.5 Schematic parallel computer organization. (a) Typical shared-memory system, where the interconnect may be either a simple bus or a sophisticated switch. (b) Distributed-memory system, which may be either a distributed shared-memory system or a simpler shared-nothing system, depending on the capabilities of the network interface (NIC).

and in the impact that this has on the performance of applications. The major choice here is between distributed memory and shared memory.

Distributed Memory

The simplest approach from the hardware perspective is the *distributed-memory*, or *shared-nothing*, model. The approach here is to use separate computers connected by a network. The typical programming model consists of separate processes on each computer communicating by sending messages (*message passing*), usually by calling library routines. This is the most classic form of parallel computing, dating back to when the computers were people with calculators and the messages were written on slips of paper [800]. The modern distributed-memory parallel computer started with the work of Seitz [845].

Distributed-memory systems are the most common parallel computers because they are the easiest to assemble. Systems from Intel, particularly the Paragon and the 512-processor Delta, were important in demonstrating that applications could make effective use of large numbers of processors. Perhaps the most successful commercial distributed-memory system is the IBM SP family. SP systems combine various versions of the successful RS6000 workstation and server nodes with different interconnects to provide a wide variety of parallel systems, from 8 processors to the 8192-processor ASCI White system. Some distributed-memory systems have been built with special-purpose hardware that provides remote memory operations such as put and get. The most successful of these are the Cray T3D and T3E systems.

Many groups have exploited the low cost and relatively high performance of commodity microprocessors to build clusters of personal computers or workstations. Early versions of these were built from desktop workstations and were sometimes referred to as NOWs, for networks of workstations. The continued improvement in performance of personal computers, combined with the emergence of open source (and free) versions of the UNIX operating system, gave rise to clusters of machines. These systems are now widely known as Beowulfs or Beowulf clusters, from a project begun by Thomas Sterling and Donald Becker at the National Aeronautics and Space Administration [897, 898]. They are real parallel machines; as of 2000, 2 of the top 100 supercomputer systems were built from commodity parts.

We note that the term *cluster* can be applied both broadly (any system built with a significant number of commodity components) or narrowly (only commodity components and open-source software). In fact, there is no precise definition of a cluster. Some of the issues that are used to argue that a system is a massively parallel processor (MPP) instead of a cluster include proprietary interconnects (various interconnects are described in Section 2.2.2), particularly ones designed for a specific parallel computer, and special software that treats the entire system as a single machine, particularly for the system administrators. Clusters may be built from personal computers or workstations (either single processors or symmetric multiprocessors (SMPs)) and may run either open-source or proprietary operating systems.

While the message-passing programming model has been successful, it emphasizes that the parallel computer is a collection of separate computers.

Shared Memory

A more complex approach ties the computers more closely together by placing all of the memory into a single (physical) address space and supporting virtual address spaces across all of the memory. That is, data are available to all of the CPUs through the load and store instructions of the ISA. Because access to the memory is through load and store operations rather than the network operations used in distributed-memory systems, access to remote memory has lower latency and higher bandwidth. These advantages come with a cost, however. The two major issues are *consistency* and *coherency*. The most serious problem (from the viewpoint of the programmer) is consistency. To understand this problem, consider the following simple Fortran program:

```
a = a + 1
b = 1
```

In a generic ISA, the part that increments the variable a might be translated into

```
  .
  .
  .
LOAD   R12, %A10  ;  Load a into register
ADD    R12, #1    ;  Add one to the value in R12
STORE R12, %A10   ;  Store the result back into A
  .
  .
  .
```

The important point here is that the single program statement a=a+1 turns into three separate instructions. Now, recall our discussion of cache memory. In a uniprocessor, the first time the LOAD operation occurs, the value is brought into the memory cache. The STORE operation writes the value from register *back into the cache*. Now, assume that another CPU, executing a program that is using the same address space, executes

```
10   if (b .eq. 0) goto 10
     print *, a
```

What value of a does that CPU see? We would like it to see the value of a after the increment. But that requires that the value has both been written back to the memory from the cache of the first CPU and read into cache (even if the corresponding cache line had previously been read into memory) on the second CPU. In other words, we want the program to execute as if the cache were not present, that is, as if every load and store operation worked directly on the memory and in the order in which it was written. The copies of the memory in the cache are used only to improve performance of memory operations; they do not change the behavior of programs that are accessing the same memory locations. Cache memory systems that accomplish this objective are called *cache coherent*. Most (but not all) shared-memory systems are cache coherent. Ensuring that a memory system is cache coherent requires additional hardware and adds to the complexity of the system. On the other hand, it simplifies the job of the programmer, since the correctness of a program doesn't depend on details of the behavior of the cache. We will see, however, that while cache coherence is necessary, it is not sufficient to provide the programmer with a friendly programming environment.

The complexity of providing cache coherency has led to different designs. One important class is called *uniform memory access* (UMA). In this design, each memory and cache is connected to all of the others; each part observes any memory opera- tion (such as a load from a memory location) and ensures that cache coherence is maintained. The name UMA derives from the fact that the time to access a location from memory (not from cache and on an unloaded or nearly idle machine) is inde- pendent of the address (and hence particular memory unit). Early implementations used a *bus*, which is a common signaling layer that connects each processor and memory. Because buses are not scalable (all devices on the bus must share a limited amount of communication), higher-performance UMA systems based on completely connected networks have been constructed. Such networks themselves are not scalable (the number of connections for p components grows as p^2), leading to another class of shared-memory designs.

The *nonuniform memory access* (NUMA) approach does not require that all memory be equally "distant" (in terms of access time). Instead, the memory may be connected by a scalable network. Such systems can be more sensitive to the details of data layout but can also scale to much larger numbers of processors. To emphasize that a NUMA system is cache coherent, the term CC-NUMA is often used. The term *distributed shared memory* (DSM) is also often used to emphasize the NUMA characteristics of this approach to building shared-memory hardware. The term *virtual shared memory*, or *virtual distributed shared memory*, is used to describe a system that provides the programmer with a shared-memory programming model built on top of distributed-memory (not DSM) hardware.

Shared-memory systems are becoming common, even for desktop systems. Most vendors include shared-memory systems among their offerings, including Compaq, HP, IBM, SGI, and Sun and many personal computer vendors. Most of these systems have between 2 and 16 processors; most of these are UMA systems. Typical CC-NUMA systems include the SGI Origin 3000 (typically up to 128 processors, and 1024 in special configurations) and the HP SuperDome (up to 64 processors). The SGI Origin uses an approach called *directory-based cache coherency* (*directory caches*, for short) [604] to distribute the information needed to maintain cache coherency across the network that connects the memory to the CPUs.

Shared-memory systems often have quite modest memory bandwidths. At the low end, in fact, the same aggregate memory bandwidth may be provided to systems with 1 to 4 or even 16 processors. As a result, some of these systems are often starved for memory bandwidth. This can be a problem for applications that do not fit in cache. Applications that are memory-access bound can even slow as processors are added in such systems. Of course, not all systems are underpowered, and the memory performance of even the low-end systems has been improving rapidly.

Memory Consistency and Programming Models

How does the programming model change when several threads or processes share memory? What are the new issues and concerns? Consider a uniprocessor CPU executing a single-user program (a single-threaded, single-process program). Programs execute simply, one statement after the other. Implicit in this is that all statements before the current statement have completed before the current statement is executed. In particular, all stores to and loads from memory issued by previous statements have completed before the current statement begins to execute. In a multiprocessor executing a single program on multiple processors, the notion of "current" statement and "completed before" is unclear—or rather, it can be defined to be clear, but only at a high cost in performance.

Section 3.2 discusses the question of when a program can be run in parallel and give correct results. The discussion focuses on the issues for software. Lamport [590] asked a similar question about the parallel computer hardware in an article titled, "How to Make a Multiprocessor Computer That Correctly Executes Multiprocess Programs." From a programmer's perspective, a parallel program should execute as if it were some arbitrary interleaving (but preserving order) of the statements in the program. This requirement is called *sequential consistency* and is essentially a "what you see (or write) is what you get" requirement for executing parallel programs. Unfortunately, while this matches the way most programmers look at their code, it imposes severe constraints on the hardware, in large part because of the high latency of memory accesses relative to the CPU speed.

Because providing sequential consistency limits performance, weaker models have been proposed. One model proposed in the late 1980s, called *processor consistency* [390], matched many of the then-current multiprocessor implementations but (usually) required some explicit action by the programmer to ensure correct program behavior. Programmers who use the thread programming model with thread locks to synchronize accesses to shared data structures satisfy this requirement because the implementation of the lock and unlock calls in the thread library ensures that the correct instructions are issued.

Some programmers prefer to avoid the use of locks, however, because of their relatively high overhead, and instead use flag variables to control access to shared data (as we used a as the flag variable in the preceding section). *Weak consistency* [295] is appropriate for such programs; like processor consistency, the programmer is required to take special steps to ensure correct operation.

Even weak consistency interferes with some performance optimizations, however. For this reason, *release consistency* [375] was introduced. This form of consistency separates synchronization between two processes or threads into an *acquire* and a *release* step.

The important point for programmers and algorithm developers is that the programming model that is most natural for programmers and which reflects the way we read programs is sequential consistency, and this model is not implemented by parallel computer hardware. Consequently, the programmer cannot rely on programs executing as some interleaved ordering of the statements. The specific consistency model that is implemented by the hardware may require different degrees of additional specification by the programmer. Language design for parallel programming may take the consistency model into account, providing ways for the compiler, not the programmer, to enforce consistency. Unfortunately, most languages (including C, C++, and Fortran) were designed for single threads of control and do not provide any mechanism to enforce consistency.

Note that if memory latency was small, providing sequential consistency would not greatly impact performance. Weaker forms of consistency would not be needed, and Lamport's title [590] would reflect real machines. In addition, these concepts address only correctness of parallel programs. Chapter 3 discusses some of the performance issues that arise in parallel computers, such as the problem of *false sharing*. Section 2.2.5 describes some of the instruction set features that are used by programming models to ensure correct operation of correct programs.

Other Approaches

Two other approaches to parallelism in memory are important. In both of these, the CPU is customized to work with the memory system. In single-instruction, multiple-data (SIMD) parallelism, simplified CPUs are connected to memory. Unlike the previous cases, in the SIMD approach, each CPU executes the *same* instruction in each clock cycle. Such systems are well suited for the *data-parallel* programming model, where data are divided up among memory systems and the same operation is performed on each data element. For example, the Fortran code

```
do i=1, 10000
   a(i) = a(i) + alpha * b(i)
enddo
```

can be converted into a small number of instructions, with each CPU taking a part of the arrays a and b. While these systems have fallen out of favor as general purpose computers, they are still important in fields such as signal processing. The most famous general purpose SIMD system was the Connection Machine (CM-1 and CM-2) [472].

The other major approach is vector computing. This is often not considered parallelism because the CPU has little explicit parallelism, but parallelism is used in the memory system. In vector computing, operations are performed on *vectors*, often groups of 64 floating-point numbers. A single instruction in a vector computer may cause 64 results to be computed (often with a pipelined floating-point unit), using vectors stored in vector registers. Data transfers from memory to vector registers make use of multiple memory *banks*; the parallelism in the memory supports very high bandwidths between the CPU and the memory. Vector computers often have memory bandwidths that are an order of magnitude or more greater than nonvector computers. We return to vector computing in Section 2.2.3 after discussing parallelism in the CPU.

Parallel vector processors represent one of the most powerful classes of parallel computer, combining impressive per processor performance with parallelism. As late as 1996, the top machines on the Top500 list of supercomputers were parallel vector processors [936], and since then only massively parallel systems with thousands of processors are faster.

The fastest of these machines may not provide full cache coherency in hardware; instead, they may require some support from the software to maintain a consistent view of memory. Machines in this category include the NEC SX-5 and Cray SV1. This is an example of the sort of tradeoff of performance versus cost and complexity that continues to face architects of parallel systems.

A distinguishing feature of vector processors and parallel vector processors is the high memory bandwidth, often 4 to 16 bytes per floating-point operation. This is reflected in the high sustained performance achieved on these machines for many scientific applications.

Parallel Random Access Memory

A great deal of theoretical work on the complexity of parallel computation has used the parallel random access memory (PRAM) model. This is a theoretical model of a shared-memory computer; different varieties of PRAM vary in the details of how memory accesses by different threads or processes to the same address are handled. In order to make the theoretical model tractable, memory access times are usually considered constant independent of the CPU performing the (nonconflicting) access; in particular, there are no caches and no factors of 100 or more difference in access times for different memory locations. While this model is valuable in understanding the limits of parallel algorithms, the PRAM model represents an abstraction that cannot be efficiently implemented in practice.

Limits to Memory System Performance

Latency can be hidden by issuing memory operations far enough ahead so that the data are available when needed. While hiding a few cycles of latency is possible, the large latencies to DRAM memory are difficult to hide. We can see this situation by applying Little's Law to memory requests. Little's Law is a result from queuing theory; applied to memory requests, it says that if the memory latency that needs to be hidden is L and the rate of requests is r, then the number of simultaneously active requests needed is rL. If this is cast in terms of clock cycles, and if the memory latency is 100 cycles and a memory request is issued every cycle, then 100 requests must be active at the same time. The consequences include the following:

1. The bandwidth of the memory system must support more requests (the number uses the same formula but uses the latency of the interconnect, which may still be around 10 cycles).
2. There must be enough independent work. Some algorithms, particularly those that use recurrence relations, do not have much independent work. This situation places a burden on the algorithm developer and the programmer.
3. The compiler must convert the program into enough independent requests, and there must be enough resources (such as registers) to hold results as they arrive (load) or until they depart (store).

Many current microprocessors allow a small number of outstanding memory operations; only the Cray MTA satisfies the requirements of Little's Law for main-memory accesses.

2.2.2 Interconnects

In the preceding section, we described the interaction of memories and CPUs. In this section, we say a little more about the interconnection networks used to connect components in a computer (parallel or otherwise).

Many types of networks have been used in the past 30 years for constructing parallel systems, ranging from relatively simple buses, to 2-D and 3-D meshes, to Clos networks, and to complex hypercube network topologies [602]. Each type of network can be described by its topology, its means of dealing with congestion (e.g., blocking or nonblocking), its approach to message routing, and its bandwidth characteristics.

For a long time, understanding details of the topology was important for programmers and algorithm developers seeking to achieve high performance. This situation is reflected both in the literature and in parallel programming models (e.g., the topology routines in message-passing interfaces). Recently, networks have improved to the point that for many users, network topology is no longer a major factor in performance. However, some of this apparent "flatness" (uniformity) in the topology comes from greatly increased bandwidth within the network. As network endpoints become faster, network topology may again become an important consideration in algorithms and programming models. Congestion in the network can still be a problem if the network performance doesn't scale with the number of processing nodes. The term *bisection bandwidth* describes the bandwidth of the network across any cut that divides the network into two parts.

Note that there is no best approach. Simple mesh networks, such as those used in the Intel TFLOPS (ASCI Red) system, provide effective scalability for many applications through low latency and high bandwidth, even though a mesh network does not have scalable performance in the sense that the bisection bandwidth of a mesh does not grow proportionally with the number of nodes. It is scalable in terms of the hardware required: there is a constant cost per node for each node added.

When interconnects are viewed as networks between computers, the performance goals have been quite modest. Fast networks of this type typically have latencies of 10 microseconds or more (including essential software overheads) and bandwidths on the order of 100 MB/s. Interconnects used to implement shared memory, on the other hand, are designed to operate at memory system speeds and with no extra software overhead. Latencies for these systems are measured in nanoseconds, and bandwidths of 1 to 10 gigabytes per second are becoming common.

Early shared-memory systems used a bus to connect memory and processors. A bus provides a single, shared connection that all devices use and is relatively inexpensive to build. The major drawback is that if k devices are using the bus at the same time, under the best of conditions, each gets $1/k$ of the available performance (e.g., bandwidth). Contention between devices on the bus can lower the available bandwidth considerably.

To address this problem, some shared-memory systems have chosen to use networks that connect each processor with each memory system. For small numbers of processors and memories, a direct connection between each processor and memory is possible (requiring p^2 connections for p devices); this is called a *full crossbar*. For larger numbers of processors, a less complete network may be used. A common approach is to build an interconnect out of several stages, each stage containing some number of full crossbars. This provides a complete interconnect at the cost of additional latency.

An interesting development is the convergence of the technology used for networking and for shared memory. The *scalable coherent interconnect* (SCI) [498] was an early attempt to provide a memory-oriented view of interconnects and has been used to build CC-NUMA systems from Hewlett-Packard. Building on work both in research and in industry, the VIA [962] and Infiniband [503] industry-standard interconnects allow data to be moved directly from one processor's memory to another along an established circuit. These provide a communication model that is much closer to that used in memory interconnects and should offer much lower latencies and higher bandwidths than older, message-oriented interconnects.

Systems without hardware-provided cache coherency often provide a way to indicate that all copies of data in a cache should be discarded; this is called *cache invalidation*. Sometimes this is a separate instruction; sometimes it is a side effect of a synchronization instruction such as test-and-set (e.g., Cray SV-1). Software can use this strategy to ensure that programs operate correctly. The cost is that *all* copies of data in the cache are discarded; hence, subsequent operations that reference memory locations stall while the cache is refilled. To avoid this situation, some systems allow individual cache lines to be invalidated rather than the entire cache. However, such an approach requires great care by the software, since the failure to invalidate a line containing data that has been updated by another processor can lead to incorrect and nondeterministic behavior by the program.

For an engaging discussion of the challenges of implementing and programming shared-memory systems, see Pfister [763].

2.2.3   CPU Parallelism

Parallelism at the level of the CPU is more difficult to implement than simple replication of CPUs and memory, even when the memory presents a single shared address space. However, modest parallelism in the CPU provides the easiest route to improved performance for the majority of applications because little needs to be done by the programmer to exploit this kind of parallelism.

Superscalar Processing

Look at Figure 2.2 again, and consider the following program fragment:

```
real a, b, c
integer i, j, k
     .
     .
     .
a = b * c
i = j + k
```

Assume that the values a, b, c, i, j, and k are already in register. These two statements use different functional units (FPU and ALU, respectively) and different register sets (FPR and GPR). A *superscalar* processor can execute both of these statements (each requiring a single register-to-register instruction) in the same clock cycle (more precisely, such a processor will "begin execution" of the two statements, since both may be pipelined). The term superscalar comes from the fact that more than one operation can be performed in a single clock cycle and that performance is achieved on nonvector code. A superscalar processor allows as much parallelism as there are functional units. Because separate instructions are executed in parallel, this is also called *instruction-level parallelism* (ILP). For ILP to be effective, it must be easy for the hardware to find instructions that do not depend on one another and that use different functional units. Consider the following example, where the CPU has one adder and one multiplier. If the CPU executes instructions in the order that they appear, then the code sequence on the left will take three cycles and the one on the right only two cycles.

```
a = b * c          a = b * c
d = e * f          i = j + k
i = j + k          d = e * f
l = m + n          l = m + n
```

Some CPUs will attempt to reorder instructions in the CPU's hardware, an action that is most beneficial to legacy applications that cannot be recompiled. It is often better, however, if the compiler *schedules* the instructions for effective use of ILP; for example, a good code-scheduling compiler would transform the code on the left to the code on the right (but breaking sequential consistency because the load/store order is not preserved!).

One major drawback of ILP, then, is that the hardware must rediscover what a scheduling compiler already knows about the instructions that can be executed in the same clock cycle.

Explicitly Parallel Instructions

Another approach is for the instruction set to encode the use of each part of the CPU. That is, each instruction contains explicit subinstructions for each of the different functional units in the CPU. Since each instruction must explicitly specify more details about what happens in each clock cycle, the resulting instructions are longer than in other ISAs. In fact, they are usually referred to as *very long instruction word* (VLIW) ISAs. VLIW systems usually rely on the compiler to schedule each functional unit. One of the earliest commercial VLIW machines was the Multiflow Trace. The Intel IA64 ISA is a descendant of this approach; the term EPIC (explicitly parallel instruction computing) is used for the Intel variety. EPIC does relax some of the restrictions of VLIW but still relies on the compiler to express most of the parallelism.

SIMD and Vectors

One approach to parallelism is to apply the same operation to several different data values, using multiple functional units. For example, a single instruction might cause four values to be added to four others, using four separate adders. We have seen this SIMD style of parallelism before, when applied to separate memory units. The SIMD approach is used in some current processors for special operations. For example, the Pentium III includes a small set of SIMD-style instructions for single-precision floating-point and related data move operations. These are designed for use in graphics transformations that involve matrix-vector multiplication by 4×4 matrices.

Vector computers use similar techniques in the CPU to achieve greater performance. A vector computer can apply the same operation to a collection of data called a *vector*; this is usually either successive words in memory or words separated by a constant offset or *stride*. Early systems such as the CDC Star 100 and Cyber 205 were vector memory-to-memory architectures where vectors could be nearly any length. Since the Cray 1, most vector computers have used vector registers, typically limiting vectors to 64 elements. The big advantage of vector computing comes from the regular memory access that a vector represents. Through the use of pipelining and other techniques such as chaining, a vector computer can completely hide the memory latency by overlapping the access to the next vector with operations on a current vector.

Vector computing is related to VLIW or explicitly parallel computing in the sense that each instruction can specify a large amount of work and that advanced compilers are needed to take advantage of the hardware. Vectors are less flexible than the VLIW or EPIC approach but, because of the greater regularity, can sustain higher performance on applications that can be expressed in terms of vectors.

Multithreading

Parallelism in the CPU involves executing multiple sets of instructions. Any one of these sets, along with the related virtual address space and any state, is called a *thread*. Threads are most familiar as a software model (see Chapter 10), but they are also a hardware model. In the usual hardware model, a thread has no explicit dependencies with instructions in any other thread, although there may be implicit dependencies through operations on the same memory address. The critical issues are (1) How many threads issue operations in each clock cycle? and (2) How many clock cycles does it take to switch between different threads?

Simultaneous multithreading (SMT) [943] allows many threads to issue instructions in each clock cycle. For example, if there are four threads and four functional units, then as long as each functional unit is needed by some thread in each clock cycle, all functional units can be kept busy every cycle, providing maximum use of the CPU hardware. The compiler or programmer must divide the program into separately executing threads. The SMT approach is starting to show up in CPU designs including versions of the IBM Power processors.

Fine-grained multithreading uses a single thread at a time but allows the CPU to change threads in a single clock cycle. Thus, a thread that must wait for a slow operation (anything from a floating-point addition to a load from main memory) can be "set aside," allowing other threads to run. Since a load from main memory may take 100 cycles or more, the benefit of this approach for hiding memory latency is apparent. The drawback when used to hide memory latency can be seen by applying Little's Law. Large numbers of threads must be provided for this approach to succeed in completely hiding the latency of main (rather than cache) memory. The Cray MTA is the only commercial architecture to offer enough threads for this purpose.

All of these techniques can be combined. For example, fine-grained multithreading can be combined with superscalar ILP or explicit parallelism. SMT can restrict groups of threads to particular functional units in order to simplify the processor design, particularly in processors with multiple FPUs and ALUs.

2.2.4   I/O and Networking for Parallel Processors

Just as in the uniprocessor case, I/O and networking for parallel processors have not received the same degree of attention as have CPU and memory performance. Fortunately, the lower performance levels of I/O and networking devices relative to CPU and memory allow a simpler and less expensive architecture. On the other hand, lower performance puts tremendous strain on the architect trying to maintain balance in the system. A common I/O solution for parallel computers, particularly clusters, is not a parallel file system but rather a conventional file system, accessed by multiple processors.

Recall that data caches are often used to improve the performance of I/O systems in uniprocessors. As we have seen, it is important to maintain consistency between the different caches and between caches and memory if correct data are to be provided to programs. Unfortunately, particularly for networked file systems such as NFS, maintaining cache consistency seriously degrades performance. As a result, such file systems allow the system administrator to trade performance against cache coherence. For environments where most applications are not parallel and do not have multiple processes accessing the same file at the nearly same time, cache coherence is usually sacrificed in the name of speed.

The redundant arrays of inexpensive disks (RAID) approach is an example of the benefits of parallelism in I/O. RAID was first proposed in 1988 [757], with five different levels representing different uses of multiple disks to provide fault tolerance (disks, being mechanical, fail more often than entirely electronic components) and performance, while maintaining a balance between read rates, write rates, and efficient use of storage. The RAID approach has since been generalized to additional levels. Both hardware (RAID managed by hardware, presenting the appearance of a single but faster and/or more reliable disk) and software (separate disks managed by software) versions exist.

Parallel I/O can also be achieved by using arrays of disks arranged in patterns different from those described by the various RAID levels. Chapter 11 describes parallel I/O from the programmer's standpoint. A more detailed discussion of parallel I/O can be found in May [657].

The simplest form of parallelism in networks is the use of multiple paths, each carrying part of the traffic. Networks within a computer system often achieve parallelism by simply using separate wires for each bit. Less tightly coupled systems, such as Beowulf clusters, sometimes use a technique called *channel bonding*, which uses multiple network paths, each carrying part of the message. GridFTP [22] is an example of software that exploits the ability of the Internet to route data over separate paths to avoid congestion in the network.

A more complex form of parallelism is the use of different electrical or optical frequencies to concurrently place several messages on the same wire or fiber. This approach is rarely used within a computer system because of the added cost and complexity, but it is used extensively in long-distance networks. New techniques for optical fibers, such as dense wavelength-division multiplexing (DWDM), will allow 100 or more signals to share the same optical fiber, greatly increasing bandwidth.

2.2.5   Support for Programming Models

Special operations are needed to allow processes and threads that share the same address space to coordinate their actions. For example, one thread may need to keep others from reading a location in memory until it has finished modifying that location. Such protection is often provided by *locks*: any thread that wants to access the particular data must first acquire the lock, releasing the lock when it is done. A lock, however, is not easy to implement with just load and store operations (although it can be done). Instead, many systems provide compound instructions that can be used to implement locks, such as test-and-set or fetch-and-increment. RISC systems often provide a "split" compound instruction that can be used to build up operations such as fetch-and-increment based on storing a result after reading from the same address only if no other thread or process has accessed the same location since the load.

Because rapid synchronization is necessary to support fine-grained parallelism, some systems (particularly parallel vector processors) use special registers that all CPUs can access. Other systems have provided extremely fast *barriers*: no process can leave a barrier until all have entered the barrier. In a system with a fast barrier, a parallel system can be viewed as sequentially consistent, where an "operation" is defined as the group of instructions between two barriers. This provides an effective programming model for some applications.

In distributed-memory machines, processes share no data and typically communicate through messages. In shared-memory machines, processes directly access data. There is a middle ground: remote memory access (RMA). This is similar to the network-connected, distributed-memory system except that additional hardware provides put and get operations to store to or load from memory in another node. The result is still a distributed-memory machine, but one with very fast data transfers. Examples are the Compaq AlphaServer SC, Cray T3D and T3E, NEC Cenju 4, and Hitachi SR8000.

2.2.6   Parallel Architecture Design Tradeoffs

Parallelism is a powerful approach to improving the performance of a computer system. All systems employ some degree of parallelism, even if it is only parallel data paths between the memory and the CPU. Parallelism is particularly good at solving problems related to bandwidth or throughput; it is less effective at dealing with latency or start-up costs (although the ability to switch between tasks provides one way to hide latency as long as enough independent tasks can be found). Parallelism does not come free, however. The effects of memory latency are particularly painful, forcing complex consistency models on the programmer and difficult design constraints on the hardware designer.

In the continuing quest for ever greater performance, today's parallel computers often combine many of the approaches discussed here. One of the most popular is distributed-memory clusters of nodes, where each node is a shared-memory processor, typically with 2 to 16 processors, though some clusters have SMP nodes with as many as 128 processors. Another important class of machine is the parallel vector processor, which uses vector-style CPU parallelism combined with shared memory.

We emphasize that hardware models and software (or programming) models are essentially disjoint; shared-memory hardware provides excellent message-passing support, and distributed-memory hardware can (at sometimes substantial cost) support a shared-memory programming model.

We close this section with a brief mention of taxonomies of parallel computers. A taxonomy of parallel computers provides a way to identify the important features of a system. Flynn [340] introduced the best-known taxonomy that defines four different types of computer based on whether there are multiple data streams and/or multiple instruction streams. A conventional uniprocessor has a single instruction stream and a single data stream and is denoted SISD. Most of the parallel computers described in this section have both multiple data and multiple instruction streams (because they have many memories and CPUs); these are called MIMD. The single instruction but multiple data parallel computer, or SIMD, has already been mentioned. The fourth possibility is the multiple-instruction, single-data category, or MISD, which is not used. A standard taxonomy for MIMD architectures has not yet emerged, but it is likely to be based on whether the memory is shared or distributed and, if it is shared, whether it is cache coherent and how access time varies. Many of the terms used to describe these alternatives have been discussed above, including UMA, CC-NUMA, and DSM.

The term *single program, multiple data* (SPMD) is inspired by Flynn's taxonomy. Because the single program has branches and other control-flow constructs, SPMD is a subset of MIMD, not a subset of SIMD programs. Using a single program, however, does provide an important simplification for software, and most parallel programs in technical and scientific computing are SPMD.

2.3   Future Directions for Parallel Architectures

In some ways, the future of parallel architectures, at least for the next 5 years, is clear. Most parallel machines will be hybrids, combining nodes containing a modest number of commodity CPUs sharing memory in a distributed-memory system. Many users will have only one shared-memory node; for them, shared-memory programming models will be adequate. In the longer term, the picture is much hazier. Many challenges will be difficult to overcome. Principal among these are memory latency and the limits imposed by the speed of light. Heat dissipation is also becoming a major problem for commodity CPUs. One major contributor to the increase in clock speeds for CPUs has been a corresponding decrease in the size of the features on the CPU chip. These feature sizes are approaching the size of a single atom, beyond which no further decrease is possible.

While these challenges may seem daunting, they offer an important opportunity to computer architects and software scientists—an opportunity to take a step that is more than just evolutionary.

As we have discussed above, one of the major problems in designing any computer is providing a high-bandwidth, low-latency path between the CPU and memory. Some of this cost comes from the way DRAMs operate: data are stored in rows; when an item is needed, the entire row is read and the particular bit is extracted, and the other bits in the row are discarded. This simplifies the construction of the DRAM (separate wires are not needed to get to each bit), but it throws away significant bandwidth. Observing that DRAM densities are increasing at a rate even faster than the rate at which commodity software demands memory, several researchers have explored combining the CPU and memory on the same chip and using the entire DRAM row rather than a single bit at a time. In fact, an early commercial version of this approach, the Mitsubishi M32000D3 processor, used a conventional, cache-oriented RISC processor combined with memory and organized so that a row of the memory was a cache line, allowing for enormous (for the time) bandwidth in memory-cache transfers. Several different architectures that exploit processors and memory in the same chip are currently being explored [275, 756], including approaches that consider vector-like architectures and approaches that place multiple processors on the same chip. Other architects are looking at parallel systems built from such chips; the IBM Blue Gene [121] project expects to have a million-processor system (with around 32 processors per node).

Superconducting elements promise clock speeds of 100 GHz or more. Of course, such advances will only exacerbate the problem of the mismatch between CPU and memory speeds. Designs for CPUs of this kind often rely on hardware multithreading techniques to reduce the impact of high memory latencies.

Computing based on biological elements often seeks to exploit parallelism by using molecules as processing elements. Quantum computing, particularly quantum computing based on exploiting the superposition principle, is a fundamentally different kind of parallelism.

2.4   Conclusion

Parallel architecture continues to be an active and exciting area of research. Most systems now have some parallelism, and the trends point to increasing amounts of parallelism at all levels, from 2 to 16 processors on the desktop to tens to hundreds of thousands for the highest-performance systems. Systems continue to be developed;

see van der Steen and Dongarra [951] for a review of current supercomputers, including large-scale parallel systems.

Access to memory continues to be a major issue; hiding memory latency is one area where parallelism doesn't provide a (relatively) simple solution. The architectural solutions to this problem have included deep memory hierarchies (allowing the use of low-latency memory close to the processor), vector operations (providing a simple and efficient "prefetch" approach), and fine-grained multithreading (enabling other work to continue while waiting for memory). In practice, none of these approaches completely eliminates the problem of memory latency. The use of low-latency memories, such as caches, suffers when the data do not fit in the cache. Vector operations require a significant amount of regularity in the operations that may not fit the best (often adaptive) algorithms, and multithreading relies on identifying enough independent threads. Because of this, parallel programming models and algorithms have been developed that allow the computational scientist to make good use of parallel systems. That is the subject of the rest of this book.

Acknowledgments

This work was supported by the Mathematical, Information, and Computational Sciences Division subprogram of the Office of Advanced Scientific Computing Research, U.S. Department of Energy, under Contract W-31-109-ENG-38.

C
H
A
P
T
E
R

3 Parallel Programming Considerations

Ken Kennedy • **Jack Dongarra** •
Geoffrey Fox • **William Gropp** •
Dan Reed

The principal goal of this chapter is to introduce the common issues that a programmer faces when implementing a parallel application. The treatment assumes that the reader is familiar with programming a uniprocessor using a conventional language, such as Fortran. The principal challenge of parallel programming is to decompose the program into subcomponents that can be run in parallel. However, to understand some of the low-level issues of decomposition, the programmer must have a simplified view of parallel machine architecture. Thus, we begin our treatment with a review of this topic, with the goal of identifying the characteristics that are most important for the parallel programmer to understand. This discussion, found in Section 3.1, focuses on two main parallel machine organizations—shared memory and distributed memory—that characterize most current machines. The section also treats hybrids of the two main memory designs.

The standard parallel architectures support a variety of decomposition strategies, such as decomposition by task (task parallelism) and decomposition by data (data parallelism). Our introductory treatment will concentrate on data parallelism because it represents the most common strategy for scientific programs on parallel machines. In data parallelism, the application is decomposed by subdividing the data space over which it operates and assigning different processors to the work associated with different data subspaces. Typically this strategy involves some data sharing at the boundaries, and the programmer is responsible for ensuring that this data sharing is handled correctly—that is, data computed by one processor and used by another are correctly synchronized.

Once a specific decomposition strategy is chosen, it must be implemented. Here, the programmer must choose the programming model to use. The two most common models are the following:

- The *shared-memory model*, in which it is assumed that all data structures are allocated in a common space that is accessible from every processor.

- The *message-passing model*, in which each processor (or process) is assumed to have its own private data space, and data must be explicitly moved between spaces as needed.

In the message-passing model, data structures are distributed across the processor memories; if a processor needs to use a data item that is not stored locally, the processor that owns that data item must explicitly "send" it to the requesting processor. The latter must execute an explicit "receive" operation, which is synchronized with the send, before it can use the communicated data item. These issues are discussed in Section 3.2.

To achieve high performance on parallel machines, the programmer must be concerned with *scalability* and *load balance*. Generally, an application is thought to be scalable if larger parallel configurations can solve proportionally larger problems in the same running time as smaller problems on smaller configurations. To understand this issue, we introduce in Section 3.3.1 a formula that defines parallel *speedup* and explore its implications. Load balance typically means that the processors have roughly the same amount of work, so that no one processor holds up the entire solution. To balance the computational load on a machine with processors of equal power, the programmer must divide the work and communications evenly. This can be challenging in applications applied to problems that are unknown in size until run time.

A particular bottleneck on most parallel machines is the performance of the memory hierarchy, both on a single node and across the entire machine. In Section 3.4, we discuss various strategies for enhancing the reuse of data by a single processor. These strategies typically involve some sort of loop "blocking" or "strip mining," so that whole subcomputations fit into cache.

Irregular or adaptive problems present special challenges for parallel machines because it is difficult to maintain load balance when the size of subproblems is unknown until run time or if the problem size may change after execution begins. Special methods involving run-time reconfiguration of a computation are required to deal with these problems. These methods are discussed in Section 3.3.3.

Several aspects of programming parallel machines are much more complicated than their counterparts for sequential systems. Parallel debugging, for example, must deal with the possibilities of race conditions or out-of-order execution (see Section 3.5). Performance analysis and tuning must deal with the especially challenging problems of detecting load imbalances and communication bottlenecks (see Section 3.6). In addition, it must present diagnostic information to the user in a format that is related to the program structure and programming model. Finally, input/output on parallel machines, particularly those with distributed memory, presents problems of how to read files that are distributed across disks in a system into memories that are distributed with the processors (see Section 3.7).

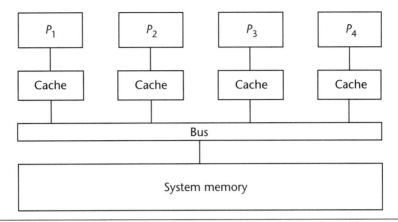

Figure 3.1 A uniform-access shared-memory architecture.

These topics do not represent all the issues of parallel programming. We hope, however, that a discussion of them will convey some of the terminology and intuition of parallel programming. In so doing, it will set the stage for the remainder of this book.

3.1 Architectural Considerations

Chapter 2 provided a detailed review of parallel computer architectures. In this chapter, we provide a simple introduction to these topics that covers most of the important issues needed to understand parallel programming.

First, as discussed in Chapter 2, we observe that most of the modern parallel machines fall into two basic categories:

1. *Shared-memory machines*, which have a single shared address space that can be accessed by any processor.

2. *Distributed-memory machines*, in which the system memory is packaged with individual nodes of one or more processors and communication is required to provide data from the memory of one processor to a different processor.

3.1.1 Shared Memory

The organization of a shared-memory machine is depicted in Figure 2.5. Figure 3.1 shows a slightly more detailed diagram of a shared-memory system with four processors, each with a private cache, interconnected to a global shared memory via a single system bus. This organization is typically called a *symmetric multiprocessor* (SMP).

In a symmetric multiprocessor, each processor can access all locations in global memory using standard load operations. The hardware ensures that the caches

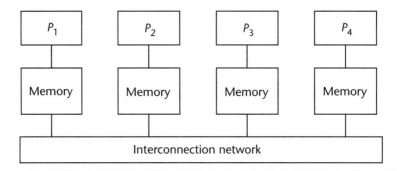

Figure 3.2 A distributed-memory architecture.

are "coherent" by watching the system bus and invalidating cached copies of any block that is written into. This mechanism is generally invisible to the user, except when different processors are simultaneously attempting to write into the same cache line, which can cause the cache line to ping-pong between two different caches, a situation known as *thrashing*. To avoid this problem, the programmer and programming system must be careful with shared data structures and nonshared data structures that can be located on the same cache block, a situation known as *false sharing*. Synchronization of accesses to shared data structures is a major issue on shared-memory systems—it is up to the programmer to ensure that operations by different processors on a shared data structure leave that data structure in a consistent state. Various memory consistency models are discussed in Section 2.2.1.

The main problem with the shared-memory system as described above is that it is not scalable to large numbers of processors. Most bus-based systems are limited to 32 or fewer processors because of contention on the bus. If the bus is replaced by a crossbar switch, systems can scale to as many as 128 processors, although the cost of the switch increases as the square of the number of processors, making this organization impractical for truly large numbers of processors. Multistage switches can be made to scale better at the cost of longer latencies to memory.

3.1.2   Distributed Memory

The scalability limitations of shared memory have led designers to use distributed-memory organizations such as the one depicted in Figure 3.2. Here the global shared memory has been replaced by a smaller local memory attached to each processor. Communication among the processor-memory configurations is over an interconnection network. These systems can be made scalable if a scalable interconnection network is used. For example, a hypercube has cost proportional to $n \lg(n)$ where n is the number of processors.

The advantage of a distributed-memory design is that access to local data can be quite fast. On the other hand, access to remote memories requires much more effort. Most distributed-memory systems support a *message-passing* programming model, in which the processor owning a datum must send it to any processor that needs it. These "send–receive" communication steps typically incur long start-up times, although the bandwidth after start-up can be high. Hence, on message-passing systems, it typically pays to send fewer, longer messages.

The principal programming problem for distributed-memory systems is management of communication between processors. Usually this means consolidation of messages between the same pair of processors and overlapping communication and computation so that long latencies are hidden. In addition, data placement is important so that as few data references as possible require communication.

3.1.3 Hybrid Systems

As seen in Chapter 2, there are various ways in which the two memory paradigms are combined. Some distributed-memory machines allow a processor to directly access a datum in a remote memory. On these *distributed shared-memory* (DSM) systems, the latency associated with a load varies with the distance to the remote memory. Cache coherency on DSM systems is a complex problem that is usually handled by a sophisticated network interface unit. Given that DSM systems have longer access times to remote memory, data placement is an important programming consideration.

For very large parallel systems, a hybrid architecture called an *SMP cluster* is common. An SMP cluster looks like a distributed-memory system in which each of the individual components is a symmetric multiprocessor rather than a single processor node. This design permits high parallel efficiency within a multiprocessor node, while permitting systems to scale to hundreds or even thousands of processors. Programming for SMP clusters provides all the challenges of both shared- and distributed-memory systems. In addition, it requires careful thought about how to partition the parallelism within and between computational nodes.

3.1.4 Memory Hierarchy

As discussed in Chapter 2, the design of memory hierarchies is an integral part of the design of parallel computer systems because the memory hierarchy is a determining factor in the performance of the individual nodes in the processor array. A typical memory hierarchy is depicted in Figure 3.3. Here the processor and a level-1 (L1) cache memory are found on-chip, and a larger level-2 (L2) cache lies between the chip and the memory.

When a processor executes a load instruction, the L1 cache is first interrogated to determine if the desired datum is available. If it is, the datum can be delivered to the processor in two to five processor cycles. If the datum is not found in the L1 cache, the processor stalls while the L2 cache is interrogated. If the desired datum is found in L2, then the stall may last for only 10 to 20 cycles. If the datum is not found in either cache, a full *cache miss* is taken with a delay of possibly 100 cycles or

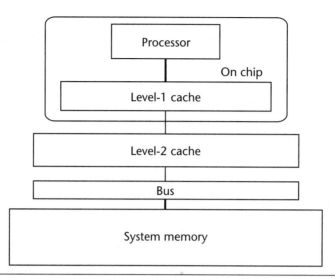

Figure 3.3   A standard uniprocessor memory hierarchy.

more. Whenever a miss occurs, the datum is saved in every cache in the hierarchy, if it is not already there. Note that on modern machines, caches transfer data in a minimum-size *cache block*, so that whenever a datum is loaded to that cache, the entire block containing that datum comes with it.

The performance of the memory hierarchy is determined by two hardware parameters: *latency,* which is the time required to fetch a desired datum from memory, and *bandwidth*, which is the number of bytes per unit time that can be delivered from the memory at full speed. Long latencies increase the cost of cache misses, thus slowing performance, while limited bandwidth can cause applications to become "memory bound," that is, continuously stalled waiting for data. These two factors are complicated by the multilevel nature of memory hierarchies, because each level will have a different bandwidth and latency to the next level. For example, the SGI Origin 2000 can deliver about 4 bytes per machine cycle from the L1 cache to the processor and 4 bytes per cycle from the L2 cache to the L1 cache, but it can deliver only about 0.8 bytes per cycle from memory to L1 cache [272].

Another important parameter that affects memory performance on a uniprocessor is the length of the standard *cache block* (or *cache line*). Most cache systems will only transfer blocks of data between levels of the memory hierarchy. If all the data transferred in a block are used, then no bandwidth is wasted. In that case, the cost of the cache miss can be amortized over all the data in the block. If only one or two data items are used, then the average latency is much higher and the effective bandwidth much lower.

There are two kinds of strategies for overcoming latency problems. *Latency hiding* attempts to overlap the latency of a miss with computation. Prefetching of cache lines is a latency-hiding strategy. *Latency tolerance*, on the other hand, attempts to restructure a computation to make it less subject to performance problems due to long latencies. The single most important latency tolerance technique is *cache blocking*, which brings accesses to the same locations closer together in time so that accesses after the first are likely to find the desired data in cache.

Strategies that improve reuse in cache also improve effective bandwidth utilization. Perhaps the most important way to ensure good bandwidth utilization is to organize data and computations to use all the items in a cache line whenever it is fetched from memory. Ensuring that computations access data arrays in strides of one is an example of how this might be done.

The memory hierarchies on parallel machines are more complicated because of the existence of multiple caches on shared-memory systems and the long latencies to remote memories on distributed-memory configurations. There may also be interference between data transfers between memories and from local memory to a processor.

3.2 Decomposing Programs for Parallelism

Given that you have decided to implement a program for a parallel machine, there are four main issues that you must deal with. First, you must have a way of identifying components of the computation that can safely be run in parallel. Second, you need to adopt a strategy for decomposing the program into parallel components. Third, you must actually write the parallel program, which requires that you choose a programming model and interface for the implementation. Finally, you must choose an implementation *style* that is effective for the given application and that works well with the chosen programming model. In this section, we discuss each of these issues and illustrate them with an extended example at the end.

3.2.1 Identification of Parallelism

The first task in a parallel implementation is to identify the portions of the code where there is parallelism to exploit. To do this we must address a fundamental question: *When can we run two different computations in parallel?* We cannot answer this question without thinking about what it means for two computations to run in parallel. Most programmers think of the meaning of a program to be defined by the sequential implementation. That is, for a parallel implementation to be correct, it must produce the same answers as the sequential version every time it is run. So the question becomes: *When can we run two computations from a given sequential program in parallel and expect that the answers will be the same as those produced by the sequential program?* By "running in parallel," we mean asynchronously, with synchronization at the end. Thus, the parallel version of the program will spawn a number of parallel processes to handle different computations, with each of the computations running until the end, when they synchronize.

The naive answer to the question is that we can run computations in parallel if they do not share data. However, we can refine this substantially. Certainly it does not cause a problem if two computations both read the same data from a shared-memory location. Therefore, for data sharing to cause a problem, one of the computations must write into a memory that the other accesses by either reading or writing. If this is the case, then the order of those memory operations is important. If the sequential program writes into a location in the first computation and then reads from the same location in the second computation, parallelizing the computation might cause the read to be executed first, leading to wrong answers. Such a situation is called a *data race*.

In the 1960s, Bernstein [101] formalized a set of three conditions capturing this notion. For the purposes of parallelization, these three conditions can be stated as follows: Two computations C_1 and C_2 can be run in parallel without synchronization if and only if none of the following holds:

1. C_1 writes into a location that is later read by C_2—a *read-after-write* (RAW) race.

2. C_1 reads from a location that is later written into by C_2—a *write-after-read* (WAR) race.

3. C_1 writes into a location that is later overwritten by C_2—a *write-after-write* (WAW) race.

We will see how these conditions can be applied in practice to common programming structures.

3.2.2   Decomposition Strategy

Another important task in preparing a program for parallel execution is to choose a strategy for decomposing the program into pieces that can be run in parallel. Generally speaking, there are two ways to do this. First, you could identify the tasks (major phases) in the program and the dependences among them and then schedule those tasks that are not interdependent to run in parallel. In other words, different processors carry out different functions. This approach is known as *task parallelism*. For example, one processor might handle data input from secondary storage, while a second generates a grid based on input previously received.

A second strategy, called *data parallelism*, subdivides the data domain of a problem into multiple regions and assigns different processors to compute the results for each region. Thus, in a 2-D simulation on a 1000×1000 grid, 100 processors could be effectively used by assigning each to a 100×100 subgrid. The processors would then be arranged as a 10×10 processor array. Data parallelism is more commonly used in scientific problems because it can keep more processors busy—task parallelism is typically limited to small degrees of parallelism. In addition, data parallelism exhibits a natural form of scalability. If you have 10,000 processors to apply to the problem above, you could solve a problem on a $10,000 \times 10,000$ cell grid, with each processor still assigned a 100×100 subdomain. Since the computation per processor remains the same, the larger problem should take only modestly longer running time than the smaller problem takes on the smaller machine configuration.

As we shall see, task and data parallelism can be combined. The most common way to do this is to use *pipelining*, a software strategy analogous to the hardware method described in Section 2.1.1, in which each processor is assigned to a different stage of a multistep sequential computation. If many independent data sets are passed through the pipeline, each stage can be performing its computation on a different data set at the same time. For example, suppose that the pipeline has four stages. The fourth stage would be working on the first data set, while the third stage would be working on the second data set, and so on. If the steps are roughly equal in time, the pipelining into four stages provides an extra speedup by a factor of four over the time required to process a single data set, after the pipeline has been filled.

3.2.3 Programming Models

Another consideration in forming a parallel program is which programming model to use. This decision will affect the choice of programming language system and library for implementation of the application. The two main choices were originally intended for use with the corresponding parallel architectures.

- In the *shared-memory* programming model, all data accessed by the application occupy a global memory accessible from all parallel processors. This means that each processor can fetch and store data to any location in memory independently. Shared-memory parallel programming is characterized by the need for synchronization to preserve the integrity of shared data structures.

- In the *message-passing* model, data are viewed as being associated with particular processors, so communication is required to access a remote data location. Generally, to get a datum from a remote memory, the owning processor must *send* the datum and the requesting processor must *receive* it. In this model, send and receive primitives take the place of synchronization.

Although these two programming models are inspired by the corresponding parallel computer architectures, their use is not restricted. It is possible to implement the shared-memory model on a distributed-memory computer, either through hardware (distributed shared memory) or software systems that simulate DSMs (e.g., Tread-Marks [31]). Symmetrically, message passing can be made to work with reasonable efficiency on a shared-memory system. In each case there may be some loss of performance. Nevertheless, for the remainder of this section we will assume that the shared-memory model is associated with SMPs and the message-passing model is used on distributed-memory systems.

3.2.4 Implementation Styles

We now turn to the issues related to the implementation of parallel programs. We begin with data parallelism, the most common form of parallelism in scientific codes. There are typically two sources of data parallelism: iterative loops and recursive traversal of tree-like data structures. Below we discuss each of these in turn. Data parallel loops are typically implemented using two styles: on shared-memory systems, they correspond to explicitly parallel loops in which the iterations are unsynchronized, while on distributed-memory systems, the *single-program, multiple-data* (SPMD) style is most often used.

Parallel Loop Programming

Loops represent the most important source of parallelism in scientific programs. The typical way to parallelize loops is to assign different iterations, or different blocks of iterations, to different processors. On shared-memory systems, this decomposition is usually coded as some kind of PARALLEL DO loop. According to Bernstein, we can do this without synchronization only if there are no data races between iterations of the loop. Thus we must examine the loop carefully to see if there are places where data sharing of this sort occurs. In the literature on compiler construction, these kinds of races are identified as *dependences* [27]. These concepts can be illustrated by a simple example. Consider the loop:

```
DO I = 1, N
   A(I) = A(I) + C
ENDDO
```

Here each iteration of the loop accesses a different element of the array A so that there is no data sharing. On the other hand, in the loop

```
DO I = 1, N
   A(I) = A(I+1) + C
ENDDO
```

there would be a write-after-read race because the element of A being read on any given iteration is the same as the element of A that is written on the next iteration. If the iterations are run in parallel, the write might take place before the read, causing incorrect results.

Thus, the main focus of loop parallelization is the discovery of loops that have no races. In some cases, it is possible to achieve significant parallelism in the presence of races. For example, consider:

```
SUM = 0.0
DO I = 1, N
   R = F(B(I),C(I))  ! an expensive computation
   SUM = SUM + R
ENDDO
```

There is a race in this loop involving the variable SUM, which is written and read on every iteration. However if we assume that floating-point addition is commutative and associative (which it isn't on most machines), then the order in which results are added to SUM does not matter. Since we assume that the computation of function F is expensive, some gain can still be achieved if we compute the values of F in parallel and then update SUM in the order in which those computations finish. To make this work, we must ensure that only one processor updates SUM at a time and each finishes before the next is allowed to begin. On shared-memory systems, *critical regions*—code segments that can be executed by only one processor at a time—are designed to do exactly this. Here is one possible realization of the parallel version:

```
SUM = 0.0
PARALLEL DO I = 1, N
   R = F(B(I),C(I)) ! an expensive computation
   BEGIN CRITICAL REGION
      SUM = SUM + R
   END CRITICAL REGION
ENDDO
```

The critical region ensures that SUM is updated by one processor at a time on a first-come, first-served basis. Because sum reductions of this sort are really important in parallel computation, most systems offer a primitive function that computes such reductions using a scheme that takes time proportional to the logarithm of the number of processors.

SPMD Programming

A programmer who wishes to perform the sum reduction above on a distributed-memory message-passing system will need to rewrite the program to use explicit message passing. As a matter of convenience, the programmer will often employ the SPMD style [246, 525]. In an SPMD program, all of the processors execute the same code, but apply the code to different portions of the data. Scalar variables are typically replicated on all of the processors and redundantly computed (to identical values) on each processor. In addition, the programmer must insert explicit communication primitives in order to pass the shared data between processors. For the sum-reduction calculation above, the SPMD program might look something like this:

```
! This code is executed by all processors
! MYSUM, MYFIRST, MYLAST, R, and I are private local variables
! MYFIRST and MYLAST are computed separately on each processor
!    to point to nonintersecting sections of B and C
! GLOBALSUM is a global collective communication primitive
MYSUM = 0.0
DO I = MYFIRST, MYLAST
   R = F(B(I),C(I)) !  an expensive computation
   MYSUM = MYSUM + R
ENDDO
SUM = GLOBALSUM(MYSUM)
```

Here the communication is built into the function GLOBALSUM, which takes one value of its input parameter from each processor and computes the sum of all those inputs, storing the result into a variable that is replicated on each processor. The implementation of GLOBALSUM typically uses a logarithmic algorithm. Explicit communication primitives and SPMD programming will be further illustrated in the pipeline parallelism example in Section 3.2.5.

Recursive Task Programming

To handle recursive parallelism in a tree-like data structure, the programmer would typically create a new process or thread whenever it is necessary to traverse two different paths down the tree in parallel. For example, a search for a particular value in an unordered tree would examine the root first. If the value were not found, it would fork a separate process to search the right subtree and then search the left subtree itself.

3.2.5   A Simple Example

We conclude this section with a discussion of a simple problem that is intended to resemble a finite-difference calculation. We show how this example might be implemented using both a shared-memory, parallel-loop model and a distributed-memory SPMD model.

Assume that we begin with a simple Fortran code that computes a new average value for each data point in array A using a two-point stencil and stores the average into array ANEW. The code might look like the following:

```
REAL A(100), ANEW(100)
.
.
.
DO I = 2, 99
   ANEW(I) = (A(I-1) + A(I+1)) * 0.5
ENDDO
```

Suppose that we wish to implement a parallel version of this code on a shared-memory machine with four processors. Using a parallel-loop dialect of Fortran, the code might look like:

```
REAL A(100), ANEW(100)
.
.
.
PARALLEL DO I = 2, 99
   ANEW(I) = (A(I-1) + A(I+1)) * 0.5
ENDDO
```

While this code will achieve the desired result, it may not have sufficient granularity to compensate for the overhead of dispatching parallel threads. In most cases, it is better to have each processor execute a block of iterations to achieve higher granularity. In our example, we can ensure that each processor gets a block of either 24 or 25 iterations by substituting a strip-mined version with only the outer loop parallel:

```
REAL A(100), ANEW(100)
  .
  .
  .
PARALLEL DO IB = 1, 100, 25
   PRIVATE I, myFirst, myLast
   myFirst = MAX(IB, 2)
   myLast =  MIN(IB + 24, 99)
   DO I = myFirst, myLast
      ANEW(I) = (A(I-1) + A(I+1)) * 0.5
   ENDDO
ENDDO
```

Here we have introduced a new language feature. The PRIVATE statement specifies that each iteration of the IB-loop has its own private value of each variable in the list. This permits each instance of the inner loop to execute independently without simultaneous updates of the variables that control the inner loop iteration. The example above ensures that iterations 2 through 25 are executed as a block on a single processor. Similarly, iterations 26 through 50, 51 through 75, and 76 through 99 are executed as blocks. This code has several advantages over the simpler version. The most important is that it should have reasonably good performance on a machine with distributed shared memory in which the arrays are stored 25 to a processor.

Finally, we turn to the message-passing version of the code. This code is written in SPMD style so that the scalar variables myP, myFirst, and myLast are all automatically replicated on each processor—the equivalent of PRIVATE variables in shared memory. In the SPMD style, each global array is replaced by a collection of local arrays in each memory. Thus the 100-element global arrays A and ANEW become 25-element arrays on each processor named Alocal and ANEWlocal, respectively. In addition, we will allocate two extra storage locations on each processor—A(0) and A(26)—to hold values communicated from neighboring processors. These cells are often referred to as *ghost cells*, *halo cells*, or *overlap areas*.

Now we are ready to present the message-passing version:

```
! This code is executed by all processors
! myP is a private local variable containing the processor number
!    myP runs from 0 to 3
! Alocal and ANEWlocal are local versions of arrays A and ANEW

IF (myP .NE. 0) send Alocal(1) to myP-1
IF (myP .NE. 3) send Alocal(25) to myP+1
IF (myP .NE. 0) receive Alocal(0) from myP-1
```

```
IF (myP .NE. 3) receive Alocal(26) from myP+1
myFirst = 1
myLast = 25
IF (myP == 0) myFirst = 2
IF (myP == 3) myLast = 24
DO I = myFirst, myLast
   ANEWlocal(I) = (Alocal(I-1) + Alocal(I+1)) * 0.5
ENDDO
```

Note that the computation loop is preceded by four communication steps in which values are sent to and received from neighboring processors. These values are stored into the overlap areas in each local array. Once this is done, the computation can proceed on each of the processors using the local versions of A and ANEW.

As we shall see later in the book, performance can be improved by inserting a purely local computation between the sends and receives in the above example. This is an improvement because the communication is overlapped with the local computation to achieve better overall parallelism. The following code fragment inserts the computation on the interior of the region before the receive operations, which are only needed for computing the boundary values.

```
! This code is executed by all processors
! myP is a private local variable containing the processor number
!      myP runs from 0 to 3
! Alocal and ANEWlocal are local versions of arrays A and ANEW

IF (myP .NE. 0) send Alocal(1) to myP-1
IF (myP .NE. 3) send Alocal(25) to myP+1
DO I = 2, 24
   ANEWlocal(I) = (Alocal(I-1) + Alocal(I+1)) * 0.5
ENDDO
IF (myP .NE. 0) THEN
   receive Alocal(0) from myP-1
   ANEWlocal(1) = (Alocal(0) + Alocal(2)) * 0.5
ENDIF
IF (myP .NE. 3) THEN
   receive Alocal(26) from myP+1
   ANEWlocal(25) = (Alocal(24) + Alocal(26)) * 0.5
ENDIF
```

3.3   Enhancing Parallel Performance

Parallel programming is difficult in part because high performance does not automatically follow from parallel implementation. To achieve the highest possible performance, the implementer must take a number of other considerations into account. First, he or she must balance the loads on the components of the computing configuration so that no single component dominates the running time. Second, solving very large problems requires that the computation scale to large numbers of parallel processors; the implementation must be crafted to achieve this goal. Third, some components of the problem, though serial, may be made faster by a partial parallelization strategy known as pipelining. Finally, the implementer may need special strategies to deal with computations that are *irregular*. Irregular computations include sparse matrix calculations and calculations defined on irregular grids, such as those that employ adaptive meshing. This section provides a brief introduction to each of these issues.

3.3.1   Scalability and Load Balance

The idealized goal of parallel computation is to have the running time of an application reduced by a factor that is inversely proportional to the number of processors used. That is, if a second processor is used, the running time should be half of what is required on one processor. If four processors are used, the running time should be a fourth. Any application that achieves this goal is said to be *scalable*. Another way of stating the goal is in terms of *speedup*, which is defined to be the ratio of the running time on a single processor to the running time on the parallel configuration. That is,

$$Speedup(n) = T(1)/T(n)$$

An application is said to be scalable if the speedup on n processors is close to n. Scalability of this sort has its limits—at some point the amount of available parallelism in the application will be exhausted, and adding further processors may even detract from performance.

This leads us to consider a second definition of scalability, called *scaled speedup*— an application will be said to be scalable if, when the number of processors and the problem size are increased by a factor of n, the running time remains the same [418]. This captures the notion that larger machine configurations make it possible to solve correspondingly larger scientific problems.

There are three principal reasons why scalability is not achieved in some applications. First, the application may have a large region that must be run sequentially. If we assume that T_S is the time required by this region and T_P is the time required by the parallel region, the speedup for this code is given by:

$$Speedup(n) = \frac{T_S + T_P}{T_S + \frac{T_P}{n}} \leq \frac{T(1)}{T_S}$$

This means that the total speedup is limited by the ratio of the sequential running time to the running time of the sequential region. Thus if 20 percent of the running time is sequential, the speedup cannot exceed 5. This observation is known as Amdahl's Law [30].

A second impediment to scalability is the requirement for a high degree of communication or coordination. In the global summation example above, if the computation of the function F is fast, then the cost of the computation is dominated by the time required to take the sum, which is logarithmic at best. This can be modeled to produce a revised speedup equation [338]:

$$Speedup(n) = \frac{T(1)}{T_S + \frac{T_P}{n} + c \lg(n)} = \mathcal{O}\left(\frac{1}{\lg(n)}\right)$$

Even if c is tiny, the logarithmic factor in the denominator will grow with the number of processors to a significant size. When the number of processors becomes large enough, the speedup will stop increasing and begin to decline.

The third major impediment to scalability is poor *load balance*. If one of the processors takes half of the parallel work, speedup will be limited to a factor of two, no matter how many processors are involved. Thus, a major goal of parallel programming is to ensure good load balance.

If all the iterations of a given loop execute for exactly the same amount of time, load balance can be achieved by giving each processor exactly the same amount of work to do. Thus, the iterations could be divided into blocks of equal number, so that each processor gets roughly the same amount of work, as in the following example:

```
K = CEIL(N/P)
PARALLEL DO I = 1, N, K
   DO ii = I, MIN(I+K-1,N)
      A(ii) = B(ii+1) + C
   ENDDO
ENDDO
```

However, this strategy fails if the work on each iteration takes a variable amount of time. On shared-memory machines, this can be ameliorated by taking advantage of the way parallel loops are scheduled. On such machines, each processor goes back to the queue that hands out iterations when it has no work to do. Thus, by reducing the amount of work on each iteration (while keeping it above threshold) and increasing the total number of iterations, we can ensure that other processors take up the slack for a processor that has a long iteration. If the same example were coded as

```
K = CEIL(N/(P*4))
PARALLEL DO I = 1, N, K
   DO ii = I, MIN(I+K-1,N)
      A(ii) = B(ii+1) + C
   ENDDO
ENDDO
```

then on average, each processor should execute four iterations of the parallel loop. However, if one processor gets stuck, the others will take on more iterations to naturally balance the load.

In cases where neither of these strategies is appropriate, such as when the computer is a distributed-memory, message-passing system or when load is not known until run time, a dynamic load-balancing scheme may be required, in which the assignment of work to processors is done at run time. Hopefully, such a load-balancing step will be required infrequently so that the cost is amortized over a number of computation steps.

3.3.2 Pipeline Parallelism

To this point, we have been dealing primarily with parallelism that is *asynchronous* in the sense that no synchronization is needed during parallel execution. (The exception was the summation example, which required a critical section.) Ideally, we should always be able to find asynchronous parallelism, because this gives us the best chance for scalability. However, even when this is not possible, some parallelism may be achievable by staggering initiation of tasks and synchronizing them so that subsections with no interdependencies are run at the same time. This strategy is known as *pipelining* because it is the software analogue of pipelining in CPU hardware, described in Section 2.1.1. To see how this works, consider the following variant of successive overrelaxation:

```
DO J = 2, N-1
   DO I = 2, N-1
      A(I,J) = (A(I-1,J) + A(I+1,J) + A(I,J-1) + A(I,J+1)) * 0.25
   ENDDO
ENDDO
```

Although neither of the loops can be run in parallel, there is some parallelism in this example, as is illustrated in Figure 3.4. All of the values on the shaded diagonal can be computed in parallel because there are no dependences between any of these elements.

Suppose, however, that we wish to compute all the elements in any column on the same processor, so that A(*,J) would be computed on the same processor for all values of J. If we compute the elements in any column in sequence, all of the dependences along that column are satisfied. However, we must still be concerned about the rows. To get the correct result, we must delay the computation on each row by enough to ensure that the corresponding array element on the previous row is completed before the element on the current row is computed. This strategy can be implemented via the use of *events*—synchronization mechanisms that make it possible for one process to "wait" for something to happen (an event that is "posted") in another process. (See Chapter 12 for more on events.) The following pseudocode demonstrates this approach:

```
EVENT READY(N,N) ! Initialized to false
PARALLEL DO I = 1, N
   POST(READY(I,1))
ENDDO
PARALLEL DO J = 2, N-1
   DO I = 2, N-1
```

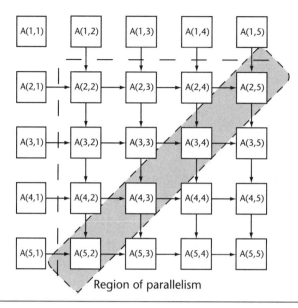

Figure 3.4 Wavefront parallelism.

```
        WAIT(READY(I,J-1))
        A(I,J) = (A(I-1,J) + A(I+1,J) + A(I,J-1) + A(I,J+1)) * 0.25
        POST(READY(I,J))
    ENDDO
ENDDO
```

Initially all the events are false—a wait on a false event will suspend the executing thread until a post for the event is executed. All of the READY events for the first column are then posted, so the computation can begin. The computation for the first computed column, A(*,2), begins immediately. As each of the elements is computed, its READY event is posted so that the next column can begin computation of the corresponding element. The timing of the computation is illustrated in Figure 3.5. Note that the event posting has aligned the region of parallelism so that all processors are simultaneously working on independent calculations.

3.3.3 Regular versus Irregular Problems

Most of the examples we have used in this chapter are regular problems—defined on a regular, fixed grid in some number of dimensions. Although a large fraction of scientific applications focus on regular problems, a growing number of applications address problems that are irregular in structure or use adaptive meshes to improve efficiency. This means that the structure of the underlying grid is usually not known until run time. Therefore, these applications present special difficulties for parallel

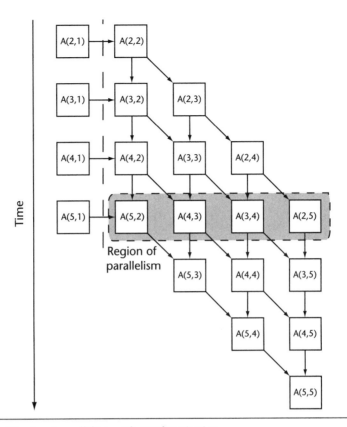

Figure 3.5 Wavefront parallelism with synchronization.

implementation because static, compile-time methods cannot be used to perform load balancing and communication planning.

To illustrate these issues we present a code fragment from a simple force calculation that might be part of a molecular dynamics code.

```
DO I = 1, NPAIRS
    F(L1(I)) = F(L1(I)) + FORCE(X(L1(I)), X(L2(I)))
    F(L2(I)) = F(L2(I)) + FORCE(X(L2(I)), X(L1(I)))
ENDDO
DO I = 1, NPART
    X(I) = MOVE(X(I), F(I))
ENNDO
```

The first loop is intended to traverse a list of particle pairs where the two particles in the pair are located at index L1(I) and index L2(I), respectively. In molecular dynamics codes, these pair lists are often constructed by taking every pair of particles that are within some cutoff distance of one another. For each pair, the force arising from the particle interaction (due to electromagnetic interaction) is calculated by function FORCE and added to an aggregate force for the particle. Finally, the aggregate forces are used to calculate the new location for each particle, represented by X(I).

This code illustrates a fundamental characteristic of irregular problems, namely the use of subscripted index variables in the index positions of the fundamental data quantities of the problem. These index arrays are computed at run time, so the actual data locations of the quantities involved in calculations in the first loop are not known until the pair list is constructed at run time. Therefore, load balancing cannot take place until the pair list is constructed. Furthermore, if communication is required, the optimization of communication must be postponed until run time as well.

To address this issue, a standard approach is to perform three steps as execution begins.

1. Read in all the data.
2. Perform load balancing by distributing data to different processors and possibly reorganizing data within a processor.
3. Step through the computation loop (without performing a computation) to determine a communication schedule, if one is needed. Schedule, if required.

The last step is known as the *inspector* because its goal is to inspect the calculation to plan communication.

In the force calculation above, the goal of load balancing would be to organize the layout of particles and force pairs so that the maximum number of particle interactions are between particles on the same processor. There are many ways to approach this problem. As an example, we will describe a simple but fairly effective strategy that uses *Hilbert curves*, often called *space-filling curves*, to lay out the data. A Hilbert curve traces through 1-D, 2-D, or 3-D space in an order that ensures that particles that are close together on the curve are usually close together in space. The particles can then be ordered in memory by increasing position on the Hilbert curve, with an equal number of particles allocated to each processor. Pairs can be allocated to processors so that it is likely that one element of the pair will reside on the processor where the pair resides. In many cases this can be accomplished by some form of lexicographic sort applied to the pairs [664]. Finally, the pairs requiring communication can be determined by an inspector that steps through the pair list to see if one of the elements of the pair is on another processor. All of the communication from the same processor can then be grouped and the data delivered in a block from each processor at the beginning of every execution step.

Although this discussion is much oversimplified, it should give the flavor of the strategies used to parallelize irregular problems. There is one further complication worth mentioning, however. In the example above, the pair list may need to be reconstructed from time to time, as the particles move around and some drift out of the cutoff area while others drift in. When this happens, it may be necessary to reorganize the data, rebalance the load, and invoke the inspector once again. However, this should be done as seldom as possible to ensure that the potentially high cost of these steps is amortized over as many execution steps as possible.

3.4   Memory-Hierarchy Management

In this section we discuss programming strategies that can help make optimal use of the memory hierarchy of a modern parallel computer system. We begin with the strategies that improve the performance of a uniprocessor node within the memory and then proceed to the issues that are complicated by parallelism.

3.4.1   Uniprocessor Memory-Hierarchy Management

As discussed in Section 2.1.2, a critical issue in getting good memory-hierarchy performance on a uniprocessor is achieving high degrees of reuse of data in both registers and cache memory. Many programmers are surprised to find that proper organization of their programs can dramatically affect the performance that they achieve.

Three principal strategies available to programmers for improving the performance of memory hierarchy are described below.

Stride-One Access

Most cache memories are organized into blocks that contain multiple data items. For example, the level-2 cache block on the SGI Origin can hold 16 double-precision floating-point numbers. On every machine, these numbers are at contiguous addresses in memory. If a program is arranged to iterate over successive items in memory, it can suffer at most one cache miss for every cache block. All successive data items in the cache block will be hits. Thus, programs in which the loops access contiguous data items are typically much more efficient than those that do not.

Blocking

Program performance can also be improved by ensuring that data remains in cache between subsequent accesses to the same memory location. As an example, consider the following code, which is a simple analogue of matrix multiplication:

```
DO I = 1, N
  DO J = 1, N
      A(I) = A(I) + B(J)
  ENDDO
ENDDO
```

Although this loop achieves a high degree of reuse for array A, missing only N/L times where L is the size of the cache block, it has a dismal performance on array B, on which it incurs N^2/L misses. The problem is that, even though access to B is stride-one, B(J) cannot remain in cache until its next use on the next iteration of the outer loop. Therefore, all N/L misses will be incurred on each iteration of the outer loop. If the loop on J is "blocked" or "strip mined" to a size where all the elements of B that it touches can remain in cache, then the following loop results:

```
DO J = 1,N,S
  DO I = 1, N
    DO jj = J, MIN(J+S,N)
      A(I) = A(I) + B(jj)
    ENDDO
  ENDDO
ENDDO
```

where S is the maximum number of elements of B that can remain in cache between two iterations of the outer loop.

In this version, we have blocked the inner loop to the size of the cache and moved the iterate-by-strip loop to the outermost loop position. In this new organization, we suffer at most N/L misses for B, because each element of B is reused N times. On the other hand, we increase the number of misses on A to $N^2/(LS)$ because we must now miss for all the elements of A on each of the N/S iterations of the outer loop. Overall, the number of misses has been reduced by a factor of S.

Data Reorganization

A third strategy for improving the behavior of a uniprocessor memory hierarchy is to reorganize the data structures so that data items that are used together are stored together in memory. For example, many older Fortran programs use multidimensional arrays to store complex data structures. In these programs, one often sees an array declaration such as:

```
DOUBLE PRECISION PART(10000,5)
```

Here the second dimension is being used to store the fields of a data structure about one of the 10,000 particles in a simulation. If the fields describing a single particle are updated together, this is the wrong data organization because Fortran uses column-major order and the five fields are likely to appear on different cache lines. This organization can reduce the effective bandwidth in the program by up to a factor of five. A much better organization for Fortran is to swap the data dimensions:

```
DOUBLE PRECISION PART(5,10000)
```

However, this requires rewriting every access to the array PART in order to ensure correctness. Thus, this task is often best left to a tool, although the programmer should be aware of this problem while writing the program initially. Data reorganization is also very effective on irregular problems, even though the reorganization must take place at run time. In irregular particle codes, the cost of misses due to bad data organization far outweighs the cost of rearranging the data at run time. Judicious use of these strategies can improve performance by integer factors. However, they are tedious to apply by hand, so they are better carried out by automatic means. In particular, cache blocking and interchange to achieve stride-one access have been built into most modern Fortran compilers, while tools for global data reorganization exist as research prototypes [273].

3.4.2 Multiprocessor Memory Hierarchies

Multiprocessors add a number of complexities to the problem of managing accesses to memory and improving reuse. In this section, we focus on three of the most significant problems.

Synchronization

In many parallel programs it is useful to have several different processors updating the same shared data structure. An example is a particle-in-cell code where the forces on a single particle are computed by a number of different processors, each of which must update the aggregate force acting on that particle. If two processors attempt two different updates simultaneously, incorrect results may occur. Thus, it is essential to use some sort of locking mechanism, such as a critical region, to ensure that when one processor is performing such an update on a given particle, all other updates for the same particle are locked out. Typically, processors that are locked out execute some sort of busy–waiting loop until the lock is reset. Most machines are designed to ensure that these loops do not cause ping-ponging of the cache block containing the lock.

Elimination of False Sharing

False sharing is a problem that arises when two different processors are accessing distinct data items that reside on the same cache block. On a shared-memory machine, if both processors attempt to write into the same block, the block can ping-pong back and forth between those processor caches. This phenomenon is known as false sharing because it has the effect of repeated access to a shared datum even though there is no real sharing. False sharing is typically avoided by ensuring that data used by different processors reside on different cache blocks. This can be achieved by the programmer or a compiler through the use of *padding* in data structures. Padding is the process of inserting empty bytes in a data structure to ensure that different elements are in different cache blocks.

Communication Minimization and Placement

Communication with a remote processor can have a number of negative effects on the performance of a computation node in a parallel machine. First, the communication itself can cause computation to wait. The typical strategy for addressing this problem is to move send and receive commands far enough apart so that the time spent on communication can be overlapped with computation. Alternatively, a program reorganization may reduce the frequency of communication, which not only reduces the number of start-up delays that must be incurred but also reduces the interference with local memory-hierarchy management. A form of blocking can be useful in this context—if large data structures are being cycled through all the processors of a distributed-memory computer, it pays to block the data so that all computations involving that data structure by one processor can be carried out at the same time. This ensures each block has to be communicated to a given processor only once.

Once again, many of the useful strategies can be automated in a compiler.

3.5   Parallel Debugging

Parallel debugging is the process of ensuring that a parallel program produces correct answers. We will say that it produces correct answers if it satisfies two criteria:

1. *Absence of nondeterminism.* It always produces the same answers on the same inputs.

2. *Equivalence to the sequential version.* It produces the same answers as the sequential program on which it is based.

These criteria are based on two underlying assumptions. First, we assume that a parallel program will typically be developed by producing and debugging the sequential version and then converting it to use parallelism. In this model the sequential program becomes a specification for the desired answers. Note that some differences from the sequential answers are considered "tolerable." For example, regrouping of sequential summations into parallel global-sum operations may produce slightly different answers due to the nonassociativity of floating-point arithmetic.

Second, we assume that nondeterminism is not a desirable property. Although there is much discussion in the literature of using nondeterminism in programming, our experience is that most scientific users want repeatability in their codes (except of course for Monte Carlo codes and the like). Because the sequential program is almost always equivalent to the parallel program run on one processor, we concentrate on the goal of eliminating nondeterminism.

In shared-memory programming models, the principal sources of nondeterminism are *data races*. A data race occurs when different iterations of a parallel loop share data, with one iteration writing to the shared location. As an example, consider the following loop.

```
PARALLEL DO I = 1, N
    A(I) = A(I+5) + B(I)
ENDDO
```

Even though this loop can be vectorized, it has a data race because if iteration 6 gets far enough ahead of iteration 1, it might store into A(6) before the value is loaded on iteration 1. This produces wrong answers because the sequential version reads the value of A(6) as it is on loop entry.

Data races are often difficult to detect because they do not show up on every execution. Thus, tools are typically required to detect them. One strategy that can be used to uncover races is to run all the parallel loops in a program backward and forward sequentially and compare the answers. Although this is not guaranteed to find all the races, it can uncover the most common ones.

A number of sophisticated tools have been developed or proposed to detect data races. These generally fall into two classes:

1. *Static analysis tools*, which use the analysis of dependence from compiler parallelization to display potential data races in parallel loops. An example from the CRPC is the ParaScope Editor [70].

2. *Dynamic analysis tools*, which use some sort of program replay with shadow variables to determine if a race might occur at run time.

In message-passing programs, the most common parallel bugs arise from messages that arrive out of order. When most message-passing programs execute receive operations from a given processor, the programmer expects that the message would be one that came from a particular send. However, if more than one message is being sent between the same pair of processors, they might arrive out of order, leading to nondeterministic results. For this reason, many message-passing libraries use "tags" to ensure that send and receive pairs match. A tag can be thought of as specifying a specific channel on which messages are to be watched for. Since there can be more than one channel between the same pair of processors, this can be used to ensure that message-out-of-order bugs do not occur.

Another problem in message-passing programs arises because it is possible to execute a receive of a message that never arrives. This can happen, for example, if the receive is always executed but the send is executed only under certain conditions. A somewhat symmetric bug occurs when more messages are sent than are received, due to mismatching conditions. This can cause messages to never be received, with resulting wrong (or at least surprising) answers. Problems of this sort can usually be detected by analyzing traces of communication operations.

3.6 Performance Analysis and Tuning

Because the primary goal of parallel computing is to obtain higher performance than is possible via sequential computation, optimizing parallel application behavior is an integral part of the program development process. This optimization requires knowledge of the underlying architecture, the application code parallelization strategy, and the mapping of the application code and its programming model to the architecture.

The basic performance tuning cycle consists of four steps:

- *Automatic or manual instrumentation.* This instrumentation typically inserts measurement probes in application code and system software, perhaps with additional software measurement of hardware performance counters.

- *Execution of the instrumented application and performance data.* Such executions record hardware and software metrics for offline analysis. The recorded data may include profiles, event traces, hardware counter values, and elapsed times.

- *Analysis of the captured performance data.* Using recorded data, analysis, either manual or automatic, attempts to relate measurement data to hardware resources and application source code, identifying possible optimization points.

- *Modification of the application source code, recompilation with different optimization criteria, or modification of run-time system parameters.* The goal of these modifications is to better match application behavior to the hardware architecture and the programming idioms for higher performance.

As a concrete example, consider an explicitly parallel message-passing code, written in C or Fortran 77 and intended for execution on a distributed-memory parallel architecture (e.g., a Linux PC cluster with a 100 MB/s Ethernet interconnect). A detailed performance instrumentation might include (a) use of a profiler to estimate procedure execution times, (b) recording of hardware instruction counters to identify operation mixes and memory-access costs, and (c) use of an instrumented version of the Message Passing Interface (MPI) standard to measure message-passing overhead.

A profile, based on program-counter sampling to estimate execution times, typically identifies the procedures where the majority of time is spent. Examining the program's static call graph often suggests the invocation pattern responsible for the overhead (e.g., showing that inlining the body of a small procedure at the end of a call chain in a loop nest would reduce overhead).

If a procedure profile is insufficient, hardware counter measurements, when associated with loop nests, can identify the types and numbers of machine instructions associated with each loop nest. For example, seeing memory reference instruction stall counts may suggest that a loop transformation or reblocking would increase cache locality.

Finally, analysis and visualization of an MPI trace (e.g., via Jumpshot) may suggest that the computation is dominated by the latency associated with transmission of many small messages. Aggregating data and sending fewer, larger messages may lead to substantially higher performance.

The problems for data-parallel or implicitly parallel programs are similar, yet different. The range of possible performance remedies differs, based on the programming model (e.g., modifying array distributions for better memory locality), but the instrumentation, execution, and analysis, and code optimization steps remain the same.

Perhaps most critically, the common theme is the need to intimately understand the relations among programming model, compiler optimizations, run-time system features and behavior, and architectural features. Because performance problems can arise at any point in the multilevel transformations of user-specified application code that precede execution, one cannot expect to obtain high performance without investing time to understand more than just application semantics.

3.7   Parallel Input/Output

Most parallel programs do more than just compute (and communicate): they must also access data on secondary storage systems, whether for input or output. And precisely because parallel computations can execute at high speeds, it is often the case that parallel programs need to access large amounts of data. High-performance I/O hence becomes a critical concern. On a parallel computer, that inevitably means *parallel* I/O; without parallelism we are reduced to reading and writing files from a single processor, which is almost always guaranteed to provide only low performance. That is, we require techniques that can allow many processors to perform I/O at the same time, with the goal of exploiting parallelism in the parallel computer's communication network and I/O system.

The parallel programmer can take two different approaches to achieving concurrency in I/O operations. One approach is for each process to perform read and write operations to a distinct file. While simple, this approach has significant disadvantages: programs cannot easily be restarted on different numbers of processors, the underlying file system has little information on which to base optimization decisions, and files are not easily shared with other programs. In general, it is preferable to perform true parallel I/O operations, which allow all processes to access a single shared file.

The parallel I/O problem is multifaceted and often quite complex. This is due to the need to deal with issues at multiple levels, including the I/O architecture of the parallel computer (e.g., each compute processor can have a local disk, or disks can be managed by distinct I/O processors), the file system that manages access to this I/O architecture, the high-level libraries that may be provided to map application-level I/O requests into file system operations, and the user-level application programming interface(s) (API) used to access lower-level functions. Fortunately, after much research, the community has succeeded in developing a standard parallel I/O interface, namely the parallel I/O functions included in the MPI-2 standard. (These are sometimes also referred to as MPI-IO.) These functions are supported on most major parallel computer platforms in the form of a vendor-supported library and the freely available ROMIO package developed at Argonne National Laboratory.

MPI-IO functions enable a set of processes to open, read, write, and eventually close a single shared file. Many of the read and write functions are collective, meaning that all processes call them together; in these operations, each process contributes part of the data that are to be read (or written). This use of collective operations allows the underlying I/O library and file system to perform important optimizations: for example, they can reorganize data prior to writing them to disk.

The following example gives the flavor of the MPI-IO interface. This code fragment first opens a file for read-only access and then calls the collective I/O function MPI_File_read_all. Each calling process will obtain a piece of the file in its local_array.

```
MPI_File_open(MPI_COMM_WORLD, ''/pfs/datafile'', MPI_MODE_RDONLY, MPI_INFO_NULL, &fh);
   :
   :
MPI_File_read_all(fh, local_array, local_array_size, MPI_FLOAT, &status);
```

A detailed discussion of parallel I/O techniques and MPI-IO is provided in Chapter 11.

3.8   Conclusion

This chapter has presented an introductory treatment of a number of the strategies and issues that a new parallel programmer must deal with, including programming models and strategies, application partitioning, scalability, pipelining, memory-hierarchy management, irregular versus regular parallelism, parallel debugging, performance tuning, and parallel I/O. These topics will be discussed in more detail in the remainder of this book. In addition, they will be tied to specific application programming interfaces, such as languages and run-time systems.

Further Reading

Later chapters in this book include in-depth coverage of many of the programming topics introduced here. Chapter 9 is an overview of the programming support technologies covered in this book. Chapter 10 surveys message-passing programming in MPI and introduces thread programming. Chapter 12 includes material on parallel loop programming with events in OpenMP. In addition, the same chapter covers SMTP programming in Co-Array Fortran, along with programming in High Performance Fortran, a distributed array language. Finally, Chapter 16 provides examples of different programming styles applied to the simple Poisson problem.

For further background on parallel programming topics, we recommend the following books:

- *Parallel Computing Works!* [358] by Fox, Williams, and Messina is a substantive repository of information about parallel computation, particularly in the early days of distributed-memory machines.

- *Designing and Building Parallel Programs* [341] by Foster provides a good tutorial introduction to parallel computing and to programming using message passing in MPI.

- *Parallel Programming in OpenMP* [183] by Chandra et al. provides an introduction to shared-memory parallel programming in the most popular programming interface for loop parallelism and its extensions.

- *Using MPI: Portable Parallel Programming with the Message Passing Interface* [406] by Gropp et al. is an excellent introduction to the most widely used message-passing programming interface. Its successor, *Using MPI-2: Advanced Features of the Message-Passing Interface* [407] by Gropp et al., covers advanced features, including the MPI-IO interface described in Section 3.7.

II Applications

4 General Application Issues

Geoffrey Fox

This chapter is the first of five devoted to application strategies and their realization in specific applications. As such it is intended to set the stage for the entire section by laying out general principles for application development.

We begin this overview by presenting the questions that an application developer should ask when considering a specific application for parallelization:

- I have an application: can, and should, it be parallelized?
- If so, how should this be done?
- What are appropriate target hardware architectures?
- What is known about clever algorithms?
- What software technologies are recommended?

By following this thought process on specific applications, we can identify general characteristics that are useful for classifying the issues in parallelization. To illustrate, I review the Poisson equation, which is the subject of Chapter 16. The goal of the analysis here is to revisit the discussions of Chapter 3 from an application, rather than a parallel programming perspective. By contrast, Chapter 16 presents sample implementations in several different programming interfaces. Although the Poisson equation is not a "real" application like the others treated in this section of the book, it can serve as a simple example to frame the discussion of general application issues.

4.1 Application Characteristics in a Simple Example

Simple 2-D electrostatic problems can be reduced to solving Laplace's or Poisson's equation. Poisson's equation (see Chapter 16) is often solved numerically by finite difference methods. These could involve adaptive meshes and hierarchical multigrid

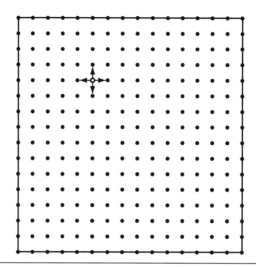

Figure 4.1 A 16 × 16 2-D mesh with an illustration of the basic nearest-neighbor update used in Jacobi's method of Chapter 16.

methods but, in the simplest formulation, they are set up as a regular grid of field values where the basic iterative update links 2-D nearest neighbors, as in Figure 4.1.

If we label points by an index pair (i, j), then Jacobi's method (see equation 16.3) can be written

$$\phi_{New}(i, j) = \left(\phi_{Left} + \phi_{Right} + \phi_{Up} + \phi_{Down} \right) / 4 \qquad (4.1)$$

corresponding to the stencil in Figure 4.2, where the subscript *Left* corresponds to index pair $(i - 1, j)$, and so on.

We note that the problem can be viewed as an algorithm (4.1) applied to a set of data points. Parallelism is naturally found by dividing the domain into parts and assigning each part to a different processor, as seen in Figure 4.3. This technique is often called "domain decomposition" or "data parallelism," but these terms already have a particular meaning in the algorithm and parallel programming fields, respectively. We will use the term "block data decomposition" instead. This is essentially the nomenclature used in High Performance Fortran (HPF).

This geometric view is appropriate for many problems from nature. In a weather simulation, for example, the atmosphere over California evolves independently from that over Indiana. So, for short time extrapolations, they can be simulated on separate processors. Eventually, information flows between these sites and their dynamics are mixed. Of course, it is the communication of data between the processors (either directly in a distributed memory or implicitly in a shared memory) that implements this eventual mixing.

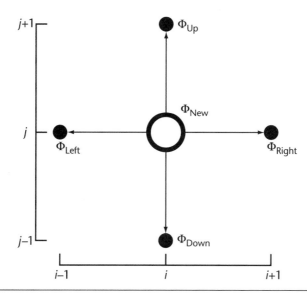

Figure 4.2 Stencil for Jacobi iteration of Figure 4.1.

Block data decompositions typically lead to a single-program, multiple-data (SPMD) structure, with each processor executing the same code on different data points and using different boundary conditions. In Figure 4.3, the processor associated with a center block (Case C) will be "in charge" of 16 points. Boundary data will be obtained by communication with the processors controlling data adjacent to the four edges of the region. Processors associated with edge blocks (Case E) must handle a mix of conventional and communication boundaries. A set of halo, or ghost, grid points (Figure 4.4) is often used to represent the communicated values. (See also Section 16.3.)

This type of data decomposition leads to the so-called owners-compute rule. We imagine that each data point is owned by the processor to which the decomposition assigns it. The owner of a given data point is responsible for performing the computation that updates its corresponding data values. Thus, the parallel program consists of a loop over iterations divided into two phases:

- *Communicate.* At the start of each iteration, communicate any outside data values needed to update the data values at points owned by this processor.

- *Compute.* Update the data values. Each processor operates without the need to synchronize with other machines.

This type of structure can be used with many complex physical simulations. The decompositions can be irregular, as long as they are fixed. Dynamic decompositions require an additional step. Data locations must be migrated between processors to

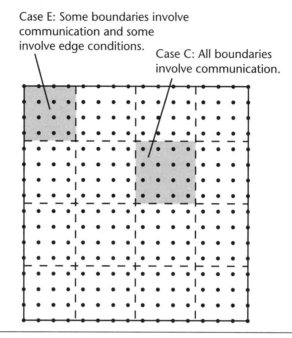

Figure 4.3 A 16×16 mesh divided among 16 processors with a 2-D grid chopped into rectangular subdomains.

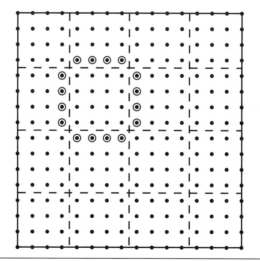

Figure 4.4 Communication structure for the Poisson equation example. The circled points are the halo or ghost grid points. Their values must be communicated across the boundary.

ensure load balance. But data migration is usually followed by similar communicate–compute phases. The communication phase synchronizes the operation of the parallel processors and provides an efficient barrier point that scales naturally.

In the previous discussion, we used terminology natural for distributed-memory hardware or message-passing programming models. When using a shared-memory model such as OpenMP, communication is implicit, and the communication phase is implemented as a barrier synchronization.

4.2 Communication Structure in Jacobi's Method for Poisson's Equation

On a distributed-memory machine, the geometrically local structure of the linked entities of Figure 4.1 leads to a classic communication structure: the communication required is proportional to the surface area of each subdomain, while computation is proportional to volume. (Note that in the 2-D example of Figure 4.3, the "surface" of the subdomain consists of the edges of the square.) One can usually "block" the communication to transmit all the needed points in a few messages. Chapters 3, 7, and 10 explain why blocking is important to reduce the effects of the latency of the messaging system. We can use our current Poisson equation example to produce some rules of thumb that allow us to estimate the performance of many parallel programs.

As shown in Figure 4.5, we characterize each node of a parallel machine by a parameter t_{float}, which is the time required to perform a single floating-point operation. Of course, t_{float} is not very well defined. It depends on the effectiveness of cache, the possible use of fused multiply–add, and other issues. This means that the measure will have some application dependence, reflecting the goodness of the match of the problem to the node architecture. We let n be the grain size—the number of data locations owned by a typical processor. In the example of Figure 4.3, n is 16; in a realistic example, n would be larger, but limited by the memory of each processor. For a hypothetical $10^3 \times 10^3 \times 10^3$ 3-D grid solved on a 1000-processor machine, n would be 10^6.

Communication performance—whether through a shared- or distributed-memory architecture—can be parameterized as

$$\text{Time to communicate } N_{comm} \text{ words} = t_{latency} + N_{comm} \cdot t_{comm}$$

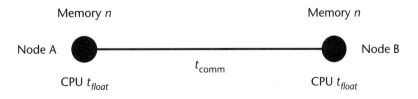

Figure 4.5 Parameters determining performance of loosely synchronous problems.

This equation ignores some issues (e.g., bus or switch contention), but it is a reasonable model in most cases. It is dangerous to quote explicit values for these parameters, as hardware is always improving. Very roughly, the value of $t_{latency}$ is around $1\mu s$ on shared-memory machines and at least an order of magnitude higher, say $40\mu s$, between remote nodes on distributed-memory machines. This latency becomes 10–$100\mu s$ between nodes of a geographically distributed metacomputer; this drastic increase in latency explains why one cannot easily use such systems for parallel computing. The parameter t_{comm} is the time required to communicate a single word and is in the range of 0.1 to $0.01\mu s$ per word. For large enough messages (N_{comm} in the range of 100 to 1000 or larger), the latency term can be ignored. So we will set $t_{latency} = 0$ in the following discussion.

Now let's generalize the problem above to N_{proc} processors arranged in an $\sqrt{N_{proc}} \times \sqrt{N_{proc}}$ grid with a total of N grid points and grain size $n = N/N_{proc}$. We will first consider measures of load balance. Let t_{calc} denote the time required to execute the basic update described in equation (4.1). Then

$$t_{calc} = 4 \cdot t_{float}$$

Since the boundary points are fixed, we only need to update the $(\sqrt{N} - 2) \times (\sqrt{N} - 2)$ array of interior points. So the sequential execution time is given by

$$T(1) = \left(\sqrt{N} - 2\right)^2 \cdot t_{calc}$$

The parallel execution time is governed by the "interior" processors, which need to update n points. So

$$T(N_{proc}) = n \cdot t_{calc} = 4 \cdot n \cdot t_{float}$$

and the speedup is given by

$$S(N_{proc}) = \frac{T(1)}{T(N_{proc})} = N_{proc} \left(1 - \frac{2}{\sqrt{n \cdot N_{proc}}}\right)^2$$

The speedup $S(N_{proc})$ is less than N_{proc} because the processors do not all update the same number of points. However, as either n or N_{proc} becomes large, this load imbalance effect becomes less noticeable.

So far, we have not considered the communication overhead. Figure 4.6 illustrates the cases $n = 16$ and $n = 64$. The processor needs to obtain values for the circled points in order to update its own data values. This means that our expression for parallel execution time now becomes

$$T(N_{proc}) = 4 \cdot n \cdot t_{float} + 4 \cdot \sqrt{n} \cdot t_{comm}$$

Since the communication term is proportional to $\sqrt{n}$, while the computation term is proportional to n, the communication overhead decreases in importance as n

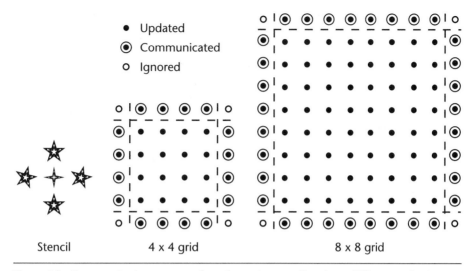

Figure 4.6 Communication structure for a five-point stencil and two different grain sizes.

increases. Adding communication overhead to the speedup formula, we get

$$S(N_{proc}) = N_{proc} \left[\frac{\left(1 - \frac{2}{\sqrt{n \cdot N_{proc}}}\right)^2}{\left(1 + \frac{t_{comm}}{\sqrt{n} \cdot t_{float}}\right)} \right] \qquad (4.2)$$

Realistic values for t_{comm}/t_{float} are in the range of 10 to 100; so the communication overhead dominates in equation (4.2). Suppose that $t_{comm}/t_{float} = 50$ and that we want to reduce the communication overhead below 0.1. Then the grain size n needs to be greater than 250,000 grid points. On some computers, it is possible to overlap communication and computation. The analysis above can be extended in a straightforward manner to handle such strategies.

To generalize the formalism above, we introduce an efficiency ε and an overhead f. Then we can write

$$S(N_{proc}) = \varepsilon \cdot N_{proc} = \frac{N_{proc}}{1 + f} \qquad (4.3)$$

The communication part of the overhead, f_{comm}, appears in equation (4.2) as

$$f_{comm} = \frac{t_{comm}}{\sqrt{n} \cdot t_{float}} \qquad (4.4)$$

In many instances, f_{comm} can be thought of as simply the ratio of parallel communication to parallel computation. Equation (4.4) can be generalized to handle almost all the problems we will later term "loosely synchronous." For those problems, the overhead in a coupled communicate phase and compute phase takes the form

$$f_{comm} = constant \cdot \frac{t_{comm}}{n^{1/d} \cdot t_{float}} \qquad (4.5)$$

Here, d is an appropriate (complexity or information) dimension. For equations based on partial differential equations, d is just the geometric dimension. The same holds for other geometrically local algorithms. For 3-D problems, $d = 3$ and $n^{1/d}$ is the surface-to-volume ratio. For full matrix problems, one finds the value $d = 2$ for the best decompositions, such as those used in ScaLAPACK (see Chapter 20).

Applying equation (4.3), we find that $S(N_{proc})$ increases linearly with N_{proc} if f_{comm} is held fixed. Since t_{comm} and t_{float} are naturally fixed, holding f_{comm} fixed implies keeping the grain size n fixed. This is scaled speedup, since the problem size $N = n \cdot N_{proc}$ also increases linearly with N_{proc}.

The continuing success of parallel computing even on very large machines can be considered a consequence of equations (4.3) and (4.5). Note that the formula for f_{comm} (whose numerical value we could aim to keep around 10% or lower) only depends on local node parameters and not on the number of processors. Here we consider the grain size n as reflecting the amount of local memory. Thus, as we scale up the number of processors, keeping the node hardware and application size n fixed, we will get scaling performance—speedup proportional to N_{proc}.

This simple problem is perhaps the one where the parallel issues are most obvious. However, it is not the one where the parallel performance is easiest to obtain, as the small computation load of the update (equation 4.1) makes the communication overhead relatively more important. There is a fortunate general rule: As one increases the complexity of a problem, the computation required grows faster than the communication overhead. I illustrate this below.

Jacobi iteration requires perhaps the least communication for problems of this class. However, it has one of largest ratios of communication to computation and correspondingly high parallel overhead. Note that one sees the same effect on a hierarchical (cache) memory machine, where problems such as Jacobi iteration for simple equations can perform poorly as the number of operations performed on each word fetched into cache is proportional to the number of links per entity, and this is small (four in the 2-D mesh considered above) for this problem class.

4.3   Communication Overhead for More General Update Stencils

It is instructive to consider in detail how the analysis above changes when a different update formula is used. First, consider using fourth-order differencing to approximate ∇^2 in Poisson's equation. Then, as illustrated in Figure 4.7, we need to communicate twice as many points into halo cells. Since the computation required to update each point is also doubled, the ratio of communication to computation is roughly the same as it was before. Hence, the overhead f_{comm} does not differ significantly from its value in equation (4.4).

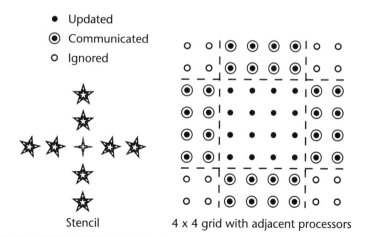

Figure 4.7   Communication structure for a nine-point stencil.

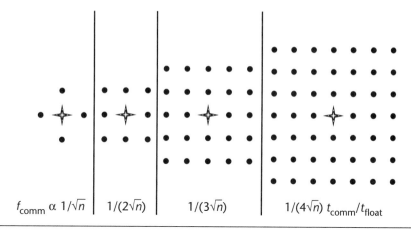

Figure 4.8   Communication structure as a function of stencil size. The stencils shown have (from left to right) range $l = 1, 1, 2,$ and 3.

We can now systematically increase the size of the stencil and find how f_{comm} changes. In the case below, the grid points are replaced by particles. Increasing the stencil size corresponds to ratcheting up the range of force between the particles.

We find that the communication overhead decreases systematically as the range of the force increases. (See Figure 4.8.) For a range of l (measured in units of grid spacings), one finds in this 2-D case that

$$f_{comm} \propto \frac{t_{comm}}{l \cdot \sqrt{n} \cdot t_{float}}$$

This equation is valid when l is large compared to 1, but smaller than the length scale corresponding to the region stored in each processor. In the interesting limit of an infinite range $(l \to \infty)$ force, redoing the analysis leads to the result

$$f_{comm} \propto \frac{t_{comm}}{n \cdot t_{float}} \qquad (4.6)$$

independent of the geometric dimension. This result has the same form as equation (4.5) for complexity dimension $d = 1$. This is the best-understood case in which the geometric and complexity dimensions are different.

The overhead formula of equation (4.6) corresponds to the computationally intense $\mathcal{O}(N^2)$ algorithms for evolving N-body problems. The amount of computation is so large that the ratio of communication to computation is extremely small. This observation is at the heart of the success of special-purpose machines such as GRAPE from the University of Tokyo (*http://grape.astron.s.u-tokyo.ac.jp/grape/*). The 1-teraflop GRAPE 4 won the Gordon Bell prize twice, and the GRAPE 5 took the cost-effectiveness award in 1999 (at $7 per megaflop). The 100-teraflop GRAPE 6 competed in 2000 and won another Gordon Bell award! The modest memory and communication needs of the N-body problem are some of the reasons enabling these powerful machines to outperform any of the more general-purpose parallel computers on this problem. Of course, the specialized GRAPE architecture limits the problems to which it is applicable.

4.4   Applications as Basic Complex Systems

We saw above that the discussion of parallel issues is the same for two different cases: particle dynamics and local discretization for partial differential equations. This is generally true, as the parallel issues depend not on the detailed science or numeric algorithm, but on overall characteristics of the application. So, it makes sense to generalize the discussion in terms of both general principles applicable to many parallel computing problems and special features of the particular 2-D structure seen in Poisson's equation. It is useful to think of an application as a "complex system," or a linked set of entities. This way of thinking can relate the parallelization strategies of seemingly very different problems.

In particular, many other applications have computational structures similar to the Laplace or Poisson equation discussed in previous sections. Consider first the 2-D Ising model, where the mesh of Figure 4.9 is now a fixed grid of spins with a nearest-neighbor connection for the interaction (forces) between them. The Ising model has a geometric structure similar to equation (4.1), but the physics and numerical procedure have many differences from Poisson's equation. The grid points in the Ising model are physically real spins; in the Poisson case, the grid points are artifacts of the numerical procedure. The nearest-neighbor local connection in the Ising case corresponds to a physical force law; it follows from the differencing approximation to a partial derivative in Poisson's case. Further, the usual numerical approach to the Ising model uses a Monte Carlo method rather than a differential equation to

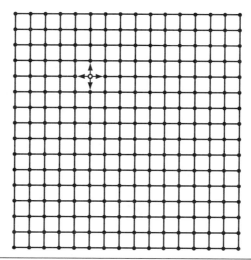

Figure 4.9 A basic complex system with a set of entities with nearest-neighbor linkage to at most four others.

express the dynamics of the system. In Poisson's equation, the iterative process is a perturbed solution to an exact matrix problem. For the Ising model, the iterator counts Monte Carlo sweeps as integration points are accumulated. This approach decreases the statistical error, which is inversely proportional to the square root of the number of sweeps. These differences, which are very important to the underlying science, have little effect on decisions involving appropriate parallelization strategies or the needed hardware and software systems.

Even closer to our Poisson equation would be an application that solved a simple wave equation (or Maxwell's equations) in a 2-D domain. Here we see an identical computational structure, with the perturbed iteration in the sparse matrix solution replaced by stepping through a discretized time variable. Yet another rather similar structure can be found in cellular automata problems.

We can extend this very simple problem in several ways; some of these are explored in Chapter 16. For instance, finite element problems have a similar mesh, but it can be quite irregular compared to the uniform geometry of most finite difference problems. This makes load balancing an important issue. Particle dynamics problems with a short-range force can exhibit structure similar to that of Figure 4.8, but with a dynamic irregular structure and a variable number of links per entity.

An obvious and important generalization of the Poisson structure is to higher dimensions, with 3- and even 4-D structures. Equation (4.5) provided a general form for the communication overhead. Applying this equation when $d = 3$, we see that overhead decreases as $n^{1/3}$. This is slower than in the 2-D case previously discussed. So a grain size $n \approx 10^6$ is needed for a 3-D problem in order to match the performance of a grain size $n \approx 10^4$ in two dimensions.

In Chapter 8, we describe two physics examples—numerical relativity and computational quantum chromodynamics (QCD)—where the basic mesh is four dimensional. The many partial differential equation applications in Chapters 5, 6, 7, and 8 have a richer structure at each grid or finite element mesh point than the single value of Poisson's equation. For instance, QCD has 3×3 complex matrices representing gluons and vectors representing quarks. Computational fluid dynamics is usually formulated in terms of five degrees of freedom at each point. Compared to the simple formula of equation (4.1), the basic updates for these examples involve much more computation. But, as we have explained, that actually tends to reduce the parallel overhead. Communication tends to scale like the number of degrees of freedom at each point. The computational update time complexity per point usually increases faster than this.

We have seen that it is helpful to consider many problems as linked entities arranged in 1-, 2-, 3-, or higher-dimensional geometries. This linkage was "short range" (a few links per entity) in the examples we discussed, but this is not always the case. Particles interacting through a long-range gravitational force require many links per entity. This example, using the simple $\mathcal{O}(N^2_{particle})$ algorithm discussed at the end of Section 4.3, has very different properties from the short-range case. In particular, the performance of this problem is excellent on both distributed- and hierarchical-memory machines. There are many (of order $N_{particle}$) computations for any point stored in cache. Even though the communication appears heavy in a distributed-memory machine, the above analysis shows a low ratio of communication to computation.

This type of long-range problem is found in a variety of fields; they may be far from particle dynamics, but they still have the same computational structure. We provide one interesting example of an $\mathcal{O}(N^2_{particle})$ algorithm in Chapter 8—the Green's function approach to the simulation of earthquakes. Such partial differential equation solvers become integral equations over the domain boundaries with full linkage between the element mesh on the boundary. Some applications involving determination of correlation functions also have this fully connected structure between the points in the computation.

The N-body example can be used to illustrate another important point. A given physical problem can look quite different in different numerical formulations. The natural $\mathcal{O}(N^2_{particle})$ algorithm is often not the best approach to the simulation of gravitating particles. For large problems, one usually adopts the so-called fast multipole method with $\mathcal{O}(N_{particle})$ or $\mathcal{O}(N_{particle} \cdot \log(N_{particle}))$ behavior. This again shows that one needs to choose parallel algorithms carefully; the lowest communication, or even the lowest communication-to-calculation ratio, may not be the best choice. A simpler application illustrating the same issue is Poisson's equation, which can often be solved by either iterative local methods, such as Jacobi or conjugate gradient, or by the Fast Fourier Transform. In both cases, the obvious approach has a simpler complex-system structure, while the fast algorithm has a more complicated tree structure. Computational scientists use their skill to convert a given application into a numerical system, and it is the structure of the latter that determines the key parallel computing issues.

4.5   Time-Stepped and Event-Driven Simulations

We noted above the rich spatial or geometric structure of applications. Two rather distinct simulation methods, time stepped and event driven, correspond to different temporal structures. Most of the examples in this book correspond to the time-stepped case; the entities in a complex system evolve together and are synchronized globally by the concept of time or something equivalent, such as an iteration or Monte Carlo sweep. This is reasonable since it is "how nature works." In the early days of parallel computing, there were concerns that the global synchronization implied by the time-stepped approach would lead to uncontrollable overhead. This is not true, for it can be seen (see the description at the end of Section 4.1 for the simplest nearest-neighbor Laplace equation) that global time synchronization is implied by the local synchronization of neighboring nodes, either by exchanging messages or the equivalent shared-memory mechanism. This synchronization mechanism is itself fully parallel (with no "hot spots" in proper implementations) and so introduces no serious parallel-computing overhead. Such efficient synchronization is present in all problems having a time or iteration count to provide algorithmic synchronization. Correct implementation of an algorithm with natural synchronization points implies that the parallel program needs no special additional synchronization. Message-passing systems such as the MPI (Message Passing Interface) standard have synchronization barriers built in naturally; other programming models (such as active messages and OpenMP) require explicit user attention to this issue.

The military makes substantial use of event-driven simulations in the field of forces modeling, and we provide an example of this in Section 8.11. Here, one tends not to simulate systems in terms of their fundamental constructs (atoms, grid points, etc.), but rather in terms of macroscopic constructs such as vehicles, mines, or battalions. The system components are naturally formulated in terms of objects interacting with events. These are queued (often in a distributed fashion) and executed either in real time (the natural case when there is "hardware in the loop") or according to a global virtual time. Here we do find potentially serious problems with the overhead of global synchronization, and very ingenious techniques have been developed. One important strategy—incorporated in the Time Warp Operating System [513]—involves simulating the system in terms of interacting timestamped events. Block data decomposition is typically used for parallelism, just as in the synchronous and loosely synchronous cases. But now there is no straightforward way to ensure that all events have been received and thus be able to decide to let the simulation proceed on a given processor. The Time Warp approach optimistically marches the simulation forward in time in each processor, using whatever events are available. Correctness is guaranteed by recording the system state from time to time. If necessary, the system state can be rolled back to an old (correct) state if an event arrives bearing a time stamp earlier than the current processor simulation time. The particular minefield simulation cable managment system (CMS) application described in Section 8.11 was successfully parallelized because the different entities in the simulation are largely independent; hence, there was essentially no difficulty with synchronization.

One of the most powerful parallel event-driven approaches is the SPEEDES system from Metron Corporation discussed in Section 8.11, and there are overall frameworks such as high-level architecture (HLA) and run-time infrastructure (RTI) defined for this field. HLA and RTI are object models similar to those described in Chapter 13. However, no software system for event-driven simulation enjoys the universal acceptance and relatively clear methodology for getting good performance shown by MPI in the time-stepped case. Some recent work at the Los Alamos National Laboratory is potentially of great importance. These researchers have shown that some applications traditionally approached by event-driven simulation (e.g., large-scale traffic models) can be tackled as loosely synchronous problems with excellent scaling of parallel performance.

Circuit simulation is an interesting application area that can be tackled by either simulation technique. Obviously, a circuit has a natural time that can be iterated over, with every device component being updated at each step. This approach can be inefficient; on most iterations, only a tiny fraction of the components are active. The event-driven approach can be more effective, as one automatically updates only those devices affected by queued events. This analysis is clear for sequential machines, but the difficult parallelism of event-based systems makes the parallel situation less clear.

4.6   Temporal Structure of Applications

It is useful to divide the temporal structure of numerical systems into four broad areas:

1. *Synchronous.* Each point can be evolved in synchronous mode, as is natural on a single-instruction multiple-data (SIMD) machine. The temporal synchronization is on a point-by-point basis. Most of the simple examples discussed above are of this type.

2. *Loosely synchronous.* The temporal synchronization is on a subdomain basis; this is the natural form of SPMD implementations, including all HPF and most MPI programs. Most of today's major applications are of this type. Nearly any serious irregularity (geometrical or otherwise) added to the model of a synchronous problem changes it into a loosely synchronous problem. In particular, finite element problems and finite difference codes with adaptive meshes are loosely synchronous. Domain decomposition (Chapter 6) has this structure, as does the fast multipole approach to particle dynamics discussed earlier. However, the simple $\mathcal{O}(N_{particle}^2)$ particle-dynamics algorithm is synchronous.

3. *Asynchronous.* Event-driven simulations fall into a class that includes problems not formulated in terms of a stepped time or iterator that is associated with each system entity. As discussed above, asynchronous problems can be very hard to parallelize, whereas in principle loosely synchronous applications always run efficiently if they are large enough.

4. *Pleasingly parallel.* The time or iteration evolution structure of a problem can greatly impact the appropriate software and hardware architecture. However, there is one important special case where this is not true—namely, cases where the entities in the system are essentially disconnected. Then each entity can be evolved more or less separately, and there is no significant synchronization overhead whatever the differences between the entities. One typically uses a "farm" architecture with worker nodes that somehow receive chunks of the simulation (entities) to do as they finish their previous assignments. There are nontrivial application-dependent implementation issues, but such problems will always parallelize well if the problem is large enough. Good examples of this problem class come from the Internet, where both large Web servers and the back-end of database search engines such as Inktomi and Google are of this type. This problem class was often termed "embarrassingly parallel" in the past.

4.7   Summary of Parallelization of Basic Complex Systems

Let us take stock of where we are. Problems are set up as computational or numerical systems. We have discussed one set of such systems, those that consist of a space of linked entities. We called these systems "basic complex systems" and characterized them by their possibly dynamic, spatial (geometric) and temporal structure. We noted the difference between the structure of the original problem and that of the computational system derived from it. We can summarize much past experience in parallelizing applications by the conclusion:

> Synchronous and loosely synchronous problems perform well on large parallel machines if the problem is large enough. For a given machine, there is a typical subdomain size (i.e., the grain size or the size of the part of the problem stored on each node) above which one can expect to get good performance. There will be a roughly constant ratio of parallel speedup to N_{proc} if one scales the problem with fixed subdomain size and total size proportional to N_{proc}.

Although this assertion is probably true in most important cases, it has proven to be very difficult to design and implement productive programming environments that allow the user to realize this goal. That is why we need to write this book even though, in principle, success is guaranteed.

4.8   Meta-Problems

Several applications can be discussed solely in terms of computational systems that fall into the basic complex-system type discussed above. This description is often incomplete, although it does properly describe key computational modules that are part of the complete application. More generally, one finds meta-problems built up from multiple modules, each of which can be classified as a basic complex system. Such meta-problems are particularly interesting today, as many of them are natural applications for distributed systems such as computational grids. One tends to run basic complex systems on classic shared- or distributed-memory machines, as these have the required low latency and high bandwidth communication. Separate modules in a meta-problem can often be run on geographically separated machines, as they tend to have much less stringent communication requirements than do simulations of basic complex systems. Important examples of meta-problems are:

- The three-way linkage of data store, simulation, and visualization subsystems forms one of the most generic meta-problems. It is seen in many different disciplines. Section 8.10 describes an application of this type with a synchrotron light source.

- As discussed in Chapter 22, there is a growing trend in modern engineering toward sophisticated systemwide optimization. For aircraft design, one might simultaneously optimize over fluid flow, structural, acoustic, and electromagnetic properties. Each of these corresponds to a separate module in the discussion above. The new DoD initiative in simulation-based acquisition (see Section 8.11) would need such meta-problems, and this type of application is illustrated in Figure 4.10.

- An early success of the CASA gigabit network was the simulation of a coupled ocean–atmosphere meta-problem. There is a general understanding that such approaches are essential for reliable long-range climate forecasts.

- The forces modeling community often builds such meta-problems; each component is a separate focused simulation. In the example of Section 8.11, one simulation engine is used to describe minefields and another describes squads of vehicles. These simulations have interesting interactions. In this field, meta-problems are called *federations*, and the basic simulations are termed *federates*. As mentioned above, this community has recently adopted sophisticated software standards (RTI and HLA) to support the federation of multiple event-driven simulations.

Note that basic complex systems often have huge potential for parallelism. A complex 3-D simulation may exhibit a billion independent degrees of freedom. These are candidates for data-parallel systems. Meta-problems are different in that

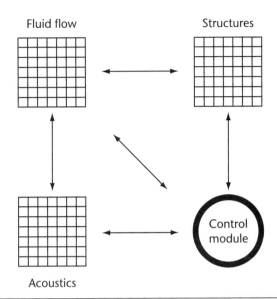

Figure 4.10 The linked modules in a typical meta-problem. We show three large-scale parallel modules that can be expected to execute individually on massively parallel systems. The control module is logically separate and may not require high-performance computing.

they typically contain only a few independent modules. In addition, the linkage of these modules is often timed asynchronously. These are naturally supported by different software concepts than the data-parallel subcomponents. One may find a meta-problem with each module using MPI, OpenMP, or HPF internally and with the modules linked together through channels using, perhaps, GridFTP (high-performance grid standard), Web services, and SOAP (W3C distributed object and message model), IIOP (CORBA), or RMI (Java). We discuss these different software models more completely in terms of object-based approaches and problem-solving environments in Chapters 13 and 14.

4.9   Conclusion

At the start of this chapter, we presented the problem of understanding the principles governing the types of applications that can be parallelized. We addressed this by first identifying basic (or "atomic") complex systems. We discussed their parallelism in terms of their spatial and temporal structure, which we summarized in Section 4.7, and in terms of the application characteristics that govern the parallelism.

The majority of large-scale scientific and engineering codes can be parallelized. We illustrated these conclusions with examples and a simple performance model given in earlier sections of the chapter. In Section 4.8, we introduced meta-problems as the general application class defined by loosely coupled aggregates of basic complex systems. We noted that this type of application was naturally suitable for distributed Grid architectures. This rather simplified discussion is complemented by the analysis of Section 8.12, which looks at some 50 particular applications and summarizes their computational structure. Chapters 5, 6, and 7 and Sections 8.1 through 8.11 describe 14 application areas in detail.

5 Parallel Computing in Computational Fluid Dynamics

Ron Henderson • Dan Meiron •
Manish Parashar • Ravi Samtaney

In this chapter we provide a very brief introduction to computational fluid dynamics (CFD), with the objective of providing a rationale for the use of high-performance parallel computation in the solution of a variety of flow problems.

The basic equations of fluid mechanics are presented, after which a brief overview is provided of some of the common physical regimes described by these equations (compressible vs. incompressible flow) and the dimensionless parameters associated with these physical regimes (Reynolds number and Mach number). The need to use high-performance computation to solve these equations in many cases of interest is then explored via some example applications.

We then focus on the particular computational difficulties associated with incompressible viscous CFD. For complex geometries that are of practical interest, special attention is paid to the application of high-order finite element methods (also called spectral element methods) and their parallel implementation. The reason for presenting the material in this way is that the finite element framework provides a unified approach to describing the equations of fluid dynamics in both simple and complex geometries. It is also easy to express low-order approximations, such as those that arise in the application of classical finite difference or finite volume methods, as well as higher-order approximations in this framework. As seen below, it turns out that in most applications, the use of the finite element method along with some simplifying assumptions makes it clear that the relevant issue in solving most time-dependent CFD problems is the need to solve efficiently several (possibly coupled) elliptic equations. Thus, for incompressible flows, efficient parallel implementations for CFD are intimately connected to efficient parallel solution procedures for elliptic partial differential equations. Therefore, many of the methods described in this volume for parallel solution of such equations are directly applicable. Unfortunately, to achieve the enormous economy of description of the finite element method, it becomes necessary to use the mathematical formalism of finite elements, which can at times be somewhat daunting.

A brief overview is then presented of approaches to the numerical simulation of compressible CFD. It is argued that the need to capture fine-scale features such as shock waves makes the use of adaptive mesh refinement essential, especially in three dimensions. The difficulty of establishing load balancing and scalability for such calculations is discussed. The chapter concludes with a brief discussion of some future computational challenges for CFD and an assessment of the computational resources required to overcome these challenges.

5.1 Introduction to Computational Fluid Dynamics

CFD is an enormous field with a vast literature, and it is basically impossible in this short chapter to provide comprehensive implementations of parallel solution strategies. At best, this chapter provides a glimpse of some of the essential issues associated with high-performance computation of both incompressible and compressible flows and attempts to provide some brief examples of the flow simulations achievable.

5.1.1 Basic Equations of Fluid Dynamics

The motion of a fluid is governed by the principles of classical mechanics and thermodynamics, namely, conservation of mass, momentum, and energy. The most general statement of these principles is carried out in integral form in a stationary frame of reference leading to the following conservation equations [593]:

$$\frac{d}{dt} \int_V \rho \, dV + \int_\Sigma (\rho \, \boldsymbol{u} \cdot \boldsymbol{n}) \, d\Sigma = 0 \tag{5.1}$$

$$\frac{d}{dt} \int_V \rho \, \boldsymbol{u} \, dV + \int_\Sigma [(\boldsymbol{n} \cdot \boldsymbol{u}) \, \rho \, \boldsymbol{u} - \boldsymbol{n}\sigma] \, d\Sigma = \int_V \mathbf{f}_e \, dV \tag{5.2}$$

$$\frac{d}{dt} \int_V \rho \, E \, dV + \int_\Sigma \boldsymbol{n} \cdot \left[\rho \, E \boldsymbol{u} - \sigma\boldsymbol{u} + \mathbf{q} \right] d\Sigma = \int_V (\mathbf{f}_e \cdot \boldsymbol{u}) \, dV \tag{5.3}$$

Here, t is time, ρ is density, $\boldsymbol{u}$ is the velocity of a material fluid particle in this frame of reference, E is the total specific energy, given by

$$E = e + \frac{1}{2} \boldsymbol{u} \cdot \boldsymbol{u}$$

where e is the specific internal energy, σ is the stress tensor, $\mathbf{q}$ is the heat flux, $\mathbf{f}_e$ is the external force per unit volume, and $\boldsymbol{n}$ is the unit outward normal to the surface Σ enclosing the fluid volume V. We ignore other sinks and sources of energy, such as those arising from chemical reactions or other phenomena.

The solutions of equations (5.1), (5.2), and (5.3) need not be continuous functions of space, and it is for this reason that the equations are written in integral form. However, if the flow density, velocity, and energy are sufficiently smooth, then these equations can be transformed into an equivalent set of partial differential equations through the use of the divergence theorem:

$$\partial_t(\rho) + \nabla \cdot (\rho \, \boldsymbol{u}) = 0$$

$$\partial_t(\rho \boldsymbol{u}) + \nabla \cdot (\rho \, \boldsymbol{u} \, \boldsymbol{u} - \sigma) = \mathbf{f}_e$$

$$\partial_t(\rho E) + \nabla \cdot (\rho \, E \, \boldsymbol{u} - \sigma \, \boldsymbol{u} + \mathbf{q}) = \mathbf{f}_e \cdot \boldsymbol{u}$$

The basic dependent variables are the density, velocity, and energy of the flow. Constitutive relations for the stress tensor σ and for the heat flux vector $\mathbf{q}$ must be added to these equations in order to form a closed system. A *Navier–Stokes* fluid is defined by the following constitutive relations:

$$\sigma = -p\,\mathbf{I} + \lambda\,(\nabla \cdot \boldsymbol{u})\,\mathbf{I} + \mu \left[(\nabla \boldsymbol{u}) + (\nabla \boldsymbol{u})^T \right]$$

Here p is the pressure, and λ, μ are coefficients of viscosity. The fluid is assumed to obey the Fourier law of heat conduction,

$$\mathbf{q} = -k\,\nabla T$$

where T is the absolute temperature and k is the thermal conductivity. Finally, since we assume that the fluid is in thermodynamic equilibrium locally, we require an equation of state for the fluid that relates, for example, the entropy of the fluid to the density and internal energy:

$$S = S(\rho, e)$$

where S is the entropy. From this and the thermodynamic identities,

$$p = -\rho^2\,T \left(\frac{\partial S}{\partial \rho} \right)_e \qquad T^{-1} = \left(\frac{\partial S}{\partial e} \right)_\rho$$

the Navier–Stokes equations become a closed system for the dynamic variables ρ, $\boldsymbol{u}$, and E.

An important special case of these equations is the flow of a perfect gas with constant specific heats C_p and C_v. For such a gas, the equation of state is the well-known ideal gas law:

$$p = (\gamma - 1)\,\rho\,e \qquad \gamma = \frac{C_p}{C_v} \qquad e = C_v\,T$$

For further details the reader is referred to Thompson [930].

5.1.2   Physical Regimes and Dimensionless Variables

The Navier–Stokes equations have been shown to be valid over a wide class of flow regimes. A useful approach to distinguishing the key regimes is to scale the physical variables and to rewrite the equations in dimensionless form. To do this, we scale all quantities relative to a reference length L, a reference velocity V^*, a reference density ρ^*, and reference values of the coefficients of the viscosity μ and thermal conductivity k. All other characteristic quantities can be derived from these basic ones, although some understanding of the various balances of terms in the equations is required to achieve meaningful results. We choose L/V^* to scale time t, $\rho^* V^{*2}$ to scale the stress σ, and so forth. In this dimensionless form, the equations remain essentially unchanged, but the constitutive laws reappear in a scaled form:

$$\sigma = -p\,\mathbf{I} + \frac{1}{Re}\left\{\lambda\,(\nabla\cdot\boldsymbol{u})\,\mathbf{I} + \mu\left[(\nabla\boldsymbol{u}) + (\nabla\boldsymbol{u})^T\right]\right\}$$

where Re is the Reynolds number and is given by $Re = V^* L \rho^* / \mu^*$.

The Reynolds number is a measure of the ratio of inertial to viscous forces acting within the fluid. A low Reynolds number signifies flow dominated by viscous effects, while a high Reynolds number indicates flows dominated by inertial effects. This would seem to imply that one could ignore the viscous terms for flows at high Reynolds numbers (e.g., for flow around an aircraft or car, which is typically in the range of $Re = 10^5$ to 10^8). However, this is not quite correct since the viscous terms become important near solid boundaries (such as the wing or body of the airplane) and must be included if one wishes to compute the fluid drag on the car or plane. In addition, in a turbulent flow the viscous terms are active at small length scales and cannot be ignored if one wants to compute how much energy is required, for example, to keep the flow moving at the characteristic velocity implied by a high Reynolds number.

If we assume the fluid is a perfect gas, then it can be shown that the heat flux is given by

$$\mathbf{q} = -\frac{\gamma}{RePr}\, k\,\nabla e$$

where $Pr = \mu^* C_p / k^*$ is the Prandtl number, which measures the relative importance of viscous to thermal diffusion. For a perfect gas with constant specific heats, the equation of state becomes

$$e = \frac{T}{\gamma\,(\gamma - 1)\,M^2}$$

where $M = V^* / \sqrt{\gamma\, R\, T^*}$ is the Mach number, which measures the ratio of the characteristic velocity to the speed of sound of the gas at temperature T^*. It can be shown that, provided the velocity of the fluid remains substantially lower than the speed of sound, the flow is essentially incompressible. This means that the density of a fluid element is simply carried along by the flow as the flow evolves. In this case the equations simplify, and the equation of state of the fluid becomes irrelevant.

For flows with velocities comparable or exceeding the local speed of sound, it is possible to generate shock waves in the fluid. These are essentially thin layers of fluid separating regions in which the flow is locally supersonic from those in which the flow is subsonic. The viscous terms again become very important in these thin shock regions.

5.1.3   The Role of High-Performance Computing

Numerical computation of fluid flows and, in particular, the use of high-performance computation plays a critical role in fluid mechanics research for several reasons. First, the equations of motion as described above are nonlinear. Exact solutions of these equations exist only for highly simplified geometries and initial conditions. Numerical computation is essential for solving general initial value problems in realistic geometries, such as the flow over an automobile or an airplane wing. In addition, the number of degrees of freedom required for accurate simulation of flows in realistic geometries rises rapidly with Reynolds number and Mach number.

To get a feel for the computational requirements, consider the simulation of turbulent flow without boundaries. It can be shown that the number of degrees of freedom required to simulate all relevant length scales in the flow properly (including the dissipation-producing length scales due to viscosity) varies as $Re^{9/4}$. For a moderate Reynolds number of 10^6, this implies a total of 3×10^{13} degrees of freedom per velocity component. Typically, this needs to be multiplied by a factor of 10 to 15 to accommodate the storage required to carry out a computation. Thus, roughly 300 terawords of memory are required simply to describe the flow. In order to integrate the flow forward in time over a typical number of time steps (with a time step on the order of $1/Re$ and thus on the order Re steps), one would need to sweep through the mesh several times per time step. The exact number of sweeps depends on the solver being used, but in any case, these simple considerations lead to an estimate of the flop count on the order 10^{19} or more for a Reynolds number of 10^6. From this simple estimate, it is clear that one requires a machine with the capability of hundreds of teraflops or even petaflops in order to perform such simulations in a reasonable time. Such architectures are only now on the horizon.

Turbulent flow is not the only application requiring high-resolution numerical simulations. Even if the flow is kept smooth and laminar, the computation of fluid flow about a solid body such as an airplane or car still requires substantial resources. At the surface of a body, the flow satisfies the "no-slip" condition and is constrained to move at the velocity of the body. The flow accommodates to this condition via a thin boundary layer in which the viscous terms are sizable. The thickness of a laminar boundary layer scales as $Re^{-1/2}$. For example, the boundary layer on a 20-foot automobile traveling at 55 miles per hour is about 1/10 of an inch. Again, a wide range of scales is required in order to capture the flow correctly.

An even more severe ratio of length scales occurs for compressible flow with shock waves. The thickness of strong shock waves is only on the order of a few molecular mean free paths for a gas. The mean free path is typically several orders of magnitude smaller than any characteristic length scale of the mean flow. In fact, it is currently impractical to perform computations of compressible flows with shock waves in which viscous effects are resolved across the shock wave except at Mach numbers near 1.

The need to resolve the enormous range of scales in the examples above makes the use of CFD essential. Even so, it is currently not possible to perform direct numerical simulations of engineering flows in which all relevant scales are resolved. In all such flows, some model of the small scales must be introduced. For turbulent flows, we introduce a turbulence model to perform the dissipation of missing scales. For strongly compressible flows, we employ modern artificial viscosities that allow us to capture correctly the large-scale effects of the shock wave.

5.2   Incompressible Flows

We begin our discussion by considering Newtonian incompressible fluids with constant density ρ and kinematic viscosity $v = \mu/\rho$, the motion of which is governed by the incompressible Navier–Stokes equations:

$$\nabla \cdot \boldsymbol{u} = 0 \quad \text{in } \Omega$$

$$\partial_t \boldsymbol{u} = \mathbf{N}(\boldsymbol{u}) - \frac{1}{\rho}\, \nabla p + \frac{1}{Re}\, \nabla^2 \boldsymbol{u} \quad \text{in } \Omega \tag{5.4}$$

where $\boldsymbol{u} = (u_1, u_2, u_3)$ is the velocity field, p is the static pressure, $Re \equiv UL/v$ is the Reynolds number, and Ω is the computational domain. Without loss of generality, we take the numerical value of $\rho = 1$, since this simply sets the scale for p. $\mathbf{N}(\boldsymbol{u})$ represents the nonlinear advection term:

$$\mathbf{N}(\boldsymbol{u}) = -(\boldsymbol{u} \cdot \nabla)\, \boldsymbol{u}$$

$$= -\frac{1}{2}\, [(\boldsymbol{u} \cdot \nabla)\, \boldsymbol{u} + \nabla \cdot (\boldsymbol{u}\,\boldsymbol{u})]$$

$$= -\frac{1}{2} \nabla\, (\boldsymbol{u} \cdot \boldsymbol{u}) - \boldsymbol{u} \times \nabla \times \boldsymbol{u}$$

We refer to these as the *convective* form, *skew-symmetric* form, and *rotational* form, respectively. These three forms for $\mathbf{N}(\boldsymbol{u})$ are mathematically equivalent but behave differently when implemented for a discrete system. As shown by Zang [1015], the skew-symmetric form is the most robust; this form is used in all calculations described here.

The Navier–Stokes equations are coupled through the incompressibility constraint $\nabla \cdot \boldsymbol{u} = 0$ and the nonlinear term $\mathbf{N}(\boldsymbol{u})$. Dealing with this coupling in an efficient and accurate manner is one of the challenges inherent in simulating incompressible flow. However, the biggest challenge for time integration actually comes from the *linear* term:

$$\mathbf{L}(\boldsymbol{u}) \equiv \frac{1}{Re}\, \nabla^2 \boldsymbol{u}$$

This term is responsible for the fastest time scales in the system and thus poses the most severe constraint on the maximum allowable time step for numerical integration of the fluid equations. Problems associated with the stiffness of the linear operator are handled by treating this term implicitly, while the nonlinear term is usually integrated with a more direct and easily implemented explicit method. Completely implicit treatments of the nonlinear term have been developed and lead to more robust simulations, especially at high flow speeds [882]. The application of an appropriate time-stepping scheme is a key part of any formulation and involves essential issues of numerical stability. For an example of some of the subtleties, see Petersson [762].

5.2.1   Semi-discrete Formulation

To solve the Navier–Stokes equations, equation (5.4) is integrated over a single time step to obtain:

$$\boldsymbol{u}(t + \Delta t) = \boldsymbol{u}(t) + \int_t^{t+\Delta t} \left[\mathbf{N}(\boldsymbol{u}) - \frac{1}{\rho} \nabla p + \mathbf{L}(\boldsymbol{u}) \right] dt$$

Next we introduce a discrete set of times $t_n \equiv n\,\Delta t$, where the solution is to be evaluated, and define $\boldsymbol{u}^n \equiv \boldsymbol{u}(\mathbf{x}, t_n)$ as the semi-discrete approximation to the velocity (discrete in time, continuous in space). For reasons that will be explained in a moment, the pressure integral is replaced with:

$$\nabla \tilde{P} \equiv \frac{1}{\Delta t} \int_{t_n}^{t_{n+1}} \frac{1}{\rho} \nabla p \, dt \tag{5.5}$$

Next we introduce appropriate integration schemes for the linear and nonlinear terms. The simplest implicit/explicit scheme would be first-order Euler time integration:

$$\int_{t_n}^{t_{n+1}} \mathbf{L}(\boldsymbol{u}) \, dt \approx \Delta t \, \mathbf{L}(\boldsymbol{u}^{n+1}) \tag{5.6}$$

$$\int_{t_n}^{t_{n+1}} \mathbf{N}(\boldsymbol{u}) \, dt \approx \Delta t \, \mathbf{N}(\boldsymbol{u}^{n}) \tag{5.7}$$

Combining (5.5)–(5.7) we get a semi-discrete approximation to the momentum equation:

$$u^{n+1} = u^n + \left[\mathbf{N}(\boldsymbol{u}^n) - \nabla \tilde{P} + \mathbf{L}(\boldsymbol{u}^{n+1}) \right] \Delta t \tag{5.8}$$

This system of equations can be solved by further splitting (5.8) into three substeps as follows:

$$
\begin{aligned}
\boldsymbol{u}^{(1)} \quad &- \quad \boldsymbol{u}^n \quad &= \quad \Delta t \mathbf{N}(\boldsymbol{u}^n) \\
\boldsymbol{u}^{(2)} \quad &- \quad \boldsymbol{u}^{(1)} \quad &= \quad -\Delta t \nabla \tilde{P} \\
\boldsymbol{u}^{n+1} \quad &- \quad \boldsymbol{u}^{(2)} \quad &= \quad \Delta t \mathbf{L}(\boldsymbol{u}^{n+1})
\end{aligned}
$$

Here $\boldsymbol{u}^{(1)}$ and $\boldsymbol{u}^{(2)}$ are intermediate velocity fields that progressively incorporate the nonlinear terms and the incompressibility constraint. The motivation for the splitting is to decouple the pressure term from the advection and diffusion terms. It should be noted that the splitting procedure constitutes only an approximate solution to the problem of solving equation (5.8) coupled to the incompressibility constraint. For many purposes, this solution is sufficiently accurate, but in certain cases errors occur at flow boundaries; these can sometimes be significant. The errors arise because the incompressibility constraint is not enforced at all points up to and including the flow boundaries. Again the reader is referred to Petersson [762] for a more complete discussion.

The classical splitting scheme proceeds by introducing two assumptions: that $u^{(2)}$ satisfies the divergence-free condition ($\nabla \cdot u^{(2)} = 0$), and that $u^{(2)}$ satisfies the correct Dirichlet boundary conditions in the direction normal to the boundary ($n \cdot u^{(2)} = n \cdot u^{n+1}$). Incorporating these assumptions, we can derive a separately solvable elliptic problem for the pressure in the form:

$$\nabla^2 \tilde{P} = \frac{1}{\Delta t} \left(\nabla \cdot u^{(1)} \right) \tag{5.9}$$

The field $\tilde{P}$ is no longer associated with thermodynamic pressure and becomes a dynamic variable that couples the divergence-free condition and the momentum equation. Neumann boundary conditions for $\tilde{P}$ come from equation (5.8), which can be simplified to the form:

$$\frac{\partial \tilde{P}}{\partial n} = n \cdot \left[\mathbf{N}(u^n) - \frac{1}{Re} \nabla \times \nabla \times u^n \right] \tag{5.10}$$

This boundary condition prevents the propagation and accumulation of time differencing errors and ensures that $\tilde{P}$ satisfies the important pressure compatibility condition [531]. Note that the linear term in equation (5.10) is derived from $\mathbf{L}(u^n)$ rather than $\mathbf{L}(u^{n+1})$. This type of first-order extrapolation is necessary to keep the pressure equation decoupled from the other substeps. The order of the extrapolation should be consistent with the overall time accuracy.

A single time step using the skew-symmetric form of the nonlinear terms requires the computation of various spatial derivatives to assemble the nonlinear term, plus the solution of one Poisson equation for the pressure, and up to three Helmholtz equations for the diffusion in each direction. Most of the computational work is associated with solving these linear systems; integration of the nonlinear terms makes only a minor contribution. The techniques outlined below can be applied directly to the solution of the various elliptic subproblems as well as computation of the nonlinear terms.

5.2.2   Spectral Element Methods

As stated above, the key steps in solving the Navier–Stokes equations are the approximation of the various operators (both linear and nonlinear) and the solution of the Poisson equation for the pressure. In this section we lay out a solution to both of these problems that uses high-order finite element or spectral element methods. The advantage of this approach is that we can address issues of accuracy as well as complex geometry. As was shown above, the solution of elliptic problems (equation (5.9), for example) is a key aspect of solving incompressible flow problems. In this domain, finite element methods also confer some advantage, as there is a well-developed theory to assess the numerical error resulting from such approximations. Finally, classical formulations of discrete solutions of the Navier–Stokes equations that are obtained via the use of lower-order finite difference methods or finite volume methods can be recovered using the finite element formulation through the use of low-order basis functions and appropriate projection operators. For details, the reader should consult the very thorough presentation of Gresho and Sani [396]. A good introduction to spectral element methods can be found in Karniadakis and Sherwin [532].

A One-Dimensional Example

It turns out that all the key aspects of the spatial approximation schemes can be described by considering the solution in one space dimension of the Poisson equation.

Suppose that we want to find u such that

$$u'' + f = 0 \quad \text{on } \Omega$$

where Ω is the unit interval $0 \le x \le 1$ and f is a given smooth function. At the endpoints, we will specify the boundary conditions

$$u(0) = g$$
$$u'(1) = h$$

This defines the *strong* form, the usual starting point for finite difference and other schemes.

Consider the following alternative formulation of the same problem. We begin with the equation for the residual,

$$R(u) = \int_\Omega w \left(u'' + f \right) \, dx \tag{5.11}$$

from which we want to find the unique function u that drives the residual to zero. The search will include all functions satisfying the boundary condition $u(0) = g$; each candidate is called a *trial* solution, and we denote the set of all trial solutions by $\mathcal{S}$. The residual is orthogonalized with respect to a second set of functions $w \in \mathcal{V}$ called *test functions* or *variations*. Each test function should satisfy $w(0) = 0$. To incorporate the Neumann boundary condition, we integrate equation (5.11) once by parts, finding that $R(u) = 0$ if

$$\int_\Omega w' u' \, dx = \int_\Omega w f \, dx + w(1) h$$

If we identify the symmetric, bilinear forms $a(w, u) = \int_\Omega w'u' \, dx$ and $(w, f) = \int_\Omega wf \, dx$, then we can state the *weak* form as follows: find $u \in \mathcal{S}$ such that, for every $w \in \mathcal{V}$,

$$a(w, u) = (w, f) + w(1) h \tag{5.12}$$

Galerkin approximation solves equation (5.12) using a finite collection of functions: find $u^h \in \mathcal{S}^h$ such that, for every $w^h \in \mathcal{V}^h$,

$$a(w^h, u^h) = (w^h, f) + w^h(1) h \tag{5.13}$$

This method reduces an *infinite*-dimensional problem to an *n*-dimensional problem by choosing a set of *n* basis functions $(\phi_1, \phi_2, \ldots, \phi_n)$ to represent each member of $\mathcal{S}^h$ and $\mathcal{V}^h$. It admits all linear combinations $w^h \in \mathcal{V}^h$ as

$$w^h = c_1 \phi_1 + c_2 \phi_2 + \ldots + c_n \phi_n$$

where each $\phi_p(0) = 0$. To generate the trial solutions, we need one additional function satisfying $\phi_{n+1}(0) = 1$, so that if $u^h \in \mathcal{S}^h$ then

$$u^h = g\,\phi_{n+1} + \sum_{p=1}^{n} d_p\,\phi_p$$

Note that, with the exception of ϕ_{n+1}, $\mathcal{S}^h$ and $\mathcal{V}^h$ are composed of the same functions. Substituting u^h for u and w^h for w, the weak form becomes

$$\sum_{p=1}^{n} c_p\,G_p = 0$$

where

$$G_p = \sum_{q=1}^{n} \left[a(\phi_p, \phi_q)\,d_q - (\phi_p, f) - \phi_p(1)\,h + a(\phi_p, \phi_{n+1})\,g \right]$$

Since this must be true for any choice of the c_p's, we require $G_p \equiv 0$. If we put the coefficients d_p into a vector $\vec{d}$, we obtain the matrix problem

$$\mathbf{A}\vec{d} = \vec{F}$$

where the matrix entries are given by $A_{pq} = a(\phi_p, \phi_q)$, and the components of the vector $\vec{F}$ are $F_p = (\phi_p, f) + \phi_p(1)h - a(\phi_p, \phi_{n+1})g$. The solution is $\vec{d} = \mathbf{A}^{-1}\vec{F}$. Quite literally, this is a best fit of the approximate solution u^h to the true solution u based on the measure of error given in equation (5.11).

Basis Functions

Galerkin approximation is "optimal" in the sense that it gives the best approximation in the restricted space $\mathcal{S}^h$. If the true solution u lies in the intersection of $\mathcal{S}^h$ and $\mathcal{S}$, then $u^h = u$. But the success of the method lies in the selection of the basis functions. If they are too complicated, it will be impossible to generate the matrix problem; too simple, and they cannot adequately describe the true solution u. The key is to combine computability and accuracy. Spectral elements accomplish this in the following manner.

First, the domain is partitioned into K nonoverlapping subintervals, where each subinterval, or *element*, is given by $\Omega^k = [a^k, b^k]$. On element k we want to introduce a set of local functions that provide accuracy of order N for the solution over that piece of the computational domain. For spectral element methods, the basis functions are invariably polynomials.

Often, the most convenient approach is to form a set of polynomials from the Lagrangian interpolants through a particular set of *nodes*. Recall that the Lagrangian interpolant takes the value one at some node x_i and is zero at all other nodes. The simplest set of nodes would be the equally spaced points $x_i = a^k + (b^k - a^k) i/N$. This turns out to be a terrible choice for a high-order method because the basis is almost linearly dependent, resulting in ill-conditioned algebraic systems. It is not the choice of Lagrangian interpolants that causes the difficulty, but the choice of nodes over which they are defined. To fix the problem, we just need to choose a "good" set of nodes. The choice of points is crucial to the success and accuracy of the spectral method. In contrast, this close connection between the sampling points and the order of the method is not present in finite difference methods.

To standardize the basis, we introduce a parent domain with the coordinates $-1 \leq \xi \leq 1$ and a coordinate transformation to the elemental nodes as

$$x_i = a^k + \frac{b^k - a^k}{2} (1 + \xi_i)$$

Now we choose the nodes ξ_i to be the solutions of $(1 - \xi^2) L'_N(\xi) = 0$, where $L_N(\xi)$ is the Legendre polynomial of degree N. With this special choice, the Lagrangian interpolants can be written down explicitly as

$$\phi_i(\xi) = -\frac{(1 - \xi^2) L'_N(\xi)}{N(N+1) L_N(\xi_i) (\xi - \xi_i)} \tag{5.14}$$

These polynomials are called the Gauss–Lobatto Legendre (GLL) interpolants. Figure 5.1 illustrates the mesh and basis functions for a typical element. We will refer to any basis defined this way as a *nodal* basis.

There are several important reasons for choosing this set of polynomials. First, the expansion of any smooth function using the GLL interpolants, $u \approx u^h = \sum d_i \phi_i(x)$, converges exponentially fast, as can be demonstrated by singular Sturm–Liouville theory [393]. Because these are Lagrangian interpolants, the coefficients d_i are simply the nodal values of the approximate solution: $d_i = u^h(x_i)$. Also, there is a set of integration weights ρ_i associated with the nodes ξ_i so that the integrals appearing in the weak form can be computed via the GLL quadrature

$$\int_{-1}^{1} f \, d\xi = \sum_{i=0}^{N} \rho_i f(\xi_i) + \epsilon_N$$

where the error $\epsilon_N \sim \mathcal{O}(f^{2N}(\zeta))$ for some point in $-1 \leq \zeta \leq 1$. As long as the integrand is a polynomial of degree less than $2N$, this quadrature rule is exact [249]. Finally, and perhaps most importantly, the interpolants, quadrature points, and weights can be generated within a computer program by recursive algorithms that are numerically stable through values of $N \sim 100$, eliminating the need to store static tables of quadrature data.

Legendre polynomials are one example of a broad polynomial class called the *generalized Jacobi polynomials*, which we denote as $P_n^{\alpha,\beta}(\xi)$. Legendre polynomials

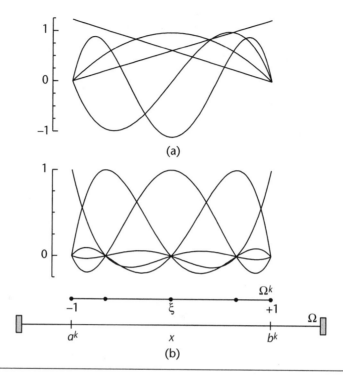

Figure 5.1   One-dimensional, spectral-element basis functions for an expansion order of $N = 4$, along with a sketch of the local and global coordinate systems: (a) modal basis constructed from $P_n^{1,1}(\xi)$; (b) Gauss–Lobatto Legendre basis and the set of nodal points that define them as Lagrangian interpolants.

correspond to the parameter values $\alpha = 0$, $\beta = 0$. Sometimes, especially in higher dimensions and on more complex domains, it is more convenient to work directly with the polynomials rather than an intermediate Lagrangian basis. Jacobi polynomials have the orthogonality property

$$\int_{-1}^{1}(1-\xi)^\alpha \, (1+\xi)^\beta \, P_i^{\alpha,\beta}(\xi) \, P_j^{\alpha,\beta}(\xi) \, \mathrm{d}\xi = \delta_{ij}$$

We can use Jacobi polynomials directly to represent a function through the expansion $u^h = \sum d_i P_i^{\alpha,\beta}(x)$. The values d_i are the coefficients of the basis functions, but they do not correspond to any set of nodal values. In practice, there is a significant advantage if most of the basis functions are orthogonal, so in the 1-D case we would use:

$$\phi_0(\xi) = \frac{1}{2}(1+\xi)$$

$$\phi_1(\xi) = \frac{1}{2}(1-\xi) \tag{5.15}$$

$$\phi_i(\xi) = \frac{1}{4}(1+\xi)(1-\xi)\,P_{i-2}^{1,1}(\xi), \quad i \geq 2$$

Figure 5.1 shows the first five basis functions constructed this way. In the nodal basis, every function is a polynomial of degree N. In the modal basis, there is a *hierarchy* of modes starting with the linear modes, proceeding with the quadratic, the cubic, and so on.

We will refer to spectral elements constructed from a nodal basis as *Lagrange spectral elements* and to those based on a modal basis as *h-p elements*. The latter were first introduced in the early 1970s by Szabo [907], who used the integrals of Legendre polynomials as a modal basis, taking $\phi_i(\xi) = \int_{-1}^{\xi} P_{i-1}^{0,0}(s)\,ds$. However, using the properties of Jacobi polynomials [3] we obtain

$$2n \int_{-1}^{\xi} P_{n-1}^{0,0}(s)\,ds = (1-\xi)(1+\xi)\,P_{n-2}^{1,1}(\xi)$$

which is the same as the basis in equation (5.15), except for the normalization.

The choice of which approach to take is somewhat arbitrary, since a nodal basis can always be transformed to an equivalent modal basis and vice versa. The Fast Fourier Transform (FFT) is one familiar example of such a transformation onto the basis $\phi_k(\xi) = \exp(ik\xi)$. Unfortunately, there are no "fast transform" methods for Jacobi polynomials, and the transforms require matrix multiplication. However, for the values of N used in practice ($N \leq 16$), this is not a serious drawback.

Discrete Equations

Returning to the problem of solving equation (5.13), we begin by noting that the integral can be broken into a sum of integrals of each element:

$$a(\phi_p, \phi_q)_\Omega = \sum_{k=1}^{K} a(\phi_p, \phi_q)_{\Omega^k}$$

Since each basis function is nonzero over a *single* element, the inner product $a(\phi_p, \phi_q)$ is nonzero only if ϕ_p and ϕ_q "belong" to the same element. This makes the global system sparse and allows us to compute only local matrices. Because of the origin of finite element methods in computational mechanics, these matrices are traditionally called:

$$\text{"mass"}\,\mathbf{M}_{pq}^k = \int_{\Omega^k} \phi_p\,\phi_q\,dx$$

$$\text{"stiffness"}\,\mathbf{A}_{pq}^k = \int_{\Omega^k} \phi_p'\,\phi_q'\,dx$$

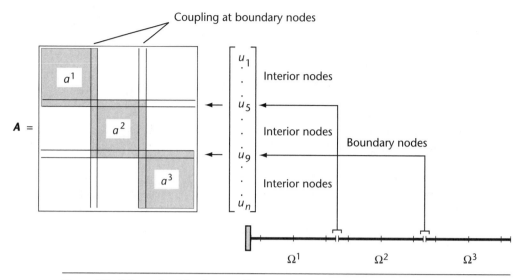

Figure 5.2   Schematic of the direct stiffness summation of local matrices A^k to form the global matrix A.

To construct the right-hand side of the matrix system, $f(x)$ is approximated by collocation at the nodal points to produce $f^h(x)$; the mass matrix provides the coefficients necessary to perform the integration. Now the *elemental* matrix system may be written as

$$\mathbf{A}^k \, \vec{v}^k = \vec{F}^k \quad (+ \text{ boundary terms})$$

Just as the integral over the entire domain can be written as a sum of the integral over each element, the global matrices can be computed by summing contributions from the elemental matrices:

$$\mathbf{A} = \sum_{k=1}^{K}{}' \mathbf{A}^k, \quad \mathbf{M} = \sum_{k=1}^{K}{}' \mathbf{M}^k$$

The symbol $\sum'$ represents "direct stiffness summation." The procedure is exemplified in the diagram for the nodal basis in Figure 5.2 that maps contributions from the boundary node shared by adjacent elements to the same row of the global matrix **A**. The global matrix system is

$$\mathbf{A}v = \mathbf{F} \quad (+ \text{ boundary terms})$$

A is banded as a result of using local basis functions, with all of its nonzero entries located in the N diagonals above and below the main diagonal. It is also symmetric, due to the symmetry of $a(\cdot, \cdot)$, and positive definite. Thus, **A** can be computed, stored, and factored economically and efficiently.

Spectral element discretizations encompass both spectral methods and finite elements. With the proper choice of basis functions and projection methods, finite difference methods can also be included. Standard approximation error estimates for Galerkin methods applied to elliptic problems on quasi-uniform meshes predict that

$$\|u - u^h\|_1 \leq \text{constant} \times h^{\mu-1} N^{-(D-1)} \|u\|_D$$

where $\mu = \min(D, N + 1)$, N is the polynomial degree appearing in the basis functions, and h is a parameter related to the element size [64]. The constant depends on the degree of mesh quasi-uniformity. D basically represents the Dth derivative of the solution and can be taken to be some fixed value. We assume that D can actually be taken to be large since we assume the flow variables are smooth and possess all derivatives. The main point of this result is that there are two ways to improve the approximation: make h smaller ($K \to \infty$), or make N and μ larger ($N \to \infty$). The latter results in *exponential* convergence for smooth solutions. If a solution varies rapidly over a small region, any polynomial fit will oscillate rapidly, and the best approach is to reduce the element size until the solution is resolved *locally*. A more effective approach is to combine the two convergence procedures, increasing both K and N simultaneously; this dual path of convergence is known as an *h-p* refinement procedure [907]. The flexibility to adapt the mesh to the solution makes spectral element methods quite robust.

Basis Functions in *d* Dimensions

A key to the efficiency of high-order methods in 2- and 3-D problems is the formation of a basis from the *tensor product* of 1-D functions. Among other things, this allows the computation of integrals and derivatives of the basis functions to be simplified through a procedure called *sum factorization* [728]. It also contributes to the sparse structure of matrix systems for multidimensional problems.

In this section, we describe the procedure for constructing an efficient, high-order basis on 2- and 3-D domains. To keep the discussion simple, we only consider the standard domains $\mathbb{R}^d$, where d is the problem dimension. Figure 5.3 defines the standard rectangle, $\mathbb{R}^2$. "Standard" here means that the coordinates are normalized to fall in the range -1 to 1. For $d = 3$, the standard domain is a hexahedral element. Isoparametric mappings can always be used to transform more general elements to these standard domains, as illustrated in Figure 5.3. On the standard element, we wish to define a polynomial basis, denoted by $\phi_{ij}(\xi_1, \xi_2)$, so that we can represent a function $u^h(\xi_1, \xi_2)$ by the expansion

$$u^h(\xi_1, \xi_2) = \sum_{i=0}^{N} \sum_{j=0}^{N} u_{ij}\, \phi_{ij}(\xi_1, \xi_2)$$

where u_{ij} is the coefficient of the basis function ϕ_{ij} and $\xi = (\xi_1, \xi_2)$ is the local coordinate within the element.

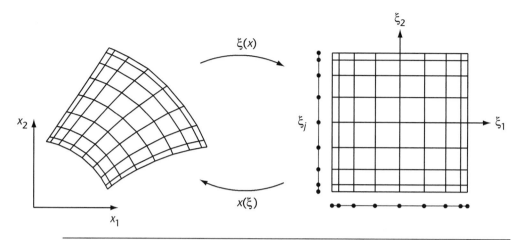

Figure 5.3 Definition of the standard quadrilateral domain $\mathbb{R}^2$. General curvilinear elements can always be mapped back to the standard element as shown.

For quadrilateral (2-D) and hexahedral (3-D) elements, the procedure is straightforward. For example, on the domain $\Omega^k = \mathbb{R}^2$, the basis would be

$$\phi_{ij}(\xi_1, \xi_2) = \phi_i(\xi_1)\,\phi_j(\xi_2)$$

where $\phi_i(\xi)$ is the one-dimensional GLL polynomial defined in equation (5.14). In this case, u_{ij} represents the function value at the node ξ_{ij}. The 3-D basis on $\mathbb{R}^3$ is exactly analogous to this one.

In the remainder of this chapter, we use the following simplified notation: every index (ijk) in the tensor product basis will be mapped to a single number as $p = i + jN + kN^2$, so that there is a one-to-one correspondence between $\phi_p(\xi)$ and $\phi_{ijk}(\xi)$. This hides the tensor product nature of the basis but makes the discrete equations much easier to write down. When necessary, we can "unroll" the p index to take advantage of the tensor product form. This expression for p is valid for quadrilateral elements only.

5.2.3 Basic Operations

Solution of the Navier–Stokes equations using spectral element methods requires the ability to perform several basic operations. In particular, we need a suitable quadrature rule for performing the integration, and we need to be able to evaluate functions or derivatives at specified points.

Integration

The general form for the evaluation of an integral by Gaussian quadrature with weights $(1 - \xi)^\alpha (1 + \xi)^\beta$ can be written as

$$\int_{-1}^{1} (1 - \xi)^\alpha (1 + \xi)^\beta u(\xi) \, d\xi = \sum_{i=0}^{N} \rho_i^{\alpha,\beta} u(\xi_i^{\alpha,\beta})$$

where $\xi_i^{\alpha,\beta}$ and $\rho_i^{\alpha,\beta}$ are the quadrature points and weights associated with the Jacobi polynomial $P_N^{\alpha,\beta}(\xi)$. The quadrature rule is exact if $u(\xi)$ is a polynomial of degree $2N + 1$ for the Gauss points, $2N$ for the Gauss–Radau points, and $2N - 1$ for the Gauss–Lobatto points.

To integrate a function defined over the standard domain $\mathbb{R}^2$, we simply use the tensor product form to reduce the integral to two 1-D quadratures. The integral of a general function is written as

$$\int_{\mathbb{R}^2} u(\xi) \, d\xi_1 d\xi_2 = \sum_{i=0}^{N} \sum_{j=0}^{N} \rho_i \rho_j \, u(\xi_{ij})$$

The extension to integrals over $\mathbb{R}^3$ is straightforward.

Projection

To apply the integration rules described above, we need to evaluate a function at a given set of quadrature points. For the nodal basis this is trivial because the basis coefficients *are* the function values at the quadrature points. For a modal basis we need an efficient way to evaluate the full solution at the quadrature points. This problem and the related problem of determining the modal expansion coefficients from a set of nodal values are both called *projections*.

A projection is the procedure for determining the coefficients u_{ijk} so that $u^h \approx u$ for some given function u. First, recall the general form of the expansion:

$$u(\xi) \approx u^h(\xi) = \sum_p u_p \, \phi_p(\xi)$$

The expansion coefficients are determined by taking the inner product with the basis functions on both sides of this equation:

$$(u, \phi_p)_{\Omega^k} = (u^h, \phi_p)_{\Omega^k} \quad \forall \phi_p \in \{\phi_{ijk}\} \tag{5.16}$$

Solving this system of equations to determine the approximation u^h is straightforward if the basis $\{\phi_{ijk}\}$ is orthogonal. Otherwise, we have to compute u^h by inverting a matrix.

To describe this for the modal basis, we introduce the following notation:

$$\vec{u}_p = \text{Vector of } P \sim N^3 \text{ expansion coefficients, } \vec{u}_p \leftarrow u_{ijk}$$

$$\tilde{\vec{u}}_q = \text{Vector of } Q \text{ function values at the quadrature points}$$

$$\tilde{\vec{u}}_q \leftarrow u(\xi_q)$$

$$\mathbf{W}_{qq} = \text{Diagonal matrix of } Q \times Q \text{ quadrature weights required}$$

$$\text{to integrate a function over } \Omega^k$$

$$\mathbf{B}_{qp} = \text{Rectangular matrix containing the value of the basis}$$

$$\text{functions at the quadrature points. There are } Q$$

$$\text{quadrature} \times P \text{ basis functions.}$$

Now we can write down the algebraic form of the inner products given in equation (5.16). First, the inner product of u with the basis functions:

$$(u, \phi_p)_{\Omega^k} \;\rightarrow\; \mathbf{B}^T \mathbf{W}\, \tilde{\vec{u}}$$

Second, the inner product of u^h with the basis functions:

$$(u^h, \phi_p)_{\Omega^k} \;\rightarrow\; \mathbf{B}^T \mathbf{W} \mathbf{B}\, \vec{u}$$

The approximation $u^h \approx u$ is determined by matching these two inner products for every basis function:

$$\mathbf{B}^T \mathbf{W}\, \tilde{\vec{u}} = \mathbf{B}^T \mathbf{W} \mathbf{B}\, \vec{u}$$

This is the fully discrete form of equation (5.16). Note that the expression on the right-hand side defines the mass matrix:

$$(\phi_i, \phi_j)_{\Omega^k} \;\rightarrow\; \mathbf{B}^T \mathbf{W} \mathbf{B}$$

or simply $\mathbf{M} = \mathbf{B}^T \mathbf{W} \mathbf{B}$.

Now we can define the discrete projection operator as

$$\vec{u} = \mathcal{P}(\tilde{\vec{u}}) \equiv \left[\mathbf{B}^T \mathbf{W} \mathbf{B} \right]^{-1} \mathbf{B}^T \mathbf{W} \tilde{\vec{u}}$$

This is also called the *forward transform* of a function from physical space (nodal values) to transform space (modal coefficients). The discrete *inverse transform* is simply the evaluation of the modal basis at a given set of points:

$$\tilde{\vec{u}} = \mathcal{P}^{-1}(\vec{u}) \equiv \mathbf{B} \vec{u}$$

Finally, we note that in the GLL nodal basis, $\mathbf{M}$ is a *diagonal* matrix. This follows directly from the discrete orthogonality of the basis functions and the fact that $\phi_p(\xi_q) = \delta_{pq}$, where ξ_q are the GLL quadrature points. A diagonal mass matrix is a tremendous simplification since multiplication by $\mathbf{M}^{-1}$ is trivial.

Differentiation

Since the basis is formed from continuous functions, derivatives can, in principle, be evaluated by simply differentiating the basis functions:

$$\frac{\partial u^h}{\partial \xi_1} = \sum_{ijk} u_{ijk} \, \frac{\partial \phi_i}{\partial \xi_1}(\xi_1) \, \phi_j(\xi_2) \, \phi_k(\xi_3)$$

In practice, we only need the derivatives at certain points, namely the quadrature points. Therefore, the solution is first transformed onto an equivalent Lagrangian interpolant basis defined over the quadrature points. We introduce the 1-D Lagrangian derivative matrix

$$\mathbf{D}_{ip} \equiv \frac{d\phi_p}{d\xi}\bigg|_{\xi_i}$$

Rather than $\mathcal{O}(N^3)$ terms, the Lagrangian interpolant basis reduces the summation to an equivalent 1-D operation. The coefficient of the derivative, u'_{ijk}, is then given by

$$u'_{ijk} = \sum_{p=0}^{N} \mathbf{D}_{ip} \, u_{pjk}$$

Since only $\mathcal{O}(N)$ operations are required per point, it takes $\mathcal{O}(N^3)$ operations to compute all derivatives in $\mathbb{R}^2$ and $\mathcal{O}(N^4)$ operations to compute all derivatives in $\mathbb{R}^3$. In the modal basis, calculation of derivatives is preceded by an inverse transform (to nodal values) and followed by a forward transform (to modal coefficients), therefore increasing the computational cost.

5.2.4   Global Matrix Operations

One of the basic principles for maintaining the sparse structure in the global matrix systems is to enforce only the minimum continuity between elements. For all of the problems we consider here, the global basis is required to be C^0 continuous, that is, only function values and not derivatives are required to be globally continuous. For discretizations with both Lagrangian and h-p basis functions, this is accomplished by choosing a unique set of global "degrees of freedom" that define the approximation space.

Global continuity in the Lagrangian basis is straightforward. Since the basis functions are defined as the Lagrangian interpolant through the elemental nodes, we only have to use the same set of nodes along the edge of adjacent elements. As long as the elements are conforming (each edge matches up exactly to one other edge) and of equal order (same number of nodes along each edge), C^0 continuity is guaranteed. Figure 5.4 shows a possible global numbering scheme for a simple quadrilateral mesh.

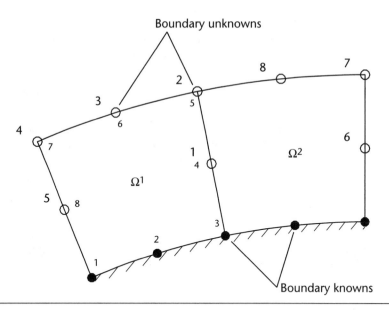

Figure 5.4   Local and global numbering for a simple domain composed of two quadrilateral elements of order $N = 2$. Points along the boundary do not constitute global "degrees of freedom" and are not assigned indices in the global index set.

An important extension to the original spectral element method was the introduction of *nonconforming* elements by Bernardi et al. [95]. Here we give only a sketch of the way the method is used to patch together a nonconforming mesh. For a full description of the method, including efficient solution techniques and numerous examples, see the references Anagnostou [32], Bernardi et al. [95], Henderson [452, 453], and Mavriplis [655].

The main idea is to use a *constrained approximation*. For a geometrically and functionally nonconforming set of elements, we cannot guarantee global C^0 continuity of the basis. Therefore, we make the basis as continuous as possible by minimizing the difference in function values across each nonconforming interface. We do this by enforcing the following weighted residual equation:

$$\int_\Gamma (u - v)\, \psi \, ds = 0 \quad \forall \psi \in P_{N-2}(\Gamma) \tag{5.17}$$

The residual is the difference between two functions u and v that we would like to be continuous, and ψ is the weight used to perform the minimization. The algebraic form of this equation is

$$\vec{u} = \mathbf{Z}\, \vec{v}$$

where $\bar{u}$ and $\bar{v}$ are the coefficients of whatever basis we choose to represent u and v, and the entries of $\mathbf{Z}$ are determined by evaluating the residual equation using numerical quadrature. We say the values of $\bar{v}$ are free and the values of $\bar{u}$ are constrained to match them such that equation (5.17) is satisfied.

To use this as a computational tool, we choose v to be the solution along the edge of some element and u to be the solution along the edge of an adjacent nonconforming element. Equation (5.17) is used to construct u from v, thereby eliminating u as an "unknown" in the mesh. Since v contributes to the global degrees of freedom in the problem, this is one type of "combining" described next in Section 5.2.5. There is an additional consistency error associated with the nonconforming discretization because the approximation space is no longer a proper subset of the solution space—it admits discontinuous solutions. As bad as this sounds, the consistency error is of the same order as other components of the approximation error, and if implemented properly the method always converges to a continuous solution if one exists.

Nonconforming elements allow quadrilateral meshes to be refined locally, without the conforming restriction propagating refinement across the mesh. It is not as important for triangular and tetrahedral elements where algorithms such as Rivara refinement [804] can be used to perform local refinement and maintain consistency in the mesh. We provide several examples that make use of nonconforming quadrilateral elements in the following sections.

5.2.5   Data Structures

Here we describe the data structures and basic operations required to implement the most common procedures in spectral element methods. We cover representation of the global system, how to transfer global data to local (element) data, direct stiffness summation, and finally the procedures for integration and differentiation of solutions defined on geometrically complex 2- and 3-D elements.

Implementation

First we start with the representation of the solution within a computer program. In this section, we give several examples as pseudocode fragments that follow basic C and C++ syntax. This is not meant to be an in-depth presentation, but simply an illustration of the most important ideas and the basic approach.

In spectral element methods, as in finite element methods, global data are stored as a flat, unstructured array. The basic data structure used to relate the mesh to entries in this array is a table that identifies the global node number of a local node within each element. Since we are interested in both nodal and modal descriptions, we replace "node" with the more general concept of a "degree of freedom" in the global solution. The table of indices can be stored as a two-dimensional array of integers:

$$\mathsf{map[k][i]} = \text{global index of local datum } i \text{ in element } k$$

Local data can be stored in any convenient, regular format. In our first version, we will assume the number of degrees of freedom in the mesh (ndof) and the number of degrees of freedom associated with each element (edof) are constant. To perform some global operation, for example to evaluate a function $v = F(u)$, we insert a layer of indirection between the unstructured global data and the structured local data. The following is a template for any such computation:

```
for (i=0; i < ndof; i++)      // Initialize v
  v[i] = 0.;
for (k=0; k < nel; k++) {      // Loop over elements
  for (i=0; i < edof; i++)     // Copy global data
    uk[i] = u[ map[k][i] ];    // --- gather
    compute (uk, vk);          // Compute v=F(u) locally
  for (i=0; i < edof; i++)     // Accumulate the result
    v[ map[k][i] ] += vk[i];   // --- scatter
}
```

Depending on the specific operation, the final result may need to be corrected in some way: rescaled with the global mass matrix, averaged based on the data multiplicity, or some similar global operation. The last loop corresponds to direct stiffness summation, and in our matrix notation we would write this same operation as:

$$\vec{v} = \sum_{k=1}^{K}{}' \vec{v}^k = \sum_{k=1}^{K}{}' F(\vec{u}^k) = F(\vec{u}) \tag{5.18}$$

To make this data structure suitable for both hierarchical bases and nonconforming elements (to be developed in Section 5.2.7), we introduce two generalizations. First, we allow the number of degrees of freedom in each element to be different by replacing the constant edof with the array edof[k]. Second, we allow each local degree of freedom to depend on an arbitrary combination of the global degrees of freedom. To implement this we need to introduce two new arrays:

idof[k][i] = number of global dependencies for local datum i in element k

combine[k][i] = array of coefficients for combining global data to get local data

And finally, we need to add a new dimension to our index table:

map[k][i][j] = global index of the jth dependency of local datum i

In effect, we are introducing a set of coefficient matrices Z^k that define a general transformation between global and local degrees of freedom. Using this approach, the global initialization, loop over the elements, and function call for the local computation shown above stay the same, but the procedure for constructing the local data is rewritten as follows:

```
for (i=0; i < edof[k]; i++)    // Initialize
  uk[i] = 0.;
for (i=0; i < edof[k]; i++) { // Combine
   real *Z  = combine[k][i];
   for (j=0; j < idof[k][i]; j++)
     uk[i] += Z[j] * u[ map[k][i][j] ];
}
```

Likewise, the accumulation of results uses a similar method for combining local contributions to the global degrees of freedom:

```
for (i=0; i < edof[k]; i++) { // Combine
  real *Z  = combine[k][i];
  for (j=0; j < idof[k][i]; j++)
    v[ map[k][i][j] ] += Z[j] * vk[i];
}
```

We also introduce a new matrix notation for this more general approach. Since the local data is $Z^k \vec{u}$, and the local contribution to the global system is $[Z^k]^T \vec{v}^k$, the equivalent procedure for assembling the global system is written as:

$$\vec{v} = \sum_{k=1}^{K}{}' [Z^k]^T \, \vec{v}^k = \sum_{k=1}^{K}{}' [Z^k]^T F(Z^k \vec{u}) = F(\vec{u}) \tag{5.19}$$

Compare this to equation (5.18) above, and note that the only change is how we transform *between* the local and global systems. The actual computations at both the local and global levels are the same.

In the remaining sections, we describe computations in terms of either the local or global system, omitting the actual "assembly" required to go between them. Equation (5.19) is always implied as the method for recovering local solutions and assembling global ones. This simplifies what would otherwise become a confusing barrage of notation. Along the way, we will give more specific information about how the coefficients for the mapping matrix Z^k are chosen. This is a very flexible scheme for storing the global solution and reconstructing the local one. The additional storage and computational overhead is simply the price we pay for new capabilities: variable order of the local basis functions and arbitrary connectivity in the mesh. However, these are the key ingredients for adaptive *h-p* refinement techniques.

Improvements

Although the scheme outlined above is complete, it is not an efficient way to implement *h-p* methods: too much of the addressing is done by indirection. One of the computational advantages of high-order elements is the natural partitioning of data into sets that can be operated on as a group. For example, local degrees of freedom are normally partitioned into several groups: vertices, edges, faces, and interior data. Data associated with any of these groups can be operated on as a single entity. For example, all the points on the interior of an element can be identified with the element number and moved around or computed on as a single unit. High-order elements provide better data locality than low-order elements because computations always involve large amounts of data that can be grouped together in memory.

The type of full indirection outlined above is only necessary for the degrees of freedom associated with the surface of an element. These data make up the loosely coupled components of the global system. This sparse global system forms the "skeleton" of the discretization and shares many characteristics with low-order finite elements. For example, the numbering system stored in the index table can be optimized to reduce its algebraic bandwidth using the same techniques applied in finite element methods (see Section 5.2.6). Unfortunately, more sophisticated data structures than can be described here are required to incorporate these simplifications.

5.2.6   Solution Techniques

In this section, we describe efficient iterative and direct methods for inverting the large algebraic systems that result from nonconforming spectral element discretizations. Iterative methods are more appropriate for steady-state calculations or calculations involving variable properties, such as a changing time step or a Helmholtz equation with a variable coefficient. For direct methods, the issue is one of memory management—storing $\mathbf{A}$ as efficiently as possible without sacrificing the performance needed for fast back-substitution. The development of fast direct and well-preconditioned iterative solvers represents a major advance toward the application of nonconforming spectral element methods to the simulation of turbulent flows on unstructured meshes.

Conjugate Gradient Iteration

Conjugate gradient methods [81] have been particularly successful with spectral elements because the tensor-product form and local structure allows the global Helmholtz inner product to be evaluated using only elemental matrices. To solve the system $\mathbf{A}\vec{u} = \vec{F}$ by the method of conjugate gradients, we use the algorithm in Figure 5.5, where k is the iteration number, r_k is the residual, and p_k is the current search direction. The matrix $\mathbf{M}$ is a preconditioner used to improve the convergence rate of the method and is discussed in detail next.

Selection of a good preconditioner is critical for rapid convergence; the preconditioner must be spectrally close to the full stiffness matrix yet easy to invert. Popular preconditioners for spectral methods include incomplete Cholesky factorization and low-order (finite element, finite difference) approximations [261, 728]. Unfortunately, these preconditioners can be as complicated to construct for an unstructured mesh as the full stiffness matrix $\mathbf{A}$. Next, we present three preconditioners that are simple to build and apply, even when the mesh is unstructured.

$k = 0; \; u_0 = 0; \; r_0 = \vec{F};$
while $r_k \neq 0$
 Solve $\mathbf{M} \, q_k = r_k; \;\; k = k + 1$
 if $k = 1$ **then**
  $p_1 = q_0$
 else
  $\beta_k = r_{k-1}^T \, q_{k-1} / r_{k-2}^T q_{k-2}$
  $p_k = q_{k-1} + \beta_k p_{k-1}$
 end
 $\alpha_k = r_{k-1}^T \, q_{k-1} / p_k^T \, \mathbf{A} p_k$
 $r_k = r_{k-1} - \alpha_k \, \mathbf{A} p_k$
 $u_k = u_{k-1} + \alpha_k p_k$
end
$\vec{u} = u_k$

Figure 5.5   Algorithm for conjugate gradient iteration.

In conjugate gradient methods, the number of iterations required to reach a given error level scales as $\sqrt{\kappa_A}$. This is only an estimate, since the actual convergence rate is determined by the *distribution* of eigenvalues—if all of $\mathbf{A}$'s eigenvalues are clustered together, convergence is much faster. To assess the effectiveness of a given preconditioner, we begin by looking at the condition number of $\mathbf{M}^{-1}\mathbf{A}$.

Each of the following methods is based on selecting a subset of entries from the full stiffness matrix. The first two preconditioners are diagonal matrices given by

$$M_{ii} = A_{ii} \qquad \text{``diagonal,'' and} \tag{5.20}$$

$$M_{ii} = \sum_{j=0}^{n_{\text{dof}}} |A_{ij}| \quad \text{``row-sum,''}$$

where $n_{\text{dof}} = \text{rank}(\mathbf{A})$; the diagonal (5.20) is sometimes called a point Jacobi preconditioner. Both are direct estimates of the spectrum of $\mathbf{A}$ and have the advantage of minimal storage and work. The third preconditioner is a block-diagonal matrix:

$$M_{ij} = \begin{cases} |A_{ij}| & \text{if } i \leq n_{\text{bof}}, \; j = i \\ 0 & \text{if } i \leq n_{\text{bof}}, \; j \neq i \\ A_{ij} & \text{otherwise} \end{cases}$$

where n_{bof} is the number of mortar nodes in the mesh. The structure of this matrix assumes that $\mathbf{A}$ is arranged in the static condensation format described in Section 5.2.6. Applying this preconditioner amounts to storing and inverting the isolated blocks of $\mathbf{A}$ associated with the degrees of freedom on the interior of each element, while applying a simple diagonal matrix to the mortar nodes.

We conclude this section by giving the memory requirements and computational complexity for a preconditioned conjugate gradient (PCG) solver. Since the elemental Helmholtz operator can be evaluated using only the 1-D Lagrangian derivative matrix, the required memory is simply storage for the nodal values and geometric factors:

$$S_I = s_1 K N^2$$

As mentioned above, the dominant numerical operations are vector–vector and matrix–vector products, although derivative calculations are folded into a more efficient matrix–matrix multiplication. The operation count for the entire solver is

$$C_I = J^\epsilon \left[c_1 K N^3 + c_2 K N^2 + c_3 K N \right]$$

where $J^\epsilon \propto \sqrt{KN^3}$ is the number of iterations required to reach a given error level ϵ. Our numerical results show that with these preconditioners J^ϵ is still proportional to KN^3, but the constant is reduced. The block matrix operations required to compute the elemental inner products provide good data locality and can be coded efficiently on both vector processors and RISC microprocessors.

Static Condensation

The static condensation algorithm is a method for reducing the complexity of the stiffness matrices arising in finite element and spectral element methods. Static condensation is particularly attractive for unstructured spectral element methods because of the natural division of equations into those for boundaries (mortar elements) and element interiors. To apply this method to the discrete 1-D Helmholtz equation, we begin by partitioning the stiffness matrix into boundary and interior points:

$$\begin{bmatrix} A_{11} & A_{12} \\ A_{21} & A_{22} \end{bmatrix}^k \begin{bmatrix} \vec{u}_b \\ \vec{u}_i \end{bmatrix}^k = \begin{bmatrix} \vec{F}_b \\ \vec{F}_i \end{bmatrix}^k$$

where A_{11} is the boundary matrix, $A_{12} = [A_{21}]^T$ is the coupling matrix, and A_{22} is the interior matrix. This system can be factored into one for the boundary (mortar) nodes and one for the interior nodes, so that on Ω^k:

$$[A_{11} - A_{21}A_{22}^{-1}A_{12}]\vec{u}_b = \vec{F}_b - [A_{21}A_{22}^{-1}]\vec{F}_i$$

$$A_{22}\,\vec{u}_i = \vec{F}_i - A_{21}\vec{u}_b$$

During a preprocessing phase, the global boundary matrix is assembled by summing the elemental matrices,

$$\mathbf{A}_{11} = \sum_{k=1}^{K}{}' \left[A_{11} - A_{21}A_{22}^{-1}A_{12} \right] \tag{5.21}$$

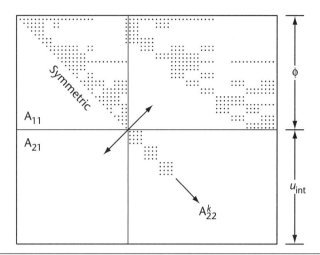

Figure 5.6 Static condensation form of the spectral element stiffness matrix. The vector $\phi = \vec{u}_b$ represents the boundary (mortar) solution, while $\vec{u}_i$ represents the interior solution.

and prepared for the solution phase by computing its LU factorization. Equation (5.21) may also be recognized as the Schur complement of A_{22} in A. As part of this phase, we also compute and store for each element the inverse of the interior matrix $[A_{22}^{-1}]$ and its product with the coupling matrix $[A_{21}A_{22}^{-1}]$. The system is solved by setting up the modified right-hand side of the global boundary equations, solving the boundary equations using back-substitution, and then computing the solution on the interior of each element using direct matrix multiplication. Because the coupling between elements is only C^0, the element interiors are independent of each other, and on a multiprocessor system this final stage can be solved concurrently.

Figure 5.6 illustrates the structure of a typical spectral element stiffness matrix factored using this approach. To reduce computational time and memory requirements for the boundary phase of the direct solver, we wish to find an optimal form of the discrete system corresponding to a minimum bandwidth for the matrix $\mathbf{A}_{11}$. This is complicated by the irregular connectivity generated by using nonconforming elements. One approach to bandwidth optimization is to think of the problem in terms of finding an optimal path through the mesh that visits "nearest neighbors." During each of the K stages of the optimization, an estimate is made of the new bandwidth that results from adding one of the unnumbered elements to the current path. The element corresponding to the largest increase is chosen for numbering, resulting in what is essentially a greedy algorithm. This basic concept is illustrated in Figure 5.7. The reduction in bandwidth translates to direct savings in memory and quadratic savings in computational cost. Note that standard methods of bandwidth reduction used for finite elements, such as the reverse Cuthill–McKee algorithm, can also be used, although they only need be applied to the boundary system.

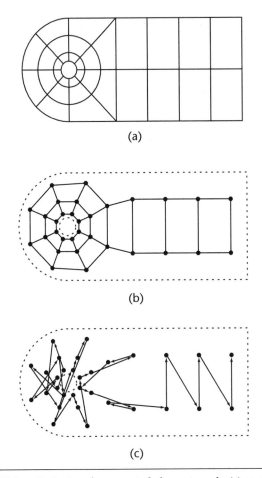

(a)

(b)

(c)

Figure 5.7 Bandwidth optimization for a spectral element mesh: (a) computational domain, (b) connectivity graph, and (c) an optimal path for numbering the boundary nodes in the mesh.

The search for an optimal numbering system can be accomplished during preprocessing, so the extra work has no impact on the simulation cost and can result in significant savings. For computers where memory is a limitation, this procedure can determine whether an in-core solution is even possible. Other simple memory optimizations include storage of only a single copy of the interior and coupling matrices for each element with the same geometry, and evaluation of the force vector $\vec{F}$ using tensor product summation instead of matrix operations. By carefully organizing matrix usage, the overall memory requirement scales as

$$S_D = \frac{1}{2}\, s_1\, K^2 N^2 + s_2\, K N^3 + s_3\, K N^4$$

As mentioned in the introduction to this section, the direct solver is advantageous only when the cost of factoring this stiffness matrix can be spread over a large number of solutions. Therefore, we consider only the cost of a back-substitution using the factored stiffness matrix, for which the operation count scales as

$$C_D = c_1 \, K^{3/2} N^2 + c_2 \, KN^4 + c_3 \, KN$$

For a well-conditioned, diagonally dominant system, this method usually results in at least a factor of two savings versus an iterative solver. For a system that is not diagonally dominant, such as the Navier–Stokes pressure equation, it can be faster by a full order of magnitude.

5.2.7 Adaptive Mesh Refinement

In this section, we look at the implementation of a high-order adaptive code based on the nonconforming spectral element method. In practice, this method is used with high-order polynomials ($p \approx 4$ to 16) and a mesh of elements that is generated adaptively by h-refinement. We will not attempt to refine both the elements and the basis functions simultaneously, as experience indicates that uniformly high p and adaptive mesh refinement leads to an efficient solution for a wide variety of problems.

The formulation based on mortar elements [95] allows completely arbitrary assembly of nonconforming elements. However, our goal is to develop automatic procedures for generating an appropriate mesh, and this calls for some compromises. To simplify the encoding of the mesh, we will require the refinement to propagate down a quadtree (2-D geometries) or oct-tree (3-D geometries). A basic description of the mesh generation procedure is provided below. This is found to be a suitable restriction for problems with smooth solutions and leads to a significant reduction in the complexity of the data structure needed to represent the many levels in the refined grid. For complex geometries, the mesh may incorporate multiple trees at the coarse level.

To give a more specific introduction to the goals of developing an adaptive spectral element method, Figure 5.8 shows a sample calculation for the impulsively started flow past a bluff plate. In this simulation, the solution field is generated by integrating the incompressible Navier–Stokes equations from an initial state of zero motion. The characteristic scales in the problem are the free-stream speed u_∞, the plate diameter d, and the kinematic viscosity of the fluid v. The Reynolds number, defined as $Re \equiv u_\infty d/v$, is set to the value $Re = 1000$. Figure 5.8(b) shows the global domain used to represent the flow around the plate. A symmetry condition is imposed along the centerline so that only one-half of the flow field needs to be computed. Figure 5.8(a) is an enlargement of the near wake region. It shows both the vorticity of the developing flow at an early time and the adaptively generated mesh. The vorticity of the flow is defined by $\omega = \nabla \times \boldsymbol{u}$ and is a measure of the rotational components of the velocity field. Each element is an 8×8 point subdomain ($p = 7$) of the global solution. A large number of separate "trees" are needed at the coarse level to correctly model the

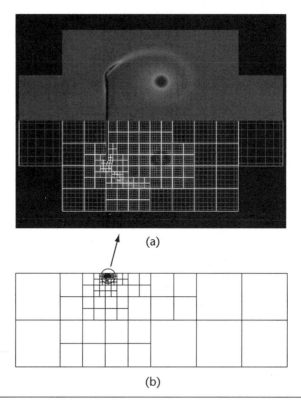

(a)

(b)

Figure 5.8   Simulation of the impulsively started flow past a bluff plate at $Re = 1000$ using an adaptive spectral element method: (a) close-up of the mesh and vorticity of the flow a short time after the impulsive start; (b) global computational domain.

beveled geometry of the finite-thickness plate. The initial stage of mesh generation is done by hand to provide the correct starting geometry. Once the problem is handed to the flow solver, the additional adaptivity in the mesh is based on a maximum allowable approximation error in the vorticity field.

Because the algorithms for time integration in problems like the one illustrated in Figure 5.8 are generally semi-implicit, the computational issues that arise are somewhat different when compared to other methods that incorporate adaptive meshes. We are interested primarily in studying *incompressible* flows governed by the Navier–Stokes and Euler equations. Because of the elliptic nature of the governing equations (due in part to the incompressibility constraint), local time stepping is not usually an option. Therefore, solving the elliptic boundary-value problems that arise in these systems is a particular challenge. Even for 2-D flows, the resolution needed to maintain sufficiently high accuracy can lead to very large systems of equations, and computational efficiency is an important issue. In the past, this meant algorithms that could be *vectorized*, while today it means algorithms that can be *parallelized*. There is a close relationship between spectral elements and finite elements. So when it comes to parallel computing, many of the same problems (e.g., load balancing) arise, and similar solutions apply. Section 5.2.8 addresses the implementation of this method for parallel computers with a programming model based on a weakly coherent shared memory that is synchronized via message passing.

Just as important as overall computational performance are the algorithms used for driving adaptive refinement. Ideally, such an algorithm would take as input an error estimate and produce as output a new discrete model or mesh that reduces the error. The basic problems are the lack of an error estimate for nonlinear systems and the unlimited ways in which such an algorithm could improve the discrete model. The latter problem is addressed by restricting "improvements" to propagating refinement down the tree. The former problem is addressed with a pseudo-heuristic error estimate based on the local polynomial spectrum as described below. Depending on the nonlinearity in the partial differential equations being solved, parts of the spectrum will give an accurate approximation to the true solution and parts will be polluted. We estimate the order of magnitude of the local error by examining the decay along the tail of the local polynomial spectrum. In a general sense, this heuristic flags locations in the mesh where the polynomial basis fails to provide a good description of the solution. For simple problems (linear, 1-D), this can be formally related to the true difference between the exact solution and the approximate solution, that is, the approximation error. For more interesting problems, it is shown to be a robust guide for driving adaptivity. The heuristic is easy to compute but is only accurate as an error estimate in computations with sufficiently high p, meaning that the local polynomial coefficients should decay like $|a_n| \sim \exp(-\sigma n)$ for $p = n \gg 1$. This is generally not true near singular points (e.g., corners), and these locations are automatically flagged for refinement. The method based on local spectra is compared to simpler heuristics such as refining in regions with strong gradients, and the two are shown to lead to quite different results. In general, the local spectrum works well and is a good match to the overall computational strategy.

Framework

In this section, we restrict our attention to 2-D problems. Most of the difficulties arise in two dimensions, and there are no fundamental barriers (other than computing power) in extending the method to three dimensions. To begin, let D be some region of space that has been partitioned into K subdomains, which we denote $D^{(k)}$. We consider two related problems:

1. Given a discretization tolerance ϵ, generate a spatial discretization $D = \{D^{(k)}\}$ that allows the tolerance to be met.

2. Given a spatial discretization $D = \{D^{(k)}\}$, generate a finite-dimensional approximation $u^h \approx u$. The function u may be given explicitly or implicitly, that is, as the solution of a boundary-value problem.

Our approach to problem 1 is to create a hierarchy of grids by forming a quadtree partition of D. This provides the computational domain for problem 2, where we apply a nonconforming spectral element method to approximate u^h.

Mesh Generation

The mesh generation problem is somewhat simpler, so we describe that first. A quadtree is a partition of 2-D space into squares. Each square is a *node* of the tree. It has up to four daughters, obtained by bisecting the square along each dimension. Each node in a quadtree has geometrical properties (spatial coordinates, size) and topological properties (parents, daughters, siblings). Geometrical properties of daughter nodes are inherited from parents, and thus the geometrical properties of the entire tree are determined by the root node.

To represent the topological aspects of the tree, we use an idea originally developed for gravitational N-body problems [824]. Every possible square $S^{(i)}$ is assigned a unique integer *key*. The root of the tree is $S^{(1)}$, with key 1. The daughters of any node are obtained by a left shift of two bits of the parent's key, followed by a binary *or* in the range 00 to 11 (binary) to distinguish each sibling. A node's parent is obtained by a two-bit right shift of its own key. Since the set of keys installed in the tree at any time is obviously much smaller than the set of all possible keys, a hash table is used for storage and lookup.

From the complete set of nodes in the tree we choose a certain subset $D^{(k)} \subseteq S^{(i)}$ to form the *active* elements of the computational domain. Figure 5.9 shows a four-level quadtree with 13 nodes and $K = 10$ active elements. Active elements in the figure are shown with a solid outline, while inactive elements are shown with a dashed outline. Inactive elements are retained so that they are available for coarsening the mesh, if necessary. The only requirement enforced on the topology of the mesh is that active elements that share a boundary segment live at most one refinement level apart, limiting adjacent elements to a two-to-one refinement ratio. This imposes a certain smoothness on the change in resolution in the mesh that is appropriate for the class of smooth functions we wish to represent.

Refinement Criteria

The adaptive mesh generation and high-order domain decomposition methods described here are coupled through refinement criteria used to drive adaptivity. Here we consider three types of refinement criteria.

The first is by far the simplest: refine everywhere that solution gradients are large. We can enforce this idea by requiring

$$\|\nabla u^{(k)}\| \le \epsilon \, \|u^h\|_1$$

everywhere in the mesh, where $\|\cdot\|$ is the L_2 norm, $\|\cdot\|_1$ is the H^1 norm, and ϵ is the discretization tolerance. This is a common refinement criterion in cases where there is simply no alternative measure of solution errors.

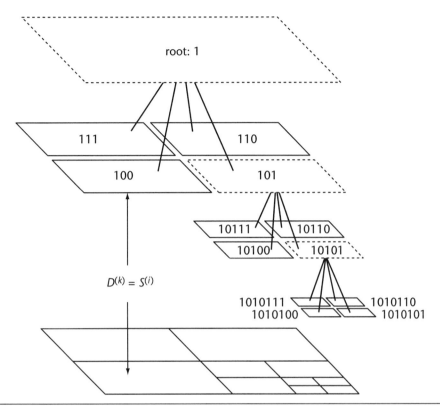

Figure 5.9 A four-level quadtree mesh, expanded to show the elements that make up each level. Each leaf node $S^{(i)}$ has a unique integer key shown in binary. Daughter keys are generated from a parent's key by a two-bit left shift, followed by a binary *or* in the range 00 to 11. The active elements $D^{(k)}$ that make up the current discretization are shown with a solid outline.

The second type takes direct advantage of the high-order polynomial basis. Consider the expansion of a given smooth function u over the domain $D = [-1, 1]^2$ in terms of Legendre polynomials:

$$u(x, y) = \sum_{n=0}^{\infty} \sum_{m=0}^{\infty} a_{n,m} P_n(x) P_m(y)$$

The expansion coefficients are given by

$$a_{n,m} = \frac{1}{c_n c_m} \int_{-1}^{1} \int_{-1}^{1} u P_n P_m |J| \, dx \, dy$$

where the normalization constant is $c_i = (2i + 1)/2$. We have included the Jacobian, $|J|$, to include the effects of element size and other geometric transformations, such as curvilinear boundaries. There is nothing magical about Legendre polynomials—they are simply a convenient orthogonal basis for projecting the approximation onto. Since our approximate solution $u^h \approx u$ is formed essentially by truncating this expansion at some finite order p, we can form an estimate of the approximation error $\|u - u^h\|$ by examining the tail of the spectrum.

To do so, we first average over polynomials in x and y to produce an equivalent 1-D spectrum:

$$\bar{a}_p = |a_{p,p}| + \sum_{i=0}^{p-1} \Big(|a_{i,p}| + |a_{p,i}| \Big)$$

Next we replace the discrete spectrum $\bar{a}_p$ with an approximation to a decaying exponential:

$$\tilde{a}(n) = \text{constant} \times \exp(-\alpha n)$$

The function $\tilde{a}(n)$ is a least squares best fit to the last four points in the spectrum $\bar{a}_p$. Our refinement criterion becomes

$$\left(\tilde{a}(p)^2 + \int_{p+1}^{\infty} \tilde{a}(n)^2 \, \mathrm{d}n \right)^{1/2} \leq \epsilon \|u^h\| \tag{5.22}$$

The only practical complication here is making sure that the decay rate $\alpha > 0$ so that the integral converges. Otherwise, the estimate is ignored and the element is flagged for immediate refinement. This method is analyzed in Mavriplis [656], where it is shown to be an effective refinement criterion for driving h-p refinement.

The third refinement criterion is similar. Since the main contribution to equation (5.22) comes from the coefficients of order p, we can simply sum along the tail of the spectrum. For an accurate representation of u, we require the spectrum to satisfy the discretization tolerance:

$$|a_{p,p}| + \sum_{i=0}^{p-1} \Big(|a_{i,p}| + |a_{p,i}| \Big) \leq \epsilon \|u^h\| \tag{5.23}$$

This method is somewhat simpler to apply and, as we will see, produces almost identical results.

To use these polynomial spectrum criteria with our spectral element method (based on GLL polynomials), we first perform a Legendre transform of the local solution $u^{(k)} \to a_{n,m}$ and then use equation (5.22) or (5.23) to decide if the element should be refined. Although we keep p fixed, the error is reduced because we approximate u over a smaller region $D^{(k)}$.

5.2.8   Implementation for Parallel Architectures

We end this section with a few additional notes on implementation. The algorithms described above have been implemented using a combination of C for the computational modules and C++ for high-level data types, such as Element $\equiv D^{(k)}$ and Field

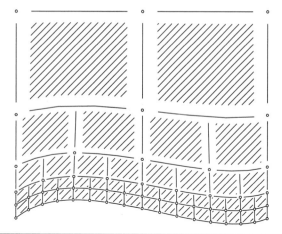

Figure 5.10 The logical structure of a spectral element mesh can be divided into three geometric parts: (o) vertices, (—) edges, and (*shaded*) interiors. Edges and vertices define the connectivity in the mesh.

$\equiv u^h$, that make up the discretization. The logic and control structures needed for most of the code are the same as in any algorithm for finite element methods. The most complex problem is maintaining the connectivity of the mesh dynamically, and the approach taken here is worth mentioning.

The geometry and topology of the mesh are closely connected. Figure 5.10 shows the three geometric elements of the discretization: vertices, edges, and interiors. Obviously, interior points are completely local to an element and play no role in the global system. All connectivity in the mesh is through the edges and vertices. Because of the method used to construct the grid, these geometric elements are interlocking. The midpoint of each nonconforming edge aligns with the shared vertex of its two adjacent elements. As discussed below, this feature is used to simplify the procedure for setting up the mesh topology.

Figure 5.10 shows another side effect of the mesh generation. Internal curvilinear boundaries are automatically propagated down the various levels of the refinement tree because of the isoparametric representation of the geometry. In the same way that a solution field is projected onto a new set of elements, the polynomial representation of the geometry can also be projected to a finer grid. On the other hand, external boundaries like the B-spline segment shown as the lower boundary in the figure are explicitly reevaluated to keep the representation as accurate as possible.

How does one represent the topology of this kind of mesh? One solution is to use pointers. This immediately runs into the problem of interpreting pointers to objects on remote processors if the computation is running in parallel. Instead, we use the concept of a *voxel database* (VDB) of geometric positions in the mesh [996]. A VDB may be thought of as a register of position–subscript pairs. To each position stored

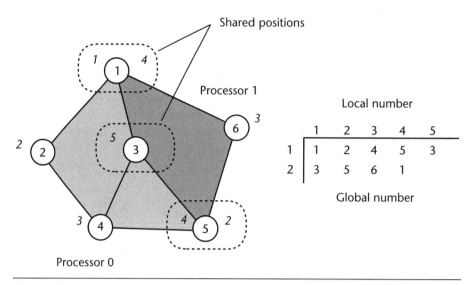

Figure 5.11   Connectivity and communications are established by building a *voxel database* (VDB) of positions. A VDB maps each position to a unique index or subscript. It also tracks points shared by multiple processors to provide a loosely synchronous shared memory. Points that share memory are those at the same geometric position.

in the VDB we assign a unique integer subscript, so that data may be associated with points in space by using the subscript as an index into an array.

The basic idea is illustrated in Figure 5.11. The number of times a position is registered is its *multiplicity*. Data objects that share positions also share memory by virtue of a common subscript. In essence, the VDB provides a natural map of the mesh geometry onto the computer's memory. This basic paradigm can be used to implement many types of finite element or finite volume methods [996].

To establish the connectivity of a mesh like the one depicted in Figure 5.10, we build two separate VDBs: one for the vertices and one for the midpoints of the edges. Every vertex with multiplicity one that does not lie along an external boundary is *virtual* and not part of the true mesh degrees of freedom. Every edge with multiplicity one that does not lie along an external boundary is *nonconforming*. For each nonconforming edge, we make a second query to the VDB using the endpoints. If there is a match, then the edge is also *virtual*, and we store the subscript of the adjacent edge. Otherwise, it is simply flagged as an internal nonconforming boundary segment.

The shared memory represented by a VDB is extended across processor boundaries by passing around a list of local positions and comparing against those registered remotely. A communications link is established for each common position. The shared memory at each point is weakly coherent and must be synchronized by explicit message passing. For example, elements on separate processors with a common boundary segment share data along an edge. Each processor may update its edge values independently and then call a synchronization routine that combines local and remote values to produce a globally consistent data set. For further details see Williams [996].

There is very little overhead for the adaptive versus nonadaptive data structure: just one integer (the node key) per element. Likewise, an iterative solver for sparse systems incurs no performance penalty just because the underlying mesh is adaptive. When approached in the right way, the conversion to a solution adaptive code is almost trivial. To a large degree, this is because of the unstructured nature of the spectral element method we built upon.

5.2.9 An Example—The Cylinder Wake

Understanding the fluid flow around a straight circular cylinder is one of the most fundamental problems in fluid mechanics. It is a model for flow around bridges, buildings, and many other nonaerodynamic objects. Recent work, both experimental and computational, has revealed some exciting new information about the nature of this flow, including intricate 3-D structures that emerge just prior to the onset of turbulence in the wake.

The system considered is an infinitely long cylinder placed perpendicular to an otherwise uniform open flow. The sole parameter for this system is then the Reynolds number: $Re \equiv U_\infty d/\nu$, where U_∞ is the free-stream velocity and d is the cylinder diameter. We describe some of the physically important behavior in this flow and then come back to details of how it can be simulated. It helps to begin with a "road map" for the sequence of bifurcations that take the flow from simple to more complex states. There are two useful quantities to form such a guide to understanding: the nondimensional shedding frequency and the mean drag coefficient C_D. Both shedding frequency and drag show distinct changes at the various bifurcation points of the wake and can be used as a guide to interpreting changes in the wake structure and dynamics as a function of Reynolds number.

In nondimensional form, the shedding frequency is referred to as the Strouhal number. It is defined as $St \equiv f\, d/u_\infty$, where f is the peak oscillation frequency of the wake. At low Reynolds number, the flow is steady ($St = 0$) and symmetric about the centerline of the wake. At $Re_1 \simeq 47$, the steady flow becomes unstable and bifurcates to a 2-D, time-periodic flow. Note that each point along the 2-D curve represents a perfectly time-periodic flow, and there is no evidence of further 2-D instabilities for Reynolds numbers up to $Re \approx 1000$. At $Re_2 \simeq 190$, the 2-D wake becomes absolutely unstable to long-wavelength spanwise perturbations and bifurcates to a 3-D flow (mode A). Experiments and computations indicate a further instability at $Re_2' \simeq 260$, marked by the appearance of fine-scale streamwise vortices.

Figure 5.12 shows the drag curve for flow past a circular cylinder for Reynolds number up to 1000. In the computations, the spanwise-averaged fluid force $\mathbf{F}(t)$ is computed by integrating the shear stress and pressure over the surface of the cylinder. The x-component of $\mathbf{F}$ is the drag; the y-component is the lift. Because C_D is determined from an average over the surface of the cylinder, it is much less

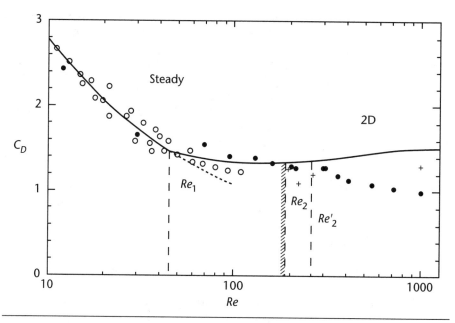

Figure 5.12   Drag coefficient as a function of Reynolds numbers for the flow past a circular cylinder. Experiments: (○,●), Wieselsberger [993]; 3-D simulations: +, Henderson [454]. The solid line is a curve fit to 2-D simulation data for Re up to 1000 [453].

sensitive to changes in the character of the wake at low Reynolds number than single-point measurements like the shedding frequency. The "textbook" version of the drag curve is generally plotted on a log–log scale, where the only discernible feature is the drag crisis at $Re = \approx (10^5)$. The flat response of C_D to changes in the Reynolds number is compounded by the fact that experimental drag measurements are extremely difficult to make at low Reynolds numbers, and subtle details of the drag curve are lost in the experimental scatter. The decrease in magnitude of C_D in the steady regime can be fitted to a power-law curve and also makes a sharp but continuous transition at Re_1. Henderson [453] gives the form and coefficients for the steady and unsteady drag curves.

This problem is extremely challenging because it combines several features that are difficult to handle numerically: unsteady separation, thin boundary layers, outflow boundary conditions, and the need for a large computational domain to simulate an open flow. If the computational domain is too small, the simulation suffers from blockage. This can have a significant impact on quantities such as the shedding frequency, generally producing higher frequencies in the simulations than are observed in experiments [533]. If resolution near the cylinder is sacrificed for the sake of a larger computational domain, then the physically important flow dynamics may not be computed accurately.

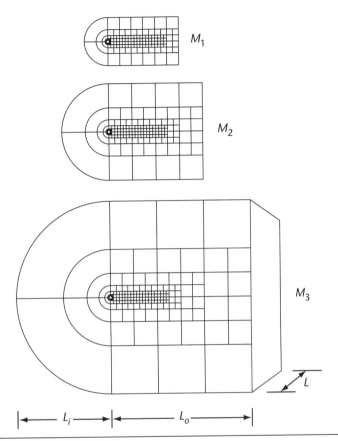

Figure 5.13 Computational domains used for simulating the flow past a circular cylinder. Each domain is a subset of the largest. The parameters L_o and L_i determine the cross-sectional size, and L determines the spanwise dimension.

Figure 5.13 shows a sequence of computational domains used to simulate both 2-D and 3-D wakes using nonconforming quadrilateral elements [454]. Boundary conditions are imposed as follows. Along the left, upper, and lower boundaries we use free-stream conditions: $(u_1, u_2, u_3) = (1, 0, 0)$. At the surface of the cylinder, the velocity is equal to zero (no-slip). Along the right boundary, we use a standard outflow boundary condition for velocity and pressure:

$$p = 0, \quad \partial_x u_i = 0$$

Along all other boundaries the pressure satisfies equation (5.10).

These domains use large elements away from the cylinder and outside the wake where the flow is smooth. Local mesh refinement is used to resolve the boundary layer, near wake, and wake regions downstream of the cylinder. In this case, the refinement is done beforehand, and the mesh is static. Clearly, from Figure 5.12 the simulations predict values of the drag that agree extremely well with experimental studies up to the point of 3-D transition. Just as important as good agreement with experiments, the simulation results are independent of the grid, as shown by a detailed *h*- and *p*-refinement study [77].

Finally, Plate 1 in the color insert shows some of the rich nonlinear behavior that can be observed as the flow over the cylinder undergoes transition to turbulence. Shown in this figure is the vorticity for the cylinder flow at various Reynolds numbers. The figure clearly shows the transition from an orderly array of vortices to the more disordered form characteristic of turbulent flows. These arrangements of the vortices actually correspond to complex "modes" of the system that have also been observed experimentally. The value of such high-resolution simulations in allowing us to see details of flow structure not easily accessible from experiment is evident from these figures.

5.3   Compressible Flows

As mentioned in Section 5.1.2, the Navier–Stokes equations for compressible flow admit solutions that, while thought to be smooth, can possess thin internal layers in which dissipative effects such as viscosity become important. These layers, however, are typically on the order of several mean-free-path lengths in thickness and thus cannot be resolved practically if one is interested in capturing features of the flow on macroscopic scales. Because of this, numerical methods for compressible flow are typically developed for the Euler equations, which can be derived from the Navier–Stokes equations by ignoring the viscous terms. In this case, shock waves are treated as true discontinuities, and the solutions to the Euler equations are not smooth. In addition, because of their character, such discontinuous solutions can appear spontaneously in the flow and typically do not disappear under the subsequent evolution of the flow.

In this section, we provide a very brief overview of numerical approaches that can be used to simulate compressible flow. The distinguishing aspects of such simulations are the need to resolve flow on time scales at or faster than the local sound speed of the fluid and the existence of nearly discontinuous flow features such as shock waves, contact discontinuities, and vortex sheets. It is impossible to be comprehensive in our coverage of numerical techniques, partly because the numerical simulation of compressible flow remains an area of active research. The chief difficulty in the simulation of compressible flow is the representation of the discontinuities. Because most numerical techniques (such as spectral element methods) are predicated on some notion of smoothness of the underlying solution, it is necessary to apply rather different strategies to correctly capture the flow features than those used in our discussion of incompressible flow.

Broadly, the numerical methodology breaks into two major approaches. The first is known as *shock tracking,* in which flow discontinuities are precisely tracked, while a more conventional numerical approach is used for those portions of the flow corresponding to smooth solutions. This approach has been shown to be viable, notably through the work of J. Glimm [193] and his collaborators in their development of front-tracking methods. However, such approaches are not widely used due to the complex machinery required to track the discontinuities and the more challenging difficulty that such discontinuities arise spontaneously in the flow due to wave focusing phenomena. Developing intelligent schemes that track the birth (and death) of such features remains a research challenge.

The second major approach is known as *shock capturing.* In this approach, various intelligent numerical viscosities are designed so as to provide the appropriate dissipation in regions of discontinuity, with the result that shocks and other discontinuities are smoothed out and captured over a few grid cells. These techniques are far more amenable to both vector and parallel computing (as well as more elaborate approaches such as adaptive mesh refinement, discussed below) and have therefore been the preferred approach for numerical simulation since the 1960s. A good overview is available in the monograph of Le Veque [606]. As a result, we will only briefly discuss shock-capturing methods in this section, with an emphasis on parallel simulation using both regular and adaptive grid methods.

5.3.1 Governing Equations of Motion

In this section we present the Euler equations of motion. These can be easily derived from our presentation in Section 5.1.1, but we repeat them here to bring out the special features of the relevant numerical schemes.

Define the solution vector $\boldsymbol{u}$ by

$$\boldsymbol{u} = \begin{bmatrix} \rho \\ u \\ v \\ w \\ E \end{bmatrix}$$

where $\rho(x, y, z, t)$ is the fluid density, u, v, w are the x-, y-, and z-components of velocity, respectively, and $E(x, y, z, t)$ is the total energy of the flow as defined in equations (5.1) to (5.3). The governing equations of motion can be written in the following *conservation* form:

$$\partial_t \boldsymbol{u} + \mathcal{F}(\boldsymbol{u})_x + \mathcal{G}(\boldsymbol{u})_y + \mathcal{H}(\boldsymbol{u})_z = 0$$

where

$$\mathcal{F} = \begin{bmatrix} \rho u \\ \rho u^2 + p \\ \rho uv \\ \rho uw \\ (E + p)u \end{bmatrix} \quad \mathcal{G} = \begin{bmatrix} \rho v \\ \rho uv \\ \rho v^2 + p \\ \rho vw \\ (E + p)v \end{bmatrix} \quad \mathcal{H} = \begin{bmatrix} \rho w \\ \rho uw \\ \rho vw \\ \rho w^2 + p \\ (E + p)w \end{bmatrix}$$

The pressure p is related to the total energy by the equation of state. In this case, we are assuming that we are dealing with a perfect gas:

$$p = (\gamma - 1)\left(E - \frac{1}{2}\rho\, \boldsymbol{u} \cdot \boldsymbol{u}\right)$$

Note that in this case the pressure is a thermodynamic variable, in contrast with the situation of incompressible flow where it acts essentially as a constraint variable. Note also, in contrast to the incompressible case, that an evolution equation can be written for the pressure (although, as we shall see below, the pressure is not typically used directly to march the evolution of the fluid forward in time).

5.3.2   Numerical Methods for Hyperbolic Conservation Laws

In order to simplify the discussion, we will focus on flow in one space and one time dimension. Incompressible flows in 1-D are trivial (corresponding to constant velocity), but because of the compressibility of the medium, compressible flows in one space dimension possess many of the features of flow in high dimensions. In addition, with some slight modification, numerical methods developed in 1-D can be applied to higher-dimensional flows. In 1-D the equations can be written as

$$\partial_t \boldsymbol{u}^* + \mathcal{F}(\boldsymbol{u}^*)_x = 0,$$

where

$$\boldsymbol{u}^* = \begin{bmatrix} \rho \\ u \\ p \end{bmatrix} \qquad \mathcal{F} = \begin{bmatrix} \rho u \\ \rho u^2 + p \\ (E + p)u \end{bmatrix}$$

Again, the equations are written in *conservation form*. It is easy to convert them from this form back to the more physically relevant integral form described in Section 5.1.1. As shall be shown, modern numerical methods respect this conservation form and effectively substitute a discrete approximation for the conservation law, which then automatically produces a discrete version of the original conservation law and at the same time applies a flow-dependent viscosity to ensure that shock waves are properly captured.

Note that away from discontinuities, such as shock waves, it is possible to apply standard numerical schemes that are appropriate for smooth solutions. However, it is impossible to know in advance where the discontinuities lie, and so modern numerical schemes typically employ special "switching" logic to sense the smoothness of the flow. Away from shocks, these schemes can provide solutions of higher-order accuracy. However, as the switching logic senses the presence of a possible shock wave, the scheme switches to a lower-order approach that provides an appropriate viscosity to capture the shock wave over as few grid cells as possible.

We illustrate these considerations by describing a scheme that provides second-order accuracy in space and time for smooth flows but reverts to a first-order accurate scheme in space near shock waves. This is typical behavior for all such schemes. To begin we express the 1-D equations in a *nonconservative form*:

$$\partial_t \mathbf{u}^* + \mathbf{A}_J \, \partial_x \mathbf{u}^* = 0 \qquad (5.24)$$

where $\mathbf{A}_J$ is the Jacobian matrix and is given by

$$\mathbf{A}_J = \begin{bmatrix} u & \rho & 0 \\ 0 & u & 1/\rho \\ 0 & \gamma p & u \end{bmatrix}$$

The system (5.24) now takes the form of a hyperbolic system of equations. Such systems typically can be decoupled by reexpressing the equations in terms of special characteristic variables determined by computing the eigenvalues and eigenvectors of the matrix $\mathbf{A}_J$. The eigenvalues of $\mathbf{A}_J$ are $u - c, u, u + c$. The left eigenfunctions of the matrix are given as the rows of the following matrix

$$\mathbf{L} = \begin{bmatrix} 0 & \rho/2 & -1/(2c) \\ c & 0 & -1/c \\ 0 & \rho/2 & -1/(2c) \end{bmatrix}$$

where $c = \sqrt{\gamma P/\rho}$ is the local sound speed. The inverse of $\mathbf{L}$ is also required in what follows and is given by

$$\mathbf{L}^{-1} = \begin{bmatrix} -1/c & 1/c & 1/c \\ 1/\rho & 0 & 1/\rho \\ -c & 0 & c \end{bmatrix}$$

The equations in (5.24) are then decoupled by defining the vector of characteristic fields $\mathbf{V} = \mathbf{L}\mathbf{u}^*$ and recasting equation (5.24) as a system of equations for $\mathbf{V}$.

The details of the method to be presented below derive from the MUSCL and PPM schemes developed by van Leer [954, 955], Colella and Woodward [206], and Colella [205]. Such schemes use the characteristic information to provide second-order (and higher) accuracy while providing adequate dissipation to prevent short wavelength spurious oscillations from arising near discontinuities. As indicated above, this is accomplished by use of a low-order scheme that deals robustly with shocks. In this case, we will use the classic Godunov method. In this approach, each pair of adjoining cells is viewed as a miniature tube with constant left and right flow states (which may be discontinuous). The discontinuity is supported by an imaginary diaphragm at the cell boundary. To complete a time step, we imagine that the diaphragm is removed and flow between the two states ensues. In this case, the resulting flow states can be expressed for a short time analytically as the solution to a set of nonlinear equations, which again are solved only for each adjoining pair of cells. This provides the needed dissipation to deal with discontinuities, while the preparation of the states using the characteristic information allows us to maintain higher-order accuracy away from shock waves. All robust numerical methods require some solution to this problem, be it approximate or exact, as in the case above.

We divide the 1-D computational domain into uniform cells of width Δx and label the cells $i = 1, 2, \ldots, N$. The ith cell has its left interface at $x = x_{i-1/2} = x_i - \Delta x/2$ and its right boundary at $x = x_{i+1/2} = x_i + \Delta x/2$. We call the left interface the ith interface. We assume that the solution $\boldsymbol{u}^*(x_i, t^n) = (\boldsymbol{u}^*)_i^n$ is known, and we wish to advance the solution one step forward to $t = t + \Delta t = t^{n+1}$. We do this by calculating the vector $\boldsymbol{u}^*$ from $\boldsymbol{u}$. We denote this as $\overline{\boldsymbol{u}^*}$ and we think of these values as representing constant average states in each cell. Our next step is to improve this approximation by creating a piecewise linear distribution in each cell to improve the spatial accuracy in regions we believe to be smooth. However, to mitigate short wavelength oscillations that will result if we adopt this procedure near shocks, we use a limiting function due to van Leer to produce a monotonicity-preserving value of the slope. Let M_i represent the slope (actually a vector of slopes) in cell i. Then define

$$M_i = \min \left[\frac{L_i(\overline{\boldsymbol{u}}^*_{i+1} - \overline{\boldsymbol{u}}^*_{i-1})}{2\Delta x_i}, \frac{L_i(\overline{\boldsymbol{u}}^*_i - \overline{\boldsymbol{u}}^*_{i-1})}{\Delta x_i}, \frac{L_i(\overline{\boldsymbol{u}}^*_{i+1} - \overline{\boldsymbol{u}}^*_i)}{\Delta x_i} \right]$$

with the proviso that if $L_i(\overline{\boldsymbol{u}}^*_{i+1} - \overline{\boldsymbol{u}}^*_i) \, L_i(\overline{\boldsymbol{u}}^*_i - \overline{\boldsymbol{u}}^*_{i-1}) < 0$, then we set $M_i = 0$. This limiting formula selects a gradient that is sensitive to the local solution and makes sure that we don't add new extrema to the solution, which would encourage oscillations in the neighborhoods of shocks. The prescription above is not unique, and many variants of these limiter functions are in use. Using the calculated gradient, we can then use the slopes in conjunction with the cell values. Define

$$V_i^n = \overline{V}_i^n + M_i(x - x_i), \quad \overline{V} = \overline{L_i \boldsymbol{u}^*_i}$$

We then solve the decoupled equations at the cell interfaces at time $t = t_{n+1/2}$. This gives us new intermediate interfacial values and allows us to apply time centering to increase the order of the time accuracy:

$$V_{k,i,RIGHT}^{n+1/2} = \begin{cases} \overline{V}_{k,i}^n - M_{k,i}(\Delta x_i + \lambda_{k,i}\Delta t)/2 & \text{if } \lambda_{k,i} < 0, \\ \overline{V}_{k,i}^n & \text{otherwise;} \end{cases}$$

$$V_{k,i,LEFT}^{n+1/2} = \begin{cases} \overline{V}_{k,i-1}^n + M_{k,i-1}(\Delta x_i - \lambda_{k,i-1}\Delta t)/2 & \text{if } \lambda_{k,i} > 0, \\ \overline{V}_{k,i-1}^n & \text{otherwise;} \end{cases}$$

where k ranges from 1 to 3 and signifies the kth element of the vector V. We then recover the values of $\boldsymbol{u}^*$ on either side of the ith interface by transforming back from characteristic variables. We now have left and right states at the intermediate time $t_{n+1/2}$. From this we solve a Riemann problem at each cell interface. In principle, this requires the solution of some nonlinear equations; in practice, there exist effective approximations to the solutions of the nonlinear Riemann problem that can be evaluated easily. Note that in order for this procedure to work, the time step over which we form this solution to the Riemann problem must be taken small enough so that the evolution of the solutions in other cells does not affect the solution of the cell under consideration. This is the essence of what is called the *CFL criterion*, which requires that the time step be limited by the local speed of the waves in each cell. This constrains Δt such that

$$\Delta t \leq \frac{\Delta x}{(u + |c|)}$$

Once the Riemann problem is solved, we can calculate the fluxes required from each cell to move the solution forward to the next time step, so that the overall effect is that the Riemann problem solution is used to generate the next time step. This is the heart of Godunov's method. The 2-D or 3-D version of this scheme is accomplished by treating each space dimension in turn as a 1-D problem and using the formulation above. However, when all this is put together, it looks formally like the following difference scheme:

$$\overline{\pmb{u}}_i^{n+1} = \overline{\pmb{u}}_i^n - \frac{\Delta t}{\Delta x_i} \left[\overline{\mathcal{F}} \left(\pmb{u}_{i+1/2}^{n+1/2} \right) - \overline{\mathcal{F}} \left(\pmb{u}_{i-1/2}^{n+1/2} \right) \right]$$

where $\overline{\mathcal{F}}$ is a flux constructed to achieve the results of the Riemann problem approach with the slope limiting discussed above. Written this way, the scheme is manifestly in conservative form, which ensures that shock waves and other discontinuities are treated correctly.

While the scheme outlined above is manifestly nonlinear, with complex logic to ensure that shock waves can be handled, from a computational point of view it is very simple. A review of the steps outlined above will reveal that the update of any given cell requires only knowledge of the values at most two cells away in either direction. Making such an algorithm parallel is, in fact, very simple. Regardless of the solver used, one important aspect of the calculation described above is that it proceeds by sweeping through the (uniform) mesh and is therefore very amenable to parallelization. In order to calculate a time step Δt that is appropriate for all cells, one takes the minimum time step resulting from an application of the CFL criterion.

On a parallel architecture it is easy to see that, if the computational mesh is partitioned into a lattice of processors, the communication pattern required is one of nearest neighbor exchange of information at each time step. Since the communication will scale according to some factor times the bounding surface of a given submesh associated with a processor, it is easy to see that, provided the problem size is kept suitably large, it is possible to achieve scalability, since the total computational labor will scale with the mesh volume. The computation of the correct time step is accomplished via a global reduction over the mesh.

5.3.3   An Application: The Richtmyer–Meshkov Instability

In this section we present an application of the ideas described above. The Richtmyer–Meshkov (RM) instability arises at an interface separating two gases when it is subject to an impulsive acceleration [802]. In the original paper, Richtmyer used a shock wave to provide the impulsive acceleration to an interface (contact discontinuity) with long wavelength perturbations and performed a linear stability analysis. Subsequently, analysis, numerical simulation, and experimental studies of the interactions of shock waves with contact discontinuities have been generically associated with the RM instability. The principal interaction parameters are the Mach number of the shock, M_s; the Atwood number across the contact, defined as $At = (\rho_2 - \rho_1)/(\rho_2 + \rho_1)$, where ρ_2, ρ_1 represent, respectively, the density ahead of and behind the interface; and the geometry of the interface. Typically, the interface is perturbed with single or multiple harmonic perturbations or with random white noise perturbations. The physical domain is a 3-D rectangular shock tube. A shock wave (called the *incident shock*) is initialized on the left of an interface and moves from left to right. The incident shock refracts at the interface and bifurcates into a reflected wave (which may be a shock or an expansion fan) and a transmitted shock. We focus here on interactions of strong shock waves ($M_s \geq 10$) with interfaces perturbed with a single harmonic in 3-D. The main object of study in RM flows is the behavior of the so-called mixing width and its growth rate. Of particular interest is the effect of *reshock* on the growth of the mixing width. Reshock refers to the fact that the transmitted shock reflects off the right boundary of the shock tube, and this reflected wave then interacts again with the interface. This typically leads to compressible turbulence and mixing and is a generic phenomenon seen in a variety of applications.

The 3-D shock tube was discretized by a uniform mesh of $1024 \times 128 \times 128$ cells. The shock Mach number was fixed at $M_s = 10$. The interface geometry was a single mode perturbation given by $A = 0.35(\cos ky)(\cos kz)$, where $k = 2\pi/\lambda$ and $\lambda = 3.2$. Two different Atwood numbers are considered here: $At = 0.5$ and $At = -0.33$. Note that a positive (resp. negative) Atwood number corresponds to the fast–slow (resp. slow–fast) case, which means that the transmitted shock speed is slower (resp. faster) than the incident shock speed. Time is scaled such that it takes a unit time for an acoustic wave in the unshocked incident gas to travel one wavelength λ.

Images of volume-rendered density fields at different times are shown in Plates 2 and 3 of the color insert, for $At = 0.5$ and $At = -0.33$, respectively. In both cases, the incident shock initially compresses the interface, which reduces the mixing width rapidly. After the passage of the incident shock, the mixing width increases due to the instability for the positive Atwood ratio interface. For the positive Atwood number interface, reshock causes a phase reversal of the interface. On the other hand, for the negative Atwood number interface, the interface undergoes a phase reversal early in the interaction, after which the mixing width grows. After reshock there is no phase reversal, and the interface mixing width continues to grow.

The calculations described above are easily parallelized (the results shown here were produced on a 512-node Cray T3E). Even larger runs of this type have been performed recently on the ASCI teraflop platforms with over 3000 processors. The examination of such compressible turbulent flows on massively parallel platforms holds the promise that detailed examination of the complex processes inherent in these flows will lead to improved understanding of turbulence in compressible fluids, which is as yet a relatively unexplored area.

5.3.4   Adaptive Mesh Refinement

The techniques outlined above are most conveniently used on regular discrete meshes, as opposed to the irregular finite element meshes outlined in the discussion on spectral element methods. The structure and resolution of the grid used to discretize a given compressible flow problem must be adjusted to properly resolve the phenomena of interest. In many cases, however, the features requiring resolution are quite localized (e.g., shock waves). One is then faced with the problem that high resolution is required to correctly capture such features, whereas lower resolution would suffice in other regions of the flow. If one uses a single uniform mesh for this purpose, then the computational workload is greatly increased, since high resolution is being applied uniformly over the whole mesh. An obvious solution to this problem is to refine the mesh only in those regions requiring refinement. For problems in which shock waves and other small-scale features are static (as occurs, for example, in the computation of steady transonic flows over a wing), this approach is viable, although it is still necessary to use a time step compatible with the smallest mesh spacing. However, for problems in which such features are dynamic, the use of a uniformly fine mesh results in a waste of resources.

An alternative is to use dynamic adaptive mesh refinement (AMR) methods, which are more efficient in their use of computational resources but also preserve the accuracy attainable with a fine mesh. The idea is to concentrate the computational effort by using locally refined meshes with higher resolution only in those areas of interest. Typically, one starts with a coarse mesh with some minimally acceptable resolution that covers the entire domain. As small-scale features evolve, regions requiring additional resolution are identified, and finer grids are overlaid on these regions. This can actually be carried out recursively, in that the finer grids can be examined and even finer grids introduced until adequate resolution is achieved. The resulting structure is an adaptive hierarchy of meshes. One common implementation of this idea was pioneered by Berger and Oliger [94] and Berger and Colella [93]. We will use this algorithm as an example of AMR methods and discuss in this section efficient parallel implementations of this approach.

An adaptive grid hierarchy is a set of dynamically overlaid grids generated by recursively refining a base grid in response to some feature in the transient solution. It can be represented as a family of grids $\{G_n^l\}$, where the subscript l ($0 \leq l \leq L$) represents the level of refinement (with 0 being the coarsest level and L the finest), and the subscript n is an index for component grids at a given level. Viewed this way, the hierarchy is actually a directed acyclic graph, and each node of the graph represents a component grid. Levels of the graph correspond to the levels of refinement, and nodes at a given level correspond to the component grids. As the solution evolves, the graph also evolves dynamically, both in the number of levels and in the number of grids at each level. The discretized equations are applied to each grid at each level independently, although communication between grids is required to provide appropriate boundary data compatible with the global solution. Thus, the algorithm used to solve the equations of motion (e.g., a conservative Godunov scheme as outlined above or any other finite difference method) can be completely reused without any fundamental changes in approach or programming.

The Berger–Oliger algorithm requires that the grid spacing of component grids at any level l of the hierarchy must be an integral multiple of the grid spacing of component grids at the next level, $(l+1)$. That is, $h_l = k h_{l+1}$, where k is some integer. An important aspect of the Berger–Oliger scheme is that the component grids must be *properly nested*, so that each component grid at level $l+1$ is contained within

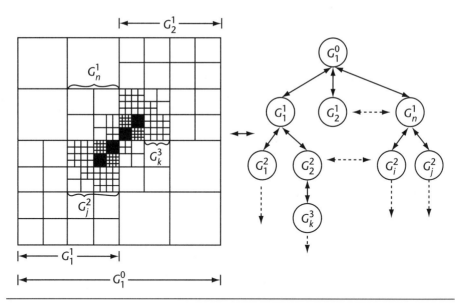

Figure 5.14   Adaptive grid hierarchy of the Berger–Oliger algorithm.

a component grid at level *l*. In fact, for this algorithm, the directed acyclic graph corresponding to the refinement hierarchy is a tree. These two views (i.e., grid based and graph based) of the algorithm are illustrated in Figure 5.14.

The AMR integration algorithm defines the order in which different levels of the grid hierarchy are integrated, the interactions between overlaying component grids at different levels, and the criterion and method for grid refinement. There are three key components of the algorithm:

1. *Time integration.* Time integration is performed on each component grid using a specified finite difference operator. Each component grid can be integrated independently (once boundary values are in place). The order of integration is defined recursively. Before advancing component grids at a particular level of refinement in time, all component grids at higher levels of refinement must be integrated to the current time of grids at that level. That is, before performing a time step at level *l* (i.e., G_i^l from some time *t* to $t + \Delta t_l$), all component grids at levels $> l$ must be integrated to *t*.

2. *Error estimation and regridding.* The error estimation and regridding component of the integration algorithm performs the following three steps:

   • Flag regions that need refinement based on error estimation.
   • Cluster the flagged points.
   • Generate the refined grid.

```
Algorithm Integrate(level)
Repeat (refine_ratio)^(level)
   if (Regrid_time) then
       do Regridding
   end
   Step dt[level] on all grids at level
   if (level+1 exists) then
       Integrate(level+1)
       Update(level, level+1)
   end
end
```

Figure 5.15   Berger-Oliger AMR algorithm.

The result may be creation or deletion of grids and must be performed in a way that maintains the proper nesting property of the meshes.

3. *Inter-grid operations*. Such operations are used to communicate solution values along the adaptive grid hierarchy. The following types of operations are required:

   • *Initialization of refined grids*. This may require transferring interior values of overlying grids or possibly using interpolated values from a coarser grid.

   • *Coarse grid update*. Where possible, fine grid values are injected onto the coarse grid so that the values used are the most accurate.

   • *Coordination of common values*. This is required whenever two grids overlap, so that their values are consistent.

Figure 5.15 contains pseudocode representation of the Berger–Oliger AMR algorithm that illustrates the recursive approach. Although such methods are clearly advantageous in terms of computational resources, their implementation, especially on parallel architectures, requires considerable effort. The main complexity actually has nothing to do with the physics of the flow field. It arises simply because one must maintain a hierarchical data structure and provide operations on this structure. For parallel implementation, the problem is compounded since the data structure is now distributed. This is similar to the difficulty encountered in implementing adaptive spectral methods discussed in Section 5.2.7.

The complexity of this approach can be substantially alleviated through the use of appropriate high-level programming abstractions that maintain the required data structure and free the implementor to concentrate only on the nature of the algorithm to be used on each component grid. These abstractions are conveniently expressed as object-oriented frameworks. Several of these are currently in existence.

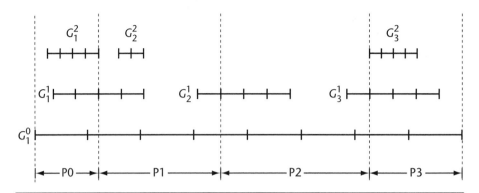

Figure 5.16   Composite distribution of the grid hierarchy in one dimension.

A notable example is the GrACE framework of Parashar [743], based on earlier work of Parashar and Browne [745]. The GrACE framework provides a distributed data structure that encapsulates the various operations such as interpolation as well as communication.

An additional critical issue is that of load balancing. As refinement takes place, the workload of a given processor increases due to the rising volume of computation. Clearly, some strategy must be employed to distribute the finer meshes to remote processors in order to even out the load. However, unless this is done carefully, meshes that are in physical proximity to one another (due to the refinement operation) will find that they are separated by large distances in terms of the processor network. This in turn leads to overhead due to communications. An example of a desirable processor/data distribution for a 1-D case is shown in Figure 5.16. Such a distribution maintains reasonable load balance while preserving physical locality. Note that this must be done repeatedly as various flow features form.

A key idea in ensuring that computational load is balanced is the use of space-filling curves to allocate grids to processors. Space-filling curves are a class of locality-preserving mappings from d-dimensional space to 1-D space. The mapping can be thought of as threading a string through the mesh hierarchy so that it fills the space. Load is then balanced by examining the length of this string and splitting the string into relatively equal pieces assigned to neighboring processors. This approach achieves load balancing, while ensuring that points that are physically close remain close in processor space. Early examples of its use can be found in the work of Salmon and Warren [824], as mentioned in Section 5.2.7. An example of the use of such a curve in 2-D is shown in Figure 5.17. The need to dynamically distribute parts of grids to remote processors in coordination with the use of space-filling curves, so as to achieve load balancing, requires the ability to distribute the data for a given grid across several processors. Thus the GrACE framework implements the graph of grids via a scalable, distributed dynamic array (SDDA), which uses extendable hashing techniques to provide dynamically extensible and globally indexed storage.

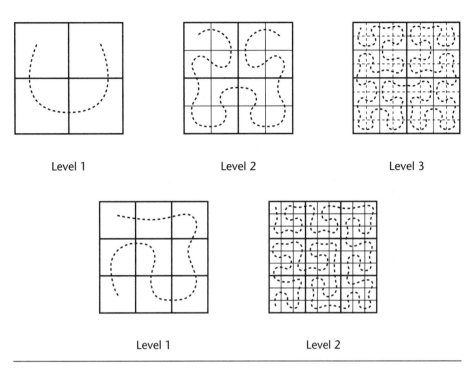

Figure 5.17   Self-similar, space-filling curves.

As an application of these ideas, we illustrate the use of AMR for the Richtmyer–Meshkov problem discussed above. In Plate 4 of the color insert, we show the solution, at various times, for the interaction of a shock wave with an inclined interface. In this case, we want not only to refine in the region of the shock wave but also to sharpen the contact discontinuity, which is where the mixing ultimately originates. It turns out that most shock-capturing schemes perform well in the presence of shocks but often smear out contact discontinuities to an unacceptable degree. The use of the AMR algorithm allows one to focus on these features and, at the same time, to reduce the deleterious effects of the dissipation inherent in modern shock-capturing schemes. In Plate 5 of the color insert, the solutions are shown at identical times, except that we have overlaid the corresponding AMR meshes. The dynamic nature of the algorithm is apparent. As further levels of refinement are used, the solution process becomes very efficient relative to a simulation using a single fine mesh.

The ability to abstract the complex data manipulations and parallel communications makes it necessary for the applications scientist to provide only the appropriate method for integration of the particular compressible flow. In the future, it is anticipated that implementation of AMR frameworks on massively parallel architectures will lead to important advances in our understanding of compressible flows.

5.4   Conclusion

In this necessarily brief overview of numerical methods for CFD, we have attempted to discuss some of the central issues associated with simulation of both incompressible and compressible flows. At best, this overview can only serve as an introduction to some of the challenges encountered in solving the Navier–Stokes and Euler equations on high-performance parallel machines. We have ignored completely a large number of crucial topics. Nevertheless, it is hoped that the reader can get some appreciation for the role parallel computing plays in facilitating high-resolution simulations of fluid phenomena.

As the available architectures become larger and more powerful, and as the required algorithmic and programming tools mature, it will soon be possible to contemplate the simulation of flows in realistic geometries at resolutions that capture most of the physically crucial scales. This will allow us, for the first time, to explore the detailed physics of complex phenomena such as turbulence and to produce models of these effects that can then be used in engineering simulations. It will then be possible to consider the use of optimization methods to tailor flows for optimal effect in a wide variety of critical applications.

6 Parallel Computing in Environment and Energy

**Mary F. Wheeler • Wonsuck Lee •
Clint N. Dawson • Dorian C. Arnold •
Tahsin Kurc • Manish Parashar •
Joel Saltz • Alan Sussman**

During the past 20 years, the impact of environmental problems on the health and well-being of humankind has become one of the top international issues. The modeling of surface water is important in predicting tidal ranges and surges, such as tsunamis and hurricanes caused by severe earthquake and storm events. In addition, groundwater and surface-water contamination affects a most vital condition of life, namely fresh water.

Cost-effective contaminant remediation is driving a new generation of environmental applications. The central challenge is to minimize costs for cleanup of a site whose properties are only poorly known and in which a variety of complex chemical and physical phenomena take place. The heart of this effort must be robust subsurface and surface-water simulators. In the case of groundwater, this must comprise coupled programs that together account for multicomponent, multiphase flow and transport through heterogeneous geological structures (porous media) and in surface-water flow models, either depth-averaged or deep ocean. For both applications, strategies optimal with respect to different objectives and subject to existing constraints are sought. During containment and remediation, real-time data need to be assimilated into the simulations and optimizations. For evaluation of longer-term effects, it is critical to couple the surface-water fluxes to models of the subsurface that account for flow, transport, and reaction of soluble contaminants.

Similarly, oil and gas production are of critical importance to the nation, since about two-thirds of U.S. energy currently comes from oil and gas, and this situation will not change much over the next few decades. Although oil can be imported, there are profound advantages to domestic production: ensuring a stable supply and price to the consumer and promoting a healthy national economy. Future production in the United States is dependent on enhanced oil recovery (EOR) and reservoir-characterization technologies. Intense computer simulation is essential for effective field management. Parallel reservoir simulators have the potential to solve larger, more realistic and practical problems faster and more economically. In this chapter, we describe some of the research on subsurface- and surface-flow models and related scientific computing problems that were facilitated collaborations by the CRPC.

One outcome is the development of a parallel problem-solving environment IPARS (Integrated Parallel Accurate Reservoir Simulator), suitable for modeling multiphase, multiphysics flow in porous media on massively parallel computers or clusters of workstations. In addition, we discuss the coupling of IPARS with NetSolve and demonstrate reservoir simulation in a grid-computing environment. We also incorporate additional functionality to IPARS by adding interactive steering and tracking capability using the software library DISCOVER (Distributed Interactive Steering and Collaborative Visualization Environment). We devote Sections 6.1 to 6.3 to this subject.

Another outcome is the coupling of Active Data Repository (ADR) and the modeling code CE-QUAL-ICM and its parallel version PCE-QUAL-ICM, which we describe in Section 6.4. CE-QUAL-ICM is a 3-D eutrophication model developed at the Department of Defense Engineer Research and Development Center (DoD-ERDC). The water quality model is semi-explicit in time and is based on an unstructured cell-centered finite volume numerical method. This sequential Fortran code was parallelized using a data/domain decomposition strategy and a single-program, multiple-data (SPMD) paradigm. PCE-QUAL-ICM, the parallel water-quality model, enhances CE-QUAL-ICM with message passing. Interprocessor communication is done using Message Passing Interface (MPI) communication libraries, and the parallel code has been ported to the CRAY-T3E, IBM-SP, and SGI O2000.

In addition, present research involves the coupling of IPARS with ADR for exploration of history-matching scenarios with uncertainty in the geological data. ADR enables integration of storage, retrieval, and processing of multidimensional multiple data sets on parallel machines and provides support for spatial queries and complex data aggregations [990].

6.1   Subsurface-Flow Modeling

Flow-in-porous-media problems are modeled by degenerate parabolic and nearly hyperbolic (i.e., advection-dominated), partial differential equations with equality and inequality constraints and are subject to hysteresis. The simulation processes occur on widely disparate time and space scales, such as the scales of reaction rates, precipitation, dissolution, and other phase changes, medium heterogeneity and fractures, and wells.

Degeneracies and hyperbolicity tend to produce flow and transport solutions with relatively steep fronts. Typically diffusion/dispersion is small. In the limit of no diffusion/dispersion, actual shocks develop, and the mathematical equations possess multiple solutions. However, only the entropy solution is physically relevant. It is difficult to approximate shocks without introducing spurious oscillations or an artificially large amount of numerical dispersion. These can smear the steep front, change its speed, and render any further computations, such as those for reactions and phase changes, suspect.

Extremely large systems of nonlinear equations result. This is due in part to the sheer size of the groundwater domain or petroleum reservoir, the number of phases and chemical species present, and the need to resolve time and space scales adequately. But it is also due to the highly coupled nonlinear nature of the equations.

Physical and mathematical considerations lead us to emphasize conservative schemes that preserve maximum and/or minimum principles, produce little or no numerical dispersion, can support adaptive local grid refinement, and give asymptotically accurate solutions of the governing equations. Mixed finite element (finite volume) methods coupled with Godunov characteristics or discontinuous Galerkin methods [805, 806] have been formulated that satisfy these criteria.

6.1.1   IPARS Motivation

The modeling of subsurface problems requires (1) a high-performance computing (HPC)–based interdisciplinary attack on the geochemical, biochemical, multiphase, compositional, and mathematical complexities that dominate subsurface flow and transport in heterogeneous porous media and (2) a problem-solving environment (PSE) for predictive simulation that uses advanced, scalable parallel algorithms and multiscale nonlinear and stochastic science to resolve these complexities and to quantify and diminish uncertainties in prediction. Key requirements include the support of high-resolution reservoir studies with millions of grid elements, ability to handle multiple physical models (e.g., CO2, surfactant, and thermal), multiple fault blocks, dynamic locally adaptive mesh refinements, and interactive tracking, visualization, and computational steering.

The main objective of the PSE is to simplify the building of flexible and efficient parallel reservoir simulators through the use of a high-level programming interface for problem specification and model composition, object-oriented programming abstractions that implement application objects, and distributed dynamic data management that efficiently supports adaptation and parallelism. Secondary objectives include developing a general framework for integrating input/output, visualization, and interactive experimentations. These objectives motivated the development of a computing framework called IPARS, suitable for massively parallel computers or clusters of PCs. This framework provides all the required memory management, message passing, table lookup, solvers, and input/output. The developer only needs to code the relevant physics. In addition, this software permits physically representative coupling of different physics or different numerical algorithms in different parts of the domain.

6.1.2   IPARS Description

The development of the subsurface-flow simulator framework IPARS, suitable for research and with possible commercial applications, has been an ongoing project for the past four years at the Center for Subsurface Modeling (CSM). The IPARS framework supports 3-D transient flow of multiple phases containing multiple components through immobile phases (rock/soil). The bulk phase of the medium (i.e., the rock plus fluid) can be regarded as compressible in order to include the elastic property of the bulk rock. Thermodynamic quantities include phase densities, compressibility factors, and viscosities. These may be represented as arbitrary functions of pressure and composition, or they may be approximated by simpler functions (e.g., constant compressibility). The initial system is isothermal, but an effort is being made to incorporate nonisothermal calculations.

The most general mathematical representation of such a system without mutual solubility between hydrocarbon and water phases is

$$\frac{\partial\left(\rho_i S_i \phi_i\right)}{\partial t} - \nabla \cdot \sum_{j}^{N_p} \frac{K\, k_{rj}\, \xi_j}{\mu_j}\, x_{ij} \left(P_j - \gamma \Delta D\right) = q_i$$

for N_c hydrocarbon phases and N_p consisting phases. ξ_j and x_{ij} denote the molar density of phase j and the mole fraction of the i-component in liquid phase j, respectively. The first term represents the change of mass of the ith phase with time. The second term represents the change due to phase transport. The right-hand side is a source/sink term.

Discretization employs mixed finite elements based on the lowest-order Raviart–Thomas spaces or cell-centered finite differences and backward differences in time [46, 818]. The simulator is designed to handle dynamic grid refinement, but this is not currently implemented.

The number of physical models used in petroleum engineering applications and environmental subsurface-flow problems is increasing. There are currently eight physical models available:

- *Implicit hydrology model.* Simulate oil–water flow system with an implicit numerical scheme.

- *IMPES hydrology model.* Simulate oil–water flow system with an explicit numerical scheme.

- *Two implicit black-oil models (different primary unknowns).* Simulate oil–gas–water petroleum reservoir flow with an implicit numerical scheme but two different choices of primary unknowns.

- *Implicit air–water model.* Air-and-water-flow simulation model for subsaturated and saturated groundwater-flow zones using an implicit method.

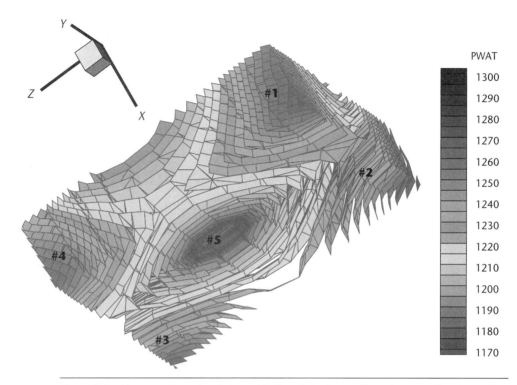

Figure 6.1 Air–water flow simulation with four injection wells and one production well.
PWAT is water pressure.

- *Implicit and explicit single-phase models.* Fully saturated groundwater-flow simulation model. One uses an implicit method; the other one is designed with
  an explicit scheme.
- *Compositional model.* Most general hydrocarbon reservoir simulation model.

Here we present examples of IPARS simulation. Figure 6.1 shows the results of an
air–water subsurface-flow model [596]. Water pressure distribution is plotted for a
five-well model. Wells #1 through #4 are water injection wells, and well #5 is producing air and/or water. With this air–water model, one can study flow in subsaturated
zones without mathematical simplification, as in Richards' equation. Unlike many
groundwater-flow simulators, the air–water model is capable of handling wells in
addition to general boundary conditions. All of the framework-supported functionalities, including parallel computation, are available without additional programming.
Also, multiblock formation is readily embedded in the air–water model. We now describe it with a more complicated three-phase flow model known as the *black-oil
model*.

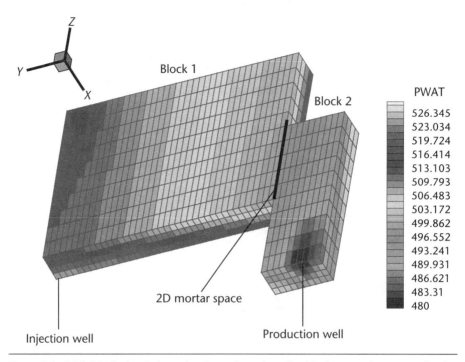

Figure 6.2   Multiblock simulation of a three-phase (two liquid phases and one gas phase) black-oil model.

The simulation domain may consist of one or more fault blocks. Each fault block can have an independent coordinate system and be exposed to different body forces. The multiblock implementation in IPARS allows one to split the domain into several fault blocks. Then each fault block can have different physical parameters and field data. Furthermore, the grids of two fault blocks are not necessarily matching. The formulation is based on the mortar formulation of the domain decomposition algorithm [1009].

Figure 6.2 demonstrates the cell-averaged water pressure at 30-days' operation over the two blocks that constitute the whole simulation domain. Two blocks with different field data are attached by a mortar space (depicted in the figure by a black solid line).

Under the IPARS framework, two or more different physical models can be run on different parts of the domain (fault blocks). This is the multiphysics capability of IPARS [990]. Thus, one can use, for instance, a black-oil model on one fault block while the other fault block is being simulated by a hydrology model.

From the beginning, IPARS was intended to solve problems involving a million or more grid elements economically, thereby greatly improving grid resolution.

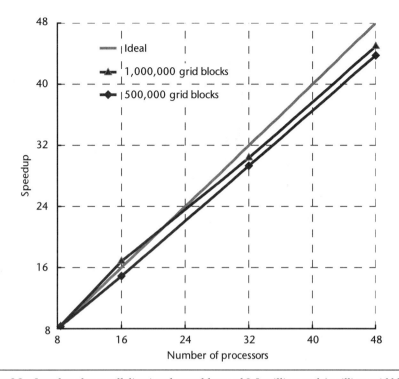

Figure 6.3   Speedups by parallelization for problems of 0.5 million and 1 million grid blocks. Black-oil model simulation.

This task can be handled efficiently by multiple-processor machines. Here we cite the work by Wheeler et al. [989]. This study considered the black-oil model. Figure 6.3 shows the scalability of the black-oil model simulation. Speedup of two cases of 500,000 grid blocks and 1,000,000 grid blocks was compared and showed close to ideal performance. Figure 6.4 indicates that the workload for each processor is almost equal, since the maximum and minimum load are very close. In other words, the dynamic load-balancing support by the IPARS framework is nearly perfect.

The grid-element-keyout capability of IPARS allows flow simulation on a domain with complicated geometry. A keyed-out cell is a grid block that does not contain fluids. The cell is removed from the flow simulation domain. Figure 6.5 shows an example of the air–water-model simulation [596] on an irregularly shaped domain where one injection well is placed in the middle of the head of a Texas longhorn.

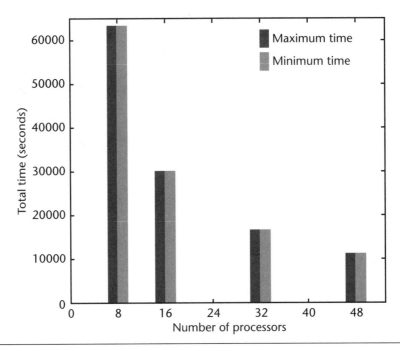

Figure 6.4 Histogram for load balancing of a parallel IPARS job.

6.2   IPARS and Grid Computing by NetSolve

In order to obtain accurate solutions in many field-scale applications, the engineer
may require access to multiple-processor machines at some distant location. Most
likely, this engineer will not be intimately familiar with the details of physically
complex simulators. Thus, a simple and user-friendly interface for accessing available
computational resources is desirable. The Grid Computing environment, NetSolve,
provides such an interface: an Internet-based global route to software. NetSolve
has been developed at the Innovative Computing Laboratory (ICL), University of
Tennessee at Knoxville. Under CRPC guidance, CSM and ICL have coupled IPARS
and NetSolve and demonstrated how a reservoir simulator may be accessed remotely
with an easy-to-use interface [48].

In the NetSolve environment, a user can access a scientific application as a
client, virtually anywhere in the world, without having to worry about obtaining,
installing, or maintaining computing resources. The IPARS-NetSolve integration was
designed so that users can initiate the simulation and examine output, including
visualization, through a Web browser's window. These tasks can be carried out with
laptop computers or with smaller devices such as a handheld PC or a cellular phone
with an Internet connection and a Web browser installed. CSM is setting up a

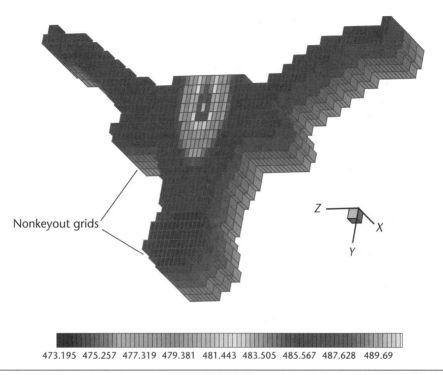

Nonkeyout grids

473.195 475.257 477.319 479.381 481.443 483.505 485.567 487.628 489.69

Figure 6.5   Demonstration of keyout capability of IPARS. Air–water model simulation on Texas longhorn shape domain.

collaborative system for several of its industrial partners based on the computing environment described below.

6.2.1   Integrating IPARS into NetSolve

In this section we describe how IPARS was integrated into the NetSolve environment. Key to the coupling of NetSolve and IPARS is a clear understanding of their respective interfaces. IPARS is designed to receive a single file input containing all the parameters and field data describing the simulation. It produces several output files. One output file describes the results and contains numerical values of the variables of the simulation in an ASCII format. The other output files contain data that are used to support visualization. Hence the answer to integration is somewhat straightforward: create interface routines for IPARS and NetSolve and embed IPARS in NetSolve servers.

First, a functional wrapper was created to initiate an IPARS job with an input and several output file names. This wrapper runs the simulation and also calls scripts external to the simulator, which uses a commercial visualization software package

TECPLOT™ to post-process the output into a series of graphical frames. These frames represent snapshots of different parameters being observed in the field of study. The UNIX utility, "convert," is then used to change the format and to attach each set of frames (corresponding to different parameters) into a single movie file for each set. These movie files, along with the ASCII output file, are stored on a server and can be accessed by users.

The NetSolve system provides a code generator that parses a NetSolve problem-description file (PDF) in order to extend the server's functional capabilities. This was the tool used to create a server with IPARS capability; a portion of the PDF file used for integration follows.

```
@PROBLEM ipars
@INCLUDE ''ipars.h''
@LIB /home/user/lib/libipars.a
@DESCRIPTION
Parallel Sub-surface Flow Simulator
@INPUT 2
@OBJECT STRING CHAR model
IPARS physical model to use
@OBJECT FILE CHAR infile
Input data file
```

Eventually, this PDF will describe the code that determines how to call the abovementioned wrapper with the inputs given from a client program. After this configuration and a compilation, the NetSolve server is ready to be attached to a NetSolve agent/system and service requests. Note that although we only mention one server cluster, it is also possible to have several IPARS-enabled server clusters or parallel machines attached to the system; the NetSolve agent would dynamically marshal requests to the best candidate, yielding better performance (Figure 6.6).

6.2.2   Client-Side Web-Browser Interface

At this point, one can now use any of the NetSolve client interfaces to access IPARS. This has two major impacts: (1) with a single installation of IPARS, many users can benefit from the simulator without having to go through the hassles of installation and maintenance; and (2) IPARS can be used from any host machine (even architectures to which IPARS has not been ported). A further result is that one can get significant speedup by accessing server clusters that are orders of magnitude faster than the available local computers. The fact that we are using the NetSolve client means that the user has access to all the functionalities of any and every NetSolve server in the system.

In order to make things even easier for the user, we take our interface a step further. We make the IPARS simulator accessible to the ever-present Web browsers.

First, a flexible and user-friendly menu for data input was developed. The menu allows the following selections: choice of one of eight physical models, including

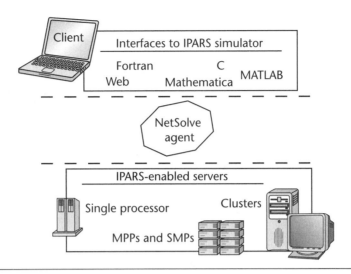

Figure 6.6 Overview of the NetSolve/IPARS integration.

physical and geological parameters; grid selection and numerical algorithmic parameters; and visualization variables.

We used HyperText Markup Language (HTML) forms and the Common Gateway Interface (CGI) to provide a complete interface to IPARS that basically sits on top of the NetSolve middleware system. The total package has all the components that every application should have: complete portability, an easy and intuitive interface, and run-time load balancing to ensure maximum performance. All of this capability is available without ever downloading or installing any components (other than the Web browser, which can be assumed to be standard). Figure 6.7 is a schematic description of the resulting Web-based computing environment of IPARS.

In the next section we show, using a library developed by computer scientists, how we have pulled IPARS to a new level: interactive tracking and simulation.

6.3 Tracking and Interactive Simulation in IPARS

Most scientific computing software does not allow users to interact during the simulation process. Thus, a scientist who finds something undesirable usually waits for termination of the simulation or stops the execution. The restart capability of a simulation program is often used to incorporate certain changes in physical situations. Scientists analyze the output files and apply new conditions by changing appropriate parameters in the input files that will be used for the restart. However, the time required to perform this tedious cyclic work is not acceptable.

There are many engineering applications that will benefit by real-time interactive simulation. Petroleum production engineers often want to change the number of

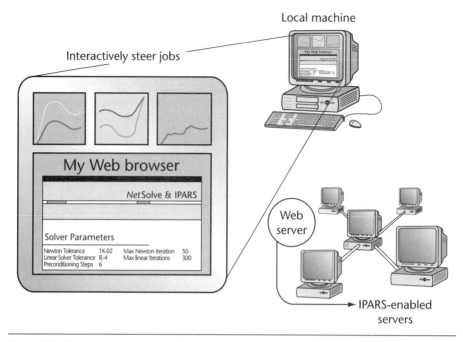

Figure 6.7   Schematic description of using IPARS in a remote setting.

active wells, their type, and conditions in field activity. Hence, an interactive computer simulation capability can be a very profitable tool. Environmental hydrologists who want to simulate the transport of groundwater over a period of dry and rainy seasons may effectively study a real-world situation by changing conditions at soil boundaries interactively.

We include tracking and steering capabilities with IPARS so that the user can monitor the simulation domain in the middle of the computation. Tracking is not an additional feature, but a necessary procedure to steer the simulation. It should give useful and essential information concerning the physical problems to scientists. During the simulation, tracked data can be reported in numerical form or represented visually so that users can decide when to steer and what parameters to change.

For safe steering, users are allowed to change only preselected variables at certain points of the simulation program. This avoids nonphysical situations and the introduction of discontinuities, which may cause the simulation to break down. Changing certain parameters in the middle of time steps may lead to an abrupt change in a variable and may make the linear system ill-conditioned.

This means that the designer of the algorithm must select the steering points and variables carefully, while allowing the user as much flexibility as possible. For IPARS, wells and boundary conditions are the candidates for steering. The variables that will be steered are chosen so that nonphysical parameters are not introduced.

We have used DISCOVER (Distributed Interactive Steering and Collaborative Visualization Environment) to provide tracking and steering in IPARS. Interaction points are inserted in the IPARS program. At an interaction point, the DISCOVER interface allows the user to pause and restart IPARS. In the following section, we describe DISCOVER and the integration of IPARS with DISCOVER to provide an interactive steering environment.

6.3.1   An Interactive Computational Collaboration: DISCOVER

DISCOVER is a Web-based collaborative interaction and steering environment that addresses each of these issues. Figure 6.8 shows an architectural overview of the system. The system supports a three-tier architecture composed of detachable thin clients at the front-end, a network of Java interaction servers in the middle, and a control network of sensors, actuators, and interaction agents superimposed on the application data network at the back-end. The interaction Web server enables clients to connect to and collaboratively interact with registered applications using a conventional browser. Furthermore, it provides access to computational and visualization servers and to simulation archives.

The application control network enables sensors and actuators to be encapsulated within and directly deployed with the computational objects, thus forming interaction objects. Interaction agents resident at each computational node register the

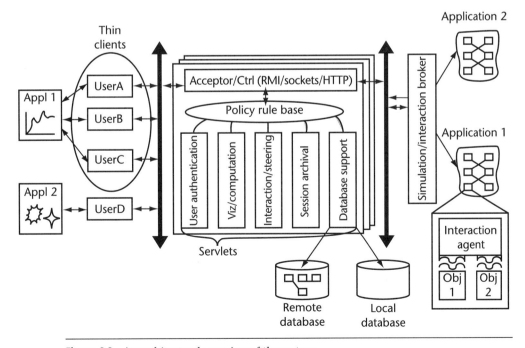

Figure 6.8   An architectural overview of the system.

interaction objects and export their interaction interfaces to the application interaction proxy, which manages the overall interaction through the control network of interaction agents and objects. The interaction proxy uses JNI to create Java proxy objects that mirror the computational objects and allow them to be accessed directly by the interaction Web server. DISCOVER is an ongoing research initiative at the Advanced Software Systems Laboratory (TASSL) at Rutgers University.

6.3.2   Integrating IPARS with DISCOVER

IPARS has been integrated with the DISCOVER framework, enabling collaborative remote interaction and steering of IPARS oil reservoir and hydrology applications. Current capabilities include application control (start, stop, and pause), checkpoint/rollback, query and control of parameters such as well diameter, pressure, oil/water injection rate, and so on. Development of the IPARS-DISCOVER iteration involved transforming IPARS data structures into interaction objects using a C++ wrapper, as described above. Each interaction object created in this way exported View/Command interfaces for interaction. Figure 6.9 shows a screen dump of plots tracking changes in well parameters of interest for an IPARS implicit hydrology model simulation.

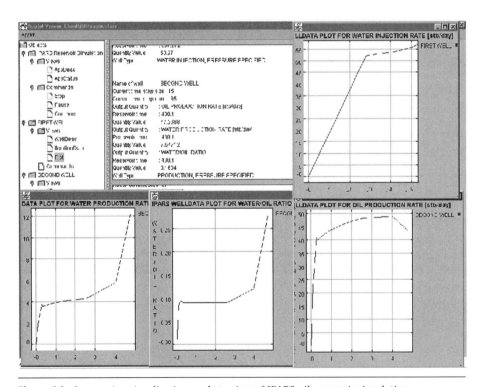

Figure 6.9   Interactive visualization and steering of IPARS oil reservoir simulations.

6.4   Surface-Water Simulation

The ability to accurately and efficiently model near-coastal waters is of extreme importance to a number of government agencies and private industries. These flows are described by the 3-D Navier–Stokes equations with a free surface. However, present limitations on computational algorithms and architecture make solving these equations numerically extremely difficult. Hence, several approximate mathematical models have been developed, including the shallow water equations (SWE). The SWE are obtained by vertically integrating the 3-D incompressible Navier–Stokes equations along with the hydrostatic pressure approximation. They can successfully model water bodies with horizontal characteristic lengths much larger than the fluid depth.

Tidal fluctuations are frequently modeled using the SWE. Such models are useful, for example, for tidal power-generation projects and for determining the periodic forces acting on offshore structures. The SWE, coupled with a pollutant and/or salinity transport algorithm, are useful for designing effective remediation strategies for polluted bays and estuaries.

However, numerical solution of the SWE is not straightforward, due to the extremely complicated geometries and the strong coupling between the fluid depth and velocities. This coupling can lead to problems with stability and spurious oscillation. Various numerical techniques have been and are being developed for this purpose.

Numerical algorithms and mathematical analysis go hand in hand. An understanding of the convergence and stability properties of a numerical model for the SWE is essential for developing robust numerical procedures. We have analyzed the generalized wave continuity equation (GWCE), developed by W. G. Gray et al., for the SWE. Both continuous-time and discrete-time a priori error estimates have been derived. We have also parallelized shallow water flow and transport simulation: the ADCIRC software, which is used on the GWCE, and CE-QUAL-ICM, a water quality model.

6.4.1   A Water Quality Model: CE-QUAL-ICM

CE-QUAL-ICM is a water quality model developed at the DoD-ERDC by Carl F. Cerco, Thomas Cole, and others [177, 178]. This numerical code can model the transport and reaction of multiple variables simultaneously. It also contains a sediment transport model and can be run in 1-, 2-, or 3-D configurations. CE-QUAL-ICM allows for inflow, no flow, and outflow boundary conditions. CE-QUAL-ICM has been used extensively in the eutrophication studies of Chesapeake Bay. The numerical method is based on an unstructured finite volume method. It is explicit in time in the horizontal direction and implicit in the vertical columns. The reader is referred to Cerco and Cole [177, 178] for a detailed description of the numerical model.

The main component of CE-QUAL-ICM is the solution of a 3-D mass conservation equation of the following form for each state variable:

$$\frac{\delta\left(V_j C_j\right)}{\delta t} = \sum_{k=1}^{n} Q_k C_k + \sum_{k=1}^{n} A_k D_k \frac{\delta C}{\delta x_k} + \sum S_j$$

The above equation represents conservation of mass in the jth control volume, and n is the number of faces attached to control volume j. Q_k, C_k, D_k, and A_k are, respectively, the volumetric flow rate, concentration, diffusion coefficient, and cross-sectional area at face k of control volume j. V_j is the volume of control volume j, and S_j are the external sources and sinks present in control volume j. $\delta C/\delta x_k$ is the spatial gradient of concentration in the direction normal to face k, and $(\delta V_j C_j)/\delta t$ is the rate of change of the total concentration in control volume j.

6.4.2   A Parallel Water-Quality Model: PCE-QUAL-ICM

In a water quality model, special interests are long-term studies, typically comprising decades. For these long-term simulations, the serial code requires hundreds of vector computer (CRAY-YMP) hours. We achieved an order of magnitude reduction in simulation times by porting the serial code to distributed-memory parallel computing platforms.

PCE-QUAL-ICM, a parallel water-quality model, is a product of this effort and has been developed at CSM in conjunction with ERDC. A data/domain decomposition strategy is employed, along with a single-program, multiple-data (SPMD) paradigm. Interprocessor communication is done through standard MPI message-passing libraries. The parallel code has been ported to the IBM-SP and CRAY-T3E, which are distributed-memory parallel computers, and to the SGI O2000, which has some shared and some distributed memory.

As stated above, CE-QUAL-ICM uses an explicit/implicit time-marching solution strategy. Within each time step itself, the solution update is broken into two separate steps. In the first step, an intermediate concentration is computed that takes into account horizontal diffusion and advection, along with all the external sources and sinks. This step is completely explicit, and there is no need to solve any system of linear equations. In the next step, the vertical diffusion and advection are incorporated in an implicit manner. This requires solution of a tridiagonal system of equations for each vertical water column.

Solution methodology plays an important role in parallelization. Not all numerical techniques are readily parallelizable. Since CE-QUAL-ICM has an explicit treatment of horizontal diffusion and advection, it easy to parallelize, and it can potentially benefit greatly from parallelization. Implicit treatment of vertical transport and explicit treatment of horizontal transport implies that we can benefit by doing domain decomposition only in the horizontal plane. For each surface block, the underlying vertical column is assigned to the same subdomain.

For computing the horizontal advective flux, the concentration C_k at face k is needed, and CE-QUAL-ICM has two ways to compute this. One is a simple first-order-accurate upwind differencing that sets C_k equal to the upstream value, with the upstream direction determined by the sign of Q_k. The other is a higher-order-accurate QUICKEST scheme that uses quadratic interpolation for computing C_k by taking two upstream cells and one downstream cell. Thus, in a traditional domain decomposition sense, we will need at least two layers of "overlap" or ghost blocks. Note that upwinding or the QUICKEST scheme is used only in the horizontal direction; in the vertical direction, a simple linear interpolation between the adjoining cells is used to compute C_k.

Either a fixed time step can be specified or an automatic time-step selection based on stability criteria can be used. If the automatic time stepping option is chosen, then the subdomains need to communicate with each other to select a global minimum time step if the computations are to remain synchronous.

6.4.3   Parallel Algorithm

From the solution algorithm of CE-QUAL-ICM already outlined above, it is clear that it is readily parallelizable. It is an explicit code and is implicit only in the vertical direction. A small tridiagonal system of equations is solved locally within each water column. Therefore, a data-parallel approach would be a natural way to parallelize this code. The original global domain is split into smaller subdomains, and each processor element (PE) works only on its local subdomain. Since the solution within a subdomain will depend on the solution in its neighboring subdomains, the PEs exchange information through message-passing communication libraries. The explicit nature of the solution algorithm in CE-QUAL-ICM implies that it is enough to do message passing once every time step. Note that this type of parallel computation does not change the global solution algorithm. Conceptually, all we are doing is splitting the work among processors. Thus, the solution we would get through parallel computation will be identical to that we would obtain if we were to solve it sequentially, up to machine precision.

The domain is decomposed in the horizontal plane alone, and all the underlying blocks in a vertical column are assigned to the same processor. This minimizes interprocessor communication, since now the implicit step involving solving a system of tridiagonal linear equations is done locally within each PE.

Domain decomposition or mesh partitioning on unstructured grids is a nontrivial task and needs to take into consideration several issues, such as load balancing and locality. C. Edwards [306, 823] developed an effective decomposition strategy based on a Hilbert space-filling curve, and this has been used with great success in parallelizing ADCIRC, an advanced coastal circulation model based on the shallow water equations [196]. A space-filling curve based domain decomposition is used in PCE-QUAL-ICM.

The basic idea behind this decomposition algorithm is to construct a map from d-dimensional space to the interval $[0,1]$ on the real line. In our case $d = 2$, since we

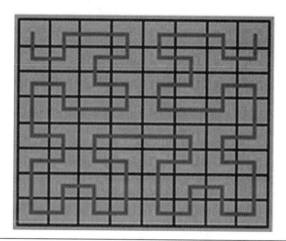

Figure 6.10   Hilbert space-filling curve on a rectangular mesh.

decompose only the surface blocks. Given a list of points in the original domain, a space-filling curve is built that passes through each point once. Since the curve is one dimensional, the position of a point along the curve determines its order in the interval [0,1]. The map is constructed so that points that are close in d-dimensional space remain close when mapped. Thus, the curve preserves locality.

A space-filling curve on a simple rectangular mesh is shown in Figure 6.10. One can also weight the points on the curve by a measure of the amount of "work" associated with that point. This weighting is useful in our application, since each surface block can have a different number of vertical blocks underneath it. In this way, better load balancing can be achieved. Once the curve is constructed, the decomposition of the domain is performed by dividing the interval [0,1] into N subintervals, where N is the desired number of processors, and mapping each subinterval to a processor. That is, the points in d-space associated with the subinterval are assigned to the processor.

6.5   A Coupled Simulation of Flow and Transport with ADR

A coupled simulation system for bays and estuaries includes a hydrodynamics simulator, which simulates the flow of water in the domain of interest, and a chemical transport simulator, which simulates both the reactions among chemicals in the bay and the transport of these chemicals. For a complete simulation system, the chemical transport simulator needs to be coupled to the hydrodynamics simulator, since the former uses the output of the latter to simulate the transport of chemicals within the domain. Note that chemical reactions and transport of chemicals do not affect the computed hydrodynamics values. Thus, the same flow values can be used by a chemical transport simulator for different simulations.

However, coupling the two simulators to form a complete system is not a straightforward process. First, the chemical transport simulator can be used to simulate changes over a long period of time (from days to hundreds of years). This requires a large amount of hydrodynamics simulation output to be stored on and retrieved from disks and/or tertiary storage. Second, the chemical transport simulator may use coarser time steps than the hydrodynamics simulator. Moreover, the grids (in two or three dimensions) used by the chemical transport simulator may be different from the grids employed by the hydrodynamics simulator.

Thus, post-processing of the output data set from the hydrodynamics simulator is required to generate the proper input to the chemical transport simulator. One post-processing operation required is averaging velocity and elevation values over several time steps of the hydrodynamics simulation to generate initial values for each time step in the chemical transport simulation. The other operation is a projection of the averaged velocity values at the grid points in the hydrodynamics simulation to flow values on the edges of the chemical transport simulator grid.

Therefore, the two crucial components of the coupled simulation system are (1) a *projection code* to perform the projection operation, and (2) a *data management infrastructure* that will provide optimized storage, retrieval, and post-processing (time averaging) of the outputs of the hydrodynamics simulator as and when needed by the chemical transport simulator.

6.5.1   The Active Data Repository

In this section we briefly describe an infrastructure, called the Active Data Repository (ADR) [186, 187, 327, 586], developed at the University of Maryland, for storing and processing multidimensional data sets, such as those generated by hydrodynamics simulators.

The ADR is an infrastructure that enables integration of storage, retrieval, and processing of multidimensional data sets on a distributed-memory parallel machine, with one or more disks attached to each processor. ADR targets scientific applications that make use of multidimensional scientific data sets.

These applications have several important common characteristics. Applications may use only a subset of all the data available in data sets. Access to data items is described by a *range query*, namely a multidimensional bounding box in the underlying multidimensional attribute space of the data set. Only the data items whose associated coordinates fall within the multidimensional box are retrieved. The processing structures of these applications also share common characteristics. The processing steps consist of retrieving input and output data items that intersect the range query, *projecting* the coordinates of the retrieved input items to the corresponding output items, and *aggregating*, in some way, all the retrieved input items mapped to the same output data items. Correctness of the output usually does not depend on the order input data items are aggregated. An intermediate data structure, referred to as an *accumulator*, can be used to hold intermediate results during processing. For example, an accumulator can be used to keep a running sum for an averaging operation.

At the end of processing, the final output is produced from the intermediate results stored in the accumulator.

Using ADR for building the data management/manipulation system of the coupled simulation system has several advantages. First, ADR is targeted toward multidimensional data sets and can simultaneously manage and process multiple data sets. The hydrodynamics simulator simulates flow patterns on an unstructured grid, and velocity and elevation values are computed at all vertices of the grid at each time step. Thus, the output of the hydrodynamics simulator is a multidimensional data set over space (the 2-D or 3-D grid) and simulation time. In addition, the capacity to handle multiple data sets enables management of data sets generated by different hydrodynamics simulators or from different runs of the same simulator. Second, ADR leverages commonality in processing requirements to seamlessly integrate data retrieval and processing. Integration of data retrieval and computations makes it possible to mask I/O latencies. Moreover, integrating the processing and data retrieval allows significant reductions in data volumes before sending the data over the network (local or wide area) to the projection code or the chemical transport simulator. Third, ADR can be customized for a wide variety of applications without compromising efficiency. This capability allows different chemical transport simulators to use the data sets stored in the database system.

6.5.2   Implementation

We have built a prototype of the coupled simulation system using ADR [587]. In our implementation of the coupled simulation system, we use a hydrodynamics simulator [628] developed to model circulation patterns in coastal seas, bays, and estuaries, and a chemical transport simulator, called UTTRANS, developed to model and simulate reactions and transport of various chemicals in bays and estuaries. The hydrodynamics simulator is ADCIRC—a circulation model [629], which was parallelized by Chippada et al. [196]. The chemical transport simulator is a sequential program and was developed at CSM. The projection operation is carried out by a code called UT-PROJ [197], also developed at CSM.

We have customized ADR to store, retrieve, and process the output of the hydrodynamics simulator on an IBM SP at the University of Maryland. The output from the hydrodynamics simulator is partitioned into chunks, each of which contains velocity and elevation values over a set of time steps at a subset of the grid points. The chunks are distributed across the disks on the SP, using default declustering methods implemented in ADR for loading data sets, so that each disk has about the same number of chunks covering approximately the same set of time steps.

A spatial index, containing a bounding box for each chunk and the locations of the chunks on the disks, is created for the entire data set. A function that performs averaging of velocity and elevation values over several time steps of the hydrodynamics simulation was registered as an aggregation function. A query from the chemical transport simulator specifies the time period of interest, the hydrodynamics data set of interest, and how to send the output back (using UNIX sockets or Meta-Chaos).

ADR performs retrieval and averaging of velocity and elevation values over the time steps of the hydrodynamics simulator that fall into the time period of interest. The results are then sent to the chemical transport code, which is a sequential program and runs on one of the processors of the SP. The chemical transport code uses the projection code UT-PROJ to perform projection of the averaged grid values for the data set specified in the query. It then uses the results to compute the transport of chemicals (e.g., an oil spill) in the bay or estuary.

Our experimental results show that a query, over a simulation time period of 225 seconds (15 time steps of the hydrodynamics simulator) on a grid modeling Galveston Bay with 2113 points, is resolved by ADR in 0.8 seconds (including 0.4 seconds to send the results back to the chemical transport simulator over the LAN) on eight SP nodes with two local disks per node. Using ADR, UT-PROJ, and UTTRANS, a 2-hour oil spill simulation with the Galveston Bay data stored in ADR takes about 300 seconds.

6.6   Conclusion

We have described and demonstrated IPARS as a PSE for applications arising in environmental and petroleum engineering. These problems are prototypical of multiscale simulations such as reactive computational fluid mechanics. Particular applications targeted include the remediation of polluted soils and aquifers and the environmentally prudent production of oil and gas energy resources. We have discussed IPARS enhancements through integration with NetSolve and DISCOVER.

Similarly, we have described parallel modeling of coupled hydrodynamic and environmental simulators for surface-water flow. The models discussed in this chapter are presently being employed in treating real-life scenarios such as dredging in Chesapeake Bay, remediating several Florida bays and the Everglades, as well as studying flood prevention in Louisiana. ADR software has proved to be useful for coupling multidimensional data between the different flow and reactive transport simulators. Instead of taking more than a year, parallel computation now allows many of these investigations to be completed in less than a month.

The infrastructure of CRPC was instrumental in the development of the science as well as the collaborations that we have described in this chapter. It is clear that CRPC can claim that the sum of the parts in these efforts has been greater than the whole.

Acknowledgments. The authors of this chapter wish to acknowledge Steven Bryant, Jack Dongarra, Victor Parr, Malgorzata Peszyńska, Joel Saltz, and John Wheeler for their contributions and fruitful discussions.

7 Parallel Computational Chemistry: An Overview of NWChem

David E. Bernholdt

Computational chemistry has a long and venerable history. With the help of improvements in computational methodology, and in computers themselves, it has been transformed into a virtually indispensable tool, used by a large cross section of the discipline. The ability to model "real-world" chemical systems with the sophistication necessary to obtain chemically meaningful results has helped produce a remarkable level of synergy between computational and experimental treatments of chemical problems. This, in turn, has fueled further interest in expanding the role of computational chemistry to even larger, more sophisticated, and more demanding simulations.

Vector supercomputers played a prominent role in the rise of computational chemistry, as chemists went beyond simple ports of existing codes, restructuring them and making important advances in algorithms. Today, few vector-based computers are still produced, but modern commodity CPUs make good use of the optimizations and algorithms originally designed for vector machines. The cutting edge of high-performance computing has shifted to parallel computers, based on those same commodity CPUs, and computational chemistry is of course following. Numerous packages can make effective use of modestly sized shared-memory parallel systems, but fewer are available for the high-end systems that use distributed-memory architectures (including those in which each node is a shared-memory multiprocessor). The two interrelated issues primarily responsible for this situation are ease of programming and scalability of algorithms.

Computational chemistry methods tend to be computationally complex and resource intensive (memory and disk as well as CPU), so parallelizing chemistry methods can be challenging, especially if scalability to large numbers of processors is required. In a shared-memory environment, programming is relatively straightforward, and reasonable parallel algorithms can provide adequate performance and scalability for many applications—sufficient for the modestly sized shared resources typically available within a research group, department, or university. However, the largest and most complex problems require the largest massively parallel processors (MPPs), which are presently distributed-memory systems. Chemistry algorithms scalable to hundreds or thousands of processors are far more challenging and often too complex to be implemented within the message-passing programming models widely used in distributed-memory environments.

Computational chemistry is a rather broad field, and a comprehensive review of the state of the art in parallel computing across the entire field would require a book of its own. In this chapter, I focus on a portion of the field in which high-performance computing has had a particularly significant impact on the day-to-day conduct of the science of chemistry: molecular quantum chemistry. I use the NWChem software package [98, 313, 411–414, 440, 557] as a representative of the current state of the art in highly scalable, fully distributed, parallel computational chemistry software, focusing on molecular structure methods. At its inception, the goal for the NWChem project was to deliver molecular modeling software that provides 10 to 100 times the effective capability of what was currently available on conventional supercomputers. This necessitated the use of algorithms that exhibit parallel scalability, both in the size of the computational resource and in the molecular system being modeled. Scalable applications must not only effectively parallelize the requisite computations but must also utilize the aggregate subsystems of the MPP. Algorithms must distribute data across the total system memory, not limiting the functional problem size by the effective memory of any single computational node. Furthermore, other MPP subsystems that algorithms exploit (i.e., communication and secondary storage) must be utilized in a scalable fashion.

The scalable modules in NWChem span a broad range of computational chemistry methods: Hartree-Fock (HF) or self-consistent field (SCF), density functional theory, *ab initio* molecular dynamics, perturbation theory, coupled cluster, multiconfiguration self-consistent field (MCSCF), configuration interaction (CI), molecular mechanics, molecular dynamics, free energy simulations, Car-Parrinello, and so on. These modules have been implemented in the environment by a collection of supporting modules providing basic computational capabilities and fundamental services required for chemical computations. After a general outline of the equations and their solution, I describe the overall architecture of the NWChem package and several critical supporting modules. I then focus on two of the NWChem chemistry methods, emphasizing their implementation in the NWChem environment and their performance. I conclude by placing the methods and tools used within NWChem in the broader context of computational chemistry and computational science in general.

7.1   Molecular Quantum Chemistry

The various methods of molecular quantum chemistry ultimately derive from the time-independent Schrödinger equation,

$$\left(T_e + T_n + V_{en} + V_{ee} + V_{nn}\right) \Psi = E \, \Psi \qquad (7.1)$$

The five terms in parenthesis at the left are components of the Hamiltonian operator, representing, respectively, the electronic and nuclear kinetic energies and the potentials due to interactions of electrons and nuclei, electrons with other electrons and nuclei with other nuclei; E is the energy of the system, and Ψ is the wavefunction. The Hamiltonian terms are

$$T_e(r) = -\frac{1}{2} \sum_i \nabla_i^2$$

$$T_n(R) = -\sum_A \frac{1}{2M_a} \nabla_i^2$$

$$V_{en}(r,R) = -\sum_{i,A} \frac{Z_A}{|r_i - R_A|}$$

$$V_{ee}(r) = \frac{1}{2} \sum_{i \neq j} \frac{1}{|r_i - r_j|}$$

$$V_{nn}(R) = \frac{1}{2} \sum_{A \neq B} \frac{Z_A Z_B}{|R_A - R_B|}$$

In these expressions, i and j refer to electrons, A and B to nuclei; R_A and r_i refer to the spatial coordinates of nucleus A and electron i, respectively; and Z_A and M_A are the charge and mass of nucleus A. The unsubscripted symbols r and R refer to the complete set of position vectors of the electrons and nuclei, respectively. Since the nuclei are about 1836 times more massive than the electrons, and therefore move much more slowly, it is common to invoke the Born–Oppenheimer approximation to separate the nuclear and electronic portions of the problem. Since the nuclei are essentially fixed in space relative to the electrons, the T_n term drops out and the V_{nn} term becomes a simple constant. The result is referred to as the *electrostatic Hamiltonian*, and, per equation (7.1), when this operator is applied to the electronic wavefunction, it gives the (scalar) electronic energy of the molecular system. Other areas of computational chemistry deal with other forms of the Schrödinger equation or with other equations entirely. Quantum dynamics methods generally start from the time-dependent Schrödinger equations, and the nuclear portion of the Hamiltonian and wavefunction are considered together with the electronic part. Molecular dynamics, on the other hand, uses a simplified "ball-and-spring" model of the molecule in which the interactions among the atoms are treated classically, and the positions of the atoms are evolved in time according to the computed forces and Newton's Laws.

The Schrödinger equation cannot be solved exactly for more than two electrons; however, it (or more commonly certain approximations) can be evaluated numerically. Numerical solution of the Schrödinger equation begins with the choice of a basis. The common choice in molecular quantum chemistry is to use 3-D Gaussian functions. These functions are usually (but not necessarily) chosen to mimic the *atomic orbital* (AO) description of atomic structure used in chemistry and physics. That is, basis functions are centered on atoms and have shapes and shell structure like the atomic *s*, *p*, *d*, etc. orbitals. A complete (infinite) basis would span all of space and thus allow an exact description of the wavefunction. In practice, however, computational resources place limits on the size of the basis that may be employed, and it is necessary to compromise between the cost of the calculation and the accuracy required. Evaluation of the Hamiltonian operator over the basis functions results in matrix elements or integrals, the most numerous of which ($\mathcal{O}(N^4)$ for N basis functions) are the two-electron integrals arising from the V_{ee} term,

$$(\mu\nu|\lambda\sigma) = \int \chi_\mu(r_1)\,\chi_\nu(r_1)\,\frac{1}{|r_1 - r_2|}\,\chi_\lambda(r_2)\,\chi_\sigma(r_2)\,d^3r_1\,d^3r_2 \tag{7.2}$$

where r_1 and r_2 are the positions of the two electrons, and the $\{\chi_\mu(r)\}$ are the basis functions.

Thus far, we have said nothing about the mathematical form of the electronic wavefunction. In molecular quantum chemistry, the usual approach is to make a "one-electron approximation," which says that we can represent the total wavefunction of the molecule as a simple product of functions representing individual electrons within the molecule. These *molecular orbitals* are represented by linear combinations of the original atomic orbital basis functions. The molecular orbitals are calculated by the Hartree–Fock self-consistent field method, and this model corresponds to the qualitative ideas about molecular orbitals often used by chemists and taught beginning at the general chemistry level. The SCF approach is at the heart of molecular quantum chemistry. It is also the basis of *semi-empirical* methods, in which instead of being computed outright, integrals are approximated by much simpler phenomenological expressions that are parameterized based on experimental data.

The SCF procedure provides a very useful qualitative description of molecules, but it is generally inadequate for quantitative applications requiring high accuracy. The method considers each electron in the *average* field of all others, which ignores the fact that the motion of each electron is instantaneously correlated with all others (due to the Pauli exclusion principle). When higher accuracy is required, it is necessary to go beyond the one-electron approximation and treat correlation effects in the system. This is usually formulated in terms of the interaction between different "configurations" of a set of one-electron functions. The SCF one-electron orbitals are used as a starting point, but electrons are placed in them in different ways. Each distinct way of placing electrons in the orbitals is a configuration, and the interaction energies between configurations can be evaluated numerically, leading to an expression for the energy and wavefunction corresponding to the particular correlated method. There are numerous correlated methods with different levels of sophistication and complexity. The interested reader may wish to refer to the classic text by Szabo and Ostlund [906] for a more in-depth presentation of the material sketched in this section and for further pointers to the classic quantum chemistry literature.

NWChem is one of many codes in this area of computational chemistry. It implements the SCF method and a number of correlated methods, as well as molecular dynamics and a variety of related methods targeted to periodic systems (i.e., solids) as opposed to isolated molecules. Because it focused from the start on parallelism and its relatively recent development, it serves as an excellent example of the current state of the art in high-performance computational chemistry software.

7.2   The NWChem Architecture

In order to meet the original goals of the project, the initial NWChem development team recognized that NWChem would be a fast-growing code, in which ease of development (a short learning curve) and the ability to rapidly prototype algorithms would be critical to its success. Consequently, we chose a highly structured approach to the design of the package, using object-oriented (OO) design throughout [96]. In deference to the fact that relatively few chemists have experience with truly object-oriented languages, we chose to implement the OO design of NWChem in a combination of Fortran77 and C. Since these languages do not provide the kind of enforcement mechanisms that are built into OO languages, such an approach relies on the developers themselves to enforce the OO design, but overall we have found it to be quite effective. Newcomers to the code who are unfamiliar with OO design concepts can easily pick up the basics required to work successfully in the NWChem environment, and they are quickly productive since they can work in familiar languages.

Figure 7.1 provides a schematic representation of the overall architecture of NWChem. The bottom two layers depict some of the fundamental tasks that NWChem can do (compute an energy or a gradient, perform Newtonian dynamics, etc.) and some of the chemistry methods with which these tasks can be carried out (i.e., MP2, SCF, and DFT). These are the two layers most directly visible to the NWChem user; the remaining modules constitute the environment or "umbrella" that allows for (relatively) easy parallel implementation of the various chemistry methods and tasks. On the left are modules that "know something about" chemistry, in other words, those providing basic objects needed for chemical calculations. On the right are modules that provide the computational infrastructure for NWChem: the parallel programming environment, parallel I/O support, and so on. While most of these modules were developed in conjunction with NWChem, they are not specific to chemistry applications. Most are freely available separately from NWChem and have been adopted by other software developers both inside and outside of chemistry.

At the heart of the NWChem programming environment is the Global Array parallel programming model, which provides the developer with the appearance of a global shared-memory environment in a portable fashion. This important component of the NWChem umbrella is described in greater detail below, along with the PeIGS parallel eigensolver. Many other components of the NWChem programming environment are relatively straightforward conveniences with the important

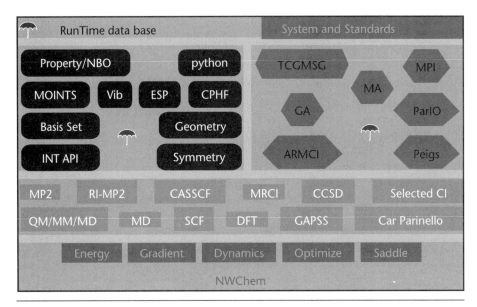

Figure 7.1   The NWChem architecture representing general functionality within NWChem, which is built upon layers of other modules, tools, chemistry APIs, and computational and computer science standards. The link between NWChem and Ecce is a loosely coupled interface. The umbrella symbol identifies some of the software described in this section.

function of facilitating general, portable, and rapid development of computational chemistry software. For example, MA is a portable memory allocator, implementing both stack and heap memory management models, which provides equal access to objects from both Fortran and C code. It also provides support for debugging and verification (especially detecting array overwriting and memory leaks). The run-time database (RTDB) provides a simple mechanism to allow the storage of name/value pairs (values can be of the basic Fortran data types, including 1-D arrays; other modules may provide convenience routines to read/write more complex data structures to the RTDB in an opaque fashion) that NWChem uses to communicate information between high-level modules and also as persistent storage between related jobs. The ParIO module is an abstraction layer that provides the user with three types of files:

- *Disk-resident arrays* (DRAs) are a simple means of providing secondary storage for global arrays, the distributed arrays provided by the global array toolkit. All operations are collective and are therefore open to additional optimizations on some parallel file systems.

- *Exclusive access files* (EAFs) are sets of process-private files that can be accessed independently. They are typically used for out-of-core computations that do not lend themselves to collective I/O operations and the use of DRAs.

- *Shared files* (SFs) are shared by all processes and can be read or written in noncollective fashion at any arbitrary location in the file.

The ParIO library is layered on top of a "device library," ELIO (for elementary I/O), which provides a portable interface to the file system and allows NWChem to take advantage of special high-performance I/O libraries that might be available on various platforms.

The chemistry-specific portion of the NWChem umbrella is similarly designed to facilitate the rapid development of chemistry software. Consistent with the object-oriented design philosophy used throughout NWChem, these modules typically expose well-defined application program interfaces (APIs) to provide the developer with access to all the information and functions of the object, while hiding the specific data structures. This helps protect the underlying data structures against manipulation (accidental or intentional) that does not conform to their API—an all-too-common occurrence in older, less well-structured chemistry software. Another distinction from older chemistry software is that, where appropriate, multiple instances of objects are supported. This allows the developer to, for example, refer explicitly to three different basis sets to be used in different aspects of a calculation by simple "handles" rather than error-prone manipulations of a single, monolithic, basis-set data structure. Two excellent examples in NWChem include the most fundamental chemical objects in quantum mechanical electronic-structure calculations are the definition of the molecular system (the "geometry" object in NWChem) and the basis set. The geometry object is a well-defined, extensible API that provides all the geometrical and atomic data for the molecular system under study (e.g., masses, atomic number, nuclear charges, coordinates, applied external fields, etc.). The basis set object is also a well-defined, extensible API that provides all the basis set functionality for all NWChem modules that utilize basis sets. The basis set object is interfaced to a library that contains a wide variety of published basis sets. The NWChem basis set library is periodically synchronized with the EMSL basis set library, which is available to the public via a Web interface [677]. Currently the NWChem library has 3762 Gaussian basis sets and 462 effective core potentials conveniently specified for the user community.

Other modules encapsulate various chemistry-specific computations used by the main chemistry methods rather than being invoked directly at the user level. Perhaps one of the most widely used within NWChem is the integral-evaluation module (*int api*). This module computes integrals of the (usually Gaussian) basis functions, possibly belonging to different basis sets, with various operators, an operation central to all quantum mechanical electronic structure methods. The module provides a uniform interface to five separate integral-evaluation codes with different capabilities and strengths. The choice of which method of integral evaluation to use is normally made within the module, based on details of the requested computation, but it can also be explicitly controlled by the software developer, or even by the NWChem user if the need arises. Because these codes are hidden behind a uniform interface, all modules that use the integral package can benefit immediately from the introduction of new methods and optimizations.

The NWChem umbrella modules are not set in stone. Although we tried to design from the start with the necessary flexibility and generality, inevitably there have been occasions that require existing objects to be modified or extended. In general, the most substantial changes have been extensions of functionality; rarely are significant changes required in existing application code. Implementation of new chemistry methods within NWChem will sometimes occasion the extension of the functionality of the existing umbrella or the development of new supporting modules. New modules are also sometimes created by abstracting the repeated use of the same or similar functionality in different places.

7.3   NWChem Parallel Computing Support

NWChem provides the user with a variety of tools for efficiency of calculation and ease of parallel model management. This section discusses the Global Array Toolkit, which is used to implement the Global Array programming model, and PeIGS, which is a parallel linear algebra library.

7.3.1   The Global Array Toolkit

The Global Array (GA) Toolkit [381, 710, 711] implements the primary parallel programming model used within NWChem, though traditional message passing is also available and is used as needed. GAs provide a portable shared-memory programming environment, which is implemented using native one-sided communications on distributed-memory systems and the common System V interface on true shared-memory systems. The shared-memory programming environment is important for two reasons. In the first place, it is much easier for the software developer to deal with, thus shortening the learning curve and facilitating development. Second, and more fundamentally, many sophisticated, highly scalable chemistry algorithms (and those in other fields) are extremely complex when written in message-passing form; others may be impossible to implement in the message-passing model because of the coordination required among processors.

Another important feature of the Global Array model is the fact that it explicitly exposes the memory hierarchy to the programmer. Specifically, global arrays distinguish between "local" and "remote" memory with difference latency and bandwidth characteristics. This is different from most shared-memory programming environments, in which all memory is presumed to have the same access characteristics, but we have found the distinction quite useful because it helps software developers create algorithms that work well on both distributed- and shared-memory systems. It is also easy to integrate this distinction into the nonuniform memory access (NUMA) hierarchy with which the most programmers are already familiar: registers, cache, local memory, remote memory, and so on. (Note that the disk-resident-array component of the ParIO module described above can be thought of as extending the hierarchy one more level, to disk storage.)

At the simplest level, the programming model using GA assumes that "remote" memory access is the rate-limiting step and that local memory access is much faster. Memory access using GA provides one-sided or asynchronous access to global data elements. Using the GA programming model, algorithms can be designed with knowledge of data locality that can be tuned for many different computational resources to essentially cover the worst-case scenario. This may require multiple algorithmic implementations to cover different ranges of bandwidth and latency. For example, suppose that one has two algorithms for a specific kernel in an application. The first algorithm has low latency requirements; the second algorithm can tolerate latency, but with a factor of four in computation. The second algorithm would likely be the mainstream choice to work on "all" machines. The first algorithm could be turned "on" after testing the viability on each system as the application is ported. This is obviously not limited to two algorithms.

Global arrays themselves are multidimensional arrays that are distributed among processors in blockwise fashion. The distribution can be completely specified by the programmer and may be regular or irregular, or a GA convenience routine can be used to quickly create a regular blocked distribution. Data may be accessed locally or remotely using block-oriented "put," "get," and "accumulate" functions. It is also possible for the programmer to inquire as to boundaries of the local block of a global array and to obtain direct access to the appropriate region of memory. This makes it convenient to write data-parallel operations using GAs. By knowing the locality of data, programmers can explicitly manage the nature of the memory hierarchy for their parallel algorithm. The operations mentioned above can be used in asynchronous or one-sided fashion by any processor. Other GA functions are collective, including creation and destruction of GAs, synchronization, and high-level linear algebra and convenience routines. The GA library also includes interfaces to a variety of external linear algebra libraries, including the PeIGS parallel eigensolver described below.

The Global Array Toolkit is implemented on top of the Aggregate Remote Memory Copy Interface (ARMCI) library [12, 708], developed jointly by researchers at the Pacific Northwest National Laboratory and the Northeast Parallel Architectures Center at Syracuse University. As the name suggests, this library provides general remote-memory-access capabilities through the use of one-sided messaging or true shared memory, according to the hardware on which it is used. From a performance viewpoint, one of the most important features of ARMCI is the ability to describe in a succinct way transfers that involve multiple noncontiguous blocks of memory and to aggregate such data automatically into a contiguous chunk before sending it over the wire and disaggregating it on the other side.

Although the primary focus of the design and development of the Global Array Toolkit has been to support NWChem, the model is suitable for a much broader range of applications (especially if it is combined with the normal message-passing model) and is freely distributed, separate from NWChem. It is not, however, suitable for all applications. General guidelines with respect to algorithmic design and usability imply that GA would be appropriate for applications

- with dynamic and irregular communication patterns
- with a need for one-sided access to shared data structures
- when data locality is important
- when a message-passing implementation is too complicated
- with a need for high-level operations on distributed arrays for out-of-core array–based algorithms
- where simulations are driven by dynamic load balancing
- when portable performance is important

GA is not necessarily appropriate for algorithms that

- have systolic or nearest-neighbor communications
- require synchronization and point-to-point message passing (e.g., Cholesky factorization)
- can be effectively parallelized using interprocedural analysis and compiler parallelization
- can use existing parallel constructs of a programming language, and robust compilers are available

GAs are being used in at least five other computational chemistry packages besides NWChem, and others have implemented similar models. It is also being used in a variety of other problem domains, including electron microscopy, geological simulations, astrophysics, parallel graphics rendering, computational fluid dynamics (CFD), financial modeling, and atmospheric chemistry. So far, it is the CFD application that is pushing GA the furthest beyond the functionality required to satisfy the chemistry community. Among the most significant requested additions are support for higher-dimensional arrays (now implemented), ghost cells around GA data blocks on individual processors, and sparse data structures [707].

7.3.2   Parallel Linear Algebra: PeIGS

PeIGS is a collection of commonly used linear algebra subroutines for computing the eigensystem of the real, standard, symmetric eigensystem problem $Ax = \lambda x$ and the general, symmetric eigensystem problem $Ax = \lambda Bx$. A and B are dense and real matrices, with B being positive definite. λ is an eigenvalue corresponding to the eigenvector x. PeIGS can also handle associated computations such as the Cholesky factorization of positive definite matrices in packed storage format and linear matrix equations involving lower and upper triangular matrices in distributed packed row or column storage.

The numerical algorithms implemented are "standard" (cf. [994] and [35]), with the exception of the subspace inverse iteration and reorthogonalization scheme for finding basis vectors for degenerate eigensubspaces [317, 318] and the Dhillon–Fann–Parlett algorithm for computing eigenvectors of a real symmetric tridiagonal matrix [262].

The current version of PeIGS has some unique features not found in any other eigensystem library:

- The Dhillon-Fann-Parlett inverse iteration algorithm
- Guaranteed orthonormal eigenvectors in the presence of large clusters of degenerate eigenvalues
- Packed storage for matrices
- Small scratch space requirements

The second feature is particularly important in quantum chemistry applications, where degenerate eigenvalues are common and orthogonality is critical.

The performance of PeIGS in sequential mode is impressive. Table 7.1 compares the current version of PeIGS with other standard solvers. The parallel performance of the three major components and the total time to solution are shown in Figure 7.2. The solution of the tridiagonal problem is scalable and fast; however, at this point, the Householder reduction and its back transform (i.e., producing the tridiagonal representation) is the identified bottleneck, accounting for over 90% of the serial performance of the solver and up to 65% at 128 nodes.

Internally, PeIGS uses the traditional message-passing programming model and a column-wrapped distribution of the matrices. PeIGS rearranges the columns into panel blocking in parts of the code for better performance. In NWChem the interface to PeIGS is hidden behind a GA-based API, where the necessary data reorganization is conveniently hidden from the application programmer. The data transformation from the GA-based global storage to that required for optimal PeIGS performance is very fast compared to the $\mathcal{O}(N^3/P)$ time required for the eigensolution operations.

Like the GA Toolkit, PeIGS is freely distributed, separately from NWChem, and can be used in other packages.

Table 7.1   Time for the solution of the tridiagonal matrix of rank 966 on a single IBM RS6000/590 processor.

Method	Time (s)
PeIGS 3.0	6
PeIGS 2.0	126
EISPACK	32
LAPACK: bisection + inverse iteration	112
LAPACK: QR	46
LAPACK: divide and conquer	20

NOTE: The tridiagonal matrix was generated via Householder reduction of the fitting basis set, overlap matrix from a resolution of the identity, second-order Møller-Plesset (RI-MP2) simulation of a fluorinated biphenyl [262].

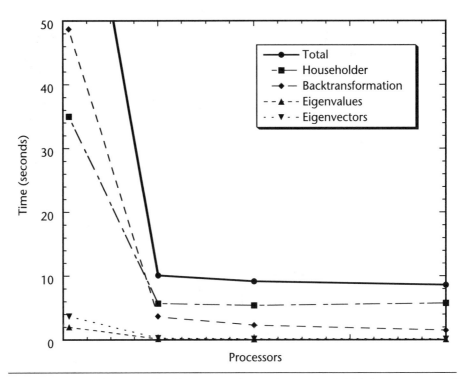

Figure 7.2   The performance of PeIGS using a tridiagonal matrix (rank 966) that was generated via Householder reduction of the fitting basis set, overlap matrix from an RI-MP2 simulation of a fluorinated biphenyl.

7.4   NWChem Chemistry Modules

NWChem implements a broad range of computational chemistry methods, emphasizing quantum-mechanics–based methods. There is insufficient space to describe all of them in detail, but I will provide a list of NWChem's current capabilities here and focus on a more detailed discussion of two methods: Hartree–Fock self-consistent field (SCF), and the resolution of the identity approximation to second-order, many-body perturbation theory (RI-MP2).

The following quantum mechanical methods are available to calculate energies and analytic first derivatives with respect to atomic coordinates. Second derivatives are computed by finite differences of the first derivatives.

- SCF or Hartree–Fock (RHF, UHF, high-spin ROHF). Code to compute analytic second derivatives is being tested.

- Gaussian-orbital–based density functional theory (DFT), using many local and nonlocal exchange-correlation potentials (RHF and UHF) with formal $\mathcal{O}(N^3)$ and $\mathcal{O}(N^4)$ scaling.

- MP2, including semi-direct using frozen core and RHF or UHF reference.
- Complete active-space SCF (CASSCF).

The following methods are available to compute energies only. First and second derivatives are computed by finite differences of the energies.

- CCSD(T), with RHF reference.
- Selected CI with second-order perturbation correction.
- MP2 fully direct with RHF reference.
- Resolution of the identity integral approximation MP2 (RI-MP2), with RHF and UHF reference (analytic first derivatives are being implemented).

For all methods, the following operations may be performed:

- Single point energy.
- Geometry optimization (minimization and transition state).
- Molecular dynamics on the fully *ab initio* potential energy surface.
- Numerical first and second derivatives automatically computed if analytic derivatives are not available.
- Normal mode vibrational analysis in Cartesian coordinates.
- Generation of an electron density file for graphical display.
- Evaluation of static, one-electron properties.
- Electrostatic potential fit of atomic partial charges (CHELPG method with optional RESP restraints or charge constraints).

In addition, interfaces are provided to:

- The COLUMBUS multireference CI package.
- The natural bond orbital (NBO) package.
- Python scripting language.
- The POLYRATE package for the computation of chemical reaction rates.

The following modules are available to compute the energy, minimize the geometry, and perform *ab initio* molecular dynamics using pseudopotential plane-wave DFT with local exchange-correlation potentials: fixed step–length steepest descent, and Car-Parinello (extended Lagrangian dynamics), with

- LDA and LSDA exchange-correlation potentials.
- (*G* point) periodic orthorhombic simulation cells.
- Hamann and Troullier–Martins norm-conserving pseudopotentials.
- Modules to convert between small and large plane-wave expansions.

A module (Gaussian Approach to Polymers, Surfaces and Solids, GAPSS) is available to compute energies by periodic Gaussian-based DFT with many local and nonlocal exchange-correlation potentials.

The following classical, molecular-simulation functionality is available:

- Single configuration energy evaluation.

- Energy minimization.

- Molecular dynamics simulation.

- Free energy simulation (multistep thermodynamic perturbation (MSTP) or multiconfiguration thermodynamic integration (MCTI) methods with options of single and/or dual topologies, double-wide sampling, and separation-shifted scaling).

NWChem also has the capability to combine classical and quantum descriptions in order to perform:

- Mixed quantum-mechanics and molecular-mechanics (QM/MM) energy minimization and molecular dynamics simulation.

- Quantum-molecular dynamics simulation by using any of the quantum mechanical methods capable of returning gradients.

The classical force field includes:

- Effective pair potentials (functional form used in AMBER, GROMOS, CHARMM, etc.).

- First-order polarization.

- Self-consistent polarization.

- Smooth particle mesh Ewald (SPME).

- Twin range energy and force evaluation.

- Periodic boundary conditions.

- SHAKE constraints.

- Consistent temperature and/or pressure ensembles.

7.4.1   Hartree–Fock Self-Consistent Field

The Hartree–Fock self-consistent field module is an essential functionality for NWChem or any quantum chemistry package. The NWChem SCF module and associated gradient module compute energies, wavefunctions, and gradients for closed-shell restricted Hartree–Fock (RHF), restricted high-spin, open-shell Hartree–Fock (ROHF), and spin-unrestricted Hartree–Fock (UHF). The algorithms are designed to use the aggregate memory available on the parallel supercomputer or cluster.

The construction of the Fock matrix is the most time-consuming part of any SCF calculation [439, 1004] and is iterated until the wavefunction reaches self-consistency. The "Fock build" provides an interesting illustration of the form that parallelism often takes in computational chemistry. The most computationally demanding part of the Fock matrix is defined by

$$F_{\mu\nu} \leftarrow D_{\lambda\sigma} \{2(\mu\nu|\lambda\sigma) - (\mu\lambda|\nu\sigma)\}$$

where D is the density matrix, and the $(\mu\nu|\lambda\sigma)$ are the two-electron integrals. See equation (7.2).

The cost of the Fock build scales with the number of integrals, which is formally $\mathcal{O}(N^4)$ for N basis functions. The NWChem SCF module was designed with a goal of 10,000 basis functions, so that the Fock and density matrices would be $10,000 \times 10,000$ and the number of two-electron integrals is formally 10^{16} (neglecting permutational symmetries of the indices and other factors).

Evaluation of the integrals occurs in irregular blocks, according to details of the basis set structure, so that a block may contain anything from a single integral to 10,000 integrals or more. The cost of each block is also highly variable and can only be crudely estimated in advance; it averages 500 FLOPs per integral value. Their cost, combined with permutational symmetries among indices, makes it most efficient to drive the Fock build with a loop over the unique integrals, making the four different contributions dictated by those symmetries at one time rather than duplicating integral evaluation. In NWChem, integral evaluation is dynamically distributed across the processors (controlled by an atomic read-and-increment counter) without regard to the distribution of the global arrays containing the density and Fock matrices. Each processor fetches into a local buffer the four patches of the density matrix it needs to contract with the integral block it has been assigned; it puts the results into another set of local buffers, which are accumulated into the proper places in the Fock matrix global array when the integral block is completed. To minimize communications, multiple integral blocks are aggregated into parallel tasks (maintaining roughly 100 tasks per processor to ensure load balance), and intelligent caching is used to avoid unnecessary communications for density and Fock matrix patches. Because of the irregular distribution, dimensions, and timings of the parallel tasks when programming the Fock build using message passing, this algorithm would be extremely challenging to implement in a message-passing environment, requiring synchronization between sender and receiver [363]. However, using the one-sided communications of the GA model, it is straightforward; and the fact that the NUMA nature of the parallel processor is exposed to the programmer leads to the aggregation of integral blocks and the use of intelligent caching, both of which provide significant performance gains.

The integrals do not change from one iteration of the SCF algorithm to the next and may be stored or recomputed. Many SCF codes offer either "conventional" or "direct" modes, in which the integrals are either stored on disk and reused or are recomputed every iteration (the relative efficiency of these two approaches depends on both hardware performance factors and the particular molecule and basis set). NWChem provides a more flexible "semi-direct" algorithm, which includes memory as well as disk storage, and can span the entire range from fully disk- (or memory-)

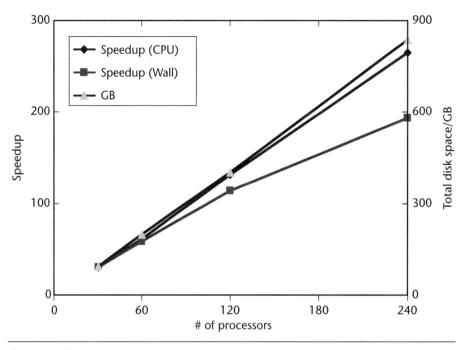

Figure 7.3   The scaling of the semi-direct SCF module for a modified crown-ether system on an IBM SP, 160 MHz nodes, 512 MB memory per node, and 3 GB of disk per node. 15 MB/sec/node sustained-read bandwidth was achieved.

based to full recomputation according to available disk and memory space, or directly under user control. In addition to the fully distributed Fock build, a replicated data algorithm (Fock and density matrices replicated, integral evaluation distributed across the machine) is also implemented to take advantage of those situations where available memory and the molecule under study allow this approach. The convergence algorithm is the quadratic SCF [1004] with both preconditioning and line-search mechanisms built in.

Figure 7.3 shows the speedup obtained for a modified crown-ether complex running on an IBM SP system using the semi-direct algorithm and taking advantage of the local secondary storage on the system. The 105-atom system, shown in Figure 7.4, has 1342 basis functions, and the calculation was completed in 5.7 hours on 240 nodes (160 MHz).

7.4.2   Resolution of the Identity Second-Order, Many-Body Perturbation Theory

This method (RI-MP2) is the result of applying the so-called resolution-of-the-identity (RI) integral approximation [331, 558, 948] to the traditional second-order, many-body perturbation theory method [437], often abbreviated MP2. MP2 is the simplest method to include the effects of dynamic electron correlation, which are

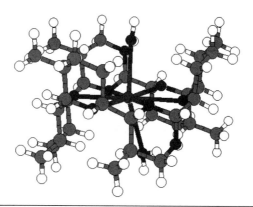

Figure 7.4 The modified crown-ether system, with 105 atoms, 1343 basis functions using the Dunning augmented cc-pVDZ basis set, and 362 electrons.

important to the proper description of many chemical phenomena, and it is also the most widely used correlated method. MP2 calculations can be systematically improved by going to higher orders of perturbation theory or to coupled cluster methods [437].

The MP2 energy can be simply expressed (in spin orbital form), as

$$E^{(2)} = \frac{1}{2} \sum_{i,j,a,b} \frac{(ia|jb)\left[(ia|jb) - (ib|ja)\right]}{\epsilon_i + \epsilon_j - \epsilon_a - \epsilon_b} \tag{7.3}$$

with the $\{\epsilon_p\}$ being the SCF orbital energies. The integrals are the same as in the SCF method, but transformed from the original "atomic orbital" (AO) basis to the "molecular orbital" (MO) basis that is one of the products of the SCF calculation. Given the MO basis integrals, the energy expression above costs $\mathcal{O}(N^4)$ to evaluate, but the transformation of the integrals from the AO to MO basis has a cost of $\mathcal{O}(N^5)$, which dominates the calculation.

The RI approximation represents the two-electron integrals in the form [948]

$$(pq|rs) = \sum_{\Delta, \Phi} (pq|\Delta) \, V_{\Delta\Phi}^{-1} (\Phi|rs) \tag{7.4}$$

involving three-center two-electron integrals

$$(pq|\Delta) = \int \phi_p(r_1) \, \phi_q(r_1) \, \frac{1}{|r_1 - r_2|} \, \alpha_\Phi(r_2) \, d^3r_1 \, d^3r_2 \tag{7.5}$$

and two-center two-electron integrals

$$V_{\Delta\Phi} = \int \alpha_\Delta(r_1) \, \frac{1}{|r_1 - r_2|} \, \alpha_\Phi(r_2) \, d^3r_1 \, d^3r_2$$

where uppercase Greek indices denote functions from a "fitting basis" introduced by this approximation. Essentially, the fitting basis $\{\alpha_\Delta(r)\}$ is used to approximate the product space of the AO basis ($\{\phi_i(r) \, \phi_j(r)\}$). To obtain the RI-MP2 energy [99, 331], equation (7.4) is simply substituted into the MP2 energy expression, equation (7.3).

$$E^{(2)} = \frac{1}{2} \sum_{i,j,a,b,\Delta,\Phi} \frac{(ia|\Delta)\, V_{\Delta\Phi}^{-1}\, (\Phi|jb) \left[(ia|\Delta)\, V_{\Delta\Phi}^{-1}\, (\Phi|jb) - (ib|\Delta)\, V_{\Delta\Phi}^{-1}\, (\Phi|ja) \right]}{\epsilon_i + \epsilon_j - \epsilon_a - \epsilon_b}.$$

The RI approximation has several important strengths. Most obviously, it replaces a fourth-rank tensor (two-electron integrals) with a combination of third- and second-rank quantities, dramatically reducing the volume of data that must be computed, stored, and manipulated. Second, as the AO basis set gets larger (for a fixed molecule), the product space will be increasingly redundant, making it possible to (nearly) span the space with a fitting set that is smaller in relative terms. In a sense, the RI approximation could be said to "take advantage of" the use of large basis sets.

RI-MP2 calculations occur in two steps: the integral transformation, followed by the energy evaluation [99, 97]. The general form of the integral transformation can be written as

$$(ai|\Delta') = (ai|\Delta)\, V_{\Delta\Phi}^{-\frac{1}{2}} = C_{\mu a}\, C_{vi}\, (\mu v|\Delta)\, V_{\Delta\Phi}^{-\frac{1}{2}}$$

where the indices μ and v represent the AO basis and C is the SCF eigenvector matrix, which defines the transformation from AOs to MOs. The $V^{-\frac{1}{2}}$ term comes from rewriting equation (7.4) in a symmetric form that further simplifies integral handling, as first suggested by Rendell and Lee [796]. This step requires $\mathcal{O}(N^4)$ operations, as opposed to the $\mathcal{O}(N^5)$ for the exact MP2 transformation. The first two transformation steps ($C_{\mu a}$ and C_{vi}) are handled, in succession, locally to each processor. The fitting basis index is distributed across processors, so that each node generates AO integrals for all μ and v and a subset of Δ. In order to make the matrix multiplications more efficient, the integral blocks are aggregated in a local buffer sized according to the available memory before the two transformations are applied. The results are accumulated into a global array with ai as the combined row index and Δ as the column index, distributed in the same fashion as the integral evaluation loop (making the accumulate a local operation). The third transformation step is carried out as a parallel matrix multiplication (ga_dgemm) of the GA just produced with another GA holding $V^{-\frac{1}{2}}$ (computed using GA and PeIGS routines). If there is insufficient total memory available to complete the entire transformation in a single pass, multiple passes are made based on the i index.

The primary data structure of the energy evaluation phase is a fourth-rank tensor representing quantities like the (approximate) four-center, two-electron integral $(ia|jab)$. It is organized as a supermatrix with row and column indices i and j, each element of which is a complete matrix labeled by a and b. The calculation is performed as a loop over i and j, blocked according to available memory. All of the GAs of this type are distributed across the machine in regularly sized blocks. For given i and j blocks, the first step of the energy evaluation is to produce the approximate integrals $(ia|jb)$ according to equation (7.4). It is implemented straightforwardly by reading in blocks of transformed three-center integrals corresponding to the i

and j ranges required and multiplying them in parallel with *ga_dgemm* in a step costing $\mathcal{O}(N^5)$. Given the approximate $(ia|jb)$, the remaining operations (formation of $(ia|jb) - (ib|ja)$, application of denominators, and the evaluation of the actual energy contributions) are carried out almost entirely in data parallel fashion—each process working with the portion of the data that it "owns." As in the exact MP2, these remaining operations cost $\mathcal{O}(N^4)$.

The RI-MP2 method illustrates a different use of the GA Toolkit than the SCF algorithm described above. The RI-MP2 integral transformation uses many of the same concepts as the Fock build, but in this case constitutes a small portion of the computational effort. The dominant cost in the RI-MP2 calculation is a simple call to the GA matrix multiplication routine. The remainder of the calculation involves mostly data parallel operations implemented variously with standard GA calls, as adaptations of standard GA routines specific to this application, or built from the lower-level utility routines provided by the GA Toolkit.

Figure 7.5 shows the parallel speedup of a large RI-MP2 calculation on an IBM RS/6000 SP parallel computer (120 MHz Power2 Super CPU, 512 MB RAM, 5 GB local scratch disk per node) [97]. The calculations were part of a study of the relative energetics of the four conformations of tetramethoxycalix[4]arene (Figure 7.6) [703],

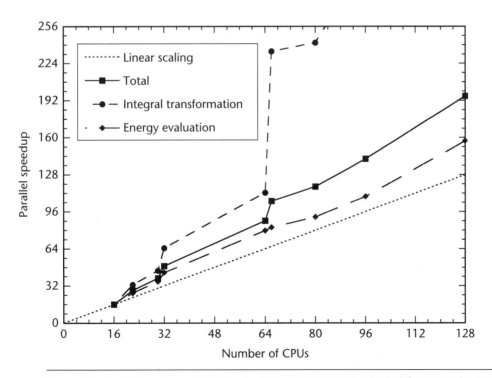

Figure 7.5 Parallel speedup of RI-MP2 calculations on tetramethoxycalix[4]arene on the IBM RS/6000 SP computer [97]. All speedups are referenced to the 16-node timings.

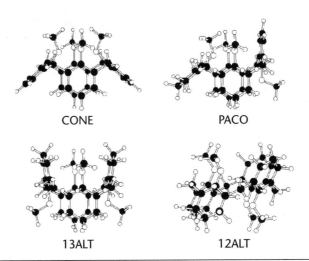

CONE   PACO

13ALT   12ALT

Figure 7.6   The four conformations of tetramethoxycalix[4]arene [703]. The molecule is composed of four anisoles linked at the meta position by methylene bridges, and conformations differ in the relative orientation of the anisoles.

in which this 68-atom molecule was treated with a modified aug-cc-pVTZ AO basis (just cc-pVTZ on the hydrogens) and the corresponding aug-cc-pVTZ-fit2-1 (cc-pVTZ-fit2-1 on H) fitting basis (2460 AO basis functions, 8260 fitting functions) [100, 302]. The total wall-clock time for the RI-MP2 calculation ranged from 55.6 hours on 16 nodes to 4.7 hours on 128 nodes. The overall scaling is quite good—the line is fairly straight and at 128 nodes shows no sign of saturation. The jumps in the curve are clearly associated with jumps in the integral transformation speedup. The overall speedup is uniformly at or above the "ideal" linear speedup line, primarily due to the fact that as the graph is presented, the 16-node calculation is implicitly assumed to be 100% efficient. If the actual efficiency (<100%) at 16 nodes were known, it would shift the entire curve downward. The apparently extraordinary speedup of the transformation arises from the fact that for 16 nodes (the reference point) the algorithm is forced to make five passes through the integrals to complete the transformation. As more nodes are added, the algorithm uses the additional memory as well as the CPU, so that the number of passes required drops to one by 66 nodes.

7.5   NWChem's Place in the Computational Chemistry Community

The primary goal of NWChem was to improve the performance and capability of computational chemistry tools by focusing on the development of scalable parallel algorithms and implementations. But of course this work did not take place in a vacuum—there are numerous other software packages, both sequential and parallel, that have some overlap with the functionality provided by NWChem. The development of NWChem began in 1993, in an environment in which the chemistry community had for some years been experimenting with parallelism, but vector computing was the norm and there was little or no use of parallelism in "production" computational chemistry. The prior experimentation had been based primarily on message-passing programming models. It showed that using parallel computers in chemistry was possible, but not easy, and had produced few enduring (i.e., scalable) algorithms.

NWChem was then, and remains today, one of the very few codes in the chemistry community designed from scratch for parallelism—in most other packages, parallelism has been included as a retrofit to existing code. This is understandable given the tremendous investment that has been put into many widely used packages over many years. (It has been estimated that more than 100 person-years of effort have gone into NWChem [301], which is still a fairly young code in this community.) On the other hand, our experience with NWChem suggests that highly scalable algorithms can be significantly different from the traditional sequential algorithms, so that "retrofit parallel" codes are generally rather limited in scalability compared to "designed parallel" codes unless the developers are willing to make more extensive changes. There is a significant gap between the size of leading-edge MPPs, which NWChem is specifically intended to exploit, and the class of parallel machines that are routinely available to researchers at a research group, department, or campus level; indeed, even state or national supercomputer centers often operate their systems to accommodate the greatest number of users or greatest throughput at the expense of being able to run the most demanding jobs with a reasonable turnaround. This, together with the extra effort typically required to obtain the best possible performance, may explain why many developers of parallel chemistry codes accept lower levels of scalability, which are nevertheless sufficient for the machines to which they have access.

Although parallel computing in this community is still far from universal, one can now find multiple parallel implementations of virtually every important method in computational chemistry and see them being used routinely in a "production" context by researchers who would not claim to be experts in parallel computing. Many factors have contributed to this transition. I believe that the principal contributions of the NWChem project in this respect have been twofold:

- It has served as a demonstration of what is possible in terms of scalability, and the types of algorithms required to achieve it.

- In the Global Array Toolkit, it has offered an efficient, easy-to-use programming model that is well suited to the expression of scalable chemistry algorithms.

It is worth noting that parallelism is not the only way to increase performance of chemical computations. In recent years, there has been significant research activity on techniques that take advantage of the size of the molecular systems that can now be treated computationally to reduce the cost of the calculation, typically by replacing some of the longer-range interactions with simpler approximations. The previously described RI-MP2 method is one example of the numerous approaches. Others often include phrases such as "linear scaling," "$\mathcal{O}(N)$," "pseudospectral," "local correlation" and "multipole expansion" in their names or descriptions. These approaches can in principle yield much greater performance improvements than can be obtained from parallelism because in some cases they can actually reduce the computational complexity of the problem in an asymptotic sense—in other words, for suitably large molecules, where "large" depends both on the computational method and characteristics of the molecule. However, no single "fast" method will provide the desired performance improvement across the entire computational chemistry problem space, and all such methods depend in some fashion on the molecule being large enough that the approximations introduced do not destroy the overall accuracy and reliability of the calculation. Therefore, "fast" methods should be viewed as complementing parallelism rather than competing with it; they are being implemented in sequential and parallel codes alike.

7.6   A Larger Perspective: Common Features of Computational Chemistry Algorithms

The two NWChem methods described earlier were chosen as examples of different patterns of use of the parallel programming environment in NWChem. In the Hartree–Fock case, task-based parallelism and dynamic distribution of those tasks are the key features. This is characteristic of algorithms that compute and (directly) process the two-electron integrals such as equation (7.2) or (7.5). Density functional theory and the transformation step in higher-level methods such as MP2 (including RI-MP2), coupled cluster theory, and configuration interaction methods are other examples of where this pattern is used.

In the RI-MP2 example, task-based parallelism is used in the transformation step, but the bulk of the work is done in parallel linear algebra calls and in essentially data-parallel (or "owner computes") code using GAs. This pattern is seen in some of the higher-level methods, where, after the required integrals are evaluated and processed (usually task-based), one is left with a number of large data structures, typically tensors of rank 4 or higher, which must be contracted in various ways and otherwise manipulated. Some other methods, such as electronic structure codes using a regular grid of plane-wave basis functions instead of Gaussians, also lead to algorithms that are predominantly data parallel plus linear algebra (in this case a 3-D FFT).

The importance of task-based parallelism comes from the irregular nature of most quantum mechanical calculations employing Gaussian basis sets. The basis functions are usually associated with the individual atoms rather than being laid out on a regular grid. Both the number and type of basis functions will vary with the atom, reflecting some basic concepts of atomic structure. This gives rise to the tremendous range of sizes and times involved in the evaluation of integrals over these basis functions, as described in Section 7.4.1, and the need for dynamic load balancing.

The irregular and dynamic nature of these computations is also what makes the shared-memory aspect of the programming model so important to the development of fully distributed data-parallel algorithms in chemistry. Message-passing models and others that implicitly synchronize communicating processes can be used in these types of algorithms, but they make the task much more complex and error prone and they can represent a significant hurdle to producing *scalable* algorithms [363]. Of course in data-parallel algorithms, the choice between message passing and shared memory becomes a lot less important. In NWChem, the majority of methods have both task- and data-parallel portions, and the shared-memory model provided by the Global Array Toolkit is convenient to use throughout. However, some methods, such as the plane-wave density functional theory module referred to above, are almost entirely data parallel and use message passing throughout. As mentioned before, the Global Array model is meant to complement message passing, not to exclude it, so this is quite natural.

Linear algebra has historically played a significant and interesting role in the development of chemistry software. In the chemistry domain, a great deal of computational effort goes into *producing* the matrix that is fed into a linear algebra code—quite often it is the production of the matrix (or subsequent processing of the linear algebra result) that is the computational bottleneck, not the linear algebra itself. In some cases, the nature of the chemical problem imposes requirements that "standard" linear algebra packages don't meet or allows optimizations they don't support. Historically, concerns about efficiency and data structures suitable to chemical applications were not always satisfied by standard linear algebra packages. As a result of all of these facts, it used to be quite common in the chemistry community for software developers to produce their own linear algebra routines as well, either by adapting them from existing libraries or creating them from scratch.

With the rise of vector computing, chemists began to recognize the performance advantages of replacing their own linear algebra routines with standard libraries, which computer vendors had an incentive to optimize for their platforms, such as BLAS, EISPACK, LINPACK, and later LAPACK. The general wisdom within the community came to be that algorithms should be couched in terms of standard linear algebra library routines wherever possible, at least for "simple" things such as BLAS, direct linear equation solvers, and eigensolvers. (Iterative solvers, in methods that require them, are still often "hand crafted.") The BLAS library has been particularly influential in the evolution of algorithms in chemistry. The "discovery" by chemists of the BLAS, particularly the level-3 matrix multiplication (xGEMM) routines, led to efforts to recast algorithms in terms of matrix multiplication operations wherever possible, and this has become the accepted wisdom in the field. Such codes benefit not only from the performance of the (often, optimized) BLAS routines themselves, but also from the fact that structuring the equations and code to make maximum use of the matrix-multiply kernel tends to result in better cache utilization outside of the BLAS routines as well.

Nevertheless, standard numerical libraries cannot satisfy all needs of the chemistry community, particularly with the move toward parallel computing, where linear algebra tools are not yet as mature as sequential libraries were when the chemistry community finally adopted them. Parallel eigensolvers are a particular example. The traditional implementation of a number of fundamental quantum chemistry methods (e.g., SCF and DFT) involves repeated diagonalization of a matrix until the iterative process reaches self-consistency. Overall, the cost of these methods scale with the fourth power of the problem size, while the diagonalization portion scales with the third power. However, at the time development of NWChem was begun, the state of the art in eigensolvers did not provide very good parallel scalability, and this portion of the calculation rapidly became the performance bottleneck on large parallel machines. The eigensolvers available at the time suffered from other problems as well. For example, they did not always provide strongly orthogonal eigenvectors and didn't easily handle situations with large clusters of degenerate eigenvalues, both of which are important in chemical applications. This has led some to develop new "diagonalization-free" methods, or to fall back on known but little-used alternative algorithms that avoid the eigenproblem as much as possible.

In the case of NWChem, we were able to take a unique twofold approach. In designing the first module implemented in NWChem, the Hartree–Fock method described in Section 7.4.1, we adopted a "quadratically convergent" algorithm, which requires only an initial and final diagonalization and elsewhere uses matrix exponentiation, instead of the traditional approach, which involves diagonalization for every iteration. At the same time, because the development team included not only chemists, but also computer scientists and numerical analysts working in close collaboration, we were able to launch a research effort to address the problems with parallel eigensolvers, which led to the PeIGS package described in Section 7.3.2. As a result, when later we began development of the density functional theory module, sufficient progress had been made on the eigensolver problem that we felt performance would be acceptable using the traditional repeated diagonalization algorithm, and we did not need to undertake the development of a DFT equivalent to the quadratically convergent SCF method.

The SCF and DFT methods are two examples where eigenproblems are prominent in the algorithms, at least in the traditional formulations of the problem, where they appear in the main iterative step of the algorithm. These methods generally use dense matrices and direct solvers, and they require all eigenvalues and eigenvectors. This kind of eigenproblem also crops up frequently in minor roles in a great many other quantum chemistry methods, and it is typically solved using libraries such as PeIGS, ScaLAPACK, LAPACK, and so on. A class of more sophisticated methods, known as configuration interaction (CI) methods, also revolve around eigensolvers, in this case iterative sparse solvers, where the interest is in a limited number of eigenpairs [869]. In these problems, the matrix-vector product required by the eigensolver is the most complex and time-consuming aspect of the calculation, and specialized data structures and storage formats supporting this aspect of the calculation usually mean that "off the shelf" library solvers are not suitable solutions. Large linear or nonlinear equations also play roles in a broad range of chemistry methods. Coupled cluster methods, similar in purpose and sophistication to the CI methods mentioned above, use a slightly different formulation of essentially the same problem and result in very large systems of nonlinear equations instead of CI's eigenproblem. As with CI, the evaluation of the matrix elements and the matrix-vector product, rather than the solver itself, is where the computational complexity lies, and the solvers tend to be relatively unsophisticated. As with eigenproblems, smaller linear and nonlinear equations also play minor roles in a great many chemical methods. Once again, for the smaller problems it is more common to use solvers from standard libraries. In codes like NWChem, there has also been some effort over time to standardize and generalize and reuse non–library solvers incorporated within the code rather than having multiple implementations. As might be expected, this process tends to start with the smaller or less important problems and work up to the larger, more prominent ones.

Sparsity, as manifested in most quantum chemistry methods, is based primarily on the distance between atoms but also depends on the details of the molecular system and the basis set. This means that a simple distance-only, "cut-off radius" does not provide a good guide as to sparsity. While the formal number of two-electron integrals (see equation (7.2)), for example, is $\mathcal{O}(N^4)$ for N basis functions, it has been shown that the actual number of nonzero values tends *asymptotically* to $\mathcal{O}((N \ln N)^2)$ [304]. However, even the largest calculations currently possible rarely reach this limit—in other words, they have more than $(N \ln N)^2$ nonzero integrals. Because basis sets are usually atom-centered and have a blocked structure on each atom, quantities such as the two-electron integrals also tend to have a blocked structure, although the size of blocks may vary over several orders of magnitude. This blocked structure is helpful to chemistry software developers, in that they can in most cases work with dense matrices and standard libraries (like the BLAS) rather than less-developed sparse matrix tools, which also tend not to make as efficient use of the memory hierarchy. A common technique is to use a local buffer to aggregate neighboring blocks into a matrix large enough to allow the CPU to obtain good performance, but small enough that it is possible to completely avoid processing large chunks of zeros. This approach is used, for example, in the integral transformation phase of the RI-MP2 computation. In some cases, particularly on parallel systems with programming environments such as Global Arrays, it is far simpler and more efficient to design the algorithm to process a large data object by making multiple passes with fully dense matrices sized according to the available memory. The RI-MP2 energy evaluation is an example of such an algorithm. Sparsity is more commonly used in disk storage of large data objects, although as mentioned in the discussion of the NWChem SCF, it is often possible to recompute certain values as fast or faster than retrieving them from disk storage. These so-called integral-direct techniques appear in many programs besides NWChem and many methods besides SCF. However, deciding a priori whether storage or recomputation will be more efficient in a particular case remains as much art and intuition as science because of the number of factors involved.

In addition to sparsity, many molecules have symmetry, which reduces the number of *unique* integrals because the symmetry properties of the atoms and the basis set are reflected in relationships among integrals and related values. Taking advantage of redundancies caused by symmetry can give a useful performance improvement, but it has a tendency to reduce the natural size of nonzero blocks and introduces relationships among values that might be far apart in either a geometrical or lexigraphical (based on their indices) sense. It is the latter factor in particular that represents the biggest hurdle to utilizing symmetry in parallel algorithms. Together with the fact that the larger a molecule is the less likely it is to possess any symmetry, many have found it easy to decide *not* to incorporate symmetry into their parallel implementations of computational chemistry methods. This was the decision made, for example, during the design of the RI-MP2 code described above.

7.7   Conclusion

I have presented an overview of NWChem as an example of the state of the art in a fully distributed, parallel computational chemistry software package. The GA programming model is at the heart of almost all of the parallel algorithms in NWChem, and parallel linear algebra libraries such as PeIGS have also proved extremely important, both for ease of development and performance. I have sketched the parallel algorithms behind two chemistry methods in NWChem, SCF and RI-MP2, which illustrate the importance of the GA programming model as well as its flexibility. Both methods have been demonstrated to be scalable to hundreds of processors and work efficiently on distributed-memory parallel systems, as have the other methods implemented in NWChem. I have also tried to provide a sense of NWChem's relationship with the larger computational chemistry community and describe in a more generic sense some of the notable features of computational problems in this domain.

The development of NWChem continues in conjunction with a variety of projects. Most of the work currently centers on extending and enhancing chemistry methods already in NWChem, and implementing new methods based on the needs of the user community. While the requirements of the chemistry have always been the primary driver for the development of NWChem's computational infrastructure, it is possible to suggest some of the ways that NWChem *might* change in the near future, from a computational viewpoint.

- First is increasing the use of scripting languages at the top levels of the package. The object-oriented scripting language Python [633, 782] is already incorporated into NWChem, so that Python scripts can be used to drive some calculations. An interface to the GAs has been created, and interfaces to other NWChem modules are under development. The use of scripting languages as (part of) the high-level control structure of a package like NWChem makes it easier for users to perform more complex calculations that would otherwise require unmaintainable "one-off" modifications to the source of NWChem itself.

- Second, with the recent release of version 3.0 of the GA Toolkit, general multidimensional arrays became available (previously, GA supported only 2-D arrays). Because they are new, they have not yet been used extensively in NWChem chemistry modules. However, they promise to be particularly useful in high-level correlated methods (perturbation theory and coupled cluster methods especially) where the primary data structures are tensors of rank 4 and 6. Expressing these data structures in their natural multidimensional form offers opportunities for the introduction of block-structured sparsity and automatic rearrangement of data to make tensor contractions more efficient.

- Third, with development tending to focus on more complex and sophisticated chemistry methods (especially CI and coupled cluster approaches) and adoption of the GA Toolkit by users from other fields, there is an increasing interest in extending the GA model to support sparsity. This could be in two basic forms: providing new objects and interfaces that support some of the common sparse data structures used in other fields, or retaining most of the current dense matrix interface, but internally using sparsity in storage and manipulation of the objects. The latter approach would obviously be a particularly convenient way to support many existing GA codes with better performance and efficiency; however, the first approach would probably allow codes from other domains to be ported to GAs more easily. Ultimately, both approaches will probably be used to varying extents.

- Finally, the current trend in large MPPs is a distributed-memory system composed of multiprocessor shared-memory nodes. While GAs can already take advantage of this type of system, the parallel algorithms in NWChem are not currently designed with explicit consideration of this new layer in the NUMA hierarchy—they assume that all memory not "local" is essentially equally "remote." One can imagine several different ways in which algorithms in NWChem might be adapted to incorporate this deeper memory hierarchy. It will be interesting to see which are most effective in terms of both performance and ease of development.

Acknowledgments. NWChem has been the work of more than 40 people since 1993 [440], under the leadership of the High Performance Computational Chemistry Group at the Pacific Northwest National Laboratory. I gratefully acknowledge their contributions to the experience described in this chapter. All opinions expressed in this chapter are mine alone and do not necessarily represent those of other NWChem developers.

The Pacific Northwest National Laboratory is a multiprogram laboratory operated by the Battelle Memorial Institute for the U.S. Department of Energy (DoE) under Contract DE-AC06-76RLO-1830, and the development of NWChem has been supported by the DoE's Office of Scientific Computing and Office of Health and Environmental Research. Work at Syracuse has also been supported by the Alex G. Nason Prize Fellowship.

Finally, I am grateful to George Fann, Rick Kendall, and Jarek Nieplocha, for their assistance with parts of this presentation.

8 Application Overviews

Geoffrey Fox

This chapter begins with a summary of the different application discussions, highlighting computational issues. Note that every discussion—whether one of the applications presented in the preceding chapters or one of the shorter notes to follow—is only a snapshot of a given field. Each article chooses a few interesting aspects of major research areas. We hope this cursory discussion will allow readers to find useful hints on ways to parallelize their applications or ways to test new computational science technologies. We encourage the reader to explore the citations for each section to get more detail.

Chapters 5, 6, and 7 contain case studies of applications in the areas of computational fluid dynamics, environment and energy, and computational chemistry, respectively. Additional applications can be found in Fox et al. [358] and Koniges [573]. Section 8.12 analyzes the computational structure of the 14 application areas in this book (Chapters 5–7 and Sections 8.1–8.11) from a common point of view. It follows with a similar analysis of the applications in [358] and [573]. This integrated analysis may help readers identify those applications of particular interest to them.

8.1 Numerical (General) Relativity
Geoffrey Fox

This field numerically solves the deceptively innocent equation proposed by Einstein in 1915:

$$G_{\mu\nu} = 8 \pi G T_{\mu\nu}$$

This equation expresses gravitation geometrically and relates the curvature of space-time (Einstein tensor $G_{\mu\nu}$) to the mass distribution (stress–energy tensor $T_{\mu\nu}$); the indices μ and ν run over four index values, corresponding to time and three spatial directions. The value of the gravitational constant, G, is extremely small, and this equation reduces to Newtonian dynamics, except in regions of extreme gravitational fields. This general theory has been tested in a few well-known cases (such as the bending of light in a stellar gravity field), but it has few direct verifiable consequences. Numerical study [69, 219, 352, 566, 653] is motivated by both intellectual curiosity (surely we must try to solve the fundamental macroscopic equations of science) and phenomenological value to new tests of the theory. Recently, both Europe and the United States have mounted major experiments to detect the gravity waves predicted by Einstein's equations. One expects binary black holes to be an important source of such waves. Binary black holes are expected to be the last hurrah of many double stars, as the insistently attractive force of gravity pulls their matter into an oblivion from which no information can escape. Einstein's equations can be solved analytically for single black holes in equilibrium, but currently only numerical methods can address two interacting black holes. This field represents the case, common in fundamental science, in which the challenge is a single very hard problem rather than complexity stemming from a coupling of many subproblems into a large system.

The equations treat space and time symmetrically and have a rather different structure from those coming from other fields simulating physical phenomena. One does get coupled partial differential equations, as in most fields studying the physical world, but they have many special features. These features both distinguish the field and put it outside most of the forefront research in the algorithm and applied mathematics community. Note that as the existence of wave solutions suggests, one can view Einstein's equations as "just" a complicated nonlinear version of Maxwell's equations. Correspondingly, electromagnetic systems are a useful test environment for some solution techniques. The following characteristics are particularly interesting:

1. There is total freedom in choosing the coordinate system, and the equations can change their nature dramatically if one uses this so-called gauge freedom. Some coordinate systems can lead to nondynamical singularities; "physical intuition" and a deep understanding of this field are needed to distinguish among "science," "numerical problems," and "coordinate system artifacts."

2. There are many formulations of the Einstein equations. In one formulation, the equations are set up as a constrained Hamiltonian system. This invokes classic time evolutions, with 12 equations (for the six components of the spatial metric, and its six momenta) with first-order time derivatives. These equations are nonlinear, and their characterization into hyperbolic, parabolic, or elliptic form depends on the coordinates chosen; some coordinate choices depend functionally on the field variables. There is an additional set of four equations (the constraints) describing the initial conditions. These represent a feasible elliptic subset of the full problem and have been successfully addressed numerically.

3. At large distances from the strong gravitational fields, one finds wavelike solutions that can be solved by expansion around the linear limit with a natural light-cone-coordinate choice. These waves are the experimental measurements, and this form represents the "boundary condition at infinity" needed by a solution in the interior region, where the strong fields probably require different coordinate choices.

4. Most distinctive is the interior boundary condition, which is optimally posed in terms of the remarkable physics of a black hole from which no information can escape. Translating this into numerically stable boundary conditions is not trivial. Physics implies that no information specified inside the black hole can propagate outside. The "event horizon" defines the true black hole surface and represents this information barrier. Since its location is unknown, one excises the singular region at the "apparent horizon," which always lies inside the black hole surface. Remarkably, physically interesting results have been obtained in a regime where no condition at the inner boundary (simple excision) is required.

The problem becomes a set of (12) field values defined on a 3-D spatial grid that has two holes excised—one for each of the black holes, cut off at the apparent horizon. At large distances, outgoing wave solutions are required. As the black holes move, this geometric structure changes. One is required to solve the equations in this geometry for given initial conditions and then to extract the gravitational wave structure as the black holes rotate around each other and eventually spiral into cosmic union. The unusual inner boundary conditions, nonlinear equations, and well-known difficulties involving numerical propagation of waves without dissipation all contribute to the numerical challenge.

8.1.1 Current Situation

As with computational electromagnetics, one can look at several solution approaches—finite difference, finite element, and spectral methods. Currently the finite difference method has gathered the most attention, although this is not the most convenient at the inner boundary conditions. Remember that spectral methods (the method of moments) produced the first reliable results in the computational electromagnetism domain. A large Grand Challenge Binary Black Hole (BBH) project recently ended [220, 654]; although much important progress was made, it did not produce a fully functional 3-D numerically stable code for the binary black hole problem. This project did use several parallel computing technologies described in other sections of the book. In fact, the distributed adaptive grid hierarchy (DAGH) distributed-data-structure programming environment was developed as part of this Black Hole Grand Challenge. We also looked at High Performance Fortran since the equations are naturally expressed as tensors, making Fortran 90 an attractive language. However, the compilers were not mature enough when choices had to be made, and DAGH was successfully adopted by the collaboration [567]. Fortran 90 continued to be used, however; a Perl interface mapped this automatically into DAGH. To a large extent, this was a programming-style question, as physicists prefer the Fortran constructs. The Fortran-to-DAGH translation via Perl proved to be too rigid to allow fast development on the Fortran side. Changes as simple as introducing another field variable required Perl-script rewriting. Adaptive meshes are needed in order to combine fine resolution near the holes with solutions that extrapolate with the wave solutions at long distances. This was recognized even when the proposal was initially written, but adaptive meshes were not used in production during the 5-year Grand Challenge project. It was difficult to take the existing applied mathematics literature and correctly apply it to these complex equations running in parallel. This illustrates the importance of producing more broadly usable software infrastructure to support parallel programming.

We have stressed the freedom available to choose coordinate systems. The BBH collaboration studied two very distinct choices—the more traditional ADM formulation and a newer "hyperbolic" method developed by York from North Carolina. It is not clear what mix of physics intuition and computer science infrastructure is most needed. Maybe a brilliant new coordinate system and ingenious physics insight to the inner boundary conditions are all that is needed. Alternatively, or more likely in addition, this field needs a powerful problem-solving environment that supports tensor notation, parallel adaptive meshes, reliable interpolation technology between regular meshes, and irregular dynamic hole boundaries. In either circumstance, one can estimate that at least teraflop-class performance will be necessary for the major computations.

In Figures 8.1 to 8.4, I show results from the work of Richard Matzner at Texas [652, 653], with four pictures showing the grazing collision of two black holes. The relative velocity is half the speed of light. For more recent results, see the Cactus Code website [946].

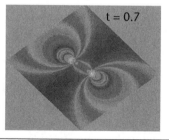

Figure 8.1   Black holes near start of the evolution. Two separate apparent horizons can be barely seen as transparent bubbles. They become clearer in following figures.

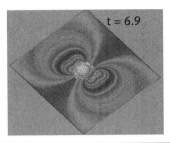

Figure 8.2   Black holes showing clearly that the separate "apparent horizons" have merged.

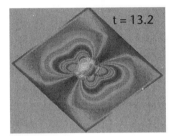

Figure 8.3   As the simulation progresses, the apparent horizon oscillates with "undisturbed space-time," in which waves propagate at "infinity."

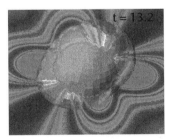

Figure 8.4   Close-up of apparent horizon in Figure 8.3.

8.2   Numerical Simulations in Lattice Quantum Chromodynamics

Urs M. Heller

The 20th century brought striking progress in our understanding of the fundamental structure of matter, beginning with quantum mechanics and culminating with the "Standard Model" of particle interactions. The dramatic successes of quantum electrodynamics (QED), verified to an accuracy of better than 1 part in 10^8 in some processes, and of the unification of electromagnetic and weak interactions explain a vast array of physical phenomena. However, traditional theoretical tools have proven very limited in the study of quantum chromodynamics (QCD), the component of the Standard Model that describes strongly interacting particles, the hadrons. The rich and complex structure of this highly nonlinear theory arises from the interactions between quarks, the constituents of protons, neutrons, and all the other hadrons, and gluons, the carriers of the strong force. QCD is quite similar to quantum electrodynamics, in which photons are the carriers of the force between electric charges. But unlike photons, gluons interact with each other, leading to the nonlinearities that make QCD so difficult to deal with.

At short distances, which correspond to high energies, the interactions in QCD are relatively weak, allowing for a perturbative treatment, an expansion in the small coupling constant. Most confirmations that QCD correctly and accurately describes the strong interactions come from high-energy experiments probing this regime. At longer distances, corresponding to lower energies, the interactions, due to the self-interactions among the gluons, become really strong. Then the nonlinearities become important, and the perturbative methods fail. But it is exactly this regime that is necessary to explain many of the properties of the hadrons: mass, decay amplitude and lifetime, stability, size, charge radius, and so on. As the distance increases, in fact, the interaction becomes so strong that the quarks are permanently confined within hadrons.

Lattice quantum chromodynamics, by way of large-scale numerical simulations, provides the only known comprehensive method for computing, with controlled systematic errors, properties of hadrons starting from the simple equations of QCD. Many of these properties, such as the hadron spectrum, are well known experimentally. Lattice QCD then aims to confirm—or disprove—QCD as the theory that explains these properties correctly.

Precise knowledge of the effects of QCD is needed to complete the determination of the basic parameters of the Standard Model, which is the central focus of current and planned high energy physics experiments, and in the search for new physics beyond the Standard Model. Prime among the basic parameters are those that describe how the weak interactions mix different species of quarks, the elements of the Cabbibo–Kobayashi–Maskawa (CKM) matrix. For heavy quark species, those matrix elements remain poorly known. Their determination requires combining experimental measurements with lattice QCD calculations.

While all experimentally known hadrons are made up of quarks and antiquarks, QCD predicts the existence of "exotic matter" that contains gluons as an essential ingredient. Finding particles such as the so-called glueballs or hybrid mesons would make a dramatic confirmation of QCD as the theory of the strong interactions. But searching for them in experiments is much like finding a needle in a haystack. Lattice QCD computations of the mass and other properties of these particles would help tremendously in experiments, such as those being performed and planned at Jefferson National Lab, by indicating promising reactions in which to search for these exotic particles.

Under normal conditions, quarks and gluons are confined inside hadrons. At sufficiently high temperature and/or pressure, a new state of matter should appear, which is a phase best described as a plasma of unconfined quarks and gluons. This quark–gluon plasma filled the entire universe until roughly 100 microseconds after the Big Bang, and it may play a role today in the cores of neutron stars. Observation of this plasma is the primary goal of heavy ion experiments at the Relativistic Heavy Ion Collider (RHIC) at the Brookhaven National Lab. Lattice QCD simulations have already provided the best estimate of the temperature at which the plasma appears, roughly 2 trillion °C. Further large-scale simulations are needed to study the detailed nature of the phase transition and to determine the equation of state for the plasma phase.

8.2.1   Lattice QCD Simulation Setup

Lattice QCD simulations started in 1979 with the seminal work of Creutz [232], who was the first to apply Monte Carlo simulation techniques to lattice QCD and to produce the first numerical evidence of confinement in QCD.

The nonperturbative solution of QCD is in many ways similar to solving fluid dynamics problems (especially when employing molecular dynamics techniques, as described below). One has a simple set of equations that implicitly contain all the information (up to the boundary conditions). Because they are very nonlinear, these equations are extremely difficult to solve. Indeed, the numerical solution of QCD appears to be one of the most challenging computational problems in physics.

The starting point of calculations in QCD is the path-integral approach to quantum field theories. To allow for a numerical attack, one first discretizes space-time into a regular 4-D grid, called a *lattice* [997], with lattice spacing a. The quarks are then described by fields $\psi(x)$—complex 3-vectors—attached to the sites of this lattice, and the gluons by special complex unitary 3×3 matrices $U_\mu(x)$, belonging to the color group $SU(3)$, attached to the links with endpoints x and $x + a\hat{\mu}$. The relation to the gluon fields $A_\mu(x)$ of the continuum field theory is given by $U_\mu(x) = \exp\{iagA_\mu(x)\}$, with g denoting the coupling constant at energy scale $1/a$. The physical observables are extracted from expectation values

$$\langle \Omega \rangle = \frac{1}{Z} \int [d\psi]\,[d\bar{\psi}]\,[dU]\,\exp\{-S(U) - \bar{\psi}\,\mathcal{M}(U)\,\psi\}\Omega(U, \psi, \bar{\psi}) \qquad (8.1)$$

The function $S(U)$ in the exponential is the gluon action, containing the gluons' kinetic term and local interactions. It consists of the sum of products of the four U-matrices on the links around elementary squares, called *plaquettes*, of the 4-D lattice, labeled by their lower left-hand corner site x and the directions $1 \le \mu < \nu \le 4$ specifying the plane in which the plaquette lies:

$$S(U) = \frac{1}{2g^2} \sum_{x,\mu<\nu} \mathrm{Tr}\left[U_\mu(x)\,U_\nu(x+\mu)\,U_\mu^\dagger(x+\nu)\,U_\nu^\dagger(x) + h.c.\right]$$

This is the simplest form that is invariant under local gauge transformations,

$$U_\mu(x) \longrightarrow U'_\mu(x) = V^\dagger(x) \, U_\mu(x) \, V(x+\mu)$$

and reduces in the limit $a \to 0$ to the continuum action,

$$S \longrightarrow \int d^4x \left(\frac{1}{2}\right) \text{Tr}\left[F^2_{\mu\nu}(x)\right] + \mathcal{O}(a^2)$$

with

$$F_{\mu\nu}(x) = \partial_\mu A_\nu(x) - \partial_\nu A_\mu(x) + g\left[A_\mu(x), A_\nu(x)\right]$$

$\mathcal{M}(U)$ in equation (8.1) contains the kinetic term of the quark fields and their interactions with the gluons. One of the most commonly used forms, known as Wilson's fermion action, is

$$\begin{aligned}
\bar{\psi} \, \mathcal{M}(U) \, \psi = \sum_x \bar{\psi}(x) \, \{ \, & (4+m) \, \psi(x) \\
& -\frac{1}{2} \sum_{\mu=1}^{4} \left[\, (1-\gamma_\mu) \, U_\mu(x) \, \psi(x+\mu) \right. \\
& \left. + \, (1+\gamma_\mu) \, U^\dagger_\mu(x-\mu) \, \psi(x-\mu) \, \right] \} \\
\to \int d^4 x \, \bar{\psi}(x) & \left[\gamma_\mu \left(\partial_\mu + g A_\mu(x)\right) \psi(x)\right] + \mathcal{O}(a)
\end{aligned}$$

(8.2)

Z in equation (8.1) is a normalization factor, often referred to as a partition function because of its similarity to partition functions in statistical mechanics. The integration is over the fields at each site and link of the lattice. The fermion fields are somewhat peculiar. They are anticommuting and therefore not representable on a digital computer. Fortunately, their integration is Gaussian and can be carried out analytically. This leads to

$$\begin{aligned}
\langle \Omega \rangle &= \frac{1}{Z} \int [dU] \, \det \mathcal{M}(U) \, \exp\{-S(U)\} \Omega(U, \mathcal{M}^{-1}(U)) \\
&= \frac{1}{Z} \int [dU] \, \exp\{-S(U) + \text{Tr} \log \mathcal{M}(U)\} \Omega(U, \mathcal{M}^{-1}(U))
\end{aligned}$$

(8.3)

The price we have to pay for the peculiarity of the quark fields now consists in the very time-consuming computation of $\det \mathcal{M}(U)$, with $\mathcal{M}(U)$ a huge, but sparse, matrix, as can be seen from equation (8.2).

We still need to do the integration over the U-field on each link of the lattice. This is typically an integral over more than 10^6 dimensions—an impossible task using any kind of standard integration method. Due to the exponential factor in equation (8.3), the contribution from most field configurations to the integral is negligible, and we can use stochastic methods. For pure gauge simulations, that is, without the fermion determinant $\det \mathcal{M}(U)$ in equation (8.3), standard Monte Carlo algorithms are adequate and widely used. These include the Metropolis algorithm and the heat bath algorithm and (slight) improvements, as used in statistical mechanics.

In full QCD simulations, because of the nonlocality of $\det \mathcal{M}(U)$, these standard Monte Carlo methods are impractical: for every local change of the gauge fields, the change in the fermion determinant would be needed. The best algorithms for the computation of equation (8.3) known to date are based on the analogue to microcanonical ensembles in statistical mechanics. One introduces momenta conjugate to the U-fields, with Gaussian distribution $\exp(-p^2/2)$ for each, and rewrites equation (8.3) as

$$\langle \Omega \rangle =$$

$$\frac{1}{Z'} \int [dU]\,[dp] \exp \left\{ -\frac{1}{2} \sum_{x,\mu} p_\mu^2(x) - S(U) + \mathrm{Tr}\,\log \mathcal{M}(U) \right\}$$

$$\Omega(U, \mathcal{M}^{-1}(U)) \tag{8.4}$$

The expression in the exponent is now viewed as (the negative of) a Hamiltonian, with $V(U) = S(U) - \mathrm{Tr}\,\log \mathcal{M}(U)$ as the potential term and $\sum p^2/2$ as the kinetic term. Introducing further a fictitious time, the U-fields and momenta are updated by integrating the corresponding equations of motion, schematically:

$$\frac{d}{dt}U = \frac{\partial}{\partial p}H = p$$

$$\frac{d}{dt}p = -\frac{\partial}{\partial U}H = -\frac{\partial}{\partial U}\left\{ S(U) - \mathrm{Tr}\,\log \mathcal{M}(U) \right\}$$

$$= -\frac{\partial}{\partial U}S(U) + \mathrm{Tr}\left[\mathcal{M}^{-1}(U)\,\frac{\partial}{\partial U}\mathcal{M}(U) \right]$$

Therefore, only a single computation of $\mathcal{M}^{-1}(U)$ is needed to update all the gauge fields simultaneously. This enormous savings in computing effort for QCD simulations makes these kinds of simulation algorithms the most effective in lattice QCD simulations.

The average in equation (8.4) is then replaced by an average over $\Omega(U(t),$ $\mathcal{M}^{-1}(U(t)))$ in fictitious time, with $U(t)$ the solution of the equations of motion resulting from the Hamiltonian. This procedure is referred to as the *molecular dynamics* algorithm. To ensure ergodicity, the momenta p are, from time to time, after what is referred to as a trajectory, replaced by new random Gaussian variables, that is, refreshed. This combination is known as the *hybrid molecular dynamics* algorithm (HMD) [292, 294]. The expectation values, equation (8.4), are then computed as simple averages

$$\overline{\Omega} = \frac{1}{N}\sum_{i=1}^{N} \Omega(\,U(t_i),\ \mathcal{M}^{-1}(U(t_i))\,)$$

with t_i, $i = 1, \ldots, N$ labeling a set of ending points of trajectories. This amounts to a stochastic estimation of $\langle \Omega \rangle$ and becomes exact only in the limit $N \to \infty$. For a finite number of trajectories, the estimate has a statistical error that decreases for large N as $1/\sqrt{N}$.

To solve the equations of motion numerically, we have to discretize the fictitious time. This introduces finite-step-size errors that have to be kept under control (e.g., kept smaller than the statistical errors). Better still would be to use a few different step sizes and then extrapolate to zero step size. Since each simulation is very time consuming, such an extrapolation is rarely possible. Usually a "leapfrog" integration scheme is used to solve the discretized equations of motion. It has the advantage of being simple and easily implemented, but it is also (up to round-off errors) explicitly time-reversal invariant. This property is important in the variant of the algorithm that compensates for the errors coming from the discretization of the equations of motion in fictitious time by performing an accept/reject Metropolis step after each trajectory. This variant is an exact algorithm called the *hybrid Monte Carlo* algorithm (HMC) [293]. While it does not suffer from finite-step-size errors, it cannot be used for all systems of interest. In those cases, one resorts to the inexact HMD algorithm and tries to control the finite-step-size errors.

The equations of motion to be solved contain a term of the form

$$\mathrm{Tr}\left\{ \frac{\partial \mathcal{M}(U)}{\partial U} \mathcal{M}^{-1}(U) \right\}$$

from the derivative of $\mathrm{Tr}\,\log \mathcal{M}$ in equation (8.3). Each step in the integration requires inversion of the large, but sparse, matrix $\mathcal{M}(U)$. This is still not practical. However, one can avoid this by noting that, for two flavors of fermions, and using that for the fermion action equation (8.2) one has that $\det \mathcal{M}^{\dagger} = \det \mathcal{M}$,

$$\exp\{2\,\mathrm{Tr}\,\log \mathcal{M}\} = \det[\mathcal{M}^{\dagger}\mathcal{M}] = \int [d\phi][d\phi^{\dagger}] \exp\{-\phi^{\dagger}[\mathcal{M}^{\dagger}\mathcal{M}]^{-1}\phi\} \tag{8.5}$$

with ϕ, $\phi^{\dagger}$ bosonic fields. During the molecular dynamics evolution of the HMD or HMC algorithm, these fields are held constant. At the beginning of each trajectory they are refreshed, like the momenta, by creating them with the distribution of equation (8.5). This can be achieved by creating Gaussian random fields χ and setting $\phi = \mathcal{M}^{\dagger}\chi$. The derivative in the molecular dynamics evolution now becomes $\phi^{\dagger}\left[\mathcal{M}^{\dagger}\mathcal{M}\right]^{-1}\partial\left[\mathcal{M}^{\dagger}\mathcal{M}\right]/\partial U\left[\mathcal{M}^{\dagger}\mathcal{M}\right]^{-1}\phi$ and involves only the computation $[\mathcal{M}^{\dagger}\mathcal{M}]^{-1}\phi$, that is, only one row of the inverse. This is still the task that makes lattice QCD simulations so expensive. The inversion is done with an iterative method, usually the conjugate gradient (CG) algorithm.

8.2.2   Computational Requirements

Here is an example of the computational demands: one iteration of the CG algorithm for a lattice size $24^3 \times 64$ requires between about $6 \cdot 10^8$ and $3 \cdot 10^9$ floating-point operations, depending on the exact way the fermion–gluon interaction was discretized on the lattice (i.e., depending on the exact form of the matrix $\mathcal{M}$). Most of the operations come from multiplying the complex 3×3 matrices on the links, representing the gluons, with complex 3-vectors on the sites, representing the quarks (see equation (8.2)). Convergence of the CG algorithm can take between 500 and, for physically more interesting parameter values, more than 1000 iterations each time. To keep the acceptance rate sufficiently high in the HMC algorithm (above 50%), or the step-size errors reasonably small in the HMD case, step sizes as small as $dt = 0.005$ to 0.01 are needed. And finally, to collect reasonable statistics for the observables, computed as fictitious time averages, the equations of motion have to be integrated for a length of 2000 to 5000 time units. Combining all these numbers, we see that a "state-of-the-art" computation requires between $3 \cdot 10^{16}$ and $3 \cdot 10^{18}$ floating-point operations, which translates to between about 1 and 100 gigaflop/s-years.

These are the resources needed for a simulation with just one set of parameters, that is, one fixed lattice spacing a, one volume, and one quark mass value. Several simulations are needed to make sure that finite-volume effects are negligible and that an extrapolation to zero lattice spacing, to the continuum limit, can be made with controlled errors. In a typical simulation, the lattice spacing is, say, 0.1 fm (1 fm = $1 \cdot 10^{-15}$ m). A proton has a charge radius of about 1 fm, and a proton therefore should fit nicely into our 24^3 box without finite-size effects, while at the same time the lattice spacing should be fine enough to give a good resolution of the proton. Nevertheless, it is known that the results of such a computation can differ from the final continuum limit by as much as 10% to 30%. This difference is referred to as *lattice* or *discretization effects*.

In addition, the quark masses in a lattice QCD simulation are typically much larger than those in nature, and therefore simulations at a few different quark masses are needed to allow an extrapolation to the almost massless up and down quarks of nature.

8.2.3   Implementation Considerations

From the requirements of a single computation described above, it is clear that the computing power of even high-end workstations is dismally inadequate for lattice QCD calculations. In a lattice QCD code, the same operations usually have to be performed on all the lattice sites of a regular fixed grid. And the data needed either reside on that site or on one of the nearest-neighbor sites in one of the directions of the 4-D grid. This is a classic case of a data-parallel situation and lends itself to rather straightforward vectorization or parallelization. Indeed, lattice-gauge theory codes are among the most efficient, both on vector and, more importantly, on massively parallel supercomputers.

I am a member of a large project, partially sponsored by the Department of Energy, known as the MIMD Lattice Calculation (MILC) Collaboration. This collaboration is using any parallel computer that it can get time on. For this, MILC has developed a family of portable MIMD codes that run on a wide variety of scalable parallel computers, from single workstations for code development and testing, to the T3E, SP systems, Origin 2000, and, more recently, PC clusters. The code is written in C and is highly portable. The only parts of the C code that are machine dependent are the communications routines. These are stored in a single file. A different version of this file exists for each machine or communications library. Standard message-passing libraries are especially interesting from the point of view of maintaining portable code, and the MILC collaboration has implemented a version of the communications routines for both PVM and MPI [676]. Older versions were running on Intel Paragons and TMC CM-5s.

8.2.4   Recent Developments and Future Prospects

Like other computational fields, lattice QCD has profited from the fast development of ever more powerful computers. The numerical algorithms used, hybrid Monte Carlo and conjugate gradient–type routines for the very frequent inversions of the large sparse quark matrices, are by now fairly standard. Tremendous progress already has been made in the last few years and can be made in the future in reducing lattice discretization errors. In the most commonly used lattice formulation of the quarks, the so-called Wilson fermions, the finite-lattice-spacing errors are of the order $\mathcal{O}(a)$. To reduce those errors by half, the lattice spacing needs to be decreased by a factor of two. The number of lattice sites for a fixed physical 4-D lattice then grows by a factor 2^4; the actual costs, in CPU time, of a simulation grow by a factor of 2^8 to 2^{10}, depending on the details of the simulation algorithm used. Therefore, reducing the discretization errors from $\mathcal{O}(a)$ to $\mathcal{O}(a^2)$ can produce enormous savings. Unfortunately, due to the intrinsic quantum nature of the problem, this is not as easy as just using a better finite difference approximation to a derivative. However, a method to achieve this goal has recently been developed [630, 631, 632, 510].

Thus far, lattice QCD computations have determined the value of the strong coupling constant at the energy scale given by the Z-boson mass, where all different determinations are usually compared (recall that the coupling decreases with increasing energy) to an accuracy of 3%, which is about the same as the best experimental determinations. The error estimates include the statistical error from the stochastic Monte Carlo computation and the systematic errors from the extrapolation to the continuum, $a \to 0$, limit [753]. The masses of the light hadrons have been computed to an accuracy of 5% to 10%, including those of the lightest exotic states, glueballs, and hybrid mesons.[1] Computations of the QCD effects on weak matrix elements, on the other hand, so far typically have errors of 20% to 40%. In many cases this is 5 to 10 times the errors of the experimental measurements with which the computations need to be combined to extract the fundamental parameters of the Standard Model.

This discrepancy has led to a considerable effort to increase the computing resources available for lattice QCD computations. If this effort is successful, the errors on the weak-matrix-element computations, for example, are expected to be reduced by a factor of two over the next 2 years. Teraflop/s scale computations, foreseen for the years 2002 to 2005, are expected to bring the errors down to be comparable with the experimental errors.

---

[1] For recent reviews on the status of lattice QCD, see "Progress in Lattice Theory," the September 1998 plenary talk by Stephen R. Sharpe at ICHEP98 in Vancouver, Canada (heplat/9811006, available at *http://arXiv.org/abs /hep-lat/9811006*); and "Lattice Gauge Theory," the July 1999 plenary talk by H. Wittig at the Europhysics Conference on High Energy Physics in Tampere, Finland (hep-ph/9911400, available at *http://arXiv.org/abs/ hep-ph/9911400*).

Acknowledgments. This work has been supported in part by DoE contracts DE-FG05-85ER250000 and DE-FG05-96ER40979.

8.3   Ocean Modeling

John Dukowicz, Richard Smith, and Robert Malone

The Parallel Ocean Program (POP) was developed at Los Alamos National Laboratory (LANL) under the sponsorship of the DoE's CHAMMP program, which brought massively parallel computers to the realm of climate modeling. POP is a descendant of the Bryan–Cox–Semtner (BCS) class of models [154, 226, 846]. A number of improvements to the standard BCS model have been developed and incorporated in POP. Although originally motivated by the adaptation of POP for massively parallel computers, in particular the Connection Machine (CM-5), many of these changes improved not only its computational performance but the model's physical representation of the ocean as well. The most significant of these improvements are summarized below. For details, see Dukowicz and Smith [299], Dukowitz et al. [300], and Smith et al. [874, 876].

The Bryan–Cox–Semtner ocean model is a 3-D model in Eulerian coordinates (latitude, longitude, and depth). The incompressible Navier–Stokes equations and the equations for the transport of temperature and salinity, along with a turbulent eddy viscosity and diffusivity, are solved subject to the hydrostatic and Boussinesq approximations. As originally formulated, the model includes a rigid-lid approximation (zero vertical velocity at the ocean surface) to eliminate fast surface waves. The presence of such waves would require use of a very short time step in numerical simulations and hence greatly increase the computational cost. The equations of motion are split into two parts: a set of 2-D *barotropic* equations describing the vertically averaged flow, and a set of 3-D *baroclinic* equations describing temperature, salinity, and deviation of the horizontal velocity components from the vertically averaged flow. (The vertical velocity component is determined from the constraint of mass conservation.) The barotropic equations contain the fast surface waves and separate them from the rest of the model.

The baroclinic equations are solved explicitly; that is, their solution involves a simple forward time-stepping scheme, which is well suited to parallel computing. On the other hand, the barotropic equations (2-D sparse-matrix equations linking nearest-neighbor grid points) are solved implicitly; that is, they are solved at each time step by iteration.

For historical reasons, the barotropic equations in the Bryan–Cox–Semtner model are formulated in terms of a stream function. Such a formulation requires solving an additional equation for each island, an equation that links all points around the island. This was not a problem when limited computing power would permit only very coarse resolution ($\geq 5°$ in latitude and longitude), because only continent-size landmasses could be resolved. As the model was pushed to higher resolution, not only were there many additional equations to solve, but each equation required "gather–scatter" memory accesses on each solver iteration. This was costly, even on machines with fast memory access, such as Cray parallel-vector-processor computers. To reduce the number of equations to solve, it was common practice to submerge islands, connect them to nearby continents with artificial land bridges, or merge an island chain into a single mass without gaps. The first modification created artificial gaps, permitting increased flow; the second and third modifications closed channels that should exist. For example, in the pioneering work of Semtner and Chervin [847, 848], of the 80 islands resolvable at the horizontal resolution employed (0.5° latitude and longitude), all but the three largest "islands" (Antarctica, Australia, and New Zealand) were eliminated by artificial changes in the bottom topography. Even then, the barotropic part of the code consumed about one-third of the total computing time when the model was executed on a Cray. On distributed-memory parallel computers, these added equations became even more costly because, on every iteration, each required gathering data from a (possibly large) set of processors to do a summation around each island. When the model was executed on a Connection Machine, about two-thirds of the total computing time was spent on the barotropic part.

8.3.1   Surface-Pressure Formulation of the Barotropic Mode

The above considerations led us to focus our efforts on speeding up the barotropic part of the code. We developed and implemented two new numerical formulations of the barotropic equations, both of which involve a surface-pressure field rather than a stream function. The surface-pressure formulations have several advantages over the stream function formulation and are more efficient on both distributed-memory parallel and shared-memory vector computers.

The first new formulation recasts the barotropic equations in terms of a surface-pressure field but retains the rigid-lid approximation. The surface pressure represents the pressure that would have to be applied to the surface of the ocean to keep it flat (as if capped by a rigid lid). The barotropic equations must still be solved implicitly, but the boundary conditions are simpler and much easier to implement. Furthermore, islands require no additional equations; any number of islands can be included in the grid at no extra computational cost. Perhaps most importantly, the surface-pressure, rigid-lid formulation, unlike the stream function, rigid-lid formulation, exhibits no convergence problems due to steep gradients in the bottom topography. The matrix operator in the surface-pressure formulation is proportional to the depth field H, whereas the matrix operator in the stream function formulation is proportional to $1/H$. Therefore, the latter matrix operator is much more sensitive than the former to rapid variations in the depth of waters over the edges of continental shelves or submerged mountain ranges. In such situations, the depth may change from several thousand meters to a few tens of meters within a few grid points. Because such a rapidly varying operator may prevent convergence to a solution, steep gradients were removed from the stream function formulation by smoothing the depth field (which also had the then-desirable effect of eliminating many islands). The surface-pressure formulation, on the other hand, converges even in the presence of steep depth gradients. Artificial smoothing of the depth field can significantly affect the accuracy of a numerical simulation of the interaction of a strong current with bottom topography. For example, the detailed course and dynamics of the Antarctic Circumpolar Current (the strongest ocean current in terms of total volume transport) is greatly influenced by its interaction with bottom topography.

As we worked with the surface-pressure, rigid-lid model, we noticed a problem in shallow isolated bays such as the Sea of Japan. In principle, we should have been able to infer the elevation of the ocean surface (relative to the mean elevation) from the predicted surface pressure. We found, however, that the surface heights so inferred were quite different from those expected, due to inflow or outflow from the bays. Removing the rigid lid solved that problem, but of course it also brought back the unwanted and unneeded surface waves. We were able to overcome that new difficulty by treating the terms responsible for the surface waves implicitly, which artificially slows the waves, whereas the rigid-lid approximation artificially speeds up the waves to infinite velocity. (Either departure from reality is acceptable. Climate modeling does not require an accurate representation of the waves because they have little effect on ocean circulation.)

8.3.2 Free-Surface Formulation

Those considerations led us next to abandon the rigid-lid approximation in favor of a free-surface formulation. The surface pressure is then proportional to the mass of water above a reference level near the surface. The benefits of the surface-pressure, free-surface model are greater physical realism and faster convergence of the barotropic solver. In particular, the revised barotropic part of the code, including 80 islands, is many times faster than the original, which included only three islands (when both are implemented on the 0.5 grid). In addition, the surface pressure is now a prognostic variable that can be compared to global satellite observations of sea-surface elevation to validate the model, and satellite data can now be assimilated into the model to improve short-term prediction of near-surface ocean conditions.

None of our revisions, of course, changed the fact that the large matrix equation in the barotropic solver must be solved implicitly. We chose to use conjugate gradient methods for that purpose because they are both effective and easily adapted to parallel computing. Conjugate gradient methods are most effective when the matrix is symmetric. Unfortunately, the presence of Coriolis terms (terms associated with the rotation of the Earth) in the barotropic equations makes the matrix non-symmetric. By using an approximate factorization method to split off the Coriolis terms, we retained the accuracy of the time discretization of the Coriolis terms and produced a symmetric matrix to which a standard conjugate gradient method may be applied. We also developed a new preconditioning method for use on massively parallel computers that is very effective at accelerating the convergence of the conjugate gradient solution. The method exploits the idea of a local approximate inverse to find a symmetric preconditioning matrix. Calculating the preconditioner is relatively expensive, but it only needs to be done once for a given computational grid.

8.3.3   Pressure Averaging

Elimination of the extra equations for islands and the associated gather–scatter memory operations greatly reduced the cost of solving the barotropic equations. Further savings can be obtained by implementing *pressure averaging,* a well-known technique in atmospheric modeling for increasing the time step [145]. After the temperature and salinity have been updated to time step $n + 1$ in the baroclinic routines, the density ρ^{n+1} and pressure p^{n+1} can be computed. By calculating the pressure gradient with a linear combination of p at three time levels ($n - 1$, n, and $n + 1$), it is possible to increase the time step by as much as a factor of two. However, at first this doubling was not obtained because something else was limiting the time step. Analysis of factors constraining the time step revealed that it was being limited by horizontal diffusion at high latitudes, as described next.

8.3.4   Latitudinal Scaling of Horizontal Diffusion

Horizontal mixing by unresolved turbulence is commonly parameterized by either Laplacian, ∇^2, or biharmonic, ∇^4, diffusion terms. These operators scale as Δx^{-m}, with $m = 2$ or 4. Here $\Delta x = a * \Delta \lambda * \cos \phi$, where ϕ and λ are latitude and longitude, respectively, and a is the radius of the Earth. Because $\cos \phi \to 0$ at the poles, these diffusion terms become very large at high latitude. Although horizontal diffusion parameterizations are intended to mimic the effects of unresolved turbulence, their essential purpose is to dissipate energy at scales near the grid resolution. Consequently, they can be arbitrarily rescaled, as long as they give sufficient dissipation to prevent the buildup of computational noise at small spatial scales. The diffusion term, $\nabla^m T$, only needs to be big enough at all latitudes to balance the advection term, $U \cdot \nabla T$, in the transport equation for tracer T. The advection term scales as Δx^{-1}, so scaling of the horizontal diffusion coefficient by $(\cos \phi)^n$ was introduced, where $n = m - 1$ ($n = 1$ for Laplacian mixing; $n = 3$ for biharmonic mixing). This scaling prevents horizontal diffusion from limiting the time step severely at high latitudes, yet keeps diffusion large enough to maintain numerical stability.

Once this scaling was introduced and the associated time-step constraint was removed, the doubling of the time step with the *pressure-averaging* method was attained. Taken together, the improved numerical stability of the surface-pressure formulations, the $(\cos \phi)^3$ tapering of the biharmonic diffusion coefficient, and pressure averaging permitted the time step to be increased by about a factor of four compared to the best calculations at that time [847, 848]. They used a time step of 15 minutes when running a standard BCS model at 0.5° resolution. With POP, it was possible to run with a 30-minute time step at 0.28° resolution, an improvement of a factor of four over the 7.5-minute time step expected by extrapolating Semtner's experience.

8.3.5   Code Designed for Parallel Computers

The code is written in Fortran 90 and can be run on a variety of parallel and serial computer architectures. It uses domain decomposition in latitude and longitude, combined with MPI for interprocessor communications on distributed memory machines. SHMEM is also available on machines that support it (SGI Origin 2000 and Cray T3E).

8.3.6   General Orthogonal Coordinates and the "Displaced-Pole" Grid

Because the code is written in Fortran 90, it was relatively easy to reformulate and discretize the equations of motion to allow the use of any locally orthogonal horizontal grid without a major rewrite of the code [876]. This generalization provides alternatives to the standard latitude–longitude grid with its singularity at the North Pole. In particular, a "displaced-pole" grid was developed, in which the singularity arising from convergence of meridians at the North Pole is moved into an adjacent landmass such as North America, Greenland, or Russia. This leaves a smooth, singularity-free grid in the Arctic Ocean, which is important for the modeling of sea ice. That grid joins smoothly at the equator with a standard Mercator grid in the Southern Hemisphere. If the singularity is moved to Greenland, distortion relative to the standard grid is minimized, but the smallness of ocean cells just off the coast of Greenland may restrict the time step excessively. Placing the singularity in either Greenland or North America increases the resolution in the Gulf Stream and the northern seas; the Gulf Stream transports warm salty water into the northern seas, where deep water is formed by wintertime convection. Both transport and convection are important aspects of the global thermohaline circulation that need to be as well resolved as possible.

The displaced-pole grid has proven to be one of the most popular features of POP, especially in fully coupled atmosphere–ocean–sea ice models. The Los Alamos sea ice model (CICE) also supports the displaced-pole grid, so no interpolation is needed between POP and CICE. A package based on conservative remapping techniques, the Spherical Coordinate Remapping and Interpolation Package (SCRIP), has been developed [523] that transforms state variables and fluxes between any pair of orthogonal grids on the sphere. SCRIP handles the transformations between the atmospheric model grid and the displaced-pole grid used by POP and CICE.

Many of the improvements first introduced in POP have been adopted in other models, even for use on parallel-vector machines.

8.3.7   High-Resolution Simulations Enabled by POP

Massively parallel computers are ideally suited to high-resolution modeling of the oceans. "Mesoscale" eddies in the oceans are 50 to 100 km in size, roughly 10 times smaller than their atmospheric analogues: high and low pressure and frontal systems. Thus, ocean models need to have finer grids than atmospheric models. Cost rises rapidly as resolution is increased: doubling the horizontal resolution increases the cost by an order of magnitude when the reduction in time step and a modest increase in vertical resolution are taken into account. At the time POP was being developed, the state of the art in high-resolution global modeling was the work of Semtner and Chervin [847, 848] at 0.5°. They were using a model with the standard rigid-lid, stream function formulation, smoothed bottom topography with only three "islands," biharmonic diffusion and no pressure averaging; the model time step was 15 minutes at 0.5° resolution. With POP running on the CM-5, it was possible to double the resolution to 0.28°, use unsmoothed bottom topography, include all 112 resolvable islands, and run with a time step of 30 minutes [642]. Although many aspects of the 0.28° global simulations were improved compared to the earlier simulations, quantitative comparisons of sea-surface height variability predicted by POP with measurements from the TOPEX/Poseidon satellite altimeter showed that the model variability was still low by a factor of two. This meant that the mesoscale eddy spectrum was still not adequately resolved. Limitations in computing power made it impractical to go to higher resolution at the global scale; however, it was feasible to go to 0.1° in the Atlantic Ocean basin only. That calculation had about the same number of horizontal grid points (992×1280) as the global 0.28° calculation (1280×896), but 40 depth levels rather than 20. The time step had to be reduced by the resolution ratio (2.8) to 10 minutes, so three times as many time steps were needed to integrate the model for a decade of simulated time. With twice as many depth levels, the 0.1° calculation was six times more expensive than a similar length 0.28° run. Four months of almost dedicated time on 512 processors of the Los Alamos National Laboratory/Advanced Computing Laboratory CM-5 were needed to complete the calculation [875]. Many important aspects of Atlantic circulation were accurately captured for the first time, including good quantitative agreement between POP and TOPEX/Poseidon. The results are so impressive that the international oceanographic community is eagerly awaiting a global simulation at the same 0.1° scale. This was impossible until 1999, when the ACL took delivery of a 2048 processor SGI Origin 2000 system with a peak rating of 1 teraflop. Benchmark tests of POP indicate that roughly 6 months of nonstop computing on 512 processors will be required to extend the 0.1° simulation to the global scale. The grid will have 3600 points in longitude, 2400 in latitude, and 40 depth levels, for a total 3.5×10^8 grid cells. With a 10-minute time step, nearly 1 million time steps will be needed.

8.4   Simulations of Earthquakes
Geoffrey C. Fox

The importance of simulating earthquakes is intuitively obvious. For instance, the Kobe, Japan, earthquake of January 16, 1995, was only a magnitude 6.9 event and yet produced an estimated \$200 billion loss. Despite an active earthquake prediction program in Japan, this event was a complete surprise. Similar and more drastic scenarios are possible, and indeed eventually likely, in Los Angeles, San Francisco, Seattle, and other urban centers around the Pacific plate boundary.

There are currently no approaches to earthquake forecasting that are uniformly reliable. The field uses phenomenological approaches, which attempt to forecast individual events, or more reliable statistical analyses giving probabilistic predictions. The development of these methods has been complicated by the fact that large events responsible for the greatest damage repeat at irregular intervals of hundreds to thousands of years, and so the limited historical record has frustrated phenomenological studies. Up to now, direct numerical simulation has not been extensively pursued due to the complexity of the problem and the (presumed) sensitivity of the occurrence of large events to detailed understanding of both Earth constituent makeup and the relevant microscale physics that determines the underlying friction laws. However, good progress has been made recently with a variety of numerical simulations, and both Earth and satellite sensors are providing an increasing volume of data that can be used to constrain and test the numerical simulations. This field is different from most other applications in this book, as it thus far has made little use of parallel computing and only now is starting its own "Grand Challenges." It is thus not known how important large-scale simulations will be in earthquake science. Maybe they will never be able to predict the "big one" on the San Andreas fault, but nevertheless it is essentially certain that they can provide a numerical laboratory of "semi-realistic" earthquakes with which other more phenomenological methods based on pattern recognition can be developed and tested. As one can use data assimilation techniques to integrate real-time measurements into the simulations, simulations provide a powerful way of integrating data into statistical and other such forecasting methods.

Although this field has some individually very difficult simulations, it has only just started to use high-performance computers. Thus, the most promising computations at this stage involve either scaling up existing simulations to large system sizes with modern algorithms or integrating several component computations with assimilated data to provide early, full-fault system simulations. The latter has important real-world applications in the area of responding to and planning for crises as one can carry the computations through from initial sensing of stress buildup through the structural simulation of building and civil infrastructure responses to propagating waves.

Earthquake science embodies a richness present in many physical sciences as there are effects that spread over 10 orders of magnitude in spatial and temporal scales (Figure 8.5). Success requires linking numerical expertise with the physical insight needed to coarse grain or average the science at a fine scale to be used phenomenologically in simulations at a given resolution of relevance to the questions addressed. Again, nonlinear fault systems exhibit a wealth of emergent, dynamic phenomena over a large range of spatial and temporal scales, including space–time clustering of events, self-organization, and scaling. An earthquake is itself a clustering of slipped fault segments, as seen in studies of critical phenomena [23, 87, 157, 267, 337, 365, 511, 839]. As in the latter field, one finds (empirically) scaling laws that include

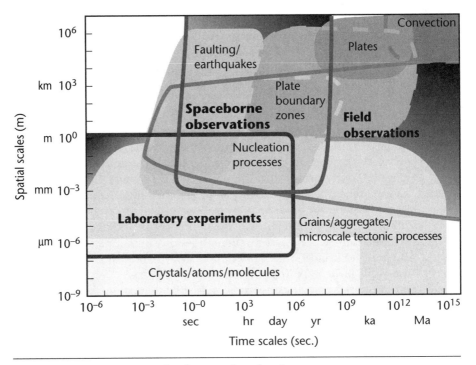

Figure 8.5   Spatial and temporal scales in earthquake science.

the well-known Gutenberg–Richter, magnitude–frequency relation, and the Omori law for aftershocks (and foreshocks). Some of the spatial scales for physical fault geometries include:

- *The microscopic scale* ($\sim 10^{-6}$ m to 10^{-1} m) associated with static and dynamic friction (the primary nonlinearities associated with the earthquake process).
- *The fault-zone scale* ($\sim 10^{-1}$ m to 10^{2} m) that features complex structures containing multiple fractures and crushed rock.
- *The fault-system scale* ($\sim 10^{2}$ m to 10^{4} m), in which faults are seen to be neither straight nor simply connected, but in which bends, offsetting jogs, and subparallel strands are common and known to have important mechanical consequences during a fault slip.
- *The regional fault-network scale* ($\sim 10^{4}$ m to 10^{5} m), where seismicity on an individual fault cannot be understood in isolation from the seismicity on the entire regional network of surrounding faults. Here concepts such as "correlation length" and "critical state" borrowed from statistical physics have led to new approaches to understanding regional seismicity.

- *The tectonic plate-boundary scale* ($\sim 10^5$ m to 10^7 m), at which planetary scale boundaries between plates can be approximated as thin shear zones and the motion is uniform at long time scales.

8.4.1   Typical Computational Problems

Many different types of codes eventually could be linked together to support either real-time response to a crisis or fundamental scientific studies [353, 357]. The process of coordinating the field in this area is happening in Japan, where major computational resources are being deployed. There is also an international effort among several Asia–Pacific nations, including the United States (the so-called Asian–Pacific Economic Cooperation initiative [44]) and a U.S. activity, known as GEM for its goal to produce a "general earthquake model" [373]. Three distinct computational problems are presented below.

Data Assimilation

The initial simulations, aimed at helping a crisis response team, would be triggered by the detection of an earthquake event by the many sensors now deployed, especially in California. Since these sensors provide incomplete information, they must be assimilated into model simulations to allow the following two model computations to attempt forecasting of possible aftershock activity and the consequent damage to civil infrastructure. The Jet Propulsion Laboratory has developed one such code (*disloc*) to process data from the large NASA-NSF-USGS SINE Sensor array. It uses finite elements and complex meshing techniques to represent the complexity of the 3-D Earth crust. It is shown in Figure 8.6 and described below as a "problem-solving environment" designed to support the earthquake-response community after events like those occurring in Turkey or Taiwan in 1999.

Earthquake Fault–System Simulations—Virtual California

With reasonable approximation, the long-term evolution of stresses and strains on interacting fault segments can be modeled with a Green's function approach [813, 814]. This method leads to a boundary-value formulation (the faults determine the boundary) that numerically looks like the long-range force problem. The faults are paneled with segments (with area of some 100 m^2 in definitive computations) that interact as though they were dipoles. The original calculations of this model used the basic $\mathcal{O}(N^2)$ algorithm, but a new set of codes will use the *fast-multipole* method briefly described in Chapter 4 for astrophysical problems. There are interesting differences between the earthquake and gravitational applications. In gravity, there are wide ranges in density and dynamical effects from the natural clustering of the gravitating particles. Earthquake "particles" are essentially fixed on complex fault geometries, and their interactions fall off faster than those in the astrophysical problem. Several variants of this model have been explored, including approximations that keep only interactions between nearby fault segments. These *cellular-automata*

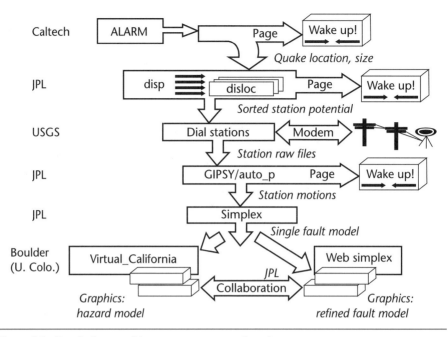

Figure 8.6   Simulations used in response to an earthquake.

or *slider-block* models look very much like statistical physics, with an earthquake corresponding to clusters of particles slipping together when the correlation length gets long near a critical point. The full Green's function approach should parallelize straightforwardly [931] in either $\mathcal{O}(N^2)$ or multipole formulation. Cellular automata models [146, 365, 815] will be harder, as we know from experience with the corresponding statistical physics case, where clustering models have been extensively studied. An interesting aspect of these simulations is that they provide a "numerical laboratory" for the study of space–time patterns in seismicity information. This type of analysis was used successfully in the climate field to aid in the prediction of El Niño phenomena. These pattern analyses may or may not need large computational resources, although they can involve determination of eigensolutions of large matrices, which is potentially time consuming. In Figure 8.6, we show Virtual California, used to help predict aftershocks and manage the consequences of actual earthquakes. This illustrates the concepts described in Chapter 25 of large simulations being used in a real-time network to address problems of importance to society.

Earthquake Engineering

The most mature computations in the field are those used to calculate the response of buildings to seismic waves. In fact, R. Clayton of the Caltech Geophysics department performed one of the very first Caltech Cosmic Cube computations to simulate the motion of earthquake waves in the Los Angeles Basin. This wave motion can, in principle, be generated from the earthquake "events" calculated in the Virtual California simulations described above. The wave motion can be used as a forcing function for structural dynamics computations of buildings, roads, and other civil infrastructure. These are large-scale, finite element problems with complex grids, and a recent National Science Foundation "Grand Challenge" was very successful in this area.

Response to an Earthquake in Southern California

In this typical scenario, which is the first part of Figure 8.6, the goal is to rapidly form a consensus among researchers concerning the characterization of the deformation field and the location, size, and direction of slip on a fault following an earthquake. This consensus can be used to guide decisions on both civil and scientific responses to the quake.

Following an earthquake in Southern California, the location and magnitude are calculated based on seismic data within minutes by Caltech/U.S. Geological Survey (USGS) and are broadcast to several users via email and pagers. The information on location and magnitude could then be automatically used to define an area wherein instruments might be expected to record a signal. Data from these stations would be given priority in retrieval and analysis. In this example, we assume that the data in question are global-positioning-system (GPS) data from the Southern California Integrated Geodetic Network (SCIGN) array. Retrieval in this case occurs via telephone modem. As soon as the list of possibly affected stations has been generated, the database at the USGS is checked. If any of the stations on the list have not had data downloaded since the quake, computers at the USGS begin dialing the selected stations and retrieving the data.

Data from these stations are then processed for rapid analysis to determine the measured displacements of the stations. If the measured displacements are large enough, emergency and scientific personnel are notified via email and pager. These displacements are then automatically fed into an inversion routine (simplex) that solves for the best-fit, single-fault displacement. This single-fault displacement is in turn fed back into a forward, elastic, half-space model that yields a preliminary map of displacements over the whole area.

At this point, this map is shared among various scientists and emergency personnel, using systems such as Tango Interactive that allow the collaboration and interaction of many people viewing and manipulating the same data set over the Internet. The emergency personnel can use the preliminary map in combination with geographical information system (GIS) data about utilities, lifelines, and so on to help assign resources to various areas. The scientists use the preliminary map to help design a strategy for collecting additional measurements. Before rerunning the inversion, they can also collaborate on refining the single-fault model, possibly breaking the single preliminary fault into several segments, introducing more realistic material properties or including more data.

This environment permits the rapid determination and dissemination of preliminary information about the earthquake and the collaborative refining of that information following an event. The rapid dissemination of information can greatly aid both the civil and scientific response to the quake. Resources can be more efficiently allocated to the areas where they are needed, and scientific measurements can be focused to provide information critical to refining our understanding of the earthquake system. Once an acceptable model of the earthquake has been determined, various models can be used to estimate the updated earthquake hazard for adjacent areas. Since there are currently several competing models for this, it will undoubtedly involve multiple runs of multiple models and significant discussion among scientific colleagues. Each of these models, as well as the various pieces of the automated processes described above, has been developed by different people under different assumptions, and each is developed, run, and maintained on computers under the control of the developer. Technologies such as CORBA and Enterprise Java Beans allow appropriate access and security mechanisms in this complex, evolving distributed system.

The Izmit, Turkey, earthquake in 1999 provided an example of how a system like this could have been useful. Following that earthquake, many geoscientists participated in a series of conference telephone calls to try to piece together what had happened and to determine an appropriate response. Initially, some participants only knew what had been reported in the media. Others knew of specific pieces of data concerning the earthquake or of actions being taken by various groups and individuals. It is safe to say that no one had a complete picture. Much of the conference call was devoted to informing everyone about all the pieces of data and all the various initiatives that people were pursuing or might pursue. Similar calls and emails occurred after the 1992 Landers and 1994 Northridge earthquakes. Having a system such as the one described above, in which participants could share maps, descriptions, programs, data sets, and graphs, and in which they could interactively and collaboratively manipulate the data and programs both synchronously and asynchronously, would immeasurably aid the rapid and accurate diagnosis of what has happened and what should be done next.

8.4.2   Computational Resource Requirements

Current evidence suggests that forecasting earthquakes of magnitude ~ 6 and greater will depend on understanding the space–time patterns displayed by smaller events, that is, the magnitude 3's, 4's and 5's. With at least 40,000 km^2 of fault area in Southern California, as many as 108 grid sites will be needed to accommodate events down to magnitude 3. Extrapolations based on existing calculations indicate that using time steps of ~ 100 s implies that ~ 108 time steps will be required to simulate several earthquake cycles. This leads to the need for teraflop-class computers. At this stage, we cannot guess how far this class of computer will take us; the systems needed to support research, crisis managers, or insurance companies assessing possible earthquake risk may require much higher performance.

8.5 Cosmological Structure Formation

Michael Norman and Greg Bryan

The universe is homogeneous and isotropic on scales exceeding 1 billion light years. But on smaller scales it is clumpy, exhibiting a hierarchy of structures, including individual galaxies, groups and clusters of galaxies, and superclusters of galaxies. Understanding the origin and cosmic evolution of these structures is the goal of *cosmological structure formation* (CSF). CSF is inherently nonlinear and multidimensional, and it involves a broad range of physical processes operating on a range of length and time scales. Numerical simulation is the only means we have of studying it in any detail.

8.5.1 The Problem to be Solved

Simulations of CSF have grown in size and complexity as computer power has grown. The largest N-body CSF simulations of the day have increased from $N = 32^3$ particles on VAXs in the mid 1980s to 1024^3 particles on today's MPPs—an astounding factor of over 32,000. Today, CSF simulations are among the largest consumers of supercomputer cycles at the National Science Foundation centers, rivaling CFD, condensed matter physics, and lattice gauge theory.

Two parallel applications described here simulate CSF in three spatial dimensions and time within an expanding background space–time consistent with our understanding of the Big Bang origin of the universe. The first code, called Kronos [153], uses a uniform Cartesian grid comoving with the expanding universe as the basis for discretizing the equations of matter and gravitational dynamics. The second code, called Enzo [150, 152, 716], adds structured, adaptive mesh refinement (SAMR) to the Kronos algorithm for improved spatial and temporal resolution in high-density regions (galaxies, clusters, etc.). Sequential and parallel versions of both codes have been developed and optimized for vector multiprocessors, SMPs, MPPs, and clusters of PCs and SMPs. The message-passing parallel version Enzo, which can be run with and without mesh refinements, is our computational workhorse and is the main focus of this report.

8.5.2 Computational Issues

Matter in the universe is of two basic types: ordinary *baryonic* matter composed of nucleons and electrons, out of which stars and galaxies are made, and nonbaryonic *dark* matter of unknown composition, which is nevertheless known to be the dominant mass constituent in the universe on scales of galaxies and larger. Kronos and Enzo self-consistently simulate both components, which evolve according to different physical laws and therefore require different numerical algorithms.

Baryonic matter is evolved using a finite volume discretization of the Euler equations of gas dynamics cast in the comoving frame, including energy source and sink terms due to radiative heating and cooling processes, as well as changes in the ionization state of the gas [153]. In some calculations involving nonequilibrium chemistry,

separate chemical/ionic species are evolved by solving their kinetic rate equations
[42]. Radiation fields are modeled as evolving, but spatially homogeneous, back-
grounds; true radiative transfer is not yet included, but is on the horizon [2].

Dark matter is assumed to behave as a collisionless phase fluid, obeying the
Vlasov–Poisson equation. Its evolution is solved using particle-mesh algorithms
for collisionless N-body dynamics [479]. Dark matter and baryonic matter interact
only through their self-consistent gravitational field. The gravitational potential is
computed by solving the Poisson equation on the uniform or adaptive grid hierarchy
using Fourier transform techniques. In generic terms, our CSF codes are 3-D hybrid
codes consisting of a multispecies hydrodynamic solver for the baryons coupled to
a particle-mesh solver for the dark matter via a Poisson solver.

Matter evolution is computed in a cubic domain of length $L = a(t)X$, where
X is the domain size in comoving coordinates and $a(t)$ is the homogeneous and
isotropic scale factor of the universe, which is an analytic or numerical solution of
the Friedmann equation, a first-order ordinary differential equation. For sufficiently
large L compared to the structures of interest, any chunk of the universe is statistically
equivalent to any other, justifying the use of periodic boundary conditions. The
speed of Fast Fourier Transform (FFT) algorithms and the fact that they are ideally
suited to periodic problems make them the Poisson solver of choice, given the large
grids employed—512^3 or larger.

CSF simulations require very large grids and particle numbers due to two competing demands: large boxes are needed for a fair statistical sample of the universe; and
high mass and spatial resolution are needed to adequately resolve the scale lengths
of the structures that form. For example, in order to adequately simulate the internal structure of galaxies and simultaneously describe their large-scale distribution in
space (large-scale structure), a dynamic range of 10^4 per spatial dimension and 10^9
in mass is needed *at a minimum*.

The largest uniform grid simulation ever done including gas and dark matter is
a Kronos simulation we carried out on 512 processors of the Connection Machine-
5 at the National Center for Supercomputing Applications in 1994 (see Plate 6 of
the color insert). The simulation used a grid of 512^3 cells and 5×10^7 particles—
far short of the requirements mentioned above. With the use of the adaptive mesh
refinement code Enzo on the current generation of terascale computing systems, the
desired resolutions are now achievable. In the next two sections, we discuss parallel
computing aspects of these two codes.

8.5.3   Parallel Unigrid Code: Kronos

The Kronos code was developed in 1992–1994 by Greg Bryan for the Connection
Machine-5 at the NCSA. The CM-5 had 512 processor nodes, each consisting of a SUN
Sparc microprocessor, four vector processors, and 32 MB of memory. The theoretical
peak speed of the system was quoted as 0.128 Gflop/s/PN $\times$ 512 PN = 65 Gflop/s,
and the total memory was 16 GB.

Kronos was implemented in the data-parallel Connection Machine Fortran (CMF) programming model. Conceptually, Kronos is the union of two codes: a 3-D Eulerian gas dynamics code (suitably modified for cosmology [153]) and a 3-D particle-mesh code (of which the FFT-based Poisson solver is a component) for the collisionless dark matter. The parallel challenges and solutions for each code are quite different, and so we discuss them individually.

The equations of gas dynamics are purely local: changes in cell quantities due to pressure forces and fluid advection involve only nearest neighbors. By assigning one virtual processor per cell in a 3-D Cartesian lattice, nearest-neighbor information was passed using the CM-5 NEWS data communication network via simple CSHIFT calls. This was the basis of our first implementation. Performance tests measured at ≈ 8 Mflops/s/PN, or about 6% of peak. The reason for this poor performance was that the communication network was invoked between every computational cell, regardless of whether they resided on the same physical processor or not.

In order to circumvent this, our second implementation abandoned the one virtual processor per cell model in favor of explicit domain decomposition. This was accomplished within the CMF data-parallel programming model by declaring 6-D arrays for the fluid field variables—for example, d(:serial, :serial, :serial, :news, :news, :news)—with the serial dimensions referring to the 3-D index of a cell within a given block and the parallel dimensions referring to the indices of the block in a 3-D block decomposition of the computational domain. This had the advantage that serial operations on d within a block could proceed in parallel without invoking the communication network. Internal boundary values were copied from neighboring processors once per time step into 5-D arrays that corresponded to the faces of the blocks. In this way, communication was isolated to one rather minor phase of the calculation. Performance improved threefold to ≈ 24 Mflop/sec or 18% of peak, which largely reflected the sustained speed of the purely local computations. Scaling tests with constant work per processor yielded ideal scaling up to $NP = 512$ nodes, confirming that communication costs were minimal.

The particle-mesh (PM) code, on the other hand, is communication intensive. The PM algorithm consists of three phases, the first and third of which involve nonlocal communication between and among the 1-D particle list and 3-D field arrays. In the first, *mass assignment*, phase, the particles' mass is assigned to a density field array via a gather operation. In the second, *field solve* phase, the Poisson equation is solved for the gravitational potential using 3-D FFTs—a nonlocal operation. The mesh force is computed from spatial differences of the potential—a local operation. In the third, *force interpolation*, phase, the mesh force is interpolated to the particle positions via a scatter operation. Obviously, finding efficient parallel implementations that minimize communication costs is essential. An additional complication is that the particle distribution becomes highly inhomogeneous due to gravitational clustering, creating load imbalances in phases one and three, even if the particle list and field arrays are uniformly distributed across processors.

We implemented the algorithm of Ferrell and Bertschinger [328], which elegantly solves all of these problems. Since the algorithm and its performance on the CM-5 are described in detail in Ferrell and Bertschinger [328], we merely summarize the key points. The gather–scatter portion of phases one and three are done in a completely load-balanced way through the use of *parallel prefix operations* on the particle list [473]. Parallel prefix operations, also referred to as *scans*, are a method of turning certain kinds of global communications into regular, mostly local, communications. Briefly, the procedure is to sort the particle list so that all particles within a given processor are contiguous. An index list is introduced that contains the processor ID for each particle. Because the list has been sorted, the processor ID is constant in a segment, changing to another value in the next segment. We then use a *segmented scan add* operation, which computes a running sum of the masses of the particles within a given segment. This operation requires $\mathcal{O}(\log NP)$ communication operations. The last element in each segment contains the total mass in the segment. We then have only one word of data to send to each virtual processor assigned to a grid cell. In step two, three components of the gravitational acceleration on the grid are computed from the gridded mass densities using Fourier transforms. For this purpose, we used the highly optimized 3-D FFT routines in the CMSSL library. The third, force interpolation, phase is essentially the inverse of the mass assignment phase. We use a *segmented scan copy* to copy the gridded forces to a segmented force list. This operation also takes $\mathcal{O}(\log NP)$ communication operations. The forces are then applied to the particles in parallel in a purely local fashion.

For a scaled work problem, the combined code exhibited linear speedup on the CM-5 to 512 processors, with a parallel efficiency of $T(1)/(NP * T(NP)) \sim 0.75$. Clearly, the communication overhead in the PM portion of the calculation is responsible for the lack of ideal scaling. Still, the fact that parallel speedup was roughly constant versus NP indicates that the combined algorithm was scalable.

8.5.4 Parallel AMR Code: Enzo

The demise of the CM-5, coupled with the need for higher resolution than afforded by uniform grids, motivated the development of Enzo. Enzo uses structured adaptive mesh refinement (SAMR) [93, 152] to achieve high resolution in gravitational condensations. The central idea behind SAMR is simple to describe but difficult to implement efficiently on parallel computers. While solving the desired set of equations on a coarse uniform grid, monitor the quality of the solution; when necessary, add an additional finer mesh over the region that requires enhanced resolution. This finer (child) mesh obtains its boundary conditions from the coarser (parent) grid or from other neighboring (sibling) grids with the same mesh spacing. The finer grid is also used to improve the solution on its parent. As the evolution continues, it may be necessary to move, resize, or even remove the finer mesh. Even finer meshes may be required, producing a tree structure that can continue to any depth.

To advance our system of coupled equations in time on this grid hierarchy, we use a recursive algorithm. For simplicity, we consider only the hydrodynamic portion of the algorithm; the dark matter dynamics and Poisson equation have a similar structure. The EvolveLevel routine is passed the level of the hierarchy that it is to work on and the new time. Its job is to march the grids on that level from the old time to the new time:

EvolveLevel(*level*, *ParentTime*)
begin
   SetBoundaryValues(all grids);
   while (*Time* < *ParentTime*)
   begin
     dt = *ComputeTimeStep*(all grids);
     SolveHydroEquations(all grids, *dt*);
     Time += *dt*;
     SetBoundaryValues(all grids);
     EvolveLevel(*level*+1, *Time*);
     RebuildHierarchy(*level*+1);
   end
end

Inside the loop that advances the grids on this level, there is a recursive call, so that all the levels above (with finer subgrids) are advanced as well. The resulting order of time steps is like the multigrid W cycle.

As with any hyperbolic equation, we must set the boundary conditions on the grids. This is done by first interpolating from a grid's parent and then copying from sibling grids, where available. Once the boundary values have been set, we evolve the hydrodynamic field equations using procedure `SolveHydroEquations`. The final task of the `EvolveLevel` routine is to modify the grid hierarchy to the changing solution. This is accomplished via the `RebuildHierarchy` procedure, which takes a level as an argument and modifies the grids on that level and all higher levels. This involves three steps: First, a refinement test is applied to the parent grids of the current level to determine which cells need to be refined. Second, rectangular regions are chosen that cover all of the refined regions, while an attempt is made to minimize the number of unnecessarily refined points. Third, the new grids are created and their values are copied from the old grids (which are deleted) or interpolated from parent grids. This process is repeated on the next refined level until the grid hierarchy has been entirely rebuilt.

8.5.5 Parallelization of Enzo

Other than the physical equations solved, Enzo bears no relation to Kronos. Virtually none of the CMF code was reusable because not only did we change algorithms, we changed programming models and languages as well. The code is mostly implemented in C++, with compute-intensive kernels in Fortran 77. Efficiently parallelizing SAMR is difficult, particularly for distributed-memory systems. Grids have a relatively short life, so information must be updated frequently. Moreover, load balancing becomes crucial since small regions of the original grid eventually dominate the computational requirements.

Enzo development proceeded in two major steps. The first step, carried out by Greg Bryan in 1994–1996, was the implementation of a shared-memory parallel code for the SGI Origin 2000 employing SGI's PowerC compiler to concurrently execute grids at a given refinement level. The powerful, mature C development environment on the SGI was a major boon. However, since the workload is typically distributed nonuniformly across levels (cf. Figure 8.8) and the algorithm dictates that levels must be processed sequentially, we found that we could not efficiently use more than about 16 processors. Therefore, a second SPMD message-passing code for distributed-memory systems was implemented in 1997–2000, wherein the root grid is domain decomposed into 3-D blocks. Each block and its complement of subgrids are assigned to different processors, which work on them in parallel. Load balancing is achieved by sending grids from overloaded processors to underloaded ones, and optionally through the use of *grid splitting* [591].

We have used the MPI library to produce a code that is portable and efficient. In particular, we have used the following optimization techniques:

- *Distributed objects*. We leveraged the object-oriented design by distributing the objects over the processors, rather than attempting to distribute an individual grid.

- *Sterile objects*. Although distributing the objects results in good load balancing, it has the potential to greatly increase the amount of communication since each processor has to probe other processors to find out about neighboring grids. We solved this problem by creating a type of object that contained information about the location and size of a grid, but did not contain the actual solution arrays. These sterile objects are small; thus, each processor can hold the entire hierarchy. Only those grids that are truly local to that processor are nonsterile.

- *Pipelined communications*. One result of distribution is that all operations between two grids (e.g., obtaining boundary values) are potentially nonlocal. We optimize this by dividing each communication stage into two steps. First, all of the data are processed and sent. Since all processors have the location of all grids locally (thanks to the sterile objects), we can order these sends such that the data that are required first are sent first. Then, in the receive stage, the data needed immediately have had a chance to propagate across the network while the rest of the sends were initiated.

8.5.6   Performance

The performance of an adaptive mesh-refinement (AMR) application is difficult to characterize because the workload and its distribution are dynamically changing throughout the calculation. The simplest measure is *time to solution* of a run versus *NP*. This necessitates running a job to completion over and over again, varying *NP*. This is computationally expensive for modest problem sizes and impractical for medium-to-large problems of interest. Nevertheless, this has been done; results are

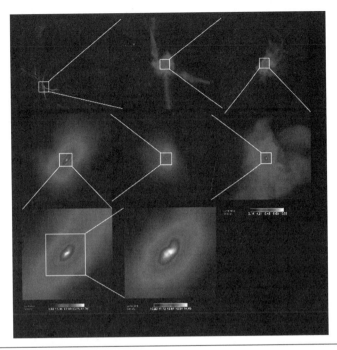

Figure 8.7 Enzo simulation of primordial star formation. Each image shows gas density in a region 10 times smaller than the previous. From Bryan et al. [149].

reported in Lan et al. [592]. We find that not only is parallel efficiency *problem-size dependent*, as expected, but also *problem dependent* as well. For example, a survey calculation involving a large root grid and no subgrids distributed over many processors will scale very differently from a calculation involving a large number of small, deeply nested subgrids focusing on a single collapsing object.

To illustrate the operation and performance of Enzo on the latter sort of problem, we show in Figure 8.7 an AMR simulation of primordial star formation that achieves a local resolution in space and time of 10^{12}. For comparison, 10^{12} is roughly the ratio of the diameter of the Earth to the size of a human cell. Temporally, 10^{12} is roughly the ratio of time since the extinction of the dinosaurs to when you woke up this morning. Over 8000 subgrids are developed at 34 levels of refinement to achieve this unprecedented dynamic range.

In Figure 8.8(a) and (b), we show how the grid hierarchy grows as time progresses. Note the slow increase in the number of grids as the protostar condenses and the final, very sudden jump in the depth of the grid tree at the end, when the core of the cloud collapses to high density. This demonstrates how the data structures themselves adapt to fit the physical solution. Note also the extremely large number of memory allocations and frees, since the entire grid hierarchy is rebuilt thousands

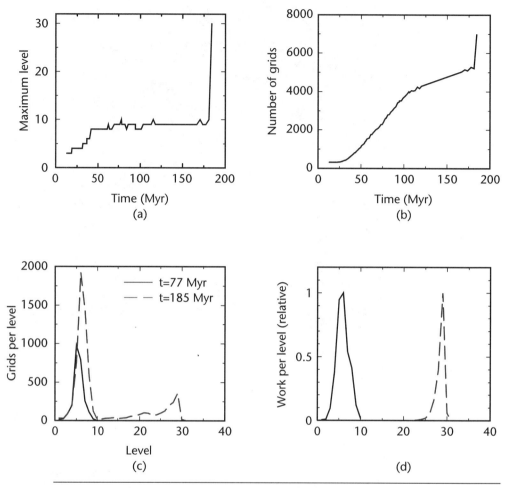

Figure 8.8 (a) Depth of the hierarchy tree and (b) number of grids as a function of time (in millions of years). (c) Number of grids per level and (d) estimate of the computational work required per level (in each case normalized so that the maximum value is unity).

of times. This kind of method represents a new class of scientific computing that places great strain on the operating system infrastructure. Total memory usage is also substantial, often reaching up to 20 GB. With outputs in the 2 to 4 GB range, we require at least 50 to 100 GB of disk storage and much more mass storage space.

In Figure 8.8(c) and (d), we have chosen two representative times and plotted the distribution of levels per grid. At early times, most of the grids are at moderate levels, representing the fact that relatively low resolution is sufficient to model the protostar. However, at late times, a large investment is required at the very highest levels of resolution.

Finally, we estimate the raw performance of the code in the following way. We have used the hardware floating-point counter on the SGI Origin 2000 to determine the speed of a similar SAMR calculation. This provides a benchmark from which we can determine the speed of this calculation, which was run on the Blue Horizon IBM SP2 system at the San Diego Supercomputer Center (SDSC). Running on 64 processors produced a speed approximately 125 times faster than a single Origin 2000 processor (105 Mflop/s), yielding a total speed of approximately 13 Gflop/s. As an exercise, we can also ask how long this calculation would have taken with a traditional static grid code and compute an effective or virtual flop rate. To do this, we assume a grid with 10^{12} cells on each side and assume that the entire calculation would have taken (quite conservatively) 10^{10} time steps. This works out to approximately 10^{50} floating-point operations. Since the entire calculation took in the order of 10^6 seconds, this converts to a virtual flop rate of 10^{44} flop/s.

8.5.7 Future Work

In the near future we intend to carry out large-scale simulations of galaxy formation resolving the internal structure of thousands of galaxies simultaneously. These will involve large global root grids (512^3 or larger) and deep mesh refinements around each forming galaxy. Computational requirements are in the sustained teraflop range, owing to the large number of time steps required, with concomitantly large RAM and disk requirements. Currently, we are porting Enzo to terascale cluster architectures, including the Compaq system at the Pittsburgh Supercomputing Center (PSC), as well as Linux clusters at NCSA. Principal needs remain mature C and Fortran compilers, debugging tools, optimized mathematical subroutine libraries, and efficient parallel I/O subsystems. We plan to explore mixed-mode parallel programming (threads plus message passing) on the IBM SP2 with Power3 SMP nodes at the SDSC. Our experience with the CM-5 has taught us, the hard way, that language solutions to massive parallelism vanish as quickly as the hardware they rode in on.

Acknowledgments. This work was carried out under the auspices of the Grand Challenge Cosmology Consortium with partial support by NSF grants ASC-9318185 and AST-9803137, as well as support from the National Center for Supercomputing Applications, University of Illinois at Urbana-Champaign, which is gratefully acknowledged.

8.6 Computational Electromagnetics

J. S. Shang

Computational electromagnetics (CEM) has a tier-structured approach for radar cross-section (RCS) prediction, antenna radiation, and coupling problems. The predictive techniques fall naturally into three general groups, according to the mathematics formulation of the physics and the frequency spectrum of interest. In essence, numerical methods are derived for dominant physical phenomena depending on whether they occur in the Rayleigh, resonance, or optical region. The collective modeling and simulation tools span a range, including the asymptotic method, the frequency-domain method (or method of moments, MoM), the time-domain method, and the more recent hybrid technique [471, 535, 647, 857]. Individually, they may be limited either by predictive accuracy or by practicality in application. As a group, these methods have been extremely productive for antenna and low-observable technology development.

In the optical region, the asymptotic methods for RCS prediction are based on ray tracing and edge diffraction [647], which are developed from both simple geometrical optics and geometrical theory of diffraction but not by solving the Maxwell equations. The scattering phenomenon is described by a set of parallel rays issued from radar and reflected from a geometric surface. The total scattering field is then determined by summing the contributions from all rays at a far-field observation point. Evaluations of these incident and reflected rays are essentially independent from each other. Thus, numerical methods of this group are extremely easy to port on massively parallel computers. In fact, scalable performance is a common feature of all ray-tracing methods. However, these methods are accurate only if the physical dimension of the scatterer is large in comparison with the incident wavelength and if it does not have small features such as wires, cracks, and cavities. In order to include effects of detailed features such as these, it is necessary to apply more accurate methods involving solution of the Maxwell equations. Unfortunately, frequency-domain (MoM) and time-domain methods are both time consuming and memory intensive.

Massively parallel computing capability has aided in the practical application of frequency-domain and time-domain methods in two ways. First, concurrent computing significantly reduces the wall-clock time required for data processing. Recent research efforts in porting CEM programs to multicomputers have recorded two orders of magnitude of speedup in the data processing rate [857].

More importantly, the distributed and the shared-distributed memory systems can now accommodate a far larger number of unknowns than were unattainable just a few years ago. This increased capacity expands the frequency range and complexity of physics that can be practically simulated.

Meanwhile, numerical algorithm improvement also redefines the application domain for CEM. For the frequency-domain method, the fast multipole algorithm has demonstrated a higher computational efficiency by reducing arithmetic operations [194]. In turn, the gain in computational efficiency enlarges the application range of MoM methods from the resonance to the optical region. Compact-difference schemes, on the other hand, also provide the means for the time-domain method to approach a spectral-like performance [854, 855]. Although a continuing research effort is still required to realize the full application potential, the progress in CEM warrants a timely assessment.

In the development of interdisciplinary modeling and simulation technology, electromagnetic phenomena are increasingly used as additional control mechanisms. In this regard, magneto-aerodynamics is truly an interdisciplinary endeavor. The interactive physical phenomenon requires the interplay of aerodynamics, electromagnetics, chemical physics, and quantum physics to describe the ionized gas flow in the presence of magnetic and electric fields. The science issues for this interdisciplinary endeavor are extremely complex, and the required knowledge base is the sparest; but the prospect for technical breakthrough is too great to be overlooked [856]. The present effort attempts to assess the progress in CEM and to identify future research needs. The major challenges for CEM simulation in the future are wide-band antenna design, real-time range profiling, synthetic-aperture radar (SAR) imaging, and ultra-wideband systems for radar remote sensing. In order to meet these challenges, additional physics must be incorporated into the predictive tools of CEM. The more complex physical description can only be accommodated by increasing the efficiency of modeling and simulation technology through improvement of numerical procedures and interdisciplinary analysis.

8.6.1   Asymptotic Methods

For high-frequency applications, the ray tracing or the shooting-and-bouncing-ray (SBR) technique is used exclusively [615, 647]. The underlying principle of this technique is based on physical optics, physical theory of diffraction, or a combination of both. For multibounce calculations, the effects of polarization, ray divergence factor, and material reflection coefficients must be taken into consideration. The scattered far field is derived from the induced surface current by physical optics integration. Therefore, the predictive accuracy is controllable by the density of the tracing rays. At present, the SBR technique for RCS and range profile calculation requires a minimum ray density of 10 rays per wavelength. Hence, the RCS of a typical fighter at an incidence elevation and azimuth angle will need about a 30-million-ray window when illuminated by radar at the X-band frequency (8 to 12 GHz). Fortunately, the SBR algorithm is naturally suitable for concurrent computing. Exceptionally high parallel-computing efficiency has been consistently demonstrated in the development of automatic target recognition (ATR) technology [647].

For the asymptotic approach, the development of pre- and post-processors is identified as the pacing item [647]. Predictive accuracy depends on the integrity of the CAD geometry file of the scatterer. It is therefore critical to be able to inspect the fidelity of the geometry data and the connectivity of the surface elements. For post-processor development, the effort needs to go beyond acquisition of an excellent graphical user interface; hybrid methods, coupling other numerical results, must be developed.

8.6.2   Frequency-Domain Methods

The progress in the method of moments (MoM) for computing efficiency improvement has been strongly impacted by incorporating advanced basis functions and the fast multipole method (FMM) [194]. The Rao–Wilson–Glisson (RWG) basis function used to discretize the surface integral kernel has substantially reduced the number of unknowns for finite element approximations [790]. On the other hand, the FMM technique relies on a hierarchical subdivision of space that encloses the source and scattering point. For the matrix–vector multiply-dominated numerical procedure, the operation count can be reduced from $\mathcal{O}(N^2)$ to $\mathcal{O}(N)$ or $\mathcal{O}(N \log N)$, depending on the spatial-distribution point density and implementation.

Research on the integral equation approach emphasizes two areas. The first is computing efficiency and memory enhancement of the basic algorithms by using either FMM or the adaptive integral method (AIM) [120]. The second is exclusively related to parallel computing and requires an extensive investment in the scalable and parallel matrix–vector multiplier library. An efficient, sparse-matrix-inversion procedure for MoM is the pacing item for large-scale electromagnetic scattering or radiating simulations.

8.6.3   Time-Domain Methods

Advances in time-domain methods have been made in porting numerical procedures to parallel computers [857], unstructured grid implementation [430], and compact-difference method developments [366, 603, 855, 1011]. Since integration with other scientific disciplines is often based on the time-domain approach, we discuss these methods in more detail.

Multicomputers, either distributed-memory or shared-distributed-memory RISC (reduced instruction set computer) systems, have provided a viable means for simulating dynamic and wide-band electromagnetic phenomena. It is well known that balancing the processor's workload and minimizing interprocessor communication are essential for effective use of multicomputers. A frequently overlooked requirement for efficient parallel computing has been identified from the programming paradigm for 3-D Maxwell equations. Cache memory, together with memory hierarchy utilization, emerges as an equally critical element for high concurrent computing performance [857]. A data processing rate exceeding 41.3% of the SGI R10000 processor specification (rated peak performance of 390 Mflops) has been achieved by enhancing the data locality feature. This performance accomplishment demonstrated that mapping numerical procedures to RISC-based multicomputers, balancing the processor's work load, minimizing interprocessor communication, and managing cache memory are procedures essential for effective use of distributed-memory multicomputers.

The key to making a computer program flexible enough for a wide range of applications lies in mapping all grid topologies onto a common framework [430, 854, 857]. Since an unstructured-grid approach represents the most general grid connectivity, grids are best converted to and stored via an unstructured-grid data composition. This conversion process requires explicit connectivity of adjacent grid points. The same requirement exists when mapping a numerical procedure to multicomputers by the domain-decomposition approach. Explicit connectivity of adjacent grid points or data blocks becomes a common feature of these two unrelated techniques. It seems logical to adopt the unstructured-grid approach for both discretizing and parallel computing. This point is unequivocally illustrated in solving a perfect, electrically conducting (PEC) sphere problem by an explicit finite-volume, time-domain (FVTD) procedure at high incident–wave frequency [430, 856]. The scattering simulation is obtained from a patched surface mesh to alleviate the mesh point clustering of the spherical polar coordinate in the polar region. The unstructured-grid approach realizes a factor of four in computing resource savings over that of conventional methods. An accurate prediction is obtained on 16 nodes of an SGI Origin 2000 system using a total 33.92 nodal hours, or a wall-clock time of 2.12 hours. The computing resource requirement is comparable to the most efficient MoM computation using the FMM procedure (20 hours on a single node) [194, 854]. The gain in numerical efficiency of unstructured-grid formulations, however, is offset by the limitation of second-order numerical algorithms.

For telecommunication and navigation, high-frequency wave packets are required to propagate over a long distance without significant phase error and amplitude modulation. A spectral-like, high numerical resolution for simulating long-distance wave propagation can be derived from high-order or compact-difference algorithms [603]. The compact-difference–based finite-volume and finite-difference methods have produced remarkably accurate results for transient electromagnetic wave propagation in waveguides [366, 603, 855, 1011]. These numerical procedures can be further optimized to minimize dissipative, dispersive, and anisotropic errors. More recently, a low-pass filter was developed to effectively control an undesirable time-instability feature of compact-difference schemes. The numerical filter eliminates the Fourier components that are unsupportable by the grid-point density used. This high-resolution numerical algorithm research, together with the concept of perfectly matched layers (PMLs) [91], will remain research foci for CEM in the time domain.

8.6.4 Hybrid Methods

A relatively new approach in the practical CEM arena for full-scale dynamic simulation is the hybrid method [535, 647]. This method is designed to simulate physics involving interactions of discontinuities on electrically large structures. Three levels of hybridization are possible by consistently combining earlier computational tools for solving time-domain, frequency-domain, and asymptotic formulation for scattering and radiation. The hybrid formulations in CEM meld the best of high-frequency asymptotics with rigorous low-frequency approaches that are based on first principles [535, 647]. In general, three types of hybridization have been derived from the concept of domain decomposition. Type 1 is developed from the Schelkunoff equivalence principle [535] to allow the combination of high-frequency asymptotes with the solution of surface integral equations. Type 2 hybridization iteratively couples physical optics with the solution of the surface integral equation. This approach can treat electrically large and intermediate size scatterers, as well as a radiator strongly dominated by interaction with surface discontinuities. Type 3 hybridization analyzes problems dominated by strong bidirectional surface-wave interactions, which are induced by widely separated, local geometrical complexities or different materials. Although hybrid methods are still in the initial stage of development, computing time savings by a factor of 20 have been realized in some numerical simulations [535]. The development of a consistent and systematic hybrid technique is a major area of emphasis for future CEM research.

8.6.5   State of the Art

Computational magneto-aerodynamics is recognized as a new frontier for interdisciplinary technology development. A key element of this technical requirement is integrating CEM in the time domain with computational fluid dynamics and computational chemical kinetics. The impact of this interdisciplinary endeavor to high-speed flight may be revolutionary.

This assessment indicates that the hybrid technique is one of the most exciting developments in expanding the application envelope for CEM. For frequency-domain methods, an efficient and scalable matrix–vector multiplier appears to be the pacing item. In order to achieve greater computational efficiency on RISC-based multicomputers, cache utilization emerges as an important requirement for high-performance computing.

8.7   Parallel Algorithms in Data Mining
Mahesh V. Joshi, Eui-Hong (Sam) Han, George Karypis, and Vipin Kumar

Recent growth in the availability of various kinds of data has been explosive. It has resulted in an unprecedented opportunity to develop automated data-driven techniques of extracting useful knowledge. Data mining, an important step in this process of knowledge discovery, consists of methods that discover interesting, non-trivial, and useful patterns hidden in the data [191, 902]. The field of data mining builds on ideas from diverse fields, such as machine learning, pattern recognition, statistics, database systems, and data visualization. But techniques developed in these traditional disciplines are often unsuitable due to some unique characteristics of today's data sets, such as their enormous sizes, high dimensionality, and heterogeneity.

To date, the primary driving force behind research in data mining has been the development of algorithms for data sets arising in various business, information retrieval, and financial applications. Businesses can use data mining to gain significant advantages in today's competitive global marketplace. For example, the retail industry is using data mining techniques to analyze buying patterns of customers, mail order businesses are using them for targeted marketing, the telecommunication industry is using them for churn prediction and network alarm analysis, and the credit card industry is using them for fraud detection. Also, the recent growth of electronic commerce is generating a wealth of online Web data, which requires sophisticated data mining techniques.

Due to the latest technological advances, very large data sets are becoming available in many scientific disciplines as well. The rate of production of such data sets far outstrips the ability to analyze them manually. For example, a computational simulation running on state-of-the-art, high-performance computers can generate terabytes of data within a few hours, whereas a human analyst may take several weeks or longer to analyze and discover useful information from these data sets. Data mining techniques hold great promise for developing new sets of tools that can be used to automatically analyze the massive data sets resulting from such simulations and thus help engineers and scientists unravel the causal relationships in the underlying mechanisms of dynamic physical processes. Some other recently emerging applications of data mining can be found in the analysis and understanding of gene functions in the field of genomics and the categorization of stars and galaxies in the field of astrophysics.

The huge size of the available data sets and their high dimensionality make large-scale data mining applications computationally very demanding, and high-performance parallel computing is becoming an essential component of the solution. Moreover, the quality of the data mining results often depends directly on the amount of computing resources available. In fact, data mining applications are poised to become the dominant consumers of supercomputing in the near future. There is a necessity to develop effective parallel algorithms for various data mining techniques. However, designing such algorithms is challenging. In the rest of this section, we describe the parallel formulations of two important data mining algorithms: discovery of association rules and induction of decision trees for classification.

8.7.1 Parallel Algorithms for Discovering Associations

An important problem in data mining [191] is the discovery of associations present in the data. Such problems arise in the data collected from scientific experiments, from monitoring of physical systems such as telecommunications networks, or from transactions at a supermarket. The problem was formulated originally in the context of transaction data at a supermarket. These *market basket* data consist of transactions made by each customer. Each transaction contains items bought by the customer (see Table 8.1). The goal is to see if the occurrence of certain items in a transaction can be used to deduce occurrence of other items, or in other words, to find associative relationships among items. If such interesting relationships can be found, then they can be put to various profitable uses: shelf management, inventory management, and so on. Thus, *association rules* were born [14]. Given a set of items, association rules predict the occurrence of some other set of items with a certain degree of confidence. The goal is to discover *all* such *interesting* rules. This problem is far from trivial because of the exponential number of ways in which items can be grouped together and the different ways in which one can define the "interestingness" of a rule. Hence, much research effort has been put into formulating efficient solutions to the problem.

Table 8.1   Supermarket transactions.

TID	Items
1	Bread, Coke, Milk
2	Beer, Bread
3	Beer, Coke, Diaper, Milk
4	Beer, Bread, Diaper, Milk
5	Coke, Diaper, Milk

Let T be the set of transactions, where each transaction is a subset of the item set I. Let C be a subset of I. We define the *support count* of C with respect to T to be:

$$\sigma(C) = |\{t| t \in T, C \subseteq t\}|$$

Thus $\sigma(C)$ is the number of transactions that contain C. An *association rule* is an expression of the form $X \xrightarrow{s,\alpha} Y$, where $X \subseteq I$ and $Y \subseteq I$. The *support* s of the rule $X \xrightarrow{s,\alpha} Y$ is defined as $\sigma(X \cup Y)/|T|$, and the confidence α is defined as $\sigma(X \cup Y)/\sigma(X)$. For example, for transactions in Table 8.1, the support of rule {Diaper, Milk} $\implies$ {Beer} is $\sigma(Diaper, Milk, Beer)/5 = 2/5 = 40\%$, whereas its confidence is $\sigma(Diaper, Milk, Beer)/\sigma(Diaper, Milk) = 2/3 = 66\%$.

The task of discovering an association rule is to find all rules $X \xrightarrow{s,\alpha} Y$ such that s is greater than or equal to a given minimum support threshold and α is greater than or equal to a given minimum confidence threshold. The association rule discovery is usually done in two phases. The first phase finds all the *frequent* item sets, that is, sets satisfying the support threshold. These are then post-processed in the second phase to find the high-confidence rules. The former phase is computationally more expensive, and much research has been done in developing efficient algorithms for it. A comparative survey of all the existing techniques is given in Joshi et al. [526]. A key feature of these algorithms lies in their method of controlling the exponential complexity of the total number of item sets ($2^{|I|}$). Briefly, they all use the antimonotone property of an item set support, which states that an item set is frequent only if all of its sub–item sets are frequent. The Apriori algorithm [16] pioneered the use of this property to systematically search the exponential space of item sets. At iteration k, it generates all the *candidate* k-item sets (of length k) such that all their $(k-1)$-subsets are frequent. The occurrences of these candidates in the transaction database are counted to determine frequent k-item sets. Efficient data structures are used to perform fast counting.

Overall, serial algorithms such as Apriori have been successful on a wide variety of transaction databases. However, many practical applications of association rules involve huge transaction databases that contain a large number of distinct items. In such situations, these algorithms running on single-processor machines may take unacceptably long times. For example, in the Apriori algorithm, if the number of candidate item sets becomes too large, then they might not all fit in the main memory, and multiple database passes would be required within each iteration, incurring expensive I/O cost. This implies that, even with the highly effective pruning method of Apriori, the task of finding all association rules can require a lot of computational and memory resources. This is true of most of the other serial algorithms as well, and it motivates the development of parallel formulations.

Various parallel formulations have been developed; a comprehensive survey can be found in Joshi et al. [526], and Zaki 1013]. These formulations are designed to effectively parallelize either or both of the computation phases: candidate generation and candidate counting. The candidate-counting phase can be parallelized relatively easily by distributing the transaction database and gathering local counts for the entire set of candidates stored on all the processors. The CD algorithm [15] is an example of this simple approach. It scales linearly with respect to the number of transactions; however, generation and storage of a huge number of candidates on all the processors becomes a bottleneck, especially when high-dimensional problems are solved for low support thresholds using a large number of processors. Other parallel formulations, such as IDD [433], have been developed to solve these problems. Their key feature is that they distribute the candidate item sets to processors so as to extract the concurrency in the candidate-generation phase as well as the counting phase. Various ways are employed in IDD to reduce the communication overhead, to exploit the total available memory, and to achieve reasonable load balance. The IDD algorithm exhibits better scalability with respect to the number of candidates. Moreover, reduction of redundant work and the ability to overlap counting computation with communication of transactions improves its scalability with respect to the number of transactions. However, it still faces problems when one desires to use a large number of processors to solve the problem. As more processors are used, the number of candidates assigned to each processor decreases. This has two implications for IDD. First, with fewer candidates per processor, it is much more difficult to achieve load balance. Second, it results in less computation work per transaction at each processor, reducing the overall efficiency. Further, lack of asynchronous communication ability may worsen the situation.

Formulations that combine the approaches of replicating and distributing candidates so as to reduce the problems of each one have been developed. An example is the HD algorithm of [433]. Briefly, it works as follows. Consider a P-processor system in which the processors are split into G equal-size groups, each containing P/G processors. In the HD algorithm, we execute the CD algorithm as if there were only P/G processors. That is, we partition the transactions of the database into P/G parts, each of size $N/(P/G)$, and assign the task of computing the counts of the candidate set C_k for each subset of the transactions to each one of these groups of processors. Within each group, these counts are computed using the IDD algorithm. The HD algorithm inherits all the good features of the IDD algorithm. It also provides good load balance and enough computation work by maintaining a minimum number of candidates per processor. At the same time, the amount of data movement in this algorithm is cut down to $1/G$ of that of IDD. A detailed parallel run-time analysis of

HD is given in Han et al. [434]. It shows that HD is scalable with respect to both the number of transactions and the number of candidates. The analysis also provides the necessary conditions under which HD can outperform CD.

Sequential Associations

The concept of association rules can be generalized and made more useful by observing another fact about transactions. All transactions have a time stamp associated with them, that is, the time at which the transaction occurred. If this information can be put to use, one can find relationships such as: *if a customer bought [The C Programming Language] book today, then he/she is likely to buy a [Using Perl] book in a few days' time*. The usefulness of this kind of rule gave birth to the problem of discovering *sequential patterns* or *sequential associations*. In general, a sequential pattern is a sequence of item sets with various timing constraints imposed on the occurrences of items appearing in the pattern. For example, (A) (C,B) (D) encodes a relationship that *event D occurs after an event-set (C,B), which in turn occurs after event A*. Prediction of events and identification of sequential rules that characterize different parts of the data are some example applications of sequential patterns. Such patterns are not only important because they represent more powerful and predictive relationships, but they are also important from the algorithmic point of view. Bringing in sequential relationships increases the combinatorial complexity of the problem enormously. The maximum number of sequences having k events is $\mathcal{O}(m^k 2^{k-1})$, where m is the total number of distinct events in the input data. In contrast, there are only $\binom{m}{k}$ size-k item sets possible when discovering nonsequential associations from m distinct items. Designing parallel algorithms for discovering sequential associations is equally important and challenging. In many situations, the techniques used in parallel algorithms for discovering standard nonsequential associations can be extended easily. However, different issues and challenges arise due to the sequential nature and various ways in which interesting sequential associations can be defined. Details of various serial and parallel formulations and algorithms for finding such associations can be found in Joshi et al. [526, 528].

8.7.2   Parallel Algorithms for Induction of Decision-Tree Classifiers

Classification is an important data mining problem. The input to the problem is a data set called the *training set,* which consists of a number of examples, each having a number of attributes. The attributes are either *continuous*, when the attribute values are ordered, or *categorical*, when the attribute values are unordered. One of the categorical attributes is called the *class label* or the *classifying attribute*. The objective is to use the training set to build a model of the class label, based on the other attributes, such that the model can be used to classify new data not from the training data set. Application domains include retail target marketing, fraud detection, and design of telecommunication service plans. Several classification models such as neural networks [617], genetic algorithms [386], and decision trees [785] have been proposed. Decision trees are probably the most popular, since they obtain reasonable accuracy [673] and are relatively inexpensive to compute.

Most of the existing induction-based algorithms such as C4.5 [785], CDP [13], SLIQ [662], and SPRINT [851] use Hunt's method [785] as the basic algorithm. Here is its recursive description for constructing a decision tree from a set T of training cases, with classes denoted $\{C_1, C_2, \dots, C_k\}$.

Case 1. T contains cases all belonging to a single class C_j. The decision tree for T is a leaf identifying class C_j.

Case 2. T contains cases that belong to a mixture of classes. A test is chosen, based on a single attribute, that has one or more mutually exclusive outcomes $\{O_1, O_2, \dots, O_n\}$. Note that in many implementations, n is chosen to be 2; this leads to a binary decision tree. T is partitioned into subsets $T_1, T_2, \dots, T_n$, where T_i contains all the cases in T that have outcome O_i of the chosen test. The decision tree for T consists of a decision node identifying the test and one branch for each possible outcome. The same tree-building machinery is applied recursively to each subset of training cases.

Case 3. T contains no cases. The decision tree for T is a leaf, but the class to be associated with the leaf must be determined from information other than T. For example, $C4.5$ chooses this to be the most frequent class at the parent of this node.

Figure 8.9 shows a training data set with four data attributes and two classes; its classification decision tree was constructed using Hunt's method. In Case 2 of Hunt's method, a test based on a single attribute is chosen for expanding the current node. The choice of an attribute is normally based on the entropy gains [785] of the attributes. The entropy of an attribute, calculated from class distribution information, depicts the classification power of the attribute by itself. The best attribute is selected as a test for node expansion.

Highly parallel algorithms for constructing classification decision trees are desirable for dealing with large data sets in a reasonable amount of time. Classification decision-tree construction algorithms have natural concurrency; once a node is generated, all of its children in the classification tree can be generated concurrently. Furthermore, the computation for generating successors of a classification-tree node can also be decomposed by performing data decomposition on the training data. Nevertheless, parallelization of the algorithms for constructing the classification tree is challenging. First, the shape of the tree is highly irregular and is determined only at run time. Furthermore, the amount of work associated with each node also varies and is data dependent. Hence, any static allocation scheme is likely to suffer from major load imbalance. Second, even though the successors of a node can be processed concurrently, they all use the training data associated with the parent node. If these data are dynamically partitioned and allocated to different processors that perform computation for different nodes, then there is a high cost for data movements. If the data are not partitioned appropriately, then performance can be bad due to this loss of locality.

Outlook	Temp (F)	Humidity (%)	Windy?	Class
sunny	75	70	true	Play
sunny	80	90	true	Don't Play
sunny	85	85	false	Don't Play
sunny	72	95	false	Don't Play
sunny	69	70	false	Play
overcast	72	90	true	Play
overcast	83	78	false	Play
overcast	64	65	true	Play
overcast	81	75	false	Play
rain	71	80	true	Don't Play
rain	65	70	true	Don't Play
rain	75	80	false	Play
rain	68	80	false	Play
rain	70	96	false	Play

(a)

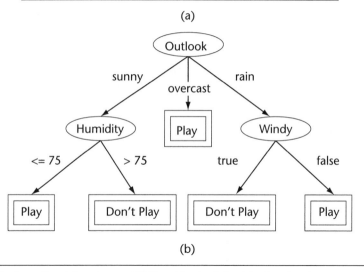

(b)

Figure 8.9   A small training data set [785] and its final classification decision tree.

Several parallel formulations of classification decision-tree construction have been proposed recently [189, 385, 527, 584, 760, 851, 893]. In this section, we present two basic parallel formulations for classification decision-tree construction and a hybrid scheme that combines good features of both of these approaches described in Srivastava et al. [893]. Most of the other parallel algorithms are similar, and their characteristics can be explained using these two basic algorithms. For these parallel formulations, we focus our presentation on discrete attributes only. Handling of continuous attributes is discussed separately. In all parallel formulations, we assume that N training cases are randomly distributed to P processors and that each processor initially has N/P cases.

Synchronous Tree-Construction Approach

In this approach, all processors construct a decision tree synchronously by sending and receiving class distribution information of local data. Figure 8.10(a) shows the overall picture. The root node has already been expanded, and the current node is the leftmost child of the root (as shown in the top part of the figure). All four processors cooperate to expand this node to have two child nodes. Next, the leftmost node of these child nodes is selected as the current node (in the bottom of the figure), and all four processors again cooperate to expand the node.

Partitioned Tree-Construction Approach

In this approach, whenever feasible, different processors work on different parts of the classification tree. In particular, if several processors cooperate to expand a node, then these processors are partitioned to expand the successors of this node. Figure 8.10(b) shows an example. First (at the top of the figure), all four processors co-operate to expand the root node just as they do in the synchronous tree-construction approach. Next (in the middle of the figure), the set of four processors is partitioned into three parts. The leftmost child is assigned to processors 0 and 1, while the other nodes are assigned to processors 2 and 3, respectively. Now these sets of processors proceed independently to expand their assigned nodes. In particular, processor 2 and processor 3 expand their part of the tree using the serial algorithm. The group containing processors 0 and 1 splits the leftmost child node into three nodes. These three new nodes are partitioned into two parts (shown in the bottom of the figure); the leftmost node is assigned to processor 0, while the other two are assigned to processor 1. From now on, processors 0 and 1 work independently on their respective subtrees.

Hybrid Parallel Formulation

The hybrid parallel formulation has elements of both schemes. The *synchronous tree-construction approach* incurs high communication overhead as the frontier gets larger. The *partitioned tree-construction approach* incurs the cost of load balancing after each step. The hybrid scheme continues with the first approach as long as the communication cost incurred by the first formulation is not too high. Once this cost becomes high, the processors and the current frontier of the classification tree are partitioned into two parts. Figure 8.11 shows one example of this parallel formulation. At the classification-tree frontier at depth 3, no partitioning has been done, and all processors are working cooperatively on each node of the frontier. At the next frontier at depth 4, partitioning is triggered, and the nodes and processors are partitioned into two partitions.

A key element of the algorithm is the criterion that triggers the partitioning of the current set of processors (and the corresponding frontier of the classification tree). If partitioning is done too frequently, then the hybrid scheme will approximate

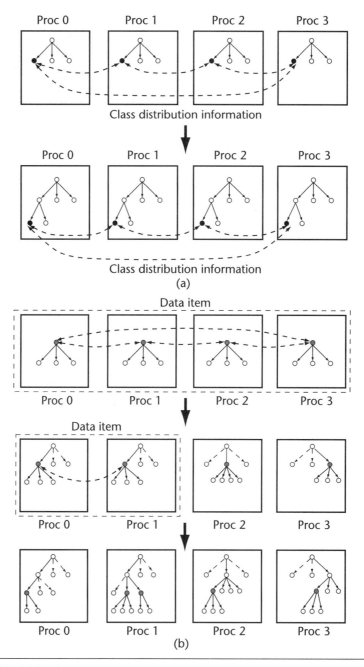

Figure 8.10   (a) Synchronous tree-construction approach and (b) partitioned tree-construction approach.

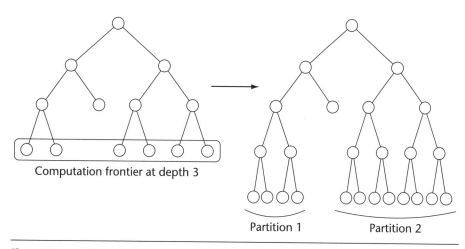

Computation frontier at depth 3

Partition 1   Partition 2

Figure 8.11   Hybrid tree-construction approach.

the partitioned tree-construction approach, and thus will incur too much data-movement cost. If the partitioning is done too late, then it will suffer from the high cost of communicating statistics generated for each node of the frontier, like the synchronized tree-construction approach. In the hybrid algorithm, splitting is performed when the accumulated cost of communication becomes equal to the cost of moving records and load balancing in the splitting phase.

The size and shape of the classification tree vary widely, depending on the application domain and training data set. Some classification trees might be shallow, and the others might be deep. Some classification trees could be skinny; others could be bushy. Some classification trees might be uniform in depth, while other trees might be skewed in one part of the tree. The hybrid approach adapts well to all types of classification trees. If the decision tree is skinny, the hybrid approach will just stay with the synchronous tree-construction approach. On the other hand, it will shift to the partitioned tree-construction approach as soon as the tree becomes bushy. If the tree has a big variance in depth, the hybrid approach will perform dynamic load balancing with processor groups to reduce processor idling.

Handling Continuous Attributes

The approaches described above concentrated primarily on how the tree is constructed in parallel with respect to the issues of load balancing and reducing communication overhead. The discussion was simplified by assuming that there were no continuous-valued attributes. Continuous attributes can be handled in two ways. One is to perform intelligent discretization, either once in the beginning or at each node as the tree is being induced, and to treat them as categorical attributes. Another, more popular approach is to use decisions of the form $A < x$ and $A \geq x$ directly on the values, x, of continuous attribute A. The decision value of x needs to be determined at each node. For efficient search of x, most algorithms require the attributes to be sorted on values, such that one linear scan can be done over all the values to evaluate the best decision. Among various different algorithms, the approach taken by the SPRINT algorithm [851], which sorts each continuous attribute only once in the beginning, is efficient for large data sets. The sorted order is maintained throughout the induction process, thus avoiding the possibly excessive costs of resorting at each node. A separate list is kept for each of the attributes; a record identifier is associated with each sorted value. The key step in handling continuous attributes is the proper assignment of records to child nodes after a splitting decision is made. Implementation of this offers a design challenge. SPRINT builds a mapping between a record identifier and the node to which it goes based on the splitting decision. The mapping is implemented as a hash table and is probed to split the attribute lists in a consistent manner.

Parallel formulation of the SPRINT algorithm falls under the category of synchronous tree-construction design. The multiple sorted lists of continuous attributes are split in parallel by building the entire hash table on all the processors. However, with this simpleminded way of achieving a consistent split, the algorithm incurs a communication overhead of $\mathcal{O}(N)$ per processor. Since the serial run time of the induction process is $\mathcal{O}(N)$, SPRINT becomes unscalable with respect to run time. It is unscalable in memory requirements also, because the total memory requirement per processor is $\mathcal{O}(N)$, as the size of the hash table is of the same order as the size of the training data set for the upper levels of the decision tree, and it resides on every processor. Another parallel algorithm, ScalParC [527], solves this scalability problem. It employs a distributed hash table to achieve a consistent split. The communication structure used to construct and access this hash table is motivated by the parallel, sparse matrix–vector multiplication algorithms. It is shown in Joshi et al. [527] that, with the proper implementation of parallel hashing, the overall communication overhead does not exceed $\mathcal{O}(N)$, and the memory required does not exceed $\mathcal{O}(N/p)$ per processor. Thus, ScalParC is scalable in run time as well as memory requirements.

8.7.3   State of the Art

This section presented an overview of parallel algorithms for two of the commonly used data mining techniques. Key issues such as load balancing, attention to locality, extracting maximal concurrency, avoiding hot spots in contention, and minimizing parallelization overhead are just as central to these parallel formulations as they are to the traditional, scientific parallel algorithms. In fact, in many cases, the underlying kernels are identical to well-known algorithms, such as the sparse matrix–vector product.

To date, the parallel formulations of many decision-tree induction and association rule–discovery algorithms are reasonably well understood. Relatively less work has been done on parallel algorithms for other data mining techniques, such as clustering, rule-based classification algorithms, deviation detection, and regression. Some possible areas of further research include parallelization of many emerging new and improved, serial data-mining algorithms; further analysis and refinements of existing algorithms for scalability and efficiency; designs targeted for shared-memory and distributed shared-memory machines equipped with symmetric multiprocessors; and efficient integration of parallel algorithms with parallel database systems.

Acknowledgments. This work was supported by National Science Foundation contract CCR-9972519, Army Research Office contract DA/DAAG55-98-1-0441, DoE grant LLNL/DOE B347714, and Army High Performance Computing Research Center (AHPCRC) contract DAAH04-95-C-0008. Access to computing facilities was provided by AHPCRC, Minnesota Supercomputer Institute. Related papers are available at *http://www.cs.umn.edu/~kumar*.

8.8 High-Performance Computing in Signal and Image Processing

D. R. Prabhu, Ashok K. Krishnamurthy, and Stanley C. Ahalt

The signal and image processing (SIP) community is extremely diverse and includes applications in geophysics, biomedical engineering, wireless communications, factory automation, speech processing, and automatic target recognition (ATR), to name a few. A general introduction to signal processing can be found in Oppenheim et al. [726], with a more advanced treatment in Zelniker and Taylor [1017]. There are also numerous excellent books focused on image processing [389, 508, 776], and multidimensional signal processing [296, 614].

Research groups within the SIP community have been working for many years on tasks that share a number of basic characteristics, and a framework has gradually emerged by which shared algorithms, software, and data can be distributed and tested. The overall aim of the community was to speed development, reduce cost, and improve the quality of fielded systems. This effort gave rise to a set of common tools being used by the majority of SIP algorithm designers and researchers. Most notably, C, C++, MATLAB, and Khoros emerged as the primary tools used in the SIP community. However, in contrast to other areas of research, much of the SIP community did not embrace the use of high-performance computing (HPC). While the reasons for this phenomenon have been debated, one significant factor was that SIP developers became accustomed to working and testing codes on interactive systems, while most HPC systems were managed as batch-oriented systems.

Thus, until recently most of the algorithm development work in the SIP community has been performed on single-processor workstations or on networks of loosely coupled workstations. Similarly, most of the deployed SIP systems have been implemented on either programmable, embedded DSP chips that are designed to run SIP algorithms or on highly specialized, closely coupled embedded architectures that could take advantage of regularization in SIP processing algorithms. Although there are isolated examples of subsets of the SIP community extensively using HPC resources, most notably the seismographic community [910], only recently have high-performance computers become more widely utilized by SIP researchers. This use of HPC resources in the SIP community has largely arisen from Department of Defense (DoD) research and engineering activities. Within DoD the need for very high-performance signal and image processing has increased dramatically in the last 5 years, particularly for automatic object recognition and related image processing tasks. In these types of applications, either computational requirements and/or streaming data (I/O) requirements dictate the use of HPC architectures.

Consequently, recent HPC work in the SIP community has focused on two themes. The first theme is the use of libraries, software components, and higher-level languages (HLLs) that allow complex SIP algorithms to be assembled, rigorously tested, and executed on commodity HPC platforms. That is, SIP algorithms are increasingly developed and tested on HPC systems, and in some cases production algorithms are executed on HPC systems in order to process massive data sets in a timely fashion. The second theme is emerging research directed at finding methods of mapping SIP algorithms to highly parallel, embedded processors. These two themes underlie the examples discussed below.

A large portion of the work in signal/image processing often involves simulation and modeling of a variety of sensors and algorithms. In a typical simulation code, there is an outer loop stepping through space or time, and the results from one iteration of the outer loop do not influence the results of subsequent iterations. Coarse-grain parallelization of such codes is fairly straightforward. The total number of outer loop iterations is divided evenly across the number of available CPUs. Each CPU computes a part of the outer loop. At the end of computation, one of the CPUs gathers results from the rest of the CPUs and creates the final outputs. It is relatively easy to distribute the first chunk of work to the first CPU, the second chunk to the second CPU, and so on. It is also relatively easy to gather results at the end with the above simple distribution. Unfortunately, this simplistic method may not be the best way of distributing work to achieve good load balance. The preferred way to distribute this type of SIP application is to deal out a tiny chunk of work to all CPUs and then have each CPU request more work when it has finished computing its part. This method, however, results in more communication.

8.8.1 Examples of HPC Use in Signal and Image Processing

Our experience with diverse SIP algorithms and SIP simulation and modeling codes is described below. Before we begin these descriptions, we note that it is critical to obtain good serial performance before any parallelization work is undertaken. For example, the developer should use the highest level of optimization that results in the best performance and yields correct outputs. Additionally, compiler flags that make full use of the available cache and software pipelines of the processors on the target platform should be used. Linking to a fast math library before linking to the regular math library can often yield a significant speedup, but one should be careful to examine the resulting precision and verify for correctness. Serial performance can sometimes be significantly improved by using certain well-written fast libraries for math computation and signal/image processing. An example of such a fast library is FFTW from the Massachusetts Institute of Technology [362].

The examples provided are representative of the increasing use of HPC in the SIP community. It should be noted that, while the examples discussed below are necessarily biased toward DoD applications, the seismographic community continues to make extensive use of SIP algorithms on virtually all HPC architectures.

Automatic Target Recognition

ATR is one of the most important military applications of signal/image processing algorithms. An ATR system typically has a variety of sensors, such as infrared, millimeter wave, and so on, and either performs onboard computations on acquired data or transmits data to a nearby ground station for analysis. A typical ATR system has severe constraints on streaming-input data rates (of signals or images) as well as latency requirements (time taken to process one signal or image).

For example, in the Predator system used for Tactical Endurance Synthetic Aperture Radar (TESAR) imagery, images vary in size and complexity with data rates up to 1 Mpixel/s depending on the radar mode, platform velocity, and imaging geometry. Thus, a fielded ATR system must be able to handle this data rate and identify targets in a timely manner for presentation on a waterfall display. Operational requirements set the time allowed for ATR computation; for example, it should be possible to command the Predator to reimage a scene of interest while still in range. This constraint typically permits a 20-second latency period for such reconnaissance ATR systems.

As an example of the impact of HPC on the development of ATR systems, an existing three-stage template-based algorithm for ATR of military ground targets in synthetic aperture radar (SAR) images was redesigned and implemented. The system was ultimately targeted to two multiprocessing configurations: (1) a 10-processor laboratory/fieldable system, and (2) an HPC system [900]. The Scalable Programming Environment (SPE) from the Naval Command, Control and Ocean Surveillance Center [754] was employed to parallelize the ATR code in a highly scalable way. Input images were distributed to several ATR processes running on multiple CPUs in a round-robin fashion. The outputs of the ATR processes were then collected by an ATR detection collector process, and made available to a waterfall-type display. Scalability was demonstrated on the fieldable system for 10 target types and on the HPC resources at the Army Research Laboratory's Major Shared Resource Center (ARL MSRC) for up to 100 different target types.

The above example demonstrates how software tools have evolved to support SIP applications on modern HPCs. SPE is a Message Passing Interface (MPI)–based tool for developing applications of parallel signal/image processing. SPE allows the construction of data-flow-type applications with simple connections. Program modules are mapped to processors, and the connections between user-denominated ports (e.g., `atr:image_input`) are made at run time, based on configuration file specifications. The programming environment is flexible and allows independently developed programs to be assembled together in different configurations as a single parallel application—without the need for recompilation. There is also an excellent interface for job control, tracing, and profiling.

Munition Simulations

The first simulation/modeling code to be described was a serial code used for scene generation in a munition hardware-in-the-loop simulation [775]. This code computes the sensor measurements in a simulated descent of widely used submunition, referred to as SADARM. For each time step, the following are computed: pose, IR, magnetometer, active mmW, passive mmW, and encounter measurements. The original nonoptimized serial code ran for approximately 9 hours on one CPU of an SGI Origin 2000 (195 MHz R10K processors) to produce a simulation output set. Prior to the parallelization, multiple copies of the serial code were run simultaneously on multiple CPUs for simulation. Each copy would take 9 hours to complete. Performing any "what-if" computation by changing inputs based on the results of a previous run required 9 hours to generate the new output set.

The optimized and parallelized code completed the same simulation run in approximately 22 minutes using 12 CPUs and in only 9 minutes using 32 CPUs on the SGI Origin 2000. Running the code on 32 CPUs of an SGI Origin 2000 with 300 MHz R12K processors further reduced the computation time to about 6 minutes. A plot of computation time versus number of CPUs is presented in Figure 8.12(a). The resulting speedup curves are shown in Figure 8.12(b). Serial optimization of the code was achieved through the use of appropriate compiler flags and through linking to a hardware-optimized, fast math library. Parallelization of the code was achieved by employing the MPI. This speedup has had a significant impact on SADARM verification and validation efforts, and it has resulted in significant cost savings to DoD.

One limitation of such a straightforward, coarse-grained, parallelization approach is that the parallel code will not scale beyond the number of outer loop iterations, where each CPU gets exactly one iteration. To achieve scalability to a larger number of processors, one would then have to examine the inner loops, if any, and then carefully distribute work among all the available processors in order to achieve load balance, while still achieving good performance.

Radar Propagation Codes

A second simulation/modeling code was coarse-grain parallelized. This code was a radar propagation code that is being developed by the Army Research Laboratory in collaboration with the University of Michigan. The code had the familiar outer loop structure with independent iterations. A typical run involved only about 30 iterations of the outer loop; consequently, the parallel code would not scale to beyond 30 processors. The serial code took about 8.75 hours on a SUN Ultra SPARC machine. The parallel code took only about 7.5 minutes to run on 30 CPUs of a

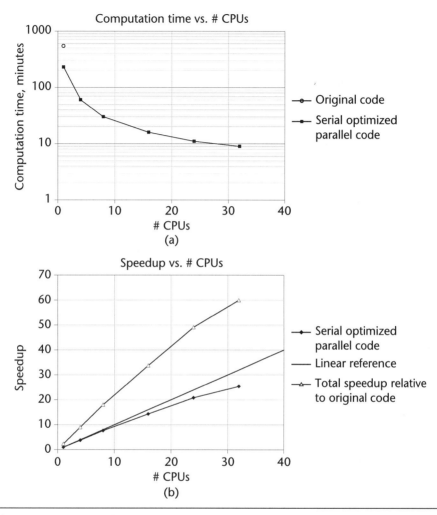

Figure 8.12   Speedup of the SADARM scene-generation code. (a) Computation time versus number of CPUs for the original and parallel versions of the SADARM scene-generation code. (b) Speedup of serial optimized parallel code versus number of CPUs. The total speedup is relative to the original nonoptimized serial code.

SUN E10K at the ARL MSRC. The speedup enables rapid what-if computations and facilitates rapid computational steering while resulting in significant cost savings.

Radar Cross-Section Codes

The third simulation/modeling code that was parallelized was a radar cross-section computation code developed at the ARL. The original code was a serial MATLAB code in m-file form. MATLAB has been identified as one of the key higher-level programming languages for algorithm development work in signal/image processing. Core MATLAB, along with numerous toolboxes for specialized applications, provides a very rich collection of functions and visualization tools for rapid code development and prototyping. The signal processing and image processing toolboxes significantly reduce algorithm development time for signal/image processing applications. Unfortunately, MATLAB is inherently serial code and is thus somewhat difficult to use on parallel machines. Some parts of MATLAB that are linked to certain vendor-provided libraries do run in multithreaded mode, but they do not result in good overall parallelization of user-developed code.

The MATLAB compiler from Mathworks, Inc. was used to convert the serial m-file into standalone C code. The serial code once again had the familiar outer loop that was stepping through all 360° of a circle in steps of 1°. The computations for any given angle were independent of those for other angles in that loop. So coarse-grain parallelization of the code was relatively straightforward. Calls to MPI functions were hand inserted in the resulting C code. The MATLAB compiler converts each variable in MATLAB to an mxArray structure in C, so one has to be careful while obtaining and setting values of variables within the automatically generated C code. The modified C code, with MPI calls, was then compiled and linked with the MPI library and run on multiple processors. The original code (vectorized and well written in MATLAB) took about 3 hours to run on a SUN Ultra SPARC machine. The parallel code took only about 9 minutes to produce identical outputs on eight CPUs of a SUN E10K at the ARL MSRC.

There are other ways of parallelizing serial MATLAB code. One approach is to use a commercial package called RTExpress from Integrated Sensors Inc. (ISI) [811]. RTExpress converts MATLAB m-files to C code, compiles the resulting C code, links with MPI libraries and ISI-developed parallel libraries for MATLAB functions, and runs the resulting parallel code on multiple CPUs. There is a small amount of input from the user through a target balancing tool (tbt), where the user assigns different parts of the code to different groups. The groups are subsequently mapped to different processors automatically by RTExpress. This environment is a fairly good rapid prototyping tool and has support for over 90% of the functionality of core MATLAB. Toolbox functions are not yet implemented. Some of the other competing products that are currently in development are MultiMATLAB at Cornell University [941] and Parallel Problems Server at MIT [496].

Sometimes, compiling m-files and producing either MEX files or standalone C programs can speed up execution times, especially if the MATLAB code has been poorly written, not vectorized, or has a lot of for loops inside it.

In addition to MATLAB, Khoros from Khoral Research Inc. [565] has also been identified as a key higher-level programming language for the development of signal/image processing algorithms. The commercially available version of Khoros is serial in nature and does not run on multiple processors. However, Advanced Khoros 2.3, which has recently completed beta testing, has a Parallel Toolbox that provides "parallel glyphs" to the user. Parallel glyphs are MPI-based modules that run on multiple CPUs and blend in seamlessly with other glyphs that can either be serial or parallel.

8.8.2 State of the Art

The signal/image processing community is largely divided into two major groups— embedded systems developers and algorithm developers. Most signal/image processing algorithms are eventually embedded into fielded systems with real-time performance constraints in addition to constraints on size, weight, and power consumption. Portability from the large HPCs to embedded systems has always been time consuming. The Vector Signal Image Processing Library (VSIPL) [840] is an emerging standard API/library for vector-signal, image processing primitives, with the goals of portability across platforms, reuse, interoperability, and reduction of development cost. The VSIPL 1.0 API standard is currently undergoing a few final finishing touches. Several vendors, including Mercury Computers, MPI Software Technology, Annapolis Microsystems, Sky Computers, and Atlantis Corporation, have already announced VSIPL products. Advanced Khoros 2.3 has some VSIPL support.

Acknowledgment. The Programming Environment and Training (PET) program at the Army Research Laboratory, Major Shared Resource Center supported the code parallelization work described in this paper.

8.9 Deterministic Monte Carlo Methods and Parallelism
Michael Mascagni

Monte Carlo methods (MCMs) have been, and continue to be, very popular algorithms for solving a wide variety of problems in science, engineering, and technology. However, they are generally methods of last resort. As Mark Kác, a probability and Monte Carlo pioneer, put it, "You use Monte Carlo methods until you understand the problem." Yet there are clearly large classes of problems that remain poorly understood in the sense of Mark Kác. This is because MCMs remain the best approaches to certain classes of problems. While it is impossible to clearly identify the problem classes where MCMs are most effective, one can generally say that most problems that rely on MCMs for their solution either live in high dimensions or have extremely complicated geometries.

Given that MCMs will continue to dominate numerical approaches in certain application areas, it behooves MCM practitioners to optimize their computational methods as much as possible. This is especially evident when one considers that the U.S. Department of Energy (DoE) has claimed that MCMs have consistently consumed up to a half of their high-performance computing cycles since the beginning of DoE's supercomputing activities. A generic problem with MCMs is their slow convergence with respect to statistical error. Since MCMs are based on statistical sampling, a quantity of interest is known only within a statistically defined confidence interval. The width of such confidence intervals generically decreases as

$\mathcal{O}(N^{-1/2})$ with N random samples. Clearly, a modest improvement in this stochastic convergence rate would have a significant impact on scientific computing.

A generic approach to the acceleration of Monte Carlo convergence is through the use of so-called quasi-random numbers (QRNs). These are numbers that are highly uniformly distributed and thus preferred in MCMs where an even sampling of the computational space is more important than randomness. The classical MCM, numerical integration, is an example of an application that in reality requires uniformity, not randomness. With pseudorandom numbers (PRNs), N samples reduce the stochastic errors by $\mathcal{O}(N^{-1/2})$, while quasi–Monte Carlo methods can produce *deterministic* errors as small as $\mathcal{O}(N^{-1})$ in numerical integration. QRNs have also been used to accelerate the Monte Carlo convergence of other applications, and so they are sought after by computational scientists.

The purpose of this section is twofold. Primarily, it is to acquaint the reader with QRNs and the advances being made with quasi–MCMs in a variety of application areas. Secondarily we describe some of the problems inherent with applying QRNs to parallel computations and provide the reader with empirical evidence that quasi–MCMs are being applied to a broad spectrum of parallel Monte Carlo applications with some success. We begin with a standard introduction to QRNs via the numerical quadrature application. This introduces the discrepancy, a measure of the deviation of a point set from uniformity, and provides us with an understanding of how well QRNs can perform. This also gives us a clear demonstration of a Monte Carlo algorithm that in reality needs uniformity rather than randomness for optimal performance. Next, a problem associated with splitting QRN sequences for use on different problems (processors) is discussed. This shows that in this particular case, the ability to combine two or more results to obtain greater accuracy is equivalent to the problem of creating a parallel QRN generator. This is a special set of circumstances where the parallelization is required to advance capabilities for serial computation as well. We then review methods of quasi-random number generation and point out the deficiencies in currently available, free QRN software. Finally, we briefly present the results of a Markov chain computation for solving a problem in linear algebra via an MCM. Here we show (1) that one can parallelize the quasi–Monte Carlo approach to the problem, (2) that the parallel efficiency of the regular Monte Carlo approach is maintained by the quasi–Monte Carlo method, and (3) that the accelerated convergence of QRNs is maintained in this parallel context.

8.9.1   Motivation for Using Quasi-Random Numbers

MCMs are based on mathematical processes that utilize random numbers. The computational requirement for random numbers in Monte Carlo applications has been satisfied with two types of computational random numbers: PRNs and QRNs. PRNs mimic the behavior of "real" random numbers in theoretical and empirical tests, whereas QRNs provide very uniformly distributed sets of numbers that may, in fact, perform poorly on tests of randomness. However, QRNs are more effective than PRNs in situations where the uniform distribution of points is important. Such applications include *the* canonical Monte Carlo application, the numerical evaluation of integrals. It is the case that many nonquadrature Monte Carlo computations can be mathematically viewed as numerical quadrature, and so many other types of Monte Carlo applications have seen performance improvement when PRNs have been carefully replaced with QRNs. In fact, many application areas that do not at face value seem to be anything like quadrature have been favorably impacted by the use of QRNs. These include simulations with random walkers in application areas as diverse as heat conduction [687], rarefied gas dynamics [165], particle transport [892], numerical linear algebra [650], and financial-instrument evaluation [166]. In addition, QRNs promise to improve the convergence of applications in quantum mechanics, materials science, biochemistry, and environmental remediation.

The mathematical motivation for QRNs can be found in the classic Monte Carlo application of numerical integration. For simplicity, we detail this for 1-D integration. Let us assume that we are interested in the numerical value of $I = \int_0^1 f(x)\,dx$, and we seek to optimize approximations of the form

$$I \approx \frac{1}{N} \sum_{n=1}^{N} f(x_n)$$

A solution to the optimization of the integration nodes, $\{x_n\}_{n=1}^{N}$, comes from the famous Koksma–Hlawka inequality. Let us define the star-discrepancy of a 1-D point set, $\{x_n\}_{n=1}^{N}$, by

$$D_N^* = D_N^*(x_1, \ldots, x_N) = \sup_{0 \leq u \leq 1} \left| \frac{1}{N} \sum_{n=1}^{N} \chi_{[0,u)}(x_n) - u \right|$$

where $\chi_{[0,u)}$ is the characteristic function of the half-open interval $[0, u)$. The term $\sum_{n=1}^{N} \chi_{[0,u)}(x_n)$ counts the number of x_n's in the interval $[0, u)$, and thus $\left| \frac{1}{N} \sum_{n=1}^{N} \chi_{[0,u)}(x_n) - u \right|$ measures the difference between the actual distribution of points in the interval $[0, u)$ and the uniform distribution on $[0, u)$. By taking the supremum, we are characterizing the distribution of the $\{x_n\}_{n=1}^{N}$ through its maximal deviation from uniformity. We thus have the remarkable theorem due to Koksma and Hlawka [571]: If $f(x)$ has bounded variation, $V(f)$, on $[0, 1)$, and $x_1, \ldots, x_N \in [0, 1]$ have star-discrepancy D_N^*, then

$$\left| \frac{1}{N} \sum_{n=1}^{N} f(x_n) - \int_0^1 f(x)\,dx \right| \leq V(f)\, D_N^*$$

This simple bound on the integration error is a product of $V(f)$, the total variation of the integrand in the sense of Hardy and Krause, and D_N^*, the star-discrepancy of the integration points. A major area of research in Monte Carlo is variance reduction, which indirectly deals with minimizing $V(f)$. QRN generation deals with minimization of the other term.

Mathematically, QRNs produce point sets and sequences that have low discrepancy. Discrepancy is a quantitative measure of the uniformity of a point set. The star-discrepancy, introduced above, is merely one of many discrepancies that are used to measure uniformity of discrete measures [706]. For example, the star-discrepancy of a point set of N "real" random numbers in one dimension is $\mathcal{O}(N^{-1/2}(\log \log N)^{1/2})$, while the discrepancy of N QRNs can be as low as (N^{-1}).[2] In $s > 3$ dimensions, it is rigorously known that the discrepancy of a point set with N elements can be no smaller than a constant depending only on s times $N^{-1}(\log N)^{(s-1)/2}$. This remarkable result of Roth [810] has motivated mathematicians to seek point sets and sequences with discrepancies as close to this lower bound as possible. Since Roth's results, there have been many constructions of low discrepancy point sets that have achieved star-discrepancies as small as $\mathcal{O}(N^{-1}(\log N)^{s-1})$. Most notably, there are the constructions of Hammersley, Halton [431], Soboĺ [139, 881], Faure [321, 351], and Niederreiter [140, 706].

While QRNs do improve the convergence of some applications, it is by no means trivial to enhance the convergence of all MCMs. Even in the case of numerical integration, enhanced convergence is by no means assured in all situations with the naive use of QRNs. This fact was demonstrated through studies of the efficacy of QRNs in numerical integration [165, 166, 688, 691,] by carefully investigating the impact of dimensionality and smoothness of the integrand on convergence. In a nutshell, their results showed that at high dimensions ($s \approx> 40$), quasi–Monte Carlo integration ceases to be an improvement over regular Monte Carlo integration. Perhaps more startling was that a considerable fraction of the enhanced convergence is lost in quasi–Monte Carlo integration when the integrand is discontinuous. In fact, even in two dimensions one can lose the approximately $\mathcal{O}(N^{-1})$ quasi–Monte Carlo convergence for an integrand that is discontinuous on a curve such as a circle. In the best cases, the convergence drops to $\mathcal{O}(N^{-2/3})$, which is only slightly better than regular Monte Carlo integration.

8.9.2   Methods of Quasi-Random Number Generation

Perhaps the best way to illustrate the difference between QRNs and PRNs is with a picture. In Figure 8.13, we plot 4096 tuples produced by successive elements from a 64-bit PRN generator from the SPRNG library [651]. These tuples are distributed in a manner consistent with real random tuples. In Figure 8.14, we see 4096 quasi-random tuples formed by taking the second and third dimensions from the Soboĺ sequence. It is clear that the two figures look very different and that Figure 8.14 is much more uniformly distributed. Both plots have the same number of points, and the largest "hole" in Figure 8.13 is much larger than that in Figure 8.14. This illustrates quite effectively the qualitative meaning of low discrepancy.

---

[2] Of course, the N optimal quasi-random points in $[0, 1)$ are the obvious: $\frac{1}{(N+1)}, \frac{2}{(N+1)}, \cdots, \frac{N}{(N+1)}$.

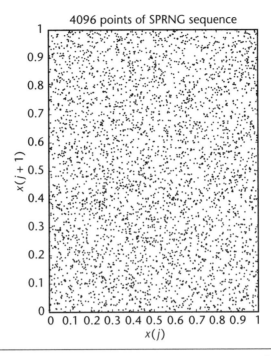

Figure 8.13 Tuples produced by successive elements from a SPRNG pseudorandom number generator.

The first QRN sequence was proposed by Halton [431] and is based on the Van der Corput sequence, with different prime bases for each dimension. The jth element of the Van der Corput sequence with base b is defined as $\phi_b(j-1)$, where $\phi_b(\cdot)$ is the radical inverse function and is computed by writing $j-1$ as an integer in base b, and then flipping the digits about the ordinal (decimal) point. Thus, if $j-1 = a_n \ldots a_0$ in base b, then $\phi_b(j-1) = 0.a_0 \ldots a_n$. As an illustration, in base $b=2$, the first elements of the Van der Corput sequence are $\frac{1}{2}, \frac{1}{4}, \frac{3}{4}, \frac{1}{8}, \frac{5}{8}, \frac{3}{8}, \frac{7}{8}$; while with $b=3$, the sequence begins with $\frac{1}{3}, \frac{2}{3}, \frac{1}{9}, \frac{4}{9}, \frac{7}{9}, \frac{2}{9}, \frac{5}{9}, \frac{8}{9}$. With $b=2$, the Van der Corput sequence methodically breaks the unit interval into halves in a manner that never leaves a gap that is too big. With $b=3$, the Van der Corput sequence continues with its methodical ways, but instead recursively divides intervals into thirds.

Another way to think of the Van der Corput sequence (with $b=2$) is to think of taking the bits in $j-1$ and associating with the ith bit the number v_i. Every time the ith bit is one, perform an exclusive-or in v_i, called the ith direction number. For the Van der Corput sequence, v_i is just a bit sequence with all zeroes except a one in the ith location counting from the left. Perhaps the most popular QRN sequence, the Soboĺ sequence, can be thought of in these terms. Soboĺ [881] found a clever way to define more complicated direction numbers than the "unit vectors" that define the

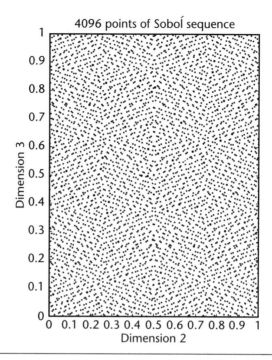

Figure 8.14   Tuples produced by the second and third dimension of the Soboĺ sequence.

Van der Corput sequence. Besides producing very good quality QRNs, the reliance on direction numbers means that the Soboĺ sequence is both easy to implement and very computationally efficient.

Since this initial work, Faure et al. [321], Niederreiter [705], and Soboĺ [881] chose alternate methods based on another sort of finite field arithmetic that utilizes primitive polynomials with coefficients in some prime Galois field. All of these constructions of quasi-random sequences have discrepancies that are $\mathcal{O}(N^{-1}(\log N)^s)$ [705]. What distinguishes them is the asymptotic constant in the discrepancy and the computational requirements for implementation. However, practice has shown that the provable size of the asymptotic constant in the discrepancy is a poor predictor of the actual computational discrepancy displayed by a concrete implementation of any of these QRN generators. There are existing implementations of the Halton, Faure, Niederreiter and Soboĺ sequences [139, 140, 351] that are computationally efficient. Each of these sequences is initialized to produce quasi-random s-tuples, and each one of these requires the initialization of s 1-D quasi-random streams. However, in practice the Soboĺ sequence has shown itself superior in quality and efficiency to these other methods. Thus, we will restrict our discussion to the Soboĺ generator.

8.9.3 A Fundamental Problem with Quasi-Random Numbers

QRNs are finely crafted mathematical objects that are hyperuniform. Recall the definition of the star-discrepancy of a set of points above. It is defined as the *supremum* of the difference between an empirical distribution of the set of points and the ideal uniform distribution. Clearly, a single misplaced point can lead to a serious degradation in this estimate. Thus, one should think of point sets (sets with N fixed numbers in them) of QRNs as sets that have completely filled all the holes in space at a given spatial scale. Similarly, sequences (sets with an extensible number of points) of QRNs are constructed so that the areas with the largest holes in space are exactly the next areas where points are to be placed.

The very highly structured nature of QRNs leads to an interesting problem. Let us perform a calculation with N QRNs from a given quasi-random sequence with given parameters and given initial values. Let's say we obtain the estimate q for some quantity of interest, Q. Theory tells us that in the best circumstances $|q - Q| = \mathcal{O}(N^{-1}(\log N)^k)$, for some k. However, the only practical way to continue this calculation is to continue with the $(N + 1)$st QRN from the same sequence. If we choose another QRN sequence, or even the same sequence starting with other than the *next* unused point, we will get no guarantee of continued accelerated Monte Carlo convergence. In fact, using incompatible QRNs can lead to circumstances where convergence to the correct answer may no longer hold.

Clearly, this problem is equivalent to the problem of finding parallel streams of QRNs that can collectively be used together in a complementary fashion. Work in this area has shown that the gist of the above paragraph seems to be true, that is, at present one can do no better than to break up a single QRN sequence into nonoverlapping blocks for use in parallel. Schmid and Uhl [837] investigated the consequences of blocking QRN sequences versus using a leapfrog technique.[3] They determined that blocking from the same sequence led to acceptable results, whereas the leapfrog technique often caused problems with the subsequences. Clearly, more flexibility than this will be required if QRNs are to be used in calculations that terminate with a stochastic convergence condition.

8.9.4 State-of-the-Art Quasi-Random Number Generators

A serious problem with using QRNs in both serial and parallel Monte Carlo applications is the lack of good quality, widely available QRN generation software. At present, good implementations of the Soboĺ, Faure, and Halton sequences exist, but there is no software that provides the facilities necessary for simple parallel use of such generators. In addition, generators with certain desirable properties are not freely available. One of the most popular application areas for QRNs is currently in

---

[3] Suppose we have k QRN subsequences of length N we wish to create. In blocking, the first subsequence consists of the first N numbers, the second subsequence of the next N numbers, and so on. When using the leapfrog technique, the ith subsequence is $\{x_i, x_{i+N}, x_{i+2N}, \ldots, x_{i+(N-1)N}\}$.

Table 8.2 Implementation using MPI of the power Monte Carlo algorithm (PMC) and power quasi–Monte Carlo algorithm (PQMC) for calculating the dominant eigenvalue of a matrix of size 2000 using PRNs and Soboĺ QRNs.

| | | Number of processors | | | | |
		1	2	3	4	5
PMC	Time (s)	168	84	56	42	33
	Efficiency		1	1	1	1.01
	λ_{max}	62.48	61.76	63.76	61.3151	61.39
PQMC	Time (s)	177	87	70	57	44
	Efficiency		1.01	0.84	0.77	0.80
	λ_{max}	64.01	64.01	64.01	64.01	64.01

Note: The number of Markov chains (realizations) used is $100,000$, and the exact value is $\lambda_{max} = 64.00$.

financial mathematics. However, some of the canonical problems are often set in very high-dimensional spaces. For example, the pricing of a mortgage-backed security made up of 30-year home mortgages is a 360-dimensional problem [689].[4] At present, there is no high-quality QRN software that produces sequences in such high dimensions. In fact, to our knowledge the only publicly available Soboĺ QRN generation software allows for sequences up to dimension 41.

8.9.5   A Parallel Quasi–Monte Carlo Application

Given this brief introduction to QRNs, we wish to illustrate their utility on a parallel application. We present our results for an MCM for the computation of the extremal eigenvalue of a sparse, square matrix [271]. The method we employ is a stochastic version of the well-known power method. It is based on the repeated application of the matrix, which is ideal for Markov-chain–based MCMs. A good description of both the MCM and the application of QRNs to this problem can be found elsewhere [648, 649, 650]. The computations presented here were implemented in parallel using MPI on an IBM SP-2 located at the Florida State University's School of Computational Science and Information Technology.

MCMs are "naturally parallel."[5] They allow us to compute with minimal communication. In our case, we need only pass the nonzero elements of the sparse matrix A to every processor (Table 8.2). Then we compute a total of N Monte Carlo realizations on p processors. Each processor gets N/p realizations, and we collect the results at the end. The only communication here is at the beginning and at the end of the

---

[4] Thirty-year mortgages are paid monthly, giving 360 payment periods during the mortgage's life. This accounts for the 360-dimensionality of the mortgage-backed security problem.
[5] This distinction of MCMs as "naturally parallel" was first used by Malvin Kalos.

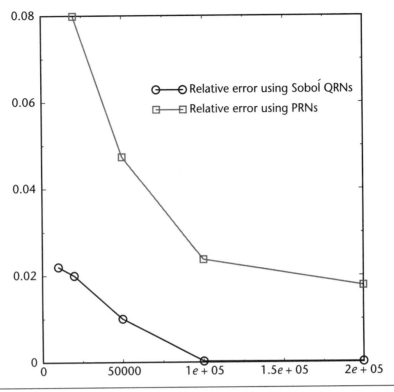

Figure 8.15   Relative errors in computing the dominant eigenvalue for a sparse matrix of size 2000×2000. Markov chains are realized using PRNs and Soboĺ QRNs.

program execution; this provides a very efficient parallel implementation. Note that in our empirical analysis, we use the standard definition of *parallel efficiency, E.*

Figure 8.15 presents the relative errors of the power MC algorithm and power quasi-Monte Carlo algorithm (using the Soboĺ sequence) for computing the dominant eigenvalue for a sparse square matrix of size 2000. Note that with 20, 000 points from our Soboĺ sequence, we achieve an accuracy that would require 100, 000 or more PRNs. The fact that QRNs can achieve accuracy similar to PRNs for this kind of calculation, while using only a fraction of the time, is the significant reason for using QRNs.

In this computation, we knew beforehand how many QRNs would be used in the entire calculation, and we neatly broke the sequences into same-sized subsequences. Clearly, it is not expected that this information will be known beforehand. Providing QRNs that can help extend calculations easily remains the major challenge to widespread parallel use of QRNs.

We have shown that one can parallelize the quasi–Monte Carlo approach to the calculation of the extremal eigenvalue of a matrix. We have also shown that the parallel efficiency of the regular Monte Carlo approach is maintained by the quasi–Monte Carlo method; however, there is some slight degradation. Finally, perhaps the most important fact is that the accelerated convergence of QRNs is maintained in this parallel context.

8.9.6   State of the Art

We have introduced the reader to the concept of quasi–MCMs and QRNs. These are powerful techniques for accelerating the convergence of ubiquitous MCMs. However, even though quasi–MCMs can often be made to converge much faster than ordinary MCMs, the ability to improve the accuracy of quasi–MCMs as readily as ordinary MCMs is not here yet. Nonetheless, for certain applications it is possible to accelerate the convergence of Monte Carlo applications with QRNs and to take advantage of their natural parallelism. At present, there are a variety of Monte Carlo applications that benefit from QRN acceleration. Most notable, perhaps, is the calculation of financial derivatives [303]. In the future, we expect to see considerable benefits to other Monte Carlo applications, and hence to scientific computing.

8.10   Quasi–Real Time Microtomography Experiments at Photon Sources

Gregor von Laszewski, Mei-Hui Su, Joseph Insley, Ian Foster, and Carl Kesselman

Computed microtomography (CMT) is a powerful tool for obtaining nondestructively a 3-D view of the internal structure of opaque objects [421]. In contrast to the widespread use of this technique in the millimeter scale as part of diagnostic procedures in hospitals, we are interested in the investigation of objects on the micrometer scale.

One application of this method is quality control during the production of 3-D semiconductor wafers. Being able to visualize the details of chip wafers in all three dimensions allows engineers to improve the chip design before production. Other examples can be found in the field of earth science, where common tasks include investigation of the interior of very small meteorites and study of the enclosures of very tiny materials in opaque diamonds formed 100,000 years ago, in order to determine more about the origin and development of the Earth.

The energy and the infrastructure necessary to conduct such experiments can be provided by using x-ray beams at synchrotrons. The use of x-rays for investigating the internal structure of materials at the micron scale has grown rapidly over the past decade as a result of the availability of synchrotron radiation sources. One such facility is the Advanced Photon Source (APS) at Argonne National Laboratory.

A typical computed microtomography experiment at the APS proceeds as follows. A sample is mounted in the experiment station, parameters are adjusted, and the sample is illuminated by a collimated beam of x-rays. Data are collected for multiple sample orientations by using a charge-coupled device. A time-consuming reconstruction process is then used to obtain a 3-D representation of the raw data with spatial resolution of as little as 1 mm. The 3-D image contains quantitative information about the x-ray attenuation coefficient at a particular x-ray energy.

The many orders of magnitude increase in brilliance now available at third-generation sources such as the APS allows dramatic improvements in temporal resolution and makes it feasible to record fully 3-D, high-resolution tomographic data on time scales of less than a second per image.

Nevertheless, a major difficulty with the current practice is the turnaround time between data acquisition and reconstruction, often due to lack of available computing power. This is especially problematic for all synchrotron-based experiments because only a limited amount of beam time is available for a user. The use of distributed supercomputing power can reduce this turnaround time to a few hours or minutes, enabling users to view the results in quasi-real time and to alter experiment conditions on the fly. This capability can greatly improve the usefulness of a synchrotron radiation facility.

8.10.1 The Computational Processing Pipeline Framework

We have provided a general framework for CMT applications that is based on the concept of a processing pipeline [966, 979]. The pipeline consists of a series of components that communicate with each other via input and output channels. Each of the components can be mapped, in principle, onto different computational resources. Thus, the framework ideally can be mapped onto computational Grids [345]. The CMT pipeline has additional properties described below.

Data Format

HDF is used to guarantee portability of the data across a variety of diverse computer platforms. In addition, it provides the ability for self-describing data, which will enable the organization of large subject-related data archives in the near future [568, 698].

Data Interchange

The Globus Nexus communication library is used to allow the support of multiple protocols as part of the message-exchange mechanism. The protocol is selected based on its availability and performance characteristics among the computational processing units connected via the channels.

Preprocessing Algorithm

To improve the quality of the reconstruction, images should be preprocessed with appropriate filters. The preprocessing algorithm usually varies from experiment to experiment. A set of predefined standard preprocessing algorithms is available that can be easily used without recompiling the code. The user can extend the available preprocessors.

Reconstruction Algorithm

Currently, we use a high-performance parallel implementation of reconstruction algorithms for microtomography data sets, based on a filtered backprojection technique.

Interleaved Reconstruction and Visualization

Resulting images are shipped in real time to a visualization unit to gradually update a 3-D rendered image during the experiment. This gradual update is important to allow decisions as to whether the experiment should continue. If the experiment does not perform as expected, it is terminated.

Integrated Visualization and Collaboration Engine

One goal of this project is to enable researchers to participate in an experiment from their home institutions rather than traveling to the APS (cf. Mercurio et al. [667]). A beamline scientist will be able to handle the experiment locally, communicating with the scientist designing the experiment. A remote video-conferencing tool allows such collaboration. In addition, the 3-D image analysis tool contains a control component that enables collaborative visualization on a variety of output devices, including graphics workstations, ImmersaDesks (Figure 8.16), and CAVEs. This allows the resulting 3-D image to be rendered rapidly. Moreover, it provides a shared control among the users participating in a collaborative session, enabling computational steering of the experiment. This general visualization framework [343] is currently used by scientists from different disciplines with similar visualization requirements (e.g., electron microscopy and astrophysics).

8.10.2   Scientific Challenges

The computational framework based on a processing pipeline presents several scientific and computational challenges.

Filtering and Reconstruction

As noted, we currently use a reconstruction algorithm based on filtered backprojection. Before the reconstruction algorithm is performed, filter operations are applied to improve the image quality. The raw projection data typically contain many artifacts resulting from beam nonuniformity and defects in the scintillator, lens, and detector. They can be effectively corrected by removing black- and white-field images with the following method:

$$f = \ln\left(\frac{f_w - f_b}{f_0 - f_b}\right)$$

where f is the filtered image, f_0 is the raw projection, and f_w and f_b are the white- and black-field images, respectively. This filtering process gives the line integral of

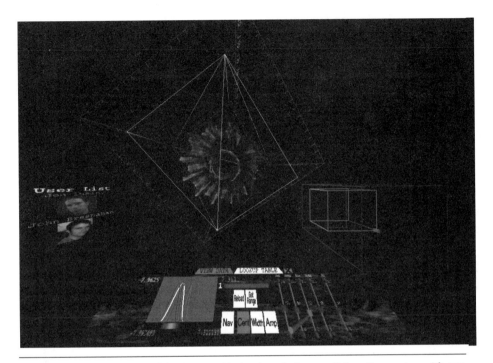

Figure 8.16   A screen shot of the ImmersaDesk taken during a collaborative session with two users. The control panel allows the user to modify parameters such as the color tables used to control the position, size, and orientation of the object. The inner markup of the object can be analyzed further with the help of cross sections and transparent masking of uninteresting features.

the absorption through the sample along the beam direction. The collection of such filtered projections $f(\theta, x, y)$ is then the Radon transform of the sample's 3-D absorption map $\rho(x, y, z)$. Some phase information is usually present in the images, but it is minimized by reducing the distance between the sample and the scintillator screen (less than 5 mm in our case). We can therefore ignore the phase information in our calculations without introducing many observable artifacts.

An outlier filter is sometimes used to remove isolated high-intensity points resulting from pixel defects in the CCD chip or from cosmic rays. It calculates the local median and standard deviation for each pixel in the image and replaces the pixel by the median if the pixel value is more than a certain number of standard deviations away from the median. A least-squares deconvolution (Wiener) filter has also been implemented to restore the images degraded by the optical system, but since the images are undersampled in most cases, it is applicable only when the $40\times$ objective is in use.

Before the projections are used in reconstruction calculations, they must be aligned to one another so that the rotation axis is located at the center of the images. We have learned that our rotation-stage bearing typically has a radial run-out error on the order of 1 μm. Therefore, for images with 1 to 2 μm resolution, each projection must be aligned individually. For the projections at 6 μm or lower resolution, however, the stage error can be ignored. We only need to determine the location of the rotation axis in one and then collectively shift them all by the same amount. A cross-correlation function is used to identify the rotation axis. We reverse the projection acquired at a 180° angle and compute the cross-correlation function with the 0° image:

$$C_{fg}(x', y') = \int_{-\infty}^{+\infty} \int_{-\infty}^{+\infty} f^{\neq}(x - x', y - y') \, g(x, y) \, dx \, dy$$

where f represents the 0° image and g represents the reversed 180° image. Ideally, f and g are the same image but shifted from each other, and the rotation center is located halfway between the shift features. The peak of the correlation function indicates the amount of shift between the two images and therefore how much each image is to be shifted. In practice, the cross-correlation function is calculated using the property

$$F(C_{fg}) = F^{\neq}(f) \, F(g)$$

where F indicates a Fourier transform. For the higher-resolution images, such cross-correlation calculations must be performed on each projection to correct for both the rotation-stage errors and the shift from the rotation center. In the special cases in which the object is of high contrast and completely located inside the imaging field, the image centroid can be computed and can serve as the alignment mark for centering.

The reconstruction programs used in our experiments are based on a code provided by Ellisman and Young from the National Center for Microscopy and Imaging Research at the San Diego Supercomputing Center [667]. Three commonly used algorithms—filtered backprojection, ART, and SIRT—have been implemented, but because of the high angular sampling rate used in our experiments, filtered backprojection is almost always used because of its higher speed. The original code has been optimized for our parallel computer and acquisition scheme. In our case, where a single rotation axis is used, the reconstruction calculation for each section is independent.

Hence, this algorithm parallelizes nicely in that each slice in a data set can be processed independently. Hence, the principal challenge is to develop efficient techniques for moving data among detector, secondary storage, supercomputers, and workstations for visualizing results.

New Acquisition and Reconstruction Strategies

Access to a large amount of computational power allows the use of new acquisition and reconstruction strategies. Traditionally, data are collected at microtomographic beamlines at constant angle offsets: for example, 0, 1, 2,... degrees if 360 samples are to be taken. In an interactive environment such as we describe here, it becomes attractive instead to use an interleaved angle list. For example, we may first gather images at 60° offsets (0, 60, 120, 180, 240, 300), then collect additional images to provide a 30° sampling, and so on until a complete 1° data set is obtained. The advantage of this strategy is that the reconstruction algorithm can be run repeatedly, once for each more detailed set of data; hence, the scientist obtains a series of more refined images and may be able to detect a flawed experimental setup early in the data collection process.

Another interesting direction that is enabled by the availability of supercomputer resources is the following. In principle, reconstruction quality can be improved by performing multiple reconstructions with different algorithms and parameter settings. We are hopeful that the enhanced compute power made accessible by grid environments will initiate a new area in the development of reconstruction algorithms for computed microtomography and other disciplines.

Computational Requirements

The data rates and compute power required to address a CMT problem are prodigious, easily reaching 1 Gb/s and 1 Tflop/s. We illustrate this statement with a scenario. A 3-D raw data set generated by a typical detector will comprise 1000 1024×1500 two-byte slices (3 GB); detectors with significantly higher resolutions will soon be available. If we assume current reconstruction techniques and make fairly optimistic scaling assumptions, reconstruction of this data set requires about 1013 floating-point operations (10 Tflops). On a 100 Mflop/s workstation, this translates to 32 hours; on a 1 Tflop/s computer, it would take 10 seconds. With current detector technologies, this data set might take 1500 seconds to acquire; however, new detectors will improve readout times considerably. Besides the computational demand resulting from the reconstruction of the 3-D object, the display of the rendered final result is also a problem with the current state-of-the-art imaging hardware. The size of the data sets generated in these experiments can be quite large, typically on the order of 1024^3 floating-point values. Currently, even the accelerated graphics hardware used by our application has trouble keeping up with volumes of this size, and the data set needs to be subsampled down to 256^3 floating-point values in order to maintain its frame rates for interactive usage.

8.10.3 Benefits of Real-Time X-Ray Microtomography Experiments

The framework described in this section offers several benefits to the end user. First, a fast reconstruction algorithm can be used to help decide whether the current experiment has to be interrupted prematurely because of an error in the setup. This will allow an increase in the number of experiments conducted per hour. In order to handle complicated and diverse supercomputing environments, it is essential to provide a simple interface giving the beamline experimentalist control over the parameter set, as well as the ability to terminate the current calculation at any time.

Besides the requirements driven by the computational aspect of the application, organizational aspects benefit from the framework described in this section. Because of the hazardous and often unpleasant environment at the beamline, remote operation is desirable. With remote operation, the facility can maintain a small but well-trained team of beamline staff experimentalists. This approach offers several advantages. It reduces the operational and user-specific cost and minimizes travel cost to the unique facility. Furthermore, it increases access time to the beamline, while minimizing the effort required by trained experts to set up experiments. With the availability of a collaborative and remote steering environment, new user communities in commercial and educational facilities are likely to use the supercomputing-enhanced light sources in remote fashion. During an experiment, multiple users using different visualization engines at geographically dispersed locations should be able to collaborate easily with each other. The details of this infrastructure will be hidden from the end users, the microtomography scientists. For these users, it is irrelevant where and how the result is achieved, as long as time and computational accuracy requirements are met. Figure 8.17 shows such a grid-enabled collaborative application.

Figure 8.17   A "grid-enabled" CMT application allows researchers to display the same state of the visualized object on all display stations participating in a collaborative session. Remote computation and steering become possible across multiple access points.

8.10.4   Future Work

In this section we described a grid-enabled real-time analysis, visualization, and steering environment for microtomography experiments. Specifically, we have provided a portable parallel framework that allows different reconstruction algorithms to be ported on the Grid. A standard data format based on HDF is defined to distribute the data among scientists in a meaningful way.

The real-time visualization environment developed fulfills the basic needs of the microtomography scientists. Moreover, with the availability of this environment, we anticipate that scientists will make algorithm improvements, for example, including a priori knowledge of a previous reconstruction in order to increase the quality of the image. The current system has been successfully used in various experiments.

In the future, we will focus on the use of new modalities in real-time reconstruction for interactive use and will explore the collaborative analysis of results. In addition, we will emphasize improvements to the usage of dynamic scheduling of computers, high-speed networking, and collaboration technologies.

Acknowledgments. This work was supported by the Mathematical, Information, and Office of Advanced Scientific Computing Research subprogram of the Office of Computational and Technology Research, U.S. Department of Energy (DoE), under contract W-31-109-Eng-38. Globus research and development are supported by the Defense Advanced Research Projects Agency, DoE, and the National Science Foundation.

We based the grid-enabled version of the code from code provided by Mark Ellisman and Steve Young from the National Center for Microscopy and Imaging Research at San Diego Supercomputing Center. We would like to thank Derrick C. Mancini, Steve Wang, Ian McNulty, Mark Rivers, and Francesco DeCarlo for conducting the experiments at the APS beamline. This truly interdisciplinary project would not have been possible without the countless hours of work performed by the Globus team: Joe Bester, Steve Fitzgerald, Brian Toonen, Steve Tuecke, Karl Czajkowski, and all the others who have helped us throughout the years.

8.11   WebHLA-Based Meta-Computing Environment for Forces Modeling and Simulation

Wojtek Furmanski

This section focuses on the use of HPC for DoD modeling and simulation, addressed by the Forces Modeling and Simulation (FMS) Computational Technology Area within the DoD HPC Modernization Program. Over the last few years, Syracuse University acted as a technical lead for the academic part, PET (Programming Environments and Training); Syracuse University provided assistance to FMS users in both the infrastructure and application development sectors. Our approach explored synergies among, and integrated distributed-object standards emerging from, industry (CORBA), Web (Java, XML) and the DoD (HLA). We developed a three-tier WebHLA environment that offered standards-based, plug-and-play support for both the back-end HPC simulation modules and the front-end Web/commodity interfaces. In this section, I provide an overview of the DoD modeling and simulation domain from the perspective of HPC, summarize the high-level architecture (HLA) standard, outline our WebHLA environment, and illustrate its use for building a meta-computing–level battlefield simulation that involves large-scale minefields (on the order of 1 million mines).

8.11.1 DoD Modeling and Simulation

Modeling and simulation (M&S) is a major, computationally intense, mission-critical domain of DoD computing. It addresses a broad range of application areas, ranging from weapons engineering to multiplayer training to campaign analysis; it includes a spectrum of granularity and fidelity levels, ranging from close combat to entity level to force-on-force simulations. Being naturally modular in terms of distributed simulation entities, DoD M & S always acted as a driving force for new distributed computing and network technologies. Based on lessons learned from SIMNET, first-generation standards emerged. These include DIS (Distributed Interactive Simulation) for real-time simulations and ALSP (Aggregate-Level Simulation Protocol) for logical-time simulations. Several large-scale joint enterprises now address various aspects of the broad field of M&S. These include JSIMS (Joint Simulation System) for training simulations, JMASS (Joint Modeling and Simulation System) for engineering simulations, and JWARS (Joint Warfare Systems) for campaign-level analytical simulations. These large-scale efforts were accompanied by numerous smaller-scale modeling and simulation activities in many DoD labs, so that the whole field was significantly fragmented until recently. New mechanisms for simulation interoperability were developed and enforced by the DMSO (Defense Modeling and Simulation Office), in terms of the HLA-based federation framework discussed below.

8.11.2 Forces Modeling and Simulation

One relatively small, but special, sector on the large DoD modeling and simulation landscape is forces modeling and simulation (FMS), focused on large-scale simulations that require HPC support. Most other computational technology areas within the DoD HPC Modernization Program, such as CFD, CSM, and CEA, are based on traditional data-parallel, time-stepped HPC simulation technologies, whereas FMS represents a special domain of object-oriented, event-driven, task-parallel HPC simulations. Parallel and distributed event-driven simulations (PDES) are often classified as either "real-time" (or "as-fast-as-possible") or "logical-time" management schemes. The former, typically used for real-time battlefield simulations (e.g., for training purposes) were usually based on the DIS protocol. In such simulations, all active objects (vehicles, troops, weapons, etc.) broadcast their entity state PDUs (protocol data units) periodically, informing all other players of their positions and internal state. Based on received PDUs, all entities update their states "as fast as possible," and the resulting simulation advances in "real time." In the logical-time management mode, simulation objects generate events and schedule them for execution at some future time instances. For example, when a missile is fired, its space–time collision point is precomputed, and the corresponding "target-hit" event is constructed and put into the time-ordered queue for future execution. Simulation time advances in discrete irregular steps, given by the time stamps of the subsequent events in the queue.

Both time-management regimes are being addressed by FMS projects. In the logical-time domain, the dominant PDES technology is based on the SPEEDES (Synchronous Parallel Environment for Emulation and Distributed Events Simulation) system developed by Metron Corporation and, more recently, by RAM Laboratories. SPEEDES uses an optimistic roll-backable, parallel-time–management scheme based on a variant of the Time Warp algorithm developed by the National Aeronautics and Space Administration/Jet Propulsion Laboratory in the late 1980s. In the real-time domain, the DIS-based battlefield simulations map naturally onto networks of workstations, and hence the use of MPPs was rather limited in this area. However, there are some specific DIS simulation problems that require HPC. One such challenge, raised recently by Ft. Belvoir, Virginia, addressed support for entity-level battlefield simulation in the large minefields (1 million or more mines) that are required by modern warfare models. We discuss this comprehensive mine simulator (CMS) application and our support for parallel CMS in the following sections. First, however, we summarize the current status in the area of simulation interoperability, represented by the HLA federation framework.

8.11.3   High-Level Architecture

HLA is a language-independent, object-based, distributed software architecture for simulation reusability and interoperability that is now being enforced DoD-wide across all individual M&S programs, systems, and simulation paradigms, including both real-time (DIS) and logical-time (event-driven) management models. HLA views distributed simulation as a *federation* of coarse-grain, opaque, semiautonomous entities called *federates* that govern, locally and independently, their simulation objects and that conform strictly to some global federation rules, specifying the information-exchange policy across the federation. The associated run-time infrastructure (RTI) offers the software bus services available to the HLA-compliant federates. These include federation, object, declaration, ownership, time, and data distribution management. The overall organization of RTI is illustrated in Figure 8.18. Federates (large circles) maintain their simulation objects (medium circles) given by attribute sets (small circles), and they interact via RTI services (rounded rectangles) managed by the RTI bus (central elongated rectangle). Both local (simulation) and global (federation) objects conform to a simple attribute-value–based entity format specified by the object model template (OMT) and are suitably grouped and maintained by the RTI as SOMs (simulation object models) or FOMs (federation object models). Federates can join or leave the federation (using federation management); they create their objects and register them with the RTI (using object management); they can publish and/or subscribe some of their objects (or their selected attributes) for sharing (using the declaration management); they can negotiate update rights for shared objects (using ownership management); they can evolve their objects in time

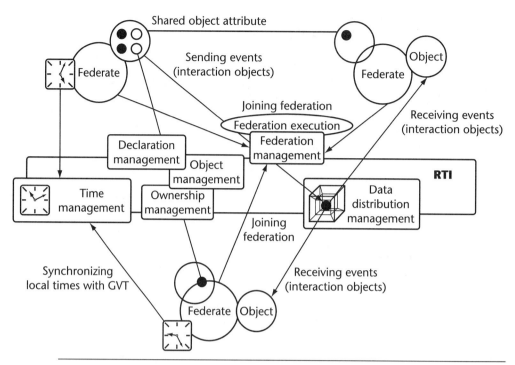

Figure 8.18 Architecture of the run-time infrastructure (RTI) software bus of the high-level architecture (HLA). Circles represent entities (such as federates, objects, and attributes); rectangles represent services.

and synchronize their local simulation clocks with the federation time (using time management); and they can build dynamic, multidimensional routing channels for optimized multicast delivery of discrete communication events called interaction objects (using data distribution management).

8.11.4 WebHLA

The main emphasis of the Defense Modeling and Simulation Office has been on supporting reusability of and HLA-enabled interoperability among diverse existing legacy codes, rather than on providing HLA-based software engineering support for new simulations that would utilize the latest Web/commodity technologies of Java, CORBA, and XML. We proposed to fill this gap in our WebHLA framework that offered open implementation of HLA in terms of a suite of emergent object standards for the Web-based distributed computing—we call it the *Pragmatic Object Web*—that integrated Java, CORBA, COM, and XML (see Figure 8.19). WebHLA is an interactive three-tier environment that includes: (1) DMSO HLA architecture and our JWORB-based Object Web RTI implementation in the *middleware*;

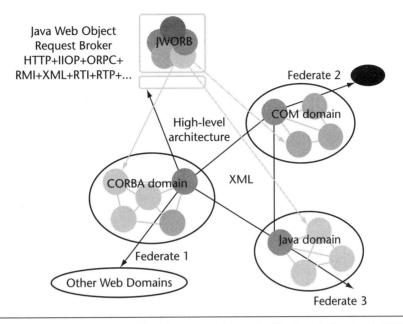

Figure 8.19   Pragmatic object Web architecture—fine-grain distributed objects of CORBA, Java, and COM interoperate as coarse-grain HLA federates linked via XML messages.

(2) Web/commodity *front-ends* (such as Web browsers or Microsoft Windows); and (3) customer- and application-specific *back-end* technologies (ranging from legacy systems such as relational databases to HPC modeling and simulation modules). Both the core components of WebHLA, such as JWORB and OWRTI, and a suite of tools and plug-and-play federates developed so far, including RtiCap, JDIS, PDUDB and SimVis, are outlined below.

JWORB (Java Web Object Request Broker) is a multiprotocol network server written in Java (see Figure 8.20). Currently, JWORB supports HTTP and IIOP protocols; that is, it can act as a Web server and as a CORBA broker or server. In the planning stage is support for the DCE RPC protocol, which would provide COM server capabilities. JWORB recognizes a particular protocol based on the anchor/magic number of the current network packet and invokes a suitable handler. JWORB is a useful middleware technology for integrating and efficiently aggregating competing distributed-object technologies and the associated network protocols of CORBA, Java, COM, and XML.

OWRTI (Object Web RTI) is an implementation of DMSO RTI 1.3 written in Java on top of the JWORB middleware, that is, packaged as a JWORB CORBA service (see Figure 8.21). In OWRTI, each of the RTI management services shown in Figure 8.18 is implemented as an independent CORBA object. Other CORBA objects in the system include: *RTIKernel*, which acts as a core top-level manager; *FederationExecution*, which

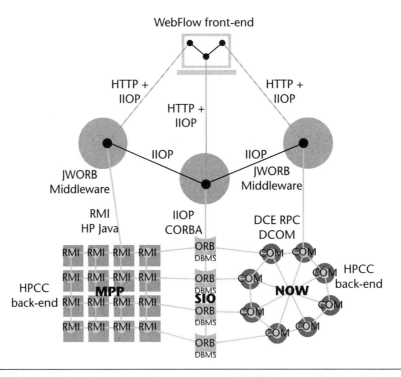

Figure 8.20 Overall architecture of the multiprotocol JWORB server—front-end browsers (orblets) connect via HTTP (IIOP), middleware is IIOP based, and legacy back-ends are linked via dedicated protocols.

represents a federation instance; *RTIAmbassador*, which acts as a client-side proxy of the RTI bus; and *FederateAmbassador*, which acts as the RTI-side proxy of a federate.

RtiCap is a library that provides RTI with a C++ programming interface, packaged as a CORBA service offering access to Java-based OWRTI from C++ federates. The RtiCap glue library uses public-domain OmniORB2 as a C++ object request broker. The RTI ambassador glue/proxy object forwards all C++ client method calls to its Java/CORBA peer, and the federate ambassador object forwards all received callbacks to its C++ peer. Versions of RtiCap library are running on Windows NT, IRIX, and SunOS platforms.

To link DIS-based legacy simulation systems such as ModSAF (Modular Semi-Automated Forces) with HLA federations, a bridge node is required to transform between different event models used in both frameworks: DIS PDUs and HLA interactions. We constructed such a bridge, called *JDIS*, in Java, starting from a public-domain DIS Java parser and completing it to support all PDUs required by the ModSAF system. JDIS can also write/read PDUs from a file or a database; hence, it can be used to log and play back sequences of simulation events. In order to fa-

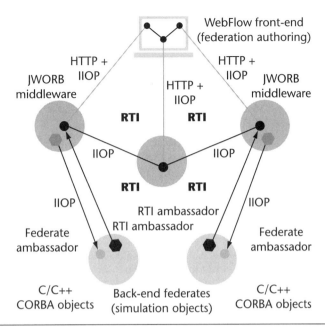

Figure 8.21   Overall architecture of OWRTI, packaged as a JWORB facility. RtiCap library is employed to link C++ simulation back-ends via RTI in terms of RTI ambassador and Federate ambassador proxies.

cilitate the transmission of PDUs and their persistent storage, we adopted XML as a uniform wire format, and we constructed suitable PDU-XML converters.

Playing the real scenario over and over again for testing and analysis is a time-consuming and tedious effort. A database of the equivalent PDU stream is often needed for selectively playing back segments of a recorded scenario. We constructed and packaged as a WebHLA federate such a PDU database, *PDUDB*, using Microsoft's Access for storage, Java servlets for loading and retrieving the data, and JDBC for servlet-database communication. The PDU logger servlet receives its input via an HTTP POST message in the form of XML-encoded PDU sequences. Such an input stream is decoded, converted to SQL, and stored in the database using JDBC. The playback is done using another servlet that sends the PDUs generated from the database as a result of a query. A common visual front-end for JDIS and PDUDB federates is shown in Figure 8.22. It supports run-time display of the PDU flow, and it offers several controls and utilities, including: (1) switches among DIS, HLA, and various I/O (file, database) modes; (2) frequency calibration for a PDU stream generated from a file or database; (3) PDU probe and sequence generators; and (4) simple analysis tools, such as statistical filters or performance benchmarks that can be performed on accumulated PDU sequences.

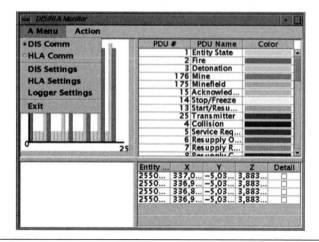

Figure 8.22   A sample screen of the JDIS and PDUDB control monitor window, illustrating the dynamic display of the PDU flow and various protocol and I/O modes (DIS vs. HLA, run time vs. playback.)

Using Microsoft Direct3D technology, we constructed a real-time battlefield visualizer, *SimVis* (see Figure 8.23) that can operate both in the DIS and HLA modes. SimVis is an NT application written in Visual C++ that extracts the battlefield information from the event stream. This information includes the state (e.g., velocity) of vehicles in the terrain, the position and state of mines and minefields, and explosions that occur (e.g., when vehicles move over and activate mines). The renderer performs the real-time visualization of the extracted information using the ModSAF terrain database; a suite of geometry objects and animation sets for typical battlefield entities, such as armored vehicles (tanks); and visual events, such as explosions. We developed these objects using the 3D Studio MAX authoring system and imported them into the DirectX/Direct3D run-time environment.

8.11.5   Example WebHLA Application: Parallel/Meta-Computing CMS

Having outlined the WebHLA framework, its application is illustrated in a particular FMS project conducted by NPAC that developed parallel and meta-computing CMS based on the CMS simulator from Ft. Belvoir. This effort included converting the CMS system from the DIS to the HLA framework, constructing a scalable, parallel CMS federate for the Origin 2000, and linking it with the ModSAF vehicle simulator and other utility federates toward a meta-computing CMS federation. In the following, I review the original CMS system, present our approach and performance results for parallel CMS, and describe our current and planned meta-computing CMS configurations.

Figure 8.23   A sample screen of SimVis, used to visualize a battlefield (including tanks propagating through terrain with a deployed minefield) associated with Parallel CMS + ModSAF simulation.

Comprehensive Mine Simulator by Ft. Belvoir

The Night Vision Lab at Ft. Belvoir conducts research and development in the area of countermine engineering, using the advanced CMS as an experimentation environment for a synthetic battlefield. Developed by the OSD-sponsored Joint Countermine Advanced Concepts Technology Demonstration (JCM ACTD), CMS is a state-of-the-art high-fidelity minefield simulator with support for a broad range of mine categories. These include conventional types, such as buried pressure-fuzed mines, antitank mines, and other types, including off-route (side attack) and wide-area (top attack) mines. CMS organizes mines in components given by regular arrays of mines of particular types. Minefields are represented as heterogeneous collections of such homogeneous components. CMS interoperates via the DIS protocol with ModSAF vehicle simulators. Mine interaction with a target is controlled by its fuze. CMS supports several fuze types, including full width, track-width fuzes, off-route fuzes, and others. CMS mines can also interact with countermine systems, including both mechanical and explosive countermeasures and detectors.

The relevance of HPC for the CMS system stems from the fact that modern warfare can require 1 million or more mines to be present on the battlefield, such as in the Korean Demilitarized Zone or the Gulf War. The simulation of such battlefield areas requires HPC support. As part of the PET FMS project, Syracuse University analyzed the CMS code and ported the system to the Origin 2000 shared-memory, parallel MPP. Below, we summarize our approach and results.

Parallel CMS: Approach

In our first attempt to port CMS to the Origin 2000, we identified performance-critical parts of the inner loop that were related to the repetitive tracking operation over all mines with respect to the vehicle positions. We tried to parallelize it using the Origin 2000 compiler pragmas (i.e., loop partition and/or data decomposition directives). Unfortunately, this approach delivered only very limited scalability for up to four processors. We concluded that the pragmas-based techniques, while efficient for regular Fortran programs, are not very practical for parallelizing complex and dynamic object-oriented, event-driven FMS simulation codes—especially the "legacy" object-oriented codes such as CMS that were developed by multiple programming teams over a long period of time and resulted in complex dynamic memory layouts of numerous objects that are now extremely difficult to decipher and properly distribute.

In the follow-on effort, we decided to explore an alternative approach based on a more direct, lower-level parallelization technique. Based on our analysis of the SPEEDES simulation kernel, which is known to deliver scalable object-oriented HPC FMS codes on the Origin 2000 (such as the Parallel Navy Simulation System under development by Metron), we constructed a similar parallel support for CMS. The base concept of this "micro SPEEDES kernel" approach, borrowed from the SPEEDES engine design but prototyped by us independently of the SPEEDES code, is to use only fully portable UNIX constructs, such as fork and shmem, for interprocess and interprocessor communication. This guarantees that the code is portable across all UNIX platforms. Hence, it can be more easily developed, debugged, and tested in the single-processor, multithreaded mode on sequential UNIX boxes.

In our microkernel, the parent process allocates a shared-memory segment using shmget(); then it forks *n* children, remaps them via execpv(), and passes the shared-memory-segment descriptor to each child via the command line argument. Each child attaches to its dedicated slice of the shared memory using shmat(), thereby establishing the highest-possible performance (no MPI overhead), fully portable (from O2 to O2K), multiprocessor communication framework. We also developed a simple set of semaphores to synchronize node programs and to avoid race conditions in critical sections of the code. On a single-processor UNIX platform, our kernel, when invoked with *n* processes, generates in fact *n* concurrent threads, communicating via UNIX shared memory. In an unscheduled Origin 2000 run, the number of threads per processor and the number of processors used are undetermined (i.e., under control of the OS). However, when executed under control of a parallel scheduler such as MISER, each child process forked by our parent is assigned to a different processor, which allows us to regain control over the process placement and to realize a natural scalable implementation of parallel CMS.

Parallel CMS: Architecture

On top of this microkernel infrastructure, we put suitable object-oriented wrappers that hide the explicit shmem-based communication under suitable higher-level abstractions, so that each node program behaves as a sequential CMS operating on a suitable subset of the full minefield. The CMS module cooperates with the ModSAF vehicle simulator running on another machine on the network. CMS continuously reads vehicle motion PDUs from the network, updates vehicle positions, and tracks all mines in the minefield in search of possible explosions. In our parallel version, the parent node 0 reads from the physical network and broadcasts all PDUs via shared memory to the children. Each child reads its PDUs from a virtual network that is a TCP/IP wrapper over the shmem communication channel.

Minefield segments are assigned to individual node programs using the scattered/cyclic decomposition, which guarantees reasonable dynamic load balancing regardless of the current number and configuration of vehicles propagating through the minefield. We found the CMS minefield parser and the whole minefield I/O sector difficult to decipher and modify to support scattered decomposition. We bypassed this problem by constructing our own Java-based minefield parser using the new powerful, public-domain Java parser technology called ANTLR, offered by the MageLang Institute. Our parser reads the large sequential minefield file and chops it into *n* files, each representing a reduced node minefield generated via scattered decomposition. All these files are fetched concurrently by the node programs when the parallel CMS starts. The subsequent simulation decomposes naturally into node CMS programs, operating on scattered sectors of the minefield and communicating via the shmem microkernel channel described above.

Parallel CMS: Performance

We performed timing runs of the Parallel CMS using the Origin 2000 systems at the Navy Research Laboratory in Washington, DC, and at the Engineer Research and Development Center's Major Shared Resource Center at Vicksburg, Mississippi. The performance results are presented in Figures 8.24 and 8.25. They illustrate that we have successfully constructed a fully scalable, parallel CMS for the Origin 2000 platform. Figures 8.24 and 8.25 present timing results of the parallel CMS for a large minefield of 1 million mines, simulated on 16, 32, and 64 nodes. The timing histogram in Figure 8.24 displays total simulation times in a 16-node run spent by each of the nodes. It demonstrates that we obtained almost perfect load balance. Higher bars on this figure represent full simulation runs with all ModSAF PDUs activated, whereas lower bars represent dry CMS runs without vehicle updates. Comparison of the two sets illustrates that communication with ModSAF vehicles took about 20% to 25% of the total simulation time and that both computation and communication parts are fully load balanced.

Figure 8.25 illustrates the speedup measured on 16, 32, and 64 nodes. Instead of $T(1)/T(n)$, we present unnormalized $1/T(n)$ in this plot, since we couldn't measure $T(1)$—when trying to run a 1-million mine simulation in one node we got a memory overflow error. The speedup plot illustrates that the parallel CMS offers almost perfect (linear) scaling over a broad range of processors.

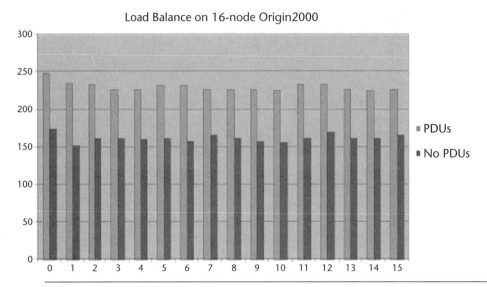

Figure 8.24   Simulation time spent by various nodes in a parallel CMS run for 1 million mines on a 16-node subset of an Origin 2000 at NRL (both for full run with vehicle PDUs and for a dry CMS-only run without PDUs). Illustrates very good load balance.

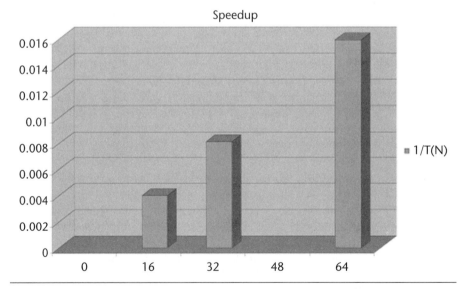

Figure 8.25   Speedup of parallel CMS on an NRL Origin 2000 for 1 million mines and 30 vehicles, measured on 16, 32, and 64 nodes. Illustrates almost perfect scalability across a broad processor range.

The timing results described above were obtained during parallel CMS runs within a WebHLA-based HPDC environment spanning three geographically distributed laboratories and utilizing most of the WebHLA tools and federates discussed above. The overall configuration of an initial meta-computing CMS environment is shown in Figure 8.26. ModSAF, JDIS, and SimVis modules were typically running on a workstation cluster at NPAC in Syracuse University. The JWORB/OWRTI-based federation manager (marked as RTI in Figure 8.26) was typically running on Origin 2000 at ERDC in Vicksburg. The parallel CMS federate was typically running on an Origin 2000 at NRL in Washington, DC. Large MISER runs at NRL need to be scheduled in a batch mode and are activated at unpredictable times, often in the middle of the night. This created some logistical problems, since ModSAF is a GUI-based legacy application that needs to be started by a human pressing the button. To bypass the need for a human operator to monitor the MISER batch queue continuously and to start ModSAF manually, we constructed a log of a typical simulation scenario with some 30 vehicles and played it repetitively from the database using our PDUDB federate. The only program running continuously (at ERDC) was the JWORB/OWRTI-based federation manager. After the parallel CMS was started by MISER at NRL, it joined a distributed federation (managed at ERDC) and automatically activated the PDUDB playback server at NPAC that started to stream vehicle PDUs to JDIS, which in turn converted them to HLA interactions and sent them (via RTI located at ERDC) to the parallel CMS federate at NRL. Each such event, received by node 0 of the parallel CMS, was multicast via shared memory to all nodes of the simulation run and used there by the node CMS programs to update the internal states of the simulation vehicles. An inner loop of each node CMS program was continuously tracking all mines scattered into this node against all vehicles in search of possible explosions.

Having constructed a fully scalable parallel CMS federate and having established a robust meta-computing, CMS experimentation environment, we conducted a set of experiments with wide-area-distributed, large-scale FMS simulations, using CMS as the application focus and testbed. In the first series of such experiments, we were able to successfully distribute large minefields containing millions of mines over several Origin 2000 machines in various DoD labs using domain decomposition, followed by the scattered decomposition of each minefield domain over the nodes of a local parallel system. In the next stage, we began replacing our simple SPEEDES microkernel, discussed above, by the full SPEEDES simulation engine, as illustrated in Figure 8.27. The goal here was to offer optimized communication among individual MPPs using the SPEEDES-based HPC RTI under development by Metron and to offer a more general-purpose platform for converting legacy M&S codes such as CMS to a well-organized programming model of SPEEDES. This ambitious and challenging plan is yet to be completed. We are currently exploring continuation of this effort within the new HPCMO PET 2 program and based on the latest DoD and Web/commodity technologies, as summarized below.

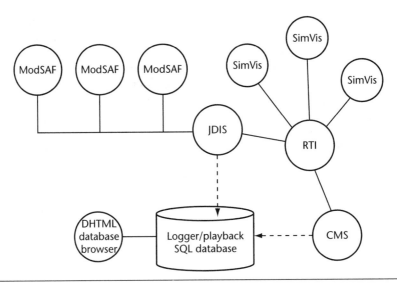

Figure 8.26   A WebHLA environment that supports parallel CMS experiments and includes ModSAF vehicles, SimVis front-ends, JDIS bridge between DIS and HLA domains, event logger and playback database, parallel CMS, and RTI federation manager.

8.11.6   Next Steps

The meta-computing FMS environment described here was built in 1997–2000 and was based on a suite of state-of-the-art DoD and commodity technologies then available. These included HLA, SPEEDES, CORBA, Java, and XML. The most important recent developments that will impact the evolution of our approach include: (1) adoption of SPEEDES as a core simulation engine by the JSIMS Enterprise; and (2) onset of a new Web/commodity technology cycle, led by the Microsoft .NET framework. Having selected SPEEDES as the HPC back-end, JSIMS will need a flexible commodity platform to deliver DoD-wide interactive and interoperable combat training systems. We therefore view our work on a commodity-based, HLA-compliant simulation integration framework as adequate for current DoD M&S needs and worth continuing. .NET—a new overarching commodity platform for the next-generation Internet—will likely play a critical role in distributed-systems engineering across various computational domains and communities. We could view .NET as either one more component within our previous pragmatic object Web framework—or rather as a system-wide integrated solution for such a framework. Within the FMS community, we try to pursue the latter approach, being encouraged by the recent efforts by Microsoft to standardize .NET via the ECMA process and by the growing interest of the open-software community to join the .NET initiative.

Porting our meta-computing FMS environment to the .NET framework is a major challenge, as .NET brings an integrated suite of technologies that effectively

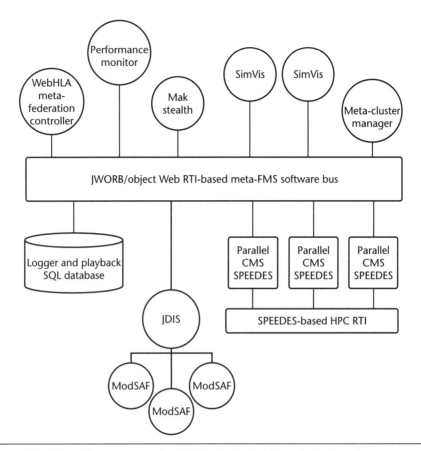

Figure 8.27   Planned meta-computing CMS with WebHLA-based distributed management similar to that of Figure 8.26 and with SPEEDES-based HPDC support for large-scale geographically distributed minefields.

replace individual components of our heterogeneous pragmatic object Web. For example, .NET Remoting brings a new powerful distributed-object model that replaces CORBA, and C# offers a new high-performance, object-oriented programming language that replaces Java. XML remains as a core communication protocol and meta-data fabric of .NET, but it is now highly structured and packaged in terms of SOAP messaging and a suitable family of self-documentation formats. Implications of .NET for HPC are yet to be explored. But the overall structure of this new powerful multilanguage framework, with the underlying common language run time, mobile high-performance, intermediate compiler formats, and JIT compilation technology, appears to be very promising, not only for general-purpose commodity computing, but also for the advanced needs of science and engineering computation. In the modeling and simulation area, .NET/C# brings several new and useful constructs, such as events and delegates, that enable an elegant high-level programming framework for event-driven simulations. It seems conceivable that, a few years down the road, FMS systems such as SPEEDES will be routinely and efficiently constructed using the C# language over the cross-platform .NET framework, rather than using C++ over traditional vendor-specific compilers, as is still being done today. We intend to initiate this process by porting our CORBA/Java-based WebHLA to an equivalent .NET/C# system—to be called HLA.NET—and by gradually moving individual federates and engines of our meta-computing FMS toward the suitable .NET technologies as they emerge, stabilize, and standardize.

8.12 Computational Structure of Applications

Here we summarize the applications of this book and two other books discussed below. We focus on the problem structure as it impacts the parallelization strategy.

8.12.1 Applications from This Book

Computational Fluid Dynamics (CFD) (Chapter 5). This chapter provides a thorough formulation of CFD with a general discussion of the importance of nonlinear terms and, most importantly, viscosity. Difficult features like shockwaves and turbulence can be traced to the small coefficient of the highest-order derivatives. Incompressible flow is approached using the spectral element method, which combines the features of finite elements (copes with complex geometries) and highly accurate approximations within each element. These problems need fast solvers for elliptic equations, and there is a detailed discussion of data and matrix structure and the use of iterative conjugate gradient methods. This is compared with direct solvers using the static condensation method for calculating the solution (stiffness) matrix. The important problem of adaptive meshes is described using the successive refinement quad/oct-tree (in two and three dimensions) method. Compressible flow methods are reviewed, and the key problem of coping with the rapid change in field variables at shockwaves is identified. One uses a lower-order approximation near a shock but preserves the most powerful high-order spectral methods in the areas where the flow is smooth. Parallel computing (using space-filling curves for decomposition) and adaptive meshes are covered.

Environment and Energy (Chapter 6). This chapter describes three distinct problem areas, each illustrating important general approaches. Subsurface flow in porous media is needed in both oil reservoir simulations and environmental pollution studies. The nearly hyperbolic or parabolic flow equations are characterized by multiple constituents and by very heterogeneous media with possible abrupt discontinuities in the physical domain. This motivates the use of domain decomposition methods where the full region is divided into blocks that can use different solution methods if necessary. The blocks must be iteratively reconciled at their boundaries (mortar spaces). The IPARS code described has been successfully integrated into two powerful problem-solving environments: NetSolve, described in Chapter 14, and DISCOVER (aimed especially at interactive steering) from Rutgers University.

The discussion of the shallow water problem uses a method involving implicit (in the vertical direction) and explicit (in the horizontal plane) time-marching methods. It is instructive to see that good parallel performance is obtained only by decomposing in the horizontal directions and keeping the hard-to-parallelize implicit algorithm sequentially implemented. The irregular mesh is tackled using space-filling curves, as also described in Chapter 5.

Finally, important code coupling (meta-problem in Chapter 4 notation) issues are discussed for oil spill simulations, where water and chemical transport require modeling in a linked fashion. ADR (active data repository) technology from Maryland is used to link the computations between water and chemical simulations. Sophisticated filtering is needed to match the output and input needs of the two subsystems.

Molecular Quantum Chemistry (Chapter 7). This chapter surveys in detail two capabilities of the NWChem package from Pacific Northwest Laboratory. It surveys other aspects of computational chemistry. This field makes extensive use of particle dynamics algorithms and some use of partial differential equation solvers. However, characteristic of computational chemistry is the importance of matrix-based methods, and these are the focus of this chapter. The matrix is Hamiltonian (energy) and is typically symmetric positive definite. In a quantum approach, the eigensystems of this matrix are the equilibrium states of the molecule being studied. This type of problem is characteristic of quantum theoretical methods in physics and chemistry; particle dynamics is used in classical nonquantum regimes.

NWChem uses a software approach, the Global Array (GA) Toolkit, a programming model that lies in between HPF and message passing and has been highly successful. GA exposes locality to the programmer but has a shared-memory programming model for accessing data stored in remote processors. Interestingly, in many cases, calculating the matrix elements dominates (over solving for eigenfunctions), and this is a pleasing parallel task. It requires very careful blocking and staging of the components used to calculate the integrals forming the matrix elements. In some approaches, parallel matrix multiplication is important in generating the matrices. The matrices typically are taken as full, and very powerful parallel eigensolvers were developed for this problem. This area of science clearly shows the benefit of linear algebra libraries (see Chapter 20) and general performance enhancements like blocking.

Numerical (General) Relativity (Section 8.1). This field involves time evolution of complex partial differential equations having similarities with the simpler Maxwell equations used in electromagnetics (see Section 8.6). Key difficulties are the boundary conditions, which are outgoing waves at infinity, and the difficult and unique, multiple-black-hole internal surface conditions. Finite difference and adaptive meshes are the usual approach.

Numerical Simulations in Lattice Quantum Chromodynamics (Section 8.2).   Monte Carlo methods are central to the numerical approaches to many fields (especially in physics and chemistry) and can consume substantial computing resources. The error in such computation decreases as the square root of the computer time used; most differential equation– and particle dynamics–based methods display power convergence. One finds Monte Carlo methods being used when problems are posed as integral equations. The often high-dimension integrals are solved by Monte Carlo methods using a randomly distributed set of integration points. Quantum chromodynamics (QCD) simulations are a classic example of large-scale Monte Carlo simulations that perform excellently on most parallel machines. Their modest communication costs and regular structure lead to good node performance. This application is straightforward to parallelize and very suitable for high-performance Fortran (HPF) as the basic data structure is an array. However, the work described here uses a portable message passing interface (MPI) code.

Advances in lattice quantum chromodynamics typically come from new physics insights that lead to more efficient numerical formulations, rather than from improvements in the Monte Carlo algorithms used. This field has generated many special-purpose facilities, as the lack of significant I/O and the CPU-intense nature of QCD allows optimized node designs. The work at Columbia [202] and Tsukuba [227] universities is well known. Adaptive load balancing and related issues involved with irregular finite element problems also appear in other irregular-geometry Monte Carlo problems.

Ocean Modeling (Section 8.3).   This section describes the issues encountered in optimizing a whole-earth ocean simulation including realistic geography and proper ocean atmosphere boundaries. Conjugate gradient solvers and MPI message passing with Fortran 90 are used for the parallel implicit solver for the vertically averaged flow.

Simulations of Earthquakes (Section 8.4).   Earthquake simulation is a relatively young field, and it is yet not known how successful forecasts of large earthquakes can be. The field has an increasing amount of real-time sensor data, requiring data assimilation techniques and automatic differentiation tools (see Chapter 24). Study of earthquake faults can use finite element techniques; with some approximation, Green's function approaches, which can use fast multipole methods, may also be applied. Analysis of the observational and simulation data use data-mining methods, as described in Section 8.7. The principal component and hidden Markov classification algorithms currently used in the earthquake field [481, 786, 816, 817, 877, 932, 944] illustrate the diversity in data-mining methods when compared with the decision-tree methods of Section 8.8.

Cosmological Structure Formation (Section 8.5).   Cosmological structure formation (CSF) is an example of a coupled particle field problem. The universe is viewed as a set of particles that generate a gravitational field obeying Poisson's equation. This field determines the force needed to evolve each particle in time. The same structure is also seen in plasma physics, where electrons create an electromagnetic field. Generating compatible particle and field decompositions is difficult. CSF exhibits large ranges in distance and temporal scale, characteristic of the attractive gravitational forces. Poisson's equation is solved by Fast Fourier Transforms, and deeply adaptive meshes are generated. The article describes both MPI and CMFortran (HPF-like) implementations. Further, it makes use of object-oriented techniques (see Chapter 13) with kernels in F77. Some approaches to this problem class use fast multipole methods.

Computational Electromagnetics (Section 8.6).   This overview summarizes several different approaches to electromagnetic simulations and notes the growing importance of coupling electromagnetics with disciplines such as aerodynamics and chemical physics. Parallel computing has been successfully applied to the three major approaches to computational electromagnetics. Asymptotic methods use ray tracing, as is done in visualization. Frequency-domain methods use moment (spectral) expansions that were the earliest uses of large parallel full-matrix solvers 10 to 15 years ago. Finally, time-domain methods use finite volume (element) methods with an unstructured mesh. As in general relativity, special attention is required in order to obtain accurate wave solutions at infinity in the time-domain approach.

Parallel Algorithms in Data Mining (Section 8.7).   Data mining is a broad field with many different applications and algorithms (see also Sections 8.4 and 8.8). This section describes important algorithms used in discovering associations among items that are likely to be purchased by the same customer. These associations can occur either in time or because the purchases tend to be in the same shopping basket. Other data-mining problems discussed include the classification problem tackled by decision trees. These tree-based approaches are parallelized effectively (as they are based on huge transaction databases), with load balance being a difficult issue.

High-Performance Computing in Signal and Image Processing (Section 8.8).   This section discusses some of the issues from this field, which currently makes surprisingly little use of parallel computing—even though good parallel algorithms often exist. The field has preferred the convenient programming model and interactive feedback of systems like MATLAB and Khoros. These are problem-solving environments, as described in Chapter 14.

Deterministic Monte Carlo Methods and Parallelism (Section 8.9).   This section describes some very important developments in the generation of "random" numbers. Quasi-random numbers are more uniformly distributed than the standard truly random numbers and, for certain integrals, lead to more rapid convergence. In particular, these methods have been applied to financial modeling, where one needs to calculate one or more functions (stock prices, their derivatives, or other financial instruments) at some future time by integrating over the possible future values of the underlying variables. These future values are given by models based on the past behavior of the stock. This can be captured in some cases by the volatility or standard deviation of the stock. The simplest model is perhaps the Black–Scholes equation, which can be derived from a Gaussian stock distribution, combined with an underlying "no-arbitrage" assumption. This asserts that the stock market is always in equilibrium instantaneously and there is no opportunity to make money by exploiting mismatches between buy and sell prices. In the language of physics, the different players in the stock market form a heat bath, which keeps the market in adiabatic equilibrium. There is a straightforward binomial method for predicting the probability distributions of financial instruments. However, Monte Carlo methods and quasi-random numbers are the more powerful approach.

Quasi–Real Time Microtomography Experiments at Photon Sources (Section 8.10). Section 8.10 describes a successful application of computational grids to accelerate the data analysis of an accelerator experiment. It is an example that can be generalized to other cases. The accelerator (here a photon source at Argonne National Laboratory) data is passed in real time to a supercomputer, where the analysis is performed. Multiple visualization and control stations are also connected to the Grid.

WebHLA-based Meta-Computing Environment for Forces Modeling and Simulation (Section 8.11). This section describes event-driven simulations, which are very common in military applications (see Chapter 4). A distributed-object approach called high-level architecture or HLA (see Chapter 13) is being used for modern problems of this class. Some run in "real time," with synchronization provided by the wall clock and humans and machines in the loop. Other cases are run in "virtual time," in a more traditional standalone fashion. This section describes integration of these military standards with Object Web ideas such as CORBA and .NET from Microsoft. One application simulated the interaction of vehicles with a million mines on a distributed Grid of computers. This work also parallelized the minefield simulator using threads (see Chapter 10).

8.12.2   Applications from *Industrial Strength Parallel Computing* [573]

Ocean Modeling and Visualization, Chapter 7 (Yi Chao, P. Peggy Li, Ping Wang, Daniel S. Katz, Benny N. Cheng, Scott Whitman). This uses a variant of the same ocean code described in Section 8.3 of this book. It describes both basic parallel strategies and the integration of the simulation with a parallel, 3-D volume renderer.

Impact of Aircraft on Global Atmospheric Chemistry, Chapter 8 (Douglas A. Rotman, John R. Tannahill, Steven L. Baughcum). This discusses issues related to those in Chapter 6 of this book in the context of estimating the impact on atmospheric chemistry of supersonic aircraft emissions. Task decomposition (code coupling) for different physics packages is combined with domain decomposition and parallel block data decomposition. Again, one keeps the vertical direction in each processor and decomposes in the horizontal plane. Nontrivial technical problems are found in the polar regions due to decomposition singularities.

Petroleum Reservoir Management, Chapter 9 (Michael DeLong, Allyson Gajraj, Wayne Joubert, Olaf Lubeck, James Sanderson, Robert E. Stephenson, Gautam S. Shiralkar, Bart van Bloemen Waanders). This addresses an application covered in Chapter 6 of this book, but focuses on a different code, Falcon, developed as a collaboration between Amoco and Los Alamos. As in other chapters of ISPC, detailed performance results are given. Particularly interesting is the discussion of the sparse matrix solver (see Chapter 21 of this book). A very efficient parallel preconditioner for a fully implicit solver was developed, based on the incomplete LU factorization approach. This rearranged the order of computation, but faithfully preserved the sequential algorithm.

An Architecture-Independent Navier-Stokes Code, Chapter 10 (Johnson C. T. Wang, Stephen Taylor). This describes parallelization of commercial code ALSINS (from Aerospace Corporation) that solves the Navier–Stokes equations (see Chapter 5 of this book) using finite difference methods in the Reynolds-averaging approximation for turbulence. Domain decomposition (Chapters 6 and 20 of this book) and MPI are used for the parallelism. The application studied involved flow over Delta and Titan launch rockets.

Gaining Insights into the Flow in a Static Mixer, Chapter 11 (Olivier Byrde, Mark L. Sawley). This chapter studies flow in commercial chemical mixers with Reynolds-averaged, Navier–Stokes equations using finite volume methods as in ISPC, Chapter 10. Domain decomposition (Chapters 6 and 20 of this book) of a block-structured code and PVM are used for the parallelism. The mixing study required parallel study of particle trajectories in the calculated flow field.

Modeling Groundwater Flow and Contaminant Transport, Chapter 12 (William J. Bosl, Steven F. Ashby, Chuck Baldwin, Robert D. Falgout, Steven G. Smith, Andrew F. B. Tompson). This presents a groundwater flow (Chapter 6 of this book) code, ParFlow, that uses finite volume methods to generate the finite difference equations. A highlight is the detailed discussion of parallel multigrid (Section 8.5, Chapter 12, and Chapter 21 of this book), which is used not as a complete solver, but as a preconditioner for a conjugate gradient algorithm.

Simulation of Plasma Reactors, Chapter 13 (Stephen Taylor, Marc Rieffel, Jerrell Watts, Sadasivan Shankar). This simulates plasma reactors used in semiconductor manufacturing plants. The direct-simulation Monte Carlo method is used to model the system in terms of locally interacting particles. Adaptive 3-D meshes (Chapter 19 of this book) are used with a novel diffusive algorithm to control dynamic load balancing (Chapter 18 of this book).

Electron-Molecule Collisions for Plasma Modeling, Chapter 14 (Carl Winstead, Chuo-Han Lee, Vincent McKoy).   This complements Chapter 13 of ISPC by studying the fundamental particle interactions in plasma reactors. It is instructive to compare the discussion of the algorithm in this chapter with that of Chapter 7 of this book. They lead to similar conclusions, with Chapter 7 naturally describing the issues more generally. Two steps—calculation of matrix elements and then a horde of matrix multiplications to transform basis sets—dominate the computation. In this problem class, the matrix solver is not a computationally significant step.

Three-Dimensional Plasma Particle-in-Cell Calculations of Ion Thruster Backflow Contamination, Chapter 15 (Robie I. Samanta Roy, Daniel E. Hastings, Stephen Taylor).   This chapter studies contamination from space-craft thruster exhaust using a 3-D particle-in-the-cell code. This involves a mix of solving Poisson's equation for the electrostatic field and evolving ions under the forces calculated from this field. There are algorithmic similarities to the astrophysics problems in this book (Section 8.5), but electromagnetic problems produce less extreme density concentrations than the purely attractive (and hence clumping) gravitational force found in astrophysics.

Advanced Atomic-Level Materials Design, Chapter 16 (Lin H. Yang).   This describes a quantum molecular-dynamics package implementing the well-known Car-Parrinello method. This is part of the NWChem package featured in Chapter 7 of this book, but not described in detail there. The computation is mostly dominated by 3-D FFTs and basic BLAS (complex vector arithmetic) calls, but has significant I/O.

Solving Symmetric Eigenvalue Problems, Chapter 17 (David C. O'Neal, Raghurama Reddy).   This describes parallel eigenvalue determination, which is covered in Section 7.3.2 and Chapter 20 of this book.

Nuclear Magnetic Resonance Simulations, Chapter 18 (Alan J. Benesi, Kenneth M. Merz, James J. Vincent, Ravi Subramanya).   This is a pleasingly parallel computation of NMR spectra obtained by averaging over crystal orientation.

Molecular Dynamics Simulations Using Particle-Mesh Ewald Methods, Chapter 19 (Michael F. Crowley, David W. Deerfield II, Tom A. Darden, Thomas E. Cheatham III).   This chapter discusses parallelization of a widely used molecular dynamics code, AMBER, and its application to computational biology. Much of the discussion is devoted to implementing a particle-mesh method aimed at fast calculation of the long-range forces. Section 8.5 of this book discusses this problem for astrophysical cases. The ISPC discussion focuses on the needed 3-D FFT.

Radar Scattering and Antenna Modeling, Chapter 20 (Tom Cwik, Cinzia Zuffada, Daniel S. Katz, Jay Parker).   This article discusses a finite element formulation of computational electromagnetics (see Section 8.6 of this book) that leads to a sparse matrix problem with multiple right-hand sides. The minimum residual iterative solver was used—this is similar to the conjugate gradient approach described extensively in this book (Chapter 20, Chapter 21, and many applications, especially Chapter 5). The complex geometries of realistic antenna and scattering problems demanded sophisticated mesh generation (Chapter 19 of this book).

Functional Magnetic Resonance Imaging Dataset Analysis, Chapter 21 (Nigel H. Goddard, Greg Hood, Jonathan D. Cohen, Leigh E. Nystrom, William F. Eddy, Christopher R. Genovese, Douglas C. Noll).   This describes a common, important type of data analysis in which raw images (MRI scans in neuroscience) need basic processing before they can be interpreted. This processing for MRI involves a pipeline of 5 to 15 steps, of which the computationally intense Fourier transforms, interpolation, and head motion corrections were parallelized. Sections 8.8 and 8.10 of this book describe related applications.

Selective and Sensitive Comparison of Genetic Sequence Data, Chapter 22 (Alexander J. Ropelewski, Hugh B. Nicholas, Jr., David W. Deerfield II).   This describes the very important genome database search problem implemented in a program called Msearch. The basic sequential algorithm involves very sophisticated pattern matching, but parallelism is straightforward because one can use pleasingly parallel approaches involving decomposing the computation over parts of the searched database.

8.12.3   Applications from *Parallel Computing Works!*

The applications in *Parallel Computing Works!* [358] are not as sophisticated as those discussed above, as they come from a time when few scientists addressed 3-D problems. Two-dimensional computations were typically the best you could do in the partial differential equation arena. To make a stark contrast, the early 1983 QCD (Section 8.2 of this book) computations in PCW were done on the Caltech hypercube, whose 64 nodes could only make it to a total of 3 megaflops when combined! Today, teraflop performance is available—almost a million times better. Nevertheless, in many applications, the parallel approaches described in this book are still sound and state of the art.

A Methodology for Computation (Chapter 3).   This chapter describes more formally the approach taken in Chapter 4 of this book.

Synchronous Applications I (Chapter 4).   This chapter describes QCD (Section 8.2 of this book) and other similar statistical physics, Monte Carlo simulations on a regular lattice. It also presents a cellular automata model for granular materials (such as sand dunes). This model has a simple, regular lattice structure, as mentioned in Section 4.4 of this book.

Synchronous Applications II (Chapter 6).   This chapter describes other regular problems, including convectively dominated flows and the flux-corrected transport differential equations. High statistics studies of 2-D statistical physics problems are used to study phase transitions (cf. Sections 8.2 and 8.9 of this book). Parallel multiscale methods are also described for various image processing algorithms, including surface reconstruction, character recognition, real-time motion field estimation and collective stereosis (cf. Section 8.8 of this book).

Independent Parallelism (Chapter 7).   This PCW chapter describes what is termed "pleasingly parallel" applications in Chapter 4 of this book. It includes a physics computation of quantum-string theory surfaces, parallel random-number generation, and ray tracing to study a statistical approach to the gravitational lensing of quasars by galaxies. A high-temperature superconductor study uses the quantum Monte Carlo method—here one uses Monte Carlo methods to generate a set of random independent paths—a different problem structure to that of Section 8.2, but a method of general importance in chemistry, condensed matter, and nuclear physics. GENESIS [132] was one of the first general-purpose, biological neural network simulators.

Full Matrix Algorithms and Their Applications (Chapter 8).   This chapter first discusses some parallel matrix algorithms (Chapter 20 of this book) and applies the Gauss–Jordan matrix solver to a chemical reaction computation. This directly solves Schrödinger's equation for a small number of particles and is different in structure from the problems in this book, Chapter 7. It reduces to a multichannel, ordinary differential equation and leads to full matrix solvers. A section on "electron-molecule collisions" describes a similar structure to the much more sophisticated simulation engines of this book, Chapter 7. Further work by this group can be found in Chapter 14 of ISPC.

Loosely Synchronous Problems (Chapter 9).   The chapters above describe synchronous or pleasingly parallel systems, in the language of Chapter 4 of this book. This chapter describes several loosely synchronous cases. Geomorphology by micromechanical simulations is a different approach to granular systems (from the cellular automata in Chapter 4 of PCW) using direct modeling of particles "bouncing off each other." Particle-in-cell simulation of an electron-beam plasma instability uses particle-in-the-cell methods, which have, of course, grown tremendously in sophistication, as seen in the astrophysics simulation of this book, Section 8.5, and the ion thruster simulations in Chapter 15 of ISPC (which uses the same approach as described in this PCW chapter). Computational electromagnetics (see Section 8.6 of this book) used finite element methods and is followed up in Chapter 20 of ISPC. Concurrent DASSL applied to dynamic distillation-column simulation uses a parallel sparse solver (Chapter 21 of this book) to tackle coupled, ordinary, differential-algebraic equations arising in chemical engineering.

This chapter also discusses the parallel adaptive multigrid for solving differential equations—an area with similarities to mesh refinement, discussed in this book Chapter 5, Section 8.5, Chapter 12, and Chapter 19. See also Chapter 9 of ISPC. Munkres's assignment algorithm was parallelized for a multitarget Kalman-filter problem (cf. Section 8.7 of this book). This PCW chapter also discusses parallel implementations of learning methods for neural networks.

DIME Programming Environment (Chapter 10).   This chapter discusses one of the earliest parallel unstructured-mesh generators and applies it to model finite element problems. Chapter 19 of this book is an up-to-date survey of this field.

Load Balancing and Optimization (Chapter 11).   This chapter describes approaches to optimization based on physical analogies, including approaches to the well-known traveling salesman problem. These physical optimization methods complement those discussed in Section 8.7 and Chapter 22 of this book.

Irregular Loosely Synchronous Problems (Chapter 12).   This chapter features some of the harder parallel scientific codes in PCW. It includes two adaptive unstructured-mesh problems that used the DIME package described in PCW, Chapter 10. One was a simulation of the electrosensory system of the fish *gnathonemus petersii* and the other transonic flow in CFD (Chapter 5 of this book). There is a full discussion of fast multipole methods and their parallelism. These were mentioned in Chapter 4 and Section 8.6 of this book. In PCW they are applied to astrophysical problems similar to those in Section 8.5 of this book and to the vortex approach to CFD. Fast multipole methods are applied to the same problem class as particle-in-the-cell codes, as they again involve interacting particles and fields. Chapter 19 of ISPC discusses another biochemistry problem of this class.

Parallel sorting is an interesting area, and this PCW chapter describes several good algorithms and compares them. The discussion of cluster algorithms for statistical physics is interesting, as these are the best sequential algorithms, but the method is very hard to parallelize. The same difficult structure occurs in some approaches to region finding in image processing and also in some models of the formation of earthquakes using cellular automata-like models. The clusters are the aligned strains that form the earthquake.

Asynchronous Applications (Chapter 14).   This chapter describes examples of the temporally asynchronous algorithms described in Chapter 4 of this book, where scaling parallelism is not easy. Melting in two dimensions illustrates a subtle point that distinguishes Monte Carlo and PDE algorithms, as one cannot simultaneously update in Monte Carlo those sites with overlapping neighbors. This complicates the loosely synchronous structure and can make problem architecture look like that of asynchronous event-driven simulations—here the events are individual Monte Carlo updates. "Detailed balance" requires that such events be sequentially (if arbitrarily) ordered, which is not easy in a parallel environment. Nevertheless, using the equivalent of multiple threads (Chapter 10 of this book), one finds an algorithm that gives good parallel performance.

Computer chess is the major focus of this chapter. Parallelism is obtained from sophisticated parallelism of the game tree. Statistical methods are used to balance the processing of the different branches of the dynamically pruned game tree. There is a shared database containing previous evaluation of positions, but otherwise the processing of the different possible moves is independent. One does need a clever ordering of the work (evaluation of the different final positions) in order to avoid a significant number of calculations being wasted because they would "later" be pruned away by a parallel calculation on a different processor. Branch-and-bound applications have parallelization characteristics that are similar to computer chess. Note that this is not the only, and in fact not the easiest, form of parallelism in computer chess. Rather, fine-grain parallelism in evaluating each position is used in all recent computer-chess championship systems. The work described in PCW is complementary to this mainstream activity.

Complex System Simulation and Analysis (Chapter 18). This chapter describes a few meta-problems, using the syntax of Section 4.8 of this book. ISIS was an interactive seismic imaging system, and there is a long discussion of one of the first large-scale, parallel military simulations mixing data and task parallelism. This involved generation of scenarios, tracking multiple ballistic missiles and a simulation of the hoped-for identification and destruction. A very sophisticated parallel Kalman filter was generated in this project.

8.13   Conclusion

In this chapter we have presented an overview of various applications that show the use of parallel computing in many disciplines. The examples include support for basic science research, support for societal needs, and engineering applications. The algorithms used by these applications include scalable methods traditionally considered particularly appropriate for solving partial differential equations and n-body problems, Monte Carlo methods, and new algorithms in areas such as data mining. One stiking feature is that parallel computers have become just another component of a scientific instrument, rather than an exotic piece of equipment. The examples given here provide a good starting point for understanding the capabilities of parallel computers and the approaches needed to use them. In the subsequent chapters, we cover in detail the algorithmic and software techniques required to design and build parallel applications.

9   Software Technologies

**Ian Foster • Jack Dongarra •
Ken Kennedy • Charles Koelbel**

While parallel computing is defined by hardware technology, it is software that renders a parallel computer usable. Parallel software technologies are the focus of both this overview chapter and the seven more comprehensive chapters that follow in Part III.

The concerns of the parallel programmer are those of any programmer: algorithm design, convenience of expression, efficiency of execution, ease of debugging, component reuse, and life-cycle issues. Hence, we should not be surprised to find that the software technologies required to support parallel program development are familiar in terms of their basic function. In particular, the parallel programmer, like any programmer, requires languages and/or application programming interfaces (APIs) that allow for the succinct expression of complex algorithms, hiding unimportant details while providing control over performance-critical issues; associated tools (e.g., performance profilers) that allow diagnosis and correction of errors and performance problems; and convenient formulations of efficient algorithms for solving key problems, ideally packaged so that they can easily be integrated into an application program.

However, despite these commonalities, the particular characteristics of parallel computers and of parallel computing introduce additional concerns that tend to complicate both parallel programming and the development of parallel programming tools. In particular, we must be concerned with the following three challenges:

1. *Concurrency and communication*. Parallel programs may involve the creation, coordination, and management of potentially thousands of independent threads of control. Interactions between concurrent threads of control may result in nondeterminism. These issues introduce unique concerns that have profound implications for every aspect of the program development process.

2. *Need for high performance.* In sequential programming, ease of expression may be as important or even more important than program performance. In contrast, the motivation for using parallel computation is almost always a desire for high performance. This requirement places stringent constraints on the programming models and tools that can reasonably be used for parallel programming.

3. *Diversity of architecture.* The considerable diversity seen in parallel computer architectures makes the development of standard tools and portable programs more difficult than is the case in sequential computing, where we find remarkable uniformity in basic architecture.

The role of parallel software is thus to satisfy the requirements listed at the beginning of this section, while simultaneously addressing in some fashion the three challenges of concurrency and communication, performance demands, and architectural diversity. This is a difficult task, and so in practice we find a variety of approaches to parallel software, each making different tradeoffs between these requirements.

In the rest of this chapter, we provide an overview of the major software and algorithmic technologies that we can call upon when developing parallel programs. In so doing, we revisit issues that were first developed at the beginning of the book relating to programming models, methodologies, and technologies, and attempt to integrate those different perspectives in a common framework. We structure the presentation in terms of two key questions that we believe will be asked by any parallel programmer:

- *How do I select the parallel programming technology (library or language) to use when writing a program?* We introduce the programming models, APIs, and languages that are commonly used for parallel program development and provide guidance concerning when these different models, APIs, and languages may be appropriate.

- *How do I achieve correct and efficient execution?* Here, we discuss issues relating to nondeterminism and performance modeling.

In each case, we provide pointers to the chapters in which these issues are discussed at greater length.

A third important question—*How do I reuse existing parallel algorithms and code?*—is addressed in Chapter 17, where we describe several techniques used to achieve code reuse in parallel algorithms.

9.1   Selecting a Parallel Program Technology

As explained in Chapter 2, a parallel computer is a collection of processing and memory elements, plus a communication network used to route requests and information among these elements. The task of the parallel programmer is to coordinate the operation of these diverse elements so as to achieve efficient and correct execution on the problem of interest.

The performance of a parallel program is determined by how effectively it maximizes *concurrency* (the number of operations that can be performed simultaneously), while minimizing the amount of *communication* required to access "nonlocal" data, transfer intermediate results, and synchronize the operation of different threads of control. Communication costs are frequently sensitive to *data distribution*, the mapping of application data structures to memory elements; a good data distribution can reduce the number of memory accesses that require expensive communication operations. If work is not distributed evenly among processors, *load imbalances* may occur, reducing concurrency and performance.

When evaluating the correctness of a parallel program, the programmer may need to take into account the possibility of *race conditions*, which occur when the executions of two or more distinct threads of control are sufficiently unconstrained that the result of a computation can vary nondeterministically, depending simply on the speed at which different threads proceed. The programmer, when faced with the task of writing an efficient and correct parallel program, can call upon a variety of parallel languages, compilers, and libraries, each of which implements a distinct programming model with different tradeoffs among ease of use, generality, and achievable performance.

In the rest of this section, we first review some of the principal programming models implemented by commonly used languages and libraries. Then, we examine each of these languages and libraries in turn and discuss their advantages and disadvantages.

9.1.1 Parallel Programming Models

We first make some general comments concerning the programming models that underlie the various languages and libraries that will be discussed subsequently. Thirty years of research have led to the definition and exploration of a large number of parallel programming models [867]. Few of these models have survived, but much experience has been gained in what is useful in practical settings.

Data Parallelism versus Task Parallelism

Parallel programs may be categorized according to whether they emphasize concurrent execution of the same task on different data elements (*data* parallelism) or the concurrent execution of different tasks on the same or different data (*task* parallelism). For example, a simulation of galaxy formation might require that essentially the same operation be performed on each of a large number of data items (stars); in this case, a data-parallel algorithm is obtained naturally by performing this operation on multiple items simultaneously. In contrast, in a simulation of a complex physical system comprising multiple processes (e.g., a multidisciplinary optimization of an aircraft might couple airflow, structures, and engine simulations), the different components can be executed concurrently, hence obtaining task parallelism.

Most programs for scalable parallel computers are data parallel in nature, for the simple reason that the amount of concurrency that can be obtained from data parallelism tends to be larger than can be achieved via task parallelism. Nevertheless, task parallelism can have an important role to play as a software engineering technique: it often makes sense to execute distinct components on disjoint sets of processors (or even on different computers) for modularity reasons. It is increasingly common for parallel programs to be structured as a task-parallel composition of data-parallel components.

Explicit versus Implicit Parallelism

Parallel programming systems can be categorized according to whether they support an explicitly or implicitly parallel programming model. An *explicitly* parallel system requires that the programmer specify directly the activities of the multiple concurrent "threads of control" that form a parallel computation. In contrast, an *implicitly* parallel system allows the programmer to provide a higher-level specification of program behavior in which parallelism is not represented directly. It is then the responsibility of the compiler or library to implement this parallelism efficiently and correctly.

Implicitly parallel systems can simplify programming by eliminating the need for the programmer to coordinate the execution of multiple processes. For example, in the implicitly parallel, primarily data-parallel language High Performance Fortran (HPF), the programmer writes what is essentially sequential Fortran 90 code, augmented with some directives. Race conditions cannot occur, and the HPF program need not be rewritten to take advantage of different parallel architectures.

Explicitly parallel systems provide the programmer with more control over program behavior and hence can often be used to achieve higher performance. For example, a Message Passing Interface (MPI) implementation of an adaptive mesh-refinement algorithm may incorporate sophisticated techniques for computing mesh distributions, for structuring communications among subdomains, and for redistributing data when load imbalances occur. These strategies are beyond the capabilities of today's HPF compilers.

A parallel programming style that is becoming increasingly popular is to encapsulate the complexities of parallel algorithm design within libraries (e.g., an adaptive-mesh-refinement library, as just discussed). An application program can then consist of just a sequence of calls to such library functions. In this way, many of the advantages of an implicitly parallel approach can be obtained within an explicitly parallel framework.

Shared Memory versus Distributed Memory

Explicitly parallel programming systems can be categorized according to whether they support a shared- or distributed-memory programming model. In a *shared-*

memory model, the programmer's task is to specify the activities of a set of processes that communicate by reading and writing shared memory. In a *distributed-memory* model, processes have only local memory and must use some other mechanism (e.g., message passing or remote procedure calls) to exchange information.

Shared-memory models have the significant advantage that the programmer need not be concerned with data-distribution issues. On the other hand, high-performance implementations may be difficult on computers that lack hardware support for shared memory, and race conditions tend to arise more easily.

Distributed-memory models have the advantage that programmers have explicit control over data distribution and communication; this control facilitates high-performance programming on large distributed-memory parallel computers.

Other Programming Paradigms

Some important aspects of programming are orthogonal to the model of parallelism, but can have a significant impact on the parallel programming process. Arguably, the most important example of this is *object-oriented programming*. Although the fundamentals of object-oriented design—including encapsulation of data and function, inheritance and polymorphism, and generic programming enabled by powerful abstraction—come from the sequential world, they are also relevant to parallel computing. In particular, appropriate abstractions can hide parallelism when it complicates programming. Good examples include C++ libraries for array expressions [798, 959], which provide a familiar interface to the programmer that can be used efficiently on both sequential and parallel computers. Abstractions can also provide "glue" to tie parallel components together. The resulting component architectures provide excellent run-time environments for building applications by composition. Chapter 13 explores object-oriented parallel programming in more detail.

Other programming paradigms are specific to parallel programming, but not to the particular model of parallelism. One of particular interest is the *single-program, multiple-data* (SPMD) approach, in which all available processors execute the same textual program. Because each processor has its own thread of control, different processors may take different paths through this program and may operate on different data. (In fact, it is usually the case that most processors take similar paths through the program, perhaps varying slightly in the number of iterations of a particular loop or the active branch of some conditionals.) Many programmers find this an intuitive model that can be used for shared or distributed memory. For example, they often write message-passing programs in this style, although it is not mandated by the MPI standard. Some explicit parallel languages make heavy use of the SPMD paradigm, as Section 12.4 describes.

9.1.2   Parallel Programming Technologies

We provide a brief summary of the major programming technologies discussed in this book and provide pointers to the chapters where they are covered in more detail. In the next subsection, we discuss the situations in which each is to be preferred.

Message Passing Interface

The Message Passing Interface (MPI) is a specification for a set of functions for managing the movement of data among sets of communicating processes. Official MPI bindings are defined for C, Fortran, and C++; bindings for various other languages have been produced as well. MPI defines functions for point-to-point communication between two processes, collective operations among processes, parallel I/O, and process management. In addition, MPI's support for *communicators* facilitates the creation of modular programs and reusable libraries. Communication in MPI specifies the types and layout of data being communicated, allowing MPI implementations to both optimize for noncontiguous data in memory and support clusters of heterogeneous systems. As illustrated in Figure 9.1, taken from Chapter 16, MPI programs are commonly implemented in terms of an SPMD model, in which all processes execute essentially the same logic. Chapter 10 provides more details on MPI, while MPI's support for parallel I/O is discussed in Chapter 11.

Analysis.   MPI is today the technology of choice for constructing *scalable* parallel programs, and its ubiquity means that no other technology can beat it for portability. In addition, a significant body of MPI-based libraries has emerged that provide high-performance implementations of commonly used algorithms. Nevertheless, given that programming in an explicit message-passing style can place an additional burden on the developer, other technologies can be useful if our goal is a modestly parallel version of an existing program (in which case OpenMP may be useful), we are using Fortran 90 (HPF), or our application is a task-parallel composition designed to execute in a distributed environment (CORBA, RMI).

Parallel Virtual Machine

Parallel Virtual Machine (PVM) represents another popular instantiation of the message-passing model that was one of the principal forerunners of MPI and the first de facto standard for implementation of portable message-passing programs. The example in Figure 9.2 shows a PVM version of the Poisson problem that was previously given in MPI. Although PVM has been superseded by MPI for tightly coupled multiprocessors, it is still widely used on networks of workstations. PVM's principal design goal was portability, even to nonhomogeneous collections of nodes, which was gained by sacrificing optimal performance. MPI, on the other hand, provides high-performance communication. MPI-1 provided only a nonflexible static process model, while MPI-2 adds a scalable dynamic process model.

Central to the design of PVM is the notion of a "virtual machine"—a set of heterogeneous hosts connected by a network that appears logically to the user as a single large parallel computer. PVM API functions provide the ability to (1) join or leave the virtual machine; (2) start new processes by using a number of different selection criteria, including external schedulers and resource managers; (3) kill a process; (4) send a signal to a process; (5) test to check that a process is responding; and (6) notify an arbitrary process if another disconnects from the PVM system.

```
use mpi
real u(0:n,js-1:je+1), unew(0:n,js-1:je+1)
real f(1:n-1, js:je), h
integer nbr_down, nbr_up, status(MPI_STATUS_SIZE), ierr

! Code to initialize f, u(0,*), u(n:*), u(*,0), and
! u(*,n) with g

h = 1.0 / n
do k=1, maxiter
  ! Send down
  call MPI_Sendrecv( u(1,js), n-1, MPI_REAL, nbr_down, k, &
                     u(1,je+1), n-1, MPI_REAL, nbr_up, k, &
                     MPI_COMM_WORLD, status, ierr )
   ! Send up
  call MPI_Sendrecv( u(1,je), n-1, MPI_REAL, nbr_up, k+1, &
                     u(1,js-1), n-1, MPI_REAL, nbr_down, k+1,&
                     MPI_COMM_WORLD, status, ierr )
   do j=js, je
     do i=1, n-1
       unew(i,j) = 0.25 * ( u(i+1,j) + u(i-1,j) + &
                            u(i,j+1) + u(i,j-1) - &
                            h * h * f(i,j) )
     enddo
   enddo
   ! Code to check for convergence of unew to u.
   ! Make the new value the old value for the next iteration
   u = unew
enddo
```

Figure 9.1   Message-passing version of the Poisson problem, as presented in Figure 16.3.

Analysis.   If an application is going to be developed and executed on a single MPP, then MPI has the advantage of expected higher communication performance. In addition, MPI has a much richer set of communication functions, so it is favored when an application is structured to exploit special communication modes, such as nonblocking send, not available in PVM. PVM has the advantage when the application is going to run over a networked collection of hosts, particularly if the hosts are heterogeneous. PVM includes resource management and process control functions that are important for creating portable applications that run on clusters of workstations and MPPs. PVM is also to be favored when fault tolerance is required. MPI implementations are improving in all of these areas, but PVM still provides better functionality in some settings.

```
real u(0:n,js-1:je+1), unew(0:n,js-1:je+1)
real f(1:n-1, js:je), h
integer nbr_down, nbr_up, rc

! Code to initialize f, u(0,*), u(n:*), u(*,0), and
! u(*,n) with g

h = 1.0 / n
do k=1, maxiter
  ! Send down
  ! Cannot do a head to head as lack of buffering will cause
  ! deadlock, so odd row sends first
  ! while even receives and then we swap
  if (odd) then
     call pvmfpsend(nbr_down, k, u(1,js),   n-1, PVM_FLOAT, rc)
     call pvmfprecv(nbr_up,   k, u(1,je+1), n-1, PVM_FLOAT, rc)
  else
     call pvmfprecv(nbr_up,   k, u(1,je+1), n-1, PVM_FLOAT, rc)
     call pvmfpsend(nbr_down, k, u(1,js),   n-1, PVM_FLOAT, rc)
  endif

  ! Send up
  ! Similar odd/even swapping to sending down
  if (odd) then
     call pvmfpsend(nbr_up,   k, u(1,je),   n-1, PVM_FLOAT, rc)
     call pvmfprecv(nbr_down, k, u(1,js-1), n-1, PVM_FLOAT, rc)
  else
     call pvmfprecv(nbr_down, k, u(1,js-1), n-1, PVM_FLOAT, rc)
     call pvmfpsend(nbr_up,   k, u(1,je),   n-1, PVM_FLOAT, rc)
  endif

  do j=js, je
    do i=1, n-1
      unew(i,j) = 0.25 * ( u(i+1,j) + u(i-1,j) + &
                           u(i,j+1) + u(i,j-1) - &
                           h * h * f(i,j) )
    enddo
  enddo
  ! code to check for convergence of unew to u.
  ! Make the new value the old value for the next iteration
  u = unew
enddo
```

Figure 9.2   A PVM formulation of the Poisson problem.

Parallelizing Compilers

Because parallel programming is so difficult, it is appealing to think that the best solution would be to let the compiler do it all. Thus, automatic parallelization—extraction of parallelism from sequential code by the compiler—has been the holy grail of parallel computing software, particularly given the success of automatic methods on vector machines. Unfortunately, automatic parallelization has never achieved success comparable to that of automatic vectorization. As explained in Chapter 12, the reasons for this failure stem from the greater complexity of compiler analysis and hardware features of parallel machines.

As a result of these difficulties, automatic parallelization has been successful primarily on shared-memory machines with small numbers of processors. The performance gains that can be expected from this technology are application dependent, but are generally small. Programmer-supplied information (typically communicated via directives) can improve the overall parallelization in some situations. However, in those cases OpenMP offers a much more portable way of specifying that information.

Analysis. Parallelizing compilers are certainly worth trying, especially when first implementing a program on a shared-memory machine where only a small degree of parallelism is required. If more parallelism or portability is needed, OpenMP or MPI is a better solution. On scalable machines, HPF may provide an acceptably simple alternative to automatic parallelization for regular, data-parallel problems coded in Fortran 90.

P-Threads

As noted above, in the shared-memory programming model, multiple threads of control operate in a single memory space. The POSIX standard threads package (p-threads) represents a particularly low-level, but widely available, implementation of this model. The p-threads library provides functions for creating and destroying threads and for coordinating thread activities via constructs designed to ensure exclusive access to selected memory locations (locks and condition variables). Chapter 10 provides a more detailed discussion of p-threads.

Analysis. We do *not* recommend the use of p-threads as a general-purpose parallel program development technology. While they have their place in specialized situations and in the hands of expert programmers, the unstructured nature of p-threads constructs makes the development of correct and maintainable programs difficult. In addition, p-threads programs are not scalable to large numbers of processors.

OpenMP

An alternative approach to shared-memory programming is to use more structured constructs such as parallel loops to represent opportunities for parallel execution. This approach is taken in the increasingly popular OpenMP, a set of compiler

```
real u(0:n,0:n), unew(0:n,0:n)
real f(1:n-1, 1:n-1), h

! Code to initialize f, u(0,*), u(n:*), u(*,0), and
! u(*,n) with g

h = 1.0 / n
do k=1, maxiter

  !$OMP PARALLEL DO DEFAULT(SHARED) PRIVATE(i)
  do j=1, n-1
    do i=1, n-1
      unew(i,j) = 0.25 * ( u(i+1,j) + u(i-1,j) + &
                           u(i,j+1) + u(i,j-1) - &
                           h * h * f(i,j) )
    enddo
  enddo
  !$OMP END PARALLEL DO

  ! Code to check for convergence of unew to u

  ! Make the new value the old value for the next iteration
  !$OMP PARALLEL WORKSHARE
  u = unew
  !$OMP END PARALLEL WORKSHARE

enddo
```

Figure 9.3   An OpenMP formulation of the Poisson problem.

directives, library routines, and environment variables that can be used to specify
shared-memory parallelism in Fortran and C/C++ programs. As illustrated in Figure 9.3, OpenMP extensions focus on the exploitation of parallelism within loops.
In the example, the outer loop of a finite-difference calculation is declared to be
parallel. Arrays u, unew, and f are shared, while the inner loop induction variable is
private. OpenMP also provides the WORKSHARE directive to exploit the data parallelism
in array assignments (and other situations not shown here).

The parallelism in OpenMP may be coarse grained (as in the do loop of Figure 9.3)
or fine grained (as in the array assignment, or as it would be if nested parallelism were
used to make every iteration of both loops parallel). A desirable feature of OpenMP
is that it preserves sequential semantics: in a legal program, you may ignore the
structured comments and a sequential program is obtained. This simplifies program

development, debugging, and maintenance. However, if the programmer makes an error and mistakenly specifies a loop to be parallel when a race condition exists, the program will produced undetermined results. Even though such a program is "noncompliant," it may be difficult to find the problem. Chapter 12 provides a more detailed discussion of OpenMP.

Analysis.   We recommend the use of OpenMP when the goal is to achieve modest parallelism on a shared-memory computer. In this environment, the simplicity of the OpenMP model and the fact that a parallel program can be obtained via the incremental addition of directives to a sequential program are significant advantages. On the other hand, the lack of support for user management of data distribution means that scalable implementations of OpenMP are unlikely to appear in the foreseeable future.

High Performance Fortran

High Performance Fortran (HPF), like OpenMP, extends a sequential base language (in this case Fortran 90) with a combination of directives, library functions, and (in the case of HPF) some new language constructs to provide a data-parallel, implicitly parallel programming model. HPF differs from OpenMP in its focus on support for user management of data distribution, so as to support portable, high-performance execution on scalable computers of all kinds, particularly in distributed-memory environments.

Figure 9.4 illustrates how structured comments are used to express the number of processors that a program is to run on and to control the distribution of data. Note that only three directives have been added to what is otherwise a pure Fortran 90 program: PROCESSORS, DISTRIBUTE, and ALIGN directives. These directives partition each of the arrays by contiguous blocks of rows, hence allocating approximately $\frac{n}{4}$ rows to each of four processors. Although the array assignment statement is explicitly parallel, the same distribution applied to a loop formulation of finite difference would be expected to achieve the same results—if the loop can be run in parallel on the assigned collection of processors, it should be. Chapter 12 provides more details on HPF.

Analysis.   When HPF works well, it is a wonderful tool: complex parallel algorithms can be expressed succinctly as Fortran 90 code. Furthermore, it captures, in a machine-independent way, the notion of data decomposition, which is essential to successful parallelization of codes for distributed-memory systems. However, current implementations of HPF are effective primarily for algorithms defined on regular grids and for dense linear algebra. Although the extended HPF-2 standard defines language extensions that would make HPF applicable to irregular computations, few compilers implement these extensions. Hence, even though there are a number of substantive applications, HPF remains a niche technology, for now at least.

```
real u(0:n,0:n), unew(0:n,0:n)
real f(1:n-1, 1:n-1), h
!HPF$ PROCESSORS pr(4)              ! Run on 4 processors
!HPF$ DISTRIBUTE u(BLOCK,*)         ! Distribute u by rows
!HPF$ ALIGN unew(i,j) WITH u(i,j) ! Distribute unew like u
!HPF$ ALIGN f(i,j) WITH u(i,j)    ! Distribute f like u

! Code to initialize f, u(0,*), u(n:*), u(*,0), and
! u(*,n) with g

h = 1.0 / n
do k=1, maxiter

  unew(1:n-1,1:n-1) =  0.25 * ( u(2:n,1:n-1) + u(0:n-2,1:n-1) + &
                       u(1:n-1,2:n) + u(1:n-1,0:n-2) - &
                       h * h * f(1:n-1,1:n-1) )

  ! code to check for convergence of unew to u.

  ! Make the new value the old value for the next iteration
  u = unew

enddo
```

Figure 9.4   An HPF formulation of the Poisson problem.

Co-Array Fortran

Co-Array Fortran [719] takes the approach of designing a language to express the single-program-multiple-data programming model. Many threads (which may correspond to physical processors) execute the same program, exchanging data by assignment statements. Unlike MPI and PVM, only one thread in the data exchange needs to specify this communication. A program accomplishes this by declaring nonlocally accessed arrays with an extra "co-dimension" and indexing that co-dimension with the thread id. Figure 9.5 shows how this works in the Poisson example program. Note the explicit synchronization (the call to synch_all) that ensures that both data copies are completed. Chapter 12 discusses Co-Array Fortran in more detail.

Analysis.   SPMD languages such as Co-Array Fortran have many potential advantages. They are often reasonably clean (as in the above example), allow low-level manipulations when necessary to tune program performance, and are not tied to particular hardware models. However, they are relatively new and not widely supported. In particular, Co-Array Fortran is not a formal standard and is not supported

```
real u(0:n,js-1:je+1)[*], unew(0:n,js-1:je+1)[*]
real f(1:n-1, js:je), h
integer nbr_down, nbr_up, nbrs(3), me

! Code to initialize f, u(0,*), u(n:*), u(*,0), and
! u(*,n) with g

h = 1.0 / n
do k=1, maxiter
  ! Send down
  u(1:n-1,je+1)[nbr_down] = u(1:n-1,js)[me]
  ! Send up
  u(1:n-1,js-1)[nbr_up] = u(1:n-1,je)[me]
  call synch_all( wait=nbrs )
  do j=js, je
    do i=1, n-1
      unew(i,j)[me] = 0.25 * ( u(i+1,j)[me] + u(i-1,j)[me] + &
                               u(i,j+1)[me] + u(i,j-1)[me] - &
                               h * h * f(i,j) )
    enddo
  enddo
  ! Code to check for convergence of unew to u
  ! Make the new value the old value for the next iteration
  u[me] = unew[me]
enddo
```

Figure 9.5 A Co-Array Fortran formulation of the Poisson problem.

on many machines. (The Cray C90 and T3E are important machines where it is supported.) Some research implementations are beginning to appear. While we hesitate to recommend such languages for production use today, the situation may improve in the future. Co-Array Fortran may also be a good choice for experimental, proof-of-concept work due to its expressiveness.

POOMA and HPC++

An alternative approach to the implementation of implicit data parallelism is to define libraries that use object-oriented techniques (in particular, inheritance and polymorphism) to abstract and encapsulate parallel operations. This is essentially the approach taken in POOMA [798] and HPC++, two libraries that define standard-use object-oriented technology to define classes that encapsulate parallelism. In POOMA, for example, we can write code such as

```
A[I][J] = 0.25*(A[I+1][J] + A[I-1][J] + A[I][J+1] + A[I][J-1] );
```

to express the data-parallel operation for which we have presented various implementations in this chapter. In this formulation, A is a 2-D field, and I and J are index
objects representing the domain of the field object. As is discussed in more detail in
Chapter 13, issues relating to distribution across processors and communication are
handled by the array objects. A more complete version of this example is presented
as Figure 9.6, which is replicated from Chapter 13. That chapter also explains how
Java can be used as an effective programming language for object-oriented libraries.

Analysis.   A significant advantage of object-oriented approaches is the great simplicity and clarity that can be obtained. Another advantage is that the developer of these
libraries can incorporate substantial "smarts" in order to obtain good performance
on parallel platforms (see Chapter 13). A disadvantage in some situations is that
because we are dealing with often complex library software, the task of debugging
performance and correctness problems can be nontrivial.

Component Models

The final programming technology that we mention briefly is the various component technologies that have been proposed and are used to facilitate the modular construction of complex software systems. CORBA, .COM, and Java Beans are
well-known examples. While various groups have experimented with the use of
these technologies within high-performance computing (e.g., [550]), lack of support
for parallelism has hindered their use for parallel computing proper. The Common Component Architecture effort [47], discussed in Chapter 13, is attempting to
overcome some of these problems. Other relevant efforts include problem-solving
environments (PSEs) and PSE toolkits such as Uintah [250], NetSolve [173], and
WebFlow [354], discussed more fully in Chapter 14. We can hope that these efforts
will produce the technology base required to support truly modular construction of
parallel software systems. In the meantime, the parallel programmer can and should
seek to apply well-established principles of modular design.

Hybrids

A variety of hybrid approaches are possible and in some cases are proving effective
and popular. For example, it is increasingly common to see applications developed
as a distributed-memory (MPI) framework with shared-memory parallelism (e.g.,
OpenMP) used within each "process." The primary motivation is a desire to write
programs whose structure mirrors that of contemporary parallel computers consisting of multiple shared-memory computers connected via a network. The technique
can have advantages: for example, a multidimensional problem can be decomposed
across processes in one dimension and within a process in a second.

Other hybrids that have been discussed in a research context include MPI and
p-threads, MPI and HPF [348, 349], and CORBA and HPF.

```
01  #include "Pooma/Arrays.h"
02
03  #include <iostream>
04
05  // The size of each side of the domain
06  const int N = 20;
07
08  int
09  main(
10      int                 argc,       // argument count
11      char*               argv[]      // argument list
12  ){
13      // Initialize POOMA
14      Pooma::initialize(argc, argv);
15
16      // The array we'll be solving for
17      Array<2,double> V(N, N);
18      V = 0.0;
19
20      // The right-hand side of the equation (spike in the center)
21      Array<2,double> b(N, N);
22      b = 0.0;
23      b(N/2, N/2) = -1.0;
24
25      // Specify the interior of the domain
26      Interval<1> I(1, N-2), J(1, N-2);
27
28      // Iterate 200 times
29      for (int iteration=0; iteration<200; ++iteration)
30      {
31          V(I,J) = 0.25*(V(I+1,J) + V(I-1,J) + V(I,J+1) + V(I,J-1) - b(I,J));
32      }
33
34      // Print out the result
35      std::cout << V << std::endl;
36
37      // Clean up POOMA and report success.
38      Pooma::finalize();
39      return 0;
40  }
```

Figure 9.6 A POOMA code that performs a Jacobi iteration with a five-point stencil.

Table 9.1 Decision rules for selecting parallel programming technologies.

Use . . .	If
Compilers	Goal is to extract moderate [$O(4$–$10)$] parallelism from existing code
	Target platform has a good parallelizing compiler
	Portability is not a major concern
OpenMP	Goal is to extract moderate [$O(10)$] parallelism from existing code
	Good quality implementation exists for target platform
	Portability to distributed-memory platforms is not a major concern
MPI	Scalability is important
	Application must run on some message-passing platforms
	Portability is important
	A substantive coding effort is acceptable to achieve other goals
PVM	All MPI conditions plus fault tolerance are needed
HPF	Application is regular and data parallel
	A simple coding style in Fortran 90 is desirable
	Explicit data distribution is essential to performance
	A high degree of control over parallelism is not critical
Co-Array	An implementation is available
Fortran	Moderate coding effort (less than MPI) is desired
	SPMD programming style is acceptable
Threads	Scalability is not important
	Program involves fine-grained operations on shared data
	Program has significant load imbalances
	OpenMP is not available or suitable
CORBA,	Program has task-parallel formulation
RMI	Interested in running in network-based system
	Performance is not critical
High-level	They address your specific problem
libraries	The library is available on the target platform

9.1.3   Decision Rules

In the preceding discussion of parallel programming models and technologies, we have made a number of points concerning the pros and cons of different approaches. Table 9.1 brings these various issues together in the form of a set of rules for selecting parallel programming models. We emphasize that this table includes only some of the available parallel technologies.

9.2   Achieving Correct and Efficient Execution

The problem of achieving *correct* and *efficient* parallel programs is made difficult by the issues noted in the introduction to this chapter: nondeterminism, concurrency, and complex parallel computer architectures. These problems can be overcome by a combination of good programming practice and appropriate tools. Tools such as debuggers, profilers, and performance analyzers are discussed in Chapter 15; we talk here about two issues of programming practice, namely, dealing with nondeterminism and performance modeling.

9.2.1   Dealing with Nondeterminism

A nondeterministic computation is one in which the result computed depends on the order in which two or more unsynchronized threads of control happen to execute. Nondeterministic interactions can sometimes be desirable: for example, they can allow us to select the "first" solution computed by a set of worker processes that are executing subtasks of unknown size. However, the presence of nondeterminism also greatly complicates the task of verifying program correctness; in principle, we need to trace every possible program execution before we can ensure that the program is correct. And in practice it can be difficult both to enumerate the set of possible executions and to reproduce a particular behavior. Hence, nondeterminism is to be avoided whenever possible. The following general techniques can be used to achieve this goal:

- When possible, use a parallel programming technology that does not permit race conditions to occur (e.g., HPF).

- If using a parallel programming technology that permits race conditions, adopt defensive programming practices to avoid unwanted nondeterminism. For example, in MPI, ensure that every "receive" call can match exactly one "send." Avoid the use of p-threads.

- When nondeterminism is required, encapsulate it within objects with well-defined semantics. For example, in a manager–worker structure, the manager may invoke a function "get next solution"; all nondeterminism is then encapsulated within this function.

9.2.2   Performance Modeling

In Chapter 15, tools are described for measuring and analyzing the performance of a parallel program. In principle, a good performance tool should be able to relate observed performance to the constructs of whatever parallel programming technology was used to write the original program. It may also seek to suggest changes to the program that can improve performance. Tools available today do not typically achieve this ideal, but they can provide useful information.

An important adjunct to any performance tool is the use of *analytic performance models* as a means of predicting likely performance and of explaining observed performance. As discussed, for example, in *Designing and Building Parallel Programs* [341], a good performance model relates parallel program performance (e.g., execution time) to key properties of the program and its target execution environment: for example, problem size, processor speed, and communication costs. Such a model can then be used for qualitative analysis of scalability. If the model is sufficiently accurate (and especially if it is calibrated with experimental data), it can also be used to explain observed performance. Performance models are also discussed in Chapter 15.

9.3   Conclusion

We conclude this chapter with a discussion of four areas in which significant progress is required—and, we believe, will occur—in parallel software concepts and technologies.

9.3.1   Clusters and DSM

While shared-memory multiprocessors are becoming increasingly common, another parallel computing technology is also seeing widespread use, namely, clusters constructed from PC nodes connected with commodity networks. Such clusters can be extremely cheap when compared with multiprocessors, but do not offer the same integrated operating system services or a convenient shared-memory programming model. Heterogeneity is another potential obstacle. However, numerous research and development activities are working to overcome these problems.

At the operating system level, we see numerous activities focused on parallel file systems, scheduling, error management, and so on. In addition, work such as Fast Messages [734] and Virtual Interface Architecture (VIA) [962] is helping to reduce communication costs to something more like MPPs.

Clusters today are almost invariably programmed with MPI. Yet experience with multiprocessors shows that shared-memory parallelism can be more convenient for applications that involve irregular data structures and data access patterns. Hence, various groups are working to develop software-based, distributed-shared-memory (DSM) systems that will allow a cluster to be treated as a shared-memory multiprocessor, with various combinations of run-time support, operating system modifications, and compiler modifications being used to provide (sometimes) efficient support for a shared-memory programming model.

9.3.2   Grids

Emerging "Computational Grid" infrastructures support the coordinated use of network-connected computers, storage systems, and other resources, allowing them to be used as an integrated computational resource [345].

Grid concepts and technologies have significant implications for the practice of parallel computing. For example, while parallel computers have been used traditionally as "batch" engines for long-running, noninteractive jobs, in Grid environments a parallel computer may need to interact frequently with other systems, whether to acquire instrument data, enable interactive control, or access remote storage systems [343]. These new modes of use are likely to require new run-time system and resource management techniques [344].

Grid infrastructures can also be used to create what might be termed "generalized clusters," enabling the dynamic discovery and assembly of collections of resources that can be used to solve a computational problem. Because so many computational resources are underutilized, this mode of use has the potential to deliver order-of-magnitude increases in available computation. However, the heterogeneous and dynamic nature of such generalized clusters introduces significant challenges for algorithms and software technologies.

9.3.3 Ultra-Scale Computers

The final architecture-based topic that we discuss relates to the software technologies required for tomorrow's extremely large-scale parallel computers—those capable of 10^{15} operations per second or more.

A variety of very different architectures have been proposed for such computers, ranging from scaled-up versions of today's commodity-based systems to systems based on processor-in-memory components and/or superconducting logic [896]. These different systems have in common a need to be able to exploit large amounts of parallelism—10^3 times more than today's largest computers—and to deal with deep memory hierarchies in which memory may be a factor of 10^3 further away (in terms of processor clock cycles) than in today's systems.

These scaling issues, which derive from trends in processor and memory technology, pose major challenges for parallel software technologies at every level.

9.3.4 Programming Productivity

One major goal for research and development in parallel computing must necessarily be to reduce the cost of writing and executing parallel programs, particularly for shared-memory multiprocessor systems. This goal becomes more difficult to achieve as the computing platforms become ever more complex. From the previous paragraphs, we can see that platforms will become even more complex in the future. With these architectural advances, we may see the day that programming for the most advanced computational facilities will become the exclusive domain of professional programmers. This would be a major setback for computational science. To avoid that setback, we need revolutionary advances in programming support technologies.

As discussed in Chapter 12, automatic methods for extracting parallelism from conventional programming languages have been only a limited success. Furthermore, it seems unlikely that these techniques will extend well to the complex architectures of the future. So, how can we support end-user programming while maintaining a high level of performance? One approach that shows considerable promise for productivity improvement is the use of high-level, domain-specific problem-solving environments. Examples of such systems include MATLAB [426], Mathematica [1002], Ellpack [490], and POOMA [53].

The difficulty with problem-solving environments as they are currently implemented is that they produce code that is not efficient enough to be used on a computation-intensive application. However, advanced techniques based on extensive library precompilation may offer a way to bring the performance of problem-solving languages up to the level of conventional languages [559]. Furthermore, by exploiting the domain knowledge contained in the language and the underlying library, it should be possible to extract the natural parallelism in the problem and tailor it to a variety of different target platforms.

9.3.5 Further Reading

An article by Skillicorn and Talia [867] provides an excellent survey of parallel programming paradigms and languages.

The book *Designing and Building Parallel Programs* [341] provides a good tutorial introduction to parallel computing, MPI, and HPF.

The book *The Grid: Blueprint for a New Computing Infrastructure* [354] provides a comprehensive review of the technologies that underlie emerging Grid infrastructures and applications. See also Foster et al. [347] and Foster [342].

10

Message Passing and Threads

**Ian Foster • William Gropp •
Carl Kesselman**

In this chapter we examine two fundamental, although low-level, approaches to expressing parallelism in programs. Over the years, numerous different approaches to designing and implementing parallel programs have been developed (e.g., see the excellent survey article by Skillicorn and Talia [867]). However, over time, two dominant alternatives have emerged: *message passing* and *multithreading*.

These two approaches can be distinguished in terms of how concurrently executing segments of an application share data and synchronize their execution. In message passing, data are shared by explicitly copying ("sending") it from one parallel component to another, while synchronization is implicit with the completion of the copy. In contrast, the multithreading approach shares data implicitly through the use of shared memory, with synchronization being performed explicitly via mechanisms such as locks, semaphores, and condition variables.

As with any set of alternatives, there are advantages and disadvantages to each approach. Multithreaded programs can be executed particularly efficiently on computers that use physically shared memory as their communication architecture. However, many parallel computers being built today do not support shared memory across the whole computer, in which case the message-passing approach is more appropriate.

From the perspective of programming complexity, the implicit sharing provided by the shared-memory model simplifies the process of converting existing sequential code to run on a parallel computer. However, the need for explicit synchronization can result in errors that produce nondeterministic race conditions that are hard to detect and correct. On the other hand, converting a program to use message passing requires more work up front, as one must extract the information that must be shared from the application data structures and explicitly move it to the desired concurrently executing program component. However, because synchronization is implicit in the arrival of the data, race conditions are generally avoided.

Both message passing and multithreading can be implemented via special-purpose programming languages (and associated compilers) or through libraries that are linked with an application written in an existing programming language, such as Fortran or C. In this chapter, we focus on the most common library-based implementations, specifically the Message Passing Interface (MPI) [878] for message-passing programs and the POSIX standard thread library (p-threads) [499] for multithreading programs. We also discuss popular alternatives, notably the Parallel Virtual Machine (PVM) [371].

10.1   Message-Passing Programming Model

Message passing is by far the most widely used approach to parallel computing, at least on large parallel systems. (Multithreading dominates on small shared-memory systems.) In the message-passing model, a computation comprises one or more processes that communicate by calling library routines to send and receive *messages*. Communication is *cooperative*: data are sent by calling a routine, and the data are not received until the destination process calls a routine to receive the data. This is in contrast to other models, such as one-sided or remote-memory operations, where communication can be accomplished by a single process.

The message-passing model has two great strengths. The most obvious to users is that programs written using message passing are highly portable. Virtually any collection of computers can be used to execute a parallel program that is written using message passing; the message-passing programming model does not require any special hardware support for efficient execution, unlike, for example, shared-memory programming models. The second strength is that message passing provides the programmer with explicit control over the location of memory in a parallel program, specifically, the memory used by each process. Since memory access and placement often determine performance, this ability to manage memory location can allow the programmer to achieve high performance. The major disadvantage of message passing is that the programmer is *required* to pay attention to such details as the placement of memory and the ordering of communication.

Numerous different message-passing models and libraries have been proposed. At their core, most support the same basic mechanisms. For *point-to-point* communication, a *send* operation is used to initiate a data transfer between two concurrently executing program components, and a matching *receive* operation is used to extract that data from system data structures into application memory space. In addition, *collective* operations such as broadcast and reductions are often provided; these implement common global operations involving multiple processes.

Specific models and libraries also differ from one another in a variety of ways. For example, the send calls may be blocking or nonblocking, as can the receives. The means by which a send and receive are matched up may also vary from implementation to implementation. The exact details of how message buffers are created, filled with data, and managed also vary from implementation to implementation.

Variations in the specifics of a message-passing interface can have a significant impact on the performance of programs written to that interface. There are three major factors that influence performance: bandwidth and latency of actual message passing and the ability to overlap communication with computation. On most modern parallel computers, latency is dominated by the message setup time rather than the actual time of flight through the communication network. Thus the software overhead of initializing message buffers and interfacing with the communication hardware can be significant. The bandwidth achieved by a specific message-passing implementation is often dominated by the number of times the data being communicated must be copied when transferring data between application components. Poorly designed interfaces can result in extra copies, reducing the overall performance of an application. The final performance concern is that of overlapping communication and computation. Nonblocking sending semantics enable the sender to continue execution even if the data have not been accepted by the receiver. Furthermore, nonblocking receives enable a receiver to anticipate the next incoming data elements, while still performing valuable work. In both situations, the performance of the resulting application is improved.

While message passing can be, and indeed has been, provided as primitives in a programming language (e.g., Occam [504], Concurrent C [372]), it is more typically implemented by library routines. In the following we focus on the two most widely used message-passing libraries: Message Passing Interface (MPI) and Parallel Virtual Machine (PVM).

10.1.1 The Message Passing Interface Standard

While the message-passing model is portable in the sense that it is easily implemented on any parallel platform, a specific program is portable only if the system that supports it is widely available. For example, programs written in C and Fortran are portable because C and Fortran compilers are widely available. In the early history of parallel computing, there were numerous different implementations of the message-passing model, with many being specific to individual vendor systems or written by research groups. This diversity of message-passing implementations prevented applications from being portable to a wide range of parallel computers.

Recognizing that a single clearly and precisely specified message-passing interface would benefit users (by making their programs portable to a larger set of machines) and vendors (by enlarging the set of applications that can run on any machine), a group of researchers, parallel computer vendors, and users came together to develop a standard for message passing. Following in the footsteps of the High Performance Fortran Forum, this group developed a standard called the Message Passing Interface [668, 879], and the group was called the MPI Forum. The standard itself is available on the web at *http://www.mpi-forum.org*.

MPI defines a library of routines that implement the message-passing model. Rather than simply codifying features of the message-passing libraries that were in common use when MPI was defined, such as PVM, Express, and p4 [133, 158], the MPI Forum incorporated best practices across a variety of different message-passing libraries. The result is a rich and sophisticated library that includes a wide variety of features, many of which are important in implementing large and complex applications.

Although MPI is a complex and multifaceted system, just six of its functions are needed to solve a wide range of problems. We focus our attention here on those functions; for a more complete tutorial discussion of MPI, see Foster [341], Gropp et al. [406, 407], and Pacheco [732].

When describing MPI functions, an all-uppercase form (e.g., MPI_INIT) is used to denote the MPI specifications. MPI function names in C use a mixed-case form (e.g., MPI_Init), while MPI function names in Fortran are commonly written in all lowercase (e.g., mpi_init). The six MPI functions that we describe here are used to initiate and terminate a computation, identify processes, and send and receive messages:

MPI_INIT	:	Initiate an MPI computation.
MPI_FINALIZE	:	Terminate a computation.
MPI_COMM_SIZE	:	Determine number of processes.
MPI_COMM_RANK	:	Determine my process identifier.
MPI_SEND	:	Send a message.
MPI_RECV	:	Receive a message.

Function parameters are detailed in Figure 10.1. In this and subsequent code blocks, the labels IN, OUT, and INOUT indicate whether the function uses but does not modify the parameter (IN), does not use but may update the parameter (OUT), or both uses and updates the parameter (INOUT).

MPI defines "language bindings" for C, Fortran, and C++ (bindings for other languages can be defined as well). Different language bindings have slightly different syntax, reflecting language peculiarities. Sources of syntactic difference include the function names themselves, the mechanism used for return codes, the representation of the *handles* used to access specialized MPI data structures such as communicators, and the implementation of the status data type returned by MPI_RECV. (The use of handles hides the internal representation of MPI data structures.)

For example, in the C language binding, function names are as in the MPI definition but with only the MPI prefix and the first letter of the function name capitalized. Status values are returned as integer return codes. The return code for successful completion is MPI_SUCCESS; a set of error codes is also defined. Compile-time constants are all in uppercase and are defined in the file "mpi.h," which must be included in any program that makes MPI calls. Handles are represented by special defined types, defined in mpi.h. These will be introduced as needed in the following. Function parameters with type IN are passed by value, while parameters with type OUT and INOUT are passed by reference (that is, as pointers).

MPI_INIT(int *argc, char ***argv)
Initiate a computation.
> argc, argv are required only in the C language binding,
>> where they are the main program's arguments.

MPI_FINALIZE()
Shut down a computation.

MPI_COMM_SIZE(comm, size)
Determine the number of processes in a computation.
IN	comm	communicator (handle)
OUT	size	number of processes in the group of comm (integer)

MPI_COMM_RANK(comm, pid)
Determine the identifier of the current process.
IN	comm	communicator (handle)
OUT	pid	process id in the group of comm (integer)

MPI_SEND(buf, count, datatype, dest, tag, comm)
Send a message.
IN	buf	address of send buffer (choice)
IN	count	number of elements to send (integer ≥ 0)
IN	datatype	data type of send buffer elements (handle)
IN	dest	process id of destination process (integer)
IN	tag	message tag (integer)
IN	comm	communicator (handle)

MPI_RECV(buf, count, datatype, source, tag, comm, status)
Receive a message.
OUT	buf	address of receive buffer (choice)
IN	count	size of receive buffer, in elements (integer ≥ 0)
IN	datatype	data type of receive buffer elements (handle)
IN	source	process id of source process, or MPI_ANY_SOURCE (integer)
IN	tag	message tag, or MPI_ANY_TAG (integer)
IN	comm	communicator (handle)
OUT	status	status object (status)

Figure 10.1   Basic MPI. These six functions suffice to write a wide range of parallel programs. The arguments are characterized as having mode IN or OUT and having type integer, choice, handle, or status. These terms are explained in the text.

All but the first two calls take a *communicator handle* as an argument. A communicator identifies the *process group* and *context* with respect to which the operation is to be performed. As we shall see later, communicators provide a mechanism for identifying process subsets when we are developing modular programs. They also ensure that messages intended for different purposes are not confused. For now, it suffices to provide the default value MPI_COMM_WORLD, which identifies *all* processes involved in a computation. Other arguments have type integer, data type handle, or status.

The functions MPI_INIT and MPI_FINALIZE are used to initiate and shut down an MPI computation, respectively. MPI_INIT must be called before any other MPI function and must be called exactly once per process. No further MPI functions can be called after MPI_FINALIZE.

The functions MPI_COMM_SIZE and MPI_COMM_RANK determine the number of processes in the current computation and the integer identifier assigned to the current process, respectively. (The processes in a process group are identified with unique, contiguous integers numbered from 0.) For example, consider the following program, expressed in pseudocode rather than Fortran or C.

```
program main
begin
  MPI_INIT()                                  Initiate computation
  MPI_COMM_SIZE(MPI_COMM_WORLD, count)        Find # of processes
  MPI_COMM_RANK(MPI_COMM_WORLD, myid)         Find my id
  print("I am", myid, "of", count)            Print message
  MPI_FINALIZE()                              Shut down
end
```

The MPI standard does not specify how a parallel computation is started. However, a typical mechanism might be a command line argument indicating the number of processes that are to be created: for example, "myprog -n 4," where myprog is the name of the executable. Additional arguments might be required, for example to specify processor names in a networked environment.

Once a computation is initiated, each of the processes created will normally execute the same program. Hence, execution of the program above gives something like the following output.

```
              I am 1 of 4
              I am 3 of 4
              I am 0 of 4
              I am 2 of 4
```

The order in which the output from the four processes appears is not defined; we assume here that the output from individual print statements is not interleaved.

Finally, we consider the functions MPI_SEND and MPI_RECV. These are used to send and receive messages, respectively. A call to MPI_SEND has the following general form:

```
MPI_SEND(buf, count, datatype, dest, tag, comm)
```

It specifies that a message containing `count` elements of the specified `datatype` starting at address `buf` is to be sent to the process with identifier `dest`. As will be explained in greater detail subsequently, this message is associated with an *envelope* comprising the specified `tag`, the source process's identifier, and the specified communicator (`comm`). An MPI data type is defined for each C data type: `MPI_CHAR`, `MPI_INT`, `MPI_LONG`, `MPI_UNSIGNED_CHAR`, `MPI_UNSIGNED`, `MPI_UNSIGNED_LONG`, `MPI_FLOAT`, `MPI_DOUBLE`, `MPI_LONG_DOUBLE`, and so forth. MPI provides similar data type names for Fortran and C++. In addition, MPI allows the user to define new data types that represent noncontiguous buffers (such as constant stride vectors or index scatter/gathers).

A call to `MPI_RECV` has the following general form.

```
MPI_RECV(buf, count, datatype, source, tag, comm, status)
```

It attempts to receive a message with an envelope corresponding to the specified `tag`, `source`, and `comm`, blocking until such a message is available. When the message arrives, elements of the specified `datatype` are placed into the buffer at address `buf`. This buffer is guaranteed by the user to be large enough to contain at least `count` elements. The `status` variable can be used subsequently to inquire about the size, tag, and source of the message.

The six functions just described can be used to express a wide variety of parallel computations. Figure 10.2 shows a simple Fortran program that sends data from the process with rank zero to the process with rank one. Note that in the message-passing model, each process is separate from all other processes. The variables in this program represent *different* memory locations for each process and may, in fact, be on computer hardware (executing on processors) located miles apart. In other words, the variable `buf` in process 0 is a different memory location than the variable `buf` in process 1.

Nonblocking Communication Operations

The MPI communication routines just described are *blocking*; when the routine returns, the user can use the data buffer. In the case of `MPI_Send`, the user can immediately change the value of data in the buffer (e.g., execute abuf = 2). In the case of `MPI_Recv`, the user can immediately use the value in the buffer, as we do in our example. This is a simple and easy-to-use model, but it has two major drawbacks. Consider the program where the two processes exchange data:

```
...
if (rank .eq. 0) then
    call mpi_send( abuf, n, MPI_INTEGER, 1, 0, MPI_COMM_WORLD, ierr )
    call mpi_recv( buf, n, MPI_INTEGER, 1, 0, MPI_COMM_WORLD, status, ierr )
else if (rank .eq. 1) then
    call mpi_send( abuf, n, MPI_INTEGER, 0, 0, MPI_COMM_WORLD, ierr )
    call mpi_recv( buf, n, MPI_INTEGER, 0, 0, MPI_COMM_WORLD, status, ierr )
endif
```

```
program main
use mpi
integer ierr, size, rank
integer abuf, buf, status(mpi_status_size)

call mpi_init(ierr)
call mpi_comm_size( mpi_comm_world, size, ierr )
call mpi_comm_rank( mpi_comm_world, rank, ierr )
if (size .lt. 2) then
   print *, 'Error - must have at least 2 processes'
   call mpi_abort( mpi_comm_world, ierr )
endif
if (rank .eq. 0) then
   abuf = 10
   call mpi_send( abuf, 1, MPI_INTEGER, 1, 0, mpi_comm_world, ierr )
elseif (rank .eq. 1) then
   buf = -1
   print *, 'Buf before recv = ', buf
   call mpi_recv( buf, 1, MPI_INTEGER, 0, 0, mpi_comm_world, status, ierr )
   print *, 'Buf after recv = ', buf
endif
call mpi_finalize(ierr)
end
```

Figure 10.2 Simple MPI: Using the six basic functions to write a program that communicates data from process 0 to process 1.

For this program to execute correctly, at least one of the processes must complete the MPI_Send call so that the matching MPI_Recv will be executed. For the MPI_Send calls to complete, the data in abuf must be copied into a system buffer. This introduces two problems. First, a data copy hurts performance; it is an operation that doesn't achieve anything other than allowing the operation to complete. Second, and more serious, there must be enough buffer space to copy the data into. In the example above, this is (usually) not a problem if n is 1, 10, or even 1000; but if n is very large (e.g., 100,000,000), there may not be enough space in the buffer. In this case, the program will never complete; it will *deadlock*.

It is always possible to reorder the send and receive operations to avoid this deadlock, but particularly for complex communication patterns, this can be so difficult as to be impractical. Hence, MPI also provides for nonblocking variants of the send and receive routines: MPI_Isend and MPI_Irecv. These calls do not wait for the communication to complete before they return. (The user can ensure that they have completed by calling MPI_Wait or any of several variants.) These routines are necessary for the *correct* operation of message-passing programs. For more discussion on this point, see Gropp et al. [406, Chapter 4].

Communicators

In the MPI interface, the message tag is used to match a send operation with a receive operation. The tag provides a simple means of separating messages at the receiver. This can be used to identify the purpose of the message or make sure that one part of a program doesn't receive a message that was not intended for it. For example, a different tag value can be used for data values and message-containing configuration options for the program.

In early message-passing libraries, the message tag was the only mechanism provided to distinguish messages. This made it difficult to write reusable program libraries. Even preallocating ranges of tags to a library is not sufficient to ensure that messages intended for one piece of code are not intercepted by another (if MPI_ANY_TAG is used). MPI addressed this problem by introducing the concept of a communication context. Each MPI communicator contains a separate communication context; this defines a separate virtual communication space. As discussed above, each MPI send and receive operation takes a communicator as an argument, and thus we can isolate an application library by providing it its own communicator when it is invoked.

Communicators do more than scope a tag name space. They also define a name space of processes, that is, the size and rank used for named endpoints of send and receive operations. Starting with MPI_COMM_WORLD, which contains all the processes in a parallel computation, new communicators are formed by either including or excluding processes from an existing communicator. Within a communicator, processes are assigned rank from zero to one minus the size of the communicator. Thus, MPI_Comm_size returns the number of processes within the specified communicator, while MPI_Comm_rank returns the identifier of the current process within the scope of the specified communicator.

Collective Operations

Parallel algorithms often call for coordinated communication operations involving multiple processes. For example, all processes may need to cooperate to transpose a distributed matrix or to sum a set of numbers distributed one per process. Clearly, these global operations can be implemented by a programmer using the send and receive functions introduced previously. For convenience, and to permit optimized implementations, MPI also provides a suite of specialized *collective communication* functions that perform commonly used operations of this type. These functions include the following:

- *Barrier.* Synchronize all processes.
- *Broadcast.* Send data from one process to all processes.

- *Gather.* Gather data from all processes to one process.
- *Scatter.* Scatter data from one process to all processes.
- *Reduction operations.* Addition, multiplication, and so on of distributed data.

These operations are all executed in a collective fashion, meaning that each process in a process group calls the communication routine.

10.1.2   Parallel Virtual Machine

At this point, it would be instructive to discuss the major message-passing library that was in common use prior to the development of MPI. The PVM [371] was a widely used library that ran on a large number of different parallel computing platforms, including networks of workstations. While there was a public domain distribution of this library, there were also vendor-supported versions on computers such as the Cray T3E and the IBM SP2. Chapter 9 illustrates the use of PVM in a simple problem.

The message-passing primitives of PVM differ from MPI in a number of significant ways. For example, there is no notion of communicators. Also, buffers are implicit to the send operation, rather than being explicitly provided by a function argument. However, PVM is still important. In addition to providing communication operations, it also provides a set of operations for manipulating the computing environment to dynamically construct a "parallel virtual machine," from which the library takes its name.

Unlike MPI, which assumes a fixed set of processes in MPI_COMM_WORLD, PVM applications can dynamically change the set of processes over which communication operations take place. Rather than sending to a process of a specific rank, PVM applications use *task identifiers (tid)* to specify the endpoints of a communication operation. While many applications can fit into the static process model of MPI, there are a number of significant applications that cannot. Addressing the needs of these more dynamic applications was one of the motivations that led to the development of MPI-2, discussed in the next section.

10.1.3   Extensions to the Message Passing Interface

Even though the MPI specification contains a large number of routines, many users found that it lacked needed features. To remedy this, the MPI Forum developed a set of extensions to the MPI specification, called MPI-2 [405, 671]. These new features fell into three major categories. In the original MPI specification (henceforth MPI-1), the number of processes in an MPI application remains fixed between the call to MPI_Init and MPI_Finalize. As experience with PVM showed, it is sometimes helpful to be able to change the number of processes available during the execution of a parallel computation. In MPI-2, the function MPI_Comm_spawn allows the user to create new processes and connect them to an MPI application; other routines allow two MPI programs to connect to each other.

Another requested feature, stimulated both by research into other parallel computing models such as active messages [965] and bulk synchronous processes (BSP) [470], and in particular by the success of the Cray shmem library, was one-sided or remote-memory operations. MPI-2 provides routines that allow a process to put or get directly into another process's memory.

Perhaps the most requested feature, however, was for parallel I/O. The MPI approach to I/O is covered later in this book in Chapter 11.

In addition, MPI-2 added bindings for C++ and Fortran 90; defined how MPI programs that make use of C, Fortran 90, and C++ communicate; and added a number of more minor (but necessary) extensions. These new features are covered in more detail in Gropp et al. [405, 407].

10.1.4 State of the Art

MPI has been a tremendously successful parallel programming system. While low level, it has provided a standard notation for parallel program design and has permitted the development of high-performance implementations. MPI-1 implementations are available on almost every parallel computer, and large numbers of applications and libraries have been developed that achieve high performance on small and large parallel systems. MPI-2 implementations are also beginning to appear. The I/O part of MPI-2 is already widely available, and several supercomputer vendors have complete MPI-2 implementations.

Equally important, MPI support for modular program construction has facilitated, almost for the first time, the development of reusable parallel program components. (The Connection Machine's library was one important precursor.) Hence, we see the development of important reusable code bases. An example is the PETSc library for scientific computing [71], which allows application programmers to develop complex parallel programs without writing any explicitly parallel code.

In summary, MPI is particularly suited for applications where portability, both in space (across different systems that exist now) and in time (across generations of computers), is important. MPI is also an excellent choice for task-parallel computations and for applications where the data structures are dynamic, such as unstructured mesh computations.

10.2 Multithreaded Programming

We now turn our attention to the multithreaded programming model. As we described above, the message-passing model assumes that each concurrently executing program component has a separate, independent address space and that data are moved explicitly among these address spaces via send and receive operations. The shared-memory programming model is the exact opposite, in that we start with the assumption that concurrently executing program components all share a single, common address space. There is no need to provide special operations for copying, as program components can exchange information simply by reading and writing to memory using normal variable assignment operations. Because the concurrent elements of the program do not have distinct address spaces, it is not correct to refer to them as processes. Instead, we say that the program consists of many independent "threads of control," or threads for short. Hence the use of the name *multithreaded programming*.

Because communication in shared-memory programs is implicit, it is generally up to the hardware platform on which the program is executing to ensure that the latest value of a variable updated in one thread is used when that same variable is accessed in another thread. This is the so-called memory coherence problem, which can be difficult to solve for a variety of reasons. Modern computer architectures tend to copy data in local, high-speed memory in order to decrease access time. Some of this memory (i.e., registers) is manipulated explicitly by the compiler, while other memory takes the form of one or more levels of cache. These are transparent to the compiler and application (except in terms of performance). If shared-memory programs are to function properly, both the hardware and the compilers used to generate and execute the multithreaded program need to make sure that the various pieces of memory in the computer remain consistent. Hardware support typically takes the form of a *cache-coherency protocol*. Many different consistency models and associated coherency protocols have been proposed, often with slightly different sharing semantics [7, 552]. Yet in spite of these sophisticated protocols, physical constraints limit the number of processors that can share memory. As a rule, shared-memory programs do not scale as well as message-passing programs.

Software-only shared-memory systems have been proposed as well. These so-called *distributed shared-memory* (DSM) systems generally try to exploit the hardware support for implementing virtual memory in order to determine when changes to memory are made and to propagate those changes to other processors [88, 102, 552, 710]. These systems typically use a message-passing layer as the means for communicating updated values throughout the system. Because memory updates are done on a page basis with hundreds or thousands of memory locations, arbitrary writing of variables can be very costly. For this reason, DSM systems typically try to enhance the locality of modifications, restrict which memory locations can be shared, or introduce specialized coherency semantics in order to reduce the number of pages that must be sent from one processor to another.

While the operations for sharing data are straightforward, multithreaded programs introduce the new problem of controlling access to a shared-memory location while values are being updated. In the message-passing model, the success of a receive operation indicates that all the data have been transferred from one process to another and that the data are now available for use. Without the intervention of some explicit synchronization operation, interleaved execution of multiple threads can result in incorrect results. For example, in many situations, partially modified data structures should not be used, and a reading thread should be delayed until the writing thread has finished updating all of the data-structure fields. Likewise, having two threads attempt to update the contents of a data structure at the same time can be disastrous, with the result being an arbitrary combination of the fields written by the competing threads.

Over the years, many different proposals have been made concerning synchronization of multithreaded programs. Some of these limit the ways in which variables can be written (e.g., functional and single-assignment languages [4, 350, 659]). Others define special synchronization operations, including monitors, locks, critical sections, condition variables, semaphores, and barriers (see André et al. [41] for an overview of these operations). There are some fundamental concepts (e.g., some notion of an atomic test-and-set operation) that underlie all of these primitives. But in many cases, one set of synchronization operations can be implemented in terms of other primitives and the choice of the set to use comes down to programming convenience and performance.

Methods for development of multithreaded programs are similar to methods for development of message-passing systems: one can produce special-purpose languages, extend existing languages, or provide purely library-based approaches. In the following, we examine two different approaches. The first is POSIX threads and is completely library based. The second, OpenMP, combines compiler support with library calls to implement its multithreading model.

10.2.1 POSIX Threads

The multithreading programming model has important uses outside of parallel programming. Multithreading proves to be a very effective programming model when a program has to respond to asynchronous requests. Such requests occur, for example, when interacting with slow I/O systems or when implementing network-based systems such as client/server architectures (specifically the server). For this reason, the set of real-time extensions defined for the POSIX operating system interface includes a thread library. Because of its wide range of intended uses, the POSIX standard thread library [499], or *p-threads* as it is often called, includes many features that are not of interest to parallel program developers. In the following, we provide a brief overview of those facilities that are germane to parallel programs.

A p-thread program starts its life with a single thread of control, just like any sequential program. New threads of control must be created explicitly by calling the pthread_create function and specifying the function to run in the newly created thread. This call creates a thread record, which is initialized by allocating a call stack and creating an initial stack frame, and sets up the call of the function to be executed in the thread. There is no restriction on the number of threads that can be created by a program. In particular, the number of threads can exceed the number of processors available in the system. To support the creation of more threads than processors, thread records are generally handed to a scheduler that arranges to execute the thread when a processor becomes available. It is interesting to note that from the perspective of concurrency, the p-thread model is fundamentally dynamic, while the MPI model is basically static.

A thread terminates when the function being executed by the thread completes or when an explicit thread exit function is called. Threads can also be explicitly terminated by specifying the thread identifier returned by a pthread_create call as an argument to the pthread_kill function.

In the POSIX model, all the memory associated with a thread is shared, including the thread's call stack, dynamically allocated heap memory, and obviously global variables. This can cause programming difficulties. Often, one needs a variable that is global to the routines called within a thread but not shared between threads. A set of p-thread functions is used to manipulate *thread local storage* to address these requirements.

Synchronization Operations

The p-threads library provides two types of synchronization primitives, one associated with the control structure (i.e., threads) and the second to synchronize access to data structures. The control-oriented synchronization enables one thread to block, waiting for the completion of a second thread. Unfortunately, this facility does not generalize to more than two threads, meaning that it cannot be used to implement the popular join/fork concurrency model (discussed below).

The data-oriented synchronization routines are based on the use of a *mutex*, short for mutual exclusion. A mutex is a dynamically allocated data structure that can be passed as an argument to the routines pthread_mutex_lock and pthread_mutex_unlock. Once a pthread_mutex_lock call is made on a specific mutex, subsequent pthread_mutex_lock calls will block until a call is made to pthread_mutex_unlock with that mutex.

Locking is generally used for fine-grain access control. To minimize the response time to an unlock operation, locks are often implemented by *spinning,* repeatedly testing the lock to see if it has been released. This has the downside of consuming 100% of the resources of the processor executing the lock operation. More coarse-grain synchronization is provided by *condition variables*, which allow a thread to wait until a Boolean predicate that depends on the contents of one or more shared-memory locations becomes true.

A condition variable associates a mutex with the desired predicate. Before the program makes its test, it obtains a lock on the associated mutex. Then it evaluates the predicate. If the predicate evaluates to false, the thread can execute a pthread_cond_wait operation, which atomically suspends the calling thread, puts the thread record on a waiting list that is part of the condition variable, and releases the mutex. The thread scheduler is now free to use the processor to execute another thread. If the predicate evaluates to true, the thread simply releases its lock and continues on its way.

If a thread changes the value of any shared variables associated with a condition variable predicate, it needs to cause any threads that may be waiting on this condition variable to be rescheduled. The pthread_cond_signal causes one of the threads waiting on the condition variable to become unblocked, returning from the pthread_cond_wait that caused it to block in the first place. The mutex is automatically reobtained as part of the return from the wait, so the thread is in the position to reevaluate the predicate immediately.

Because condition variables enable atomic evaluation of arbitrary predicates, they are quite flexible and can be used to implement a range of different synchronization structures, including semaphores, barriers, critical sections, and so on.

10.2.2 OpenMP

As we discussed above, support for parallel programming was only one of the factors that was considered in the design of p-threads. Not surprisingly, compromises were made that affect both programmability and performance. The OpenMP interface [725] is an alternative multithreading interface specifically designed to support high-performance parallel programs.

OpenMP differs from p-threads in several significant ways. Where p-threads is implemented purely as a library, OpenMP is implemented as a combination of library calls and a set of compiler directives or pragmas. These directives instruct the compiler to create threads, perform synchronization operations, and manage shared memory. OpenMP does require specialized compiler support in order to understand and process these directives. However, an increasing number of vendors are producing OpenMP versions of their Fortran, C, and C++ compilers.

In p-threads, there is almost no structure or a priori relationship between threads, short of the ability of one thread to wait for the termination of another thread. While such lack of structure is essential to the design of servers, which typically consist of a number of independent threads, the need for structure in the design of programs is well understood. Because OpenMP was designed specifically for parallel applications, the use of threads is highly structured, following what is known as the fork/join model. This is a block-structured approach to introducing concurrency. A single thread of control splits into some number of independent threads (the fork), and the end of the block is reached when all the threads have completed execution of their specified tasks (the join). In OpenMP, a fork/join block is indicated by a *parallel region*, indicated by PARALLEL and END PARALLEL directives. The number of threads assigned to a region is defined by the user, either globally or on a region-by-region basis, and each thread executes the code enclosed by the PARALLEL directives. Because of the way OpenMP is defined, a PARALLEL region does not imply the creation of a new thread. Thus, if an existing thread is available, it can be used to execute a parallel region, allowing the OpenMP implementation to amortize thread start-up costs. Parallel blocks can be nested, with the implementation figuring out when the threads in each nested region have completed. Clearly, the use of parallel regions can significantly decrease the potential for error.

The PARALLEL region enables a single task to be replicated across a set of threads. However, in parallel programs it is very common to distribute different tasks across a set of threads, such as parallel iteration over the index set of a loop. To support this common need, a PARALLEL region can be augmented with an additional set of directives that enable each thread to execute a different task. This is called *worksharing*. The most useful form of worksharing is a parallel do loop, which is specified by inserting a DO directive in front of a do loop and enclosing the entire thing in a PARALLEL declaration. During execution, the parallel region creates some number of independent threads, and the worksharing declaration causes the compiler to generate code that distributes the iterations (which can be greater in number than the number of threads) to the threads for execution.

OpenMP synchronization primitives are also more application-oriented than the p-thread synchronization primitives. OpenMP synchronization primitives include the following:

- *Critical sections*, which ensure that only one thread at a time executes the enclosed code (critical sections are similar to p-thread mutexes).
- *Atomic updates*, which behave like critical sections, but can be optimized on some hardware platforms.
- *Barriers*, which synchronize all threads in a parallel region.
- *Master selection*, which ensures that the enclosed code only executes in one thread, even if the code is part of a parallel region.

This selection of synchronization primitives makes it easier to write parallel programs. Certainly, each of these operations can be implemented in terms of p-thread mutex and condition variables. However, by including these as basic OpenMP operations, it is possible for an OpenMP implementation to generate code that is more efficient than the equivalent p-thread code.

The final place where OpenMP differs from p-threads is in its treatment of shared memory. Recall that in p-threads, all memory is shared with the exception of thread local storage. Unlike p-threads, OpenMP does not allow sharing of stack variables. Again, this makes it possible to generate better optimized code. OpenMP also provides thread local storage. However, because of the block-structured nature of PARALLEL regions, OpenMP threads can access local variables that are defined by the routine or block in which the PARALLEL region occurs (this is not an issue in p-threads because p-threads has no concept of nesting). Sometimes it is advantageous for each thread to have its own private copy of these variables, and OpenMP allows variables to be annotated as being PRIVATE.

In summary, OpenMP does not define a new programming language, but rather consists of a set of annotations that are interpreted by an OpenMP-enabled compiler, or preprocessor. OpenMP annotations can be included in Fortran programs as directives, or in C and C++ programs as pragmas. By focusing specifically on the needs of parallel programs, OpenMP can result in a more convenient and higher-performance implementation of multithreaded parallel programs.

10.3   Conclusion

In the preceding sections, we discussed the message-passing and multithreaded approaches to parallel programming in isolation. Given that many recent large-scale parallel computers are built as clusters of multiprocessor (i.e., shared-memory) nodes, there is a strong motivation to combine message passing and multithreading in a single application. The hybrid approach has the potential to optimize program performance by using multithreaded structures within a multiprocessor node and message-passing primitives for communication between nodes.

In principle, there is no reason why message passing and parallel programming cannot be combined in a single application program. In practice, we find that many implementations of message passing are not thread-safe; that is, it is not safe for two threads to make message-passing calls at the same time. This can be caused by a number of different factors: the message-passing interface may have been designed so as to preclude a thread-safe implementation (e.g., requiring that state be stored in the implementation), or an otherwise thread-safe API may not have been implemented in a thread-safe manner, or the low-level interfaces to the message-passing hardware may not be thread-safe. These caveats aside, MPI was designed to be thread-safe and thread-safe implementations of MPI exist. These implementations can be combined with multithreading approaches such as p-threads or OpenMP to produce hybrid programs.

There are a variety of approaches that can be used to merge the message-passing and multithreading styles. The most common is to use a single thread (the main thread) for all MPI communication and to use other threads for computational tasks; this is the case when OpenMP is used to parallelize loops that do not contain any MPI calls. Most MPI implementations (even those that are not thread-safe) may be used in this way with threads. Another method is to perform sends from any thread, but receives within a single receiver thread. This thread would be responsible for integrating receive buffers into shared memory. It would then either notify waiting threads or create new threads to process the new data. Alternatively, one could perform receives from an arbitrary thread. This can be a good approach if there is a collection of worker threads, and any one of them can process the data from an incoming message. A modification is to perform send and receive operations between specific thread pairs [326]. For this to work, one must assume that threads are long lived, as performing a send to a thread that no longer exists would result in an error. MPI communicators can be very helpful in implementing this type of hybrid model. A final approach is that taken by special-purpose communication libraries, such as Nexus [346], in which the arrival of data causes the automatic creation of a new thread of control to process that data.

While tools and techniques that support both message passing and multithreading are important, the significant challenge lies not in the tools but in the application itself. For these hybrid techniques to be useful, one must be able to exploit the heterogeneous characteristics, in terms of bandwidth and latency, found in shared-memory and message-passing systems [324, 580, 611, 905].

11

Parallel I/O

Rajeev Thakur • William Gropp

Many parallel applications need to access large amounts of data. In such applications, the I/O performance can play a significant role in the overall time to completion. Although I/O is always much slower than computation, it is still possible to achieve good I/O performance in parallel applications by using a combination of a sufficient amount of high-speed I/O hardware, appropriate file-system software, the appropriate application programming interface (API) for I/O, a high-performance implementation of the API, and by using that API the right way. We explain these points in further detail in this chapter.

We begin by explaining what parallel I/O means, how it arises, and why it is a problem. We give an overview of the infrastructure that currently exists for parallel I/O on modern parallel systems, including I/O architecture, parallel file systems, high-level libraries, and APIs for parallel I/O. We explain how the API plays a key role in enabling (or preventing) high performance and how the lack of an appropriate standard API for parallel I/O has hindered performance and portability.

Much of the research in parallel I/O over the last several years has contributed to the definition of the new standard API for parallel I/O that is part of the MPI-2 standard [670]. We discuss the evolution and emergence of this API, often just called MPI-IO, and introduce it with a simple example program. We also describe some optimizations enabled by MPI-IO that are critical for high performance. Finally, we provide guidelines on what users can do to achieve high I/O performance in their applications.

Our focus is mainly on the type of parallel I/O commonly seen in high-end scientific computing and not on the I/O that arises in databases, transaction processing, and other commercial applications. I/O in parallel scientific computing often involves large data objects, such as a single large array, that is distributed across hundreds of processors. In contrast, while the amount of data stored and accessed in a commercial database may be larger than the data stored as a result of a scientific simulation, each record in a commercial database is usually very small.

Any application, sequential or parallel, may need to access data stored in files for many reasons, such as reading the initial input, writing the results, checkpointing for later restart, data analysis, and visualization [367]. In this chapter we are concerned mainly with *parallel* applications consisting of multiple processes (or threads[1]) that need to access data stored in files. We define parallel I/O as concurrent requests from multiple processes of a parallel program for data stored in files. Accordingly, at least two scenarios are possible:

- Each process accesses a separate file; that is, no file is shared among processes.
- All processes access a single shared file.

While the former scenario can be considered as parallel I/O in some sense because it represents I/O performed by a parallel program, it is actually just sequential (uniprocess) I/O performed independently by a number of processes. The latter case, where all processes access a shared file, is true parallel I/O and represents what the term *parallel I/O* means as used in this chapter. In other words, the I/O is parallel from the application's perspective.

In recent years, although great advances have been made in the CPU and communication performance of parallel machines, similar advances have not been made in their I/O performance. The densities and capacities of disks have increased significantly, but improvement in performance of individual disks has not followed the same pace. Although parallel machines with peak performance of 1 Tflop/s or more are available, applications running on parallel machines usually achieve I/O bandwidths of at most a few hundred Mbytes/s. In fact, many applications achieve less than 10 Mbytes/s [229].

As parallel computers get bigger and faster, scientists are increasingly using them to solve problems that not only need a large amount of computing power but also need to access large amounts of data. (See del Rosario and Choudary [253], Kotz [577], Scalable I/D Initiative [830] for a list of many such applications.) Since I/O is slow, the I/O speed, and not the CPU or communication speed, is often the bottleneck in such applications. For parallel computers to be truly usable for solving real large-scale problems, the I/O performance must be scalable and balanced with respect to the CPU and communication performance of the system.

The rest of this chapter is organized as follows. In Section 11.1, we describe the existing infrastructure for parallel I/O, including architecture, file systems, and high-level libraries. We also discuss the issue of application programming interfaces (APIs) for parallel I/O and explain how the lack of an appropriate standard API has hindered performance and portability in the past. In Section 11.2, we introduce the new

---

[1] The discussion in this chapter refers to multiple processes rather than threads because our focus is on the MPI-IO model for parallel I/O. Nonetheless, the issues we discuss apply equally well to a parallel programming model based on multiple threads within a process.

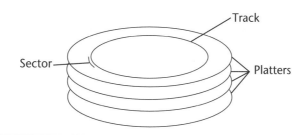

Figure 11.1   Schematic of a typical disk.

MPI-IO standard API, which has the potential to solve the API problem and deliver performance and portability. In Section 11.3, we describe some optimizations that are critical to parallel I/O performance. In Section 11.4, we provide some guidelines on how users can achieve high I/O performance in their applications. We summarize the chapter in Section 11.5.

11.1   Parallel I/O Infrastructure

In this section we give a brief overview of the infrastructure for parallel I/O that currently exists on parallel machines. We begin by reviewing basic nonparallel I/O.

11.1.1   Basic Disk Architecture

The most common secondary-storage device is a *disk*. A disk consists of one or more *platters* coated with a magnetic medium. The disk spins at a relatively high rate; 5000 to 10000 RPMs (revolutions per minute) are common. A platter is divided into a number of concentric *tracks*, which are themselves divided into smaller arcs called *sectors*. A sector is the smallest addressable unit on the disk, and a typical sector size is 512 bytes [435]. Data are read by one or more *heads* that can move across the platters. A schematic of a disk is shown in Figure 11.1.

Data from a disk are typically accessed in multiples of sectors stored contiguously, sometimes called a *cluster*. On commodity disks, a minimum of 32 sectors (16 Kbytes) or more are accessed in a single operation. As a result, reading or writing a single byte of data from or to a disk actually causes thousands of bytes to be moved. In other words, there can be a huge difference between the amount of data logically accessed by an application and the amount of data physically moved, as demonstrated in Simitci and Reed [863]. In addition, a substantial latency is introduced by the need to wait for the right sector to move under a read or write head—even at 10,000 RPM, it takes 6 milliseconds for the disk to complete one revolution. To avoid accessing the disk for each I/O request, an operating system typically maintains a cache in main memory, called the *file-system cache*, that contains parts of the disk that have been recently accessed. Data written to the cache are periodically flushed to the disk by an operating-system daemon. Despite the cache, an application that performs

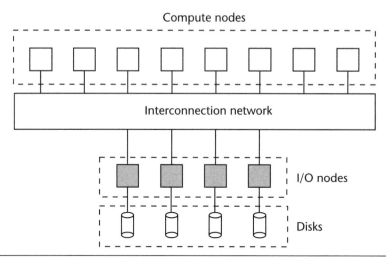

Figure 11.2   General parallel I/O architecture of distributed-memory systems.

a large number of small reads or writes usually performs poorly. Applications that need high I/O performance must ensure that I/O operations access large amounts of data.

Further details about disk architecture can be found in Chen et al. [192] and The Hard Disk Drive Guide [435].

11.1.2   Parallel I/O Architecture

Let us now consider the I/O architectures of parallel machines. We first consider distributed-memory machines, examples of which include the IBM SP, ASCI Red (Intel Tflops), Cray T3E, clusters of workstations, and older machines such as the Thinking Machines CM-5, Intel Paragon, and iPSC hypercubes. Figure 11.2 shows the general I/O architecture of a distributed-memory machine. In addition to the compute nodes, the machine has a set of I/O nodes. The I/O nodes are usually connected to each other and to the compute nodes by the same interconnection network that connects the compute nodes. Each I/O node is connected to one or more storage devices, each of which could be either an individual disk or an array of disks, such as a RAID (redundant array of inexpensive disks) [192, 757]. The I/O nodes function as servers for the parallel file system. The parallel file system typically stripes files across the I/O nodes and disks by dividing the file into a number of smaller units called *striping units* and assigning the striping units to disks in a round-robin manner. File striping provides higher bandwidth and enables multiple compute nodes to access distinct portions of a file concurrently.

Usually, but not always, the I/O nodes are dedicated for I/O, and no compute jobs are run on them. On many machines, each of the compute nodes also has a local disk of its own, which is usually not directly accessible from other nodes. These disks are not part of the common "parallel I/O system," but are used to store scratch files local to each process and other files used by the operating system.

This kind of architecture allows concurrent requests from multiple compute nodes to be serviced simultaneously. Parallelism comes about in multiple ways: parallel data paths from the compute nodes to the I/O nodes, multiple I/O nodes and file-system servers, and multiple storage devices (disks). If each storage device is a disk array, it provides even more parallelism.

Shared-memory machines typically do not have this kind of I/O architecture; they do not have separate I/O nodes. Examples of such machines are the SGI Origin 2000, Cray T90, HP Exemplar, and NEC SX-4. On these machines, the operating system schedules the file-system server on the compute nodes. Nonetheless, these machines can be configured with multiple disks, and the file system can stripe files across the disks. The disks are connected to the machine via SCSI or Fibre Channel connections, just as they are in distributed memory machines.

For further information on parallel I/O architecture, see the excellent surveys in Feitelson [322] and Kotz [578].

A relatively new area of research is that of network-attached storage devices (NASD) [376]. In NASD, storage devices are not directly connected to their host systems via a specialized I/O bus, but instead communicate with their host systems through a high-performance network such as Fibre Channel [333]. This approach has the potential to improve performance and scalability by providing direct data transfer between client and storage and eliminating the server, which can be a bottleneck.

11.1.3   File Systems

A number of commercial and research file systems have been developed over the last few years to meet the needs of parallel I/O. We briefly describe some of them below and provide pointers to additional information.

One of the first commercial parallel file systems was the Intel Concurrent File System (CFS) for the Intel iPSC hypercubes. It had a UNIX-like API with the addition of various file-pointer modes [766]. CFS evolved into the Parallel File System (PFS) on the Intel Paragon, but retained the same API. The CM-5, nCUBE, and Meiko CS-2 also had their own parallel file systems [322]. A different API was introduced by the Vesta file system, developed at the IBM Watson Research Center [224]. Vesta provided the initial parallel file system for the IBM SP. The unique feature of Vesta was that it supported logical file views and noncontiguous file accesses— a departure from the traditional UNIX API. Vesta evolved into an IBM product called PIOFS, which remained the parallel file system on the SP until recently. The current parallel file system on the IBM SP is called GPFS [394], which interestingly is not backward compatible with PIOFS. It does not support PIOFS file views or noncontiguous file accesses; instead, it supports the POSIX I/O interface [500]. However, for noncontiguous accesses, users can use the MPI-IO interface on top of GPFS by using either IBM's implementation of MPI-IO or other implementations, such as ROMIO [807]. Shared-memory multiprocessors also have high-performance file systems that allow concurrent access to files. Examples of such file systems are XFS on the SGI Origin 2000, HFS on the HP Exemplar, and SFS on the NEC SX-4. Sun has developed a parallel file system, Sun PFS, for clusters of Sun SMPs [998].

A number of parallel file systems have also been developed by various research groups. The Galley parallel file system developed at Dartmouth College supports a 3-D file structure consisting of files, subfiles, and forks [712]. PPFS is a parallel file system developed at the University of Illinois for clusters of workstations [494]. The developers use it as a testbed for research on various aspects of file-system design, such as caching/prefetching policies and automatic/adaptive policy selection [634, 635]. PVFS is a parallel file system for Linux clusters developed at Clemson University [742]. PVFS stripes files across the local disks of machines in a Linux cluster and provides the look-and-feel of a single UNIX file system. The regular UNIX commands, such as rm, ls, and mv, can be used on PVFS files, and the files can be accessed from a (parallel) program by using the regular UNIX I/O functions. PVFS is also packaged in a way that makes it very easy to download, install, and use.

Distributed/networked file systems are a rich area of research. Examples of such file systems are xFS [38], AFS/Coda [204], and GFS [382]. We do not discuss them in this chapter; interested readers can find further information in the papers cited above.

11.1.4   The API Problem

Most commercial parallel file systems have evolved out of uniprocessor file systems, and they retain the same API, namely, the UNIX I/O API. The UNIX API, however, is not an appropriate API for parallel I/O for two main reasons: it does not allow noncontiguous file accesses, and it does not support collective I/O. We explain these reasons below.

The UNIX read/write functions allow users to access only a single contiguous piece of data at a time.[2] While such an API may be sufficient for the needs of uniprocess programs, it is not sufficient for the kinds of access patterns common in parallel programs. Many studies of the I/O access patterns in parallel programs have shown that each process of a parallel program may need to access several relatively small, noncontiguous pieces of data from a file [86, 229, 713, 871, 870, 917]. In addition, many or all processes may need to access the file at about the same time, and although the accesses of each process may be small and noncontiguous, the accesses of different processes may be interleaved in the file and together may span large

---

[2] UNIX does have functions readv and writev, but they allow noncontiguity only in memory and not in the file. POSIX has a function lio_listio that allows users to specify a list of requests at a time, but each request is treated internally as a separate asynchronous I/O request, the requests can be a mixture of reads and writes, and the interface is not collective.

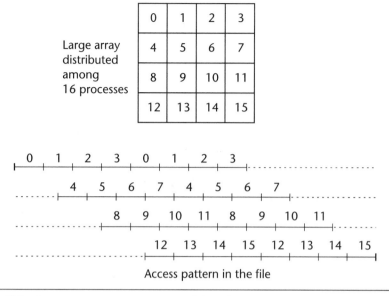

Figure 11.3   Common access pattern in parallel applications: distributed-array access. The numbers on the line indicate the process that needs a particular portion of the file.

contiguous chunks. Such access patterns occur because of the manner in which data stored in a shared file is distributed among processes. With the UNIX I/O interface, the programmer has no means of conveying this "big picture" of the access pattern to the I/O system. Each process must seek to a particular location in the file, read or write a small contiguous piece, then seek to the start of the next contiguous piece, read or write that piece, and so on. The result is that each process makes hundreds or thousands of requests for small amounts of data. Numerous small I/O requests arriving in any order from multiple processes results in very poor performance, not just because I/O latency is high but also because the file-system cache gets poorly utilized.

The example in Figure 11.3 illustrates this point. The figure shows an access pattern commonly found in parallel applications, namely, distributed-array access. A 2-D array is distributed among 16 processes in a (block, block) fashion. The array is stored in a file corresponding to the global array in row-major order, and each process needs to read its local array from the file. The data distribution among processes and the array storage order in the file are such that the file contains the first row of the local array of process 0, followed by the first row of the local array of process 1, the first row of the local array of process 2, the first row of the local array of process 3, then the second row of the local array of process 0, the second row of the local array of process 1, and so on. In other words, the local array of each process is not located contiguously in the file. To read its local array with a UNIX-like API, each process must seek to the appropriate location in the file, read one row, seek to the next row, read that row, and so on. Each process must make as many read requests as the number of rows in its local array. If the array is large, the file system may receive thousands of read requests.

Instead, if the I/O API allows the user to convey the entire access information of each process as well as the fact that all processes need to access the file simultaneously, the implementation (of the API) can read the entire file contiguously and simply send the right pieces of data to the right processes. This optimization, known as *collective I/O*, can improve performance significantly [252, 579, 843, 919]. The I/O API thus plays a critical role in enabling the user to express I/O operations conveniently and also in conveying sufficient information about access patterns to the I/O system so that the system can perform I/O efficiently.

Another problem with commercial parallel–file-system APIs is the lack of portability. Although parallel file systems have UNIX-like APIs, many vendors support variations of the UNIX (or POSIX [500]) API, and, consequently, programs written with these APIs are not portable.

11.1.5   I/O Libraries

A number of I/O libraries have also been developed over the last several years, mostly as part of research projects. These libraries either provide a better API than UNIX I/O and perform I/O optimizations enabled by the API or provide some convenience features useful to applications that file systems do not provide. We list some of these libraries below.

The PASSION library, developed at Syracuse University, supports efficient access to arrays and sections of arrays stored in files [916]. It uses data sieving, two-phase collective I/O, and (recently) compression as the main optimizations. The Panda library, developed at the University of Illinois, also supports high-performance array access [843]. It uses server-directed collective I/O and chunked storage as the main optimizations. SOLAR is a library for out-of-core linear algebra operations developed at IBM Watson Research Center [933]. The ChemIO library, developed at Pacific Northwest National Laboratory, provides I/O support for computational chemistry applications [709].

HDF [698], netCDF [702], and DMF [842] are libraries designed to provide an even higher level of I/O support to applications. For example, they can directly read/write meshes and grids. These libraries are very popular among application developers because they provide a level of abstraction that application developers need. Until recently, these libraries did not perform parallel I/O and consequently did not achieve high performance. Newer versions of these libraries, particularly HDF-5, are being implemented to use parallel I/O (via MPI-IO). Because all the libraries mentioned here support their own API, usually much different from the UNIX I/O API, they do not solve the API portability problem.

11.1.6   Language-Based Parallel I/O

Some efforts have been made to support parallel I/O directly in the parallel programming language. For example, the Fortran D and Fortran 90D research projects
explored the use of language-based parallel I/O with a combination of compiler direc-
tives and run-time library calls [130, 131, 735]. CM Fortran from Thinking Machines
Corporation also supported reading and writing of parallel arrays. Although parallel
I/O was discussed during the deliberations of the High Performance Fortran (HPF)
Forum, it does not appear in the final HPF standard. In all, language-based parallel
I/O remains mainly a research effort.

11.2   Overview of MPI-IO

Although great strides were made in parallel I/O research in the early 1990s, there
remained a critical need for a single, standard, language-neutral API designed specifically for parallel I/O performance and portability. Fortunately, such an API now
exists. It is the I/O interface defined as part of the MPI-2 standard, often referred to
as MPI-IO [407, 670].

In this section, we give a brief overview of MPI-IO, describe its main features,
and elaborate on one important feature—the ability to specify noncontiguous I/O
requests by using MPI's derived data types.

MPI-IO originated in an effort begun in 1994 at IBM Watson Research Center to
investigate the impact of the (then) new MPI message-passing standard on parallel
I/O. A group at IBM wrote an important paper [779] that explores the analogy
between MPI message passing and I/O. Roughly speaking, one can consider reads
and writes to a file system as receives and sends of messages. This paper was the
starting point of MPI-IO in that it was the first attempt to exploit this analogy by
applying the (then relatively new) MPI concepts for message passing to the realm of
parallel I/O.

The idea of using message-passing concepts in an I/O library appeared successful,
and the effort was expanded into a collaboration with parallel I/O researchers from
the NASA Ames Research Center. The resulting specification appeared in [223]. At
this point a large email discussion group was formed, with participation from a wide
variety of institutions. This group, calling itself the MPI-IO Committee, pushed the
idea further in a series of proposals, culminating in Version 0.5 [692].

During this time, the MPI Forum had resumed meeting to address a number of
topics that had been deliberately left out of the original MPI standard, including
parallel I/O. The MPI Forum initially recognized that both the MPI-IO Committee
and the Scalable I/O Initiative [829] represented efforts to develop a standard parallel
I/O interface and therefore decided not to address I/O in its deliberations. In the
long run, however, the three threads of development—by the MPI-IO Committee,
the Scalable I/O Initiative, and the MPI Forum—merged because of a number of
considerations. The result was that, from the summer of 1996, the MPI-IO design
activities took place in the context of the MPI Forum meetings. The MPI Forum used

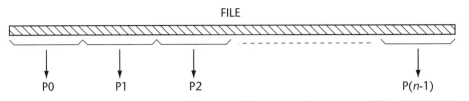

Figure 11.4 Each process needs to read a chunk of data from a common file.

the latest version of the existing MPI-IO specification [692] as a starting point for the
I/O chapter in MPI-2. The I/O chapter evolved over many meetings of the Forum and
was released in its final form along with the rest of MPI-2 in July 1997 [670]. MPI-IO
now refers to this I/O chapter in MPI-2.

11.2.1   Simple MPI-IO Example

To get a flavor of what MPI-IO looks like, let us consider a simple example: a parallel
program in which processes need to read data from a common file. Let us assume that
there are n processes, each needing to read $(1/n)$th of the file as shown in Figure 11.4.
Figure 11.5 shows one way of writing such a program with MPI-IO. It has the usual
functions one would expect for I/O: an open, a seek, a read, and a close. Let us look
at each of the functions closely.

MPI_File_open is the function for opening a file. The first argument to this function
is a communicator that indicates the group of processes that need to access the file
and that are calling this function. This communicator also represents the group of
processes that will participate in any collective I/O operations on the open file. In this
simple example, however, we don't use collective I/O functions. We pass MPI_COMM_
WORLD as the communicator, meaning that all processes need to open and thereafter
access the file. The file name is passed as the second argument to MPI_File_open.
The third argument to MPI_File_open specifies the mode of access; we use MPI_MODE_
RDONLY because this program only reads from the file. The fourth argument, called the
info argument, allows the user to pass hints to the implementation. In this example,
we don't pass any hints; instead, we pass a null info argument, MPI_INFO_NULL. MPI_
File_open returns a *file handle* in the last argument. This file handle is to be used for
future operations on the open file.

After opening the file, each process moves its local file pointer, called an *individual
file pointer,* to the location in the file from which the process needs to read data. We
use the function MPI_File_seek for this purpose. The first argument to MPI_File_seek
is the file handle returned by MPI_File_open. The second argument specifies the offset
in the file to seek to, and the third argument MPI_SEEK_SET specifies that the offset
must be calculated from the head of the file. We specify the offset to MPI_File_seek
as a product of the rank of the process and the amount of data to be read by each
process.

```
/* Read from a common file using individual file pointers */
#include "mpi.h"

#define FILESIZE (1024 * 1024)

int main(int argc, char **argv)
{
    int *buf, rank, nprocs, nints, bufsize;
    MPI_File fh;
    MPI_Status status;

    MPI_Init(&argc,&argv);
    MPI_Comm_rank(MPI_COMM_WORLD, &rank);
    MPI_Comm_size(MPI_COMM_WORLD, &nprocs);

    bufsize = FILESIZE/nprocs;
    buf = (int *) malloc(bufsize);
    nints = bufsize/sizeof(int);

    MPI_File_open(MPI_COMM_WORLD, "/pfs/datafile",
                  MPI_MODE_RDONLY, MPI_INFO_NULL, &fh);
    MPI_File_seek(fh, rank*bufsize, MPI_SEEK_SET);
    MPI_File_read(fh, buf, nints, MPI_INT, &status);
    MPI_File_close(&fh);

    free(buf);
    MPI_Finalize();
    return 0;
}
```

Figure 11.5 Simple MPI-IO program to perform the I/O needed in Figure 11.4.

We use the function MPI_File_read for reading data. On each process, this function reads data from the current location of the process's individual file pointer for the open file. The first argument to MPI_File_read is the file handle. The second argument is the address of the buffer in memory into which data must be read. The next two arguments specify the amount of data to be read. Since the data are of type integer, we specify them as a count of the number of integers to be read. The final argument is a status argument, which is the same as the status argument in MPI communication functions, such as MPI_Recv. One can determine the amount of data actually read by using the functions MPI_Get_count or MPI_Get_elements on the status object returned by MPI_File_read, but we don't bother to do so in this example. MPI_

File_read increments the individual file pointer on each process by the amount of data read by that process. Finally, we close the file using the function MPI_File_close.

The five functions, MPI_File_open, MPI_File_seek, MPI_File_read, MPI_File_write, and MPI_File_close, are actually sufficient to write any I/O program. The other MPI-IO functions are for performance, portability, and convenience. Although these five functions[3] can be used as a quick start to using MPI-IO and for easily porting UNIX I/O programs to MPI-IO, users must not stop here. For the real benefits of using MPI-IO, users must use its special features, such as support for noncontiguous accesses and collective I/O. This issue is discussed further in Section 11.4 and in Gropp et al. [407].

11.2.2   Main Features of MPI-IO

MPI-IO is a rich interface with many features specifically intended for portable, high-performance parallel I/O. It has bindings in three languages: C, Fortran, and C++.

MPI-IO supports three kinds of basic data-access functions: using an explicit offset, individual file pointer, and shared file pointer. The explicit-offset functions take as argument the offset in the file from which the read/write should begin. The individual-file-pointer functions read/write data from the current location of a file pointer that is local to each process. The shared-file-pointer functions read/write data from the location specified by a common file pointer shared by the group of processes that together opened the file. In all these functions, users can specify a noncontiguous data layout in memory and file. Both blocking and nonblocking versions of these functions exist. MPI-IO also has collective versions of these functions, which must be called by all processes that together opened the file. The collective functions enable an implementation to perform collective I/O. A restricted form of nonblocking collective I/O, called *split collective I/O,* is supported.

A unique feature of MPI-IO is that it supports multiple data-storage representations: native, internal, external32, and also user-defined representations. native means that data are stored in the file as they are in memory; no data conversion is performed. internal is an implementation-defined data representation that may provide some (implementation-defined) degree of file portability. external32 is a specific, portable data representation defined in MPI-IO. A file written in external32 format on one machine is guaranteed to be readable on any machine with any MPI-IO implementation. MPI-IO also includes a mechanism for users to define a new data representation by providing data-conversion functions, which MPI-IO uses to convert data from file format to memory format and vice versa.

MPI-IO provides a mechanism, called *info,* that enables users to pass hints to the implementation in a portable and extensible manner. Examples of hints include

---

[3] The reader familiar with threads will note that the seek operation is not thread-safe: it effectively sets a global variable (the position in the file) that another thread could change before the subsequent read or write operation. MPI-IO has thread-safe variants of MPI_File_read and MPI_File_write, called MPI_File_read_at and MPI_File_write_at, that combine the seek and read/write operation.

parameters for file striping, prefetching/caching information, and access-pattern information. Hints do not affect the semantics of a program, but they may enable the MPI-IO implementation or underlying file system to improve performance or minimize the use of system resources [169, 758].

MPI-IO also has a set of rigorously defined consistency and atomicity semantics that specify the results of concurrent file accesses.

For details of all these features, we refer readers to Gropp et al. [405, 407], and to the MPI-2 document [670]. We elaborate further on only one feature—the ability to access noncontiguous data with a single I/O function by using MPI's derived data types—because it is critical for high performance in parallel applications. We emphasize this point because achieving high performance requires both a proper API and proper use of that API by the programmer. Other I/O efforts have also addressed the issue of accessing noncontiguous data; one example is the low-level API [225] developed as part of the Scalable I/O Initiative [829]. MPI-IO, however, is the only widely deployed API that supports noncontiguous access.

11.2.3   Noncontiguous Accesses in MPI-IO

In MPI, the amount of data a function sends or receives is specified in terms of instances of a *data type* [669]. Data types in MPI are of two kinds: basic and derived. Basic data types are those that correspond to the basic data types in the host programming language—integers, floating-point numbers, and so forth. In addition, MPI provides data type-constructor functions to create derived data types consisting of multiple basic data types located either contiguously or noncontiguously. The data type created by a data type constructor can be used as an input data type to another data type constructor. Any noncontiguous data layout can therefore be represented in terms of a derived data type.

MPI-IO uses MPI data types for two purposes: to describe the data layout in the user's buffer in memory and to define the data layout in the file. The data layout in memory is specified by the data type argument in each read/write function in MPI-IO. The data layout in the file is defined by the *file view*. When the file is first opened, the default file view is the entire file; that is, the entire file is visible to the process, and data will be read/written contiguously starting from the location specified by the read/write function. A process can change its file view at any time by using the function MPI_File_set_view, which takes as argument an MPI data type, called the *filetype*. From then on, data will be read/written only to those parts of the file specified by the filetype; any "holes" will be skipped. The file view and the data layout in memory can be defined by using any MPI data type; therefore, any general, noncontiguous access pattern can be compactly represented.

11.2.4   MPI-IO Implementations

Several implementations of MPI-IO are available, including portable and vendor-specific implementations. ROMIO is a freely available, portable implementation that we have developed at the Argonne National Laboratory [807, 920]. It runs on most parallel computers and networks of workstations and uses the native parallel/high-performance file systems on each machine. It is designed to be used with multiple MPI-1 implementations. Another portable MPI-IO implementation is PMPIO from the NASA Ames Research Center [335]. A group at Lawrence Livermore National Laboratory has implemented MPI-IO on the HPSS mass-storage system [524]. Most vendors either already have an MPI-IO implementation or are actively developing one. SGI and HP have included ROMIO in their MPI product. Sun [998] and Fujitsu have their own (complete) MPI-IO implementations. IBM, Compaq (DEC), NEC, and Hitachi are in various stages of MPI-IO development.

11.3   Parallel I/O Optimizations

In this section we describe some key optimizations in parallel I/O that are critical for high performance. These optimizations include data sieving, collective I/O, and hints and adaptive file-system policies. With the advent of MPI-IO, these optimizations are now supported in the API in a standard, portable way. This in turn enables a library or file system to actually perform these optimizations.

11.3.1   Data Sieving

As mentioned above, in many parallel applications each process may need to access small, noncontiguous pieces of data. Since I/O latency is very high, accessing each contiguous piece separately is very expensive: it involves too many system calls for small amounts of data. Instead, if the user conveys the entire noncontiguous access pattern within a single read or write function, the implementation can perform an optimization called *data sieving* and read or write data with much higher performance. Data sieving was first used in PASSION in the context of accessing sections of out-of-core arrays [914, 916]. We use a very general implementation of data sieving (for any general access pattern) in our MPI-IO implementation, ROMIO. We explain data sieving in the context of its implementation in ROMIO [919].

To reduce the effect of high I/O latency, it is critical to make as few requests to the file system as possible. Data sieving is a technique that enables an implementation to make a few large, contiguous requests to the file system even if the user's request consists of several small, noncontiguous accesses. Figure 11.6 illustrates the basic idea of data sieving. Assume that the user has made a single read request for five noncontiguous pieces of data. Instead of reading each noncontiguous piece separately, ROMIO reads a single contiguous chunk of data starting from the first requested byte up to the last requested byte into a temporary buffer in memory. It then extracts the requested portions from the temporary buffer and places them in the user's buffer. The user's buffer happens to be contiguous in this example, but it could well be noncontiguous.

A potential problem with this simple algorithm is its memory requirement. The temporary buffer into which data is first read must be as large as the *extent* of the

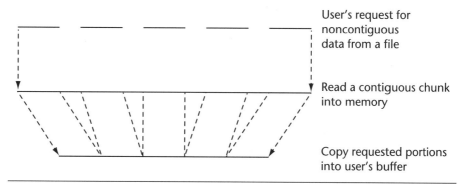

Figure 11.6 Data sieving.

user's request, where extent is defined as the total number of bytes between the first and last byte requested (including holes). The extent can potentially be very large—much larger than the amount of memory available for the temporary buffer—because the holes (unwanted data) between the requested data segments could be very large. The basic algorithm, therefore, must be modified to make its memory requirement independent of the extent of the user's request.

ROMIO uses a user-controllable parameter that defines the maximum amount of contiguous data that a process can read at a time during data sieving. This value also represents the maximum size of the temporary buffer. The user can change this size at run time via MPI-IO's hints mechanism. If the extent of the user's request is larger than the value of this parameter, ROMIO performs data sieving in parts, reading only as much data at a time as defined by the parameter.

The advantage of data sieving is that data are always accessed in large chunks, although at the cost of reading more data than needed. For many common access patterns, the holes between useful data are not unduly large, and the advantage of accessing large chunks far outweighs the cost of reading extra data. In some access patterns, however, the holes are so large that the cost of reading the extra data outweighs the cost of accessing large chunks. An "intelligent" data-sieving algorithm can handle such cases as well. The algorithm can analyze the user's request and decide whether to perform data sieving or access each contiguous data segment separately. We plan to add this feature to ROMIO.

Data sieving can similarly be used for writing data. A read-modify-write must be performed, however, to avoid destroying the data already present in the holes between contiguous data segments. The portion of the file being accessed must also be locked during the read-modify-write to prevent concurrent updates by other processes. The size of the write buffer can also be changed by the user via hints.

One could argue that most file systems perform data sieving anyway because they perform caching. That is, even if the user makes many small I/O requests, the file system always reads multiples of disk blocks and may also perform a read-ahead.

The user's requests, therefore, may be satisfied out of the file-system cache. Our experience, however, has been that the cost of making many system calls, each for small amounts of data, is extremely high, despite the caching performed by the file system. In most cases, it is more efficient to make a few system calls for large amounts of data and extract the needed data.

11.3.2   Collective I/O

In many cases, the data to be read or written represent a single object, distributed across many processors. An example is a single array, distributed across all processes in a parallel application. As we have seen, when this array is written to a file, each process must write many relatively small segments. Yet once the data are in the file, the array is stored in a single, contiguous block in the file. How can we exploit the fact that all the data to be written fills a large contiguous block in the file?

If the entire noncontiguous access information of all processes is known, an implementation can optimize the access even further. Instead of reading large chunks and discarding the unwanted data as in data sieving, the unwanted data can be communicated to other processes that need them. Such optimization is broadly referred to as *collective I/O*, and it has been shown to improve performance significantly [252, 579, 843, 919, 998].

Collective I/O can be performed in different ways and has been studied by many researchers in recent years. It can be done at the disk level (disk-directed I/O [579]), at the server level (server-directed I/O [843]), or at the client level (two-phase I/O [252] or collective buffering [714]). Each method has its advantages and disadvantages. Since ROMIO is a portable, user-level library with no separate I/O servers, ROMIO performs collective I/O at the client level using a generalized version of two-phase I/O. We explain the basic concept of two-phase I/O below; details of ROMIO's implementation can be found in Thakur et al. [919].

Two-Phase I/O

Two-phase I/O was first proposed in del Rosario et al. [252] in the context of accessing distributed arrays from files. The basic idea in two-phase I/O is to avoid making lots of small I/O requests by splitting the access into two phases: an I/O phase and a communication phase. Let us consider the example of reading a (block, block) distributed array from a file using two-phase I/O, illustrated in Figure 11.7. In the first phase of two-phase I/O, all processes access data assuming a distribution that results in each process making a single, large, contiguous access. In this example, such a distribution is a row-block or (block,*) distribution. In the second phase, processes redistribute data among themselves to the desired distribution. The advantage of this method is that by making all file accesses large and contiguous, the I/O time is reduced significantly. The added cost of interprocess communication for redistribution is (almost always) small compared with the savings in I/O time. The overall

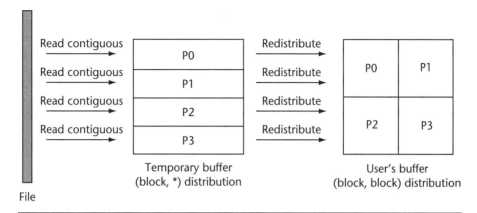

Figure 11.7   Reading a distributed array by using two-phase I/O.

performance, therefore, is close to what can be obtained by making large I/O requests in parallel.

The basic two-phase method was extended in Thakur and Choudary [915] to access sections of out-of-core arrays. An even more general version of two-phase I/O is implemented in ROMIO [919]. It supports any access pattern, and the user can also control via hints the amount of temporary memory that ROMIO uses as well as the number of processes that actually perform I/O in the I/O phase.

11.3.3   Hints and Adaptive File-System Policies

Parallel applications exhibit such a wide variation in access patterns that any single file-system policy (regarding file-striping parameters, caching/prefetching, etc.) is unlikely to perform well for all applications. Two solutions exist for this problem: either the user can inform the file system (via hints) about the application's access pattern, the desired striping parameters, or the desired caching/prefetching policies, or the file system can be designed to automatically detect and adapt its policies to the access pattern of the application. Various research efforts have demonstrated the benefits of such optimization [169, 634, 635, 758].

As mentioned above, hints can also be used to vary the sizes of temporary buffers used internally by the implementation for various optimizations. Choosing the right buffer size can improve performance considerably, as demonstrated in Section 11.4.2 and in Wisniewski et al. [998].

The hints mechanism in MPI-IO also allows users to specify machine-specific options and optimizations in a portable way. That is, the same program can be run everywhere, and the implementation will simply ignore the hints that are not applicable to the machine on which the program is being run. An example of the use of machine-specific hints are the hints ROMIO accepts for using "direct I/O" on

SGI's XFS file system. Direct I/O is an XFS option that can be specified via the 0_
DIRECT flag to the open function. In direct I/O, the file system moves data directly
between the user's buffer and the storage devices, bypassing the file-system cache
and thereby saving an extra copy. Another advantage is that, in direct I/O, the file
system allows writes from multiple processes and threads to a common file to proceed
concurrently rather than serializing them as it does with regular buffered I/O. Direct
I/O, however, performs well only if the machine has sufficient I/O hardware for high
disk bandwidth. If not, regular buffered I/O through the file-system cache performs
better. ROMIO, therefore, does not use direct I/O by default. It uses direct I/O only if
the user (who knows whether the machine has high disk bandwidth) recommends it
via a hint. On the Argonne Origin 2000 configured with 10 Fibre Channel controllers
and a total of 100 disks, we obtained bandwidths of around 720 MBytes/s for parallel
writes and 650 MBytes/s for parallel reads with the direct I/O hint specified. Without
this hint, the bandwidth was only 100 MBytes/s for parallel writes and 300 MBytes/s
for parallel reads.

Direct I/O can be used only if certain restrictions regarding the memory alignment
of the user's buffer, minimum and maximum I/O sizes, alignment of file offset, and
so on are met. ROMIO determines whether these restrictions are met for a particular
request and only then uses direct I/O; otherwise it uses regular buffered I/O (even
if the user specifies the direct I/O hint). We plan to add an optimization to ROMIO
in which even though the user's request does not meet the restrictions, ROMIO will
try to meet the restrictions by reorganizing the data internally, at least in the case of
collective I/O routines.

11.4   How Can Users Achieve High I/O Performance?

In this section, we provide general guidelines for achieving high I/O performance
and some specific guidelines for achieving high performance with MPI-IO.

11.4.1   General Guidelines

Following are some general guidelines for achieving high I/O performance. Although
many of them seem obvious, the reason for poor performance is often that one or
more of these simple guidelines are not being followed.

- *Buy Sufficient I/O hardware for the machine.* Machines tend to be purchased for
  high computation and communication performance but are often undercon-
  figured for the I/O requirements of the applications being run on them. It
  is impossible to achieve good I/O performance with insufficient I/O hardware
  (e.g., too few disks). It is difficult to say how much I/O hardware is sufficient—it
  depends on the application's requirements, system architecture, performance
  of the I/O hardware, and so on. The vendor of the machine may be able to
  provide guidance in this regard. Some useful guidelines on how to configure
  an I/O subsystem are provided in Feitelson et al. [322].

- *Use fast file systems, not NFS.* On many installations of high-performance machines, the home directories of users are NFS (Network File System [899]) mounted so that they can be accessed directly from other machines. This is a good convenience feature, but users must not use the same directory for reading or writing large amounts of data from parallel applications, because NFS is terribly slow. They must use the directory that corresponds to the native high-performance file system on the machine.

- *Do not perform I/O from one process only.* Many parallel applications still perform I/O by having all processes send their data to one process that gathers all the data and writes it to a file. Application developers have chosen this approach because of historical limitations in the I/O capabilities of many parallel systems: either parallel I/O from multiple processes to a common file was not supported, or if supported, the performance was poor. On modern parallel systems, however, these limitations no longer exist. With sufficient and appropriately configured I/O hardware and modern high-performance file systems, one can achieve higher performance by having multiple processes directly access a common file. The MPI-IO interface is specifically designed to support such accesses and to enable implementations to deliver high performance for such accesses.

- *Make large requests wherever possible.* I/O performance is much higher for large requests than for small requests. Application developers must therefore make an attempt to write their programs in a way that they make large I/O requests rather than lots of small requests, wherever possible.

- *Use MPI-IO and use it the right way.* MPI-IO offers great potential in terms of portability and high performance. It gives implementations an opportunity to optimize I/O. Therefore, we recommend that users use MPI-IO and use it the right way. The right way is explained in more detail below, but in short, whenever each process needs to access noncontiguous data and multiple processes need to perform such I/O, users must use MPI-derived data types, define a file view, and use a single collective I/O function. They must not access each small contiguous piece separately as they would with UNIX I/O.

11.4.2   Achieving High Performance with MPI-IO

Let us examine the different ways of writing an application with MPI-IO and see how this choice affects performance.[4] Any application has a particular "I/O access pattern" based on its I/O needs. The same I/O access pattern, however, can be presented to the I/O system in different ways, depending on which I/O functions the application uses and how. The different ways of expressing I/O access patterns in

---

[4] This section is reprinted with permission from *Using MPI-2: Advanced Features of the Message Passing Interface*, by William Gropp, Ewing Lusk, and Rajeev Thakur (MIT Press, Cambridge, MA, 1999).

```
MPI_File_open(..., "filename", ..., &fh)
for (i=0; i<n_local_rows; i++){
    MPI_File_seek(fh, ...)
    MPI_File_read(fh, row[i], ...)
}
MPI_File_close(&fh)
```

Level 0
(many independent, contiguous requests)

```
MPI_File_open(MPI_COMM_WORLD,
    "filename", ..., &fh)
for (i=0; i<n_local_rows; i++){
    MPI_File_seek(fh, ...)
    MPI_File_read_all(fh, row[i], ...)
}
MPI_File_close(&fh)
```

Level 1
(many collective, contiguous requests)

```
MPI_Type_create_subarray(..., &subarray, ...)
MPI_Type_commit(&subarray)
MPI_File_open(..., "filename", ..., &fh)
MPI_File_set_view(fh, ..., subarray, ...)
MPI_File_read(fh, local_array, ...)
MPI_File_close(&fh)
```

Level 2
(single independent, noncontiguous request)

```
MPI_Type_create_subarray(.., &subarray, ...)
MPI_Type_commit(&subarray)
MPI_File_open(MPI_COMM_WORLD,
    "filename", ..., &fh)
MPI_File_set_view(fh, ..., subarray, ...)
MPI_File_read_all(fh, local_array, ...)
MPI_File_close(&fh)
```

Level 3
(single collective, noncontiguous request)

Figure 11.8   Pseudocode that shows four ways of accessing the data in Figure 11.3 with MPI-IO.

MPI-IO can be classified into four *levels*, level 0 through level 3 [918]. We explain this classification with the help of the same example we considered in previous sections, namely, accessing a distributed array from a file (Figure 11.3). The principle applies to other access patterns as well.

Recall that in this example the local array of each process is not contiguous in the file; each row of the local array is separated by rows of the local arrays of other processes. Figure 11.8 shows four ways in which a user can express this access pattern in MPI-IO. In level 0, each process does UNIX-style accesses—one independent read request for each row in the local array. Level 1 is similar to level 0 except that it uses collective I/O functions, which indicate to the implementation that all processes that together opened the file will call this function, each with its own access information. Independent I/O functions, on the other hand, convey no information about what other processes will do. In level 2, each process creates a derived data type to describe the noncontiguous access pattern, defines a file view, and calls independent I/O functions. Level 3 is similar to level 2 except that it uses collective I/O functions.

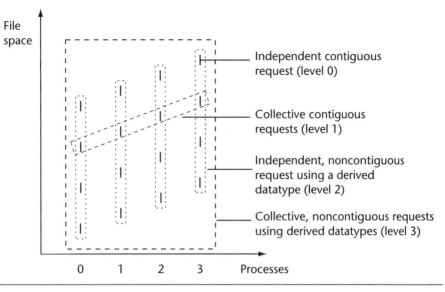

Figure 11.9 The four levels representing increasing amounts of data per request.

The four levels represent increasing amounts of data per request, as illustrated in Figure 11.9.[5] The more the amount of data per request, the greater the opportunity for the implementation to deliver higher performance. How good the performance is at each level depends, of course, on how well the implementation takes advantage of the extra access information at each level. ROMIO, for example, performs data sieving for level-2 requests and collective I/O for level-3 requests. However, it cannot perform these optimizations if the user does not express the access pattern in terms of level-2 or level-3 requests. Users must therefore strive to express their I/O requests as level 3 rather than level 0. Figure 11.10 shows the detailed code for creating a derived data type, defining a file view, and making a level-3 I/O request for the distributed-array example of Figure 11.3.

If an application needs to access only large, contiguous pieces of data, level 0 is equivalent to level 2, and level 1 is equivalent to level 3. Users need not create derived data types in such cases, as level-0 requests themselves will likely perform well. Many real parallel applications, however, do not fall into this category [86, 229, 713, 870, 871, 917].

We note that the MPI standard does not *require* an implementation to perform any of these optimizations. Nevertheless, even if an implementation does not perform

---

[5] In this figure, levels 1 and 2 represent the same amount of data per request, but in general, when the number of noncontiguous accesses per process is greater than the number of processes, level 2 represents more data than level 1.

```
gsizes[0] = num_global_rows;
gsizes[1] = num_global_cols;
distribs[0] = distribs[1] = MPI_DISTRIBUTE_BLOCK;
dargs[0] = dargs[1] = MPI_DISTRIBUTE_DFLT_DARG;
psizes[0] = psizes[1] = 4;
MPI_Comm_rank(MPI_COMM_WORLD, &rank);
MPI_Type_create_darray(16, rank, 2, gsizes, distribs, dargs,
                       psizes, MPI_ORDER_C, MPI_FLOAT,
                       &filetype);
MPI_Type_commit(&filetype);
local_array_size = num_local_rows * num_local_cols;
MPI_File_open(MPI_COMM_WORLD, "/pfs/datafile", MPI_MODE_RDONLY,
              MPI_INFO_NULL, &fh);
MPI_File_set_view(fh, 0, MPI_FLOAT, filetype, "native",
                  MPI_INFO_NULL);
MPI_File_read_all(fh, local_array, local_array_size,
                  MPI_FLOAT, &status);
MPI_File_close(&fh);
```

Figure 11.10   Detailed code for the distributed-array example of Figure 11.3 using a level-3 request.

any optimization and instead translates level-3 requests into several level-0 requests to the file system, the performance would be no worse than if the user directly made level-0 requests. Therefore, there is no reason not to use level-3 requests (or level-2 requests where level-3 requests are not possible).

Performance Results

We present some performance results to demonstrate how the choice of level of request affects performance. We wrote the distributed-array access example using level-0, level-2, and level-3 requests and ran the three versions *portably* on five different parallel machines—HP Exemplar, SGI Origin 2000, IBM SP, Intel Paragon, and NEC SX-4—using ROMIO. (For this particular application, level-1 requests do not contain sufficient information for any useful optimizations, and ROMIO therefore internally translates level-1 requests into level-0 requests.) We used the native file systems on each machine: HFS on the Exemplar, XFS on the Origin 2000, PIOFS on the SP, PFS on the Paragon, and SFS on the SX-4.

We note that the machines had varying amounts of I/O hardware. Some of the differences in performance results among the machines are due to these variations. Our goal in this experiment was to compare the performance of the different levels of requests on a given machine, rather than comparing the performance of different machines.

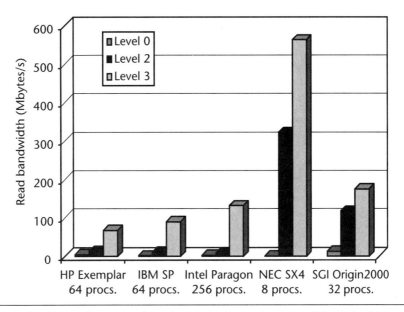

Figure 11.11 Read performance of distributed array access (array size $512 \times 512 \times 512$ integers $= 512$ MB).

Figures 11.11 and 11.12 show the read and write bandwidths. The performance with level-0 requests was, in general, very poor because level-0 requests result in too many small read/write calls. For level-2 requests—for which ROMIO performs data sieving—the read bandwidth improved over level-0 requests by a factor ranging from 2.6 on the HP Exemplar to 453 on the NEC SX-4. Similarly, the write bandwidth improved by a factor ranging from 2.3 on the HP Exemplar to 121 on the NEC SX-4. The performance improved considerably with level-3 requests because ROMIO performs collective I/O in this case. The read bandwidth improved by a factor of as much as 793 over level-0 requests (NEC SX-4) and as much as 14 over level-2 requests (Intel Paragon). Similarly, with level-3 requests, the write performance improved by a factor of as much as 721 over level-0 requests (NEC SX-4) and as much as 40 over level-2 requests (HP Exemplar). It is clearly advantageous to use level-3 requests rather than any other kind of request.

We obtained similar results with other applications as well; see Thakur et al. [919] for details.

Upshot Graphs

We present some graphs that illustrate the reduction in time obtained by using level-2 and level-3 requests instead of level-0 requests for writing a 3-D distributed array of size $128 \times 128 \times 128$ on 32 processors on the Intel Paragon at Caltech. We

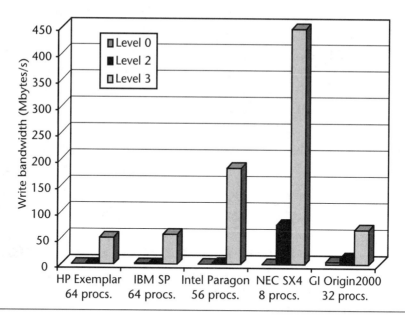

Figure 11.12   Write performance of distributed array access (array size $512 \times 512 \times 512$ integers $= 512$ MB).

instrumented the ROMIO source code to measure the time taken for each file-system call made by ROMIO and also for the computation and communication required for collective I/O. The instrumented code created trace files, which we visualized using a performance visualization tool called Upshot [464].

Plate 7 of the color insert shows the Upshot plot for level-0 requests, where each process makes a separate write function call to write each row of its local array. The numerous small bands represent the numerous writes in the program, as a result of which the total time taken is about 125 seconds. The large white portions are actually lots of writes clustered together, which become visible when you zoom in to the region using Upshot.

Plate 8 of the color insert shows the Upshot plot for level-2 requests, for which ROMIO performs data sieving. In this case, it performed data sieving in blocks of 4 MBytes at a time. Note that the total time has decreased to about 16 seconds compared with 125 seconds for level-0 requests. For writing with data sieving, each process must perform a read-modify-write and also lock the region of the file being written. Because of the need for file locking and a buffer size of 4 MBytes, many processes remain idle waiting to acquire locks. Therefore, only a few write operations take place concurrently. It should be possible to increase parallelism, however, by decreasing the size of the buffer used for data sieving. Plate 9 of the color insert shows the results for a buffer size of 512 KBytes. Since more I/O operations take place in parallel, the total time decreased to 10.5 seconds. A further reduction in buffer size to 64 KBytes (Plate 10 of the color insert) resulted in even greater parallelism, but the I/O time increased because of the smaller granularity of each I/O operation. The performance of data sieving can thus be tuned by varying the size of the buffer used for data sieving, which can be done via the hints mechanism in MPI-IO.

Plate 11 of the color insert shows the Upshot plot for level-3 requests, for which ROMIO performs collective I/O. The total time decreased to about 2.75 seconds, which means that level-3 requests were about 45 times faster than level-0 requests and about four times faster than the best performance with level-2 requests. The reason for the improvement is that the numerous writes of each process were coalesced into a *single* write at the expense of some extra computation (to figure out how to merge the requests) and interprocess communication. With collective I/O, the actual write time was only a small fraction of the total I/O time; for example, file open took longer than the write.

11.5 Conclusion

I/O on parallel computers has always been slow compared with computation and communication. As computers get larger and faster, I/O becomes even more of a problem. In this chapter we have provided a general introduction to the field of parallel I/O. Our emphasis has been on the practical aspects of *using* parallel I/O and achieving high performance. By following the guidelines presented, we believe that users *can* achieve high I/O performance in parallel applications.

Acknowledgments. This work was supported by the Mathematical, Information, and Computational Sciences Division subprogram of the Office of Advanced Scientific Computing Research, U.S. Department of Energy, under contract W-31-109-Eng-38.

12

Languages and Compilers

Ken Kennedy • Charles Koelbel

Because parallel computing is significantly more complicated than serial computing, it places significant burdens on the application developer. In addition to developing a correct problem solution, the user must also control and coordinate the uses of parallelism in the solution program. This is even more complicated because the methodology and mechanisms for exerting control may differ from target platform to target platform.

As a result, high-performance parallel computing presents significant challenges and opportunities for programming language designers, compiler implementors, and run-time system developers. If program development support software can make it easier for programmers to design, implement, debug, and tune parallel programs on a variety of target platforms, parallelism may become accessible to the larger community of application developers.

To understand the nature of the challenge for programming support software, we must consider the process for development of parallel applications. The implementor must be able to find opportunities for parallelism in his or her application, express the parallelism in a machine-independent way, and debug and tune the resulting application for a particular parallel platform. In designing language and compiler support for this process, we must keep three goals firmly in mind:

- *Programming should be as easy as possible.* The end user should experience only slightly more complexity than for development of uniprocessor programs.

- *The resulting programs should be portable across platforms with modest effort.* It should not be necessary to maintain multiple source versions of the same program. Rather it should be possible to move the same source to each platform, adjust some tuning parameters, and run with nearly the full performance available on the machine.

- *The programmer should retain as much control over performance as possible.* If performance problems develop, it should be possible for the programmer to address them within the high-level programming model—that is, without having to resort to modification of low-level code generated from the high-level representation.

These seemingly conflicting goals will be difficult to achieve because parallelism presents significant challenges to the application developer. To achieve these goals, the programming system will need to solve three fundamental problems:

1. It must find extensive parallelism in the application presented by the user. It must then package and coordinate that parallelism during execution. Finding parallelism may involve a transfer of information from the user, but it must be possible to get this information without forcing a complete revision of the application.

2. It must overcome performance penalties due to the complex memory hierarchies on modern parallel computers. This could involve extensive program transformations to increase locality. This is more challenging on parallel computers because there is often a tradeoff between increasing parallelism and finding locality.

3. It must support migration of parallel programs to different architectures with only modest changes. This will entail development of a programming interface that is not machine specific and strategies for optimizing and tuning applications for different architectures.

In designing strategies for support of parallel programming, we must keep in mind the principle that each component of the system should do what it does best.

- The *application developer* should be able to concentrate on problem analysis and decomposition at a fairly high level of abstraction.

- The *system*, including the programming language and compiler, should handle the details of mapping the abstract decomposition onto the computing configuration available at any given moment.

- The *application developer and the system* should work together to produce a correct and efficient program through the use of execution monitoring, debugging, and tuning tools.

This chapter explores four technologies that have been reasonably successful in meeting the goals of parallel programming support for scientific computation: automatic parallelization; data-parallel languages (High Performance Fortran); shared-memory, parallel programming interfaces (OpenMP); and single-program, multiple-data (SPMD) languages (Co-Array Fortran). (Parallel object-oriented programming is considered in Chapter 13.) The intent of our presentation is to give a somewhat tutorial introduction to these technologies, while providing background on the intellectual development that led to them and an assessment of their usefulness.

12.1 Automatic Parallelization

From the user's perspective, the most appealing approach to program decomposition is automatic parallelization. If a fully automatic system could efficiently parallelize applications, the user would be free to concentrate on *what* is being computed rather than *how* it is being computed. However, to be acceptable, a fully automatic scheme must generate code that achieves performance competitive with programs hand-coded by experts. Object-program performance has been a significant factor in the acceptance of new programming languages since the original Fortran I compiler. This observation is based on strong evidence, including this reflection by John Backus [66]:

> It was our belief that if FORTRAN, during its first months, were to trans-late any reasonable "scientific" source program into an object program only half as fast as its hand-coded counterpart, then acceptance of our system would be in serious danger. . . . To this day I believe that our em-phasis on object program efficiency rather than on language design was basically correct. I believe that had we failed to produce efficient pro-grams, the widespread use of languages like FORTRAN would have been seriously delayed.

Automatic parallelization research began in the 1970s as *automatic vectorization*, a technology to support portable programming on vector processors. The important technological tool used in automatic vectorization is *dependence analysis*, which seeks to determine whether pairs of references to the same data structure (usually a subscripted variable) may access the same memory location [582, 583]. An example loop suggests how this can be done:

```
REAL A(1000,1000)
DO J = 2, N
  DO I = 2, N
    A(I,J) = (A(I,J+1)+ 2*A(I,J) + A(I,J-1))*0.25
  ENDDO
ENDDO
```

Any particular element in the interior of the array, say $A(m_1,m_2)$ will be accessed on three iterations of the loop nest: $(I = m_1, J = m_2 - 1)$, $(I = m_1, J = m_2)$, and $(I = m_1, J = m_2 + 1)$. Iteration $(I = m_1, J = m_2)$ also assigns to that element. Therefore, the J loop iterations must execute in the correct order, for a fixed value of I, to avoid overwriting the element while the "old" value is still needed. However, the I loop iterations never interfere with each other and therefore can execute in any order, including overlapped execution. In other words, the I loop is vectorizable while the J loop is not. Dependence analysis formalizes this test.

Returning to our example above, we see that there are two dependences from the assignment to itself—a dependence from the store to a use of A(I,J-1) on the next iteration and an *antidependence* (needed to ensure that loads do not move before stores) from the use of A(I,J+1) to the store into A(I,J) on the next iteration. These two dependences arise from the iteration of the loop on index J, so we say that they are *carried* by that loop. In terms of dependence, the test for vectorization can be stated as follows: A statement can be vectorized with respect to a given loop if that statement is not part of a dependence cycle carried by that loop. Hence, we see in the example above that the J-loop is not vectorizable, but the I-loop is. The code can therefore be rewritten in Fortran 90 as follows:

```
REAL A(1000,1000)
DO J = 2, N
  A(2:N,J) = (A(2:N,J+1)+ 2*A(2:N,J) + A(2:N,J-1))*0.25
ENDDO
```

Vectorizers based on dependence analysis matured into extremely useful tools by the mid-1980s and came to be standard on all vector machines [26, 1001]. Yet in spite of the sophistication of vectorizing compilers, it was still not possible to present a naively coded Fortran program to any of them with the expectation of achieving high performance. Some subscripts simply cannot be fully checked by compile-time dependence analysis. In particular, references such as A(IND(I)) require run-time information not available to the compiler. Virtually every program had to be rewritten so that the computationally intensive loops were vectorizable. One can therefore characterize the contribution of vectorizing compilers as defining a subdialect of Fortran—the "vectorizable loop" subdialect—for which high performance would be achieved on virtually every vector machine.

Building on the success of vectorization, the research and development community turned its attention to automatic parallelization for multiple-instruction, multiple-data (MIMD) architectures with shared memory [24, 25, 28, 75, 582, 1000, 1001]. For configurations with modest numbers of processors, the technology of automatic vectorization could be employed with good results. However, parallel computers soon moved to distributed-memory architectures, as described in Chapter 2. This made the automatic parallelization problem far more complex; the compiler now had the additional task of determining how to partition data to the memories of a processor in a way that maximized the number of local memory accesses and minimized communication, which was relatively expensive on such machines [29, 168, 171, 1019]. Moreover, the compiler and run-time system had the task of arranging the communication operations themselves, which were far more complex than the simple loads and stores needed on shared-memory machines.

Another important implication of the new architectures was that, even on shared-memory parallel computers, the regions of parallel execution had to be large enough to compensate for the overhead of initiating and synchronizing the parallel computation. This led to research on how the compiler could find larger program regions to run in parallel. Dependence analysis, which worked so well for vectorization, now had to be applied over larger regions of the program, even across procedure boundaries. This led to research on *interprocedural analysis and optimization*, by which a program and all its subroutines are analyzed as a whole [76, 82, 156, 221, 222, 428, 429, 942].

Through the use of increasingly complex analysis and optimization technologies, research compilers have been able to parallelize a number of interesting programs. However, due to the complexity of the techniques, the long compiler running times, and the small number of successful demonstrations, there exist few commercial compilers that attempt to parallelize whole applications on scalable parallel machines. Although this research has yielded many important new compilation techniques, it is now widely believed that automatic parallelization, by itself, is not enough to solve the parallel programming problem.

As a result of these observations, research has turned increasingly to language-based strategies that can get more information from the user, while exploiting techniques from automatic parallelization to lessen the burden of programming.

12.2 Data-Parallel Programming in High Performance Fortran

Early in the research efforts on parallel computing, Fox and others observed that the key to achieving high performance on distributed-memory machines is to allocate data to the various processor memories to maximize locality and minimize communication [358]. Once this is done, if each computation in a program is performed on the processor where most of the data involved in that computation resides, the program can be executed with high efficiency.

A second important observation is that if parallelism is to scale to hundreds or thousands of processors, *data parallelism* must be effectively exploited. Data parallelism is parallelism that derives from subdividing the (presumably large) data domain in some manner and assigning the subdomains to different processors. This strategy provides a natural fit with data layout, because the data layout falls naturally out of the division into subdomains.

These observations are the foundation for data-parallel languages, which provide mechanisms for supporting data parallelism, particularly through data layout. A number of such languages were developed in the late 1980s and early 1990s, including Fortran D [356, 475], Vienna Fortran [188, 1018], CM Fortran [921], C* [432], data-parallel C, and PC++ [641]. These research efforts were the precursors of informal standardization activities leading to High Performance Fortran (HPF) [468]. (A similar informal standardization effort led to HPC++ [516], described in Chapter 13.)

The idea behind High Performance Fortran, an extended version of Fortran 90 generated by an informal standardization process in the early 1990s, is to automate most of the details of managing data. It accomplishes this goal by providing a set of directives that the user inserts to describe the data layout. The compiler and run-time system translate these high-level directives into the complex low-level operations that actually communicate the data and synchronize processors when needed. An important quality of the layout directives is that they have no effect on the meaning of the program—they merely provide advice to the compiler on how to assign elements of the program arrays and other data structures to different processors for high performance. This layout specification is relatively machine independent; once it exists, the program can be tailored by the compiler to run on any of a variety of distributed-memory machines.

HPF provides fairly fine-grained control over data layout of arrays through directives, encoded as structured comments that extend the variable type declarations. We illustrate this by extending the example of the last section:

```
REAL A(1000,1000), B(1000,1000)
DO J = 2, N
  DO I = 2, N
    A(I,J) = (A(I,J+1)+ 2*A(I,J) + A(I,J-1))*0.25 &
            + (B(I+1,J)+ 2*B(I,J) + B(I-1,J))*0.25
  ENDDO
ENDDO
```

The DISTRIBUTE directive specifies how to partition a data array onto the memories of a real parallel machine. In this case, it is most natural to distribute the first dimension, since iterations over it can be performed in parallel. For example, the programmer can distribute data in contiguous chunks across the available processors by inserting the directive

```
!HPF$ DISTRIBUTE A(BLOCK,*)
```

after the declaration of A. HPF also provides other standard distribution patterns, including CYCLIC in which elements are assigned to processors in round-robin fashion, or CYCLIC(K) by which blocks of K elements are assigned round-robin to processors. Generally speaking, BLOCK is the preferred distribution for computations with nearest-neighbor elementwise communication, while the CYCLIC variants allow finer load balancing of some computations. Also, in many computations (including the example above), different data arrays should use the same or related data layouts. The ALIGN directive specifies an elementwise matching between arrays in these cases. For example, to give array B the same distribution as A, the programmer would use the directive

```
!HPF$ ALIGN B(I,J) WITH A(I,J).
```

Integer linear functions of the subscripts are also allowed in ALIGN and are useful for matching arrays of different shapes.[1]

In addition to the distribution directives, HPF has special directives that can be used to assist in the identification of parallelism. Because HPF is based on Fortran 90, it also has array operations to express elementwise parallelism directly. These operations are particularly appropriate when applied to a distributed dimension, in which

---

[1] In fact, other alignments would produce better performance for our example. However, we use the direct alignment above to illustrate points about communication later.

case the compiler can (relatively) easily manage the synchronization and data movement together. Using array notation in this example produces the following:

```
REAL A(1000,1000), B(1000,1000)
!HPF$ DISTRIBUTE A(BLOCK,*)
!HPF$ ALIGN B(I,J) WITH A(I,J)
DO J = 2, N
  A(2:N,J) = (A(2:N,J+1)+ 2*A(2:N,J) + A(2:N,J-1))*0.25 &
           + (B(3:N+1,J)+ 2*B(2:N,J) + B(1:N-1,J))*0.25
ENDDO
```

Alternately, the programmer could retain the loop notation but explicitly identify the
inner loop as parallel. The INDEPENDENT directive specifies that the loop that follows
is safe to execute in parallel. In our example, this appears as

```
REAL A(1000,1000), B(1000,1000)
!HPF$ DISTRIBUTE A(BLOCK,*)
!HPF$ ALIGN B(I,J) WITH A(I,J)
DO J = 2, N
  !HPF$ INDEPENDENT
  DO I = 2, N
    A(I,J) = (A(I,J+1)+ 2*A(I,J) + A(I,J-1))*0.25 &
           + (B(I+1,J)+ 2*B(I,J) + B(I-1,J))*0.25
  ENDDO
ENDDO
```

Many compilers can detect this fact for themselves using the dependence analysis
discussed in Section 12.1. However, the directive ensures that all compilers to which
the program is presented can do so. The INDEPENDENT directive is even more important for loops that are theoretically unanalyzable; often the programmer will have
application-specific knowledge that allows the loop to be executed in parallel.

Using either of the above notations (or relying on the compiler dependence analysis) puts the burden of efficiently executing the loop on the HPF implementation.
A typical implementation would distribute the computations in loop iterations according to the *owner-computes* rule, by which the processor owning the array element
on the left-hand side of the assignment statement would perform the computation
for each iteration. In the above example, if there are 25 processors, the first processor
would handle iterations 2 through 40, the second would handle 41 through 80, and
so on. These calculations would be done completely in parallel. Note, however, that
the references to B(I-1,J) and B(I+1,J) give rise to communication when I is equal
to $40k$ and $40k+1$, respectively. The compiler would generate this communication
automatically and would package the communication to optimize performance. On
distributed-memory machines, this packaging would generally consist of sending all
required values of B before the start of the loop body, thus avoiding repeated message
start-ups.

The HPF compiler must often go to substantial lengths to preserve the meaning of the underlying Fortran 90 program. For example, we might code a sum reduction loop as follows:

```
REAL A(10000)
!HPF$ DISTRIBUTE A(BLOCK)
X = 0.0
DO I = 1, 10000
   X = X + A(I)
ENDDO
```

Although this is much simpler than the equivalent message-passing program written in MPI, it has a downside—the compiler must do a substantial amount of work to generate a program that displays reasonable efficiency. In particular, it must recognize that the main calculation is a sum reduction and replicate the values of X on each processor. Then it must generate the final parallel sum at the end. HPF provides directives that make it possible for the user to help the system recognize such opportunities.

In the example above, the usual INDEPENDENT directive would not be applicable because the repeated assignments to X create a data dependence. However, because reduction is a common operation with special properties that allow parallelization, HPF provides an additional clause for the directive to handle it:

```
REAL A(10000)
!HPF$ DISTRIBUTE A(BLOCK)
X = 0.0
!HPF$ INDEPENDENT, REDUCTION(X)
DO I = 1, 10000
   X = X + A(I)
ENDDO
```

This version is easier for the compiler to process into an efficient program. We note in passing that there is also a standard intrinsic function available for this reduction:

```
REAL A(10000)
!HPF$ DISTRIBUTE A(BLOCK)
X = SUM(A)
```

The compiler can implement this as a library function or by expanding the sum in-line. In either case, the generated code will operate as described above.

As a final example, we present a simple HPF code fragment that is intended to model parts of a multigrid method. All arrays are aligned to a "master," which is the finest grid level; that grid is distributed in both dimensions to get maximal locality. We use INDEPENDENT directives to ensure portability across compilers that might not recognize the parallelism in the computation loops; we could equally well have used array syntax.

```
REAL A(1023,1023), B(1023,1023), APRIME(511,511)
!HPF$ ALIGN B(I,J) WITH A(I,J)
!HPF$ ALIGN APRIME(I,J) WITH A(2*I-1,2*J-1)
!HPF$ DISTRIBUTE A(BLOCK,BLOCK)

!HPF$ INDEPENDENT, NEW(I)
DO J = 2, 1022  ! Multigrid Smoothing (Red-Black)
   !HPF$   INDEPENDENT
   DO I = MOD(J,2)+2, 1022, 2
      A(I,J) = 0.25*(A(I+1,J) + A(I-1,J) + &
               A(I,J-1) + A(I,J+1)) + B(I,J)
   ENDDO
ENDDO

!HPF$ INDEPENDENT, NEW(I)
DO J = 2, 510   ! Multigrid Restriction
   !HPF$   INDEPENDENT
   DO I = 2, 510
      APRIME(I,J) = 0.05*(A(2*I-2,2*J-2) + &
         4*A(2*I-2,2*J-1) + A(2*I-2,2*J) + &
         4*A(2*I-1,2*J-2) + 4*A(2*I-1,2*J) + &
         A(2*I,2*J-2) + 4*A(2*I,2*J-1) + &
         A(2*I,2*J))
   ENDDO
ENDDO
```

In the example, the qualifier NEW(I) is used in the INDEPENDENT directive for the outer loop to ensure that the inner loop induction variable I is replicated on each group of processors that execute different iterations of the outer loop. This is roughly equivalent to the PRIVATE directive in other parallel dialects.

HPF compilation has been the subject of substantial research and development [9, 33, 45, 134, 135, 138, 417, 438, 475, 956, 1019]. Eleven companies currently offer HPF products, and over 30 applications have been or are being written in it, including some having over 100,000 lines.

A major drawback of HPF is its limited support for problems defined on irregular meshes, which represent a fairly large fraction of important science and engineering applications. To address this and other problems, the HPF Forum completed a second round of HPF standardization to produce HPF 2.0 [468], which includes important irregular distributions such as distribution indirectly via a run-time array and the generalized block distribution, which allows blocks to be of different sizes.

12.3   Shared-Memory Parallel Programming in OpenMP

Although HPF provides excellent facilities for specifying data distribution, its mechanisms for specifying explicit parallelism are fairly limited. Principal among these is the INDEPENDENT directive discussed in the previous section. Control of the parallelism in HPF is *implicit*; the system, not the programmer, assigns work to processors. Moreover, the control is linked to the partitioning of data among processor memories. On machines where the entire system memory is shared among all processors, such implicit methods seem obscure. Furthermore, types of parallelism other than data parallelism are often profitable on such machines, but not well supported by HPF.

Although a number of machine vendors produced mechanisms for explicit specification of parallelism in the late 1980s, there was no widely accepted parallel language standard for shared-memory parallel machines. To address this deficiency, the Parallel Computer Forum began an open standardization process that led to the definition of PCF Fortran [740] and eventually to the ANSI abstract interface standard X3H5 [43]. PCF Fortran combined the facilities of two programming models: loop parallelism and task parallelism. PCF Fortran included a feature called *parallel regions*, which were constructs within which tasks could be defined and concurrently executed. Standalone parallel loops were also included in the specification as a shorthand for a parallel region that exactly brackets a work-distribution loop.

The PCF/X3H5 standard lay fallow until 1997, when an industry consortium led by Silicon Graphics refined and simplified these ideas to produce OpenMP, an informal standard parallel-programming interface with bindings to Fortran 77 and C. The consortium later extended those bindings to include Fortran 95 and is studying additions for C++. OpenMP drew strongly on the ideas from PCF Fortran, and it adopted the directive conventions as in HPF to specify parallelism in the program. As in HPF, OpenMP directives in a standard-conforming program can be ignored as comments by a uniprocessor compiler with no difference in results. In this section, we focus on OpenMP because it is the most recent and widely used of these systems; however, many of the technical ideas were common to the PCF Fortran and ANSI X3H5 dialects.

Perhaps the simplest way to specify parallelism in OpenMP is via an explicitly parallel loop, bracketed by the PARALLEL DO and the END PARALLEL DO directives. The PARALLEL DO directive can have a number of qualifying clauses that permit the specification of variables that are private to threads executing individual loop iterations and variables that are used in a reduction. The following example of a PARALLEL DO loop computes a simple relaxation step:

```
!$OMP PARALLEL DO
DO I = 2, N
   APRIME(I) = (A(I+1) +2*A(I) + A(I-1))*0.25
ENDDO
```

Note here that the loop induction variable I is private by default. The END PARALLEL DO directive is optional. OpenMP provides mechanisms for specifying how the iterations of a parallel loop are to be assigned to threads within a team. The following variant will assign contiguous blocks of iterations to a single thread at compile time.

```
!$OMP PARALLEL DO SCHEDULE(STATIC)
DO I = 2, N
   APRIME(I) = (A(I+1) +2*A(I) + A(I-1))*0.25
ENDDO
```

Under this specification, each thread would get a single contiguous block of iterations. This is roughly equivalent to the effect that would be achieved in HPF by declaring APRIME to have a BLOCK distribution. The effect of a BLOCK(K) distribution can be achieved by explicitly specifying a chunk size:

```
!$OMP PARALLEL DO SCHEDULE(STATIC,10)
DO I = 2, N
   APRIME(I) = (A(I+1) +2*A(I) + A(I-1))*0.25
ENDDO
```

This loop will hand out chunks of 10 iterations to threads in round-robin fashion in the order of the thread number. If the keyword STATIC is replaced by DYNAMIC in the above loop, chunks would be distributed to threads at run-time as those threads became ready to execute. OpenMP also permits GUIDED scheduling, in which chunk sizes decrease as the remaining number of iterations decreases, and RUNTIME scheduling, in which the scheduling and chunk size can be selected at run-time by setting environment variables. This permits the algorithm to make dynamic choices based on conditions discovered in the data.

To illustrate the reduction mechanism, we present the global sum example from HPF, rewritten to use the OpenMP directives:

```
REAL A(10000)
X = 0.0
!$OMP PARALLEL DO REDUCTION(+: X)
DO I = 1, 10000
   X = X + A(I)
ENDDO
```

This example is strikingly similar to its HPF counterpart. The REDUCTION clause specifies that the final value of variable X is determined by summing the final values in all of the threads executing iterations of the loop.

Task parallelism can be achieved in OpenMP through the PARALLEL SECTIONS directive. The following example illustrates its usage on a two-processor version of a routine to find the maximum of a set of numbers:

```
!$OMP PARALLEL SECTIONS PRIVATE(I), LASTPRIVATE(MAX1,MAX2)
!$OMP SECTION
```

```
     IF (N>=1) THEN MAX1 = 1 ELSE MAX1 = 0
     DO I = 2, N/2
        IF(A(I)>A(MAX1)) THEN MAX1 = I
     ENDDO
!$OMP SECTION
     IF (N>=N/2+1) THEN MAX2 = N/2+1 ELSE MAX2 = 0
     DO I = N/2+2,N
        IF(A(I)>A(MAX2)) THEN MAX2 = I
     ENDDO
!$OMP END PARALLEL SECTIONS
     IF (MAX1>0) THEN
        IF (A(MAX2)>A(MAX1)) THEN IMAX = MAX2 ELSE IMAX = MAX1
     ELSE
        IMAX = 0
     ENDIF
```

The LASTPRIVATE clause on the SECTIONS directive indicates that MAX1 and MAX2 are private to threads that execute the sections, but they retain their last value on exit from the clause. Indeed, these variables are tested outside the region to determine which is the index of the larger value.

OpenMP also provides lock variables to allow fine-grain synchronization between threads. We illustrate this by an example of parallelizing a simple relaxation code using wavefront parallelism. The scalar computation looks like this:

```
PARAMETER (N  = 2048) ! Total number of elements
REAL A(N,N)

DO J = 2, N-1
  DO I = 2, N-1
    A(I,J) = 0.25*(A(I+1,J) + A(I-1,J) + A(I,J-1) + A(I,J+1))
  ENDDO
ENDDO
```

A simple PARALLEL DO cannot be used in this case, because both the J and I loops carry data dependences. However, the computation can be partially parallelized in pipeline fashion as follows. Partition each column (by blocks) among the threads. At the beginning of each processor's section of the column, force the calculation of A(I,J) to wait until the thread computing A(I-1,J) finishes that calculation, so that it can get the correct input value. Lock variables do exactly this type of waiting; only one thread may hold a lock at any given time, forcing others to delay until it is finished. A 2-D array of OpenMP locks can therefore handle the synchronization as follows:

```
PARAMETER (NP = 8)     ! # of processors
PARAMETER (NEP = 256)  ! # of elements per processor
PARAMETER (N  = NP*NEP) ! Total # of elements
```

```
REAL A(N,N)
INTEGER LCK(NP,N)

!$OMP PARALLEL PRIVATE(ME,JLO,JHI,I,J)
ME = OMP_GET_THREAD_NUM()+1    ! This thread's id
ILO = MAX( 2, (ME-1)*NEP+1 )   ! Thread's starting point
IHI = MIN( N-1, ME*NEP )        ! Thread's ending point

! Initialize the locks
DO J = 2, N-1
   CALL OMP_INIT_LOCK( LCK(ME,J) ) ! Leaves lock unset
   IF (ME>1) CALL OMP_SET_LOCK( LCK(ME,J) )
ENDDO
! Make sure other threads have done their initialization
!$OMP BARRIER

! Execute this thread's portion of the loop nest
DO J = 2, N-1
   IF (ME>1) THEN
      ! Wait to acquire lock, then go forward
      CALL OMP_SET_LOCK(LCK(ME-1,J)) ! Waits for lock unset
      CALL OMP_UNSET_LOCK(LCK(ME-1,J))
   ENDIF
   DO I = ILO, IHI
      A(I,J) = 0.25*(A(I+1,J) + A(I-1,J) + A(I,J-1) + A(I,J+1))
   ENDDO
   CALL OMP_UNSET_LOCK( LCK(ME,J) )
ENDDO

!$OMP END PARALLEL
```

We should note that this code is likely to be impractical on most implementations because of the overhead in time and space of managing so many locks. We can reduce the number of locks by synchronizing groups of columns, rather than one at a time. This sacrifices some parallelism (by delaying the start of the pipeline on some processors) in exchange for reducing the overall overhead. The optimal number of columns to group in this way will depend on the parameters of the machine, but the outline of the blocked code would always be similar to the following:

```
PARAMETER (NP = 8)        ! # of processors
PARAMETER (NB = 16)       ! # of blocks
PARAMETER (NEB = 16)      ! # of elements per block
PARAMETER (NEP = NB*NEB)  ! # of elements per processor
PARAMETER (N  = NP*NEP)   ! Total # of elements
```

```
      REAL A(N,N)
      INTEGER LCK(NP,NB)

!$OMP PARALLEL  PRIVATE(ME,JLO,JHI,I,J,JJ,JLO,JHI)
      ME = OMP_GET_THREAD_NUM()+1    ! This thread's id
      ILO = MAX( 2, (ME-1)*NEP+1 )
      IHI = MIN( N-1, ME*NEP )


      ! Initialize the locks
      DO JJ = 1, NB
         CALL OMP_INIT_LOCK( LCK(ME,JJ) )
         IF (ME>1) CALL OMP_SET_LOCK( LCK(ME,JJ) )
      ENDDO
!$OMP BARRIER

      ! Execute this thread's portion of the loop nest
      DO JJ = 1, NB
        JLO = MAX( 2, (JJ-1)*NEB+1 )
        JHI = MIN( N-1, JJ*NEB )
        IF (ME>1) THEN
           ! Wait to acquire lock, then go forward
           CALL OMP_SET_LOCK(LCK(ME-1,JJ))
           CALL OMP_UNSET_LOCK(LCK(ME-1,JJ))
        ENDIF
        DO J = JLO, JHI
          DO I = ILO, IHI
            A(I,J) = 0.25*(A(I+1,J) + A(I-1,J) + A(I,J-1) + A(I,J+1))
          ENDDO
        ENDDO
        CALL OMP_UNSET_LOCK( LCK(ME,JJ) )
      ENDDO

!$OMP END PARALLEL
```

OpenMP is an excellent programming interface for uniform-access, shared-memory machines. However, it provides the user with no way to specify locality in machines with nonuniform shared memory or distributed memory. On clusters of multiprocessor workstations, it is often used in conjunction with MPI, with OpenMP used for nodes and MPI used for message passing among nodes. A mixture of OpenMP and HPF directives seems a promising way to provide programming support for modern machines with a mixture of shared-memory and distributed-memory parallelism. An alternate approach is found in single-program, multiple-data languages discussed in the next section.

12.4   Single-Program, Multiple-Data Programming in Co-Array Fortran

Single-program, multiple-data (SPMD) programming, introduced in Section 3.2, is a common strategy for implementing parallel programs. The basic idea is that all the processors or threads available to the program execute the entire program. This execution is redundant[2] unless and until the threads encounter a special work-distribution construct or synchronization operation. The exact synchronization operations differ from language to language. One advantage of the SPMD strategy is that each thread builds up its own replicated copy of the program state in local memory, enhancing the locality of references in the code. It is also conceptually clear to most programmers and conveniently implemented by generating and loading the same object code for all processors.

Starting in the 1980s, early SPMD systems such as The Force [525] and IBM's VM/EPEX [245, 246] implemented this idea on shared-memory computers. Access to shared data structures such as arrays required synchronization, either through the work-sharing constructs such as parallel loops or through explicit operations such as locks, to avoid race conditions. Lessons from these languages found their way into other shared-memory languages, as we saw in Section 12.3. At the time, the full implications of cache-coherence protocols had not been grasped, and therefore the languages generally assumed a coherent underlying memory. With the advent of distributed-memory architectures in the 1990s, message-passing programs were generally written in SPMD style, although not in a new SPMD language. That is, programs using the MPI library [878] or PVM library [371] typically assumed that all processes (or processors) ran the identical program. Chapter 10 discusses such message-passing programs in more detail. Here, we simply note that for these SPMD programs, all data was local to a process and all communication was explicit. At about the same time, a new generation of languages such as Split-C [235] and AC [172] was including support for asynchronous memory operations. These reflected the relaxed consistency models described in Section 2.2.1, and again used an SPMD programming paradigm. This meant that there were primitives for synchronization and access to shared data, but with a different set of assumptions about how the access was carried out. Co-Array Fortran [719] (originally known as F--) borrows from all of these influences.

As with all SPMD languages, Co-Array Fortran assumes that multiple copies of the program (called *images*) execute asynchronously. By default, data objects are replicated in all images and may have different values in the different images. However, an array declared with an additional co-dimension specified in square brackets becomes a co-array that is accessible by all the images. The extent of the co-dimension is the same as the number of images. For example, the following

---

[2] For simplicity of presentation, we temporarily ignore the race conditions caused by "redundant" execution of assignments to shared data.

declarations define co-arrays X, Y, and Z whose local sections in each image are a 10-element vector, a 4×4 matrix, and a $\frac{1000}{\text{NUM\_IMAGES()}} \times 1000$ matrix:

```
REAL X(10)[*], Y(4,4)[*]
REAL Z(1000/NUM_IMAGES(),1000)[*]
```

Because NUM_IMAGES is an intrinsic function returning the number of images, the last example is roughly equivalent to the HPF array with (BLOCK,*) distribution discussed earlier. A co-array can have more than one co-dimension to reflect multidimensional processor layouts.

Programs can use the co-dimension as they would any other dimension. This allows simple expressions to communicate data between images. For example, here is the extended grid smoothing example from Section 12.3 rewritten in Co-Array Fortran:

```
PARAMETER(MY_N = 1000/NUM_IMAGES())
REAL A(0:MY_N+1)[*], APRIME(0:MY_N+1)[*]
ME = THIS_IMAGE()
IF (ME > 1) THEN
  MY_LO = 1
  A(0)[ME] = A(MY_N)[ME-1]
ELSE
  MY_LO = 2
ENDIF
IF (N > ME*MY_N) THEN
  MY_HI = MY_N
  A(MY_N+1)[ME] = A(1)[ME+1]
ELSE
  MY_HI = N - (ME-1)*MY_N
ENDIF
DO I = MY_LO, MY_HI
  APRIME(I)[ME] = (A(I+1)[ME] + 2*A(I)[ME] + A(I-1)[ME])*0.25
ENDDO
```

The explicit computations of the local bounds for the I loop are similar in form and function to those in message-passing programs. The [ME] designation in the co-array references means that each image updates only its own data. In other words, this example uses the owner-computes rule discussed in Section 12.2, although doing so is not a requirement of the language. The references to A(MY_N)[ME-1] and A(1)[ME+1] bring in the data from other images. Although this example was somewhat trivial, much more complex communications operations can easily be specified using regular section notation. Note that only one image needs to specify the communication, rather than the two-sided protocols described in Chapter 10. If Co-Array Fortran is implemented on hardware that does not support one-sided communication, then the compiler or run-time system must insert appropriate communication calls in the executing code. The analysis to do this is similar to that needed to generate communication in HPF.

It is important to note that synchronization is not automatic in Co-Array Fortran. Repeated smoothing operations would need synchronization operations, perhaps as follows:

```
! declarations, ME, MY_LO, MY_HI set as above
DO J = 1, NITER
 CALL SYNCH_ALL()
 IF (ME > 1)      A(0)[ME] = A(MY_N)[ME-1]
 IF (N > ME*MY_N) A(MY_N+1)[ME] = A(1)[ME+1]
 DO I = MY_LO, MY_HI
  APRIME(I)[ME] = (A(I+1)[ME] + 2*A(I)[ME] + A(I-1)[ME])*0.25
 ENDDO
 A(:)[ME] = APRIME(:)[ME]
ENDDO
```

The SYNCH_ALL call forces all images to wait for the previous iteration to finish on other images, as the OpenMP PARALLEL DO construct does by default. Co-Array Fortran also provides SYNCH_TEAM and SYNCH_MEMORY to synchronize subsets of the images with less global overhead.

Co-Array Fortran uses the standard Fortran 90 reduction operations to perform global reductions. For example, the sum of a co-array can be computed as follows:

```
PARAMETER(MY_N = 10000/NUM_IMAGES())
REAL A(MY_N)[*]
ME = THIS_IMAGE()
X = SUM(A(:)[:])
```

The co-dimension subscript [:] specifies that all images contribute to the global operation. In this case, the compiler would emit a collective communications operation. Some other uses of intrinsic reductions would require communications, such as gathering data into a single image.

Co-Array Fortran generally makes communication and synchronization requirements more explicit than HPF and OpenMP. This allows greater tuning, but sometimes requires detailed coding. Perhaps this is best appreciated by examining the Co-Array Fortran version of the final examples from Sections 12.2 and 12.3.

Translating the HPF multigrid code fragment (in Section 12.2) into Co-Array Fortran yields the following:

```
PARAMETER( N = 1023 )
PARAMETER( NP = NUM_IMAGES() )
PARAMETER( NP1 = 2**(LOG2_IMAGES()/2), NP2 = NP/NP1 )
PARAMETER( NEP1 = (N+1)/NP1, NEP2=(N+1)/NEP2 )
PARAMETER( MEP1 = (N+1)/(2*NP1), MEP2=(N+1)/(2*NP2) )
REAL A(0:NEP1+1,0:NEP2+1)[NP1,*]
```

```
REAL B(NEP1,NEP2)[NP1,*]
REAL APRIME(MEP1,MEP2)[NP1,*]
INTEGER NBR1(3), NBR2(3)

ME=THIS_IMAGE(); ME1=MOD(ME,NP1)+1; ME2=ME/NP1+1

! Initial assignments to overlap areas
CALL SYNCH_ALL()
NNBR1 = 1; NBR1(1) = ME
IF (ME1>1) THEN
  A(0,1:NEP2)[ME1,ME2] = A(NEP1,1:NEP2)[ME1-1,ME2]
  NNBR1 = NNBR1+1; NBR1(NNBR1) = ME1-2 + NP1*(ME2-1)
ELSE
  A(0,1:NEP2)[ME1,ME2] = -1.0 ! dummy value
ENDIF
IF (ME1<NP1) THEN
  A(NEP1+1,1:NEP2)[ME1,ME2] = A(1,1:NEP2)[ME1+1,ME2]
  NNBR1 = NNBR1+1; NBR1(NNBR1) = ME1 + NP1*(ME2-1)
ELSE
  A(NEP1+1,1:NEP2)[ME1,ME2] = -2.0 ! dummy value
ENDIF
NNBR2 = 1; NBR2(1) = ME
IF (ME2>1) THEN
  A(1:NEP1,0)[ME1,ME2] = A(1:NEP1,NEP2)[ME1,ME2-1]
  NNBR2 = NNBR2+1; NBR2(NNBR2) = ME1-1 + NP1*(ME2-2)
ELSE
  A(1:NEP1,0)[ME1,ME2] = -3.0 ! dummy value
ENDIF
IF (ME2<NP2) THEN
  A(1:NEP1,NEP2+1)[ME1,ME2] = A(1:NEP1,1)[ME1,ME2+1]
  NNBR2 = NNBR2+1; NBR2(NNBR2) = ME1-1 + NP1*(ME2)
ELSE
  A(1:NEP1,NEP2+1)[ME1,ME2] = -4.0 ! dummy value
ENDIF

IF (ME2>1) THEN JLO=1 ELSE JLO=2 ENDIF
IF (ME2<NP2) THEN JHI=NEP2 ELSE JHI=NEP2-2 ENDIF
DO J = JLO, JHI ! Multigrid Smoothing (Red-Black)
   DO I = MOD(J,2)+2, NEP1-1, 2
      A(I,J)[ME1,ME2] = 0.25*(A(I+1,J)[ME1,ME2] + &
             A(I-1,J)[ME1,ME2] + A(I,J-1)[ME1,ME2] + &
             A(I,J+1))[ME1,ME2] + B(I,J)[ME1,ME2]
   ENDDO
ENDDO
```

```
! Update new values of A from adjoining images
CALL SYNCH_ALL( WAIT=NBR1(1:NNBR1) )
IF (ME1>1) A(0,1:NEP2)[ME1,ME2] = A(NEP1,1:NEP2)[ME1-1,ME2]
IF (ME1<NP1) A(NEP1+1,1:NEP2)[ME1,ME2] = A(1,1:NEP2)[ME1+1,ME2]
CALL SYNCH_ALL( WAIT=NBR2(1:NNBR2) )
IF (ME2>1) A(0:NEP1+1,0)[ME1,ME2] = A(0:NEP1+1,NEP2)[ME1,ME2-1]
IF (ME2<NP2) A(0:NEP1+1,NEP2+1)[ME1,ME2] = A(0:NEP1+1,1)[ME1,ME2+1]


IF (ME2>1) THEN JLO=1 ELSE JLO=2 ENDIF
IF (ME2<NP2) THEN JHI=MEP2 ELSE JHI=MEP2-2 ENDIF
IF (ME1>1) THEN ILO=1 ELSE ILO=2 ENDIF
IF (ME1<NP2) THEN IHI=MEP1 ELSE IHI=NEP2-2 ENDIF
DO J = JLO, JHI    ! Multigrid Restriction
   DO I = ILO, IHI
      APRIME(I,J)[ME1,ME2] = 0.05*(A(2*I-2,2*J-2)[ME1,ME2] + &
         4*A(2*I-2,2*J-1)[ME1,ME2] + A(2*I-2,2*J)[ME1,ME2] + &
         4*A(2*I-1,2*J-2)[ME1,ME2] + 4*A(2*I-1,2*J)[ME1,ME2] + &
         A(2*I,2*J-2)[ME1,ME2] + 4*A(2*I,2*J-1)[ME1,ME2] + &
         A(2*I,2*J)[ME1,ME2])
   ENDDO
ENDDO
```

Although clearly more complex than the HPF version, the conceptual changes can be readily explained.

1. The PARAMETER and array declarations must now reflect only the local section of the array (a $\frac{1024}{\sqrt{NP}} \times \frac{1024}{\sqrt{NP}}$ subsection of the original array). The expansion to 1024 elements in each dimension is needed to make the size divisible by the number of processors. This and our assumption that the number of processors is a power of two have greatly simplified the subscript calculations.

2. Because Co-Array Fortran makes data movement explicit, calls to SYNCH_ALL and data copying statements (noted as assignments to the overlap areas in the code) must appear in the code. The HPF compiler would generate these automatically.

3. The manipulation of the NBR1 and NBR2 arrays allows each image to wait only for the images that will supply it with data. This is a detail that is not required by the Co-Array Fortran language, but it adds substantial efficiency.

The Co-array Fortran version of the OpenMP pipelining example (in Section 12.3) is as follows:

```
PARAMETER (NP = NUM_IMAGES()) ! # of processors
PARAMETER (N  = 2048)          ! Total # of elements
```

```
PARAMETER (NEP = N/NP)          ! # of elements per image
PARAMETER (NEB = 16)            ! # of elements per block
PARAMETER (NB = NEP/NEB)        ! # of blocks
REAL A(0:NEP+1,N)[*]

ME = THIS_IMAGE()

! Initialize (upper) overlap areas
A( NEP+1, 2:N-1 )[ME] = A( 1, 2:N-1 )[ME+1]

! Execute this thread's portion of the loop nest
IF (ME>1) THEN ILO = 1 ELSE ILO = 2 ENDIF
IF (ME<NP) THEN IHI = NEP ELSE IHI = NEP-1 ENDIF
DO JJ = 1, NB
  JLO = MAX( 2, (JJ-1)*NEB+1 )
  JHI = MIN( N-1, JJ*NEB )
  IF (ME>1) THEN
      ! Wait for image ME-1, then go forward
      CALL SYNCH_TEAM( (/ ME, ME-1 /) )
  ENDIF
  DO J = JLO, JHI
    DO I = ILO, IHI
      A(I,J)[ME] = 0.25*(A(I+1,J)[ME] + A(I-1,J)[ME] + &
                         A(I,J-1)[ME] + A(I,J+1)[ME])
    ENDDO
  ENDDO
  IF (ME<NP) THEN
      ! Set (lower) overlap area for next block
      A( 0, JLO:JHI )[ME+1] = A( NEP, JLO:JHI )[ME]
      ! Release image ME+1 for next block
      CALL SYNCH_TEAM( (\ ME+1, ME \) )
  ENDIF
ENDDO
```

Comparing this to the OpenMP version of the code, the key differences are as follows:

1. Addressing of the A array uses local coordinates. That is, each image "sees" a $NEP + 2 \times N$ local array (indexed from 0 in the first dimension) rather than the $N \times N$ global array.

2. Computations of the first subscript of A are modified to account for the local addressing.

3. Explicit data-copying operations—the assignments to A(NEP+1,2:N-1)[ME] and A(0,JLO:JHI)[ME+1]—are needed to transfer the data for the pipeline. Note that the second data-copying operation performed an assignment on a remote image, which in this case is more convenient to program (and more efficient on some architectures).

4. The intrinsic synchronization operation SYNCH_ALL is arguably higher level than the OpenMP lock operations. However, the same threads/images must interact with each other.

SPMD languages such as Co-Array Fortran have many advantages for explicit parallel programming. They allow low-level manipulations when necessary, but provide some high-level operations for common cases. Implementations can be relatively simple if the hardware supports Co-Array Fortran operations such as one-sided communication. More research is needed, however, to determine how portable the performance of these languages is. In particular, there seems to be some scope for compiler optimizations, but the asynchronous operations that SPMD entails may make analysis difficult. As of this writing, the jury is still out on the best language(s) to use for parallel programming.

12.5 Supporting Technologies

To support the goal of making it possible to provide the user with a high level of abstraction without denying the opportunity to have fine-grained control over performance, the programming system must provide mechanisms for understanding the performance of applications and for overcoming any bottlenecks that are discovered in the tuning process. In addition, certain functions that are used over and over again in parallel programs need to be pretuned for execution on each parallel platform. This requires certain component technologies be developed along with the language compilers. Two of these—tools and tuned libraries—are of critical importance to the success of new languages.

12.5.1 Programming Support Tools

All of the strategies envisioned for application development establish a complex relationship between the source version of the program and the version that runs on the actual machine. Science and engineering users need to have ways to understand performance of a given program and to tune it when it is unacceptable. Chapter 15 discusses these requirements in more detail. Furthermore, the explanation of program behavior must be presented in terms of the source rather than the object version. Otherwise, the advantages provided by language abstraction will be lost. This becomes particularly challenging when some of the compilation process is done at run time.

The HPF experience has established that the compiler must generate two things to support performance analysis and tuning [11]: (1) calls to the performance monitoring system at critical points, where what is "critical" must be decided by some combination of user and system; and (2) information on how to map performance information back to the source of the program when it becomes available after execution.

In addition, the compiler and language must provide mechanisms that permit the program performance to be improved once the bottlenecks have been identified. These performance-improving changes must typically be made in the program source, so they will be preserved for the next run. Thus the tools must understand the relationship between the structure of the program and typical performance problems, and they must be able to make transformations based on that understanding.

12.5.2 Libraries

There are many functions that are common in parallel programming yet difficult to implement efficiently for different platforms without hand tuning. It has been common to encapsulate these functions in programming support libraries. HPF was one of the first languages to specify an extensive library as a part of the language, and Java has followed suit with a large collection of special-purpose library interfaces. The advantage of a library is that it can be hand tuned to achieve optimal performance on each target platform. The disadvantage is that, without such tuning, performance is likely to suffer. One of the most important impediments to widespread acceptance of HPF has been problems with the library implementations. This has been compounded by the absence of a well-developed, portable math library such as the CMSSL, which was developed for the Connection Machine. To be truly useful, all of the standard libraries must be capable of accepting the data types provided in the language—scientific programmers expect no less.

One area of importance in the future will be methodologies for development of libraries that can be easily and efficiently integrated into applications via transformations in the compiler. This will be discussed further in the next section.

12.6 Future Trends

As of this publication, the research community and commercial vendors have been actively working on programming support for parallel computer systems for over 15 years, yet the improvements in ease of programming have been only modest. In our opinion, this has been because designers have been exclusively focused on making it possible to write parallel programs that can be ported to a variety of parallel computing platforms. With technologies such as MPI, PVM, p-threads, HPF, OpenMP, and Java, these problems have been well addressed. However, as new parallel computing platforms emerge, they will bring new challenges for compiler developers.

Over the next decade we see two major challenges for research on programming systems:

- *Programming support for the computational Grid.* There is great emerging interest in using the global information infrastructure as a computing platform. By drawing on the power of high-performance computing resources across the world, it may be possible to solve problems that cannot currently be attacked by any single computer system, parallel or otherwise. However, the so-called Computational Power Grid, or *Grid* for short, presents nightmarish problems for the application developer because of the dynamic nature of the underlying computing and communications resources. The critical issues are how to build applications that are tolerant of the changes in resource base and how to construct execution environments that can deliver reliable progress on a given application. One strategy being pursued by a number of CRPC researchers in the Grid Application Development Software (GrADS) Project is to implement an execution environment that constantly monitors progress of an application and automatically reconfigures it whenever performance falls below certain specifications. To implement this strategy, compilers and libraries will need to be developed with the notion of reconfigurability built in from the outset.

- *Problem-solving environments and high-level programming systems.* Programming for parallel execution environments is still clearly an expert's game. If parallel computing is ever to become more widely used, we need ways to make it easier for end users to develop programs. One strategy that promises to become more prominent over the next few years is the use of sophisticated problem-solving environments (PSEs). In such environments, domain-specific macro operations could be encapsulated as language primitives and programs written in high-level, easy-to-use scripts. Visual Basic, MATLAB, and database query languages are three examples of such systems. If script-based PSEs are to be used for applications where efficiency and performance are critical factors, the compilation systems will need to be able to automatically integrate the macro operations with scripts and translate the resulting global program to make effective use of scalable parallelism. PSEs are discussed in more detail in Chapter 14.

If substantive progress is made on these two issues over the next decade, it should be possible to come much closer to the dream of making the collection of networked computers into a problem-solving system for ordinary users, much as the Internet has become the common person's information system. Such a goal is worthy of a major national effort.

12.7 Conclusion

Parallel computation is a challenging activity because, at the lowest level, the application developer must discover parallel work and coordinate the activities of multiple processors carrying it out. The goal of high-level language and compiler strategies is to make this job easier by doing as much as possible for the user. In this chapter, we described three key technologies developed over the past 15 years for support of high-level parallel programming:

1. *Automatic parallelization*, in which the compiler translates a sequential program to a parallel one. Although this is the ideal strategy from the point of view of the end user, it has not been successful in achieving acceptable degrees of scalability. Nevertheless, the techniques of automatic parallelization are fundamental to the support of most other high-level strategies.

2. *Data-parallel languages*, as exemplified by HPF. Data-parallel languages support a style of parallelism derived from decomposing array data structures across the processors of distributed-memory machines. HPF provides a set of data-decomposition directives that serve as hints to the compiler on how to achieve high locality and implicit parallelism on such systems.

3. *Shared-memory parallel programming interfaces,* as exemplified by OpenMP. Shared-memory parallelism is primarily concerned with work decomposition, since the ideal target systems for such interfaces have a uniform-access, shared global memory. OpenMP is the most prominent example of such systems. It uses a system of directives that specify where multiple threads should be applied and how to assign work to those threads.

4. *Single-program, multiple-data languages,* as exemplified by Co-Array Fortran. This style of language directly programs each asynchronous process of a parallel computation. This has advantages for control, but typically requires low-level programming for certain operations.

These four strategies represent the most promising results of the research conducted by the community on support for parallel computing over the lifetime of CRPC. Although they represent fairly modest advances, we believe they have set the stage for much more dramatic improvements that will come in the near future.

Further Reading

For more information on the topics covered in this chapter, the following works are recommended:

- *Parallel Computing Works!* [358], by Fox, Williams, and Messina, compiles an enormous amount of information about parallel computation, particularly in the early days of distributed-memory machines.

- *High Performance Compilers for Parallel Computing* [1001], by Wolfe, covers most of the vectorization and parallelization subjects.

- *Languages, Compilation Techniques and Run Time Systems for Scalable Parallel Systems* [739], edited by Santosh Pande and Dharma P. Agrawal, contains a collection of articles on compiling for modern parallel machines.

- *Optimizing Compilers for Modern Architectures* [27], by Allen and Kennedy, provides in-depth coverage of automatic methods of vectorization, parallelization, and management of memory hierarchies.

- The survey article "Interprocedural Analysis and Optimization" [221], by Cooper, Hall, Kennedy, and Torczon, provides a fairly comprehensive overview of whole-program compilation technologies.

- The article "Requirements for Data-Parallel Programming Environments" [8], by Adve et al., gives an overview of considerations in designing programming tools that are integrated with the language compiler system.

13 Parallel Object-Oriented Libraries

**John Reynders • Dennis Gannon •
K. Mani Chandy**

In Chapter 20, Dongarra, Eijkhout, and Sorensen describe the challenges and progress that have been made on scalable, parallel numerical libraries. In this chapter, we approach the design of libraries for parallel scientific computation from a different, but complementary, perspective.

Object-oriented programming has taught us the power of abstraction through encapsulation of data and function. By learning to organize software in ways that exploit inheritance and polymorphism, we gain in our ability to maintain and reuse important code. This is made possible because object-oriented design allows us to separate the interface of an object from its implementation, and it also gives us a more powerful tool for factoring a computation into multiple levels of functionality. Generic programming takes us in a seemingly different direction. It encourages us to think about algorithms in a manner that is independent of the data structure we use to represent information. In scientific computing, this concept is reflected in the numerical templates approach [81], where one is shown the "generic" design of an algorithm such as conjugate gradient in a manner that is independent of the implementation of the matrices and vectors. It is also reflected in the work of Chandy on archetypes [185]. But it was the work of Stepanov that pioneered the use of generic programming in C++, with the introduction of the standard template library (STL) [695]. And it was the work of Veldhuizen that showed us how to use the C++ template library to write "template expressions" [959] that could run as fast as optimized Fortran.

This chapter is intended to illustrate how these ideas can be used in the design of scientific and engineering applications. In particular, there are four distinct ways of using object-oriented technology in the design of high-performance scientific computations. The first section of the chapter describes the design of parallel libraries as object-oriented application frameworks. In this section, we look at object-oriented data structure libraries and frameworks that encapsulate algorithm archetypes. In addition, we consider the role of abstraction, encapsulation of parallelism, generic programming, and design patterns in the construction of these libraries.

In the second section we take a look at the role of Java. We begin with a brief examination of how Java with parallelism is encapsulated in data structure libraries. In the third section of the chapter, we consider the explicit parallel programming in multithreaded, shared-memory environments and the incorporation of this model with distributed-computing concepts to build wide-area scientific applications. We briefly describe a C++ library called HPC++ that is based on Compositional C++ [184] and Java. In the last section of the chapter, we describe how these technologies can be used to build a component-based framework, where new applications can be built by composing existing parallel modules.

13.1   Object-Oriented Parallel Libraries

Significant agility in software development has been required these past 5 years to follow the high-performance computing platforms through vector processing, massively parallel, and clustered shared-memory processor (SMP) architectures. Object-oriented (OO) approaches have eased these transitions by encapsulating the complexities of parallel simulation in science-based software components, and generic programming has contributed new insight into the way scientific libraries can be designed and optimized.

Although there are many impressive serial OO/generic libraries, such as Blitz++ [960] and the MTL [844], we will focus here on the particular challenges in developing parallel object-oriented libraries for scientific computing. Issues of language, abstractions, parallelism, design, generic programming, and components will be examined. To bring the discussion to life, we draw examples from the Parallel Object-Oriented Methods and Applications (POOMA) Framework [798], a significant object-oriented library that has been used in multiple large-scale parallel applications over the past 5 years.

13.1.1   Abstraction

One of the great strengths in object-oriented programming for scientific simulation development is the ability to develop a logical set of physics objects that act in a manner intuitive to users. Historically, physics applications have been data-centric—large blocks of data are accessed by a variety of subroutines and functions to execute a simulation. Object-oriented programming binds data and actions together into objects that interact in a prescribed fashion to execute a simulation. The POOMA framework (Figure 13.1) provides several physics-based objects that represent arrays, particles, fields, meshes, and solvers. These objects not only contain data, they also provide a logical set of operations that act on the data. For example, arrays have indexing and mathematical operations to represent partial differential equations, whereas particle objects have attribute operators, interaction functions, and interpolator objects to

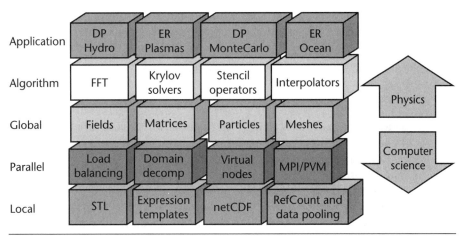

Figure 13.1 The POOMA library.

manipulate the behavior of particle groups in a simulation. Developing a consistent set of behaviors for an object and a consistent pattern of interaction with other objects in an object-oriented scientific library is one of the most important aspects of object-oriented library design.

C++ provides non–object-oriented features that are very convenient for scientific code development—the most notable being overloaded operators. This allows library builders to do more than develop physics-based classes, such as arrays, meshes, particles, and matrices. The builder can also deploy a set of accompanying operators, so that a physicist utilizing the library is able to write code that is very similar to the actual physics equations under consideration—except for all those semicolons.

As an example, the simple diffusion equation

$$\frac{\partial}{\partial t}\mathbf{u}\,(\mathbf{x},\mathbf{t}) = -\nabla \cdot \nu\,\mathbf{u}\,(\mathbf{x},\mathbf{t})$$

can be cast into a finite-difference form

$$\frac{u_{ijk}^{n+1} - u_{ijk}^{n-1}}{2dt} = -\frac{\nu_x\left(u_{i+1,j,k}^{n} - u_{i-1,j,k}^{n}\right)}{2dx}$$

which, in turn, is represented in POOMA by the following line of code.

```
u = uPrev - 2 * dt * div<Cell>(v * u);
```

It is important to note that the representation in POOMA is very similar to the original equation. An interesting feature of this representation is the parameterization of the divergence operator on `Cell`. This highlights a very useful feature of C++ in scientific computing. The finite-difference centerings (e.g., cell centered or vertex centered) have been cast into the type system through template parameterization. Thus, operators can be combined and correctness, in terms of the difference centering of any given equation, checked at compile time rather than run time.

13.1.2   Parallelism

There are many aspects to writing a parallel simulation that have made high-performance code development a far more formidable task than was the case a decade ago. Whereas high-performance computer architectures in the late 1980s were mostly serial machines that required some vector programming and perhaps some multitasking, today's supercomputers are typically distributed-memory machines with deep hierarchies of memory and communication. Furthermore, the nodes on these machines are typically populated by many processors with nonuniform memory access rates. This clustered shared-memory processing architecture requires the parallel library developer to consider data distributions, load balancing, data movement, messaging, task concurrency, and cache performance. Many library writers have turned to object-oriented techniques for parallel library development to hide the architectural complexities of parallelism from the end user.

The POOMA framework provides users with array and field abstractions to enable data-parallel operations across many processors. For example, given a 2-D field, A, and a pair of index objects, I and J, which represent the domain of the field object, the data-parallel expression

```
A[I][J] = 0.25*(A[I+1][J] + A[I-1][J] + A[I][J+1] + A[I][J-1] );
```

executes an averaging operation across an arbitrary number of processors for any given domain size represented by the index pair I and J, up to the memory limit of the parallel computer. The issues of data movement based on the field domain decomposition across the processors and the indexing operations on the processor boundaries are handled internally by the array objects. For example, given a four-processor machine and index objects, each with a range from 1 to 8, Figure 13.2 represents how the domain decomposition and data movement would occur. Since the data-parallel expression above has a stencil with an extent of one, the overloaded "equals" operator will cause a border swap of ghost cells one cell deep. All of these operations change automatically, depending on the number of processors and the communication requirements of each data-parallel expression. Optimizations in the POOMA framework enable deferred evaluation and data movement, so that communications can be ganged together and optimized. All of these parallel operations and optimizations, however, occur underneath a powerful abstraction barrier which presents the user with a simple array class.

Today's supercomputers are typically composed of multiple memory subsystem layers (multiple cache levels and nonuniform memory access rates in main memory). The rate at which CPU clock speeds are increasing is progressing much faster than the rate at which clocks on memory subsystems are progressing, causing significant penalties to simulations that are not able to operate on data in cache for as

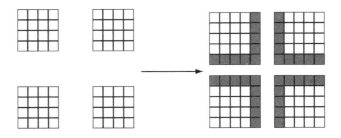

Figure 13.2 Domain decomposition and adding of ghost cells.

long as possible. Data-parallel constructs, such as the Array abstraction in POOMA, tend to exacerbate this problem by running through all data in an array during the course of a single array statement. If an object in the array statement is reused in the next expression, the cache needs to be reloaded from main memory at a performance hit. The POOMA framework is working with the Shared-Memory Asynchronous Run-Time System (SMARTs) [949] to enable microdata flow scheduling of lightweight threads. Combined with a scalable expression-dependence analyzer within the framework, data-parallel statements can be broken down into fine-grained pieces and efficiently scheduled on processors, caches, and communications hardware. Utilization of lightweight user-level threads for fast context switching and memory-affinity calculations are crucial for scientific computing and have enabled small POOMA kernels to run with out-of-order execution to obtain a factor-five speedup over simple data-parallel expressions based solely on a message-passing substrate.

13.1.3 Encapsulation

The above example emphasizes the use of object-oriented techniques to encapsulate the complexity of a parallel system. Taking different approaches, the above libraries are able to hide the details of parallel computing from the end user, enabling scientists to spend more time focusing on their science of interest rather than on the details of programming a complex parallel architecture. Furthermore, the use of encapsulation enables the library developer to try different techniques with minimal perturbation to the user interface. For example, the POOMA framework moved from a message-passing implementation to a mixed-model messaging and threaded system with minimal impact to the user interface. As the complexity of computer architectures grows, the use of object-oriented techniques to encapsulate the intricacies of parallel code development has become a promising approach to increasing the speed at which scientists are able to develop scalable, efficient simulations.

In object-oriented, parallel-library development, one seeks ideally to provide optimal performance while encapsulating all aspects of parallel computing, including the number of processors being used, the system topology, the memory hierarchies, and other details of the parallel system. However, application performance typically depends critically on how an application is laid out on a system. Hence, object-oriented libraries seek to provide layers of encapsulation—the highest layer providing full defaults so that a developer may completely ignore the underlying architecture and concentrate on physics development. At this level of abstraction, an object-oriented library such as POOMA enables a developer to build an application on a serial workstation and move the simulation to a parallel machine with no changes to source code. For example, it is possible to run POOMA codes in a serial mode on a workstation to develop physics modules and then, with only a recompile, retarget the code to a parallel supercomputer. Furthermore, POOMA is able to employ a variety of parallel optimization techniques without perturbing user applications, since the parallelism is an aspect of the object implementation, not the object interface.

As developers become more comfortable with a parallel machine and demand greater performance, POOMA provides high-level tools to affect data layout, task execution, and load balancing. This enables the user to concisely express aspects of the application that can be optimally mapped to the underlying machine. Most object-oriented libraries enable developer access to library implementation to explicitly invoke features and utilize inheritance to extend library functionality for a particular required optimization. For example, the POOMA library allows arrays to be instantiated with a variety of user-directed layouts to optimize for a given application. This ability to penetrate down into different layers of a framework or library is critical to enable the necessary extensions most users are going to require to obtain a desired level of performance and specific functionality.

Finally, many scientific simulations have a high degree of complexity, not only in terms of the target parallel architecture, but also in terms of the physics under exploration. Object-oriented libraries help in simultaneously encapsulating both the architectural complexities of parallelism and the algorithmic and geometric complexities of multiphysics applications. For example, the POOMA framework provides a set of parallel particle, field, and spectral transform classes that have been used to develop complex plasma physics simulations. Parallel object-oriented libraries, such as POOMA, provide the user with high-level physics-based abstractions that enable the development of complex physics applications with little detailed knowledge of the target supercomputer.

13.1.4   Generic Programming

One of the distinguishing features of the POOMA framework is its heavy use of generic programming techniques that allow software components to adapt to different uses through language-supported, compile-time methods. The C++ template facility provides for generic compile-time polymorphism, wherein the best algorithm or data structure for a particular set of requirements known at compile time can be deployed. For example, POOMA fields are array-like structures that differentiate themselves from other array classes by providing template parameters for the field class and functions acting on fields that specialize in mesh geometry, dimension, and centering of field values on the mesh. This approach selects and in-lines the optimal data structures and operators for a given mesh, dimension, and centering at compile time rather than at run time. The user can thus write geometry- and dimension-independent code without a run-time penalty. Furthermore, the framework utilizes an engine pattern wherein arrays are simply interface classes, and the data representation is provided by a template parameter. In this manner, dense, sparse, and parallel arrays all have the same interface and can all be used interchangeably. Thus, an algorithm written with POOMA arrays can efficiently utilize different data representations by only changing a template parameter and recompiling. This generic programming use of compile-time rather than run-time optimization affords the user significant performance advantages, while minimally impacting the user code.

Another important capability afforded by generic programming techniques is the utilization of expression templates (ETs) with large data-parallel objects to obtain significant performance advantages in comparison to overloaded operator implementations. ETs are classes formed at compile time that transform data-parallel expressions into single objects that iterate over all elements of the expression and execute the operations within a single loop. This compile-time transformation of a large expression into a tight loop provides the back-end optimizer a good representation for pipelining and generating efficient assembly. The POOMA framework utilizes expression templates in object-overloaded operators and has been able to obtain significant performance speedups—in some cases within 90% of equivalent hand-coded C and Fortran kernels.

13.1.5   A POOMA Example

Before moving on to object-oriented parallel programming in Java, we provide a full example written in POOMA. This and many more examples using the POOMA framework (carefully crafted by Greg Wilson) are available at *www.acl.lanl.gov*.

Below we show a POOMA code that performs a Jacobi iteration with a five-point stencil.

```
01  #include "Pooma/Arrays.h"
02
03  #include <iostream>
04
05  // The size of each side of the domain
06  const int N = 20;
07
08  int
09  main(
10      int                 argc,          // argument count
```

```
11       char*                    argv[]              // argument list
12    ){
13        // Initialize POOMA
14        Pooma::initialize(argc, argv);
15
16        // The array we'll be solving for
17        Array<2,double> V(N, N);
18        V = 0.0;
19
20        // The right-hand side of the equation (spike in the center)
21        Array<2,double> b(N, N);
22        b = 0.0;
23        b(N/2, N/2) = -1.0;
24
25        // Specify the interior of the domain
26        Interval<1> I(1, N-2), J(1, N-2);
27
28        // Iterate 200 times
29        for (int iteration=0; iteration<200; ++iteration)
30        {
31            V(I,J) = 0.25*(V(I+1,J) + V(I-1,J) + V(I,J+1) + V(I,J-1) - b(I,J));
32        }
33
34        // Print out the result
35        std::cout << V << std::endl;
36
37        // Clean up POOMA and report success
38        Pooma::finalize();
39        return 0;
40    }
```

In lines 1 through 12 we have the obligatory includes, constant initializations, and main routine. Line 14 is a required static call that starts all the POOMA machinery. Line 17 instantiates the array that will be used in the Jacobi iteration. Note that the dimension and type of the array are template parameters and thus cause all the machinery for a 2-D array of doubles to be formed at compile time. The first and second parameter of the array constructor represent the size of the array in each dimension. Line 18 initializes the array to zeros in every element. Lines 21 and 22 likewise instantiate another array and initialize each element to zero. Line 23 now adds a single spike into the center of the array b. Line 26 introduces a new object called an Interval object—this is used to specify the interior of the domain and limit the places where the calculation occurs in the body of the array. The integer template argument to Interval specifies the interval's rank, while the constructor arguments specify the bounds of the interval's value. At line 29, we enter into the iteration and perform data-parallel operations across all elements of the array. As discussed earlier, an expression template is formed during compilation to perform the inner loop of this stencil operation efficiently. Likewise, all of the necessary domain decomposition, data distribution, and data movement occur at each iteration as dictated by the stencil operations. Note that the assignment on line 31 automatically creates a temporary copy of the array V, so that values are not read while they are being overwritten.

Finally, the entire code above will run a 20×20 simulation on your laptop; or you can perform a 20 million $\times$ 20 million simulation on a 1000-node supercomputer—with no change to the above source other than the constant on line 6.

13.2   Object-Oriented Parallel Programming in Java

Engineers select programming languages based on many attributes of software systems, including performance, problem structure, portability across multiple platforms, speed of development, reliability and maintainability, and availability of tools and trained engineers. In the next paragraph, we explore questions such as: What attributes are important in parallel scientific computing, and what attributes are important for Internet computing applications such as e-commerce and e-service? What aspects of Java make it the language of choice for certain problems?

Often, in parallel scientific computing, performance is valued more than other attributes. Indeed, the primary reason for executing programs on parallel machines is to get results quickly. Many problems that have received attention in computational science have relatively regular data structures. A primary motivating idea in High Performance Fortran (HPF) is the recognition of the importance of regular data structures in scientific computing. Of course, scientific computing covers a vast domain, and the kinds of data structures employed within this domain are rich and varied. Many, but certainly not all, computational science problems compute a function from input to output: these programs carry out a computation on the input to produce an output. Such programs are not reactive, in the sense that they do not have to continuously interact with multiple computers, instruments, and people. Web browsers play a larger role as input/output devices in Internet applications than in computational science because inputs and outputs are complex and voluminous in science problems.

Java is a language of choice for Internet applications, and some of the features that make it attractive in this domain also make it attractive for scientific computing. Some design choices that make Java ideal for Internet applications are potentially problematic for computational science, and we address them first.

- *Write once, run everywhere.* Java implementations are designed to be portable. Portability is achieved by interpreting Java byte code on a virtual machine.

Porting a Java program from one computing system to another is straight-forward, provided the target system has an appropriate JVM (Java Virtual Machine). Of course, users must take steps such as ensuring that class–path directories are set appropriately, but on the whole porting Java programs is often easier than porting programs written in other languages (such as C++). Interpreted Java programs usually run somewhat slower than compiled programs. Execution times can be improved in two ways: (a) use a JIT (just-in-time) compiler that executes byte code faster than direct interpretation, or (b) compile Java to the target machine and do not use a JVM. JITs and Java compilers continue to improve, and the performance loss by using a JIT is often outweighed by the flexibility of using a virtual machine. Why not compile Java just as Fortran and C++ are compiled? The virtual machine provides flexibility at run time, such as the ability to load classes from anywhere on the Internet. Also, with a JVM, an object can use reflection to determine the signature (public methods and variables) of another object at run time. Indeed, run-time flexibility is one of the attributes that makes Java so attractive for Internet applications. These features, however, are not essential for many computational science problems.

- *Ease of memory management.* Java collects garbage, whereas C++ does not. Should managing memory be the user's responsibility? Giving users control over deallocation of memory can result in highly optimized programs. It can also result in programs that "leak memory" and that have bad performance as a consequence. Programmers do have to be concerned with memory usage, even in Java. For instance, rapid and continuous creation and deletion of threads in Java can cause garbage to be generated very fast, and this can lead to poor performance. There are effective ways of managing memory in Java, such as using thread pools, and there are effective tools for dealing with memory leaks in C++. In many cases, effective memory management is easier in Java than in C or C++. However, C and C++ allow memory management solutions tailored to a given problem.

- *Support for parallelism.* Threads are an integral part of Java, so designing multi-threaded programs is relatively easy in Java. Programmers do not have to deal with different thread libraries and different operating systems. Java does not support data-parallel operations directly. Of course, data-parallel operations can be implemented on top of threads, in a style similar to the implementation of the parallel STL in HPC++ and in the HP-Java effort. Java allows interprocess communication by using RMI (remote method invocation) and message passing via sockets. At this point, RMI seems relatively slow, probably because it offers a great degree of run-time flexibility. The simplest way to develop parallel Java programs is to use threads within a shared-memory multiprocessor system. However, local and remote method invocation can be combined within a program. Likewise, message passing can be combined with threads in a straightforward way and completely within Java. The Infospheres system, for instance, allows processes to have mailboxes to which other processes send messages (and, of course, threads can be used within each process), and message types do not have to be determined at compile time. Java is a language of choice when computations and data structures are dynamic and irregular. Computational scientists with pure data-parallel computations may find that HPF is more suitable for their computations.

- *Interfaces*. Java does not support multiple inheritance. Java offers interfaces as a simple way of dealing with some of the features offered by multiple inheritance. Java does not support templates, such as those in C++. Computational scientists, most notably the POOMA group at Los Alamos National Laboratory, have put multiple inheritance and templates to excellent use. Parameterized types will be part of the next major release of Java, but it is not yet clear that they will have the same optimization features that have made templates such a success in C++.

- *Numerics*. The first version of Java included a floating-point model that stressed "bit-for-bit" reproducibility and run-time checks on array bounds. Unfortunately, these features proved to limit Java for high-performance applications where speed is a primary concern. Recognizing this problem, a group supported by Sun, called Java Grande, was organized to address this and other issues important to large-scale science and engineering. The Java Grande group has proposed a new model for floating-point operations that is under consideration by Sun and the Java standards group. In addition, Java Grande has proposed ideas for numerical linear algebra APIs, better multidimensional arrays, a binding for MPI, a repository of scientific benchmarks written in Java, and requirements for primitives such as Complex. (Details about all of this can be found on the Java Grande website, *www.javagrande.org*.)

Java has features such as beans that allow the use of graphical interfaces for composing program components. Java database drivers; database systems with embedded Java stored procedures; JVMs for palm devices and Windows CE handheld devices and information appliances, and tools for using XML and XSL (extended markup languages and extended style sheets); and EJBs (Enterprise Java Beans) that encapsulate business logic, make Java ideal for many Internet applications. These features are also useful in some scientific problems, such as steering a complex computation while it is in execution, controlling a distributed set of scientific instruments, and executing complex man-in-the-loop simulations.

The central concept, relevant to parallel scientific computation, that Java has (in common with other object-oriented languages) is encapsulation. For instance, data structures that support data-parallel operations are encapsulated as classes. Threads and messages are hidden, encapsulated by classes. This allows programmers to focus their attention on their algorithms rather than on details of parallelism implementation. Of course, the efficiency of the program will depend on the efficiency of

the implementation of the classes on the target machine. Performance parameters
such as block size and number of threads may have to be tailored to each machine,
resulting in additional steps in porting a program from one machine to another.

Examples

One approach to the shortcomings of the standard Java arrays for multidimensional
applications is to design special array classes. A research team at IBM has designed a
family of Java array classes that the IBM compiler can recognize and optimize. For
example, the following method illustrates a matrix–matrix multiply using a matrix–
vector multiply provided in a different method. The code illustrates the use of the
array section operators and the use of a Range object to describe a sequence of index
values.

```
public static doubleArray2D matmul(doubleArray2D A, doubleArray2D B)
    throws NonconformingArrayException, InvalidArrayShapeException,
        InvalidArrayAxisException, InvalidRangeException {

    /*
     * Compute the product of two matrices, A and B, represented
     * as 2-D array. If A is mxn and B is nxp, then
     * the resulting matrix C is mxp.
     */
    int m = A.size(0);
    int n = A.size(1);
    if (n != B.size(0)) throw new NonconformingArrayException();
    int p = B.size(1);

    doubleArray2D C = new doubleArray2D(m,p);

    /*
     * Column j of C is the product of matrix A by column j of B:
     *      C(0:m-1,j) = A * B(0:n-1,j).
     */
    for (int j=0; j<p; j++) {
        doubleArray1D column = matvec(A,B.section(new Range(0,n-1),j));
        C.section(new Range(0,m-1),j).assign(column);
    }
    return C;
}
```

To illustrate how one may apply multithreaded parallelism to this example,
consider the for loop in the statement above. First, place this loop into a thread
class of the following form.

```
public class ColumnBlock extends Thread{
    doubleArray2D A, B, C;
    int l, h;
    public ColumnBlock(doubleArray2D LeftOp, doubleArray2D RightOp,
                doubleArray2D Target, int low, int hi){
        A = leftOp; B = rightOp, C = Target;
        l = low; h = high;
        }
    public run(){
  for (int j=1; j<h; j++) {
      doubleArray1D column = matvec(A,B.section(new Range(0,n-1),j));
      C.section(new Range(0,m-1),j).assign(column);
  }
};
```

The loop in the matmul method may now be replaced by the following Java code that blocks the loop into segments whose size is provided by the parameter blockSize.

```
ColumnBlock thread[];
int numThreads = 0;
for(j = 0; j < p; j = j+blockSize){
    int h = min(j+blockSize, p);
    thread[numThread] = new ColumnBlock(A,B,C,j,h);
    thread[numThread++].start();
    }
for(j = 0; j < numThread; j++)
    thread[j].join();
```

When run on a JVM that supports the native threads on a multiprocessor, this version of the matmul method will exploit the "outer loop" parallelism in matrix multiply. The actual performance of this parallel version of the program will depend on many factors. First, the execution time of the two loops above is bounded below by the overhead cost $T_{ov} = numThread * (T_{ts} + T_j)$ where T_{ts} is the time to create and start a thread and T_j is the time for the synchronizing join operation. Hence the overhead grows linearly in the number of threads launched. On the other hand, if the number of columns p is very large and the number of threads is kept to a modest level, the computational work in each thread will dominate the start-up overhead. In other words, for large-enough problem sizes, this scheme will yield good performance on a modest-sized shared-memory multiprocessor.

There are other scaling issues that must be considered when applying a multi-threaded parallelization to Java programs. For example, access to the shared array objects in the example above does not have conflicts. However, some class objects may only be accessed by *synchronized* methods, and parallel accesses by multiple threads will be serialized. Very little research has been done on how well the JVM scales to large numbers of processors on SMP systems. Consequently, most approaches to large-scale parallelism in Java are focused on SPMD programming using the new Java binding for MPI.

In the next section, we show how this multithreaded execution model may also be used in C++ and describe how distributed-object system ideas in both Java and C++ may be used to support parallel computations.

13.3   Multithreaded Computation in C++

The computing landscape is often described as a pyramid with the largest super-computers at the very top. These machines are located at government laboratories and a few universities, and they each contain thousands of processors organized in clusters of two to a few dozen processor "nodes." The programming model for these systems consists of HPF- and MPI-based libraries such as those described in other chapters in this book. These machines are required for our largest and most challenging computations.

At the next level of the pyramid are a very large number of shared-memory, multiprocessor systems. While not typically called "supercomputers," these large "servers" exist in great number and are connected by high-speed networks over a very wide geographical area. With from 8 to 64 processors each and very large, shared memories, these systems provide the computational power for applications that range from high-traffic e-commerce sites to corporate engineering analysis and advanced visualization.

In this section, we consider object-oriented parallel programming for this second level of the pyramid. In particular, we focus on the following problems:

- How does one program a shared-memory parallel computer for dynamic and irregularly structured applications that are not well suited to an SPMD compu-tational model?

- How can one harness the power of a set of shared-memory parallel systems connected together by a high-performance, wide-area network?

The approach described here is derived from many sources. In 1993, Chandy and Kesselman designed an extension to C++ called Compositional C++ (CC++) [184]. This language added some very simple primitives to the core C++ language that would enable the design of parallel programming using threads and remote objects. About the same time, languages such as pC++ [123], which was based on SPMD programming for distributed-memory supercomputers, were released. In Japan, the Real World Computing Project (RWCP) had a very large project using object-oriented software design in construction of languages, operating systems, and hardware for parallel computing. One of the results of the RWCP project was a set of language extensions and a C++ template library called MPC++ [507]. MPC++ incorporated several ideas from CC++, but showed how the C++ template mechanism could be used to implement them, thus avoiding the need for several of the CC++ language extensions. In the following we use HPC++ [142], which was released in 1997. HPC++ draws upon CC++, MPC++, and pC++ ideas and constructs in the form of a C++ template library.

Java was introduced to the computing world at large in 1995, and it had a huge impact on the design of HPC++. The fact that Java had standard library support for threads meant that generations of new programmers were going to be trained to think about concurrency in those terms. Because many scientific computations were becoming more irregular and adaptive in their structure and organization, it was becoming apparent that multithreaded design would be a good approach to exploiting shared-memory multiprocessors. The HPC++ designers decided that adopting a "Java"-style thread library would be the most attractive to future programmers.

Java was originally designed, and has continued to evolve, as a language that supports distributed computing. The addition of the Java Remote Method Invocation (RMI) has enabled new distributed-computing technologies such as Jini [307] and Enterprise Java Beans [924].

13.3.1 The Execution Model

There are three conventional modes of executing an HPC++ program. The first is as a single multithreaded program that runs within one shared memory context. Parallelism comes from the dynamic creation of threads. Sets of threads can be bound into groups, and there are collective operations, such as reductions and prefix operators, that can be applied to synchronize the threads within a group. This model of programming is very well suited to modest levels of parallelism (about 32 processors) and where memory locality is not a serious factor.

The second mode of program execution is an explicit single-program, multiple-data (SPMD) model, where n copies of the same program are run on n different contexts. This programming model is similar to that of programs based on MPI, in which data are distributed among multiple memory contexts and the synchronization of accesses to that data must be managed by the programmer. HPC++ differs from typical MPI programs in that for HPC++ the computation on each context can also be multithreaded, and the synchronization mechanisms for thread groups extend to sets of thread groups running in multiple contexts.

The third, and perhaps most often used, model for HPC++ programming is where multiple HPC++ programs communicate via RMIs. This is the basis of our component architecture work and is described in the last section of this chapter.

13.3.2   Thread and Synchronization

HPC++ uses a model of threads that is based on a Thread class that is, by design, similar to the Java thread system. More specifically, there are two basic classes that are used to instantiate a thread and get it to do something. Basic thread objects encapsulate a thread and provide a private unique name space for that thread to use. The public interface to the thread is the HPC++ counterpart to the Java thread.

There are two ways to create a thread and give it work to do. One is based on the Java-style Runnable interface, and the other is the direct instantiation of a subclass of HPCxx_Thread. For example, to create two simple threaded "hello world" objects one can write:

```
class MyThread: public HPCxx_Thread{
      char *x;
   public:
      MyThread(char *y): x(y), HPCxx_Thread(){}
      void run(){
            printf(x);
            }
};
int main(int argv, char *argc){
      HPCxx_Group *g;
      hpcxx_init(&argv, &argc, g);

      MyThread *t1 = new MyThread(''hello.'');
      MyThread *t2 = new MyThread(''hi there!'');
      t1->start(); t2->start();
      t1->join();  t2->join();
      return hpcxx_exit(g);
}
```

This program prints

```
hello.hi there!
```

The initialization function hpcxx_init() initializes the object g of type HPCxx_Group that is used for synchronization purposes and is described in greater detail later. The join() operator will cause the caller to suspend until the target thread terminates. The termination function hpcxx_exit() is a final cleanup routine.

Thread and Data Synchronization

The join operator described above is an example of a primitive synchronization operation in HPC++. There are two types of synchronization mechanisms used in this HPC++ implementation: primitive synchronization objects and collective operator objects. The primitive synchronization objects are used for thread synchronization, while the collective operations can be used for collective operations on a set of threads and/or contexts.

In addition to thread join, there are five basic synchronization classes in the library. None of these is very remarkable, as they are intended to be easily recognized and used by the programmer. With the exception of the first, most are based on p-threads standards.

- *Sync.* CC++ introduced a special *sync* modifier for providing protected access to class members. In HPC++, we approximate this with a templated type. A HPCxx_Sync<T> object is a variable of base type T that can be written to once and read as many times as you want, but only read after the write.

- *Sync queue class.* Another template called HPCxx_SyncQ<T> provides a dual "queue" of values of type T.

- *The Mutex class.* Unlike languages such as Java and CC++, a library cannot support synchronized methods or atomic members through the template mechanism. However, in HPC++ a simple Mutex object with two functions lock() and unlock() provides the basic capability required for primitive mutual exclusion.

- *Condition variables.* Whereas the HPCxx_Mutex class allows threads to synchronize by controlling their access to data via a locking mechanism, the HPCxx_Cond class allows threads to synchronize on the value of the data. Cooperating threads wait until data reach some particular state or until some particular event occurs.

These synchronization types are "classic" concurrency control constructs. They are appropriate for the management of small numbers of threads. However, for large-scale parallelism one needs collective operations for barrier synchronization, reductions, and broadcasts. Similar operations are found in MPI. However, HPC++ provides a mechanism for collective operations on SPMD computations where each "node" of a program is running multiple threads.

The most basic collective operation is the HPCxx_Barrier that is a degenerate form of a more general operation known as a *reduction*. For example, suppose you want to calculate the sum of integer values computed by each of a number of threads. We can follow the generic programming style and define a function class as follows:

```
class intAdd{
   public:
      int & operator()(int &x, int &y) { x += y; return x;}
};
```

To create an object that can be used to form the sum-reduction of one integer from each thread, the declaration takes the form

```
HPCxx_Reduct<int, intAdd> reduction_object(group);
```

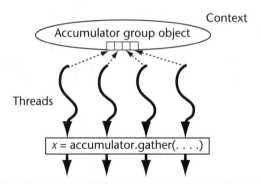

Figure 13.3 The collective gather operation synchronizes the operations of all threads that are members of the group associated with that collective.

This object has an overloaded ( ) operator that takes the form

```
T operator()(int thread_key,  T argument)
```

where T is the type of the operands in the binary operator (in this case int) and thread_key is a unique identifier assigned by the group to each member thread. Each thread provides its key value and one argument. The collective reduction operator applies the binary operator to build a binary reduction tree and then propagates the result to all waiting participant threads.

Often, threads need to coordinate so that one thread may share a value with the other threads or so that a number of threads can concatenate subvectors into one vector. Both of these operations are instances of a function we call *gather* that is a parallel-prefix concatenation operation and is a member of the HPCxx_Collective class (Figure 13.3).

```
template <class T>
class HPCxx_Collective{
 public:
   HPCxx_Collective(HPCxx_Group *g);
   int acquireKey();
   T * gather(int threadKey, T* thread_data, int &size);
   ...
};
```

The gather operation allows each thread to contribute a vector of data of arbitrary size and returns the vector of concatenated subvectors (whose size is given by the value of the reference parameter size when the call completes). (A broadcast is simply a special case of the gather operation, where all but one thread contribute a vector of length 0.)

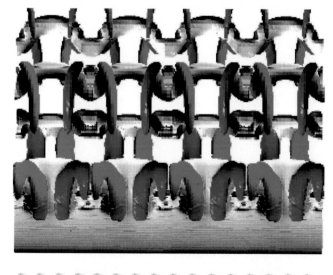

(a)

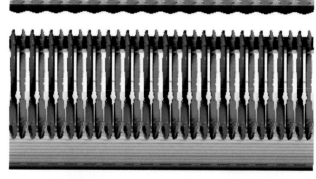

(b)

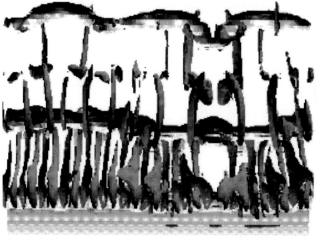

(c)

PLATE 1

Flow visualization of the three-dimensional vorticity field due to secondary instability in the wake of a circular cylinder: (a) $Re = 195$, (b) $Re = 265$, and (c) $Re = 265$ [457].

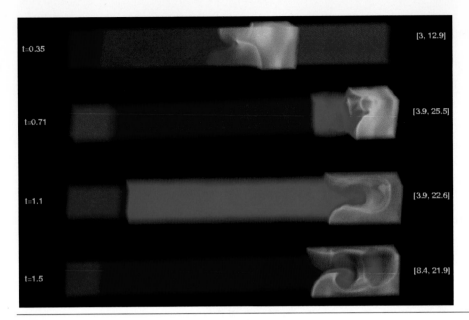

t=0.35 [3, 12.9]

t=0.71 [3.9, 25.5]

t=1.1 [3.9, 22.6]

t=1.5 [8.4, 21.9]

PLATE 2

Images of volume-rendered density field at various times for Richtmyer–Meshkov instability. The Atwood ratio $At = 0.5$. The color-map varies from purple-blue to red with increasing density. The minimum and maximum density values for the color-scale are shown in brackets at the right of each image. The ratio of the initial perturbation amplitude to wavelength is 0.109. The shock Mach number is $M_s = 10$.

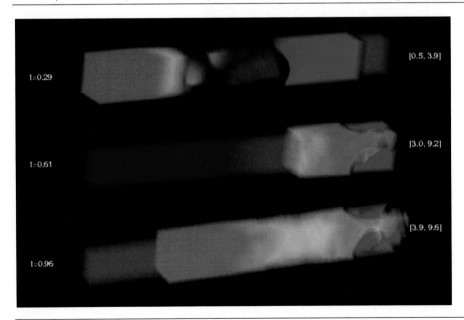

t=0.29 [0.5, 3.9]

t=0.61 [3.0, 9.2]

t=0.96 [3.9, 9.6]

PLATE 3

Images of volume-rendered density field at various times for Richtmyer–Meshkov instability. The Atwood ratio $At = -0.33$. The color-map varies from purple-blue to red with increasing density. The minimum and maximum density values for the color-scale are shown in brackets on the right of each image. The ratio of the initial perturbation amplitude to wavelength is 0.109. The shock Mach number is $M_s = 10$.

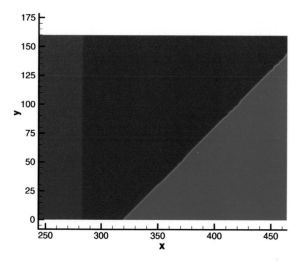

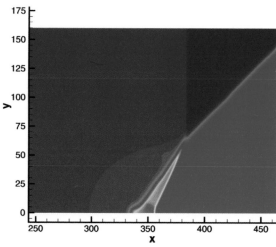

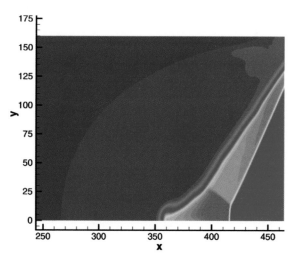

PLATE 4

Solution of a shock-contact interaction using parallel AMR.

PLATE 5

The dynamic mesh structure associated with the solution of a shock-contact interaction using AMR.

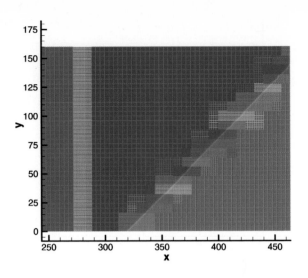

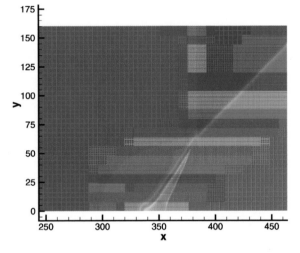

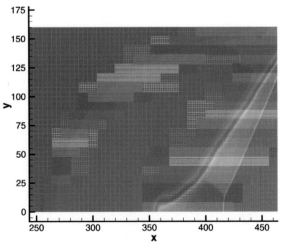

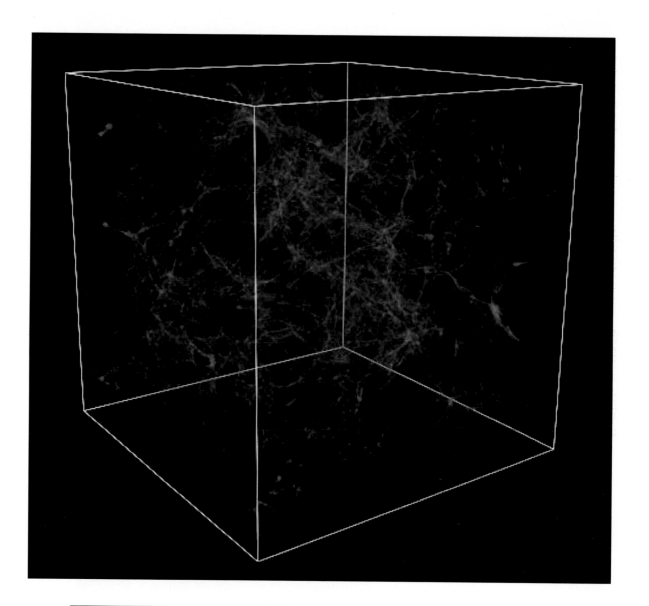

PLATE 6

Kronos simulation of large-scale cosmological structure. Shown is the distribution of gas density in a volume of a half-billion light years on a side. From [151].

PLATE 7

Writing a 128 × 128 × 128 distributed array on the Intel Paragon using level-0 requests (Unix-style independent writes). Elapsed time = 125 seconds.

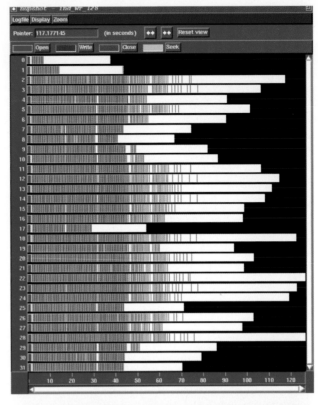

PLATE 8

Writing a 128 × 128 × 128 distributed array on the Intel Paragon using level-2 requests, with the buffer size for data sieving = 4 Mbytes. Elapsed time = 16 seconds.

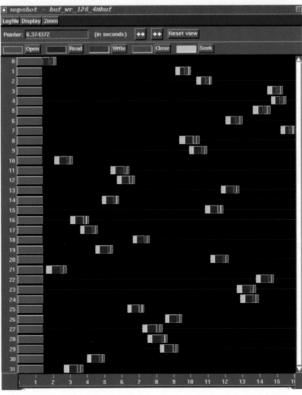

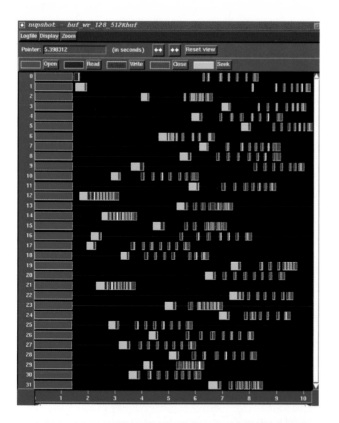

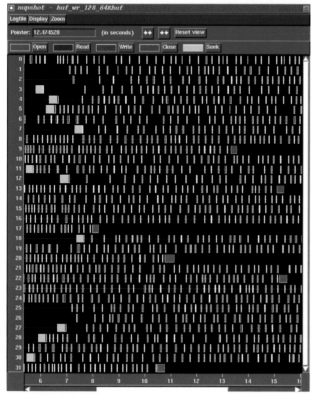

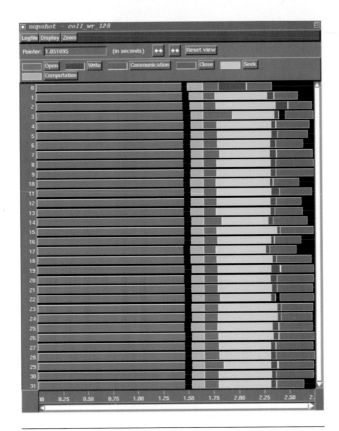

PLATE 11

Writing a $128 \times 128 \times 128$ distributed array on the Intel Paragon using level-3 requests. Elapsed time = 2.75 seconds.

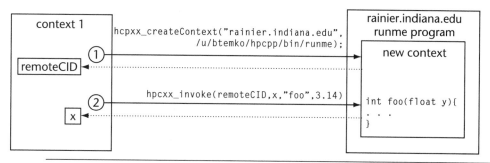

Figure 13.4 A thread in context 1 creates a new remote context on host *rainier.indiana.edu*. The returned ContextID object is used in context 1 to execute the remote function foo in the new context.

13.4 Remote Function Calls, Global Pointers, and Java RMI

Java was originally designed, and has continued to evolve, as a language that supports distributed computing. The addition of RMI to Java has enabled new distributed-computing technologies such as Jini [307] and Enterprise Java Beans [924]. Java RMI is based on the concept of remote reference, which is not that far from the global pointer in CC++. In HPC++, the global pointer takes the form of a template, and it has been implemented to allow interoperability with Java RMI.

An HPC++ program running in one context can invoke another HPC++ program and start it running in another context by a call of the form

```
HPCxx_ContextID *remoteCID =
  hpcxx_createContext(''remote-host.somewhere.com'',
                    ''/home/me/programs/executable'');
```

where the executable path is the location on the named host of a compiled HPC++ "server" program. The server is like any other HPC++ program, but it has a main program that suspends prior to termination. At the point of suspension, the remote, creating program receives a "ContextID" that is a proxy for the newly created and suspended object. As illustrated in Figure 13.4, this ContextID is a handle to use to execute remote function calls that may take the form

```
T  returned_val;
hpcxx_invoke(*remoteCID, returned_val, function_identifier,
            arg1, arg2, ... );
```

In this template, function_identifier is a special unique identifier for the remote function (which is obtained by a special function-registration operation), and all arguments are supplied by value.

In the case of remote objects, remote method calls are based on the HPC++ global pointer that is, in turn, based on the CC++ global pointer. A global pointer is a generalization of the C pointer type to support pointers to objects that exist in other address spaces. It is closely linked to the idea of a global reference, which is an object that is a proxy for a remote object. The HPC++ library implements this with a HPCxx_ GlobalPtr template, as is done in the RWCP MPC++ Template Library.

In most ways, a global pointer can be treated exactly as a pointer to a local object. The primary difference between a global pointer and a regular one is that global pointers can be passed from one context to another. For example, they can be returned as a result of a gather operation or returned as a result of a remote function call.

For objects of the simple type, a global pointer can be dereferenced like any other pointer. However, for objects of the class type, the situation is more complex. To allow remote method invocation through a global pointer to a remote object, HPC++ has two approaches. The most direct method is to register all the members of each class and invoke them with a version of the hpcxx_invoke template function. Most programmers find this to be an awkward way of programming.

An alternative method is to describe the interface to the class in CORBA IDL. For example, suppose that one has a set of classes whose public interfaces can be described with the IDL as

```
//  IDL declaration
module SimpleExample {
  interface Shape{
    attribute float length;
    attribute float breadth;
    readonly attribute long bitsRequired;
    float getLength();
    float getBreadth();
    double getArea(in float length, in float breadth);
  };
  interface Rectangle : Shape{
    long amIaSquare();
  };
};
```

The IDL-to-HPC++ compiler will generate a C++ subclass of the global pointer class that will allow remote invocation of methods of classes implementing these interfaces. For example, if one knows that a remote server process named *rectangles* registered on the host *myhost.indiana.edu* at port 7000 has provided an instance of the rectangle class, then one can fetch a global pointer to the rectangle instance and make remote method invocations as follows:

```
// HPC++ code
gpRectangle rectPtr;
lookupToRegistry(''myhost.indiana.edu'', ''rectangles'', 7000, RectPtr);
float len = rectPtr->getLength();
long result = rectPtr->amIaSquare();
```

Furthermore, the implementation of the remote object can be programmed in either Java or HPC++, and this language interoperability goes both ways. The standard Java RMI code below can be used to access the same remote object.

```
// Java code
String registryHost = ''myhost.indiana.edu'';
String serverName = ''rectangles'';
private int PORT = 7000;
Rectangle rectRef = Naming.lookup(''rmi://''+registryHost+'':'' +
                                  PORT + ''/'' + serverName);
float len = rectRef.getLength();
long result = rectRef.amIaSquare();
```

This interoperability between Java RMI and the HPC++ global pointer allows an object-level interaction between Java front-ends and HPC++ remote multithreaded parallel computations. This property is heavily used in one implementation of the DOE Common Component Architecture described in the next section.

13.5   Component-Based Software Design

Experience with many object-oriented libraries has shown that users are hesitant to utilize large software systems that require them to "buy in" to an entire system in order to assemble their simulation. Although the object-oriented design of scientific libraries is appealing, without careful consideration of physical design factorization [589], libraries can be built that require the user to link in everything and the kitchen sink—regardless of how small the library component that is needed. Users desire only the minimal set of necessary components from an object-oriented library. This has been a large stumbling block to getting object-oriented libraries into the hands of users.

POOMA has been undergoing a "componentization" of sorts; through generic programming techniques and efficient object factorization, the framework may be reduced to a set of interacting components that can be used in minimal sets as needed. For example, the infrastructure for the data-parallel objects has recently been extended with a generic array-mapping abstraction between arbitrary domains and ranges that will enable efficient general communication patterns, including indirect addressing across arbitrarily varying layouts in expressions. These features will provide the user a factored set of objects to develop unstructured grid simulations, particle methods, and nonaligned, structured grid applications with the same set of framework abstractions. Furthermore, the use of the engine pattern is a modularization of the POOMA framework to further separate the interface and implementation, while preserving efficiency. This, and other physical design optimizations, will allow users to develop code with appropriate subsets of the framework rather than the entire class library.

13.5.1   The DOE Common Component Architecture

The most significant advance in software reuse has come from the design of software component architectures. A component architecture is a set of rules and behaviors that define the way objects interact, the way they are composed, and the run-time environment in which they operate. Component systems are divided into two basic elements. Components are the reusable software parts from which applications are built. They constitute the encapsulated bits of application logic that can be specified and implemented independent of the rest of the system. The second basic element of every component architecture is the framework. Frameworks consist of the component "containers" and the software glue that allows us to bind components together to make an application. Each component architecture provides a set of design rules that a software engineer must follow to create a new component. These rules specify how a framework can create an instance of a component and learn about the interfaces implemented by the component. The rules also specify standards that must be followed to allow a new component access to the services provided by the framework. A component architecture does not require new software technology; it is a set of precise software engineering rules that assure component interoperability.

Component-based software design is now a standard practice in the commercial software world. All Microsoft applications are based on something called the Component Object Model (COM) [850], which allows them to interoperate on the desktop and over the network. Within the Java programming world, the Java Beans component programming model has become the standard for building graphical-user-interface applications, and Enterprise Beans is the extension of this component model to distributed application. In 1999, the Object Management Group (OMG) approved a new standard for CORBA components [720] that encompass the Enterprise Bean specification [924] .

In 1997, a group of researchers from each of the DOE laboratories and several universities came together as part of the DOE 2000 project to define a standard component model for scientific computing. The result of this design effort is the CCA [47] specification.

By design, CCA is consistent with the emerging CORBA component model. However, there are large differences in the way the specification is presented. The initial specification of the CCA model is completely in terms of the requirements of the component builder, that is, those rules of behavior that a component must follow so that it may be reused in any CCA-compliant framework. The second phase of the specification process will define the run-time environment and common services each CCA framework will support and the interoperability protocol that will allow a component instance running in one framework to communicate with another component running in a different framework.

A CCA component is defined by two types of interface *ports*:

- *Provides Ports* are references to objects internal to the component that implement a well-defined interface of functions. These references are the handles to the methods and may be invoked on the component by external agents. Each interface may contain several functions, and a component may provide several different ports, or none at all.
- *Uses Ports* are references to objects, external to the component, whose methods are called by the component. Each such referenced object is defined by an interface that describes the methods the component may call on that external object.

Typically, a Uses Port on one component is connected to a Provides Port on another component. A Uses Port may be connected to one or more providers, and each Provides Port may be used by zero or more users. The ability for two ports to be connected is defined by the type compatibility of their interfaces.

A typical CCA framework is defined by the services it provides to components for their internal use. Examples of services might include:

- *Directory services* that allow a component to discover other components by port interface type or by resource requirements. The directory is also used to discover running instances of other components that are available to provide services.
- *Creation services* can be invoked by a component to instantiate a component on a given compute server.
- *Connection services* can be used by one component to connect a Uses Port of a second component to a third.
- *Event services* allow components to publish or subscribe to local or global event streams.

The exact list of services that each CCA framework will support and the way a component accesses these services are topics that are still under consideration.

Another important CCA component property is the concept of a parallel port. This is a "collective port" that will allow a component implemented as a parallel SPMD object to connect over parallel communication channels to another parallel component of possibly different "parallel rank." The future of CCA will include interoperability with other scientific component frameworks such as WebFlow [354] and other technologies to provide a link between the desktop and the supercomputer. The primary goal should be to make it easier to build applications for science and engineering (Figure 13.5).

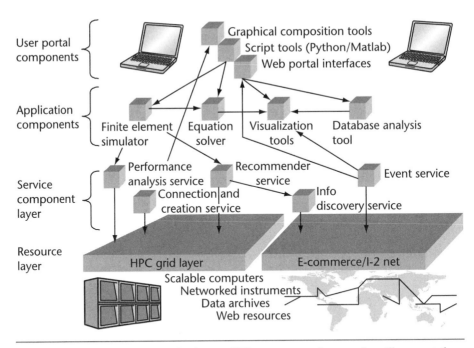

Figure 13.5   It is hoped that in the future, CCA component frameworks will support the construction of application workbenches on the emerging high-performance Grid, as well as interact with the component frameworks of e-commerce and the next-generation Internet.

13.6   Conclusion

This chapter has described four ways in which object-oriented technology can be used in parallel scientific computation.

- *Parameterized data structure libraries* such as POOMA provide a powerful set of generic distributed-data containers for arrays, fields, and particles. Libraries in this class have a set of associated overloaded operators and other methods that can be highly optimized at compile time. POOMA hides the details of parallel computation in a flexible "evaluator" architecture. For the user, this means that a program can be written in a highly abstract data-parallel form, tested and debugged in serial mode, and then run in parallel with very little effort.

- *Algorithmic frameworks* such as SAMRAI [483] take a family of algorithmically related computations and recast them as a set of building blocks with well-defined interfaces. When the building blocks are reassembled, they define a generic representative of the computational family. By extending the base classes and adding application-specific data types and computational kernels, new instances of this archetype can be easily created.

- *Explicit thread and remote object* libraries such as HPC++ and languages such as Java provide a direct approach to writing parallel code for SMP systems and for coordinating the computations of distributed-object systems.

- *Component architectures* provide a software-engineering methodology for building applications by composition. Components encapsulate data and functionality and are defined by their exposed interfaces and the services they require to operate. Component frameworks provide the run-time environment in which components can be instantiated and composed. A framework may operate over a wide-area Grid or completely within a massively parallel computer. In many cases component frameworks are programming-language neutral, and components written in different programming languages can be easily composed. For example, a component designed using POOMA can be composed with a SAMRAI-based component, provided they both adhere to the component framework rules.

Each of these four paradigms plays an important and distinct role in scientific computation. However, the best metric of success for any object-oriented library or framework is the application and user base it supports. The libraries discussed in this chapter have been deployed to many application domains, including hydrodynamics, plasma physics, combustion modeling, fire modeling, electronic structures, molecular dynamics, radiation transport, turbulence modeling, and accelerator dynamics. All the libraries have been ported to several parallel architectures, and some have demonstrated scaling over thousands of processors. The most difficult part of gaining widespread use of these libraries has been the close interaction required with the application domain. Using object-oriented libraries is a new endeavor for many computational physicists. No matter how good the documentation, example codes, and software quality, breaking through the cultural barrier of moving from a procedural to an object-oriented/generic approach to simulation requires significant interaction and collaboration. The key to most successful object-oriented libraries is a set of dedicated, forward-looking users working closely with the library developers.

Several of the strategic simulation efforts underway at large national centers are now based on C++ and Java and build on object-oriented libraries. The growing maturity of both languages and the widespread availability of efficient compilers over the past 5 years has substantially increased the rate of object-oriented library development. Furthermore, the new scientists coming into the scientific computing field tend to be better trained in object-oriented programming techniques than in procedural techniques, further influencing the move toward object-oriented library development for scientific computing.

14 Problem-Solving Environments

Geoffrey Fox • **Jack Dongarra** •
Dorian Arnold • **Henri Casanova** •
Ann Christine Catlin • **Tomasz Haupt** •
Elias Houstis • **John R. Rice**

Problem-solving environments (PSEs) have been studied over the last 30 years and have always suffered from a certain impreciseness in their definition. However, we can follow a pioneer in this field (John Rice from Purdue) and use his 1994 description (*http://www.cs.purdue.edu/research/cse/pses*):

> A PSE is a computer system that provides all the computational facilities needed to solve a target class of problems. These features include advanced solution methods, automatic and semiautomatic selection of solution methods, and ways to easily incorporate novel solution methods. Moreover, PSEs use the language of the target class of problems, so users can run them without specialized knowledge of the underlying computer hardware or software. By exploiting modern technologies such as interactive color graphics, powerful processors, and networks of specialized services, PSEs can track extended problem-solving tasks and allow users to review them easily. Overall, they create a framework that is all things to all people: they solve simple or complex problems, support rapid prototyping or detailed analysis, and can be used in introductory education or at the frontiers of science.

This definition first appeared in *Computer as Thinker/Doer: Problem-Solving Environments for Computational Science* by E. Gallopoulos, E. Houstis and J. R. Rice (*IEEE Computational Science and Engineering*, Summer 1994). According to these authors, the birth of PSEs can be traced to the 1963 proposal of Culler and Fried for an "Online Computer Center for Scientific Problems." In 1967, over 300 people attended an Association for Computing Machinery (ACM) conference on a PSE as an "Interactive System for Experimental Applied Mathematics." The most well-known example of a PSE is probably MATLAB, which has been a popular commercial system in the linear algebra and signal processing fields. Khoros is another well-known PSE in the latter field. Purdue also produced a high-level interface PDELab for solving 2-D and 3-D partial differential equations. The latest Web-based implementation of PDELab is described in Section 14.4. In general, however, the PSE area languished for some 20 years. It was realized that such complex systems were outside the scope of available hardware and software. This situation has changed recently. Not only has hardware performance increased dramatically, but the Web has provided both rich information resources and a powerful software framework, Object Web technology. In fact, a PSE is naturally implemented as a *Web portal to computational science*, to use popular parlance. Other names for PSEs are *scientific workbenches* or *toolkits*.

When discussing PSEs, it is useful to distinguish the PSE itself, which is typically aimed at a particular scientific computing domain, from a PSE Toolkit, which is the group of technologies within some software architectures that can build multiple PSEs. In this chapter, we discuss two CRPC contributions to the PSE toolkit: NetSolve from the University of Tennessee and WebFlow from Syracuse University. Although both are Web based, we will see that they address different needs and have in mind rather different computational models. In each case, we discuss some of the application areas to which these two PSE toolkits have been applied to build domain-specific PSEs. In Section 14.3, we contrast these CRPC systems with the higher-level WebPDELab, which supports special tools aimed at solving partial differential equations on parallel or sequential machines.

PSEs require several major subsystems to provide capabilities such as language/ programming support, access to existing libraries and applications, and intelligent aids to both the science and the computer science. All of this must be tied together with a "software bus or glue." The rest of the chapters in Part III discuss many of the components that are linked together in a PSE. PSEs support interfaces to tools; ability to request particular load-balancing algorithms; mesh generation; linkage of libraries and services, such as access to job status; and, most importantly, security. Input and output data should be specified, and many applications may need to be linked together to solve a single problem. We describe how the two toolkits enable convenient, flexible integration of these services. In Chapter 9 and Section 14.4.1, we discuss computational grids and the Globus toolkit. Comparing systems like Globus with NetSolve and Legion, we see different views of the same dream of building a geographically dispersed linked set of resources to support computational science grand challenges. Globus starts with basic hardware and software capabilities and builds out to the user; NetSolve and WebFlow start with the user and build inward. These complementary roles will be seen in some later examples, where NetSolve and WebFlow provide high-level interfaces to computational grids constructed with Globus. Both the systems described adopt a similar three-tier approach, the client–server–service shown in Figure 14.1.

NetSolve uses agent technology to allow clients to choose the most appropriate service provider for a networked solver, such as a parallel matrix-algebra package. Diverse clients are supported, including Web browsers as well as library calls from user code or packages such as MATLAB. WebFlow supports a distributed object for

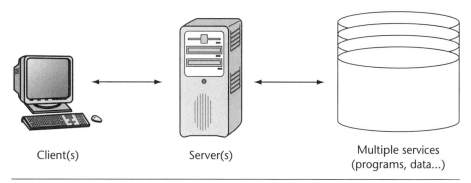

Client(s)　　　　　　Server(s)　　　　　Multiple services
(programs, data...)

Figure 14.1 Idealized three-tier computing model.

program and data components; it uses Java or CORBA object brokers for the server layer. The client level is a Web interface to the distributed objects and supports a visual or scripted specification of the composition of computational objects. WebFlow separates control functions implemented in the server layer from computation and high-performance data transfer in the back-end service layer. This strategy avoids well-known performance limitations in CORBA by using this commodity object technology only to control proxies for coarse-grain HPCC components. WebPDELab establishes a PELLPACK PDE Solver environment on the server and uses the Virtual Network Computing (VNC) [800] system to replicate the PELLPACK user interface on the client.

In Sections 14.1 through 14.3 we describe NetSolve, WebFlow, and WebPDELab. Section 14.4 contrasts these systems with other approaches to computational grids and so-called seamless (Web browser) interfaces to back-end computing resources.

14.1   NetSolve: Network-Enabled Solvers

The current software usage model entails three basic phases: (1) obtaining the software (locating and/or purchasing, investigating licensing, import and export restrictions, etc.); (2) installing the software; and finally, (3) using the software. In addition to these mundane tasks, maintenance of the software system is also necessary to ensure that the latest versions are being used and to obtain patches and bug fixes. The NetSolve project, underway at the University of Tennessee at Knoxville and the Oak Ridge National Laboratory, had very humble beginnings. Its original goal was to free domain scientists from having to perform these tedious tasks when they needed to use numerical software, particularly on multiple platforms. NetSolve began with a single interface, MATLAB, and allowed access to solver routines from the LAPACK library. The first major release was in 1995.

Today, NetSolve has evolved into one of the leading research projects in the area of Grid computing. Its various interfaces provide uniform access to an assortment of software toolkits and libraries. These libraries come from diverse spheres of influence, ranging from mathematical solvers to more eclectic domains such as microbiology and image visualization. The NetSolve system receives continual enhancements and feature upgrades. NetSolve software is freely available and can be downloaded, along with additional documentation and related papers, at *http://www.cs.utk.edu/netsolve*.

14.1.1 The NetSolve Philosophy

As research scientists continue efforts to harness as much computational resources and power as possible, NetSolve continues to position itself in the midst of it all. As the system becomes more enhanced and, unfortunately, more complicated, there are certain fundamentals that we try to maintain. First, the system should be easy to deploy and use. The user wants the software and hardware resources that the middleware makes available and should not have to be concerned about the way these resources are accessed. On the other hand, the interface must be complex enough to meet the full needs of its users. So, NetSolve attempts to do the impossible: to be simple, yet complicated at the same time. We have managed to achieve what we believe to be an adequate, if not perfect, balance between the two.

Another feature of NetSolve involves the integration and usage of other Grid-computing infrastructure. Rather than reinventing the wheel, we try to leverage the accomplishments of the Grid-computing community at large. But our design ensures that we are dependent on none of these systems. Should their resources be available in any of our users' domains, we gladly take advantage of them; but the NetSolve system can, and most often does, stand alone without infrastructure native to the NetSolve system.

14.1.2 NetSolve Infrastructure

As depicted Figure 14.2, NetSolve reflects a client/agent/server design. The client issues requests to agents; the agents allocate servers to service those requests; and the servers receive inputs for the problem, do the computation, and return the output parameters to the client. The NetSolve client-user gains access to limitless software resources without the tedium of installation and maintenance. Furthermore, NetSolve facilitates remote access to computer hardware, including high-performance supercomputers, with complete opacity. Users need no knowledge of computer networking in order to use NetSolve—they don't even have to know that remote resources are involved. Features such as fault tolerance and load balancing further enhance the NetSolve system. In the sections below, we offer a brief discussion of the three aforementioned components.

The Client Interfaces

A major goal in designing NetSolve was to provide users with a choice of interfaces. NetSolve can be invoked via C, Fortran, MATLAB, or Mathematica interfaces (the Mathematica interface is available only on Win32 client platforms). In the past, we

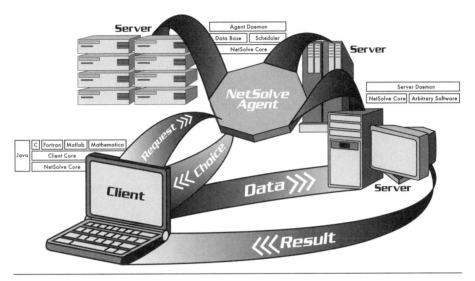

Figure 14.2   NetSolve system.

supported a Java application programming interface (API) and Web-based graphical user interface (GUI). We are upgrading these interfaces to operate with the current version of NetSolve. Another goal was to implement interfaces that were simple to use, but which allowed the user as much control as possible of remote procedure execution.

Each interface provides two basic functions. The first allows synchronous or blocking requests. These do not return until remote execution is complete (or failure is detected). The second provides more nontraditional asynchronous or nonblocking requests. These return immediately, giving the user a "handle" that can be used to query the readiness of and/or obtain the solution set. In addition to these, we provide functions in the API to do error reporting. We also provide the capability to dynamically query a NetSolve system to receive information about either the hardware or software resources. Such queries are used primarily to determine which problems are available and the number, type, and description of the input and output parameters that each problem requires. Interfaces using command-line interpreters such as MATLAB and Mathematica implement these in the form of functions; for the compiled interfaces C and Fortran, compiled executables are used.

The NetSolve Agent

Keeping track of the software resources available and the servers on which they are located is perhaps the most fundamental task of the NetSolve agent. The agent keeps a *database* that maps software resources to hardware components in the NetSolve system. It thus has a complete picture of the capabilities of both the individual servers and the NetSolve system as a whole. The agent can report this information to the client via the interfaces (see above); this aids the user in setting up the problem on top of the NetSolve middleware. The protocol that NetSolve uses to maintain this database is fairly straightforward: upon initialization, a new server sends a "problem description" for each problem that it can solve to the agent with which it was configured to register. This description contains, among other things, the location of the server and the particulars of the function(s) being contributed. Eventually the server is integrated into the system and can be used to service users' requests.

In order to service user requests expeditiously, the agent must use certain criteria to *choose* the best-suited computational server for each incoming request. There are two basic choices: (1) static scheduling—at compile time, the agent is programmed to use an a priori scheme such as round-robin scheduling; and (2) dynamic scheduling— the agent uses run-time information to decide which server component should be used to service a request. NetSolve employs dynamic scheduling, making use of both static and dynamic information. Static information includes speed and number of processors and complexity of the solution algorithm. Dynamic information includes server loads, network delays and transmission rates, and input data sizes. The agent uses this information to rank the servers from best to worst. This list is passed to the client, and the client makes its request to each server in turn, until either the problem has been successfully solved or the list has been exhausted.

The protocol described above emphasizes high throughput rather than *balancing the load* among the servers. Consider a scenario in which NetSolve receives several simultaneous requests. First, suppose that the available servers are a high-performance supercomputer and some mediocre standalone workstations. Assuming that the supercomputer is determined to be the component that will finish the service quickest, then most of the requests will be sent there. Now suppose that all server resources are of approximately the same rating. Then the load will be balanced evenly among the servers, since this will yield the highest throughput.

For *fault tolerance,* NetSolve ensures that a user request will be completed unless every single resource capable of servicing the request has failed. When a client sends a request to a NetSolve agent, it receives a sorted list of computational servers to try. When one of these servers has been contacted successfully, the computation starts. If the contacted server fails during the computation, then another server is contacted and the computation restarts. This entire procedure is transacted independently of, and possibly unbeknownst to, the client user. Although effective, this primitive fault-tolerant mechanism needs to be enhanced. In the next section, where we discuss current developments, we describe our research into employing more advanced fault tolerance.

The Computational Server

One of the challenges in building the NetSolve system was to design a suitable model for the computational servers. For the user to be able to invoke numerical software directly through our servers, three major features seemed mandatory for the servers:

- *Uniform access to the software.* The NetSolve servers should present the interfaces with an illusion of uniformity among the various integrated packages. The critical point is to try to maintain high levels of consistency among and within the different sets of subroutines/functions provided to the user. This allows the user to focus on the particular problem being solved rather than on the peculiarities of the software package being used. This also eliminates long learning phases when using new features.

- *Configurability.* Since the server should not be confined to any particular software, we had to provide a framework that permitted the addition of functionality to a computational server. This framework needed to be general, so that any software toolkit could be integrated with any NetSolve server and made accessible to the client interfaces. In addition, the framework needed to be as intuitive as possible.

- *Preinstallation.* As stated above, we wished to free the user from the burden of software installation. Therefore, in the NetSolve paradigm, the client user is not responsible for installing any software directly; software is made available via the NetSolve servers in a ready-to-use fashion. It is also possible for the NetSolve system to dynamically install and compile routines without any intervention at the user level.

The NetSolve server addresses and successfully resolves all these issues. The server can be configured with a set of preinstalled software libraries to provide uniform access to the subroutines provided. This is done through the use of what we call a *problem description file* (PDF), which describes the particulars of a function to be added. Examples of the information provided in a PDF are the name to be given to the problem, the calling sequence to the NetSolve client interface, and the libraries or archives containing the underlying functions being integrated. The PDF really describes a wrapper that is used to receive or send input and output parameters from and later back to the client interface. Somewhere in these networking transactions is a call to the routine that will actually perform the service that was requested.

Although network interactions are involved, neither the client nor the writer of the PDF needs be concerned with this. The NetSolve system carefully encapsulates and hides these interactions from the user. These wrappers are parsed and compiled into source codes that are compiled with the library archives into NetSolve-specific executables. The appropriate executable is initiated by the server daemon whenever it needs to service a client request.

14.1.3   Some Applications of NetSolve

In this section, we give a brief description of the integration of NetSolve into Grid computing systems and describe some of the applications that have taken advantage of NetSolve's features. In Section 14.4, we discuss some of the other meta-computing resources that NetSolve has used to leverage itself.

MCell

MCell is a general Monte Carlo simulator of cellular microphysiology. MCell uses Monte Carlo diffusion and chemical reaction algorithms in three dimensions to simulate the complex biochemical interactions of molecules inside and outside of living cells. MCell is a collaborative effort between the Terry Sejnowski Lab at the Salk Institute and the Miriam Salpeter Lab at Cornell University. NetSolve is very well suited to MCell's needs, and this project involves writing a NetSolve-based framework to support large MCell runs. One of the central pieces of that framework is a scheduler that takes advantage of MCell input data requirements to minimize turnaround time. This scheduler is part of the larger AppLeS at the University of California-San Diego. The use of NetSolve isolates the scheduler from the resource management details and allows researchers to focus only on the design of the scheduler.

IPARS

IPARS is a framework, described in Chapter 6, for developing parallel models of subsurface flow and transport through porous media. It currently can simulate single-phase (water only), two-phase (water and oil), or three-phase (water, oil, and gas) flow through a multiblock 3-D porous medium. IPARS can model water table decline due to overproduction near urban areas or enhanced oil and gas recovery in industrial applications. IPARS is being made into a fully functional NetSolve server. The goal of the project is to allow this server to be accessible via a Web browser using the Common Gateway Interface on top of NetSolve's C interface. The server will also render animated graphics via a destination Web page. Web accessibility means that those wanting to see IPARS simulations will only have to provide some simple input parameters defining the simulation.

SCIRun

SCIRun is a scientific programming environment that allows the interactive construction, debugging, and steering of large-scale scientific computations. SCIRun can be used interactively in (1) changing 2-D and 3-D geometry models (meshes); (2) controlling and changing numerical simulation methods and parameters; and (3) performing scalar and vector field visualization. Currently, NetSolve is being integrated into SCIRun as the broker for computational resources. This integration will allow for increased parallelism and performance in the SCIRun paradigm.

LUCAS

LUCAS is a system that helps natural resource specialists evaluate the consequences of alternative land management scenarios. It uses computer modeling to integrate both biological and socioeconomic data. The geographic information system GRASS is used to represent and manipulate spatial data on workstations. There is an ongoing effort to integrate NetSolve to harness the computational cycles for LUCAS. This will prove especially useful when LUCAS is used to spawn several "replicates," which normally would compute in serial on the local machine. Using NetSolve, the computations would be done in parallel, possibly on machines specialized for high-performance computing.

DIPS

DIPS is a software tool, developed at the Computer Graphics and Vision unit of the Graz University of Technology in Austria, that allows remote computing for image processing. DIPS extends the Image/J Java image-processing application to provide remote access to the high-performance ImageVision library by Silicon Graphics. At its core, DIPS uses NetSolve as its meta-computing resource to provide unprecedented computing power by aggregating distributed resources on the Internet to a single system.

14.1.4 Current Developments and Future Research

Here we offer insight into a few of the developments that we have made with NetSolve over the past few months. The area of Grid Computing is still relatively fresh, and Net Solve will continue to evolve, as will the Grid, in the years to come.

Dynamic Server-Software Enhancements

In the current NetSolve design and implementation, there is a tight coupling between the server's hardware and software components. The server is statically configured (at compile time) to solve a particular problem set. Although we have provided tools that allow this problem set to be expanded easily, this can only be done during initial configuration. Increasing a running server's capability entails a shutdown, reconfigure, and restart loop. This will not be the case in the next major release of NetSolve. We are providing the capability of storing NetSolve-specific software binaries (see Section 14.1.2) in a software repository whose location is known to the NetSolve agent. At request time, should a particular server not possess the appropriate binaries, it will be directed to the repository for a download. This paradigm will not replace, but will enhance, the current protocol in which the server is statically binded with software.

Fault Tolerance

As explained in Section 14.1.2, the fault tolerance possessed by the NetSolve system incorporates only a retry and restart mechanism. We are presently developing servers enhanced with checkpointing capabilities. As they run, the servers will take frequent checkpoints (via a core dump mechanism). Should one of these servers fail, they will be restarted from the state represented by the core image of the most recent checkpoint, rather than from the beginning. Homogeneous migration will also be possible; a process may be restarted on a different machine of similar architecture and operating system. As this feature becomes more advanced, we will investigate heterogeneous migration and, possibly, checkpointing parallel programs.

Request Sequencing

We recently finished research that would allow us to minimize the network traffic between client and servers in a single-client program making numerous requests to NetSolve. We noticed that, in many cases, data dependencies exist between these requests. We have implemented a feature that allows the client user to bracket together multiple requests to NetSolve. The NetSolve system then analyzes data dependencies and sends only the minimal data necessary to the servers. Inputs to later requests that were outputs of a previous request(s) need not be obtained from the client again. The server makes this data persistent and uses it across all requests as necessary. In our current model, all requests must execute on a single server. Future research will yield a model to use systems such as the Internet Backplane Protocol (IBP) and other distributed storage facilities to stage data as requests are serviced on multiple servers.

Win32 Servers

The Distributed Component Object Model (DCOM) is a protocol that enables software components to communicate directly over a network in a reliable, secure, and efficient manner. DCOM is based on the Open Software Foundation's DCE-RPC and is a standard similar to that of the Common Object Request Broker Architecture (CORBA). We will be developing a version of the NetSolve server that acts as a gateway to problem-solving libraries and systems optimized for the NT platform. The server will be built using the DCOM protocol to manage its networking interactions.

14.2 WebFlow-Object Web Computing

In Figure 14.3, we expand the basic network server picture in Figure 14.1 to show how one of the middle-tier servers acts as a broker between any client and a collection of interesting services. Note that we view the services as being provided by a collection of (distributed) objects. We adopt what we call the *pragmatic object Web* philosophy, where realistic systems are likely to involve aspects of the four leading distributed object technologies: CORBA, COM, Java, and XML [106, 354, 355]. Appropriate

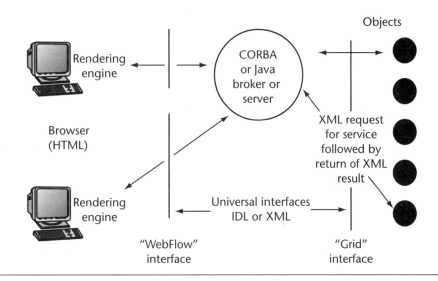

Figure 14.3   More detailed three-tier architecture.

middleware allows these different approaches to interoperate. In particular, WebFlow now uses XML to specify all object interfaces, and these are termed the WebFlow and Grid interfaces for the user and system view, respectively. This two-interface model was adopted at meetings of the Computing Portals group in 1998–1999. As an example, the WebFlow Interface defines an abstract task such as "run a chemistry problem using an HPF simulation code with given data," and the middle-tier server matches this with the back-end objects. The latter are defined by the Grid interface, which can use the Globus resource language RSL. This matching then instantiates a real job to solve the chemistry problem on one or more of the back-end resources. WebFlow originally used Java Servers but now uses CORBA object servers. One simply takes the XML object specifications and uses these to generate the appropriate RMI or CORBA interfaces necessary for the chosen middle tier. This use of XML object specification linked to different object run times is very common in modern commercial systems. Figure 14.4 takes the general architecture of the previous diagram and highlights the capabilities of WebFlow in each of the three tiers. This will be described in more detail in Section 14.2.1. (See also Akarsu et al. [18, 19], Gateway Project [370], Haupt et al. [443, 445], and WebFlow Project [985].)

In the three-tier diagram, WebFlow contributes to the client and middle tiers, as these are the PSE layers where one integrates the components composed of the basic HPCC tools, algorithms, and applications. The WebFlow client tier can be constructed in several ways, but one distinctive capability (which gives the system its name) is the WebFlow composition tool. Here a WebFlow front-end editor applet offers an intuitive click-and-drag metaphor for instantiating middleware or back-end modules. The modules are represented as visual icons in the active editor area;

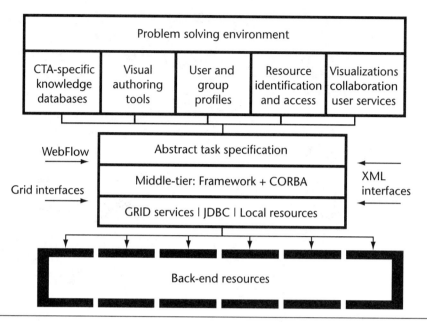

Figure 14.4   WebFlow system architecture.

WebFlow interconnects them visually in the form of computational graphs, familiar to AVS [6] and Khoros [565] users. WebFlow middleware was originally provided by a mesh of Java Web servers, custom extended with servlet-based support for the WebFlow session implementing module and connection managers. These then implemented the middleware logic to support both this general distributed-data-flow computing model and a more general linked-object model. Both models are represented as abstract tasks in XML, allowing scripted as well as visual invocation of programs. This computational paradigm is very popular in some fields (such as signal processing with Khoros). It is seen in research systems such as Arcade from ICASE, which is designed to support multidisciplinary applications such as those arising in structures and fluid flow programs controlled by an optimization module. The WebFlow toolkit also includes the general capability to link to back-end resources, as illustrated by its support of Globus.

Note that WebFlow uses CORBA (or more generally, commodity distributed-object technology) only to manipulate proxies for back-end entities. Thus, it is not impacted by performance limitations of commodity technology. WebFlow's front-end supports visual proxies to specify the problem, while the middle-tier functional proxies support needed control logic. WebFlow relies on classic HPCC back-end capabilities for high-performance computing and communication.

This WebFlow toolkit has been applied to build several problem-solving environments. In Section 14.2.2, we describe two focused examples. The first, LMS, used a custom Java applet front-end instead of the composition tool to control particular linked applications for environmental modeling. A second application of WebFlow is quantum Monte Carlo simulations, developed in collaboration with the National Center for Supercomputing Applications/Condensed Matter Physics Laboratory. Here simulations are linked together and the results stored on many different computers. The output file of one application in the chain is the input of the next one, after a suitable format conversion. This was a natural place to use the WebFlow composition tool.

Recently, we have used WebFlow technology in the so-called Gateway project for the DoD high-performance computing program [765]. Gateway is designed to build a seamless access to the suite of different machines in a computer center. In this case, we needed to address security and fault tolerance more carefully and so reimplemented the WebFlow middle tier using the industry-standard, distributed-object technologies, JavaBeans and CORBA, and industry-standard secure communication protocols based on SSL.

14.2.1 WebFlow Architecture

The WebFlow system is implemented as an object Web three-tier system, as shown in Figure 14.4. Tier 1 is a high-level front-end for visual programming, steering, run-time data analysis, and visualization. It is built on top of the Web and OO commodity standards. A distributed object-based, scalable, and reusable Web server and object broker middleware form tier 2. Back-end services comprise tier 3. In particular, high-performance services are implemented using the Globus meta-computing toolkit.

Front-End

Different classes of applications require different functionality from the front-end. We have therefore designed the WebFlow system to support many different front-ends, from very flexible authoring tools and PSEs that allow for dynamic creation of meta-applications from preexisting modules to highly specialized and customized front-ends to meet the needs of specific applications. Also, we support many different computational paradigms, from general object-oriented to data-flow to a simple "command-line" approach. This flexibility is achieved by allowing as a WebFlow front-end any program implementing the WebFlow API described below.

WebFlow and Grid Interfaces (APIs)

The WebFlow API allows the user's task to be specified in the form of an abstract task descriptor (ATD), following the current computing portals' recommendations. The ATD is constructed recursively and may comprise an arbitrary number of subtasks. The lowest level, or atomic, task corresponds to the atomic operation in the middle tier. These include instantiation of an object and establishing interactions between two objects through event binding. In many cases, such details should be hidden from the end user and even from the front-end developer. Thus, the WebFlow API provides interfaces to higher-level functionality, such as submitting a single job or making a file transfer. When specifying a task, the user does not have to specify the resources to be used to complete the task, but instead may specify requirements that the target resource must satisfy in order to be capable of executing the job. The identification and allocation of the resources are left to the discretion of the system. Typically, the middle tier delegates these tasks to the meta-computing services (such as Globus [383, 398]) or an external scheduler (such as PBS). Once the resources are identified, the abstract task descriptor becomes a job specification.

Middle Tier

A mesh of CORBA-based WebFlow servers currently makes up the WebFlow middle tier. A dedicated gatekeeper server, as shown in Figure 14.4, facilitates a secure access to the system. A general WebFlow server maintains the sessions within which the users create and control their applications. The middle-tier services provide the means to control the life cycles of modules and to establish communication channels among them. The modules can be created locally or on remote hosts. In the latter case, the task of module instantiation and initialization is transparently delegated to a peer WebFlow server on the selected host, and the communication channels are adjusted accordingly. The services provided by the middle tier include methods for submitting and controlling jobs; file manipulation; providing access to databases and mass storage; and querying the status of the system, of the users' applications, and of their components.

Gatekeeper Server

The gatekeeper comprises three logical components: a (secure) Web server, the AKENTI server [694], and a CORBA-based WebFlow server. The user accesses the WebFlow system through a portal Web page from the gatekeeper Web server. The portal implements the first component of WebFlow security: user authentication and generation of the user credentials that eventually will be used to grant access to resources. The AKENTI server controls the authorization process. For each authorized user, the Web server creates a session (i.e., it instantiates the user context in the WebFlow server, as described below) and gives permission to download the front-end applet. The applet is used to create or restore, run, and control user applications. The applet, using the IIOP protocol, communicates directly with the CORBA-based WebFlow server.

To implement the WebFlow server, we use the ORBacus (formerly known as OmniBroker) secure ORB [721], for which we have obtained a free research license. The security services are implemented on top of the IAIK SSL library, which is already used by the Jigsaw Web server.

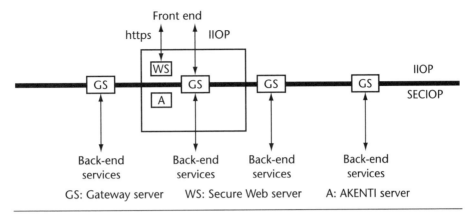

Figure 14.5 WebFlow middle tier with gateway servers (GS); secure Web server (WS), and authentication (AKENTI) server A.

WebFlow Server

The WebFlow server initializes the ORB and several generic CORBA and specific WebFlow services. The main function of the WebFlow server is to manage WebFlow sessions. A session is established automatically after the authorized user is connected to the gatekeeper by creating a user context. The user context is a container object that stores the user applications. The application is another container object that stores components of the user application. The application component is either a single WebFlow module or another, finer-grain, application context. This way, the WebFlow server can simultaneously manage many sessions; and within each session, the user can define many applications, hierarchically composed of many modules.

WebFlow Modules

The WebFlow modules are CORBA objects conforming to the Java Beans model, whose implementation is described in detail in Akarsu [17]. The functionality of a module is implemented either directly in the body of the module, or the module serves as a proxy of specific back-end services, such as database or high-performance computing and communication (HPCC) services. We expect to support the standards for HPCC back-end services under development by the Grid Forum. For databases, we support the industry standard JDBC (Java database connectivity).

Interactions between WebFlow Modules

The WebFlow modules follow the Java Beans model, and they interact with each other by using Java Beans methods through event binding, property binding, and vetoable property binding. With Java Beans, events are used to communicate information about the changing state of a bean. Events form a core component of the Java Beans architecture, in that they are largely responsible for enabling beans to be plugged together as building blocks in an application builder. Event notification in Java works using method invocation. The object that is a source of an event calls a method on the destination object for one event when the event is triggered. The destination of the message must implement the method (or methods) to be notified when the event occurs. The event object encapsulates all the information about an event.

Event targets are connected to event sources through a registration mechanism. WebFlow applications are created dynamically from independently developed WebFlow modules. Therefore, we provide support for a dynamical event binding based on the standard CORBA dynamic interface invocation (DII) and dynamic stub invocation (DSI) mechanisms. This is implemented by introducing an event adapter associated with the application context. The adapter maintains a binding table to associate the event sources with the actual event destinations. Note that we choose not to use the important commodity Enterprise Java Bean middle-tier containers, as currently they appear difficult to implement consistently with our security requirements.

14.2.2   WebFlow Applications

WebFlow has been used successfully in several applications. These include the Landscape Management System, Quantum Simulations, and the Gateway system for seamless access. Each of these is discussed briefly in this section.

Landscape Management System

The Landscape Management System (LMS) project [442] was sponsored by the U.S. Army Corps of Engineers Waterways Experiment Station (ERDC) Major Shared Resource Center (MSRC) at Vicksburg, Mississippi, under the DoD HPC modernization program, Programming Environment and Training (PET). The application can be idealized as follows. A decision maker (the end user of the system) wants to evaluate changes in vegetation, caused by a short-term disturbance such as a fire or human activities, in some geographical region over a long time period. One of the critical parameters of the vegetation model is soil condition at the time of the disturbance. This, in turn, is dominated by the rainfall that occurs at that time. Consequently, as shown in Figure 14.6, implementation of this project requires the following activities:

- Data retrieval from remote sources, including DEM (data elevation model) data, land use maps, soil textures, and dominant flora species and their growing characteristics. The data are available from many different sources. These include public services such as U.S. Geological Survey Web servers and proprietary data-

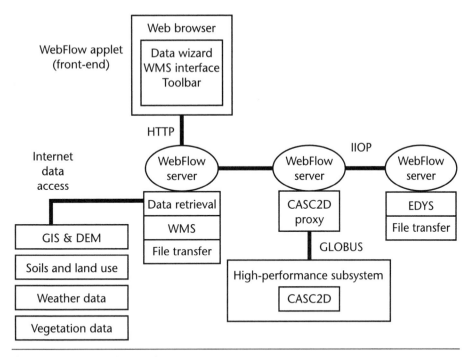

Figure 14.6   LMS problem-solving environment.

bases. The data come in different formats and with different spatial resolutions. Without WebFlow, the data must be manually prefetched.

- Data preprocessing to prune and convert the raw data to a format expected by the simulation software. This preprocessing is performed interactively using the WMS (Watershed Modeling System) package [999].

- Execution of two simulation programs: EDYS [195] for vegetation simulation including the disturbances and CASC2D [722] for watershed simulations during rainfall. The latter generates maps of soil conditions after the rainfall. The initial conditions for CASC2D are set by EDYS just before the rainfall event, and the output of CASC2D after the event is used to update parameters of EDYS. The data transfer between the two codes has to be performed several times during one simulation. EDYS is not CPU demanding, and it is implemented only for Windows 95/98/NT systems. On the other hand, CASC2D is very computationally intensive and typically is run on powerful back-end supercomputer systems.

- Visualization of the results of the simulation. Again, WMS is used for this purpose.

One requirement of this project was to demonstrate the feasibility of implementing a system that would allow launching and controlling the complete simulation from a networked laptop. We successfully implemented it using WebFlow, with WMS and EDYS encapsulated as WebFlow modules running locally on the laptop and CASC2D executed by WebFlow on remote hosts. The existing codes were not modified; instead, the WebFlow PSE used object wrappers to construct a powerful integrated application-specific environment. Further, the applications involved showed a typical mix of HPCC and computationally less demanding PC codes.

For this project, we developed a custom front-end that allows interactive selection of the region of interest. The user draws a rectangle on a map, selects the data type to be retrieved, launches WMS to preprocess the data and make visualizations, and finally launches the simulation with CASC2D running on a host of choice.

Quantum Simulations

A major goal of the quantum simulation (QS) activity was to demonstrate the feasibility of layering WebFlow on top of the Globus meta-computing toolkit. This way, WebFlow serves as a job broker for Globus. Globus (or more precisely, GRAM-keeper) takes responsibility for the actual resource allocation, which includes authentication and authorization of the WebFlow user to use computational resources under Globus control.

This application [783] can be characterized as follows. A chain of high-performance applications (including commercial packages such as GAUSSIAN or GAMESS and custom-developed packages) is run repeatedly for different data sets. Each application can be run on several different (multiprocessor) platforms, so input and output files must be moved between machines. Output files are visually inspected by the researcher; if necessary, applications are rerun with modified input parameters. The output file of one application in the chain is the input of the next one, after a suitable format conversion. The logical structure of the application is shown in Figure 14.7. GAUSSIAN and GAMESS are run as Globus jobs on Origin 2000 or Convex Exemplar at NCSA, while all file editing and format conversions are performed on the user's desktop.

Unlike LMS, for QS we are using the WebFlow program composition editor as the front-end. This WebFlow editor provides an intuitive environment to visually compose (click-drag-and-drop) a chain of data-flow computations from preexisting modules (as shown in Figure 14.8). In the edit mode, modules can be added to or removed from the existing network and connections between the modules can be updated. Once created, the network can be saved (on the server side) for later restoration. The workload can be distributed among several WebFlow nodes (WebFlow servers), with the interprocessor communications handled by the middle-tier services. Moreover, thanks to the interface to the Globus system in the back-end, execution of particular modules can be delegated to powerful HPCC systems. In the run mode, the meta-application represented by the visually constructed graph is

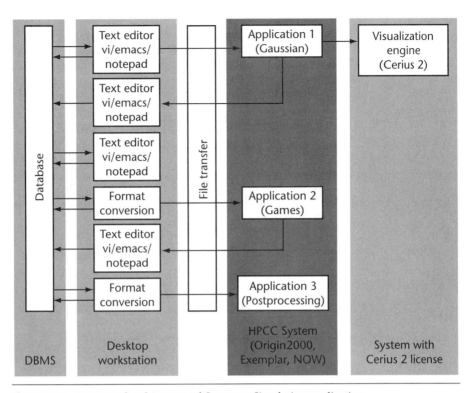

Figure 14.7 Functional architecture of Quantum Simulation application.

passed to the middle tier by sending a series of requests (module instantiation, in-termodule communications) to the middle-tier services.

Control of module execution involves more than just sending relevant data through the input ports of the module. Most of the modules developed so far require some additional parameters that can be entered via "module controls," which are Java applets displayed in a card panel of the main WebFlow applet. The communication channels between the back-end implementation of a module and its front-end module controls are generated automatically during the instantiation of the module.

Gateway Seamless Access

Exploiting our experience developing the WebFlow PSEs described above, we designed a new system, Gateway, to provide seamless and secure access to computational resources at DoD modernization sites—in particular, first at the ASC Major Shared Resource Center at Wright Patterson Air Force Base in Dayton, Ohio [765]. While preserving the original three-tier architecture, we reengineered the implementation of each tier in order to conform to the XML-based standards indicated

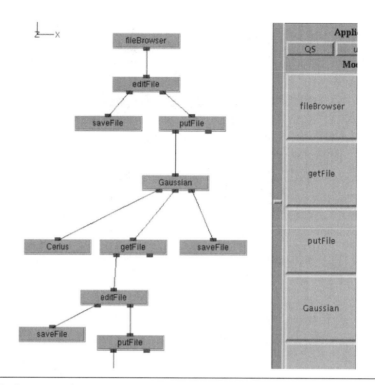

Figure 14.8   Fragment of quantum simulation WebFlow composition tool.

in Figures 14.3 and 14.5. We developed for this application the CORBA and the Java Beans model to build a new middle tier, which facilitates seamless integration of commodity software components. The security system supports the Kerberos and SecurID system adopted by DoD for their modernization program. This new technology is being retrofitted to the applications described above and is used in newly developed applications.

Gateway's architecture includes provision for visualization. We are working with NCSA (VisBench) [701] and ARL (DICE) [263] to design visualization subsystems supporting the WebFlow distributed-object model. In the first two PSEs discussed above, we integrated existing visualization systems such as WMS (for LMS) and Cerius (for the QS case) with WebFlow. We also prototyped XML specifications of collaboration. When combined with the WebFlow API, these can generate collaborative portals to computing.

Initially, Gateway is designed with a custom chemistry front-end developed by the Ohio Supercomputer Center (OSC). It handles job submission (to the scheduler PBS via Globus), choice of multiple applications, and basic WebFlow file services. The front-end is arranged in layers: entry, problem description, code, and results with well-defined (XML) interfaces. This approach appears to generalize to other applications.

At present, Gateway development is focused on supporting the areas of earthquake science [353] and structural mechanics [765].

14.3 WebPDELab

WebPDELab is a Web server that provides access to PELLPACK [175], a sophisticated problem-solving environment for partial differential equation (PDE) problems. Users can connect to the WebPDELab site at *http://webpellpack.cs.purdue.edu/* with any Java-enabled browser for information, demonstrations, cases studies, and PDE problem-solving service.

14.3.1 The WebPDELab Server

The scenario illustrated in Figure 14.9 shows how a user on the Internet accesses WebPDELab services. A new PELLPACK session is initiated for each user who connects to the WebPDELab server, and a unique identification and private file space for

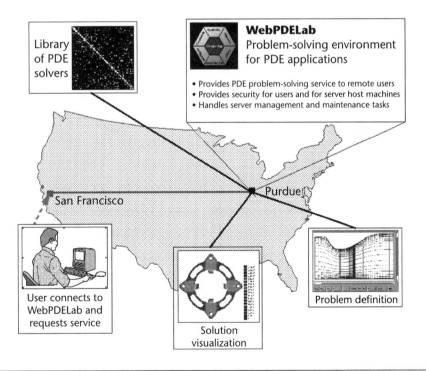

Figure 14.9 View of the WebPDELab system operating over the Internet.

the session are created. The file space is available until the user disconnects from the service, at which time the session is terminated and the user's files are deleted. Users may download files generated by PELLPACK to their own machines before terminating the session, and they may upload files to WebPDELab at the start of subsequent server sessions. When the server invokes the PELLPACK system software, the entire PDE problem-solving environment described in Houstis et al. [488] is presented to the user. This environment is described only briefly in Section 14.3.1. For a detailed description of the functionality and operation of the PELLPACK software, all or part of the user guide (400 pages) [175] can be downloaded from the website. PELLPACK is a comprehensive system for modeling physical objects based on PDEs. It has been used by hundreds of students and faculty, both inside and outside of Purdue University, for solving problems in physics (liquid crystal droplets, proton flux propagation), thermal field analysis, fluid dynamics, semiconductors, geophysical research, electromagnetic field analysis, thermo-elasticity, structural analysis, and other scientific and engineering applications. PELLPACK has a user-friendly interface, and even first-time users can solve interesting problems by following the fully documented, step-by-step descriptions of the problem-solving process presented in Getting Started at the WebPDELab site.

The PELLPACK Problem-Solving Environment

WebPDELab is an Internet-based, client-server implementation of the PELLPACK software. PELLPACK is a system that allows users to specify and solve PDE problems on a target computational platform and to visualize the solution. PELLPACK provides a graphical user interface for defining the PDE model and selecting solution methods (Figure 14.10) and is supported by the Maxima symbolic system and well-known numerical libraries. The graphical interface is implemented on top of a very high-level PDE language. Users can specify their PDE problem and its solution visually using the graphical interface or textually using the "natural" language. PELLPACK has incorporated over 100 solvers of various types that cover all the common PDE applications in two and three dimensions.

In the PELLPACK system, a problem is represented by the PDE objects involved: PDE model or equations, domain, conditions on the domain boundary, solution methods, and output requirements. The PELLPACK interface consists of many graphical tools and supporting software to assist users in building a problem definition. A textual specification of these objects comprises PELLPACK's natural PDE language, and the language representation of each object is generated by the object editors/tools. The language definition of a user's problem (the .e file) is automatically passed to PELLPACK's language processor, which translates the problem into a Fortran driver program and then compiles and links it with numerical libraries containing the user-specified solver methods. Sequential or parallel program execution is a one-step process; the program is executed on one or more machines in the supporting i86pc host cluster. Problem solutions are passed to the PELLPACK visualization system for solution display and analysis.

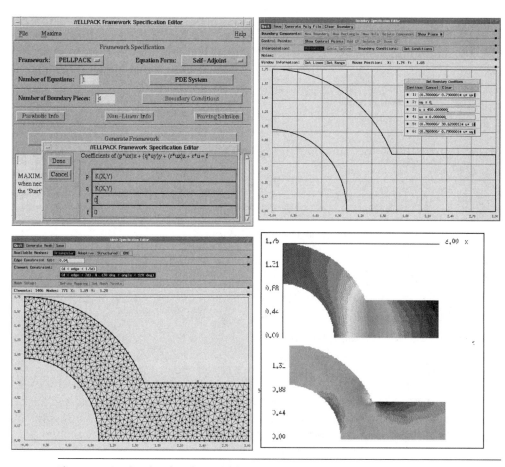

Figure 14.10   Graphical tools available in the PELLPACK problem-solving environment.

The WebPDELab Interface

The WebPDELab server is accessed from the WebPDELab website. This website is an instructional source for anyone interested in solving PDE applications. It provides information about PDE problem solving in general and about the process of solving PDE problems with PELLPACK in particular. A collection of fully documented case studies is available at the site (Figure 14.11), presenting step-by-step solutions of common PDE applications (flow, heat transfer, electromagnetism, conduction), with every user action and PELLPACK result described with images and detailed text.

Users who request the PDELab problem-solving service must first register with WebPDELab (Figure 14.12). After the user-registration information is validated and the server connects to a host machine, WebPDELab presents a framed HTML page.

Steady–state Heat Diffusion in a Slice of Reactor Dome.

The Problem.
We want to solve the heat transfer problem on a 2–D slice of reactor dome constructed from two materials: steel and concrete. The self–adjoint form of the heat equation models the temperature distribution :
$(K(x,y)*T_x)_x + (K(x,y)*T_y)_y = 0$
where $K(x,y)$ is the thermal conductivity of the materials. The PDE problem with domain and boundary conditions is shown to the right. Click <u>here</u> to see a physical description of the problem. We will generate a uniform triangular mesh, and we select the

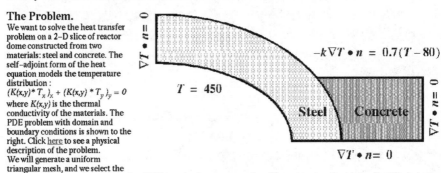

bi–linear FEM discretizer with the Jacobi CG iterative linear system solver. We want to store the solution T and its derivatives Tx and Ty.

Use PDELab to ...

- <u>Define the Problem</u>
- <u>Specify the Solution</u>
- <u>Execute the Problem</u>
- <u>Visualize the Solution</u>

Figure 14.11   Sample case study from `Getting Started` at the website.

There is a control panel in the top frame (Figure 14.13), consisting of four buttons: `Upload Files`, `Download Files`, `Start Server`, and `Exit Server`. The bottom frame contains the user identification number, host connection information, and instructions for using the buttons of the control panel in the top frame. At this point, the WebPDELab server has already created the user's directory space, so that users can upload files to their directories using the Upload button. Generally, users upload PELLPACK problem-definition files, such as .e files, mesh files, and solution files, from previous WebPDELab sessions. Users can upload up to 20 files to their assigned directory space, but files may no longer be uploaded once a user clicks on the Start Server button.

The Download button returns a listing of the user's directory contents. Files in this directory can be viewed or downloaded from the listing. Since users' directories are password protected, no other directories can be viewed or entered. The Download button is available throughout the user's PELLPACK session. Users should look here frequently during the session to check on PELLPACK-generated problem, solution, and trace files. The Start Server button invokes the password-protected PELLPACK software. After the password is entered and verified (Figure 14.14), the top-level window of the PELLPACK system appears in the bottom frame of the browser window, as shown in Figure 14.15. A collection of sample problems has been placed in the user's directory, so users can load an example into the PELLACK session or begin their own problem definition. The PELLPACK session in Figure 14.16 is in the bottom frame of the WebPDELab server. The buttons of the control panel are

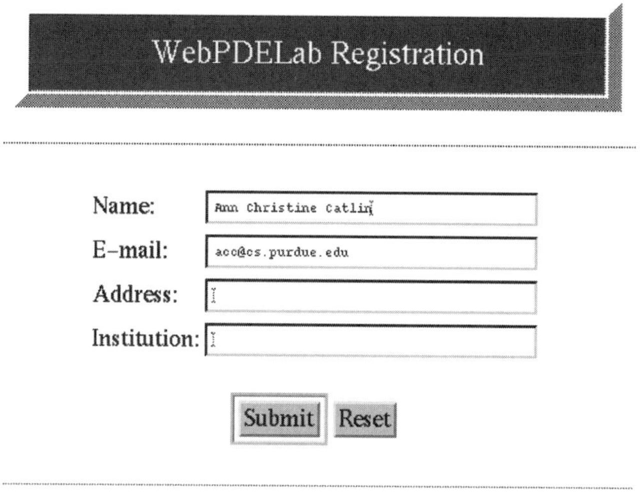

Figure 14.12   WebPDELab registration.

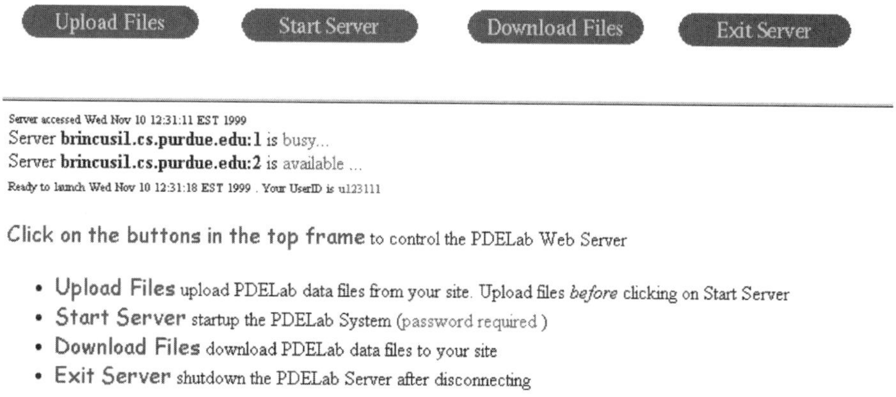

Figure 14.13   WebPDELab server with control panel in the top frame and panel instructions and connection information in the bottom frame.

still available in the top frame, but only the Download and Exit Server buttons are enabled. The Upload and Start Server buttons remain disabled while the PELLPACK software is running in the bottom frame.

During the PELLPACK session, WebPDELab is passing the display of the remotely executing PELLPACK environment to the user's browser window. The graphical

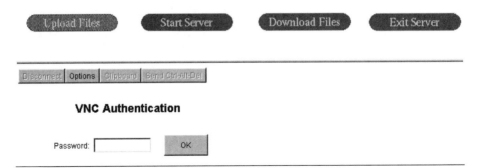

Figure 14.14   Password entry for the PELLPACK system, showing the control panel in the top frame.

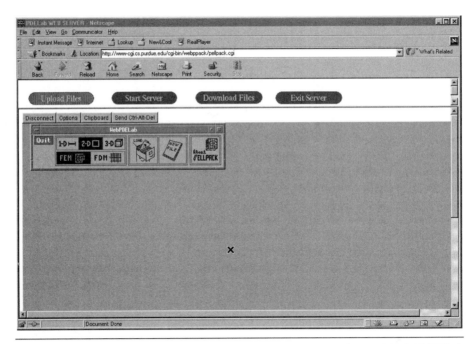

Figure 14.15   The PELLPACK top-level window appears in the bottom frame of the WebPDELab browser window. It is ready for user interaction.

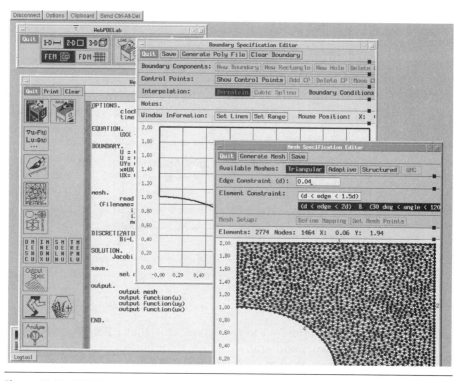

Figure 14.16   PELLPACK session running inside the WebPDELab browser window.

interface displayed on the user's screen belongs to PELLPACK and is not described in this paper. When a user clicks on Exit Server, the PELLPACK session is terminated and the user's directory is removed.

WebPDELab traces all user activities from the start of the server session until its termination. Users' files are secure from other users, but WebPDELab "looks at" the contents of every file uploaded to WebPDELab or created by the user from within the PELLPACK system. WebPDELab protective mechanisms implemented for the security of the WebPDELab server and host cluster are discussed in Section 14.3.2.

WebPDELab Implementation

WebPDELab is the PELLPACK problem-solving environment implemented as a Web server using virtual network computing (VNC) [800]. VNC is a remote display system which allows users to view a computing "desktop" environment from anywhere on the Internet using a wide variety of machine architectures. VNC consists of a server that runs the applications and generates the display, a viewer that draws the display on the client screen, and a TCP/IP connection between them. The server is started on the machine where the desktop resides; after this any number of viewers can

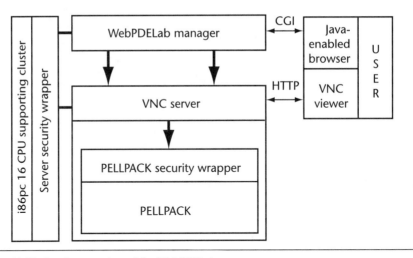

Figure 14.17   Implementation of the WebPDELab server.

be started and connected to the server. This allows the client user to access the applications, data, and entire desktop environment provided by the server. The viewer is a small, shareable, platform-independent, and stateless system that runs on the client machine.

In the WebPDELab implementation, a new VNC UNIX server is started for each user who accesses the WebPELab Web server from a Java-enabled browser (see Figure 14.17). The VNC Java viewer is started from the user's browser, allowing the user to display and interact with the PELLPACK environment, which consists of X-windows programs and libraries compiled and running on the i86pc SunOS 5.6 host machines. Within this framework, any user worldwide who is connected to the Internet and has access to a Java-capable browser can run WebPDELab.

The WebPDELab *manager* is the collection of CGI scripts (Common Gateway Interface protocol for browser-to-server communication) that control all user activity once the PDELab Server button at the WebPDELab web site is pressed. When a user accesses the server, the manager collects information on all currently running VNC servers from the host machines. The manager then asks the potential user to enter registration information, including a valid email address. After the email address is validated, a unique user ID is generated for the new user, and a log file is set up to track registration information, user access/exit times, and user activities while running the PELLPACK software. The host machine with the lightest traffic is selected by the manager for running the VNC server and subsequently the PELLPACK software. A protective client-server application is used to launch the VNC server, so that users are never logged in to any machine in the host cluster. The VNC server start-up invokes the PELLPACK system; the manager creates the user directory, sends the control panel to the user, and monitors the user's interaction with the control panel buttons (Upload Files, Download Files, Start Server, and Exit Server).

Upload Files is implemented using copyrighted public domain code at *http://stein .cshl.org/WWW/software/CGI* (Lincoln D. Stein, 1998). The code has been modified to operate with the WebPDELab/VNC user-directory privacy restrictions. The Download Files button is implemented as a standard link to the user's file space, but additional password security protects a user's assigned directory from all other users on the Internet. Start Server connects the VNC client user to the VNC server that has been instantiated for the caller on the selected host for a specific VNC server.

After control has passed to the VNC client, the manager waits for a VNC disconnect or an Exit Server button click. When signaled to start exit processing, the manager saves the trace of user activities to the log database, kills the VNC server, and removes the user's directory. The manager also checks all executing VNC servers periodically for sessions running longer than 10 hours, and these sessions are terminated. When the manager has finished exit processing, control is returned to the WebPDELab home page.

14.3.2   WebPDELab Security Issues

All Internet-based services must be concerned with security issues and must strive to protect their network and host environments from unauthorized access. WebPDELab implements measures to provide such a secure environment by enforcing common rules of best practice that are used to secure UNIX machines, taking advantage of the strength and flexibility of the UNIX operating system. WebPDELab maintains several levels of security provided by the operating system, the WebPDELab and VNC servers, and protective language processing software built on top of the PELLPACK system. These security measures are described in this section.

When a user logs in to the WebPDELab server, a CGI script is executed that generates a unique UID (user identification) for that user and requests one of the cluster host machines to invoke a VNC X-server. The WebPDELab CGI scripts reside on an isolated machine dedicated to serving CGI requests. This machine has no NFS-mounted disks; an attacker attempting to take advantage of vulnerable CGI scripts is locked into the cgi-bin directory and cannot gain access to any other machines or disks. All parameters passed to WebPDELab CGI scripts are scanned to ensure that they contain precisely the expected values (argument number, length, and contents); otherwise, the request is terminated. The cluster machines listen on a fixed port for start-up requests from the CGI machine. If an attempt to connect to this port does not originate from the CGI host, the connection is immediately terminated. All cluster machines run a daemon that listens for socket connections on a specified port and spawns a child process to serve the request; the parent continues to listen for other connections so that requests can be served simultaneously. A client program is invoked by the CGI script to contact the cluster machine and request that a new VNC X-server be launched. The client may only specify the VNC X-server start-up parameters, since the launching of the VNC X-server binary is hard-coded in the configuration file of the daemon serving requests originating from the CGI host. The VNC server itself is protected by a challenge–response password scheme.

The cluster machines run the VNC X-server as owned by a dedicated account whose root directory is the account's home directory (using the UNIX maintenance chroot command). All the required binaries are located the chroot-ed directory. If a user discovers vulnerabilities in one of the cluster machines, the user is locked into the home directory of the account and is unable to cause harm to other accounts or disks. In order to protect the machine from unauthorized Fortran code inserted by a user into the PELLPACK .e file, specialized filters have been built into the original PELLPACK system. The original PELLPACK language processor already restricted the location of Fortran code to specialized segments within the PELLPACK problem definition file; these segments are now re-parsed by filters that identify inserted Fortran statements for unauthorized code.

Every user is provided with a unique directory for uploading and downloading files, thus facilitating the option of saving and retrieving material. This directory is created by the CGI script after the registration information is entered and validated. Users' directories are password protected, securing each user from all other users. Every user file, however, is opened and checked by WebPDELab for legal content as it is uploaded or saved by the user from inside PELLPACK.

14.3.3   WebPDELab Features and Issues

In this section, we list the significant benefits resulting from the implementation of the WebPDELab server described in Section 14.3.1:

- *Generality*. Any machine connected to the Internet can use the PELLPACK environment without concerns about language or machine compatibility.
- *Interaction*. Users can specify the PDE with normal interaction speeds for the client machine, since data entry is done locally. The amount of code exported to support the user interface is substantial (several megabytes), but it is only a fraction of the PELLPACK system. If the user has no graphics capability, then the text-based interface tools must be used; these are less convenient but still practical to use.

   As the PDE problem is being specified, information is sent to the server. The server might request additional information, but once the problem is completely specified, it is solved on the server's host machines. After the PDE is solved, the user can either view output generated by the server or request that the solution (normally a large data set) be sent for local use.
- *Access to high-performance computers*. Any user can access machines with sufficient power to solve the PDE problem. Even if the solution is too large to be sent to the user (or if there are no local visualization tools), the solution can be explored over the Internet.

- *No code-portability problems.* Users do not need to have the code in the local machine language, since the software infrastructure operates only on the server's host machines.

There are several concerns and technical issues involved in the service provided by WebPDELab.

- *Performance of the user interface.* There is a clear tradeoff in user interface performance between exporting code to the user's machine and executing code on the server. Our existing prototype shows that communicating each mouse click back to the server for processing provides unsatisfactory interactive performance due to network delays. Our analysis indicates that almost all of the interaction can be run locally by exporting a moderate amount of code. The user interface does use tools that are both time consuming to execute and too large to export. Examples are Maxima (used to transform mathematical equations) and domain processors (used to create meshes or grids in geometric domains). These tools usually require pauses in response even without a network, and the added delay due to networks is unlikely to be significant.

- *Security for the server.* While we control the material received from a user, the server is clearly subject to attack. We place the server on a separate subnet and access licensed software through a gateway. Since we know exactly what is to be sent via an RPC, it is possible to protect this licensed software. Even if a user succeeds in becoming "root," access to other machines is not possible. Of course, network file systems and similar tools are not used. Our process of "registering" users when we give them accounts provides us with a chance to screen users before providing them access to WebPDELab.

- *Security for the user.* This requires each user to be completely isolated from all others. Each user on the server runs in a virtual file system using a login with no access privileges. Thus, each user appears to have the entire machine, and the protection mechanisms between machines protects users from one another. This approach provides security at the cost of using much more memory than would normally be necessary.

- *Software ownership and fair use.* We prevent the copying of software by placing, if necessary, source code on another machine or another network and using secure RPC.

- *Payment for computing services.* The WebPDELab server is provided free to users as is time on associated servers used for security purposes. We do not foresee a need to charge users for time on these machines. If large numbers of users contend for service, then they will be queued and the cost of the servers is clearly limited. However, there is a real problem when we access parallel machines that act as compute servers. Initially, WebPDELab uses local machines (a 140-processor Paragon, a 64-processor SP-2, a PC cluster with 32 PCs, and an SGI Origin 2000 with 32 processors), and a user can easily pose a problem that uses several hours on one of these machines. We intend to access off-site machines in the future. When the usage of these compute servers becomes a problem, we will require users to obtain accounts on them. This is a nuisance now, but we believe that the Internet infrastructure will evolve soon to simplify such administrative problems.

There are three technical issues considered in the deployment of WebPDELab as a successful server. First, the user interface must be clearly separated from the rest of the system. Our system is very modular in nature, and we have already essentially completed this task. Second, the user interface must be efficient and exportable. We have already made a prototype exportable user interface that is neither efficient nor general. It assumes the user has an X-windows server and it requires excessive network communication. We have studied Java implementation and believe we can use it to obtain both efficiency and generality on the network.

Third, the user interface must deal with the visualization of very large data sets over the network. Using WebPDELab, a person with a simple PC can generate a PDE solution consisting of millions of data points in 3-D. In our own group, we have 155 Mbit/s asynchronous transport mode (ATM) networks and expensive graphics workstations to visualize such solutions. We see two ways to provide visualization service to the user, neither of which is always satisfactory. First, we have visualization tools to slice, rotate, color, and otherwise manipulate data for viewing. We could send these images back over the Internet, but the user might have a slow network connection or a black-and-white display. In that case, the viewing process would be painfully slow. Second, we can send the data set to the user. A 2-million-point solution is not rare, and its data set would be at least 25 to 50 MBytes. The transmission time could be prohibitive if the user has slow network connections. In addition, the user might not have space to store the solution or might not have any visualization tools that can handle the data. We believe that visualization over the Internet will be a serious problem for some users, and it is one for which we currently have no solution. We believe that this is a common problem and that the Internet infrastructure will provide solutions in a few years.

14.4   Other Grid-Computing Environments

There are additional Grid-computing environments available. These include Meta-computing systems, such as Globus, CONDOR, Ninf, and Legion, as well as projects providing seamless access to remote resources.

14.4.1   Meta-Computing Systems

Meta-computing systems provide support in developing whole applications for distributed computing environments. Here we discuss four of the most prominent of these.

Globus [383] is a software system that provides infrastructure for computations that leverage distributed computational and informational resources. It is being developed at the Argonne National Laboratory and the University of Southern California's Information Sciences Institute. Currently, the NetSolve system uses a component of Globus referred to as the Heart Beat Monitor (HBM). The HBM allows NetSolve to easily detect failed server hosts and update the agent's database. We are also testing a new NetSolve proxy-client that allows Globus-enabled NetSolve client users to access and use Globus computational resources through the NetSolve interface. We have discussed extensively the integration of WebFlow with Globus. Recent developments of the Globus Group—especially the COG Kit [215] for linking Globus services automatically to middle-tier servers—have extended greatly the capability of Globus to support PSEs.

The CONDOR system, of the University of Wisconsin, takes advantage of the fact that many CPU cycles go wasted on idle workstations at times when the primary user is not using the machine. The system assigns tasks submitted to the CONDOR system to "registered" host machines as long as these machines are idle. Should the owner return to the machine, the task is immediately halted and assigned to another host. CONDOR pools can be used as NetSolve servers. In essence, the request for service is forwarded to the CONDOR system, which then assigns the task to an idle workstation for completion. CONDOR has not yet been used with WebFlow, but it should be straightforward to use CONDOR at the back-end tier in the same way that Globus is used in the examples of Section 14.2.2.

Ninf is a system very similar to NetSolve. Developed at the Electrotechnical Laboratory in Tsukuba, Japan, it provides an interface that allows for remote execution of functional components. In a collaborative effort, a NetSolve-Ninf bridge has been built that allows each system to utilize servers provided to the other. Administrators of NetSolve and Ninf systems can then join forces to create an even bigger computational Grid.

Legion is an object-based meta-systems software project at the University of Virginia. Its goal is to tie together host systems with high-speed links and present the illusion of a single computer with access to varied physical resources. The NetSolve client-user can use the NetSolve interface while leveraging the meta-computing resources of Legion. The NetSolve client side uses Legion data-flow graphs to keep track of data dependencies. We hope to study the linkage of Legion and WebFlow, but as both have object models, the integration is not as straightforward as for Globus and WebFlow.

14.4.2 Seamless Access and Application Integration

Several other projects address the problem of seamless access to remote resources. A comprehensive list of these is available from the Java Grande and Computing Portals websites [397, 512]. The NCSA Alliance has started an effort (The Common Portal Architecture) that will build on many of the ideas discussed above to provide a common framework for building Web-based portals to the large computational science application efforts at the NSF supercomputer centers.

The UNICORE project [945] introduces an excellent model for the abstract task descriptor that was well received at Computing Portals meetings [397] and, consequently, we are taking a similar approach. The UNICORE middle tier is given by a network of Java Web servers (Jigsaw). The WebSubmit project from the National Institute of Standards and Technology [986] implements Web access to remote high-performance resources through CGI scripts. Both projects use the https protocol for user authentication (as we do) and implement custom solutions for access control. The ARCADE project [661] is aimed at multidisciplinary applications (especially those of interest to the National Aeronautics and Space Administration and aerospace applications), and its designers intend to use CORBA to implement the middleware. Indiana University has developed application integration tools built on the ideas of the Department of Energy's common component architecture (CCA) [176, 216].

14.5   Conclusion

Problem-solving environments represent an active and expanding area of research, with the potential for a wide impact on high-performance computing. PSEs provide software tools and expert assistance to the user and serve as an easy-to-use interface to high-performance computing resources, thereby allowing the rapid prototyping of ideas, detailed analysis, and higher productivity. Utilizing and managing distributed high-performance computing resources is important for a PSE to meet the requirements of large-scale simulations. These types of PSE have the potential for profoundly changing the way high-performance computing resources are used to solve problems. In the future, PSEs may be the primary way in which high-performance computing resources are accessed. As PSEs expand to encompass the use of the Web, Internet, and the Grid as platforms for computing, we will see more demand for PSEs to provide seamless access to a wide range of services and resources.

15 Tools for Performance Tuning and Debugging

Daniel A. Reed • Ruth A. Aydt

Scalable parallel systems and PC clusters with hundreds or even thousands of processors have displaced traditional vector supercomputers as the hardware platform of choice for high-performance computing. This architectural change has created a plethora of new and complex performance tuning and debugging problems for application developers.

First, large-scale parallelism means that new software bugs may arise from the complex interactions among large numbers of parallel software components. Moreover, these bugs may have high latency, with their effects not manifest in executing software until long after the erroneous condition(s) occurred. Equally importantly, they may be subtly dependent on timing conditions that can rarely be reproduced. This means that locating and eliminating software bugs can be extraordinarily tedious and time consuming, with users forced to trace software component interactions for long periods to identify the root causes of logical errors.

Even if the parallel code is logically correct, users of parallel systems often complain that it is difficult to achieve a high fraction of the theoretical performance peak. Moreover, the sensitivity of parallel system performance to slight changes in application code, together with the large number of potential application performance problems (e.g., load balance, data locality, or input/output) and continually evolving system software, make application tuning complex and often counterintuitive.

Both debugging and performance analysis involve monitoring of software execution. Hence, both are prey to the same theoretical and pragmatic pitfalls as other experimental sciences. In particular, they must not unduly perturb the measured system, or else the experimental data will not reflect the system's nominal behavior. However, the data must be sufficiently detailed to capture the phenomenon of interest, either the application error or performance bottleneck.

Aspects of the *uncertainty principle* also apply—the debugging or measurement infrastructure usually is a part of the system, making it impossible to accurately capture certain phenomena using only internal capabilities. For example, one cannot unobtrusively measure an input/output system if the instrumentation system must rely on that same input/output system to record the measurement data. Similarly, debugger threads can change application thread schedules, masking synchronization errors.

There are many reasons for all of these difficulties, but most are rooted in the relation of application programming models to complex, multilevel hardware and software. From the application creator's perspective, the underlying parallel architecture is viewed through the lens of the parallel programming model chosen for application development. Based on the programming model, compilers or run-time systems may dramatically transform the code written by the software developer. When debugging and tuning the application's execution behavior, the programmer has only the original code as his or her frame of reference.

To be successful, software tools must relate both run-time performance measures and debugging queries to the original source code. Without such inverse transformations, the parallel application developer has little recourse but to learn the idiosyncrasies of the multilevel hardware/software transformations. In the serial domain, this is analogous to requiring Fortran or C developers to read compiler-generated assembly code for debugging and performance tuning.

Despite the complexity of relating performance metrics and debugging queries to source code, the associated parallel software tools must be simple and intuitive to use. Unless compelled by circumstances, most users are unwilling to invest great time and effort to learn the syntax and semantics of new software tools; they often view debugging and performance optimization as unavoidable evils. Hence, portability and ease of use are critical to the acceptance of new software tools. Simply put, the goal of parallel software tools is to provide insight into application behavior and performance bottlenecks by efficiently capturing and intuitively presenting relevant data.

In this chapter, we review basic techniques for both correctness debugging and performance instrumentation and analysis. We illustrate these techniques using representative tools that bridge the gap between application source code and parallel execution behavior. Finally, we conclude with some thoughts on the state of the art and open problems.

15.1 Correctness and Performance Monitoring Basics

Although apparently dissimilar, debugging and performance tuning rely on many of the same monitoring techniques and share a similar goal—identifying the root cause for a particular execution phenomenon. For debugging, the goal is achieving the desired program behavior. For performance tuning, the goal is satisfying some performance criterion.

Users debug sequential programs for many reasons. These range from uncovering program logic errors that produce incorrect results, through identifying and removing the cause of infinite loops, to correcting program crashes due to memory corruption.

Parallel execution shares these pitfalls but also includes task and data coordination and interaction (e.g., via shared variables, synchronization, or message passing). Moreover, behavior during an execution may not be repeatable; subtle variations in resource availability may skew event timing across tasks. Good debugging tools should aid users in identifying problems and, ideally, suggest possible solutions.

The sources of performance problems are just as diverse as those for correctness, ranging from a mismatch of application needs and available resources through load imbalances. Performance-monitoring tools should identify bottlenecks, suggest possible remedies, and relate performance problems to application source code.

Historically, monitoring approaches have included counting and sampling, interval timing, event tracing, and breakpoint insertion for code stepping. Conceptually, each strikes a different balance between monitoring overhead, data volume, and detail. Many of these approaches have multiple possible implementation techniques, ranging from completely extrinsic (e.g., an external hardware monitor that counts cache misses via connections to a set of probe points) to completely intrinsic (e.g., inserted code in an application program to compute a histogram of procedure activation lifetimes or test program correctness assertions).

Typically, performance tuning and debugging are iterative processes. One begins with global, but coarse-grained probes to identify performance bottlenecks or task interactions. One then enables more intrusive (expensive) probes to expose behavior in the bottleneck regions. Of course, performance bottlenecks or correctness errors may be caused by behavior in other code regions (e.g., a bottleneck procedure may appear as a bottleneck due to improper or excessive invocation from a calling site).

Event counts can identify how many times different code regions are invoked. Many times, seeing these counts or stepping through code via breakpoints is enough to suggest a problem or confirm correct behavior. Similarly, comparing execution time profiles across tasks can highlight load imbalances. Event tracing enables detailed analysis of program behavior. Comparing event time lines across tasks can highlight problematic interactions and performance problems.

To summarize, the appropriate monitoring apparatus is determined by the desired data and the experimental environment. The best combination is dependent on both the parallel system and the software context.

15.1.1   Profiling and Program-Counter Sampling

A common monitoring method is program-counter sampling. The widely used UNIX prof and gprof [395] utilities display profiles of program execution time taken from histogram data collected by periodically sampling the program counter during execution.

When profiling is enabled, program initialization automatically creates a buffer to hold the histogram data. The histogram bins correspond to equally sized subdivisions of the program's address space. During program execution, profile-timer interrupts occur at regular intervals, every few milliseconds. At each interrupt, the system samples the program counter and increments the appropriate histogram bin. When the program exits, the histogram data are saved to a file.

The object file's symbol table, which contains the starting and ending addresses of each procedure, is used to identify the procedure associated with each histogram bin. Because sampling occurs at known intervals, histogram bin height can be used to estimate the amount of time spent in each procedure.

Profiling depends on an external sampling task, making its granularity necessarily coarse. To obtain accurate profiles, the total program execution time must be sufficiently high to accumulate a statistically meaningful set of samples.

As an example, Figure 15.1 shows a profile of *one* process from a Message Passing Interface (MPI) code on a SUN workstation cluster. This example code computes a parallel Jacobi iteration on a 2-D square mesh, with horizontal strip partitions.

Figure 15.2 shows the high-level structure of the code. Each task locally computes a new submesh, computes the local convergence data, and then participates in a global reduction to determine global convergence. Note that the profile fails to capture the parallel behavior of the MPI code; the profile reports data for only one task because each monitoring file contains data for a single MPI process. Moreover, the profile does not report data on any overlap across processes.

15.1.2   Event Counting

Event counting redresses the limitations of sampling, albeit at some cost. Because counting is not a statistical measure, the observed frequencies are accurate.[1] Typically, event counting is used to compute the number of times procedures or other source-code fragments are executed. At a more detailed level, compilers can insert counters in basic blocks to generate statement-execution counts and dynamic machine-instruction frequencies.

To support unobtrusive capture of hardware performance data, most microprocessor vendors now include on-chip hardware counters. These counters can be read and reset under software control, but are incremented automatically when certain hardware operations occur. The Intel Pentium, Compaq Alpha, HP PA-Risc, IBM POWER series, and MIPS R12000 [505, 1012, 495, 269, 987] all include an array of instruction and cache operation counters.

These microprocessor hardware counters draw on lessons from earlier counters such as the Cray Hardware Performance Monitor (HPM) [594]. The HPM included multiple counter groups that recorded such things as memory references,

---

[1] This is not true if the code has timing-dependent behavior. In this case, invasive instrumentation can change code execution paths, and the actual counts may have been different had the instrumentation been less intrusive.

%Time	Seconds	Cumsecs	#Calls	msec/call	Name
79.5	7.81	7.81	1	7810.	main
14.4	1.42	9.23	364242	0.0039	_read
1.5	0.15	9.38	3290	0.046	_write
0.9	0.09	9.47	3249	0.028	_poll
0.7	0.07	9.54	1127473	0.0001	_mcount
0.5	0.05	9.59	360476	0.0001	_cerror
0.4	0.04	9.63	1624	0.025	_so_recv
0.3	0.03	9.66	360498	0.0001	___errno
0.2	0.02	9.68			_libc_threads_interface
0.2	0.02	9.70	1	20.	_fileno_unlocked
0.2	0.02	9.72			net_recv
0.2	0.02	9.74			PMPI_Recv
0.1	0.01	9.75			p4_recv
0.1	0.01	9.76			__pthread_cleanup_push
0.1	0.01	9.77			MPID_Msg_rep
0.1	0.01	9.78	4	2.	_libc_fork
0.1	0.01	9.79			MPID_CH_Check_incoming
0.1	0.01	9.80			MPIR_ToPointer
0.1	0.01	9.81			MPID_CH_Eagerb_recv_short
0.1	0.01	9.82	226	0.04	strcpy
0.1	0.01	9.83			PMPI_Bcast
0.0	0.00	9.83	500	0.00	_sqrt

Figure 15.1 Sun cluster profile for Jacobi MPI example (one process).

```
while (NOT Globally Converged) {
  Exchange partition boundary points with neighboring tasks
      using MPI_Send() and MPI_Recv()
  for (i,j)
    xnew[i][j] = (x[i+1][j] + x[i-1][j] + x[i][j+1] +
                          x[i][j-1]) * 0.25
  endfor
  for (i,j)
    x[i][j] = xnew[i][j];
  endfor

  Compute local convergence data
  Compute global convergence using MPI_Allreduce() then sqrt()
  }
```

Figure 15.2 MPI pseudocode for parallel Jacobi iteration.

instructions issued, and floating-point operations. Each counter was updated automatically by the processor hardware, with no software overhead for recording.

Even with such hardware counters, to obtain timing data one must periodically time stamp and record the counts (i.e., one must sample the counter values). Hence, software counting requires either passive monitoring (e.g., via an external hardware monitor) or invasive instrumentation (e.g., via software instrumentation of program control flow to count execution of code fragments).

As an example, Figure 15.3 shows software-sampled hardware counter values from SGI Speedshop. In the figure, cycle counts are shown for each procedure in the upper left panel, and for source code lines in the lower panel.

15.1.3   Interval Timing

Interval timing combines counts with elapsed-time measurements. Intuitively, interval timing is the measured analogue of interval sampling. Rather than sampling the program counter periodically to compute the amount of time spent in code fragments, interval timing brackets code fragments with a pair of calls to a timing routine.

The first invocation records the time of entry; the second uses the current time and the previous time to determine the elapsed time. The timing data can be used to compute the code fragment's total execution time by summing the intervals, histograms of code fragment execution time by binning the data, or execution time moments (i.e., mean, variance, and higher moments) by summing the data and recording counts. Alternatively, one can simply record the magnitude of each interval and post-process the data.

However, for large-scale parallel systems, recording each interval on each task can quickly produce large amounts of data. Hence, interval timing is most often used either to time large code sections that dominate execution or to sum the time intervals spent in frequently invoked, but small, code fragments.

15.1.4   Event Tracing

Unlike counting, which naturally abstracts the occurrence of specific events, or interval timing, which abstracts the frequency of specific events, event tracing generates a complete sequence of events, their time of occurrence, and ancillary data about the time-evolutionary system state. As an example, the event-tracing instrumentation in Figure 15.4 would generate two events on each invocation of the procedure, in this case an MPI message send [405]. On a parallel system, the recorded data for each event would include the event identifier, the time the event occurred, the task identifier, and any data related to the event (e.g., current variable values).

Event tracing has been widely used to debug and tune the performance of message-passing parallel programs [448, 637, 639, 795]. Typically, a modified version of the message-passing library intercepts each message-passing call, records relevant

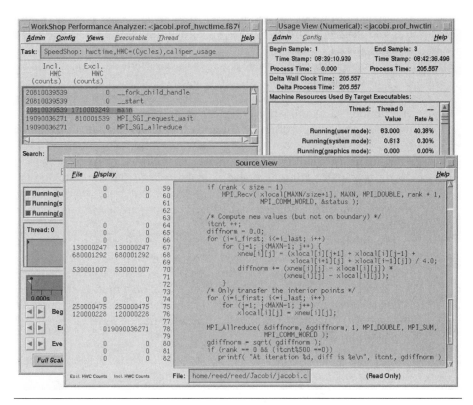

Figure 15.3 SGI Speedshop hardware counter performance display.

```
MPI_Send(void * Buffer, const int Count,
         MPI_Datatype Datatype, int Destination,
         int Tag, MPI_comm Handle)
{
   TraceEvent(MPI_SEND_ENTRY_EVENT, EventRelatedData);

   PMPI_Send(Buffer, Count, Datatype, Destination,
             Tag, Handle);

   TraceEvent(MPI_SEND_EXIT_EVENT, EventRelatedData);
}
```

Figure 15.4 Event-tracing instrumentation example.

parameters from the call, and invokes the actual message-passing routine. Indeed, the MPI message-passing standard [405] defines a profiling interface for precisely this purpose.

Given event traces, one can visualize causal event dependencies in a variety of ways. Widely used academic and commercial tools such as ParaGraph [448], Pablo [793], Jumpshot [1014], and Vampir [736] process raw event traces and produce visualizations and animations of event types, durations, and dependences. In Section 15.5, we describe some of these and other representative tuning and debugging tools.

In summary, event tracing is a more general monitoring technique than either counting or interval timing; from an event trace, one can compute counts or times—the converse is not true. Moreover, parallel event traces can be used to debug software component interactions by analyzing the partial event order for unexpected patterns.

The disadvantage of tracing is the potential monitoring intrusion. Because each event must be time stamped and recorded separately, the potential data volume is large, and the input/output requirements are substantial. For example, a trace of MPI events for the Jacobi iteration of Figure 15.2 on a modest-size, 384×384 mesh generates tens of thousands of events for 500 iterations. Although useful for tuning applications with small, test data sets, detailed tracing must be used sparingly with large-scale production runs.

15.1.5   Control Breakpoints

A common mechanism for program correctness debugging is the breakpoint debugger. Typically, a monitoring process controls execution of the application process(es) via system calls, such as ptrace() on UNIX systems. Using compiler symbol table information and system calls, the breakpoint debugger control process interrogates stack frames of the executing code, allowing users to examine and change variables, start and stop processes, and trace execution paths.

For parallel programs, breakpoint debuggers must coordinate the execution states, starting and stopping the code at consistent points. As parallelism levels rise to hundreds or thousands of parallel processes and threads, this distributed coordination becomes increasingly complex.

In addition to handling the process coordination issues, the breakpoint debugger must also provide a simple and intuitive user interface to the parallel processes. Without such an interface, the user will be overwhelmed by data and complexity, and the debugger will not be usable. For example, simple debugger commands such as print X have many possible interpretations, ranging from display of the variable value in the current process context to display of all copies of the variable.

If the variable X is a global array in a data-parallel language like High Performance Fortran (HPF), then the debugger may have to gather subsets of the array from multiple processes before printing. Addressing many of these challenges requires deep integration of compilers, run-time libraries, and system software.

One of the few research or commercial breakpoint debuggers to support parallel program analysis at truly large scale is TotalView [315], which has been extended via the U.S. Accelerated Strategic Computing Initiative (ASCI) for systems with thousands of parallel tasks. In Section 15.5, we examine TotalView in more detail.

15.2   Measurement and Debugging Implementation Challenges

In general, counting, timing, tracing, and breakpoint management occupy different points in the continuum of detail and measurement overhead. The choice of a particular approach is dictated by the desired data and the constraints of the underlying instrumentation implementation—some measurements are not feasible in some environments. Two of the most basic implementation challenges concern clocks and event orders.

15.2.1   Clocks and Timing

Both interval timing and event tracing require clock access. The clock being accessed need not have the resolution of the processor clock (i.e., a 500-MHz microprocessor need not have a user-accessible, 2-ns clock), but the clock resolution should be sufficiently high that the measured times of successive events differ. Also, the cost of clock access should be small relative to the frequency of events.

Unfortunately, many systems fail to satisfy these standard constraints on clock features. As microprocessor clock speeds have increased, the resolution of many PC and workstation clocks has not increased at the same rate. This disparity in workstation speed and clock resolution makes it more difficult to obtain accurate timing measurements.

On a 1-MIP processor, a clock with 1-ms resolution can accurately measure code fragments as small as a few thousand instructions. An equivalent clock on a 100-MIP machine can accurately measure only instruction sequences of a few hundred thousand instructions.

High software overhead for clock access is as debilitating as low clock resolution—one cannot measure frequently occurring events without grossly perturbing system behavior. Under these circumstances, it is best to map hardware cycle counters into the application address space. This makes it possible to read the counters and compute cycle counts with only a handful of hardware instructions.

15.2.2   Event Orders and Time

Monitoring overhead can change the times when events of interest occur. More subtly, on a parallel system it can also change the *order* in which events occur. This can change observed performance and mask behavioral bugs.

In contrast to the total order that exists in the single task of a sequential program, the events across tasks in a parallel program are partially ordered. Concretely,

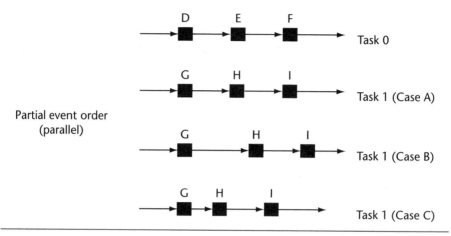

Figure 15.5   Event orders.

consider the example in Figure 15.5. In the figure, the events on task 0 are totally ordered, as are the events on task 1. Instrumentation or breakpoint overhead cannot change the event order on either task unless the code contains time-dependent actions. Similarly, it cannot change program correctness unless the program contains a logical error.

However, overhead can change the total event order *across* tasks. For example, in MPI programs, performance instrumentation or debugging breakpoints can change the order that receivers who wait for messages from multiple senders receive those messages. In turn, this can change execution behavior in the receiving process. Likewise, in thread-based programs, instrumentation can change thread execution times, leading to different thread schedules and behavior.

Even if one assumes no time-dependent code exists, the global, total order of events for the pair of tasks depends strongly on the absolute times of events in multiple tasks. In Figure 15.5, a shift in the time that event H occurs can change the total order of the events E and H across tasks to EH or HE. Moreover, the effects of this change may be propagated to future events; by shifting their starting times, their relation to events in other tasks may change as well.

Because it is impossible to eliminate instrumentation or breakpoint overhead, instrumentation is subject to an *uncertainty principle*—the act of observing the system may change the event order. Under restricted circumstances, it is possible to post-process an event trace and recover the actual event order (i.e., the event order that occurs without instrumentation) [638, 640]. In general, however, the observed event order cannot be exactly recovered, and event-order perturbations must be minimized by reducing instrumentation overhead or reducing the number of events that are instrumented.

A consistent global time base is implicit in the assumption of event order across tasks. Lest this statement seem pedantic, many parallel systems have been built with local clocks on each processor; PC clusters are the most recent example. Not only are these clocks independent, but manufacturing variances in the clock crystals mean that they tick at slightly different rates. The only clock synchronization present on most PC clusters is based on the network time protocol, which yields resolution too poor to maintain full causality for low-latency communication libraries.

The absence of a global time base can lead to causality violations. For example, if one were to instrument a message-passing code to record both the time a message was sent and the time it was received, the message would appear to have been received before it was sent if the sender's clock were faster than that of the receiver. To redress this problem, most current parallel systems contain a globally synchronized clock. Unfortunately, the resolution of the global clock is typically less than that of the local clock and the access time is greater.

15.3   Deep Compiler Integration

Most performance-analysis and debugging tools target the collection and presentation of application behavior when the parallelism and interprocessor communication are explicit (e.g., in message-passing or shared-memory threaded codes). To support high-level languages that rely on compilers to infer such details from data-decomposition directives, tools for debugging and performance analysis require an increased level of sophistication and integration with other components in the programming system.

The use of high-level languages and sophisticated parallelizing compilers means that an application-software developer's mental model of a program and the actual code that executes on a particular parallel system can be quite different. For analysis tools to provide relevant data and suggestions for debugging and performance improvements at the level of an abstract, high-level program, they must integrate data from dynamic program execution with data recorded by the high-level language compiler that describes the mapping from the high-level source to the resulting low-level explicitly parallel code.

15.3.1   A Motivating Example

The need for integrated compilation systems and performance-analysis environments is best illustrated by considering the steps that currently must be followed to compile and analyze the performance of data-parallel HPF code on distributed-memory parallel systems using decoupled compilation and performance-analysis tools. Similar problems exist for other languages and systems with high-level abstractions (e.g., Java, parallel C++, or MATLAB).

```
! Original HPF Code

REAL A(10000), APRIME(10000)
!HPF$ DISTRIBUTE A(BLOCK)
!HPF$ DISTRIBUTE APRIME(BLOCK)

DO I = 2, N
    APRIME(I) = (A(I+1) + 2*A(I) + A(I-1)) * 0.25
ENDDO

! Generated SPMD Code (Assuming 100 Processors)

REAL A(100), APRIME(100)
REAL TMP

send A(1) to task K-1
send A(100) to task K+1
receive LOW from task K-1
receive HIGH from task K+1

APRIME(1) = (A(2) + 2*A(1) + LOW) * 0.25
APRIME(100) = (HIGH + 2*A(100) + A(99)) * 0.25

DO I = 2, 99
    APRIME(I) = (A(I+1) + 2*A(I) + A(I-1)) * 0.25
ENDDO
```

Figure 15.6   HPF and generated SPMD code.

As an example, consider the HPF code fragment in Figure 15.6. In a distributed-memory parallel system, an HPF compiler must translate the data-distribution directives and Fortran array operations into parallel, message-passing code. First, the compiler distributes portions of arrays across the processor memories, then maps a subset of the array operations to each processor, and finally, synthesizes message-passing calls to realize the illusion of shared memory.

In the example of Figure 15.6, the compiler must generate temporary variables and communication to share the boundary elements of the subarrays across processors. As a consequence of this translation, there is a large semantic gap between the data-parallel programming model and the compiler-generated SPMD message-passing model, much as there is between code expressed in a sequential language like C and the assembly language code generated by a C compiler.

Because the goal of high-level, data-parallel languages like HPF is to insulate the software developer from the idiosyncrasies of message passing, performance tuning should not require the developer to understand the details of the compiler-synthesized, message-passing code. Instead, compilers and performance tools should work together to "invert" the compiler transformations and relate performance data from the generated code to the original data-parallel source code.

The difficulty of this inverse mapping is exacerbated by the range of possible compiler optimizations. A data-parallel compiler may inline procedures, distribute or fuse loops, vectorize and pipeline communication, and apply a host of other optimizations. The greater the sophistication of the compiler, the more complex the inverse mapping from generated code to data-parallel source code, and the lower the likelihood that a unique inverse mapping exists.

Even if the programmer successfully maps dynamic performance data back to the data-parallel source code, he or she has succeeded only in identifying why the code executed inefficiently. Understanding how to modify the data-parallel source to increase performance remains problematic—the inverse mapping of performance data to data-parallel source code is not predictive! The HPF programmer can affect performance only by changing data distributions and other HPF code fragments and needs estimates of the relative merits of code changes.

Unfortunately, there are no extant commercial compilers and tools that fully provide guidance on the possible effects of high-level code changes. Indeed, as explained below, this is an area of active research, with new algorithms and techniques needed to better support predictive performance tuning.

15.3.2 Performance Modeling and Prediction

Developers often invest substantial intellectual effort in designing and coding a parallel program, only to discover upon execution that it yields a mere fraction of peak system performance. At this *postmortem* stage, software-performance tuning begins in an effort to locate and remove bottlenecks in the original design and implementation.

Unfortunately, even on a single parallel architecture, observed application performance may vary substantially as a function of input parameters. Furthermore, if the application code is portable across multiple parallel architectures, it is highly unlikely that it will achieve high performance on all architectures. This sensitivity to input parameters and architecture makes the task of tuning code to perform well in general, based on the observed behavior for a particular run, extremely difficult.

Ideally, an integrated modeling and measurement environment would allow designers to "mix and match" software and hardware components, validating performance design goals against a composition of calibrated models of proposed components and measurements of extant components *prior* to detailed design and software construction. Although easily stated, providing such guidance is difficult.

Important performance-prediction questions include determining how application performance changes with variations in the parallel system configuration or application problem size, and identifying which code fragments will become the performance-limiting bottlenecks as hardware or application parameters change. Not only do performance prediction and scalability share many challenges and problems with deep compiler integration, namely the need for data on compiler transformations and the relation of source and executable code, prediction and scalability also require accurate models of diverse hardware and software components, including I/O systems, networks, memory managers, and schedulers.

In principle, one could combine compiler-derived data on symbolic program variables and performance measurements from selected executions of the compiler-generated code to generate scalability predictions. These models consist of symbolic expressions representing the execution complexity of individual program sections. Combining predictions for program sections with control flow data yields aggregate program predictions. Despite the attraction of symbolic performance prediction and ongoing research [10, 666, 794], at present there are no symbolic prediction systems suitable for use with large-scale parallel applications.

Hence, several vendors and groups are exploring alternate techniques based on pattern matching, expert systems, and machine learning; all rely on detailed data from compilation systems. Cray's ATExpert (AutoTasking Expert) [231] was one of the first tools to embody developer experience on the best approaches to parallelizing codes for Cray vector systems. ATExpert predicts and reports dedicated autotasking performance (i.e., that obtained by automatically distributing loop iterations across processors) based on data collected from a single execution on a nondedicated system. Its successor, the Cray MPP Apprentice [230], provides a superset of these features.

More recently, SGI's PCP (Performance Co-Pilot) [862] and Miller's Paradyn Consultant [530] built on these ideas by attempting to classify performance problems based on execution signatures. Using these signatures, the tools suggest possible performance problems and trigger solutions. For example, PCP includes an inference engine that can trigger alarms based on anomalous behavior or initiate corrective system actions.

15.4   Software Tool Interfaces and Usability

The effectiveness of tools for debugging and performance tuning is ultimately determined by use; sophisticated software and hardware to support monitoring and analysis provide no insight unless they are used. Surveys [737] have shown that scientific application software developers will eschew powerful, but complex tools in favor of inferior, but easily understood tools. Unless compelled by circumstances, most users are unwilling to invest much time and effort to learn the syntax and semantics of new performance or debugging tools. Unlike compilers, where users have no choice, most users have "home grown," ad hoc debugging and tuning techniques of their own.

Within the parallel computing community, the Parallel Tools Consortium [741] has been a leader in identifying user needs and promoting the development of tools that address those needs. Top priorities include ease of use, portability across architectures, scalability, and control over the level of monitoring and the detail of presentation.

15.4.1 Tool Scalability

Scalability is a key characteristic of commodity parallel systems; by adding processors one can incrementally increase performance without replacing existing hardware or changing the underlying software. Software tool scalability not only implies that the environment must be capable of capturing and analyzing data from very large numbers of processors, it must also be capable of presenting the data in ways that are intuitive and instructive.

Many debugging and performance presentation techniques represent the states of individual tasks (e.g., by a colored square or debugging window for each task) and do not scale to thousands of concurrent entities [448, 736]. Likewise, displays of interprocessor communication patterns are limited by workstation-screen real estate. For example, the Jumpshot display of Figure 15.7, though invaluable for analyzing communication patterns, cannot readily display detailed patterns for thousands of tasks.

Fortunately, for most scalable parallel systems and their associated applications, task behaviors often form a small number of equivalence classes; it frequently suffices to see aggregate behavior with detail for equivalence class representatives and outliers. Hence, both new analysis techniques that identify such equivalence classes [704] and new display idioms are needed if software tools are to scale with parallel system size. Many of the more recent tools described in Section 15.5 provide just such capabilities.

15.4.2 User Expectations and Recommendations

Based on the experience of tool designers and developers, there are three classes of potential software tool users: novice, intermediate, and expert. Each is often loosely correlated with the class of parallel system they may use: small-scale SMP, moderately parallel system, or terascale parallel system with hundreds or thousands of processors.

Novice users know relatively little about parallel system software or hardware, nor do they wish to learn more than the minimum necessary to debug and optimize the performance of their application codes. They want tools that are simple and easy to use and that will quickly identify performance bottlenecks or program errors. Equally importantly, they are much more interested in acceptable performance rather than in achieving optimal performance. For these users, profiling tools often strike the right balance among tool complexity, ease of use, and problem identification.

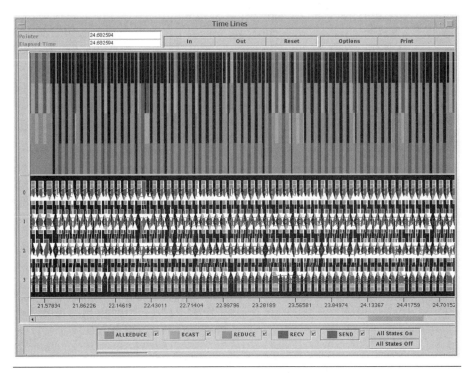

Figure 15.7 Jumpshot event visualization.

In contrast, intermediate users often wish to conduct performance experiments, asking such questions as, What caused this behavior? or How do these performance metrics interrelate? Although they are unlikely to be willing to extend the software tool by writing new software, these users do want a modicum of control over the environment's behavior. For example, they may wish to compute new performance metrics from the measured data and to compare them to other metrics. This intermediate user class needs an environment toolkit whose components can be assembled in a wide variety of ways. Tools such as the SGI Performance Co-Pilot [862] provide such capabilities.

Finally, expert users are intimately acquainted with the parallel architecture and system software. Indeed, they may wish to use the performance environment to study the effects of system software modifications. These users need the broadest latitude, subsuming the needs of both the novice and intermediate users. Not only will they wish to reassemble the existing components of the environment toolkit, they will want to add new toolkit components. Moreover, they expect the added components to integrate seamlessly with extant elements.

Ideally, performance and debugging tools would accommodate all three user classes. In keeping with the dictum that the common case should be easy, well-designed software tool interfaces allow users to proceed from the simple to the complex. For debugging, this means testing first for global conditions across all tasks, then allowing related-task or per-task queries. For performance analysis, this means that high-level, aggregate performance data should be presented first, followed by increasing detail as the user explores the causes for poor performance.

Following these guidelines, profiles are an excellent entree to performance analysis. They are intuitive, easily displayed, and involve minimal instrumentation. Once the user has identified the performance bottleneck, more detailed metrics, such as processor utilizations or aggregate interprocessor communication patterns, can provide additional insight. Finally, in certain instances, detailed examination of task interaction patterns may be appropriate for selected tasks; presenting detailed data from all tasks is both computationally prohibitive and graphically cumbersome.

15.5   Software Tool Examples

Below, we describe four systems, two academic and two commercial, that provide simple, yet powerful interfaces for specifying instrumentation, analyzing data, and debugging applications. These systems were chosen as representatives of current techniques and user interfaces. Other companies, including IBM, SGI, KAI Software, and Pallas provide similar analysis tools, and a host of other academic projects are exploring a diverse set of instrumentation and data-presentation techniques.

15.5.1   Jumpshot Event Visualization

Jumpshot [1014] shares many features with commercial event-visualization tools like Vampir [736]. Other academic trace-visualization tools such as ParaGraph [448] also provide similar functionality.

Instrumentation and Analysis

Jumpshot relies on event-trace data generated via the MPI profiling interface, as described in Section 15.1.4. Using MPI traces, Jumpshot displays execution activity in each parallel task as a time line. As an example, Figure 15.7 shows the message-passing activity of the Jacobi iteration code shown previously.

Jumpshot supports two display modes, "mountain range" and event time line, shown in the top and bottom panes of Figure 15.7, respectively. The "mountain range" mode at the top of the figure uses colors to show the message-passing state of each task. The event time line is similar, but it also shows communication patterns by connecting message senders and receivers.

To accommodate large message-passing traces from long-running codes, Jumpshot includes a scaling mode via which users can choose the time scale of the displayed data, ranging from an entire execution to a small time window. Finally, one can display histograms of message sizes and durations.

Assessment

Jumpshot focuses on tuning of applications written using one of the most common models—message passing via MPI. As such, it provides detailed views of intertask communication, time spent in different states, and message-passing overhead. Its biggest limitation is the lack of support for compiler-assisted source code correlation, although this was not one of its design goals.

15.5.2   SvPablo Source Code Correlation

As noted earlier, correlating data-parallel source code with dynamic performance data from both software and hardware measurements, while still providing a portable, intuitive, and easily used interface, is a challenging task [738]. The Sv-Pablo (Source View Pablo) graphical environment draws on lessons from several generations of performance-tool development.

SvPablo supports application source code instrumentation, performance data capture and analysis, and browsing of dynamic performance metrics for applications written in a variety of languages and executing on both sequential and parallel systems [259, 260]. In addition, SvPablo exploits hardware support for performance counters.

Following execution, performance data from each task is integrated, additional statistics are computed, and the resulting metrics are correlated with application source code, creating a *performance file* that is represented via the Pablo self-describing data format (SDDF) [792]. This file is the specification used by SvPablo's browser to display application source code and correlated performance metrics.

SvPablo Performance Instrumentation

Interactive instrumentation provides detailed control, allowing users to specify precise points at which data should be captured, albeit at the possible expense of excessive perturbation and inhibition of compiler optimizations. In contrast, automatic instrumentation relies on the compiler or run-time system to insert probes in compiler-synthesized code.

Currently, SvPablo supports interactive instrumentation of C, Fortran 77, and Fortran 90 and automatic instrumentation of data-parallel High Performance Fortran (HPF). As noted earlier, instrumenting the data-parallel source code can potentially inhibit any or all of these optimizations, dramatically reducing performance and, equally importantly, resulting in performance measurements that are not typical of normal execution. Hence, SvPablo relies on the HPF compiler to emit instrumented code.

SvPablo Performance Analysis

One of the design goals for SvPablo was to create an intuitive, cross-architecture, language-independent, performance analysis interface. Realizing such a design

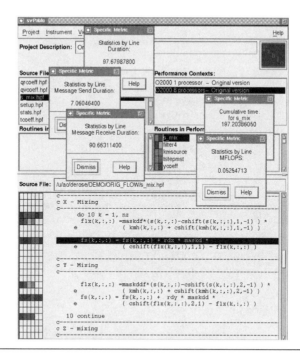

Figure 15.8 Baseline performance data (MSTFLOW HPF code).

would allow users and performance analysts to learn a single set of source code navigation skills and then apply those skills to application codes written in a variety of languages and executing on a diverse set of architectures.

Hence, the SvPablo implementation relies on a single interface for performance instrumentation and visualization. If the program is interactively instrumented, the user can refine the performance analysis by reinstrumenting the source code while visualizing performance data from earlier executions. Regardless of the instrumentation mode, one can access and load performance data from multiple prior executions, including different numbers of processors and hardware platforms.

As an example, Figure 15.8 shows the SvPablo interface, together with code and performance data from an HPF program. In the figure, the leftmost scrollbox shows the set of files comprising the HPF program, with all previously measured executions of this code shown in the scrollbox to the right. Here, the user has loaded a performance data context (i.e., a measured execution) for an eight-processor SGI Origin 2000. After selecting a performance context, the list of procedures in the application code, together with two color-coded metrics, is shown below the performance contexts scrollbox in the area labeled *Routines in Performance Data*. The two colored columns summarize, over all processes, the average number of calls and average cumulative time for the routines.

Clicking on a routine name loads the associated source code in the bottom pane of Figure 15.8, together with color-coded metrics beside each source line. By default, the SvPablo interface displays one column for each metric. However, the user can select only a subset of the metrics to appear in the color-coded columns. Clicking the mouse on a colored box, either in the routine list or beside a source code line, creates a dialog box displaying the maximum value associated with the selected metric. In addition, pop-up dialogs showing other statistics and detailed information about a particular routine or source code line, including individual process metrics, can be obtained by clicking the mouse on the routine name or the source code line.

Assessment

Like other tools, SvPablo has both strengths and weaknesses. Although the user interface is language neutral, one cannot "drill down" for additional levels of performance data (e.g., examining compiler-synthesized message-passing code). Moreover, it does not integrate debugging and performance analysis, nor does it include a performance advisor or distributed-computation assessment.

15.5.3 Thinking Machines Prism

Although Thinking Machines Corporation (TMC) no longer builds or sells parallel systems, many of the ideas of and approaches to large-scale performance analysis and debugging were exemplified by the TMC Prism environment. Moreover, portions of Sun's HPC ClustersTools software for performance tuning and debugging are based on Prism.[2]

Performance Instrumentation

As Figure 15.9 suggests, Prism was first developed as an integrated breakpoint debugger and performance-analysis system for the CM-2 and CM-5 [922]. On Sun systems, one captures application performance data by compiling the code with a profile flag. This directs the compiler to generate code whose performance can be measured via standard profiling tools such as gprof.

On the CM-5, performance data were captured via interval timers. In this case, profiles were *measured*, rather than statistical (i.e., the execution time of each code fragment was measured and a profile was computed from cumulative execution time, rather than via program-counter sampling).[3]

The CM-5 supported both message passing and data-parallel programming. Prism was initially developed to support the data-parallel model, which was common to both the SIMD CM-2 and the MIMD CM-5, with a later version supporting TMC's

---

[2] Sun acquired rights to much of TMC's software, including Prism, and several TMC staff joined Sun.
[3] The CM-5 supported standard UNIX prof and gprof as well, and the Sun version of Prism relies on Solaris support for performance data.

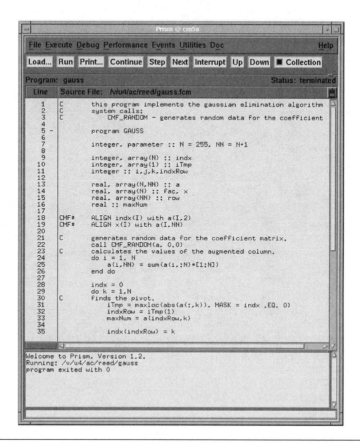

Figure 15.9 Thinking Machines Prism interface.

message-passing library. Sun versions of Prism now support analysis of data-parallel code written in HPF, as well as message-passing codes based on MPI, Fortran 77, Fortran 90, C, and C++.

As one might expect, the choice of a programming model has profound implications for what data are captured, how the data are reduced, and how the data are presented. The message-passing model is a direct reflection of the TMC CM-5's underlying distributed-memory architecture and the clustered nature of Sun's networked servers. Logically, the data-parallel model is "higher level"—it is implemented using message passing. In both cases, compiler-generated instrumentation captures the performance of the executed code. For the data-parallel model, performance data from all the nodes must be combined and related to the user's code. For message passing, the behavioral variance across nodes is potentially large, and it is desirable to examine the performance of each node separately.

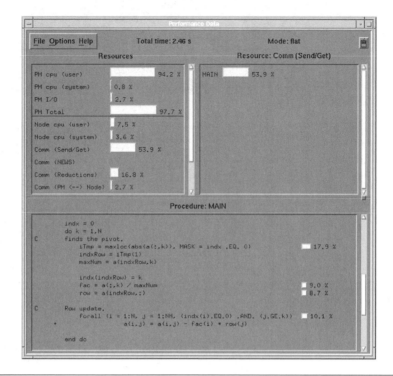

Figure 15.10   Thinking Machines Prism performance data.

Performance Analysis

Figure 15.10 shows the display created by Prism in response to a user selection from the Performance menu of Figure 15.9. This display contains three panes, and each pane shows a separate performance view. The panes in the upper left, upper right, and bottom show resource use, procedure statistics, and source line statistics, respectively. In all three cases, the statistics are displayed as simple bar graphs, with options to sort metrics magnitudes based on time or utilization.

For each of the resource use metrics in the top left pane, one can display the distribution of this time across procedures in the procedure pane to the right; this can be either a flat display such as is produced by the UNIX prof utility or a hierarchical display like that produced by gprof. In the hierarchical display mode, one can navigate the hierarchy by clicking on a procedure to see more detail. In Figure 15.10, the top right pane has been configured to show the time spent in message passing. In this example, the code contains no procedures other than the main program; hence the display in Figure 15.10 is degenerate.

Finally, the source code pane at the bottom of Figure 15.10 shows the source code for a procedure and the amount of time in each code fragment. Because one selects the procedure to display by clicking on it in the procedure pane above, the metric displayed is the same—message passing in this example.

Breakpoint Debugging

In addition to support for performance analysis, both the TMC and Sun versions of Prism include a breakpoint debugger. Originally, the most notable feature of this debugger was its support for process sets. By allowing users to specify groups of logically related processes, Prism can be used to debug parallel applications with large numbers of parallel tasks.

Assessment

TMC Prism's simplicity was both its greatest advantage and its greatest limitation. Integration of performance analysis with the breakpoint debugger ensures that the performance analysis interface will be well understood by users before they begin performance tuning. Likewise, the fixed set of performance data reductions and presentations means that the user need not endure a complex configuration process prior to examining the performance data. The simplicity of the Prism interface, together with the undeniable utility of the presented data, made Prism very popular.

15.5.4   Etnus TotalView

TotalView [315] is one of the few commercially available, multiplatform debuggers. A breakpoint debugger, TotalView uses system services to start, stop, and manipulate collections of processes. Initially developed by BBN Technologies in the late 1980s for the BBN Butterfly, TotalView has been ported to almost all parallel and vector platforms, including the IBM SP, SGI Origin, Sun and Compaq clusters, Cray, Fujitsu, NEC, and Hitachi vector machines. In addition, it supports the common languages and programming models, including C, C++, Fortran 77, Fortran 90, HPF, MPI, PVM, and OpenMP.

Debugging and Visualization

Like Prism, TotalView supports interactive data visualization. By taking slices of arrays and displaying array subsets based on specified conditions (e.g., IEEE "not-a-number" or numerical ranges), users can analyze changes in array values throughout execution. *Seeing* scalars and arrays take on unexpected values is one of the most powerful analysis techniques—it enables debugger users to test their mental model of code execution against actual execution.

TotalView also supports the notion of process groups—groups of related processes that execute the same code. The TotalView interface then allows users to operate on process groups as if they were single processes, allowing scalable debugging of hundreds or thousands of parallel tasks.

Moreover, TotalView supports debugging of hybrid applications (i.e., those written using multiple languages and programming models) that execute on distributed clusters of systems. For MPI applications and application components, one can examine the MPI message queues to identify possible causes for message deadlock. Similarly, for HPF applications and components one can visualize arrays and their processor distributions and even examine and debug the generated Fortran 77 code.

Assessment

The major strength of TotalView is its support for almost all common parallel hardware platforms and programming models. By providing a standard look-and-feel, users can migrate codes across platforms and still use the same debugger interface.

15.6 Challenges and Open Problems

Although there are several commercial and academic software tools for performance tuning and debugging, tool developers continue struggling to support evolving system features and programming models. New architectural features (e.g., out-of-order instruction execution, deep memory hierarchies, and network-attached storage) and programming models (e.g., hybrids based on combinations of OpenMP and MPI) create new performance problems and change optimization criteria.

More perniciously, experience has shown that first-generation tools are rarely as effective as those that build on lessons learned from user studies and feedback. Hence, the rapid pace of hardware and software change means that tool developers have little opportunity to capture and embody experience with common programming idioms.

15.7 Conclusion

Parallel systems continue to change rapidly, and each poses a different set of performance-analysis and debugging problems. However, a set of standard instrumentation techniques for parallel systems has begun to emerge. Although the implementation of profiling, counting, interval timing, event tracing, and breakpoint debugging differs across systems, all implementations require high-resolution, low-overhead clocks and efficient data-extraction mechanisms. Open instrumentation questions include techniques for automatically identifying the causes of performance bottlenecks and locating tasks with anomalous behavior, and developing additional mechanisms for relating low-level performance data to high-level, data-parallel languages.

The state of data-presentation techniques is more nascent. Scalable parallel systems mandate presentation of higher-level, less-detailed performance data—

otherwise, the user is overwhelmed by the volume of data. For example, many current graphical performance-presentation techniques represent the states of individual tasks and do not scale to thousands of processors. An ideal performance data presentation should proceed from high-level, aggregate metrics that involve all processors and the entire computation to successively more detailed metrics for a subset of the processors and portion of the execution.

15.8   Further Reading

- Margaret L. Simmons, Ann H. Hayes, Jeffrey J. Brown and Daniel A. Reed, *Debugging and Performance Tuning for Parallel Computing Systems*, IEEE Computer Society Press, 1996. Summarizes a workshop on performance tools for parallel computing. With chapters on academic, national laboratory, and vendor software tool efforts, it is both a checkpoint of the state of the art and an analysis of the challenges faced by software tool developers.

- Vikram S. Adve, John Mellor-Crummey, Mark Anderson, Ken Kennedy, Jhy-Chun Wang, and Daniel A. Reed, "An Integrated Compilation and Performance Analysis Environment for Data Parallel Programs," *Supercomputing '95*, December 1995. Describes the problems inherent in building a performance-analysis environment that can relate dynamic performance data to data-parallel source code.

- Daniel A. Reed and Randy L. Ribler, "Performance Analysis and Visualization," in *Computational Grids: The Future of High-Performance Distributed Computing*, Ian Foster and Carl Kesselman (eds.), Morgan-Kaufmann, 1998. A review of the history of performance data visualization, emphasizing the evolution from postmortem optimization to real-time analysis and tuning.

- Daniel A. Reed, David A. Padua, Ian T. Foster, Dennis B. Gannon, and Barton P. Miller, "Delphi: An Integrated, Language Directed Performance Prediction, Measurement, and Analysis Environment," *The 7th Symposium on the Frontiers of Massively Parallel Computation*, February 1999. A look at compiler-aided performance prediction for complex parallel and distributed applications.

Acknowledgments. Portions of the work described here were conducted by members of the Pablo research group at the University of Illinois over a period of many years. We express special thanks for insights and ideas from Luiz DeRose, Allen Malony, Celso Mendes, and Jhy-chun Wang. Much of the work in deep compiler integration described in Section 15.3 was done by Vikram Adve, Ken Kennedy, and John Mellor-Crummey, members of the D System project. In addition, the members of the Delphi project, Ian Foster, Dennis Gannon, Bart Miller, and David Padua, are the source of many of the approaches to performance prediction described in Section 15.3.2.

This work was supported in part by the Defense Advanced Research Projects Agency under contracts F30602-96-C-0161, DABT63-96-C-0027, and N66001-97-C-8532. Support also came from the National Science Foundation (NSF) under grants CDA 94-01124, ASC 97-20202, and the NSF Partnerships for Advanced Computational Infrastructure cooperative agreement, and the Department of Energy under contracts B-341494, W-7405-ENG-48, and 1-B-333164.

16 The 2-D Poisson Problem

William Gropp

In this chapter I briefly describe how an approximate solution to the simple partial differential equation introduced in Chapter 4 can be found when using parallel computing. This allows us to illustrate the issues involved in parallelizing an application and to contrast the two major approaches: message passing and shared memory. The presentation complements and builds on the material in Chapter 4, which discusses the same problem from the perspective of parallel algorithms and performance modeling issues, and on Chapter 9, where we reviewed other parallel programming systems.

16.1 The Mathematical Model

The Poisson problem is a simple elliptic partial differential equation. The Poisson problem occurs in many physical problems, including fluid flow, electrostatics, and equilibrium heat flow. In 2-D, the Poisson problem is given by the following equations:

$$\frac{\partial^2 u(x,y)}{\partial x^2} + \frac{\partial^2 u(x,y)}{\partial y^2} = f(x,y) \quad \text{in the interior} \tag{16.1}$$

$$u(x,y) = g(x,y) \quad \text{on the boundary}$$

To compute an approximate solution to this problem, we define a discrete mesh of points (x_i, y_j) on which we will approximate u. To keep things simple, we assume that the mesh is uniformly spaced in both the x and y directions and that the distance between adjacent mesh points is h, that is, $x_{i+1} - x_i = h$ and $y_{j+1} - y_j = h$. We can then use a simple centered-difference approximation to the derivatives in equation (16.1) [506] to get

$$
\begin{aligned}
&\frac{u(x_{i+1}, y_j) - 2u(x_i, y_j) + u(x_{i-1}, y_j)}{h^2} \\
&\quad + \frac{u(x_i, y_{j+1}) - 2u(x_i, y_j) + u(x_i, y_{j-1})}{h^2} = f(x_i, y_j)
\end{aligned}
\tag{16.2}
$$

at each point (x_i, y_j) of the mesh. To simplify the rest of the discussion, we replace $u(x_i, y_j)$ with $u_{i,j}$.

16.2   A Simple Algorithm

Many numerical methods have been developed for approximating the solution of the partial differential equation in equation (16.1) and for solving the approximation in equation (16.2). In this section we will describe a very simple algorithm so that we can concentrate on the issues related to the parallel version of the algorithm. In practice, the algorithm we describe here is obsolete and should not be used (because it converges very slowly and better methods exist). However, many of the more modern algorithms use the same approach to achieve parallelism, such as those described in Chapters 20 and 21.

The algorithm that we use is called the *Jacobi method*. This method is an iterative approach for solving equation (16.2) that can be written as

$$
u_{i,j}^{k+1} = \frac{1}{4} \left(u_{i+1,j}^k + u_{i-1,j}^k + u_{i,j+1}^k + u_{i,j-1}^k - h^2 f_{i,j} \right)
\tag{16.3}
$$

This equation defines the value of $u(x_i, y_j)$ at the $k + 1$st step in terms of u at the kth step; it also ignores the boundary conditions.

We can translate this into a simple Fortran program by defining the array u(0:n,0:n) to hold u^k and unew(0:n,0:n) to hold u^{k+1}. This is shown in Figure 16.1; details of initialization and convergence testing have been left out.

16.3   Parallel Solution of Poisson's Equation

In this section, I discuss two different approaches to changing the sequential program above into a parallel program.

16.3.1   Message Passing and the Distributed-Memory Model

One of the two major classes of parallel programming models is the distributed-memory model, as discussed in Chapter 3. In this model, a parallel program is

```
real u(0:n,0:n), unew(0:n,0:n), f(1:n, 1:n), h

! Code to initialize f, u(0,*), u(n:*), u(*,0), and
! u(*,n) with g

h = 1.0 / n
do k=1, maxiter
  do j=1, n-1
    do i=1, n-1
      unew(i,j) = 0.25 * ( u(i+1,j) + u(i-1,j) + &
                           u(i,j+1) + u(i,j-1) - &
                           h * h * f(i,j) )
    enddo
  enddo
  ! Code to check for convergence of unew to u
  ! Make the new value the old value for the next iteration
  u = unew
enddo
```

Figure 16.1   Sequential version of the Jacobi algorithm.

made up of many processes,[1] each of which has its own address space and (usually) variables. Because each process has its own address space, special steps must be taken to communicate information between processes. One of the most widely used approaches is *message passing*. In message passing, information is communicated between processes using a cooperative approach; both the sender and the receiver make subroutine calls to arrange for the transfer of data between them. Variables in one process are not directly accessible by any other process.

In creating a parallel program for this programming model, the first question to ask is, What data structures in my program must be *distributed* or *partitioned* among these processes? In our example, in order to achieve any parallelism, each process must do part of the computation of unew. This suggests that we should distribute u, unew, and f. One such partition is shown in Figure 16.2(a). The part of the distributed data structure that is held by a particular process is said to be *owned* by that process.

Note that the code to compute unew(i,j) requires u(i,j+1) and u(i,j-1). This means that, in addition to the part of u and unew that each process has (as part of the

---

[1] In this chapter we are careful to refer to processes rather than processors. A processor is a piece of hardware; zero, one, or more processes may be running on a processor. In most parallel programs of the type described in this book, at most one thread should be running on each processor; in the simplest programming models, there is one thread per process, allowing the terms "process" and "processor" to be used interchangably. However, the difference between process and processor is real and important, and process rather than processor will be used in this chapter.

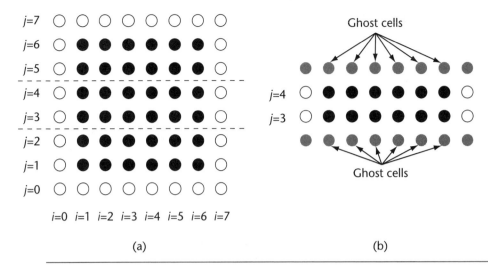

Figure 16.2   Simple decomposition of the mesh across processes. (a) Entire mesh, divided among three processes. Open circles correspond to points on the boundary. (b) Part of this array owned by the second process; the gray circles represent the ghost or halo cells.

decomposition), it also needs a small amount of data from its neighboring processes. These data are usually copied into a slightly expanded array that holds both the part of the distributed array managed (or *owned*) by a process with *ghost* or *halo* points that hold the values of these neighbors. This is shown in Figure 16.2(b). A process gets these values by communicating with its neighbors.

The code in Figure 16.3 shows the distributed-memory, message-passing version of our original code in Figure 16.1.

The values of js and je are the values of j for the bottom and top of the part of u owned by a process. The routine MPI_Sendrecv is part of the MPI message-passing standard [668]; it both sends and receives data. In this case, the first call sends the values u(1:n-1,js) to the process below or down, where it is received into u(1:n-1,je+1).

Note that although each process has variables js, je, u, and so on, these are all *different* variables (precisely, they are different memory locations).

There are many other ways to describe the communication needed for this algorithm and algorithms like it. See Gropp et al. [406, Chapter 4] for more details.

16.3.2   The Single Name-Space, Distributed-Memory Model

High Performance Fortran (HPF) [569] provides an extension of Fortran (Fortran 90) to distributed-memory parallel environments. Unlike the message-passing model, a single variable may be declared as distributed across all processes. For example, rather than declaring the part of the u variable owned by each process, in HPF the program

```
use mpi
real u(0:n,js-1:je+1), unew(0:n,js-1:je+1)
real f(1:n-1, js:je), h
integer nbr_down, nbr_up, status(MPI_STATUS_SIZE), ierr

! Code to initialize f, u(0,*), u(n:*), u(*,0), and
! u(*,n) with g


h = 1.0 / n
do k=1, maxiter
  ! Send down
  call MPI_Sendrecv( u(1,js), n-1, MPI_REAL, nbr_down, k &
                     u(1,je+1), n-1, MPI_REAL, nbr_up, k, &
                     MPI_COMM_WORLD, status, ierr )
  ! Send up
  call MPI_Sendrecv( u(1,je), n-1, MPI_REAL, nbr_up, k+1, &
                     u(1,js-1), n-1, MPI_REAL, nbr_down, k+1,&
                     MPI_COMM_WORLD, status, ierr )
  do j=js, je
    do i=1, n-1
      unew(i,j) = 0.25 * ( u(i+1,j) + u(i-1,j) + &
                           u(i,j+1) + u(i,j-1) - &
                           h * h * f(i,j) )
    enddo
  enddo
  ! Code to check for convergence of unew to u.
  ! Make the new value the old value for the next iteration
  u = unew
enddo
```

Figure 16.3 Message-passing version of Figure 16.1.

simply declares u in the same way as for the sequential program, and adds an HPF *directive* that describes how the variable should be distributed across the processes. All communication required to access neighbor values is handled for the programmer by the HPF compiler. The HPF version of the Jacobi iteration is shown in Figure 16.4.

Variables that are not specifically distributed by the programmer with an HPF directive behave just like variables in the message-passing program: each process has a separate version of the variable. For example, the variable h is in a different memory location on each process (even though we give it the same value).

Note also that the details of the distribution are controlled by HPF: the BLOCK distribution is specifically defined by HPF and does not exactly match the decomposition shown in Figure 16.2. For values of n that are much greater than the number

```
   real u(0:n,0:n), unew(0:n,0:n), f(0:n, 0:n), h
!HPF$ DISTRIBUTE u(:,BLOCK)
!HPF$ ALIGN unew WITH u
!HPF$ ALIGN f WITH u

   ! Code to initialize f, u(0,*), u(n:*), u(*,0),
   ! and u(*,n) with g

   h = 1.0 / n
   do k=1, maxiter
     unew(1:n-1,1:n-1) = 0.25 * &
                     ( u(2:n,1:n-1) + u(0:n-2,1:n-1) + &
                       u(1:n-1,2:n) + u(1:n-1,0:n-2) - &
                         h * h * f(1:n-1,1:n-1) )
     ! Code to check for convergence of unew to u.

     ! Make the new value the old value for the next iteration
     u = unew
   enddo
```

Figure 16.4   HPF version of the Jacobi algorithm.

of processes (the only case where parallelism makes any sense), however, the HPF choice is as good as any.

An advantage of HPF is that by changing the single line

```
!HPF$ DISTRIBUTE u(:,BLOCK)
```

to

```
!HPF$ DISTRIBUTE u(BLOCK,BLOCK)
```

we can change the distribution of the arrays to that shown in Figure 16.5. This distribution is more scalable than that in Figure 16.2 because the amount of data communicated per process decreases as the number of processes increases. The relative advantages of different decompositions is discussed in more detail in Chapter 18.

We call this the single name-space, distributed-memory model because all communication between processes is handled with variables (like u) that are declared globally; that is, they are declared as if they were accessible to all processes. This allows many programs to be written so that they are very similar to the sequential version of the same program. In fact, the HPF version of the program in Figure 16.4 is nearly identical to Figure 16.1, particularly if the i and j loops in Figure 16.1 are replaced with the Fortran 90 array expression used in Figure 16.4.

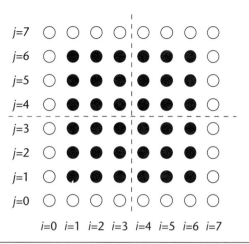

Figure 16.5 Decomposition of the mesh across a 2-D array of four processes, corresponding to an HPF BLOCK,BLOCK distribution.

16.3.3 The Shared-Memory Model

The shared-memory model, in contrast to the distributed-memory model, has only one process, but multiple threads. All threads can access all memory of the process. This means that there is only a single version of each variable. This is very convenient; in some cases, a parallel, shared-memory version of Figure 16.1 looks exactly the same: the compiler may be able to create a parallel version directly from the sequential code.

However, it can be helpful, both in terms of code clarity and the generation of efficient parallel code, to include some code that describes the desired parallelism. One method that was designed for this kind of code is OpenMP [725]. The OpenMP version is shown in Figure 16.6. In this example, the code between the comments !$omp parallel and !$omp end parallel is executed in parallel using multiple threads. The comment !$omp do indicates that the next line describes a do loop that should be *work shared*; that is, the iterations specified by this do statement will be executed by a collection of threads.

See Chapter 10 for a more detailed discussion of OpenMP. A complete OpenMPI code for the Jacobi example is available at the OpenMP website [724].

OpenMP handles many of the details of multithreaded programming for the user. It is also possible to use threads directly; it may be necessary in cases where an OpenMP-enabled compiler is not available. For UNIX systems, p-threads (i.e., POSIX threads [500]) defines a library interface to threads. In this approach, the code to be executed by a thread is placed into a separate routine; the name of that routine is passed to a thread-creation routine (e.g., pthread_create), which then starts that routine in a separate thread. The pthread_join routine is used to wait for the routine

```
      real u(0:n,0:n), unew(0:n,0:n), f(1:n-1, 1:n-1), h

      ! Code to initialize f, u(0,*), u(n:*), u(*,0),
      ! and u(*,n) with g

      h = 1.0 / n
      do k=1, maxiter
!$omp parallel
!$omp do
      do j=1, n-1
        do i=1, n-1
          unew(i,j) = 0.25 * ( u(i+1,j) + u(i-1,j) + &
                               u(i,j+1) + u(i,j-1) - &
                               h * h * f(i,j) )
        enddo
      enddo
!$omp enddo
      ! Code to check for convergence of unew to u

      ! Make the new value the old value for the next iteration
      u = unew
!$omp end parallel
      enddo
```

Figure 16.6   OpenMP (shared-memory) version of the Jacobi algorithm.

running in a thread to return. Using explicit threads allows you to work with any compiler, but requires a great deal of care on the part of the programmer. In addition, thread libraries are often not intended for scalable parallel computing and may not provide scalable performance.

Another approach for shared-memory parallelism is to use a language that provides explicit parallelism constructs for both data and tasks. Two examples of such languages are Co-Array Fortran and UPC. Chapter 9 shows an example of the Poisson problem using Co-Array Fortran.

16.3.4   Comments

Thus far, I have described very briefly the steps required when parallelizing code to approximate the solution of a partial differential equation. While the algorithm used in this discussion is inefficient by modern standards, the approach to parallelism is very similar to what is needed by state-of-the-art approaches for both implicit and explicit solution methods. Other chapters in this book discuss more modern techniques.

Because of the simplicity of the algorithm and data structures, these examples fail to address many of the issues that can arise in more complex situations. These include unstructured grids, dynamic (run-time) allocation and management of data structures, and more complex data dependencies between shared data structures (either between processes or threads). Some of these issues are discussed in more detail in Chapter 21 and other chapters.

The algorithm above did not specify the test for convergence. The result of such a test is a single value that all processes/threads contribute to and that must be available to all processes. Computing it scalably and correctly requires care. Each of the programming models illustrated above provides special features to handle this and similar problems. These are discussed in the next section.

Another discussion that focuses on some of the more subtle issues, particularly for the shared-memory case, is given in Pfister [763]. Suggestions for choosing among different approaches to expressing parallel programs are given in Chapter 9.

16.4   Adding Global Operations

The examples above showed how to compute with an array distributed across many processes. Sometimes, all processes or threads will need access to a single value. In this section, I discuss how each approach to parallel computing provides this operation by describing the implementation of a convergence test.

A simple convergence test is to compute the two-norm of the difference between two successive iterations. In the serial case, this can be accomplished with the code shown in Figure 16.7.

16.4.1   Collective Operations in MPI

In the MPI case, computing the two-norm of the difference of unew and u requires two steps. First, the sum of the squares of the differences of the local part of unew and u

```
real u(0:n,0:n), unew(0:n,0:n), twonorm

! ...
  twonorm = 0.0
  do j=1, n-1
    do i=1, n-1
      twonorm = twonorm + (unew(i,j) - u(i,j))**2
    enddo
  enddo
  twonorm = sqrt(twonorm)
  if (twonorm .le. tol) ! ... declare convergence
```

Figure 16.7   Sequential code to compute the two-norm of the difference between two iterations of the Jacobi algorithm.

```
      use mpi
      real u(0:n,js-1:je+1), unew(0:n,js-1:je+1), twonorm
      integer ierr

      ! ...

        twonorm_local = 0.0
        do j=js, je
          do i=1, n-1
            twonorm_local = twonorm_local + &
                         (unew(i,j) - u(i,j))**2
          enddo
        enddo
        call MPI_Allreduce( twonorm_local, twonorm, 1, &
                   MPI_REAL, MPI_SUM, MPI_COMM_WORLD, ierr )
        twonorm = sqrt(twonorm)
        if (twonorm .le. tol) ! ... declare convergence
```

Figure 16.8   Message-passing version of Figure 16.7.

is computed. These are then combined with the contributions from all of the other processes and summed together. Because the operation of combining values from many processes is common and important and because efficient implementations of this operation can require very system-specific code and algorithms, MPI provides a special routine, MPI_Allreduce, to combine a value from each process and return to all processes the result. This is shown in Figure 16.8.

This operation is called a *reduction* because it combines values from many sources into a single value. MPI provides many routines for communication and computation on a collection of processes; these are called *collective operations*.

16.4.2   Reductions in HPF

Fortran 90 and hence HPF contain built-in functions for computing the sum of all of the values in an array. In HPF, these functions work with distributed arrays, so the code is very simple, as shown in Figure 16.9.

16.4.3   Reductions in OpenMP

The approach taken in OpenMP is somewhat different from that in HPF. Like MPI, OpenMP recognizes that reductions are a common operation. In OpenMP, you can indicate that the result of a variable is to be formed by a reduction with a particular operator. This is shown in Figure 16.10.

```
    real u(0:n,0:n), unew(0:n,0:n), twonorm
!HPF$ DISTRIBUTE u(:,BLOCK)
!HPF$ ALIGN unew with u
!HPF$ ALIGN f with u

    ! ...
      twonorm = sqrt ( &
              sum ( (unew(1:n-1,1:n-1) - u(1:n-1,1:n-1))**2) )
      if (twonorm .le. tol) ! ... declare convergence
    enddo
```

Figure 16.9   HPF version of the convergence test for the Jacobi algorithm.

```
    real u(0:n,0:n), unew(0:n,0:n), twonorm

    ! ..
      twonorm = 0.0
!$omp parallel
!$omp do private(ldiff) reduction(+:twonorm)
      do j=1, n-1
        do i=1, n-1
          ldiff = (unew(i,j) - u(i,j))**2
          twonorm = twonorm + ldiff
        enddo
      enddo
!$omp enddo
!$omp end parallel
      twonorm = sqrt(twonorm)
    enddo
```

Figure 16.10   OpenMP (shared-memory) version of the convergence test for the Jacobi algorithm.

The effect of the reduction(+:twonorm) statement is to cause the OpenMP compiler to create a separate, private version of twonorm in each thread. When the enclosing scope ends, OpenMP combines the contributions in each thread using the specified operation to form the final value.

This code also illustrates the directive private to create a variable that is private to each thread (i.e., not shared). Without this directive, the value of ldiff added to the thread-private value of twonorm could come from the "wrong" thread. This also illustrates a difference in the OpenMP and HPF programming models. In OpenMP, most variables are shared by default, while in HPF, most variables are not.

16.4.4   Conclusion

All of the above approaches to finding the two-norm exploit the associativity of real arithmetic. Unfortunately, computers don't use real numbers; they use an approximation called floating-point numbers. Operations with floating-point numbers are nearly, but not exactly, associative. (See any introductory book on numerical analysis.) Because of this lack of associativity, the value computed by these methods may be different. In a well-designed algorithm, the difference will be small (in relative terms). However, this difference can sometimes be unexpected and hence confusing. It is also important to ensure that each process computes the *same* result for the reduction, since each process uses this value to decide whether to stop. Carefully designed routines for reduction operations will guarantee this result; programming models such as MPI, HPF, and OpenMP also guarantee that all processes receive the same result.

IV Enabling Technologies and Algorithms

17

Reusable Software and Algorithms

**Jack Dongarra • Ian Foster •
Ken Kennedy**

The ability to reuse existing algorithms and software is critical to an application programmer's productivity: without it, no programmer can build on prior experience, and every programming project must start from scratch. Effective reuse requires both *cataloging* so that programmers can locate algorithms and techniques that meet their needs and *reuse technologies* that allow these algorithms and techniques to be encapsulated in a reusable fashion—whether as design patterns, functions, libraries, components, objects, or whatever.

This book is not intended to serve as a comprehensive catalog of parallel algorithms. Nevertheless, the various application chapters of Part II and the more detailed technology chapters of Part III do collectively present a broad spectrum of algorithms. For more detailed discussions of parallel algorithm design, see Kumar et al. [585], Leighton [602], and Foster [341].

The technologies and techniques used to achieve reuse are discussed in several chapters. We provide here a brief review of three major approaches: the definition of templates, the development of data-distribution-neutral libraries, and standard libraries and components. We also introduce automatic differentiation, a technique that allows us to avoid code development altogether in one particular area.

17.1 Templates: Design Patterns for Parallel Software

In sequential programming, the concept of a *design pattern* has emerged as an approach to cataloging and communicating basic programming techniques [368]. For example, *divide and conquer* is a design pattern with relevance to a variety of problems. A specification of this pattern might specify the problem-independent structure and note where problem-specific logic must be supplied. This specification does not provide any executable code but provides a basic structure that can guide a programmer in developing an implementation.

The design pattern concept has considerable relevance to parallel programming, as in practice we find that there are only a fairly small number of basic parallel algorithm techniques. For example, the manager/worker structure is often appropriate when a large number of independent tasks need to be executed. A single *manager* process generates tasks and allocates those tasks to a number of *worker* processes; each worker repeatedly requests tasks from the manager and executes the problem-specific code required to perform those tasks (returning results to the manager) until the manager signals that no tasks remain. Variants of this basic pattern may create a hierarchy of managers, in order to avoid a bottleneck at the central manager, and/or allow for constant input data to be cached within workers, hence avoiding redundant communication.

Other common patterns include the *butterfly*, used, for example, to perform parallel summations in time proportional to the log of the number of processors (see Chapter 20), and *domain decomposition*, which is of course fundamental to the data-parallel programming model discussed earlier in Chapters 3 and 9.

The design-pattern concept turns up at various points in this book but is discussed in particular within Chapter 13, where the concept of *templates* is introduced. A template can be thought of as a reusable algorithm that includes the algorithm itself, along with information about how it is to be used, where specific computational specialization can occur, and how the algorithm can be tuned. A template may also include some sample implementations in different languages and pointers to background information.

17.2   Communicators and Data Structure Neutrality

The development of truly reusable parallel libraries is difficult (outside the somewhat constrained world of languages such as OpenMP and HPF) because of additional complexities associated with concurrency and data distribution:

- An unfortunate consequence of *concurrency* is that two processes or functions that execute correctly in isolation may not execute correctly when composed, because of race conditions.

- *Data-distribution* issues can lead to both correctness and performance problems. If a function expects data to be distributed in one fashion and receives it in another, then either the function will execute incorrectly (in the worst case) or an expensive redistribution operation may be required.

A consequence of these complexities is that until recently there were relatively few examples of successful reusable parallel libraries. Those libraries that did exist (e.g., ScaLAPACK) could only deal with a small number of data distributions and required that these data distributions be specified via cumbersome argument lists.

Two recent advances have led to a new generation of libraries that can be composed and reused relatively easily, thanks to two techniques:

- MPI's *communicators* mechanism allows the programmer to encapsulate communications that are "internal" to a function, hence avoiding race conditions that might occur if communications intended for one function are intercepted by another. This mechanism makes it easier to construct components so that interactions occur only via well-defined interfaces.

- Improved software engineering techniques allow data distribution issues to be separated from other aspects of function logic. What are sometimes called *data-structure-neutral* libraries allow an application to invoke an operation on a parallel data structure without regard to how the data structure is distributed; the distribution should impact performance but not correctness [73].

A contemporary example of a library that incorporates these two techniques is the PETSc collection of numerical solvers, described in Chapter 21.

17.3   Standard Libraries and Components

The increasing availability of advanced-architecture computers is having a significant effect on all spheres of scientific computation, including algorithm research and software development. One significant outcome of this work is the development of substantial bodies of "standard" code that are seeing significant use. We review briefly in the following the contents of the principal chapters in this book that deal with this topic.

17.3.1   Load Balancing and Grid Generation

Algorithms that find good partitionings of unstructured and irregular graphs are critical for the efficient execution of scientific simulations on high-performance parallel computers. In these simulations, computation is performed iteratively on each element of a physical 2-D or 3-D mesh, and then information is exchanged between adjacent mesh elements. Efficient execution of these simulations requires a mapping of the computational mesh to the processors such that each processor gets a roughly equal number of elements and the amount of interprocessor communication required to exchange the information between connected mesh elements is minimized. Such a mapping is commonly found using the traditional graph-partitioning problem. Many scientific simulations require the solutions of large sparse linear systems of equations. The solution of a sparse system of linear equations $Ax = b$ via iterative methods on a parallel computer gives rise to a graph partitioning problem. A key step in each iteration of these methods is the multiplication of a sparse matrix and a (dense) vector. A good partitioning of the graph corresponding to matrix A can significantly reduce the amount of communication in parallel sparse matrix–vector multiplication. These issues are addressed in Chapter 18.

17.3.2   Mesh Generation

Mesh generation is an essential element for the computational simulation of field phenomena such as fluid mechanics, heat and mass transfer, structural mechanics, plasmadynamics, electromagnetics, and other such physical processes that occur over a region of space. Mesh generation is the means by which the domain of interest is discretized into a collection of discrete points or volumes on which the governing equations can be represented and then solved computationally. The mesh thus provides the framework on which the solution is computed and subsequently visualized. Chapter 19 deals with tools for mesh generation.

17.3.3   Software for Scalable Solution of PDEs

The numerical approximation of the solution of partial differential equations (PDEs), which can be used to model physical, chemical, and biological phenomena, is an important application of parallel computers. Many issues arise in designing a parallel program to approximate the solution to a PDE. These include the choice of numerical algorithms and the distribution of data. The layout of data and specifics of data access in the numerical algorithms are also extremely important for achieving good performance on each individual processing node; high-performance parallel computing requires high-performance sequential kernels. Another issue is effective management of the interrelationships among software for the various facets of the overall simulation, including tools for time evolution, algebraic nonlinear and linear solution, adaptive mesh manipulations, optimization, and data analysis, since total computational efficiency can be only as good as its weakest link. These issues are addressed in Chapter 21.

17.3.4   Parallel Continuous Optimization

Optimization has broad applications in engineering, science, and management. Many of these applications either have large numbers of variables or require expensive function evaluations. In some cases, there may be many local minimizers, and the user naturally wants to know how solutions found by the algorithm compare to other local solutions. These factors contribute to the need for more intensive computation than traditional architectures can support. High-performance computing provides powerful tools for solving these problems with a degree of practicality that would otherwise be impossible. Chapter 22 covers parallel continuous optimization in detail.

17.4   Automatic Differentiation

Automatic differentiation (AD)—also known as computational differentiation or algorithmic differentiation—is a maturing technology for computing derivatives of computer simulations. AD is an automatic technique for augmenting computer programs with code to compute derivatives accurately and efficiently. As an automatic technique, AD has the potential to eliminate the need to explicitly develop code to compute derivatives. Not only can AD reduce the time required to develop a differentiated code, it also reduces the total amount of code that needs to be maintained and allows developers to focus on the underlying computational simulation. The ideas underlying automatic differentiation are not new—in high school calculus, most students realize that differentiation is an essentially mechanical procedure. There have been more than 60 automatic differentiation software packages developed since the 1950s. The great majority of these software packages were developed for use by their developers for specialized applications. These issues are addressed in Chapter 24.

17.5 Templates and Numerical Linear Algebra

Large-scale problems of engineering and scientific computing often require solutions of linear algebra problems. Half a century ago, it might have been sufficient to recommend inverting a matrix or forming a characteristic polynomial and then computing its roots. These mathematicians' methods were only practical for very small problems. The time is ripe to organize descriptions of the many modern practical methods including advice on how to wisely choose among them, and how to interpret the results.

A computational scientist interested in solving a large sparse linear algebra problem might have to search among books, the research literature, and online or library software. The search can be daunting. Software may be found in well-maintained libraries available commercially or publicly, other libraries distributed with texts or other books, individual subroutines tested and published by organizations such as the Association for Computing Machinery (ACM), and even more software is available from individuals on individual Web pages, or publicly maintained pages such as Netlib (*http://www.netlib.org*). Sometimes the software may be hard to find or come without support. Although we admit that some challenging numerical linear algebra problems still await satisfactory solutions, many excellent methods do exist from a plethora of sources.

But the sheer number of algorithms and their implementations makes it hard even for experts, let alone general users, to find the best solution for a given problem. This has led to the development of various online search facilities for numerical software. One has been developed by NIST the (National Institute of Standards and Technology), and is called GAMS (Guide to Available Mathematical Software, *http://gams.nist.gov*); another is part of Netlib. These facilities permit searches based on library names, subroutine names, keywords, and a taxonomy of topics in numerical computing. But for the general user in search of advice as to which algorithm or which subroutine to use for her particular problem, they offer relatively little advice.

Furthermore, many challenging problems cannot be solved with existing "black-box" software packages in a reasonable time or space. This means that more special-purpose methods must be used and tuned for the problem at hand. Tuning is a great challenge, since there are a large number of tuning options available, and for many problems it is a challenge to get any acceptable answer at all or to have confidence in what is computed. The expertise regarding which options are likely to work in a specific application area is distributed among many experts.

Thus, there is a need for tools to help users pick the best algorithm and implementation for their numerical problems, as well as expert advice on how to tune them.

The approach we have taken in CRPC is that of algorithm templates, with a decision tree to help choose among them. Specifically, the decision tree uses information about the structure of the problem, the kind of solution that is desired, and the kind of computer available to identify one or more suitable algorithm templates. A template will include some or all of the following: (1) a high-level description of an algorithm; (2) a description of when it is effective, including conditions on the input, and estimates of the time, space, or other resources required; (3) a description of available refinements and user-tunable parameters, as well as advice on when to use them; (4) pointers to complete or partial implementations, perhaps in several languages or for several architectures (such as different parallel architectures); (5) a way to assess the accuracy; (6) numerical examples, on a common set of examples, illustrating both easy cases and difficult cases; (7) troubleshooting advice; and (8) pointers to texts or journal articles for further information.

For the past 20 years or so, there has been a great deal of activity in the area of algorithms and software for solving scientific problems. The linear algebra community has long recognized the need for help in developing algorithms into software libraries, and several years ago, as a community effort, put together a de facto standard identifying basic operations required in linear algebra algorithms and software. The hope was that the routines making up this standard, known collectively as Basic Linear Algebra Subprograms [283, 284, 595], would be efficiently implemented on advanced-architecture computers by many manufacturers, making it possible to reap the portability benefits of having them efficiently implemented on a wide range of machines. This goal has been largely realized.

The key insight of the approach to designing linear algebra algorithms for advanced-architecture computers is that the frequency with which data are moved between different levels of the memory hierarchy must be minimized in order to attain high performance. Thus, our main algorithmic approach for exploiting both vectorization and parallelism in our implementations is the use of block-partitioned algorithms, particularly in conjunction with highly tuned kernels for performing matrix–vector and matrix–matrix operations. In general, the use of block-partitioned algorithms requires data to be moved as blocks, rather than as vectors or scalars, so that although the total amount of data moved is unchanged, the latency (or start-up cost) associated with the movement is greatly reduced because fewer messages are needed to move the data. A second key idea is that a user can tune the performance of an algorithm by varying the parameters that specify the data layout. On shared-memory machines, this is controlled by the block size, while on distributed-memory machines it is controlled by the block size and the configuration of the logical process mesh.

More details on templates for numerical linear algebra are provided in Chapter 20.

17.6 Conclusion

Within the last few years, many who work on the development of numerical algorithms have come to realize the need to get directly involved in the software development process. Issues such as robustness, ease of use, and portability are standard fare in any discussion of numerical algorithm design and implementation. The portability issue, in particular, can be very challenging. As new and exotic architectures evolve, they will embrace the notions of concurrent processing, shared memory, pipelining, and so on in order to increase performance. The portability issue becomes formidable indeed as different architectural designs become reality. In fact, it is very tempting to assume that an unavoidable byproduct of portability must be an unacceptable degradation in the level of efficiency on a given variety of machine architecture. We contend that this assumption is erroneous and that its widespread adoption could seriously hamper the ability to effectively utilize machines of the future.

Architectures of future machines promise to offer a profusion of computing environments. The existing forerunners have already given many software developers cause to reexamine the underlying algorithms for efficiency's sake. However, it seems to be an unnecessary waste of effort to recast these algorithms with only one computer in mind, regardless of how fast that one may be. The efficiency of an algorithm should not be discussed in terms of its realization as a computer program. Even within a single architecture class, the features of one system may improve the performance of a given program, while features of another system may have just the opposite effect.

Software developers should begin to identify classes of problems suitable for parallel implementation and to develop efficient algorithms for each of these areas. With such a wide variety of computer systems and architectures in use or proposed, the challenge for people designing algorithms is to develop algorithms, and ultimately software, that are both efficient and portable. To address this challenge, there appear to be three approaches. They are not mutually exclusive, but each can contribute to provide an effective solution. The first approach is to express the algorithms in terms of modules at a high level of granularity. When moving software from one architecture to another, the basic algorithms are the same, but the modules are changed to suit the new architectures. A second approach is to create a model of computation representing the computing environment. This model should be characterized by the salient features of a given architectural category. Software is written for the model and then transformed to suit a particular realization of an architecture that fits the model. The general categories of multiple instruction, multiple data (MIMD) and single instruction, multiple data (SIMD) are of course too crude, but additional details could be specified. For example, an MIMD model might be characterized by the number of processors, communication vehicle, access to shared memory, and synchronization primitives. Software written for such a model can be transformed to software for a specific machine by a macro processor or a specially designed pre-processor. As a third approach, the software can be written in high-level language constructs, such as array-processing statements. Again, a preprocessor can be written to generate the "object" code suitable for a particular architecture.

Of the three approaches, expressing the algorithms in terms of modules with a high level of granularity seems preferable where it is applicable. In particular, it would seem applicable to certain basic software library subroutines that are expected to shoulder the bulk of the work in a wide variety of numerical calculations. Where successful, the effect of this will enhance both the maintenance and use of the software. Software maintenance would be enhanced because more of the basic mathematical structure would be retained within the formulation of the algorithm. The fine computational detail required for efficiency would be isolated within the high-level modules. Software users would benefit through the ability to move existing codes to new environments and experience a reasonable level of efficiency with minimal effort. A key issue in the success of this approach is to identify a level of granularity that will permit efficient implementations across a wide variety of architectural settings. Individual modules can then be dealt with separately, retargeting them for efficiency on quite different architectures. This will have the effect of concealing the peculiarities of a particular machine from a potential user of the software and will allow him to concentrate his effort on his application rather than on the computing environment.

Of course, the approach described above has limited application. One area where it works well is in linear algebra, and hence it may be effective in any application that is dominated by these calculations. In areas where this approach will not work, there is a need to develop algorithms that focus on the architectural features at a deeper level. However, the goal in these efforts must be to exploit the key features of the architecture and not the particular realization. This is where the approach based upon a model of computation can be useful. As multiprocessor designs proliferate, research efforts should focus on "generic" algorithms that can be easily transported across various implementations of these designs. If a code has been written in terms of high-level synchronization and data-management primitives, which are expected to be supported by every member of the model of computation, then these primitives only need to be customized to a particular realization. A very high level of transportability may be achieved through automating the transformation of these primitives. The benefit to software maintenance, particularly for large codes, is in the isolation of synchronization and data-management peculiarities.

18 Graph Partitioning for High-Performance Scientific Simulations

Kirk Schloegel • **George Karypis** • **Vipin Kumar**

Algorithms that find good partitionings of unstructured and irregular graphs are critical for the efficient execution of scientific simulations on high-performance parallel computers. In these simulations, computation is performed iteratively on each element (and/or node) of a physical 2-D or 3-D mesh. Information is then exchanged between adjacent mesh elements. For example, computation is performed on each triangle of the 2-D irregular mesh shown in Figure 18.1. Then information is exchanged for every face between adjacent triangles. Efficient execution of such simulations on distributed-memory machines requires a mapping of the computational mesh onto the processors that equalizes the number of mesh elements assigned to each processor and minimizes the interprocessor communication required to perform the information exchange between adjacent elements. Such a mapping is commonly found by solving a graph partitioning problem. For example, a graph partitioning algorithm was used to decompose the mesh in Figure 18.1. Here, the mesh elements have been shaded to indicate the processor to which they have been mapped. Simulations performed on shared-memory multiprocessors also benefit from partitioning, as this increases data locality and thus leads to better cache performance.

In many scientific simulations, the structure of the computation evolves from time step to time step. These simulations require decompositions of the mesh prior to the start of the simulation (as described above) and periodic load balancing during the course of the simulation. Other classes of simulations (i.e., multiphase simulations) consist of a number of computational phases separated by synchronization steps. These require that each of the phases be individually load balanced. Still other scientific simulations model multiple physical phenomena (i.e., multiphysics simulations) or employ multiple meshes simultaneously (i.e., multimesh simulations).

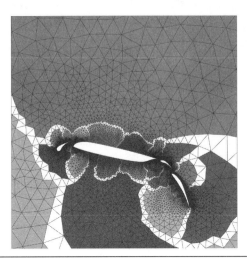

Figure 18.1   A partitioned 2-D irregular mesh of an airfoil. The shading of a mesh element indicates the processor to which it is mapped.

These impose additional requirements that the partitioning algorithm must take into account. Traditional graph partitioning algorithms are not adequate to ensure the efficient execution of these classes of simulations on high-performance parallel computers. Instead, generalized graph partitioning algorithms have been developed for such simulations.

This chapter presents an overview of graph partitioning algorithms used for scientific simulations on high-performance parallel computers. Recent developments in graph partitioning for adaptive and dynamic simulations, as well as partitioning algorithms for sophisticated simulations such as multiphase, multiphysics, and multimesh computations are also discussed. Specifically, Section 18.1 presents the graph partitioning formulation used to model the problem of mapping computational meshes onto processors. Section 18.2 describes numerous static graph partitioning algorithms. Section 18.3 discusses the adaptive graph-partitioning problem and describes a number of repartitioning schemes. Section 18.4 discusses the issues involved with the parallelization of static and adaptive graph partitioning schemes. Section 18.5 describes a number of important types of applications for which the traditional graph partitioning problem is inadequate. This section also describes generalizations of the graph partitioning problem that are able to effectively model these applications as well as algorithms for computing partitionings based on these new formulations. Finally, Section 18.6 presents concluding remarks, discusses areas of future research, and charts the functionality of a number of publicly available graph partitioning software packages.

18.1   Modeling Mesh-Based Computations as Graphs

In order to compute a mapping of a mesh onto a set of processors via graph partitioning, it is first necessary to construct the graph that models the structure of the computation. In general, computation of a scientific simulation can be performed on the mesh nodes, the mesh elements, or both of these. If the computation is mainly performed on the mesh nodes, then this graph is straightforward to construct. A vertex exists for each mesh node, and an edge exists on the graph for each edge between the nodes. We refer to this as the *node* graph. However, if the computation is performed on the mesh elements, then the graph is such that each mesh element is modeled by a vertex, and an edge exists between two vertices whenever the corresponding elements share an edge (in 2-D) or a face (in 3-D). We refer to this as the *dual* graph. Figure 18.2 illustrates a 2-D example. Figure 18.2(a) shows a finite-element mesh, and Figure 18.2(b) shows the corresponding node graph. Figure 18.2(c) shows the dual graph that models the adjacencies of the mesh elements. Partitioning the vertices of these graphs into k disjoint subdomains provides a mapping of either the mesh nodes or the mesh elements onto k processors. If the partitioning is computed such that each subdomain has the same number of vertices, then each processor will have an equal amount of work during parallel processing. The total volume of communications incurred during this parallel processing can be estimated by counting the number of edges that connect vertices in different subdomains. Therefore, a partitioning should be computed that minimizes this metric (which is referred to as the *edge-cut*).

The objective of the graph partitioning problem is to compute just such a partitioning (i.e., one that balances the subdomains and minimizes the edge-cut). More formally, the graph partitioning problem is as follows. Given a weighted, undirected graph $G = (V, E)$, for which each vertex and edge has an associated weight, the k-way graph partitioning problem is to split the vertices of V into k disjoint subsets

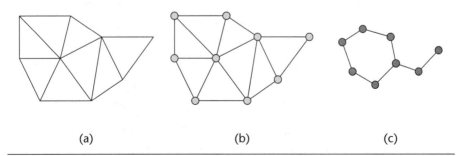

(a)   (b)   (c)

Figure 18.2   (a) 2D irregular mesh and (b and c) corresponding graphs. The graph in (b) models the connectivity between the mesh nodes. The graph in (c) models the adjacency of the mesh elements.

(or *subdomains*) such that each subdomain has roughly an equal amount of vertex weight (referred to as the *balance constraint*), while minimizing the sum of the weights of the edges whose incident vertices belong to different subdomains (i.e., the edge-cut).

In some cases, it is beneficial to compute partitionings that assign each subdomain a specified amount of vertex weight. This may be necessary for scientific simulations performed on a cluster of heterogeneous workstations. The subdomain weights should result in more work being assigned to the faster machines and less work to the slower machines. Subdomain weights can be specified by using a vector of size k in which each element of the vector indicates the fraction of the total vertex weight that the corresponding subdomain should contain. In this case, the graph partitioning problem is to compute a partitioning that splits the vertices into k disjoint subdomains such that each subdomain has the specified fraction of total vertex weight and such that the edge-cut is minimized.

It is important to note that the edge-cut metric is only an approximation of the total communications volume incurred by parallel processing [455]. It is not a precise model of this quantity. Consider the example in Figure 18.3. Here, three subdomains, A, B, and C, are shown. The edge-cut of the (three-way) partitioning is seven. During parallel computation, the processor corresponding to subdomain A will need to send the data for vertices 1 and 3 to the processor corresponding to subdomain B and the data for vertex 4 to the processor corresponding to subdomain C. Similarly, B needs to send the data for 5 and 7 to A and the data for 7 and 8 to C. Finally, C needs to send the data for 9 to B and the data for 10 to A. This equals nine units of data to be sent, while the edge-cut is seven. Edge-cut and total communication volume are not the same because the edge-cut counts every edge cut, while data are required to be sent only one time if two or more edges of a single vertex are cut by the same subdomain. (This is the case, for example, for vertex 3 and subdomain B in Figure 18.3.) It should also be noted that total communication volume alone cannot accurately predict interprocessor communication overhead. A more precise measure is the maximum time required by any of the processors to perform communication (assuming that computation and communication occur in alternating phases). This depends on a number of factors, including the amount of data to be sent out of any one processor, as well as the number of processors with which a processor must communicate. In particular, on message-passing architectures, minimizing the maximum number of message start-ups that any one processor must perform can sometimes be more important than minimizing the communications volume [456]. Nevertheless, there still tends to be a strong correlation between edge-cuts and interprocessor communication costs for graphs of uniform degree (i.e., graphs in which most vertices have about the same number of edges). This is a typical characteristic of graphs derived from scientific simulations. Therefore, the min-cut partitioning problem is a reasonable model for minimizing the interprocessor communications of parallel scientific simulations.

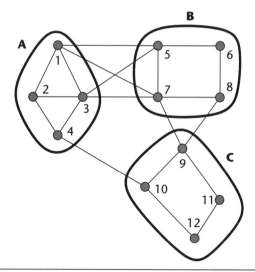

Figure 18.3   A partitioned graph with an edge-cut of seven. Here, nine communications are incurred during parallel processing.

18.1.1   Computing a k-Way Partitioning via Recursive Bisection

Graphs are frequently partitioned into k subdomains by recursively computing two-way partitionings (i.e., *bisections*) of the graph [92]. This method requires the computation of $k-1$ bisections. If k is not a power of two, then for each bisection, the appropriate subdomain weights need to be specified in order to ensure that the resulting k-way partitioning is balanced.

For a large class of graphs derived from scientific simulations, recursive bisection algorithms are able to compute k-way partitionings that are within a constant factor of the optimal solution [866]. Furthermore, if the balance constraint is sufficiently relaxed, then recursive bisection methods can be used to compute k-way partitionings that are within $\log p$ of the optimal for all graphs [866]. Since the direct computation of a good k-way partitioning is harder in general than the computation of a good bisection (although both problems are NP-complete), recursive bisection has become a widely used technique.

18.2   Static Graph-Partitioning Techniques

The graph partitioning problem is known to be NP-complete. Therefore, in general it is not possible to compute optimal partitionings for graphs of interesting size in a reasonable amount of time. This fact, combined with the importance of the problem, has led to the development of numerous heuristic approaches [50, 51, 80, 92, 155,

218, 265, 334, 374, 379, 384, 415, 423, 424, 441, 449, 460, 459, 538, 542, 560, 674, 678, 718, 755, 767, 774, 773, 787, 865, 970, 1003]. These can be classified as either geometric techniques [92, 379, 449, 674, 718, 755, 767, 787], combinatorial techniques [50, 51, 265, 334, 374, 384, 424, 560], spectral techniques [459, 460, 773, 774, 865], combinatorial optimization techniques [80, 423, 1003], or multilevel methods [155, 218, 415, 441, 538, 542, 678, 970]. In this section, we discuss several of these classes and describe the important schemes from them.

18.2.1   Geometric Techniques

Geometric techniques [92, 379, 449, 674, 718, 755, 767, 787] compute partitionings based solely on the coordinate information of the mesh nodes. Since these techniques do not consider the connectivity between the mesh elements, there is no concept of edge-cut here. In order to minimize the interprocessor communications incurred due to parallel processing, geometric schemes are usually designed to minimize a related metric, such as the number of mesh elements that are adjacent to nonlocal elements (i.e., the size of the subdomain boundary). Usually, these techniques partition the mesh elements directly, rather than the graphs that model the structures of the computations. Because of this distinction, they are often referred to as *mesh-partitioning* schemes.

Geometric techniques are applicable only if coordinate information exists for the mesh nodes. This is usually true for meshes used in scientific simulations. Even if the mesh is not embedded in a k-dimensional space, there are techniques that are able to compute node coordinates automatically, based on the connectivity of the mesh elements [427]. Typically, geometric partitioners are extremely fast. However, they tend to compute partitionings of lower quality than schemes that take the connectivity of the mesh elements into account. For this reason, multiple trials are usually performed, with the best partitioning of these being selected.

Coordinate Nested Dissection

Coordinate nested dissection (CND) (also referred to as recursive coordinate bisection) is a recursive bisection scheme that attempts to minimize the boundary between the subdomains (and therefore, the interprocessor communications) by splitting the mesh in half normal to its longest dimension. Figure 18.4 illustrates how this works. Figure 18.4(a) gives a mesh bisected normal to the x-axis. Figure 18.4(b) gives the same mesh bisected normal to the y-axis. The subdomain boundary in Figure 18.4(a) is much smaller than that in Figure 18.4(b). This is because the mesh is longer in the direction of the x-axis than in the direction of y-axis.

The CND algorithm works as follows. The centers of mass of the mesh elements are computed, and these are projected onto the coordinate axis that corresponds to the longest dimension of the mesh. This gives an ordering of the mesh elements. (Note that this scheme can result in multiple mesh elements being projected onto the same point along the selected dimension. Such "ties" in ordering can be broken

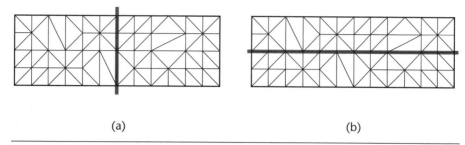

(a)   (b)

Figure 18.4 Two mesh bisections normal to the coordinate axes. (a) Mesh is bisected normal to the x-axis. (b) Mesh is bisected normal to the y-axis. The subdomain boundary in (a) is smaller than that in (b).

arbitrarily.) The ordered list is then split in half to produce a bisection of the mesh elements.[1] Each subdomain can then be recursively subdivided by the same technique [92]. Figure 18.5 illustrates an eight-way partitioning computed by this method. Figure 18.5(a) shows the centers of mass of the mesh elements and the computed recursive bisections. First, the solid line bisected the entire mesh. Then, the dashed lines bisected the two subdomains. Finally, the dashed-and-dotted lines bisected the resulting subdomains. Figure 18.5(b) shows the mesh elements shaded according to their subdomains.

The CND scheme is extremely fast, requires little memory, and is easy to parallelize. In addition, partitionings obtained by this scheme can be described quite compactly (just by the splitters used at each node of the recursive bisection tree). However, partitionings computed via CND tend to be of low quality. Furthermore, for complicated geometries CND tends to produce partitionings that contain disconnected subdomains. Figure 18.6 gives an example of this. Here, the upper- and lower-left subdomains are both disconnected. Several variations of CND have been developed that attempt to address its disadvantages [449]. However, even the most sophisticated variants tend to produce worse quality partitionings than more sophisticated schemes.

Recursive Inertial Bisection

The CND scheme can only compute bisections that are normal to one of the coordinate axes. In many cases, this restriction can limit the quality of the partitioning. Figure 18.7 gives an example. The mesh in Figure 18.7(a) is bisected normal to the longest dimension of the mesh. However, the subdomain boundary is still quite long. This is because the mesh is oriented at an angle to the coordinate axes. To achieve a smaller subdomain boundary, the algorithm must orient the bisection in

---

[1] Alternatively, the mesh *nodes* can be ordered and split in half instead of the mesh elements.

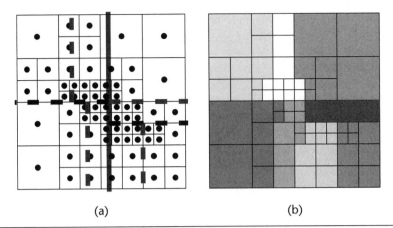

(a)   (b)

Figure 18.5 An eight-way partitioning of a mesh computed by a CND scheme. First, the solid bisection was computed. Then the dashed bisections were computed for each of the subdomains. Finally, the dashed-and-dotted bisections were computed. (a) Centers of mass of the mesh elements. (b) Mesh elements are shaded to indicate their subdomains.

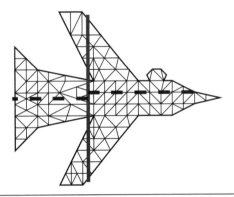

Figure 18.6 A four-way partitioning computed by a CND scheme. First, the solid bisection was computed. Then the dashed bisections were computed for each of the subdomains. The upper- and lower-left subdomains are disconnected.

a way that takes the angle into account. One way to do this is to treat the mesh elements as point masses and to compute the principal inertial axis of the mass distribution. If the mesh is convex, then this axis will align with the overall orientation of the mesh. A bisection line that is orthogonal to this will often result in a small subdomain boundary, as the mesh will tend to be thinnest in this direction [772].

The recursive inertial bisection (RIB) algorithm improves upon the CND scheme by making use of this idea as follows. The inertial axis of the mesh is computed, and

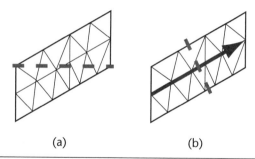

(a)   (b)

Figure 18.7   Bisections for a mesh are computed by the CND and RIB schemes. (a) Mesh is bisected by the CND scheme. (b) Mesh is bisected by the RIB scheme, which results in a significantly smaller subdomain boundary.

an ordering of the elements is produced by projecting their centers of mass onto this axis. The ordered list is then split in half to produce a bisection. The scheme can be applied recursively to produce a k-way partitioning [718]. As an example, the bisection of the mesh in Figure 18.7(b) is computed using the RIB algorithm. The solid arrow indicates the inertial axis of the mesh. The dashed line is the bisection. Here, the subdomain boundary is much smaller than that produced by the CND scheme in Figure 18.7(a).

Space-Filling Curve Techniques

The CND and RIB algorithms find orderings of the mesh elements and then split the ordered list in half to produce a bisection. In these schemes, orderings are computed by projecting the elements onto either the coordinate or inertial axes. A disadvantage of these techniques is that orderings are computed based on a single dimension at a time. A scheme that considers more than one dimension may produce better partitionings.

One such method orders the mesh elements according to the positions of their centers of mass along a space-filling curve [731, 755, 767, 980] (or a related self-avoiding walk [451]). Space-filling curves are continuous curves that completely fill higher-dimensional spaces such as squares or cubes. A number of such curves have been defined that fill space in a locality-preserving way (e.g., Peano–Hilbert curves [469]). These produce orderings of mesh elements that have the desirable characteristic that elements that are near each other in space are likely to be ordered near each other as well. After the ordering is computed, the ordered list of mesh elements is split into k parts resulting in k subdomains. Figure 18.8 illustrates a space-filling curve method for computing an eight-way partitioning of a quad-tree mesh.

Space-filling curve partitioners are fast and generally produce partitionings of somewhat better quality than either the CND or RIB schemes. They tend to work particularly well for classes of simulations in which the dependencies between the

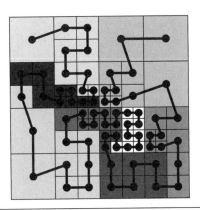

Figure 18.8   A Peano–Hilbert space-filling curve is used to order the mesh elements. The eight-way partitioning that is produced by this ordering is shown.

computational nodes are governed by their spatial proximity to one another as in *n*-body computations using hierarchical methods [980].

Sphere-Cutting Approach

Miller et al. [674] proposed a new class of graphs, called *overlap* graphs, that contains all *well-shaped* meshes, as well as all planar graphs. Meshes are considered well shaped if the angles and/or aspect ratios of their elements are bounded within some values. Most of the meshes used in scientific simulations are well shaped according to this definition. Miller et al. proved that overlap graphs have $O(n^{(d-1)/d})$ vertex separators. In doing so, they extended results by Lipton and Tarjan [619] and others [675]. Note that a vertex separator is a set of vertices that, if removed, splits the graph into two roughly equal-sized subgraphs, such that no edge connects the two subgraphs. That is, instead of partitioning the graph between the vertices (and so cutting edges), the graph is partitioned along the vertices. For this formulation, the sum weight of the separator vertices should be minimized.

Miller et al. used the concept of a *neighborhood system* to define an overlap graph. A *k*-ply neighborhood system is a set of *n* spheres in a *d*-dimensional space such that no point in space is encircled by more than *k* of the spheres. An (α, k)-overlap graph contains a vertex for each sphere, with an edge existing between two vertices if the corresponding spheres intersect when the smaller of them is expanded by a factor of α. Figure 18.9 illustrates these concepts. Figure 18.9(a) shows a set of points in a 2-D space. Figure 18.9(b) shows a three-ply neighborhood system for these points. Figure 18.9(c) shows the (1, 3)-overlap graph constructed from this neighborhood system.

Gilbert et al. [379] describe an implementation of a geometric bisection scheme based on these results. This scheme projects each vertex of a *d*-dimensional (α, k)-

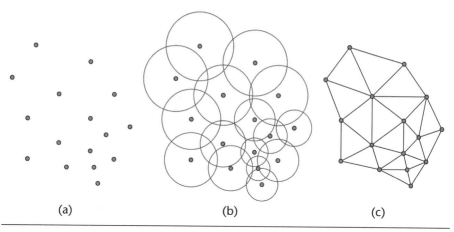

Figure 18.9 (a) Nodes of a finite-element mesh. (b) Three-ply neighborhood systems for the nodes. (c) The (1, 3)-overlap graph for the mesh.

overlap graph onto the unit $(d+1)$-dimensional sphere that encircles it. A random great circle of the sphere has a high probability of splitting the vertices into three sets A, B, and C, such that no edge joins A and B, A and B each have at most $\frac{d+1}{d+2}n$ vertices, and C has only $O(\alpha k^{1/d} n^{(d-1)/d})$ vertices [674]. Therefore, by selecting a few great circles at random and picking the best separator from these, the algorithm can compute a vertex separator of guaranteed quality (in asymptotic terms) with high probability.

The sphere-cutting scheme is unique among those described in this chapter in that it guarantees the quality of the computed bisection for well-shaped meshes. But it is not guaranteed to compute perfectly balanced bisections. It is proven in Miller et al. [674] that the larger subdomain will contain no more than $\frac{d+1}{d+2}n$ vertices. However, experiments cited in Gilbert et al. [379] on a small number of test graphs indicate that, in three dimensions, splits as bad as $2:1$ are rare, and most are within 20%. Gilbert et al. [379] suggest a modification of the scheme that will result in balanced bisections by shifting the separating plane normal to its orientation.

18.2.2 Combinatorial Techniques

When computing a partitioning, geometric techniques attempt to group together vertices that are spatially near each other, whether or not these vertices are highly connected. Combinatorial partitioners, on the other hand, attempt to group together highly connected vertices, whether or not these are near each other in space. That is, combinatorial partitioning schemes compute a partitioning based only on the adjacency information of the graph; they do not consider the coordinates of the vertices. For this reason, the partitionings produced typically have lower edge-cuts and are less likely to contain disconnected subdomains than partitionings produced by geometric schemes. However, combinatorial techniques tend to be slower than geometric partitioning techniques and are not as amenable to parallelization.

Levelized Nested Dissection

A partitioning will have a low edge-cut if adjacent vertices are usually in the same subdomain. The levelized nested dissection (LND) algorithm attempts to put connected vertices together. It starts with a subdomain containing a single vertex and incrementally adds adjacent vertices [374].

More precisely, the LND algorithm works as follows. An initial vertex is selected and assigned the number 0. Then all of the vertices that are adjacent to the selected vertex are assigned the number 1. Next, all of the vertices that are not assigned a number and are adjacent to any vertex that has been assigned a number are assigned that number plus 1. This process continues until half of the vertices have been assigned a number. At this point, the algorithm terminates. The vertices that have been assigned numbers are in one subdomain, and the vertices that have not been assigned numbers are in the other subdomain. Figure 18.10 illustrates the LND algorithm. It shows the numbering starting with the extreme lower-right vertex. Here, the solid line shows a bisection with an edge-cut of eight computed by the LND algorithm.

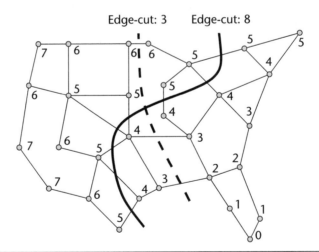

Figure 18.10   A graph partitioned by the LND algorithm. The vertex in the extreme bottom right was selected and labeled 0. Then, the vertices were labeled in a breadth-first manner according to how far they are from the 0 vertex. After half of the vertices had been labeled, a bisection (solid line) was constructed such that the labeled vertices are in one subdomain and the unlabeled vertices are in another subdomain. This figure also shows a higher-quality bisection (dashed line) for the same graph.

This scheme tends to perform better when the initial seed is a pseudo-peripheral vertex (i.e., one of the pairs of vertices that are approximately the greatest distance from each other in the graph) as in Figure 18.10. Such a vertex can be found by a process that is similar to the LND algorithm. A random vertex is initially selected to start the numbering of vertices. Here, all vertices are numbered. The vertex (or one of the vertices) with the highest number is likely to be in a corner of the graph. This vertex can be used either as an input to find another corner vertex (at the other end of the graph) or as the seed vertex for the LND scheme.

The LND algorithm ensures that at least one of the computed subdomains is connected (as long as the input graph is fully connected). It tends to produce partitionings of comparable or better quality than geometric schemes. However, even with a good seed vertex, the LND algorithm can sometimes produce poor quality partitionings. For example, the graph in Figure 18.10 contains a natural bisector shown by the dashed line. However, the LND algorithm was unable to find this bisection. For this reason, multiple trials of the LND algorithm are often performed, and the best partitioning from these is selected. Several variations and improvements of levelized nested dissection schemes are studied in Chung and Ranka [203], Goehring and Saad [384], and Sadayappan and Ercal [822].

Kernighan–Lin/Fiduccia–Mattheyses Algorithm (KL/FM)

Closely related to the graph partitioning problem is that of partition refinement. Given a graph with a suboptimal partitioning, the problem is to improve the partition quality while maintaining the balance constraint. This differs from the graph partitioning problem only in that it requires an initial partitioning of the graph. Indeed, a refinement scheme can be used as a partitioning scheme simply by using a random partitioning as its input.

Given a bisection of a graph that separates the vertices into sets A and B, a powerful means of refining the bisection is to find two equal-sized subsets, X from A and Y from B, such that swapping X to B and Y to A yields the greatest possible reduction in the edge-cut. This type of swapping can be repeated until no further improvement is possible [560]. However, the problem of finding optimal sets X and Y is intractable itself (just like the graph partitioning problem). For this reason, Kernighan and Lin [560] developed a greedy method of finding and swapping near-optimal sets X and Y (referred to as Kernighan–Lin or KL refinement).

The KL algorithm consists of a small number of passes through the vertices. During each pass, the algorithm repeatedly finds a pair of vertices, one from each of the subdomains, and swaps their subdomains. The pairs are selected so as to give the maximum improvement in the quality of the bisection (even if this improvement is negative). Once a pair of vertices has been moved, neither is considered for movement in the rest of the pass. When all of the vertices have been moved, the pass ends. At this point, the state of the bisection at which the minimum edge-cut was achieved is restored. (That is, all vertices that were moved after this point are moved back to their original subdomains.) Another pass of the algorithm can then

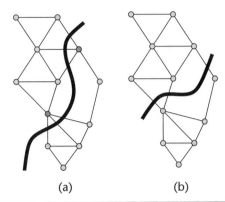

(a)   (b)

Figure 18.11   A bisection of a graph refined by the KL algorithm. The two shaded vertices will be swapped by the KL algorithm in order to improve the quality of the bisection (a). The resulting bisection is shown in (b).

be performed by using the resulting bisection as the input. The KL algorithm usually takes a small number of such passes to converge. Each pass of the KL algorithm takes $\mathcal{O}(|V|^2)$. Figure 18.11 illustrates a single swap made by the KL algorithm. In Figure 18.11(a), the two dark gray vertices are selected to switch subdomains. Figure 18.11(b) shows the bisection after this swap is made.

Fiduccia and Mattheyses present a modification of the KL algorithm [334] (called Fiduccia–Mattheyses or FM refinement) that improves its run time without significantly decreasing its effectiveness (at least with respect to graphs arising in scientific computing applications). This scheme differs from the KL algorithm in that it moves *only a single vertex* at a time between subdomains instead of swapping *pairs* of vertices. The FM algorithm makes use of two priority queues (one for each subdomain) to determine the order in which vertices are examined and moved. As in KL, the FM algorithm consists of a number of passes through the vertices. Prior to each pass, the *gain* of every vertex is computed (i.e., the amount by which the edge-cut will decrease if the vertex changes subdomains). Then it is placed into the priority queue that corresponds to its current subdomain and ordered according to its gain. During a pass, the vertices at the top of each of the two priority queues are examined. If the top vertex in only one of the priority queues is able to switch subdomains while still maintaining the balance constraint, then that vertex is moved to the other subdomain. If the top vertices of both of the priority queues can be moved while maintaining the balance, then the vertex that has the highest gain among these is moved. Ties are broken by selecting the vertex that will most improve the balance. When a vertex is moved, it is removed from the priority queue and the gains of its adjacent vertices are updated. (Therefore, these vertices may change their positions in the priority queue.) The pass ends when neither priority queue has a vertex that can be moved. At this point, the highest quality bisection that was found during the pass is restored. With the use of appropriate data structures, the complexity of each pass of the FM algorithm is $\mathcal{O}(|E|)$.

KL/FM-type algorithms are able to escape from some types of local minima because they explore moves that temporarily increase the edge-cut. Figure 18.12 illustrates this process. Figure 18.12(a) shows a bisection of a graph with an edge-cut of 6. Here, the weights of the vertices and edges are 1. There are 20 vertices in the graph. Therefore, a perfectly balanced bisection will have subdomain weights of 10. However, in this case we allow the subdomains to be up to 10% imbalanced. Therefore, subdomains of weight 11 are acceptable.[2] Figure 18.12(b) shows the gain of each vertex. Since all of the gains are negative, moving any vertex will result in the edge-cut increasing. Therefore, the bisection is in a local minimum. However, the algorithm will still select one of the vertices with the highest gain and move it. The white vertex is selected. Figure 18.12(c) shows the new bisection, as well as the updated vertex gains. There are now two positive-gain vertices. However, neither of these can be moved at this time. The black vertex has just moved, and so it is ineligible to move again until the end of the pass. The other vertex with +1 gain is unable to move, as this will violate the balance constraint. Instead, one of the highest negative-gain vertices (shown in white) from the left subdomain is selected. Figure 18.12(d) shows the result of this move. Now there are two positive-gain vertices that are able to move and two that are ineligible to move. The white vertex is selected. Figure 18.13 shows the results of continued refinement. By Figure 18.13(d), the bisection has reached another minimum with an edge-cut of 2. The refinement algorithm has succeeded in climbing out of the original local minimum and reducing the edge-cut from 6 to 2.

While KL/FM schemes are able to escape from certain types of local minima, this ability is still limited. Therefore, the quality of the final bisection obtained by KL/FM schemes is highly dependent on the quality of the input bisection. Several techniques have been developed that try to improve these algorithms by allowing the movement of larger sets of vertices together (i.e., more than just a single vertex or vertex pair) [51, 265, 424]. These schemes improve the effectiveness of KL/FM refinement at the cost of increased algorithm complexity. KL/FM-type refinement algorithms tend to be more effective when the average degree of the graph is large [155]. Furthermore, they perform much better when the balance constraints are relaxed. When perfect balance is desired, these schemes are quite constrained as to the refinement moves that can be made at any one time. As the imbalance tolerance increases, they are allowed greater freedom in making vertex moves and can provide higher-quality bisections.

---

[2] It is common for KL/FM-type algorithms to tolerate a slight amount of imbalance in the partitioning in an attempt to minimize the edge-cut.

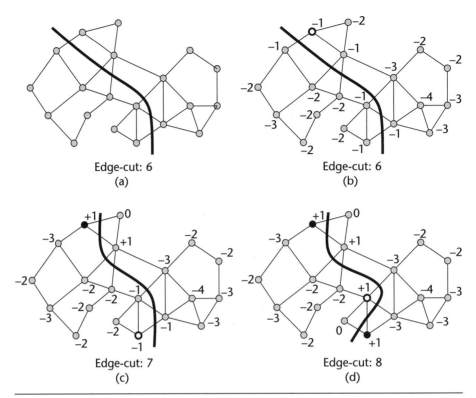

Figure 18.12 Bisection of a graph refined by a KL/FM algorithm. The white vertices indicate those selected to be moved. (a) The partitioning is in a local minimum. (b) The algorithm explores moves that increase the edge-cut. In (c) and (d) the edge-cut is increased, but now there are edge-cut reducing moves to be made.

18.2.3   Spectral Methods

Another method of solving the bisection problem is to formulate it as the optimization of a discrete quadratic function. However, even with this new formulation, the problem is still intractable. For this reason, a class of graph partitioning methods, called *spectral* methods, relaxes this *discrete* optimization problem by transforming it into a *continuous* one. The minimization of the relaxed problem is then solved by computing the second eigenvector of the discrete Laplacian of the graph.

More precisely, spectral methods work as follows. Given a graph G, its discrete Laplacian matrix L_G is defined as

$$(L_G)_{qr} = \begin{cases} 1, & \text{if } q \neq r, \ q \text{ and } r \text{ are neighbors,} \\ -deg(q), & \text{if } q = r, \\ 0, & \text{otherwise.} \end{cases}$$

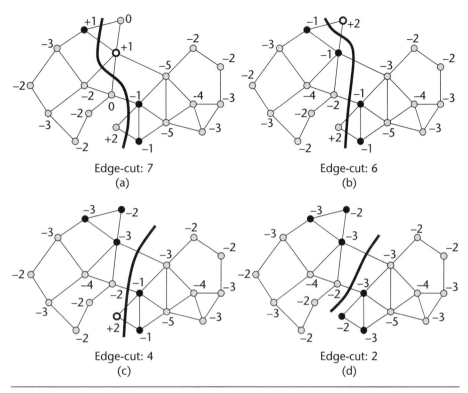

Figure 18.13 The KL/FM algorithm from Figure 18.12 is continued here. (a through d) Edge-cut reducing moves. By (d), the refinement algorithm has reached a local minimum.

L_G is equal to $A - D$, where A is the adjacency matrix of the graph and D is a diagonal matrix in which $D[i, i]$ is equal to the degree of vertex i. The discrete Laplacian L_G is a negative semidefinite matrix. Furthermore, its largest eigenvalue is 0 and the corresponding eigenvector consists of all ones. Assuming that the graph is connected, the magnitude of the second largest eigenvalue gives a measure of the connectivity of the graph. The eigenvector corresponding to this eigenvalue (referred to as the *Fiedler* vector), when associated with the vertices of the graph, gives a measure of the distance (based on connectivity) between the vertices. Once this measure of distance is computed for each vertex, these can be sorted by this value, and the ordered list can be split into two parts to produce a bisection [459, 773, 774]. A k-way partitioning can be computed by recursive bisection. Figure 18.14 illustrates the spectral bisection technique. It shows a graph along with its adjacency matrix A, degree matrix D, Laplacian L_G, and the resulting bisected graph.

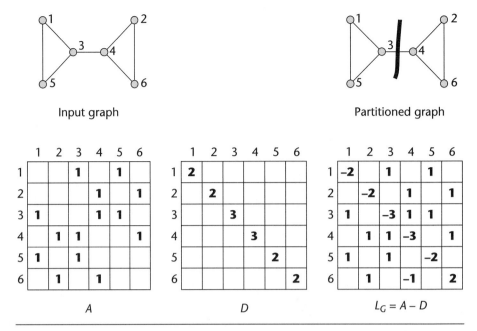

Figure 18.14 A graph, along with its adjacency matrix A, degree matrix D, and Laplacian L_G. The Fiedler vector of L_G associates a value with each vertex. The vertices are then sorted according to this value. A bisection is obtained by splitting the sorted list in half.

While the recursive spectral bisection algorithm typically produces higher-quality partitionings than geometric schemes, calculating the Fiedler vector is computationally intensive. This process dominates the run time of the scheme and results in overall times that are several orders of magnitude higher than geometric techniques. For this reason, great attention has been focused on speeding up the algorithm. First, the improvement of methods, such as the Lanczos algorithm [748], for approximating eigenvectors has made the computation of eigenvectors practical. Multilevel methods have also been employed to speed up the computation of eigenvectors [79].[3] Finally, spectral partitioning schemes that use multiple eigenvectors in order to divide the computation into four and eight parts at each step of the recursive decomposition have been investigated [459]. Since the computation of the additional eigenvectors is relatively inexpensive, this scheme has a smaller net cost, while producing partitionings of comparable or better quality, compared to bisecting the graph at each recursive step.

---

[3] Note that multilevel eigensolver methods are not the same as the multilevel graph partitioning techniques discussed in Section 18.2.4.

18.2.4   Multilevel Schemes

Recently, a new class of partitioning algorithms has been developed [155, 218, 415, 441, 460, 538, 542, 678, 971] that is based on the multilevel paradigm. This paradigm consists of three phases: graph coarsening, initial partitioning, and multilevel refinement. In the graph-coarsening phase, a series of graphs is constructed by collapsing together selected vertices of the input graph in order to form a related coarser graph. This newly constructed graph then acts as the input graph for another round of graph coarsening, and so on, until a sufficiently small graph is obtained. Computation of the initial bisection is performed on the coarsest (hence smallest) of these graphs and so is very fast. Finally, partition refinement is performed on each level graph, from the coarsest to the finest (i.e., original graph) using a KL/FM-type algorithm. Figure 18.15 illustrates the multilevel paradigm.

A common method for graph coarsening is collapsing together the pairs of vertices that form a matching. A matching of the graph is a set of edges, no two of which are incident on the same vertex. Vertex matchings can be computed by a number of methods. Widely used schemes include random matching, heavy-edge matching [538], maximum weighted matching [364], and approximated maximum weighted matching [678]. As an example, Figure 18.16(a) shows a random matching along

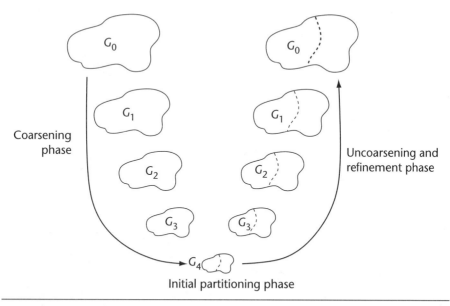

Figure 18.15   The three phases of the multilevel graph partitioning paradigm. During the coarsening phase, the size of the graph is successively decreased. During the initial partitioning phase, a bisection is computed. During the uncoarsening and refinement phase, the bisection is successively refined as it is projected to the larger graphs. G_0 is the input graph, which is the finest graph. G_{i+1} is the next level coarser graph of G_i. G_4 is the coarsest graph.

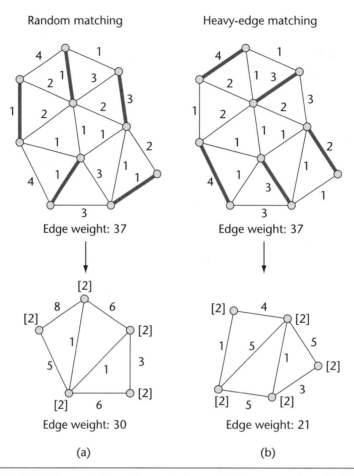

Figure 18.16   (a) Random matching of a graph along with the coarsened graph. (b) The same graph is matched (and coarsened) with the heavy-edge heuristic in. The heavy-edge matching minimizes the exposed edge weight.

with the coarsened graph that results from collapsing together vertices incident on every matched edge. Figure 18.16(b) shows a heavy-edge matching that tends to select edges with higher weights [538].

The multilevel paradigm works well for two reasons. First, a good coarsening scheme can hide a large number of edges on the coarsest graph. Figure 18.16 illustrates this point. The original graphs in Figures 18.16(a) and (b) have total edge weights of 37. After coarsening is performed on each, their total edge weights are reduced. Figures 18.16(a) and (b) show two possible coarsening heuristics, random and heavy-edge. In both cases, the total weight of the visible edges in the coarsened graph is less than that on the original graph. Note that by reducing the exposed edge weight, the task of computing a good-quality partitioning becomes easier. For exam-

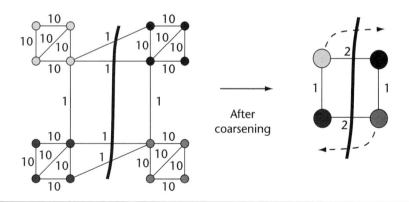

Figure 18.17 An example of a partitioned graph (with edge weights) before and after coarsening. The partitioning for the uncoarsened graph is in a local minimum, while the partitioning for the coarsened graph is not.

ple, a worst-case partitioning (i.e., one that cuts every edge) of the coarsest graph will be of higher quality than the worst-case partitioning of the original graph. Also, a random bisection of the coarsest graph will tend to be better than a random bisection of the original graph.

The second reason that the multilevel paradigm works well is that incremental refinement schemes such as KL/FM become much more powerful in the multilevel context. Here, the movement of a single vertex across the subdomain boundary in one of the coarse graphs is equivalent to the movement of a large number of highly connected vertices in the original graph, but is much faster. The ability of a refinement algorithm to move groups of highly connected vertices all at once allows the algorithm to escape from some types of local minima. Figure 18.17 illustrates this phenomenon. It shows a partitioned graph (included are the edge weights for the graph) both before and after coarsening. The partitioning for the uncoarsened graph (on the left-hand side) is in a local minimum. However, the partitioning for the coarsened graph (on the right side) is not. That is, edge-cut reducing moves can be made here. As discussed in Section 18.2.2, modifications of KL/FM schemes have been developed that attempt to move sets of vertices at once in order to improve the effectiveness of refinement [51, 265, 424]. However, computing good sets to move is computationally intensive. Multilevel schemes benefit from moving multiple vertices at the same time without having to compute these sets.

Preliminary theoretical work that explains the effectiveness of the multilevel paradigm has been done by Karypis and Kumar [537].

Multilevel Recursive Bisection

The multilevel paradigm was developed independently by Bui and Jones [155], in the context of computing fill-reducing matrix reorderings; by Hendrickson and Leland [460], in the context of finite-element mesh partitioning; and by Hauck and Borriello

[441] (called Optimized KLFM) and by Cong and Smith [218], for hypergraph partitioning.[4] Karypis and Kumar studied this paradigm extensively [538] by evaluating a variety of coarsening, initial partitioning, and refinement schemes in the context of graphs from many different application domains. Their evaluation showed that the overall paradigm is quite robust and consistently outperformed the spectral partitioning method in both speed and quality of partitioning. The evaluation also showed that the heavy-edge matching heuristic is very effective in hiding edges in the coarsest graph. Figure 18.16 gives an example of this. The random matching in Figure 18.16(a) results in a total exposed edge weight of 30, while the heavy-edge matching in Figure 18.16(b) results in a total exposed edge weight of only 21. When heavy-edge matching is used, the initial partitioning that is computed on the coarsest graph is often not too different from the final partitioning obtained after multilevel refinement. This allows the use of greatly simplified (and therefore fast) variants of KL/FM schemes during the uncoarsening phase. These simplified schemes significantly speed up refinement without compromising the quality of the partitioning. Furthermore, these simplified variants are much more amenable to parallelization than the original KL/FM heuristic that is inherently serial [380]. Karypis and Kumar [537] also showed that as long as a good matching scheme is used and KL/FM refinement is performed on each level graph, the method of computing the initial partitioning on the coarsest graph does not have much impact on the final solution quality.

Multilevel recursive bisection partitioning algorithms are available in several public domain libraries, such as Chaco [458], METIS [540], and Scotch [761], and are used extensively for graph partitioning in a variety of domains. Additional variations of the heavy-edge heuristic are presented in Karypis and Kumar [545] in the context of hypergraph partitioning. These variations are implemented in the hMETIS [539] library for partitioning hypergraphs.

Multilevel *k*-Way Partitioning

Karypis and Kumar [542] present a scheme for refining a *k*-way partitioning that is a generalization of simplified variants of the KL/FM bisection refinement algorithm. Using this *k*-way refinement scheme, Karypis and Kumar present a *k*-way multilevel partitioning algorithm in [542] whose run time is linear in the number of edges (i.e., $\mathcal{O}(|E|)$); whereas the run time of multilevel recursive bisection schemes is $\mathcal{O}(|E| \log k)$. Experiments on a large number of graphs arising in various domains (including finite element methods, linear programming, VLSI, and transportation) show that this scheme produces partitionings that are of comparable or better quality than those produced by multilevel recursive bisection, while requiring substantially less time. For example, partitionings of graphs containing millions of vertices can be computed

---

[4] A hypergraph is a generalization of a graph in which edges can connect not just two, but an arbitrary number of vertices.

in only a few minutes on a typical workstation. For many of these graphs, the process of graph partitioning takes less time than the time to read the graph from disk into memory. Compared with multilevel spectral bisection [460, 773, 774], multilevel *k*-way partitioning is usually two orders of magnitude faster and produces partitionings with generally smaller edge-cuts. The run times of multilevel *k*-way partitioning algorithms are usually comparable to the run times of small numbers (two to four) of runs of geometric recursive bisection algorithms [379, 449, 674, 718, 787] but tend to produce higher-quality partitionings for a variety of graphs, including those originating in scientific simulation applications.

Multilevel *k*-way graph partitioning algorithms are available in the Jostle [968] and METIS [540] software packages.

18.2.5 Combined Schemes

All of the graph partitioning techniques discussed in this section have individual advantages and disadvantages. Combining different types of schemes intelligently can maximize the advantages without suffering all of the disadvantages. In this section, we briefly describe a few commonly used combinations.

KL/FM-type algorithms are often used to improve the quality of partitionings that are computed by other methods. For example, an initial partitioning can be computed by a fast geometric method, and then the relatively low-quality partitioning can be refined by a KL/FM algorithm. Multilevel schemes use this technique, as well, by performing KL/FM refinement on each coarsened version of the graph after an initial partitioning is computed (by either LND [538], spectral [460], or other methods [415]). As another example, spectral methods can be used to compute coordinate information for vertices [427]. These coordinates can then be used by a geometric scheme to partition the graph [865].

18.2.6 Qualitative Comparison of Graph Partitioning Schemes

The large number of graph partitioning schemes reviewed in this section differ widely in the edge-cut quality produced, run time, degree of parallelism, and applicability to certain kinds of graphs. Often, it is not clear as to which scheme is better under different scenarios. In this section, we categorize properties of graph partitioning algorithms commonly used in scientific simulation applications. This task is quite difficult, as it is not possible to precisely model the properties of the graph partitioning algorithms. Furthermore, for most of the schemes, sufficient data on the edge-cut quality and run time for a common pool of benchmark graphs are not available. The relative comparison of different schemes draws upon the experimental results in [379, 449, 459, 538]. We try to make reasonable assumptions whenever enough data are not available. For the sake of simplicity, we have chosen to represent each property in terms of a small discrete scale. In the absence of extensive data, it is not possible to do much better than this in any case.

	Number of trials	Needs coordinates	Quality	Local view	Global view	Run time	Degree of parallelism
Recursive spectral bisection	1	no	●●●●	○	●●●●	■■■■	▲▲
Multilevel spectral bisection	1	no	●●●●	○	●●●●	■■■	▲▲
Mulitlevel spectral bisection-KL	1	no	●●●●●●	●●	●●●●	■■■	▲▲
Multilevel partitioning	1	no	●●●●●●	●●	●●●●	■■	▲▲
Levelized nested dissection	1	no	●●	○	●●	■■	▲▲
Kernighan-Lin	1	no	●●	●●	○	■■	▲
	10	no	●●●◐	●●	●◐	■■■	▲▲
	50	no	●●●●	●●	●●	■■■■◻	▲▲
Coordinate nested dissection	1	yes	●	○	●	■	▲▲▲
Recursive inertial bisection	1	yes	●●	○	●●	■	▲▲▲
Recursive inertial bisection-KL	1	yes	●●●●	●●	●●	■■	▲
Geometric sphere-cutting	1	yes	●●	○	●●	■	▲▲▲
	10	yes	●●●◐	○	●●●●	■■	▲▲▲
	50	yes	●●●●	○	●●●●	■■◻	▲▲▲
Geometric sphere-cutting-KL	1	yes	●●●●	●●	●●	■■	▲
	10	yes	●●●●●◐	●●	●●●◐	■■■	▲▲
	50	yes	●●●●●●	●●	●●●●	■■■■◻	▲▲

Figure 18.18 Graph partitioning schemes rated with respect to quality, run time, degree of parallelism, and related characteristics.

Figure 18.18 compares three variations of spectral partitioners [79, 460, 774, 773], a multilevel algorithm [542], an LND algorithm [374], a KL algorithm (with random initial partitionings) [560], a CND algorithm [449], two variations of the RIB algorithm [458, 718], and two variations of the geometric sphere-cutting algorithm [379, 674].

For each graph partitioning algorithm, Figure 18.18 shows a number of characteristics. The first column shows the number of trials that are performed for each partitioning algorithm. For example, for the KL algorithm, different trials can be performed each starting with a different random partitioning of the graph. Each trial is a different run of the partitioning algorithm, and the best of these is selected. As we can see from this table, some algorithms require only a single trial, either because multiple trials will give the same partitioning or a single trial gives very good results (as in the case of multilevel graph partitioning). However, for some schemes (e.g., KL and geometric partitioning), different trials yield significantly different edge-cuts. Hence, these schemes usually require multiple trials in order to produce good-quality partitionings. For multiple trials, we only show the case of 10 and 50 trials, as often the quality saturates beyond 50 trials or the run time becomes too large.

The second column shows whether the partitioning algorithm requires coordinates for the vertices of the graph. Some algorithms such as CND and RIB are applicable only if coordinate information is available. Others (e.g., combinatorial schemes) only require the sets of vertices and edges.

The third column of Figure 18.18 shows the relative quality of the partitionings produced by the various schemes. Each additional circle corresponds to roughly 10% improvement in the edge-cut. The edge-cut quality for CND serves as the base, and it is shown with one circle. Schemes with two circles for quality should find partitionings that are roughly 10% better than CND. This column shows that the quality of the partitionings produced by the multilevel graph partitioning algorithm and the multilevel spectral bisection with KL is very good. The quality of geometric partitioning with KL refinement is equally good when 50 or more trials are performed. The quality of the other schemes is worse than the above three by various degrees. Note that for both KL partitioning and geometric partitioning, the quality improves as the number of trials increases.

The reason for the differences in the quality of the various schemes can be understood if we consider the degree of quality as a sum of two quantities that we refer to as *local view* and *global view*. A graph partitioning algorithm has a local view of the graph if it is able to do localized refinement. According to this definition, all the graph partitioning algorithms that perform KL/FM-type refinement possess this local view, whereas the others do not. Global view refers to the extent that the graph partitioning algorithm takes into account the structure of the graph. For instance, spectral bisection algorithms take into account only global information of the graph by minimizing the edge-cut in the continuous approximation of the discrete problem. On the other hand, a single trial of the KL algorithm does not utilize information about the overall structure of the graph, since it starts from a random bisection. For schemes that require multiple random trials, the degree of the global view increases as the number of trials increases. The global view of multilevel graph partitioning is among the highest. This is because multilevel graph partitioning captures global graph structure in two ways. First, it captures global structure through the process of coarsening; second, it captures global structure during initial graph partitioning by performing multiple trials.

The sixth column of Figure 18.18 shows the relative time required by different graph partitioning schemes. CND, RIB, and geometric sphere-cutting (with a single trial) require relatively small amounts of time. We show the run time of these schemes by one square. Each additional square corresponds to roughly a factor of 10 increase in the run time. As we can see, spectral graph partitioning schemes require several orders of magnitude more time than the faster schemes. However, the quality of the partitionings produced by the faster schemes is relatively poor. The quality of these schemes can be improved by increasing the number of trials and/or by using the KL/FM refinement, both of which increase the run time of the partitioner. On the other hand, multilevel graph partitioning requires a moderate amount of time and produces partitionings of very high quality.

The degree of parallelizability of different schemes differs significantly and is depicted by a number of triangles in the seventh column of Figure 18.18. One triangle means that the scheme is largely sequential, two triangles means that the scheme can exploit a moderate amount of parallelism, and three triangles means that the scheme can be parallelized quite effectively. Schemes that require multiple trials are inherently parallel, as different trials can be done on different (groups of) processors. In contrast, a single trial of KL is very difficult to parallelize and appears inherently serial [380]. Multilevel schemes that utilize relaxed variations of KL/FM refinement and the spectral bisection scheme are moderately parallel in nature.

18.3   Load Balancing of Adaptive Computations

For large-scale scientific simulations, the computational requirements of techniques relying on globally refined meshes become very high, especially as the complexity and size of the problems increase. By locally refining and de-refining the mesh either to capture flow-field phenomena of interest [116] or to account for variations in errors [755], adaptive methods make standard computational methods more cost effective. One such example is numerical simulations for improving the design of helicopter blades [116] (see Figure 18.19). In order to capture flow-field phenomena of interest accurately, the finite element mesh must be extremely fine both around the helicopter blade and in the vicinity of the sound vortex created by the blade. It should be coarser in other regions of the mesh for maximum efficiency. As the simulation progresses, neither the blade nor the sound vortex remains stationary. Therefore, the new regions of the mesh that these enter need to be refined, while those regions that are no longer of key interest should be de-refined. These dynamic adjustments to the mesh result in some processors having significantly more (or less) work than others and thus cause load imbalance. Similar issues exist for problems in which the amount of computation associated with each mesh element changes over time [274]. For example, in particles-in-cells methods that advect particles through a mesh, large temporal and spatial variations in particle density can introduce substantial load imbalance.

In both of these types of applications, it is necessary to dynamically load balance the computations as the simulation progresses. This dynamic load balancing can be achieved by using a graph partitioning algorithm. In the case of adaptive finite-element methods, the graph either corresponds to the mesh obtained after adaptation or else corresponds to the original mesh with the vertex weights adjusted to reflect error estimates [755]. In the case of particles-in-cells, the graph corresponds to the original mesh with the vertex weights adjusted to reflect the particle density.

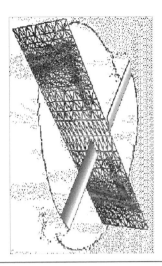

Figure 18.19   A helicopter blade rotating through a mesh. As the blade spins, the mesh is adapted by refining it in the regions that the blade has entered and de-refining it in the regions that are no longer of interest. (Figure courtesy of Rupak Biswas, NASA Ames Research Center.)

We refer to this problem as *adaptive graph partitioning* to differentiate it from the static graph-partitioning problem that arises when the computations remain fixed.

Adaptive graph partitioning shares most of the requirements and characteristics of static graph partitioning but also adds an additional objective. That is, the amount of data that needs to be redistributed among the processors in order to balance the load should be minimized. In order to accurately measure this cost, we need to consider not only the weight of a vertex, but also its *size* [723]. Vertex weight is the computational cost of the work represented by the vertex, while size reflects its redistribution cost. Thus, the repartitioner should attempt to balance the partitioning with respect to vertex weight while minimizing vertex migration with respect to vertex size. Depending on the representation and storage policy of the data, size and weight may not necessarily be equal [723].

Oliker and Biswas [723] studied various metrics for measuring data redistribution costs. They presented the metrics TOTALV and MAXV. TOTALV is defined as the sum of the sizes of vertices that change subdomains as the result of repartitioning. TOTALV reflects the overall volume of communications needed to balance the partitioning. MAXV is defined as the maximum of the sums of the sizes of those vertices that migrate into or out of any one subdomain as a result of repartitioning. MAXV reflects the maximum time needed by any one processor to send or receive data. Results show that measuring the MAXV can sometimes be a better indicator of data redistribution overhead than measuring the TOTALV. However, many repartitioning schemes [723, 832, 833, 974] attempt to minimize TOTALV instead of MAXV for the following reasons:

1. TOTALV can be minimized during refinement by the use of relatively simple heuristics; minimizing MAXV tends to be more difficult.

2. The MAXV is lower bounded by the amount of vertex weight that needs to be moved out of the most overweight subdomain (or into the most underweight subdomain). For many problems, this lower bound can dominate the MAXV and so no improvement is possible.

3. Minimizing TOTALV often tends to do a fairly good job of minimizing MAXV.

Repartitioning Approaches

A repartitioning of a graph can be computed by simply partitioning the new graph from scratch. Since no consideration is given to the existing partitioning, it is unlikely that vertices will be assigned to their original subdomains with this method. Therefore, this approach will tend to require much more data redistribution than is necessary in order to balance the load.

An alternate strategy is to attempt to perturb the input partitioning just enough to balance it. This can be accomplished trivially by the following *cut-and-paste repartitioning* method: excess vertices in overweight subdomains are simply swapped into one or more underweight subdomains (regardless of whether these subdomains are adjacent) in order to balance the partitioning. While this method will optimally minimize data redistribution, it can result in significantly higher edge-cuts compared with more sophisticated approaches and will typically result in disconnected subdomains. For these reasons, it is usually not considered a viable repartitioning scheme for most applications. A better approach is to use a diffusion-based repartitioning scheme. These schemes attempt to minimize the data redistribution costs while significantly decreasing the possibility that subdomains become disconnected.

Figure 18.20 illustrates these methods for a graph whose vertices and edges have weights of 1. The shading of a vertex indicates the original subdomain to which it belongs. In Figure 18.20(a), the original partitioning is imbalanced because subdomain 3 has a weight of 6, while the average subdomain weight is only 4. The edge-cut of the original partitioning is 12. In Figure 18.20(b), the original partitioning is ignored and the graph is partitioned from scratch. This partitioning also has an edge-cut of 12. However, 13 out of 20 vertices are required to change subdomains. That is, TOTALV is 13; MAXV is 6. In Figure 18.20(c), cut-and-paste repartitioning was used. Here, only two vertices are required to change subdomains and MAXV is also 2. The edge-cut of this partitioning is 16, and subdomain 1 is now disconnected. Figure 18.20(d) gives a diffusive repartitioning that presents a compromise between those in Figure 18.20(b) and (c). Here, TOTALV is 4, MAXV is 2, and the edge-cut is 14.

18.3.1   Scratch-Remap Repartitioners

The example in Figure 18.20(b) illustrates how partitioning from scratch resulted in the lowest edge-cut of the three repartitioning methods. This is expected since it is possible to use a state-of-the-art graph partitioner to compute the new par-

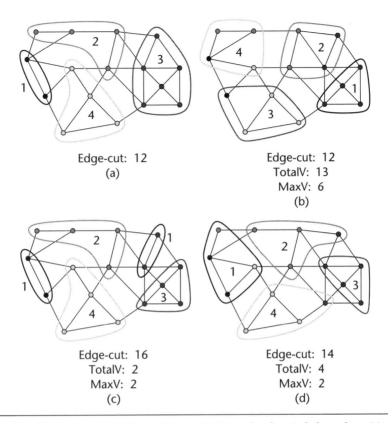

Edge-cut: 12
(a)

Edge-cut: 12
TotalV: 13
MaxV: 6
(b)

Edge-cut: 16
TotalV: 2
MaxV: 2
(c)

Edge-cut: 14
TotalV: 4
MaxV: 2
(d)

Figure 18.20 Various repartitioning schemes. (a) Example of an imbalanced partitioning. This partitioning is balanced by partitioning the graph (b) from scratch, (c) cut-and-pasted repartitioning, and (d) diffusive repartitioning.

titioning from scratch. However, this repartitioning resulted in the highest data redistribution costs. To understand this, it is necessary to examine the partitionings in Figures 18.20(a) and (b). Note that in Figure 18.20(a), subdomain 1 is on the left, subdomain 3 is on the right, and subdomain 4 is on the bottom. For the partitioning in Figure 18.20(b), subdomain 1 is on the right, subdomain 3 is on the bottom, and subdomain 4 is on the top left. A large amount of the data redistribution required for the partitioning in Figure 18.20(b) is brought about because the subdomains are labeled suboptimally. Simply changing the subdomain labels of the new partitioning in accordance with the old partitioning (without otherwise modifying the partitioning) can significantly reduce the data redistribution cost [884].

Oliker and Biswas [723] present a number of repartitioning schemes that compute new partitionings from scratch and then intelligently map the subdomain labels to those of the original partitionings in order to minimize the data redistribution costs. We refer to this method as *scratch-remap* repartitioning. Partition remapping is performed as follows:

1. Construct a similarity matrix, S, of size $k \times k$. A similarity matrix is one in which the rows represent the subdomains of the old partitioning, the columns represent the subdomains of the new partitioning, and each element, S_{qr}, represents the sum of the sizes of the vertices that are in subdomain q of the old partitioning and in subdomain r of the new partitioning.

2. Select k elements such that every row and column contains exactly one selected element and such that the sum of the selected elements is maximized. This corresponds to the remapping in which the amount of overlap between the original and the remapped partitionings is maximized, and hence, the total volume of data redistribution required in order to realize the remapped partitioning is minimized.

3. For each element S_{qr} selected, rename domain r to domain q on the remapped partitioning.

Figure 18.21 illustrates such a remapping process. Here, similarity matrix S has been constructed based on the example in Figure 18.20. The first row of S indicates that subdomain 1 on the old partitioning (Figure 18.20(a)) consists of 0 vertices from subdomains 1 and 2 on the new partitioning (Figure 18.20(b)) and 1 vertex from each of subdomains 3 and 4 on the new partitioning. Likewise, the second row indicates that subdomain 2 on the old partitioning consists of 2 vertices from each of subdomains 2 and 4 on the new partitioning and 0 vertices from the other two subdomains. The third and fourth rows are constructed similarly. In this example, we select underlined elements S_{14}, S_{22}, S_{31}, and S_{43}. This combination maximizes the sum of the sizes of the selected elements. Running through the selected elements, subdomain 1 on the newly computed partitioning is renamed 3, and subdomains 2, 3, and 4 are renamed 2, 4, and 1, respectively. Figure 18.21(c) shows the remapped partitioning. Here, TOTALV is 6 and MAXV is 3.

Although the remapping phase reduces the data redistribution costs (without affecting the edge-cut), scratch-remap schemes still tend to result in higher redistribution costs than schemes that attempt to balance the input partitioning by minimal perturbation (e.g., cut-and-paste and diffusion-based schemes). For example, if the newly adapted graph is only slightly different from the original graph, then partitioning from scratch could produce a new partitioning that is still substantially different from the original and requires many vertices to be moved even after the remapping phase. On such a graph, the imbalance could easily be corrected by moving only a small number of vertices. Figure 18.22 illustrates an example of this. The partitioning in Figure 18.22(a) is slightly imbalanced. The upper-right subdomain has five vertices, while the average subdomain weight is 4. In Figure 18.22(b), the partitioning is balanced by moving a single vertex from the upper-right subdomain to the lower-right subdomain. Therefore, both TOTALV and MAXV are 1. Figure 18.22(c) shows a new partitioning that has been computed from scratch and then optimally

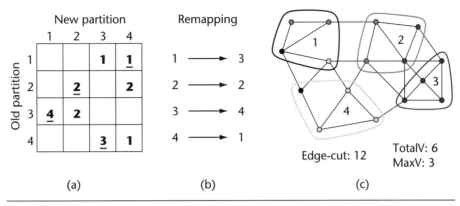

Figure 18.21 A similarity matrix, the corresponding remapping, and the remapped partitioning from Figure 18.20(b).

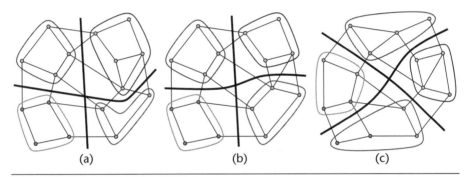

Figure 18.22 An imbalanced partitioning and two repartitioning techniques. (a) Partitioning is imbalanced. It is balanced by (b) an incremental method and by (c) a scratch-remap method.

remapped to the partitioning in Figure 18.22(a). Despite this optimal remapping, the repartitioning has a TOTALV of 7 and a MAXV of 2. All three of the partitionings have similar edge-cuts.

The reason that the scratch-remap scheme does so poorly here with respect to data redistribution is because the information that is provided by the original partitioning is not utilized until the final remapping process. At this point, it is too late to avoid high data redistribution costs even if we compute an optimal remapping. The problem in our example is that the partitioning in Figure 18.22(a) is shaped like a plus symbol (+), while the partitioning in Figure 18.22(c) forms an "X". Both of these are of equal quality, so a static partitioning algorithm could easily compute either of these. However, we would like the partitioning algorithm used in a scratch-remap repartitioner to drive the computation of the partitioning toward that of the original partitioning, whenever possible, without affecting the quality. A scratch-remap algorithm can potentially do this if it is able to extract and use the information implicit in the original partitioning during the computation of the new partitioning. An algorithm called locally matched multilevel scratch-remap (LMSR) that tries to accomplish this is presented in Schloegel et al. [833]. LMSR decreases the amount of data redistribution required to balance the graph compared to naive scratch-remap schemes, particularly for slightly imbalanced graphs [833].

18.3.2   Diffusion-Based Repartitioners

Diffusive load-balancing schemes attempt to minimize the difference between the original partitioning and the final repartitioning by making incremental changes in the partitioning to restore balance. Subdomains that are overweight in the original partitioning export vertices to adjacent subdomains. These may further export vertices to their neighbors in an effort to reach global balance. By limiting the movement of vertices to neighboring subdomains, these schemes attempt to minimize the edge-cut and maintain connected subdomains. As an example, the repartitioning in Figure 18.20(d) is obtained by a diffusive process. In this case, subdomain 3 migrates a vertex to each of subdomains 2 and 4. This causes the recipient subdomains to become overweight. Each next migrates a vertex to subdomain 1.

Any diffusion-based repartitioning scheme needs to address two questions:

1. How much work should be transferred between processors?
2. Which tasks should be transferred?

The answer to the first question tells us how to balance the partitioning, while the answer to the second tells us how to minimize the edge-cut as we do this. A lot of work has focused on answering the first question in the context of balancing unrelated tasks that are unevenly distributed among processors [124, 242, 264, 484, 492, 493, 982, 1006]. These take the machine architecture, but not the interdependencies of the tasks, into consideration when computing the amount of work to transfer between processors. More recently, in the context of adaptive computational simulations, work has focused not only on how much, but also which tasks to transfer [274, 730, 731, 755, 768, 832, 833, 883, 953, 961, 973, 974]. In the rest of this section, we focus on these schemes.

Schemes for determining how much work to transfer between processors can be grouped into two categories. Diffusion schemes that base the exchange of work among the processors only on their respective workloads (and not on the loads of distant processors) [832] are called *local* diffusion algorithms. Other schemes [274, 730, 731, 755, 768, 832, 833, 883, 953, 961, 973, 974], use global views of the processor loads to balance the partitioning. We call these *global* diffusion schemes. Most global diffusion schemes either perform diffusion in a recursive bisection manner [274, 883, 961], utilize space-filling curves [731, 755, 768], or compute *flow solutions* [730, 832, 833, 973, 974] that prescribe the amount of work to be moved between pairs of processors.

Recursive bisection diffusion schemes [274, 883, 961] split the subdomains into two groups and then attempt to balance these groups. Next, both of the (balanced) groups are split in two and the algorithm recurses on these subgroups.

Adaptive space-filling curve partitioners [731, 755, 768] can compute repartitionings by maintaining the original ordering of the mesh elements. Here, the weights associated with the ordered mesh elements are changed to reflect the structural changes in the computation. All that is required to compute a repartitioning is to recompute the k-way splitting of the ordered list with respect to the new weights.

Flow solutions are usually computed in order to optimize some objective. Ou and Ranka [730] present a global diffusion scheme that optimally minimizes the one-norm of the flow using linear programming. Such a scheme will minimize TOTALV provided that the weights and sizes of the vertices are equal. Hu and Blake [493] present a method that optimally minimizes the two-norm of the flow. They prove that such a flow solution can be obtained by solving the linear equation $(-L)\lambda = b$, where b is the vector containing the load of each subdomain minus the average subdomain load, L is the Laplacian matrix (as defined in Section 18.2.3) of the graph that models the subdomain connectivity (i.e., the *subdomain connectivity graph*), and λ, the flow solution, is a vector with k elements. An amount of vertex weight equal to $\lambda_q - \lambda_r$ needs to be moved from subdomain q to subdomain r for every r that is adjacent to q in order to balance the partitioning.

Figure 18.23 illustrates the difference between one- and two-norm minimization of the flow solution. This figure shows the subdomain connectivity graph for a nine-way partitioning along with the two different flow solutions. Here, the two dark subdomains are overweight by 10, while the two white subdomains are underweight by 10. The weight of the rest of the subdomains equals the average subdomain weight. The flow solution in Figure 18.23(a) minimizes the one-norm of the data movement. The flow solution in Figure 18.23(b) minimizes the two-norm of the data movement. The one-norm minimization solution can minimize TOTALV, but will not in general minimize MAXV, as most of the flow is sent through a few links. The two-norm minimization solution more evenly distributes the flow through the links (and thus tends to result in lower values for MAXV), but requires greater total flow (and therefore, worse TOTALV), compared to the one-norm solution.

The flow solution indicates how much vertex weight needs to be transferred between each pair of adjacent subdomains. The second problem is to determine exactly which vertices to move so as to minimize the edge-cut of the resulting partitioning. One possibility is to repeatedly transfer layers of vertices along the subdomain boundary until the desired amount of vertex weight has been transferred [730, 961]. A more precise scheme is to move one vertex at a time across the subdomain boundary, each time selecting the vertex that will result in the smallest edge-cut [973]. This scheme, like the KL/FM algorithm, utilizes only a local view of the graph and can make (globally) poor selections. This problem can be corrected if the transfer of vertices is performed in a multilevel context [832, 974]. Such schemes, called *multilevel diffusion* algorithms, perform graph coarsening and then begin diffusion on the coarsest graph. During the uncoarsening phase, vertices are

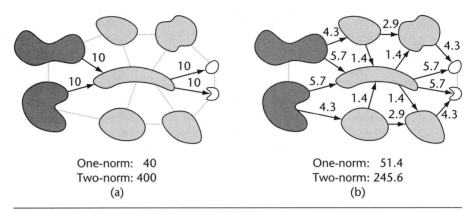

One-norm: 40   One-norm: 51.4
Two-norm: 400   Two-norm: 245.6
(a)   (b)

Figure 18.23 Two different flow solutions for the subdomain graph of an imbalanced partitioning. (a) One-norm of the data migration is minimized. (b) Two-norm of the data migration is minimized.

moved to achieve (or maintain) load balance, while also trying to improve the edge-cut. By beginning diffusion on the coarsest graph, these algorithms are able to move large chunks of highly connected vertices in a single step. Thus, the bulk of the work required to balance the partitioning is done quickly. Furthermore, by moving highly connected vertices together, high-quality edge-cuts can often be maintained. Experimental results show that multilevel diffusion can compute partitionings of higher quality than schemes that perform diffusion only on the original graph [832, 974] and is often faster.

For partitionings that are highly imbalanced in localized areas, diffusion-based schemes require vertex flow to propagate over long distances. For this class of problems, it is beneficial to determine not only *how much* and *which* vertices to move, but also *when* vertices should move [264]. A diffusion algorithm, called *wavefront diffusion,* that determines the best time to migrate vertices is presented in [833]. In wavefront diffusion, the flow of vertices moves in a wavefront starting from the most overweight subdomains. This method guarantees that all subdomains will contain the largest possible selection of vertices when it is their turn to export vertices. Thus, subdomains are able to select those vertices for migration that will best minimize edge-cut and data redistribution costs. Wavefront diffusion obtains significantly lower data redistribution costs while maintaining similar or better edge-cut results compared to diffusion schemes that do not determine the best time to migrate vertices, especially for partitionings that are highly imbalanced in localized areas [833].

Tradeoff between Edge-Cut and Data Redistribution Costs

Often, the objective of minimizing the data redistribution cost is at odds with the objective of minimizing the edge-cut. For applications in which the mesh is frequently adapted or the amount of state associated with each element is relatively high, minimizing the data redistribution cost is preferred over minimizing the edge-cut. For applications in which repartitioning occurs infrequently, the key objective of a repartitioning scheme will be obtaining the minimal edge-cut.

While a number of coarsening and refinement heuristics have been developed [832, 969] that can control the tradeoffs between these two objectives to some extent, most adaptive partitioners naturally minimize one in preference to the other. For example, wavefront diffusion tends to minimize data redistribution costs better than the LMSR algorithm. However, the LMSR algorithm tends to minimize the edge-cut of the repartitioning better than wavefront diffusion. As such, the two provide the user with a limited control of the tradeoffs among these objectives. A new scheme, called the *unified repartitioning* algorithm [836], has been developed that gives the user a more fine-tuned control of the tradeoffs among the objectives. Experimental results on a variety of problems show that the unified repartitioning algorithm is able to reduce the sum of the interprocessor communication overhead incurred during the iterative mesh-based computation and the data redistribution costs required to balance the load as well as or better than other repartitioning schemes.

18.4 Parallel Graph Partitioning

The ability to perform partitioning in parallel is important for many reasons. The amount of memory on serial computers is often not enough to allow the partitioning of graphs corresponding to large problems that can now be solved on massively parallel computers and workstation clusters. A parallel graph partitioning algorithm can take advantage of the significantly higher amount of memory available in parallel computers to partition very large graphs. Also, as heterogeneous systems of parallel machines are integrated into a single system of systems (e.g., the NASA Information Power Grid [517]), the role of graph partitioning will change. Here, the exact number of processors and/or the architectural characteristics of the hardware assigned to a computation will not be known until immediately before the computation is permitted to execute. Parallel graph partitioning is crucial for efficiency in such an environment. In the context of adaptive graph partitioning, the graph is already distributed among processors, but needs to be repartitioned due to the dynamic nature of the underlying computation. In such cases, having to bring the graph to one processor for repartitioning can create a serious bottleneck that could adversely impact the scalability of the overall application.

Work in parallel graph partitioning [78, 380, 449, 543, 546, 788, 970] has been focused on geometric [449, 788], spectral [78], and multilevel partitioning schemes [543, 546, 970]. Geometric graph partitioning algorithms tend to be quite easy to parallelize. Typically, these require a parallel sorting algorithm. Spectral and multilevel partitioners are more difficult to parallelize. Their parallel asymptotic run times are the same as that of performing a parallel matrix–vector multiplication on a randomly partitioned matrix [546]. This is because the input graph is not well distributed across the processors. If the graph is first partitioned and then distributed across the processors accordingly, the parallel asymptotic run times of spectral and multilevel partitioners drop to that of performing a parallel matrix–vector multiplication on a well-partitioned matrix. Thus, performing these partitioning schemes efficiently in parallel requires a good partitioning of the input graph [546, 970]. In the case of static graph partitioning, we cannot expect the input graph to be partitioned already, since this is exactly what we are trying to do. However, for the adaptive graph partitioning problem, we can expect the input partitioning to be of high quality (i.e., have a low edge-cut, even though it will be imbalanced). For this reason, parallel adaptive graph partitioners [833, 974] tend to run significantly faster than static partitioners.

Since the run times of most parallel geometric partitioning schemes are not affected by the initial distribution of the graph, they can be used to compute a partitioning for multilevel (or spectral) partitioning algorithms. That is, a rough partitioning of the input graph can be computed by a fast geometric approach. This partitioning can be used to redistribute the graph prior to performing parallel multilevel (or spectral) partitioning [547]. Use of this "boot-strapping" approach significantly increases the parallel efficiency of the more accurate partitioning scheme by providing it with data locality.

Parallel multilevel algorithms for graph partitioning are available in the ParMETIS [547] and Jostle [968] libraries.

18.5   Multiconstraint, Multiobjective Graph Partitioning

In recent years, with advances in the state of the art of scientific simulation, sophisticated classes of computations such as multiphase, multiphysics, and multimesh simulations have become commonplace. For many of these, the traditional graph partitioning formulation is not adequate to ensure their efficient execution on high-performance parallel computers. Instead, new graph partitioning formulations and algorithms are required to meet the needs of these. In this section, we describe some important classes of scientific simulation that require more generalized formulations of the graph partitioning problem in order to ensure their efficiency on high-performance machines; we discuss these requirements; and we describe new, generalized formulations of the graph partitioning problem as well as algorithms for solving these problems.

Multiphysics Simulations

In multiphysics simulations, a variety of materials and/or processes are simulated together. The result is a class of problems in which the computation as well as the memory requirements are not uniform across the mesh. Existing partitioning schemes can be used to divide the mesh among the processors such that either the amount of computation or the amount of memory required is balanced across the processors. However, they cannot be used to compute a partitioning that simultaneously balances both of these quantities. Our inability to do so can either lead

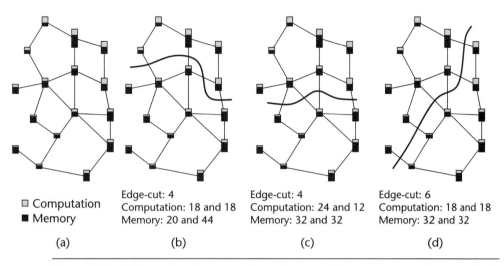

□ Computation
■ Memory

Edge-cut: 4	Edge-cut: 4	Edge-cut: 6
Computation: 18 and 18	Computation: 24 and 12	Computation: 18 and 18
Memory: 20 and 44	Memory: 32 and 32	Memory: 32 and 32

(a)   (b)   (c)   (d)

Figure 18.24 (a) Example of a computation with nonuniform memory requirements. Each vertex in the graph is split into two amounts. The size of the lightly shaded portion represents the amount of computation associated with the vertex, while the size of the dark portion represents the amount of memory associated with the vertex. (b) Bisection balances the computation. (c) Bisection balances the memory. (d) Bisection balances both memory and computation.

to significant computational imbalances, limiting efficiency, or significant memory imbalances, limiting the size of problems that can be solved using parallel computers. Figure 18.24 illustrates this problem. It shows three possible partitionings of a graph in which the amount of computation and memory associated with a vertex can be different throughout the graph. The partitioning in Figure 18.24(b) balances the computation among the subdomains, but creates a serious imbalance for memory requirements. The partitioning in Figure 18.24(c) balances the memory requirement, while leaving the computation imbalanced. The partitioning in Figure 18.24(d), which balances both of these, is the desired solution. In general, multiphysics simulations require the partitioning to satisfy not just one, but a multiple number of balance constraints. (In this case, the partitioning must balance two constraints: computation and memory.)

Multiphase Simulations

Multiphase simulations consist of m distinct computational phases, each separated by an explicit synchronization step. In general, the amount of computation performed for each element of the mesh is different for different phases. The existence of the synchronization steps between the phases requires that each phase be individually load balanced. That is, it is not sufficient to simply sum up the relative times required for each phase and to compute a decomposition based on this sum.

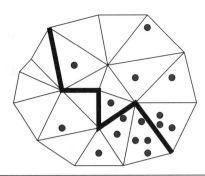

Figure 18.25 A mesh for a particle-in-cell computation. Here, both the mesh elements and the particles should be balanced across the subdomains.

Doing so may lead to some processors having too much work during one phase of the computation (these may still be working after other processors are idle) and not enough work during other phases (these may be idle while other processors are still working). Instead, it is critical that every processor have an equal amount of work from all of the phases of the computation. A traditional partitioning scheme can be used to balance the load across the processors for a single phase of the computation. However, the load may be seriously imbalanced for the other phases. Another method is to use *m* distinct partitionings, each of which balances the load of a single phase only. This method requires that costly data redistribution be performed after each phase in order to realize the partitioning corresponding to the next phase. A better method is to compute a single partitioning that simultaneously balances the work performed in each of the phases. In this case, no redistribution of the data is necessary, and all of the phases are well balanced.

Figure 18.25 gives an example. It shows the mesh for a simulation of particles moving through space. This computation is composed of two phases. The first phase is a mesh-based computation. The second phase is a particle-based computation. In order to load balance such an application, each processor must have a roughly equal amount of both the mesh computation and the particle computation. One such bisection is shown. It splits both the mesh elements and the particles in half.

Figure 18.26 shows another example. This is the mesh associated with the numerical simulation of the ports and the combustion chamber of an internal combustion engine. In this particular problem, the overall computation is performed in six phases. (Each corresponds to a different shade in the figure.) In order to solve such a multiphase computation efficiently on a parallel machine, every processor should contain an equal number of mesh elements of each different shade. Figure 18.27 shows two subdomains of an eight-way partitioning of the mesh in Figure 18.26. This partitioning balances all six phases while also minimizing the interprocessor communications. (Note that not all of the shades are visible in Figures 18.26 and 18.27.)

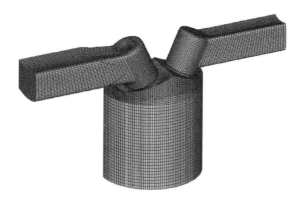

Figure 18.26 An internal combustion engine simulation is an example application whose computation is performed in multiple phases. Each shade represents elements active during a different phase. (Figure courtesy of Analysis and Design Application Company Limited.)

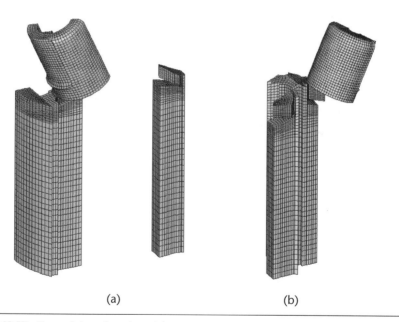

(a)　　　　　　　　　　　　　　　(b)

Figure 18.27 Two subdomains of an eight-way partitioning computed by the multiconstraint graph partitioner implemented in METIS 4.0 are shown. Note that the subdomains have an equal number of elements of each shade (although they are not all visible). (Figure courtesy of Analysis and Design Application Company Limited.)

Multimesh Computations

An important class of emerging numerical methods is multimesh computations. Multiple meshes arise in several settings that use grids to discretize partial differential equations. For example, some operations are innately more efficient on structured grids, such as radiation transport sweeps or FFTs. However, complex geometries are better fitted with unstructured meshes. In some simulations, both kinds of grids may be used throughout the computation. Similarly, various codes that solve for multiple physical quantities may use separate grids to solve the appropriate equations for each variable. For example, consider a simulation of the welding of a joint between two parts, a process in which the parts are pressed together and thermally annealed [770]. One grid could be used for the solution of the stress–strain relations that mediate the mechanical deformation of the parts. A second grid could be used to solve the heat equation for thermal conduction in the system. Since the regions of high strain may be distinct from those with high thermal gradients, each grid can be individually tailored to accurately represent the relevant physics.

Now consider the implementation of such a multiphysics example on a distributed-memory parallel machine. A typical time step consists of computing a solution on the first mesh, interpolating the result to the second mesh, computing a solution on the second mesh, interpolating it back to the first mesh, and so on. One way of performing this type of computation in parallel is to partition the meshes separately so that every processor has a portion of each mesh. This approach will balance the computations and minimize the communications during each of the solution phases. However, because the different meshes are partitioned independently, there is no assurance that an individual processor will own portions of the meshes that spatially overlap. Therefore, the amount of communication performed during the interpolation and transfer of the solution data can be quite high, even if an efficient approach is used to manage this communication [770]. Ideally, we would like to partition the different meshes such that each processor performs an equal amount of work for every mesh. At the same time, we would like to minimize the amount of interprocessor communications required during the computations of the solutions, as well as that required during the interpolation and transfer of the solutions.

Domain Decomposition-Based Preconditioners

The two keys to the efficient solution of systems of sparse linear equations via iterative methods are (1) the ability to perform the matrix–vector multiplication efficiently in parallel, and (2) minimizing the number of iterations required for the method to converge. The matrix–vector multiplication is typically implemented by first reordering the sparse matrix to minimize the number of nonzero elements that are off of the block diagonal. Then a striped partitioning of the matrix and the vector is used. Here, an interprocessor communication is required for every nonzero element off of the block diagonal. A high-quality partitioning of the graph corresponding to the sparse matrix provides a reordering such that the number of interprocessor communications is minimized. Use of various preconditioners can minimize the number of iterations required for the solution to converge. There are a number of preconditioning schemes that construct a preconditioner of each block of the block diagonal separately. These are combined to form a preconditioner for the entire matrix. Examples are block-diagonal preconditioners and local ILU preconditioners. These preconditioners ignore the intrasubdomain interactions that are represented by the nonzero elements off of the block diagonal.

Since the matrix reordering is commonly obtained by a graph partitioner, this ensures that the *number* of nonzeros that are ignored in the preconditioner is relatively small. Therefore, the matrix–vector multiplications will be computed efficiently. However, this ordering does not attempt to minimize the *magnitude* of these ignored nonzeros. Therefore, it could be the case that while the number of nonzero elements is small, the sum of the ignored nonzeros is quite large. The consequence of this is that the preconditioner may not be as effective as it could be if the sum of the ignored elements was minimized [563]. That is, the number of iterations for the method to converge may not be minimized. The magnitude of the ignored elements could be minimized directly by a partitioning that is computed using the magnitude of the elements as the edge weights of the graph. However, such an approach will not minimize the communication overhead incurred by the matrix–vector multiplication. This is because an ordering computed in this way would not minimize the number of ignored elements. Ideally, we would like to obtain an ordering that minimizes both the number of intra-domain interactions (reducing the communication overhead) and the numerical magnitude of these interactions (potentially leading to a better preconditioner).

Figures 18.28 through 18.30 illustrate this problem. Figure 18.28 shows a partitioning of a graph that minimizes the edge-cut and the corresponding matrix ordered with respect to this partitioning. Here, there are only a small number of ignored nonzero entries off of the diagonal. However, their magnitudes are high compared to the other elements. Figure 18.29 shows a partitioning of a graph that minimizes the magnitude of the ignored entries and the matrix ordered accordingly. Here, there are quite a bit more ignored entries compared to the ordering shown in Figure 18.28. However, the magnitudes of these entries are small. Figure 18.30 shows the partitioning that attempts to minimize both the number and the magnitude of the ignored entries as well as the corresponding matrix.

18.5.1 A Generalized Formulation for Graph Partitioning

The common characteristic of these problems is that they require the computation of partitionings that satisfy an arbitrary number of balance constraints and/or an arbitrary number of optimization objectives. Traditional graph partitioning techniques have been designed to balance only a single constraint (i.e., the vertex weight) and to minimize only a single objective (i.e., the edge-cut). An extension of the graph partitioning formulation that can model these problems is to assign a weight vector of size m to each vertex and a weight vector of size l to each edge. The problem becomes that of finding a partitioning that minimizes the edge-cuts with respect to all

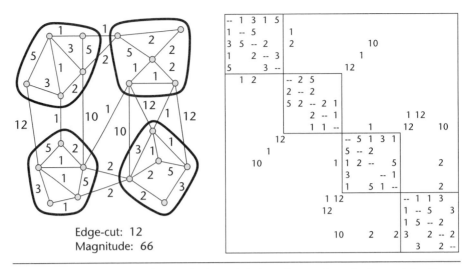

Figure 18.28 Partitioning of a graph that minimizes the number of edges cut by the partitioning along with the associated sparse matrix ordered accordingly.

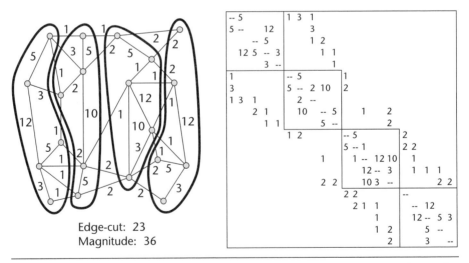

Figure 18.29 Partitioning of a graph that minimizes the sum magnitude of the edges cut by the partitioning along with the associated sparse matrix ordered accordingly.

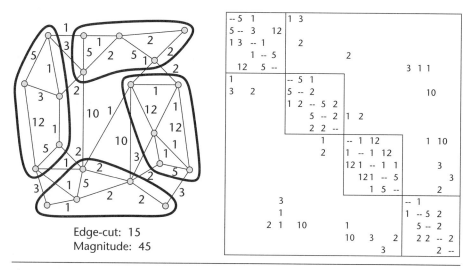

Edge-cut: 15
Magnitude: 45

Figure 18.30 Partitioning that minimizes both the number and the magnitude of the edges cut by the partitioning along with the associated sparse matrix ordered accordingly.

l weights, subject to the constraints that each of the m weights is balanced across the subdomains. This *multiconstraint, multiobjective* graph partitioning problem is able to model all of the problems described above effectively.

For example, the problem of balancing computation and memory can be modeled by associating a vector of size 2 with each vertex (i.e., a two-constraint problem), where the elements of the vector represent the computation and memory requirements associated with the vertex. Similarly, the problem of computing an ordering for a system of sparse linear systems preconditioned by a block-diagonal method can be modeled by assigning a vector of size 2 to each edge (i.e., a two-objective problem), where the elements of the vector represent the number of nonzero entries (all ones in this case) and the magnitude of these entries.

Computing decompositions for multimesh computations is a multiconstraint, multiobjective problem. Figure 18.31 illustrates an example for a simple case with two meshes. Figure 18.31(a) shows a pair of overlapping graphs (one with light, circular vertices and dotted edges and the other with dark, square vertices and solid edges). Additionally, dashed lines are included that show the interactions required in order to facilitate the interpolation and transfer process. Figure 18.31(b) shows the graph that models this problem. Here, the two graphs (and additional edges) from Figure 18.31(a) are combined. Every square vertex is given a weight of (1, 0) and every circular vertex is given a weight of (0, 1). Solid edges are weighted (1, 0, 0). Dotted edges are weighted (0, 1, 0). Dashed edges are weighted (0, 0, 1). (Note that not all of the vertices and edges are labeled here.) Figure 18.32 gives a four-way

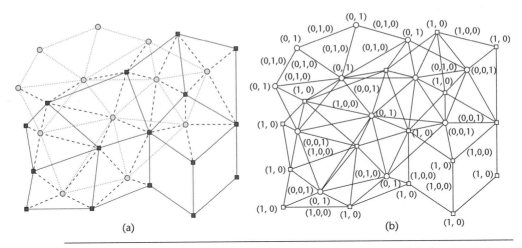

(a)

(b)

Figure 18.31 (a) Example of two overlapping meshes (light circles and dark squares) along with dashed interpolation edges and, (b) corresponding multiconstraint, multiobjective formulation.

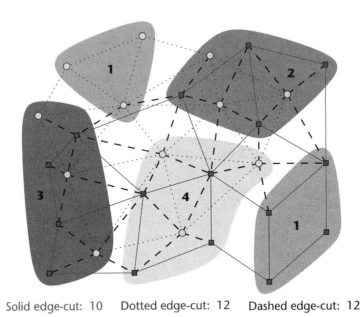

Solid edge-cut: 10   Dotted edge-cut: 12   Dashed edge-cut: 12

Figure 18.32 The partitioned meshes from Figure 18.31.

partitioning of this graph. Here, both types of vertices are balanced and their edge-cuts are minimized. At the same time, minimizing the number of dashed edges cut has helped to ensure that regions from the two graphs that spatially overlap tend to be in the same subdomain. This minimizes the communications incurred by the interpolation and transfer process.

Multiconstraint Graph Partitioning

Theoretical work relating to multiconstraint graph partitioning includes the ham-sandwich theorem and its generalization [901]. This theorem states that a single plane can divide three bounded and connected regions in half in a 3-D space. If two of the regions are interpreted as slices of bread and one as a slice of ham, then the conclusion is that a single stroke of a knife can evenly divide the sandwich in two so that all three slices are cut exactly in half. Also, Djidjev and Gilbert [276] proved that if a vertex separator theorem holds for a class of graphs (for example, Lipton and Tarjan's planar separator theorem [619]), then the theorem also holds for graphs in which the vertices have an arbitrary number of distinct weights.

Multiconstraint graph partitioning algorithms have recently been developed by a number of researchers [541, 771, 835, 976, 981]. These vary in their generality and complexity. A method is presented in Walshaw et al. [976] that utilizes a slight modification of a traditional graph partitioner as a black box in order to compute partitionings for multiphase computations. This method partitions disjoint subsets of vertices sequentially. Vertices are grouped together depending on the first phase of the multiphase computation in which they are active. After a set of vertices is partitioned, their subdomains are locked. Subsequent partitioning of other sets of vertices are influenced by the locked vertices. In this way, free vertices that are highly connected to locked vertices are likely to be assigned to the same subdomains as their neighbors. This scheme is sufficient for partitioning the multiphase mesh shown in Figure 18.26.

A more complex and more general algorithm is presented in Karypis and Kumar [541]. This is a multilevel scheme that extends the coarsening and refinement phases to handle multiple balance constraints. A key component of this algorithm is the initial partitioning algorithm. Here, a partitioning needs to be computed that balances multiple constraints. The authors present a lemma that proves that a set of two-weight objects can be partitioned into two disjoint subsets such that the difference between either of the weights of the two sets is bounded by twice the maximum weight of any object. They further show that this bound can be generalized to m weights. However, maintaining the weight bound depends on the presence of sufficiently many objects with certain weight characteristics (an assumption that usually holds for medium- to large-size graphs). The lemma leads to an algorithm for computing such a bisection. This scheme is sufficient for a wide range of multiphase, multiphysics, and multimesh simulations (including all of the examples described in this section).

A parallel formulation of the multiconstraint partitioner [541] is described in Schloegel et al. [835]. Experimental results show that this formulation can efficiently compute partitionings of similar quality to the serial algorithm and scales to very large graphs. For example, the parallel multiconstraint graph partitioner is able to compute a three-constraint 128-way partitioning of a 7 million–vertex graph in about 7 seconds on 128 processors of a Cray T3E.

Multiobjective Graph Partitioning

For any single-objective optimization problem (such as the traditional graph partitioning problem), an optimal solution exists in the feasible solution space. In multiobjective optimization, there is no single overall optimal solution, although there is an optimal solution for each one of the objectives. Consider the set of solution points for the two-objective optimization problem shown in Figure 18.33. The optimally minimal values for the two objectives are shown by the dashed lines. In this set, two unique points have the (same) optimal value for the first objective. However, their values for the second objective differ. Clearly, we would prefer the lightly shaded point over the black point, as this one is equal with respect to the first objective and has a better (smaller) value for the second objective. In this set of solution points, we can quickly determine that most of the points are not of interest. The solutions that are of interest are those that are not dominated by any other solution, regardless of whether they have optimal values for any of the objectives. These are called the *Pareto optimal* points. A solution is Pareto optimal if there is no feasible solution for which one can improve the value of any objective without worsening the value of at least one other objective [636]. In Figure 18.33,

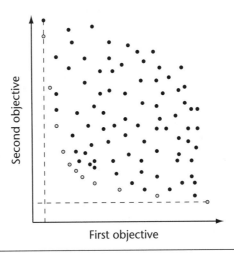

Figure 18.33   A number of solution points for a two-objective optimization problem. The lightly shaded points are Pareto optimal.

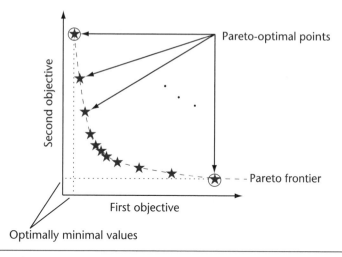

Figure 18.34 The Pareto frontier for a two-objective optimization problem. The optimally minimal values of each objective are also shown.

the lightly shaded points (and only these points) are Pareto optimal. The set of all Pareto-optimal points is called the *Pareto frontier* [636] (see Figure 18.34). In general, multiobjective optimization problems have many Pareto-optimal solutions. One of the implications of multiple Pareto-optimal solutions is that the definition of the *desired solution* becomes ambiguous. Every multiobjective optimization scheme requires that some method be used in order to disambiguate the definition of a desired solution. In the context of multiobjective graph partitioning, the user should specify the area along the Pareto frontier in which they are interested, and by doing so, control the tradeoffs among the objectives.

The key challenge in solving the multiobjective partitioning problem is to allow the user to control the tradeoffs among the different objectives. This is particularly difficult when the objectives are dissimilar in nature, as such objectives cannot readily be combined. A new method of reformulating the multiobjective graph partitioning problem so that it can be solved using a traditional (i.e., single-objective) partitioner is presented in [834]. This method provides the user with a fine-tuned control of the tradeoffs among the objectives, results in predictable partitionings, and is able to handle dissimilar objectives. Specifically, the algorithm computes a multiobjective partitioning based on a user-specified preference vector. This vector describes how the tradeoffs among the objectives should be enforced. For example, if there are two objectives and the user supplies a preference vector of $(1, 1)$, then the algorithm will allow one objective to move away from its optimal value by some amount only if the other objective moves toward its optimal value by more than that amount. For the case of three objectives with a preference vector of $(6, 2, 1)$, the algorithm will prefer a new solution only if $6x + 2y + z > 0$, where x is the gain with respect to the first objective, y is the gain with respect to the second objective, and z is the gain with respect to the third objective.

A number of multiconstraint and multiobjective graph partitioning algorithms, as well as some of their parallel formulations, have been implemented in the METIS [540] and ParMETIS [547] libraries. Serial and parallel multiphase partitioning algorithms [976] are implemented in the Jostle [968] library.

18.6   Conclusion

The state of the art in graph partitioning for high-performance scientific simulations has improved dramatically over the past decade. Improvements in the speed, accuracy, generality, and scalability of graph partitioners have led to significant milestones. For example, extremely large graphs (over 0.5 billion vertices) have been partitioned on machines consisting of thousands of processors in only a couple of minutes [551]. However, despite impressive achievements, there is still work to be done in the field. In this section, we discuss some of the limitations of current graph partitioning problem formulations (many of which were highlighted by Hendrickson and Kolda [456]), as well as areas of future work. We end this chapter by charting the functionality of some of the publicly available graph partitioning software packages.

18.6.1   Limitations of the Graph-Partitioning Problem Formulation

As discussed previously, the edge-cut metric is not a precise model of the interprocessor communication costs incurred by parallel processing. Nor is it even a precise model of the total communications volume [455]. While the min-cut formulation has proved effective for the well-shaped meshes that are common to scientific simulations, alternative formulations are still needed for more general cases. As an example of recent work in this area, Catalyurek and Aykanat [174] have developed a hypergraph partitioning formulation that precisely models total communication volume. Experimental results comparing the hypergraph partitioning model to the traditional graph partitioning model show that for graphs of nonuniform degree, using the hypergraph model can significantly decrease the interprocessor communication costs compared to using the graph model. However, for graphs of uniform degree, the hypergraph model provides only a modest improvement and requires more runtime compared to state-of-the-art graph partitioners [174]. While the hypergraph partitioning formulation allows us to precisely minimize communications volume, it does not allow us to minimize other important components of interprocessor communication cost such as the message start-up time or the time required for the processor with the most communication (i.e., minimize the maximum processor communication time). Developing new formulations and algorithms that do so is an open area of research in the field.

18.6.2 Other Application Modeling Limitations

In addition to being imprecise, the traditional partitioning formulation is inadequate for many important classes of scientific simulation. For example, the standard graph partitioning formulation can effectively model only square, symmetric sparse matrices. However, general rectangular and unsymmetric matrices are required for solving linear systems, least-squares problems, and linear programs [457]. Bipartite graph partitioning [457] and multiconstraint graph partitioning [541, 835] can be effective for these types of applications. Also, minimizing the edge-cut of a partitioning does not ensure the *numerical scalability* of iterative methods. Numerical scalability means that as the number of processors increases, the convergence rate of the iterative solver remains constant. Vanderstraeten et al. [957] have shown that the numerical scalability of a class of iterative solvers can be maintained if partitionings are computed such that their subdomains have low average aspect ratios. The traditional partitioning formulation does not optimize subdomain aspect ratios. Walshaw et al. [972] developed graph partitioning schemes that attempt to minimize the average aspect ratio of the subdomains. Experimental results show that these schemes are able to compute partitionings with significantly better subdomain aspect ratios than traditional partitioners. However, they often result in worse edge-cuts. While these results are promising, it is desirable for a partitioning to minimize both of these objectives (edge-cut and aspect ratio) simultaneously. Recent work in multiobjective graph partitioning [834] may also be relevant here to control the tradeoff between these two objectives.

18.6.3 Architecture Modeling Limitations

When traditional graph partitioners are used for mapping computations onto parallel machines, there is an assumption that the target architecture is flat and homogeneous [266, 456]. While it is true that many current architectures display similar computing powers, bandwidths, and latencies regardless of the processors involved, heterogeneous and hierarchical architectures are becoming increasingly commonplace. For example, consider the problem of decomposing a mesh for parallel processing on an architecture that consists of a cluster of heterogeneous workstations connected by a high-speed, high-latency network to a distributed-memory multiprocessor in which each node consists of a four-processor, shared-memory machine. Here, both the computational and communicational speeds depend on the specific processors involved. Standard graph partitioners do not take such considerations into account when computing a partitioning. Partitioning for heterogeneous and hierarchical architectures is especially important in meta-computing environments [517]. In such an environment, it may be impossible to predict the type (or types) of machines or even the exact number of processors that a simulation will be executed on until immediately prior to execution. In this case, both computational speeds and communication costs can fluctuate widely, even between repeated executions of the same simulation. Alternative (e.g., hierarchical and other [190, 912, 975]) partitioning methods are starting to be applied to such problems, but more work still needs to be done.

18.6.4   Functionality of Available Graph Partitioning Packages

Many of the graph partitioning schemes described in this chapter have been implemented in publicly available software packages. Figure 18.35 charts the functionality of some of the more widely used packages. These include Chaco [458], Jostle [968], METIS [540], ParMETIS [547], Party [777], Scotch [761], and S-Harp [883].

Acknowledgments. We would like to thank Rupak Biswas, Bruce Hendrickson, Abani Patra, Robert Preis, and Chris Walshaw as well as the CRPC book reviewers for their insightful comments on earlier drafts of this chapter. This work was supported by DoE contract number LLNL B347881, NSF grants CCR-9972519, EIA-9986042, and ACI-9982274, Army Research Office contract DA/DAAG55-98-1-0441, and Army High Performance Computing Research Center cooperative agreement number DAAH04-95-2-0003/contract number DAAH04-95-C-0008; content does not necessarily reflect the position or the policy of the government, and no official endorsement should be inferred. Additional support was provided by the IBM Partnership Award and by the IBM SUR equipment grant. Access to computing facilities was provided by AHPCRC and the Minnesota Supercomputer Institute.

	Chaco	Jostle	METIS	ParMETIS	PARTY	Scotch	S-Harp
Geometric schemes	●				●		●
Coordinate nested dissection					●		
Recursive inertial bisection	●						●
Space-filling curve methods				●			
Spectral methods	●						●
Recursive spectral bisection	●						
Multilevel spectral bisection	●						
Combinatorial schemes	●				●	●	
Levelized nest dissection					●	●	
KL/FM	●				●	●	
Multilevel schemes	●	●	●	●		●	
Multilevel recursive bisection	●		●			●	
Multilevel k-way partitioning		●	●	●			
Multilevel fill-reducing ordering			●	●			
Dynamic repartitioners		●		●			●
Diffusive repartitioning		●		●			●
Scratch-remap repartitioning				●			
Parallel graph partitioners		●		●			●
Parallel static partitioning		●		●			●
Parallel dynamic partitioning		●		●			●
Other formulations		●	●	●			
Multiconstraint graph partitioning		●	●	●			
Multiobjective graph partitioning			●				

Figure 18.35   Functionality of a number of publicly available software packages.

19 Mesh Generation

Bharat K. Soni • Joe F. Thompson

Mesh generation is an essential infrastructure element—an enabling technology—for the computational simulation of field phenomena such as fluid mechanics, heat and mass transfer, structural mechanics, plasmadynamics, electromagnetics, and other such physical processes that occur over a region of space. Mesh generation is the means by which the domain of interest is discretized into a collection of discrete points or volumes on which the governing equations can be represented and then solved computationally. The mesh thus provides the framework on which the solution is computed and subsequently visualized.

Fundamentally, mesh generation operates by distributing points throughout the volume of the physical region, as well as on the boundary surfaces. Connecting the points forms the mesh and subdivides the physical region into a filling set of discrete volume elements. The governing equations may be represented discretely on the points, with derivatives being represented by finite differences, or in the more fundamental integral form on the volume elements, with integrals being represented by discrete sums. In either case, the resulting set of simultaneous algebraic equations constitutes a matrix problem that is solved computationally by some direct, factored or iterative method.

The time required for mesh generation is much more a question of person time than computation time. Thus, there is also the need to make the mesh generation process easier for the user.

The real needs in mesh generation emerge as the following:

- Capability for bigger meshes, that is, more points
- Compatibility of data structure with solution codes
- More ease of user operation, that is, more automation
- Capability for macros, editing, and script-based operation

All facets of mesh generation have recently been addressed—from the standpoint of application and best practices—in the *Handbook of Grid Generation*, edited by J. Thompson and B. Soni of Mississippi State University and N. Weatherill of the University of Wales, Swansea [928]. The present chapter, therefore, defers to that work for details and focuses on a brief overview of strategies and technology, examples of application, and aspects of parallel operation.

19.1   Mesh-Generation Strategies and Techniques

Mesh-generation strategies can be classified as Cartesian, structured, unstructured, hybrid (generalized), and meshless. The techniques employed in these strategies and the state of the art and state of the practice are discussed in the following sections.

19.1.1   Cartesian Meshes

In this approach, a network of mesh lines with uniform spacing is defined in a rectangle (2-D) or a rectangular box (3-D) in the domain in question. The size of the box is determined as a function of the dimensions of solid geometric components associated with the simulation. The discretization associated with solid geometrical components is decoupled from the mesh. The boundary condition implementation is established by "cutting" the interior geometrical entities with mesh lines.

This approach is the simplest and most straightforward way of discretizing the given domain. The entire mesh-generation process and boundary-condition specification can be automated. The governing equations can be discretized using a cell-based or node-based approach; however, the cell-to-cell or node-to-node connectivity at solid boundaries/surfaces is not known a priori, which adds complexity to the discretization of the governing equations. Also, a special data structure is needed to describe conservation of volume.

The Cartesian approach has been used to solve a variety of problems [665]. Developments in computer science, involving search algorithms, quadtree–octree data structures, polygon clipping schemes, and adaptive refinement [94] based on isotropic subdivision, have shown potential in the application of this approach to complex configurations automatically without user intervention. However, validation and practical application of this approach to Navier–Stokes simulations involving viscous boundary layers and simulations associated with complex physics involving disparate time and length scales require more research.

19.1.2   Structured Meshes

If the points are placed in a logically rectangular pattern, so that adjacent points are readily recognizable, the mesh is said to be "structured." This automatic neighbor recognition greatly simplifies both the data structure and the discrete representation of derivatives and integrals and generally results in an orderly, sparse matrix problem. This structure comes at the price of geometric flexibility, however. Although great strides have been made in the generation of structured meshes, the most complex geometrical configurations can be difficult to treat with this approach. Block-structured generation has extended the range of application of structured meshes to quite complicated configurations, but the goal of automation has not yet been achieved. In fact, the large number of blocks that must necessarily result with most complicated configurations makes these meshes unstructured in the global sense.

The structured mesh is represented by a network of curvilinear coordinate lines such that a one-to-one mapping can be established between physical and computational space. The curvilinear mesh points conform to the solid surfaces/boundaries and, hence, provide the most economical and accurate way for specifying boundary conditions. For complicated geometrical configurations, the physical region is divided into subregions; a structured mesh is generated within each of these. The resulting submeshes may be patched together at common interfaces, overlapped or overlaid (commonly referred to as a *chimera mesh*). The transfer of solution information at the block interface is very critical for successful simulation.

Structured meshes can be generated algebraically or as the solution of partial differential equations (PDEs). Algebraic mesh generation [391, 886] is simply an interpolation of interior points from boundary points—the variants just use different kinds of interpolation. The most fundamental and versatile form—and the one now commonly incorporated in mesh-generation codes—is TFI (transfinite interpolation). Algebraic mesh generation based on TFI is the fastest procedure for generating structured meshes and is also commonly used to generate an initial mesh in generation systems based on PDEs. Meshes generated algebraically may, however, have problems with smoothness and may overlap strongly convex portions of boundaries. Generation systems based on PDEs can produce smoother meshes with fewer problems with boundary overlap. Such generation systems are, therefore, often used to smooth algebraic meshes.

TFI can be mathematically described as a Boolean sum of interpolation projectors in all three coordinate directions:

$$P_\xi \oplus P_\eta \oplus P_\zeta = P_\xi + P_\eta + P_\zeta - P_\xi P_\eta - P_\eta P_\zeta - P_\zeta P_\xi + P_\xi P_\eta P_\zeta$$

Here, the interpolation projectors represent linear, Lagrange, Hermite, Bezier, B-spline, NURBs, or any other interpolation selected by the developer.

Since mesh generation is essentially a boundary-value problem, meshes can be generated from point distributions on boundaries by solving elliptic PDEs in the field. The smoothness properties and extremum principles inherent in some PDE systems can serve to produce smooth meshes without boundary overlap. The PDE solution is generally done by iteration, and, therefore, elliptic mesh generation is not as fast as algebraic mesh generation.

The elliptic PDEs employed for mesh generation are not unique, of course, but must be designed. This design has converged over the years to the elliptic system that forms the basis for most mesh-generation codes today. This formulation incorporates control functions that are determined from the boundary point distribution. These functions control the mesh line spacing and orientation in the field so that the latter is compatible with that on the boundary.

Evaluation of these control functions is the key factor to achieving mesh smoothness and orthogonality. This technology is well developed, and a good quality mesh can be generated for very complex arbitrary regions [926]. The elliptic system typically employed is of the form:

$$\sum_{i=1}^{3}\sum_{j=1}^{3} g^{ij} r_{\xi i} r_{\xi j} + \sum_{k=1}^{3} \phi_k r_{\xi k} = 0$$

where

$$g^{il} = \frac{1}{g} \left(g_{jm} g_{km} - g_{jn} g_{kn} \right),$$

$$i = 1, 2, 3; \quad j = 1, 2, 3 \quad\quad (i, j, k), (l, m, n) \text{ cyclic}$$

This elliptic system can be rewritten in the following form for evaluation of the control functions:

$$\sum_{i=1}^{3}\sum_{j=1}^{3} g^{ij} (g_{iq})_{\xi j} + \sum_{k=1}^{3} \phi_k g_{kq}$$

$$- \sum_{i=1}^{3}\sum_{j=1}^{3} g^{ij} \left(\frac{(g_{ij})_{\xi q} - (g_{jq})_{\xi i} + (g_{iq})_{\xi j}}{2} \right) = 0$$

with $q = 1, 2, 3$. Assuming orthogonality, the control functions can be derived as

$$\phi_k = \frac{1}{2} \frac{d}{d\xi^k} \left(\ln \left(\frac{g_{kk}}{g_{ii} g_{jj}} \right) \right)$$

with (i, j, k) cyclic and $k = 1, 2, 3$.

This definition of the control functions is straightforward and has been found to be most effective with respect to improving orthogonality and smoothness in structured meshes.

An alternative approach to mesh generation via PDEs is to use a hyperbolic generation system [895] rather than an elliptic system. Elliptic equations admit boundary conditions, that is, mesh point distributions, on all boundaries of a region. Hyperbolic systems, however, can take boundary conditions only on a portion of the boundary. Therefore, while elliptic mesh-generation systems produce a mesh in the volume from point distributions of the entire boundary, hyperbolic systems generate the mesh by marching outward from a portion of the boundary. Hyperbolic mesh-generation systems, therefore, cannot be used to generate a mesh in the entirety of a volume defined by a complete boundary.

Hyperbolic generation is very useful for external flow problems and for generating component meshes in the case of overlaid meshes. The following equations are linearized and then solved numerically to generate hyperbolic meshes:

$$r_\zeta \cdot r_\xi = \sqrt{g_{11} g_{33}} \cos(\phi)$$

$$r_\zeta \cdot r_\eta = \sqrt{g_{22} g_{33}} \cos(\psi)$$

$$r_\zeta \cdot (r_\xi \times r_\eta) = V$$

The usual practice is to enforce orthogonality by assuming ϕ and ψ in these equations to be 90°. Structured meshes are not generally made orthogonal, although orthogonality at boundaries is often incorporated, as has been noted above. In fact, 3-D orthogonality is not generally possible without imposing certain conditions on the meshes on the boundary surfaces. Even in 2-D, orthogonality imposes severe restrictions on the mesh distribution. Transformed PDEs, however, take a much more simple form on orthogonal meshes, providing some incentive for their use when feasible: with relatively simple boundary configurations and physical problems without strong localized gradients.

Various approaches are documented in the literature [887] that combine the best features of algebraic–elliptic–hyperbolic techniques to accomplish quality static and adaptive/dynamic mesh generation. Another approach that is utilized, especially in 2-D applications, is based on variational functionals [136].

A powerful and versatile alternative to block-structured meshes is the overset mesh approach (originally called *chimera,* after the composite monster of Greek mythology). With this approach, individual structured meshes are generated around separate boundary components, such as bodies, and these separate meshes simply overlap each other in some hierarchy. Data are transferred between overlapping meshes by interpolation. The chimera meshes [660] offer the flexibility to address moving-body problems that require dynamic meshing.

The structured, multiblock mesh represents a widely utilized strategy for practical computational field simulation (CFS) applications. The major issue here is automation. The generation of multiblock meshes is extremely time consuming, especially for very complex geometrical configurations. User ingenuity and user experience govern the response time in mesh generation. In the past few years, various research activities [244, 747] have been dedicated to developing algorithms to perform automatic blocking and mesh generation; however, user interactions and graphical interfaces remain extremely important for generation of structured meshes.

19.1.3   Unstructured Meshes

"Unstructured" meshes are just that: no logical connection of adjacent points is self-evident. Rather, a connectivity table must be constructed and preserved for use in the numerical simulation. The representation of derivatives and integrals is also more complicated, and the resulting matrix problem is more dense and less orderly. The solution algorithm in this approach becomes more complex, but with a significant gain in the ability to treat truly complex configurations automatically.

Unstructured meshes are composed of triangles or quadrilaterals (2-D) and tetrahedrals or hexahedrals (3-D). The mesh information is represented by a set of coordinates (nodes) and the connectivity between the nodes. The explicit connectivity table specifies the connections and appropriate neighborhood information between nodes and cells.

Triangular/tetrahedral unstructured mesh generation is accomplished by point creation and/or point connection [983]. These methods are usually classified into three categories: quadtree–octree based subdivision algorithms, Delaunay triangulation, and advancing-front methods. The subdivision-based algorithms are applicable to field simulations needing uniform cells. The Delaunay triangulation is based on the creation of Dirichlet tessellations [967] in the convex region. The advancing-front scheme [624] is based, however, on the generation of triangles/tetrahedra by marching, as a front, from the initial geometry toward the interior. This process enables the generation of elements of variable size with desired stretching.

The generation of quadrilateral (2-D) meshes is accomplished by appropriately utilizing methods for structured meshes and unstructured triangular meshes. However, the point insertion methods (e.g., Delaunay-type methods), which are widely utilized, very successfully, in the generation of tetrahedral unstructured meshes, are not applicable to hexahedral mesh generation. Hence, hexahedral unstructured meshes are difficult and cumbersome to generate. The block-decomposition methods and superposition methods are usually applied in the generation of hexahedral meshes. The block-decomposition methods include structured grid-generation methodologies with techniques to decompose the domain of interest into blocks where boundary-conforming, coordinate mapping can be applied. The concept of medial-axis [778] superposition methods involves similar strategies. However, instead of decomposing the domain, the complex domain is superpositioned with a regular region on which structured grid–based coordinate transformation can be performed. Geometric techniques are then applied to remove points outside the desired domain and in generating near-boundary hexahedral elements. The whisker-weaving algorithm [911] developed by the CUBIT team at the Sandia National Laboratory uses paving and plastering advancing-front–like methods. However, this methodology is not applicable to general, very complex configurations.

Unstructured meshes offer greater geometric flexibility, and quality meshes can be generated, especially for Euler simulations. Data structures play an important role in handling unstructured meshes. The development of the AFLR (advancing-front local reconnection) scheme [646] offers the best features of both Delaunay and advancing-front schemes. However, unstructured meshes potentially suffer from accuracy problems due to the skewness of high-aspect-ratio tetrahedra in viscous regions. The concept of using hexahedra meshes in the viscous regions is being explored by various researchers. In general applications, the fact that one hexahedral volume requires five tetrahedral elements makes hexahedra attractive in view of mesh size efficiency. Also, in finite element analysis, quadrilatral/hexahedra meshes are preferred in view of numerical accuracy. For example, in applications involving elastic–plastic material, hexhedral mesh is significantly better. Additionally, as reported by Shaw [859], there are concerns regarding the efficiency of the unstructured mesh approach.

Unstructured meshes are now being utilized in computational field simulations (CFS); however, the generation of quality meshes, especially for simulations requiring high-aspect-ratio cells, is still a bottleneck. The major advantage of unstructured meshes is the potential for automation and greater geometric flexibility.

19.1.4   Hybrid/Generalized Meshes

Structured meshes enabled the great advances in aerospace computational fluid dynamics (CFD) in the 1970s and 1980s; unstructured meshes came to the fore in the 1990s, driven significantly by automotive applications. There are, of course, hybrid combinations of structured and unstructured meshes that build on the strengths of each. Further, generalized grid algorithms have been developed that remove all restrictions on cell topology.

The hybrid/generalized meshes allow polygonal cells with differing numbers of sides. The usual practice is to generate structured meshes near solid components where high-aspect-ratio cells are required and to fill in the remaining void with an unstructured mesh. Finite volume algorithms using generalized meshes to numerically simulate CFS problems [574] offer a greater potential for geometric flexibility and high-quality meshes with automation, especially in the regions where high-aspect-ratio cells are needed. The generation of such generalized meshes, however, is a formidable task, and algorithms are still being developed. An example of a hybrid/generalized mesh is demonstrated in Figure 19.1.

Experience would seem to indicate that no one mesh-generation technique is optimal for all problems. It is attractive, therefore, to explore utilizing a generalized mesh approach in which modules for the generation of structured and unstructured meshes can be combined within one data structure and software framework to

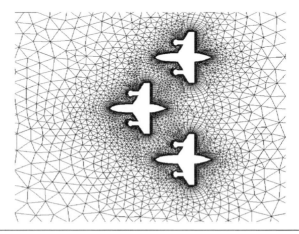

Figure 19.1   Example of a hybrid mesh.

provide comprehensive mesh capability. Such a system has been developed for applications in 2-D and is now widely used within a research environment [574]. Depending on the problem at hand, either a structured, unstructured, or hybrid (combination of structured and unstructured) mesh can be used. As with mesh types, it also seems clear that for maximum flexibility and efficiency, several forms of mesh adaptivity will be required for general problems. It follows, therefore, that for a generalized mesh and field system, all mesh types should be available for use, and these should be coupled with modules for mesh adaptation using h-refinement, de-refinement, and point movement.

19.1.5   Meshless Methods

The meshless method of mesh generation facilitates the numerical treatment of governing equations without requiring explicit connectivity between points. A cloud of points is placed in the field, and the discretized numerical scheme is developed based on the points registered in the neighborhood of each point. The development of this technology is in its infancy and has a long way to go before utilization in practical industrial applications. However, techniques for simulating Euler flows have been developed by various researchers [85, 621].

19.2   Mesh-Generation Process and Geometry Preparation

Regardless of which strategy is being considered, creation of a computational mesh requires:

- *Computational mapping.* Establishing an appropriate mapping from physical to computational space, allowing proper multiblock strategies (in the case of structured and hybrid meshes) or establishing an ordering of nodes (in the case of unstructured meshes and hybrid meshes).

- *Geometry generation.* Defining an accurate numerical description of all solid components (surfaces), in conjunction with associated computational mapping criteria and a desired distribution of points.

- *Computational modeling.* Generating an "appropriate" mesh around these surfaces according to some criteria, usually with a specified multiblock strategy, point distribution, smoothness, and orthogonality (in the case of structured meshes) and desired background mesh representative of the required point distribution (in the case of unstructured meshes).

The relationship of geometry to the mesh-generation process is analogous to the relationship between boundary conditions and the solution of the governing equations. An accurate construction of the geometry, with the proper distribution of points, usually consumes 85% to 90% of the total time spent on the mesh-generation process. The geometry specification associated with mesh generation involves:

- Determination of the desired distribution of mesh points, which depends on the expected field characteristics.

- Evaluation of boundary segments and surface patches to be defined, in order to resolve an accurate mathematical description of the geometry in question.

- Selection of the geometry tools to be utilized to define these boundary segments/surface patches.

- Following an appropriate logical path to blend the aforementioned tasks to obtain the desired discretized mathematical description of the geometry with properly distributed points.

The parametric-based, nonuniform rational B-spline (NURBS) is a widely utilized representation for geometrical entities in CAD/CAM/CAE systems. The convex hull, local support, shape-preserving forms, affine invariance, and variation-diminishing properties of NURBS are extremely attractive in engineering design applications. The IGES format [502] has become the de facto standard I/O (input/output) for exchanging data between various CAD/CAM and CAE systems. Recently, the IGES entities 126 (NURBS curve) and 128 (NURBS surface) have become increasingly popular in mesh generation, CFS, and in general CAE analysis and simulation systems.

Most of the geometrical configurations of interest to practical CFS problems are designed in CAD/CAM systems and are available to analysts in an IGES format. Geometry preparation, which is considered the most critical and labor-intensive part of CFS, involves the discrete-sculptured definition of all boundaries/surfaces with a desired point distribution and smoothness and orthogonality criteria associated with the domain of interest.

The NURBS-based geometry preparation for addressing complex CFS problems encountered in an industrial environment involves:

- Transformation of widely utilized explicitly/implicitly/discretely defined IGES geometric entities into common data structures involving NURBS.

- Surface reparametrization for poorly defined surfaces and repairing of faulty surfaces (the most common faults involve gaps, overlaps, and undesired discontinuity between neighboring surface patches) and pertinent geometric entities.

- Geometrical operations allowing projections, intersections (surface–surface intersections), composition, union, and other related transformations essential for surface mesh generation with desired topological criteria.

- Mesh point distribution with desired stretching and quality criteria on domain boundaries/surfaces.

The algorithms for transforming geometric entities into NURBS, composition of curves and surfaces and their respective NURBS definitions, mesh point distribution, and surface/volume reparametrization are well documented in the literature.

19.3   Adaptive Mesh Generation

There are three basic strategies that may be employed in dynamically adaptive meshes [136] coupled with the solution of the physical problem. The first approach is to redistribute a fixed number of points. In this approach, points move from regions of relatively small error to regions of large error. While the global order of the approximation cannot be increased by such movement of points [136], it is possible to improve the approximation locally. As long as the redistribution of points does not seriously deplete the number of points in other regions, this is a viable approach [311, 885, 925]. The second approach involves local refinement. In this approach, points are added (or removed) locally in a fixed-point structure in regions of relatively large error. There is, of course, no depletion of points in other regions and, therefore, no formal increase of error occurs. However, the computer time and storage increase with refinement, and the data structures can be difficult to implement. This approach is well suited to unstructured meshes [887, 984]. In the last approach, the solution algorithm is changed locally to a higher-order approximation in regions of relatively large error. This, again, increases the formal global accuracy but involves great complexity of implementation in flow solvers. This approach has not had any significant application in CFD in multiple dimensions.

19.3.1   Structured Mesh Adaptation

With structured meshes, the adaptive strategy based on redistribution is by far the most simple to implement, requiring only regeneration of the mesh and interpolation of field properties at the new mesh points at each adaptive stage. No modification of the field solver is required unless time accuracy is desired. Time accuracy can be achieved, as far as the mesh is concerned, by simply transforming the time derivatives by adding convective-like terms that do not alter the basic conservation of PDEs.

Adaptive redistribution of points traces its roots to the principle of equidistribution of error [137], by which a point distribution is set so as to make the product of the spacing and a weight function constant over the points:

$$w \, \Delta x = constant$$

With the point distribution defined by a function ξ_i, where ξ varies by a unit increment between points, the equidistribution principle can be expressed as

$$w \, x_\xi = constant$$

This 1-D equation can be applied in each direction in an alternating fashion [311]. A direct extension to multiple dimensions using algebraic [885], variational, and elliptic [925] systems has been developed.

Weight Function

The weight function is a very important part of the adaptive process. A generalized weight function applicable to various field characteristics has been developed. The weights are computed in all computational directions and then coupled adaptation is applied. A linear combination,

$$\left[1 + \left(\sum_{j=1}^{N} \lambda_j w_j \right) wtf \right] disf, \ \sum \lambda_j = 1 \tag{19.1}$$

where

$\quad\quad N =$ number of flow variables (e.g., pressure, temperature, or density)

$\quad\quad \lambda_j =$ weighting factor associated with flow parameter

$\quad\quad\quad w_j - \alpha_j q_j \oplus \beta_j k_j = \alpha_j q_j + \beta_j k_j - (\alpha_j + \beta_j - 1) q_j k_j$

$\quad\quad q_j =$ scaled gradient of the flow variable j such that $0 \le q_j \le 1$

$\quad\quad k_j =$ scaled curvature values of the flow variable j such that $0 \le k_j \le 1$

$\quad\quad wtf =$ weight factor that enhances the total effect of heavily weighted areas

$\quad\quad disf =$ distribution factor that can keep the original distribution

and

$$0 \le \alpha_j \le 1 \quad\quad 0 \le \beta_j \le 1$$

is formulated as a weight function utilizing the Boolean sum of contributions from scaled gradients and curvatures. The value of the contribution is controlled by the weight factors and is at a maximum when gradients and/or curvature values are at a maximum. An appropriate scaling scheme [885] for the weight factors α_j and β_j has been developed to ensure a proper distribution of mesh points.

Algebraic Technique

The redistributed algebraic mesh is generated by utilizing a surface/volume distribution mesh as the reparametrized space associated with NURBS surface/volume representation. The application of the inverse NURBS formulation [885] allows reevaluation of control points, which influences the fidelity of solid surface geometry during the redistribution process.

Elliptic Technique

The elliptic generation system,

$$\sum_{i=1}^{3} \sum_{j=1}^{3} g^{ij} r_{\xi^i \xi^j} + \sum_{k=1}^{3} g^{kk} P_k r_{\xi^k} = 0 \tag{19.2}$$

where

$$r = \text{position vector}$$

$$g^{ij} = \text{contravariant metric tensor}$$

$$\xi^i = \text{curvilinear coordinate}$$

$$P_k = \text{control function}$$

is widely utilized for mesh generation [929]. The control of the characteristics and distribution of a mesh system can be achieved by varying the values of the control functions P_k in equation (19.2) [929]. The application of the 1-D form of equation (19.2) with equation (19.1) results in the definition of the control functions in three dimensions,

$$P_i = \frac{W_{\xi^i}}{W}, \quad i = 1, 2, 3$$

These control functions were generalized by Eiseman [311] as

$$P_i = \sum_{j=1}^{3} \frac{g^{ij}}{g^{ij}} \frac{(W_i)_{\xi^i}}{W_i}, \quad i = 1, 2, 3$$

In order to conserve the geometrical characteristics of the existing mesh, the definition of the control functions is extended as

$$P_i = \left(P_{initial\ geometry} \right)_i + c_i \left(P_{wt} \right), \quad i = 1, 2, 3$$

where

$$P_{initial\ geometry} = \text{control function based on initial mesh geometry}$$

$$P_{wt} = \text{control function based on gradient of flow parameter}$$

$$c_i = \text{constant weight factors}$$

These control functions are evaluated based on the current mesh at the adaptation step and can be formulated as

$$P_i^{(n)} = P_i^{(n-1)} + c_i \left(P_{wt} \right)^{(n-1)}, \quad i = 1, 2, 3$$

where

$$P_i^{(1)} = \left(P_{initial\ geometry} \right)^{(0)} + c_i \left(P_{wt} \right)^{(0)}, \quad i = 1, 2, 3$$

A flow solution is first obtained with an initial mesh. Then the control function is evaluated in accordance as indicated above, which is a combination of the geometry of the current mesh and the weight functions associated with the current flow solution.

19.3.2 Generalized Mesh Adaptation

In the generalized mesh approach, algebraic and elliptic, partial-differential equation methods [645] have been used for the generation of structured meshes, and Delaunay triangulation has been used for unstructured meshes of triangles. It is possible, by utilizing a combination of these techniques, to generate high-quality meshes for a variety of aerospace configurations. A data structure based on a modified quadtree format has been used to combine, in a unified form, the various mesh types.

Flow Algorithm

A finite-volume algorithm to solve the equations for viscous compressible flows on generalized meshes has been developed. It is based on the Runge–Kutta scheme of Jameson [509]. This approach has been well documented. Here, only the aspects of our implementation that make it applicable to all mesh types will be highlighted.

The flow of a viscous compressible fluid is governed by the Navier–Stokes equations. They represent conservation of mass, momentum, and energy. For 2-D, unsteady flow, the integral form is

$$\frac{\partial}{\partial t} \iint_\Omega w \, dx \, dy + \int_{\partial\Omega} (F \, dy - G \, dx) = 0$$

where x and y are the Cartesian coordinates, and the integrals are taken over a control volume Ω, with boundary $\partial\Omega$. The conserved variable vector is $w = [(\rho, \rho u, \rho v, \rho e)]$, where ρ, u, v, and e are the density, the components of velocity, and the energy, respectively. Further details of the equations are not relevant to this discussion and can be found elsewhere.

The flux integral above is approximated by defining a residual R_j. Several possible interpretations can be given. The option selected is to treat the residual on an element-by-element basis and, hence, the residual, as the net flux for each cell, is

$$R_j = \sum_{i=1}^{m} \left[F(w_j)\Delta y - G(w_j)\Delta x \right]$$

where the summation is carried out over the m edges that define the cell j, with Δx and Δy consistent with an anticlockwise line integration around the cell. Note that this definition for the residual is dependent on the number of edges that define the cell and not specifically on whether the cell is a triangle or quadrilateral. This statement motivated Jameson to construct an edge-based data structure in which the flux across an edge in a mesh is sent, with the appropriate sign, to the two cells that it separates. Such a data structure is ideal for an algorithm for generalized meshes.

To ensure stability, it is necessary to augment the governing flow equations with terms that represent artificial dissipation. Two terms, D_o^1, a diffusive Laplacian smoothing to capture shock waves, and D_o^2, a bi-harmonic diffusive smoothing acting as a low-level background dissipation to reduce odd–even decoupling, are introduced. A simple way to introduce these dissipation operators is to construct a Laplacian operator by taking the difference between the values at a given cell and its nearest neighbors. This objective is accomplished by looping over all edges. Recycling along edges, the values for the Laplacian, leads to a form for the bi-harmonic contribution. For cell o, we have

$$D_o^1 = \sum_{i=1}^{m} \varepsilon_{ko}^1 (w_i - w_o) \qquad D_o^2 = \sum_{i=1}^{m} \varepsilon_{ko}^2 (E_i - E_o) ; \quad E_o = D_o^1$$

The summations taken over the m edges of cell o and the coefficients ε_{ko}^1 and ε_{ko}^2 incorporate pressure sensors. These two terms are then summed to produce the dissipative term, which is added to the residual. Again, no assumption is made in this formulation about the type of cell. In a similar way, the edge data structure can be used to compute the areas of cells and the time appropriate for the explicit scheme in a general manner. The area, for example, of a region bounded by $\partial\Omega$ is

$$A = \int_{\partial\Omega} x \, dy$$

which can be approximated as

$$A = \sum_{edges} x \, \Delta y$$

where x and y are interpreted as edge quantities.

Given the solution and residuals for a point at time level n, the solution at the new time level $n + 1$ is obtained from the multistage scheme. For example, a three-stage scheme is

$$w^1 = w^n - \left(\frac{0.6 \, \Delta t \, R}{A}\right) w^n$$

$$w^2 = w^1 - \left(\frac{0.6 \, \Delta t \, R}{A}\right) w^1$$

$$w^{n+1} = w^2 - \left(\frac{\Delta t \, R}{A}\right) w^2$$

where Δt is the time step and is taken as the minimum of the time steps admitted by the Courant number for each cell, and A is the corresponding area of the control volume. The time integration is again seen to be independent of the geometrical shape of the cell.

From the outline given, it can be seen that a general algorithm can be constructed that, given the edge-based data structure, will be applicable to any generalized mesh. The incorporation of mesh adaptation also does not afford any major problems. H-refinement on a structured mesh leads to the introduction of nodes that are not fully connected and are termed *hanging nodes*. These types of nodes can also be introduced on h-refined triangular meshes if a particular subdivision strategy is used.

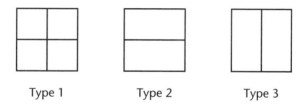

Type 1   Type 2   Type 3

Figure 19.2 Types of quadrilateral subdivision.

Figure 19.3 Subdivision of a triangle.

H-Refinement and De-refinement

The basic subdivisions for a structured quadrilateral mesh are shown in Figure 19.2 [928]. Repeated application of these subdivisions, or combinations of these subdivisions, results in meshes that contain polygonal cells. However, these cells are treated as a collection of edges, and the solution algorithm is not aware of the order of the polygons.

Figure 19.3 shows the strategy that has been adapted for the subdivision of triangles.

The order of the polygon does not interfere with the operation of the algorithm. However, the discontinuity in spacing caused by embedding can result in unsmooth solutions on these mesh interfaces. The rapid change of the size of the mesh influences the field solver in both the computation of fluxes and the artificial diffusion terms. These computations need to be modified accordingly. With reference to Figure 19.4, a typical weighting [984] that can be used in the computation of the variable at the edges from the cell-center data is

$$w_{edge} = \frac{1}{a+b} \left(bw_o + aw_1 \right)$$

Node Movement

In addition to h-refinement, node movement has been found to be necessary for an efficient implementation of mesh adaptation. Node movement can be applied in the form

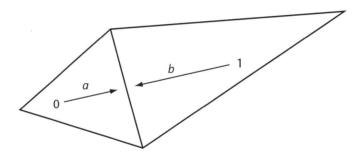

Figure 19.4   Weighted average for the computation of edge values from cell-centered values.

$$r_o^{n+1} = r_o^n + \omega_i \left[\frac{\sum\limits_{i=1}^{m} C_{io} \left(r_i^n - r_o^n \right)}{\sum\limits_{i=1}^{m} C_{io}} \right]$$

where $r = (x, y)$, r_o^{n+1} is the position of node o at relaxation level $n + 1$, C_{io} is the adaptive weight function between nodes i and o, and ω is the relaxation parameter [984]. A commonly used adaptive weight function takes the form

$$C_{io} = k_1 + k_2 \left| \frac{\phi_i - \phi_o}{\phi_i + \phi_o} \right|$$

where ϕ is the driving variable (e.g., pressure, density, Mach number), k_1 and k_2 act to damp out noise, and k_2 amplifies the gradients along the edges. In practice, this is implemented in a form that guarantees positive-area cells after movement, even in regions close to a wall. For viscous meshes, these can have very small volumes.

Adaptation Criterion

For the present solution-adaptive mesh-generation procedure, an error indicator is required that detects and locates appropriate features in the flow field [984]. In order to provide flexibility in isolating varying features, multiple error indicators are used. Each can isolate a particular type of feature. The error indicators are set to the negative and positive components of the gradient in the direction of the velocity vector, as given by

$$e_1 = \min (V \cdot \nabla u, \ 0)$$
$$e_2 = \max (V \cdot \nabla u, \ 0)$$

and the magnitude of the gradient in all directions normal to the velocity is given by

$$e_3 = \left| \nabla u - V \frac{(V \cdot \nabla u)}{V \cdot V} \right|$$

where V is the velocity vector and u is any suitable flow property. Typically, density is used as the basis for the error indicator. The first two error indicators represent expansions and compressions in the flow direction, and the third represents gradients normal to the flow direction. The indicators can be scaled by the relative element size. Length scaling can improve detection of weak features on a coarse mesh with the present procedure. Each error indicator is treated independently, allowing particular features in the flow field to be isolated. For each error indicator, an error is determined from

$$e_{lim} = e_m + c_{lim} \cdot e_s$$

where e_{lim} is the error limit, e_m is the mean of the error indicator, e_s is the standard deviation of the error indicator, and c_{lim} is a constant. Typically, a value near 1 is used for the constant. The error indicators are used to control the local reduction in relative element size during mesh generation.

An example of the mesh adaptation using the weighted Laplacian approach is shown in Figure 19.5. An unstructured mesh for a scramjet engine geometry is considered for this purpose. The inlet Mach number is taken to be 3, and the resultant pressure distribution together with initial mesh are shown in Figure 19.5(a). The

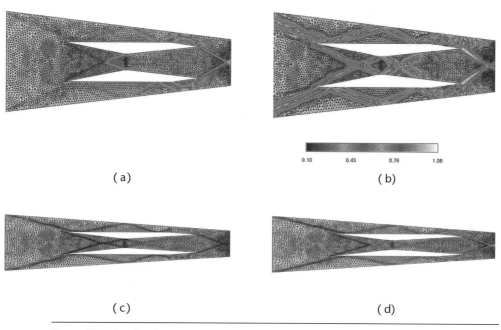

Figure 19.5 Mesh adaptation for unstructured mesh using weighted Laplacian approach. (a) Initial mesh and pressure distribution. (b) Initial mesh and weight functions. (c) Adapted mesh. (d) Pressure distribution on adapted mesh.

weight function is calculated based on the conserved variables and is plotted in Figure 19.5(b). The resultant adapted mesh and the solution on the adapted mesh are shown in Figure 19.5(c) and Figure 19.5(d). It can be seen from the pictures that the shocks and expansion fans are captured clearly as compared to the unadapted mesh.

19.4   Parallel Mesh Generation

Interest in parallel mesh generation is directly related to the need for more points and for the mesh data structure to be compatible with parallel operation of solution codes. Structured mesh generation is not nearly as computer-intensive as are the field solutions performed on the mesh. Therefore, there is no real need for parallel operation of the structured mesh generator just to increase the speed of the mesh-generation code. It is storage that creates the real need for multiprocessor operation of the structured mesh-generation code. However, this is not true for unstructured meshes. In simulation applications where unstructured remeshing is required due to geometry movements/deformations, mesh generation may consume more than 50% of the CPU time taken to solve the associated field equations. The call for parallel mesh generation is, thus, actually reflective of the need to increase the storage available and to have the mesh compatible with parallel, partial-differential-equation (PDE) solution codes. Additional incentive for speeding up the mesh generator appears only for unstructured meshes. With the advent of powerful parallel computers, computational field simulation on several million points has become a common practice. The usual practice is to generate the mesh in a sequential manner and split the mesh later for the simulation of the field problems on parallel machines. The drawback of this approach is that the overhead due to file I/O and data movement between these stages is about 90% of the total execution time. In order to avoid this problem and to speed up the mesh-generation process, the mesh-generation and partitioning problems have been cast into a single paradigm. The two most widely used unstructured mesh-generation approaches are the Delaunay triangulation and the advancing-front method. In the case of Delaunay triangulation, a new point is introduced into an existing triangulation based on the boundary discretization, and the new point is connected to the existing point such that it satisfies the Delaunay properties [967]. In the case of the advancing-front method, new elements are added one at a time. These two approaches can be parallelized efficiently. The two existing heuristics for mesh partitioning are (1) global or direct and (2) local or incremental [201]. In the first case, full information about the mesh is required before partitioning the mesh. In the latter approach, the partitioning starts with an initial partitioning that is iteratively refined. This incremental approach is more suitable for parallel unstructured mesh generation. The parallel Delaunay triangulation starts with the partitioning of an initial coarse mesh. The Bowyer–Watson algorithm, which is used to reconnect the points after the addition of new points in the process of Delaunay triangulation, is purely local in nature and enables the user to add points simultaneously in different domains without disturbing the global Delaunay property. When new points are inserted in different domains or submeshes, the voids created by the addition of new points are triangulated separately. In some cases, addition of points near the interface of one subdomain makes the tetrahedron in the neighboring domain non-Delaunay. In these cases, the cavities extend to two or more blocks and are retriangulated. The new elements are assigned to blocks that have a smaller number of predicted elements in each block. The prediction of the number of elements is done using (1) the current number of elements, (2) the current number of bad elements, and (3) the current mesh quality of each block that shares the interface cavity [201]. A parallel advancing-front mesh generation in the shared-memory paradigm has been reported in Lohner and Cebral [623]. In the advancing-front algorithm, one element at a time is introduced by eliminating the face in the front that produces the smallest element. Different elements can be added simultaneously using different processes if the elements added are sufficiently far apart. An octree is used to split the domain into different boxes, and elements are introduced into these boxes using different processors. During this process, the boxes that contain the regions where the smallest new elements are being added are considered. After the boxes are meshed, a new octree is generated, and the process is repeated. The large number of active faces in the advancing front from different boxes is reduced by shifting the boxes slightly and remeshing them [623]. Load balancing is obtained by grouping different boxes so that the total load in each process is the same. This process is done using a marching-cube procedure [623]. Depending on the list of active faces and the size of the box, the box is divided into a number of small cubes called *voxels*. An average surface normal is estimated for each voxel that cuts the active front. Depending on this normal, the rest of the voxels are marked as inside or outside the domain. The workload in each box is estimated based on the number of expected elements in each of the voxels that are inside the domain. Using this information, different boxes are grouped together such that each process will have approximately the same workload.

19.5   Mesh Software

In this section, we list some of the mesh software currently available.

- *ADMesh version 0.95.*   A program for processing triangulated solid meshes. Currently, ADMesh only reads the STL file format that is used for rapid prototyping applications, although it can write STL, VRML, OFF, and DXF files. *(http://www.varlog.com/products/admesh/).*

- *Automatic mesh generation of CAD and discrete data models.*   A collection of quadtree/octree-based, mesh-generation tools. *(http://scorec.rpi.edu/programs /modeling/meshing/Meshing.html).*

- *BAMG.*   A mesh generator for isotropic or anisotropic triangular meshes. *(http://www-rocq.inria.fr/gamma/cdrom/www/bamg/eng.htm).*

- *CAGI (Computer-aided grid interface) version 1.0.*   A mesh generation package with a NURBS database. *(http://WWW.ERC.MsState.Edu/ccs/docs/cagi/).*

- *CAMINO (Cardinal's advanced mesh innovation with octree).*   An octree process and device simulation. *(http://www-tcad.stanford.edu/tcad/bios/tchen.html).*

- *EAGLE mesh generation code.*   Eglin arbitrary geometry-implicit, Euler, multi-block, mesh-generation code and steady-state-flow solver system. *(http://www .erc.msstate.edu/~jiang/eagle.html).*

- *EAGLEView mesh generation code.*   Interactive surface and mesh generation software that combines the surface and volume mesh-generation codes of EAGLE under one GUI. *(http://www.erc.msstate.edu/~jiang/ev.html).*

- *EasyMesh version 1.4.*   Two-dimensional quality mesh generator, constrained Delaunay triangulations. *(http://www-dinma.univ.trieste.it/~nirftc/research /easymesh/).*

- *FELISA (Unstructured volume mesh generator and inviscid flow solution package) version 1.1.*   A surface-and volume-triangulation and mesh-adaption software. *(http://abweb.larc.nasa.gov:8080/~kbibb/felisa.html).*

- *femmesh.*   A UNIX/OpenWindows program designed to interactively generate 2-D FEM meshes composed of three-noded triangular elements. *(http://www .ucl.ac.uk/MedPhys/toast/femmesh/intro.htm).*

- *FIST (Fast, industrial-strength triangulation).*   A robust polygon-triangulation code (ear clipping) that can handle many kinds of degenerate data. *(http://www .andrew.cmu.edu/user/sowen/software/FIST.html).*

- *GENIE++.*   Part of a family of software to GENerate computational meshes for internal-external flow configurations. GENIE++ generates 3D, structured, multiblock meshes. *(http://www.erc.msstate.edu/ccs/docs/genie/).*

- *GiD: academic version.*   A universal, adaptive, and user-friendly graphical user interface for geometrical modeling, data input, and visualization of results for all types of numerical simulation programs. The academic version is completely functional but meshes are limited to 700 2-D elements and 3000 3-D elements. *(http://www.gid.cimne.upc.es/download/index.html).*

- *GJK-engine.*   The "heart" of SOLID, a general-purpose software library for collision detection of 3-D objects. GJK-engine is a fast and robust implementation of the Gilbert–Johnson–Keerthi algorithm. SOLID uses the GJK algorithm for testing intersections, determining common points, and computing pairs of closest points of convex objects. The GJK-engine is released as a separate library, without the application programming interface (API) and bounding-box structures of SOLID. The library is written in standard C++ and relies on STL. Currently, it compiles under GNU ++ version 2.8.1 and Visual C++ 5.0. The source code and documentation are released under the terms of the GNU Library General Public License. *(http://www.win.tue.nl/~gino/solid/).*

- *GEOMESH/LaGriT.*   Unstructured finite-element mesh generation for geological applications. *(ftp://ftp.cs.ualberta.ca:/pub/geompack/).* A mathematical software package written in standard Fortran 77 for the generation of 2-D and 3-D triangular/tetrahedral, finite-element meshes using GEOMetric algorithms. *(http://ees-www.lanl.gov/EES5/geomesh/).*

- *GMSH (Geometry mesh and post processing).* A Delaunay-based mesh generator that generates adapted meshes for lines, surfaces, and volumes. *(http://www .montefiore.ulg.ac.be/~geuzaine/gmsh.html).*

- *GridTool.* A tool for structured and unstructured mesh generation. *(http://geolab.larc.nasa.gov/GridTool/).*

- *GRUMMP.* Generation and refinement of unstructured, mixed-element meshes in parallel. *(http://tetra.mech.ubc.ca/GRUMMP/).*

- *IBG.* Octree-based, triangular- and tetrahedral-element mesh generation. *(ftp://ftp.wias-berlin.de/pub/ibg/doc/ibg.html).*

- *LaGriT.* An unstructured mesh generation and optimization software package used for semiconductor device modeling, computational fluid dynamics, and porous flow modeling. *(http://www.t12.lanl.gov/~lagrit/).*

- *Mesh-Maker version 0.2.* A program for generating unstructured meshes over a prespecified topography. *(http://www.lec.leeds.ac.uk/~jason/Mesh-Maker/).*

- *Meshme3D.* An automatic mesh generator in 3-D. Uses Delaunay–Voronoi methods to generate a 3-D, tetrahedral-element mesh using the surface mesh as an input. *(http://www.arc.umn.edu/~johnson/meshme.html).*

- *mesh2d.* Triangular/tetrahedral mesh generators, suitable for parallel implementation. An efficient combination of Delaunay and advancing-front methods. *(http://www.andrew.cmu.edu/user/sowen/software/mesh2d.html).*

- *MG (Mesh Generator) version 4.0.* A system for the generation of 3-D finite-element meshes with interactive graphics capabilities. *(http://www.tecgraf.puc-rio.br/~lula/mg/index.html).*

- *NCSA MinMaxer Overview.* A 2-D triangulation tool with an optional graphic user interface. The program implements several optimal 2-D triangulation algorithms and can be used to aid mesh generation and visualization. *(http://www .ncsa.uiuc.edu/SDG/Software/Brochure/Overview/MinMaxer.overview.html).*

- *NGP (National Grid Project) version 3.0.* Comprehensive numerical mesh-generation software system developed at the National Science Foundation Engineering Research Center for computational field simulation (CFS) at Mississippi State University. *(http://www.erc.msstate.edu/ccs/docs/ngp/)* .

- *PMAG (Parallel multiblock adaptive grid system).* Mesh-generation system based on the solution of elliptic, partial differential equations. Also capable of generating smooth orthogonal meshes on complex multiblock domains. *(http://www.erc.msstate.edu/~bsoni/pmag).*

- *Qhull.* A general-dimension code for computing convex hulls, Delaunay triangulations, Voronoi vertices, and half-space intersections. *(http://www.geom .umn.edu/software/qhull/).*

- *QMG version 1.1* Finite-element mesh generation in 2-D and 3-D (triangles/tetrahedra), integrated into MATLAB. *(http://simon.cs.cornell.edu/Info /People/vavasis/qmg1.1/qmg1_1_home.html).*

- *SD (Super Delaunay).* A fully dynamic, constrained, Delaunay triangulation engine for real-time triangulation. *(http://www.dlc.fi/~dkpa/).*

- *SolidMesh.* Unstructured mesh-generation system that enables the user to create both 2-D and 3-D unstructured meshes. Surface meshes can be created in parametric space on the NURBS or by using a 3-D point insertion method iterating between parametric space and physical space. *(http://www.erc.msstate.edu /simcenter/docs/solidmesh/).*

- *3DMAGGS.* (3-D multiblock advanced grid generation system). Elliptic volume-mesh generator used to generate computational domains for CFD analysis of aerodynamic vehicles. *(http://abweb.larc.nasa.gov:8080/~salter /3DMAGGS.html).*

- *TIGER.* Mesh-generation software that exclusively generates 3-D structured meshes for all classes of turbo machines with external, internal, and external–internal flow fields. *(http://www.erc.msstate.edu/ccs/docs/tiger/).*

- *UNAMALLA version 2.0.* Mesh generation over irregular polygonal regions using discrete functionals. *(http://www.mathmoo.unam.mx/unamalla/).*

- *VGM (Volume grid manipulator).* Alters, adapts, smooths, and even generates surface and volume meshes based on existing 2-D and 3-D data. VGM bridges the gaps between CAD systems, mesh-generation packages, and a deliverable/usable high-fidelity surface or volume mesh to be used for CFD simulations. *(http://abweb.larc.nasa.gov:8080/~salter/VGM-web.html).*

19.6   Mesh Configurations

The application of chimera/overset, structured mesh generation to very complex complete configurations is presented in Figure 19.6 and Figure 19.7. The mesh demonstrated in Figure 19.6 represents surface mesh over an entire space launch vehicle, and the configuration in Figure 19.7 displays particle traces demonstrating complex dynamic flow behavior near the V22 Osprey blade-tip. This dynamic simulation was performed using the chimera structured grid system. The demonstration of hybrid and generalized mesh is provided in Figure 19.8 and Figure 19.9. Both of these meshes are generated automatically from given boundary/surface distribution.

The mesh shown in Figure 19.10 was made using VMESHns and required 4 days to complete (geometry acquisition to completed mesh). The power of unstructured meshes is demonstrated with this case: there are 120,360 surface triangles on the SR-71 body but only 1029 triangles on the outer boundaries. The symmetry plane contained 50,179 triangles [935]. Figure 19.11 shows an unstructured mesh

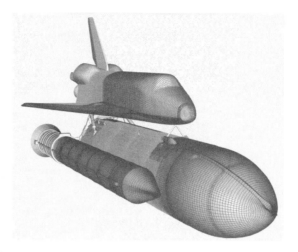

Figure 19.6 Chimera mesh system for space shuttle launch vehicle. (Figure courtesy of R. Gomez, NASA/Johnson Space Center [388].)

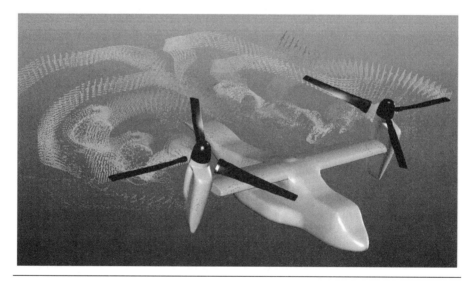

Figure 19.7 Particle trace on V22 Osprey blade-tip. (Courtesy, R. Meakin/NASA ARC [658].)

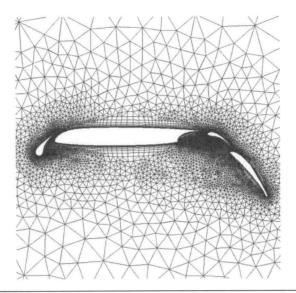

Figure 19.8   Hybrid mesh for a cross section of a wing configuration.

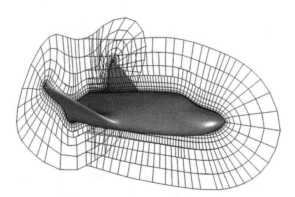

Figure 19.9   Generalized mesh for a space shuttle–like geometry.

generated using VMESHns that contains 6.62 million tetrahedral cells. The symmetry plane and a fuselage station are shown in Figure 19.11(a). Figure 19.11(b) shows the mesh clustering near the stores in carriage. Figure 19.11(c) is a close-up of the Joint Direct Attack Munition (JDAM); note the geometric complexities modeled including the strake and the notches in the strakes. Figure 19.11(c) also shows the surface triangulation on the JDAM, fuel tank, pylons, and part of the wing [934].

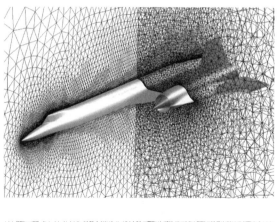

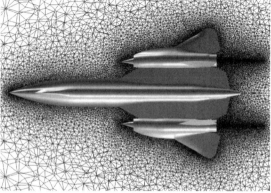

Figure 19.10 SR-71 mesh: unstructured mesh containing 6.99 million tetrahedra, approximately 4.2 million cells in the boundary layer. (Figure courtesy of Tomoro and Wurtzler [935].)

19.7 Mesh Web Sites

More information about mesh generation may be obtained from the following websites.

- International Society of Mesh Generation *http://www.isgg.org*
- Association of Computing Machinery *http://www.acm.org/*
- CFD Online *http://www.cfd-online.com/*
- Mesh and mesh generation on the Web *http://www-users.informatik.rwth-aachen .de/~roberts/meshgeneration.html*

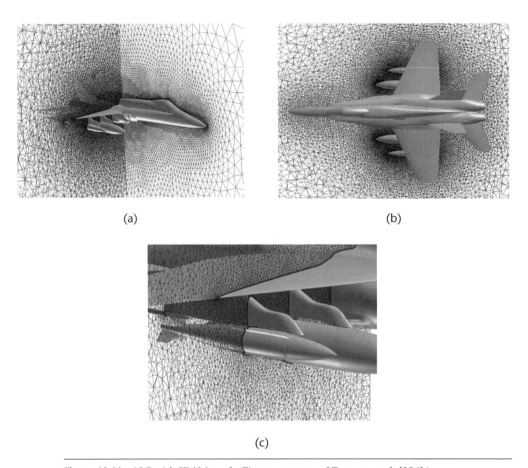

(a)   (b)

(c)

Figure 19.11   18C with JDAM mesh (Figure courtesy of Tomoro et al. [934].)

- Meshing Research Corner *http://www.andrew.cmu.edu/user/sowen/mesh.html*
- NASA's Steering Committee for Surface Modeling and Grid Generation *http://geolab.larc.nasa.gov/SMAGG/*
- Paul Heckbert's collection of mesh-generation links *http://almond.srv.cs.cmu.edu /afs/cs/user/ph/www/mesh.html*
- NSF Engineering Research Center for Computational Field Simulation *http://www.erc.msstate.edu*
- Numerical mesh generation—foundations and applications *http://www.erc .msstate.edu/publications/gridbook/*

19.8   The Pacing Obstacle: Geometry/Mesh Generation

Computational simulation in engineering analysis and design requires that the geometrical configuration be represented accurately by software. This representation must allow ease of modification in order to enable the simulation to function efficiently and effectively in multidisciplinary design optimization cycles. Also required is the efficient generation of a mesh covering surfaces and filling the volumetric regions to form the infrastructure on which the computational solution is accomplished. The representation of the geometrical configuration and the generation of the mesh are intimately coupled. This task continues to be the pacing item in the application of computational simulation in engineering analysis and design in industry—requiring too much person-time to produce the geometry/mesh for new or modified configurations and thus significantly delaying and lengthening the design process. In general, 80% to 90% of the mesh-generation labor is spent on the geometry preparation and surface mesh generation. In most CFS applications, these surfaces are defined in the CAD/CAM system as a composite of explicit or implicit analytical entities, semianalytical parametric entities, and/or a sculptured discrete set of points. The standard common interface for geometry exchange is IGES (International Graphics Exchange Standard), which is based on the curve and surface definition of geometric entities. These entities are not suitable for the treatment of trimmed curves, which widely appear in industrial CAD definitions. Research concentration has been placed in the past few years on using CAGD (computer-aided geometric design) techniques and NURBS (nonuniform rational B-splines) for modeling geometrical entities. NURBS allow a common data structure to represent all geometrical entities with various other (shape preserving, local control, convex hull, etc.) desirable properties. The CAD industry, however, is moving in the direction of using solid-modeling–based geometrical entities. A new international standard, STEP, is under development for solid modeling based on entities. The ultimate goal should be to develop mesh technology based on solid models. A multitude of general-purpose, mesh-generation codes to address complex structured–unstructured, mesh-generation needs are available in the public domain or as proprietary commercial codes. The mesh-generation strategies, especially in the structured–unstructured area, are well developed and validated. Rapid turnaround, geometric flexibility, accuracy, affordability, and robustness are the key requirements that must be addressed for CFS to play its rightful role in industrial multidisciplinary design environments. However, the present mesh-generation process needs to address various issues to fulfill these requirements. A chart representing these issues and their past, present, and future states with ultimate goals is presented in Figure 19.12.

The major concern is response time. In general, only for the simplest of configurations can a geometry be prepared and mesh be generated quickly or easily to fulfill industrial needs. The ultimate industrial goal [928] is to perform complex mesh generation in 1 hour and the entire field simulation in 1 day. Today, with a clean geometry definition in a desired format, a structured multiblock mesh (for a Navier–Stokes simulation) around complex aircraft can be developed within 2 to 3 weeks. An

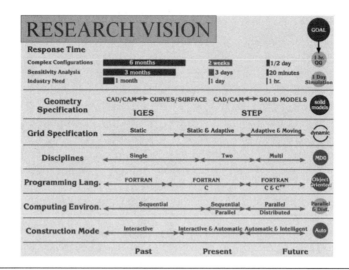

Figure 19.12   Mesh generation research vision.

unstructured mesh, however, can be developed in a day (for a Euler simulation) and a Cartesian mesh could be developed in a matter of hours (for a Euler simulation). The unstructured and Cartesian mesh strategies fulfill today's industrial need for Euler simulations. The demand for simulations in industry, however, is for complex turbulent Navier–Stokes models with chemical reactions and multiphase, multispecies physics that are provided by a simulation system allowing structured, multiblock meshes. The unstructured, Cartesian technology, in the context of field simulation, is still being developed for complex physics. The response time chart presents the average time required to perform mesh generation, sensitivity analysis (mesh generation with minor geometric-distribution perturbation), and the expectations of industry. In view of affordability and accuracy requirements, it is important to develop quality meshes based on field characteristics (adaptive meshes) and/or based on the movement of geometrical components in the field (moving meshes). There is an increasing demand for dynamic (adaptive/moving) meshes. The dynamic mesh algorithms, at present, are limited to simple configurations. Techniques are needed to enhance the applicability of adaptive schemes pertaining to complex configurations. The dynamic meshing capability, however, is inherent in the construction of unstructured and Cartesian meshes. The industrial environment is also rapidly moving into parallel/distributed computing with an object-oriented environment. CFS must play its role in this computing environment by contributing to industrial multidisciplinary design and analysis optimization (MDAO) applications. One goal for the mesh-generation community, with respect to MDAO applications, should be to develop algorithms for automatic and intelligent meshes (without visual interactions) for complex configurations. In spite of repeatedly citing the geometry/mesh problem by industry as continually being the major pacing item as the capability of computational simulation has advanced, this fundamental obstacle remains: cross-cutting applications in Departments of Defense and Energy, and industry in general. The geometry/mesh concerns have been less of a factor in many of the scientific Grand Challenges where the focus was more on complex physics than on complex geometry. In engineering analysis and design, however, geometry can be complex and is of overriding importance, and, thus, at the heart of the entire problem. The computational realization of geometrical representation and mesh generation may be said to be a major "engineering" Grand Challenge that has yet to be addressed adequately by any initiative, as well as a major obstacle impacting directly on both economic competitiveness and national security.

19.9   Desiderata

The major driving factors in comprehensive mesh-generation codes must first be automation and then graphical user interaction. Since design is the paramount application, the efficacy of a mesh code is measured primarily by the person-time it takes to generate a series of geometrically related meshes for complex configurations. The coupling with CAD systems on the front-end and with solution systems on the back-end must be seamless and effective. The ideal is not to make it easy for a person to generate a mesh but rather to remove the person from the process—that is, not to make it interactive, but to make it automatic. Present mesh-generation codes enable and rely on extensive graphical user interaction rather than automation; they require considerable user experience and effort. The goal of an automated mesh-generation system that will produce a suitable mesh with little user interaction and effort has not yet been achieved in any current code, commercial or freeware. Mesh-generation tools must be designed to be applied by design engineers rather than mesh-generation specialists. There is also the problem that the more powerful of these mesh codes now require considerable training and experience for effective use. This latter factor sometimes causes users to continue to use tools that are less powerful but familiar, rather than moving to newer and more effective tools.

Mesh-generation systems must be capable of handling large-scale variations, such as those occurring in high-Reynolds-number flow. This precludes any approach not encompassing large aspect-ratio cells with good numerical properties. There is a clear need for interaction with commercial CAD vendors.

CAD codes were developed before the onset of mesh-generation technology and widespread application. In order to become truly effective in multidisciplinary design optimization, CAD tools must be redesigned to target computational analysis as well as tooling and material formation. Additionally, there is the fact that comprehensive mesh codes are very large software systems; however, the real market is not yet large enough to encourage development to the extent that has been attained by commercial CAD systems. The development of an entirely new mesh code is a multiyear, multi-million-dollar effort. All of this argues for the creation of a toolbox or library for geometry/mesh generation: a set of interfacing components that are reliable and readily usable and that can be assembled to effectively and efficiently address the demands of different applications and different users of computational simulation for engineering analysis and design in DoD, DoE, and industry. This geometry/mesh toolkit/library should have the following characteristics:

- Object oriented for modularity
- Java-based for portability
- Scalable parallel operation
- Incorporation of existing useful components
- Extendable to incorporate emerging technology
- Automated operation, with user intervention
- User configurable for compatibility with applications
- Built-in, Web-based training facility and documentation

Further, it should incorporate the following features:

- Interface with CAD systems, solution systems, and visualization systems
- Internal CAD capability for geometry generation, repair, and modification
- Block-structured meshes, including overset and hybrid
- Unstructured meshes, both tetrahedral and hexahedral
- Surface and volume mesh systems
- Quality assessment, display, and control
- Dynamic adaptive coupling with solution systems
- Macros, editing, and script-based operation capability

The development of this geometry/mesh generation toolkit/library system should proceed as follows:

1. Establishment of a collaborative framework.
2. Definition of all needed capability, with DoD/DoE/industry users.
3. Encapsulation of all capability into components (objects/operations).
4. Identification of existing components.
5. Identification of components to be developed.
6. Design of library infrastructure and data structure.
7. Design of documentation and training structure.
8. Implementation.

19.10 Conclusion

A brief overview of mesh generation—an essential infrastructure element for CFS—is presented in this chapter. Static and dynamic mesh generation strategies and methodologies and their applicability to general CFS problems are discussed. Motivation for addressing very complex engineering Grand Challenge applications is developed in parallel mesh generation and mesh configurations discussions. Sections on mesh software and websites provide references for very useful mesh-related information. The characteristics and ingredients of the future information-technology–based, mesh-generation system are described. This chapter provides a very brief and concise description of the current state of the art and state of the practice in mesh generation.

20 Templates and Numerical Linear Algebra

Jack Dongarra • Victor Eijkhout •
Dan Sorensen

The increasing availability of advanced-architecture computers has a significant effect on all spheres of scientific computation, including algorithm research and software development in numerical linear algebra. Linear algebra—in particular, the solution of linear systems of equations—lies at the heart of most calculations in scientific computing. This chapter discusses some of the recent developments in linear algebra designed to exploit these advanced-architecture computers. We discuss two broad classes of algorithms: those for dense matrices and those for sparse matrices. A matrix is called sparse if it has a substantial number of zero elements, making specialized storage and algorithms necessary.

Much of the work in developing linear algebra software for advanced-architecture computers is motivated by the need to solve large problems on the fastest computers available. In this chapter, we focus on four basic issues: (1) motivation for the work; (2) development of standards for use in linear algebra and the building blocks for libraries; (3) aspects of algorithm design and parallel implementation; and (4) future directions for research.

As representative examples of dense matrix routines, we consider the Cholesky and LU factorizations; and these will be used to highlight the most important factors that must be considered in designing linear algebra software for advanced-architecture computers. We use these factorization routines for illustrative purposes not only because they are relatively simple, but also because of their importance in several scientific and engineering applications that make use of boundary element methods. These applications include electromagnetic scattering and computational fluid dynamics problems, as discussed in more detail in Section 20.1.2.

For the past 15 years or so, there has been a great deal of activity in the area of algorithms and software for solving linear algebra problems. The goal of achieving high performance on codes that are portable across platforms has largely been realized by the identification of linear algebra kernels, the Basic Linear Algebra Subprograms (BLAS). We will discuss the EISPACK, LINPACK, LAPACK, and ScaLAPACK libraries, which are expressed in successive levels of the BLAS.

The key insight of our approach to designing linear algebra algorithms for advanced-architecture computers is that the frequency with which data are moved between different levels of the memory hierarchy must be minimized in order to attain high performance. Thus, our main algorithmic approach for exploiting both vectorization and parallelism in our implementations is the use of block-partitioned algorithms, particularly in conjunction with highly tuned kernels for performing matrix–vector and matrix–matrix operations (Levels 2 and 3 of BLAS).

20.1   Dense Linear Algebra Algorithms

Common operations involving dense matrices are the solution of linear systems

$$Ax = b$$

the least-squares solution of over- or underdetermined systems

$$\min_x \|Ax - b\|$$

and the computation of eigenvalues and eigenvectors

$$Ax = \lambda x$$

Although these problems are formulated as matrix–vector equations, their solution involves a definite matrix–matrix component. For instance, in order to solve a linear system, the coefficient matrix is first factored as

$$A = LU$$

(or $A = U^t U$ in the case of symmetry) where L and U are lower and upper triangular matrices, respectively. It is a common feature of these matrix–matrix operations that they take, on a matrix of size $n \times n$, a number of operations proportional to n^3, a factor n more than the number of data elements involved.

Thus, we are led to identify three levels of linear algebra operations:

- *Level 1*. Vector–vector operations such as the update $\bar{y} \leftarrow \bar{y} + \alpha \bar{x}$ and the inner product $d = \bar{x}^t \bar{y}$. These operations involve (for vectors of length n) $\mathcal{O}(n)$ data and $\mathcal{O}(n)$ operations.

- *Level 2*. Matrix–vector operations such as the matrix–vector product $y = Ax$. These involve $\mathcal{O}(n^2)$ operations on $\mathcal{O}(n^2)$ data.

- *Level 3*. Matrix–matrix operations such as the matrix–matrix product $C = AB$. These involve $\mathcal{O}(n^3)$ operations on $\mathcal{O}(n^2)$ data.

These three levels of operations have been realized in a software standard known as the Basic Linear Algebra Subprograms (BLAS) [283, 284, 595]. Although BLAS routines are freely available on the Internet, many computer vendors supply a tuned, often assembly-coded, BLAS library optimized for their particular architectures. See also Section 20.3.1.

The relation between the number of operations and the amount of data is crucial for the performance of the algorithm. We discuss this in detail in Section 20.2.1.

20.1.1 Loop Rearranging

The operations of BLAS Levels 2 and 3 can be implemented using doubly and triply nested loops, respectively. With simple modifications, this means that for Level 2 each algorithm has two different implementations; for Level 3 there are six. For instance, solution of a lower triangular system $Lx = y$ is usually written

for $i = 1 \ldots n$
$\quad t = 0$
$\quad$ for $j = 1 \ldots i - 1$
$\quad\quad t \leftarrow t + \ell_{ij} x_j$
$\quad x = \ell_{ii}^{-1}(y_i - t)$

but can also be written as

for $j = 1 \ldots n$
$\quad x_j = \ell_{jj}^{-1} y_j$
$\quad$ for $i = j + 1 \ldots n$
$\quad\quad y_i \leftarrow y_i - \ell_{ij} x_j.$

(The latter implementation overwrites the right-hand-side vector y, but this can be eliminated.)

While the two implementations are equivalent in terms of numbers of operations, there may be substantial differences in performance due to architectural considerations. We note, for instance, that the inner loop in the first implementation uses a row of L, whereas the inner loop in the second traverses a column. Since matrices are usually stored with either rows or columns in contiguous locations, with column storage the historical default inherited from the Fortran programming language, the performance of the two can be radically different. We discuss this point further in Section 20.2.1.

20.1.2 Uses of LU Factorization in Science and Engineering

A major source of large dense linear systems is the collection of problems involving the solution of boundary integral equations. These are integral equations defined on the boundary of a region of interest. All examples of practical interest compute some intermediate quantity on a 2-D boundary and then use this information to compute the final desired quantity in 3-D space. The price one pays for replacing three dimensions with two is that the original sparse problem in $\mathcal{O}(n^3)$ variables is replaced by a dense problem in $\mathcal{O}(n^2)$.

Dense systems of linear equations are found in numerous applications, such as the following:

- Airplane wing design
- Radar cross-section studies
- Flow around ships and other offshore constructions
- Diffusion of solid bodies in a liquid
- Noise reduction
- Diffusion of light through small particles

The electromagnetics community is a major user of dense linear-system solvers. Of particular interest to this community is the solution of the so-called radar cross-section problem. In this problem, a signal of fixed frequency bounces off an object; the goal is to determine the intensity of the reflected signal in all possible directions. The underlying differential equation may vary, depending on the specific problem. In the design of stealth aircraft, the principal equation is the Helmholtz equation. To solve this equation, researchers use the *method of moments* [436, 977]. In the case of fluid flow, the problem often involves solving the Laplace or Poisson equation. Here, the boundary integral solution is known as the *panel method* [465, 466], so named from the quadrilaterals that discretize and approximate a structure such as an airplane. Generally, these methods are called *boundary element methods*.

Use of these methods produces a dense linear system of size $\mathcal{O}(N) \times \mathcal{O}(N)$, where N is the number of boundary points (or panels) being used. It is not unusual to see size $3N \times 3N$, representing three physical quantities of interest at every boundary element.

A typical approach to solving such systems is to use LU factorization. Each entry of the matrix is computed as an interaction of two boundary elements. Often, many integrals must be computed. In many instances, the time required to compute the matrix is considerably larger than the time for solution.

The builders of stealth technology who are interested in radar cross-sections are using direct Gaussian elimination methods for solving dense linear systems. These systems are always symmetric and complex, but they are not Hermitian.

For further information on various methods for solving large, dense, linear algebra problems that arise in computational fluid dynamics, see the report by Edelman [305].

20.1.3   Block Algorithms and Their Derivation

It is comparatively straightforward to recode many of the dense linear-algebra algorithms so that they use Level-2 BLAS. Indeed, in the simplest cases the same floating-point operations are done, possibly even in the same order: it is just a matter of reorganizing the software. To illustrate this point, we consider the Cholesky factorization algorithm, which factors a symmetric positive definite matrix as $A = U^T U$.

We consider Cholesky factorization because the algorithm is simple, and no pivoting is required on a positive definite matrix.

Suppose that after $j - 1$ steps the block A_{00} in the upper left corner of A has been factored as $A_{00} = U_{00}^T U_{00}$. The next row and column of the factorization can then be computed by writing $A = U^T U$ as

$$\begin{pmatrix} A_{00} & b_j & A_{02} \\ \cdot & a_{jj} & c_j^T \\ \cdot & \cdot & A_{22} \end{pmatrix} = \begin{pmatrix} U_{00}^T & 0 & 0 \\ v_j^T & u_{jj} & 0 \\ U_{02}^T & w_j & U_{22}^T \end{pmatrix} \begin{pmatrix} U_{00} & v_j & U_{02} \\ 0 & u_{jj} & w_j^T \\ 0 & 0 & U_{22} \end{pmatrix}$$

where b_j, c_j, v_j, and w_j are column vectors of length $j - 1$, and a_{jj} and u_{jj} are scalars. Equating coefficients of the jth column, we obtain

$$b_j = U_{00}^T v_j$$

$$a_{jj} = v_j^T v_j + u_{jj}^2$$

Since U_{00} has already been computed, we can compute v_j and u_{jj} from the equations

$$U_{00}^T v_j = b_j$$

$$u_{jj}^2 = a_{jj} - v_j^T v_j$$

The computation of v_j is a triangular system solution, a Level-2 BLAS operation. Thus, a code using this will have a single call replacing a loop of Level 1 calls or a doubly nested loop of scalar operations.

This change by itself is sufficient to result in large gains in performance on a number of machines—for example, from 72 to 251 Megaflops for a matrix of order 500 on one processor of a CRAY Y-MP. Since this is 81% of the peak speed of matrix–matrix multiplication on this processor, we cannot hope to do very much better by using Level-3 BLAS.

We can, however, restructure the algorithm at a deeper level to exploit the faster speed of the Level-3 BLAS. This restructuring involves recasting the algorithm as a *block algorithm*—that is, an algorithm that operates on *blocks* or submatrices of the original matrix.

Deriving a Block Algorithm

To derive a block form of Cholesky factorization, we partition the matrices so that the diagonal blocks of A and U are square, but of differing sizes. We assume that the first block has already been factored as $A_{00} = U_{00}^T U_{00}$ and that we now want to determine the second block column of U, consisting of the blocks U_{01} and U_{11}:

$$\begin{pmatrix} A_{00} & A_{01} & A_{02} \\ \cdot & A_{11} & A_{12} \\ \cdot & \cdot & A_{22} \end{pmatrix} = \begin{pmatrix} U_{00}^T & 0 & 0 \\ U_{01}^T & U_{11}^T & 0 \\ U_{02}^T & U_{12}^T & U_{22}^T \end{pmatrix} \begin{pmatrix} U_{00} & U_{01} & U_{02} \\ 0 & U_{11} & U_{12} \\ 0 & 0 & U_{22} \end{pmatrix}$$

Equating submatrices in the second block of columns, we obtain

$$A_{01} = U_{00}^T U_{01}$$

$$A_{11} = U_{01}^T U_{01} + U_{11}^T U_{11}$$

Hence, since U_{00} has already been computed, we can compute U_{01} as the solution to the equation

$$U_{00}^T U_{01} = A_{01}$$

by a call to the Level-3 BLAS routine STRSM; and then we can compute U_{11} from

$$U_{11}^T U_{11} = A_{11} - U_{01}^T U_{01}$$

This involves first updating the symmetric submatrix A_{11} by a call to the Level-3 BLAS routine SSYRK and then computing its Cholesky factorization. Since Fortran does not allow recursion, a separate routine must be called, using Level-2 BLAS rather than Level 3. In this way, successive blocks of columns of U are computed.

20.2   The Influence of Computer Architecture on Performance

Differences in computer architecture can markedly affect the performance of software for the solution of systems of linear equations. In this section, we introduce the architectural features that influence the choice of algorithm and suggest some simple implementation strategies for obtaining the best performance on the target architecture.

20.2.1   Discussion of Architectural Features

In Section 20.1.1 we noted that for BLAS Levels 2 and 3 several equivalent implementations of the operations exist. These differ, for instance, in whether they access a matrix operand by rows or columns in the inner loop. In Fortran, matrices are stored by columns, so accessing a column corresponds to accessing consecutive memory elements. On the other hand, as one proceeds across a row, the memory references jump across memory, the length of the jump being proportional to the length of a column.

We now provide a simplified discussion of the various architectural issues that influence the choice of algorithm. The following is, of necessity, a simplified account of the state of affairs for any particular architecture.

At first, we concentrate only on "nonblocked" algorithms. In blocked methods, discussed in more detail below, every algorithm has two levels on which we can consider loop arranging: the block level and the scalar level. Often, the best arrangement on one level is not the best on the other. The next two subsections are focused on the scalar level.

Using Consecutive Elements

Matrix elements should be traversed in a way that accesses elements that are consecutive in storage. There are at least three architectural reasons for this.

Page swapping.   By using consecutive memory elements, instead of elements at some stride distance from each other, the amount of memory-page swapping is minimized.

Memory banks.   If the processor cycle is faster than the memory cycle, and memory consists of interleaved banks, consecutive elements will be in different banks. By contrast, taking elements separated by a distance equal to the number of banks, all elements will come from the same bank. This will reduce the effective performance of the algorithm to the memory speed instead of the processor speed.

Cache lines.   Processors with a memory cache typically do not bring in single elements from memory to cache, but move them one "cache line" at a time. A cache line consists of a small number of consecutive memory elements. Thus, using consecutive memory-storage elements means that a next element will already be in cache and does not have to be brought into cache. This cuts down on memory traffic.

Whether consecutive elements correspond to rows or columns in a matrix depends on the programming language used. In Fortran, columns are stored consecutively, whereas C has row elements contiguous in memory.

The effects of column orientation are quite dramatic: on systems with virtual or cache memories, the LINPACK library codes (Section 20.3.2), which are written in Fortran and are column oriented, will significantly outperform Fortran codes that are not column oriented. In the C language, however, algorithms should be formulated with row orientation. We note that textbook examples of matrix algorithms are usually given in a row-oriented manner.

Cache Reuse

In many contemporary architectures, memory bandwidth is not enough to keep the processor working at its peak rate. Therefore, the architecture incorporates some cache memory, a relatively small store of faster memory. The memory-bandwidth problem is now shifted to bringing the elements into cache, and this problem can be obviated almost entirely if the algorithm can reuse cache elements.

Consider, for instance, a matrix–vector product $y = Ax$. The doubly nested loop has an inner statement

$$y_i \leftarrow y_i + a_{ij} x_j$$

implying three reads and one write from memory for two operations. If we write the algorithm as

$$y_* = x_1 a_{1*} + x_2 a_{2*} + \cdots$$

we see that, keeping y in cache[1] and reusing the elements of x, we only need to load the column of A, making the asymptotic demand on memory one element load once x and y have been brought into cache.

Blocking for Cache Reuse

Above, we saw in the Cholesky example how algorithms can be written naturally in terms of Level-2 operations. In order to use Level-3 operations, a more drastic rewrite is needed.

Suppose we want to perform the matrix–matrix multiplication $C = AB$, where all matrices are of size $n \times n$. We divide all matrices into subblocks of size $b \times b$, and let for simplicity's sake b divide n: $n = bm$. Then the triply nested scalar loop becomes, in one possible rearrangement

for $i = 1 \ldots m$
    for $k = 1 \ldots m$
        for $j = 1 \ldots m$
            $C_{ij} \leftarrow C_{ij} + A_{ik}B_{kj}$

where the inner statement is now a size b matrix–matrix multiplication.

If the cache is large enough for three of these smaller matrices, we can keep C_{ij} and A_{ik} in cache,[2] while successive blocks B_{kj} are being brought in. The ratio of memory loads to operations is then (ignoring the loads of the elements of C and A, which are amortized) b^2/b^3, that is, $1/b$.

Thus, by blocking the algorithm and arranging the loops so that blocks are reused in cache, we can achieve high performance in spite of a low memory bandwidth. We often see as much as an order of magnitude increase in performance by using these techniques.

20.2.2   Target Architectures

The EISPACK and LINPACK software libraries were designed for supercomputers used in the 1970s and early 1980s, such as the CDC-7600, Cyber 205, and Cray-1. These machines featured multiple functional units pipelined for good performance [480]. The CDC-7600 was basically a high-performance scalar computer, while the Cyber 205 and Cray-1 were early vector computers.

The development of LAPACK in the late 1980s was intended to make the EISPACK and LINPACK libraries run efficiently on shared-memory, vector supercomputers. The ScaLAPACK software library, first released in 1995, extends the use of LAPACK to distributed-memory concurrent supercomputers.

---

[1] Since many Level-1 caches are write-through, immediately writing the information to memory, we wouldn't actually keep y in cache, but rather would keep a number of elements of it in register and reuse these registers by unrolling the $*$ loop.
[2] Again, with a write-through Level-1 cache, one would try to keep C_{ij} in registers.

The underlying concept of both the LAPACK and ScaLAPACK libraries is the use of block-partitioned algorithms to minimize data movement among different levels in hierarchical memory. Thus, the ideas discussed in this chapter for developing a library for dense linear algebra computations are applicable to any computer with a hierarchical memory that (1) imposes a sufficiently large start-up cost on the movement of data between different levels in the hierarchy, and for which (2) the cost of a context switch is too great to make fine-grain-size multithreading worthwhile. Our target machines are, therefore, medium- and large-grain-size, advanced-architecture computers. These include "traditional" shared-memory, vector supercomputers, such as the Cray C-90 and T-90, and MIMD distributed-memory concurrent supercomputers, such as the SGI Origin 2000, IBM SP, Cray T3E, and HP/Convex Exemplar concurrent systems.

Future advances in compiler and hardware technologies are expected to make multithreading a viable approach for masking communication costs. Since the blocks in a block-partitioned algorithm can be regarded as separate threads, our approach will still be applicable on machines that exploit medium- and coarse-grain-size multithreading.

20.3 Dense Linear Algebra Libraries

In this section, we discuss four well-known linear algebra packages: LINPACK, EISPACK, LAPACK, and ScaLAPACK. All of these employ the basic linear algebra subprograms (BLAS) to enhance performance and portability across a variety of machines.

20.3.1 The BLAS as the Key to Portability

At least three factors affect the performance of compilable code.

1. *Vectorization/cache reuse.* Designing vectorizable algorithms in linear algebra is usually straightforward. Indeed, for many computations there are several variants, all vectorizable, but with different characteristics in performance (see, for example, Dongarra [280]). Linear algebra algorithms can approach the peak performance of many machines—principally because peak performance depends on some form of chaining of vector addition and multiplication operations or cache reuse, and this is just what the algorithms require. However, when the algorithms are realized in straightforward Fortran 77 or C code, the performance may fall well short of the expected level, usually because Fortran compilers fail to minimize the number of memory references—that is, the number of vector load and store operations—or effectively reuse cache.

2. *Data movement.* What often limits the actual performance of a vector or scalar floating-point unit is the rate of transfer of data between different levels of memory in the machine. Examples include the transfer of vector operands in and out of vector registers, the transfer of scalar operands in and out of a high-

speed cache, the movement of data between main memory and a high-speed cache or local memory, paging between actual memory and disk storage in a virtual-memory system, and interprocessor communication on a distributed-memory concurrent computer.

3. *Parallelism.* The nested loop structure of most linear algebra algorithms offers considerable scope for loop-based parallelism. This is the principal type of parallelism that LAPACK and ScaLAPACK presently aim to exploit. On shared-memory concurrent computers, this type of parallelism can sometimes be generated automatically by a compiler, but it often requires the insertion of compiler directives. On distributed-memory concurrent computers, data must be moved between processors. This is usually done by explicit calls to message-passing routines, although parallel language extensions, such as Coherent Parallel C [323] and Split-C [235] do the message passing implicitly.

These issues can be controlled, while obtaining the levels of performance that machines can offer, through use of the BLAS, introduced in Section 20.1.

The Level-1 BLAS are used in LAPACK, but for convenience rather than for performance: they perform an insignificant fraction of the computation, and they cannot achieve high efficiency on most modern supercomputers. Also, the overhead entailed in calling the BLAS reduces the efficiency of the code. This reduction is negligible for large matrices, but it can be quite significant for small matrices. Fortunately, the Level-1 BLAS can be removed from the smaller, more frequently used LAPACK codes in a short editing session.

The Level-2 BLAS can achieve near-peak performance on many vector processors, such as a single processor of a CRAY X-MP or Y-MP, or Convex C-2 machine. However, on other vector processors such as a CRAY-2 or an IBM 3090 VF, the performance of the Level-2 BLAS is limited by the rate of data movement between different levels of memory.

The Level-3 BLAS have overcome this limitation. This third level of BLAS performs $\mathcal{O}(n^3)$ floating-point operations on $\mathcal{O}(n^2)$ data, whereas the Level-2 BLAS perform only $\mathcal{O}(n^2)$ operations on $\mathcal{O}(n^2)$ data. The Level-3 BLAS also allow us to exploit parallelism in a way that is transparent to the software that calls them. While the Level-2 BLAS offer some scope for exploiting parallelism, greater scope is provided by the Level-3 BLAS, as Table 20.1 illustrates.

The BLAS can provide portable high performance through being a standard that is available on many platforms. Ideally, the computer manufacturer has provided an assembly-coded BLAS tuned for that particular architecture, but there is a standard implementation available that can simply be compiled and linked. Using this standard, BLAS may improve the efficiency of programs when they are run on non-optimizing compilers. This is because doubly subscripted array references in the inner loop of the algorithm are replaced by singly subscripted array references in the appropriate BLAS. The effect can be seen for matrices of rather small order, and for large orders the savings are quite significant.

Table 20.1 Speed in Mflop/s of Level-2 and Level-3 BLAS operations on a CRAY C90

Number of processors	1	2	4	8	16
Level 2: $y \leftarrow \alpha Ax + \beta y$	899	1780	3491	6783	11207
Level 3: $C \leftarrow \alpha AB + \beta C$	900	1800	3600	7199	14282
Level 2: $x \leftarrow Ux$	852	1620	3063	5554	6953
Level 3: $B \leftarrow UB$	900	1800	3574	7147	13281
Level 2: $x \leftarrow U^{-1}x$	802	1065	1452	1697	1558
Level 3: $B \leftarrow U^{-1}B$	896	1792	3578	7155	14009

NOTE: All matrices are of order 1000; U is upper triangular.

Today's microprocessors have peak execution rates ranging from 300 Mflop/s to 1.2 Gflop/s. However, straightforward implementation in Fortran or C of computations based on simple loops rarely results in such high performance. To realize such peak rates of execution for even the simplest of operations has required tedious, hand-coded, programming efforts.

Since their inception, the use of de facto standards like the BLAS [283, 284] has been a means of achieving portability and efficiency for a wide range of kernel scientific computations. While these BLAS are used heavily in linear algebra computations, such as solving dense systems of equations, they have also found their way into the basic computing infrastructure of many applications. The BLAS are high-quality, "building-block" routines for performing basic vector and matrix operations. Level-1 BLAS do vector–vector operations, Level-2 BLAS do matrix–vector operations, and Level-3 BLAS do matrix–matrix operations. Because the BLAS are efficient, portable, and widely available, they are commonly used in the development of high-quality linear algebra software, such as LAPACK [34] and ScaLA-PACK [119].

In general, the existing BLAS have proven to be very effective in facilitating the production of portable, efficient software for sequential, vector, and shared-memory, high-performance computers. However, hand-optimized BLAS are expensive and tedious to produce for any particular architecture. In general, they will only be created when there is a large enough market, which is not true for all platforms. The process of generating an optimized set of BLAS for a new architecture or a slightly different machine version can be a time-consuming process. The programmer must understand the architecture, how the memory hierarchy can be used to provide data in an optimal fashion, how the functional units and registers can be manipulated to generate the correct operands at the correct time, and how best to use the compiler optimization. Care must be taken to optimize the operations to account for many parameters such as blocking factors, loop unrolling depths, software pipelining strategies, loop ordering, register allocations, and instruction scheduling.

A goal is to develop a methodology for automatic generation of highly efficient, basic linear algebra routines for today's microprocessors. In particular, the present effort is targeted for platforms possessing an on-chip cache and a reasonable C compiler. One approach, called *automatically tuned linear algebra software* (ATLAS), has been able to match or exceed the performance of the vendor-supplied version of matrix multiply in almost every case.

Atlas Approach

This section describes a general methodology that may be used to support the Level-3 BLAS. For the moment, consider the operation matrix multiply, which can be described as $C \leftarrow \alpha\, op(A)op(B) + \beta C$, where $op(X) = X$ or X^T. C is an $M \times N$ matrix, and A and B are matrices of size $M \times K$ and $K \times N$, respectively.

In the ATLAS approach, the machine-specific features of the operation to several routines, all of which deal with performing an optimized, on-chip (i.e., in level-1 cache), matrix multiply of the form $C \leftarrow A^T B + C$, are isolated. This section of code is automatically created by a code generator that uses timings to determine the correct blocking and loop-unrolling factors to perform an optimized on-chip multiply. The user may supply the code generator with as much detail as desired (i.e., the user may explicitly indicate the level-1 cache size, the blocking factor(s) to try, etc.); if such details are not provided, the generator will determine appropriate settings via timings.

The rest of the code does not change across architectures (other than perhaps including preprocessor information discovered by the code generator), and handles blocking for higher-level caches (if any) and the necessary overhead required to build the complete matrix–matrix multiply from the on-chip multiply.

At this point, we consider how the general method outlined in this section can be extended to other BLAS. All Level-3 BLAS can naturally be expressed in terms of the previously mentioned on-chip matrix multiply. This means that no more system-specific code must be generated to support these routines, which in turn implies that our installation time should not increase when these additional BLAS are supported. Support of these routines should require only the development of the off-chip codes. In the meantime, a gemm-based or "poor-man's BLAS" [529] may be utilized in order to generate a wider set of Level-3 BLAS.

The Level-1 and Level-2 BLAS require a different approach. In Level 3, the luxury of $\mathcal{O}(N^3)$ operations allows us to perform data copies, thereby concentrating most optimization, and thus system-specific code, in a few routines. When the order of operations to be done is the same as the data, this is not feasible. This means that code must be directly generated for each transpose case, for instance (since we can no longer coerce all transpose settings to one with a data copy). This turns out not to be too burdensome, since Level-2 BLAS routines are relatively simple compared to those of Level 3.

20.3.2   Overview of Dense Linear Algebra Libraries

Over the past 25 years, we have been directly involved in the development of several important packages of dense linear algebra software: EISPACK, LINPACK, LAPACK, and the BLAS. In addition, we are currently involved in the development of ScaLAPACK, a scalable version of LAPACK for distributed-memory concurrent computers. In this section, we give a brief review of these packages—their history, advantages, and limitations on high-performance computers.

EISPACK

EISPACK is a collection of Fortran subroutines that compute the eigenvalues and eigenvectors of nine classes of matrices: complex general, complex Hermitian, real general, real symmetric, real symmetric banded, real symmetric tridiagonal, special real tridiagonal, generalized real, and generalized real symmetric matrices. In addition, two routines are included that use singular value decomposition to solve certain least-squares problems.

EISPACK is primarily based on a collection of Algol procedures developed in the 1960s and collected by J. H. Wilkinson and C. Reinsch in a volume entitled *Linear Algebra* in the *Handbook for Automatic Computation* [995] series. This volume was not designed to cover every possible method of solution; rather, algorithms were chosen on the basis of their generality, elegance, accuracy, speed, or economy of storage.

Since the release of EISPACK in 1972, over 10,000 copies of the collection have been distributed worldwide.

LINPACK

LINPACK is a collection of Fortran subroutines that analyze and solve linear equations and linear least-squares problems. The package solves linear systems whose matrices are general, banded, symmetric indefinite, symmetric positive definite, triangular, and tridiagonal square. In addition, the package computes the QR and singular value decompositions of rectangular matrices and applies them to least-squares problems.

LINPACK is organized around four matrix factorizations: LU factorization, pivoted Cholesky factorization, QR factorization, and singular value decomposition. The term *LU factorization* is used here in a very general sense to mean the factorization of a square matrix into a lower triangular part and an upper triangular part, perhaps with pivoting. These factorizations will be treated at greater length later, when the actual LINPACK subroutines are discussed. But first, a digression on organization and factors influencing LINPACK's efficiency is necessary.

LINPACK uses column-oriented algorithms to increase efficiency by preserving locality of reference. By column orientation we mean that the LINPACK codes always reference arrays down columns, not across rows. This works because Fortran stores arrays in column-major order. This means that as one proceeds down a column of an array, the memory references proceed sequentially in memory. Thus, if a program references an item in a particular block, the next reference is likely to be in the same block. For further information, see Section 20.2.1.

LINPACK uses the Level-1 BLAS; see Section 20.3.1.

LAPACK

LAPACK [254] provides routines for solving systems of simultaneous linear equations, linear least-squares problems, eigenvalue problems, and singular value problems. The associated matrix factorizations (LU, Cholesky, QR, SVD, Schur, generalized Schur) are also provided, as are related computations, such as reordering of the Schur factorizations and estimating condition numbers. Dense and banded matrices are handled, but not general sparse matrices. In all areas, similar functionality is provided for real and complex matrices, in both single and double precision.

The original goal of the LAPACK project was to make the widely used EISPACK and LINPACK libraries run efficiently on shared-memory vector and parallel processors. On these machines, LINPACK and EISPACK are inefficient because their memory access patterns disregard the multilayered memory hierarchies of the machines, thereby spending too much time moving data instead of doing useful floating-point operations. LAPACK addresses this problem by reorganizing the algorithms to use block matrix operations, such as matrix multiplication, in the innermost loops [37, 254]. These block operations can be optimized for each architecture to account for the memory hierarchy [36], and so provide a transportable way to achieve high efficiency on diverse modern machines. Here we use the term "transportable" instead of "portable" because, for fastest possible performance, LAPACK requires that highly optimized, block matrix operations be already implemented on each machine. In other words, the correctness of the code is portable, but high performance is not—if we limit ourselves to a single Fortran source code.

LAPACK can be regarded as a successor to LINPACK and EISPACK. It has virtually all the capabilities of these two packages and many more besides. LAPACK improves on LINPACK and EISPACK in four main respects: speed, accuracy, robustness, and functionality. While LINPACK and EISPACK are based on the vector operation kernels of the Level-1 BLAS, LAPACK was designed at the outset to exploit the Level-3 BLAS—a set of specifications for Fortran subprograms that do various types of matrix multiplication and the solution of triangular systems with multiple right-hand sides. Because of the coarse granularity of the Level-3 BLAS operations, their use tends to promote high efficiency on many high-performance computers, particularly if specially coded implementations are provided by the manufacturer.

LAPACK is designed to give high efficiency on vector processors, high-performance "superscalar" workstations, and shared-memory multiprocessors. LAPACK in its present form is less likely to give good performance on other types of parallel architectures (e.g., massively parallel SIMD machines, or MIMD distributed-memory machines), but the ScaLAPACK project, described in Section 20.3.2, is intended to adapt LAPACK to these new architectures. LAPACK can also be used satisfactorily on all types of scalar machines (PCs, workstations, mainframes).

LAPACK, like LINPACK, provides LU and Cholesky factorizations of band matrices. The LINPACK algorithms can easily be restructured to use Level-2 BLAS, although restructuring has little effect on performance for matrices of very narrow bandwidth. It is also possible to use Level-3 BLAS, at the price of doing some extra work with zero elements outside the band [286]. This process becomes worthwhile for large matrices and semibandwidth greater than 100 or so.

ScaLAPACK

The ScaLAPACK software library extends the LAPACK library to run scalably on MIMD, distributed-memory, concurrent computers [199, 200]. For such machines the memory hierarchy includes the off-processor memory of other processors, in addition to the hierarchy of registers, cache, and local memory on each processor. Like LAPACK, the ScaLAPACK routines are based on block-partitioned algorithms in order to minimize the frequency of data movement between different levels of the memory hierarchy. The fundamental building blocks of the ScaLAPACK library are distributed-memory versions of the Level-2 and Level-3 BLAS, and a set of Basic Linear Algebra Communication Subprograms (BLACS) [281, 289] for communication tasks that arise frequently in parallel linear-algebra computations. In the ScaLAPACK routines, all interprocessor communication occurs within the distributed BLAS and the BLACS, so the source code of the top software layer of ScaLAPACK looks very similar to that of LAPACK.

We envisage a number of user interfaces to ScaLAPACK. Initially, the interface will be similar to that of LAPACK, with some additional arguments passed to each routine to specify the data layout. Once this is in place, we intend to modify the interface so that the arguments to each ScaLAPACK routine are the same as in LAPACK. This will require information about the data distribution of each matrix and vector to be hidden from the user. This may be done by means of a ScaLAPACK initialization routine. This interface will be fully compatible with LAPACK. Provided "dummy" versions of the ScaLAPACK initialization routine and the BLACS are added to LAPACK, there will be no distinction between LAPACK and ScaLAPACK at the application level, although each will link to different versions of the BLAS and BLACS. Following on from this, we will experiment with object-based interfaces for LAPACK and ScaLAPACK, with the goal of developing interfaces compatible with Fortran 90 [199], and C++ [288].

20.3.3 Available Software

Table 20.2 lists the characteristics of software packages implementing algorithms for the solutions to dense linear algebra problems. Each of these packages is available from Netlib (*http://www.netlib.org*).

Table 20.2 Available dense linear algebra software.

Package	Language binding	Type	Sequential	Parallel
BLAS[1]	Fortran and C	Real and complex	Sequential	
ATLAS[2]	Fortran and C	Real and complex	Sequential	Threaded
LAPACK[3]	Fortran and C	Real and complex	Sequential	
ScaLAPACK[4]	Fortran and C	Real and complex		MPI

NOTE: URLs for the packages discussed in the table:
1. *http://www.netlib.org/blas/*
2. *http://www.netlib.org/atlas/*
3. *http://www.netlib.org/lapack/*
4. *http://www.netlib.org/scalapack/*

20.4   Sparse Linear Algebra Methods

A system of linear equations is called sparse if its coefficient matrix contains a substantial number of zero elements. Such systems arise naturally in mathematical models of many physical problems of interest. Linear algebra algorithms can be designed to take advantage of this special structure, allowing very large problems to be solved efficiently.

20.4.1   Origin of Sparse Linear Systems

The most common source of sparse linear systems is the numerical solution of partial differential equations (PDEs). Many physical problems, such as fluid flow or elasticity, can be described by partial differential equations. These are implicit descriptions of a physical model, describing some internal relation such as stress forces. In order to arrive at an explicit description of the shape of the object or the temperature distribution, we need to solve the PDE, and for this we need numerical methods.

Discretized Partial Differential Equations

Several methods for the numerical solution of PDEs exist, the most common ones being the methods of finite elements, finite differences, and finite volumes. A common feature of these is that they identify discrete points in the physical object and yield a set of equations relating these points.

Typically, only points that are physically close together are related to each other in this way. This gives a matrix structure with very few nonzero elements per row, and the nonzeros are often confined to a "band" in the matrix.

Sparse Matrix Structure

Matrices from discretized partial differential equations contain so many zero elements that it pays to find a storage structure that avoids storing these zeros. The resulting memory savings, however, are offset by an increase in programming complexity and by decreased efficiency of even simple operations, such as the matrix–vector product.

More complicated operations, such as solving a linear system, with such a sparse matrix present the next level of complication. Neither the inverse nor the LU factorization of a sparse matrix is as sparse as the original and needs considerably more storage. Specifically, the inverse of the type of sparse matrix we are considering is a full matrix, and factoring such a sparse matrix fills in the band completely. An example follows: Central differences in d dimensions, n points per line, matrix size $N = n^d$, bandwidth $q = n^{d-1}$ in natural ordering, number of nonzero $\sim n^d$, and number of matrix elements $N^2 = n^{2d}$, number of elements in factorization $N^{1+(d-1)/d}$.

20.4.2 Basic Elements in Sparse Linear Algebra Methods

Methods for sparse systems use, like those for dense systems, vector–vector, matrix–vector, and matrix–matrix operations. However, there are some important differences.

For iterative methods, discussed in section 20.6, there are almost no matrix–matrix operations. See Jones and Plassmann [519] for an exception. Since most modern architectures prefer these Level-3 operations, the performance of iterative methods will be limited from the outset.

An even more serious objection is that the sparsity of the matrix implies that indirect addressing is used for retrieving elements. For example, in the popular row-compressed matrix storage format, the matrix–vector multiplication looks like this:

for $i = 1 \ldots n$
    $p \leftarrow$ pointer to row i
    for $j = 1, n_i$
        $y_i \leftarrow y_i + a(p+j)x(c(p+j))$

where n_i is the number of nonzeros in row i, and $p(\cdot)$ is an array of column indices. A number of such algorithms for several sparse data formats are given in Barrett et al. [81].

Direct methods can have a Level-3 BLAS component if they are a type of dissection method. However, in a given sparse problem, the more dense the matrices are, the smaller they are on average. They are also not general full matrices, but only banded. Thus, we don't expect very high performance on such methods either.

20.5 Direct Solution Methods

One way of solving a linear system is to factor the coefficient matrix by a direct method, that is, by some variant of Gaussian elimination. As remarked above, for a sparse matrix, this fills in many elements in the band in which the nonzero elements are contained. In order to minimize the storage needed for the factorization, research has focused on finding suitable orderings of the matrix.

There are several issues to be distinguished here:

- For a symmetric, positive-definite matrix, we know that the pivots can be found on the diagonal, so we can limit ourselves to symmetric permutations (i.e., $P^t A P$) performed solely for reduction of the fill-in.

- In general, a factorization will have to perform pivoting for numerical stability, in addition to the symmetric permutations for fill reduction. A two-part approach is popular (used in such packages as SuperLU [612]) where the matrix is first ordered, using for instance a multiple minimum-degree ordering, but during the factorization additional row permutations may be performed for partial pivoting in the pivot column.

- Given a permutation of the matrix, there are still several factorization algorithms possible. The choice among them is dictated by performance considerations. Many packages these days focus on finding applications for Level-3 BLAS kernels in the factorization phase.

20.5.1   Matrix Orderings

The most convenient way of talking about matrix orderings or permutations is to consider the matrix "graph" [752]. (See Chapter 18 for additional information on matrix ordering and graph partitioning.) We introduce a node for every physical variable, and nodes i and j are connected in the graph if the (i, j) element of the matrix is nonzero. A symmetric permutation of the matrix then corresponds to a numbering of the nodes, while the connections stay the same. With these permutations, one hopes to reduce the "bandwidth" of the matrix, and thereby the amount of fill generated by the factorization.

Cuthill–McKee Ordering

A popular ordering strategy is the Cuthill–McKee ordering, which finds levels or wavefronts in the matrix graph. This algorithm is easily described:

1. Take any node as starting point, and call that "level 0."
2. Now successively take all nodes connected to the previous level, and group them into the next level.
3. Iterate until all nodes are grouped into some level; the numbering inside each level is of secondary importance.

This ordering strategy often gives a smaller bandwidth than the natural ordering, and there are further advantages to having a level structure (e.g., for out-of-core solution or for parallel processing). Often, one uses the "reverse Cuthill–McKee" orderings [622].

Cuthill–McKee orderings reduce bandwidth, but do not in general reduce fill-in by any substantial amount. However, there is value in the observation that any level works as a separator between two domain halves. This fact was used in SDCpack [789].

Minimum Degree

An explicit reduction of bandwidth is effected by the minimum-degree ordering, which at any point in the factorization chooses the variable with the smallest number of connections. More sophisticated strategies use *minimum deficiency:* they choose the pivot that will add the lowest number of fills. Since the pivot choice is usually not unique, factors such as the size of the resulting fill-in are used as a tiebreaker.

Minimum-degree methods can be made parallel by having multiple eligible pivots be processed in parallel. This method is called the *multiple minimum-degree* ordering.

Nested Dissection

Instead of trying to minimize fill-in by reducing the bandwidth, one could try a direct approach. The *nested-dissection* ordering recursively splits the matrix graph in two, thus separating it into disjoint subgraphs. Somewhat more precisely, given a graph, this algorithm relies on the existence of a *separator,* that is, a set of nodes such that the other nodes fall into two mutually unconnected subgraphs. The fill from factoring these subgraphs before factoring the separator is likely to be lower than for other orderings.

For PDEs in 2-D, this method can be shown to have a storage requirement that is within a log-factor of that for the matrix itself; that is, it is very close to optimal [374]. This proof is easy for PDEs on rectangular grids, and with enough graph theory it can be generalized [618, 620]. However, for problems in 3-D, the nested dissection method is no longer optimal.

An advantage of dissection-type methods is that they lead to large numbers of uncoupled matrix problems. Thus, to an extent, parallelization of such methods is easy. However, the higher levels in the tree quickly have fewer nodes than the number of available processors. In addition to this, they are also the larger subproblems in the algorithm, thereby complicating the parallelization of the method.

Another practical issue is the choice of the separator set. In a model case this is trivial, but in practice, and in particular in parallel, this is a serious problem, since the balancing of the two resulting subgraphs depends on this choice.

Recently, methods based on the *Fiedler vector,* the eigenvector of the second-smallest eigenvalue of a singular M-matrix based on the matrix graph, have become popular for this [774]. Such methods are based on the fact that this eigenvector is zero on a "line" through the domain. This line gives a separator for two halves of the domain. This method is known as *spectral bisection.*

Finding the Fiedler vector can be done in parallel, by performing a Lanczos iteration process. However, the accuracy of solution is critical in finding a separator that properly balances the domain halves. Thus, for large systems and for finding multiple separators, the cost of this stage can become quite high. For such reasons, hybrid methods are becoming popular. A small number of separators is found, and then a multiple minimum-degree ordering takes over on the subdomains.

Multifrontal Factorization of a Sparse Matrix

The multifrontal method, proposed in Duff and Reid [298], forms a tree of multiple fronts—that is, nodes allowing simultaneous, independent elimination. Proceeding from one node to the nodes connected to it gives a *front* and a frontal matrix. Frontal matrices quickly become dense, so high performance can be reached handling them.

20.5.2   Use of Level-3 BLAS Kernels

It is generally recognized that high performance results mostly from the use of Level-3 BLAS kernels, specifically the matrix–matrix multiply. Through their reuse of cached data, these kernels mask the gap between high processor speed and lower bandwidth to memory. In order for them to be applicable, dense subblocks have to be found in the factorization.

First, any *clique* of nodes (i.e., a fully connected group of nodes) can be permuted so that the matrix shows a dense diagonal block.

Second, recent efforts have focused on more general *supernodal* techniques. These identify blocks of columns that have an identical nonzero structure. In a left-looking factorization, one could then let supernodes in the already factored columns update supernodes in the destination columns, thus enabling the use of Level-2 BLAS kernels, instead of (sparse) Level-1 BLAS.

Almost Level-3 BLAS performance can be reached by using supernodes to let blocks of pivot columns be updated. This approach is taken in SuperLU [612]; the authors call their kernels BLAS 2/, 1/2.

20.5.3   Available Software

There are several direct sparse solver packages freely available. However, because of the effort involved in writing them, the best packages are probably commercial or even proprietary.

Standalone software for graph partitioning and matrix reordering exists. As remarked above, this most often applies in the case of symmetric, positive definite matrices.

METIS/ParMETIS.   These packages (ParMETIS is an MPI-based version of the Metis algorithms) use *multilevel k-way partitioning* [544]. By first coarsening the mesh down to small size, they find an initial partitioning in k parts. This partitioning is then gradually extended to the original mesh by projecting it upward. A fill-reducing ordering is computed by first finding a p-way partitioning (where p is the number of processors) as described above. A multiple minimum-degree ordering is then used on each of the subdomains.

Chaco.   This package [459, 460] uses a multilevel approach with spectral graph partitioning on the lowest level.

Some of the free solver packages are listed below:

Pspases. This package [416] uses METIS/ParMETIS (see above) as a preprocessing stage. Then it uses a multifrontal method with block-cyclic distribution of the matrix and subtree-to-subcube mapping to achieve high performance. Because of the separate ordering and factorization phases, this package is limited to matrices that allow diagonal pivoting.

Spooles. This package [49, 52] provides minimum-degree, nested dissection, and multisection orderings. It can run serially, multithreaded, and in parallel using MPI. It supports pivoting for numerical stability and uses Level-3 BLAS kernels for high performance.

SuperLU. This solver [612] is available in single-processor and multithreaded versions, with a parallel version announced. By use of supernodes and panel updates, which enable the use of Level-3 BLAS kernels, it achieves a high performance. This package can handle fairly general matrices.

UMFpack. This is a general unsymmetric, multifrontal, systems-solver package.

Table 20.3 lists the characteristics of some of the available software for the direct solution of sparse linear algebra problems.

Table 20.3 Direct sparse solver packages

Package	Language Binding	Arithmetic	Sequential	Parallel	Type of matrix
MA28	Fortran [1]	Real	Sequential		SPD and General
MFACT	Fortran [2]	Complex	Sequential		SPD
MP_Solve	Fortran and C [3]	Real and complex		MPI	General
Pspases	Fortran [4]	Real		MPI	SPD
Sparse	Fortran and C [5]	Real and complex	Sequential		SPD and general
Sparseqr	Fortran [6]	Real	Sequential		SPD and general
Spooles	Fortran and C [7]	Real and complex	Sequential	MPI	SPD and general
SuperLU	Fortran and C [8]	Real and complex	Sequential		SPD and general
UMFpack	Fortran and C [9]	Real and complex	Sequential		SPD and general
Y12M	Fortran [10]	Real	Sequential		SPD and general

NOTE: URLs for the packages discussed in the table.
 1. *http://www.netlib.org/harwell/index.html*
 2. *http://www.netlib.org/atlas/*
 3. *http://www.cs.utk.edu/~padma/mfact.html*
 4. *http://www.cs.umn.edu/~mjoshi/pspases/index.html*
 5. *http://www.netlib.org/sparse/index.html*
 6. *http://www.arc.unm.edu/~trobey/*
 7. *http://www.netlib.org/linalg/spooles/*
 8. *http://www.netlib.org/scalapack/prototype/index.html*
 9. *http://www.netlib.org/linalg/umfpack2.2.tgz*
10. *http://www.netlib.org/y12m/index.html*

20.6   Iterative Solution Methods

Direct methods, as sketched above, have some pleasant properties. Foremost is the fact that their time to solution is predictable, either a priori or after determining the matrix ordering. This is due to the fact that the method does not rely on numerical properties of the coefficient matrix but only on its structure. On the other hand, the amount of fill can be substantial, and with it the execution time. For large-scale applications, the storage requirements for a realistic size problem can simply be prohibitive.

Iterative methods have far lower storage demands. Typically, the storage, and the cost per iteration with it, is of the order of the matrix storage. However, the number of iterations strongly depends on properties of the linear system and is at best known up to an order estimate; for difficult problems, the methods may not even converge due to accumulated round-off errors.

20.6.1   Stationary Iterative Methods

In each iteration, an iterative method locates an approximation to the solution of the problem, measures the error between the approximation and the true solution, and based on the error measurement improves on the approximation by constructing a next iterate. This process repeats until the error measurement is deemed small enough.

The simplest iterative methods are the *stationary iterative methods*. They are based on finding a matrix M that is, in some sense, "close" to the coefficient matrix A. Instead of solving $Ax = b$, which is deemed computationally infeasible, we solve $Mx_1 = b$. The true measure of how well x_1 approximates x is the error $e_1 = x_1 - x$. Since we do not know the true solution x, this quantity is not computable. Instead, we look at the *residual*, $r_1 = Ae_1 = Ax_1 - b$, which is a computable quantity. One easily sees that the true solution satisfies $x = A^{-1}b = x_1 - A^{-1}r_1$. So, replacing A^{-1} with M^{-1} in this relation, we define $x_2 = x_1 - M^{-1}r_1$.

Stationary methods are easily analyzed: we find that $r_i \to 0$ if all eigenvalues $\lambda = \lambda(I - AM^{-1})$ satisfy $|\lambda| < 1$. For certain classes of A and M, this inequality is automatically satisfied [422, 958].

20.6.2   Krylov Space Methods

The most popular class of iterative methods nowadays is that of *Krylov space methods*. The basic idea is to construct the residuals such that the nth residual r_n is obtained from the first by multiplication by some polynomial in the coefficient matrix A, that is,

$$r_n = P_{n-1}(A)r_1$$

The properties of the method then follow from the properties of the actual polynomial [61, 108, 182].

Most often, these iteration polynomials are chosen such that the residuals are orthogonal under some inner product. From this, one usually obtains some minimization property, though not necessarily a minimization of the *error*.

Since the iteration polynomials are of increasing degree, it is easy to see that the main operation in each iteration is one matrix–vector multiplication. Additionally, some vector operations, including inner products in the orthogonalization step, are needed.

The Issue of Symmetry

Krylov method residuals can be shown to satisfy the equation

$$r_n \in \text{span}\{Ar_{n-1}, r_{n-1}, \dots, r_1\}$$

This brings up the question as to whether all $\{r_{n-1}, \dots, r_1\}$ need to be stored in order to compute r_n. The answer is that this depends on the symmetry of the coefficient matrix. For a symmetric problem, the r_n vectors satisfy a three-term recurrence. This was the original conjugate gradient method [467].

For nonsymmetric problems, on the other hand, no short recurrences can exist [316], and therefore, all previous residuals need to be stored. Some of these methods are OrthoDir and OrthoRes [1010].

If the requirement of orthogonality is relaxed, one can derive short-recurrence methods for nonsymmetric problems [339]. In the biconjugate gradient method, sequences $\{r_n\}$ and $\{s_n\}$ are derived, which are mutually orthogonal and satisfy three-term recurrences.

A disadvantage of this latter method is that it needs application of the transpose of the coefficient matrix. In environments where the matrix is only operatively defined, this method may be excluded from consideration. Recently developed methods, mostly based on the conjugate gradient squared [888] and biconjugate gradients stabilized [952] methods, obviate this consideration. Furthermore, they can theoretically have double the convergence speed of other CG-like methods.

True Minimization

The methods mentioned so far minimize the error (over the subspace generated) in some matrix-related norm, but not in the Euclidean norm. We can effect a true minimization by finding a minimizing convex combination of the residuals generated so far. This leads to one of the most popular methods today: GMRES [821]. It will always generate the optimal iterate, but it requires storage of all previous residuals. In practice, truncated or restarted versions of GMRES are popular.

Parallelism in the Iterative Method

Conjugate gradient–type methods are largely parallelizable. Vector updates are fully parallel, and the matrix–vector product involves only local communication for most sparse problems. Calculation of norms and inner products takes global operation, but the amount of data involved is small, and the cost is usually negligible compared to the matrix–vector product and, especially, the preconditioner application.

20.6.3   Preconditioners

The matrix M that appeared in the section on stationary iterative methods can also play a role in Krylov space methods. There, it is called a *preconditioner,* and it acts to improve spectral properties of the coefficient matrix that determine the convergence speed of the method. In a slight simplification, one might say that we replace the system $Ax = b$ by

$$(AM^{-1})(Mx) = b$$

(The inner product is typically changed as well.) It is generally recognized that a good preconditioner is crucial to the performance of an iterative method.

The requirements on a preconditioner are that it should be easy to construct, a system $Mx = b$ should be simple to solve, and in some sense M should be an approximation to A. These requirements need to be balanced: a more accurate preconditioner is usually harder to construct and more costly to apply, so any decrease in the number of iterations has to be set against a longer time per iteration, plus an increased setup phase.

The holy grail of preconditioners is finding an *optimal* preconditioner—one for which the number of operations required to apply it is of the order of the number of variables, while the resulting number of iterations is bounded in the problem size. There are very few optimal preconditioners.

Simple Preconditioners

Some preconditioners need no construction at all. For instance, the Jacobi preconditioner is simply the matrix diagonal D_A. In PDE applications, the largest elements are on the diagonal, so one expects some degree of accuracy from this. By partitioning the matrix in blocks instead of scalars, this generalizes to the block Jacobi method, which usually gives faster convergence than the point method.

An even more accurate method results from using the whole lower triangular part $D_A + L_A$ of the coefficient matrix. This is called the *Gauss–Seidel method* or, introducing a damping parameter as in $D_A + \omega L_A$, the *SOR method*. Since this triangular matrix is nonsymmetric, it is usually balanced with the upper triangular part as $(D_A + L_A)D_A^{-1}(D_A + U_A)$, which is called the *SSOR method*.

While the Jacobi method is trivially parallel, the SOR and SSOR methods are not. Since they have the same logical structure as incomplete factorizations, this point will be tackled in the next section.

Incomplete Factorizations

A successful strategy for preconditioners results from mimicking direct methods, but applying some approximation process to them. Thus, the so-called *incomplete factorization* methods ignore fill elements in the course of the Gaussian elimination process. Two strategies are to ignore elements in fixed positions, or to drop elements that are deemed small enough to be negligible. The aim is to preserve at least some of the sparsity of the coefficient matrix in the factorization, while providing something that is close enough to the full factorization.

Incomplete factorizations can be very effective, but there are a few practical problems. For the class of M-matrices, these methods are well defined [663]. For other, even fairly common, classes of matrices, there is a possibility that the algorithm breaks down [515, 562, 644].

Also, factorizations are inherently recursive. Coupled with the sparseness of the incomplete factorization, this gives very limited parallelism in the algorithm using a natural ordering of the unknowns. It has been established that different orderings affect the number of iterations [297] and that very little parallelism is possible without sacrificing convergence speed [308]. However, once we reconcile ourselves to the extra iterations incurred, it is possible to attain a large degree of parallelism by using orderings based on multicoloring [519]. Such factorizations can even be constructed in parallel.

Analytically Inspired Preconditioners

In recent years, a number of preconditioners more directly inspired by the continuous problem have gained in popularity. For a matrix from an elliptic PDE on a rectangular grid, one can use a so-called *fast solver* as preconditioner [217, 312, 992].

A particularly popular class of preconditioners based on the continuous problem is that of *domain-decomposition* methods. If the continuous problem is elliptic, then decomposing the domain into simply connected pieces leads to elliptic problems on these subdomains. These are tied together by internal boundary conditions of some sort.

For instance, in the Schur complement-domain-decomposition method [118], thin strips of variables function as an interface region. The original problem reduces to fully independent problems on the subdomains, connected by a system on the interface that is both smaller and better conditioned, but more dense, than the original one. While the subdomains can trivially be executed in parallel, the interface system poses considerable problems.

Choosing overlapping instead of separated subdomains leads to the class of Schwarz methods [616]. The original Schwarz method on two domains proposed solving one subdomain, deriving interface conditions from it for the other subdomain, and solving the system there. Repetition of this process can be shown to converge. In a more parallel variant of this method, all subdomains solve their systems simultaneously, and the solutions on the overlap regions are added together.

Multilevel methods do not operate by decomposing the domain. Rather, they work on a sequence of nested discretizations, solving the coarser ones as a starting point for solving the finer levels. The idea behind multilevel methods is that relaxation, using a simple method such as SOR, on the coarse grid, reduces the high frequency error, while restriction to the remaining grid points solves the lower-frequency error terms by recursive application of this process. The result is a *V-cycle*. By judicious choice of the smoother and the restriction/prolongation operators, work proportional to the number of unknowns can be attained.

Classically, multilevel methods were based on the problem geometry [420]. However, from a point of view of library software, there is a large interest in purely algebraic multilevel methods that require only the matrix as input. Under certain conditions, such methods can be also shown to be close to optimal [62, 63, 812]. In both cases, these methods can be parallelized by distributing each level over the processors, but this may not be trivial, and there are several unsolved research questions left.

20.6.4   Libraries and Standards in Sparse Methods

Unlike the case of dense methods, there are few standards for iterative methods. This is chiefly due to the fact that sparse storage is more complicated, more varied, and therefore less standardized. Whereas the (dense) BLAS has been accepted for a long time, sparse BLAS is not more than a proposal under research.

Storage Formats

As is apparent from the matrix–vector example in Section 20.4.2, storage formats for sparse matrices include both the matrix elements and pointer information describing where the nonzero elements are placed in the matrix. The following storage formats are in common use (for more details, see Barrett et al. [81]):

Aij format.   In the *Aij* format, three arrays of the same length are allocated: one containing the matrix elements; the other two containing the i and j coordinates of these elements. No particular ordering of the elements is implied.

Row/column compressed.   In addition to storing the matrix elements, the row-compressed format allocates an integer array containing the column indices of the nonzero elements. Since all elements in the same row are stored contiguously, a second, smaller, array can be used to specify the starting points of the rows in the two larger arrays.

Compressed diagonal.   If the nonzero elements of the matrix are located, roughly or exactly, along subdiagonals, one could use contiguous storage for these diagonals. There are several diagonal storage formats. In the simplest, describing a contiguous block of subdiagonals, only the array of matrix elements is needed; two integers are sufficient to indicate which diagonals have been stored.

Blocked versions of these formats exist. These are used for matrices that can be partitioned into small, square subblocks.

Software Libraries for Sparse Systems Solvers

Since sparse formats are more complicated than dense matrix storage, sparse libraries have an added level of complexity. In the parallel case, additional indexing information is needed to specify which matrix elements are on which processor.

There are two fundamentally different approaches for handling this complexity. Some sparse libraries require the user to set up the matrix and supply it to the library; all handling is performed by the library. Since the user must store data in a format dictated by the library, this might involve considerable work.

On the other hand, the library might do even the matrix setup internally, hiding all data from the user. This gives total freedom to the user, but it requires the library to supply sufficient access functions so that the user can perform certain matrix operations without having access to the object itself.

This issue and others are discussed in Eijkhout [309], which contains a fairly comprehensive survey of freely available iterative packages. Here we mention just two:

Aztec.   In this package [497], the user distributes the matrix and passes the distributed parts to the library, using the global numbering. A preprocessing transform call then localizes the matrix, but no new allocation is performed. Aztec offers a range of iterative methods and preconditioners.

PETSc.   This library [73] completely hides all data from the user. Data are available only through access routines. To construct objects such as matrices, the user passes individual elements to the library; distribution of the matrix is left to the library. PETSc, in addition to offering iterative methods and preconditioners, has a large number of lower-level service routines; thus, it can be used as a toolbox for parallel linear algebra. ParPre [181, 310] is an add-on library of parallel preconditioners for PETSc that includes domain decomposition and algebraic multilevel methods.

Templates for Iterative Methods

Researchers who want to use iterative methods and insist on high performance are faced with a dilemma. They can read the technical papers and invest a great deal of energy in coming up with their own implementations that are tuned to their architectures and applications. Alternatively, they can use software libraries and settle for not exactly the desired method, imperfect integration in their applications, or less-than-optimal performance on their particular platforms. One solution to this problem has proved fruitful in the past: the *template* approach.

A template for an iterative method—Barrett et al. [81] is a good example—contains a number of ingredients. First, it contains enough basic theory to make a user aware of the applicability and limitations of the method. Second, it contains a reference implementation that is complete in a model sense: it abstracts away from data structures tuned to a particular application and uses, for instance, dense matrices. In Barrett et al., each algorithm is given as meta-code and as MATLAB and Fortran source. Third, a template indicates the elements of the code that can be altered or tuned to a particular application. Issues such as data structures and stopping tests fall under this item.

20.6.5   Available Software

Table 20.4 lists the characteristics of some of the availble software for the iterative solution of sparse linear algebra problem.

Table 20.4   Sparse linear solvers

Package	Language binding	Arithmetic	Sequential	Parallel	Type of matrix
BILUM	Fortran [1]	Real	Sequential		SPD and general
BlockSolve95	Fortran, C, C++	Real		MPI	SPD and general
BPKIT	Fortran, C, C++ [3]	Real			Preconditioners
IML++	Fortran, C, C++ [4]	Real	Sequential		SPD and general
ISIS++	C++ [5]	Real		MPI	SPD and general
ITPACK	Fortran [6]	Real	Sequential		SPD and general
LASPack	C [7]	Real	Sequential		SPD and general
ParPre	C [8]	Real		MPI	Preconditioners
PCG	Fortran, C, C++ [9]	Real		PVM	SPD
PETSc	Fortran, C [10]	Real and complex	Sequential	MPI	SPD and general
PIM	Fortran [11]	Real and complex	Sequential	MPI/PVM	SPD and general
P-SparsLIB	Fortran [12]	Real		MPI	General
QMRPACK	Fortran [13]	Real and complex	Sequential		SPD and general
SPLIB	Fortran [14]	Real	Sequential		SPD and general
SPOOLES	Fortran, C [15]	Real and complex	Sequential	MPI	SPD and general
Templates	Fortran, C [16]	Real	Sequential		SPD and general

NOTE: URLs for the packages discussed in the table.
1. *http://www.cs.uky.edu/~jzhang/bilum.html*
2. *http://www.mcs.anl.gov/sumaa3d/BlockSolve/index.html*
3. *http://www-users.cs.umn.edu/~chow/bpkit.html/*
4. *http://math.nist.gov/iml++*
5. *http://z.ca.sandia.gov/isis/*
6. *http://www.netlib.org/itpack/*
7. *http://www.tu-dresden.de/mwism/skalicky/laspack/laspack.html*
8. *http://www.cs.utk.edu/~eijkhout/parpre.html*
9. *http://www.cfdlab.ae.utexas.edu/pcg/index.html*
10. *http://www-unix.mcs.anl.gov/petsc/petsc-page.html*
11. *ftp://unix.hensa.ac.uk/pub/misc/netlib/pim*
12. *http://www.cs.umn.edu/Research/arpa/p_sparslib/psp-abs.html*
13. *http://www.netlib.org/linalg/qmrpack.tgz*
14. *ftp://ftp.cs.indiana.edu/pub/bramley/splib.tar.gz*
15. *http://www.netlib.org/linalg/spooles/*
16. *http://www.netlib.org/templates/index.html*

20.7 Sparse Eigenvalue Problems

The past decade has produced several significant advances in the solution of large eigenvalue problems. The most significant of these has been the development of methods and software for computing a selected subset of the eigenvalues and eigenvectors of a large nonsymmetric matrix A. This section will present a method developed during the course of the CRPC project. This approach, called the *implicitly restarted Arnoldi method,* has led to the software package ARPACK and the parallel version P_ARPACK. These packages are widely considered to be the state of the art for this problem.

20.7.1 Algorithms and Software for Large Eigenvalue Problems $Ax = \lambda x$

ARPACK and P_ARPACK are now used throughout the world on a variety of applications. Nonsymmetric problems arise in bifurcation and stability analysis in computational fluid dynamics, waveguide design, semiconductor device modeling, and many others. Currently, problems on the order of 1 million variables are being solved using P_ARPACK at Sandia National Laboratory [598]. Symmetric problems arise in structural analysis, semiconductor laser design, computational chemistry, and many other areas. Symmetric problems of order 10M variables are now being solved.

A third capability, the computation of a partial singular-value decomposition, has an endless number of applications. The leading few singular values and vectors are used to obtain a low-rank representation of the original data matrix. This finds application in Web-based search engines, 3-D image reconstruction from 2-D data, principal component analysis, reduced-basis techniques for dynamical systems, graph partitioning, and so on.

Basic Methods

Typically, in these large-scale applications, one desires the computation of a selected subset of eigenvalues and corresponding eigenvectors with specified properties. For example, in bifurcation analysis one is only interested in a few eigenvalues near the imaginary axis. The size of the problem usually makes it intractable to compute all eigenvalues and vectors to select the desired ones. Instead, we seek methods that require a minimal amount of storage proportional to $n \cdot k$, where n is the matrix order and k is the desired number of eigenvalues. We also require that the method take advantage of sparsity or structure of the given matrix.

In this context, we shall discuss the solution of the standard linear eigenvalue problem

$$Ax = \lambda x$$

The most successful numerical algorithms for (small) dense eigenvalue problems are based on the Schur decomposition. It states that every square matrix is *unitarily similar* to an upper triangular matrix.

Every square matrix A may be decomposed in the form

$$AV = VR$$

where V is unitary ($V^*V = I$) and R is upper triangular. The diagonal elements of R are the eigenvalues of A.

Dense algorithms, such as those found in LAPACK, compute all of the eigenvalues and corresponding eigenvectors by applying a sequence of dense unitary similarity transformations that transform the original matrix A to upper triangular form R, hence producing the Schur decomposition.

This is not suitable for the large-scale setting. Keeping our goals in mind, we instead seek a method that will compute a partial Schur decomposition. The key here is that there is a Schur decomposition with the eigenvalues of A appearing in any specified order on the diagonal of R.

If V_k represents the leading k columns of V and R_k the leading principal $k \times k$ submatrix of R, then

$$AV_k = V_k R_k$$

and $Range(V_k)$ is an invariant subspace of A with the k eigenvalues of R_k (i.e., the leading k eigenvalues of R) being the eigenvalues of A with respect to this subspace. If $R_k y = \lambda y$, then $Ax = \lambda x$ with $x = V_k y$.

We refer to this as a *partial Schur decomposition* of A. Since there is a Schur decomposition with the eigenvalues of A appearing on the diagonal in any given ordering, there is always a partial Schur decomposition of A with the diagonal elements of R_k consisting of any specified subset of k eigenvalues of A.

Implicit restarting provides a means to compute this leading portion of the Schur decomposition (a partial Schur decomposition) without having to apply dense similarity transformations to A, and hence without destroying the sparsity or structure of A. Typically, the only requirement of A is a matrix–vector product.

Single-Vector Methods

Single-vector methods, such as the power method, are the simplest and most storage-efficient ways to compute a single eigenvalue and its corresponding eigenvector. The simple power method and its rapidly convergent variant, the inverse power method, form the foundation for understanding the behavior of the more sophisticated projection methods used today.

However, the power method may be slow to converge (or may fail to converge). The inverse power method works with a spectral transformation of the original problem using $(A - \sigma I)^{-1}$ in place of A to rapidly compute eigenvalues near the shift point σ. While the inverse power method can overcome the slow convergence, neither method can compute more than one eigenvalue and corresponding eigenvector without employing deflation techniques that can be quite difficult to control.

Factor $AV = VH$
for $j = 1, 2, 3, \ldots$ **until** convergence
    $\mu = select\_shift(H);$
    Factor $QR = H - \mu I;$
    $H \leftarrow Q^*HQ; \quad V \leftarrow VQ;$
end

_____

Figure 20.1   The Shifted QR method.

The QR Algorithm

At the other algorithmic extreme are methods for finding all of the eigenvalues and vectors of a given matrix. Typically, these are unsuitable for large problems because they involve a sequence of dense similarity transformations that quickly destroy any sparsity or structure of the original matrix A.

Certainly, when it is possible to use it, the well-known implicitly shifted QR-algorithm [359, 360] is the method of choice as a general algorithm for finding all of the eigenvalues and vectors. It actually computes a Schur decomposition by producing a sequence of unitary similarity transformations that iteratively reduce A to upper triangular form.

The algorithm begins with an initial unitary similarity transformation of A to the condensed form $AV = VH$, where H is upper Hessenberg (tridiagonal in case $A = A^*$) and V is unitary. Then the iteration shown in Figure 20.1 is performed.

In this scheme, Q is unitary and R is upper triangular (i.e., the QR factorization of $H - \mu I$). It is easy to see that H is unitarily similar to A throughout the course of this iteration. The iteration is continued until the subdiagonal elements of H converge to zero, that is, until a Schur decomposition has been (approximately) obtained.

Subspace Projection Methods

We are striving for something in between a single-vector method and the QR algorithm that will be suitable for computing a selected subset of the spectrum of A. A class of methods called _Krylov subspace-projection_ methods provide the basis for meeting this goal. In the case of the standard problem $Ax = \lambda x$, Krylov subspace projection results in the Lanczos/Arnoldi class of methods. These methods may be viewed as systematic ways to extract additional eigen-information from the sequence of vectors produced by a power iteration.

If one hopes to obtain additional information through various linear combinations of the power sequence, it is natural to formally consider the _Krylov_ subspace,

$$\mathcal{K}_k(A, v_1) = span\{v_1, Av_1, A^2v_1, \ldots, A^{k-1}v_1\}$$

and to attempt to formulate the best possible approximations to eigenvectors from this subspace. Approximate eigenpairs are constructed from this subspace by imposing a Galerkin condition. Given any k-dimensional subspace S of $\mathbf{C}^n$, we define a vector $x \in S$ to be a *Ritz vector*, with corresponding *Ritz value* θ, if the Galerkin condition

$$\langle w, Ax - x\theta \rangle = 0, \quad \text{for all } w \in S$$

is satisfied, with $< \cdot, \cdot >$ denoting some inner product on $\mathbf{C}^n$. In this setting, we are interested in $S = \mathcal{K}_k(A, v_1)$. From its definition, we see that every $w \in \mathcal{K}_k$ is of the form $w = \phi(A)v_1$ for some polynomial ϕ of degree less than k and also that $\mathcal{K}_{j-1} \subset \mathcal{K}_j$ for $j = 2, 3, \cdots, k$. Thus, if we have constructed a sequence of orthogonal bases $V_j = [v_1, v_2, \cdots, v_j]$ with $\mathcal{K}_j = Range(V_j)$ and $V_j^* V_j = I_j$, then it is fairly straightforward to see that $v_j = p_{j-1}(A)v_1$, where p_{j-1} is a polynomial of degree $j - 1$. To extend the basis for $\mathcal{K}_k$ to one for $\mathcal{K}_{k+1}$, we must construct a new vector that has a component in the direction of $A^k v_1$ and then orthogonalize this with respect to the previous basis vectors. The only basis vector available with a component in the direction of $A^{k-1}v_1$ is v_k, and thus a convenient way to obtain the direction of the new vector v_{k+1} will be given by

$$f_k = Av_k - V_k h_k,$$
$$v_{k+1} = f_k / \|f_k\|$$

where the vector h_k is constructed to achieve $V_k^* f_k = 0$. Of course, the orthogonality of the columns of V_k gives the formula $h_k = V_k^* Av_k$.

This construction provides a crucial fact concerning f_k:

$$\|f_k\| = \min_h \|Av_k - V_k h\| = \min \|p(A)v_1\|$$

where the second minimization is over all polynomials p of degree k with the same leading coefficient as p_{k-1}.

The only opportunity for failure here is when $f_k = 0$. However, when this happens it implies that

$$AV_k = V_k H_k$$

where $H_k = V_k^* AV_k = [h_1, h_2, \cdots, h_k]$ (with a slight abuse of notation). Hence, this "good breakdown" happens precisely when $\mathcal{K}_k$ is an invariant subspace of A.

Of course, we must ask the question: When can $f_k = 0$ happen? Well, if $v_1 = \sum_{i=1}^k q_j \gamma_j$ where $Aq_j = q_j \lambda_j$, then $p(A)v_1 = 0$ with $p(\tau) = \prod_{i=1}^k (\tau - \lambda_j)$. Since this polynomial can be normalized to have the same leading coefficient as p_{k-1}, the minimization property implies that $f_k = 0$.

The Arnoldi Factorization

The construction we have just derived provides a relation between the matrix A, the basis matrix V_k, and the residual vector f_k of the form

$$AV_k = V_k H_k + f_k e_k^*$$

where $V_k \in \mathbf{C}^{n \times k}$ has orthonormal columns, $V_k^* f_k = 0$, and $H_k \in \mathbf{C}^{k \times k}$ is upper Hessenberg with nonnegative subdiagonal elements. We shall call this a *k-step Arnoldi factorization* of A. It is easily seen from the construction that $H_k = V_k^* A V_k$ is upper Hessenberg. When A is Hermitian, this implies H_k is real, symmetric, and tridiagonal, and the relation is called a *k-step Lanczos factorization* of A. The columns of V_k are referred to as the *Arnoldi vectors* or *Lanczos vectors*, respectively.

The discussion of the previous section implies that Ritz pairs satisfying the Galerkin condition are immediately available from the eigenpairs of the small projected matrix H_k.

If $H_k s = \theta s$, then the vector $x = V_k s$ satisfies

$$\|Ax - \theta x\| = \|(AV_k - V_k H_k)s\| = |\beta_k e_k^* s|$$

Observe that if (x, θ) is a Ritz pair, then

$$\theta = s^* H_k s = (V_k s^*) A (V_k s) = x^* A x$$

is a Rayleigh quotient (assuming $\|s\| = 1$) and the associated Rayleigh quotient residual $r(x) \equiv Ax - x\theta$ satisfies

$$\|r(x)\| = |\beta_k e_k^* s|$$

When A is Hermitian, this relation may be used to provide computable rigorous bounds on the accuracy of the eigenvalues of H_k as approximations to eigenvalues [749] of A. When A is non-Hermitian, we can only say that the residual is small if $|\beta_k e_k^* s|$ is small without further information. In any case, if $f_k = 0$ these Ritz pairs become exact eigenpairs of A.

The explicit steps needed to form a k-step Arnoldi factorization are given in Figure 20.2.

$v_1 = v / \|v\|;$
$w = Av_1; \alpha_1 = v_1^* w;$
$f_1 \leftarrow w - v_1 \alpha_1;$
$V_1 \leftarrow (v_1); H_1 \leftarrow (\alpha_1);$
for $j = 1, 2, 3, \ldots k - 1,$
$\quad \beta_j = \|f_j\|; v_{j+1} \leftarrow f_j / \beta_j;$
$\quad V_{j+1} \leftarrow (V_j, v_{j+1});$
$\quad \hat{H}_j \leftarrow \begin{pmatrix} H_j \\ \beta_j e_j^* \end{pmatrix};$
$\quad w \leftarrow A v_{j+1};$
$\quad h \leftarrow V_{j+1}^* w;$
$\quad f_{j+1} \leftarrow w - V_{j+1} h;$
$\quad H_{j+1} \leftarrow (\hat{H}_j, h);$
end

Figure 20.2 *k*-step Arnoldi factorization.

The dense matrix–vector products $V_{j+1}^* w$ and $V_{j+1} h$ may be expressed with the Level-2 BLAS operation _GEMV. As discussed previously, this provides a significant performance advantage on virtually every platform from workstation to supercomputer. Moreover, considerable effort has been made within the ScaLAPACK project to optimize these kernels for a variety of parallel machines.

The mechanism used here to orthogonalize the new information Av_k against the existing basis V_k is the classical Gram Schmidt process (CGS). It is notoriously unstable and will fail miserably in this setting without modification. One remedy is to use the modified Gram Schmidt process (MGS). Unfortunately, this will also fail to produce orthogonal vectors in the restarting situation we are about to discuss, and it cannot be expressed with Level-2 BLAS in this setting. Fortunately, the CGS method can be rescued through a technique proposed by Daniel, Gragg, Kaufman, and Stewart (DGKS) [243]. This scheme provides an excellent way to construct a vector f_{j+1} that is numerically orthogonal to V_{j+1}. It amounts to computing a correction

$$c = V_{j+1}^* f_{j+1} \qquad f_{j+1} \leftarrow f_{j+1} - V_{j+1} c \qquad h \leftarrow h + c$$

just after the initial CGS step if necessary. A simple test is used to avoid this DGKS correction if it is not needed. The correction needs to be computed only if $\|h\| < \eta(\|h\|^2 + \|f\|^2)^{1/2}$, where $0 < \eta < 1$ is a specified parameter. The test assures that the new vector Av makes an angle greater than $\cos^{-1}(\eta)$ with the existing Krylov subspace. This mechanism maintains orthogonality to full working precision at very reasonable cost. The special situation imposed by the restarting scheme we are about to discuss makes this modification essential for obtaining accurate eigenvalues and numerically orthogonal Schur vectors (eigenvectors in the Hermitian case).

Failure to maintain orthogonality leads to several numerical difficulties. In the Hermitian case, Paige [733] showed that the loss of orthogonality occurs precisely when an eigenvalue of H_j is close to an eigenvalue of A. In fact, the Lanczos vectors lose orthogonality in the direction of the associated approximate eigenvector. Moreover, failure to maintain orthogonality results in spurious copies of the approximate eigenvalue produced by the Lanczos method. Implementations based on selective and partial orthogonalization [404, 751, 864] monitor the loss of orthogonality and perform additional orthogonalization steps only when necessary. The methods developed in [238, 239, 750] use the three-term recurrence with no reorthogonalization steps. Once a level of accuracy has been achieved, the spurious copies of computed eigenvalues are located and deleted. Then the Lanczos basis vectors are regenerated from the three-term recurrence and Ritz vectors are recursively constructed in place. This is a very competitive strategy when the matrix–vector product $w \leftarrow Av$ is relatively inexpensive.

Restarting the Arnoldi Process

An unfortunate aspect of the Lanczos/Arnoldi process is that there is no way to ascertain in advance how many steps will be needed to determine the eigenvalues of interest within a specified accuracy. We have tried to indicate with our brief theoretical discussion that the eigen-information obtained through this process is completely determined by the choice of the starting vector v_1. Unless there is a very fortuitous choice of v_1, eigen-information of interest probably will not appear until k gets very large. Clearly, it becomes intractable to maintain numerical orthogonality of V_k. Extensive storage will be required, and repeatedly finding the eigensystem of H_k also becomes intractable at a cost of $\mathcal{O}(k^3)$ flops.

The obvious need to control this cost has motivated the development of restarting schemes. Restarting means replacing the starting vector v_1 with an "improved" starting vector v_1^+ and then computing a new Arnoldi factorization with the new vector. Our brief theoretical discussion about the structure of f_k serves as a guide: our goal is to iteratively force v_1 to be a linear combination of eigenvectors of interest. A more general and, in fact, a better numerical strategy is to force the starting vector to be a linear combination of Schur vectors that span the desired invariant subspace.

Explicit restarting schemes have a history going back to the original Lanczos method [237, 387, 536, 733]. More recently, a restarting scheme for eigenvalue computation was proposed by Saad based on the polynomial acceleration scheme originally introduced by Manteuffel [643] for the iterative solution of linear systems. Saad [819] proposed to restart the factorization with a vector that has been preconditioned so that it is more nearly in a k-dimensional invariant subspace of interest.

Implicit Restarting

There is another approach to restarting that offers a more efficient and numerically stable formulation. This approach, called *implicit restarting*, is a technique for combining the implicitly shifted QR scheme with a k-step Arnoldi or Lanczos factorization to obtain a truncated form of the implicitly shifted QR iteration. The numerical difficulties and storage problems normally associated with Arnoldi and Lanczos processes are avoided. The algorithm is capable of computing a few (k) eigenvalues with user-specified features, such as largest real part or largest magnitude, using $2nk + \mathcal{O}(k^2)$ storage. The computed Schur basis vectors for the desired k-dimensional eigenspace are numerically orthogonal to working precision.

Implicit restarting provides a means to extract interesting information from large Krylov subspaces while avoiding the storage and numerical difficulties associated with the standard approach. It does this by continually compressing the interesting information into a fixed-size k-dimensional subspace. This is accomplished through the implicitly shifted QR mechanism. An Arnoldi factorization of length $m = k + p$,

$$AV_m = V_m H_m + f_m e_m^*$$

is compressed to a factorization of length k that retains the eigen-information of interest. This is accomplished using QR steps to apply p shifts implicitly. The first stage of this shift process results in

$$AV_m^+ = V_m^+ H_m^+ + f_m e_m^* Q \tag{20.1}$$

where $V_m^+ = V_m Q$, $H_m^+ = Q^* H_m Q$ and $Q = Q_1 Q_2 \cdots Q_p$. Each Q_j is the orthogonal matrix associated with the shift μ_j used during the shifted QR algorithm. Because of the Hessenberg structure of the matrices Q_j, it turns out that the first $k - 1$ entries of the vector $e_m^* Q$ are zero (i.e., $e_m^* Q = (\sigma e_k^*, \hat{q}^*)$). This implies that the leading k columns in equation (20.1) remain in an Arnoldi relation. Equating the first k columns on both sides of equation (20.1) provides an updated k-step Arnoldi factorization

$$AV_k^+ = V_k^+ H_k^+ + f_k^+ e_k^*$$

with an updated residual of the form $f_k^+ = V_m^+ e_{k+1} \hat{\beta}_k + f_m \sigma$. Using this as a starting point, it is possible to apply p additional steps of the Arnoldi process to return to the original m-step form.

There are many ways to select the shifts $\{\mu_j\}$ that are applied by the QR steps. Virtually any explicit polynomial restarting scheme could be applied through this implicit mechanism. Considerable success has been obtained with the choice of *exact shifts*. This selection is made by sorting the eigenvalues of H_m into two disjoint sets of k "wanted" and p "unwanted" eigenvalues and using the p unwanted ones as shifts. With this selection, the p shift applications result in H_k^+ having the k wanted eigenvalues as its spectrum. As convergence takes place, the subdiagonals of H_k tend to zero, and the most desired eigenvalue approximations appear as eigenvalues of the leading $k \times k$ block of R in a Schur decomposition of A. The basis vectors V_k tend to orthogonal Schur vectors.

There are important implementation details concerning the deflation (setting to zero) of subdiagonal elements of H_m and the purging of unwanted but converged Ritz values. These details are quite important for a robust implementation, but they are beyond the scope of this discussion. Complete details of these numerical refinements may be found in Lehoucq [597] and Lehoucq and Sorensen [600].

This implicit scheme costs p rather than the $k + p$ matrix–vector products the explicit scheme would require. Thus, the exact shift strategy can be viewed both as a means to damp unwanted components from the starting vector and also as directly forcing the starting vector to be a linear combination of wanted eigenvectors. See Sorensen [889] for information on the convergence of IRAM and Baglama et al. [68] and Stathopoulos [894] for other possible shift strategies for Hermitian A. The reader is referred to Lehoucq and Scott [599] and Morgan [686] for studies comparing implicit restarting with other schemes.

Eigenvalue Software: ARPACK and P_ARPACK

ARPACK is a collection of Fortran 77 subroutines designed to solve large-scale eigenvalue problems. ARPACK stands for ARnoldi PACKage. ARPACK software is capable of solving large-scale, non-Hermitian (standard and generalized) eigenvalue problems from a wide range of application areas. Parallel ARPACK (P_ARPACK) is provided as an extension to the current ARPACK library and is targeted for distributed-memory message-passing systems. The message-passing layers currently supported are BLACS and MPI.

This software is based on the implicitly restarted Arnoldi method (IRAM) presented in Section 20.7.1. When the matrix A is symmetric, it reduces to a variant of the Lanczos process called the implicitly restarted Lanczos method (IRLM). For many standard problems, a matrix factorization is not required; only the action of the matrix on a vector is needed.

The important features of ARPACK and P_ARPACK follows:

- A reverse communication interface.

- Ability to return k eigenvalues that satisfy a user-specified criterion such as largest real part, largest absolute value, largest algebraic value (symmetric case), and so on.

- A fixed predetermined storage requirement of $n \cdot \mathcal{O}(k) + \mathcal{O}(k^2)$ words will typically suffice throughout the computation. No auxiliary storage is required.

- Sample driver routines are included that may be used as templates to implement various spectral transformations to enhance convergence and to solve the generalized eigenvalue problem. Also, there is an SVD driver.

- Special consideration is given to the generalized problem $Ax = Bx\lambda$ for singular or ill-conditioned symmetric positive semidefinite M.

- A numerically orthogonal Schur basis of dimension k is always computed. These are also eigenvectors in the Hermitian case, and orthogonality is to working precision. Eigenvectors are available on request in the non-Hermitian case.

- The numerical accuracy of the computed eigenvalues and vectors is user specified. Residual tolerances may be set to the level of working precision. At working precision, the accuracy of the computed eigenvalues and vectors is consistent with the accuracy expected of a dense method such as the implicitly shifted QR iteration.

- Multiple eigenvalues offer no theoretical difficulty. This is possible through deflation techniques similar to those used with the implicitly shifted QR algorithm for dense problems. With the current deflation rules, a fairly tight convergence tolerance and sufficiently large subspace will be required to capture all multiple instances. However, since a block method is not used, there is no need to "guess" the correct block size that would be needed to capture multiple eigenvalues.

Reverse Communication Interface

The reverse communication interface is one of the most important aspects of the design of ARPACK, both for interfacing with user application codes and for parallel decomposition. This interface avoids having to express a matrix–vector product through a subroutine with a fixed calling sequence. This means that the user is free to choose any convenient data structure for the matrix representation. Also, the user has the choice of (and responsibility for) partitioning the matrix–vector product in the most favorable way for parallel efficiency. Moreover, if the matrix is not available explicitly, the user is free to express the action of the matrix on a vector through a subroutine call or a code segment. It is not necessary to conform to a fixed format for a subroutine interface, and hence there is no need to communicate data through the use of COMMON.

A typical usage of this interface is illustrated as follows:

```
10   continue
     call snaupd (ido, bmat, n, which,...,workd,..., info)
     if (ido .eq. newprod) then
        call matvec ('A', n, workd(ipntr(1)), workd(ipntr(2)))
     else
        return
     endif
     go to 10
```

This shows a code segment of the routine that the user must write to set up the reverse communication call to the top level ARPACK routine snaupd to solve a nonsymmetric eigenvalue problem. As usual, with reverse communication, control is returned to the calling program when interaction with the matrix A is required. The action requested of the calling program is simply to perform ido. (In this case, multiply the vector held in the array workd beginning at location ipntr(1) and insert the result into the array workd beginning at location ipntr(2)). Note that the call to the subroutine matvec in this code segment is simply meant to indicate that this matrix–vector operation is taking place. One only needs to supply the action of the matrix on the specified vector and put the result in the designated location. This reverse communication feature also provides a convenient way to use ARPACK with another language such as C or C++.

Reverse communication is a mechanism that is well suited to software written in Fortran 77. There are other mechanisms for encapsulating matrix–vector operations available in other languages. See Chapters 13 and 21 for examples.

Parallelizing ARPACK

The parallelization paradigm found to be the most effective for ARPACK on distributed-memory machines was to provide the user with a single-program multiple data (SPMD) template. The reverse communication interface is one of the most important aspects in the design of ARPACK, and this feature lends itself to a simplified SPMD parallelization strategy. This approach was used for previous parallel implementations of ARPACK [890] and provides a fairly straightforward interface for the user. Reverse communication allows the P_ARPACK codes to be parallelized internally, without imposing a fixed parallel decomposition on the matrix or the user-supplied matrix–vector product. Memory and communication management for the matrix–vector product $w \leftarrow Av$ can be optimized independently of P_ARPACK.

This feature enables the use of various matrix storage formats as well as calculation of the matrix elements on the fly.

The calling sequence to ARPACK remains unchanged except for the addition of the BLACS context (or MPI communicator). Inclusion of the context (or communicator) is necessary for global communication as well as managing I/O. The addition of the context is new to this implementation and reflects the improvements and standardizations being made in message passing [290, 668].

Data Distribution of the Arnoldi Factorization

The numerically stable generation of the Arnoldi factorization

$$AV_k = V_k H_k + f_k e_k^T$$

coupled with an implicit restarting mechanism [889], is the basis of the ARPACK codes. The simple parallelization scheme used for P_ARPACK follows.

- H_k is replicated on every processor.
- V_k is distributed across a 1-D processor grid (blocked by rows).
- f_k and workspace are distributed accordingly.

The SPMD code looks very much like the serial code. It differs in that the local block of the set of Arnoldi vectors, V_{loc}, is passed in place of V, and n_{loc}, the dimension of the local block, is passed instead of n.

With this approach there are only two communication points within the construction of the Arnoldi factorization inside P_ARPACK: computation of the two-norm of the distributed vector f_k and the orthogonalization of f_k to V_k using classical Gram Schmidt with DGKS correction [243]. Additional communication will typically occur in the user-supplied matrix–vector product operation as well. Ideally, this product will only require nearest-neighbor communication among the processes. Typically the blocking of V coincides with the parallel decomposition of the matrix A. The user is free to select an appropriate blocking of V to achieve optimal balance between the parallel performance of P_ARPACK and the user-supplied matrix–vector product.

The SPMD parallel code looks very similar to that of the serial code. Assuming a parallel version of the subroutine matvec, an example of the application of the distributed interface is illustrated as follows:

```
10  continue
      call psnaupd (comm, ido, bmat, nloc, which, ..., Vloc , ... lworkl, info)
      if (ido .eq. newprod) then
        call matvec ('A', nloc, workd(ipntr(1)), workd(ipntr(2)))
      else
        return
      endif
      go to 10
```

1. $\beta_k \leftarrow gnorm(\|f_k^{(*)}\|); \; v_{k+1}^{(j)} \leftarrow f_k^{(j)} \cdot \dfrac{1}{\beta_k}$

2. $w^{(j)} \leftarrow (Aloc)v_{k+1}^{(j)}$

3. $\begin{pmatrix} h \\ \alpha \end{pmatrix}^{(j)} \leftarrow \begin{pmatrix} V_k^{(j)T} \\ v_{k+1}^{(j)T} \end{pmatrix} w^{(j)}; \; \begin{pmatrix} h \\ \alpha \end{pmatrix} \leftarrow gsum \left[\begin{pmatrix} h \\ \alpha \end{pmatrix}^{(*)} \right]$

4. $f_{k+1}^{(j)} \leftarrow w^{(j)} - (V_k, v_{k+1})^{(j)} \begin{pmatrix} h \\ \alpha \end{pmatrix}$

5. $H_{k+1} \leftarrow \begin{pmatrix} H_k & h \\ \beta_k & e_k^T \end{pmatrix}$

6. $V_{k+1}^{(j)} \leftarrow (V_k, v_{k+1})^{(j)}$

Figure 20.3   The explicit steps of the CGS process responsible for the jth block.

In this segment, nloc is the number of rows in the block Vloc of V that has been assigned to this node process.

The blocking of V is generally determined by the parallel decomposition of the matrix A. For parallel efficiency, this blocking must respect the configuration of the distributed memory and interconnection network. Logically, the V matrix will be partitioned by blocks

$$V^T = (V^{(1)T}, V^{(2)T}, \dots, V^{(nproc)T})$$

with one block per processor and with H replicated on each processor. The explicit steps of the CGS process taking place on the jth processor are shown in Figure 20.3.

Note that the function $gnorm$ at step 1 is meant to represent the global reduction operation of computing the norm of the distributed vector f_k from the norms of the local segments $f_k^{(j)}$, and the function $gsum$ at step 3 is meant to represent the global sum of the local vectors $h^{(j)}$ so that the quantity $h = \sum_{j=1}^{nproc} h^{(j)}$ is available to each process on completion. These are the only two communication points within this algorithm. The remainder is perfectly parallel. Additional communication will typically occur at step 2. Here the operation $(Aloc)v$ is meant to indicate that the user-supplied, matrix–vector product is able to compute the local segment of the matrix–vector product Av that is consistent with the partition of V. Ideally, this would only involve nearest-neighbor communication among the processes.

Since H is replicated on each processor, the implicit restart mechanism described previously remains untouched. The only difference is that the local block $V^{(j)}$ appears in place of the full matrix V. Operations associated with implicit restarting are perfectly parallel with this strategy. They consist of the steps in Figure 20.4 that occur independently on each processor.

for $i = 1, 2, \ldots, p,$
    Factor $[Q_i, R_i] = \mathrm{qr}(H_m - \mu_i I)$;
    $H_m \leftarrow Q_i^* H_m Q_i$;
    $Q \leftarrow Q Q_i$;
end
$V_m^{(j)} \leftarrow V_m^{(j)} Q$;

Figure 20.4   Implicit restart on jth block

All operations on the matrix H are replicated on each processor. Thus, there is no communication overhead. However, the replication of H and the shift selection and application to H on each processor represents a serial bottleneck that limits the scalability of this scheme when k grows with n. Nevertheless, if k is fixed as n increases, then this scheme scales linearly with n, as we shall demonstrate with some computational results. In the actual implementation, separate storage is not required for the Q_i. Instead, each is represented as a product of 2×2 Givens or 3×3 Householder transformations that are applied directly to update Q. On completion of this accumulation of Q, the operation $V_m^{(j)} \leftarrow V_m^{(j)} Q$ is performed independently on each processor j, using the Level-3 BLAS operation _GEMM.

The main benefit of this approach is that the changes to the serial version of ARPACK are very minimal. Since the change of dimension from matrix order n to its local distributed block size nloc is invoked through the calling sequence of the subroutine psnaupd, there is no fundamental algorithmic change within the code. Only eight routines were affected in a minimal way. These routines required either a change in norm calculation to accommodate distributed vectors (step 1 of the CGS process), modification of the distributed dense matrix–vector product (step 4), or inclusion of the context or communicator for I/O (debugging/tracing). More specifically, the commands are changed from

```
rnorm = sdot (n, resid, 1, workd, 1)
rnorm = sqrt(abs(rnorm))
```

to

```
rnorm = sdot (n, resid, 1, workd, 1)
call sgsum2d(comm,'All',' ',1, 1, rnorm, 1, -1, -1 )
rnorm = sqrt(abs(rnorm))
```

where sgsum2d is the BLACS global sum operator. The MPI implementation uses the MPI_ALLREDUCE global operator. Similarly, the computation of the matrix–vector product operation $h \leftarrow V^T w$ requires a change from

```
call sgemv ('T', n, j, one, v, ldv, workd(ipj), 1, zero, h(1,j), 1)
```

to

```
call sgemv ('T', n, j, one, v, ldv, workd(ipj), 1, zero, h(1,j), 1)
call sgsum2d( comm, 'All', ' ', j, 1, h(1,j), j, -1, -1 )
```

Another strategy that was tested was to use Parallel BLAS (PBLAS) [198] software developed for the ScaLAPACK project to achieve parallelization. The function of the PBLAS is to simplify the parallelization of serial codes implemented on top of the BLAS. The ARPACK package is very well suited for testing this method of parallelization since most of the vector and matrix operations are accomplished via BLAS and LAPACK routines.

Unfortunately, this approach required adding other parameters to the calling sequence (the distributed matrix descriptors) as well as redefining the workspace data structure. Although there is no significant degradation in performance, the additional code modifications, along with the data decomposition requirements, make this approach less favorable. As our parallelization is only across a 1-D grid, the functionality provided by the PBLAS was more sophisticated than we required. The current implementation of the PBLAS (ScaLAPACK version 1.1) assumes the matrix operands to be distributed in a block-cyclic decomposition scheme.

Message Passing

One objective for the development and maintenance of a parallel version of the ARPACK [601] package was to construct a parallelization strategy whose implementation required as few changes as possible to the current serial version. The basis for this requirement was not only to maintain a level of numerical and algorithmic consistency between the parallel and serial implementations, but also to investigate the possibility of maintaining the parallel and serial libraries as a single entity.

On many shared-memory MIMD architectures, a level of parallelization can be accomplished via compiler options alone without requiring any modifications to the source code. This is rather ideal for the software developer. For example, on the SGI Power Challenge architecture the MIPSpro F77 compiler uses a POWER FORTRAN Accelerator (PFA) preprocessor to automatically uncover the parallelism in the source code. PFA is an optimizing Fortran preprocessor that discovers parallelism in Fortran code and converts those programs to parallel code. A brief discussion of implementation details for ARPACK using PFA preprocessing may be found in Debicki et al. [251]. The effectiveness of this preprocessing step is still dependent on how suitable the source code is for parallelization. Since most of the vector and matrix operations for ARPACK are accomplished via BLAS and LAPACK routines, access to efficient parallel versions of these libraries alone will provide a reasonable level of parallelization.

Unfortunately, for distributed-memory architectures the software developer is required to do more work. For distributed-memory implementations, message passing between processes must be explicitly addressed within the source code, and numerical computations must take into account the distribution of data. In addition, for the parallel code to be portable, the communication interface used for message pass-

Table 20.5 Internal scalability of P_ARPACK

Number of nodes	Problem size	Total time (s)	Efficiency
1	100,000 * 1	40.53	
4	100,000 * 4	40.97	0.98
8	100,000 * 8	42.48	0.95
12	100,000 * 12	42.53	0.95
16	100,000 * 16	42.13	0.96
32	100,000 * 32	46.59	0.87
64	100,000 * 64	54.47	0.74
128	100,000 * 128	57.69	0.70

ing must be supported on a wide range of parallel machines and platforms. For P_ARPACK, this portability is achieved via the Basic Linear Algebra Communication Subprograms (BLACS) [290] developed for the ScaLAPACK project and Message Passing Interface (MPI) [668].

Parallel Performance

To illustrate the potential scalability of Parallel ARPACK on distributed-memory architectures, some example problems have been run on the Maui HPCC SP2. The results shown in Table 20.5 attempt to illustrate the potential internal performance of the P_ARPACK routines, independent of the user's implementation of the matrix–vector product.

In order to isolate the performance of the ARPACK routines from the performance of the user's matrix–vector product and also to eliminate the effects of a changing problem characteristic as the problem size increases, the tests involved replicating the same matrix repeatedly to obtain a block diagonal matrix. This completely contrived situation allows the workload to increase linearly with the number of processors. Since each diagonal block of the matrix is identical, the algorithm should behave as if *nproc* identical problems are being solved simultaneously (provided an appropriate starting vector is used). For this example, we use a starting vector of all "1's." The only obstacles that prevent ideal speedup are the communication costs involved in the global operations and the "serial bottleneck" associated with the replicated operations on the projected matrix H. If neither of these were present, then one would expect the execution time to remain constant as the problem size and the number of processors increase.

The matrix used for testing is a diagonal matrix of dimension $100,000$ with uniform random elements between 0 and 1, with four of the diagonal elements separated from the rest of the spectrum by adding an additional 1.01 to these elements. The problem size is then increased linearly with the number of processors by adjoining an additional diagonal block for each additional processor. For these timings we used the nonsymmetric P_ARPACK code pdnaupd with the following parameter selections: mode is set to 1, number of Ritz values requested is 4, portion of the spectrum is "LM," and the maximum number of columns of V is 20.

Availability and Portability

The codes are available by anonymous ftp from *ftp.caam.rice.edu* or by connecting directly to the website at *http://www.caam.rice.edu/software/ARPACK*.

To get the software by anonymous ftp, connect by ftp to *ftp.caam.rice.edu* and login as anonymous. Then change directories to software/ARPACK or connect directly to the above website and follow the instructions in the README file in that directory. The ARPACK software is also available from Netlib in the directory ScaLAPACK.

The implementation of P_ARPACK is portable across a wide range of distributed-memory platforms. Portability of P_ARPACK is achieved by utilization of the BLACS and MPI. With this strategy, it takes very little effort to port P_ARPACK to a wide variety of parallel platforms. So far, P_ARPACK has been tested on an SGI Power Challenge cluster using PVM-BLACS and MPI, on a Cray T3D using Cray's implementation of the BLACS, on an IBM SP2 using MPL-BLACS and MPI, on an Intel Paragon using NX-BLACS and MPI, and on a network of Sun stations using MPI and MPI-BLACS.

20.7.2   Additional Available Software and Future Directions

Table 20.6 lists software that is freely available, along with website addresses and software characteristics.

We also wish to mention new approaches to the large-scale eigenproblem that essentially approximate the shift-invert spectral transformation to achieve accelerated convergence. Two approaches of note are the Jacobi–Davidson approach of Sleijpen and Van der Vorst [868] and the Truncated RQ approach of Sorensen and Yang [891].

Table 20.6   Sparse Eigenvalue solvers

Package	Language binding	Arithmetic	Sequential	Parallel	Type of matrix
LASO[1]	Fortran	Real	Sequential		Symmetric
P_ARPACK[2]	Fortran, C, C++	Real and complex	Sequential	MPI	Symmetric and general
PLANSO[3]	Fortran	Real	Sequential	MPI	Symmetric
TRLAN[4]	Fortran	Real	Sequential		Symmetric

NOTE: URLs for the packages discussed in the table.
1. *http://www.netlib.org/laso/index.html*
2. *http://www.caam.rice.edu/software/ARPACK/*
3. *http://www.nersc.gov/research/SIMON/planso.html*
4. *http://www.nersc.gov/research/SIMON/trlan.html*

Both of these offer a means to effectively combine low-accuracy, iterative linear-system solvers with subspace projection methods.

20.8 Conclusion

The sparse linear systems that result from PDEs need very different techniques from those used for dense matrices. While direct methods have the virtue of reliability, they also take copious amounts of space and time. Iterative methods of one type or another are considerably more frugal in their space demands. But on difficult problems their convergence may be slow, and it is not even guaranteed.

20.8.1 Future Research Directions in Dense Algorithms

Traditionally, large general-purpose mathematical software libraries have required users to write their own programs that call library routines to solve specific subproblems arising during a computation. Adapted to a shared-memory parallel environment, this conventional interface still offers some potential for hiding underlying complexity. For example, the LAPACK project incorporates parallelism in the Level-3 BLAS, where it is not directly visible to the user.

But when going from shared-memory systems to the more readily scalable distributed-memory systems, the complexity of the distributed data structures required is more difficult to hide from the user. Not only must the problem decomposition and data layout be specified, but different phases of the user's problem may require transformations between different distributed data structures.

These deficiencies in the conventional user interface have prompted extensive discussion of alternative approaches for scalable parallel software libraries of the future. Possibilities include:

1. Traditional function libraries (i.e., minimum possible change to the status quo in going from serial to parallel environment). This will allow protection of the programming investment that has been made.

2. Reactive servers on the network. A user would be able to send a computational problem to a server that was specialized for dealing with that problem. This fits well with the concepts of a networked, heterogeneous computing environment with various specialized hardware resources (or even the heterogeneous partitioning of a single homogeneous parallel machine).

3. General interactive environments like MATLAB or Mathematica, perhaps with "expert" drivers (i.e., knowledge-based systems). With the growing popularity of the many integrated packages based on this idea, this approach would provide an interactive graphical interface for specifying and solving scientific problems. Both the algorithms and data structures are hidden from the user; the package itself is responsible for storing and retrieving the problem data in an efficient, distributed manner. In a heterogeneous networked environment,

such interfaces could provide seamless access to computational engines that would be invoked selectively for different parts of the user's computation, according to which machine is most appropriate for a particular subproblem.

4. Domain-specific, problem-solving environments, such as those for structural analysis. Environments like MATLAB and Mathematica have proven to be especially attractive for rapid prototyping of new algorithms and systems that may subsequently be implemented in a more customized manner for higher performance.

5. Reusable templates (i.e., users adapt "source code" to their particular applications). A template is a description of a general algorithm rather than the executable object code or the source code more commonly found in a conventional software library. Nevertheless, although templates are general descriptions of key data structures, they offer whatever degree of customization the user may desire.

Novel user interfaces that hide the complexity of scalable parallelism will require new concepts and mechanisms for representing scientific computational problems and for specifying how those problems relate to one another. Very high-level languages and systems, perhaps graphically based, would not only facilitate the use of mathematical software from the user's point of view, but they would also help automate the determination of effective partitioning, mapping, granularity, data structures, and so on. However, new concepts in problem specification and representation may also require new mathematical research on the analytic, algebraic, and topological properties of problems (e.g., existence and uniqueness).

We have already begun work on developing such templates for sparse matrix computations. Future work will focus on extending the use of templates to dense matrix computations.

We hope the insight we gained from our work will influence future developers of hardware, compilers, and systems software so that they provide tools to facilitate development of high-quality, portable numerical software.

21

Software for the Scalable Solution of Partial Differential Equations

Satish Balay • **William D. Gropp** •
Lois Curfman McInnes • **Barry F. Smith**

Partial differential equations (PDEs) can be used to model physical, chemical, and biological phenomena. Numerical approximation of the solution of PDEs is an important application of parallel computers, as we have seen in previous chapters and as is discussed in Koniges [573]. Early efforts to build programs to solve PDE problems had to start from scratch, building code for each algorithm used in the solution process. This custom approach has two major drawbacks: it limits the use of parallel computers to a small number of groups that have the resources and expertise to develop these codes, and it hampers the ability to take advantage of developments in parallel algorithms. In conventional, serial programming, both of these drawbacks were partially solved by developing libraries of routines that contained the best numerical analysis and implementation techniques. The same route is being followed for parallel libraries, although parallelism introduces additional complications. Handling these complications has caused many groups to rethink the structure of numerical libraries, leading to better software even for uniprocessor applications. In this chapter, we will cover some of the issues and solutions in the context of the Portable, Extensible Toolkit for Scientific Computation (PETSc), a collection of tools for the numerical solution of PDEs and related problems [72, 74].

Many issues arise in designing a parallel program to approximate the solution to a PDE. A key issue is managing *software complexity*, or the interrelationships among code for the various facets of the overall simulation. Three additional critical issues are *numerical algorithms*, *data distribution*, and *data access patterns*. Ironically, these are exactly the same issues of importance for sequential solution; only the scale is different.

We begin by asking how we can organize our program to exploit parallelism, manage the complexity of the parallel application, and use the available computing resources effectively. The approach that we take in this chapter is to start at the top, organizing the program around the mathematics of the approximation. As we will see, this single organizing principle not only provides a method for effectively distributing the computation across the processors, but also allows us to change algorithms easily. We can then incorporate new methods as they become available. Such capabilities enable numerical software developers to better serve the needs of computational scientists. Users can leverage expertise encapsulated within existing libraries without needing to commit to a particular solution strategy and to risk making premature choices of data structures and algorithms. Engaging application scientists in library use without requiring excessive commitment on their part is a critical facet of overcoming the all-too-frequent perception that applications must implement from scratch all facets of modeling to achieve good performance. In fact, the "roll-your-own" approach is undesirable. It requires implementation decisions to be made a priori, before experimentation with realistically sized problems can determine a code's most serious bottlenecks. Using abstractions in library design provides the flexibility for application programmers to use library-provided functionality from the beginning of an application's development. New algorithms and data structures (which may be written by library developers, the application scientists themselves, or third parties) may be injected during the lifetime of the application code.

The remainder of this chapter is organized as follows. Section 21.1 presents an overview of background for the numerical solution of PDEs, while Section 21.2 explains in more detail the challenges in parallel computations for PDE-based models. Section 21.3 overviews various possible solution strategies and lays out the territory for the remaining discussion in this chapter. Section 21.4 discusses the approach used within the PETSc software, with emphasis on the use of mathematical abstractions as an organizing principle that can help to address issues in algorithmic flexibility, efficient use of computational resources, and composability with external tools. Section 21.5 provides an overview of recent work throughout the high-performance computing community in parallel PDE software. We conclude in Section 21.6 with some observations and recommendations.

21.1   PDE Background

PDEs that model scientific applications span the complete range of elliptic, parabolic, and hyperbolic types and combinations thereof. As discussed in Heath [450], hyperbolic PDEs describe time-dependent physical processes, such as wave motion, that are not evolving toward a steady state; parabolic PDEs describe time-dependent physical processes, such as heat diffusion, that are evolving toward a steady state; and elliptic PDEs describe processes that have already reached a steady state, or equilibrium, and hence are independent of time. Problems can also be of mixed type, varying by region or being multicomponent in a single region (e.g., a parabolic system with an elliptic constraint). Generally, elliptic equations are easy to discretize, but challenging to solve because their Green's functions are global: the solution at each point depends upon the data at all other points. Conversely, hyperbolic equations are challenging to discretize because they support discontinuities, but easy to solve when addressed in characteristic form [549].

Many applications are based on replacing an infinite-dimensional, continuous PDE system with an approximate finite-dimensional discrete system that can be solved numerically. A wide range of numerical algorithms can be employed for such problems (see, e.g., Heath et al. [450] and Morton and Mayers [690]). We often categorize approaches as being explicit or implicit, depending on whether the algorithm computes the solution at a given mesh point using only past iterates or using current information from other mesh points as well. Explicit algorithms update the solution vector by using discretization information from neighboring mesh points; no global linear or nonlinear solves are used. Explicit methods are relatively straightforward to implement in parallel, since communication is generally needed only for global reductions (e.g., vector norms) and ghost-point transfers for local discretization. In contrast, implicit methods update all (or most) variables in a single global linear or nonlinear solve. Since they propagate information throughout the global problem domain at each iteration, implicit methods can often converge in fewer time steps than do explicit methods, particularly for large-scale problems. Unfortunately, the challenges in parallel implementations of implicit methods are considerable, due to the inherently global nature of the operators.

Intermediate between these extremes are semi-implicit methods, in which subsets of variables (e.g., pressure) are updated with global solves, and predictor-corrector methods, which use (usually explicit) accurate approximations to the solution (this is the predictor step), followed by a few applications of a corrector (also usually explicit). Most of the remaining discussion in this chapter will focus on issues arising in implicit and semi-implicit methods, since these can be especially effective for large-scale problems and are arguably more difficult to implement in parallel than explicit techniques.

21.2 Challenges in Parallel PDE Computations

A common approach for solving a PDE system is to replace the partial derivatives within the system (e.g., spatial and time derivatives) with discrete approximations based on finite differences, volumes, or elements and then to solve the resulting algebraic system of (time-dependent, nonlinear) equations numerically. Already, parallelism introduces an issue: how is the solution vector distributed among the processors? This question may seem straightforward, but it leads immediately to deeper issues regarding data access patterns as well as interrelationships among software for various facets of parallel PDE solution, such as interfaces between partitioning tools and algebraic solvers. We must somehow manage this complexity without sacrificing good performance; these dueling tradeoffs are particularly challenging when using the distributed memory resources and multilevel memory hierarchies of modern architectures.

21.2.1   Software Complexity

We recognize immediately that software for parallel numerical PDEs (e.g., tools for time evolution and algebraic nonlinear and linear solution) cannot be developed in isolation, but rather must be considered in relationship to tools that partition the problem domain. Further consideration reveals that typical scientific simulations need many additional capabilities. These include mesh generation, PDE discretization, derivative computations, adaptive mesh refinement and coarsening, optimization, sensitivity analysis, data management, visualization, and parallel performance analysis. Moreover, each computational phase may have a different preferred data representation. We must consider tradeoffs in computation time and storage space when transitioning between phases.

In recent years the high-performance computing community has developed a variety of software packages for these phases. However, the combined use of multiple software packages in a given application is a continuing challenge because of incompatibilities in data structures and interfaces. In fact, the situation appears much simpler when considering individual facets of PDE simulations; the more difficult challenges arise when considering multiple phases simultaneously. Understanding the relationships among these phases is critical for the design of efficient software because, within the realm of complete PDE-based simulations, no single software component performs in isolation. Moreover, no single research group can expect to encompass the expertise for cutting-edge capabilities in all areas. Composability and interoperability of different tools via well-defined abstract interfaces are critically important. As further discussed in Section 21.4.3, this area is now receiving considerable attention throughout the high-performance computing community.

21.2.2   Data Distribution and Access

As we saw in Chapter 2, the performance of CPUs has increased far faster than the performance of the computer's memory. In contemporary systems it can take 100 clock cycles or more to access main (as opposed to cache) memory. As a result, the performance of many applications is bounded by the performance of the main memory system, not the CPU [408], even on single-processor systems. Achieving high performance on these systems requires careful attention to the use of memory. For example, it is common in applications to use separate variables for different physical variables, such as p for pressure and v for velocity. However, implicit solver codes that access these variables in a loop over a mesh can suffer significant performance problems. Instead (at least on RISC-based systems), it is important for implicit solvers to *interlace* the variables: define a single variable where the first index (in Fortran) indicates the physical quantity (e.g., pressure or velocity) and the following indices refer to the mesh. In this way, a loop over the mesh accesses memory in a more efficient fashion. Similarly, it is important not to create algorithms that replace a single multicomponent problem with a collection of single-component (or scalar) problems. While both formulations may involve roughly the same number of floating-point operations, the collection of solvers will often involve far more memory motion and thereby lead to poor efficiencies.

These problems are exacerbated in parallel computers. In addition to the large latency of access to main memory, there is an even larger latency, coupled with significantly lower bandwidth, to the memory on remote nodes or processors. Thus, even greater attention must be paid to both the location of data (data distribution) and the mode by which it is accessed. A simple example of this is given in Chapter 16, where different distributions of data to different processes lead to different efficiencies. That example is one case of a more general principle: minimizing the surface-to-volume ratio of the data distribution. This principle arises because, for PDE calculations, the most common operations involve communicating neighbor data to processes that contain adjacent elements of the mesh. Minimizing the data that must be moved between processes is accomplished by minimizing the area of the joints between adjacent processes, relative to the mesh of unknowns. In practical terms, for a regular 2-D mesh, this means that the mesh should be divided into squares (a 2-D decomposition) rather than strips (a 1-D decomposition). Organizing the numerical algorithm to limit accesses to remote data can also have a significant beneficial effect on performance; for iterative solutions to linear equations, this is often accomplished by choosing a preconditioner that uses only or mostly data local to a process.

The large latency of access to remote memory also has implications for both algorithm and software design. In order to reduce the impact of latency, the simplest approach is to aggregate data transfers so that a single operation moves many data items. This approach encourages a software design that follows a two-phase model: in the first phase, as much data as possible is requested; in the second phase, the computation waits until the data arrives. This technique allows the memory system and interprocess communication system to move the data more efficiently than does the more common model of requesting a single item and then waiting until it is available. One concrete example of this situation arises in the assembly of a sparse matrix (see Balay et al. [73] for a detailed discussion). The most obvious approach is to add one element at a time to the matrix, updating the sparse matrix data structures as each entry is added. However, even for a single process, it is often more efficient to wait to update the sparse matrix data structures until many (possibly all) elements have been added to the matrix. As we have indicated, in the multiprocess case it is even more important to defer updating the matrix data structures until many elements can be communicated with each operation. These considerations apply to both message-passing and thread-based models of parallelism, since they reflect the costs to access remote memory. Under the thread-based model, smaller aggregates can be used because the latency is lower than in the message-passing model; however, the latency is still large relative both to local memory operations and to floating-point operations.

21.2.3   Portability, Algorithms, and Data Redistribution

If the above were not enough, any significant application must be prepared to evolve over time. Both raw computer speed and the performance of algorithms have grown tremendously over the past 30 years (see Figure 1.1). Hence, an application must be written to exploit both new computing systems and new algorithms.

Portability

To exploit new computers, an application must be portable. At the very least, the application should be written in a standard computer language (such as Fortran or C, without extensions) and be careful in its assumptions about the computing environment (e.g., a C program should not assume that an int is a particular length). Parallel programs should use standards such as MPI, OpenMP, or HPF to maintain portability. Even with such standards, the much more difficult goal of *performance portability* (portability without sacrificing performance) can be challenging to achieve, particularly over a wide range of computer architectures [285]. However, the benefits of portability are enormous. Computer performance continues to increase by leaps and bounds; portable applications can quickly take advantage of the fastest computers, independent of any particular vendor.

Algorithms

Algorithmic improvements have been at least as important as advances in computer speed for many applications. Thus, it is important that an application be portable to new algorithms as well as to new hardware. Unfortunately, there are no standards (yet) to which applications can write that will guarantee that the newest algorithm can quickly be inserted into an application. Much of the rest of this chapter discusses an approach for this problem based on developing interfaces between the application and the algorithms that it uses. These interfaces reflect the problem being solved, rather than an interface to a specific algorithm. A discussion of particular algorithms for PDEs is beyond the scope of this chapter; various issues are discussed, for example, in Heath [450], Keyes et al. [564], Morton and Mayers [690], Quarteroni and Valli [784], Saad [820], and Smith et al. [872].

Even with continual improvement in algorithms, it is not always possible to identify the best algorithm in advance. For example, preconditioned iterative methods for linear systems are powerful and effective, but their efficiency can be sensitive to details of the problem. Thus, even for an application that is not expected to be used for many years, it is important to have the ability to experiment with different methods and algorithms. This need also encourages an application design where the code interfaces to techniques that solve problems, rather than to a particular choice of algorithm.

Data Redistribution

The concerns discussed above apply to both sequential and parallel programs. Among the complexities that parallelism adds is that of data redistribution. As often noted, achieving high performance requires paying close attention to memory locality. In fact, many parallel algorithms have been developed that specify the distribution of the data for maximum efficiency. Unfortunately, the optimal data distribution for one step in an application may not be optimal for the succeeding step. For example, one popular method for solving certain kinds of PDEs is the alternating-direction implicit (ADI) method. In this method, the solution of a 3-D PDE is approximated by successively solving 1-D problems in each of the three coordinate directions. The fastest algorithms for each of these 1-D solves requires that the data be decomposed so that all of the data along the direction being solved are on the same processor. Switching from one coordinate direction to another requires transposing the data (an all-to-all communication). An alternative approach involves the development of more complex algorithms that minimize the time over all three coordinate directions, not just a single direction. Many parallel methods for PDEs suffer from varying degrees of scaling problems due to imperfect data distribution. Algorithms and software must work together to control the cost and complexity of data redistribution.

21.3 Parallel Solution Strategies

Chapters 9 and 17 review various approaches that deal with these challenges, including parallel languages, parallelizing compilers and compiler directives, computer-assisted parallelization tools, parallel libraries, and problem-solving environments. We briefly discuss issues pertaining to parallel PDE work, mention some recent research in parallel libraries for PDEs, and then explain where our work fits within this spectrum.

The complexity of PDE-based simulations makes automated analysis extremely difficult for distributed-memory parallel systems. While parallel languages and parallel compilers have worked well on shared-memory computers, particular hardware platforms (e.g., CM-5) [923], or specific problems, these approaches have not yet been able to demonstrate general applicability. For example, High Performance Fortran (HPF) [569] is not yet up to the performance of message-passing codes, except in limited settings with much structure to the memory addressing [446]. Hybrid HPF/MPI codes are possible steps along the evolutionary process, with high-level languages automating the expression and compiler detection of structured-address concurrency at lower levels of the PDE modeling. Automated source-to-source parallel translators, such as the University of Greenwich CAPTools project [501] (which adds MPI calls to a sequential Fortran 77 input), can facilitate the parallelization of legacy applications. Such tools may attain 80% to 95% of the benefits of the best manual practice, but the result is limited to the concurrency extractable from the original algorithm. In many cases, the legacy algorithm should be replaced. Similar comments apply to OpenMP and hybrid OpenMP/MPI approaches.

Beyond the capabilities of parallel languages, parallel compilers, and computer-assisted parallelization tools, we still need encapsulation of expertise for parallel PDEs in forms that are usable by the scientific computing community at large. We also must allow application programmers to leverage as much of their existing legacy code as possible, thereby enabling a gradual transition from the more traditional approach of "the application code does everything" to "the application code uses building blocks within software tools."

As illustrated by Figure 21.1, we can consider numerical libraries and problem-solving environments (PSEs) as fitting within a spectrum of different levels of abstraction. At one end of the spectrum, software presents only an application-specific interface to the user. The software handles all other facets of computation, from mesh generation to discretization to complete solution with numerical methods and data analysis. While this level of abstraction is appealing in the simplicity presented to the application scientist, there is little compile-time flexibility. At the other end of the spectrum are low-level computational kernels, which offer enormous flexibility, although the complexity of interactions is difficult to manage at this level. In the intermediate range, we tend to compromise based on the strengths of both ends. No one abstraction choice is right or wrong; different tradeoffs can be made depending on particular design objectives. PSEs, which are further discussed in Chapter 14, tend to build application-oriented abstraction layers both above and below numerical library levels. Because there is no precise definition of PSEs in use in general practice, the term PSE itself does not convey sufficient information regarding the category of software of a PSE product. Examples can range from lower-level class libraries to complete environments such as engineering tools like Nastran [693].

The approach used within PETSc focuses on abstractions for algorithms and discrete mathematics. Such abstractions range throughout a hierarchy, where software for sophisticated PDE algorithms can be designed upon lower-level building blocks of parallel data structures. Various groups have used similar approaches in leveraging abstractions at the PDE level for the development of parallel PDE software, including DAGH [744], Diffpack [148, 268], KeLP [67, 336], Overture [144, 463], SAMRAI [482, 570], POOMA [53, 625], and UG [84, 947]. Some of this work is discussed in Chapter 12 within the context of data structure libraries.

21.4   PETSc Approach to Parallel Software for PDEs

Now that we have abstractly discussed the various challenges in PDE solution and possible strategies for tackling them, we present concrete details of one approach. In particular, this section introduces a set of techniques used within the Portable, Extensible Toolkit for Scientific Computation (PETSc) [72, 74] for the development of algorithms and data structures for large-scale PDE-based problems. Paramount goals are managing software complexity and addressing issues in portable, scalable

Application-specific interface

- Programmer manipulates objects associated with the application
- beam, plate, shell, ...

High-level mathematics interface

- Programmer manipulates mathematical objects, such as PDEs and boundary conditions

- $\int_\Omega \nabla^2 u = f$

- $u\big|_{\delta\Omega} = g$

Algorithmic and discrete mathematics interface

- Programmer manipulates mathematical objects (sparse matrices, nonlinear equations), algorithmic objects (solvers), and discrete geometry (meshes)

- matrix A
- vectors x, b
- solve $Ax = b$

Low-level computational kernels

- e.g., BLAS-type operations

-
```
do i=1,n
    x[i] = a*y[i] + x[i]
enddo
```

Figure 21.1   Levels of abstraction in mathematical software.

performance across a range of parallel environments, from networks of workstations to traditional massively parallel processors to clusters of symmetric multiprocessors. Our approach uses a distributed-memory (or "shared-nothing") model, where we hide within parallel objects the details of communication, and the user orchestrates communication at a higher abstract level than message passing. We note that underneath these layers, data are generally communicated via message passing.

We introduce in Section 21.4.1 some sample motivating applications that lead to discussion in Section 21.4.2 of software design based on their mathematical formulations. Section 21.4.3 discusses issues in interoperability among software tools for the various phases of solving PDE-based systems. Finally, we explain in Section 21.4.4 how the flexibility in both algorithms and data structures afforded by this design enables us to better address issues in achieving high performance.

21.4.1   Sample Applications

Before describing the PETSc approach, we present two applications that we will use as examples. We begin with a linear 2-D problem and then consider a nonlinear PDE.

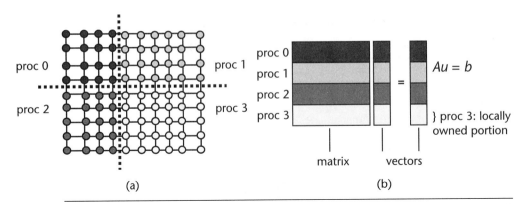

Figure 21.2   Partitioning of a rectangular mesh and a corresponding linear system so that each process "owns" a unique subset of the mesh and the corresponding unknowns of the problem, u. The matrix A and vector b are partitioned accordingly.

A Linear Elliptic Example

To enable concrete discussion of these issues and begin to explain our approach, we consider the linear elliptic PDE, $\nabla^2 u = b$, in a 2-D domain Ω with homogeneous Dirichlet boundary conditions; details of this model are discussed in Chapter 16. In subsequent sections, we discuss additional complexities that arise in nonlinear and time-dependent problems. As discussed in Chapter 9, various parallel programming models can be used, and for such a simple model all would be well suited. We focus discussion on an SPMD approach, in which all processes execute essentially the same logic, although on a subset of the global problem domain, because this approach has proven quite effective for more complicated PDE computations and is the approach discussed in Section 21.4.2.

The parallel numerical solution process begins by generating a discrete mesh of points that replaces the continuous domain of the equation. We partition the mesh and associated data at run time across the participating processes so that each process "owns" a unique subset of the mesh and the corresponding unknowns of the problem, as illustrated in Figure 21.2 for a regular rectangular mesh that is distributed across four processes. Partitioning and mesh generation are important phases for practical models beyond this simple example; these issues are discussed in Chapters 18 and 19, respectively. The next phase, discretization of the PDE over the mesh, typically follows the basic philosophy of "owner computes." For efficient distributed-memory computations, the process that stores mesh and associated data for a particular region of the global problem domain calculates most, though not necessarily all, of the entries of the corresponding local part of the discretized linear operator (or matrix), A, and the right-hand-side vector, b, that define the linear system $Au = b$.

As we further discuss in Section 21.4.2, a natural abstraction for representing this mathematical problem in numerical software libraries follows this form: given the inputs A and b, compute as output the approximate solution u. Note that at this level of abstraction, we do not specify details about the internal representation of the matrix A or the vectors u and b. Instead, use of an abstract interface and possibly multiple underlying implementations enables the application code to remain simple—no details about storage formats need to be directly specified or even understood by beginning users, although advanced users can customize these choices. This approach also affords flexibility; library writers can develop a variety of implementations, each of which may be appropriate in different circumstances (e.g., matrix formats that exploit sparsity and/or special structure). Moreover, when coupled with interoperability strategies discussed in Section 21.4.3, such abstractions help to enable the seamless introduction of newly developed implementations into existing code.

A Nonlinear PDE Example

To present the approach used in PETSc, we focus on the discrete framework for an implicit PDE solution algorithm, with pseudo-time stepping to advance toward a steady state. This algorithm has the form

$$\frac{u^l}{\Delta t^l} + F(u^l) = \frac{u^{l-1}}{\Delta t^l}$$

where $\Delta t^l \to \infty$ as $l \to \infty$, u represents a fully coupled vector of unknowns, and the steady-state solution satisfies $F(u) = 0$. We choose this problem because it is often used in large-scale CFD models, including two aerodynamics applications that we discuss in some detail, namely, a compressible flow over an airplane wing using a structured mesh [409] and both compressible and incompressible flow using an unstructured mesh [549]. While we will present computational results for these representative large-scale applications, we illustrate software design and usage via the simpler nonlinear elliptic PDE,

$$F(u) = -\nabla^2 u - \lambda e^u = 0 \qquad (21.1)$$

where $u = 0$ on the boundary of the problem domain and λ is a constant. This formulation, which is known as the Bratu problem, is taken from the MINPACK-2 test problem collection [59]. The PETSc software distribution includes parallel implementations of this model that can be used to explore the software functionality.

We explain the software design used to support pseudo-transient continuation of inexact Newton methods to advance these models toward a steady state. While this discussion will focus on the SNES (scalable nonlinear equations solvers) component, which provides a level of abstraction that is convenient for these particular applications, these design principles apply equally to the linear solvers and time-stepping algorithmic components as well.

21.4.2   Mathematical Formulation

Key considerations when designing user interfaces for algorithmic software components include the following:

- What are the mathematical formulations of the target problem classes?
- What numerical algorithms will we use to solve these problems?

The combination of these two features helps to identify abstractions for components such as solvers and time steppers as well as the mathematical operators and operands that serve as their primary inputs and outputs. As explained below, sufficiently flexible abstract interfaces can support a variety of implementations of data structures and algorithms and therefore can provide good models for exploring algorithmic interchangeability and software interoperability among multiple tools developed by different groups. Such capabilities are critical for making high-performance numerical software adaptable to the continual evolution of parallel and distributed architectures and the research community's discovery of new algorithms that exploit their features.

Mathematical Abstractions: Vectors, Matrices, Index Sets, and Solvers

The mathematical formulations for a particular class of models present natural and intuitive abstractions that can be used in software interfaces. PETSc is built around a variety of mathematical and algorithmic objects; the application programmer works directly with these objects rather than concentrating on the underlying (rather complicated) data structures. Two of the basic abstract data objects in PETSc are *vectors* and *matrices*, which were introduced for a linear problem in Section 21.4.1. A PETSc vector (Vec) is an abstraction of an array of values that represent a discrete field (e.g., coefficients for the solution of a PDE), and a matrix (Mat) represents a discrete linear operator that maps between vector spaces. Each of these abstractions has several representations in PETSc. For example, PETSc currently provides three sequential, sparse matrix-data formats, four parallel, sparse matrix-data structures, and a dense representation; each is appropriate for particular classes of problems. In addition, the same matrix interface supports matrix-free approaches, in which matrices need not be explicitly stored, but rather certain functionalities (e.g., the application of the linear operator to a vector) can be provided in an encapsulated form.

While vectors and matrices are rather straightforward mathematical abstractions regardless of parallelism, we introduce the concept of an *index set* to deal with the need for aggregation in efficient distributed-memory computations. An index set (IS) is a generalization of a set of integer indices that can be used for selecting, gathering, and scattering subsets of vector and matrix elements. The index set abstraction provides users complete control to manipulate subsets of matrix and vector elements in aggregation. While one can certainly manipulate individual matrix and vector

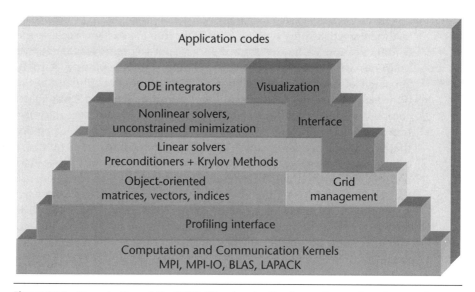

Figure 21.3   Organization of the PETSc libraries. Application codes can interface to whatever levels of abstraction are most appropriate for their needs.

elements, this approach is not a parallel expression and cannot exploit aggregation and other optimizations.

Built on top of this foundation are various classes of solvers, including linear (SLES), nonlinear (SNES), and time-stepping (TS) solvers. These solvers encapsulate virtually all information regarding the solution procedure for a particular class of problems, including the local state and various options. Application codes can interface directly to any level of the numerical library hierarchy, as shown in Figure 21.3. In addition, new software tools for other facets of scientific simulations can be built using selected parts of this hierarchy. For example, the Toolkit for Advanced Optimization (TAO) [89, 90] employs PETSc infrastructure for parallel linear algebra in the construction of parallel optimization software.

Parallelism

As explained in Balay et al. [73], we believe that use of the message-passing model within carefully designed and implemented parallel numerical libraries is an effective approach to the problem of efficiently using large-scale distributed memory, as well as clustered and NUMA (nonuniform memory access) shared-memory computers. This approach enables us to face the explicit tradeoffs that must be made to balance the code's performance (computational efficiency) and ease of use (programmer efficiency). Most important, this combination allows the gradual process of improving performance by the addition of new computational kernels, while retaining the remainder of the correctly working libraries and application code.

The PETSc 2.0 package uses object-oriented programming to conceal the details of the message passing, without concealing the parallelism. Because the details of communication are hidden from the user, approaches such as pure OpenMP or an MPI/OpenMP hybrid can be used in place of message passing. A strength of the approach of message passing combined with numerical libraries is that application codes written with this model will also run well on NUMA shared-memory computers—often as well as codes custom written for a particular machine. This translation occurs because even shared-memory machines have a memory hierarchy that message-passing programs inherently respect. For the small number of code locations where taking explicit advantage of the shared memory can lead to improved performance, alternative library routines that bypass the message-passing system may easily be provided, thus retaining a performance-portable library.

In general, the data for any PETSc object (vector, matrix, mesh, linear solver, etc.) are distributed among several processes. The distribution is handled by an MPI communicator (called MPI_Comm in MPI syntax), which represents a group of processes. When an object is created, for example, with the commands

C interface:

```
VecCreate(MPI_Comm c,int m,Vec* v);
MatCreate(MPI_Comm c,int m,int n,Mat *A);
SLESCreate(MPI_Comm c,SLES *ls);
```

Fortran interface:

```
call VecCreate(MPI_Comm c,integer m,Vec v,integer ir)
call MatCreate(MPI_Comm c,integer m,int n,Mat A,integer ir)
call SLESCreate(MPI_Comm c,SLES ls,integer ir)
```

the first argument specifies the communicator, thus indicating which processes share the object. The creation routines are collective over all processes in the communicator.

This approach does not attempt to completely conceal parallelism from the application programmer. The user initiates combinations of sequential and parallel phases of computations, but the library handles the detailed (data-structure-dependent) message passing required during the coordination of the computations. This provides a good balance between ease of use and efficiency of implementation. Six of our main guiding design principles are listed below and discussed in detail in Balay et al. [73]; the first four focus on allowing the application programmer to achieve high performance, while the last two focus on ease of use of the libraries.

- Overlapping communication and computation
- Determining within the library the details of various repeated communications and optimizing the resulting message-passing code
- Allowing the user to dictate exactly when certain communication is to occur
- Allowing the user to aggregate data for subsequent communication

- Allowing the user to work efficiently with parallel objects without specific regard for what portion of the data is stored on each processor

- Managing communication, whenever possible, within the context of higher-level operations on a parallel object or objects instead of working directly with lower-level message-passing routines

Note that the first four principles are chiefly related to reducing the number of messages, minimizing the amount of data that needs to be communicated, and hiding the latency and limitations of the bandwidth by sending data as soon as possible, *before* it is required by the receiving processor. The six guiding principles, embedded in a carefully designed object-oriented library, enable the development of highly efficient application codes without requiring a large effort from the application programmer.

Implicit Solution of Nonlinear PDEs: An Application Code Perspective

The examination of families of algorithms reveals what input and output parameters are needed within abstract interfaces. For example, to solve discretized steady-state nonlinear PDEs of the form $F(u) = 0$, where $F : \mathbb{R}^n \to \mathbb{R}^n$ (as given in equation (21.1)), a variety of algorithms can be used, including explicit, semi-implicit, and fully implicit techniques. We explore the interface of the SNES component of PETSc, which solves systems of this form using implicit Newton-type methods (see, e.g., [257, 715]), including line-search and trust-region variants. These methods can be expressed in the form

$$u_{k+1} = u_k - [F'(u_k)]^{-1}F(u_k), \quad k = 0, 1, \dots$$

where u_0 is an initial approximation to the solution and $F'(u_k)$ is nonsingular. In practice, the Newton iteration is implemented by the following two steps:

1. (Approximately) solve $F'(u_k)\Delta u_k = -F(u_k)$
2. Update $u_{k+1} = u_k + \Delta u_k$

A coarse diagram of the calling tree of a typical nonlinear PDE application appears in Figure 21.4. The top-level user routine performs I/O related to initialization, restart, and post-processing; it also calls PETSc subroutines to create data structures for vectors and matrices and to initiate the nonlinear solver. As shown by this diagram, a basic reason why the design of nonlinear equation solver libraries is fundamentally different from classical numerical linear algebra subroutine libraries such as LINPACK, EISPACK, and LAPACK is that the application code must perform certain operations for the library. The simplest such example is evaluating the nonlinear function $F(u)$ at given state vectors u; another typical requirement is approximating the associated Jacobian matrix, $F'(u)$. In addition, the software must somehow deal with application-specific data and data structures that are not known and cannot be predicted by the library writers. Auxiliary information required for the evaluation of $F(u)$ and $F'(u)$ that is not carried as part of u is communicated

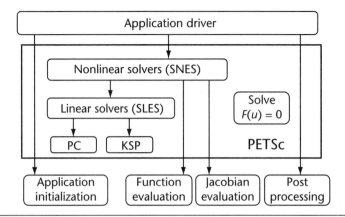

Figure 21.4 Coarsened calling tree of nonlinear PDE application, showing the user-supplied main program and call-back routines for providing the initial nonlinear iterate, computing the nonlinear residual vector at a library-requested state, and evaluating the Jacobian (preconditioner) matrix.

through PETSc via a user-defined "context" that encapsulates application-specific data. (Such information would typically include dimensioning data, mesh geometry data, physical parameters, and quantities that could be derived from the state u but are most conveniently stored instead of recalculated, such as constitutive quantities.)

Figure 21.5 illustrates the basic SNES user interface, which is both simple to use and inherently flexible. In particular, this single interface is identical for the uniprocessor and parallel cases, serves both real and complex numbers, and supports a range of different algorithms. The primary phases of solver usage are (1) instantiating the solver via the routine SNESCreate(); (2) specifying a vector data structure and callback routine for evaluation of the nonlinear function $F(u)$ via SNESSetFunction() (and optionally the matrix data structure and associated routine for evaluation of the Jacobian $F'(u)$ via SNESSetJacobian()); (3) selecting various run-time options via SNESSetFromOptions(); (4) solving the nonlinear system via SNESSolve(); and (5) destroying the solver and freeing associated memory via the routine SNESDestroy().

Note that the SNES user interface employs abstractions for vectors (Vec), matrices (Mat), and nonlinear solver algorithms (SNES). This interface reveals nothing about the particular data structures that may be used at run time. In fact, the actual algorithms, including line-search and trust-region variants of inexact Newton methods, are implemented in a data-structure-neutral format using these same abstractions. This data-structure-neutral approach [873] allows the natural storage formats for vectors and matrices to be dictated by the user's application. Since issues regarding the selection of storage formats for parallel, sparse linear algebra are usually quite complicated, this feature is critical to the software's performance.

```
SNES    snes;            /* nonlinear solver */
Mat     J;               /* Jacobian matrix */
Vec     x, f;            /* solution and residual vectors */
int     n, its;          /* problem dimension, number of iterations */
AppCtx  usercontext;     /* user-defined application context */

 .
 .
 .

/* Create matrix and vectors */
MatCreate(MPI_COMM_WORLD,n,n,&J);
VecCreate(MPI_COMM_WORLD,n,&x);
VecDuplicate(x,&f);

/* Create nonlinear solver */
SNESCreate(MPI_COMM_WORLD,SNES_NONLINEAR_EQUATIONS,&snes);

/* Set routines for evaluation of the nonlinear function and Jacobian */
SNESSetFunction(snes,f,EvaluateFunction,usercontext);
SNESSetJacobian(snes,J,EvaluateJacobian,usercontext);

/* Set run-time options */
SNESSetFromOptions(snes);

/* Solve the nonlinear system */
SNESSolve(snes,x,&its);

/* Destroy objects when finished */
SNESDestroy(snes); MatDestroy(J); VecDestroy(x); VecDestroy(f);
```

Figure 21.5 Sample SNES application code interface.

Figure 21.6 presents sample code that evaluates the nonlinear function within equation (21.1) in parallel on a 2-D regular mesh with a finite difference discretization. The problem is partitioned according to Figure 21.2, where each process owns a unique subset of the mesh and the corresponding data objects. The approach for parallel computation of the nonlinear function and Jacobian is "owner computes," with message merging and overlapping communication with computation where possible via split transactions. Each processor "ghosts" its stencil dependencies on its neighbors' data. Grid functions are mapped from a global (user-defined) ordering into contiguous local orderings, which may be designed to maximize spatial locality for cache line reuse. Scatter/gather operations are created between local sequential vectors and global distributed vectors. This example uses distributed arrays (DA) within PETSc to handle ghost-point communication; the more general

```
/*  FormFunction - Evaluates nonlinear function, F(X)

    Input Parameters:                    Output Parameter:
    snes - the SNES context              F - vector containing
    X    - input vector                      newly evaluated
    ptr  - optional user-defined context     nonlinear function
*/
int FormFunction(SNES snes,Vec X,Vec F,void *ptr)
{
 AppCtx  *a = (AppCtx *) ptr;
 int     ierr, i, j, row, mx, my, xs, ys, xm, ym, gxs, gys, gxm, gym;
 double  two = 2.0, one = 1.0, lambda, hx, hy, hxdhy, hydhx, sc;
 Scalar  u, uxx, uyy, *x, *f;
 Vec     localX = a->localX, localF = a->localF;

 mx = a->mx;             my = a->my;             lambda = a->param;
 hx = one/(double)(mx-1); hy = one/(double)(my-1);
 sc = hx*hy*lambda;      hxdhy = hx/hy;          hydhx = hy/hx;

 /* Scatter ghost points to local vector */
 ierr = DAGlobalToLocalBegin(a->da,X,INSERT_VALUES,localX); CHKERRQ(ierr);
 ierr = DAGlobalToLocalEnd(a->da,X,INSERT_VALUES,localX); CHKERRQ(ierr);

 /* Get pointers to vector data */
 ierr = VecGetArray(localX,&x); CHKERRQ(ierr);
 ierr = VecGetArray(localF,&f); CHKERRQ(ierr);

 /* Get local grid boundaries */
 ierr = DAGetCorners(a->da,&xs,&ys,PETSC_NULL,&xm,&ym,PETSC_NULL);
 CHKERRQ(ierr);
 ierr = DAGetGhostCorners(a->da,&gxs,&gys,PETSC_NULL,&gxm,&gym,
      PETSC_NULL); CHKERRQ(ierr);

 /* Compute function over the locally owned part of the grid */
 for (j=ys; j<ys+ym; j++) {
   row = (j - gys)*gxm + xs - gxs - 1;
   for (i=xs; i<xs+xm; i++) {
     row++;
     if (i == 0 || j == 0 || i == mx-1 || j == my-1)
        {f[row] = x[row]; continue;}
```

Figure 21.6 Sample parallel nonlinear function evaluation code for equation (21.1), using a finite difference discretization on a 2-D regular mesh and distributed arrays for ghost-point communication.

```
      u = x[row];
      uxx = (two*u - x[row-1] - x[row+1])*hydhx;
      uyy = (two*u - x[row-gxm] - x[row+gxm])*hxdhy;
      f[row] = uxx + uyy - sc*exp(u);
    }
  }


  /* Restore vectors */
  ierr = VecRestoreArray(localX,&x); CHKERRQ(ierr);
  ierr = VecRestoreArray(localF,&f); CHKERRQ(ierr);


  /* Insert values into global vector */
  ierr = DALocalToGlobal(a->da,localF,INSERT_VALUES,F); CHKERRQ(ierr);
  return 0;
}
```

Figure 21.6   *(continued)*

VecScatter tool could be used for unstructured meshes. Alternatively, one could
employ tools that provide parallel discretization capabilities at higher levels of
abstraction, such as Overture [144]. In fact, we have recently developed "object
wrappers" that allow all Overture and PETSc objects to coexist and interoperate in
the same application.

   Both a procedural interface (i.e., routine calls) and a command-line interface
(i.e., argc/argv program input parameters) may be used to specify particular choices
for algorithms, parameters, and data structures. The procedural interface provides
a great deal of control on a usage-by-usage basis within a single application. For
example, one can select a line-search or trust-region variant of Newton's method
by calling SNESSetType(snes,ls) or SNESSetType(snes,tr), respectively. Alternatively,
these choices can be specified by the corresponding run-time option (e.g., -snes_
type [ls,tr]); the run-time option approach applies the same rules to all queries
via a database and thereby enables the user to have complete control at run time
with no extra coding. A typical usage scenario employs the procedural interface to
indicate defaults (that may be different from those specified by the library) within a
given application code and then uses the command-line interface to override these
defaults for experimentation with a variety of alternatives.

21.4.3   Composability and Interoperability

As discussed in Section 21.2.1, the high-fidelity multiphysics applications of interest
within high-performance scientific computing often require the combined use of
software tools that encapsulate the expertise of multidisciplinary research teams.
Current-generation software tools have demonstrated good success in direct pairwise

interfaces, whereby one tool directly calls another by using well-defined interfaces that are known at compile time. For example, we have developed two-way interfaces between PETSc and PVODE, which provides higher-order, adaptive ODE schemes and robust nonlinear solvers [474]. However, more flexible and dynamic capabilities are needed than predefined interfaces that use a succession of subroutine calls. This is especially important because we must support incremental shifts in parallel algorithms and programming paradigms that inevitably occur during the lifetimes of scientific application codes.

Consequently, various research groups within the high-performance computing community are exploring the ideas of *component programming*, based on encapsulating units of functionality and providing a meta-language specification of their interfaces (see, e.g., Broy et al. [147] and Szyperski [908]). Component-based software development can be considered an evolutionary step beyond object-oriented design. Object-oriented techniques have been quite successful in managing the complexity of modern software, but they have not resulted in significant amounts of cross-project code reuse. Sharing object-oriented code is difficult because of language incompatibilities, the lack of standardization for interobject communication, and the need for compile-time coupling of interfaces. Component-based software development addresses issues of language independence—seamlessly combining components written in different programming languages—and component frameworks define standards for communication among components.

The Common Component Architecture (CCA) Forum, whose current membership is drawn from various Department of Energy national laboratories and collaborating academic institutions, is working to specify a component architecture for high-performance scientific computing [47, 216]. We are currently incorporating new features within the PETSc software to enable compliance with this evolving specification.

21.4.4   Performance Issues

As discussed by Anderson et al. [40], achieving sustained high performance for PDE-based simulations involves three aspects. The first is a scalable algorithm in the sense of convergence rate; the second is good per-processor performance on contemporary cache-based microprocessors; and the third is a scalable implementation, in the sense of time per iteration as the number of processors increases. This section demonstrates that the flexible software design presented in this chapter enables application codes to address all three of these issues and to avoid premature optimization for particular algorithmic and data structure choices by experimenting with a range of options for realistic problems.

Algorithmic Experimentation

Now that we have covered the basic principles of design and seen what some of the issues are for parallel PDE computations, we examine a specific application to demonstrate how this approach enables investigation of open research issues. In particular, we explore the standard 3-D aerodynamics test case of transonic flow over an ONERA M6 wing using the frequently studied parameter combination of a freestream Mach number of 0.84 with an angle of attack of 3.06°. The robustness of solution strategies is particularly important for this model because of the so-called λ-shock that develops on the upper wing surface. The basis for our implementation, as discussed in Gropp et al. [409], is a legacy sequential Fortran 77 code by Whitfield and Taylor [991] that uses a mapped structured C-H mesh. This application demonstrates the use of the nonlinear solvers within SNES in the legacy context, where we retain the original code's discretization as embodied in flux balance routines for steady-state residual construction and finite-difference Jacobian construction. The function evaluations are undertaken to second order in the upwinding scheme, and the Jacobian matrix (used mainly as a preconditioner) is evaluated to first order. We parallelize the logically regular, mapped mesh using the distributed array tools of PETSc.

We consider Newton–Krylov–Schwarz methods, which combine a Newton–Krylov method with a Schwarz-based preconditioner. From a computational point of view, one of the most important characteristics of a Krylov method for the linear system $Ax = b$ is that information about the matrix A needs to be accessed only in the form of matrix–vector products in a relatively small number of carefully chosen directions. Newton–Krylov methods are suited for nonlinear problems in which it is unreasonable to compute or store a true, full Jacobian, where the action of A can be approximated by discrete directional derivatives. However, if the Jacobian A is ill conditioned, the Krylov method will require an unacceptably large number of iterations. The system can be transformed into the equivalent form $B^{-1}Ax = B^{-1}b$ through the action of a preconditioner, B, whose inverse action approximates that of A, but at smaller cost. It is in the choice of preconditioning where the battle for low computational cost and scalable parallelism is usually won or lost. In Schwarz preconditioning methods (see, e.g., Smith et al [872]), the operator is introduced on a subdomain-by-subdomain basis through a conveniently computable approximation to a local Jacobian. Such Schwarz-type preconditioning provides good data locality for parallel implementations over a range of parallel granularities, allowing significant architectural adaptability.

Figure 21.7 shows a sample script that can be used to automate experimentation with this hierarchy of tunable algorithms. The script demonstrates the use of both line-search and trust-region variants of Newton's method on various numbers of processors. Several Krylov methods are considered, including GMRES, BiCGStab, and transpose-free QMR, in conjunction with additive Schwarz preconditioners with various degrees of overlap. This script facilitates the investigation of which preconditioning and Krylov methods are most effective for particular problem sizes and processor configurations. Additional run-time options could also be invoked to investigate a range of other issues, including linear and nonlinear convergence parameters, blocked matrix data structures, and derivative computations via sparse finite differences and automatic differentiation.

```csh
#! /bin/csh
#
# Sample script: Experimenting with nonlinear solver options
# Can be used with, e.g., petsc/src/snes/examples/tutorials/ex5.c
#
foreach np (8 16 32 64)                     # number of processors
  foreach snestype (ls tr)                  # nonlinear solver
    foreach ksptype (gmres bcgs tfqmr)      # Krylov solver
      foreach overlap (1 2 3 4)             # level of overlap for ASM
        echo '****** Beginning new run ******'
        mpirun -np $np ex2 -snes_type $snestype -ksp_type $ksptype \
          -pc_type asm -pc_asm_overlap $overlap
      end
    end
  end
end
```

Figure 21.7   Sample script for Newton–Krylov–Schwarz algorithmic experimentation.

Preconditioner quality dramatically affects the overall efficiency of the parallel Newton–Krylov–Schwarz methodology, as demonstrated in Figure 21.8 for various degrees of overlap for the restricted additive Schwarz method (RASM) [167], which eliminates interprocess communication during the interpolation phase of the additive Schwarz technique. The graphs within these figures compare convergence rate (in terms of relative residual norm) with both nonlinear iteration number (Figure 21.8(a)) and time (Figure 21.8(b)) for a mesh of dimension $98 \times 18 \times 18$ with five degrees of freedom per node, on 16 processors of an IBM SP2. We note that the nonlinear model employs a subtle form of continuation in boundary conditions by activating full characteristic boundary conditions at the impermeable wing surface only after the 10th nonlinear iteration. (This accounts for the spikes seen in the residual norm histories.) All runs plotted in this figure use preconditioned restarted GMRES with a Krylov subspace of maximum dimension 30 and a fixed, relative convergence tolerance of 10^{-2}; each processor hosts a single preconditioner block, which is solved via point-block ILU(0). We see that for this model, two-cell overlap provides a good balance in terms of power and cost. Less overlap trades off cheaper cost per iteration for a preconditioner that does not allow the nonlinear iterations to converge as rapidly, while more overlap is costly to apply and does not contribute to faster nonlinear convergence. While this example is a relatively small problem, similar behavior was observed for other problem sizes and processor configurations, even when using different criteria to determine linear inner iteration convergence.

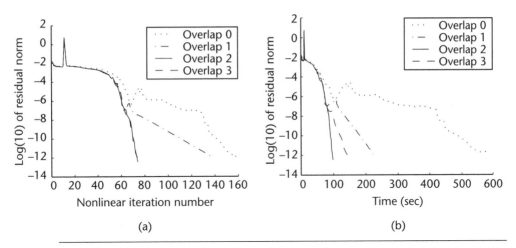

Figure 21.8   Comparison of four domain-decomposed preconditioners: subdomain block Jacobi and restricted additive Schwarz with overlap of one, two, and three cells. All methods solve point-block ILU(0) on 16 subdomains on an IBM SP2.

Data Structures and Orderings for Fast Local Performance

A key consideration in algorithms and data structures is the management of multi-level memory hierarchies. To demonstrate some of these issues, we consider another application, FUN3D, which is a tetrahedral, vertex-centered, unstructured mesh code originally developed for uniprocessors by W. K. Anderson of the NASA Langley Research Center for compressible and incompressible Euler and Navier–Stokes equations [39]. FUN3D uses a control volume discretization with variable-order Roe schemes for approximating the convective fluxes and a Galerkin discretization for the viscous terms. The application was parallelized using the VecScatter tools within PETSc for ghost-point communication and the nonlinear solvers within SNES [548].

We can view PDE computations predominantly as a mix of loads and stores with embedded floating-point operations (flops) [40]. Since flops are cheap relative to memory references, we concentrate on minimizing the memory references and emphasize strong sequential performance as one of the factors needed for efficient aggregate performance. Data storage patterns for primary and auxiliary fields should adapt to hierarchical memory through (1) interlacing, (2) structural blocking degrees of freedom that are defined at the same point in point-block operations, and (3) reordering of edges for reuse of vertex data. Interlacing allows efficient reuse of cached operands, since components at the same point interact more intensely with each other than do the same fields at other points. Similarly, blocking reduces the number of loads significantly and enhances reuse of data items in registers. Also, edge reordering for vertex reuse reflects the fact that nearby points interact more intensely than distant points. Applying these techniques within FUN3D required whole-program transformations of certain loops of the original vector-oriented application

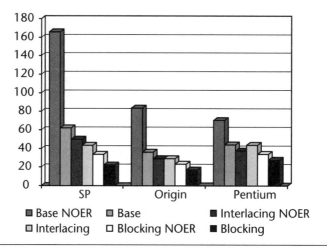

Figure 21.9 Effect of cache optimizations of the average execution time for one nonlinear iteration of the FUN3D application. *Base* denotes the case without any optimizations, and *NOER* denotes no edge reordering. The performance improves by a factor of about 2.5 on the Pentium and 7.5 on the IBM SP. The processor details are 120 MHz IBM SP (P2SC "thin," 128 KB L1), 250 MHz Origin 2000 (R1000, 32 KB L1, and 4 MB L2), and 400 MHz Pentium II (running Windows NT 4.0, 16 KB L1, and 512 KB L2).

but, as shown in Figure 21.9, raised the per-processor performance by a factor of between 2.5 and 7, depending on the microprocessor and optimizing compiler. We note that the use of the abstract interface for PETSc matrix assembly enabled the change from a compressed, sparse, row-point storage format to the block variant without changing a single line of the matrix assembly code.

Because of the cost and difficulty of architectural tuning for new environments, some recent efforts have focused on automating this process for numerical kernels. In particular, ATLAS (Automatically Tuned Linear Algebra Software) [988] and PHiPAC (Portable High Performance ANSI C) [107] are packages for automatically producing high-performance BLAS, in particular matrix–matrix multiplication routines, for machines with complicated memory hierarchies and functional units.

Scalability

Having first assured attention to good per-processor performance for the FUN3D application, we are now ready to discuss the scalability of this aerodynamic model. In Figure 21.10 we demonstrate several metrics of the code's parallel scalability, which uses pseudo-time stepping and the Newton–Krylov–Schwarz implementations in PETSc, for a fixed-size mesh with 2.8 million vertices running on up to 1024 Cray T3E processors. We see that the implementation efficiency of parallelization (i.e., the efficiency on a per-iteration basis) is 82% in going from 128 to 1024 processors.

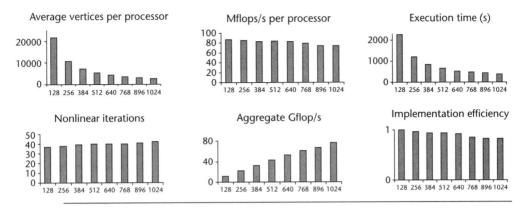

Figure 21.10   Parallel performance of the FUN3D application for a fixed-size mesh of 2.8 million vertices (over 11 million unknowns) run on up to 1024 Cray T3E 600 MHz processors.

The number of nonlinear iterations is also fairly flat over the same eightfold range of processors (rising from 37 to 42), reflecting reasonable algorithmic scalability. This is much less serious degradation than predicted by the linear elliptic theory (see Smith et al. [872]); pseudo-time stepping, required by the nonlinearity, is responsible. The overall efficiency is the product of the implementation efficiency and the algorithmic efficiency. The computational rates per processor are also close to flat over this range, even though the relevant working sets in each subdomain vary by nearly a factor of eight. This emphasizes the requirement of good serial performance for good parallel performance.

21.5   Software for PDEs

As discussed throughout the chapter, the development of scalable scientific application codes involving the solution of large-scale PDEs requires attention to complex issues, including algorithmic choices and the management of multilevel memory hierarchies. Application developers may wish to leverage software packages that can assist with various facets of solution. We now provide a brief overview of PDE-related software.

- *DAGH* [744]. DAGH (Distributed Adaptive Grid Hierarchy) provides a program development infrastructure for the implementation of solutions of PDEs using adaptive mesh-refinement algorithms.
- *Diffpack* [148, 268]. Diffpack is an object-oriented framework for solving PDEs.
- *DOUG* [425]. DOUG (Domain Decomposition on Unstructured Grids) is a black box parallel iterative solver for finite element systems arising from elliptic PDEs.

- *FFTW* [332]. FFTW is a collection of Fast Fourier Transform routines, including routines for parallel computers. FFTs are often used in solving certain classes of linear PDEs, and can be used as preconditioners for more general PDEs.

- *KeLP* [67, 336]. KeLP (Kernel Lattice Parallelism) is a framework for implementing portable scientific applications on distributed-memory parallel computers. It is intended for applications with special needs, in particular, those that adapt to data-dependent or hardware-dependent conditions at run time.

- *MUDPACK* [5]. MUDPACK includes a suite of portable Fortran programs that automatically discretize and use multigrid techniques to generate second- and fourth-order approximations to elliptic PDEs on rectangular regions.

- *Overture* [144, 463]. Overture is an object-oriented code framework for solving PDEs; it provides a portable, flexible software development environment for applications that involve the simulation of physical processes in complex moving geometry.

- *Parallel ELLPACK* [487, 489]. Parallel ELLPACK is a problem-solving environment for PDE-based applications.

- *PARASOL* [746]. PARASOL is an integrated environment for parallel, sparse matrix solvers. PARASOL is written in Fortran 90 and uses MPI for communication.

- *PETSc* [72, 73]. PETSc (Portable, Extensible Toolkit for Scientific Computing) is a collection of tools for the parallel numerical solution of PDEs and related problems.

- *POOMA* [53, 625] POOMA (Parallel Object-Oriented Methods and Applications) is an object-oriented framework for applications in computational science requiring high-performance parallel computers.

- *SAMRAI* [482, 570]. SAMRAI is an object-oriented code framework that provides general and extensible software support for rapid prototyping and development of parallel structured adaptive mesh-refinement applications.

- *UG* [84, 947]. UG (Unstructured Grids) is a flexible software tool for the numerical solution of partial differential equations on unstructured meshes in two and three space dimensions using multigrid methods.

- *VECFEM* [410]. VECFEM is a package for the solution of nonlinear boundary value problems by the finite element method.

Additional pointers may be available through the following online resources:

- *MGNet* [291]. MGNet is a repository for information related to multigrid, multilevel, multiscale, aggregation, defect correction, and domain-decomposition methods, including links to software packages.

- *NHSE* [699]. The National High-Performance Software Exchange is a distributed collection of software, documents, data, and information of interest to the high-performance and parallel-computing community.

21.6   Conclusion

As discussed in Chapter 2, future computing technology will likely be characterized by highly parallel, hierarchical designs. This trend in design is a fairly straightforward consequence of two other trends: a desire to work with increasingly large data sets at increasing speeds and the imperative of cost effectiveness. Fortunately, data use in most PDE-based applications has sufficient temporal and spatial locality to map reasonably well to distributed- and hierarchical-memory systems. To achieve good performance, this locality can be exploited by a combination of the application programmer at the algorithmic level, the system software at the compiler and run-time levels, and the hardware.

This chapter presented some ideas for addressing these issues in PDE software at the level of numerical library writers and application programmers. In particular, we discussed how organizing applications around the mathematics of models enables the writing of applications that can be run without change with a wide variety of different algorithms and data structures. This facilitates exploiting parallelism, managing complexity within the application, and effectively using the available computing resources. Using these techniques, applications have run scalably on thousands of processors, achieving performance in the teraflop range. We conclude with a few additional recommendations for application scientists.

- Design application codes around abstract concepts, not particular algorithms or data structures. Expect the best algorithms to change over the lifetime of an application.

- Take advantage of modern programming languages; for example, use features of Fortran 90 rather than minimalistic Fortran 77.

- Use programming models that offer portable performance, such as MPI or OpenMP. Use vendor-specific features or extensions only when the benefit clearly outweighs the loss of portability.

- Communicate and compute on aggregates, not individual elements.

- Use libraries whenever possible; when libraries do not provide the needed functionality, contact the authors with suggestions and recommendations.

- Give the largest possible problem to the numerical library. For example, if the library offers suitable nonlinear solvers as well as linear solvers, use the nonlinear solvers rather than building a simple nonlinear iteration yourself and using the library's linear solvers. This approach gives the library the best opportunity to maximize performance (see Section 21.2.3).

Acknowledgments. We were supported by the Mathematical, Information, and Computational Sciences Division subprogram of the Office of Advanced Scientific Computing Research, U.S. Department of Energy, under contract W-31-109-Eng-38.

22 Parallel Continuous Optimization

J. E. Dennis, Jr. • **Zhijun Wu**

Optimization has broad applications in engineering, science, and management. Many of these applications either have large numbers of variables or require expensive function evaluations. In some cases, there may be many local minimizers, and the user naturally wants to know how solutions found by the algorithm compare to other local solutions. These factors contribute to the need for more intensive computation than traditional architectures can support. High-performance computing provides powerful tools for solving these problems with a degree of practicality that would otherwise be impossible.

Example applications where parallel optimization can play an important role include aircraft shape design [228] and macromolecular modeling [681].

In aircraft shape design, one attempts to match an ideal pressure distribution by manipulating the shape variables. The number of shape variables is on the order of hundreds at most, but they are constrained by at least two systems of partial differential equations (PDEs). This is typical of many important applied optimization problems. There may not be so many decision variables for the optimizer, but there may be many ancillary variables that must be determined to compute the objective function and constraints. In order to obtain a feasible solution, the systems must match the input of each with the output of the others, in addition to satisfying side constraints such as range. The systems require expensive PDE solves for millions of grid points and different grids for different PDEs; and there is at least one PDE to be solved for the air flow and one to be solved for the structural deflection.

This problem is computationally intensive because there is a great deal of linear and nonlinear algebra going on at each function and constraint evaluation. We describe some domain-decomposition–type methods for this problem. As in that case, the *sequential* efficiency of the parallel optimization procedure can be an improvement over more traditional methods.

649

In macromolecular modeling, one attempts to determine molecular structure by minimizing a given potential energy function. One of the most important applications is the determination of protein structures in structural molecular biology. The challenge in solving this problem is that the potential energy function has many local minimizers, while the structure to be determined is believed to correspond to a global or nearly global optimal solution to the minimization problem. Global optimization algorithms have been developed to solve the problem. Not surprisingly, they rely heavily on using computing power that only parallel high-performance architectures can provide.

Substantial research efforts on parallel optimization have been made in the past 20 years. In the past 10 years or so, some have borne fruit by focusing on special applications and others by exploring more general parallel schemes.

Optimization has close relationships with numerical linear algebra and partial differential equations. For example, a typical optimization procedure requires solving a linear system at every iteration to predict a step to a better approximate solution; function or constraint evaluation often requires solving a PDE. Thus, parallel optimization algorithms and software development certainly benefit from advances in parallel numerical linear algebra and PDEs.

General algorithms have also been developed such as parallel direct-search methods by Dennis and Torczon [258], Hough et al. [485, 572] and Torczon [937]. Audet and Dennis [57] extend the methods to allow for so-called categorical variables, which are unordered discrete variables that must always have discrete values for the function values to be defined. Even more general are the evolutionary algorithms [841], which allow any sort of variables at all. For more traditional derivative-based optimization, there are parallel methods for optimization of linked subsystems by Dennis and Lewis [256] and Dennis et al. [255], and variable and constraint distribution schemes by Ferris and Mangasarian [329, 330], as well as many others based more or less or parallelizing the linear algebra involved in computing an optimization step.

Parallel global optimization has been one of the most active areas in parallel continuous optimization. Work in this area is motivated by important applications in chemical and biological disciplines such as cluster simulation and protein modeling. Algorithms and software developed in recent years include parallel stochastic global optimization algorithms for molecular conformation and protein folding by Byrd and Schnabel [160, 162]; parallel global continuation software (DGSOL) for protein structure determination with nuclear magnetic resonance (NMR) distance data by Moré and Wu [681, 682, 683, 685]; and parallel, effective-energy-simulated annealing for protein potential-energy minimization by Coleman et al. [211, 212].

Optimization problems take different forms arising from the motivating applications. They can be linear or nonlinear, constrained or unconstrained, and local or global. They can be either large and sparse or small but very expensive to evaluate. This means that quite different parallel algorithms may be required and quite different architectures may be appropriate. For example, if the problem is large but sparse, a shared-memory system may be a good choice, for otherwise the distribution of a sparse, irregular structure over multiprocessors may cause load imbalance and severe communication overhead. On the other hand, most global optimization algorithms are coarsely parallel. They can be implemented on distributed-memory architectures, or even loosely connected networks of workstations, and still maintain scalability.

In the following sections, we discuss various parallel optimization methods in greater detail. We describe optimization problems and algorithms and their associated parallelism at different computational levels: function evaluation, algebraic calculation, and optimization. In particular, we review parallel methods for local and global optimization, and we compare strategies for large, sparse versus small but expensive problems. Parallel techniques including parallel direct search, optimization of linked subsystems, and variable and constraint distribution are introduced. Future research directions are discussed at the end.

22.1   Local Optimization

Let us consider the problem of minimizing a nonlinear function, $f(x)$, where f is continuous and differentiable for all $x \in \mathbb{R}^n$. Generally, we would be given some incumbent approximate minimizer x^0. The most popular methods for this problem construct a quadratic model for the objective function (and a linear model of the constraints if they are present). This model problem is intended to represent the problem of interest in some neighborhood of x^0. Generally this is true because the model is built by using at least the first-order Taylor series term. Often finite difference approximations to the derivatives are used, and this is an obvious opportunity for parallelism. In fact, the kind of parallelism used is one of the most useful for optimization, in that values of the true function are obtained in parallel (see discussions in Byrd et al. [164]).

Since the model is thought to represent the problem locally, one hopes that by finding a really good minimizer for the model, one will obtain a point that improves the real objective function. Thus, Newton or quasi-Newton algorithms choose a putative next iterate by solving the model problem. The difficulty with this procedure is that the solution to the model problem may be outside the region about x^0 where the model represents the problem well.

If the iterate found in this way is a better solution, then one moves to it and iterates the procedure. It will not surprise the reader that this procedure is likely to find the bottom of the same function valley one starts in. That is, a nearby local minimizer x^*, assuming there is one, in the sense that for any x in a neighborhood of x^*, $f(x)$ is greater than or equal to $f(x^*)$.

If the pure iteration does not succeed in finding a better point, then it resorts to a globalization strategy. In this sense, globalization means convergence to some solution from any point, not solution to the global minimizer.

The two main classes of globalization algorithms for this problem are line searches and trust regions. Trust regions adaptively estimate a region in which the local model can be "trusted" to adequately represent the true function. The next iterate is chosen by approximately minimizing the model over the trust region. Line-search algorithms backtrack (usually) from the solution of the model problem along the direction from the incumbent. Each approach has its place in the optimization toolbox, and each has its own opportunities for parallelism.

Trust-region algorithms can use parallelism in the linear algebra needed to solve the trust-region subproblem—minimize the model in the region where it is trusted to represent the function (see Santos and Sorensen [825] and Rendl and Wolkowicz [797]). Line-search algorithms can use parallel linear algebra to compute the solution of the model problem, and they can also use parallel function evaluations to find the best step along the direction they compute. Parallel multiple line searches [697] and parallel inexact Newton step computation [696] can be applied here.

For large-scale optimization, it is often useful to take advantage of the property of partial separability. That is, the objective function can be written in the following form,

$$f(x) = \sum_{i=1}^{m} f_i(x)$$

where f_i is called an element function of f and depends only on a small subset of the variables. This class of functions can be computed in parallel by distributing the element functions to the processors. Each processor will then be responsible for computing only the contributions of the element functions to the whole function, gradient, and Hessian.

Let processor i compute element functions $f_{i_1}, \ldots, f_{i_{max}}$. Then the function, gradient, and Hessian can be computed in the following procedure,

initialize f, ∇f, $\nabla^2 f$
on processor i:
    do for $j \in \{i_1, \ldots, i_{max}\}$
        $f = f + f_j$
        $\nabla f = \nabla f + \nabla f_j$
        $\nabla^2 f = \nabla^2 f + \nabla^2 f_j$
    end do
end

where updates to f, ∇f, and $\nabla^2 f$ require global reduction on distributed-memory machines or access to shared variables on shared-memory machines. However, the updates for the gradient and the Hessian can be done efficiently by updating only the elements for which the corresponding elements of ∇f_j and $\nabla^2 f_j$ are nonzero [60, 680].

The computation of the step, or its direction, with methods using the Hessian or Hessian approximations can be parallelized in several ways. In general, this is a place where a "plug-and-play" approach can be used by calling existing parallel linear algebra software such as LAPACK or ScaLAPACK [35, 119]. For example, a parallel direct solver with Cholesky factorization can be used to compute the search direction $[B(x^i)]^{-1} \nabla f(x^i)$ at any iterate x^i if the Hessian or its approximation $B(x^i)$

is symmetric positive definite; a parallel matrix–vector multiplication routine can be used for computing all matrix–vector products in the truncated Newton or trust-region subproblem solves. Byrd et al. [164] showed that the quasi-Newton step can be obtained by using inverse BFGS updates, which then require only matrix–vector multiplications and can be parallelized straightforwardly with a parallel matrix–vector multiplication routine.

If one wishes to exploit sparsity, the above parallelization becomes more complicated. Several issues arise. First, an iterative solver can always be used for either a line-search or trust-region algorithm in the truncated Newton's method. This requires a preconditioner, which not only depends on the problem but also is more difficult to parallelize. Work on this issue was done by Balay et al. [73] and Jones and Plassmann [518, 520, 521, 522], who developed a parallel incomplete Cholesky factorization algorithm that seems efficient in practice.

Second, parallel direct-sparse solves are difficult on distributed-memory machines, because data and computation are tricky to distribute to balance the load among processors. A symbolic factorization phase is a potential serial bottleneck in addition to the sparse triangular system solves. Coleman and Sun [213] developed a group of parallel direct-sparse solvers for optimization using a multifrontal approach.

Bokhari and Mavriplis [125], Feo et al. [325], and Zaslavsky et al. [1016] demonstrated that the Tera multithreaded architecture is particularly good for parallel sparse and irregular calculations. However, there is no general sparse-matrix software available yet on this architecture. Finally, sparsity patterns often change from application to application. Classes of optimization problems having the same sparsity patterns, like some large linear programming problems, need to be identified, and special parallel sparse solvers targeted to these classes of problems can then be developed. Work in this direction includes Bixby and Martin [117], Schneider and Wise [838], and Coleman and Wright [207].

22.2   Global Optimization

Research on global optimization has increased dramatically in recent years. An important reason is that the increasing power of parallel high-performance architectures makes it possible to attack many large, difficult global optimization problems of practical interest. Ten years ago, work in this area was still limited to toy problems of about 10 variables, but now, with the help of parallel computing, advanced algorithms have been developed and applied to problems with hundreds or even thousands of variables in such applications as cluster simulation [159, 160, 161, 162, 211, 212, 858, 1007, 1008], protein folding [163, 214, 234, 575, 576, 613, 727, 764, 781, 852, 853], and molecular docking [270, 672].

A global optimization problem requires a local minimizer with the lowest function value among all local optimizers. Certain classes of problems, like convex programming problems, have only one local minimum. But most functions arising in applications are nonconvex, and they may have many local minima, constrained or unconstrained.

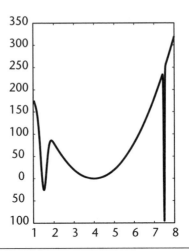

Figure 22.1   A function with three local minimizers.

It is quite easy to see that general smooth-continuous, global optimization problems are intractable. Furthermore, even if one has the global minimizer in hand, it is an intractable problem to verify that it is anything more than a local minimizer.

Nevertheless, the fact that a problem is impossible to solve in general does not preclude useful research in the area. Often practical problems are posed as global optimization problems because that is the nearest model problem in the optimization toolkit to what the user really wants, and modern global optimization methods can find valuable solutions that satisfy the user.

This point is far less subtle than it may seem at first. To see this, consider a hypothetical problem in engineering design. The designer wishes to find the best design for a widget in terms of a single design variable that is constrained to lie in a bounded interval. Suppose that there are three local minimizers, as in Figure 22.1. The left-hand local minimizer and the wide shallow middle minimizer will be found by a good global optimization algorithm. On the other hand, the wide shallow middle minimizer is likely to be the only one found by a local algorithm. However, the narrow right-hand local minimizer, which is also the global minimizer, is unlikely to be found without an impractical amount of effort by any algorithm.

In practice, this may not be important at all; such a narrow minimum for the function is likely to have little practical value because if the process for manufacturing the widget leads to any variability in the decision variable, then the actual design criterion for the finished good will end up high on the narrow valley at a much worse value than that in the more stable left-hand valley. Of course, decision makers would want to make that decision for themselves in possession of the location of the true global optimizer. Our point is that the more difficult a given global optimizer is to find, the less important it is likely to be to find it.

We describe some applications areas and related parallel, global optimization work below.

22.2.1   Protein Folding

Protein folding is a fundamental unsolved problem in structural molecular biology. The problem is to determine how the protein amino acids fold to a unique 3-D structure. There are no direct physical means to detect this. X-ray crystallography and NMR spectroscopy have been used to derive approximate structures, but this requires months, or even years, of laboratory effort for each protein.

The goal is to determine the structure, with only the knowledge of the amino acid sequence of the protein, by finding a structure corresponding to the global potential energy minimum. While this is possible in theory, it is computationally intense since it requires solving a global optimization problem with many thousands of degrees of freedom.

The potential energy function usually is given in an empirical form. It includes energy terms for such atomic interactions in proteins as electrostatic, van der Waal's, bonded, torsional, and so on. Typically, the total energy E has the following form:

$$E = E_{elec} + E_{vand} + E_{bond} + E_{angl} + E_{tors}$$

where

$$E_{elec} = \sum_{ij/electro} \frac{q_i q_j}{\epsilon r_{ij}}$$

$$E_{vand} = \sum_{ij/vander} \left(\frac{\sigma_{ij}}{r_{ij}}\right)^{12} - 2\left(\frac{\sigma_{ij}}{r_{ij}}\right)^{6}$$

$$E_{bond} = \sum_{ij/bonded} k_{ij}(r_{ij} - r_{ij}^0)^2$$

$$E_{angl} = \sum_{\theta/bonded} k_{\theta}(\theta - \theta^0)^2$$

$$E_{tors} = \sum_{\phi/torsional} k_{\phi}[1 + \cos(n\phi - \phi^0)]$$

and, where θ, ϕ, and r_{ij} are bond angle, torsional angle, and pairwise distance, respectively, and depend on the atomic positions, and all other indicated quantities are given parameters.

Note that the potential energy function is defined in terms of the atomic positions x_i, $i = 1, \ldots, n$, where n is the number of the atoms in the protein and usually is in the range of 1000 to 100,000. Recent work to develop special methods for this problem includes Scheraga et al. [575, 576, 764, 831], Straub et al. [904], Coleman et al. [211, 212], and Byrd and Schnabel [162, 163, 234, 858].

22.2.2   Cluster Simulation

Another class of global optimization problems comes from the emerging field of cluster science [419, 799]. Clusters important for material design include argon clusters [476, 477, 478], various metal clusters [369, 514], and clusters of carbon molecules such as the famous carbon 60, the Buckyball [581]. A key research problem is to find the most stable configuration for any given cluster. The clusters may not exist in nature or may be hard to observe. However, given a potential energy function, its global minimizer corresponds to the most stable configuration for that model of potential energy. As an example, the potential energy function for simulating argon clusters is

$$E_{argon} = \sum_{ij} \frac{1}{\|x_i - x_j\|^{12}} - \frac{2}{\|x_i - x_j\|^6}$$

where x_i and x_j are positions of the atoms.

Note that this function is very similar to the van der Waal term in the protein potential energy function. As a matter of fact, they are indeed models of the same type of potentials due to the so-called van der Waal weak forces between pairs of atoms. The potential energy function for the argon cluster is simpler than for proteins, but it is by no means easy to minimize. Hoare and Pal [478] estimated that this function has exponentially many local minimizers that grow as a function e^{n^2} of the number of atoms n in the cluster. Recent work on this problem includes Northby [717], Xue [1007], Byrd and Schnabel [160], Coleman et al. [211, 212], and many others.

22.2.3   Distance Geometry

Strong motivation for solving distance geometry problems is their application in NMR macromolecular modeling, where a protein structure can be determined by solving a distance geometry problem using the NMR distance data.

These problems can be formulated as global nonlinear, least-squares optimization problems [233], or, from a graph-theoretic point of view, they are a class of NP-complete, graph-embedding problems [461, 681, 827, 828]. Recent attempts to solve these problems on parallel high-performance architectures are by Hendrickson [462], Moré and Wu [683], and Byrd et al. [1020].

A simple version of the distance geometry problem is to find a set of points to realize a given set of distances between some of the points. A more general version is to satisfy a given set of bounds on the distances. Mathematically, the problem is to find a set of points $x_i \in \mathbb{R}^3$, $i = 1, \ldots, n$ such that the distance $\|x_i - x_j\|$ between points x_i and x_j is equal to a given distance d_{ij} or in between a given pair of bounds l_{ij} and u_{ij} of the distance. It can be formulated as a global optimization problem as follows. If d_{ij} are given,

$$\min \sum_{(i,j) \in S} (\|x_i - x_j\|^2 - d_{ij}^2)^2$$

where S is a given set of (i, j) pairs. If l_{ij} and u_{ij} are given,

$$\mathbf{min} \sum_{(i,j) \in S} \min^2 \left\{ \frac{\|x_i - x_j\|^2 - l_{ij}^2}{l_{ij}^2}, 0 \right\} + \max^2 \left\{ \frac{\|x_i - x_j\|^2 - u_{ij}^2}{u_{ij}^2}, 0 \right\}$$

Note that S may have (i, j) ranging from only a few to all possible pairs. For less than n pairs, the problem can be trivial. For all possible pairs, the problem still can be solved in polynomial time [122, 233]. However, in practice, S is sparse, and the problem is hard to solve.

22.2.4 Stochastic Global Optimization

A stochastic global optimization method was proposed by Rinnooy Kan and Timmer [803]. Byrd and Schnabel [162] developed a parallel version. The method has these basic steps. A set of points is chosen in the problem domain, and the objective function is evaluated at the points. A subset of the points with low function values are selected as starting points for local minimization, which then is performed.

If one of the local minimizers is accepted as the global minimizer, the algorithm stops. Otherwise, the process is repeated. Each time the starting points are selected from all previous, as well as current, sampled points. Therefore, as the algorithm proceeds, more and more points are sampled, and there are increasing chances to find the global minimizer.

Rinnooy Kan and Timmer [803] showed that with probability one, the algorithm converges to a global minimizer in a finite number of iterations. Byrd and Schnabel [162] developed a parallel version of the algorithm by sampling starting points and performing local minimizations, all in parallel. The problem domain is divided into smaller regions, each of which is assigned to a processor. Some regions are further refined if lower function values or local minima are found, and the subregions are reassigned to other processors when necessary to achieve load balance.

Although it requires dynamic load balancing, the stochastic global optimization algorithm is easy to parallelize and performs well on both shared- and distributed-memory architectures. Byrd and Schnabel [162] reported development of the algorithm on KSR-1 and IBM SP2 and performance results on protein and related molecular conformation problems. The algorithm has also been used by research groups in other institutions, including some at the CRPC.

22.2.5 Effective-Energy Simulated Annealing

The effective-energy simulated–annealing algorithm was developed by Coleman et al. [211]. The algorithm was parallelized and implemented on Intel iPSC/860 and IBM SP2. We describe the parallel implementation of this algorithm to show a general parallelization strategy for all simulated-annealing–type algorithms.

A physical annealing process starts at a high temperature and then cools down by stages gradually to the zero temperature, where the system reaches the ground state. The process has to proceed slowly so that at each cooling stage the system has enough time to reach equilibrium, for otherwise it will be trapped in a local state.

A simulated-annealing algorithm tries to mimic this process by considering the objective function of the global minimization problem as the energy function of a simulated system. A parameter corresponds to the temperature and is decreased by stages. At each stage, function values are randomly sampled. Each time a point of lower potential energy is found, it is accepted as the current point. Otherwise, a point is accepted or rejected randomly using the Metropolis criterion, which depends on the temperature: if the temperature is higher, the probability of accepting the point is also higher. This property allows the algorithm to sample and accept more points at high temperature, while gradually settling down at lower temperatures to smaller regions where the lowest point of potential energy may be located. It has been proved that the sequence of the points sampled by the simulated-annealing algorithm form a Boltzmann distribution and converges to a global minimizer with probability one as the temperature goes to zero [1].

The effective-energy simulated-annealing algorithm is similar to the simulated annealing algorithm except that a class of objective functions, called *effective energy* functions, are used, one at each temperature. The higher the temperature, the smoother the corresponding objective function. Coleman et al. [211] demonstrated experimentally that this algorithm converges faster, with fewer function evaluations than the standard simulated annealing algorithm.

As in all simulated-annealing–type algorithms, the effective-energy simulated-annealing algorithm can be parallelized by sampling and evaluating all the points in parallel at every cooling stage. A general strategy is that at each cooling stage, each processor generates its own sequence of points (i.e., random walks), compares the results with other processors, and chooses the lowest point among all processors as the starting point in the next stage. Coleman et al. [211] demonstrated scalable performance of the algorithm using this strategy on the Intel iPSC/860 with application to molecular-cluster conformation problems.

22.2.6   Global Continuation

Global continuation algorithms, as named in Moré and Wu [682], are a class of homotopy-type algorithms applied to global optimization problems. A special integral transform is used to generate the homotopy. A set of curves tracing the solutions to the homotopy at each parameter value is then traced to locate a global solution at the end. The special transform makes the function smoother, with fewer local minimizers. Also, the local minimizers are concentrated in regions with low function values, where a global minimizer is likely to be located. Therefore, by tracing the local minimizers on the smoothed functions back to the original function, there is a good chance that at least one curve will lead to a global minimizer of the original function [682, 1005].

Global continuation algorithms have been studied by several research groups, including Kostrowicki et al. [575], Shalloway [852, 853], Coleman et al. [211], Straub

[903, 904], Moré and Wu [681, 682, 683, 685]), and Shao et al. [858], each having slightly different transforms. In particular, Moré and Wu [682, 684] developed a class of parallel, global continuation algorithms for solving distance geometry problems with application to NMR macromolecular modeling.

The algorithms are pleasingly parallel: multiple solution curves are traced in parallel. The best solution found by the processors is selected at the end. The computation on each processor is intensive since it involves a sequence of local minimizations. However, the load on all processors is almost the same, and little communication is required, except at the beginning and end of the computation. The algorithms have been implemented on several parallel architectures as a parallel software package called DGSOL, available through the Network Enabled Optimization System (NEOS) at Argonne National Laboratory. This parallel implementation has been used to solve large distance geometry problems of practical interest.

22.3   Direct Search Methods

Direct search (pattern search) methods are longtime favorites of users, but they have only recently become interesting to optimization researchers. One of the reasons is that direct search methods are more interesting to try to parallelize than Newton methods. The work in a Newton method usually is dominated by the cost of the function evaluations and the linear algebra required to solve the underlying local model problem. Direct search methods require essentially no linear algebra, but they are profligate users of function evaluations. This is because there is no underlying local model to suggest where a better next iterate is likely to be found as in a Newton method. Instead, direct search methods sample the function to find the next iterate. Of course, Newton methods use function evaluations to confirm or reject a suggested next iterate, but direct search methods use function values to explore for a next iterate. This exploration phase makes it possible to invent new intrinsically parallel, direct search methods rather than simply to parallelize an existing method as in Newton's method. Again, the same thing can be said of evolutionary algorithms [841], although we will not explore them further since they seem to be practical only for very inexpensive functions, or for problems with completely general variables, and in our opinion, their convergence theory is less satisfying.

This approach led to the parallel direct-search (PDS) method [258, 937], and to the novel convergence theory for more general pattern search methods [55, 607, 608, 609, 610, 938, 939]. Audet [54] gives interesting examples to illustrate the limitations of any convergence theory for these methods. Lewis and Torczon [609] and Audet and Dennis [56] extended these methods and the convergence analysis to problems with nonlinear constraints. Audet and Dennis [56] extend the algorithms and analysis to nonlinear problems with discrete as well as continuous variables. Hough and Meza [486] proposed using the PDS method for the trust-region subproblem and developed a parallel trust-region algorithm for nonlinear optimization.

Hough et al. [485] developed a variant of PDS called APPS. The APPS software, available at *http://csmr.ca.sandia.gov/projects/apps.html*, is not only asynchronous, but also fault tolerant. The motivation is to adapt parallel pattern search to environments where the simulation times associated with individual function evaluations may vary appreciably. The idea is that each process is in charge of one or more of the search directions. The process carries out a pattern search from the best point it knows along the directions for which it is responsible. Whenever a search produces a better point, the process updates its own best point. It then sends a nonblocking message to all the other processes with the better point, its function value, and the step size that produced the better point. Meanwhile, the other processes continuously check their inboxes for messages with new candidates for best point. Each time a process finishes computing any function value, it checks its copy of the best point to see if it was changed as a consequence of a message sent by another process. If so, then the search is moved to the new best point and adopts a consistent step size.

Clearly this algorithm is asynchronous. It also is fault tolerant. If a process goes down, the orphaned search directions are reassigned to other processors. Kolda and Torczon [572] have provided a global convergence analysis for APPS. APPS may perform more function evaluations a than standard pattern search, perhaps in part because it searches only on a ray from each point, but the overall solution time still may be reduced, and we understand that users report good experience with the code.

The sequential version of PDS, called MDS or multidirectional direct search, was a "sequentialization" of PDS, rather than the usual way around. In order to discuss some practical parallel aspects of the algorithm, with its more general variants, we will give the algorithm for continuous variables and no constraints. Thus, we consider

$$\min_{x \in \mathbb{R}^n} f(x) \tag{22.1}$$

The formulation of generalized pattern search (GPS) in Figure 22.2 is from Booker et al. [129]. It differs from Torczon's original formulation in [939], but it is equivalent. For simplicity, we say that if there are constraints, and if either x is infeasible or if $f(x)$ cannot be evaluated successfully, then we set $f(x) = \infty$. Note that both steps have ample opportunities for parallel evaluations of the objective function and constraints. Indeed, one would certainly tailor the search step to the number of function evaluations it would be convenient to compute in parallel. There is also a nice place here for hierarchical parallelism if the evaluation of a single $f(x)$ is already a parallel program.

Step 2 provides the safeguard that guarantees convergence, as in the following result from Audet and Dennis [57], which extends Torczon [939]. The extension of GPS to GMIPS (x has some discrete components) differs from GPS in the definition of the poll set X_k, and the convergence result is a bit different, though equally satisfying:

If f is continuously differentiable, then there are infinitely many unsuccessful iterates produced by any GPS method, and some limit point of the unsuccessful iterates is a stationary point for problem 22.1.

Let M_0 denote a mesh on $\mathbb{R}^n$ and suppose that $x_0 \in M_0$ has been given. (Typically, $x_0 \approx x^*$, where x^* is a preliminary baseline solution, but any choice of $x_0 \in M_0$ is allowed.) Let $X_0 \subset M_0$ contain x_0 and any $2n$ points adjacent to x_0 for which the differences between those points and x_0 form a maximal positive basis (composed of multiples of the coordinate vectors for $\mathbb{R}^n$). As the algorithm generates $x_k \in M_k$, let $X_k \subset M_k$ be defined in the same way. For $k = 0, 1, \ldots,$ do the following:

1. **Search.** Employ some finite strategy to try to choose $x_{k+1} \in M_k$ such that $f(x_{k+1}) < f(x_k)$. If such an x_{k+1} is found, declare the **Search** successful, set $M_{k+1} = M_k$, and increment k;

2. **else Poll.** If x_k minimizes $f(x)$ for $x \in X_k$, then declare the **Poll** unsuccessful, set $x_{k+1} = x_k$, and refine M_k to obtain M_{k+1} by halving the mesh size (write this as $M_{k+1} = M_k/2$); else declare the **Poll** successful, set x_{k+1} to a point in X_k at which $f(x_{k+1}) < f(x_k)$, and set $M_{k+1} = M_k$.
   Increment k.

Figure 22.2 Algorithm for generalized pattern search (GPS).

This result says that one need only monitor the unsuccessful iterates of GPS to find a stationary point, and this is without regard to how naive the search strategy is in step 1. In practice, of course, the search strategy matters a lot to the number of function values required to find a good optimizer.

We now turn to using global model functions as surrogates for $f(x)$ to try to **Search** with greater parsimony and thereby reduce the total number of objective function evaluations, or parallel objective function evaluations. Intuitively, surrogate methods use global models to predict where to find a successful next iterate in just the way that Newton methods use local models. Of course, the local models must be first-order accurate for Newton methods to work—but then they work very well indeed. It is unrealistic to expect much accuracy of a global model, and that is one reason why we avoid calling them approximations. The **Poll** step has the same opportunities for parallelism as before, but parallel function evaluations of the inexpensive surrogate can allow a sort of rough, global surrogate optimization in the search strategy. One can return a number of candidates for x_{k+1}, evaluate them in parallel, and accept the best.

22.3.1 The Surrogate Management Framework

The description of the surrogate management framework (SMF) that we present in Figure 22.3 is a set of strategies for using approximations in both the **Search** and **Poll** steps of a GPS algorithm. For greater clarity, we have also identified a separate **Evaluate/Calibrate** step. In what follows, we assume that a family of approximating functions has been specified, that an initial approximation has been constructed,

Given s_0, an initial approximation of f, and $x_0 \in M_0$, let $X_0 \subset M_0$ contain x_0 and any $2n$ points adjacent to x_0 for which the differences between those points and x_0 form a maximal positive basis (composed of multiples of the coordinate vectors) for $\mathbb{R}^n$. As the algorithm generates $x_k \in M_k$, let $X_k \subset M_k$ be defined in the same way. For $k = 0, 1, \ldots$, do the following:

1. **Search.** Use any method to choose a trial set $T_k \subset M_k$. If $T_k \neq \emptyset$ is chosen, then it is required to contain at least one point at which $f(x)$ is not known. If $T_k = \emptyset$, then go to **Poll**.

2. **Evaluate/Calibrate.** Evaluate f on elements in T_k until either it is found that x_k minimizes f on T_k or until $x_{k+1} \in T_k$ is identified for which $f(x_{k+1}) < f(x_k)$. If such an x_{k+1} is found, then declare the **Search** successful. Recalibrate s_k with the new values of f computed at points in T_k.

3. If **Search** was successful, then set $s_{k+1} = s_k$, $M_{k+1} = M_k$, and increment k; else return to **Search** with the recalibrated s_k, but without incrementing k.

4. **Poll.** If x_k minimizes $f(x)$ for $x \in X_k$, then declare the **Poll** unsuccessful, set $x_{k+1} = x_k$, and set $M_{k+1} = M_k/2$; else declare the **Poll** successful, set x_{k+1} to a point in X_k at which $f(x_{k+1}) < f(x_k)$, and set $M_{k+1} = M_k$. Recalibrate s_k with the new values of f computed at points in X_k. Set $s_{k+1} = s_k$. Increment k.

Figure 22.3   Algorithm for the surrogate management framework (SMF).

and that an algorithm to recalibrate the approximation is available. (See Booker et al. [127, 129] and Serafini [849] for more details.)

22.3.2   Asynchronous Parallel Search

In general, the PDS algorithm assumes a homogeneous and tightly coupled parallel system, and it synchronizes in every iteration to compare the function values among all processors. The problem is that, in practice, the available machines are most likely loosely coupled and heterogeneous. Synchronization may force many of the processors to remain idle while others are busy. The problem can be more serious when the cost of function evaluation varies with the point at which the function is evaluated. Then the load will not be balanced among processors.

The asynchronous version of the PDS by Hough et al. [485] can be used to overcome the difficulty that the PDS algorithm has for synchronization and load balancing. In the asynchronous algorithm (APDS) shown in Figure 22.4, each processor takes an independent direction to search for a decreasing point. It broadcasts the point when it finds one or returns to the next iteration when informed that a decreasing point has been found elsewhere. Communication among the processors is managed by some daemon processes, and the cost is justified by the much better balance of computation across all processors.

On each processor, define x_+, x_{best}, x_{trial} to be current, best, and trial iterates, respectively, and let f_+, f_{best}, f_{trial} and $\Delta_+, \Delta_{best}, \Delta_{trial}$ be corresponding function values and step sizes. Let *tol* be a small tolerance for the step size.

1. Consider each incoming triplet $\{x_+, f_+, \Delta_+\}$ received from another processor. If $f_+ < f_{best}$, then $\{x_{best}, f_{best}, \Delta_+\} \leftarrow \{x_+, f_+, \Delta_+\}$, $\Delta_{trial} \leftarrow \Delta_{best}$.

2. Compute $x_{trial} \leftarrow x_{best} + \Delta_{trial} d$ and evaluate $f_{trial} = f(x_{trial})$, where d is the local direction.

3. Set $\{x_+, f_+, \Delta_+\} \leftarrow \{x_{trial}, f_{trial}, \Delta_{trial}\}$.

4. If $f_+ < f_{best}$, then $\{x_{best}, f_{best}, \Delta_{best}\} \leftarrow \{x_+, f_+, \Delta_+\}$, $\Delta_{trial} \leftarrow \Delta_{best}$, and broadcast $\{x_{best}, f_{best}, \Delta_{best}\}$. Else $\Delta_{trial} \leftarrow \frac{1}{2}\Delta_{trial}$.

5. If $\Delta_{trial} > tol$, go to step 1. Else broadcast a local convergence message.

6. Wait until either (a) enough of processes have converged for this point or (b) a better point is received. In case (a), exit. In case (b), go to step 1.

Figure 22.4   Algorithm for asynchonous parallel direct search (APDS).

22.4   Optimization of Linked Subsystems

The formulation we discuss in this section applies to a class of optimization problems arising in multidisciplinary design optimization (MDO). In MDO, the design variables and the system variables are correlated through coupled nonlinear subsystems, each of which may involve expensive calculations such as PDE solves. The idea here is that parallelism can be exploited at the coupling level where the subsystems can be solved independently, if an appropriate MDO formulation is employed. The technique we employ is related closely to domain decomposition for PDE or multiple shooting for ODE.

A general MDO problem can be formulated as the following nonlinear optimization problem:

$$\text{min} \quad f(x, u(x))$$
$$\text{s.t.} \quad g(x, u(x)) \geq 0 \qquad (22.2)$$

where x is a set of design variables and $u(x)$, the vector of system or ancillary variables, is defined implicitly by the blocked system of equations,

$$A_1(x, u_1(x), \dots, u_N(x)) = 0$$
$$\vdots \qquad\qquad (22.3)$$
$$A_N(x, u_1(x), \dots, u_N(x)) = 0$$

This system represents the linking of all the subsystems, and the act of solving it numerically for $u(x)$, given x, is known as *multidisciplinary analysis* (MDA). This terminology is in line with the standard engineering terminology that a disciplinary *analysis* is a single-disciplinary simulation run.

The most conventional approach to problem (22.2) is sometimes called the *control theory* or *closed equations* or *black-box* approach, which formulates the problem as

$$\textbf{min} \quad \hat{f}(x)$$
$$\text{s.t.} \quad \hat{g}(x) \geq 0 \tag{22.4}$$

where $\hat{f}(x) \equiv f(x, u(x))$ and $\hat{g}(x) \equiv g(x, u(x))$.

At each iteration of an optimization procedure applied to problem (22.4), any call to the function routines causes the design variable x to be passed to the MDA solver, and the linked system problem (22.3) is solved for $u(x)$. This reduces the optimization problem to its essential decision variables x, which can be large when x is a distributed parameter, but it is often an order of magnitude lower dimensional than the dimension of u.

To get a better idea of the expense of solving problem (22.3), think of MDA as solving a perhaps huge nonlinear system of equations, which will have to be done iteratively, whose residuals at a given iterate $u(x)_k$ can only be evaluated in blocks, and where evaluating the ith block may require doing a single-discipline analysis for the discipline represented by A_i perhaps several times in every iteration. Even more scary is thinking about the problem of computing derivative approximations in order to use a Newton-type method for MDA. Even getting derivatives to use in an optimization algorithm applied to problem (22.4) is expensive. For example, if one is to use finite differences, then $\nabla \hat{f}(x)$ for any x will cost dim(x) MDA solves. One can try to find and use adjoint formulations, but that is generally not practical if the dimension of the range of g is at all large.

The MDA system problem (22.3) is naturally decomposed into disciplinary equations, which can be distributed to multiprocessors and solved in parallel. For example, A_1 is solved for u_1 on processor 1, A_2 for u_2 on processor 2, and so on. However, given x, u_1 depends on x as well as other u_i, and so on for $u_2, \ldots, u_N$. Thus, this procedure is just a block nonlinear Jacobi iteration, which is problematic at best, although it easily allows parallel, single-disciplinary analyses. Of course, in many cases, load balancing is a problem because of the different cost of executing different single-disciplinary analyses.

Probably the most often used procedure is the almost equally problematic, and less parallel, Gauss–Seidel or successive replacements procedure; that is, first assume some values for x and u_i, solve A_1 for u_1; then with the new value for u_1 along with given values for x and other u_i, solve A_2 for u_2, and so on until a new set of values for all u_i is found. The procedure then repeats until the whole system reaches equilibrium, or in other words, converges to u that satisfies all the equations. This method can only be executed sequentially, and as with the Jacobi procedure, there is no reason to believe it will converge for a given problem. Still, the method does not require a system Jacobian for problem (22.3), and sometimes intuition helps to order the single-discipline solves to obtain convergence.

At the other end of the spectrum of formulations is the *simultaneous analysis and design* or *nonlinear programming* or *open equations* formulation. This formulation can best be seen by rewriting problem (22.2) as

$$\begin{aligned} \min \quad & f(x,u) \\ \text{s.t.} \quad & g(x,u) \geq 0 \\ & A(x,u) = 0 \end{aligned}$$

where x, u are both treated as independent variables, and the inclusion of the MDA equations as a constraint ensures that $u = u(x)$ at all feasible points. There are many reasons why this is the ideal formulation for most problems, but it is likely to be extremely large and to need special linear algebra techniques to handle the linear algebra for a sequential quadratic-programming implementation. A major difficulty is that one must be able to open up the single-discipline analysis codes and extract the residual computations for the equations solved by that code.

Recent work on MDO—for example, Cramer et al. [228], Dennis and Lewis [256], and Alexandrov and Lewis [21]—demonstrated that the MDA equations, as well as the MDO problem, can be solved in parallel if appropriate formulations and algorithms are used. We describe some of the ideas in the following.

For simplicity, consider a two-discipline MDO problem,

$$\begin{aligned} \min \quad & f(x_0; R_1(u_1); R_2(u_2)) \\ \text{s.t.} \quad & g_0(x_0; S_1(u_1); S_2(u_2)) \geq 0 \\ & g_1(x_0; x_1; u_1) \geq 0 \\ & g_2(x_0; x_2; u_2) \geq 0 \end{aligned}$$

where u_1 and u_2 depend on x_0, x_1, and x_2 through the MDA system,

$$\begin{aligned} A_1(x_0; x_1; u_1; T_1(u_2)) &= 0 \\ A_2(x_0; x_2; u_2; T_2(u_1)) &= 0 \end{aligned}$$

Here the design variable x is partitioned into $x = (x_0; x_1; x_2)$ with x_1 and x_2 specific to discipline 1 and 2, respectively, and x_0 shared by both. The function g_0 is called the design constraint, g_1 and g_2 are the disciplinary design constraints, and A_1 and A_2 are the disciplinary analysis constraints.

As we have discussed before, a major difficulty is that the disciplinary analysis constraints are coupled through variables u_1 and u_2. A very important property that generally holds is that the coupling through T_1, T_2 may involve small subvectors of u_1 and u_2. This is analogous to the domain decomposition approach to PDE solutions where at most a band around the boundary values at the subdomain interfaces are exchanged between subdomain solves. Thus, without making the problem too much larger than problem (22.4), we can introduce new variables u_{12} and u_{21} to replace $T_1(u_2)$ and $T_2(u_1)$ and add new constraints to make u_{12} equal to $T_1(u_2)$ and u_{21} to

$T_2(u_1)$. Again, a feasible point will satisfy problem (22.3). This gives one of the IDF formulations for the MDO problem by Cramer et al. [228]:

$$\min \quad f(x_0; R_1(u_1); R_2(u_2))$$
$$\text{s.t.} \quad g_0(x_0; S_1(u_1); S_2(u_2)) \geq 0$$
$$g_1(x_0; x_1; u_1) \geq 0$$
$$g_2(x_0; x_2; u_2) \geq 0$$
$$u_{12} - T_1(u_2) = 0 \tag{22.5}$$
$$u_{21} - T_2(u_1) = 0 \tag{22.6}$$

where u_1 and u_2 depend on x_0, x_1, and x_2 through the MDA system,

$$A_1(x_0; x_1; u_1; u_{12}) = 0$$
$$A_2(x_0; x_2; u_2; u_{21}) = 0$$

Note that in this formulation, u_{12} and u_{21} are considered as independent variables; therefore, given x_0, x_1, x_2, u_{12} and u_{21}, A_1 and A_2 can be solved in parallel for u_1 and u_2. The coupling between the two equations is handled by the consistency constraint equations (22.5) and (22.6) at the MDO level. Thus, a complete MDA is not required at each iteration of a standard SQP optimizer. A major point is that the individual discipline solver codes are used as they are.

The model we show above is for a two-discipline MDO problem, but the technique for decoupling or decomposing the MDO/MDA system into parallel, independent subsystems can be extended to problems with more than two disciplines, especially when they are loosely coupled, that is, each equation/constraint is connected with only a few other equations/constraints, and thus only a small number of auxiliary variables will be required.

MDO or linked subsystem problems are one of the "grand challenges" of scientific computation. There is little hope of solving realistic problems without significant advances in automatic differentiation.

Finally, we remark that Braun [141] and Sobieski and Kroo [880] suggested a way of posing linked subsystem problems called *collaborative optimization* (CO). Only in special circumstances is this problem equivalent to problem (22.2), but there are other ways to pose optimization with linked subsystems than the straightforward problem (22.2), and CO has the comforting feature of mimicking the way "parallel" teams of disciplinary specialists would attach such problems.

22.5   Variable and Constraint Distribution

Ferris and Mangasarian [329, 330] developed two classes of parallel algorithms for constrained optimization problems. Algorithms of the first class distribute the variables on multiple processors. Each processor updates its own variables in parallel while allowing the other variables to change in a restricted fashion. Once a new step is obtained, all processors communicate and combine the steps to obtain the new iterate in the whole space. The second class of algorithms distributes the constraints over the processors instead. Each processor then solves a subproblem with a subset of constraints and a modified objective function. The processors then exchange Lagrange multipliers and repeat.

Ferris and Mangasarian [329, 330] presented algorithms of these classes designed for various types of optimization problems, gave a convergence theory, and provided preliminary performance results. We refer the reader to these works for more details.

22.5.1 Variable Distribution

Consider the problem

$$\min_{x \in \mathcal{X}} f(x) \tag{22.7}$$

where $\mathcal{X}$ is a nonempty closed convex set in $\mathbb{R}^n$ and f a continuous and differentiable function. The variable distribution algorithm first distributes p blocks $x_1, \ldots, x_p$ of variable x, where $x_l \in \mathbb{R}^{n_l}$, $\sum_{l=1}^{p} n_l = n$, over p processors. At iteration i with an iterate $x^i \in \mathbb{R}^n$, processor l updates block x_l^i by solving a subproblem,

$$\min_{x_l, \lambda_l} \; f(x_l, x_{\bar{l}}^i + D_{\bar{l}}^i \lambda_{\bar{l}}) \tag{22.8}$$

$$\text{s.t.} \quad (x_l, x_{\bar{l}}^i + D_{\bar{l}}^i \lambda_{\bar{l}}) \in \mathcal{X}$$

where $\bar{l}$ denotes the complement of l in $1, \ldots, p$, $\lambda_{\bar{l}} \in \mathbb{R}^{p-1}$. The matrix $D_{\bar{l}}^i$ is an $n_{\bar{l}}$-by-$(p-1)$ matrix. It is formed by taking arbitrary direction $d^i \in \mathbb{R}^n$, breaking it into blocks of $d_l^i \in \mathbb{R}^{n_l}$, $l = 1, \ldots, p$, consistent with the distribution of the variables, and placing these vectors along the block diagonal of $D_{\bar{l}}^i$,

$$D_{\bar{l}}^i = \mathbf{diag}(d_1^i, \ldots, d_{l-1}^i, d_{l+1}^i, \ldots, d_p^i)$$

Let $(y_l^i, \lambda_{\bar{l}}^i)$ be the optimal solution of problem (22.8), and $x^{il} = (y_l^i, \lambda_{\bar{l}}^i)$. Then after all processors obtain their x^{il}, $l = 1, \ldots, p$, the next iterate x^{i+1} for the original problem (22.7) can be obtained by solving the subproblem,

$$\min_{\mu_0, \ldots, \mu_p} \; f(\mu_0 x^i + \sum_{k=1}^{p} \mu_k x^{ik}) \tag{22.9}$$

$$\text{s.t.} \quad \mu_0 x^i + \sum_{k=1}^{p} \mu_k x^{ik} \in \mathcal{X}, \sum_{k=0}^{p} \mu_k = 1$$

with x^{i+1} set to $\mu_0 x^i + \sum_{k=1}^{p} \mu_k x^{ik}$.

Note that the subproblem (22.8) is to solve the problem in the subspace spanned by its allocated variables. Since each involves only its own local variables, all can be solved in parallel. The subproblem (22.9) is again to solve the problem on a subspace, but now it is the subspace spanned by the steps from the current iterate to each of the subspace optima found at the previous level. Since these steps were computed on different processors, a synchronization step among processors is required for solving problem (22.9). Clearly, this process can be applied to generate multiple levels until a good fit is found for the given problem on the given machine.

The variable distribution method can be used for unconstrained optimization problems and problems with block separable constraints. Ferris and Mangasarian [330] showed that the algorithms for these problems converge with certain optimality conditions. They also tested the algorithms with a subset of optimization problems in CUTE [126] and obtained reasonable speedups on CM-5 with up to 32 processors.

22.5.2   Constraint Distribution

The constraint distribution method applies to quadratic programs with strictly convex objective functions. It can also be extended to general convex programs, but with relatively weaker convergence results.

In general, consider the following convex program,

$$\textbf{min}\quad f(x)$$
$$\textbf{s.t.}\quad g_1(x) \le 0, \dots, g_p(x) \le 0$$

where f is a strictly convex function, and g_l are convex functions from $\mathbb{R}^n$ to $\mathbb{R}^{m_l}$, $l = 1, \dots, p$. The method distributes the block constraints to p processors. On processor l, a subproblem with only constraint block $g_l(x) \le 0$ and a modified objective function is solved. Then the solutions and the Lagrange multipliers are shared among processors, and the whole process is repeated. Note that the modified objective function on one processor is composed of the original function plus some augmented Lagrangian terms formed by the constraints assigned to other processors.

For illustrative purposes, consider a quadratic program with three blocks of inequality constraints,

$$\textbf{min}\quad c^T x + \frac{1}{2} x^T Q x$$
$$\textbf{s.t.}\quad A_l x \le a_l, \quad l = 1, 2, 3$$

where $c \in \mathbb{R}^n$, $Q \in \mathbb{R}^{m_l \times n}$, $a_l \in \mathbb{R}^{m_l}$, and Q is symmetric and positive definite. A constraint distribution algorithm for this problem would first distribute the constraints to three processors, with constraint l to processor l. Then at iteration i, a subproblem can be solved on each processor in parallel, that is, on processor l:

$$\textbf{min}_{x_l}\quad c^T x_l + \frac{1}{2} x_l^T Q x_l$$
$$+ \frac{1}{2\gamma} \left[\sum_{j=1, j\neq l}^{3} \|(\gamma(A_j x_l - a_j) + p_{jl}^i\|^2 \right] + x_l^T r_l^i$$
$$\textbf{s.t.}\quad A_l x_l \le a_l \qquad\qquad (22.10)$$

where γ is a positive number and p_{jl}^i and r_l^i, $j, l = 1, 2, 3$ are parameters to be determined. The p_{jl}^i play the roles of the multipliers and converge to the optimal multipliers eventually, while r_l^i replaces estimates of the multipliers by their most recent values obtained from each of the other subproblems. Note that the objective functions for the subproblems in problem (22.10) are quadratic, augmented Lagrangian functions perturbed by the linear terms $x_l^T r_l^i$. Thus, in each subproblem, some constraints are treated explicitly as constraints while the remaining ones are terms in the augmented Lagrangian objective function.

Given the values for all the parameters, each subproblem in problem (22.10) can be solved in parallel. However, the parameters are updated using their most recent values from other processors. Therefore, communication is required at certain points. Ferris and Mangasarian [329] showed the convergence results for the constraint distribution algorithm for strictly convex quadratic programs and extended them to general convex programs. Five small quadratic programming problems were tested with the algorithm on the Sequent Symmetry S-81, and encouraging results were obtained.

22.6   Conclusion

Despite much effort and some solid developments, the use of parallelism in general optimization has not been as fruitful as its use in other areas of numerical computation, such as numerical linear algebra. There are special successful applications, and some software packages available, but not much performance analysis or benchmarking work. One of the possible reasons is that practical optimization problems often have many ancillary variables, but only a few decision variables. The great opportunities for finding parallelism might then lie in parallelizing the computation of the ancillary variables by using domain decomposition to solve a PDE, for example. If tools for hierarchical parallelism become more generally available, this situation may change.

Another reason for our slow progress may be the tradition favoring inherently sequential Newton-like methods where one carefully builds local models and extracts all the information one can before evaluating a trial step. After all, in local modeling methods, there is generally a clearly preferred trial step, and if that is not successful, then the fallback strategies use information obtained from the failure. Methods such as parallel line searches or sector searches have not been great successes, probably because they kludge one paradigm onto another rather than finding a single, consistent algorithmic paradigm.

Global optimization methods attracted more and more attention as usable parallel and high-performance computing resources became available. Indeed, there are many cases where scientific problems of an interesting size have been solved by these methods. Still, the general global-optimization problem is intractable, even for infinitely smooth functions. Empirically, the computing time needed to get a reasonable solution using a general global-optimization algorithm seems to grow exponentially with the problem size, while the speedup can at best be counted on to be linear with the number of processors. Thus, the future of global optimization is in the development of efficient and reliable algorithms for specific classes of problems. Without such algorithms, problem sizes will remain limited despite gains from parallel computation.

Parallel direct-search methods are another successful development in the quest for parallel optimization algorithms. The theory is developing rapidly, and they are easy to use either as sequential or parallel algorithms. There are many successful applications, but the methods are slower than Newton methods, and as with all derivative-free methods, it is difficult to know when to terminate. Thus, the algorithm is more suitable for small problems with uncertain accuracy in the function. Constraints are problematic for these algorithms as well. If one has no derivatives, then Lagrange multipliers, a mainstay of constrained optimization, are not available. However, algorithms for constraints and large-scale applications are interesting research directions.

We call the problem class MDO in Section 22.4, but in fact, it is much more general than design. As simulation is used to aid decision makers in more and more areas, such as crisis management, instances of these problems will arise. Picture a library of standard simulation codes, such as fluid flow, thermal conductivity, structures, and so on. One might want to make decisions concerning systems governed by coupling various choices from among these systems. It may not be practical to have special simulations in the library for all these combinations. Here, we provide a completely equivalent formulation for the original problem for which this would not be necessary because the separate "closed" subsystems could be linked numerically for each required x without recoding to obtain a solver that works for any x. However, since the method is relatively new, and the computational demands for MDO are so high, computational experiments are limited. Indeed, this field is in its infancy.

The variable- and constraint-distribution algorithms are interesting. Different from many other algorithms, which are obtained by parallelizing their serial counterparts, these algorithms are developed with parallel computation in mind. Therefore, standard optimization components, like computation of a search direction, are designed as parallel procedures. Convergence results have also been established for the algorithms. They have not been extensively tested or applied in practice. Further research on these algorithms and their applications can be promising and fruitful. For example, parallel variable distribution and parallel direct searches seem an interesting pairing for extending the latter to larger problems. Partial separability seems also to be clearly related to parallel variable distribution.

23

Path Following in Scientific Computing and Its Implementation in AUTO

H. B. Keller • E. J. Doedel

Essentially all of the equations used to describe and explore phenomena in science and technology are approximations. They represent the current state of knowledge about the phenomena they purport to explain. As experiments and experience extend our understanding, the "best" theory, and hence the set of equations, is altered to encompass the latest results. This is how science and technology advance. Unfortunately, this dynamic inherent in the pursuit of knowledge is frequently submerged, and the current theories are presented as, or believed to be, the "laws of nature." Whatever their formulations, we usually cannot determine explicit formulas expressing the consequences of these basic theories, and thus we must resort to approximations of their solutions. So, in practice one deals with approximate solutions to the current (approximate) theories. Implicit in this brief account is the hidden suggestion that there is indeed a final correct theory of everything. Why this should be so is not clear, nor is it necessary for the continual attempts to improve whatever the current theories are. Furthermore, we continue to improve the methods that yield the approximate solutions—that is what research in scientific computing is all about.

In order to obtain approximate solutions, the equations of interest are discretized—that is, they are replaced by a finite set of relations among a finite set of unknowns. This discretization process can be carried out in many ways: finite differences, finite elements, spectral and pseudospectral methods, collocation, and combinations of the above. Each of these "methods" includes a host of different approximation procedures, and it is not possible to list or categorize all of them. Further, there is no general theory that ensures the convergence or accuracy of the approximations. In many special cases, there is such a theory. But the researcher must do the best she can and proceed as if the convergence theory were applicable to the approximate problem and seek its solutions. This is what path following is all about. The discretization of most problems in science and technology leads to large systems of nonlinear equations containing one or more free parameters. Solutions are invariably required for some ranges of the parameters. Thus, if $u \in \mathbb{R}^N$ represents the values of the unknowns that satisfy the discretized problem, say

$$G(u, \lambda) = 0 \qquad (23.1)$$

and $\lambda \in \mathbb{R}$ is a parameter, then $u = u(\lambda)$ traces out some *path* in $\mathbb{R}^N$ as λ varies over some interval I. Path following is the study, development, and application of efficient numerical procedures to determine such paths. In many current applications $N \geq 10^6$, and so parallel processors may be imperative.

Of course, as the path $\Gamma : \{u = u(\lambda) \in \mathbb{R}^N, \ \lambda \in I\}$ is traversed, difficulties may arise due to the occurrence of some singular behavior. There are many various kinds of singularities that can occur, even more if the parameter $\lambda \in \mathbb{R}^p$ with $p > 1$. Methods for exploring the singular phenomena and circumventing it, if possible, have been devised. Indeed, it is frequently the case that the location and nature of the singular points on a solution path are of most interest to the scientist or engineer who proposed the problem.

The parameters λ that occur in computational problems (equation 23.1) are of three types:

1. A physical or geometric quantity explicitly entering into the formulation of the problem (the Reynolds number in a flow, the length of a structure, the resistance of a circuit element, the magnitude of an applied force).

2. An intrinsic quantity not germane to the problem formulation but perhaps useful in the solution procedure (arclength along a solution path, the magnitude or norm of some variable of the problem, time in a steady-state problem).

3. An "artificial" quantity introduced to aid in the determination of a solution; we call these *homotopy* parameters.

To clarify type 3 parameters, we illustrate a simple but pervasive homotopy procedure. Suppose we are given a problem that is somehow known to be hard to solve, say:

$$H(u) = 0$$

But we also know, or can construct, a related problem that is easy to solve, say:

$$E(u) = 0$$

"Related" means that their variables u are both of the same type; that is, flow quantities in the same geometric domain, concentrations of the same species, and so on. Then we consider the *homotopy* problem:

$$G(u, \lambda) \equiv \lambda H(u) + (1 - \lambda) E(u) = 0 \qquad (23.2)$$

For $\lambda = 0$, we can solve the problem "easily," and we need only to continue that solution along the path $u(\lambda)$ over $0 \leq \lambda \leq 1$. If this can be done, we get the solution to the hard problem: $u(1)$. A crucial aspect of this simple procedure is to be able to ensure that such a path exists. The naive view of this homotopy is that the *monotone* increase of λ from 0 to 1 will do the job. However, this is frequently not the case, and path-following techniques have been developed, as we shall see, to circumvent these difficulties.

There are many other ways in which homotopy parameters can be introduced. For example, simply multiply some or all nonlinear terms in the problem by λ and then consider continuation from $\lambda = 0$ to $\lambda = 1$.

23.1   Local Continuation

By "local continuation" we mean the ability to compute a nearby solution at a nearby parameter value when we know the solution, say u, at some parameter value, say λ. The basic idea here is the simple notion of continuity. That is, when

$$G(u, \lambda) = 0 \text{ has solution } u = u(\lambda)$$

and

$$G(u, \lambda + \delta) = 0 \text{ has solution } u = u(\lambda + \delta)$$

then for $|\delta|$ small we expect that[1]

$$\|u(\lambda + \delta) - u(\lambda)\| = \mathcal{O}(\delta)$$

is also small. Thus, we expect $u(\lambda)$ to be a good approximation to $u(\lambda + \delta)$, and we can use it as the initial iterate in some iterative procedure to compute $u(\lambda + \delta)$.

Indeed, under the appropriate hypothesis, the ideas above can be justified to yield the Implicit Function Theorem. The specific iterative procedure used to prove these results is the *chord method* or *special Newton method:*

(a) $u_0(\lambda + \delta) = u(\lambda)$

(b) $G_u(u(\lambda), \lambda) \, \Delta u_\nu(\lambda + \delta) = -G(u_\nu(\lambda + \delta), \lambda + \delta)$

(c) $u_{\nu+1}(\lambda + \delta) = u_\nu(\lambda + \delta) + \Delta u_\nu(\lambda + \delta)$ (23.3)

The hypotheses require that the Jacobian matrix $G_u(u(\lambda), \lambda)$ be nonsingular and that $|\delta|$ be sufficiently small. The scheme (equations 23.3) can be used quite effectively to compute $u(\lambda + \delta)$ as accurately as required. When this procedure is completed, we increase $\lambda + \delta$, say to $\lambda + 2\delta$, and continue the recursion. In this way, m points on the path Γ are approximated by $\{u(\lambda + k\delta)\}_{k=1}^m$.

The above procedure becomes less "local" as we carry out more steps in the continuation. That is, we depart from a small neighborhood of the original solution

---

[1] Here we have assumed the solution to be Lipschitz continuous.

$[u(\lambda), \lambda]$ at which G_u was known (or assumed) to be nonsingular, and the iterations may no longer converge. We discuss some of the questions regarding *global continuation* in the next section. But several points regarding methods for local continuation are suggested by the above observations.

The step size, δ, for incrementing the parameter, λ, can be varied. As convergence proceeds well, δ can be increased and, conversely, as it slows, δ should be reduced. Empirical formulas for doing this have been devised.

Better initial estimates of the solution $u(\lambda + \delta)$ can be derived, say, by using differentiability in place of continuity. So, rather than equation (23.3(a)), we can try

$$u_0(\lambda + \delta) = u(\lambda) + \delta \, \dot{u}(\lambda) \tag{23.4}$$

the first two terms in a Taylor expansion. This is the tangent, or Euler, approximation. Using this we get an $\mathcal{O}(\delta^2)$ error, rather than the previous $\mathcal{O}(\delta)$ error, to start the scheme. Obviously, even higher-order expansions could be employed; but then higher-order derivatives would have to be evaluated.

To obtain the tangent vector, $\dot{u}(\lambda)$, to the solution path Γ, we need only differentiate (23.1) with respect to λ to get:

$$G_u \, (u(\lambda), \lambda) \, \dot{u}(\lambda) = -G_\lambda \, (u(\lambda), \lambda) \tag{23.5}$$

Then if $G_u(u(\lambda), \lambda)$ is nonsingular, we can solve for $\dot{u}(\lambda)$. Indeed, this suggests that we might approximate the solution path, $u(\lambda)$, $\lambda \in I$ by solving the differential equation (23.5) subject to some initial condition, say

$$u(\lambda^0) = u^0$$

provided (u^0, λ^0) is some root of (23.1) and $\lambda^0 \in I$. This is a very old idea, due to Davidenko [248], and does not seem to be in current use. Since equation (23.5) is not in explicit form, numerical integration would be quite costly for N large. But a host of schemes are suggested by this idea, since there are so many ordinary differential equation (ODE) solution methods.

But perhaps the best local procedure is to use the Euler–Newton method in place of the special Newton or chord method of equation (23.3); that is,

(a) $u_0(\lambda + \delta) = u(\lambda) + \delta\dot{u}(\lambda)$

(b) $G_u(u_\nu(\lambda + \delta), \lambda + \delta) \, \Delta u_\nu(\lambda + \delta) = -G(u_\nu(\lambda + \delta), \lambda + \delta)$

(c) $u_{\nu+1}(\lambda + \delta) = u_\nu(\lambda + \delta) + \Delta u_\nu(\lambda + \delta)$ $\qquad$ (23.6)

Here we have replaced equation (23.3(a)) by the Euler initial estimate, equation (23.4). The correction $\Delta u_\nu(\lambda + \delta)$ is computed from equation (23.6(b)) using the updated Jacobian matrix, $G_u(u_\nu(\lambda + \delta), \lambda + \delta)$, rather than the fixed previously determined one, $G_u(u(\lambda), \lambda)$. The main advantage of Newton's method is that it converges quadratically, that is,

$$\| u_{\nu+1}(\lambda + \delta) - u(\lambda + \delta) \| \leq K \, \| u_\nu(\lambda + \delta) - u(\lambda + \delta) \|^2$$

for some constant K, under appropriate conditions not much more restrictive than those of the Implicit Function Theorem. The quadratic convergence can even be observed in the computations, since $\|\Delta u_\nu(\lambda + \delta)\|$ also decays quadratically.

Of course, Newton's method is also quite costly for large N, since a linear system of that order must be solved at each iteration. Thus, a host of "approximate Newton methods" have been devised. These use approximation to $G_u(u_\nu(\lambda + \delta), \lambda + \delta)$ that can be inverted in a less costly manner (say by iteration). These methods are particularly popular in the optimization literature and, although they are not quadratically convergent, many of them are superlinearly convergent.

We point out that Chapter 20 is concerned with efficient methods for solving the possibly large-order linear systems that are encountered in equations (23.3), (23.5), and (23.6). Furthermore, these systems are usually sparse or have some regular structure that can be exploited to aid in these methods. Note also that in all of the above cases, the large matrices in question are Jacobians of the nonlinear system $G(u, \lambda)$, which must be evaluated in the solution procedure. Thus, it could be advantageous to employ the automatic differentiation techniques of Chapter 24 to evaluate these Jacobians.

New methods for local continuation are being devised all the time. We have merely scratched the surface in the above account. In fact, "adaptive methods" that change the iterative procedure being employed must also be mentioned. Depending on what the convergence behavior is, or on the cost of solving the linear systems replacing equation (23.6(b)), we can devise schemes that seek to be optimal in some measure of effectiveness.

23.2 Global Continuation and Degree Theory

The existence of global solution paths of equation (23.1) can be insured when $G(u, \lambda)$ is sufficiently smooth, and the maximal rank condition

$$\text{Rank } G'(u, \lambda) \equiv \text{Rank} \left(\frac{\partial G(u, \lambda)}{\partial (u, \lambda)} \right) \tag{23.7}$$

$$\equiv \text{Rank} \left(G_u(u, \lambda), \ G_\lambda(u, \lambda) \right) = N$$

holds. In fact, it can then be shown by repeated use of the Implicit Function Theorem that

$$G^{-1}(0) \equiv \{(u, \lambda) \in \mathbb{R}^N \times \mathbb{R} \quad \text{such that } G(u, \lambda) = 0\}$$

is a set of smooth arcs or simple closed curves. Each such arc or closed curve can be represented as $\{u(s), \lambda(s)\}$, where s is arclength along the path. Using this in equation (23.1), we get the following identity for all s in some interval I:

$$G(s) \equiv G(u(s), \lambda(s)) = 0$$

The tangent to the path is given by $\{\dot{u}(s), \dot{\lambda}(s)\}$, and by differentiating the above identity we see that

$$G_u(s)\,\dot{u}(s) + G_\lambda(s)\,\dot{\lambda}(s) = 0 \qquad (23.8)$$

Also, since s is to be arclength, we must have

$$\|\dot{u}(s)\|^2 + \dot{\lambda}^2(s) = 1 \qquad (23.9)$$

This system (equations 23.8 and 23.9) can be written in $(N+1) \times (N+1)$ matrix form as

$$\begin{pmatrix} G_u(s) & G_\lambda(s) \\ \dot{u}^T(s) & \dot{\lambda}(s) \end{pmatrix} \begin{pmatrix} \dot{u}(s) \\ \dot{\lambda}(s) \end{pmatrix} \equiv \mathcal{A}(s) \begin{pmatrix} \dot{u}(s) \\ \dot{\lambda}(s) \end{pmatrix} = \begin{pmatrix} 0 \\ 1 \end{pmatrix} \qquad (23.10)$$

It is not difficult to prove that, as a consequence of expressions (23.7) along the path, the matrix $\mathcal{A}(s)$ is nonsingular. Then by applying Cramer's Rule to expression (23.10), we can solve for $\dot{\lambda}(s)$ to get:

$$\dot{\lambda}(s) = \frac{\det G_u(s)}{\det \mathcal{A}(s)} \qquad (23.11)$$

Since $\det \mathcal{A}(s) \neq 0$ along the solution path, equation (23.11) implies that $\dot{\lambda}(s)$ and $\det G_u(s)$ both change sign at the same points along the path. We refer to this result as the *Sign Change Lemma*.

We can use the above result to prove the Homotopy Invariance of Degree, which in turn yields a superb tool for solving a huge variety of nonlinear systems of equations. First we define the degree of a mapping, $G(u, \lambda) : \mathbb{R}^{N+1} \to \mathbb{R}^N$, for a domain $\Omega \subset \mathbb{R}^N$ as follows:

$$D\{G(\cdot, \lambda), \Omega\} \equiv \sum_{\begin{Bmatrix} u \in \Omega \\ G(u, \lambda) = 0 \end{Bmatrix}} \text{Sign det } G_u(u, \lambda)$$

Note that if the degree is nonzero, it implies that $G(u, \lambda) = 0$ has a solution in Ω for the given value of λ. The homotopy invariance says that the value of the degree does not change as λ varies over some interval, say $\lambda_0 < \lambda < \lambda_F$. In addition to some smoothness and the maximal rank condition (expressions 23.7) at all roots, we require that $G(u, \lambda) \neq 0$ on $\partial\Omega \times [\lambda_0, \lambda_F]$, a cylindrical surface in $\mathbb{R}^{N+1}$ (see Figure 23.1). To prove the invariance, we note that there are at most four classes of solution paths in $\Omega \times [\lambda_0, \lambda_F]$:

   I. Paths starting at $\lambda = \lambda_0$ and ending at $\lambda = \lambda_0$

   II. Paths starting at $\lambda = \lambda_F$ and ending at $\lambda = \lambda_F$

   III. Paths starting at $\lambda = \lambda_0$ and ending at $\lambda = \lambda_F$

   IV. Closed paths that never touch the bases $\lambda = \lambda_0$ or $\lambda = \lambda_F$

None of the paths can touch the cylindrical boundary. On paths of type I and II, $\dot{\lambda}(s)$ can change sign only an *odd* number of times. Thus, by the sign change lemma,

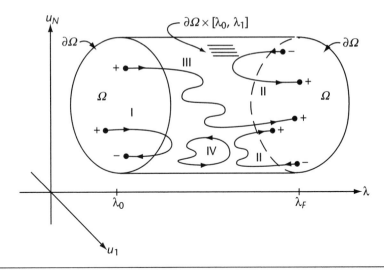

Figure 23.1 Homotopy invariance of degree. Signs ($\pm$) of $\dot{\lambda}(s)$ are shown at the bases, and $\lambda(s)$ varies as indicated by arrows. Paths of type I, II, and IV cannot contribute to the degree, but III can. Degree in this example is 1.

det $G_u(u, \lambda)$ changes sign an odd number of times on each such path. Hence, these paths can make no contribution to the degree, as there are as many contributions ($+1$) as there are contributions (-1) on them. However, paths of type III must have an even number of sign changes of $\dot{\lambda}(s)$ and hence of det $G_u(u, \lambda)$. Hence, they propagate without change the contribution that a root at $\lambda = \lambda_0$ makes to the degree along the entire path ending at $\lambda = \lambda_F$. The closed paths also have an even number of sign changes, but they never contribute a nonzero sum since they do not contact any boundaries.

If we employ the homotopy method indicated in equation (23.2) to solve a hard problem and can ensure all the hypotheses required above and, in addition, we make sure that the easy problem, $E(u) = 0$, has only one solution, then the above homotopy invariance theorem ensures us that the hard problem has at least one solution. Further, we can compute that solution by following the solution path starting from the easy solution. Methods to follow the path are discussed in Section 23.4.

23.3 Folds and Bifurcations

Any smooth solution path $\{u(s), \lambda(s)\}$ on which the maximal rank condition (expressions 23.7) holds is called a *regular path*. Thus, all of those paths used in the analysis of Section 23.2 are regular. However, those points at which $\dot{\lambda}(s_0) = 0$ are "singular" in that $G_u(u(s_0), \lambda(s_0))$ is singular. These points are known as *folds*, and they are the generic type of singularity that occurs on a solution path. The other types of singularities that can occur are *bifurcations*, at which the matrix $A(s)$ in expression (23.10) is singular. At such points, $\dot{\lambda}(s)$ may or may not vanish, and the solution path containing bifurcations cannot be regular. At fold points, the solution path usually folds back, as shown in the paths of types I and II in Figure 23.1; that is, $\ddot{\lambda}(s_0) \neq 0$. It is easy to locate and traverse fold points, as we shall see in Section 23.4. Note also that on a regular path at which $\dot{\lambda}(s_0) = 0$, we must have that $G_\lambda(s_0) \notin \mathcal{R}\{G_u(s_0)\}$. If this were not so, $G'(u(s_0), \lambda(s_0))$ could not have maximal rank N, since $G_u(s_0)$ is singular (see expressions (23.7)). It is also of interest to note that at such a fold point, the component $\dot{u}(s_0)$ of the tangent to the solution path is also a right null vector of $G_u(s_0)$, as follows from equation (23.8), and dim $\mathcal{N}\{G_u(s_0)\} = 1$.

   A bifurcation point $[u(s_0), \lambda(s_0)]$ on a smooth path $\{u(s), \lambda(s)\}$ has, by definition, the property that every ball about the point contains solutions of equation (23.1) that are not on the path. The usual way that this occurs is that some other smooth solution path intersects the given path, and their point of intersection is a bifurcation point on both paths. When a path is parameterized by the natural parameter λ, the homotopy invariance theory can be used to justify a very important test for the occurrence of bifurcation. Namely, if over some interval, $[\lambda_1, \lambda_2]$, a smooth solution path, $u(\lambda)$, is such that det $G_u(u(\lambda), \lambda)$ changes sign within the interval, then a bifurcation from $u(\lambda)$ occurs at the sign change. This basic test is proven by contradiction. If a sign change occurs and the only solutions are those on the smooth path, then a small cylinder can be placed about the path, centered at the position of sign change, and the path will only cut the cylinder at its two bases. But the degree of the mapping will differ on the two bases, since the determinant changed sign in the interior. This contradicts the homotopy invariance, and so a bifurcation must occur; that is, some solution path must touch the cylindrical surface about the original path (see Figure 23.2).

   The test indicated above can also be used to accurately locate the bifurcation point on the solution path using the method of bisection. That is, if a sign change occurs in $[\lambda_1, \lambda_2]$, then evaluate the determinant at the midpoint $\lambda_3 = \frac{1}{2}(\lambda_1 + \lambda_2)$. Now repeat this procedure in whichever interval $[\lambda_1, \lambda_3]$ or $[\lambda_3, \lambda_2]$ contains the sign change.

   It is important to note that this test requires a sign change in the *interior* of some λ-interval. Thus, it could fail to find a pitchfork type of bifurcation if the path being followed is the one that folds at the bifurcation point. Fortunately, there are other techniques that can be used to locate such bifurcations, but we do not go into such details here. An important feature that distinguishes bifurcation points from folds is that in the former $G_\lambda(s_0) \in \mathcal{R}\{G_u(s_0)\}$. Since this range has dimension less than N, we see that folds are generic and bifurcations are not.

   There are quite different bifurcations that occur in dynamical problems. These are the Hopf bifurcations that occur on steady-state solution branches, say $\{u(\lambda), \lambda\}$, when, as the natural parameter λ varies, a complex pair of eigenvalues of the Jacobian $G_u(u(\lambda), \lambda)$ crosses the imaginary axis. The bifurcating branch consists of periodic solutions. To compute them, the equations must contain appropriate time-derivative terms. Such terms must be adjoined, or it is quite possible that they have been

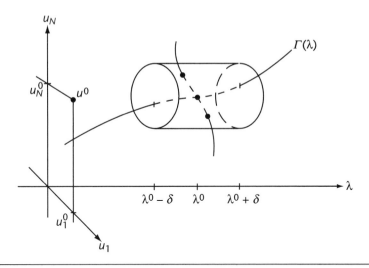

Figure 23.2 The point (u^0, λ^0), at which det G_u^0 changes sign as λ varies on $\Gamma(\lambda)$, is a *bifurcation point*. If not, the degrees at $\lambda^0 \pm \delta$ could not agree.

included in the formulation (23.1) and the "steady" solution paths $\{u(\lambda), \lambda\}$ are actually paths of periodic solutions. When a Hopf bifurcation occurs, either from a true steady path or a path of periodic solutions, the new path starts with a frequency given by the value of the purely imaginary eigenvalue (where the complex pair crosses the imaginary axis). To detect Hopf bifurcations, we must thus approximate the eigenvalues of a possibly large matrix or be able to determine a change in the number of eigenvalues in one of the half-planes as λ values. Again, the material in Chapter 20 can be of great help in these calculations.

23.4 Practical Path Following

The basic approach in computing solution paths is to use some local continuation procedure while recursively increasing or decreasing λ and monitoring to see if some singular behavior is lurking nearby. When trouble is sensed, the local procedure is altered to circumvent the singularity; afterward, the original procedure can be resumed. We will briefly describe several such methods.

As mentioned in Section 23.1, the Euler–Newton continuation procedure of equations (23.6) is extremely effective. But if a fold point lies on the path, this method will degrade as the Jacobian G_u becomes increasingly ill conditioned as it approaches singularity. Since folds are the generic type of singular point, it is most important to be able to traverse paths through them. The difficulty is clearly shown in Figure 23.3, where a fold occurs at $\lambda = \lambda_C$ and three Euler–Newton steps are attempted; the last one must fail, as there is no nearby solution at $\lambda = \lambda_4$. Of course,

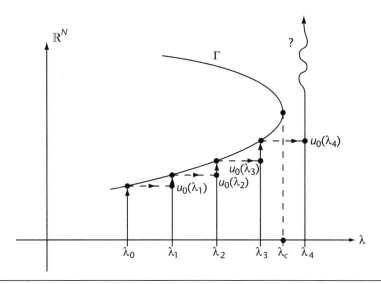

Figure 23.3   Failure of continuation in λ at a fold point at λ_C on the path Γ. The first three steps succeed, but at $\lambda_4 > \lambda_C$ it fails.

tests will have shown trouble approaching, and subsequently the λ-step lengths δ_j would have been reduced. But it is clear from the figure that small steps cannot remedy the difficulty.

The basic trouble is that the solution path in the neighborhood of the fold cannot be represented smoothly as a function of the natural parameter λ. Thus the remedy must be to use some other parameter to specify the solution path in (u, λ)-space. As we have indicated in Section 23.2, arclength along the path is naturally suggested. However, we will take a more general view and show how several alternatives can be formulated in a common framework. The idea is to introduce an *augmented* system in place of equation (23.1), namely:

(a) $G(u, \lambda) = 0,\quad G:\quad \mathbb{R}^{N+1} \to \mathbb{R}^N$

(b) $N(u, \lambda, s) = 0, N:\quad \mathbb{R}^{N+2} \to \mathbb{R}$ \hfill (23.12)

Here we allow λ to be an unknown, just like the components of u, and a new scalar parameter s (not necessarily arclength) is introduced in the arbitrary scalar *normalization* expression (23.12(b)) that is adjoined to the original system. We will show several choices for $N(\cdots)$ and their geometric interpretations.

But first we indicate why an augmented system may work at a solution (u^0, λ^0, s^0) where $G_u^0 \equiv G_u(u^0, \lambda^0)$ is singular. The Jacobian of the system (23.12) with respect to the unknowns (u, λ) is, at (u^0, λ^0, s^0),

$$\mathcal{A}^0 \equiv \begin{pmatrix} G_u^0 & G_\lambda^0 \\ N_u^0 & N_\lambda^0 \end{pmatrix}$$ \hfill (23.13)

This Jacobian is a *bordered matrix* about G_u^0, having an additional row and column. It is not difficult to show that if G_u^0 is singular with

$$\text{(a)} \quad \mathcal{N}\{G_u^0\} = \text{span}\{\phi\} \qquad \mathcal{N}\{G_u^{0T}\} = \text{span}\{\psi\}$$

and   (23.14)

$$\text{(b)} \quad \psi^T G_\lambda^0 \neq 0 \qquad N_u^0 \phi \neq 0$$

then $\mathcal{A}^0$ is nonsingular. So, if the normalization condition is chosen appropriately, Newton's method can be applicable to the augmented system (23.12) near (u^0, λ^0, s^0), while it fails on the original system (23.1) near (u^0, λ^0).

A general class of normalizations can be written as:

$$N(u, \lambda, s) \equiv v_0^T(u - u^0) + v_0(\lambda - \lambda^0) - (s - s^0) = 0 \qquad (23.15)$$

Here (u^0, λ^0, s^0) is assumed to be a solution of system (23.12), not necessarily at a fold point, and $v_0 \in \mathbb{R}^N$ and $v_0 \in \mathbb{R}$ determine the geometric significance of the constraint. If v_0 and v_0 are given constants, then expression (23.15) is linear in (u, λ) and represents a hyperplane in $\mathbb{R}^{N+1}$ that is orthogonal to the vector (v_0, v_0) and a distance $(s - s^0)$ from the point (u^0, λ^0, s^0).

The first example will be to take

$$v_0 = \dot{u}^0 \qquad v^0 = \dot{\lambda}^0 \qquad (23.16)$$

where $(\dot{u}^0, \dot{\lambda}^0)$ is the tangent to the path at (u^0, λ^0). Then s is an approximation to arc length along the solution path; we call this choice *pseudo-arclength continuation*. Note that if we use equations (23.16) in expression (23.15), divide by $(s - s^0)$, and let $s \to s^0$, we obtain equation (23.9) at $s = s^0$. The geometric significance is shown in Figure 23.4.

The Jacobian expression (23.13) becomes, with expressions (23.15) and (23.16),

$$\mathcal{A}^0 \equiv \begin{pmatrix} G_u^0 & G_\lambda^0 \\ v_0^T & v_0 \end{pmatrix} = \begin{pmatrix} G_u^0 & G_\lambda^0 \\ \dot{u}^{0T} & \dot{\lambda}^0 \end{pmatrix}$$

At a simple fold point, we get from system (23.14) that the above $\mathcal{A}^0$ is nonsingular. Clearly, as shown in Figure 23.4, this pseudo-arclength continuation method easily follows around the fold with no difficulties, consistent with the fact that $A(s)$ remains nonsingular in some neighborhood of the fold.

Another useful choice is to use:

$$v_0 = u^0 - u^{-1} \qquad v_0 = \lambda^0 - \lambda^{-1}$$

where (u^{-1}, λ^{-1}) is the solution obtained before (u^0, λ^0). This procedure replaces the tangent to the path at (u^0, λ^0) by a secant through it. With this "secant predictor," we need not compute the tangent vector, but smaller steps in s may be required.

Still another frequently suggested idea would employ:

$$v_0 = e_j, \text{ the } j\text{th unit vector in } \mathbb{R}^N; \quad v_0 = 0$$

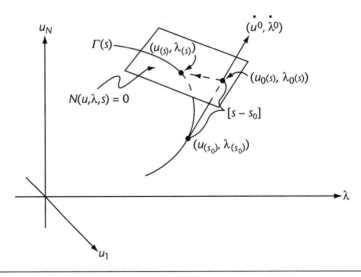

Figure 23.4   Pseudo–arc length continuation past a fold on a path $\Gamma(s)$. The fold lies on $\Gamma(s)$ between the solutions $(u(s_0), \lambda(s_0))$ and $(u(s), \lambda(s))$.

The resulting procedure simply replaces continuation in λ by continuation in u_j, the jth component of $u \in \mathbb{R}^N$. Which component should be employed is by no means clear, and for $N \gg 1$, there are many choices.

Of course, the original natural parameter continuation can be recovered by simply using

$$\dot{v}_0 = 0 \qquad \dot{v}_0 = 1$$

Finally, expression (23.15) can be nonlinear in u and λ if we use

$$\dot{v}_0 = u - u^0 \qquad \dot{v}_0 = \lambda - \lambda^0$$

In this case, the constraint becomes

$$\|u - u^0\|^2 + |\lambda - \lambda^0|^2 = (s - s^0)$$

and we call this *norm continuation*. Of course, we can replace $(s - s^0)$ here by $|s - s^0|^2$. One problem with this procedure is that it is not clear that it will converge to a new solution; it might simply return a point on the previously traversed part of the solution path. But by taking an initial guess in the proper direction, this difficulty can be avoided. In all of the other procedures, it is clear that an *orientation* is (or can be) given to the solution path, so that the procedure will not reverse and return previously computed path segments.

A very important practical consideration regarding the augmented systems of this section is the fact that bordered matrices of the form (23.13) have been thoroughly studied. Very efficient methods for solving linear systems with such coefficient matrices have been devised. Even when G_u^0 is poorly conditioned (i.e., nearly singular), these methods perform well [553, 554].

23.5   Branch Switching at Bifurcations

Near bifurcation points there are two (or more) distinct solution branches of expression (23.1),

$$\Gamma_I(s) : \{u = u_I(s),\ \lambda = \lambda_I(s)\}$$
$$\Gamma_{II}(t) : \{u = u_{II}(t),\ \lambda = \lambda_{II}(t)\}$$

For some value of the continuation parameters, say s_0 and t_0, they intersect at a bifurcation point:

$$u_I(s_0) = u_{II}(t_0) \qquad \lambda_I(s_0) = \lambda_{II}(t_0)$$

To locate a bifurcation point on $\Gamma_I(s)$ or $\Gamma_{II}(t)$ as continuation proceeds, we use the bisection procedure described in Section 23.3. However, at a bifurcation point, $\mathcal{A}_I(s_0)$ or $\mathcal{A}_{II}(t_0)$ is singular. When continuing in the natural parameter, $G_u(u_I^0, \lambda_I^0)$ or $G_u(u_{II}^0, \lambda_{II}^0)$ is singular. Thus, Newton's method and most other iterative procedures would seem to fail at such a point. It is true that the "sphere of convergence" about a point on the solution path has a radius that decreases as the point approaches the bifurcation point. Thus, there is a *convergence cone* about the path with vertex at the bifurcation point. But at a point close to the vertex, the tangent vector to the path departs from one cone segment, passes over the vertex, and enters the other cone segment, as shown in Figure 23.5. Thus, when using the Euler predictor, the computational procedure can easily oscillate back and forth across the bifurcation to facilitate the bisection method. The step size must not be too small, or the initial iterate could lie outside the convergence cone.

Having accurately located a bifurcation point on one of the paths, say $\Gamma_I(s)$, we need to compute the path $\Gamma_{II}(t)$ that emanates from that point. We indicate three methods for doing this. The first is *tangent continuation*. It uses the fact that there are two distinct tangents at the bifurcation point, one for each of the paths that meet there:

$$(\dot{u}_I^0, \dot{\lambda}_I^0) \quad \text{and} \quad (\dot{u}_{II}^0, \dot{\lambda}_{II}^0) \tag{23.17}$$

From the details of bifurcation theory, it turns out that these tangents are determined in terms of two distinct roots of the so-called *algebraic bifurcation equation*, which is generally quadratic. The coefficients of this quadratic can be approximated by means of some messy additional calculations involving left and right null vectors of G_u^0 (i.e., the ϕ and ψ of expression (23.14(a))) and the form $\psi^T G_{uu}^0 \phi \phi$. Of course, one of the tangents should be known, since Γ_I passing through the bifurcation point has been computed. Then the other tangent is determined and used in expressions (23.16) and (23.15) to compute $\Gamma_{II}(t)$ from the bifurcation point (see Figure 23.6).

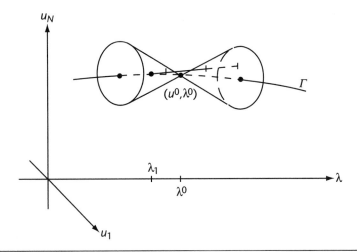

Figure 23.5   Convergence cone about a path with a bifurcation at (u^0, λ^0). The tangent at $\lambda_1 < \lambda^0$ may depart from the cone before λ^0 and reenter the cone beyond λ^0, thus enabling continuation past the bifurcation.

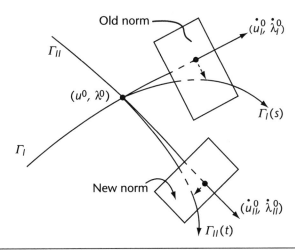

Figure 23.6   Tangent switching at the bifurcation point (u^0, λ^0).

A second method, called *parallel search*, uses a hyperplane that is parallel to the tangent to $\Gamma_I(s_0)$ and perpendicular to the plane of the two tangents in (23.17). This hyperplane is used in equation (23.15) by setting

$$v_0 = \dot{u}_\perp^0 \qquad v_0 = \dot{\lambda}_\perp^0$$

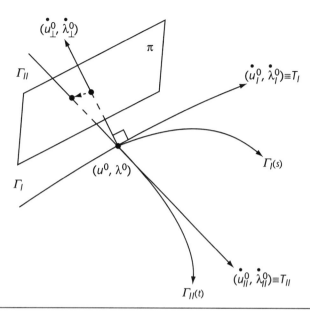

Figure 23.7 Parallel search. The plane π is parallel to T_I and orthogonal to the plane of T_I and T_{II}, so it will intersect the path Γ_{II} near the bifurcation point (u^0, λ^0).

where the normal vector $\mathbf{n}_\perp \equiv (\dot{u}^0_\perp, \dot{\lambda}^0_\perp)$ is

$$\mathbf{n}_\perp = a\left(\dot{u}^0_I, \dot{\lambda}^0_I\right) + b\left(\dot{u}^0_{II}, \dot{\lambda}^0_{II}\right)$$

with

$$a = \frac{z}{\sqrt{1-z^2}} \qquad b = \frac{-1}{\sqrt{1-z^2}} \qquad z = [\dot{u}^0_I \cdot \dot{u}^0_{II}] + \dot{\lambda}^0_I \dot{\lambda}^0_{II}$$

The geometry of this method is sketched in Figure 23.7.

The final method, called *perturbed bifurcation*, is based on the fact that, if equation (23.1) has a pair of bifurcating solution paths, then for almost any random unit vector $\tau \in \mathbb{R}^N$, the problem

$$G(u, \lambda) = \epsilon \tau \tag{23.18}$$

will have regular solution paths for all $\epsilon \neq 0$. This is based on the theory of regular and critical values of smooth functions. In particular, Sard's Lemma says that almost all values of sufficiently smooth functions are regular. It then follows that the paths on which these regular values are taken are regular paths. Thus, the solutions of equation (23.18) for $\epsilon \neq 0$ are sets of smooth nonintersecting arcs or simple closed curves. Of course, away from the bifurcation points of equation (23.1), these paths

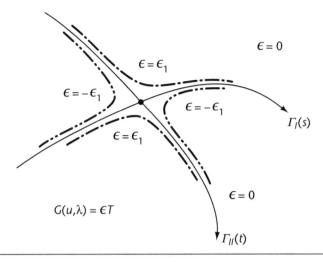

Figure 23.8   Perturbed bifurcation paths for $\epsilon \neq 0$ can occur in either of two forms, as shown.

must be close to the solution paths of equation (23.18) for ϵ sufficiently small, by the Implicit Function Theorem.

To use the above, we continue through a bifurcation point, say on $\Gamma_I(s)$. We then back off from that point and start solving equation (23.18) using continuation in ϵ with λ fixed. After departing a bit from $\Gamma_I(s)$, we fix ϵ and allow continuation in λ. This path stays close to $\Gamma_I(s)$ or to $\Gamma_{II}(t)$ for ϵ small, and thus it turns near the bifurcation point departing from Γ_I and trailing near Γ_{II}. When λ on this path is sufficiently different from λ_I^0, we keep it fixed and do continuation in ϵ back to zero. The resulting solution point of equation (23.1) will be on Γ_{II}. This behavior is depicted in Figure 23.8.

23.6   Computational Examples: AUTO

Several of the general techniques described in the preceding sections of this chapter have been incorporated into the software AUTO [277]–[279]. This program, which has a wide range of capabilities, has been used extensively in scientific and engineering computations. Some of its capabilities have been incorporated into related software, such as DsTool [65], XPPAUT [314], CONTENT [588], and POLYRED [791].

The main strength of AUTO lies in its algorithms for the numerical bifurcation analysis of boundary value problems in ordinary differential equations. Specifically, the boundary value problems are of the form

$$u'(t) = f(u(t), \lambda) \qquad t \in [0, 1], \ u(\cdot), f(\cdot, \cdot) \in \mathbb{R}^N, \ \lambda \in \mathbb{R}^{n_\lambda} \qquad (23.19)$$

with boundary conditions

$$b_i(u(0), u(1), \lambda) = 0 \qquad i = 1, 2, \dots, n_b$$

and integral constraints

$$\int_0^1 q_i \left(u(t), \lambda\right) \, dt = 0 \qquad i = 1, 2, \cdots, n_q$$

It is assumed that $n_\lambda = n_b + n_q - n + 1$, which generically leads to solution branches, rather than isolated solutions.

An important example of a system of the above form arises from the numerical continuation of periodic solutions. A boundary value formulation of the problem of computing stable and unstable periodic solutions is given by the time-scaled ODE,

$$u'(t) = T f \left(u(t), \lambda\right)$$

where T denotes the actual period, subject to the periodicity condition,

$$u(0) = u(1)$$

and a phase condition,

$$\int_0^1 u(t)^* \, \hat{u}'(t) \, dt = 0$$

This integral constraint, where $\hat{u}$ is a nearby *reference solution*, is a necessary condition for the "phase-shift distance" $D(\sigma) \equiv \int_0^1 \|u(t + \sigma) - \hat{u}(t)\|^2 dt$ to be minimized over σ.

AUTO also contains algorithms for the detection of folds, period-doubling bifurcations, and torus bifurcations along branches of periodic solutions. Moreover, these bifurcations can subsequently be continued in two problem parameters.

Another example of an ODE boundary-value problem arising from dynamical systems is the numerical computation and continuation of *connecting orbits*, that is, orbits that connect fixed points of a vector field. An important case is the *homoclinic orbit*, which connects a fixed point to itself. These orbits are important in, for example, the study of transition to chaos and in the study of traveling wave phenomena. Although such orbits have infinite period, their computation can be reduced to a problem on a finite interval by means of appropriate asymptotic boundary conditions [105, 361, 605]. The continuation of connecting orbits has been incorporated into AUTO. The software also contains algorithms for the detection and continuation of homoclinic bifurcations. In fact, the software fully incorporates the algorithms that were originally implemented as an application under the name HOMCONT [179, 180].

There are several software packages for the numerical bifurcation analysis of ODEs. Those based on global solution techniques (as opposed to "shooting") and orthogonal collocation with piecewise polynomial functions (as opposed to standard finite differences) generally perform very well on difficult problems. Here "difficult" refers to boundary or interior layers, strong relaxation phenomena, sharp fronts, near-homoclinic periodic orbits, "bursting" oscillations, and so on.

23.6.1   Bursting Oscillations

Our first example illustrates one of the many capabilities of AUTO, namely, the detection of period-doubling bifurcations and associated branch switching. The differential equation we consider is Plant's model [769] of bursting nerve cells. A system is said to exhibit *bursting* when it changes back and forth between a quiescent state and a rapidly oscillating state.

Plant's five-variable ODE model is of the form

$$\dot{V} = \left[g_I s_I^3(V)\, y_I + g_T\, x_T \right] [V_I - V]$$
$$+ \left[g_K\, x_K^4 + g_P\, c\, \left(K_p + c \right)^{-1} \right] [V_K - V] + g_L\, [V_L - V]$$
$$\dot{x}_T = [s_T(V) - x_T] / (\zeta \tau_{xT})$$
$$\dot{x}_K = [s_K(V) - x_K] / (\zeta \tau_{xK})$$
$$\dot{y}_I = \left[z_I(V) - y_I \right] / (\zeta \tau_{yI})$$
$$\dot{c} = \rho \left[K_c\, x_T \left(V_{Ca} - V \right) - c \right]$$

Detailed expressions for the various functions in this model and for parameter values can be found in Plant's paper. We let g_I be the bifurcation parameter. Figure 23.9 shows a portion of a branch of periodic solutions. The quantity *Norm*, which is used as a convenient solution measure, is here defined as

$$\|(V, x_T, x_K, y_I, c)\| \equiv \left\{ \frac{1}{T} \int_0^1 V(t)^2 + x_T(t)^2 + x_K(t)^2 + y_I(t)^2 + c(t)^2 dt \right\}^{\frac{1}{2}}$$

where T denotes the period of the oscillation. For different ranges of g_I, the qualitative behavior of the periodic orbits is characterized by the number of spikes. Between these intervals are very narrow regions where one spike is added as g_I increases. Figure 23.9 shows a blowup of the bifurcation diagram in a neighborhood of such a transition region. To the left of this region, there is one spike; to the right, there are two spikes per period. There is no branching process involved in the transition from one spike to two spikes. There are, however, cascades of period-doubling bifurcations. A typical periodic orbit on the first period-doubled branch is shown in Figure 23.10. Note that the orbit alternates between one spike and two spikes.

Plant's model is used here to illustrate how complicated, rapidly varying periodic solutions can be very effectively computed using our continuation methods, boundary value approach, high-order accurate discretization, and adaptive meshes. Many related models can be found in the literature—for example, models of the electrophysiology of pacemaker cells in the heart. The dimension of recent models of the electrical activity of a single cell is much larger than the five equations in Plant's model. Moreover, one often wants to study the collective behavior of assemblages of such cells. This task poses formidable computational challenges.

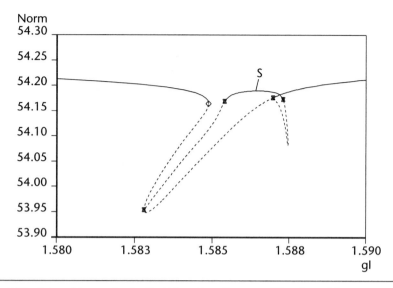

Figure 23.9 A transition region in the bifurcation diagram of Plant's model.

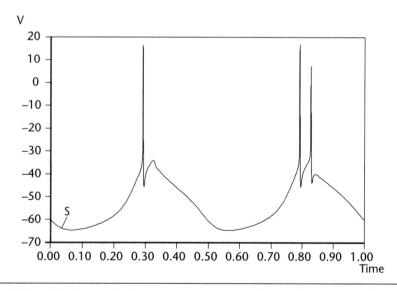

Figure 23.10 $V(t)$ versus scaled time t for the period-doubled solution marked with an "S" in the bifurcation diagram.

23.6.2   Some Navier–Stokes Flows

New techniques employing concurrent computing have been devised to solve a variety of incompressible flow problems. We sketch two such applications: Taylor–Couette flow between concentric rotating cylinders and Kolmogorov flow in a periodic box with periodic shearing forces. In both cases, a variety of bifurcations occur as the Reynolds numbers are varied. In the latter flow, the onset of turbulent worms is detected.

The incompressible Navier–Stokes equations in dimensionless coordinates are

$$\text{(a)}\quad \partial\mathbf{u}/\partial t + (\mathbf{u}\cdot\nabla)\mathbf{u} = -\nabla p + R^{-1}\Delta\mathbf{u} + \mathbf{F}$$
$$\text{(b)}\qquad\qquad \nabla\cdot\mathbf{u} = 0 \tag{23.20}$$

where $\mathbf{u}$ is the velocity, p is the pressure, R is the Reynolds number, and $\mathbf{F}$ is an external body force applied to the fluid. Solutions are sought over some domain $\Omega \subset \mathbb{R}^3$, on the boundary of which, $\partial\Omega$, appropriate conditions are imposed. We may seek steady states, with $\partial\mathbf{u}/\partial t \equiv 0$; periodic solutions, with $\mathbf{u}(t,\mathbf{x}) = \mathbf{u}(t+T,x)$ for some unknown period T; or transient solutions over some time interval $0 \leq t \leq t_F$. Frequently, steady states are computed as transients by letting $t_F \to \infty$. It would seem that only stable steady states can be computed in this way, but by employing our Recursive Projection Method (RPM) [861], we do obtain unstable states as well.

Using an appropriate spatial grid or simplicial partition of Ω, we devise a spatial discretization of system (23.20) by means of finite differences, finite elements, spectral or pseudospectral expansions or any combination of these methods. The resulting semi-discretized system can be represented as

$$\text{(a)}\quad du/dt = H(u) - Gp \equiv f(u,p),$$
$$\text{(b)}\qquad b = Du \tag{23.21}$$

Here $u(t)$ and $p(t)$ are vectors yielding approximations to the velocity and pressure, respectively, at time t and at locations $x \in \Omega$ determined by the details of the discretization. For example, using finite differences with N mesh points in Ω, we have $u(t) \in \mathbb{R}^M$, $p(t) \in \mathbb{R}^N$ with $M \doteq 3N$, the gradient is approximated by $G \in \mathbb{R}^{M\times N}$ and the divergence by $D \in \mathbb{R}^{N\times M}$. The inhomogeneous term b in equation (23.21(b)) represents possible boundary values of velocity when $u(t)$ represents only internal values in Ω. The term $H(u)$ in expression (23.21(a)) is the discretization of $[-(\mathbf{u}\cdot\nabla)\mathbf{u} + R^{-1}\Delta\mathbf{u}]$.

The system (23.21) is a set of *semi-explicit differential algebraic equations*. A brief treatment of such systems is given in Keller and von Sosen [556], and a more thorough theory is developed in Keller [555]. We sketch here the result of applying these techniques to our problems.

If the semi-discretized velocity vector has components $\mathbf{u}$, $\mathbf{v}$, and $\mathbf{w}$ in the coordinate directions, then

$$u = \begin{bmatrix} \mathbf{u} \\ \mathbf{v} \\ \mathbf{w} \end{bmatrix}$$

where we assume $\mathbf{u}, \mathbf{v}, \mathbf{w} \in \mathbb{R}^N$ and $M = 3N$. The discretized continuity equation can be decomposed using, for example, in *cylindrical coordinates*:

$$D \equiv [D_r, D_\theta, D_z] \qquad D_r \in \mathbb{R}^{N \times N}, \quad [D_\theta, D_z] \in \mathbb{R}^{N \times 2N} \qquad (23.22)$$

Our theory shows that we can impose a constraint introducing $2N$ parameters α, which we do as follows:

$$C(u, \alpha) \equiv \alpha - [0, I_{2N}] \begin{bmatrix} \mathbf{u} \\ \mathbf{v} \\ \mathbf{w} \end{bmatrix} = 0$$

Thus, our new parameters are simply the θ- and z-velocity components that is,

$$\alpha = \begin{bmatrix} \mathbf{v} \\ \mathbf{w} \end{bmatrix}$$

The radial velocity is obtained by solving the continuity equation (23.21(b)) using coordinates (23.22) to get:

$$\mathbf{u} = -D_r^{-1} [D_\theta \mathbf{v} + D_z \mathbf{w} - b]$$

This is used along with α to solve for the pressure, which satisfies, from expression (23.21(a)) on applying D, the discretized Poisson equation:

$$DGp - DH(u) = 0$$

Then it follows from the theory that $\alpha(t)$ is the solution of

$$\frac{d\alpha}{dt} \equiv \begin{bmatrix} d\mathbf{v}/dt \\ d\mathbf{w}/dt \end{bmatrix} = \begin{bmatrix} \mathbf{f}_\theta(u, p) \\ \mathbf{f}_z(u, p) \end{bmatrix} \equiv G(\alpha) \qquad (23.23)$$

Here we have used the fact that u and p are determined as above in terms of α. If we seek steady-state solutions, setting $d\alpha/dt = 0$ in expression (23.23) will do. The dependence on dimensionless parameters has been neglected here but will be introduced as required. The above derivation covers Taylor–Couette flows but has to be modified slightly for Kolmogorov flows. We turn to that case next.

23.6.3   Kolmogorov Flows

For the Kolmogorov flows the body force has the form

$$\mathbf{F} \equiv \chi \, \sin(ky) \, \mathbf{e}_x$$

where $\mathbf{e}_x$ is the unit vector in the x-direction and χ is the amplitude of the force. The periodic box has sides of lengths L_x, L_y, and L_z. To ensure periodicity, it is necessary that

$$k = \frac{2\pi m}{L_y}$$

for some positive integer m. The coordinates are scaled by L_x, L_y, and L_z to get a dimensionless unit cube, and the Reynolds number based on the maximum speed, $\chi/\nu k^2$, of the trivial shear flow solution is

$$R \equiv \frac{\chi}{\nu^2 k^3}$$

Other dimensionless parameters enter as the aspect ratios, $A \equiv L_y/L_x$ and $B \equiv L_y/L_z$, and the wave number $\gamma \equiv kL_y$. In particular, we consider bifurcations from the specific shear flow solution given by

$$u_0 = \sin(\gamma y) \qquad v_0 = 0 \qquad w_0 = 0 \qquad p_0 = 0$$

Seeking bifurcating solutions of the form $\mathbf{u} = \mathbf{u}_0 + \mathbf{u}_1$ we get, assuming that $\mathbf{u}_1 = e^{irx} \cdot e^{isz} \cdot V(y)$ and setting $\alpha \equiv Ar$, $\beta \equiv Bs$, that the linearized equations for $\mathbf{u}_1$ give

$$i\alpha \sin(\gamma y) \left(\frac{d^2 V}{dy^2} + [\gamma^2 - \alpha^2 - \beta^2]V \right) = \frac{1}{\gamma R} \left(\frac{d^2}{dy^2} - [\alpha^2 + \beta^2] \right)^2 V \qquad (23.24)$$

The boundary conditions require periodicity:

$$V(0) = V(1) \qquad\qquad (23.25)$$

In addition, there are two degrees of freedom in the problem (23.24), since the phase and amplitude of $V(y)$ are arbitrary. We thus impose two constraints, introducing two parameters (η, μ) as

$$\int_0^1 \left\{ \|V(y)\|^2 + \|V'(y)\|^2 + \|V''(y)\|^2 + \|V'''(y)\|^2 \right\} dy = \eta \qquad (23.26)$$

and adding the term

$$-\mu \sin(2\pi y) \qquad\qquad (23.27)$$

to the right-hand side of equation (23.24). The resulting two-point boundary value problem with constraints is solved using AUTO. These results obtained in Love [626] are reproduced in Figures 23.11 through 23.13.

To examine the solutions bifurcating from the basic Kolmogorov flow as R is varied, spectral collocation methods are used since the domain is a periodic cube. For steady states, the discrete solutions are computed using continuation with Newton's method. Of course, the linear systems to be solved are so large that iterative methods are used to obtain the Newton corrections. To make this practical, distributed-memory computers are used via procedures described in van de Velde [950].

To compute periodic solutions, which arise from Hopf bifurcations, and for traveling wave solutions, the problems can be reformulated to yield steady-state problems. Then the same procedures as indicated above are applicable. Results from such calculations are presented by Love [626] and Love and Keller [627].

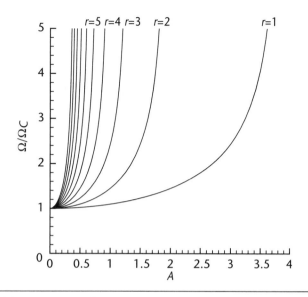

Figure 23.11   Bifurcation curves for $B = 1$, $s = 0$.

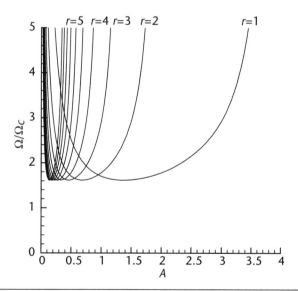

Figure 23.12   Bifurcation curves for $B = 1$, $s = 1$.

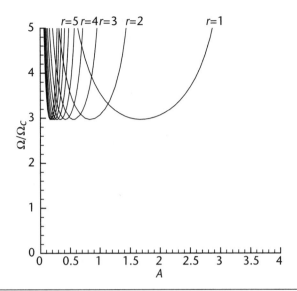

Figure 23.13   Bifurcation curves for $B = 1$, $s = 2$.

23.7   Parallel AUTO

The orthogonal collocation method with piecewise polynomials can be briefly described as follows. Introduce a mesh $\{0 = t_0 < t_1 < \cdots < t_N = 1\}$, $\Delta t_j \equiv t_j - t_{j-1}$, $(1 \leq j \leq N)$. For each mesh interval $[t_{j-1}, t_j]$, introduce the Lagrange basis polynomials $w_{j,i}(t)$, defined by

$$w_{j,i}(t) = \prod_{k=0, k \neq i}^{m} \frac{t - t_{j-\frac{k}{m}}}{t_{j-\frac{i}{m}} - t_{j-\frac{k}{m}}}$$

for $j = 1, \cdots, N$, $i = 0, 1, \cdots, m$, where

$$t_{j-\frac{i}{m}} \equiv t_j - \frac{i}{m} \Delta t_j$$

The collocation method now consists of finding, for each $j = 1, 2, \cdots, N$,

$$p_j(t) = \sum_{i=0}^{m} u_{j-\frac{i}{m}} w_{j,i}(t)$$

such that

$$p_j'(z_{j,i}) = f(p_j(z_{j,i}), \lambda) \qquad i = 1, 2, \cdots, m \tag{23.28}$$

where in each subinterval $[t_{j-1}, t_j]$ the points $\{z_{j,i}\}_{i=1}^{m}$ are the zeros of the mth-degree Legendre polynomials relative to that subinterval. With the above choice of basis, u_j and $u_{j-\frac{i}{m}}$ approximate the solution $u(t)$ of the continuous problem at t_j and

$t_{j-\frac{i}{m}}$, respectively. The discrete boundary conditions are $b_i(p_1(0), p_N(1), \lambda) = 0$, $i = 1, 2, \cdots, n_b$, that is,

$$b_i(u_0, u_N, \lambda) = 0 \qquad i = 1, 2, \cdots, n_b \tag{23.29}$$

The integrals can be discretized by a quadrature formula. A natural choice is the composite quadrature formula obtained by approximate integration over each of the subintervals $[t_{j-1}, t_j]$. This gives

$$\sum_{j=1}^{N} \sum_{i=0}^{m} w_{j,i}\, q_k(u_{j-\frac{i}{m}}, \lambda) = 0 \qquad k = 1, 2, \cdots, n_q \tag{23.30}$$

where the quantities $w_{j,i}$ are the Lagrange quadrature coefficients. Apart from a scaling factor, these are independent of j. For pseudo-arclength continuation we need to add the equation

$$\int_0^1 \left(u(t) - u_0(t)\right)^* \dot{u}_0(t)\, dt + (\lambda - \lambda_0)^* \dot{\lambda}_0 - \Delta s = 0$$

where (u_0, λ_0) is the previously computed point on the solution branch and $(\dot{u}_0, \dot{\lambda}_0)$ is the normalized direction of the branch at that point. Upon discretization, the pseudo-arclength equation becomes

$$\sum_{j=1}^{N} \sum_{i=0}^{m} w_{j,i} \left(u_{j-\frac{i}{m}} - (u_0)_{j-\frac{i}{m}}\right)^* (\dot{u}_0)_{j-\frac{i}{m}} + (\lambda - \lambda_0)^* \dot{\lambda}_0 - \Delta s = 0 \tag{23.31}$$

The complete set of discrete equations for taking one step along a branch of solutions therefore consists of solving the system of $mnN + n_b + n_q + 1$ nonlinear equations (23.28) through (23.31) for the unknowns $\{u_{j-\frac{i}{m}}\} \in \mathbb{R}^{mnN+n}$, $\lambda \in \mathbb{R}^{n_\lambda}$. This is done by a Newton or Newton–Chord iteration. After linearization via Newton's method, the matrix J in Figure 23.14 is obtained.

This matrix is structured and sparse with borders at the bottom and on the right. The corresponding linearized system has the form

$$J\,x = f \tag{23.32}$$

This system must be solved for each Newton iteration for each step along a solution branch. For example, in the numerical analysis of the bursting behavior of Plant's model in Section 23.6.1, the system (23.32) must be solved thousands of times. Thus, efficient solution techniques are desirable.

23.7.1 Parallel Implementation

Here we describe a parallel direct solver developed by Wang [978] for the sparse linear system (23.32). The matrix is shown in Figure 23.14, with right-hand side $f = (F_1, F_2, \cdots, F_N, FC)^T$. (In the illustrations we use $N = 8$.) To simplify the presentation, we do not describe pivoting, even though the actual implementation uses restricted

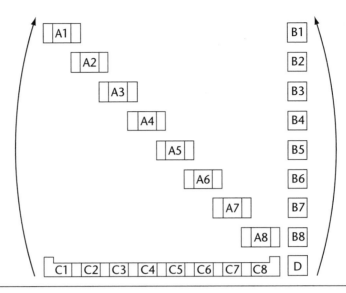

Figure 23.14   Structure of the Jacobian matrix J.

row and column pivoting. For full details, see Wang and Doedel [978]. The two main components of the solution procedure are *condensation of parameters* and *nested dissection*, which are described in some detail below.

Assume that the total number of processors is P. (In the illustrations we use $P = 8$.) We define one *data unit* as $\{A_i, B_i, C_i, F_i, D, FC\}$, where $i = 1, 2, \cdots, N$. We partition the Jacobian matrix J and the right-hand side f into P *data groups*, one data group per processor. If the number of data units is divisible by P, then each data group will contain k data units. Otherwise, some data groups will contain $k + 1$ data units.

A Gauss elimination scheme, applied concurrently in each of the processors, results in the modified Jacobian shown in Figure 23.15. Note how the scheme, known as *condensation of parameters,* has eliminated part of the center portion of each A_i. Communication needs correspond to the eliminations in the bottom rows of J, that is, for the C_i's, for D, and for the right-hand-side component FC. The C_i's require communication because the right part of C_i in node p_i overlaps with the left part of C_{i+1} in node p_{i+1}. D and FC require communication because they are shared by all nodes.

Note how the shaded portion of the matrix in Figure 23.15 corresponds to a reduced, decoupled set of equations in a correspondingly reduced set of unknowns. The decoupled matrix, shown separately in Figure 23.16, is smaller by a factor of approximately m (the number of collocation points) compared to the matrix in Figure 23.15.

The system corresponding to the matrix in Figure 23.16 is solved using nested dissection, as illustrated in Figures 23.16 through 23.19 for the case of eight mesh

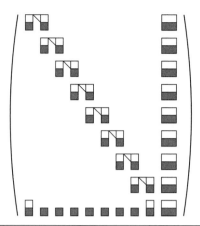

Figure 23.15   The Jacobian *J* after condensation of parameters.

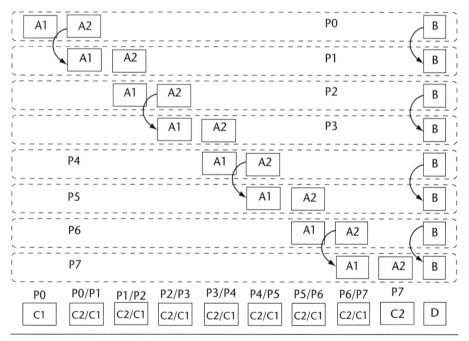

Figure 23.16   Initial state of nested dissection.

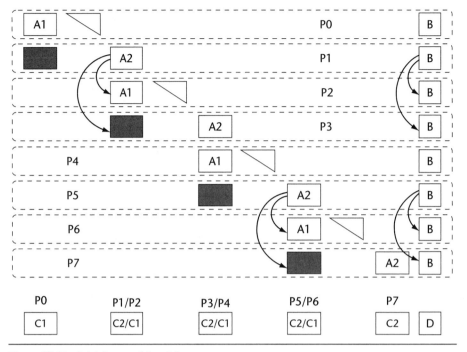

Figure 23.17   Initial state of Level 2.

intervals and eight processors. This procedure results in a further reduced subsystem, namely the system corresponding to the shaded area in Figure 23.19, which is decoupled from the full system and can be solved independently. We obtain the solution corresponding to the matrix in Figure 23.16 by a concurrent back-substitution process that first requires the solution of the final subsystem to be sent to all nodes. In order to obtain the final solution of the full system (23.32), we also need to back-substitute in the condensation of parameters process. This can be done concurrently without communication.

The timing results in Table 23.1 were obtained on the Intel Delta, consisting of 512 Intel iPSC/860 nodes connected by a mesh network. The example used for the numerical experiments is the AUTO demo *tim.f*, which defines a first-order system of n ordinary differential equations with n boundary conditions, where n can be chosen. This test problem has one integral constraint, namely the integral arising from the pseudo-arclength equation. The test run is set up so that it requires 10 decompositions and 10 back-substitutions by the linear equation solver. In the test runs we have selected the dimension of the system of differential equations to be $n = 24$, using $N = 64$ mesh intervals, with $m = 4$ Gauss collocation points per interval.

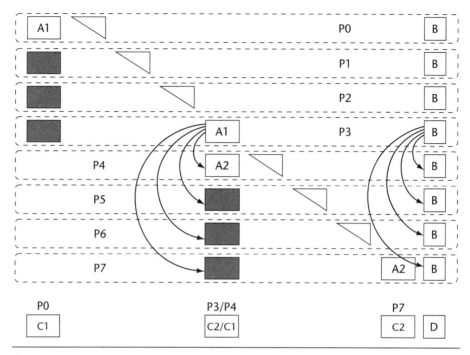

Figure 23.18 Initial state of Level 3.

23.8 Conclusion

Path following is an important capability in computational science. The techniques in this chapter enable discovery of families of solutions to differential equations and make possible solutions to difficult sets of equations by following a path from a simpler problem (homotopy). It is often the singular points along these solution paths where the most interesting information resides and where standard solution methods have the most difficulty. The AUTO software is designed to handle just such eventualities. This tool solves nonlinear boundary-value problems with integral constraints, in particular following a path of such solutions. Additionally, AUTO provides analysis of singular points, such as solution folds or bifurcations encountered along the way. Some parallel algorithms have been implemented for the solution of linear equations arising from path following, but this continues to be an area for further investigation.

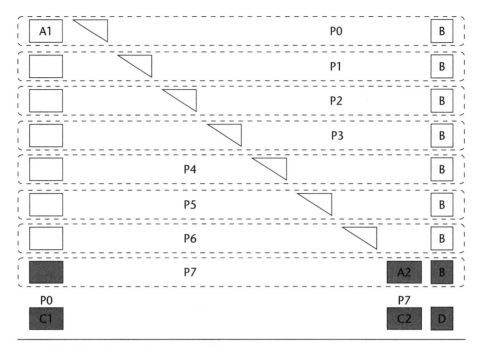

Figure 23.19   Final state after the nested dissection.

Table 23.1   Intel Delta timing results for $n = 24$, $N = 64$, $m = 4$

Number of nodes	Execution time	Speedup	Efficiency
1	0.601E+03	1	100%
2	0.314E+03	1.91	95.70%
4	0.166E+03	3.62	90.51%
8	0.923E+02	6.51	81.39%
16	0.536E+02	11.21	70.08%
32	0.310E+02	19.39	60.58%
64	0.246E+02	24.43	38.17%

24 Automatic Differentiation

Alan Carle

Derivatives play a key role in the development and subsequent use of high-performance computer simulations. Principal uses of derivatives include the following:

- Solution of *inverse problems* to calibrate the initial state of a computer model to match experimentally observed data.

- *Sensitivity analysis* to verify robustness of the simulation with respect to small changes to the input parameters and to verify that computer models behave as suggested by experimental data.

- *Uncertainty analysis* to identify the primary sources of uncertainty in the results of the simulation.

- *Design optimization* activities to identify optimal settings of design parameters to minimize a cost function [20, 170].

With regard to the computation of derivatives, developers of high-performance computer simulations fall into the following camps:

- Developers who know they need derivatives and are convinced that they can use finite-difference approximations to compute them. Finite-difference approximations evaluate a function f at x and $x + h$ for some h, and then compute $(f(x + h) - f(x))/h$ to approximate $f'(x)$. If the function to be differentiated has n inputs, then at least $n + 1$ function evaluations will be needed to approximate all of the derivatives. Since all of these $n + 1$ evaluations can be performed simultaneously, the entire process is "pleasingly parallel," given sufficient resources. Unfortunately, unless h is selected with extreme caution and sufficiently high-precision numerics are used to compute f, finite-difference approximations can be quite poor.

- Developers who know they need derivatives and explicitly introduce code into their programs to analytically compute derivatives. Four-dimensional data assimilation merges real-world observations into complex computational simulations of climate. Both the ocean and weather modeling communities invest considerable effort in the development of *adjoint codes* that compute the derivatives needed for data assimilation [700, 909, 913]. Adjoint-code development is slow, tedious work, but the efficiency of the resulting derivative code can be exceptional.

- Developers who need derivatives, but do not know that they do. Developers who are focused on achieving high performance may not realize that their simulations will ultimately need to be calibrated with experimental data by solving an inverse problem, need to be validated through a series of sensitivity and uncertainty studies, or need to be used in an optimization-based design process.

- Developers who know that they have no need for derivatives. Developers of discrete or otherwise nondifferentiable functions and developers of differentiable, but noisy, functions have little need for derivatives. For noisy functions, "trends" in the data tend to be more useful than actual derivatives. In fact, if the noise in the data has a sufficiently low amplitude, then finite-difference approximations may be an appropriate way to quantify the trends in the data.

This chapter focuses on a maturing technology for computing derivatives of computer simulations that goes by the several names: *automatic differentiation, computational differentiation* or *algorithmic differentiation* [103, 400]. Automatic differentiation, (AD) is an automatic technique for augmenting computer programs with code to compute derivatives accurately and efficiently. As an automatic technique, AD has the potential to eliminate the need to explicitly develop code to compute derivatives. Not only can AD reduce the time required to develop a differentiated code, it also reduces the total amount of code that needs to be maintained and allows developers to focus on the underlying computational simulation.

The ideas underlying automatic differentiation are not new—in high school calculus, most students realize that differentiation is an essentially mechanical procedure. A. Griewank has constructed a history of AD software that chronicles more than 60 AD software packages developed since the 1950s. The great majority of these software packages were created for use by their developers for specialized applications. In the last 10 years, however, an important change has come to the field of AD: several groups across the world have put a great deal of effort into developing general-purpose AD software—software capable of differentiating arbitrary programs written in a commonly used programming language with little or no effort by the users of the AD software.

This chapter covers the following topics:

- *Overview.* This section outlines the basic mathematics underlying AD.

- *Implementation techniques.* This section describes the two basic techniques for implementing AD—source-to-source code transformation and operator overloading.

- *Software.* In order to give a feel for AD, this section describes the design and use of two AD packages: ADOL-C, which supports AD of C and C++ programs, and Adifor 3.0, which supports AD of Fortran 77 programs.

- *Message-passing programs.* This section outlines the issues underlying the AD of programs that contain message-passing operations.

- *Advanced use.* This section describes several techniques that can be used to improve the efficiency of derivative codes.

24.1 Overview of Automatic Differentiation

Before describing the techniques underlying AD, it is useful to introduce some terminology. The goal of applying an AD tool to a function is to compute the derivatives of a specified set of *dependent variables* (a subset of the outputs of the function) with respect to a specified set of *independent variables* (a subset of the inputs of the function). An *active variable* is either: (1) an independent or dependent variable or (2) an intermediate variable that depends on the independent variables and is used to compute values for the dependent variables. AD augments the function code with additional code to compute derivatives for all of the active variables.

For a vector function F from R^n to R^m that takes times $t(F)$ and memory $m(F)$ to evaluate, the *first-order forward mode of AD* can deliver the full $m \times n$ Jacobian in $\mathcal{O}(n * t(F))$ time and $\mathcal{O}(n * m(F))$ space. For problems with $n \ll m$, the forward mode can provide accurate derivatives at a cost that is comparable to that of finite differences.

The *first-order reverse mode of AD* can deliver the full Jacobian in $\mathcal{O}(m * t(F))$ time. This mode of AD computes derivatives also referred to as *adjoint values* during a reverse pass over the function. Unfortunately, reversing the flow of the program requires $\mathcal{O}(t(F))$ space to implement, unless checkpointing strategies (see Section 24.5.5) are used to reduce this potentially immense space requirement. Assuming that the space issue can be successfully addressed, for problems with $n \gg m$ (such as the evaluation of a gradient of an objective function for use in optimization), the reverse mode is ideal, far outperforming finite differences.

In addition to computing first-order derivatives, the techniques underlying AD naturally compute various matrix products involving Jacobians. For example, for a matrix R with p columns, the forward mode computes the matrix product $J * R$, where J is the Jacobian, to give p directional derivatives in $\mathcal{O}(p * t(F))$ time. Similarly, for a matrix L with q rows, the reverse mode computes the matrix product $L * J$ in $\mathcal{O}(q * t(F))$ time, but again using a potentially huge amount of space.

The forward and reverse modes can be easily extended to compute higher-order derivatives, although at a cost higher than that required to compute the first-order derivatives.

24.1.1   How Automatic Differentiation Works

The functionality of the forward and reverse modes is achieved by associating a *derivative object* consisting of one or more new floating-point variables, with each of the floating-point variables in the original program. For the forward mode, program control flow remains unchanged. Derivative code for each assignment statement is inserted immediately before or after that assignment statement. The inserted derivative code computes values for each component of the derivative object associated with the left-hand side of the original assignment statement. For the reverse mode, more substantial changes are made to the control-flow structure of the program to ensure that the program can be executed in reverse and to ensure that the partial derivatives for each assignment statement are available. Then, derivative code is inserted to compute values for the derivative objects associated with variables appearing on the right-hand side of the original assignment statement. Reiterating, control flow in the forward mode is precisely the control flow of the original function, and control flow in the reverse mode is precisely the reverse of the control flow of the original function.

We now describe how each assignment statement in the original function code is differentiated. To simplify this presentation, we assume that assignment statements have the simple form

$$z = f(x, y)$$

where f is a basic operation $(+, *, /, -, \ldots)$ or an intrinsic operation (*sin, tan, sqrt*, ...), and z is distinct from x and y. If necessary, an automatic-differentiation tool can introduce new temporary variables and assignment statements to ensure that every assignment statement has this form.

Consider a simple pseudocode fragment:

```
    x = f1(independent_variables)
    y = f2(independent_variables)
    .
    .
    .
100 z = x * y
    .
    .
    .
    dependent_variable = f3(z)
```

Applying the forward mode of AD to this simple example is straightforward. We assume that we have associated a derivative object g_x with x, g_y with y, and g_z with

z, and, at the time the statement labeled with 100 is reached, g_x and g_y are vectors containing the derivatives of x and y with respect to all of the independent variables, respectively.

A simple vector operation that computes g_z can be introduced after the assignment to z as follows:

```
100  z = x * y
     g_z(:) = g_x(:) * y + x * g_y(:)
```

Applying the reverse mode of AD to this example is a less straightforward but still entirely mechanical process. We first look at the process mathematically and then generate the source code to reflect the appropriate derivative calculations. Linearizing the nonlinear operation

$$z = x * y$$

gives

$$dz_a = dx_b * y + x * dy_b$$

which can be written as matrix operation as

$$\begin{pmatrix} dx_a \\ dy_a \\ dz_a \end{pmatrix} = \begin{pmatrix} 1 & 0 & 0 \\ 0 & 1 & 0 \\ y & x & 0 \end{pmatrix} \begin{pmatrix} dx_b \\ dy_b \\ dz_b \end{pmatrix}$$

where $d?_a$ represents the derivative of variable ? after the assignment to z has been completed, and $d?_b$ represents the derivative of variable ? prior to the assignment to z. Transposing this matrix assignment and relabeling variables gives the new matrix operation

$$\begin{pmatrix} ax_b \\ ay_b \\ az_b \end{pmatrix} = \begin{pmatrix} 1 & 0 & y \\ 0 & 1 & x \\ 0 & 0 & 0 \end{pmatrix} \begin{pmatrix} ax_a \\ ay_a \\ az_a \end{pmatrix}$$

where $a?_a$ now represents the "adjoint" of variable ? after the assignment to z has been completed, and $a?_b$ represents the "adjoint" of variable ? prior to the assignment to z. (The *adjoint* of a variable at a particular location in the program is defined to be the derivative of the dependent variable with respect to the variable at the specified program location.) Note that the transposed matrix operation describes how to compute the adjoints of variables prior to the assignment to z, given adjoint values of variables after the assignment to z and partial derivatives of the assignment statement itself.

We can now generate two new pseudocode fragments that implement this new operation.[1] The first fragment is executed during a forward pass through the program. The forward pass records the values of partial derivatives for the assignment statement by pushing them onto a stack and then executes the assignment.

```
call push(z)
call push(y)      ! dz/dx
call push(x)      ! dz/dy
z = x * y
```

The second fragment pops the partial derivative values off of the stack and then uses them to update the adjoint values for this assignment statement during a reverse pass over the function.

```
call pop(pzy)     ! dz/dy
call pop(pzx)     ! dz/dx
a_x = a_x + pzx * a_z
a_y = a_y + pzy * a_z
a_z = 0
call pop(z)
```

Hybrid combinations of the forward and reverse modes sometimes make sense [115]. For example, the Adifor 3.0 system described below, when differentiating a program in the forward mode, actually applies the reverse mode to each assignment statement to compute the required partial derivatives. An example of code generated by this hybrid technique is shown in Section 24.2.2.

24.1.2   When Automatic Differentiation Works

AD is a purely local technique for enhancing a program with code to compute derivatives. Typical proofs of the correctness of AD start by demonstrating that AD correctly computes the derivatives of straight-line sequences of assignment statements that have the property that all operators and built-in functions are continuously differentiable on open domains and that those operators and built-in functions are evaluated at points in their domains. Straight-line sequences of assignments that meet these criteria can easily be shown to be differentiable. These proofs are then extended to deal with programs that contain *active* conditional branches by requiring that the code guarded by those conditional branches and its derivative be smooth. The following example meets this branch criterion, since both statements L1 and L2, when evaluated at $x = 0$, yield $y = 0$ and $y' = 0$:

```
       if (x < 0) then
L1:        y = x^2
```

---

[1] We can drop the "a" and "b" subscripts from the names of the adjoint variables, as long as we generate the new derivative code in the appropriate sequence.

```
        else
L2:     y = 3 * x^2
        endif
```

In contrast, the next example fails to meet the branch criterion and will lead AD astray:

```
if (x = 1) then
  y = 1
else if (x = 2) then
  y = 4
else
  y = x^2
endif
```

The derivatives of each of the constant assignments to y are 0, even though the derivative of $y = x^2$ at $x = 1$ is 2 and the derivative of $y = x^2$ at $x = 2$ is 8. Empirically we have rarely seen any problems introduced by the way AD handles branches.

Before we discuss AD implementation techniques, we need to raise two additional issues. First, since derivatives may be scaled differently than function values, overflow and underflow may arise during the evaluation of derivatives of functions that do not themselves generate overflows and underflows. On machines with IEEE arithmetic, the standard handling of overflows and underflows will make it clear when these sorts of exceptions have occurred.

Second, computer simulations almost always approximate solutions to some mathematical problem. Mathematically, there is no guarantee that differentiating an approximation to a function gives the same result as approximating (or, more simply, computing) the derivative of the function. A small example demonstrates this point. Approximate $y = x^2$ using the following code:

```
c = floor(x^2/h)
y = c * h
```

Clearly, ignoring mundane issues such as overflow, as $h \to 0$, y becomes an ever better approximation to x^2. However, in reality, c is a step function whose derivative is 0 everywhere except where it is undefined (i.e., when x^2/h is an integer value) and h is independent of x, so its derivative is 0. Therefore, for all values of x where x^2/h is not an integer value, the derivative of y is 0 and not $2x$, as might be expected.

24.2   Automatic-Differentiation Implementation Techniques

This section describes two AD implementation techniques that are used by various AD packages to perform the AD code-augmentation process: (1) operator overloading and (2) source-to-source transformation.

24.2.1   AD via Operator Overloading

Operator overloading extends elementary operations (such as multiply and divide) and elementary functions (such as sine and cosine) to compute their derivatives in addition to their usual values. This technique can be applied in any language that implements operator overloading. To use an AD tool based on operator overloading, users must modify the types of the active variables in their programs and then compile the new code along with implementations of the overloaded operations. AD tools that use the operator overloading approach include ADOL-C [401], ADOL-F [860], ADO1 [780], and OPTIMA [83]. A simple example of an implementation of the forward mode is given in Gorlen et al. [392].

Despite the elegance of the operator overloading approach, its major disadvantage is one of granularity—only individual unary and binary operations can be overloaded. When an operator overloading–based AD tool sees

```
z = x(1) * x(2) * x(3) * x(4)
```

in the forward mode, it carries out operations that correspond to the following:

```
t1 = x(1) * x(2)
g_t1(:) = g_x(:,1) * x(2) + x(1) * g_x(:,2)
t2 = t1 * x(3)
g_t2(:) = g_t1(:) * x(3) + t1 * g_x(:,3)
t3 = t2 * x(4)
g_t3(:) = g_t2(:) * x(4) + t2 * g_x(:,4)
z   = t3
g_z(:) = g_t3(:)
```

For a relatively small number of independent variables, the cost of this code is dominated by the cost of the four vector assignment statements. By taking program context into account, as shown in the next section, the cost of this derivative calculation can be significantly reduced.

24.2.2   AD via Source-to-Source Transformation

Source-to-source transformation is a compiler-based technique for transforming a computer code into a new code that explicitly includes statements that compute derivatives. This technique can be applied to programs written in any programming language. To use an AD tool based on source-to-source transformation, users present their source code and a description of the derivatives that they need to the AD tool. The AD tool then parses each of the source code modules in the program, identifies the active variables, and then transforms the source code into a new code that contains new source code that implements the required derivative computation. ADIC [113], Adifor [109, 111], ODYSSEE [808, 809], and TAMC [377, 378] all implement source-to-source techniques to enhance programs to compute derivatives.

The advantage of this approach is that the entire program context is available at compile time. The disadvantage is that the AD tool must contain a competent parser (maps source code into an internal representation), semantic analyzer (collects information from the internal representation), and unparser (maps the transformed internal representation back to source code). A serious development effort is required to create the underlying infrastructure to implement such a tool.

Taking program context into account allows the derivative computation for the example in the previous section to be performed using only a single-vector operation by transforming the assignment statement as follows (cryptic names in the following code fragment provided for your enjoyment courtesy of Adifor 3.0):

```
r_tmp_val_0 = x(1) * x(2)
r_tmp_val_1 = r_tmp_val_0 * x(3)
r_tmp_val_0_a = x(4) * x(3)
r_tmp_s_2_a = x(4) * r_tmp_val_0
r_tmp_s_0_a = r_tmp_val_0_a * x(2)
r_tmp_s_1_a = r_tmp_val_0_a * x(1)
g_y(:) = r_tmp_val_1 * g_x(:,4) + r_tmp_s_2_a * g_x(:,3)
         + r_tmp_s_1_a * g_x(:,2) + r_tmp_s_0_a * g_x(:,1)
y = r_tmp_val_1 * x(4)
```

This code demonstrates the use of the reverse mode within an assignment statement to compute derivatives that are propagated from statement to statement using the forward mode.

24.3 Automatic-Differentiation Software

We now present descriptions of two AD packages that are available to developers of high-performance simulations. The first, ADOL-C, uses operator overloading to implement AD. The second, Adifor 3.0, uses source-to-source code transformation. Other AD packages are available as well.

24.3.1 ADOL-C

ADOL-C is a C++ package for evaluating first- and higher-order derivatives of function codes written in C or C++.[2] ADOL-C uses the operator overloading facility in C++ to redefine the basic arithmetic operators and intrinsic calls in the function code to record the sequence of calculations involving active variables that occurs during the evaluation of a function. The sequence of calculations is recorded on a sequential, and possibly out-of-core, data structure that is usually referred to as a *tape.*

---

[2] C code is handled by compiling it with the C++ compiler.

The ADOL-C user must take the following steps to modify a program to create a tape:

1. Redeclare active variables in the program using special types *adouble, adoublev,* and *adoublem* for active scalars, vectors of active scalars, and matrices of active scalars, respectively.

2. Insert calls to the functions trace_on and trace_off to indicate when tape creation should start and stop.

3. Insert special assignment statements to indicate which of the active variables in the program are to be treated as independent variables and dependent variables.

After making these modifications to a function code, the user inserts a call to one of a number of different high-level drivers to obtain the desired derivatives. A partial list of high-level drivers includes gradient (to compute a gradient), jacobian (to compute a Jacobian), hessian (to compute a Hessian), or jac_vec (to compute the product of a Jacobian and a vector). Other drivers are provided for use in solving ordinary differential equations, computing higher derivative tensors, computing derivatives of implicit and inverse functions, and for detecting sparsity in Jacobian matrices.

24.3.2   Adifor 3.0

The Adifor 3.0 system is a major revision and extension of Adifor 2.0. Adifor 2.0, an AD tool for Fortran 77, was awarded the Wilkinson Prize for Numerical Computing in 1995 and was then released to the public for downloading from CRPC websites. Adifor 2.0 provided first-order, forward-mode AD for "dusty-deck" Fortran codes. Since 1995, Adifor 2.0 has been significantly revised and extended to create the Adifor 3.0 system. Adifor 3.0 provides five basic derivative modes: gradient (computes first-order derivatives using the forward mode), adjoint (computes first-order derivatives using the reverse mode), hessian_symmetric (computes matrix products of the form VHV), hessian_unsymmetric (computes matrix products of the form $W^T HV$), and taylor (computes sets of elements of Hessians by propagating two-term univariate Taylor series). Like ADOL-C's high-level drivers, Adifor 3.0 provides a large number of "high-level interfaces" that are constructed from the five basic AD modes. Both Adifor 2.0 and Adifor 3.0 use source-to-source transformation to implement AD.

Adifor 3.0 users must take the following steps to augment a code to compute derivatives:

- Create a *specification* file that specifies values for various options including AD_TOP (the name of the procedure to be differentiated), AD_MODE (the name of one of the five basic derivative modes), AD_IVARS (the names of the independent variables), AD_DVARS (the names of the dependent variables), and the names of the Fortran source files to be differentiated.

- Run Adifor 3.0 to generate new derivative-enhanced source modules for each of the modules in the original program.

- Insert calls to the generated derivative code to compute the required derivatives.

- Compile and link the generated derivative code into the program to create a derivative-enhanced executable.

24.4 Automatic Differentiation of Message-Passing Parallel Codes

In the last several years, efforts have been made to provide AD tools for message-passing parallel languages. For example, ODYSSEE [319, 320] provides support for Fortran 77 extended with (a subset of) MPI in the forward and reverse modes, and Adifor 3.0 provides support for Fortran 77 extended with (a subset of) MPI in both the forward and reverse modes. Hovland [491] describes some of the issues that must be addressed by an AD tool for parallel programs. The three key issues that must be addressed by any AD tool for message-passing parallel codes are described below.

24.4.1 Activity Analysis

Users of AD tools like ODYSSEE and Adifor 3.0 specify the sets of independent and dependent variables and let the AD tool carry out an *activity analysis* procedure to identify the other variables in the code that are active. In the presence of message-passing operations, it becomes necessary to establish pathways from the independent variables to the dependent variables that pass through *send* and *receive* operations. Only in very simple cases is it possible to determine a precise mapping between these send and receive operations. Adifor 3.0 forces all floating-point variables that occur in send and receive operations to be active. This ensures that the code generated by Adifor 3.0 will be correct, although not optimal. Efficiency could be improved by allowing users to annotate their programs with directives to indicate the precise mapping between the send and receive operations.

24.4.2 Differentiation of Communication Operations

Consider the following code fragments:

```
if (myid = 1) then
  call send(2, x)  // send array to process 2
else
  call recv(1, y) // recv array from process 1
endif
  .
  .
  .
```

The above fragment, in a strong sense, is equivalent to the following fragment:

```
if (myid = 1) then
  ether = x
else
```

```
    y = ether
  endif
    .
    .
    .
```

That is, we can interpret the *send* of x to be an assignment of x to a unique, globally available variable that we have chosen to call ether. The *recv* operation then becomes an assignment from ether to y. From this, it is possible to generate correct forward and reverse mode derivative code. Differentiating the example using the forward mode gives

```
  if (myid = 1) then
    ether = x
    g_ether(:) = g_x(:)
  else
    y = ether
    g_y(:) = g_ether(:)
  endif
```

The above results are then transformed into the familiar looking code,

```
  if (myid = 1) then
    call g_send(x, g_x, 2)
  else
    call g_recv(y, g_y, 1)
  endif
    .
    .
    .
```

Here, procedure g_send becomes responsible for sending x and g_x to process 2, and procedure g_recv becomes responsible for receiving the values sent by process 1 into y and g_y.

Differentiating the example using the reverse mode is even more interesting:

```
// forward pass of the reverse mode
    .
    .
    .
  b = (myid = 1)
  if (b) then
    call push(ether)
    ether = x
  else
    call push(y)
    y = ether
  endif
  call push(b)
```

```
                .
                .
                .
// reverse pass of the reverse mode
     call pop(b)

     if (b) then
       a_x = a_z + a_ether
       a_ether = 0.0
       call pop(ether)
     else
       a_ether = a_ether + a_y
       a_y = 0.0
       call pop(y)
     endif
```

These results are then mapped back to calls to procedures a_send and a_recv that implement the appropriate forward and reverse pass for send and recv to give:

```
// forward pass of the reverse mode
                .
                .
                .
     b = (myid = 1)
     if (b) then
       call a_send(''fwd'', x, a_x)  // a_x unused on fwd pass
     else
       call push(y)
       call a_recv(''fwd'', y, a_y)  // a_y unused on fwd pass
     endif
     call push(b)
                .
                .
                .
// reverse pass of the reverse mode
     call pop(b)

     if (b) then
       call a_send(''rev'', x, a_x)
     else
       call a_recv(''rev'', y, a_y)  // a_y unused on fwd pass
       call pop(y)
     endif
```

Most importantly, note that the a_recv operation is responsible for receiving adjoint values and then adding them into adjoint variables in the process that invoked the receive operation.

24.4.3   Differentiation of Reduction Operations

Message-passing libraries often provide a suite of reduction operations to compute the sum (product, min, max, or . . .) of all of the entries in a distributed array. Reduction operations combine communication and computation and must be differentiated accordingly. It is easy to differentiate reduction operations if all of the communication and computation is exposed to the AD tool. Ideally, however, differentiating a reduction operation would lead to a new reduction operation that could be implemented using the same high-level mechanism for reductions. For sum reductions, this is the case; for product reductions, it is not.

24.5   Advanced Use of Automatic Differentiation

This section describes ways in which the basic techniques of automatic differentiation may be modified under certain circumstances in order to compute derivatives more efficiently. Special techniques are available to handle sparse Jacobians. Additionally, parallel processing may be applied to speed up the computation in some cases.

24.5.1   Computing Sparse Jacobian Matrices with Known Sparsity

Computing the Jacobian matrix $f'(x)$ of a mapping $f : \mathbb{R}^m \to \mathbb{R}^n$ when $f'(x)$ is large and sparse can be a daunting task. In this section, we discuss a technique that can significantly reduce this cost when the sparsity pattern of $f'(x)$ is known. The technique was first used to reduce the cost of approximating sparse Jacobians using finite differences. To use this *compression* technique, it is necessary to compute Jacobian–vector products of the form $f'(x)v$, for any $v \in \mathbb{R}^n$. Using finite differences, we can approximate $f'(x)v$ by using

$$\frac{f(x + h_v v) - f(x)}{h_v}$$

with some suitable parameter h_v. AD naturally supports the computation of $f'(x)v$.

We now *partition* the columns of $f'(x)$ into groups such that columns in a group do not have nonzeros in the same row position. For example, if a function $f : \mathbb{R}^4 \to \mathbb{R}^4$ has a Jacobian matrix $f'(x)$ with the structure (symbols denote nonzeros, and zeros are not shown)

$$f'(x) = \begin{pmatrix} \diamondsuit & & & \\ \diamondsuit & & & \heartsuit \\ \clubsuit & & & \heartsuit \\ \clubsuit & \spadesuit & & \\ \clubsuit & \spadesuit & & \end{pmatrix}$$

then columns 1 and 2 can be placed in one group, while columns 3 and 4 can be placed in another group. The key idea is to identify *structurally orthogonal* columns of $f'(x)$, that is, columns whose inner product is zero, independent of x.

Given a partitioning of the columns of $f'(x)$ into p groups of structurally orthogonal columns, we can determine $f'(x)$ with p evaluations of $f'(x)v$. For each group we compute $f'(x)v$, where $v_i = 1$ if the ith column is in the group, and $v_i = 0$ otherwise. In the above example, we would compute $f'(x)v_i$ for $v_1 = e_1 + e_2$ and $v_2 = e_3 + e_4$, and obtain

$$f'(x)\, v_1 = \begin{pmatrix} \diamondsuit \\ \diamondsuit \\ \clubsuit \\ \clubsuit \\ \clubsuit \end{pmatrix} \qquad f'(x)\, v_2 = \begin{pmatrix} \heartsuit \\ \heartsuit \\ \spadesuit \\ \spadesuit \end{pmatrix}$$

at the cost of only two evaluations of $f'(x)v$ (versus four for the naive approach). Because of the structural orthogonality property, we can still uniquely extract all entries of the Jacobian matrix.

Instead of performing p evaluations of $f'(x)v_i$, it is usually more efficient to assemble the vectors v_i into a matrix V and compute $f'(x)V$ with one evaluation of the AD-augmented derivative code. In the example, we would set

$$V = \begin{pmatrix} 1 & 0 \\ 1 & 0 \\ 0 & 1 \\ 0 & 1 \end{pmatrix}$$

Curtis et al. [241] were the first to note that a partitioning of the columns into p structurally orthogonal groups allows the approximation of the Jacobian matrix with p function evaluations. Curtis et al. were interested in approximating the Jacobian matrix, and thus they approximated $f'(x)v$ by differences of function values. However, as made clear above, the same ideas apply if we compute $f'(x)v$ implicitly using AD.

In the algorithm proposed by Curtis et al. (CPR algorithm) the groups are formed one at a time by scanning the columns in the natural order, including a column in the current group if it has not been included in a previous group and if it does not have a nonzero in the same row position as another column already in the group. Coleman and Moré [210] showed that the partitioning problem could be analyzed as a *graph-coloring* problem, and that by looking at the problem from the graph-coloring point of view, it is possible to improve the CPR algorithm by scanning the columns in a carefully selected order.

Coleman et al. [208, 209] describe software for the partitioning problem. Given a representation of the sparsity structure of $f'(x)$, these algorithms produce a partitioning of the columns of $f'(x)$ into p structurally orthogonal groups. For many sparsity patterns, p is small and independent of n. For example, if the sparsity structure has bandwidth β, then $p \le \beta$. We also note that discretization of an infinite dimensional problem also leads to sparsity patterns where p is independent of the mesh size.

Averick et al. [58] describe the computation of large sparse Jacobians using graph coloring–based compression with Adifor 2.0.

24.5.2   Computing Sparse Jacobian Matrices with Unknown Sparsity

Computationally, the most expensive kernel of first-order, forward-mode derivative code is the *linear combination of vectors* operation, which can be defined as follows:

$$w = \sum_{i=1}^{k} \alpha_i v_i \qquad (24.1)$$

where w and the v_i are derivative vectors of length p, the α_i are the scalar multipliers, and k is the arity.

For problems where the derivative vectors in the above operation are known to be mostly sparse, it is worth considering using data structures and algorithms that can take advantage of this "local sparsity" to reduce the run time and memory requirements for the overall derivative computation. Such techniques may have a considerable impact on the cost of computing derivatives, even for codes whose derivatives are not sparse. For example, consider the computation of gradients of partially separable functions. Partially separable functions [403] can be represented in the form

$$f(x) = \sum_{i=1}^{np} f_i(x)$$

where each of the component functions f_i has *limited support*. Limited support means that each component function depends on only a small subset of the independent variables. This implies that the gradients ∇f_i are sparse even though the final gradient ∇f is dense. It can be shown [403] that any function with a sparse Hessian is partially separable.

This local sparsity can be exploited in a completely transparent fashion, that is, without the a priori knowledge of the sparsity pattern of the Jacobian required for graph coloring. Given the appropriate options, Adifor 3.0 generates derivative code that invokes the SparsLinC (Sparse Linear Combination) library [110, 111] to perform all of the vector linear combinations using a suite of data structures and algorithms that take advantage of sparsity. By ignoring zeros introduced by cancellation, SparsLinC delivers the sparsity structure of the Jacobian as a byproduct of the derivative computation.

24.5.3   Strip-Mining of Derivative Computations

For a sequential code with a large number of independent variables, parallel processing can be used to reduce the overall time required to compute the needed derivatives. As mentioned in the previous section, the kernel computation for first-order derivative computations is a vector linear combination. The kernel computation for higher-order derivative computations is a higher-order analogue to the vector linear combination. Therefore, to compute derivatives of a program with respect to n independent variables on p processors, assuming for simplicity that p evenly divides n, it is sufficient to compute the p Jacobian-matrix products $J * R_i$, where R_i is the

Figure 24.1 Sequential evaluation of function codes.

matrix consisting of the n/p basis vectors $e_{1+(i-1)*(n/p)} \cdots e_{i*(n/p)}$. This strip-mined derivative computation is "almost pleasingly parallel"—it is quite easy to distribute the derivative computation across p processors, but the speedup is not perfect, since each processor will be required to compute the function in addition to its strip of derivatives [112].

24.5.4 Exploiting Coarse-Grained Chain Rule Associativity

Consider the pipeline of codes shown in Figure 24.1. In the figure, code f reads its input r, performs its computation, and then passes its output s on to code g, which performs its computation and then passes its output t to code h to compute the final outputs u of the system. The derivatives of h's output u with respect to f's inputs r can be computed in one of two ways:

1. Use the forward mode of AD and propagate derivatives sequentially through f, g and h. That is, first compute ds/dr, then compute $dt/ds * ds/dr$ by using the forward mode of AD to compute $J * R$ with $J = dt/ds$ and $R = ds/dr$, and finally compute $du/dr = du/dt * (dt/ds * ds/dr)$ by using the forward mode of AD to compute $J * R$ with $J = du/dt$ and $R = (dt/ds * ds/dr)$.

2. Apply the forward mode of AD to f, g, and h and then perform two matrix multiplies. That is, compute ds/dr, dt/ds, and du/dt and then explicitly form the product $du/dt * (dt/ds * ds/dr)$ to get du/dr. Using this strategy, it is possible to compute the derivatives for each of the codes f, g, and h in parallel to compute the desired derivatives. This strategy is shown in Figure 24.2. If sufficient parallel resources are available, then this strategy can be very effective at reducing the total time required to compute the derivatives for the system.

Bischof and Wu [114] describe the application of this coarse-grained strategy to parallelize the derivative computation for a time-stepping sequential code.

24.5.5 Checkpointing for the Reverse Mode

The reverse mode of AD has been referred to as a "slam dunk" for computing gradients of functions with large numbers of independent variables because of its ability to compute the derivatives in time proportional to the time required to evaluate the function. The memory requirements of the reverse mode, though, substantially reduce its applicability. To increase the usability of the reverse mode, Griewank [399], based on results published by Volin and Ostrovski [963], devised and analyzed a scheme that uses additional time to reduce the memory requirements. We

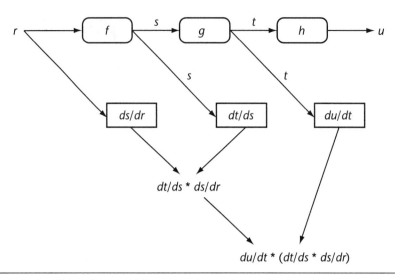

Figure 24.2   Parallel evaluation of derivatives for sequence of codes.

can demonstrate Griewank's approach using the example from the previous section. Figure 24.3 is intended to show the following sequence of events:

1. Evaluate f without taping.
2. Evaluate g without taping.
3. Evaluate h with taping.
4. Compute du/dt using reverse mode on h.
5. Evaluate g with taping.
6. Compute du/ds using reverse mode on g.
7. Evaluate f with taping.
8. Compute du/dr using reverse mode on f.

By evaluating g and h twice, we have eliminated the need to simultaneously store the trace for f, g, and h. If f, g, and h all have roughly the same cost, then this strategy has reduced the memory requirements to one-third of what they were previously at the cost of less than one function evaluation. By applying this same technique on a finer grain, Griewank is able to achieve a logarithmic reduction in the space requirements with a concomitant logarithmic growth in the time required to perform the reverse-mode computation. Greiwank and Walther [402] have developed an implementation of checkpointing for the reverse mode of AD that can be used in conjunction with the various AD tools described above.

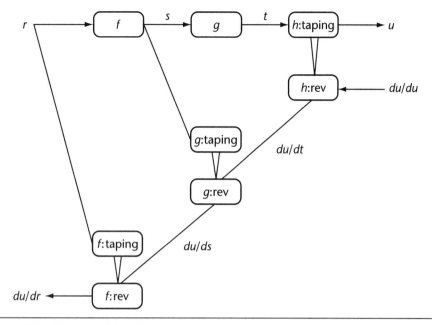

Figure 24.3 Checkpoint-based reverse mode.

24.6 Conclusion

AD provides a way to compute derivatives of computer codes ranging in size from the very small to the very large, running on machines ranging from individual workstations to full-scale computational grids. We believe that the efficiency and accuracy of the derivative-enhanced codes that can be created by using AD tools in conjunction with the advanced techniques described in this chapter, and others that have not been mentioned, make it well worth your time to become acquainted with AD.

P
A
R
T

V

Conclusion

Chapter 25   **WRAP-UP AND SIGNPOSTS TO THE FUTURE**

Andy White, *Los Alamos National Laboratory* •
Ken Kennedy, *Rice University*

<table>
<tr><td>C</td></tr>
<tr><td>H</td></tr>
<tr><td>A</td></tr>
<tr><td>P</td></tr>
<tr><td>T</td></tr>
<tr><td>E</td></tr>
<tr><td>R</td></tr>
</table>

25 Wrap-Up and Signposts to the Future

Andy White • Ken Kennedy

"That's the signpost up ahead. Your next stop . . . "
—Rod Serling, *The Twilight Zone*

This book provides a broad, often detailed look at the state of parallel computing in hardware, software, and applications. Our view has naturally focused on the work of the institutions and individuals that were brought together in the National Science Foundation's Center for Research on Parallel Computation. In this final chapter, we briefly review the central issues in each section and look for general principles among the previous discussions. Finally, we try to anticipate some of the signposts that you may catch a glimpse of over the next few years.

25.1 Computational Resources

Parallelism is a primary method for accelerating the total power that can be applied to any problem. That is, in addition to continuing to develop the performance of a technology, multiple copies are deployed that provide some of the advantages of an improvement in raw performance, but not all. Of course, for the commercial side of the house, increased volume (aka commodity market) has its own reward. The symmetric multiprocessor (SMP) provided a straightforward environment for accessing moderate levels of parallelism. However, requirements for more memory (accuracy) and more speed (response time) drove systems beyond the point at which SMPs could maintain their flat memory architecture. Another simple model of computation is data parallelism, an intuitive programming standard for many physical problems defined on $\mathbb{R}^3 \times t$. Systems and languages (e.g., CM-5, CMFortran) that implemented this model were easily mastered by both computer and computational scientists. Unfortunately, substantial reductions in the size of the high-end market and difficulty in dealing with unstructured problems slowed interest in this promising technology.

Employing parallelism to solve large-scale problems is not without its price. While Flatland, represented in hardware by SMPs and in software by data parallelism, is an appealing concept, the complexity of building parallel computers with thousands of processors to solve real-world problems requires a hierarchical approach—associating memory closely with CPUs. Consequently, the central problem faced by parallel codes is managing a complex memory hierarchy, ranging from local registers to far-distant processor memories. It is the communication of data and the coordination of processes within this hierarchy that represent the principal hurdles to effective, correct, and widespread acceptance of parallel computing. Thus, today's parallel computing environment has architectural complexity layered upon a multiplicity of processors. Scalability, the ability for hardware and software to maintain reasonable efficiency as the number of processors is increased, is the key metric.

The future will be more complex yet. Distinct computer systems will be networked together into the most powerful systems on the planet. The pieces of this composite whole will be distinct in hardware (e.g., CPUs), software (e.g., OS), and operational policy (e.g., security). This future is most apparent when we consider geographically distributed computing on the Computational Grid. However, heterogeneity also has advantages for concentrated computing within a single computer center. The fact is that there are fundamental difficulties inherent in the acquisition of large monolithic systems when procurement lasts longer than the doubling time of the technology itself. Progress toward even more complexity in hardware platforms will paradoxically also drive broad uniformity in software environments and will drive the community toward recognition that the software framework, not the hardware, must define the computing environment. This increased complexity has at least one interesting side effect—superlinear speedup is possible on heterogeneous systems, provided that the architectural diversity is sufficiently rich.

25.2 Applications

Computational physics applications have been the primary drivers in the development of parallel computing over the last 20 years. This set of problems has a number of features in common, despite the substantial specific differences in problem domain.

1. Applications were often defined by a set of partial differential equations (PDEs) on some subset of $\mathbb{R}^3 \times t$.

2. Multiphysics often took the form of distinct physical domains with different processes dominant in each.

3. The life cycle of many applications was essentially contained within the computer room, building, or campus.

These characteristics focused attention on discretizations of PDEs, the corresponding notion of resolution = accuracy, and solution of the linear and nonlinear equations generated by these discretizations. Data parallelism and domain decomposition provided an effective programming model and a ready source of parallelism. Multiphysics, for the most part, was also amenable to domain decomposition and could be accomplished by understanding and trading information about the fluxes among the physical domains. Finally, attention was focused on the parallel computer, its speed and accuracy; relatively little attention was paid to I/O beyond the confines of the computer room.

Over the last few years, parallel applications have changed. Many socially, politically, or economically relevant applications (e.g., marketing, crisis management, and war fighting) are significantly different than the PDE-defined problems that preceded them. Some of the most apparent differences include:

1. Problems are often naturally defined on graphs (e.g., transportation, communication) rather than on discretizations of $\mathbb{R}^3$.

2. Interaction among components is often global; thus, composition cannot be accomplished by understanding fluxes at boundaries.

3. Definition of a formal trust structure—for example, verification and validation in ASCI—for the hardware, software, simulation, and human interface is critical for problems whose consequences transcend the usual science application.

Data, rather than computation, will be the transformational element in many applications of the future. In fact, the existence of vast, new data sets has already transformed many applications, including marketing, bioscience, and earthquake research. I/O will be critical in accessing observational and experimental data for validation, in providing real-time surveillance for crisis and military applications, and in allowing an effective, trusted interface with the ultimate user of these simulations. Further afield still, the issues of data security, ownership, and privacy will raise significant technological, administrative, legal, and ethical questions.

25.3 Software

The holy grail for software is *portable performance*. That is, software should be reusable across different platforms and provide significant performance, say, relative to peak speed, for the end user. Often, these two goals seem to be in opposition each to the other. The classic programming environment is pictured in Figure 25.1. Standard languages (e.g., Fortran, C), language extensions (e.g., OpenMP, HPF), and libraries (e.g., MPI, Linpack) allow the programmer to access or expose parallelism in a variety of standard ways. By employing standards-based, optimized libraries, the programmer can sometimes achieve both portability and high performance. Tools (e.g., svPablo, Prism) allow the programmer to determine the correctness and performance of their code and, if falling short in some ways, suggest various remedies.

The problem-solving environment (PSE) (Figure 25.2) is yet another level removed from the computational resources. Some PSEs that were discussed here were MAT-LAB (linear algebra), NWChem (computational chemistry), and PETSc (solution of PDEs). The PSE's interface is focused on the application domain and, insofar as possible, employs the objects and language of the target application. Thus, on top of

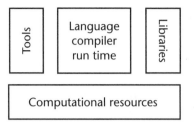

Figure 25.1   The classic programming environment.

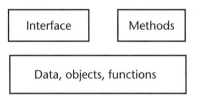

Figure 25.2   The problem-solving environment.

the middleware layers are two additional, user-accessible layers: the high-level application programming interface and a collection of high-level methods specific to the application domain. A well-constructed PSE also allows the user to transparently achieve platform-portable performance. It is often difficult, however, to reuse pieces of a PSE, because it is specifically constructed using data, objects, and functions particular to the target application. PSE toolkits, such as WebFlow, provide a more general framework for constructing specific PSEs.

Object-oriented design methodology calls for applications to be constructed by composing reusable, standards-compliant components. Component architectures, such as Java Beans and CORBA, are commonplace in the commercial marketplace, but not yet in technical computing, although the Common Component Architecture is making progress in that direction. Components are defined by their interfaces, functionality, and communication protocols. This generalized notion allows components to be reusable within a broader setting than OO libraries, such as POOMA.

Software has always followed hardware. However, there is considerable pressure to reverse this relationship. First, large-scale application codes must be trivially or, at worst, easily portable across a variety of platforms. Second, the computing environment in the future will be significantly heterogeneous. These two issues require moving toward a software-centric worldview. Abstraction, away from the details of the hardware and system software, is necessary for ease of use, particularly for those not trained in the arcane ways of computer and computational science. Reusable libraries and components are necessary to leverage the time and talents of systems programmers and to provide performance across a wide variety of platforms.

It is difficult to understand how competing armies of proprietary software will accomplish this.

25.4 Templates, Algorithms, and Technologies

Templates are an effective method of providing information about a particular technology, technique, or set of algorithms. In general, a template will discuss the basic theoretical foundation for the subject, will explore the major algorithmic or implementation issues, will provide high-level pseudocode for the principal techniques, and will list or provide links to libraries or packages that incorporate these ideas. The templates in Part IV discuss a number of important software technologies.

1. *Graph partitioning* algorithms are used to segment an irregular or unstructured graph in such as way as to equipartition a particular variable or operation defined on this graph (e.g., interprocessor communication).

2. *Mesh generation* is an important capability in accurately representing complex geometries (e.g., an automobile engine) and complex physical processes (e.g., shocks in a fluid).

3. *Numerical linear algebra*, whether with full or sparse matrices, whether standing alone or as part of a nonlinear iteration, is often the critical component of an efficient application code.

4. *Parallel optimization* is an emerging area that will become increasingly important as applications move more toward multiphysics and multidisciplinary design problems.

5. *Path following* provides a useful technique for obtaining difficult-to-find solutions to ordinary and PDEs.

6. *Automatic differentiation* is a unique capability for providing accurate derivatives of application codes themselves in order to examine their sensitivity and stability.

25.5 Signposts

We have discussed many of the innovations in parallel computation over the last decade or so. However, interspersed within these discussions have been glimpses, perhaps fleeting, of possible futures. There are a number of such signposts that we might see over the next few years, and even though we might decide to disregard Yogi Berra's advice to take the fork in the road, a half-dozen of them are well worth emphasizing here.

- *Heterogeneous hardware environments.* Hardware environments will be composed of multiple platforms that differ in performance, size, and vendor trademark. This is most easily envisioned in the context of distributed, Grid computing, but is also under discussion in the concentrated (single-site) computing arena. The primary difficulty will be increased complexity for both application and system software.

- *Software architecture.* Throughout the evolution of scientific computing, the computing environment has been defined by the hardware. There are indications that software—components and frameworks, high-level languages and compilers, PSRs, scripting languages, operating systems—will define the computing environment of the future. The primary difficulties will be validation in the face of increasing complexity and making certain that inertia does not retard the development of new capabilities, algorithms, techniques, and interfaces.

- *Open source.* Proprietary, vendor-specific software predominates in high-end computing. However, the triad of programmer productivity, hardware heterogeneity, and system reliability will place significant pressure on this community to consider an open-source infrastructure. However, this will not be without its difficulties and detractors due to such issues as development schedules, a viable economic model, and security.

- *New applications.* Computational physics has driven the development of parallel software, algorithms, and methods over the last 2 decades. However, new applications, many directly applicable to societal issues, will increasingly share the market space with traditional applications. Such meta-applications will require real-time data access, will simulate processes described only by their phenomenology, and will often be defined on graphs or have no natural structure at all. These applications will place a new focus on real-time I/O, trusted human interfaces, and ethical, legal, and jurisdictional issues.

- *Verification and validation.* The consequences of misuse or mistrust of socially relevant applications (e.g., safety and performance of nuclear weapons, global climate, critical infrastructure assurance) requires the development and deployment of formal, trusted systems—verification, validation, and quantification of uncertainty. This trust must extend to all aspects of the process: surveillance, experiment, theory, model, application code, software, hardware, and human interface. Among the difficulties are imposing formality on a complex, science-based process and accelerating acceptance of simulation-based, decision-making tools.

- *Data.* Access to data—observation, experiment, and real-time surveillance—is transforming entire disciplines (e.g., bioscience, geophysics, Stockpile Stewardship) and their projections onto computational science. These data will be of varying format, type, and quality, and the totality will be overwhelming to currently available I/O systems. In addition, socially relevant applications are making validation of application codes critically important. The difficulties will be I/O from real-time sources, data quality, and assimilation, verification, security and ownership of data, privacy, and person-machine interface.

The editors of this volume believe that these signposts, taken together, will have an impact on the future of high-performance computing similar in weight to the impact that parallel computing has had in the last fifteen years. Perhaps some of the editors will be the subjects of coordinated research efforts similar in breadth to the efforts carried out by the Center for Research on Parallel Computation from 1989 to 2000.

REFERENCES

[1]   E. Aarts and J. Korst. *Simulated Annealing and Boltzmann Machines*. John Wiley & Sons, Chichester, 1989.

[2]   T. Abel, M. L. Norman, and P. Madau. Photon-conserving radiative transfer around point sources in multidimensional numerical cosmology. *The Astrophysical Journal*, 523(1):66–71, Sep 1999.

[3]   M. Abramowitz and I. A. Stegun, eds. *Handbook of Mathematical Functions*. Dover, New York, 1970.

[4]   W. B. Ackerman. Data flow languages. *Computer*, 15(2):15–25, Feb 1982.

[5]   J. C. Adams. MUDPACK: Multigrid Software for Elliptic Partial Differential Equations (A New Portable Parallel Version), Sep 1999. Available at *http://www.scd.ucar.edu/css/software /mudpack*.

[6]   Advanced Visual Systems. Available at *http://www.avs.com/*.

[7]   S. V. Adve and K. Gharachorloo. Shared Memory Consistency Models: A Tutorial. Technical Report 9512. Department of Electrical and Computer Engineering, Rice University, Sep 1995. (Also available as Western Research Laboratory Research Report 95/7. Available at *http://www.research.digital.com/wrl/publications/abstracts/95.7.html*)

[8]   V. Adve, A. Carle, E. Granston, S. Hiranandani, K. Kennedy, C. Koelbel, U. Kremer, J. Mellor-Crummey, S. Warren, and C. W. Tseng. Requirements for data-parallel programming environments. *IEEE Parallel and Distributed Technology*, 2(3):48–58, Fall 1994.

[9]   V. Adve and J. Mellor-Crummey. Advanced code generation for High Performance Fortran. In S. Pande and D. P. Agrawal, eds., *Compiler Optimizations for Scalable Parallel Systems: Languages, Compilation Techniques and Run Time Systems for Scalable Parallel Systems*, 553–596, Springer-Verlag, Heidelberg and New York, 2001.

[10]   V. Adve and R. Sakellariou. Application representations for multiparadigm performance modeling of large-scale parallel scientific codes. *The International Journal of High Performance Computing Applications*, 14(4):304–316, Winter 2000.

[11]   V. Adve, J. Mellor-Crummey, M. Anderson, K. Kennedy, J.-C. Wang, and D. Reed. An integrated compilation and performance analysis environment for data parallel programs. In *Proceedings of Supercomputing '95*, ACM Press, New York, 1995.

[12]   Aggregate Remote Memory Copy Interface. Web page. Available at *http://www.emsl.pnl.gov :2080/docs/parsoft/armci/*.

[13]   R. Agrawal, T. Imielinski, and A. Swami. Database mining: A performance perspective. *IEEE Transactions on Knowledge and Data Engineering*, 5(6):914–925, Dec 1993.

[14]   R. Agrawal, T. Imielinski, and A. Swami. Mining association rules between sets of items in large databases. In *Proceedings of the 1993 ACM–SIGMOD International Conference on Management of Data*, 207–216, ACM Press, New York, 1993.

[15]   R. Agrawal and J. C. Shafer. Parallel mining of association rules. *IEEE Transactions on Knowledge and Data Engineering*, 8(6):962–969, Dec 1996.

[16]   R. Agrawal and R. Srikant. Fast algorithms for mining association rules. In J. B. Bocca, M. Jarke, and C. Zaniolo, eds., *Proceedings of the 20th International Conference on Very Large Data Bases*, 487–499, Morgan Kaufmann, San Francisco, 1994.

[17]   E. Akarsu. Integrated Three-Tier Architecture for High Performance Commodity Metacomputing. PhD diss., Syracuse University, Dec 1999.

[18]   E. Akarsu, G. C. Fox, W. Furmanski, and T. Haupt. WebFlow—high-level programming environment and visual authoring toolkit for high performance distributed computing. In *Proceedings of Supercomputing '98*, Nov 1998, IEEE Computer Society Press, Los Alamitos, CA. (Also available at *http://old-npac.ucs.indiana.edu/users/haupt/WebFlow/papers/SC98/INDEX .HTM*.)

[19]   E. Akarsu, G. Fox, T. Haupt, A. Kalinichenko, K.-S. Kim, P. Sheethaalnath, and C.-H. Youn. Using gateway system to provide a desktop access to high performance computational resources. In *Proceedings of the Eighth IEEE International Symposium on High Performance Distributed Computing Conference*, 294–298, IEEE Computer Society Press, Los Alamitos, CA 1999. (Also available at *http://www.computer.org/proceedings/hpdc/0287/0287toc.html*.)

[20]   N. M. Alexandrov and M. Y. Hussaini, eds. *Multidisciplinary Design Optimization: State of the Art*. SIAM, Philadelphia, PA, Feb 1997.

[21]   N. M. Alexandrov and R. M. Lewis. Comparative Properties of Collaborative Optimization to MDO. Technical Report ICASE TR99-24, Institute for Computer Applications in Science and Engineering, NASA Langley Research Center, Hampton, VA, Jul 1999.

[22]   W. Allcock, J. Bester, J. Bresnahan, A. Chervenak, L. Liming, and S. Tuecke. GridFTP: Protocol Extensions to FTP for the Grid, Mar 2001. Available at *http://www-fp.mcs.anl.gov/dsl/GridFTP-Protocol-RFC-Draft.pdf*.

[23]   C. Allègre, J. L. Le Mouel, and A. Provost. Scaling rules in rock fracture and possible implications for earthquake prediction. *Nature*, 297(5861):47–49, May 1982.

[24]   F. Allen, M. Burke, P. Charles, R. Cytron, and J. Ferrante. An overview of the PTRAN analysis system for multiprocessing. *Journal of Parallel and Distributed Computing*, 5(5):617–640, Oct 1988.

[25]   J. R. Allen, D. Callahan, and K. Kennedy. Automatic decomposition of scientific programs for parallel execution. In *Proceedings of the 14th Annual ACM SIGACT-SIGPLAN Symposium on Principles of Programming Languages*, 63–76, ACM Press, New York, 1987.

[26]   R. Allen and K. Kennedy. Automatic translation of Fortran programs to vector form. *ACM Transactions on Programming Languages and Systems*, 9(4):491–542, Oct 1987.

[27]   R. Allen and K. Kennedy. *Optimizing Compilers for Modern Architectures*. Morgan Kaufmann, San Francisco, 2002.

[28]   S. P. Amarasinghe, J. M. Anderson, M. S. Lam, and C.-W. Tseng. An overview of the SUIF compiler for scalable parallel machines. In *Proceedings of the Seventh SIAM Conference on Parallel Processing for Scientific Computing*, 662–667, SIAM, Philadelphia, PA, 1995.

[29]   S. P. Amarasinghe and M. S. Lam. Communication optimization and code generation for distributed memory machines. In *Proceedings of the ACM SIGPLAN '93 Conference on Programming Language Design and Implementation*, 126–138, ACM Press, New York, 1993.

[30]   G. M. Amdahl. Validity of the single processor approach to achieving large scale computing capabilities. In *AFIPS Conference Proceedings,* vol. 30, 483–485, AFIPS Press, Reston, VA, 1967.

[31]   C. Amza, A. L. Cox, S. Dwarkadas, P. Keleher, H. Lu, R. Rajamony, W. Yu, and W. Zwaenepoel. TreadMarks: Shared memory computing on networks of workstations. *Computer*, 29(2):18–28, Feb 1996.

[32]   G. Anagnostou. Nonconforming Sliding Spectral Element Methods for the Unsteady Incompressible Navier–Stokes Equations. PhD diss., Massachusetts Institute of Technology, 1991.

[33]   C. Ancourt, F. Coelho, F. Irigoin, and R. Keryell. A linear algebra framework for static HPF code distribution. In *Proceedings of the Fourth Workshop on Compilers for Parallel Computers*, Delft, The Netherlands, Dec 1993.

[34]   E. Anderson, Z. Bai, C. Bischof, L. S. Blackford, J. Demmel, J. Dongarra, J. Du Croz, A. Greenbaum, S. Hammarling, A. McKenney, and D. Sorensen. *LAPACK Users' Guide (Software, Environments and Tools)*, 3rd ed. SIAM, Philadelphia, PA, 2000.

[35]   E. Anderson, Z. Bai, C. Bischof, J. Demmel, J. Dongarra, J. Du Croz, A. Greenbaum, S. Hammarling, A. McKenney, S. Ostrouchov, and D. Sorensen. *LAPACK Users' Guide,* 2nd ed. SIAM, Philadelphia, PA, 1995.

[36]   E. Anderson and J. Dongarra. Results from the initial release of LAPACK. LAPACK Working Note #16 (ut-cs-89-89), Department of Computer Science, University of Tennessee, Knoxville, 1989. (Also available at *http://www.netlib.org/lapack/lawns/lawn16.ps*.)

[37]   E. Anderson and J. Dongarra. Evaluating block algorithm variants in LAPACK. LAPACK Working Note #19 (ut-cs-90-103), Department of Computer Science, University of Tennessee, Knoxville, Nov 1990. (Also available *http://www.netlib.org/lapack/lawns/lawn19.ps*.)

[38]   T. E. Anderson, M. D. Dahlin, J. M. Neefe, D. A. Patterson, D. S. Roselli, and R. Y. Wang. Serverless network file systems. In *Proceedings of the Fifteenth ACM Symposium on Operating Systems Principles*, 109–126, ACM Press, New York, 1995.

[39]   W. K. Anderson and D. L. Bonhaus. An implicit upwind algorithm for computing turbulent flows on unstructured grids. *Computers and Fluids*, 23(1):1–21, Jan 1994.

[40]   W. K. Anderson, W. D. Gropp, D. K. Kaushik, D. E. Keyes, and B. F. Smith. Achieving high sustained performance in an unstructured mesh CFD application. In *Proceedings of Supercomputing '99*, ACM Press, New York, 1999.

[41] F. André, D. Herman, and J.-P. Verjus. *Synchronization of Parallel Programs*. Translated by J. Howlett. MIT Press, Cambridge, MA, 1985.

[42] P. Anninos, Y. Zhang, T. Abel, and M. Norman. Cosmological hydrodynamics with multispecies chemistry and nonequilibrium ionization and cooling. *New Astronomy*, 2(3):209–224, Aug 1997.

[43] ANSI Working Committee. *Parallel Processing Model for High Level Programming Languages*, ANSI X3H5 Document Number X3H5/94 SD2, Apr 1994.

[44] APEC Cooperation for Earthquake Simulation (ACES). Available at *http://www.quakes.uq.edu.au/ACES/*.

[45] Applied Parallel Research. *Forge High Performance Fortran xhpf User's Guide, Version 2.1*, Applied Parallel Research, Sacramento, CA, 1995.

[46] T. Arbogast, C. N. Dawson, and M. F. Wheeler. A parallel algorithm for two phase multicomponent contaminant transport. *Applications of Mathematics*, 40(3):163–174, 1995.

[47] R. Armstrong, D. Gannon, A. Geist, K. Keahey, S. Kohn, L. McInnes, S. Parker, and B. Smolinski. Toward a common component architecture for high-performance scientific computing. In *Proceedings of the 8th IEEE International Symposium on High Performance Distributed Computing*, 115–124, IEEE Computer Society Press, Los Alamitos, CA, 1999. (Also available as Preprint P759-0699, Argonne National Laboratory, Argonne, IL, Mathematics and Computer Science Division.) Available at *http://www.computer.org/proceedings/hpdc/0287/0287toc.html*.

[48] D. C. Arnold, J. Dongarra, W. Lee, and M. F. Wheeler. Providing infrastructure and interface to high-performance applications in a distributed setting. In *Proceedings of High Performance Computing Symposium 2000*, 248–253, SCS, 2000.

[49] C. Ashcraft and R. Grimes. SPOOLES: An object-oriented sparse matrix library. In *Proceedings of the 9th SIAM Conference on Parallel Processing for Scientific Computing*, SIAM, Philadelphia, PA, 1999. (CDROM).

[50] C. Ashcraft and J. Liu. A Partition Improvement Algorithm for Generalized Nested Dissection. Technical Report BCSTECH-94-020, York University, North York, Ontario, Canada, 1994.

[51] C. Ashcraft and J. Liu. Using Domain Decomposition to Find Graph Bisectors. Technical Report CS-95-08. Department of Computer Science, York University, North York, Ontario, Canada, Nov 1995.

[52] C. Ashcraft and J. W.-H. Liu. Robust ordering of sparse matrices using multisection. *SIAM Journal on Matrix Analysis and Applications*, 19(3):816–832, Jul 1998.

[53] S. Atlas, S. Banerjee, J. C. Cummings, P. J. Hinker, M. Srikant, J. V. W. Reynders, and M. Tholburn. POOMA: A high-performance distributed simulation environment for scientific applications. In *Proceedings of Supercomputing '95*. ACM Press, New York, 1995.

[54] C. Audet. Convergence Results for Pattern Search Algorithms Are Tight. Technical Report CRPC TR-98779. Center for Research on Parallel Computation, Rice University, Houston, TX, Nov 1998.

[55] C. Audet and J. E. Dennis, Jr. Analysis of Generalized Pattern Searches. Technical Report TR00-07. Department of Computational and Applied Mathematics, Rice University, Houston, TX, 2000.

[56] C. Audet and J. E. Dennis, Jr. A Pattern Search Filter Method for Nonlinear Programming without Derivatives. Technical Report TR00-09. Department of Computational and Applied Mathematics, Rice University, Houston, TX, 2000.

[57] C. Audet and J. E. Dennis, Jr. Pattern search algorithms for mixed variable programming. *SIAM Journal on Optimization*, 11(3):573–594, 2000.

[58] B. M. Averick, J. J. Moré, C. H. Bischof, A. Carle, and A. Griewank. Computing large sparse Jacobian matrices using automatic differentiation. *SIAM Journal on Scientific Computing*, 15(2):285–294, Mar 1994.

[59] B. M. Averick, R. G. Carter, and J. Moré. The MINPACK-2 Test Problem Collection. Technical Report ANL/MCS-TM-150. Argonne National Laboratory, Argonne, IL, 1991.

[60] B. M. Averick and J. Moré. Evaluation of large-scale optimization problems on vector and parallel architectures. *SIAM Journal on Optimization*, 4(4):708–721, 1994.

[61] O. Axelsson and V. A. Barker. *Finite Element Solution of Boundary Value Problems. Theory and Computation*. Academic Press, Orlando, FL, 1984.

[62] O. Axelsson and V. Eijkhout. The nested recursive two-level factorization method for nine-point difference matrices. *SIAM Journal on Scientific and Statistical Computing*, 12(6):1373–1400, Nov 1991.

[63] O. Axelsson and P. S. Vassilevski. Algebraic multilevel preconditioning methods, I. *Numerische Mathematik*, 56(2–3):157–177, 1989.

[64] I. Babuška and M. Suri. The *p* and *h-p* versions of the finite element method, basic principles and properties. *SIAM Review*, 36(4):578–632, Dec 1994.

[65] A. Back, J. Guckenheimer, M. R. Myers, F. J. Wicklin, and P. A. Worfolk. DsTool: Computer assisted exploration of dynamical systems. *Notices of the American Mathematical Society*, 39(4):303–309, 1992.

[66] J. Backus. The history of FORTRAN I, II and III. *ACM SIGPLAN Notices*, 13(8):165–180, Aug 1978.

[67] S. Baden. The KeLP Programming System. Available at *http://www-cse.ucsd.edu/groups/hpcl/scg/kelp/*.

[68] J. Baglama, D. Calvetti, and L. Reichel. Iterative methods for the computation of a few eigenvalues of a large symmetric matrix. *BIT Numerical Mathematics*, 36(3):400–421, Sep 1996.

[69] J. Baker, S. Brandt, M. Campanelli, C. O. Lousto, E. Seidel, and R. Takahashi. Nonlinear and perturbative evolution of distorted black holes: Odd-parity modes. *Physical Review D*, 62(12):127701/1–4, Dec 2000.

[70] V. Balasundaram, K. Kennedy, U. Kremer, K. McKinley, and J. Subhlok. The ParaScope editor: An interactive parallel programming tool. In *Proceedings of Supercomputing '89*, 540–550, ACM Press, New York, 1989.

[71] S. Balay, K. Buschelman, W. Gropp, D. Kaushik, M. Knepley, L. C. McInnes, B. Smith, H. Zhang. *PETSc Users Manual (ANL-95/11 REvision 2.1.3)*. Argonne National Laboratory, Argonne, IL, May, 2002. (Also available at *http://www.mcs.anl.gov/petsc /docs*.)

[72] S. Balay, W. D. Gropp, L. C. McInnes, and B. F. Smith. PETSc Web page. Available at *http://www.mcs.anl.gov/petsc*.

[73] S. Balay, W. D. Gropp, L. C. McInnes, and B. F. Smith. Efficient management of parallelism in object-oriented numerical software libraries. In E. Arge, A. M. Bruaset, and H. P. Langtangen, eds., *Modern Software Tools in Scientific Computing*, 163–202. Birkhauser, Boston, 1997.

[74]   S. Balay, W. D. Gropp, L. C. McInnes, and B. F. Smith. PETSc 2.0 Users Manual. (Revision 2.0.28.) Technical Report ANL-95/11. Argonne National Laboratory, Argonne, IL, Mar 2000.

[75]   U. Banerjee, R. Eigenmann, A. Nicolau, and D. Padua. Automatic program parallelization. *Proceedings of the IEEE*, 81(2):211–243, Feb 1993.

[76]   J. Banning. An efficient way to find the side effects of procedure calls and the aliases of variables. In *Proceedings of the 6th ACM SIGPLAN SIGACT Symposium on the Principles of Programming Languages*, 29–41, ACM Press, New York, 1979.

[77]   D. Barkley and R. D. Henderson. Three-dimensional Floquet stability analysis of the wake of a circular cylinder. *Journal of Fluid Mechanics*, 322:215–241, Sep 1996.

[78]   S. T. Barnard. PMRSB: Parallel Multilevel Recursive Spectral Bisection. In *Proceedings of Supercomputing '95*, ACM Press, New York, 1995.

[79]   S. Barnard and H. Simon. A fast multilevel implementation of recursive spectral bisection for partitioning unstructured problems. In *Proceedings of the Sixth SIAM Conference on Parallel Processing for Scientific Computation*, 711–718, SIAM, Philadelphia, PA, 1993.

[80]   E. R. Barnes, A. Vannelli, and J. Q. Walker. A new heuristic for partitioning the nodes of a graph. *SIAM Journal on Discrete Mathematics*, 1(3):299–305, 1988.

[81]   R. Barrett, M. Berry, T. F. Chan, J. Demmel, J. M. Donato, J. Dongarra, V. Eijkhout, R. Pozo, C. Romine, and H. van der Vorst. *Templates for the Solution of Linear Systems: Building Blocks for Iterative Methods*. SIAM, Philadelphia, PA, 1994. (Also available at *http://www.netlib.org/templates/templates.ps*).

[82]   J. M. Barth. A practical interprocedural data flow analysis algorithm. *Communications of the ACM*, 21(9):724–736, Sep 1978.

[83]   M. Bartholomew-Biggs. OPFAD—A User's Guide to the OPtima Forward Automatic Differentiation Tool. Technical report. Numerical Optimization Centre, University of Hertfordshire, Hatfield, Hertfordshire, UK, 1995.

[84]   P. Bastian, K. Birken, K. Johannsen, S. Lang, N. Neuss, H. Rentz-Reichert, and C. Wieners. UG—A flexible software toolbox for solving partial differential equations. *Computing and Visualization in Science*, 1(1):27–40, 1997.

[85]   J. T. Batina. A gridless Euler/Navier–Stokes solution algorithm for complex-aircraft applications. In *Proceedings of the 31st AIAA Aerospace Sciences Meeting*, Reno, NV, Jan 1993. (AIAA Paper 93-21107.)

[86]   S. J. Baylor and C. E. Wu. Parallel I/O workload characteristics using Vesta. In R. Jain, J. Werth, and J. Browne, eds., *Input/Output in Parallel and Distributed Computer Systems*, 167–185, Kluwer, Dordrecht, 1996.

[87]   Y. Ben-Zion. Stress, slip and earthquakes in models of complex single-fault systems incorporating brittle and creep deformations. *Journal of Geophysical Research*, 101(B3):5677–5706, Mar 1996.

[88]   J. K. Bennett, J. B. Carter, and W. Zwaenepoel. Munin: Distributed shared memory based on type-specific memory coherence. In *Proceedings of the Second ACM SIGPLAN Symposium on Principles and Practice of Parallel Programming*, 168–176, Seattle, WA, Mar 1990, ACM Press, New York, 1990.

[89]   S. Benson, L. C. McInnes, and J. Moré. TAO: Toolkit for Advanced Optimization. Available at *http://www.mcs.anl.gov/tao*.

[90]   S. Benson, L. C. McInnes, and J. Moré. GPCG: A Case Study in the Performance and Scalability of Optimization Algorithms. Technical Report ANL/MCS-P768-0799. Mathematics and Computer Science Division, Argonne National Laboratory, 1999.

[91]   J.-P. Berenger. A perfectly matched layer for the absorption of electromagnetic waves. *Journal of Computational Physics*, 114(2):185–200, Oct 1994.

[92]   M. J.Berger and S. H. Bokhari. A partitioning strategy for nonuniform problems on multiprocessors. *IEEE Transactions on Computers*, C-36(5):570–580, May 1987.

[93]   M. J. Berger and P. Colella. Local adaptive mesh refinement for shock hydrodynamics. *Journal of Computational Physics*, 82(1):67–84, May 1989.

[94]   M. J. Berger and J. Oliger. Adaptive mesh refinement for hyperbolic partial differential equations. *Journal of Computational Physics*, 53(3):484–512, 1984.

[95]   C. Bernardi, Y. Maday, and A. T. Patera. A new nonconforming approach to domain decomposition: The mortar element method. In H. Brezis and J. L. Lions, eds., *Nonlinear Partial Differential Equations and Their Applications. Collège de France Seminar, Vol. XI (Paris, 1989–1991)*, 13–51, Longman Scientific, New York, 1994.

[96]   D. E. Bernholdt. Object oriented methods without object oriented languages. In M. E. Henderson, C. R. Anderson, and S. L. Lyons, eds., *Proceedings of the SIAM Workshop on Object Oriented Methods for Inter-Operable Scientific and Engineering Computing*, 40–49, SIAM, Philadelphia, PA, 1999.

[97]   D. E. Bernholdt. Scalability of correlated electronic structure calculations on parallel computers: A case study of the RI-MP2 method. *Parallel Computing*, 26(7–8):945–963, July 2000.

[98]   D. E. Bernholdt, E. Aprà, H. A. Früchtl, M. F. Guest, R. J. Harrison, R. A. Kendall, R. A. Kutteh, X. Long, J. B. Nicholas, J. A. Nichols, H. L. Taylor, A. T. Wong, G. I. Fann, R. J. Littlefield, and J. Nieplocha. Parallel computational chemistry made easier: The development of NWChem. *International Journal of Quantum Chemistry*, Quantum Chemistry symposium, 29:475–483, 1995.

[99]   D. E. Bernholdt and R. J. Harrison. Large-scale correlated electronic structure calculations: The RI-MP2 method on parallel computers. *Chemical Physics Letters*, 250(5–6):477–484, Mar 1996.

[100]   D. E. Bernholdt and R. J. Harrison. Fitting basis sets for the RI-MP2 approximate second-order many-body perturbation theory method. *The Journal of Chemical Physics*, 109(5):1593–1600, Aug 1998.

[101]   A. J. Bernstein. Analysis of programs for parallel processing. *IEEE Transactions on Electronic Computers*, 15(5):757–763, Oct 1966.

[102]   B. N. Bershad, M. J. Zekauskas, and W. A. Sawdon. The Midway distributed shared memory system. In *Proceedings of the 38th IEEE International Computer Conference*, 528–537. IEEE Computer Society Press, Los Alamitos, CA, 1993.

[103]   M. Berz, C. Bischof, G. Corliss, and A. Griewank, eds. *Computational differentiation: Techniques, applications, and tools.* In *Proceedings of the 2nd International Workshop.* SIAM, Philadelphia, PA, 1996.

[104]   S. E. Best, V. O. Ivchenko, K. J. Richards, R. D. Smith, and R. C. Malone. Eddies in numerical models of the Antarctic Circumpolar Current and their influence on the mean flow. *Journal of Physical Oceanography*, 29(3):328–350, Mar 1999.

[105] W.-J. Beyn. The numerical computation of connecting orbits in dynamical systems. *IMA Journal of Numerical Analysis*, 10(3):379–405, Jul 1990.

[106] D. Bhatia, V. Burzewski, M. Camuseva, G. Fox, W. Furmanski, and G. Premchandran. WebFlow—A visual programming paradigm for Web/Java based coarse grain distributed computing. *Concurrency: Practice and Experience*, 9(6):555–577, Jun 1997.

[107] J. A. Bilmes, K. Asanovic, R. Vudoc, S. Iyer, J. Demmel, C. Chin, and D. Lam. The PHiPAC (Portable High Performance ANSI C) page for BLAS3-Compatible Fast Matrix Multiply. Available at *http://www.icsi.berkeley.edu/~bilmes/phipac/*.

[108] G. Birkhoff and R. E. Lynch. *Numerical Solution of Elliptic Problems*. SIAM, Philadelphia, PA, 1984.

[109] C. Bischof, A. Carle, G. Corliss, A. Griewank, and P. Hovland. ADIFOR: Generating derivative codes from Fortran programs. *Scientific Programming*, 1(1)11–29, 1992.

[110] C. H. Bischof, P. M. Khademi, A. Bouaricha, and A. Carle. Efficient computation of gradients and Jacobians by dynamic exploitation of sparsity in automatic differentiation. *Optimization Methods and Software*, 7(1):1–39, Jul 1996.

[111] C. Bischof, P. Khademi, A. Mauer, and A. Carle. Adifor 2.0: Automatic differentiation of Fortran 77 programs. *IEEE Computational Science and Engineering*, 3(3):18–32, Fall 1996.

[112] C. Bischof, L. Green, K. Haigler, and T. Knauff. Parallel calculation of sensitivity derivatives for aircraft design using automatic differentiation. In *Proceedings of the 5th AIAA/USAF/NASA/ISSM Symposium on Multidisciplinary Analysis and Optimization*, Panama City Beach, FL, Sep 1994, American Institute of Aeronautics and Astronautics. (Also available as AIAA Paper 94-4261.)

[113] C. H. Bischof, L. Roh, and A. J. Mauer-Oats. ADIC: An extensible automatic differentiation tool for ANSI-C. *Software: Practice and Experience*, 27(12):1427–1456, Dec 1997.

[114] C. Bischof and P.-T. Wu. Time-Parallel Computation of Pseudo-Adjoints for a Leapfrog Scheme. Technical Report ANL/MCS-P639-0197. Mathematics and Computer Science Division, Argonne National Laboratory, Argonne, IL, 1997.

[115] C. H. Bischof and M. R. Haghighat. On hierarchical differentiation. In M. Berz, C. Bischof, G. Corliss, and A. Griewank, eds., *Computational Differentiation: Techniques, Applications, and Tools*, 83–94, SIAM Philadelphia, PA, 1996. (Also available as CRPC TR-96647 and Technical Report ANL/MCS-P571-0396.)

[116] R. Biswas and R. C. Strawn. A new procedure for dynamic adaptation of three-dimensional unstructured grids. *Applied Numerical Mathematics*, 13(6):437–452, Feb 1994.

[117] R. E. Bixby and A. Martin. Parallelizing the dual simplex method. Technical Report CRPC-TR95706. Center for Research on Parallel Computation, Rice University, Houston, TX, Dec 1995. (Revised Jul 1997.)

[118] P. E. Bjørstad and O. B. Widlund. Iterative methods for the solution of elliptic problems on regions partitioned into substructures. *SIAM Journal on Numerical Analysis*, 23(6):1097–1120, Dec 1986.

[119] L. S. Blackford, J. Choi, A. Cleary, E. D'Azevedo, J. Demmel, I. Dhillon, J. Dongarra, S. Hammarling, G. Henry, A. Petitet, K. Stanley, D. Walker, and R. Whaley. *ScaLAPACK Users' Guide*, 2nd ed. SIAM, Philadelphia, PA, 1998.

[120] E. Bleszynski, M. Bleszynski, and T. Jarosszewicz. AIM: Adaptive integral method for solving large-scale electromagnetic scattering and radiation problems. *Radio Science*, 31(5):1225–1251, Sep/Oct 1996.

[121] Blue Gene. Available at *http://www.research.ibm.com/bluegene/*.

[122] L. M. Blumenthal. *Theory and Applications of Distance Geometry*. Oxford University Press, Oxford, 1953.

[123] F. Bodin, P. Beckman, D. Gannon, S. Narayana, and S. X. Yang. Distributed pC++: Basic ideas for an object parallel language. *Scientific Programming*, 2(3):7–22, Fall 1993.

[124] J. E. Boillat. Load balancing and Poisson equations in a graph. *Concurrency: Practice and Experience*, 2(4):289–313, Dec 1990.

[125] S. H. Bokhari and D. J. Mavriplis. The TERA Multithreaded Architecture and Unstructured Meshes. Icase interim report no. 33, Institute for Computer Applications in Science and Engineering, NASA Langley Research Center, Hampton, VA, Dec 1998.

[126] I. Bongartz, A. R. Conn, N. Gould, and P. Toint. Constrained and Unconstrained Optimization Testing Environment. Technical Report 93/10. Départment de Mathématique, Facultés Universitaires Notre-Dame de la Paix, Namur, Belgium, 1993.

[127] A. J. Booker, J. E. Dennis, Jr., P. D. Frank, D. W. Moore, and D. B. Serafini. Managing surrogate objectives to optimize a helicopter rotor design—Further experiments. In *Proceedings of the Seventh AIAA/USAF/NASA/ISSM—Symposium on Multidisciplinary Analysis and Optimization*, St. Louis, MO, 1998.

[128] A. J. Booker, J. E. Dennis, Jr., P. D. Frank, D. B. Serafini, and V. Torczon. Optimization using surrogate objectives on a helicopter test example. In J. T. Borggaard, J. Burns, E. Cliff, and S. Sherk, eds., *Computational Methods for Optimal Design and Control,* Birkhauser, Boston, 1998.

[129] A. J. Booker, J. E. Dennis, Jr., P. D. Frank, D. B. Serafini, V. Torczon, and M. W. Trosset. A rigorous framework for optimization of expensive functions by surrogates. *Structural Optimization*, 17(1):1–13, Feb 1999.

[130] R. Bordawekar. Techniques for Compiling I/O Intensive Parallel Programs. PhD diss., Syracuse University, 1996. (Also available as Caltech Technical Report CACR-118.)

[131] R. Bordawekar, A. Choudhary, K. Kennedy, C. Koelbel, and M. Paleczny. A model and compilation strategy for out-of-core data parallel programs. In *Proceedings of the Fifth ACM SIGPLAN Symposium on Principles and Practices of Parallel Programming*, 1–10, ACM Press, New York, 1995.

[132] J. M. Bower and D. Beeman. *The Book of GENESIS: Exploring Realistic Neural Models with the GEneral NEural SImulation System*. TELOS, Santa Clara, CA, 1994.

[133] J. Boyle, R. Butler, T. Disz, B. Glickfeld, E. Lusk, R. Overbeek, J. Patterson, and R. Stevens. *Portable Programs for Parallel Processors*. Holt, Rinehart, & Winston, New York, 1987.

[134] Z. Bozkus, A. Choudhary, G. Fox, T. Haupt, and S. Ranka. A compilation approach for Fortran 90D/HPF compilers on distributed money MIMD computers. In *Proceedings of the Sixth International Workshop on Languages and Compilers for Parallel Computing*, 200–215, Springer-Verlag, Berlin, 1994.

[135] Z. Bozkus, L. Meadows, S. Nakamoto, V. Schuster, and M. Young. PGHPF—An optimizing High Performance Fortran compiler for distributed memory machines. *Scientific Programming*, 6(1):29–40, Spring 1997.

[136] J. U. Brackbill. An adaptive grid with directional control. *Journal of Computational Physics*, 108(1):38–50, Sep 1993.

[137] J. U. Brackbill and J. S. Saltzman. Adaptive zoning for singular problems in two dimensions. *Journal of Computational Physics*, 46:342, 1982.

[138] T. Brandes. Compiling data parallel programs to message passing programs for massively parallel MIMD systems. In *Proceedings of the Working Conference on Massively Parallel Programming Models*, 100–107, IEEE Computer Society Press, Los Alcunitos, CA 1993. (Also available at *ftp://ftp.gmd.de/gmd/adaptor/docs/compiling.ps.Z*.)

[139] P. Bratley and B. L. Fox. Algorithm 659: Implementing Sobol's quasirandom sequence generator. *ACM Transactions on Mathematical Software*, 14(1):88–100, Mar 1988.

[140] P. Bratley, B. L. Fox, and H. Niederreiter. Implementation and tests of low-discrepancy sequences. *ACM Transactions on Modeling and Computer Simulation*, 2(3):195–213, Jul 1992.

[141] R. D. Braun. An Architecture for Large-Scale Distributed Design. PhD diss., Stanford University, 1996.

[142] F. Breg, S. Diwan, J. Villacis, J. Balasubramanian, E. Akman, and D. Gannon. Java RMI performance and object model interoperability: Experiments with Java/HPC++ distributed components. *Concurrency: Practice and Experience*, 10(11-13):941–955, Sep-Nov, 1998.

[143] E. Brooks. The attack of the killer micros. Presentation during the Teraflop Computing Panel Discussion at Supercomputing '89, Reno, NV, Nov 1989.

[144] D. L. Brown, W. D. Henshaw, and D. J. Quinlan. Overture: Object-oriented tools for solving CFD and combustion problems in complex moving geometry. Available at *http://www.llnl.gov/CASC/Overture*.

[145] J. A. Brown, Jr. and K. A. Campana. An economical time-differencing system for numerical weather prediction. *Monthly Weather Review*, 106(18):1125–1136, Aug 1978.

[146] S. R. Brown, C. J. Scholz, and J. B. Rundle. A simplified spring-block model of earthquakes. *Geophysical Research Letters*, 18(2):215–218, Feb 1991.

[147] M. Broy, A. Deimel, J. Henn, K. Koskimies, F. Plášil, G. Pomberger, W. Pree, M. Stal, and C. Szyperski. What characterizes a (software) component? *Software—Concepts and Tools*, 19(1):49–56, 1998.

[148] A. M. Bruaset and H. P. Langtangen. A comprehensive set of tools for solving partial differential equations: Diffpack. In *Numerical Methods and Software Tools in Industrial Mathematics*, 61–90, Birkhauser, Boston, 1997.

[149] G. Bryan, T. Abel, and M. Norman. Achieving extreme resolution in numerical cosmology using adaptive mesh refinement: Resolving primordial star formation. In *Proceedings of Supercomputing 2001*, Nov 2001.

[150] G. L. Bryan. Fluids in the universe: Adaptive mesh refinement in cosmology. *Computing in Science and Engineering*, 1(2):46–53, Mar–Apr 1999.

[151] G. L. Bryan and M. L. Norman. Statistical properties of x-ray clusters: Analytic and numerical comparisons. *The Astrophysical Journal*, 495(1):80–99, Mar 1998.

[152] G. L. Bryan and M. L. Norman. A hybrid AMR application for cosmology and astrophysics. In S. B. Baden, N. P. Chrisochoides, D. Gannon, and M. L. Norman, eds., *Structured Adaptive Mesh Refinement (SAMR) Grid Methods*, 165–170, Institute for Mathematics and its Applications (IMA), Springer-Verlag, New York, 2000.

[153] G. L. Bryan, M. L. Norman, J. M. Stone, R. Cen, and J. P. Ostriker. A piecewise parabolic method for cosmological hydrodynamics. *Computer Physics Communication*, 89(1–3):149–168, Aug 1995.

[154] K. Bryan. A numerical method for the study of the circulation of the world ocean. *Journal of Computational Physics*, 4(3):347–376, Oct 1969. (Reprinted in *Journal of Computational Physics,* 135(2): 154–169, 1997.)

[155] T. Bui and C. Jones. A heuristic for reducing fill in sparse matrix factorization. In *Proceedings of the Sixth SIAM Conference on Parallel Processing for Scientific Computing*, 445–452, SIAM, Philadelphia, PA, 1993.

[156] M. Burke and R. Cytron. Interprocedural dependence analysis and parallelization. In *Proceedings of the SIGPLAN '86 Symposium on Compiler Construction*, 162–175, ACM Press, New York , 1986.

[157] R. Burridge and L. Knopoff. Model and theoretical seismicity. *Bulletin of the Seismological Society of America*, 57:341–371, 1967.

[158] R. M. Butler and E. L. Lusk. Monitors, message, and clusters: The p4 parallel programming system. *Parallel Computing*, 20(4):547–564, Apr 1994.

[159] R. H. Byrd, T. Derby, E. Eskow, K. P. B. Oldenkamp, and R. B. Schnabel. A new stochastic/perturbation method for large-scale global optimization and its application to water cluster problems. In W. Hager, D. Hearn, and P. Pardalos, eds., *Large-Scale Optimization: State of the Art*, 69–81, Kluwer Dordrecht, 1994.

[160] R. H. Byrd, E. Eskow, and R. B. Schnabel. A New Large-Scale Global Optimization Method and Its Application to Lennard-Jones Problems. Technical Report CU-CS-630-92. Department of Computer Science, University of Colorado, Boulder, CO, 1992. (Revised 1995.)

[161] R. H. Byrd, E. Eskow, and R. B. Schnabel. A Large-Scale Stochastic-Perturbation Global Optimization Method for Molecular Cluster Problems. Technical report. Department of Computer Science, University of Colorado, Boulder, 1999. (Available at *http://www.cs.colorado.edu /~bobby/papers/cluster.ps.*)

[162] R. H. Byrd, E. Eskow, R. B. Schnabel, and S. L. Smith. Parallel global optimization: Numerical methods, dynamic scheduling methods, and application to molecular configuration. In B. Ford and A. Fincham, eds., *Parallel Computation*, 187–207, Oxford University Press, Oxford, 1993.

[163] R. H. Byrd, E. Eskow, A. van der Hoek, R. B. Schnabel, C.-S. Shao, and Z. Zou. Global optimization methods for protein folding problems. In P. Pardalos, D. Shalloway, and G. Xue, eds., *Global Minimization of Nonconvex Energy Functions: Molecular Conformation and Protein Folding*, 29–39, American Mathematical Society, Providence, RI, 1996.

[164] R. H. Byrd, R. B. Schnabel, and M. H. Shultz. Parallel Quasi-Newton Methods for Unconstrained Optimization. Technical report. Department of Computer Science, University of Colorado, Boulder, 1990.

[165] R. E. Caflisch. Monte Carlo and quasi-Monte Carlo methods. *Acta Numerica*, 7:1–49, 1998.

[166] R. E. Caflisch, W. Morokoff, and A. Owen. Valuation of mortgage backed securities using Brownian bridges to reduce effective dimension. *Journal of Computational Finance*, 1(1):27–46, Fall 1997.

[167] X.-C. Cai and M. Sarkis. A restricted additive Schwarz preconditioner for general sparse linear systems. *SIAM Journal on Scientific Computing*, 21(2):792–797, 1999.

[168]   D. Callahan and K. Kennedy. Compiling programs for distributed-memory multiprocessors. *Journal of Supercomputing*, 2(2):151–169, Oct 1988.

[169]   P. Cao, E. W. Felten, A. R. Karlin, and K. Li. Implementation and performance of integrated application-controlled file caching, prefetching, and disk scheduling. *ACM Transactions on Computer Systems*, 14(4):311–343, Nov 1996.

[170]   A. Carle, M. Fagan, and L. L. Green. Preliminary results from the application of automated adjoint code generation to CFL3D. In *Proceedings of the 7th AIAA/USAF/NASA/ISSMO Symposium on Multidisciplinary Analysis and Optimization*, St. Louis, MO, Sep 1998. (Also available as AIAA Paper 98-4807.)

[171]   A. Carle, K. Kennedy, U. Kremer, and J. Mellor-Crummey. Automatic data layout for distributed-memory machines in the D programming environment. In *Proceedings of AP'93 International Workshop on Automatic Distributed Memory Parallelization, Automatic Data Distribution and Automatic Parallel Performance Prediction*, 108–123, Saarbrücken, Germany, Mar 1993.

[172]   W. W. Carlson and J. M. Draper. Distributed data access in AC. In *Fifth ACM SIGPLAN Symposium on Principles and Practice of Parallel Programming*, 39–47, ACM Press, New York, 1995.

[173]   H. Casanova and J. Dongarra. NetSolve: A network-enabled server for solving computational science problems. *The International Journal of Supercomputer Applications and High Performance Computing*, 11(3):212–223, 1997.

[174]   Ü. V. Catalyürek and C. Aykanat. Hypergraph-partitioning-based decomposition for parallel sparse-matrix vector multiplication. *IEEE Transactions on Parallel and Distributed Systems*, 10(7):673–693, Jul 1999.

[175]   A. C. Catlin, S. Weerawarana, E. N. Houstis, and M. Gaitatzes. *The PELLPACK User Guide*. Department of Computer Sciences, Purdue University, Lafayette, IN, 2000.

[176]   CCAT: Indiana University research group in common component architecture. Available at *http://www.extreme.indiana.edu/ccat/index.html*.

[177]   C. F. Cerco and T. Cole. Three-Dimensional Eutrophication Model of Chesapeake Bay. Technical Report CETR EL-94-4. U.S. Army Corps of Engineers Waterway Experiment Station, Vicksburg, MS, 1994.

[178]   C. F. Cerco and T. Cole. User's Guide to the CE-QUAL-ICM Three-Dimensional Eutrophication Model, Release Version 1.0. Technical Report CETR EL-95-15. U.S. Army Corps of Engineers Waterway Experiment Station, Vicksburg, MS, Mar 1995.

[179]   A. R. Champneys and Y. A. Kuznetsov. Numerical detection and continuation of codimension-two homoclinic bifurcations. *International Journal of Bifurcation and Chaos in Applied Sciences and Engineering*, 4(4):795–822, Aug 1994.

[180]   A. R. Champneys, Y. A. Kuznetsov, and B. Sandstede. HomCont: An AUTO86 Driver for Homoclinic Bifurcation Analysis, version 2.0. Technical report. CWI, Amsterdam, 1995.

[181]   T. Chan and V. Eijkhout. Design of a Library of Parallel Preconditioners. Technical Report UCLA CAM TR97–58. Department of Mathematics, University of California at Los Angeles, 1997.

[182]   T. Chan and H. van der Vorst. Linear system solvers: Sparse iterative methods. In D. Keyes et al., ed., *Proceedings of the ICASW/LaRC Workshop on Parallel Numerical Algorithms*, 91–118, Kluwer Academic Publishers, Dordrecht, The Netherlands, May 1997.

[183] R. Chandra, D. Kohr, R. Menon, L. Dagum, D. Maydan, and J. McDonald. *Parallel Programming in OpenMP*. Morgan Kaufmann, San Francisco, 2000.

[184] K. M. Chandy and C. Kesselman. CC++: A declarative concurrent object-oriented programming notation. In G. Agha, P. Wegner, and A. Yonezawa, eds., *Research Directions in Concurrent Object Oriented Programming*, 281–313, MIT Press, Cambridge, MA, 1993.

[185] M. Chandy, B. Massingill, D. Meiron, and R. Samtaney. Parallel programming archetypes and scientific computing. *CRPC Newsletter*, Fall 1995.

[186] C. Chang, A. Acharya, A. Sussman, and J. Saltz. T2: A customizable parallel database for multi-dimensional data. *ACM SIGMOD Record*, 27(1):58–66, Mar 1998.

[187] C. Chang, R. Ferreira, A. Sussman, and J. Saltz. Infrastructure for building parallel database systems for multi-dimensional data. In *Proceedings of the 13th International Parallel Processing Symposium* and *10th Symposium on Parallel and Distributed Processing IPPS/SPDP 1999*, 582–587, IEEE Computer Society Press, Los Alamitos, CA, 1999.

[188] B. Chapman, P. Mehrotra, and H. Zima. Programming in Vienna Fortran. *Scientific Programming*, 1(1):31–50, Fall 1992.

[189] J. Chattratichat, J. Darlington, M. Ghanem, Y. Guo, H. Huning, M. Kohler, J. Sutiwaraphun, H. W. To, and D. Yang. Large scale data mining: Challenges and responses. In *Proceedings of the Third International Conference on Knowledge Discovery and Data Mining*, 143–146, AAAI Press, Menlo Park, CA, 1997.

[190] J. Chen and V. Taylor. ParaPART: Parallel mesh partitioning tool for distributed systems. In *Proceedings of the 6th International Symposium on Solving Irregularly Structured Problems in Parallel*, Springer-Verlag, Heidelberg, 1999.

[191] M. S. Chen, J. Han, and P. S. Yu. Data mining: An overview from a database perspective. *IEEE Transactions on Knowledge and Data Engineering*, 8(6):866–883, Dec 1996.

[192] P. M. Chen, E. K. Lee, G. A. Gibson, R. H. Katz, and D. A. Patterson. RAID: High-performance, reliable secondary storage. *ACM Computing Surveys*, 26(2):145–185, Jun 1994.

[193] I.-L. Chern, J. Glimm, O. McBryan, B. Plohr, and S. Yaniv. Front tracking for gas dynamics. *Journal of Computational Physics*, 62(1):83–110, Jan 1986.

[194] W. C. Chew, J. M. Jin, C. C. Lu, E. Michielssen, and J. M. Song. Fast solution methods in electromagnetics. *IEEE Transactions on Antennas and Propagation*, 45(3):533–543, Mar 1997.

[195] M. Childress. EDYS Code. U.S. Army Corps of Engineers, Engineer Research and Development Center, Vicksburg, MS. Available at *http://www.wes.hpc.mil*.

[196] S. Chippada, C. N. Dawson, M. L. Martinez, and M. F. Wheeler. Parallel computing for finite element models of surface water flow. In *Computational Methods in Water Resources XI*, Vol. 2 of *Computational Methods in Surface Flow and Transport Problems*, 63–70, Computational Mechanics Publications, Southhampton, UK, 1996.

[197] S. Chippada, C. N. Dawson, M. L. Martínez, and M. F. Wheeler. A Projection Method for Constructing a Mass Conservative Velocity Field. Technical Report TICAM TR97-09. Texas Institute for Computational and Applied Mathematics, University of Texas, Austin, Jun 1997.

[198] J. Choi, J. Dongarra, S. Ostrouchov, A. Petitet, D. Walker, and R. C. Whaley. A Proposal for a Set of Parallel Basic Linear Algebra Subprograms. LAPACK Working Note #100 (ut-cs-95-292). Department of Computer Science, University of Tennessee, Knoxville, May 1995.

[199] J. Choi, J. J. Dongarra, R. Pozo, and D. W. Walker. ScaLAPACK: A scalable linear algebra library for distributed memory concurrent computers. In *Proceedings of the Fourth Symposium on the Frontiers of Massively Parallel Computation*, 120–127, IEEE Computer Society Press, Los Alamitos, CA, 1992.

[200] J. Choi, J. Dongarra, and D. Walker. The design of scalable software libraries for distributed memory concurrent computers. In J. Dongarra and B. Tourancheau, eds., *Environments and Tools for Parallel Scientific Computing*, Elsevier Science Publishers, New York, 1993.

[201] N. Chrisochoides and D. Nave. Simultaneous mesh generation and partitioning for Delaunay meshes. In *Proceedings of the 8th International Meshing Round Table*, 55–66, South Lake Tahoe, California, Oct 1999.

[202] N. Christ. Computational Quantum Field Theory at Columbia. Available at *http://www.phys.columbia.edu/~cqft*.

[203] Y. C. Chung and S. Ranka. Mapping finite element graphs on hypercubes. *Journal of Supercomputing*, 6(3):257–282, Dec 1992.

[204] Coda File System. Available at *http://www.coda.cs.cmu.edu*.

[205] P. Colella. A direct Eulerian MUSCL scheme for gas dynamics. *SIAM Journal on Scientific and Statistical Computing*, 6(1):104–117, Jan 1985.

[206] P. Colella and P. R. Woodward. The piecewise parabolic method (PPM) for gas-dynamical simulations. *Journal of Computational Physics*, 54(1):174–201, Apr 1984.

[207] T. F. Coleman, J. Czyzyk, C. Sun, M. Wagner, and S. J. Wright. pPCx: Parallel software for linear programming. In *Proceedings of the Eighth SIAM Conference on Parallel Processing for Scientific Computing*, SIAM, Philadelphia, PA, 1997.

[208] T. F. Coleman, B. S. Garbow, and J. J. Moré. Software for estimating sparse Jacobian matrices. *ACM Transactions on Mathematical Software*, 10(3):329–345, Sep 1984.

[209] T. F. Coleman, B. S. Garbow, and J. J. Moré. Software for estimating sparse Hessian matrices. *ACM Transactions on Mathematical Software*, 11(4):363–377, Dec 1985.

[210] T. F. Coleman and J. J. Moré. Estimation of sparse Jacobian matrices and graph coloring problems. *SIAM Journal on Numerical Analysis*, 20(1):187–209, Feb 1983.

[211] T. Coleman, D. Shalloway, and Z. Wu. Isotropic effective energy simulated annealing searches for low energy molecular cluster states. *Computational Optimization and Applications*, 2(2):145–170, Oct. 1993.

[212] T. Coleman, D. Shalloway, and Z. Wu. A parallel build-up algorithm for global energy minimizations of molecular clusters using effective energy simulated annealing. *Journal of Global Optimization*, 4(2):171–185, 1994.

[213] T. F. Coleman and C. Sun. Parallel orthogonal factorizations of large sparse matrices on distributed-memory multiprocessors. In *Proceedings of the Sixth SIAM Conference on Parallel Processing for Scientific Computing*, SIAM, Philadelphia, PA, 1993.

[214] T. F. Coleman and Z. Wu. Parallel continuation-based global optimization for molecular conformation and protein folding. *Journal of Global Optimization*, 8(1):49–65, 1996.

[215] Commodity Grid Kits Based on Globus (CoG Kit). Available at *http://www.globus.org/cog/*.

[216] Common Component Architecture Forum. CCA Forum Web page. Available at *http://www.acl.lanl.gov/cca-forum*.

[217] P. Concus and G. H. Golub. Use of fast direct methods for the efficient numerical solution of nonseparable elliptic equations. *SIAM Journal on Numerical Analysis*, 10(6):1103–1120, Dec 1973.

[218] J. Cong and M. Smith. A parallel bottom-up clustering algorithm with applications to circuit partitioning in VLSI design. In *Proceedings of the 30th ACM/IEEE Design Automation Conference*, 755–760, ACM Press, New York, 1993.

[219] G. B. Cook and S. A. Teukolsky. Numerical relativity: Challenges for computational science. *Acta Numerica*, 8:1–45, 1999.

[220] G. Cook et al. (Binary Black Hole Grand Challenge Alliance). Boosted three-dimensional black-hole evolutions with singularity excision. *Physical Review Letters*, 80(12):2512–2516, Mar 1998.

[221] K. D. Cooper, M. W. Hall, K. Kennedy, and L. Torczon. Interprocedural analysis and optimization. *Communications in Pure and Applied Mathematics*, 48:947–1003, 1995.

[222] K. D. Cooper and K. Kennedy. Interprocedural side-effect analysis in linear time. In *Proceedings of the SIGPLAN '88 Conference on Programming Language Design and Implementation*, 57–66, ACM Press, New York, 1988.

[223] P. Corbett, D. Feitelson, Y. Hsu, J.-P. Prost, M. Snir, S. Fineberg, B. Nitzberg, B. Traversat, and P. Wong. MPI-IO: A parallel FILE I/O interface for MPI. Technical Report RC 19841(#87784). IBM T. J. Watson Research Center, Yorktown Heights, NY, Nov 1994.

[224] P. F. Corbett and D. G. Feitelson. The Vesta parallel file system. *ACM Transactions on Computer Systems*, 14(3):225–264, Aug 1996.

[225] P. Corbett, J.-P. Prost, C. Demetriou, G. Gibson, E. Reidel, J. Zelenka, Y. Chen, E. Felten, K. Li, J. Hartman, L. Peterson, B. Bershad, A. Wolman, and R. Aydt. Proposal for a Common Parallel File System Programming Interface, Version 1.0, Sep 1996. Available at *http://www.cs.arizona.edu/sio/api1.0.ps*.

[226] M. D. Cox. A baroclinic numerical model of the world ocean: Preliminary results. In *Numerical Models of Ocean Circulation*, 107–118, National Academy of Sciences, Washington, DC, 1975.

[227] CP-PACS: Computational Physics by Parallel Array Computer System. Center for Computational Physics, University of Tsukuba, Tennodai, Tsukubashi, Japan. Web page. Available at *http://www.rccp.tsukuba.ac.jp/ccp/cp-pacs.html*.

[228] E. J. Cramer, J. E. Dennis, Jr., P. D. Frank, R. M. Lewis, and G. R. Shubin. Problem formulation for multidisciplinary optimization. *SIAM Journal on Optimization*, 4(4):754–776, 1994.

[229] P. E. Crandall, R. A. Aydt, A. A. Chien, and D. A. Reed. Input/output characteristics of scalable parallel applications. In *Proceedings of Supercomputing '95*, ACM Press, New York, 1995.

[230] Cray Research. *Introducing the MPP Apprentice Tool*. Publication IN-25112.0, Cray Research, Seattle, WA, 1997.

[231] Cray Research. *Optimizing Code on Cray PVP Systems*. Publication S6-2192-3.0, Cray Research, Seattle, WA, 1997.

[232] M. Creutz. Confinement and the critical dimensionality of space-time. *Physical Review Letters*, 43(8):553–556, Aug 1979. (Erratum, *Physical Review Letters* 43(12):890, 1979.)

[233] G. M. Crippen and T. F. Havel. *Distance Geometry and Molecular Conformation*. John Wiley & Sons, New York, 1988.

[234] S. Crivelli, R. H. Byrd, E. Eskow, R. B. Schnabel, R. Yu, T. Phillips, and T. Head-Gordon. A Global Optimization Strategy for Predicting Protein Tertiary Structure: α–Helical Proteins. Technical report. Department of Computer Science, University of Colorado, Boulder, 1998.

[235] D. E. Culler, A. Dusseau, S. C. Goldstein, A. Krishnamurthy, S. Lumetta, T. von Eicken, and K. Yelick. Introduction to Split-C: Version 0.9. Technical report. Computer Science Division—EECS, University of California, Berkeley, Feb 1993.

[236] D. E. Culler, J. P. Singh, and A. Gupta. *Parallel Computer Architecture: A Hardware/Software Approach*. Morgan Kaufmann, San Francisco, 1999.

[237] J. Cullum and W. E. Donath. A block Lanczos algorithm for computing the q algebraically largest eigenvalues and a corresponding eigenspace for large, sparse symmetric matrices. In *Proceedings of the 1974 IEEE Conference on Decision and Control*, 505–509, IEEE, New York, 1974.

[238] J. Cullum and R. A. Willoughby. Computing eigenvalues of very large symmetric matrices— An implementation of a Lanczos algorithm with no reorthogonalization. *Journal of Computational Physics*, 44(2):329–358, Dec 1981.

[239] J. K. Cullum and R. A. Willoughby. *Lanczos Algorithms for Large Symmetric Eigenvalue Computations, Volume 1, Theory*. Birkhauser, Boston, 1985.

[240] V. Cuppu, B. Jacob, B. Davis, and T. Mudge. High-performance DRAMs in workstation environments. *IEEE Transactions on Computers*, 50(11):1133–1153, Nov 2001.

[241] A. Curtis, M. Powell, and J. Reid. On the estimation of sparse Jacobian matrices. *Journal of the Institute of Mathematics and Its Applications*, 13:117–119, 1974.

[242] G. Cybenko. Dynamic load balancing for distributed memory multiprocessors. *Journal of Parallel and Distributed Computing*, 7(2):279–301, Oct 1989.

[243] J. W. Daniel, W. B. Gragg, L. Kaufman, and G. W. Stewart. Reorthogonalization and stable algorithms for updating the Gram–Schmidt QR factorization. *Mathematics of Computation*, 30(136):772–795, Oct 1976.

[244] J. F. Dannenhoffer. A new method for creating grid abstractions for complex configurations. In *Proceedings of the 31st AIAA Aerospace Sciences Meeting*, Reno, NV, Jan 1993. (Also available as AIAA Paper 93-0428.)

[245] F. Darema, D. A. George, V. A. Norton, and G. F. Pfister. A single-program-multiple-data computational model for EPEX/FORTRAN. *Parallel Computing*, 7(1):11–24, Apr 1988.

[246] F. Darema-Rogers, D. A. George, V. A. Norton, and G. F. Pfister. VM/EPEX—A VM environment for parallel execution. Technical Report RC 11225(#49161). IBM T. J. Watson Research Center, Yorktown Heights, NY, Jan 1985.

[247] F. Daube, P. Highnam, J. Ullo, and B. Schlum. Geophysical applications of parallel computing. In *Proceedings of the SPE Petroleum Computer Conference*, 115–124, Society of Petroleum Engineers, Inc., New Orleans, LA, 1993.

[248] D. F. Davidenko. On a new method of numerical solution of systems of nonlinear equations. *Doklady Natsional Akademii Nauk, SSSR(N.S))*, 88:601–602, 1953. (Russian)

[249] P. J. Davis and P. Rabinowitz. *Methods of Numerical Integration*, 2nd ed., Academic Press, Orlando, FL, 1984.

[250] D. de St. Germain, J. McCorquodale, S. G. Parker, and C. R. Johnson. Uintah: A massively parallel problem solving environment. In *Proceedings of the 9th IEEE International Symposium on High Performance Distributed Computation*, 33–41, IEEE Computer Society Press, Los Alamitos, CA, 2000.

[251] M. P. Debicki, P. Jedrzejewski, J. Mielewski, P. Przybyszewski, and M. Mrozowski. Application of the Arnoldi method to the solution of electromagnetic eigenproblems on the multiprocessor Power Challenge architecture. Preprint 19/95. Department of Electronics, Technical University of Gdansk, Gdansk, Poland, 1995.

[252] J. M. del Rosario, R. Bordawekar, and A. Choudhary. Improved parallel I/O via a two-phase run-time access strategy. In *Proceedings of the Workshop on I/O in Parallel Computer Systems at IPPS '93*, 56–70, Apr 1993. (Also available in *Computer Architecture News*, 21(5):31–38, Dec 1993.)

[253] J. M. del Rosario and A. N. Choudhary. High performance I/O for massively parallel computers: Problems and prospects. *Computer*, 27(3):59–68, Mar 1994.

[254] J. Demmel. LAPACK: A portable linear algebra library for supercomputers. In *Proceedings of the 1989 IEEE Control Systems Society Workshop on Computer-Aided Control System Design*, Dec 1989.

[255] J. E. Dennis, Jr. and R. M. Lewis. Problem formulations and other optimization issues in multidisciplinary optimization. In *Proceedings of the AIAA/NASA/USAF/ISSMO Symposium on Fluid Dynamics*, 1994. (AIAA Paper 94-2196.)

[256] J. E. Dennis, Jr., G. Li, and K. A. Williamson. Optimization Algorithms for Parameter Identification. Technical Report CRPC=TR92277. Center for Research on Parallel Computation, Rice University, Houston, TX, 1992.

[257] J. E. Dennis, Jr. and R. B. Schnabel. *Numerical Methods for Unconstrained Optimization and Nonlinear Equations*. Prentice-Hall, Englewood Cliffs, NJ, 1983.

[258] J. E. Dennis, Jr. and V. Torczon. Direct search methods on parallel machines. *SIAM Journal on Optimization*, 1(4):448–474, Nov 1991.

[259] L. De Rose, M. Pantano, R. A. Aydt, E. Shaffer, B. Schaeffer, S. Whitmore, and D. A. Reed. An approach to immersive performance visualization of parallel and wide-area distributed applications. In *Proceedings of the Eighth IEEE International Symposium on High-Performance Distributed Computing*, 247–254, Aug 1999.

[260] L. De Rose and D. A. Reed. SvPablo: A multi-language architecture-independent performance analysis system. In *Proceedings of the 1999 International Conference on Parallel Processing*, 311–318, IEEE Computer Society Press, Los Alamitos, CA, 1999.

[261] M. Deville and E. Mund. Chebyshev pseudospectral solution of second order elliptic equations with finite element preconditioning. *Journal of Computational Physics*, 60(3):517–533, Sep 1985.

[262] I. Dhillon, G. Fann, and B. Parlett. Application of a new algorithm for the symmetric eigenproblem to computational quantum chemistry. In *Proceedings of the Eighth SIAM Conference on Parallel Processing for Scientific Computing*. SIAM, 1997.

[263] DICE: Distributed Interactive Computing Environment. Army Research Laboratory, Aberdeen, MD. Web page. Available at *http://www.arl.hpc.mil/SciVis/dice/index.html*.

[264] R. Diekmann, A. Frommer, and B. Monien. Efficient schemes for nearest neighbor load balancing. *Parallel Computing*, 25(7):789–812, Aug 1999.

[265] R. Diekmann, B. Monien, and R. Preis. Using helpful sets to improve graph bisections. In D. F. Hsu, A. L. Rosenberg, and D. Sotteau, eds., *Interconnection Networks and Mapping and Scheduling Parallel Computations*, 57–73, American Mathematical Society, Providence, RI, 1995.

[266] R. Diekmann, B. Monien, and R. Preis. Load balancing strategies for distributed memory machines. *Parallel and Distributed Processing for Computational Mechanics: Systems and Tools*, 1998.

[267] J. Dieterich. A constitutive law for rate of earthquake production and its application to earthquake clustering. *Journal of Geophysical Research*, 99(B2):2601–2618, Feb 1994.

[268] Diffpack Web page. Available at *http://www.nobjects.com/Diffpack/*.

[269] Digital Equipment Corporation. *pfm—The 21064 Performance Counter Pseudo-Device*, DEC, 1995.

[270] K. A. Dill, A. T. Phillips, and J. B. Rosen. CGU: An algorithm for molecular structure prediction. In L. T. Biegler, T. Coleman, A. R. Conn, and F. N. Santosa, eds., *Large-Scale Optimization with Applications, Part III: Molecular Structure and Optimization*, 1–21, Springer-Verlag, Heidelberg and New York, 1997.

[271] I. Dimov and A. Karaivanova. Parallel computations of eigenvalues based on a Monte Carlo approach. *Monte Carlo Methods and Applications*, 4(1):33–52, 1998.

[272] C. Ding and K. Kennedy. Memory bandwidth bottleneck and its amelioration by a compiler. In *Proceedings of the 14th International Parallel and Distributed Processing Symposium*, 181–189, IEEE Computer Society Press, Los Alamitos, CA, 2000.

[273] C. Ding and K. Kennedy. Improving effective bandwidth through compiler enhancement of global cache reuse. In *Proceedings of the 15th International Parallel and Distributed Processing Symposium*, IEEE Computer Society Press, Los Alamitos, CA, 2001.

[274] P. Diniz, S. Plimpton, B. Hendrickson, and R. Leland. Parallel algorithms for dynamically partitioning unstructured grids. *Proceedings of the 7th SIAM Conference on Parallel Processing for Scientific Computation*, 615–620, SIAM, Philadelphia, PA, 1995.

[275] DIVA (Data IntensiVe Architecture) Web page. Available at *http://www.isi.edu/asd/diva/*.

[276] H. Djidjev and J. Gilbert. Separators in graphs with negative and multiple vertex weights. *Algorithmica*, 23(1):57–71, Jan 1999.

[277] E. J. Doedel, A. R. Champneys, T. F. Fairgrieve, Y. A. Kuznetsov, B. Sandstede, and X.-J. Wang. AUTO97: Continuation and Bifurcation Software for Ordinary Differential Equations. Technical report. Department of Computer Science, Concordia University, Montreal, Canada, 1997. (Also available at *ftp.cs.concordia.ca/pub/doedel/auto*.)

[278] E. Doedel, H. B. Keller, and J.-P. Kernévez. Numerical analysis and control of bifurcation problems: I—Bifurcation in finite dimensions. *International Journal of Bifurcation and Chaos in Applied Sciences and Engineering*, 1(3):493–520, 1991.

[279] E. Doedel, H. B. Keller, and J. P. Kernévez. Numerical analysis and control of bifurcation problems: II—Bifurcation in infinite dimensions. *International Journal of Bifurcation and Chaos in Applied Sciences and Engineering*, 1(4):745–772, 1991.

[280] J. Dongarra. Increasing the performance of mathematical software through high-level modularity. In *Proceedings of the Sixth International Symposium on Computing Methods in Applied Sciences and Engineering*, 239–248, North-Holland, Amersterdam, 1984.

[281] J. Dongarra. Workshop on the BLACS (Basic Linear Algebra Communication Subprograms). LAPACK Working Note #34 (ut-cs-91-134). Department of Computer Science, University of Tennessee, Knoxville, May 1991. (Also available at *http://www.netlib.org/lapack/lawns /lawn34.ps.*)

[282] J. Dongarra. Performance of Various Computers Using Standard Linear Equations Software. Technical Report CS TR-89-85. Department of Computer Science, University of Tennessee, Knoxville, Sep 2002. (Also available at *http://www.netlib.org/benchmark/performance.ps*).

[283] J. J. Dongarra, J. Du Croz, S. Hammarling, and I. Duff. A set of level 3 basic linear algebra subprograms. *ACM Transactions on Mathematical Software*, 16(1):1–17, Mar 1990.

[284] J. J. Dongarra, J. Du Croz, S. Hammarling, and R. J. Hanson. An extended set of FORTRAN basic linear algebra subroutines. *ACM Transactions on Mathematical Software*, 14(1):1–17, Mar 1988.

[285] J. J. Dongarra, F. G. Gustavson, and A. Karp. Implementing linear algebra algorithms for dense matrices on a vector pipeline machine. *SIAM Review*, 26(1):91–112, Jan 1984.

[286] J. J. Dongarra, P. Mayes, and G. Radicati di Brozolo. The IBM RISC System/6000 and linear algebra operations. *Supercomputer*, 8(4):15–30, 1991.

[287] J. Dongarra, H. W. Meuer, and E. Strohmaier. TOP500 Supercomputer Sites. Available at *http://www.top500.org*.

[288] J. Dongarra, R. Pozo, and D. Walker. An object oriented design for high performance linear algebra on distributed memory architectures. In *Proceedings of the Object Oriented Numerics Conference*, 1993.

[289] J. Dongarra and R. A. van de Geijn. Two-Dimensional Basic Linear Algebra Communication Subprograms. LAPACK Working Note #37. Department of Computer Science, University of Tennessee, Knoxville, Oct 1991.

[290] J. J. Dongarra and R. C. Whaley. A User's Guide to the BLACS, Version 1.0. LAPACK Working Note #94 (ut-cs-95-281), Department of Computer Science, University of Tennessee, Knoxville, Mar 1995.

[291] C. C. Douglas. MGNet Web page. Available at *http://www.mgnet.org*.

[292] S. Duane. Stochastic quantization versus the microcanonical ensemble: Getting the best of both worlds. *Nuclear Physics B*, 257(5):652–662, Oct 1985.

[293] S. Duane, A. D. Kennedy, B. J. Pendleton, and D. Roweth. Hybrid Monte Carlo. *Physics Letters B*, 195(2):216–222, Sep 1987.

[294] S. Duane and J. B. Kogut. The theory of hybrid stochastic algorithms. *Nuclear Physics B*, B275(3):398–420, Nov 1986.

[295] M. Dubois, C. Scheurich, and F. Briggs. Memory access buffering in multiprocessors. In *Proceedings of the 13th Annual International Symposium on Computer Architecture, Computer Architecture News*, 434–442, IEEE Computer Society Press, Los Alamitos, CA, 1986.

[296] D. E. Dudgeon and R. M. Mersereau. *Multidimensional Digital Signal Processing*. Prentice-Hall, Englewood Cliffs, NJ, 1984.

[297] I. S. Duff and G. A. Meurant. The effect of ordering on preconditioned conjugate gradients. *BIT Numerical Mathematics*, 29(4):635–657, 1989.

[298] I. S. Duff and J. K. Reid. The multifrontal solution of indefinite sparse symmetric linear equations. *ACM Transactions on Mathematical Software*, 9(3):302–325, Sep 1983.

[299] J. K. Dukowicz and R. D. Smith. Implicit free-surface method for the Bryan–Cox–Semtner ocean model. *Journal of Geophysical Research*, 99(C4):7991–8014, Apr 1994.

[300] J. K. Dukowicz, R. D. Smith, and R. C. Malone. A reformulation and implementation of the Bryan–Cox–Semtner ocean model on the connection machine. *Journal of Atmospheric and Oceanic Technology*, 10(2):195–208, Apr 1993.

[301] T. H. Dunning, Jr. Private communication.

[302] T. H. Dunning, Jr. Gaussian basis sets for use in correlated molecular calculations. I. The atoms boron through neon and hydrogen. *The Journal of Chemical Physics*, 90(2):1007–1023, Jan 1989.

[303] B. Dupore, ed. *Monte Carlo: Methodologies and Applications for Pricing and Risk Management*. Risk Publications, London, 1998.

[304] V. Dyczmons. No N^4-dependence in the calculation of large molecules. *Theoretica Chimica Acta* 28(3):307–310, 1973.

[305] A. Edelman. Large dense numerical linear algebra in 1993: The parallel computing influence. *International Journal Supercomputer Applications*, 7(2):113–128, Summer 1993.

[306] H. C. Edwards. A Parallel Infrastructure for Scalable Adaptive Finite Element Methods and Its Application to Least Squares C^∞ Collocation. PhD diss., University of Texas, Austin, 1997.

[307] W. K. Edwards. *Core Jini*. Prentice-Hall, Englewood Cliffs, NJ, 1999.

[308] V. Eijkhout. Analysis of parallel incomplete point factorizations. *Linear Algebra and Its Applications*, 154/156:723–740, 1991.

[309] V. Eijkhout. Overview of Iterative Linear System Solver Packages. LAPACK Working Note #171 (ut-cs-98-411). Department of Computer Science, University of Tennessee, Knoxville, Jul 1998.

[310] V. Eijkhout and T. Chan. ParPre: A Parallel Preconditioners Package: Reference Manual for Version 2.0.17. Technical Report CAM 97-24. Department of Mathematics, University of California at Los Angeles, 1997.

[311] P. R. Eiseman. Alternating direction adaptive grid generation. In *Proceedings of the 21st AIAA Aerospace Sciences Meeting*, Reno, NV, Jan 1983. (AIAA Paper 83-1937.)

[312] H. C. Elman and M. H. Schultz. Preconditioning by fast direct methods for nonself-adjoint nonseparable elliptic equations. *SIAM Journal on Numerical Analysis*, 23(1):44–57, Feb 1986.

[313] Environmental Molecular Sciences Laboratory. NWChem Web page. Pacific Northwest National Laboratory, Richland, WA. Available at *http://www.emsl.pnl.gov:2080/docs/nwchem/*.

[314] B. Ermentrout. XPPAUT1.61—The differential equations tool. Technical report. Department of Mathematics, University of Pittsburgh, Pittsburgh, PA, 1995.

[315] Etnus, LLC. *TotalView Multiprocess Debugger,* Software. Etnos, Framingham, MA, May 1999.

[316] V. Faber and T. A. Manteuffel. Orthogonal error methods. *SIAM Journal on Numerical Analysis*, 24(1):170–187, Feb 1987.

[317] G. Fann and R. Littlefield. Parallel inverse iteration with reorthogonalization. In *Proceedings of the 6th SIAM Conference on Parallel Processing for Scientific Computing*, 409–413, SIAM Philadelphia, PA, 1993.

[318] G. I. Fann, R. J. Littlefield, and D. M. Elwood. Performance of a fully parallel dense real symmetric eigensolver in quantum chemistry applications. In *Proceedings of High Performance*

Computing '95: Simulation Multiconference, 329–336, Society for Computer Simulation, San Diego, CA, 1995.

[319] C. Faure and P. Dutto. Extension of Odyssée to the MPI Library—Direct mode. Rapport de recherche 3715, Institut National de Recherche en Informatique et en Automatique, Voluceau, Rocquencourt, France, 1999.

[320] C. Faure and P. Dutto. Extension of Odyssée to the MPI library—Reverse mode. Rapport de recherche 3774, Institut National de Recherche en Informatique et en Automatique, Voluceau, Rocquencourt, France, 1999.

[321] H. Faure. Discrépance de suites associées à un système de numération (en dimension s). *Acta Arithmetica*, 41(4):337–351, 1982. (French)

[322] D. G. Feitelson, P. F. Corbett, S. J. Baylor, and Y. Hsu. Parallel I/O subsystems in massively parallel supercomputers. *IEEE Parallel and Distributed Technology*, 3(3):33–47, Fall 1995.

[323] E. W. Felten and S. Otto. Coherent parallel C. In G. Fox, ed., *Proceedings of the Third Conference on Hypercube Concurrent Computers and Applications*, 440–450, ACM Press, New York, 1988.

[324] E. Felton and D. McNamee. Improving the performance of message-passing applications by multithreading. In *Proceedings of the 1992 Scalable High Performance Computing Conference*, 84–89, IEEE Computer Society Press, Los Alamitos, CA, 1992.

[325] J. Feo, S. Kahan, and Z. Wu. Crash analysis on the Tera MTA. *IEEE Computational Science & Engineering*, 5(4):53–59, Oct–Dec 1998.

[326] A. Ferrari and V. S. Sunderam. TPVM: Distributed Concurrent Computing with Lightweight Processes. Technical Report CSTR-940802. University of Virginia, Knoxville, 1994.

[327] R. Ferreira, T. Kurc, M. Beynon, C. Chang, A. Sussman, and J. Saltz. Object-relational queries into multidimensional databases with the active data repository. *Parallel Processing Letters*, 9(2):173–195, Jun 1999.

[328] R. Ferrell and E. Bertschinger. Particle-mesh methods on the Connection Machine. *International Journal of Modern Physics C*, 5(6):933–956, Dec 1994.

[329] M. C. Ferris and O. L. Mangasarian. Parallel constraint distribution. *SIAM Journal on Optimization*, 1(4):487–500, 1991.

[330] M. C. Ferris and O. L. Mangasarian. Parallel variable distribution. *SIAM Journal on Optimization*, 4(4):815–832, 1994.

[331] M. Feyereisen, G. Fitzgerald, and A. Komornicki. Use of approximate integrals in ab initio theory: An application in MP2 energy calculations. *Chemical Physics Letters*, 208(5–6):359–363, Jun 1993.

[332] FFTW software Web page. Available at *http://www.fftw.org/*.

[333] Fibre Channel Industry Association (FCIA) Web page. Available at *http://www.fibrechannel .com.*

[334] C. M. Fiduccia and R. M. Mattheyses. A linear-time heuristic for improving network partitions. In *Proceedings of the 19th IEEE Design Automation Conference*, 174–181, IEEE, 1982.

[335] S. A. Fineberg, P. Wong, B. Nitzberg, and C. Kuszmaul. PMPIO—A portable implementation of MPI-IO. In *Proceedings of the Sixth Symposium on the Frontiers of Massively Parallel Computation*, 188–195, IEEE Computer Society Press, Los Alamitos, CA, 1996.

[336] S. J. Fink, S. B. Baden, and S. R. Kohn. Flexible communication mechanisms for dynamic structured applications. In *Proceedings of the Third International Workshop on Parallel Algorithms for Irregularly Structured Problems*, 203–215, Springer-Verlag, Berlin, 1996.

[337] D. S. Fisher, K. Dahmen, S. Ramanathan, and Y. Ben-Zion. Statistics of earthquakes in simple models of heterogeneous faults. *Physical Review Letters*, 78(25):4885–4888, Jun 1997.

[338] H. Flatt and K. Kennedy. Performance of parallel processors. *Parallel Computing*, 12(1):1–20, Oct 1989.

[339] R. Fletcher. Conjugate gradient methods for indefinite systems. In G. A. Watson, ed., *Numerical Analysis Dundee 1975*, 73–89, Springer-Verlag, New York, 1976.

[340] M. Flynn. Very high speed computing systems. *Proceedings of the IEEE*, 1901–1909, Dec 1966.

[341] I. Foster. *Designing and Building Parallel Programs: Concepts and Tools for Parallel Software Engineering*. Addison-Wesley, Reading, MA, 1995. (Also available at *http://www.mcs.anl.gov /dbpp/*.)

[342] I. Foster. The Grid: A new infrastructure for 21st century science. *Physics Today*, 55(2):42–47, Feb 2002.

[343] I. Foster, J. Insley, G. von Laszewski, C. Kesselman, and M. Thiebaux. Distance visualization: Data exploration on the Grid. *Computer*, 32(12):36–43, Dec 1999.

[344] I. Foster and C. Kesselman. Globus: A metacomputing infrastructure toolkit. *International Journal of Supercomputer Applications*, 11(2):115–128, Summer 1997.

[345] I. Foster and C. Kesselman, eds. *The Grid: Blueprint for a New Computing Infrastructure*. Morgan Kaufmann, San Francisco, 1999.

[346] I. Foster, C. Kesselman, and S. Tuecke. The Nexus approach to integrating multithreading and communication. *Journal of Parallel and Distributed Computing*, 37(1):70–82, Aug 1996.

[347] I. Foster, C. Kesselman, and S. Tuecke. The anatomy of the Grid: Enabling scalable virtual organizations. *The International Journal of High Performance Computing Applications*, 15(3):200–222, 2001. (Also available at *www.globus.org/research/papers/anatomy.pdf*.)

[348] I. Foster, D. R. Kohr Jr., R. Krishnaiyer, and A. Choudhary. Double standards: Bringing task parallelism to HPF via the Message Passing Interface. In *Proceedings of Supercomputing '96*, ACM Press, New York, 1996.

[349] I. Foster, D. R. Kohr Jr., R. Krishnaiyer, and A. Choudhary. A library-based approach to task parallelism in a data-parallel language. *Journal of Parallel and Distributed Computing*, 45(2):148–158, Sep 1997.

[350] I. Foster and S. Taylor. *Strand: New Concepts in Parallel Programming*. Prentice-Hall, Englewood Cliffs, NJ, 1990.

[351] B. L. Fox. Algorithm 647: Implementation and relative efficiency of quasirandom sequence generators. *ACM Transactions on Mathematical Software*, 12(4):362–376, Dec 1986.

[352] G. Fox. Lectures on Numerical Relativity for Computational Science Class: Detailed Discussion of Numerical Formulation and Solution of Collision of Two Black Holes, 1996. Available at *http://old-npac.ucs.indiana.edu/users/gcf/cps713nr96/index.html*.

[353] G. Fox, S.-H. Ko, M. Pierce, O. Balsey, J. Kim, S. Oh, X. Rao, M. Varank, H. Bulut, G. Gunduz, X. Qiu, S. Pallickara, A. Uyar, and C. Youn. Grid services for earthquake science. *Concurrency and Computation: Practice and Experience*, 14(6–7):371–393, May-June, 2002.

[354] G. Fox and W. Furmanski. High-performance commodity computing. In C. Kesselman and I. Foster, eds., *The Grid: Blueprint for a New Computing Infrastructure*, Morgan Kaufmann, San Francisco, 1998.

[355] G. C. Fox, W. Furmanski, H. T. Ozdemir, and S. Pallickara. High performance commodity computing on the pragmatic object Web. In *Technology Assessment Report for RCI, Ltd.*, RCI, Toronto, Canada, Oct 1998. Available at *http://www.new-npac.org/users/fox/documents/rcihpccoct98/rcinpacpaperoct98.html*.

[356] G. Fox, S. Hiranandani, K. Kennedy, C. Koelbel, U. Kremer, C.-W. Tseng, and M. Wu. The Fortran D Language Specification. Technical Report TR90-141. Department of Computer Science, Rice University, Houston, TX, Dec 1990.

[357] G. Fox, K. Hurst, A. Donnellan, and J. Parker. Introducing a new paradigm for computational earth science—A Web-object-based approach to earthquake simulations. In J. Rundle, D. Turcotte, and W. Klein, eds., *GeoComplexity and the Physics of Earthquakes*, 219–245, American Geophysical Union, Washington, DC, 2000.

[358] G. C. Fox, R. D. Williams, and P. C. Messina. *Parallel Computing Works!* Morgan Kaufmann, San Francisco, 1994.

[359] J. G. F. Francis. The QR transformation: A unitary analogue to the LR transformation—Part 1. *The Computer Journal*, 4(3):265–271, Oct. 1961.

[360] J. G. F. Francis. The QR transformation—Part 2. *The Computer Journal*, 4(4):332–345, Jan 1962.

[361] M. J. Friedman and E. J. Doedel. Numerical computation and continuation of invariant manifolds connecting fixed points. *SIAM Journal on Numerical Analysis*, 28(3):789–808, Jun 1991.

[362] M. Frigo and S. G. Johnson. The fastest Fourier transform in the west. Technical Report MIT-LCS-TR-728. Laboratory for Computer Science, Massachusetts Institute of Technology, Cambridge, MA, Sep 1997.

[363] T. R. Furlani and H. F. King. Implementation of a parallel direct SCF algorithm on distributed memory computers. *Journal of Computational Chemistry*, 16(1):91–104, Jan 1995.

[364] H. Gabow. Data structures for weighted matching and nearest common ancestors with linking. In *Proceedings of the First Annual ACM-SIAM Symposium on Discrete Algorithms*, 434–443, SIAM, Philadelphia, PA, 1990.

[365] A. Gabrielov, W. Newman, and L. Knopoff. Lattice models of failure: Sensitivity to the local dynamics. *Physical Review E*, 50(1):188–197, Jul 1994.

[366] D. Gaitonde and J. S. Shang. Optimized compact-difference-based finite-volume schemes for linear wave phenomena. *Journal of Computational Physics*, 138(2):617–643, Dec 1997.

[367] N. Galbreath, W. Gropp, and D. Levine. Applications-driven parallel I/O. In *Proceedings of Supercomputing '93*, 462–471, ACM Press, New York, 1993.

[368] E. Gamma, R. Helm, R. Johnson, and J. Vlissides. *Design Patterns: Elements of Reusable Object-Oriented Software*. Addison-Wesley, Reading, MA, 1995.

[369] I. L. Garzón and J. Jellinek. Melting of gold microclusters. *Zeitschrift für Physik D*, 20(1–4):235–238, 1991.

[370] Gateway Project Web page. Available at *http://www.osc.edu*.

[371] A. Geist, A. Beguelin, J. Dongarra, W. Jiang, B. Manchek, and V. Sunderam. *PVM: Parallel Virtual Machine—A Users' Guide and Tutorial for Network Parallel Computing*. MIT Press, Cambridge, MA, 1994.

[372] G. A. Geist and C. H. Romine. LU factorization algorithms on distributed-memory multiprocessor architectures. *SIAM Journal on Scientific and Statistical Computing*, 9(4):639–649, 1988.

[373] General Earthquake Models (GEM) Web page. Available at *http://milhouse.jpl.nasa.gov/gem/*.

[374] A. George and J. W.-H. Liu. *Computer Solution of Large Sparse Positive Definite Systems*. Prentice-Hall, Englewood Cliffs, NJ, 1981.

[375] K. Gharachorloo, D. Lenoski, J. Laudon, P. Gibbons, A. Gupta, and J. Hennessy. Memory consistency and event ordering in scalable shared-memory multiprocessors. In *Proceedings of the 17th Annual Symposium on Computer Architecture (17th ISCA'90)*, 15–26, Seattle, Jun 1990. IEEE Computer Society Press, Los Alamitos, CA, 1990.

[376] G. A. Gibson, D. P. Nagle, K. Amiri, F. W. Chang, E. Feinberg, H. Gobioff, C. Lee, B. Ozceri, E. Riedel, and D. Rochberg. A Case for Network-Attached Secure Disks. Technical Report CMU-CS-96-142. Carnegie-Mellon University, Pittsburgh, PA, Jun 1996.

[377] R. Giering. *Tangent Linear and Adjoint Model Compiler, Users Manual 1.2*, 1997. (TAMC 5.2 available at *http://puddle.mit.edu/~ralf/tamc*.)

[378] R. Giering and T. Kaminski. Recipes for adjoint code construction. *ACM Transactions on Mathematical Software*, 24(4):437–474, Dec 1998.

[379] J. R. Gilbert, G. L. Miller, and S. H. Teng. Geometric mesh partitioning: Implementation and experiments. In *Proceedings of the 9th International Parallel Processing Symposium*, 418–427, IEEE Computer Society Press, Los Alamitos, CA, 1995.

[380] J. R. Gilbert and E. Zmijewski. A parallel graph partitioning algorithm for a message-passing multiprocessor. *International Journal of Parallel Programming*, 16(6):427–449, Dec 1987.

[381] Global Array Toolkit. Web page. Available at *http://www.emsl.pnl.gov:2080/docs/global/ga.html*.

[382] The Global File System. Web page. Available at *http://www.sistina.com/gfs*.

[383] Globus Metacomputing Toolkit. Web page. Available at *http://www.globus.org*.

[384] T. Goehring and Y. Saad. Heuristic Algorithms for Automatic Graph Partitioning. Technical Report UMSI-94-29. University of Minnesota Supercomputing Institute, Minneapolis, MN, 1994.

[385] S. Goil, S. Aluru, and S. Ranka. Concatenated parallelism: A technique for efficient parallel divide and conquer. In *Proceedings of the 8th Symposium of Parallel and Distributed Processing*, IEEE Computer Society Press, Los Alamitos, CA, 1996.

[386] D. E. Goldberg. *Genetic Algorithms in Search, Optimizations and Machine Learning*. Addison-Wesley, Reading, MA, 1989.

[387] G. H. Golub and R. Underwood. The block Lanczos method for computing eigenvalues. In J. R. Rice, ed., *Mathematical Software III*, 361–377, Academic Press, New York, 1977.

[388] R. J. Gomez and E. C. Ma. Validation of a large scale Chimera grid system for space shuttle launch vehicle. In *Proceedings of the 12th AIAA Applied Aerodynamics Conference*, Colorado Springs, CO, Jun 1994. (Also available as AIAA Paper 94-1859.)

[389] R. C. Gonzalez and R. E. Woods. *Digital Image Processing*. Addison-Wesley, Reading, MA, 1992.

[390] J. R. Goodman. Cache Consistency and Sequential Consistency. Technical Report 61. IEEE Scalable Coherence Interface Working Group, Mar 1989. (Also available as Technical Report TR #1006, Computer Sciences Department, University of Wisconsin, Madison.)

[391] W. J. Gordon and L. C. Thiel. Transfinite mappings and their application to grid generation. In J. F. Thompson, ed., *Numerical Grid Generation,* North-Holland, Amsterdam, 1982.

[392] K. Gorlen, S. Orlow, and P. Plexico. *Data Abstraction and Object-Oriented Programming in C++.* John Wiley & Sons, New York, 1990.

[393] D. Gottlieb and S. A. Orszag. *Numerical Analysis of Spectral Methods: Theory and Applications.* SIAM, Philadelphia, PA, 1977.

[394] An introduction to GPFS 1.2. IBM. Available at *http://www.almaden.ibm.com/cs/gpfs.html.*

[395] S. L. Graham, P. B. Kessler, and M. K. McKusick. gprof: A call graph execution profiler. In *Proceedings of the SIGPLAN '82 Symposium on Compiler Construction,* 120–126, ACM Press, New York, 1982.

[396] P. M. Gresho and R. L. Sani. *Incompressible Flow and the Finite Element Method*: *Advection-Diffusion and Isothermal Laminas Flow.* John Wiley & Sons, New York, 1998.

[397] Grid Computing Environments Research Group. Computing Portals Web page. Available at *http://www.computingportals.org.*

[398] Grid Forum. Web page. Available at *http://www.gridforum.org/.*

[399] A. Griewank. Achieving logarithmic growth of temporal and spatial complexity in reverse automatic differentiation. *Optimization Methods and Software,* 1(1):35–54, May 1992.

[400] A. Griewank and G. F. Corliss, eds. *Automatic Differentiation of Algorithms: Theory, Implementation, and Application.* SIAM, Philadelphia, PA, 1991.

[401] A. Griewank, D. Juedes, and J. Utke. Algorithm 755: ADOL-C, a package for the automatic differentiation of algorithms written in C/C++. *ACM Transactions on Mathematical Software,* 22(2):131–167, Jun 1996.

[402] A. Griewank and A. Walther. Treeverse: An Implementation of Checkpointing for the Reverse or Adjoint Mode of Computational Differentiation. Preprint IOKOMO-04-1997, Technische Universitat, Dresden, 1997.

[403] A. Griewank and P. L. Toint. On the unconstrained optimization of partially separable functions. In M. J. D. Powell, ed., *Nonlinear Optimization, 1981,* 301–312, Academic Press, London, 1981.

[404] R. G. Grimes, J. G. Lewis, and H. D. Simon. A shifted block Lanczos algorithm for solving sparse symmetric generalized eigenproblems. *SIAM Journal on Matrix Analysis and Applications,* 15(1):228–272, 1994.

[405] W. Gropp, S. Huss-Lederman, A. Lumsdaine, E. Lusk, B. Nitsberg, W. Saphir, and M. Snir. *MPI—The Complete Reference: Volume 2, The MPI Extensions.* MIT Press, Cambridge, MA, 1998.

[406] W. Gropp, E. Lusk, and A. Skjellum. *Using MPI: Portable Parallel Programming with the Message-Passing Interface,* 2nd ed. MIT Press, Cambridge, MA, 1999.

[407] W. Gropp, E. Lusk, and R. Thakur. *Using MPI-2: Advanced Features of the Message-Passing Interface.* MIT Press, Cambridge, MA, 1999.

[408] W. D. Gropp, D. K. Kaushik, D. Keyes, and B. F. Smith. Toward realistic performance bounds for implicit CFD codes. In A. Ecer *et al.*, eds., *Proceedings of Parallel CFD '99*, Elsevier Science, New York and Amsterdam, 1999.

[409] W. Gropp, D. Keyes, L. C. McInnes, and M. D. Tidriri. Globalized Newton–Krylov–Schwarz algorithms and software for parallel implicit CFD. *The International Journal of High Performance Computing Applications*, 14(2):102–136, Summer 2000. (Also available as ICASE-TR98-24, August 1998.)

[410] L. Grosz. VECFEM—VECtorized Finite Element Method, Version 3. Web page. Available at *http://www.rz.uni-karlsruhe.de/Uni/RZ/Forschung/Numerik/vecfem/index_old.html.*

[411] M. F. Guest, E. Aprà, D. E. Bernholdt, H. A. Früchtl, R. J. Harrison, R. A. Kendall, R. A. Kutteh, X. Long, J. B. Nicholas, J. A. Nichols, H. L. Taylor, A. T. Wong, G. I. Fann, R. J. Littlefield, and J. Nieplocha. High performance computational chemistry: NWChem and fully distributed parallel algorithms. In J. J. Dongarra, J. S. Kowalik, L. Grandinetti, and G. R. Joubert, eds., *High Performance Computing: Technology, Methods, and Applications*, 395–427, Elsevier, Amsterdam, 1995.

[412] M. F. Guest, E. Aprà, D. E. Bernholdt, H. A. Früchtl, R. J. Harrison, R. A. Kendall, R. A. Kutteh, X. Long, J. B. Nicholas, J. A. Nichols, H. L. Taylor, A. T. Wong, G. I. Fann, R. J. Littlefield, and J. Nieplocha. Advances in parallel distributed data software; computational chemistry and NWChem. In J. Wasniewski, J. Dongarra, and K. Madsen, eds., *Applied Parallel Computing. Computations in Physics, Chemistry and Engineering Science*, 278–294, Springer-Verlag, Heidelberg, 1996.

[413] M. F. Guest, E. Aprà, D. E. Bernholdt, H. A. Fruchtl, R. J. Harrison, R. A. Kendall, R. A. Kutteh, X. Long, J. B. Nicholas, J. A. Nichols, H. L. Taylor, A. T. Wong, G. I. Fann, R. J. Littlefield, and J. Nieplocha. High-performance computing in chemistry: NWChem. *Future Generation Computer Systems*, 12(4):273–289, Dec 1996.

[414] M. F. Guest, E. Aprà, D. E. Bernholdt, H. A. Früchtl, R. J. Harrison, R. A. Kendall, R. A. Kutteh, J. B. Nicholas, J. A. Nichols, M. S. Stave, A. T. Wong, R. J. Littlefield, and J. Nieplocha. High performance computational chemistry: Towards fully distributed parallel algorithms. In A. M. Tentner, ed., *Proceedings of the 1995 Simulation Multiconference—High Performance Computing 1995: Grand Challenges in Computer Simulation*, 511–521, Society for Computer Simulation, San Diego, CA, 1995.

[415] A. Gupta. Fast and effective algorithms for graph partitioning and sparse matrix ordering. *IBM Journal of Research and Development*, 41(1/2):171–183, Jan–Mar 1997.

[416] A. Gupta, G. Karypis, and V. Kumar. Highly scalable parallel algorithms for sparse matrix factorization. *IEEE Transactions on Parallel and Distributed Systems*, 8(5):502–520, May 1997.

[417] M. Gupta, S. Midkiff, E. Schonberg, V. Seshadri, D. Shields, K. Wang, W. M. Ching, and T. Ngo. An HPF compiler for the IBM SP2. In *Proceedings of Supercomputing '95*, ACM Press, New York, Dec 1995.

[418] J. L. Gustafson. Reevaluating Amdahl's Law. *Communications of the ACM*, 31(5):532–533, May 1988.

[419] H. Haberland, ed. *Clusters of Atoms and Molecules*. Springer-Verlag, Heidelberg, 1994.

[420] W. Hackbusch. *Multi-Grid Methods and Applications*. Springer-Verlag, Heidelberg and New York, 1985.

[421] W. S. Haddad, I. McNulty, J. E. Trebes, E. H. Anderson, R. A. Levesque, and L. Yang. Ultra high resolution X-ray tomography. *Science*, 266:1213–1215, Nov 1994.

[422] L. A. Hageman and D. M. Young. *Applied Iterative Methods*. Academic Press, New York, 1981.

[423] W. W. Hager and Y. Krylyuk. Graph partitioning and continuous quadratic programming. *SIAM Journal on Discrete Mathematics*, 12(4):500–523, 2000.

[424] W. W. Hager, S. C. Park, and T. A. Davis. Block exchange in graph partitioning. In P. M. Pardalos, ed., *Approximation and Complexity in Numerical Optimization: Continuous and Discrete Problems*, 298–307, Kluwer, Dordrecht, The Netherlands, 2000.

[425] M. J. Hagger and L. Stals. DOUG: Domain Decomposition on Unstructured Grids. Web page. Available at *http://www.maths.bath.ac.uk/~parsoft/doug/*.

[426] B. D. Hahn. *Essential MATLAB for Scientists and Engineers*. Arnold, London, and Wiley, New York, 1997.

[427] K. M. Hall. An *r*-dimensional quadratic placement algorithm. *Management Science*, 17(3):219–229, Nov 1970.

[428] M. W. Hall, J. Mellor-Crummey, A. Carle, and R. Rodriguez. FIAT: A framework for interprocedural analysis and transformation. In *Proceedings of the Sixth International Workshop on Languages and Compilers for Parallel Computing*, 522–545, Springer-Verlag, Berlin, 1993.

[429] M. W. Hall, B. R. Murphy, S. P. Amarasinghe, S. Liao, and M. S. Lam. Interprocedural analysis or parallelization. In *Proceedings of the Eighth Workshop on Language and Compilers for Parallel Computing*, 61-80, Springer-Verlag, Berlin, 1995.

[430] W. F. Hall, V. Shankar, and S. Palaniswamy. Algorithmic aspects of wave propagation through stretched unstructured cells for problems in computational electromagnetics. In *Proceedings of the 13th AIAA Computational Fluid Dynamics Conference*, Snowmass Village, CO, Jun–Jul 1997. (Also available as AIAA Paper 97-2089.)

[431] J. H. Halton. On the efficiency of certain quasi-random sequences of points in evaluating multi-dimensional integrals. *Numerische Mathematik*, 2:84–90, 1960.

[432] L. Hamel, P. Hatcher, and M. Quinn. An optimizing C* compiler for a hypercube multicomputer. In J. Saltz and P. Mehrotra, eds., *Languages, Compilers, and Run-Time Environments for Distributed Memory Machines*, North-Holland, Amsterdam, 1992.

[433] E.-H. Han, G. Karypis, and V. Kumar. Scalable parallel data mining for association rules. In *Proceedings of the 1997 ACM–SIGMOD International Conference on Management of Data*, 277–288, ACM Press, New York, 1997. (Also available as Technical Report, Department of Computer Science, University of Minnesota, Minneapolis, 1997.)

[434] E.-H. Han, G. Karypis, and V. Kumar. Scalable parallel data mining for association rules. *IEEE Transactions on Knowledge and Data Engineering*, 12(3):337–352, May/Jun 2000. (Also available at *http://dlib.computer.org/tk/books/tk2000/pdf/k0337.pdf*.)

[435] The Hard Disk Drive Guide. Web page. Available at *http://www.storagereview.com*.

[436] R. Harrington. Origin and development of the method of moments for field computation. *IEEE Antennas and Propagation Magazine*, 32(3):31–35 Jun 1990.

[437] F. E. Harris, H. J. Monkhorst, and D. L. Freeman. *Algebraic and Diagrammatic Methods in Many-Fermion Theory*. Oxford University Press, New York, 1992.

[438] J. Harris, J. M. Bircsak, M. R. Bolduc, J. A. Diewald, I. Gale, N. W. Johnson, S. Lee, C. A. Nelson, and C. D. Offner. Compiling High Performance Fortran for distributed-memory systems. *Digital Technical Journal*, 7(3):5–23, Dec 1995.

[439] R. J. Harrison, M. F. Guest, R. A. Kendall, D. E. Bernholdt, A. T. Wong, M. Stave, J. L. Anchell, A. C. Hess, R. R. Littlefield, G. I. Fann, J. Nieplocha, G. S. Thomas, D. Elwood, J. L. Tilson, R. L. Shepard, A. F. Wagner, I. T. Foster, E. Lusk, and R. Stevens. High performance computational chemistry. II. A scalable SCF program. *Journal of Computational Chemistry*, 17:124–132, Jan 1996.

[440] R. J. Harrison, J. A. Nichols, T. P. Straatsma, M. Dupuis, E. J. Bylaska, G. I. Fann, T. L. Windus, E. Apra, J. Anchell, D. Bernholdt, P. Borowski, T. Clark, D. Clerc, H. Dachsel, B. de Jong, M. Deegan, K. Dyall, D. Elwood, H. Früchtl, E. Glendenning, M. Gutowski, A. Hess, J. Jaffe, B. Johnson, J. Ju, R. Kendall, R. Kobayashi, R. Kutteh, Z. Lin, R. Littlefield, X. Long, B. Meng, J. Nieplocha, S. Niu, M. Rosing, G. Sandrone, M. Stave, H. Taylor, G. Thomas, J. van Lenthe, K. Wolinski, A. Wong, and Z. Zhang. *NWChem, A Computational Chemistry Package for Parallel Computers, Version 4.0*. Pacific Northwest National Laboratory, Richland, WA, 2000.

[441] S. Hauck and G. Borriello. An evaluation of bipartitioning technique s. In *Proceedings of the Sixteenth Conference on Advanced Research in VLSI*, IEEE Computer Society Press, Los Alamitos, CA, 1995.

[442] T. Haupt, E. Akarsu, and G. Fox. Landscape Management System: A WebFlow Application. Technical report. Engineering Research and Development Center, U.S. Army Corps of Engineers, University of Mississippi, Vicksburg, Aug 1999. (Available at *http://www.new-npac.org/users/fox/documents/LMSERDCC425/C425LMSrep2.html*.)

[443] T. Haupt, E. Akarsu, G. Fox, and W. Furmanski. Web based metacomputing, 1999. Future Generation Computing Systems, 15(5–6):735–743, Oct 1999.

[444] T. Haupt, E. Akarsu, G. Fox, A. Kalinichenko, K.-S. Kim, P. Sheethalnath, and C.-H. Youn. The Gateway system: Uniform Web based access to remote resources. In *Proceedings of High-Performance Computing and Networking '99*, Amsterdam, Apr 1999.

[445] T. Haupt, E. Akarsu, G. Fox, A. Kalinichenko, K.-S. Kim, P. Sheethalnath, and C.-H. Youn. The Gateway system: Uniform Web based access to remote resources. In *Proceedings of the ACM 1999 Conference on Java Grande*, 1–7, ACM Press, New York, 1999.

[446] M. E. Hayder, D. E. Keyes, and P. Mehrotra. A comparison of the PETSc library and HPF implementations of an archetypal PDE computation. *Advances in Engineering Software*, 29(3–6):415–424, Apr–Jul 1998.

[447] E. F. Hayes et al. Report of the Task Force of the Future of the NSF Supercomputer Centers Program. Report nsf 9646, National Science Foundation, Washington, DC, Sep 1995. Available at *http://www.nsf.gov/pubs/1996/nsf9646.htm*.

[448] M. Heath and J. A. Etheridge. Visualizing the performance of parallel programs. *IEEE Software*, 8(5):29–39, Sep 1991.

[449] M. T. Heath and P. Raghavan. A Cartesian parallel nested dissection algorithm. *SIAM Journal on Matrix Analysis and Applications*, 16(1):235–253, Jan 1995.

[450] M. T. Heath. *Scientific Computing: An Introductory Survey*. McGraw-Hill, New York, 1997.

[451] G. Heber, R. Biswas, and G. R. Gao. Self-avoiding walks over adaptive unstructured grids. *Concurrency: Practice and Experience*, 12(2-3):85–109, Feb–Mar 2000.

[452] R. D. Henderson. Unstructured Spectral Element Methods: Parallel Algorithms and Simulations. PhD diss., Princeton University, 1994.

[453] R. D. Henderson. Details of the drag curve near the onset of vortex shedding. *Physics of Fluids*, 7(9):2102–2104, Sep 1995.

[454] R. D. Henderson. Nonlinear dynamics and pattern formation in turbulent wake transition. *Journal of Fluid Mechanics*, 352:65–112, Dec 1997.

[455] B. Hendrickson. Graph partitioning and parallel solvers: Has the emperor no clothes? In A. Ferreira, J. Rolim, H. Simon, and S.-H. Teng, eds., *Proceedings of the Fifth International Symposium on Solving Irregularly Structured Problems in Parallel*, 218–225, Springer-Verlag, Heidelberg and New York, 1998.

[456] B. Hendrickson and T. G. Kolda. Graph partitioning models for parallel computing. *Parallel Computing*, 26(12):1519–1534, Nov 2000.

[457] B. Hendrickson and T. G. Kolda. Partitioning rectangular and structurally nonsymmetric sparse matrices for parallel processing. *SIAM Journal on Scientific Computing*, 21(6):2048–2072, 2000.

[458] B. Hendrickson and R. Leland. The Chaco User's Guide, Version 2.0. Technical Report SAND 94-2692. Sandia National Laboratories, Albuquerque, NM, 1994.

[459] B. Hendrickson and R. Leland. An improved spectral graph partitioning algorithm for mapping parallel computations. *SIAM Journal on Scientific Computing*, 16(2):452–469, Mar 1995.

[460] B. Hendrickson and R. Leland. A multilevel algorithm for partitioning graphs. In *Proceedings of Supercomputing '95*, ACM Press, New York, 1995.

[461] B. A. Hendrickson. The Molecule Problem: Determining Conformation from Pairwise Distances. PhD diss., Cornell University, 1991.

[462] B. Hendrickson. The molecule problem: Exploiting structure in global optimization. *SIAM Journal on Optimization*, 5(4):835–857, 1995.

[463] W. D. Henshaw, D. L. Brown, and D. J. Quinlan. Overture: An object-oriented framework for solving partial differential equations on overlapping grids. In *Proceedings of the SIAM Workshop on Object Oriented Methods for Inter-Operable Scientific and Engineering Computing*, 215–224, SIAM, Philadelphia, PA, 1999.

[464] V. Herrarte and E. Lusk. Studying Parallel Program Behavior with Upshot. Technical Report ANL-91/15. Argonne National Laboratory, Argonne, IL, 1991.

[465] J. L. Hess. Panel methods in computational fluid dynamics. *Annual Reviews of Fluid Mechanics*, 22:255–274, 1990.

[466] J. L. Hess and M. O. Smith. Calculation of potential flows about arbitrary bodies. In D. Küchemann, ed., *Progress in Aeronautical Sciences, Volume 8*, Pergamon Press, Oxford and New York, 1967.

[467] M. R. Hestenes and E. Stiefel. Methods of conjugate gradients for solving linear systems. *Journal of Research of the National Bureau of Standards*, 49:409–436, 1952.

[468] High Performance Fortran Forum. High Performance Fortran language specification. *Scientific Programming*, 2(1–2):1–170, Spring–Summer 1993. (Also available as CRPC-TR92225.)

[469] D. Hilbert. Über die stetige Abbildung einer Linie auf ein Flachenstuck. *Math Annalen*, 38, 1891.

[470] J. M. D. Hill, B. McColl, D. C. Stefanescu, M. W. Goudreau, K. Lang, S. B. Rao, T. Suel, T. Tsantilas, and R. H. Bisseling. BSPlib: The BSP programming library. *Parallel Computing*, 24(14):1947–1980, Dec 1998.

[471] K. C. Hill, M. I. Sancer, and S. Bindiganavale. Assessment of development of fast CEM solvers. In *Proceedings of the 29th Plasmadynamics and Lasers Conference*, Albuquerque, NM, Jun 1998. (AIAA Paper 98-2474.)

[472] W. D. Hillis. *The Connection Machine*. MIT Press, Cambridge, MA, 1985.

[473] W. D. Hillis and G. L. Steele, Jr. Data parallel algorithms. *Communications of the ACM*, 29(12):1170–1183, Dec 1986.

[474] A. Hindmarsh et al. PVODE. Lawrence Livermore National Laboratory, Berkeley, CA. (See SUNDIALS web page, available at *http://www.llnl.gov/CASC/Sundials/*)

[475] S. Hiranandani, K. Kennedy, and C.-W. Tseng. Compiling Fortran D for MIMD distributed-memory machines. *Communications of the ACM*, 35(8):66–80, Aug 1992.

[476] M. R. Hoare. Structure and dynamics of simple microclusters. *Advances in Chemical Physics*, 40:49–135, 1979.

[477] M. R. Hoare and J. McInnes. Statistical mechanics and morphology of very small atomic clusters. *Faraday Discussions of Chemical Society*, 61:12–24, 1976.

[478] M. R. Hoare and P. Pal. Statistics and stability of small assemblies of atoms. *Journal of Crystal Growth*, 17:77–96, 1972.

[479] R. W. Hockney and J. W. Eastwood. *Computer Simulation Using Particles*. A. Hilger, Philadelphia, PA, 1988.

[480] R. W. Hockney and C. R. Jesshope. *Parallel Computers*. Adam Hilger Ltd., Bristol, UK, 1981.

[481] P. Holmes, J. L. Lumley, and G. Berkooz. *Turbulence, Coherent Structures, Dynamical Systems, and Symmetry*. Cambridge University Press, Cambridge, 1996.

[482] R. Hornung and S. Kohn. The use of object-oriented design patterns in the SAMRAI structured AMR framework. In *Proceedings of the SIAM Workshop on Object-Oriented Methods for Interoperable Scientific and Engineering Computing*, 235–244, SIAM, Philadelphia, PA, 1999.

[483] R. D. Hornung and S. R. Kohn. The use of object-oriented design patterns in the SAMRAI structured AMR framework. In *Proceedings of the SIAM Workshop on Object-Oriented Methods for Interoperable Scientific and Engineering Computing*, Yorktown Heights, NY, Oct 1998. (Also available as Lawrence Livermore National Laboratory Technical Report UCRL-JC-131825.)

[484] G. Horton. A multi-level diffusion method for dynamic load balancing. *Parallel Computing*, 19(2):209–218, Feb 1993.

[485] P. D. Hough, T. G. Kolda, and V. J. Torczon. Asynchronous parallel pattern search for nonlinear optimization. *SIAM Journal on Scientific Computing*, 23(1):134–156, Jun 2001.

[486] P. D. Hough and J. C. Meza. A Class of Trust-Region Methods for Parallel Optimization. Technical Report TR SAND 98-8245. Sandia National Laboratory, Albuquerque, NM, 1998.

[487] E. Houstis, J. Rice, and A. Hadjidimos. Parallel ELLPACK Research Project. Web page. Available at *http://www.cs.purdue.edu/research/cse/pellpack/*.

[488] E. N. Houstis, J. R. Rice, S. Weerawarana, A. C. Catlin, P. Papachiou, K. Y. Wang, and M. Gaitatzes. PELLPACK: A problem solving environment for PDE-based applications on multicomputer platforms. *ACM Transactions on Mathematical Software*, 24(1):30–73, Mar 1998.

[489] E. N. Houstis, S. B. Kim, S. Markus, P. Wu, N. E. Houstis, A. C. Catlin, S. Weerawarana, and T. S. Papatheodorou. Parallel ELLPACK elliptic PDE solvers. In *Proceedings of INTEL Supercomputer Users' Group Conference*, Albuquerque, NM, 1995.

[490] E. N. Houstis and J. R. Rice. The engineering of modern interfaces for PDE solvers. In E. N. Houstis, J. R. Rice, and R. Vichnevetsky, eds., *Proceedings of the Symbolic Computation: Applications to Scientific Computing*, 89–94, North-Holland, Amsterdam, 1992.

[491] P. Hovland. Automatic Differentiation of Parallel Programs. PhD diss., University of Illinois at Urbana-Champaign, 1997.

[492] Y. F. Hu and R. J. Blake. An improved diffusion algorithm for dynamic load balancing. *Parallel Computing*, 25(4):417–444, Apr 1999.

[493] Y. F. Hu, R. J. Blake, and D. R. Emerson. An optimal migration algorithm for dynamic load balancing. *Concurrency: Practice and Experience*, 10(6):467–483, May 1998.

[494] J. Huber, A. A. Chien, C. L. Elford, D. S. Blumenthal, and D. A. Reed. PPFS: A high performance portable parallel file system. In *Proceedings of the 9th International Conference on Supercomputing*, 385–394, 1995, ACM Press, New York, 1995.

[495] D. Hunt. Advanced performance features of the 64-bit PA-8000. In *Proceedings of the 40th IEEE International Computer Conference: Technologies for the Information Superhighway*, 123–128, IEEE Computer Society Press, Los Alamitos, CA, Mar 1995.

[496] P. Husbands and C. Isbell. The parallel problems server. In *Proceedings of the 1998 MIT Student Workshop on High-Performance Computing in Science and Engineering*, 1998. (Also available as MIT-LCS-TR-737.)

[497] S. A. Hutchinson, J. N. Shadid, and R. S. Tuminaro. Aztec User's Guide, Version 1.1. Technical Report SAND 95-1559. Sandia National Laboratories, Albuquerque, NM, 1995.

[498] IEEE Standard for Scalable Coherent Interface (SCI), 1596-1992, 1992.

[499] IEEE. IEEE P1003.1c/D10: Draft Standard for Information Technology—Portable Operating Systems Interface (POSIX), Sep 1994.

[500] IEEE. IEEE/ANSI Standard 1003.1: Portable Operating System Interface (POSIX)—Part 1: System Application Program Interface (API) [C Language], 1996.

[501] C. S. Ierotheou, S. P. Johnson, M. Cross, and P. F. Leggett. Computer aided parallelization tools (CAPTools)—Conceptual overview and performance on the parallelization of structured mesh codes. *Parallel Computing*, 22(2):163–195, Apr 1996.

[502] IGES/PDES Organization. *Initial Graphics Exchange Specification (IGES), Version 5.3*. National Computer Graphics Association, Fairfax, VA, 1995.

[503] InfiniBand Trade Association. Web page. Available at *http://www.infinibandta.org/home*.

[504] INMOS Ltd. *occam Programming Manual*. Prentice-Hall, Englewood Cliffs, NJ, 1984.

[505] Intel Corporation. *IA-32 Intel Architecture Software Developer's Manual, Volume 3: System Programming Guide (Preliminary)*, 2000.

[506] E. Isaacson and H. B. Keller. *Analysis of Numerical Methods*. John Wiley & Sons, New York, 1966.

[507] Y. Ishikawa, A. Hori, H. Tezuka, M. Matsuda, H. Konaka, M. Maeda, T. Tomokiyo, and J. Nolte. MPC++. In G. V. Wilson and P. Lu, eds., *Parallel Programming Using C++*, 429–464, MIT Press, Cambridge, MA, 1996.

[508]   A. K. Jain. *Fundamentals of Digital Image Processing*. Prentice-Hall, Englewood Cliffs, NJ, 1989.

[509]   A. Jameson, T. J. Baker, and N. P. Weatherill. Calculation of inviscid transonic flow over a complete aircraft. In *Proceedings of the 24th AIAA Aerospace Sciences Meeting*, Reno, NV, Jan 1986. (AIAA Paper 86-0103.)

[510]   K. Jansen and R. Sommer. O(a) improvement of lattice QCD with two flavors of Wilson quarks. *Nuclear Physics B*, B530(1–2):185–203, Oct 1998.

[511]   S. C. Jaume and L. R. Sykes. Changes in state of stress on the southern San Andreas Fault resulting from the California earthquake sequence of April to June 1992. *Science*, 258:1325–1328, Nov 1992.

[512]   Java Grande Forum. Available at *http://www.javagrande.org*.

[513]   D. Jefferson, B. Beckman, F. Wieland, L. Blume, M. DiLoreto, P. Hontalas, P. Laroche, K. Sturdevant, J. Tupman, V. Warren, J. Wedel, H. Younger, S. Bellenot. Distributed simulation and the Time Warp operating system. In *Proceedings of the 11th ACM Symposium on Operating Systems Principles*, ACM Press, New York, 1987.

[514]   J. Jellinek. Theoretical dynamical studies of metal clusters and cluster-ligand systems. In N. Russo, ed., *Metal-Ligand Interactions: Structure and Reactivity*. Kluwer, Dordrecht, 1995.

[515]   A. Jennings and G. M. Malik. Partial elimination. *Journal of the Institute of Mathematics and Its Applications*, 20(3):307–316, 1977.

[516]   E. Johnson, D. Gannon, and P. Beckman. HPC++: Experiments with the parallel standard template library. In *Proceedings of the 11th International Conference on Supercomputing*, 124–131, ACM Press, New York, 1997.

[517]   W. Johnston, D. Gannon, and B. Nitzberg. Grids as production computing environments: The engineering aspects of NASA's information power grid. In *Proceedings of the Eighth IEEE International Symposium on High Performance Distributed Computing*, 197–204, IEEE Computer Society Press, Los Alamitos, CA, 1999. Available at *http://www.computer.org/proceedings/hpdc /0287/0287toc.html*.

[518]   M. T. Jones and P. E. Plassmann. An efficient parallel iterative solver for large sparse linear systems. In A. George, J. Gilbert, and J. W.-H. Liu, eds., *Graph Theory and Sparse Matrix Computation*, 229–245, Springer, New York, 1993.

[519]   M. T. Jones and P. E. Plassmann. Parallel solution of unstructured, sparse systems of linear equations. In R. F. Sincovec, D. E. Keyes, M. R. Leuze, L. R. Petzold, and D. A. Reed, eds., *Proceedings of the Sixth SIAM Conference on Parallel Processing for Scientific Computing*, 471–475, SIAM, Philadelphia, PA, 1993.

[520]   M. T. Jones and P. E. Plassmann. Scalable iterative solution of sparse linear systems. *Parallel Computing*, 20(5):753–773, May 1994.

[521]   M. T. Jones and P. E. Plassmann. Algorithm 740: Fortran subroutines to compute improved incomplete Cholesky factorizations. *ACM Transactions on Mathematical Software*, 21(1):18–19, 1995.

[522]   M. T. Jones and P. E. Plassmann. An improved incomplete Cholesky factorization. *ACM Transactions on Mathematical Software*, 21(1):5–17, Mar 1995.

[523]   P. W. Jones. First- and second-order conservative remapping schemes for grids in spherical coordinates. *Monthly Weather Review*, 127(9):2204–2210, Sep 1999.

[524] T. Jones, R. Mark, J. Martin, J. May, E. Pierce, and L. Stanberry. An MPI-IO interface to HPSS. In *Proceedings of the Fifth NASA Goddard Conference on Mass Storage Systems*, I:37–50, College Park, MD, Sep 1996. (Also available at *http://esdis-it.gsfc.nasa.gov/MSST/conf1996.html*.)

[525] H. F. Jordan. The Force. In L. H. Jamieson, D. B. Gannon, and R. J. Douglass, eds., *The Characteristics of Parallel Algorithms*, MIT Press, Cambridge, MA, 1987.

[526] M. V. Joshi, E.-H. Han, G. Karypis, and V. Kumar. Efficient parallel algorithms for mining associations. In M. J. Zaki and C.-T. Ho, eds., *Lecture Notes in Computer Science: Lecture Notes in Artificial Intelligence (LNCS/LNAI)*, Vol. 1759, Springer-Verlag, Heidelberg, 2000.

[527] M. V. Joshi, G. Karypis, and V. Kumar. ScalParC: A new scalable and efficient parallel classification algorithm for mining large datasets. In *Proceedings of the International Parallel Processing Symposium*, 573–579, IEEE Computer Society Press, Los Alamitos, CA, 1998.

[528] M. V. Joshi, G. Karypis, and V. Kumar. Universal Formulation of Sequential Patterns. Technical Report TR-99-021. Department of Computer Science, University of Minnesota, Minneapolis, 1999.

[529] B. Kågström, P. Ling, and C. Van Loan. Portable high performance GEMM-based Level 3 BLAS. In *Proceedings of the Sixth SIAM Conference on Parallel Processing for Scientific Computing*, 339–346, SIAM, Philadelphia, 1993.

[530] K. L. Karavanic and B. P. Miller. Improving online performance diagnosis by use of historical performance data. In *Proceedings of Supercomputing '99*, ACM Press, New York, Nov 1999.

[531] G. E. Karniadakis, M. Israeli, and S. A. Orszag. High-order splitting methods for the incompressible Navier–Stokes equations. *Journal of Computational Physics*, 97(2):414–443, Dec 1991.

[532] G. E. Karniadakis and S. J. Sherwin. *Spectral/hp Element Methods for CFD*. Oxford University Press, New York, 1999.

[533] G. E. Karniadakis and G. S. Triantafyllou. Three-dimensional dynamics and transition to turbulence in the wake of bluff objects. *Journal of Fluid Mechanics*, 238:1–30, May 1992.

[534] A. H. Karp. Bit reversal on uniprocessors. *SIAM Review*, 38(1):1–26, Mar 1996.

[535] J. Karty, D. Car, K. Jacobs, R. Pearlman, J. Roedder, and T. Blalock. The HyPACED code: A new generation of hybrid analysis for electromagnetics. In *Proceedings of the 29th Plasmadynamics and Lasers Conference*, Albuquerque, NM, Jun 1998. (Also available as AIAA Paper 98-2473.)

[536] W. Karush. An iterative method for finding characteristics vectors of a symmetric matrix. *Pacific Journal of Mathematics*, 1:233–248, 1951.

[537] G. Karypis and V. Kumar. Analysis of multilevel graph partitioning. In *Proceedings of Supercomputing '95*, ACM Press, New York, Dec 1995.

[538] G. Karypis and V. Kumar. A fast and high quality multilevel scheme for partitioning irregular graphs. *SIAM Journal on Scientific Computing*, 20(1):359–392, 1998. (Also available at *http://www.cs.umn.edu/~karypis*; a short version appears in *Proceedings of the International Conference on Parallel Processing*, 1995.)

[539] G. Karypis and V. Kumar. HMETIS 1.5: A Hypergraph Partitioning Package. Technical report. Department of Computer Science, University of Minnesota, Minneapolis, 1998. (Also available at *http://www.users.cs.umn.edu/~karypis/metis*.)

[540] G. Karypis and V. Kumar. METIS 4.0: Unstructured Graph Partitioning and Sparse Matrix Ordering System. Technical report. Department of Computer Science, University of Minnesota, Minneapolis, 1998. (Also available at *http://www.users.cs.umn.edu/~karypis/metis*.)

[541] G. Karypis and V. Kumar. Multilevel algorithms for multi-constraint graph partitioning. In *Proceedings of Supercomputing '98*, IEEE Computer Society Press, Los Alamitos, CA, 1998.

[542] G. Karypis and V. Kumar. Multilevel k-way partitioning scheme for irregular graphs. *Journal of Parallel and Distributed Computing*, 48(1):96–129, Jan 1998. (Also available at *http://www.cs.umn.edu/~karypis*.)

[543] G. Karypis and V. Kumar. A parallel algorithm for multilevel graph partitioning and sparse matrix ordering. *Journal of Parallel and Distributed Computing*, 48(1):71–95, Jan 1998. (Also available at *http://www.cs.umn.edu/~karypis*.)

[544] G. Karypis and V. Kumar. A fast and high quality multilevel scheme for partitioning irregular graphs. *SIAM Journal on Scientific Computing*, 20(1):359–392, 1999. (Also available as Technical Report TR 95-035, Department of Computer Science, University of Minnesota, 1995, and at *http://www.cs.umn.edu/~karypis*; a short version appears in *Proceedings of the International Conference on Parallel Processing*, 1995.)

[545] G. Karypis and V. Kumar. Multilevel k-way hypergraph partitioning. In *Proceedings of the 36th ACM/IEEE Design Automation Conference*, 343–348, ACM Press, New York, 1999.

[546] G. Karypis and V. Kumar. Parallel multilevel k-way partitioning scheme for irregular graphs. *SIAM Review*, 41(2):278–300, 1999.

[547] G. Karypis, K. Schloegel, and V. Kumar. ParMETIS 1.0: Parallel Graph Partitioning and Sparse Matrix Ordering Library. Technical Report TR-97-060, Department of Computer Science, University of Minnesota, 1997. (Also available at *http://www.users.cs.umn.edu/~karypis/metis*.)

[548] D. K. Kaushik, D. Keyes, and B. F. Smith. On the interaction of architecture and algorithm in the domain-based parallelization of an unstructured grid incompressible flow code. In J. Mandel et al., ed., *Proceedings of the 10th International Conference on Domain Decomposition Methods*, 311–319, Wiley, New York, 1997.

[549] D. K. Kaushik, D. Keyes, and B. F. Smith. Newton–Krylov–Schwarz methods for aerodynamic problems: Compressible and incompressible flows on unstructured grids. In C.-H. Lai et al., ed., *Proceedings of the 11th International Conference on Domain Decomposition Methods*, Domain Decomposition Press, Bergen, 1999.

[550] K. Keahey and D. Gannon. PARDIS: A parallel approach to CORBA. In *Proceedings of the Sixth IEEE Symposium on High Performance Distributed Computing*, 31–39, IEEE Computer Society Press, Los Alamitos, CA, 1997.

[551] J. Keasler. Partitioning challenges in ALE3D, 1999. Lecture presented at Workshop on Graph Partitioning and Applications: Current and Future Directions, Army High Performance Computer Research Center, University of Minnesota, Minneapolis, 1999.

[552] P. Keleher, A. Cox, and W. Zwaenepoel. Lazy release consistency for software distributed shared memory. In *Proceedings of the 19th International Symposium on Computer Architecture*, 13–21, ACM Press, New York, 1992.

[553] H. B. Keller. Practical procedures in path following near limit points. In R. Glowinsky and J. L. Lions, eds., *Computing Methods in Applied Sciences and Engineering, V*, 177–183, North-Holland, Amsterdam, 1982.

[554] H. B. Keller. The bordering algorithm and path following near singular points of higher nullity. *SIAM Journal on Scientific and Statistical Computing*, 4(4):573–582, Dec 1983.

[555] H. B. Keller. A rank theory for differential algebraic equations. In *Proceedings of the International Symposium on Differential Equations and Their Applications*, Oct 1999.

[556] H. B. Keller and H. von Sosen. New methods in CFD: DAE and RPM. In *Proceedings of the First Asian CFD Conference*, 1995.

[557] R. A. Kendall, E. Aprà, D. E. Bernholdt, E. J. Bylaska, M. Dupuis, G. I. Fann, R. J. Harrison, J. Ju, J. A. Nichols, J. Nieplocha, T. P. Straatsma, T. L. Windus, and A. T. Wong. High performance computational chemistry: An overview of NWChem, a distributed parallel application. *Computer Physics Communications*, 128(1–2):260–283, 2000. (Available at *http://www.elsevier.nl/gej-ng/10/15/40/58/25/43/article.pdf* .)

[558] R. A. Kendall and H. A. Früchtl. The impact of the resolution of the identity approximate integral method on modern ab initio algorithm development. *Theoretical Chemistry Accounts*, 97(1–4):158–163, Oct 1997.

[559] K. Kennedy. Telescoping languages: A compiler strategy for implementation of high-level domain-specific programming systems. In *Proceedings of the 14th International Parallel and Distributed Processing Symposium 2000*, 297–304, IEEE Computer Society Press, Los Alamitos, CA, 2000.

[560] B. W. Kernighan and S. Lin. An efficient heuristic procedure for partitioning graphs. *The Bell System Technical Journal*, 49(2):291–307, Feb 1970.

[561] R. A. Kerr. Forecasters learning to read a hurricane's mind. *Science*, 284(5414):563–565, Apr 1999.

[562] D. S. Kershaw. The incomplete Cholesky–conjugate gradient method for the iterative solution of systems of linear equations. *Journal of Computational Physics*, 26(1):43–65, Jan 1978.

[563] D. Keyes. Personal communication. 1998.

[564] D. E. Keyes, A. Sameh, and V. Venkatakrishnan, eds. *Parallel Numerical Algorithms*. Kluwer, Dordrecht, 1997. (Papers from the workshop held in Hampton, VA, May 23–25, 1994.)

[565] Khoros Web page. Available at *http://www.khoral.com/khoros/*.

[566] S. Klasky. Lectures on Numerical Relativity for Computational Science Class: Binary Black Hole Collision, 1996. Available at *http://old-npac.ucs.indiana.edu/users/gcf/slitex/bbhklasky /index.html*.

[567] S. Klasky, T. Haupt, and G. Fox. MPI HPF and DAGH for Parallelization of Black Hole Codes, 1997. Available at *http://old-npac.ucs-indiana.edu/users/gcf/bbhdaghhpfmar97/index.html*. (Also appears as "Is Message Passing Obsolete?" in *Proceedings of the 1997 SIAM Workshop*, Minneapolis, MN, March 1997.)

[568] P. Klosowski, M. Koennecke, J. Z. Tischler, and R. Osborn. NeXus: A common format for the exchange of neutron and synchrotron data. *Physica B*, 241–243:151–153, Dec. 1997.

[569] C. Koelbel, D. B. Loveman, R. S. Schreiber, G. L. Steele Jr., and M. E. Zosel. *The High Performance Fortran Handbook*. MIT Press, Cambridge, MA, 1993.

[570] S. Kohn, X. Garaiza, R. Hornung, and S. Smith. SAMRAI: Structured Adaptive Mesh Refinement Applications Infrastructure. Lawrence Livermore National Laboratory, Berkeley, CA. Available at *http://www.llnl.gov/CASC/SAMRAI*.

[571] J. F. Koksma. Een algemeene stelling uit de theorie der gelijkmatige verdeeling modulo 1. *Mathematica B (Zutphen)*, 11:7–11, 1942/43.

[572] T. G. Kolda and V. J. Torczon. On the convergence of asynchronous parallel pattern search. 2002.

[573] A. E. Koniges, ed. *Industrial Strength Parallel Computing*. Morgan Kaufmann, San Francisco, 2000.

[574] R. P. Koomullil, B. K. Soni, and H. Chih-Ti. Navier–Stokes simulation on hybrid grids. In *Proceedings of the 34th AIAA Aerospace Sciences Meeting*, Reno, NV, Jan 1996. (Also available as AIAA Paper 96-767.)

[575] J. Kostrowicki, L. Piela, B. J. Cherayil, and H. A. Scheraga. Performance of the diffusion equation method in searches for optimum structures of clusters of Lennard–Jones atoms. *Journal of Physical Chemistry*, 95(10):4113–4119, May 1991.

[576] J. Kostrowicki and H. A. Scheraga. Application of the diffusion equation method for global optimization to oligopeptides. *Journal of Physical Chemistry*, 96(18):7442–7449, Sep 1992.

[577] D. Kotz. Applications of Parallel I/O, Release 1. Technical Report PCS-TR96-297. Department of Computer Science, Dartmouth College, Hanover, NH, Oct 1996. (Also available at *http://www.cs.dartmouth.edu/reports/abstracts/TR96-297*.)

[578] D. Kotz. Introduction to multiprocessor I/O architecture. In R. Jain, J. Werth, and J. C. Browne, eds., *Input/Output in Parallel and Distributed Computer Systems*, 97–123, Kluwer Dordrecht, 1996.

[579] D. Kotz. Disk-directed I/O for MIMD multiprocessors. *ACM Transactions on Computer Systems*, 15(1):41–74, Feb 1997.

[580] D. Kranz, K. Johnson, A. Agarwal, J. Kubiatowicz, and B.-H. Lim. Integrating message-passing and shared-memory: Early experience. In *Proceedings of the Fourth ACM SIGPLAN Symposium on Principles and Practice of Parallel Programming*, 54–63, ACM Press, New York, 1993.

[581] H. W. Kroto, J. R. Heath, S. C. O'Brien, R. F. Curl, and R. E. Smalley. C_{60}: Buckminsterfullerene. *Nature*, 318(6042):162–163, Nov 1985.

[582] D. Kuck, R. Kuhn, B. Leasure, and M. J. Wolfe. Analysis and transformation of programs for parallel computation. In *Proceedings of COMPSAC 80, the 4th International Computer Software and Applications Conference*, 709–715, IEEE, New York, 1980.

[583] D. Kuck, R. Kuhn, D. Padua, B. Leasure, and M. J. Wolfe. Dependence graphs and compiler optimizations. In *Proceedings of the 8th ACM SIGPLAN-SIGACT Symposium on the Principles of Programming Languages*, 207–218, AMC Press, New York, 1981.

[584] R. Kufrin. Decision trees on parallel processors. In J. Geller, H. Kitano, and C. B. Suttner, eds., *Parallel Processing for Artificial Intelligence 3*, Elsevier Science, Amsterdam and New York, 1997.

[585] V. Kumar, A. Grama, A. Gupta, and G. Karypis. *Introduction to Parallel Computing: Design and Analysis of Algorithms*. Addison-Wesley, Reading, MA, 1994.

[586] T. Kurc, C. Chang, R. Ferreira, A. Sussman, and J. Saltz. Querying very large multi-dimensional datasets in ADR. In *Proceedings of Supercomputing '99*, ACM Press, New York, 1999.

[587] T. Kurc, A. Sussman, and J. Saltz. Coupling multiple simulations via a high performance customizable database system. In *Proceedings of the Ninth SIAM Conference on Parallel Processing for Scientific Computing*, SIAM, Philadelphia, PA, 1999.

[588] Y. A. Kuznetsov and V. V. Levitin. CONTENT, A Multiplatform Continuation Environment. Technical report. CWI Amsterdam, 1996.

[589] J. Lakos. *Large-Scale C++ Software Design*. Addison-Wesley, Reading, MA, 1996.

[590] L. Lamport. How to make a multiprocessor computer that correctly executes multiprocess programs. *IEEE Transactions on Computers*, C-28(9):690–691, Sep 1979.

[591] Z. Lan, V. Taylor, and G. Bryan. Dynamic load balancing for adaptive mesh refinement. In *Proceedings of the 30th International Conference on Parallel Processing*, Sep 2001.

[592] Z. Lan, V. Taylor, and G. Bryan. Dynamic load balancing of SAMR applications on distributed systems. In *Proceedings of Supercomputing 2001*, Nov 2001. Available at *www.supercomp.org*.

[593] L. D. Landau and E. M. Lifshitz. *Fluid Mechanics*. Pergamon Press, London, and Addison-Wesley, Reading, MA, 1959.

[594] J. Larson. Cray X-MP hardware performance monitor. *Cray Channels*, 1985.

[595] C. L. Lawson, R. J. Hanson, D. R. Kincaid, and F. T. Krogh. Basic linear algebra subprograms for Fortran usage. *ACM Transactions on Mathematical Software*, 5(3):308–323, Sep 1979.

[596] W. Lee, M. H. Noh, and M. F. Wheeler. Air-water flow simulation in unsaturated porous media. In *Proceedings of the XIII International Conference on Computational Methods in Water Resources*, 93–100, A. A. Balkema, Rotterdam, 2000.

[597] R. B. Lehoucq. Analysis and Implementation of an Implicitly Restarted Iteration. PhD diss., Rice University, Houston, TX, 1995. (Also available as CAAM TR95-13.)

[598] R. B. Lehoucq and A. G. Salinger. Large-Scale Eigenvalue Calculations for Stability Analysis of Steady Flows on Massively Parallel Computers. Technical report. Department of Applied Mathematics, Computer Science Division, Sandia National Laboratory, Albuquerque, NM, Jun 1999.

[599] R. B. Lehoucq and J. A. Scott. An Evaluation of Software for Computing Eigenvalues of Sparse Nonsymmetric Matrices. Preprint MCS-P547-1195. Argonne National Laboratory, Argonne, IL, 1996.

[600] R. B. Lehoucq and D. C. Sorensen. Deflation techniques for an implicitly restarted Arnoldi iteration. *SIAM Journal on Matrix Analysis and Applications*, 17(4):789–821, Oct 1996.

[601] R. B. Lehoucq, D. C. Sorensen, and C. Yang. *ARPACK Users' Guide: Solution of Large Scale Eigenvalue Problems with Implicitly Restarted Arnoldi Methods*. SIAM, Philadelphia, PA, 1998.

[602] F. T. Leighton. *Introduction to Parallel Algorithms and Architectures: Arrays, Trees, Hypercubes*. Morgan Kaufmann, San Mateo, CA, 1992.

[603] S. K. Lele. Compact finite difference schemes with spectral-like resolution. *Journal of Computational Physics*, 103(1):16–42, Nov 1992.

[604] D. Lenoski, J. Laudon, K. Gharachorloo, W.-D. Weber, A. Gupta, J. Hennessy, M. Horowitz, and M. S. Lam. The Stanford Dash multiprocessor. *Computer*, 25(3):63–79, Mar 1992.

[605] M. Lentini and H. B. Keller. Boundary value problems over semi-infinite intervals and their numerical solution. *SIAM Journal on Numerical Analysis*, 17(4):557–604, Aug 1980.

[606] R. J. Le Veque. *Numerical Methods for Conservation Laws*, 2nd ed. Birkhäuser, Basel, 1992.

[607] R. M. Lewis and V. Torczon. Pattern Search Algorithms for Bound Constrained Minimization. Technical Report ICASE TR 96-20. Institute for Computer Applications in Science and Engineering, NASA Langley Research Center, Hampton, VA, 1996.

[608] R. M. Lewis and V. Torczon. Rank Ordering and Positive Bases in Pattern Search Algorithms. Technical Report ICASE TR 96-71. Institute for Computer Applications in Science and Engineering, NASA Langley Research Center, Hampton, VA, Dec 1996.

[609] R. M. Lewis and V. J. Torczon. A Globally Convergent Augmented Lagrangian Pattern Search Algorithm for Optimization with General Constraints and Simple Bounds. Technical Report ICASE TR 98-31. Institute for Computer Applications in Science and Engineering, NASA Langley Research Center, Hampton, VA, Jul 1998.

[610] R. M. Lewis and V. J. Torczon. Pattern Search Methods for Linearly Constrained Minimization. Technical Report ICASE TR 98-3. Institute for Computer Applications in Science and Engineering, NASA Langley Research Center, Hampton, VA, Jan 1998.

[611] K. Li. Shared virtual memory on loosely coupled multiprocessors. In *Proceedings IEEE CS 1986, International Conference on Computer Languages*, 98–106, Oct 1986.

[612] X. S. Li. Sparse Gaussian Elimination on High Performance Computers. PhD diss., University of California at Berkeley, 1996.

[613] Z. Li and H. A. Scheraga. Monte Carlo approach to the multiple-minima problem in protein folding. In *Proceedings of the National Academy of Sciences*, 84(19):6611–6615, 1987.

[614] J. S. Lim. *Two-Dimensional Signal and Image Processing*. Prentice-Hall, Englewood Cliffs, NJ 1990.

[615] H. Ling, R. C. Chou, and S. W. Lee. Shooting and bouncing rays: Calculating the RCS of an arbitrarily shaped cavity. *IEEE Transactions on Antennas and Propagation*, 37(2):194–205, Feb 1988.

[616] P.-L. Lions. On the Schwarz alternating method. I. In R. Glowinski, G. H. Golub, G. Meurant, and J. Periaux, eds., *Proceedings of the First International Symposium on Domain Decomposition Methods for Partial Differential Equations*, 1–42, SIAM, Philadelphia, PA, 1988.

[617] R. Lippmann. An introduction to computing with neural nets. *IEEE ASSP Magazine*, 4(22), Apr 1987.

[618] R. J. Lipton, D. J. Rose, and R. E. Tarjan. Generalized nested dissection. *SIAM Journal on Numerical Analysis*, 16(2):346–358, Apr 1979.

[619] R. J. Lipton and R. E. Tarjan. A separator theorem for planar graphs. *SIAM Journal on Applied Mathematics*, 36(2):177–189, Apr 1979.

[620] R. J. Lipton and R. E. Tarjan. A separator theorem for planar graphs. *SIAM Journal on Applied Mathematics*, 36:177–189, 1979.

[621] J.-L. Liu and S.-J. Su. A potential gridless solution method for the compressible Euler/Navier–Stokes equations. In *Proceedings of the 34th AIAA Aerospace Sciences Meeting*, Reno, NV, Jan 1996. (AIAA Paper 96-0526.)

[622] J. W.-H Liu and A. H. Sherman. Comparative analysis of the Cuthill–McKee and the reverse Cuthill–McKee ordering algorithms for sparse matrices. *SIAM Journal on Numerical Analysis*, 13(2):198–213, Apr 1973.

[623] R. Lohner and J. R. Cebral. Parallel advancing front grids generation. In *Proceedings of the 8th International Meshing Round Table*, 67–74, South Lake Tahoe, CA, Oct 1999.

[624]   R. Lohner and P. Parikh. Generation of three-dimensional unstructured grid by the advancing-front method. *International Journal for Numerical Methods in Fluids*, 8(10):1135–1149, Oct 1988.

[625]   Los Alamos National Laboratory. POOMA: Parallel Object-Oriented Methods and Applications. Available at *http://www.acl.lanl.gov/pooma*.

[626]   P. Love. Bifurcations in Kolmogorov and Taylor-Vortex Flows. PhD diss., California Institute of Technology, 1998. (Also available as Caltech CRPC TR-98-2.)

[627]   P. Love and H. B. Keller. Bifurcations from Kolmogorov flow. 2002.

[628]   R. A. Luettich, J. J. Westerink, and N. W. Scheffner. ADCIRC: An Advanced Three-Dimensional Circulation Model for Shelves, Coasts, and Estuaries. Technical report, Department of the Army, U.S. Army Corps of Engineers, Washington, DC, 1991.

[629]   R. A. Luettich, J. J. Westerink, and N. W. Scheffner. ADCIRC: An Advanced Three-Dimensional Circulation Model for Shelves, Coasts, and Estuaries. Report 1: Theory and methodology of ADCIRC-2DDI and ADCIRC-3DL. Technical report, DRP-92-6, U.S. Army Corps of Engineers, Waterways Experiment Station Vicksburg, MS.

[630]   M. Lüscher, S. Sint, R. Sommer, and P. Weisz. Chiral symmetry and O(a) improvement in lattice QCD. *Nuclear Physics B*, B478(1–2):365–397, Oct 1996.

[631]   M. Lüscher, S. Sint, R. Sommer, P. Weisz, and U. Wolff. Non-perturbative O(a) improvement of lattice QCD. *Nuclear Physics B*, B491(1–2):323–343, Apr 1997.

[632]   M. Lüscher, S. Sint, R. Sommer, and H. Wittig. Non-perturbative determination of the axial current normalization constant in O(a) improved lattice QCD. *Nuclear Physics B*, B491(1–2):344–361, Apr 1997.

[633]   M. Lutz. *Programming Python*. O'Reilly & Associates, Sebastopol, CA, 1996.

[634]   T. M. Madhyashtha and D. A. Reed. Exploiting global input/output access pattern classification. In *Proceedings of Supercomputing '97*, ACM Press, New York, 1997.

[635]   T. M. Madhyastha and D. A. Reed. Intelligent, adaptive file system policy selection. In *Proceedings of the Sixth Symposium on the Frontiers of Massively Parallel Computation*, 172–179, IEEE Computer Society Press, Los Alamitos, CA, 1996.

[636]   M. Makowski. Methodology and a Modular Tool for Multiple Criteria Analysis of LP Models. Technical Report IIASA WP-94-102. International Institute for Applied Systems Analysis, Laxenburg, Austria, Dec 1994.

[637]   A. D. Malony, J. L. Larson, and D. A. Reed. Tracing application program execution on the Cray X-MP and Cray 2. In *Proceedings of Supercomputing '90*, 60–73, IEEE Computer Society Press, Los Alamitos, CA, 1990.

[638]   A. D. Malony and D. A. Reed. Models for performance perturbation analysis. In *Proceedings of the ACM/ONR Workshop on Parallel and Distributed Debugging*, 15–25, ACM Press, New York, and Office of Naval Research, Arlington VA, 1991.

[639]   A. D. Malony, D. A. Reed, and D. C. Rudolph. Integrating performance data collection, analysis, and visualization. In M. Simmons and R. Koskela, eds., *Parallel Computer Systems: Performance Instrumentation and Visualization*, 73–97, Addison-Wesley Reading, MA, 1990.

[640]   A. D. Malony, D. A. Reed, and H. A. G. Wijshoff. Performance measurement intrusion and perturbation analysis. *IEEE Transactions on Parallel and Distributed Systems*, 3(4):433–450, Jul 1992.

[641]   A. Malony, B. Mohr, P. Beckman, D. Gannon, S. Yang, F. Bodin, and S. Kesavan. Implementing a parallel C++ runtime system for scalable parallel systems. In *Proceedings of Supercomputing '93*, 588–597, ACM Press, New York 1993.

[642]   M. E. Maltrud, R. D. Smith, A. J. Smith, A. J. Semtner, and R. C. Malone. Global eddy-resolving ocean simulations driven by 1985–1995 atmospheric winds. *Journal of Geophysical Research*, 103 (C13):30825–30853, Dec 1998.

[643]   T. A. Manteuffel. Adaptive procedure for estimating parameters for the nonsymmetric Tchebychev iteration. *Numerische Mathematik*, 31(2):183–208, 1978.

[644]   T. A. Manteuffel. An incomplete factorization technique for positive definite linear systems. *Mathematics of Computation*, 34(150):473–497, Apr 1980.

[645]   M. J. Marchant and N. P. Weatherill. The construction of nearly orthogonal multiblock grids for compressible flow simulation. *Communications in Numerical Methods in Engineering*, 9(7):567–578, Jul 1993.

[646]   D. L. Marcum. Generation of unstructured grids for viscous flow applications. In *Proceedings of the 33rd AIAA Aerospace Sciences Meeting and Exhibit*, Reno, NV, Jan 1995. (Also available as AIAA Paper 95-0212.)

[647]   B. Marsolf, S. Kosanovich, D. Andersh, and J. Hughes. Large scale multidisciplinary electromagnetics computations. In *Proceedings of the 29th Plasmadynamics and Lasers Conference*, Albuquerque, NM, Jun 1998. (Also available as AIAA Paper 98-2475.)

[648]   M. Mascagni and A. Karaivanova. Matrix computations using quasirandom sequences. In *Proceedings of the Second International Conference on Numerical Analysis and Applications*, 2000.

[649]   M. Mascagni and A. Karaivanova. A quasi-Monte Carlo method for computing external eigenvalues. In *Proceedings of the 2000 International Conference on Parallel and Distributed Processing Techniques and Applications (PDPTA'00)*, 2000.

[650]   M. Mascagni and A. Karaivanova. What are quasirandom numbers and are they good for anything besides integration? In *Proceedings of the Advances in Reactor Physics and Mathematics and Computation into the Next Millennium (PHYSOR2000)*, 2000.

[651]   M. Mascagni and A. Srinivasan. Algorithm 806: SPRNG: A scalable library for pseudorandom number generation. *ACM Transactions on Mathematical Software*, 26(3):436–461, Sep 2000.

[652]   R. A. Matzner, M. F. Huq, and D. Shoemaker. Initial data and coordinates for multiple black hole systems. *Physical Review D*, 59:24015/1-6, Jan 1999.

[653]   R. A. Matzner. Computational black holes. In V. Gorini, ed., *Proceedings of the First SIGRAV Graduate School in Contemporary Relativity and Gravitational Physics*, Institute of Physics Press, Villa Olmo, Como, Italy, Apr 1998.

[654]   R. Matzner et al. Binary Black Hole Grand Challenge Alliance Web page, 2000. Available at *http://old-npac.ucs.indiana.edu/projects/bh/*.

[655]   C. Mavriplis. Nonconforming Discretizations and A Posteriori Error Estimates for Adaptive Spectral Element Techniques. PhD diss., Massachusetts Institute of Technology, 1989.

[656]   C. Mavriplis. Adaptive mesh strategies for the spectral element method. *Computer Methods in Applied Mechanics and Engineering*, 116(1–4):77–86, 1994.

[657]   J. M. May. *Parallel I/O for High Performance Computing*. Morgan Kaufmann, San Francisco, CA, 2001.

[658] W. J. McCroskey, J. D. Beader, R. L. Meakin, V. Raghavan, and G. R. Srinivasan. Aerodynamics and acoustics of rotorcraft. In *Proceedings of the NAS Technical Summary, Numerical Aerodynamic Simulation Program*, Mar 1992–Feb 1993.

[659] J. McGraw, S. Skedzielewski, S. Allan, R. Oldenhoeft, J. Glauert, C. Kirkham, W. Noyce, and R. Thomas. SISAL: Streams and Iteration in a Single Assignment Language: Language Reference Manual. Technical Report M-146. Lawrence Livermore National Laboratory, Berkeley, CA, Mar 1985.

[660] R. Meakin. A DoD CHSSI core project: Scalable implementations of dynamic Chimera methods for unsteady aerodynamics. In *Proceedings of the 4th Symposium on Overset Composite Grid and Solution Technology*, Aberdeen, MD, Sep 1998.

[661] P. Mehrotra, M. Zubair, and K. Maly. Arcade computational portal. Available at *http://www.cs .odu.edu/~ppvm*.

[662] M. Mehta, R. Agrawal, and J. Rissanen. SLIQ: A fast scalable classifier for data mining. In *Proceedings of the Fifth International Conference on Extending Database Technology*, 18–32, Springer-Verlag, Berlin, 1996.

[663] J. A. Meijerink and H. A. van der Vorst. An iterative solution method for linear systems of which the coefficient matrix is a symmetric m-matrix. *Mathematics of Computation*, 31(137):148–162, Jan 1977.

[664] J. Mellor-Crummey, D. Whalley, and K. Kennedy. Improving memory hierarchy performance for irregular applications. In *Proceedings of the 13th International Conference on Supercomputing*, 425–433, ACM Press, New York, 1999.

[665] J. E. Melton, M. J. Berger, M. J. Aftosmis, and M. J. Wong. 3D applications of a Cartesian grid Euler method. In *Proceedings of the 33rd AIAA Aerospace Sciences Meeting*, Reno, NV, Jan 1995. (Also available as AIAA Paper 95-0853.)

[666] C. L. Mendes and D. A. Reed. Integrated compilation and scalability analysis for parallel systems. In *Proceedings of the International Conference on Parallel Architectures and Compilation Techniques (PACT '98)*, 385–392, IEEE Computer Society Press, Los Alamitos, CA, 1998.

[667] P. J. Mercurio, T. T. Elvins, S. J. Young, P. S. Cohen, K. R. Fall, and M. H. Ellisman. The distributed laboratory: An interactive visualization environment for electron microscopy and 3-D imaging. *Communications of the ACM*, 35(6):54–63, Jun 1992.

[668] Message Passing Interface Forum. MPI: A message-passing interface standard. *International Journal of Supercomputer Applications and High Performance Computing*, 8(3/4):165–414, 1994. (Special issue on MPI, also available at *ftp://www.netlib.org/mpi/mpi-report.ps*.)

[669] Message Passing Interface Forum. MPI: A Message-Passing Interface Standard, Version 1.1, Jun 1995. Available at *http://www.mpi-forum.org/docs/docs.html*.

[670] Message Passing Interface Forum. MPI-2: Extensions to the Message-Passing Interface, Jul 1997. Available at *http://www.mpi-forum.org/docs/docs.html*.

[671] Message Passing Interface Forum. MPI-2: A Message Passing Interface standard. *International Journal of High Performance Computing Applications*, 12(1–2):1–299, 1998.

[672] J. C. Meza, T. D. Plantenga, and R. S. Judson. Novel applications of optimization to molecular design. In L. T. Biegler, T. Coleman, A. R. Conn, and F. N. Santosa, eds., *Large-Scale Optimization with Applications, Part III: Molecular Structure and Optimization*, 73–97, Springer, New York, 1997.

[673] D. Michie, D. J. Spiegelhalter, and C. C. Taylor, eds. *Machine Learning, Neural and Statistical Classification*. Ellis Horwood, New York, 1994.

[674] G. L. Miller, S.-H Teng, W. Thurston, and S. A. Vavasis. Automatic mesh partitioning. In A. George, J. R. Gilbert, and J. W.-H. Liu, eds., *Graph Theory and Sparse Matrix Computation*, 57–84, Springer-Verlag, Heidelberg and New York, 1993.

[675] G. L. Miller and S. A. Vavasis. Density graphs and separators. In *Proceedings of the Second Annual ACM–SIAM Symposium on Discrete Algorithms*, 331–336, ACM Press, New York, 1991.

[676] MIMD Lattice Computation (MILC) Collaboration. MILC QCD Code. Available at *http://cliodhna.cop.uop.edu/~hetrick/milc/*.

[677] Molecular Science Computing Facility. Extensible Computational Chemistry Environment Basis Set Database. Environmental Molecular Science Laboratory, Pacific Northwest Laboratory, Richland, WA. Available at *http://www.emsl.pnl.gov:2080/forms/basisform.html*.

[678] B. Monien, R. Preis, and R. Diekmann. Quality Matching and Local Improvement for Multilevel Graph-Partitioning. Technical report. University of Paderborn, Paderborn, Germany, 1999.

[679] G. E. Moore. Cramming more components onto integrated circuits. *Electronics Magazine*, 38(8):114–117, Apr 1965.

[680] J. Moré, B. Walenz, and Z. Wu. Configuration of Large, Confined Ionic Systems by Potential Energy Minimization. Preprint MCS-P627-1296. Mathematics and Computer Science Division, Argonne National Laboratory, Argonne, IL, 1996.

[681] J. J. Moré and Z. Wu. ε-optimal solutions to distance geometry problems via global continuation. In P. M. Pardalos, D. Shalloway, and G. Xue, eds., *Global Minimization of Nonconvex Energy Functions: Molecular Conformation and Protein Folding*, 151–168, American Mathematical Society, Providence, RI, 1995.

[682] J. Moré and Z. Wu. Global Continuation for Distance Geometry Problems. Preprint MCS-P505-0395. Argonne National Laboratory, Argonne, IL, 1995.

[683] J. Moré and Z. Wu. Issues in Large-scale Global Molecular Optimization. Preprint MCS-P539-1095. Argonne National Laboratory, Argonne, IL, 1995.

[684] J. Moré and Z. Wu. Distance Geometry Optimization for Protein Structures. Preprint MCS-P628-1296. Argonne National Laboratory, Argonne, IL, 1996.

[685] J. Moré and Z. Wu. Smoothing techniques for macromolecular global optimization. In G. Di Pillo and F. Giannessi, eds., *Nonlinear Optimization and Applications*, 297–312, Plenum Press, New York, 1996.

[686] R. B. Morgan. On restarting the Arnoldi method for large nonsymmetric eigenvalue problems. *Mathematics of Computation*, 65(215):1213–1230, Jul 1996.

[687] W. J. Morokoff and R. E. Caflisch. A quasi-Monte Carlo approach to particle simulation of the heat equation. *SIAM Journal on Numerical Analysis*, 30(6):1558–1573, Dec 1993.

[688] W. J. Morokoff and R. E. Caflisch. Quasi-Monte Carlo integration. *Journal of Computational Physics*, 122(2):218–230, Dec 1995.

[689] W. J. Morokoff and R. E. Caflisch. Quasi-Monte Carlo simulation of random walks in finance. In *Monte Carlo and Quasi-Monte Carlo Methods 1996*, 340–352, Springer, New York, 1996.

[690] K. W. Morton and D. F. Mayers. *Numerical Solution of Partial Differential Equations*. Press Syndicate of the University of Cambridge, Cambridge, 1994.

[691] B. Moskowitz and R. E. Caflisch. Smoothness and dimension reduction in quasi-Monte Carlo methods. *Mathematical and Computer Modelling*, 23(8/9):37–54, Apr/May 1996.

[692] The MPI-IO Committee. MPI-IO: A Parallel File I/O Interface for MPI, Version 0.5.

[693] MSC Software Corporation. NASTRAN Web page. Available at *http://www.mscsoftware.com /products/products_detail.cfm?S=74&PI=7&M=0*.

[694] S. S. Mudumbai, W. Johnston, M. R. Thompson, A. Essiari, G. Hoo, and K. Jackson. Akenti—A distributed access control system. Available at *http://www-itg.lbl.gov/Akenti*.

[695] D. Musser and A. Saini. *STL Tutorial and Reference Guide*: C++ *Programming with the Standard Template Library*. Addison-Wesley, Reading, MA, 1996.

[696] S. G. Nash and A. Sofer. Block truncated-Newton methods for parallel optimization. *Mathematical Programming*, 45(3, Sep.13):529–546, 1989.

[697] S. G. Nash and A. Sofer. A general-purpose parallel algorithm for unconstrained optimization. *SIAM Journal on Optimization*, 1(4):530–547, 1991.

[698] National Center for Supercomputing Applications. The NCSA HDF Web page: Information, Support, and Software from the Hierarchical Data Format (HDF) Group of NCSA, 1999. Available at *http://hdf.ncsa.uiuc.edu/*.

[699] National HPCC Software Exchange. NHSE Web page. Available at *http://www.nhse.org*.

[700] I. M. Navon and X. Zou. Application of the adjoint model in meteorology. In A. Griewank and G. F. Corliss, eds., *Automatic Differentiation of Algorithms: Theory, Implementation, and Application*, 202–207, SIAM, Philadelphia, PA, 1991.

[701] NCSA Visualization and Virtual Environments group. VisBench and NCSA Visualization Activities. Web page. Available at *http://www.ncsa.uiuc.edu/SCD/Vis/*.

[702] NetCDF Web page. Available at *http://www.unidata.ucar.edu/packages/netcdf*.

[703] J. B. Nicholas, D. E. Bernholdt, and B. P. Hay. On the conformational energetics of tetramethoxycalix[4]arene: RI-MP2 benchmark calculations. *Journal of the American Chemical Society*, 2002. In press.

[704] O. Y. Nickolayev, P. C. Roth, and D. A. Reed. Real-time statistical clustering for event trace reduction. *International Journal of Supercomputer Applications and High Performance Computing*, 11(2):144–159, Summer 1997.

[705] H. Niederreiter. Low-discrepancy and low-dispersion sequences. *Journal of Number Theory*, 30(1):51–70, Sep 1988.

[706] H. Niederreiter. *Random Number Generation and Quasi-Monte Carlo Methods*. SIAM, Philadelphia, PA, 1992.

[707] J. Nieplocha. Private communication.

[708] J. Nieplocha and B. Carpenter. ARMCI: A portable remote memory copy library for distributed array libraries and compiler run-time systems. In J. Rolim, ed., *Parallel and Distributed Processing*, 533–546, Springer-Verlag, Heidelberg, 1999.

[709] J. Nieplocha, I. Foster, and R. Kendall. ChemIO: High-performance parallel I/O for computational chemistry applications. *The International Journal of High Performance Computing Applications*, 12(3):345–363, Fall 1998. (Also available in a special issue on I/O in *Parallel Applications*, 12(3–4)).

[710] J. Nieplocha, R. J. Harrison, and R. J. Littlefield. Global arrays: A portable "shared-memory" programming model for distributed memory computers. In *Proceedings of Supercomputing '94*, 340–349, IEEE Computer Society Press, Los Alamitos, CA, 1994.

[711] J. Nieplocha, R. J. Harrison, and R. J. Littlefield. Global arrays: A nonuniform memory access programming model for high-performance computers. *Journal of Supercomputing*, 10(2):169–189, 1996.

[712] N. Nieuwejaar and D. Kotz. The Galley parallel file system. *Parallel Computing*, 23(4–5):447–476, May 1997.

[713] N. Nieuwejaar, D. Kotz, A. Purakayastha, C. S. Ellis, and M. L. Best. File-access characteristics of parallel scientific workloads. *IEEE Transactions on Parallel and Distributed Systems*, 7(10):1075–1089, Oct 1996.

[714] B. Nitzberg and V. Lo. Collective buffering: Improving parallel I/O performance. In *Proceedings of the Sixth IEEE International Symposium on High Performance Distributed Computing*, 148–157, IEEE Computer Society Press, Los Alamitos, CA, 1997.

[715] J. Nocedal and S. J. Wright. *Numerical Optimization*. Springer-Verlag, New York, 1999.

[716] M. L. Norman and G. L. Bryan. Cosmological adaptive mesh refinement. In S. Miyama and K. Tomisaka, eds., *Numerical Astrophysics*, 19–28, Kluwer, Dordrecht, 1999.

[717] J. A. Northby. Structure and binding of Lennard–Jones clusters: $13 \leq N \leq 147$. *Journal of Chemical Physics*, 87(10):6166–6177, Nov 1987.

[718] B. Nour-Omid, A. Raefsky, and G. Lyzenga. Solving finite element equations on concurrent computers. In A. K. Noor, ed., *Proceedings of the Parallel Computations and Their Impact on Mechanics*, 291–307, American Society of Mechanical Engineers, New York, 1986.

[719] R. W. Numrich and J. K. Reid. Co-Array Fortran for parallel programming. *ACM SIGPLAN Fortran Forum*, 17(2):1–31, Aug 1998.

[720] Object Management Group. Corba Component Model, 2000. Available at *http://www.omg.org/cgi-bin/doc?orbos/97-06-12*.

[721] Object Oriented Concepts, Inc. ORBacus SSL. Available at *http://www.iona.com/products/orbacus_home.htm*.

[722] F. Ogden. CASC2D Code. Engineer Research and Development Center, U.S. Army Corps of Engineers, University of Mississippi, Vicksburg. Available at *http://www.wes.hpc.mil*.

[723] L. Oliker and R. Biswas. PLUM: Parallel load balancing for adaptive unstructured meshes. *Journal of Parallel and Distributed Computing*, 52(2):150–177, Aug 1998.

[724] OpenMP. Sample Program: jacobi.f. *http://www.openmp.org/index.cgi?samples+samples/jacobi.html*.

[725] OpenMP Web page, Oct 1997. Available at *http://www.openmp.org*.

[726] A. V. Oppenheim, R. W. Schafer, and J. R. Buck. *Discrete-Time Signal Processing*. Prentice-Hall, Englewood Cliffs, NJ, 1989.

[727] M. Orešič and D. Shalloway. Hierarchical characterization of energy landscapes using Gaussian packet states. *Journal of Chemical Physics*, 101(11):9844–9857, Dec 1994.

[728] S. A. Orszag and L. C. Kells. Transition to turbulence in plane Poiseuille flow and plane Couette flow. *Journal of Fluid Mechanics*, 96(1):159–205, Jan 1980.

[729] J. P. Ostriker and M. L. Norman. Cosmology of the early universe viewed through the new infrastructure. *Communications of the ACM*, 40(11):84–94, Nov 1997.

[730] C.-W. Ou and S. Ranka. Parallel incremental graph partitioning using linear programming. *Proceedings of Supercomputing '94*, 458–467, IEEE Computer Society Press, Los Alamitos, CA, 1994.

[731] C.-W. Ou, S. Ranka, and G. Fox. Fast and parallel mapping algorithms for irregular problems. *Journal of Supercomputing*, 10(2):119–140, Jun 1996.

[732] P. S. Pacheco. *Parallel Programming with MPI*. Morgan Kaufmann, San Francisco, 1997.

[733] C. C. Paige. The Computation of Eigenvalues and Eigenvectors of Very Large Sparse Matrices. PhD diss., University of London, 1971.

[734] S. Pakin, M. Lauria, and A. Chien. High performance messaging on workstations: Illinois fast messages (FM) for Myrinet. In *Proceedings of Supercomputing '95*, ACM Press, New York, 1995.

[735] M. Paleczny, K. Kennedy, and C. Koelbel. Compiler support for out-of-core arrays on data parallel machines. In *Proceedings of the Fifth Symposium on the Frontiers of Massively Parallel Computation*, 110–118, Feb 1995.

[736] Pallas GmbH. Vampir 2.0: Visualization and analysis of MPI programs, Oct 1999.

[737] C. M. Pancake. Establishing standards for HPC system software and tools. *NHSE Review*, Nov 1997. Online journal available at *http://softlib.rice.edu/NHSEreview/97-1.html*.

[738] C. M. Pancake, M. L. Simmons, and J. C. Yan. Performance evaluation tools for parallel and distributed systems. *IEEE Computer*, 28(11):16–19, Nov 1995.

[739] S. Pande and D. P. Agrawal, eds. *Languages, Compilation Techniques and Run Time Systems for Scalable Parallel Systems*. Springer-Verlag, Heidelberg and New York, 1997.

[740] Parallel Computing Forum. PCF: Parallel Fortran extensions. ACM SIGPLAN *Fortran Forum*, 10(3), Sep 1991.

[741] Parallel Tools Consortium. Ptools Web page. Available at *http://www.ptools.org*.

[742] The Parallel Virtual File System. Web page. Available at *http://www.parl.clemson.edu/pvfs*.

[743] M. Parashar. Integrated data management for computational steering. In *Proceedings of the IEEE Conference on Information Technology*, 61–64, IEEE Computer Society Press, Los Alamitos, CA, 1998.

[744] M. Parashar and J. C. Browne. DAGH: Data Management for Parallel Adaptive Mesh-Refinement Techniques. Available at *http://www.caip.rutgers.edu/~parashar/DAGH/*.

[745] M. Parashar, J. C. Browne, C. Edwards, and K. Klimkowski. A computational infrastructure for parallel adaptive methods. In *Proceedings of the Symposium on Parallel Adaptive Methods, 4th U.S. National Congress on Computational Mechanics*, San Francisco, Aug 1997.

[746] PARASOL Web page. Available at *http://www.parallab.uib.no/parasol/*.

[747] S. Park and K. Lee. A new approach to automated multiblock decomposition for grid generation: A hypercube ++ approach. In J. F. Thompson, B. K. Soni, and N. P. Weatherill, eds., *Handbook of Grid Generation*, CRC Press, Boca Raton, FL, 1999.

[748] B. N. Parlett, H. Simon, and L. M. Stringer. On estimating the largest eigenvalue with the Lanczos algorithm. *Mathematics of Computation*, 38(137):153–165, Jan 1982.

[749] B. N. Parlett. *The Symmetric Eigenvalue Problem*. Prentice-Hall, Englewood Cliffs, NJ, 1980.

[750] B. N. Parlett and J. K. Reid. Tracking the progress of the Lanczos algorithm for large symmetric eigenproblems. *IMA Journal of Numerical Analysis*, 1(2):135–155, Apr 1981.

[751] B. N. Parlett and D. S. Scott. The Lanczos algorithm with selective orthogonalization. *Mathematics of Computation*, 33(145):217–238, Jan 1979.

[752] S. Parter. The use of linear graphs in Gauss elimination. *SIAM Review*, 3(2):119–130, Apr 1961.

[753] Particle Data Group (C. Caso et al). Review of particle physics. *The European Physical Journal C*, 3(1–4):1–794, 1998.

[754] P. Partow and D. Cottel. Scalable Programming Environment. Technical Report NCCOSC-TR1672, Rev 1. Naval Command Control and Ocean Surveillance Center, San Diego, CA, Sep 1995.

[755] A. Patra and D. Kim. Efficient mesh partitioning for adaptive *hp* finite element methods. In *Proceedings of the International Conference on Domain Decomposition Methods*, Greenwich, UK, 1998.

[756] D. Patterson, T. Anderson, N. Cardwell, R. Fromm, K. Keeton, C. Kozyrakis, R. Thomas, and K. Yelick. A case for Intelligent RAM. *IEEE Micro*, 17(2):34–44, Mar/Apr 1997.

[757] D. A. Patterson, G. Gibson, and R. H. Katz. A case for redundant arrays of inexpensive disks (RAID). In *Proceedings of the 1988 ACM SIGMOD International Conference on Management of Data*, 109–116, ACM Press, New York, 1988.

[758] R. H. Patterson, G. A. Gibson, E. Ginting, D. Stodolsky, and J. Zelenka. Informed prefetching and caching. In *Proceedings of the 15th Symposium on Operating System Principles*, 79–95, ACM Press, New York, Dec 1995.

[759] D. A. Patterson, and J. L. Hennessy. *Computer Architecture: A Quantitative Approach*. Morgan Kaufmann, San Mateo, CA, 1990.

[760] R. A. Pearson. A coarse-grained parallel induction heuristic. In H. Kitano, V. Kumar, and C. B. Suttner, eds., *Parallel Processing for Artificial Intelligence 2*, 207–226, Elsevier Science, Amsterdam and New York, 1994.

[761] F. Pellegrini and J. Roman. SCOTCH: A software package for static mapping by dual recursive bipartitioning of process and architecture graphs. In *Proceedings of the 4th International Conference on High Performance Computing and Networking Europe*, 493–498, Springer-Verlag, Berlin, 1996.

[762] N. A. Petersson. Stability of pressure boundary conditions for Stokes and Navier-Stokes equations. *Journal of Computational Physics*, 172(1):40–70, Sep 2001.

[763] G. F. Pfister. *In Search of Clusters*, 2nd ed. Prentice-Hall, Englewood Cliffs, NJ, 1998.

[764] L. Piela, J. Kostrowicki, and H. A. Scheraga. The multiple-minima problem in the conformational analysis of molecules: Deformation of the protein energy hypersurface by the diffusion equation method. *Journal of Physical Chemistry*, 93:3339–3346, 1989.

[765] M. E. Pierce, C. Youn, and G. Fox. The gateway computational web portal. *Concurrency and Computation: Practice and Experience in Grid Computing Environments*. Special Issue, 2002. In press. Available at *http://aspen.ucs.indiana.edu/gce/C543pierce/c543gateway.pdf*.

[766] P. Pierce. A concurrent file system for a highly parallel mass storage subsystem. In *Proceedings of the Fourth Conference on Hypercubes, Concurrent Computers and Applications*, 155–160, Golden Gate Enterprises, Los Altos, CA, 1989.

[767] J. Pilkington and S. Baden. Partitioning with Space Filling Curves. Technical Report CS94-349. Department of Computer Science and Engineering, University of CA, San Diego, California, 1994.

[768] J. Pilkington and S. Baden. Dynamic Partitioning of Non-Uniform Structured Workloads with Space Filling Curves. Technical report. Department of Computer Science and Engineering, University of California, San Diego, 1995.

[769] R. E. Plant. Bifurcation and resonance in a model for bursting nerve cells. *Journal of Mathematical Biology*, 11(1):15–32, Jan 1981.

[770] S. Plimpton, B. Hendrickson, and J. Stewart. A parallel rendezvous algorithm for interpolation between multiple grids. In *Proceedings of Supercomputing '99*, IEEE Computer Society Press, Los Alamitos, CA, 1999. *http://www.supercomp.org/sc98.TechPapers/sc98_Full Abstracts/Plimpton644/*.

[771] A. A. Poe and Q. F. Stout. Load balancing 2-phased geometrically based problems. In *Proceedings of the Ninth SIAM Conference Parallel Processing for Scientific Computing*, SIAM, Philadelphia, 1999.

[772] A. Pothen. Graph partitioning algorithms with applications to scientific computing. In D. Keyes, A. Sameh, and V. Venkatakrishnan, eds., *Parallel Numerical Algorithms*, 323–368, Kluwer Dordrecht, 1996.

[773] A. Pothen, H. Simon, L. Wang, and S. Barnard. Towards a fast implementation of spectral nested dissection. In *Proceedings of Supercomputing '92*, 42–51, IEEE Computer Society Press, Los Alamitos, CA, 1992.

[774] A. Pothen, H. D. Simon, and K.-P. Liou. Partitioning sparse matrices with eigenvectors of graphs. *SIAM Journal on Matrix Analysis and Applications*, 11(3):430–452, Jul 1990.

[775] D. R. Prabhu. Speed-up of SADARM scene-generation code for hardware-in-the-loop simulation. In *Proceedings of the Multi-Spectral Scene Generation and Projection Workshop*, Apr 1999.

[776] W. K. Pratt. *Digital Image Processing*, 2nd ed. Wiley, New York, 1991.

[777] R. Preis and R. Diekmann. PARTY—A software library for graph partitioning. In B. Topping, ed., *Advances in Computational Mechanics with Parallel and Distributed Processing*, 63–71, Civil-Comp Press, Stirling, UK, 1997.

[778] M. A. Price, C. G. Armstrong, and M. A. Sabin. Hexahedral mesh generation by medial axis subdivision: I. Solids with convex edges. *International Journal for Numerical Methods in Engineering*, 38:3335–3359, 1995.

[779] J.-P. Prost, M. Snir, P. Corbett, and D. Feitelson. MPI-IO, a Message-Passing Interface for Concurrent I/O. Technical Report RC 19712 (#87394). IBM T. J. Watson Research Center, Yorktown Heights, NY, Aug 1994.

[780] J. Pryce and J. Reid. *AD01—A Fortran 90 Code for Automatic Differentiation*. Rutherford Appleton Laboratory, Oxon, UK, 1996.

[781] E. O. Purisima and H. A. Scheraga. An approach to the multiple-minima problem in protein folding by relaxing dimensionality. *Journal of Molecular Biology*, 196:697–709, 1987.

[782] Python Language Web Site. Available at *http://www.python.org*.

[783] Quantum simulations of condensed matter systems. Web page. Available at *http://www.ncsa.uiuc.edu/Apps/CMP/cmp-homepage.html*.

[784] A. Quarteroni and A. Valli. *Domain Decomposition Methods for Partial Differential Equations*. Oxford University Press, New York, 1999.

[785] J. R. Quinlan. *C4.5: Programs for Machine Learning*. Morgan Kaufmann, San Mateo, CA, 1993.

[786] L. R. Rabiner. A tutorial on hidden Markov models and selected applications in speech recognition. *Proceedings of the IEEE*, 77(2):257–286, Feb 1989.

[787] P. Raghavan. Line and Plane Separators. Technical Report UIUCDCS-R-93-1794. Department of Computer Science, University of Illinois, Urbana, IL, Feb 1993.

[788] P. Raghavan. Parallel Ordering Using Edge Contraction. Technical Report CS-95-293. Department of Computer Science, University of Tennessee, Knoxville, 1995.

[789] P. Raghavan. DSCPack: A Domain-Separator Cholesky Package. Technical report. University of Tennessee, Knoxville, 1999.

[790] S. M. Rao, D. R. Wilton, and A. W. Glisson. Electromagnetic scattering by surfaces of arbitrary shapes. *IEEE Transactions on Antennas and Propagation*, AP-30(3):409–418, May 1982.

[791] W. H. Ray. POLYRED—POLYmerization REactor Design. Department of Chemical Engineering, University of Wisconsin, Madison. (Also available at *http://whr008.che.wisc.edu/polyred/*.)

[792] D. A. Reed, R. A. Aydt, R. J. Noe, P. C. Roth, K. A. Shields, B. W. Schwartz, and L. F. Tavera. Scalable performance analysis: The Pablo performance analysis environment. In A. Skjellum, ed., *Proceedings of the Scalable Parallel Libraries Conference*, 104–113, IEEE Computer Society Press, Los Alamitos, CA, 1993.

[793] D. A. Reed, R. D. Olson, R. A. Aydt, T. M. Madhyastha, T. Birkett, D. W. Jensen, B. A. Nazief, and B. K. Totty. Scalable performance environments for parallel systems. In *Proceedings of the Sixth Distributed Memory Computing Conference*, 562–569, IEEE Computer Society Press, Los Alamitos, CA, 1991.

[794] D. A. Reed, D. A. Padua, I. T. Foster, D. B. Gannon, and B. P. Miller. Delphi: An integrated, language-directed performance prediction, measurement, and analysis environment. In *Proceedings of the 7th Symposium on the Frontiers of Massively Parallel Computation*, 156–159, IEEE Computer Society Press, Los Alamitos, CA, 1999.

[795] D. A. Reed and D. C. Rudolph. Experiences with hypercube operating system instrumentation. *International Journal of High-Speed Computing*, 1(4):517–542, Dec 1989.

[796] A. P. Rendell and T. J. Lee. Coupled-cluster theory employing approximate integrals: An approach to avoid the input/output and storage bottlenecks. *The Journal of Chemical Physics*, 101(1):400–408, Jul 1994.

[797] F. Rendl and H. Wolkowicz. A Semidefinite Framework to Trust-Region Subproblem with Applications to Large-scale Minimization. Technical Report CORR TR94-32. Department of Combinatorics and Optimization, University of Waterloo, Waterloo, Canada, 1994.

[798] J. V. W. Reynders and J. Cummings. The POOMA framework. *Computers in Physics*, 12(5):453–459, Sep/Oct 1997.

[799] P. J. Reynolds, ed. *On Clusters and Clustering: From Atoms to Fractals*. North-Holland, Amsterdam, 1993.

[800] T. Richardson, Q. Stafford-Fraser, K. R. Wood, and A. Hopper. Virtual network computing. *IEEE Internet Computing*, 2(1):33–38, Jan–Feb 1998.

[801] L. F. Richardson. *Weather Prediction by Numerical Process*. Cambridge University Press, Cambridge, 1922.

[802] R. D. Richtmyer. Taylor instability in shock acceleration of compressible fluids. *Communications in Pure and Applied Mathematics*, 13:297–319, 1960.

[803] A. H. G. Rinnooy Kan and G. T. Timmer. Global optimization. In G. L. Nemhauser, A. H. G. Rinnooy Kan, and M. J. Todd, eds., *Optimization*, 631–662, North-Holland, Amsterdam, 1989.

[804] M.-C. Rivara. Selective refinement/derefinement algorithms for sequences of nested triangulations. *International Journal for Numerical Methods in Engineering*, 28(12):2889–2906, 1989.

[805] B. Rivière, M. F. Wheeler, and V. Giraut. Part I: Improved Energy Estimates for Interior Penalty, Constrained and Discontinuous Galerkin Methods for Elliptic Problems. Technical Report TICAM TR99-09. Texas Institute for Computational and Applied Mathematics, University of Texas, Austin, Apr 1999.

[806] B. Rivière, M. F. Wheeler, and C. Baumann. Part II: Discontinuous Galerkin Method Applied to a Single Phase Flow in Porous Media. Technical Report TICAM TR99-10. Texas Institute for Computational and Applied Mathematics, University of Texas, Austin, Apr 1999.

[807] ROMIO: A high-performance, portable MPI-IO implementation. Available at *http://www.mcs.anl.gov/romio*.

[808] N. Rostaing, S. Dalmas, and A. Galligo. Automatic differentiation in Odyssée. *Tellus*, 45a(5):558–568, Oct 1993.

[809] N. Rostaing-Schmidt and E. Hassold. Basic functional representation of programs for automatic differentiation in the Odyssée system. In F.-X. Le Dimet, ed., *Proceedings of the Workshop on High-Performance Computing in the Geosciences*, Kluwer, Dordrecht, 1994.

[810] K. F. Roth. On irregularities of distribution. *Mathematika*, 1:73–79, 1954.

[811] RTExpress. Web page. Available at *http://www.rtexpress.com*.

[812] J. W. Ruge and K. Stüben. Algebraic multigrid. In S. F. McCormick, ed., *Multigrid Methods*, 73–130, SIAM, Philadelphia, PA, 1987.

[813] J. B. Rundle. A physical model for earthquakes, 2: Application to Southern California. *Journal of Geophysical Research*, 93:6255–6274, 1988.

[814] J. B. Rundle and D. D. Jackson. Numerical simulation of earthquake sequences. *Bulletin of the Seismological Society of America*, 67(5):1363–1377, Oct 1977.

[815] J. B. Rundle and W. Klein. New ideas about the physics of earthquakes. *Reviews of Geophysics (Supplement)*, 33(1):283–286, Jul 1995. (Also available as American Geophysical Union Quadrennial Report to the International Union of Geodesy and Geophysics.)

[816] J. B. Rundle, W. Klein, K. F. Tiampo, and S. Gross. Dynamics of seismicity patterns in systems of earthquake faults. In J. B. Rundle, D. L. Turcotte, and W. Klein, eds., *Geocomplexity and the Physics of Earthquakes*, 127–146, American Geophysical Union, Washington, DC, 2000. (Geophysical Monograph 120.)

[817] J. B. Rundle, W. Klein, K. Tiampo, and S. Gross. Linear pattern dynamics in nonlinear threshold systems. *Physical Review E*, 61(3):2418–2431, Mar 2000.

[818] T. F. Russell and M. F. Wheeler. Finite element and finite difference methods for continuous flows in porous media. In R. E. Ewing, ed., *The Mathematics of Reservoir Simulation*, 35–105, SIAM, Philadelphia, PA, 1983.

[819] Y. Saad. Chebyshev acceleration techniques for solving nonsymmetric eigenvalue problems. *Mathematics of Computation*, 42(166):567–588, Apr 1984.

[820] Y. Saad. *Iterative Methods for Sparse Linear Systems*. PWS Publishing, Boston, 1996.

[821] Y. Saad and M. H. Schultz. GMRes: A generalized minimal residual algorithm for solving nonsymmetric linear systems. *SIAM Journal on Scientific and Statistical Computing*, 7(3):856–869, Jul 1986.

[822] P. Sadayappan and F. Ercal. Mapping of finite element graphs onto processor meshes. *IEEE Transactions on Computers*, C-36:1408–1424, Dec 1987.

[823] H. Sagan. *Space-Filling Curves*. Springer-Verlag, Heidelberg, 1994.

[824] J. K. Salmon, M. S. Warren, and G. S. Winckelmans. Fast parallel tree codes for gravitational and fluid dynamical N-body problems. *International Journal of Supercomputer Applications*, 8(2):129–142, Summer 1994.

[825] S. A. Santos and D. C. Sorensen. A New Matrix-Free Algorithm for the Large-scale Trust-Region Subproblem. Technical Report CAAM TR95-20. Department of Computational and Applied Mathematics, Rice University, Houston, TX, 1995.

[826] A. Sathye, M. Xue, G. Bassett, and K. Droegemeier. Parallel weather modeling with the advanced regional prediction system. *Parallel Computing*, 23(14):2243–2256, Dec 1997.

[827] J. B. Saxe. Embeddability of Weighted Graphs in k-space Is Strongly NP-Hard. Technical report. Department of Computer Science, Carnegie-Mellon University, Pittsburgh, PA, 1979.

[828] J. B. Saxe. Embeddability of weighted graphs in k-space is strongly NP-hard. In *Proceedings of the 17th Allerton Conference in Communications, Control and Computing*, 480–489, 1979.

[829] Scalable I/O Initiative Web page. Available at *http://www.cacr.caltech.edu/SIO*.

[830] Scalable I/O Initiative, Applications Working Group. Preliminary Survey of I/O Intensive Applications, 1994. Available at *http://www.cacr.caltech.edu/SIO/SIOpubslist.html*.

[831] H. A. Scheraga. Predicting three-dimensional structures of oligopeptides. In K. B. Lipkowitz and D. B. Boyd, eds., *Reviews in Computational Chemistry*, Volume 3, 73–142. Wiley–VCH, 1992.

[832] K. Schloegel, G. Karypis, and V. Kumar. Multilevel diffusion schemes for repartitioning of adaptive meshes. *Journal of Parallel and Distributed Computing*, 47(2):109–124, Dec 1997.

[833] K. Schloegel, G. Karypis, and V. Kumar. Wavefront Diffusion and LMSR: Algorithms for Dynamic Repartitioning of Adaptive meshes. Technical Report TR 98-034. Department of Computer Science and Engineering, University of Minnesota, Minneapolis, 1998.

[834] K. Schloegel, G. Karypis, and V. Kumar. A new algorithm for multi-objective graph partitioning. In *Proceedings of Euro-Par '99*, 322–331, Springer-Verlag, Berlin, 1999.

[835] K. Schloegel, G. Karypis, and V. Kumar. Parallel Multilevel Algorithms for Multi-Constraint Graph Partitioning. Technical Report TR 99-031. Department of Computer Science and Engineering, University of Minnesota, Minneapolis, 1999.

[836] K. Schloegel, G. Karypis, and V. Kumar. A unified algorithm for load-balancing adaptive scientific simulations. In *Proceedings of Supercomputing '00*, IEEE Computer Society Press, Los Alamitos, CA, 2000.

[837] W. C. Schmid and A. Uhl. Parallel quasi-Monte Carlo integration using (t, s)–sequences. In P. Zinterhof, M. Vajtersic, and A. Uhl, eds., *Parallel Computation: 4th International ACPC Conference*, 96–106, Springer, Berlin and New York, 1999.

[838] J. Schneider and T. H. Wise. Airline crew scheduling: Supercomputers and algorithms. In G. Astfalk, ed., *Applications on Advanced Architecture Computers*, SIAM, Philadelphia, PA, 1996.

[839] C. H. Scholz. *The Mechanics of Earthquakes and Faulting*. Cambridge University Press, Cambridge, 1990.

[840] D. Schwartz. Implementation implications, performance opportunities, and random musings on Tisdale's. In *An Application Programmer's Interface to the VSIP Library for ANSI C*, HRL Laboratories, Malibu, CA, Jun 1997. Also available at *http://www.vsipl.org*.

[841] H.-P. Schwefel. *Evolution and Optimum Seeking*. Wiley, New York, 1995.

[842] Scientific Data Management Web page. Available at *http://www.ca.sandia.gov/asci-sdm*.

[843] K. Seamons, Y. Chen, P. Jones, J. Jozwiak, and M. Winslett. Server-directed collective I/O in Panda. In *Proceedings of Supercomputing '95*, ACM Press, New York, 1995.

[844] J. G. Seik and A. Lumsdaine. The Matrix Template Library: A generic programming approach to high-performance numerical linear algebra. In D. Caromel, R. R. Oldehoeft, and M. D. Tholburn, eds., *Computing in Object-Oriented Parallel Environments*, Lecture Notes in Computer Science 1505, Springer-Verlag, Heidelberg and New York, 1998.

[845] C. L. Seitz. The cosmic cube. *Communications of the ACM*, 28(1):22–33, Jan 1985.

[846] A. J. Semtner. An Oceanic General Circulation Model with Bottom Topography. Technical Report 9. Department of Meteorology, University of California, Los Angeles, 1974.

[847] A. J. Semtner, Jr. and R. M. Chervin. A simulation of the global ocean circulation with resolved eddies. *Journal of Geophysical Research*, 93(C12):15502–15522, Dec 1988.

[848] A. J. Semtner and R. M. Chervin. Ocean general circulation from a global eddy-resolving model. *Journal of Geophysical Research—Oceans*, 97(C4):5493–5550, Apr 1992.

[849] D. B. Serafini. A Framework for Managing Models in Nonlinear Optimization of Computationally Expensive Functions. PhD diss., Rice University, Houston, TX, Nov 1998. (Revised Jan 1999, also available as CRPC-TR98781-S.)

[850] R. Sessions. *COM and DCOM: Microsoft's Vision for Distributed Objects*. John Wiley & Sons, New York, 1997.

[851] J. Shafer, R. Agrawal, and M. Mehta. SPRINT: A scalable parallel classifier for data mining. In T. M. Vijayaraman, A. P. Buchmann, C. Mohan, and N. L. Sarda, eds., *Proceedings of 22nd International Conference on Very Large Data Bases*, 544–555, Morgan Kaufmann, San Francisco, 1996.

[852] D. Shalloway. Application of the renormalization group to deterministic global minimization of molecular conformation energy functions. *Journal of Global Optimization*, 2(3):281–311, 1992.

[853] D. Shalloway. Packet annealing: A deterministic method for global minimization, application to molecular conformation. In C. Floudas and P. M. Pardalos, eds., *Recent Advances in Global Optimization*, 433–477, Princeton University Press, Princeton, NJ, 1992.

[854] J. S. Shang. Challenges for computational electromagnetics in the time domain. In *Proceedings of the 1997 IEEE International Symposium on Antennas and Propagation*, Vol. 1, 94–97, IEEE, New York, 1997.

[855] J. S. Shang. High-order compact-difference schemes for time-dependent Maxwell equations. *Journal of Computational Physics*, 153(2):312–333, Aug 1999.

[856] J. S. Shang, J. A. Camberos, and M. D. White. Advances in time-domain computational electromagnetics. In *Proceedings of the 30th Plasmadynamics and Laser Conference*, Norfolk, VA, Jun–Jul 1999. (Also available as AIAA Paper 99-3731.)

[857] J. S. Shang, M. Wagner, Y. Pan, and D. C. Blake. Strategies for adopting FVTD on multicomputers. *IEEE Computing in Science and Engineering*, 2(1):10–21, Jan–Feb 2000.

[858] C. Shao, R. H. Byrd, E. Eskow, and R. B. Schnabel. Global optimization for molecular clusters using a new smoothing approach. In L. T. Biegler, T. Coleman, A. R. Conn, and F. N. Santosa, eds., *Large-Scale Optimization and Applications, Part III: Molecular Structure and Optimization*, 163–199, Springer-Verlag, Heidelberg and New York, 1997.

[859] J. A. Shaw. Hybrid grids. In J. F. Thompson, B. K. Soni, and N. P. Weatherill, eds., *Handbook of Grid Generation*, CRC Press, Boca Raton, FL, 1999.

[860] D. Shiriaev and A. Griewank. ADOL-F: Automatic differentiation of Fortran codes. In M. Berz, C. Bischof, G. Corliss, and A. Griewank, eds., *Proceedings of the Computational Differentiation: Techniques, Applications, and Tools*, 375–384, SIAM, Philadelphia, PA, 1996.

[861] G. M. Shroff and H. B. Keller. Stabilization of unstable procedures: The recursive projection method. *SIAM Journal on Numerical Analysis*, 30(4):1099–1120, Aug 1993.

[862] Silicon Graphics. *Performance Co-Pilot User's and Administrator's Guide*. Silicon Graphics, Mountain View, CA, 1999.

[863] H. Simitci and D. A. Reed. A comparison of logical and physical parallel I/O patterns. *The International Journal of High Performance Computing Applications*, 12(3):364–380, Fall 1998. (Also available in a special issue on I/O in *Parallel Applications*, 12(3–4).)

[864] H. D. Simon. Analysis of the symmetric Lanczos algorithm with reorthogonalization methods. *Linear Algebra and Its Applications*, 61:101–131, 1984.

[865] H. D. Simon, A. Sohn, and R. Biswas. HARP: A fast spectral partitioner. In *Proceedings of the Ninth Annual ACM Symposium on Parallel Algorithms and Architectures*, 43–52, ACM Press, New York, 1997.

[866] H. D. Simon and S.-H. Teng. How good is recursive bisection? *SIAM Journal on Scientific Computing*, 18(5):1436–1445, Sep 1997.

[867] D. Skillicorn and D. Talia. Models and languages for parallel computation. *ACM Computing Surveys*, 30(2):123–169, Jun 1998.

[868] G. L. G. Sleijpen and H. A. van der Vorst. A Jacobi–Davidson iteration method for linear eigenvalue problems. *SIAM Journal on Matrix Analysis and Applications*, 17(2):401–425, Apr 1996.

[869] G. L. G. Sleijpen and H. A. van der Vorst. A Jacobi–Davidson iteration method for linear eigenvalue problems. *SIAM Review*, 42(2):267–293, 2000.

[870] E. Smirni, R. A. Aydt, A. A. Chien, and D. A. Reed. I/O requirements of scientific applications: An evolutionary view. In *Proceedings of the Fifth IEEE International Symposium on High*

Performance Distributed Computing, 49–59, IEEE Computer Society Press, Los Alamitos, CA, 1996.

[871] E. Smirni and D. A. Reed. Lessons from characterizing the input/output behavior of parallel scientific applications. *Performance Evaluation*, 33(1):27–44, Jun 1998.

[872] B. F. Smith, P. E. Bjørstad, and W. D. Gropp. *Domain Decomposition: Parallel Multilevel Methods for Elliptic Partial Differential Equations*. Cambridge University Press, New York, 1996.

[873] B. F. Smith and W. D. Gropp. The design of data-structure-neutral libraries for the iterative solution of sparse linear systems. *Scientific Programming*, 5(4):329–336, Winter 1996.

[874] R. D. Smith, J. K. Dukowicz, and R. C. Malone. Parallel ocean general circulation modeling. *Physica D*, 60(1–4):38–61, Nov 1992.

[875] R. D. Smith, M.E. Maltrud, F. O. Bryan, and N. W. Hecht. Numerical simulation of the North Atlantic Ocean at $\frac{1}{10}°$. *Journal of Physical Oceanography*, 30(7):1532–1561, Jul 2000.

[876] R. D. Smith, S. Kortas, and B. Meltz. Curvilinear Coordinates for Global Ocean Models. Technical Report LA-UR-95-1146. Los Alamos National Laboratory, Los Alamos, NM, 1995.

[877] P. Smyth. Model selection for probabilistic clustering using cross-validated likelihood. *Statistics and Computing*, 10(1):63–72, Jan 2000.

[878] M. Snir, S. W. Otto, S. Huss-Lederman, D. W. Walker, and J. Dongarra. *MPI: The Complete Reference*. MIT Press, Cambridge, MA, 1996.

[879] M. Snir, S. Otto, S. Huss-Lederman, D. Walker, and J. Dongarra. *MPI—The Complete Reference: Volume 1, The MPI Core*, 2nd ed. MIT Press, Cambridge, MA, 1998.

[880] I. Sobieski and I. Kroo. Aircraft design using collaborative optimization. In *Proceedings of the 34th AIAA Aerospace Sciences Meeting*, Reno, NV, 1996. (Also available as AIAA Paper 96-0715.)

[881] I. M. Soboĭ. Distribution of points in a cube and approximate evaluation of integrals. *Žhurnal Vyčislitel'noĭ Matematiki i Matematičeskoĭ Fiziki*, 7(4):784–802, Jul 1967. (Russian.)

[882] W. Y. Soh and J. Goodrich. Unsteady solution of the incompressible Navier–Stokes equations. *Journal of Computational Physics*, 79(1):113–134, Nov 1988.

[883] A. Sohn. S-HARP: A Parallel Dynamic Spectral Partitioner. Technical Report CIS-97-20. Department of Computer and Information Science, New Jersey Institute of Technology, Newark, Sep 1997.

[884] A. Sohn and H. Simon. JOVE: A Dynamic Load Balancing Framework for Adaptive Computations on an SP-2 Distributed-Memory Multiprocessor. Technical Report 94–60. Department of Computer and Information Science, New Jersey Institute of Technology, Newark, 1994.

[885] B. Soni and J. Yang. General purpose adaptive grid system. In *Proceedings of the 30th Aerospace Sciences Meeting*, Reno, NV, Jan 1992. (Also available as AIAA Paper 92-0664.)

[886] B. K. Soni. Grid generation for internal flow configurations. *Computer & Mathematics with Applications*, 24(5/6):191–201, Sep 1992.

[887] B. K. Soni, J. F. Thompson, J. Hauser, and P. R. Eiseman, eds. *Numerical Grid Generation in Computational Field Simulations*. ERC Press, Mississippi State University, Starkville, 1996.

[888] P. Sonneveld. CGS, a fast Lanczos-type solver for nonsymmetric linear systems. *SIAM Journal on Scientific and Statistical Computing*, 10(1):36–52, Jan 1989.

[889] D. C. Sorensen. Implicit application of polynomial filters in a *k*-step Arnoldi method. *SIAM Journal on Matrix Analysis and Applications*, 13(1):357–385, 1992.

[890] D. C. Sorensen. Implicitly restarted Arnoldi/Lanczos methods for large scale eigenvalue calculations. In D. Keyes, A. Sameh, and V. Venkatakrishnan, eds., *Parallel Numerical Algorithms*, 119–166, Kluwer, Dordrecht, 1997.

[891] D. C. Sorensen and C. Yang. A truncated RQ-iteration for large scale eigenvalue calculations. *SIAM Journal on Matrix Analysis and Applications*, 19(4):1045–1073, 1998.

[892] J. Spanier. Quasi-Monte Carlo methods for particle transport problems. In H. Niederreiter and P. J.-S. Shiue, eds., *Monte Carlo and Quasi-Monte Carlo Methods in Scientific Computing*, 121–148, Springer-Verlag, New York, 1995.

[893] A. Srivastava, E.-H. Han, V. Kumar, and V. Singh. Parallel formulations of decision-tree classification algorithms. *Data Mining and Knowledge Discovery*, 3(3):237–261, Sep 1999. (Also available at *http://www.cs.umn.edu/~kumar*.)

[894] A. Stathopoulos, Y. Saad, and K. Wu. Dynamic thick restarting of the Davidson, and the implicitly restarted Arnoldi methods. *SIAM Journal on Scientific Computing*, 19(1):227–245, Jan 1998.

[895] J. L. Steger and D. S. Chaussee. Generation of body-fitted coordinates using hyperbolic partial differential equations. *SIAM Journal on Scientific and Statistical Computing*, 1(4):431–437, 1980.

[896] T. Sterling, P. Messina, and P. Smith. *Enabling Technologies for Petaflops Computing*. MIT Press, Cambridge, MA, 1995.

[897] T. Sterling, D. Savarese, D. J. Becker, J. E. Dorband, U. A. Ranawake, and C. V. Packer. BEOWULF: A parallel workstation for scientific computation. In *Proceedings of the 24th International Conference on Parallel Processing, Vol. 1: Architecture*, 11–14, CRC Press, Boca Raton, FL, 1995.

[898] T. L. Sterling, J. Salmon, D. J. Becker, and D. F. Savarese. *How to Build a Beowulf: A Guide to the Implementation and Application of PC Clusters*. MIT Press, Cambridge, MA, 1999.

[899] H. Stern. *Managing NFS and NIS*. O'Reilly, Sebastopol, CA, 1991.

[900] G. H. Stolovy and D. R. Prabhu. Multiple-target ATR for synthetic aperture radar imagery. In *Proceedings of ITEA Conference*, Jul 1998.

[901] A. H. Stone and J. Tukey. Generalized "sandwich" theorems. In *The Collected Works of John W. Tukey*. Wadsworth, Belmont, CA, 1990.

[902] M. Stonebraker, R. Agrawal, U. Dayal, E. J. Neuhold, and A. Reuter. DBMS research at a crossroads: The Vienna update. In R. Agrawal, S. Baker, and D. A. Bell, eds., *Proceedings of the 19th International Conference on Very Large Data Bases*, 688–692, Morgan Kaufmann, San Francisco, 1993.

[903] J. E. Straub. Optimization Techniques with Applications to Proteins. Preprint. Department of Chemistry, Boston University, 1994.

[904] J. E. Straub, J. Ma, and P. Amara. Simulated annealing using coarse-grained classical dynamics: Fokker-Planck and Smoluchowski dynamics in the Gaussian density approximation. *Journal of Chemical Physics*, 103(4):1574–1581, Jul 1995.

[905]   J. Subhlok, J. Stichnoth, D. O'Hallaron, and T. Gross. Exploiting task and data parallelism on a multicomputer. In *Proceedings of the Fourth ACM SIGPLAN Symposium on Principles and Practice of Parallel Programming*, 13–22, ACM Press, New York, 1993.

[906]   A. Szabo and N. S. Ostlund. *Modern Quantum Chemistry: Introduction to Advanced Electronic Structure Theory*, rev. 1st ed., McGraw-Hill, New York, 1989.

[907]   B. Szabó and I. Babuska. *Finite Element Analysis*. John Wiley & Sons, New York, 1991.

[908]   C. Szyperski. *Component Software: Beyond Object-Oriented Programming*. ACM Press, New York, 1998.

[909]   O. Talagrand. The use of adjoint equations in numerical modeling of the atmospheric circulation. In A. Griewank and G. F. Corliss, eds., *Automatic Differentiation of Algorithms: Theory, Implementation, and Application*, 169–180, SIAM, Philadelphia, PA, 1991.

[910]   M. C. Tanis and B. A. Smith. Finite-difference migration of 3-D seismic data with a parallel algorithm. In *Proceedings of the 67th Annual Meeting of the SEG (Expanded Abstracts)*, 1422–1425, Society of Exploration Geophysics, Tulsa, OK, 1997.

[911]   T. J. Tautges and S. Mitchell. Progress report on the whisker weaving all-hexahedral meshing algorithm. In B. K. Soni, J. F. Thompson, J. Hauser, and P. R. Eiseman, eds., *Proceedings of the 5th International Conference on Numerical Grid Generation in Computational Field Simulations*, 659–670, ERC, Mississippi State University, Starkville, 1996.

[912]   J. Teresco, M. Beall, J. Flaherty, and M. Shephard. Hierarchical Partition Model for Adaptive Finite Element Computation. Technical report. Department of Computer Science, Rensselaer Polytechnic Institute, Troy, NY, 1998.

[913]   W. C. Thacker. Automatic differentiation from an oceanographer's perspective. In A. Griewank and G. F. Corliss, eds., *Automatic Differentiation of Algorithms: Theory, Implementation, and Application*, 191–201, SIAM, Philadelphia, PA, 1991.

[914]   R. Thakur, R. Bordawekar, A. Choudhary, R. Ponnusamy, and T. Singh. PASSION runtime library for parallel I/O. In *Proceedings of the 1994 Scalable Parallel Libraries Conference*, 119–128, IEEE Computer Society Press, Los Alamitos, CA, 1994.

[915]   R. Thakur and A. Choudhary. An extended two-phase method for accessing sections of out-of-core arrays. *Scientific Programming*, 5(4):301–317, Winter 1996.

[916]   R. Thakur, A. Choudhary, R. Bordawekar, S. More, and S. Kuditipudi. Passion: Optimized I/O for parallel applications. *Computer*, 29(6):70–78, Jun 1996.

[917]   R. Thakur, W. Gropp, and E. Lusk. An experimental evaluation of the parallel I/O systems of the IBM SP and Intel Paragon using a production application. In *Proceedings of the 3rd International Conference of the Austrian Center for Parallel Computation ACPC with Special Emphasis on Parallel Databases and Parallel I/O*, 24–35. Springer-Verlag, Heidelberg and New York, Sep 1996.

[918]   R. Thakur, W. Gropp, and E. Lusk. A case for using MPI's derived data types to improve I/O performance. In *Proceedings of Supercomputing '98*, IEEE Computer Society Press, Los Alamitos, CA, 1998.

[919]   R. Thakur, W. Gropp, and E. Lusk. Data sieving and collective I/O in ROMIO. In *Proceedings of the 7th Symposium on the Frontiers of Massively Parallel Computation*, 182–189, IEEE Computer Society Press, Los Alamitos, CA, 1999.

[920] R. Thakur, W. Gropp, and E. Lusk. On implementing MPI-IO portably and with high performance. In *Proceedings of the 6th Workshop on I/O in Parallel and Distributed Systems*, 23–32, ACM Press, New York, 1999.

[921] Thinking Machines Corporation. *CM Fortran Reference Manual, Version 1.0*. Thinking Machines Corporation, Cambridge, MA, Feb 1991.

[922] Thinking Machines Corporation. *CM5 Technical Summary*. Thinking Machines Corporation, Cambridge, MA, Oct 1991.

[923] Thinking Machines Corporation. *Users Manual for CM-Fortran*. Thinking Machines Corporation, Cambridge, MA, 1993.

[924] A. Thomas and P. S. Group. Enterprise JavaBeans technology: Server component model for the Java platform, Dec 1998. Available at *http://java.sun.com/products/ejb/white_paper.html*.

[925] J. F. Thompson. A survey of dynamically-adaptive grids in the numerical solution of partial differential equations. *Applied Numerical Mathematics*, 1(1):3–27, Jan 1985.

[926] J. F. Thompson. A general three-dimensional elliptic grid generation system on a composite block structure. *Computer Methods in Applied Mechanics and Engineering*, 64(1–3):377–411, Oct 1987.

[927] J. F. Thompson. A reflection on grid generation in the 90's: Trends, needs, and influences. In B. K. Soni, J. F. Thompson, J. Hauser, and P. R. Eiseman, eds., *Proceedings of the 5th International Conference on Numerical Grid Generation in Computational Field Simulations*, 1029, ERC Press, Mississippi State University, Engineering Research Center, Starkville, 1996.

[928] J. F. Thompson, B. K. Soni, and N. P. Weatherill, eds. *Handbook of Grid Generation*. CRC Press, Boca Raton, FL, 1999.

[929] J. F. Thompson, Z. U. A. Warsi, and C. W. Mastin. *Numerical Grid Generation: Foundations and Applications*. North-Holland, New York, 1985.

[930] P. A. Thompson. *Compressible-Fluid Dynamics*. McGraw-Hill, New York, 1988.

[931] K. F. Tiampo, J. B. Rundle, S. Gross, and S. McGinnis. Parallelization of a large-scale computational earthquake simulation program. *Concurrency and Computation: Practice and Experience*, 2002. In press.

[932] K. F. Tiampo, J. B. Rundle, S. McGinnis, S. Gross, and W. Klein. Observation of systematic variations in non-local seismicity patterns from Southern California. In J. B. Rundle, D. L. Turcotte, and W. Klein, eds., *Geocomplexity and the Physics of Earthquakes*, 211–218, Geophysical Monograph 120, American Geophysical Union, Washington, DC, 2000.

[933] S. Toledo and F. G. Gustavson. The design and implementation of SOLAR, a portable library for scalable out-of-core linear algebra computations. In *Proceedings of the Fourth Workshop on Input/Output in Parallel and Distributed Systems*, 28–40, ACM Press, New York, 1996.

[934] R. F. Tomaro, W. Z. Strang, and F. C. Witzeman. A solution on the F-18C for store separation simulation using Cobalt60. In *Proceedings of the 37th Aerospace Sciences Meeting and Exhibit*, Reno, NV, Jan 1999. (AIAA Paper 99-0122.)

[935] R. F. Tomaro and K. E. Wurtzler. High-speed configuration aerodynamics: SR-71 to SMV. In *Proceedings of the 17th AIAA Applied Aerodynamics Conference*, Norfolk, VA, Jun 1999. (AIAA Paper 99-3204.)

[936] Top 500 supercomputers, Nov 1996. Available at *http://www.top500.org/lists/1996/11/*.

[937] V. Torczon. Multi-Directional Search: A Direct Search Algorithm for Parallel Machines. PhD diss., Rice University, 1990. (Also available as CAAM TR90-7.)

[938] V. Torczon. On the convergence of the multidirectional search algorithm. *SIAM Journal on Optimization*, 1(1):123–145, Feb 1991.

[939] V. Torczon. On the convergence of pattern search algorithms. *SIAM Journal on Optimization*, 7(1):1–25, Feb 1997.

[940] TRansportation ANalysis Simulation System (TRANSIMS) Web page. Available at *http://transims.tsasa.lanl.gov*.

[941] A. E. Trefethen, V. S. Menon, C.-C. Chang, G. J. Czajkowski, C. Meyers, and L. N. Trefethen. MultiMATLAB: MATLAB on Multiple Processors, 1996. Available at *http://users.comlab.ox.ac.uk/nick.trefethen/multimatlab.html*.

[942] R. Triolet, F. Irigoin, and P. Feautrier. Direct parallelization of CALL statements. In *Proceedings of the SIGPLAN '86 Symposium on Compiler Construction*, Palo Alto, CA, Jun 1986.

[943] D. M. Tullsen, S. J. Eggers, and H. M. Levy. Simultaneous multithreading: Maximizing on-chip parallelism. In *Proceedings of the 22nd Annual International Symposium on Computer Architecture*, 392–403, ACM Press, New York, 1995.

[944] N. Ueda and R. Nakano. Deterministic annealing variant of the EM algorithm. *Neural Networks*, 11(2):271–282, Mar 1998.

[945] UNICORE: Uniform Access to Computing Resources. *http://www.fz-juelich.de/unicore*.

[946] University of Potsdam. Web page for the Cactus Problem Solving Environment for Numerical Relativity (and Other Areas), 2000. Available at *http://www.cactuscode.org/*.

[947] Unstructured Grids Web page. Available at *http://cox.iwr.uni-heidelberg.de/~ug/*.

[948] O. Vahtras, J. Almlöf, and M. W. Feyereisen. Integral approximations for LCAO-SCF calculations. *Chemical Physics Letters*, 213(5–6):514–518, Oct 1993.

[949] S. Vajracharya, P. Beckman, S. Karmesin, K. Keahey, R. Oldehoeft, and C. Rasmussen. A programming model for cluster of SMPs. In *Proceedings of the 1999 International Conference on Parallel and Distributed Processing Techniques and Applications (PDPTA'99)*, Monte Carlo Resort, Las Vegas, NV, Jun–Jul 1999.

[950] E. F. van de Velde. *Concurrent Scientific Computing*. Springer-Verlag, Heidelberg and New York, 1994.

[951] A. J. Van der Steen and J. J. Dongarra. Overview of recent supercomputers, 2000. Available at *http://www.phys.uu.nl/~steen/web00/overview00.html*.

[952] H. A. van der Vorst. Bi-CGSTAB: A fast and smoothly converging variant of Bi-CG for the solution of nonsymmetric linear systems. *SIAM Journal on Scientific and Statistical Computing*, 13(2):631–644, Mar 1992.

[953] R. van Driessche and D. Roose. Dynamic Load Balancing of Iteratively Refined Grids by an Enhanced Spectral Bisection Algorithm. Technical report. Department of Computer Science, K. U. Leuven, Leuven, Belgium, 1995.

[954] B. van Leer. Towards the ultimate conservative difference scheme IV: A new approach to numerical convection. *Journal of Computational Physics*, 23(3):276–299, Mar 1977.

[955] B. van Leer. Towards the ultimate conservative difference scheme V: A second order sequel to Godunov's methods. *Journal of Computational Physics*, 32(1):101–136, Jul 1979. (Reprinted in *Journal of Computational Physics*, 135(2):227–248, Aug 1997)

[956] K. van Reeuwijk, W. Denissen, H. J. Sips, and E. M. R. M. Paalvast. An implementation framework for HPF distributed arrays on message-passing parallel computer systems. *IEEE Transactions on Parallel and Distributed Systems*, 7(9):897–914, Sep 1996.

[957] D. Vanderstraeten, R. Keunings, and C. Farhat. Beyond conventional mesh partitioning algorithms and the minimum edge cut criterion: Impact on realistic applications. In *Proceedings of the Seventh SIAM Conference on Parallel Processing for Scientific Computing*, 611–614, SIAM, Philadelphia, PA, 1995.

[958] R. S. Varga. *Matrix Iterative Analysis*. Prentice-Hall, Englewood Cliffs, NJ, 1962.

[959] T. Veldhuizen. Expression templates. *C++ Report*, 7(5):26–31, Jun 1995.

[960] T. Veldhuizen. Blitz++: Object oriented scientific computing, 2000. Available at *http://oonumerics.org/blitz/*.

[961] A. Vidwans, Y. Kallinderis, and V. Venkatakrishnan. Parallel dynamic load-balancing algorithm for three-dimensional adaptive unstructured grids. *AIAA Journal*, 32:497–505, 1994.

[962] Virtual Interface (VI) Developer Forum Web page. Available at *http://www.vidf.org*.

[963] Y. Volin and G. Ostrovskiĭ. Automatic computation of derivatives with the use of the multilevel differentiation technique. I. Algorithmic Basis *Computers & Mathematics with Applications*, 11(11):1099–1114, Nov 1985.

[964] T. von Eicken, A. Basu, V. Buch, and W. Vogels. U-Net: A user-level network interface for parallel and distributed computing. In *Proceedings of the 15th ACM Symposium on Operating Systems Principles (SOSP)*, 40–53, ACM Press, New York, 1995.

[965] T. von Eicken, D. E. Culler, S. C. Goldstein, and K. E. Schauser. Active messages: A mechanism for integrated communication and computation. In *Proceedings of the 19th International Symposium on Computer Architecture*, 256–266, ACM Press, New York, 1992. (Also available as Technical Report UCB/CSD 92/675, Computer Science Division, University of California at Berkeley.)

[966] G. von Laszewski, M.-H. Su, J. A. Insley, I. Foster, J. Bresnahan, C. Kesselman, M. Thiebaux, M. L. Rivers, S. Wang, B. Tieman, and I. McNulty. Real-time analysis, visualization, and steering of microtomography experiments at photon sources. In *Proceedings of the Ninth SIAM Conference on Parallel Processing for Scientific Computing*, Apr 1999. (Also available at *http://www.mcs.anl.gov/xray*.)

[967] G. Voronoi. Nouvelles applications des parametres continus à la theorie des formes quadratiques, recherches sur les parallelloedres primitifs. *Journal für die reine und angewandte Mathematik*, 134, 1908.

[968] C. Walshaw. *Parallel JOSTLE User Guide, Version 1.2.9*. University of Greenwich, London, 1998.

[969] C. Walshaw and M. Cross. Load-balancing for parallel adaptive unstructured meshes. In M. Cross et al., eds., *Proceedings of the Sixth International Conference on Numerical Grid Generation in Computational Field Simulations*, 781–790, International Society of Grid Generation, Mississippi State University, Starkville, 1998.

[970] C. Walshaw and M. Cross. Parallel Optimisation Algorithms for Multilevel Mesh Partitioning. Technical Report 99/IM/44. University of Greenwich, London, 1999.

[971] C. Walshaw and M. Cross. Mesh partitioning: A multilevel balancing and refinement algorithm. *SIAM Journal on Scientific Computing*, 22(1):63–80, 2000.

[972] C. Walshaw, M. Cross, R. Diekmann, and F. Schlimbach. Multilevel Mesh Partitioning for Optimising Domain Shape. Technical Report 98/IM/38. School of Computing and Mathematical Sciences, University of Greenwich, London, 1998.

[973] C. Walshaw, M. Cross, and M. Everett. Dynamic Mesh Partitioning: A Unified Optimisation and Load-Balancing Algorithm. Technical Report 95/IM/06. Centre for Numerical Modelling and Process Analysis, University of Greenwich, London, 1995.

[974] C. Walshaw, M. Cross, and M. G. Everett. Parallel dynamic graph partitioning for adaptive unstructured meshes. *Journal of Parallel and Distributed Computing*, 47(2):102–108, Dec 1997.

[975] C. Walshaw, M. Cross, M. G. Everett, S. Johnson, and K. McManus. Partitioning and mapping of unstructured meshes to parallel machine topologies. In A. Ferreira and J. Rolim, eds., *Proceedings of the Second International Symposium on Parallel Algorithms for Irregularly Structured Problems*, 121–126, Springer-Verlag, Heidelberg and New York, 1995.

[976] C. Walshaw, M. Cross, and K. McManus. Multiphase Mesh Partitioning. Technical Report 99/IM/51. University of Greenwich, London, 1999.

[977] J. H. Wang. *Generalized Moment Methods in Electromagnetics: Formulation and Computer Solution of Integral Equations*. John Wiley & Sons, New York, 1991.

[978] X. J. Wang and E. J. Doedel. AUTO94P: An Experimental Parallel Version of AUTO. Technical Report CRPC-95-2. Department of Applied Mathematics, California Institute of Technology, Pasadena, 1995.

[979] Y. Wang, F. de Carlo, I. Foster, J. Insley, C. Kesselman, P. Lane, G. von Laszewski, D. C. Mancini, I. McNulty, M.-H. Su, and B. Tieman. A quasi-realtime X-ray microtomography system at the advanced photon source. In *Proceedings of the SPIE's 44th Annual Meeting & Exhibition: The International Symposium on Optical Science, Engineering, and Instrumentation*, Vol. 3772, 301–309, Denver, CO, Jul 1999.

[980] M. S. Warren and J. R. Salmon. A parallel hashed oct-tree N-body algorithm. In *Proceedings of Supercomputing '93*, 12–21, ACM Press, New York, 1993.

[981] J. Watts, M. Rieffel, and S. Taylor. A load balancing technique for multi-phase computations. In *Proceedings of the High Performance Computing '97: Grand Challenges in Computer Simulation*, 15–20, 1997.

[982] J. Watts and S. Taylor. A practical approach to dynamic load balancing. *IEEE Transactions on Parallel and Distributed Systems*, 9(3):235–248, Mar 1998.

[983] N. P. Weatherill. Unstructured grids: Procedures and applications. In J. F. Thompson, B. K. Soni, and N. P. Weatherill, eds., *Handbook of Grid Generation*, CRC Press, Boca Raton, FL, 1999.

[984] N. P. Weatherill, O. Hassan, and D. L. Marcum. Adaptive inviscid flow solutions for aerospace geometries on efficiently generated unstructured tetrahedral meshes. In *Proceedings of the 31st AIAA Aerospace Sciences Meeting and Exhibit*, Reno, NV, Jan 1993. (AIAA Paper 93-0341.)

[985] WebFlow Project Web page. Available at *http://old-npac.ucs.indiana.edu/users/haupt /WebFlow/demo.html*.

[986] WebSubmit: A Web-Based Interface to High-Performance Computing Resources. Available at *http://www.math.nist.gov/mcsd/savg/websubmit/websubmit.html*.

[987] E. H. Welbon, C. C. Chan-Nui, D. J. Shippy, and D. A. Hicks. The POWER2 performance monitor. *IBM Journal of Research and Development*, 38(5):545–554, Sep 1994.

[988] R. C. Whaley and J. Dongarra. Automatically Tuned Linear Algebra Software (ATLAS). Available at *http://www.netlib.org/atlas/* and *http://math-atlas.sourceforge.net/*.

[989] M. F. Wheeler, M. Peszyńska, X. Gai, and O. El-Domeiri. Modeling Subsurface Flow on PC Clusters. In *Proceedings of the High Performance Comuting Symposium 2000*, 318–323, SCS, San Diego, CA, 2000.

[990] M. F. Wheeler, J. Wheeler, and M. Peszyńska. A distributed computing portal for coupling multi-physics and multiple domains in porous media. In *Proceedings of the XIII International Conference on Computational Methods in Water Resources*, 167–174, A. A. Balkema, Rotterdam, 2000.

[991] D. L. Whitfield and L. K. Taylor. Discretized Newton-relaxation solution of high resolution flux-difference split schemes. In *Proceedings of the AIAA Tenth Annual Computational Fluid Dynamics Conference*, 134–145, 1991. (AIAA Paper 91-1539.)

[992] O. Widlund. On the use of fast methods for separable finite difference equations for the solution of general elliptic problems. In D. J. Rose and R. A. Willoughby, eds., *Sparse Matrices and Their Applications*, 121–134, Plenum Press, New York, 1972.

[993] C. Wieselsberger. Neuere Feststellungen über die Gesetze des Flüssigkeits-und Luftwider-stands. *Physikalische Zeitschrift*, 22:321–328, 1921. (For translation, see NACA Technical Note #84.)

[994] J. H. Wilkinson. *The Algebraic Eigenvalue Problem*. Oxford University Press, Oxford, 1965.

[995] J. H. Wilkinson and C. Reinsch. *Handbook for Automatic Computation: Volume II—Linear Algebra*. Springer-Verlag, New York, 1971.

[996] R. D. Williams. Voxel databases: A paradigm for parallelism with spatial structure. *Concurrency: Practice and Experience*, 4(8):619–636, Dec 1992.

[997] K. G. Wilson. Confinement of quarks. *Physical Review D*, 10(8):2445–2459, Oct 1974.

[998] L. Wisniewski, B. Smisloff, and N. Nieuwejaar. Sun MPI I/O: Efficient I/O for parallel applications. In *Proceedings of Supercomputing '99*, ACM Press, New York, Nov 1999.

[999] WMS code. Engineering Research and Development Center, U.S. Army Corps of Engineers, University of Mississippi, Vicksburg. Available at *http://www.wes.hpc.mil*.

[1000] M. E. Wolf and M. Lam. A loop transformation theory and an algorithm to maximize parallelism. *IEEE Transactions on Parallel and Distributed Systems*, 2(4):452–471, Oct 1991.

[1001] M. J. Wolfe. *Optimizing Supercompilers for Supercomputers*. MIT Press, Cambridge, MA, 1989.

[1002] S. Wolfram. *The Mathematica Book*. 4th ed. Cambridge University Press, New York, 1999.

[1003] H. Wolkowicz and Q. Zhao. Semidefinite Programming Relaxations for the Graph Partitioning Problem. Technical Report CORR Report 96-17. Department of Combinatorics, University of Waterloo, Waterloo, Ontario, Canada 1996.

[1004] A. T. Wong and R. J. Harrison. Approaches to large-scale parallel self-consistent field calculations. *Journal of Computational Chemistry*, 16(10):1291–1300, Oct 1995.

[1005] Z. Wu. The effective energy transformation scheme as a special continuation approach to global optimization with application to molecular conformation. *SIAM Journal on Optimization*, 6(3):748–768, Aug 1996.

[1006] C.-Z. Xu and F. C. M. Lau. The generalized dimension exchange method for load balancing in *k*-ary *n*-cubes and variants. *Journal of Parallel and Distributed Computing*, 24(1):72–85, Jan 1995.

[1007] G. L. Xue. Improvement on the Northby algorithm for molecular conformation: Better solutions. *Journal of Global Optimization*, 4(4):425–440, 1994.

[1008] G. L. Xue, R. S. Maier, and J. B. Rosen. Minimizing the Lennard–Jones Potential Function on a Massively Parallel Computer. AHPCRC preprint 91-115. Army-High Performance Computing Research Center, University of Minnesota, Minneapolis, 1991.

[1009] I. Yotov. Mixed Finite Element Methods for Flow in Porous Media. PhD diss., Rice University, 1996.

[1010] D. M. Young and K. C. Jea. Generalized conjugate-gradient acceleration of nonsymmetrizable iterative methods. *Linear Algebra and Its Applications*, 34:159–194, Dec 1980.

[1011] J. L. Young, D. Gaitonde, and J. S. Shang. Towards the construction of a fourth-order difference scheme for transient EM wave simulation: Staggered grid approach. *IEEE Transactions on Antennas and Propagation*, 45(11):1573–1580, Nov 1997.

[1012] M. Zagha, B. Larson, S. Turner, and M. Itzkowitz. Performance analysis using the MIPS R1000 performance counters. In *Proceedings of Supercomputing '96*, ACM Press, New York, 1996.

[1013] M. J. Zaki. Parallel and distributed association mining: A survey. *IEEE Concurrency*, 7(4):14–25, Oct–Dec 1999.

[1014] O. Zaki, E. Lusk, W. Gropp, and D. Swider. Toward scalable performance visualization with Jumpshot. *International Journal of High Performance Computing Applications*, 13(3):277–288, Fall 1999.

[1015] T. A. Zang. On the rotation and skew-symmetric forms for incompressible flow simulations. *Applied Numerical Mathematics*, 7(1):27–40, Jan 1991.

[1016] L. Y. Zaslavsky, S. H. Kahan, B. H. Elton, K. J. Macshoff, and L. G. Stern. A scalable approach for solving irregular sparse linear systems on the Tera MTA multithreaded parallel shared-memory computer. In *Proceedings of the Ninth SIAM Conference on Parallel Processing for Scientific Computing*, p. 9, SIAM, Philadelphia, PA, 1999.

[1017] G. Zelniker and F. J. Taylor. *Advanced Digital Signal Processing: Theory and Applications*. Marcel Dekker, New York, 1994.

[1018] H. Zima, H.-J. Bast, and M. Gerndt. SUPERB: A tool for semi-automatic MIMD/SIMD parallelization. *Parallel Computing*, 6(1):1–18, Jan 1988.

[1019] H. Zima and B. Chapman. Compiling for distributed-memory systems. *Proceedings of the IEEE*, 81(2):264–287, Feb 1993.

[1020] Z. Zou, R. H. Byrd, and R. B. Schnabel. A Stochastic/Perturbation Global Optimization Algorithm for Distance Geometry Problems. Technical Report CU-CS-825-96. Department of Computer Science, University of Colorado, Boulder, 1996.

INDEX

scratch-remap repartitioners, 518–522
  defined, 520
  edge-cuts, 521
  illustrated, 521
  LMSR, 522, 525
  performing, 520
  poor performance, 521
  remapped partitioning, 520, 521
  remapping, 520, 521
  similarity matrix, 520, 521
  See also repartitioning
SD (Super Delaunay), 564
segmented scan add, 222
segmented scan copy, 222
self-consistent field (SCF), 168, 170, 190,
    191
  algorithm, 181
  codes, 181
  one-electron orbitals, 170
  procedure, 170
  quadratic, 182
  semidirect module, 182
semi-explicit differential algebraic
    equations, 690
sensitivity analysis, 701
sequential consistency, 31
SFS, 336
shared files (SFs), 173
shared memory, 4, 28–30
  bandwidth, 30
  consistency problem, 28–29
  defined, 28
  distributed (DSM), 30, 47
  distributed memory vs., 296–297
  issues, 28
  parallel programming, 366–370
  parallel programming interfaces, 358,
    380
  system bus, 34
  use of, 30
  virtual, 30
  See also distributed memory; memory
Shared-Memory Asynchronous Run-Time
    System (SMARTs), 45–46, 387
shared-memory model, 297, 475–476
  advantage, 297
  defined, 44, 51, 475

  example, 54–55
  implicit sharing, 313
  OpenMP, 79
shared-memory processor (SMP)
    architectures, 384
shared-memory systems, 45–46
  critical regions, 53
  defined, 45
  nondeterminism, 66
  programming, 45–46
  scalability and, 46
  synchronization, 46
  uniform-access, 45
S-Harp, 540, 541
shedding frequency, 129, 130
shock capturing, 133
  defined, 133
  schemes, 143
shock tracking, 132–133
  defined, 132–133
  viability, 133
shooting-and-bouncing-ray (SBR)
    technique, 229
Sign Change Lemma, 676
signal and image processing (SIP)
  algorithm development work, 243
  community, 243
  processing algorithms, 244
  simulation and modeling, 244
  See also SIP HPC
signposts, 727–728
simulated annealing algorithm, 658
simulations
  ADR, 162–165
  air-water flow, 149
  black-oil, 150–151
  circuit, 88
  cluster, 656
  complex system, 290
  compressible CFD, 94
  CSF, 220, 549
  cylinder wake, 131
  earthquake, 212–218
  flow and transport, 162–165
  high-resolution, 132, 211–212
  lattice QCD, 199–207
  molecular dynamics simulations, 286

ABOUT THE AUTHORS

Stanley C. Ahalt (sca@ee.eng.ohio-state.edu) is professor of electrical engineering at Ohio State University. His research interests include digital signal and image processing, pattern recognition, and high-performance computing.

Dorian C. Arnold (darnold@cs.wisc.edu) is a Ph.D. student in the Computer Sciences Department at the University of Wisconsin-Madison. His research interests include distributed systems, computer networks and protocols, and parallel performance tools.

Ruth Aydt (aydt@ncsa.uiuc.edu) is a Senior Research Programmer at the National Center for Supercomputing Applications. Her research interests include the use of cluster and Grid computing platforms for data mining, and the performance study of applications on those platforms.

Satish Balay (balay@mcs.anl.gov) is a Senior Scientific Programmer in the Mathematics and Computer Science Division of Argonne National Laboratory. He is one of the chief developers of the PETSc software.

David E. Bernholdt (bernholdtde@ornl.gov) is a member of the R&D staff at Oak Ridge National Laboratory. His research interests include high-performance computational chemistry and computer science issues in large-scale computational science.

Greg Bryan (gbryan@astro.ox.ac.uk) is a Lecturer in the Physics Department of the University of Oxford, and Fellow of New College, Oxford. His research interests include computational astrophysics and cosmology.

Alan Carle (carle@rice.edu) is a Faculty Fellow in the Department of Computational and Applied Mathematics at Rice University. His research interests include automatic differentiation, compiler construction, scientific programming environments, and high-performance computing.

Henri Casanova (casanova@cs.ucsd.edu) is an Assistant Research Scientist at the San Diego Supercomputer Center and an Adjunct Assistant Professor in the Computer Science and Engineering Department at the University of California, San Diego. His research interests include parallel computing, Grid computing, and Internet computing.

Charlie Catlett (catlett@mcs.anl.gov) is a Senior Fellow at the Computation Institute at Argonne National Laboratory and the University of Chicago. His research interests include advanced networks and Grid software architecture.

Ann Christine Catlin (acc@cs.purdue.edu) is a Research Associate in the Computer Science Department at Purdue University. Her research interests include problem-solving environments for PDE-based applications, network computing, and agent-based PDE-solving environments.

K. Mani Chandy (mani@cs.caltech.edu) is the Simon Ramo Professor of Computer Science at the California Institute of Technology. His research interests include distributed computing, verification of concurrent programs, parallel programming languages, and performance models of computing and communication systems.

Clint Dawson (clint@ticam.utexas.edu) is Professor of Aerospace Engineering and Engineering Mechanics at The University of Texas at Austin. His research interests include finite element methods and parallel algorithms, with applications to flow through porous media and shallow water systems.

John Dennis (dennis@caam.rice.edu) is Noah Harding Professor Emeritus and Research Professor at Rice University. His current research interests involve nonsmooth optimization algorithms for practical engineering design problems.

Eusebius Doedel (doedel@cs.concordia.ca) is Professor of Computer Science at Concordia University in Montreal. His research interests include numerical algorithms and software for the study of bifurcation phenomena in dynamical systems.

Jack Dongarra (dongarra@cs.utk.edu) holds an appointment as University Distinguished Professor in the Computer Science Department at the University of Tennessee. He is the director of the 40-member research group called the Innovative Computing Laboratory and the director of the Center for Information Technology Research, one of the nine University's Centers of Excellence. He also is an Adjunct R&D Participant at Oak Ridge National Laboratory and an Adjunct Professor at Rice University. He specializes in numerical algorithms in linear algebra, use of advanced-computer architectures, programming methodology, and tools for parallel computers. Other current research involves the development, testing, and documentation of high-quality mathematical software. He was involved in the design and implementation of the open source software packages EISPACK, LINPACK, the BLAS, LAPACK, ScaLAPACK, Netlib, PVM, MPI, NetSolve, ATLAS, PAPI, and Harness; and he is currently involved in the design of algorithms and techniques for high-performance computer architectures. He is a Fellow of the AAAS, ACM, and IEEE, and a member of the National Academy of Engineering.

John Dukowicz (duk@lanl.gov) is an Associate Laboratory Fellow in the Theoretical Division at Los Alamos National Laboratory. Among his various areas of interest, he has been most active in computational fluid dynamics, gasdynamics, combustion, and most recently, ocean and sea ice modeling, with particular emphasis on numerical methods.

Victor Eijkhout (eijkhout@cs.utk.edu) is a Research Assistant Professor in the Department of Computer Science of the University of Tennessee. His research interests include numerical linear algebra, parallel processing, and performance optimization.

Ian Foster (foster@mcs.anl.gov) is Senior Scientist and Associate Director in the Mathematics and Computer Science Division at Argonne National Laboratory, Professor of Computer Science at the University of Chicago, and Senior Fellow in the Argonne/University of Chicago Computation Institute. He has published four books and over 200 papers and technical reports on a variety of topics in parallel and distributed processing, software engineering, and computational science. He currently coleads the Globus project with Dr. Carl Kesselman of USC/ISI, which was awarded the 1997 Global Information Infrastructure "Next Generation" award and a 2002 R&D 100 award, and which provides protocols and services used by many distributed computing projects worldwide. He also coleads the GriPhyN and Earth System Grid projects, which are extending and applying Grid concepts in challenging application domains, and the GRIDS Center, which is developing a national middleware infrastructure. He cofounded the influential Global Grid Forum and coedited the book *The Grid: Blueprint for a New Computing Infrastructure*.

Geoffrey C. Fox (gfc@indiana.edu) is Professor of Computer Science, Informatics, and Physics at Indiana University. He is also director of the Community Grids Laboratory of the Pervasive Technology Laboratories at Indiana University and cochairs the Grid Computing Environment (GCE) working group of the Grid Forum. He previously held positions at Caltech, Syracuse University, and Florida State University.

Dr. Fox has worked in a variety of applied computer science fields, with his work on computational physics evolving into contributions to parallel computing, initially involving the hypercube architecture. He has worked on computing issues in several application areas, and he is currently focusing on Earthquake Science. Over the last four years, a major activity has been the use of Object Web technologies to build collaboration systems and their application in an integrated approach to synchronous and asynchronous distance education. Current activities include the architecture of collaborative Web services and formulation of audio-video conferencing as a Web service. He has led activities to develop prototype high-performance Java and Fortran compilers and their runtime support. His research group has pioneered use of CORBA and Java for both collaboration and distributed computing. In particular, the Gateway computational portal was one of the earliest systems to integrate object and grid technologies. He helped set up the Java Grande forum to encourage use of Java in large-scale computing. Dr. Fox is a proponent of the development of computational science and related areas such as "Informatics" and "Intermetics" as academic disciplines and scientific methods.

Wojtek Furmanski (furm@ecs.syr.edu) is Research Professor in the Department of Electrical Engineering and Computer Science at Syracuse University. His research interests include software technologies, development of large software systems, and information technologies related to the Internet and the World Wide Web.

Dennis Gannon (gannon@cs.indiana.edu) is Chair of the Department of Computer Science at Indiana University and Science Director for the Pervasive Technology Labs at Indiana University. His current research involves the design of software component architectures for distributed scientific applications and the study of the architecture of Grid systems.

William Gropp (gropp@mcs.anl.gov) is a Senior Computer Scientist and Associate Director of the Mathematics and Computer Science Division at Argonne National Laboratory. He is also a Senior Scientist in the Department of Computer Science at the University of Chicago and a Senior Fellow in the Argonne/University of Chicago Computation Institute.

Dr. Gropp's research interests are in parallel computing, software for scientific computing, and numerical methods for partial differential equations. He has played a major role in the development of the MPI message-passing standard. He is coauthor of MPICH, the most widely used implementation of MPI, and was involved in the MPI Forum as a chapter author for both MPI-1 and MPI-2. He has written many books and papers on MPI, including *Using MPI* and *Using MPI-2*. He has developed adaptive mesh refinement and domain decomposition methods with a focus on scalable parallel algorithms; these algorithms and their application to significant scientific problems are discussed in a book he coauthored, entitled *Parallel Multilevel Methods for Elliptic Partial Differential Equations*. He is also one of the designers of the PETSc parallel numerical library and has developed efficient and scalable parallel algorithms for the solution of linear and nonlinear equations. In addition, he is involved in several advanced computing projects, including performance modeling, data structure modification for ultra-high-performance computers, and development of component-based software to promote interoperability among numerical toolkits.

As testimony to his leadership in advanced computing, Dr. Gropp (with his colleagues) received the 1999 Gordon Bell prize for the application of an unstructured mesh technique to computational fluid dynamics problems. The following year he (with a colleague) received honorable mention in the Beale-Orchard-Hays Competition for Excellence in Computational Mathematical Programming for work on optimization environments; this was the first time such an award was granted by the Mathematical Programming Society in this competition.

Eui-Hong (Sam) Han (han@cs.umn.edu) is Scientist at iXmatch Inc. and is also Research Associate at the Army High Performance Computing Research Center at the University of Minnesota. His research interests include data mining, information retrieval, and parallel processing.

Tomasz Haupt (haupt@erc.msstate.edu) is Research Professor at the Engineering Research Center, Mississippi State University. His research interests include high-performance computing, Internet applications, and object-oriented, distributed systems. His current research focuses on Web-based metacomputing, seamless access to remote high-performance resources, software integration, support for distributed computing, and computational Web portals.

Urs M. Heller (heller@csit.fsu.edu) is a Scientist/Scholar at the School of Computational Science & Information Technology at Florida State University. His research interests include large-scale numerical simulations of quantum field theories, in particular quantum chromodynamics, the theory of the strong interactions in particle physics, also known as high-energy physics.

Ronald D. Henderson (rdh@its.caltech.edu) is a Senior Research Associate at the California Institute of Technology. His research interests include spectral and spectral element methods for simulating turbulence and transition.

Elias N. Houstis (enh@cs.purdue.edu) is Professor of Computer Science at Purdue University. His research interests include mathematical software, problem-solving environments, high-performance computing, and recommender systems.

Joseph Insley (insley@mcs.anl.gov) is a Scientific Programmer in the Mathematics and Computer Science Division at Argonne National Laboratory. His research interests include Grid computing and visualization of distributed systems.

Mahesh Joshi (mjoshi@cs.umn.edu) is a Research Associate at IBM T. J. Watson Research Center, New York. He is also pursuing his doctoral studies in Computer Science at the University of Minnesota, Minneapolis. His current research interests are in data mining, bioinformatics, and high-performance parallel computing.

Aneta Karaivanova (aneta@csit.fsu.edu) is Associate Professor of CLPP at the Bulgarian Academy of Sciences. Her research interests include Monte Carlo and quasi-Monte Carlo methods and parallel algorithms.

George Karypis (karypis@cs.umn.edu) is Assistant Professor in the Department of Computer Science at the University of Minnesota, Minneapolis. His current research interests are in the areas of parallel algorithm design, data mining, bioinformatics, scientific computing, and sparse matrix.

H. B. Keller (hbk@caltech.edu) is Professor of Applied Mathematics, Emeritus at the California Institute of Technology (CALTECH). His research interests include numerical analysis, bifurcation theory, scientific computing, path following, computational fluid dynamics, and dynamical systems.

Ken Kennedy (ken@rice.edu) is the John and Ann Doerr University Professor of Computer Science and Director of the Center for High Performance Software Research (HiPerSoft) at Rice University. He is a fellow of the Institute of Electrical and

Electronics Engineers, the Association for Computing Machinery, and the American Association for the Advancement of Science and he has been a member of the National Academy of Engineering since 1990. From 1997 to 1999, he served as cochair of the President's Information Technology Advisory Committee (PITAC). For his leadership in producing the PITAC report on funding of information technology research, he received the Computing Research Association Distinguished Service Award (1999) and the RCI Seymour Cray HPCC Industry Recognition Award (1999).

Professor Kennedy has published over one hundred fifty technical articles and supervised thirty-four Ph.D. dissertations on programming support software for high-performance computer systems. In 1989, he established the Center for Research on Parallel Computation (CRPC), a NSF Science and Technology Center, and he directed it throughout its eleven-year lifetime. His current research focuses on programming tools for parallel computer systems and high-performance microprocessors, seeking to develop new strategies for supporting architecture-independent parallel programming, especially in science and engineering. He directs the GrADS Project, a collaborative eight-institution research effort started in 1999 with NSF support, which is focused on application development support for computational Grids. He is also the project director of the academic partner contract for the Los Alamos Computer Science Institute, which is located at Los Alamos National Laboratory. In recognition of his contributions to software for high performance computation, he received the 1995 W. Wallace McDowell Award, the highest research award of the IEEE Computer Society. In 1999, he was named the third recipient of the ACM SIGPLAN Programming Languages Achievement Award.

Carl Kesselman (carl@isi.edu) is the Director of the Center for Grid Technologies at the Information Sciences Institute and a Research Associate Professor of Computer Science at the University of Southern California. His current research interests are in all aspects of Grid computing, including Grid architecture, resource management, security, and application development environments.

Charles Koelbel (chk@cs.rice.edu) is a Research Scientist at Rice University. His research interests include compilers for parallel and distributed systems, programming paradigms, and programming tools.

Ashok Krishnamurthy (akk@ee.eng.ohio-state.edu) is Associate Professor in the Department of Electrical Engineering at Ohio State University. His research interests include digital signal processing, speech perception and recognition, and computational models of the auditory system.

Vipin Kumar (kumar@cs.umn.edu) is Director of the Army High Performance Computing Research Center and Professor of Computer Science and Engineering at the University of Minnesota. His current research interests include high performance computing, parallel algorithms for scientific computing problems, and data mining.

Tahsin Kurc (kurc-1@medctr.osu.edu) is Assistant Professor of Biomedical Informatics at Ohio State University. His research interests include methods and software frameworks for data-intensive computing in distributed environments.

Wonsuck Lee (wonsuck@research.bell-labs.com) is a Member of Technical Staff at the Computing Science Research Center, Bell Laboratories. His research interests include computational fluid dynamics, computational photonics, and PDE/ODE constrained optimization.

Robert Malone (rcm@lanl.gov) is Deputy Leader of the Methods for Advanced Scientific Simulations Group in the Computer and Computational Sciences Division and Leader of the Climate, Ocean, and Sea Ice Modeling Project at Los Alamos National Laboratory.

Michael Mascagni (mascagni@cs.fsu.edu) is Professor of Computer Science at Florida State University. His research interests include Monte Carlo methods, random number generation, and parallel and distributed computing.

Lois Curfman McInnes (mcinnes@mcs.anl.gov) is a researcher in the Mathematics and Computer Science Division of Argonne National Laboratory and is one of the developers of PETSc and the optimization software, TAO. Her research interests include parallel algorithms and software for large-scale PDEs and interoperability issues for high-performance scientific software.

Dan Meiron (dim@its.caltech.edu) is currently Professor of Applied and Computational Mathematics and Computer Science at the California Institute of Technology. His research interests include computational fluid dynamics, computational materials science, and high-performance computing.

Michael Norman (mlnorman@ucsd.edu) is Professor of Physics at the University of California, San Diego. His research interests include computational astrophysics and cosmology, parallel computing, and scientific visualization.

Manish Parashar (parashar@caip.rutgers.edu) is Associate Professor of Electrical and Computer Engineering at Rutgers, The State University of New Jersey. His research interests include parallel, distributed and Grid computing, computer-supported collaboration, and software engineering.

D. R. Prabhu (dev.prabhu@oracle.com) is Senior Development Manager of Collaboration Products at Oracle Corporation. His research interests include parallel computation, artificial neural networks, signal/image processing, web technologies, and online collaboration.

Daniel Reed (reed@ncsa.uiuc.edu) is the Edward William and Jane Marr Professor at the University of Illinois and Director of the National Center for Supercomputing Applications (NCSA). His research interests include experimental performance analysis, performance analysis tools and techniques, and parallel I/O optimization and tuning.

John Reynders (John.Reynders@celera.com) is Vice-President for Informatics at Celera Genomics, where he is responsible for algorithm development, software engineering, computer science, and computational sciences. His research interests including parallel algorithms, object-oriented frameworks, bioinformatics, and high-performance computing.

John R. Rice (rice@cs.purdue.edu) is Distinguished Professor of Computer Science at Purdue University. His research interests include mathematical software, problem solving environments, computational mathematics, and computer security.

Joel Saltz (saltz-1@medctr.osu.edu) is Professor of Biomedical Informatics and Computer and Information Science at the Ohio State University, Columbus, Ohio and Senior Fellow, Ohio Supercomputer Center, Columbus, Ohio. His research interests include development of database tools to aggregate information from distributed data sources and to efficiently explore, analyze, and visualize large multi-resolution datasets such as those generated by numerical simulations.

Ravi Samtaney (ravi@galcit.caltech.edu) is a computational scientist in the Computational Plasma Physics Group at the Princeton Plasma Physics Laboratory, Princeton University. His research interests include computational physics, numerical analysis, and high-performance computing.

Kirk Schloegel (kirk.schloegel@honeywell.com) is a Research Scientist at Honeywell International. His research interests include parallel computing, load balancing, and automatic code generation from graphical design models.

Joseph Shang (jshang@cs.wright.edu) is a Research Professor of Mechanical and Materials engineering at the Wright State University. His research interests include computational fluid dynamics, electromagnetics, and magneto-aerodynamics.

Barry Smith (bsmith@mcs.anl.gov) is a Computer Scientist at Argonne National Laboratory. His research focuses on the scalable solution of partial differential equations.

Richard D. Smith (rdsmith@lanl.gov) is a Staff Scientist in the Fluid Dynamics Group in the Theoretical Division at Los Alamos National Laboratory. His research interests include numerical ocean modeling, global climate modeling, and turbulence parameterizations in geophysical flows.

Bharat Soni (bsoni@ERC.MsState.Edu) is Professor of Aerospace Engineering and Director, Center for Computational Systems, Engineering Research Center, Mississippi State University.

Danny C. Sorensen (sorensen@rice.edu) is Noah G. Harding Professor of Computational and Applied Mathematics at Rice University. His research interests include large-scale eigenvalue problems, reduced order models for dynamical systems, and parallel algorithms for scientific computing.

Rick Stevens (stevens@mcs.anl.gov) is Director of the Mathematics and Computer Science (MCS) Division at Argonne National Laboratory and Professor of Computer Science at the University of Chicago. His research focuses on collaborative environments, high-performance architectures, and large-scale scientific applications.

Mei-Hui Su (mei@isi.edu) is a Systems Programmer at the Information Sciences Institute, University of Southern California. Her research interests include distributed Grid computing.

Alan Sussman (als@cs.umd.edu) is an Assistant Professor of Computer Science at the University of Maryland. His research interests include high-performance database systems, compilers and runtime systems for distributed memory parallel machines, and parallel supercomputer applications.

Rajeev Thakur (thakur@mcs.anl.gov) is a Computer Scientist in the Mathematics and Computer Science Division at Argonne National Laboratory. His research interests are in high-performance computing in general and high-performance networking and I/O in particular.

Joe Thompson (joe@ERC.MsState.Edu) is Distinguished Professor of Aerospace Engineering and Director, Center for DoD Programming Environment & Training, Engineering Research Center, Mississippi State University.

Linda Torczon (linda@rice.edu) is a Research Scientist in the Department of Computer Science and Executive Director of the Center for High Performance Software Research (HiPerSoft) at Rice University. Additionally, she serves as Executive Director of the GrADS project, an eight-institution research effort funded by the National Science Foundation (NSF) to explore scientific and technical problems underlying support for Grid application development. She also serves as an executive director of the Los Alamos Computer Science Institute. From 1990 to 2000, she served as Executive Director of the Center for Research on Parallel Computation (CRPC), an NSF Science and Technology Center. In this capacity, she coordinated extensive research efforts, education and outreach programs, and technology transfer activities. In collaboration with CRPC researchers, she initiated and was actively involved in numerous activities intended to increase the number of women and underrepresented minorities entering mathematics and science-related fields.

Linda Torczon is also a member of the scalar compiler research group at Rice University. Her research interests include code generation, interprocedural data-flow analysis and optimization, programming environments, and adaptive compilation. Techniques resulting from her research are widely used in industrial and research compilers. Her current work includes applying techniques from artificial intelligence to the problem of producing high-quality compilers for a variety of processors, applications, performance environments, and end-user criteria. In addition, with Keith Cooper, she is coauthoring another Morgan Kaufmann book, *Engineering a Compiler*. It is intended as a textbook for senior-level courses on compiler construction and as a resource for compiler implementors.

Gregor von Laszewski (gregor@mcs.anl.gov) is an Assistant Scientist at the Mathematics and Computer Science Division at Argonne National Laboratory. His research interests include Grid computing, Commodity Grid Kits, and the application of Grid technologies for scientific computing.

Mary Fanett Wheeler (mfw@ticam.utexas.edu) is the Ernest and Virginia Cockrell Professor of Engineering at The University of Texas at Austin. Her research interests include numerical solution of partial differential equations, modeling flow in porous media, and parallel computation.

Andrew B. (Andy) White, Jr. (abw@lanl.gov) is the Special Projects Director for the Weapons Physics Directorate at Los Alamos National Laboratory. This new Laboratory enterprise focuses on research issues in computer and computational sciences associated with employing the largest, most complex computational resources to address important national issues such as stockpile stewardship, energy and environment, systems biology, nanotechnology and crisis management. From 1989 to 1998, he was founder and Director of the Advanced Computing Laboratory at Los Alamos, as well as the Program Manager for DOE's HPCC (High Performance Computing and Communications) program. He has been an Associate Director of the NSF Science and Technology Center for Research on Parallel Computation (CRPC), a member of the ad hoc Task Force on the Future of the NSF Supercomputing Centers (Hayes Committee), Principal Investigator for the DOE High Performance Computing Research Center at Los Alamos, and at various times assistant, deputy, and acting Division Leader of the Laboratory's computing division. His research interests are in the areas of applied mathematics, high-performance computing, computational simulation and modeling, and predictive computational capabilities.

Zhijun Wu (zhijun@iastate.edu) is Associate Professor of Mathematics at Iowa State University. His research interests include numerical linear algebra and optimization, parallel high-performance computing, and computational biology.